GunDigest®

2023

77th EDITION

EDITED BY

PHILIP P. MASSARO

Published by

Gun Digest® Books, an imprint of Caribou Media Group, LLC

Gun Digest Media
5600 W. Grande Market Drive, Suite 100
Appleton, WI 54913
gundigest.com

To order books or other products call 920.471.4522
or visit us online at gundigeststore.com

CAUTION: Technical data presented here, particularly technical data on handloading and on firearms adjustment and alteration, inevitably reflects individual experience with particular equipment and components under specific circumstances the reader cannot duplicate exactly. Such data presentations therefore should be used for guidance only and with caution. Caribou Media accepts no responsibility for results obtained using these data.

ISBN-13: 978-1-951115-62-3

Edited by Phil Massaro and Corey Graff
Cover Design by Gene Coo
Interior Design by Jon Stein and Joey Meyers

Printed in the United States of America

10 9 8 7 6 5 4 3 2 1

41st ANNUAL

John T. Amber LITERARY AWARD

The John T. Amber Literary Award is named for the editor of *Gun Digest* from 1950 to 1979, a period that could be called the heyday of gun and outdoor writing. Amber worked with many of the legends in the business during his almost 30 years with the book, including the great shooting and hunting writer Townsend Whelen. In 1967, Amber instituted an annual award, which he named for Whelen, to honor an outstanding author from the previous year's *Gun Digest* edition. In 1982, three years after Amber's retirement, the award was renamed in his honor.

Dave Fulson

When you find someone passionate about their chosen line of work, it can be very inspiring. Being an unabashed aficionado of all things Africa, and spending countless hours watching hunting television and movies, when I finally got to meet Dave Fulson — who, with partner Tim Danklef, heads up Safari Classics Productions — I was stoked. If you've met Dave, you already know, but if you haven't, he is the kind of guy you feel that you've known for years, just after a few minutes.

Fulson has been behind the camera for some of the most inspiring hunting footage. He's a man who has spent his time in the trenches. Not only that, Fulson is an ardent global hunter (don't get him started about turkey hunting) and is equally passionate about hunters' rights, both at home and around the world. He is active in the Dallas Safari Club's (DSC) efforts to maintain the rights of hunters everywhere and works tirelessly on worldwide habitat preservation. But Dave is much more than that — he's a talented author who can concisely get the point across in a conversational manner. Oh, and Dave is from Texas. You don't have to ask him; he's gonna tell you.

I am honored to present Dave Fulson with the 41st Annual John T. Amber Literary Award, named in honor of the long-time Editor-in-Chief of this prestigious tome, for his feature article "I Dreamed of Double Rifles," which appeared in the 76th Edition.

I reached out to Dave, and he had this to say: *"Africa has thrilled me and very nearly killed me, but she will always be the destination that pulls me back until finance or physical failure make it impossible to return to her. But even then, I will write about my love of her wildlife and wild places in an effort to encourage others to experience her magic spell."*

Dangerous game, be it the giant stuff of Africa, the massive buffalo of Australia or the big bears of Alaska, has been a constant love of Fulson for thirty-five of his sixty-two years. He has no plans of slowing down on that special passion. Even so, he is never far removed from his native Texas and his great love for hunting big whitetails and calling spring turkeys. And Dave knows what makes for good, ethical hunting television. I've had the opportunity to be a guest host on several episodes of *DSC's Tracks Across Africa* and *Trijicon's World of Sports Afield.* He and his company demand a level of respectability revered by viewers.

"*Writing for the* Gun Digest Annual *was a personal thrill, as well as a professional compliment that I am very grateful for. My article "I Dreamed of Double Rifles" covered a subject and firearm classification I have always been passionate about. It gives me deep satisfaction that the readers embraced it to a degree that I would be considered for the prestigious John T. Amber Literary Award. The talent pool writing for* Gun Digest *is beyond deep, and to be named as the recipient of this year's award is a very surprising, yet cherished honor,"* Fulson related.

If you enjoy Fulson's writing as I do, you'll find that he is a regular contributor to DSC's *Game Trails* magazine, highlighting many aspects of global hunting. And if you'd like to meet Dave, he can be found high-stepping through the aisles of the Dallas Safari Club annual convention in early January on one mission or another. Make him take a breather to say hello.

Phil Massaro, Editor-in-Chief

GunDigest 2023

FEATURES

Photo: Wayne van Zwoll

TESTFIRE

ONE GOOD GUN

REPORTS FROM THE FIELD

2023 FIREARMS CATALOG

INTRODUCING THE Gun Digest 2023 77th Edition

PHILIP P. MASSARO
EDITOR-IN-CHIEF

Welcome to the 77th Edition of the World's Greatest Gun Book! The last few years have been a challenge, to say the least. Still, at last, it seems that things are returning to normal, with ammunition returning to the shelves and some reloading components are available again. We're seeing innovative cartridges and interesting new projectiles, and some of our favorite manufacturers have risen from the ashes to put smiles on shooters' faces once again. All in all, I'm hopeful that the return to normal is underway, though I feel confident in saying that we would all appreciate the pre-Covid ammunition prices returning.

The collective love of the long-range shooting game has grown over the last year (I have a friend who says that 1,000 yards is the new 100 yards), and the gear for that job has continued to grow with it. Our rifles continue to evolve as manufacturing techniques and styles change.

We've got a fantastic lineup in this year's edition. Look at Thomas Gomez's feature on chassis rifles; you may find yourself customizing your next rifle to your personal taste from the ground up. At the opposite end of the spectrum, Terry Wieland runs us through the gamut of duelling pistols, transporting us to that era when a challenge might have cost you your life. As you'll see, the classic duel, as portrayed by Hollywood, was entirely different from reality.

We've got some anniversaries to celebrate in this edition! Federal celebrates its centennial in 2022, and the prestigious firm of Griffin & Howe also turns 100 in 2023. In addition, the American Custom Gunmakers Guild — a brainchild of our own editor emeritus, the late John T. Amber — turns the ripe old age of 40.

For those fans of the scattergun, Joe Coogan walks us through a lifetime's worth of experiences with a shotgun in hand, and Steve Gash reviews the new Stevens M301 .410 Turkey Gun. At the same time, our own managing editor Corey Graff introduces you to Benelli's fast-swinging little 828U 20-gauge shotgun. Larry Weishuhn — Mr. Whitetail himself — relates his experiences with all sorts of different single-shot pistols, using them on game animals from as small as javelina up through deer, elk and moose, all the way to the largest and most dangerous game animals on earth. And speaking of dangerous game, international hunter Craig Boddington discusses the merits of the double rifle vs. the bolt action for those situations where your life, as a hunter, is on the line.

In the history department, famed Alaskan bear guide Phil Shoemaker weighs in on the variety of bolt-action rifles available in the early 20th century. Pierre van der Walt takes us through the history of the Brno/CZ rifles. And if famous historical rifles are your thing, I will point you to my own article on a fantastic opportunity I was given to handle and shoot the rifle collection of Mr. Bill Jones, which may rate as one of the most amazing experiences I've ever had at a rifle range, or anywhere else for that matter.

Marlin rifles are back in production, though produced under the Ruger roof, and Andy Larsson gives us a full review of the Model 1985 SBL in .45-70 Government. Jim House takes us back a few years with his write-up about the Winchester Model 94 Big Bore in .356 Winchester. Shane Jahn waxes poetically on the vintage .33 Winchester cartridge; there is plenty of love for the lever gun within the covers of the 77th Edition.

Will Brantley shows economical choices for the deer hunter looking to fill the freezer with venison on a budget. For fans of Browning who may or may not have the BuckMark tattooed on their person, Mike Dickerson examines the history of the X-Bolt, one of the most popular rifles ever to come off Browning's assembly line.

I'm particularly proud of our Reports from the Field section, where some talented writers bring you the latest and greatest guns, optics, ammunition and more. Though many of our firearms and ammunition companies have been struggling to meet the high demands of the last couple of years, there are still some interesting new developments in the market. Among these are the .338 Weatherby Rebated Precision Magnum rifle cartridge and Federal's new .30 Super Carry pistol round. Winchester's Super-X line of ammo, a staple in my world in the late 1980s, turns 100 this year. Federal's issued some commemorative boxes to celebrate, and Remington ammunition has made its way back to the shelves of sporting goods stores.

If the obscure interests you, Mike Haskew will introduce you to the German Sturmgewehr 44 and, going even further down the rabbit hole, Jim Dickson sheds some light on the rare Nepalese Gehendra rifle. Ron Spomer acquaints you with the M704 rifle action — an action I've used myself for several years that is both interesting and unique.

For the lovers of cartridges and ballistics, Wayne van Zwoll discusses the conformation of rifle projectiles, and Stan Trzoniec brings a baker's dozen of wildcats to the table. Michael Shea revisits the ensemble of rimfire cartridges, while Sheriff Jim Wilson discusses techniques to master the double-action revolver as a defensive weapon.

There is an eclectic and diverse range of topics inside this year's edition, keeping in the World's Greatest Gun Book tradition, equally embracing that which has come before and that which is new and shiny. So, without further delay, I proudly present to you the 77th Edition of the *Gun Digest*. I truly hope you enjoy it. GD

GUN DIGEST STAFF

JIM SCHLENDER | Group Publisher
PHILIP P. MASSARO | Editor-In-Chief
COREY GRAFF | Features Editor

DEPARTMENT CONTRIBUTORS

Wayne van Zwoll | Rifles
Todd Woodard | AR Rifles
Robert Sadowski | Semi-Auto Pistols
Shane Jahn | Revolvers & Others
Kristin Alberts | Shotguns
Bob Campbell | Muzzleloaders
Joe Arterburn | Optics
Jim House | Airguns
Philip P. Massaro | Ammo, Reloading & Ballistics
Tom Turpin | Custom & Engraved Guns

About the Cover

Springfield Armory is a name that is American as apple pie. While the origins of the name date to 1777, when General George Washington oversaw its creation to store ammunition and gun carriages, its governmental affiliation ended in 1968. The Reese family resurrected the name in 1974 to produce the finest firearms ever to come out of Springfield Armory, namely the M1 Garand, the 1911-A1 and the M14. The latter — though the semi-auto Springfield Armory model is referred to as the M1A — adorns our cover. While operating out of Illinois instead of Massachusetts, Springfield Armory nonetheless has a stellar reputation among the aficionados of those models.

Springfield Armory M1A Loaded .308 Rifle

The Springfield Armory M1A Loaded .308 Rifle is an excellent example of a military-style autoloading rifle and offers many excellent features serious shooters will appreciate immediately, including its legendary reliability in all conditions. From a distance, the familiar lines of the classic rifle are all there, with its blued steel finish and walnut stock, but upon inspection, you'll find more than a few premium upgrades. A 22-inch National Match six-groove barrel features a 1:11 twist rate and is equipped with a flash suppressor at the business end. A National Match .062-inch blade front sight mates with a match-grade rear peep, with a .0520-inch aperture giving you ½-MOA adjustments for windage and 1-MOA adjustments for elevation. A tuned two-stage National Match trigger breaks at 4 ½ pounds, allowing for precise shot placement, and the rifle comes supplied with a 10-round magazine. Weighing in just under 10 pounds, the aptly named M1A Loaded .308 is chambered in the classic .308 Winchester cartridge, long associated with the Camp Perry matches and other serious shooting competitions. The M1A Loaded has an MSRP of $1,998. *springfield-armory.com*

Leupold Mark 3HD 3-9x40 P5 Illuminated TMR Firedot Scope

Leupold's riflescopes have always been a staple among American shooters, and of late, its products have gotten nothing but better. The HD series — including the VX-5HD, VX-6HD and the newly released VX-3HD — has been extended to include the Mark 3HD line. The Mark 3 HD line offers a rugged, simple and dependable scope to those who need mil-based adjustments. With a very useable 3-9x magnification range, a capped windage turret and a boldly marked elevation turret, the Mark 3HD 3-9x40mm P5 Illuminated TMR Firedot has a 30mm main tube for

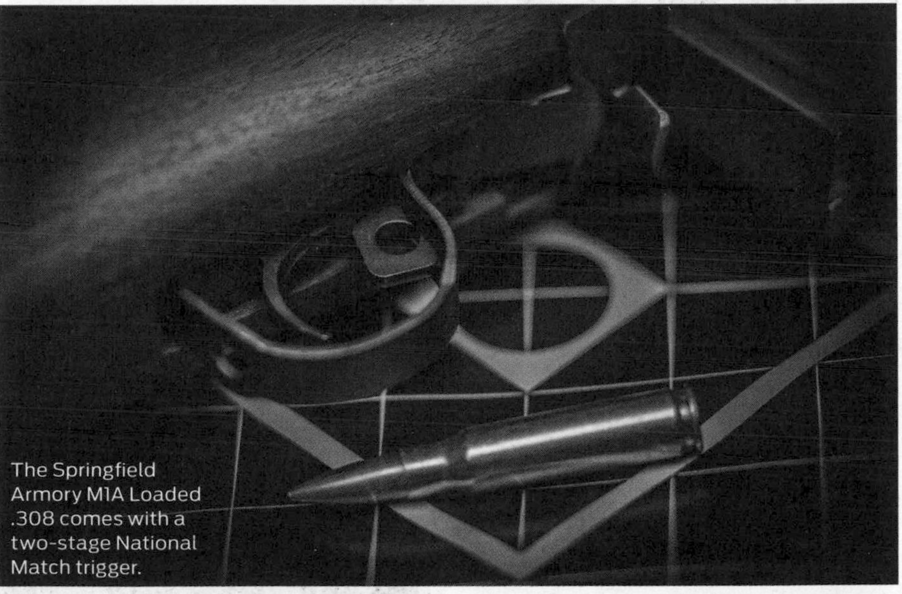
The Springfield Armory M1A Loaded .308 comes with a two-stage National Match trigger.

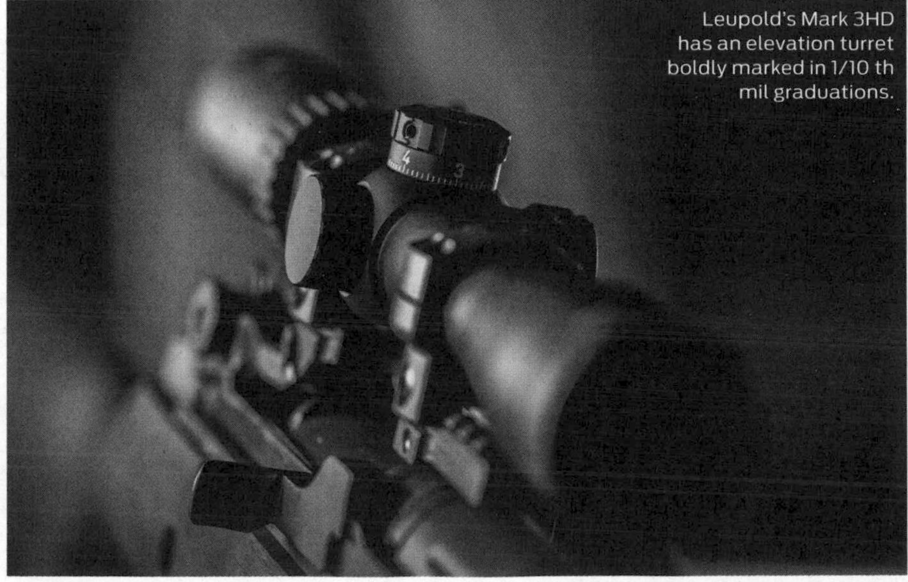
Leupold's Mark 3HD has an elevation turret boldly marked in 1/10 th mil graduations.

The National Match front sight of the Springfield M1A Loaded has a .062-inch front blade sight.

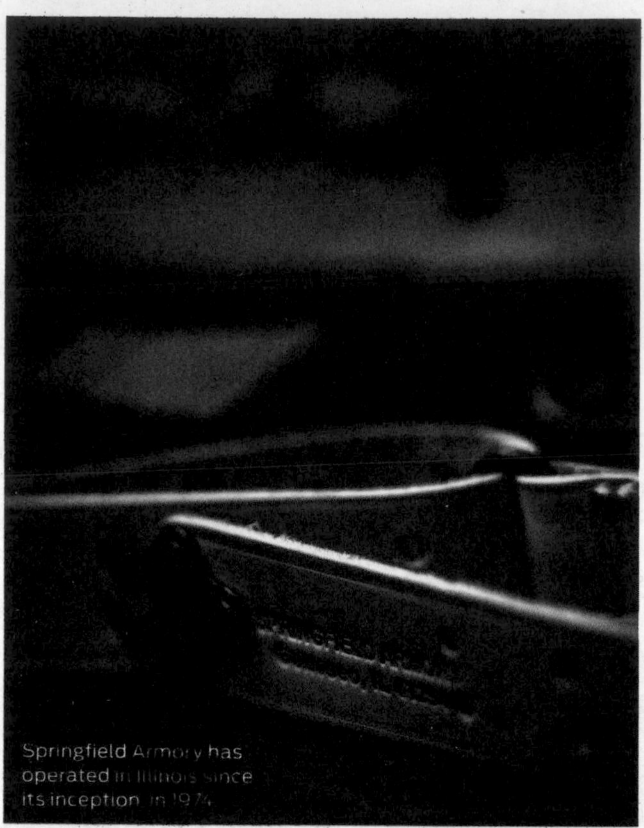

Springfield Armory has operated in Illinois since its inception in 1974.

plenty of elevation adjustment — perfect for those long-range shooting sessions. The 40mm objective lens allows the scope to be mounted low to the bore, while the Leupold lens coating delivers a bright, crisp image from edge to edge in different light conditions.

Weighing just under a pound, the Leupold Mark 3HD 3-9x40 won't destroy the balance of your rifle, yet will resist even the harshest recoil. The Leupold Elite Optical System of lenses and coatings needs to be seen to be believed and belies the price point; it offers glare reduction, crisp resolution and among the best light transmission on the market. The scope's power selector has an integrated throw lever, and like Leupold's tactical scopes, the trademark Gold Ring is replaced with a black matte ring, matching the finish of the scope body.

The Illuminated Firedot TMR reticle is a graduated crosshair subtending the prescribed distance when the riflescope is set at maximum power. With 5 mils of hash marks in ½-mil graduations in each direction from the center set in .30- and .40-mil widths, its reticle is useful yet not overly complicated. There is a red illuminated center dot with adjustable intensity via a knob on the left of the turret housing. Illumination is powered by a CR2032 battery.

Providing 36 mils of elevation adjustment and Leupold's rock-solid performance, the Mark 3HD 3-9x40mm P5 Illuminated TMR Firedot is equally at home in the whitetail blind, the competition course or at the range. MSRP $699.99. *leupold.com*

Federal Gold Medal Sierra MatchKing Ammo

Celebrating its centennial in 2022, Federal has long been famous for using other companies' projectiles in its factory-loaded ammunition. Perhaps the most famous instance is the use of the excellent Sierra MatchKing bullet (part no. 2200) in the Gold Medal Match line of target ammunition. Long before the world regularly used the word 'Creedmoor,' the standard formula for accuracy was the .308 Winchester cartridge loaded with a 168-grain Sierra MatchKing bullet. That famous boattail hollowpoint bullet has a well-deserved reputation for consistency and pinpoint accuracy, and when 1,000 yards seemed an impossible distance, it would deliver the goods.

Federal's Gold Medal Match ammunition is fueled by a specially formulated propellant and sparked by the benchrest-quality Federal Gold Medal Match primer. The proprietary primer sealant keeps things nice and dry inside the case.

Looking at the case capacity of the .308 Winchester, the 168-grain boattail bullet represents what many consider to be the perfect balance of Ballistic Coefficient and case capacity. Generations of shooters have relied on Federal Gold Medal Match ammunition to win competitions and deliver serious accuracy. Driven to a muzzle velocity of 2,650 fps, Federal's Gold Medal Match ammunition will make the most of a rifle like the Springfield Armory M1A Loaded. Sold in 20-count boxes. *federalpremium.com*

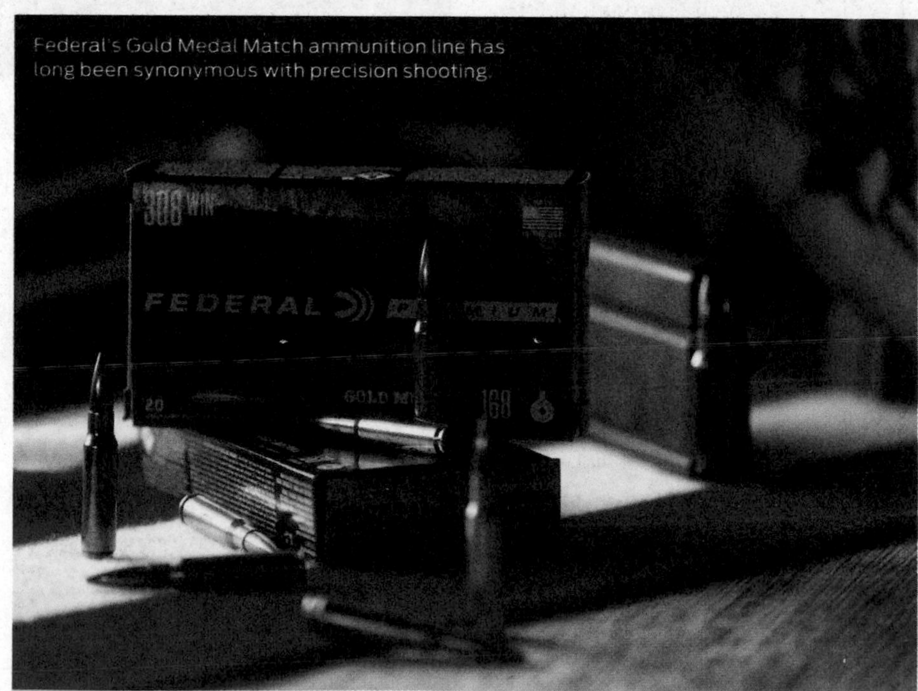

Federal's Gold Medal Match ammunition line has long been synonymous with precision shooting.

Griffin & Howe the Early Years

As one of America's premier firearms companies celebrates its centennial year, it's only fitting that we look back at its beginnings.

›RICK HACKER

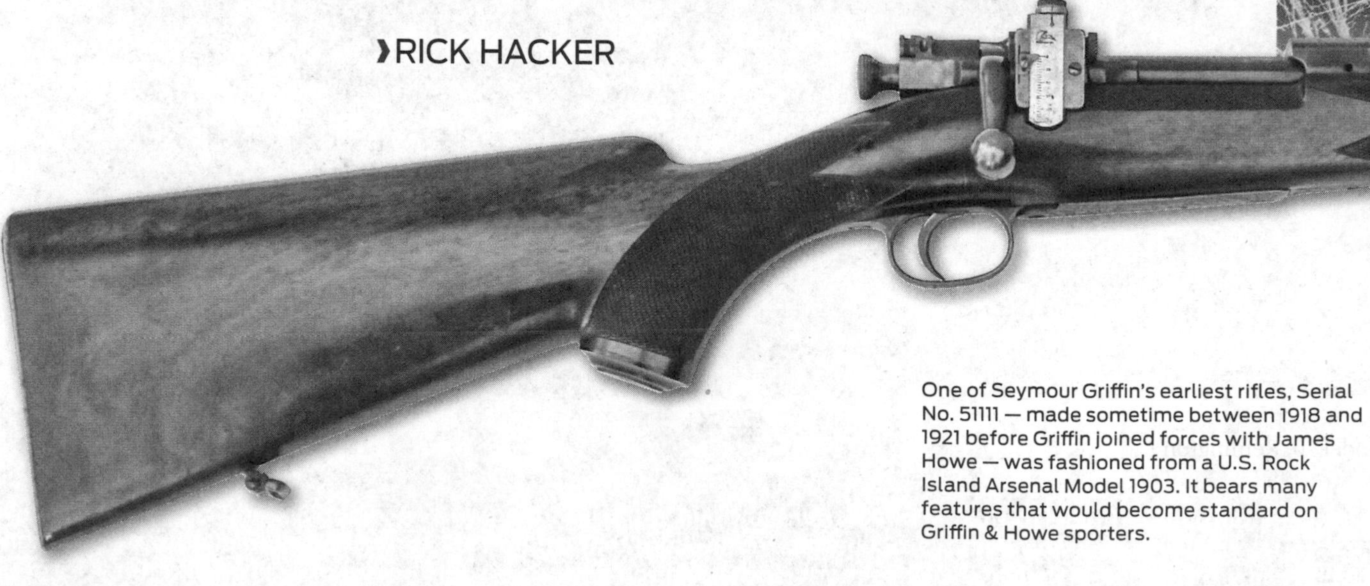

One of Seymour Griffin's earliest rifles, Serial No. 51111 — made sometime between 1918 and 1921 before Griffin joined forces with James Howe — was fashioned from a U.S. Rock Island Arsenal Model 1903. It bears many features that would become standard on Griffin & Howe sporters.

Ernest Hemingway takes careful aim with his cherished Griffin & Howe Springfield .30-06, G&H Serial #1956. He routinely used it without a scope to take numerous quarry on two East African safaris and on many hunts in Wyoming, Idaho and Montana. "Comes up naturally as pointing your finger," he once remarked, "... most beautifully made and finished and simple, practical gun I've ever seen." Sadly, it was stolen from his son's home in the 1970s and has become lost in obscurity. Photo: Griffin & Howe

Some of our classic 20th-century American bolt-action rifles were destined for immortality when they were first spotted in magazine ads, gun catalogs or dealer's gun racks. Of the many contenders, the Winchester Model 70, Remington Model 700 and Weatherby Mark V are three that immediately come to mind. But aside from the fact that all three of these examples are U.S.-made, they also have one more thing in common: they are, in essence, mass-produced factory-made guns. That is not a criticism, for they are relatively affordable and accessible to many appreciative riflemen. But as good as they are, they would still need additional individual human interaction to elevate them — and their prices — into the realm of truly custom sporting rifles.

However, as we entered the 20th century, and before the three rifles mentioned above existed, lever-action repeaters and single shots were the norm in hunting camps and on target ranges. That was also when the American shooting scene was transitioning from blackpowder to smokeless ammunition, and bolt-action rifles were becoming known. World War I significantly accelerated the exposure and appeal of the crank-handled rifle as American doughboys, accustomed to Winchesters, Marlins, Ballards, and Sharps, were issued the United

States Rifle, Caliber .30-06, Model 1903, or simply, the 1903 Springfield, as it was better known. Meanwhile, the Germans were firing back with the Gewehr 98, or the Model 1898 Mauser bolt-action rifle from the other side of the trenches.

Needless to say, after the Armistice on November 11, 1918, there was suddenly and not unexpectedly a tremendous surplus of 1903 Springfields and 1898 Mausers that flooded the civilian market and were eagerly snatched up at bargain prices by eager hunters and other assorted riflemen. But this also created an opportunity for more than a few enterprising gunsmiths to start experimenting with customizing these war surplus rifles for sporting use. Previously, a few firms, such as John Rigby & Company of London, used the standard Mauser 98 action to create stunning showpieces for wealthy sportsmen planning African and Asian safaris. But over on this side of the pond, the quarry was realistically focused on black bears, whitetails, and similar big game. And for these, the .30-06 Springfield was admirably suited.

This focus on hunting gave rise to several talented rifle makers, such as Charles Newton, R.F. Sedgley and Frank Hoffman. They all used WWI surplus Springfields and Mausers to create highly accurate and often very individualized customized sporters. Indeed, by the 1920s, this cottage industry had become an impressive part of the shooting scene.

One of the many talented individuals not immune to the newfound American trend was a young and talented New York cabinet maker and gun hobbyist named Seymour R. Griffin. Griffin was plying his cabinet-making trade out of Hotel Bretton Hall, a relatively new (at the time) apartment-hotel located at 2350 Broadway in Manhattan.

Back in 1910, Griffin had read Theodore Roosevelt's just-published book, *African Game Trails*, in which the popular ex-president vividly recounted his recent African safari. Within its pages, Roosevelt wrote glowingly about the sporterized 1903 Springfield rifle he and his son Kermit had used on the Dark Continent. This, of course, was well before the sporterization of military rifles had caught on. Nonetheless, captivated by Roosevelt's

This early photo shows the steadfast determination and pride that a dapper Seymour Griffin (1885–1966), undoubtedly exhibited as a gun maker. Photo: Griffin & Howe

Griffin & Howe still makes custom rifles. This Winchester Super Grade Model 70 in .458 Winchester Magnum was originally customized by the firm and carved in the style of the late Al Biesen at the request of a member of a prominent gun powder company. Note the company's trajectory readings engraved on the floorplate, also at the original owner's request.

praise of the rifle, Griffin immediately purchased one of the 1903 Springfields to sporterize it to mimic Roosevelt's gun. Of course, being a skilled woodworker, he selected a premium grade of Circassian walnut to carve an exquisitely shaped new stock for his Springfield. But its ownership was short-lived, for as soon as a friend saw Griffin's handiwork, he offered him a price for the rifle that the cabinet maker couldn't turn down.

Undaunted, Griffin immediately purchased another government Springfield and made a finely carved stock for it. But once again, he was subsequently offered an impressive sum of money for it, an amount that again he couldn't refuse. Eventually, by the time WWI ended, Seymour Griffin was augmenting his cabinet-making income by turning Springfield and Rock Island Arsenal surplus rifles into stylish sporters for a small but affluent and growing coterie of serious shooters. His well-finished guns were especially sought after due to their finely crafted inletting. They also featured Schnabel forends and Griffin's trademark — a sharply sloped cutaway in the stock by the bolt, ostensibly to aid ejection of spent cases but more of a decorative touch.

With a rifleman's sense of form and balance coupled with his shaping and checkering proficiency, Griffin continued using Circassian walnut for most of his stocks, further enhanced with a hand-rubbed linseed oil finish. He also had many of his guns re-barreled by Harry M. Pope, a close friend who also just happened to be one of the best barrel makers in the country, although the Griffin barrels were never marked as having been made by Pope. Other barrels were supplied by the equally famous Niedner Rifle Corporation. In addition, most of Griffin's rifles were expertly engraved on the floorplates and triggerguards by R.J. Kornbrath, the legendary master engraver who also embellished guns for companies such as Colt and Hoffman. Interestingly, Griffin did not mark his work until 1922, when he began stamping them — usually on the forward part of the floorplate or occasionally on the triggerguard or around the floorplate release — with a small "S.R. Griffin New

The author used his 1930's vintage Griffin & Howe .30-06 to drop this trophy Rambouillet-Navajo ram. Unfortunately, a Central California taxidermist never delivered the mount to the author.

Griffin & Howe's Scope Mount held a riflescope in place with just two levers, which could be pushed up for quick removal. Repositioning the scope and rotating the levers downward locked the scope in place with no loss of zero.

The typical slanted cut parallel to the bolt that Griffin put on all his bolt-action rifles. Before he teamed up with James Howe, this specimen was one of Seymour Griffin's first rifles.

The author's Griffin & Howe .30-06, built from an original Springfield '03 sometime during the 1930s, with gold-inlaid initials "CSC" that the original owner had specified for this rifle. It is as much at home in the field as in a display case.

York" banner.

One of Seymour Griffin's earliest rifles (as authenticated by Guy A. Bignell, a past Griffin & Howe President, Paul Chapman Griffin & Howe Vice President, Director of Gunsmithing, and Joe Prather, Griffin & Howe Chairman Emeritus), is a Rock Island Arsenal Model 1903 bearing the serial number 51111, which is in the author's collection. It has been estimated that Griffin sporterized this rifle sometime between 1918 and 1921.

"Some of these characteristics which Mr. Griffin incorporated into rifle #51111," the company stated in a letter referencing this particular rifle, "include 1) the ultra-fine hand checkering and checkering pattern itself, 2) precise inletting of the action to stock, 3) distinctive profile of the Griffin-carved stock, 4) downward angled plane cut into the stock parallel to the bolt ejection port, 5) Griffin Schnabel forend, and 6) cross-hatched steel butt plate with trapdoor…. These features set the tone for the Griffin & Howe rifles that were subsequently made by that firm." In addition, this rifle still retains its original Lyman No. 48 receiver sight.

Eventually, Griffin's sporterizing skills came to the attention of Major Townsend Whelen, a prolific and highly influential gun writer of the day and a noted firearms book author. Townsend began his career during the blackpowder era and was now the commanding officer at Frankford Arsenal and the director of research and development at Springfield Armory. Whelen was impressed with Griffin's skills and praised his workmanship to a far-ranging audience in nationally published articles. Writing in a 1921 issue of *Arms & The Man* (the forerunner to *American Rifleman*), Whelen stated, "…I think he [Griffin] is doing the best work of any of the gunsmiths." Since Griffin did not advertise and had become known only by word of mouth and referrals, he could not have hoped for a better champion than Whelen, whose articles

Since inception, a standard feature unless specified otherwise on Griffin & Howe rifles was a trapdoor buttplate to store additional cartridges. Photo: Griffin & Howe

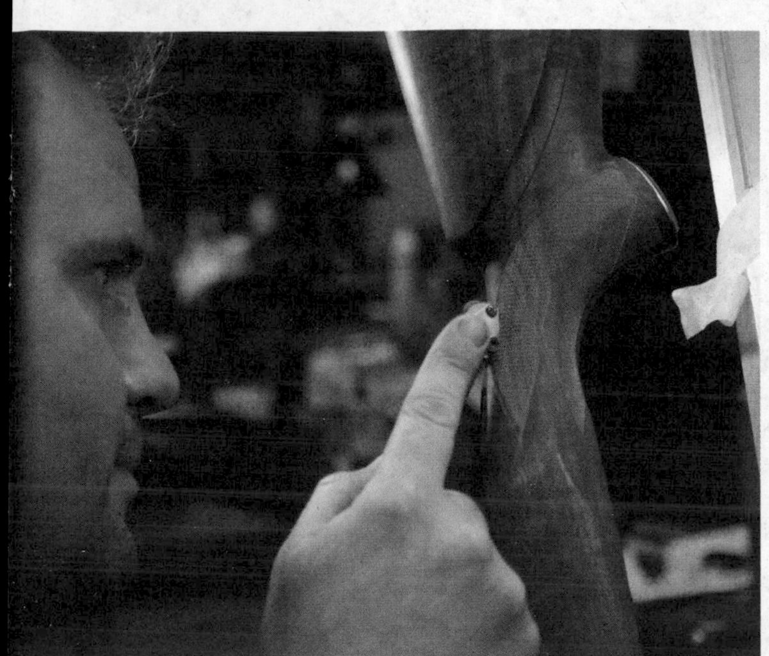

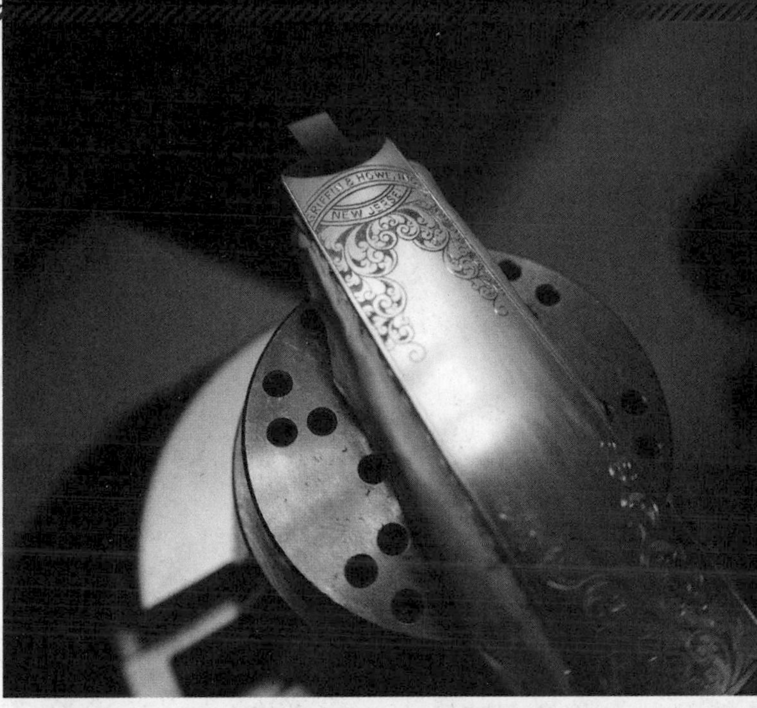

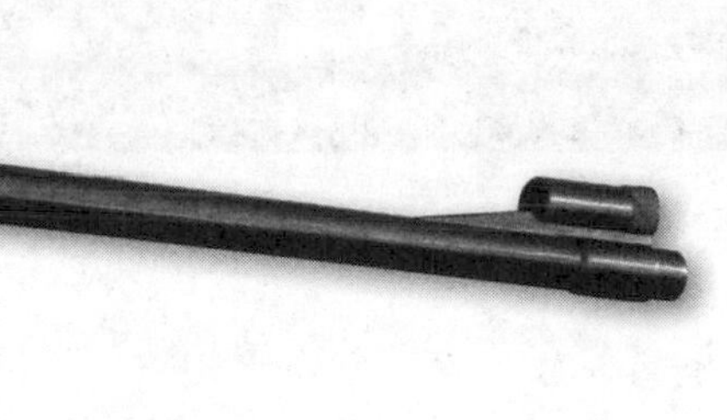

Above: In the current Griffin & Howe workshop, Dan Rossiter applies his hand-checkering skills to a rifle. Photos: Griffin & Howe

Top Right: The engraving skills of Chris Rossiter, the brother of G&H stock checkerer Dan Rossiter (both brothers are members of the American Custom Gunmakers Guild).

Right: Brett Jansen carefully inlets a bolt action into a G&H stock.

introduced the young riflesmith to even more shooters across the country. But Griffin's career was soon destined to take an even greater leap forward, again due to Whelen's involvement.

In 1921, as the commanding officer at Frankford Arsenal, Whelen encountered another talented individual, a somewhat irascible but skilled machine shop foreman from Pennsylvania named James Virgil Howe, whose specialty was metalworking. At the time, Howe headed up the armory's Small Arms Experimental Department, which also fell under Whelen's jurisdiction, and not coincidently, had developed a necked-up .30-06 cartridge he subsequently dubbed the .35 Whelen. This combination of flattery and skill undoubtedly prompted Whelen to suggest that Griffin and Howe combine their respective woodworking and metalworking talents to create a company. It could be called Griffin & Howe, which could turn out some of the finest bolt-action sporting rifles, based

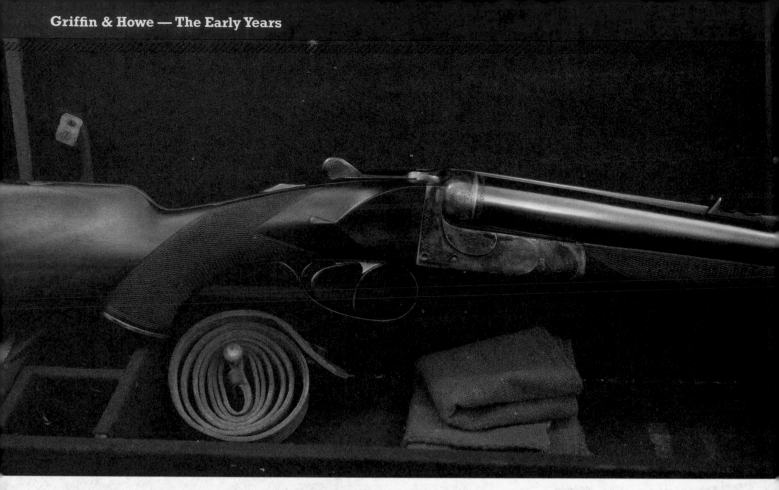

This exquisite 1928 boxlock double rifle in .470 Nitro Express was made in Belgium for Griffin & Howe and imported to its New York showroom for a customer. It came complete with a luggage-type traveling case, leather sling and accessories. In 2021, it was sold by Lock, Stock & Barrel online auctioneers (lsbauctions.com) for $12,024.99. Photo: Lock, Stock & Barrel

on Mauser 98 and Springfield 03 actions, that the world had ever seen.

Both Griffin and Howe agreed to this proposal. Whelen served as an overall advisor and was aided by additional startup capital provided by Griffin's investors James M. Holsworth and James L. Gerry. On June 1, 1923, the firm of Griffin & Howe opened for business, working out of a loft at 234 East 39th Street in New York City. However, this newfound partnership was short-lived because less than four months later, in September of that year, Howe quit the firm that bore his name and went to work for a competitor, the Hoffman Arms Company of Cleveland, Ohio.

"He only stayed long enough to get his name on the door," noted Paul Chapman, Griffin & Howe's current Vice President, Director of Gunsmithing.

No doubt, Whelen must have felt somewhat disappointed and perhaps even a little betrayed. But Griffin was not about to let this opportunity go to waste.

A carefully contoured Schnabel forend was standard on most early Griffin & Howe rifles.

Undaunted and keeping the Griffin & Howe name, he worked alone building custom rifles for the next seven years while assembling a small but highly skilled group of American and European gunmakers and engravers to assist him. Combining their various areas of expertise, they firmly established Griffin & Howe's now-iconic reputation for building some of the world's finest custom bolt-action sporting rifles in a relatively short time. Superbly grained walnut stocks, fine line checkering, folding leaf express sights, intricate engraving, and gold, silver, and platinum inlaid motifs, initials and coats of arm became the norm.

Adding to this distinction, in 1927, Griffin & Howe developed and patented an ingenious detachable scope side mount, which the company subsequently improved upon in 1931. By simply flipping up two levers, the scope could be quickly lifted off the rifle for transportation or transition to the open sights. By repositioning the scope and rotating the levers back down, the scope would be locked in place, with absolutely no zero loss. This scope mount was later adapted by Griffin & Howe for M1 sniper rifles during World War II and, in fact, is still in the line today.

With its reputation firmly established, owning a Griffin & Howe rifle became *de rigueur* for anyone who wanted the best bolt-action rifle and could afford the price. That lofty group encompassed some of the most newsworthy celebrities of the day and some of Hollywood's biggest stars. In fact, one of Griffin & Howe's most ardent fans was two-time Academy Award winner Gary Cooper, a dedicated hunter and gun collector. Cooper often took his personal guns to various outdoor movie sets to engage in a bit of target practice between scenes (one of his Griffin & Howe rifles briefly appears in his 1935 motion picture, "The Lives of a Bengal Lancer"). Cooper owned at least two Griffin & Howe rifles that we know of. One of these, a .30-06 Springfield with a silver oval on the underside of the stock and marked with the initials "GC," was originally a .220 Swift but was converted by Griffin & Howe to .30-06. As described by Rock Island Auction Company (rockislandauction.com) in its catalog listing this rifle:

"Of important note, the original caliber marking on the left side of the barrel at the breech was milled off, likely by Griffin & Howe, and replaced with a '.30-06' caliber marking on a flat surface; indicating the rechambering of the heavy barrel from its original .220 Swift chambering. Top of the barrel marked 'No. 1476 GRIFFIN & HOWE INC. NEW YORK.' Beaded blade front sight. Matted receiver ring. Fitted with a Griffin & Howe left side mount and Zeiss scope, right side mounted Lyman receiver sight base currently fitted with a blue Williams ladder with no peep for scope clearance, jeweled bolt and follower, and knurled bolt handle. Deluxe checkered shadow line cheekpiece stock with horn forend cap, blue steel grip cap, checkered and border engraved steel buttplate with trap, containing the original ladder with peep for the Lyman rear sight."

On September 11, 2021, Rock Island Auction's final hammer price for this rifle was $21,850. On that same date, Rock Island auctioned off Cooper's Zeiss-scoped .22 Hornet rifle that was also custom-built for him by Griffin & Howe, complete with a similar silver oval on the underside of the stock inscribed with the initials "GC." Estimated to bring $9,000 to $14,000, it sold for a whopping $34,500. To quote from the Rock Island Auction catalog:

"In between acting, Cooper spent a lot of his free time tinkering with rifles in his gun room to prepare for his next hunt. He went on multiple safaris in Africa in which he was credited with over sixty big game kills, including a rhinoceros, two lions, and various antelopes. His safari experiences in Africa profoundly influenced Cooper and intensified his love of the wilderness. Ernest Hemingway, the famous American novelist and sportsman, became Cooper's closest friend. Pg. 171 of the book 'Gary Cooper American Hero' by Jeff Meyers states, 'Their twenty-year friendship, sustained by Cooper's amiable temperament, was unusual for Hemingway, who became impatient with old friends and tended to break with them. For Cooper, Hemingway had a rare combination of qualities. Quite outside the world of Hollywood, he was an intel-

Part of the skilled craftsmen that Seymour Griffin assembled to build some of the finest and most elegant hunting rifles the world had ever seen. This photo dates from the late 1920s or early '30s.

The old Griffin & Howe showroom in New York, during the late 1920s or early '30s. Photos: Griffin & Howe

ligent man who understood him and could talk about personal matters.' Pg. 173 states, 'Hemingway coveted Cooper's favorite rifle, a .22 Hornet with a German telescopic sight, and asked: 'Coop, if you die before I do, are you going to will me that Hornet?' Cooper promised to do so, and then said: 'Hell, I might just decide to give it to you now so I can watch you enjoy it.'"

Obviously, that probably never happened. But then, Hemingway had his own Griffin & Howe, a much-favored .30-06 built on a match-grade Springfield-barreled action acquired for him by Whelen. The rifle came with a scope, but Hemingway removed it, preferring open sights. Nonetheless, "Papa" used this rifle on numerous western hunts and two African safaris, making an estimated 300-yard shot on a Rhino with the rifle's open sights. Sadly, this rifle has been lost to obscurity, as it was stolen from the family well after Hemingway's death. Here is the story of Hemingway's missing Griffin & Howe rifle, as relayed by Guy Bignell, former Griffin & Howe President:

"In 1929, when the young Ernest Hemingway was ready for his first big-game rifle, Col. Townsend Whelen himself picked out a National Match-quality Springfield barreled action and shipped it to Manhattan, where Seymour Griffin paid $30 for it and finished it to Hemingway's specifications in .30-06 caliber. Bearing G&H Serial No. 956, it did tremendous work in the Rocky Mountains and on two long safaris in East Africa, taking several Cape Buffalo amongst other species. By the late 1970s, it had found its way to Ernesto's son Patrick Hemingway's home in Montana. Sadly it was stolen from here, it is believed by a gang of American/Irish Pro IRA supporters, who shipped it to Ireland where it probably resides today without anyone knowing its provenance, or if captured, destroyed by the British Army or Constabulary."

As Griffin & Howe's fame spread, it eventually began selling its own brand of ammunition, in addition to established commercial offerings. More than 14 different chamberings were produced (although customers could have any caliber they desired), including propriety cartridges such as the .350 G&H Magnum (a necked-down .375 H&H), Col. Whelen's .400 Whelen and of course, the .35 Whelen.

Ironically, for all its gun-making skills and reputation, the late Michael Petrov, author of *Custom Gunmakers of the 20th Century*, estimated that Griffin & Howe produced fewer than two-thousand rifles between 1923 and World War II, which effectively put the firm's gun-making on hold. Although born during the affluent Roaring 20s, the stock market crash of 1929 and the Great Depression hit G&H especially hard, as its rifles were scarcely fit for the shooter on a budget. In 1930,

Seymour Griffin explored importing fine British shotguns to expand the inventory and appeal to smoothbore aficionados to bolster income.

Still, Griffin must have given a sigh of relief when, that same year, he was approached by James S. Cobb, president of the well-known sporting goods outfitter Abercrombie & Fitch, with an offer to assimilate Griffin & Howe into the more secure A&F stronghold. And thus, the early years' chapter of Griffin & Howe ended. It moved its headquarters to 202 E. 44th Street in New York City two years later. There it maintained gunsmithing services and continued building and customizing rifles for a distinguished clientele that included Bing Crosby, Clark Gable, Jack O'Connor, and Robert Ruark, to name but a few of the many proud owners of its guns.

When Abercrombie & Fitch liquidated in 1976, an entrepreneur and longtime employee named Bill Ward purchased Griffin & Howe. When Ward overexpanded in 1986, the firm was acquired by businessman-sportsman Joe Prather and another investor, and its headquarters were relocated to Bernardsville, New Jersey. In 1999, the company opened a second location in Greenwich, Connecticut, and, in 2003, a new showroom and outfitting location opened in Andover, New Jersey, alongside its shooting school. Prather continued to serve as president until he retired and became Chairman Emeritus. He was succeeded in March 2007 by Guy A. Bignell, who had been associated with the company since 1993. Bignell, who remains with Griffin & Howe as its Fine Sporting Arms Specialist, stepped down as CEO on June 1, 2017, and handed the reins of G&H president and CEO to another longtime employee, Steve Polanish. The latter is now the sixth president in Griffin & Howe's history, as the company enters its centennial year in 2023 with additional services, special commemorative rifles and a new logo.

Today, to quote from Griffin & Howe's website, "Griffin & Howe still builds a limited number of America's finest custom rifles the way we have for the past century. We incorporate the classic shape and proportion of the European walnut stock with a cheek piece and a hand rubbed oil finish, the Griffin & Howe quarter rib with standing bar and folding leaves, the Lyman 48 sight and all other Griffin & Howe features that have been the hallmark of the company from the very beginning.

"We also offer an extensive line of sporting shotguns, rifles and double rifles, built to our specifications by fine European makers, as well as being the official agents and U.S. representatives for James Purdey & Sons, Boss & Co, Lebeau Courally, David McKay Brown, Verney Carron, Fabbri, Blaser, Krieghoff, B. Rizzini, Beretta, Zoli, and Perazzi, to name a few of many others.

"We continue to expand, creating new products and enhancing our services, to serve our growing customer base. Our Griffin & Howe Highlander, All American and custom sporter rifles, plus our shooting academy and gunsmithing department are testament to Griffin and Howe's commitment to our clients."

Indeed, as it begins its second century on June 1, 2023, Griffin & Howe — its products and history — remain steadfast examples of constant and unwavering dedication to the best rifles and shotguns that an American shooter can aspire to own. GD

Gary Cooper with a "bobkitty," as he called this January 1948 winter kill bobcat, which he dispatched near Sun Valley, Idaho using his Griffin & Howe .30-06. The rifle had been converted by G&H for Cooper in 1936 from an original .220 Swift. Photo: Rock Island Auction Company

Scattergun Adventures

The author draws a bead on an airborne rooster with the Benelli 20-gauge Ultra Light.

I've always taken advantage of opportunities that put a shotgun in my hands.

JOE COOGAN

Long before I hunted with a rifle, I was an enthusiastic and dedicated shotgunner. My fascination with shotguns began early, which I'm sure contributed significantly to my enjoyment of outdoor pursuits. While still too young to shoot, I remember watching my father swing his big Winchester Model 12 at doves in Texas. It was pure delight to run out and retrieve the birds that fell to its commanding 12-gauge boom. Back then, Dad's Poly-Choked Model 12 did it all, no matter the bird or circumstance.

Remembering the excitement of my first duck hunt with Dad pitching out decoys in the headlights of the family Chevy, I was still not yet old enough to handle a shotgun. Back in the blind, I watched Dad place a red, paper-hull shotshell in the Model 12 receiver and then heard that wonderful metallic *chink* as he slid the forend forward, chambering the round and then pushing two more shells into the tubular magazine.

Coogan with the Franchi Veloce.

Back in the '60s, the author hunted Florida quail with his cousin, Don Corwin, who used a Browning A-5 20 gauge, while the author carried a Winchester M12, also 20 gauge.

In 1967, the author and Cocoa Beach neighborhood friends (from left; Ron Rubino, Mike Brennan, the author, Ken Brennan and Mike Wolfe) collected their limits of ducks on the Florida opener that traditionally starts on the Saturday before Thanksgiving.

The author used his Model 12 pump gun and Winchester Western's Mark 5 Super Speed loads to collect a bag of black-faced sandgrouse.

At first light, we were hunkered down, watching ducks winging across an orange dawn sky. I held my breath at their cup-winged approach to the decoys, and when they banked overhead, Dad raised up and fired twice — folding a pair that splashed down among the dekes. I inhaled that wonderful smell from the fired hulls, forever a part of the memory of those days. I could only dream of the day when I, too, would shoulder a shotgun.

WINCHESTER'S MODEL 12 & MODEL 42

It was Christmas 1962 when I received the greatest gift I could ever imagine — a beautiful little Winchester Model 42, .410-gauge shotgun. We lived in Cocoa Beach, Florida, then, and I learned to handle and shoot the little pump gun safely during the remainder of that duck season. The first duck I dropped with it was a colorful green-winged teal drake, a wall mount of which was part of a most memorable Christmas gift. There have been countless teal since taken with various shotguns, but none stand out in my memory like that first one brought down with the slim Model 42.

I soon grew into a Model 12 20 gauge, and by the time I was in high school, I was shooting the big "Twelve." Our backyard was the Banana River, a thriving saltwater estuary full of fish and birdlife that provided a venue for incomparable activities and recreation. My friends and I cruised the waters in outboard skiffs and runabouts like most kids race around their neighborhoods on bicycles. We enjoyed shooting doves after school during the cooler months, while the weekends were devoted to hunting ducks amongst a maze of mangrove islands that hosted flocks of wintering waterfowl. Those halcyon days established duck hunting as one of my life's great passions.

Winchester's Model 12 was, and still is, a special gun for me with a long history and faithful following. Winchester introduced the hammerless slide-action shotgun in 1912, which superseded the successful Model 1897, a John Moses Browning-designed pump gun with an external hammer. The Model 1912 was designed by Winchester engineer T.C. Johnson, who developed a slide-action hammerless shotgun for Winchester in 1907. The Model 1912 was initially introduced in 20 gauge, with 12- and 16-gauge models becoming available in late 1913

As Benelli USA's marketing manager, the author traveled to many hunt destinations to field-test the various shotgun brands. The author and Marc Pierce of Warm Springs Productions enjoy a successful mallard hunt in Montana with Benelli's Super Black Eagle II semi-auto shotgun.

and were included in the 1914 catalog.

According to George Madis in his book, *The Winchester Model Twelve*, twenty-nine months of intensive labor from the time of the production order were required before the first Model 1912 came off the line. "Dies, jigs, fixtures, gauges and all of the hundreds of special tools had to be made. Machines had to be purchased or moved and converted to new uses for the new model. Many small parts, which could have been made from standard steel stock, were forged, trimmed, machined and polished instead of being made in a less expensive manner. Each part was inspected after each operation. According to T.C. Johnson, there were 2,739 separate inspections performed on each Model 1912 before the final proof testing. This resulted in much higher quality, but also raised the cost of manufacture."

As the features editor for *Petersen's Hunting* magazine in 1995, the author field-tested Beretta's gas-operated AL390 Silver Mallard and Federal's new Tungsten load during a duck and dove hunt in Argentina. Ducks taken during the hunt included Fulvous tree ducks, rosy-billed pochards and silver teal.

The newly-introduced Model 1912, a 20 gauge, sold for $24.

In 1919, the barrel designation changed from "Mod. 1912" to "Model 12." By the time production ended in May 1964, more than 2 million Model 12s had been made. They were still available by special order from Winchester's Custom Shop from 1964 until 1972 and from 1976 to 1980. The Model 12's replacement was the Model 1200, which, within a few years, transitioned to the Model 1300, which is no longer made. The last Model 12 — serial number 2026721 — was reached in 1980, making the Winchester Model 12 the all-time, longest-selling pump action in shotgun history.

The Model 42, made specifically for the .410 shotshell, was introduced in 1933. Always considered the most elegant of the Winchester slide actions,

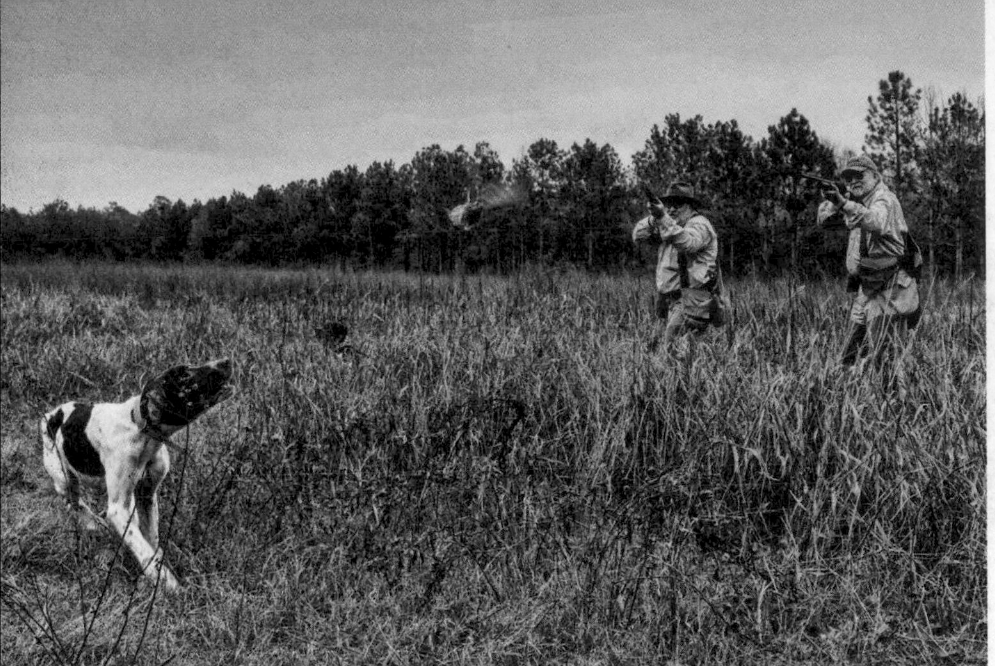

Outdoor writer Bryce Towsley (left) and the author during a quail hunt in South Georgia. Towsley used a Franchi over & under 20-gauge gun while the author shouldered a 20-gauge Franchi semi-auto.

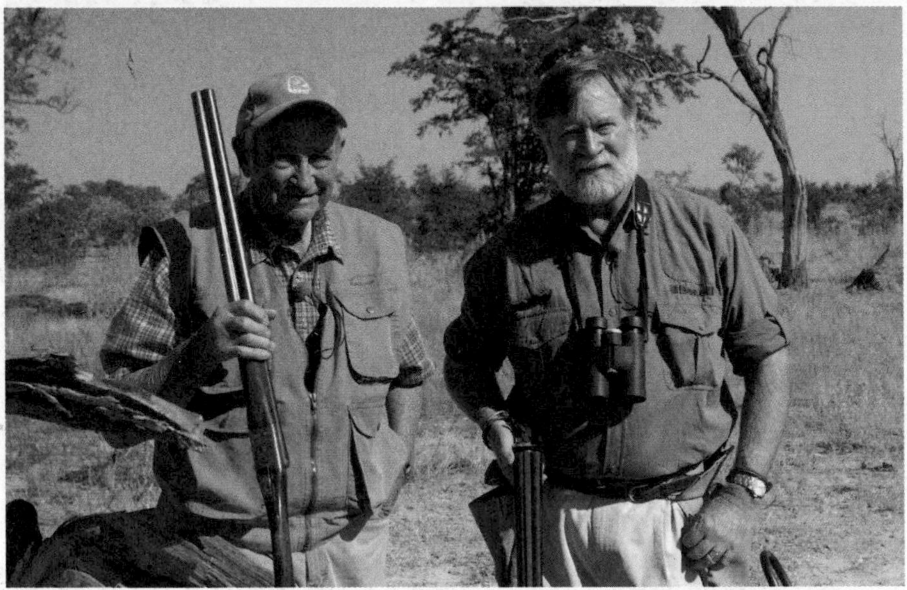

Harry Selby (left) holds a double-barrel 12-gauge Webley & Scott shotgun given to him by Robert Ruark, but Selby's favorite shotgun was a Browning Superposed 20 gauge.

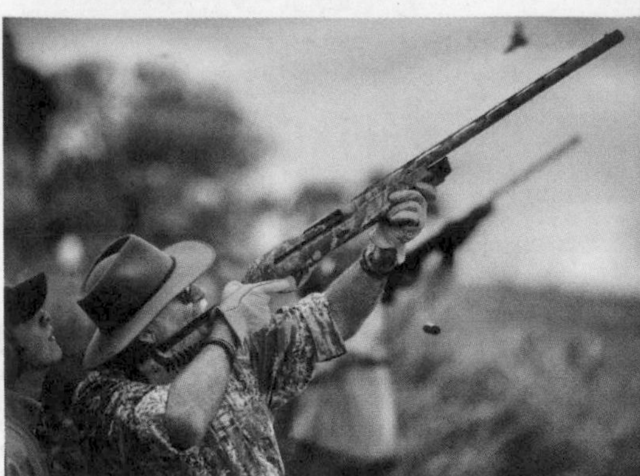

Benelli's introduction of the Vinci included a field test, which was more like a torture test on doves in Cordoba, Argentina. At the end of three days of non-stop shooting, the consensus of six writers all agreed that the Vinci was a pleasure to shoot with no faults experienced.

the Model 42 outwardly appears to be a scaled-down version of the Model 12. Still, it's distinctly different and designed to accommodate the smaller cartridge. The Model 42 was offered in five different configurations, with nearly 160,000 Model 42s built through 1963, when production ended.

I completed a modest but personally pleasing collection of Model 12s with the addition of a 1950s-vintage 16-gauge Model 12. The guns are just as attractive as they ever were and perform reliably, even though their duck blind days are over. But the little Model 42 is still one of my favorites, providing a lot of challenges with little margin for error when tackling doves riding a tailwind or quail behind dogs or close-in greenheads in flooded timber.

WINCHESTER MODEL 101

In 1964, Dad purchased a Winchester Model 101 12 gauge shortly after Winchester introduced the over/under as competition for Browning's Superposed. At the time, we lived in Okinawa, Japan, where the cost of a field grade Model 101 with 26-inch barrels and fixed chokes was around $125 at the Navy Base Exchange.

Back then, skeet and trap ranges located on Okinawa's U.S. military bases charged $1 for a round of skeet, with another $2 covering the cost of a box of Winchester AA target loads. Given those prices, along with liberal range hours, trap and skeet were very popular sports on the island. I shot skeet with both the Model 12 and Model 101 but found the pump action more to my liking and always shot better scores.

Model 101s were made in Japan by Olin Kodensha from 1963 through 1987 and were available in 12, 20 and 28 gauges. Winchester offered the Model 101 in several configurations, including Field Grade, Pigeon Grade and Diamond Grade. Higher grades, such as the Pigeon Grade, were well made and worth the money. Today, Winchester Model 101s are made by FN in Belgium and come with choke tubes and a low-profile receiver.

Back in Florida, the cost of skeet shooting was dramatically higher than it had been overseas, so that, combined with limited range times, my shotgunning refocused on nearby dove fields and duck marshes. After graduation from high school, the Model 12 accompanied me to college, where I kept it in my dorm room

Benelli's Legacy Model is a semi-auto shotgun with a finely figured walnut stock offered in 20 and 28 gauge. The Legacy is a lightweight semi-auto, an especially well-suited upland gun for flushing birds like quail and pheasant.

closet for the dove and quail hunting opportunities available in central Florida.

A RARE FIND

When my family moved to Kenya in the late '60s, the venerable Model 12 was among the guns we took to Africa. To keep guns in Kenya required having a police-inspected, lockable gun safe, which had to be permanently attached to a wall with heavy-duty lag screws. During Kenya's Mau Mau uprising in the early 1950s, many terrorists armed themselves with guns stolen from relaxed households where firearms were unlocked. When it was realized how easily the Mau Mau had obtained stolen guns, a new law made it a serious offense to lose one to theft, punishable with jail time.

A Benelli M2 semi-auto 20 gauge stoked with Federal's Premium High Density load was just the ticket for dropping a pair of blue-winged teal on a Florida duck hunt for the Benelli On Assignment TV show.

My father located a gun safe for sale in Mombasa that came with a fascinating story. An elderly Goan lady, Mrs. Robin Pereira, then in her late 80s, owned the gun safe for which she had no further need. The sale would take effect as long as whoever bought the safe would also purchase the single firearm still residing in it. Dad was delighted to discover the gun was a Westley Richards .410 double-barrel shotgun, and his only question to Mrs. Pereira was, how much? He happily paid her whatever price she asked.

Mrs. Pereira's story was fascinating. She was born in Goa, a state in western India with coastlines stretching along the Arabian Sea and a long history as a Portuguese colony until 1961. She was a young girl in the late 1800s when her family arranged with the Pereira family of Mombasa for her to marry their son, Robin, who was somewhat older than she. Arrangements were finalized, and she traveled to Mombasa by steamship, arriving there as a child bride-to-be — only then laying eyes on her future husband for the first time.

The Uganda Railway was completed in 1901, and she remembered train trips between Mombasa and Nairobi when passengers carried their sporting firearms aboard. When game or birds of interest were encountered within sight of the train, the engineer would stop the train upon request, and willing passengers would jump off to pursue

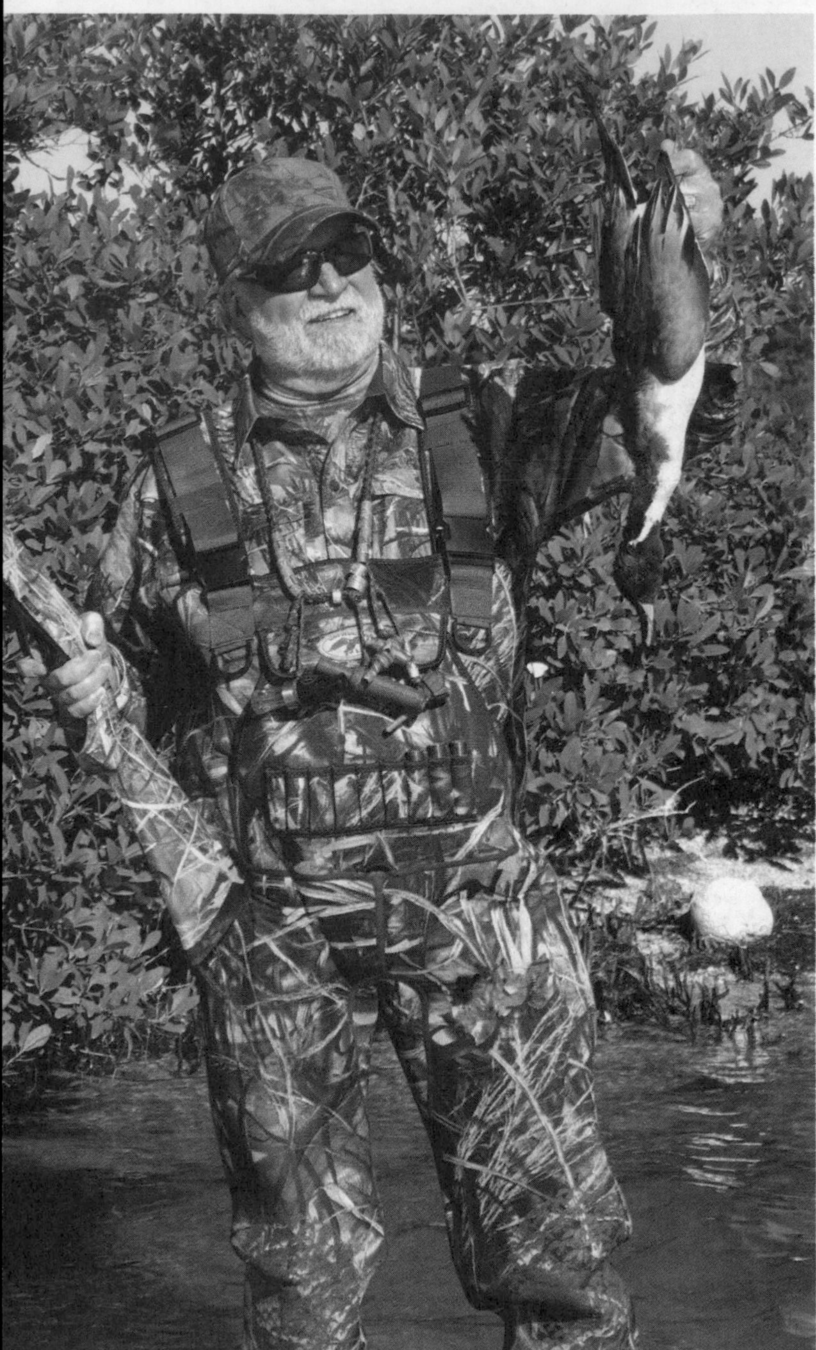

The author admires a "bull sprig" pintail he bagged during a Texas coastal duck hunt with a Realtree camo-patterned Franchi Affinity in 12 gauge.

whatever quarry had been spotted. She told us that her husband particularly enjoyed shooting guinea fowl with the little Westley Richards .410. During his occasional train trips, he always collected several guineas. In addition to enjoying the challenge of sprinting after them for the sporting shots they offered, he was particularly fond of guinea fowl curry.

Mrs. Pereira offered to come over to our house and prepare a proper curry if we would provide the birds. We took her up on that offer and the authentic curry that Mrs. Pereira prepared, complete with homemade chapatis, fresh-fried papadums, all the condiments and topped with mango chutney and desiccated coconut, was one of the best I've ever tasted.

AFRICAN GAME BIRDS

While big game captured most hunters' attention in Kenya's hunting blocks, the variety and numbers of game birds were also impressive. Pitching camp in the heart of big game country meant sharing the bush and plains with herds of elephant, buffalo, wildebeest, zebra and giraffe, not to mention the myriad of game birds. These include several doves, pigeons, sandgrouse, francolin, guinea fowl, spurfowl, bustards, ducks, and geese.

Standing near a waterhole at dawn was as much a visual treat as it was a shooting experience. Doves flocking to water by the hundreds twisted, swerved and darted to fill the sky. As the dove swarm tapered off an hour or so later, a sound as delicate as the tinkle of wine glasses heralded the arrival of sandgrouse. Like a choreographed ballet, flocks of sandgrouse maneuvered with the precision of baitfish dodging a barracuda. On cupped wings, they dropped like stones to the water's edge, and it didn't take long to collect a half-dozen or so birds necessary for preparing a delicious grilled sandgrouse dinner that evening.

Ground birds such as spurfowl, francolin and guinea fowl were like chickens on the road, running and flushing ahead of the Land Rover as we drove along. We were fortunate to have the distinctly unique vulturine guineas, named for their vulture-looking heads, occurring in several areas we hunted. When only their heads and necks were visible, they resembled a herd of snakes racing through knee-high grass. The helmeted guinea fowl, named for the bony casques on top of their heads, were commonly found throughout Masailand, Tanzania. Both species weigh as much as three pounds or more.

With good cover, we enjoyed some fast-paced walkup shooting punctuated by explosive flushes with lots of attendant excitement and action. When the birds launched themselves, the air whistled with wing beats as they fought for altitude. With luck, a couple of quick shots might connect, and by the time a bird or two thumped to the ground, no more than a few frantic seconds had passed. In the middle of the excitement, the possibility of stumbling into a lion, elephant or buffalo in thick bush necessitated having a wingman nearby carrying a heavy rifle and keeping a sharp eye out.

BERETTA AL390 SILVER MALLARD

Over the years, I've enjoyed many bird

The Westley Richards "Federal" Model

Westley Richards, one of England's oldest traditional gunmakers, is still going strong today. Among the guns it built back in the 1920s was a basic, plain double-barrel shotgun with few embellishments listed as the "Federal" model. The gun was intended for export to the colonies, and our Westley Richards .410 bore was one such model. On June 4, 1923, it was sold to Davis & Soper LTD, London, export merchants for Africa and countries of the Middle and the Far East, and exported to Kenya gun dealers either in Nairobi or Mombasa.

This Westley Richards "Federal" model .410-bore shotgun is nearly 100 years old. The gun was produced during the 1920s, designed for the colonies as a basic double barrel with few embellishments.

According to the Westley Richards' factory ledger, the manufacture of our .410 was noted: ".410 Double 27" Steel, Left Choke, A & D, No Projection, Straight Hand, Snap Forend." This translates to the gun being of .410 bore with 27-inch steel barrels, a choked left barrel, a non-ejector Anson & Deeley box-lock action with a straight-grip stock and a snap-on forend.

Several decades spent in Mombasa's hot, humid coastal environment extracted a toll on the little gun. The metalwork was rust-pitted, and the stock was thoroughly oil-soaked from years of combating the humidity with copious amounts of gun oil, causing it to appear almost pitch black in color.

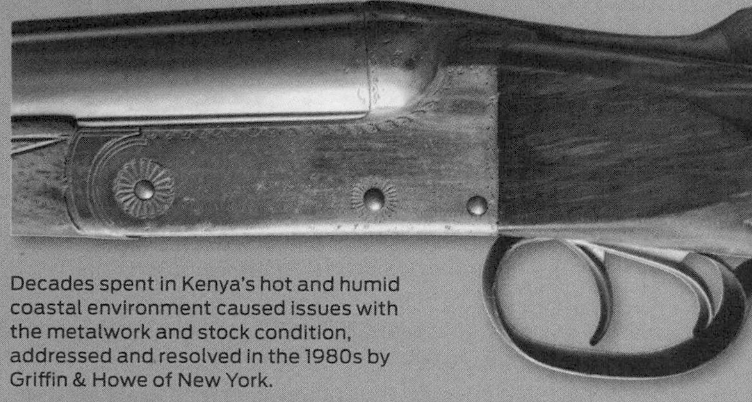

Decades spent in Kenya's hot and humid coastal environment caused issues with the metalwork and stock condition, addressed and resolved in the 1980s by Griffin & Howe of New York.

As we were allowed to keep only one shotgun in Kenya, we shipped the .410 back to the States. Years later, with quail in mind, I handed the gun over to Bill Ward of Griffin & Howe in New York to address and rectify the metal and stock issues. G&H did what it could for the metalwork and then, using heat, slowly and painstakingly leeched as much oil from the wood as possible. Eventually, the grain of walnut appeared on the stock, and with fresh bluing on the metal, the gun was deemed field-ready. I was pleased to introduce it to some classic quail hunts over dogs in northern Florida, South Georgia and Texas. Shooting the little .410 was like "pointing your finger" at birds that dropped to the shot with surprising regularity.

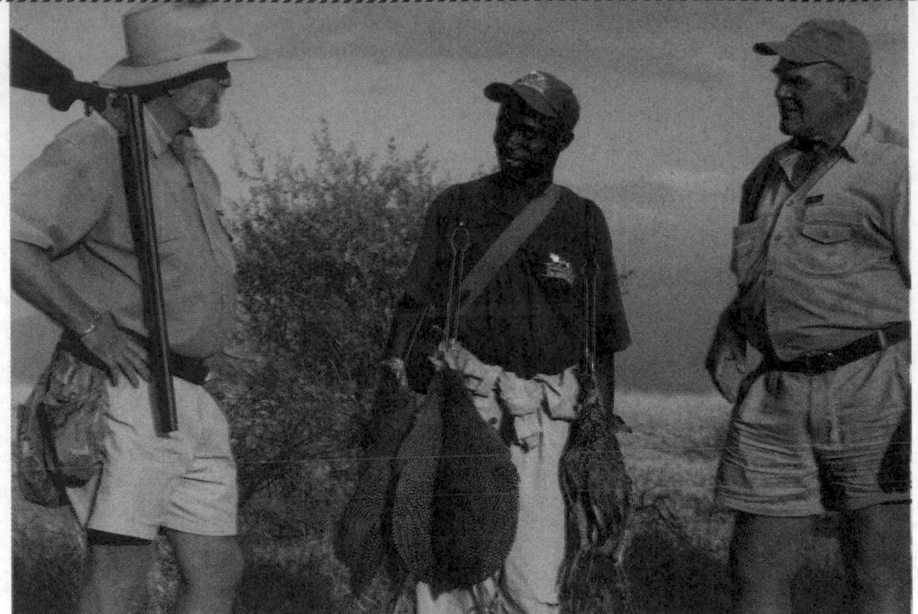

Following a successful walkup for red-necked spurfowl and helmeted guinea fowl taken in Masailand, Tanzania, with a Franchi Veloce Grade II over & under, the author (left) speaks with the tracker, Sebo (center) and Soren Lindstrom.

The author holds up a vulturine guinea fowl he bagged with a Franchi Instinct, a new-model 20-gauge over & under. During a 2011 bird shoot in Kenya, the hunt took place to introduce and field test Franchi's new line of over/under and semi-auto shotguns with a group of six outdoor writers.

shoots using semi-autos, such as Benelli's inertia-driven shotguns and Beretta's gas-operated models. (The only two brands of shotguns tough enough to hold up to the relentless stress of 1,000-round days in Cordoba, Argentina, the Dove Shooting Capital of the World.)

I first hunted in Argentina in 1997 as part of a group of shooters field-testing Federal's then-new Tungsten/Iron load on Argentine waterfowl — mostly rosy-billed pochards, yellow-billed pintails, Brazilian ducks, Fulvous and black-bellied whistling ducks along with various types of teal. I was very impressed when I shot Beretta's AL390 Silver Mallard 12 gauge for that hunt. After three days of spectacular duck shooting without a hiccup from either gun or ammo, we relocated to Cordoba. During three more days of non-stop shooting, I tried to find a chink in the AL390's armor but only succeeded in wearing myself out. I was swayed enough by the gun's performance to send Beretta a check and put the AL390 in my gun rack upon arriving in the States. The AL390 still handles and shoots like a new gun with many duck seasons behind it.

Introduced sometime around 1990, Beretta's 390 series of semi-auto shotguns featured a breakthrough in gas-system recoil technology that made shooting any load reliable and pleasant. That was possible through a self-regulating pressure valve, which was an improvement over the proven Beretta gas system of the Model 303, a design that had been state-of-the-art. It featured a single moving part, a stainless steel piston that involved no other parts that could break, jam or wear out.

The AL390 system took this a step further with a self-compensating gas system, incorporating a unique self-regulating valve that ensured there would always be sufficient pressure to drive the action. The valve utilizes cylinder-contained expanding gases to drive the piston and action but remains closed when light field and target loads are fired. Excess gases partly open the valve with medium to heavy loads, allowing enough gas pressure to drive the piston. Any excess pressure is expelled downward, away from the barrel — and the shooter. Magnum loads open the valve fully, which rapidly expels the excess gases, resulting in less wear and tear on the shotgun and the shooter.

BENELLI ON ASSIGNMENT

In 2006, I joined Benelli USA, which was charged with marketing and sales responsibilities for not only the flagship brand, Benelli, but also the guns of Franchi, Stoeger and Uberti. One of my responsibilities as the Brand Marketing Manager was hosting the Benelli On Assignment (BOA) TV show. The show featured writers from national publications on assignment, field testing the various brands and guns of Benelli USA during destination hunts. Each episode aimed to showcase a specific firearm and show how the writer obtained the material and details they needed for photographing and writing an objective article.

This Browning Superposed 20-gauge over/under shotgun, originally belonging to Harry Selby, was passed on to the author. In keeping with Selby's wishes, the author "exercises" this special Superposed wherever doves, quail or pheasants concentrate from Kentucky to Texas to Florida.

Near the end of the *BOA* series, we featured the launch of a new line of Franchi shotguns in Kenya, East Africa, where I hunted as a teenager. Although Kenya had banned big game hunting in 1977, bird shooting, in fact, had remained open. A more fascinating or exciting place for a shotgun introduction would be hard to find.

We gathered an experienced group of writers to spend 10 days in the Kenya bush with guns in hand and report the results. Kenya proved an ideal setting to test Franchi's latest shotguns by offering an unusual combination of classic sporting history, demanding conditions, and challenging shooting. Those included a new semi-auto called the Affinity, utilizing an inertia-driven action, and an over & under called the Instinct, designed along classical lines with improved ergonomics. Both guns were offered in 12- and 20-gauge configurations.

Besides talcum powder-like dust, the African bush is full of gun-scratching rocks and stock-grabbing thorns that will quickly mar a fine shotgun. In addition, climbing in and out of vehicles several times a day and shooting various shotshell loads also takes a toll on guns. Given the rugged conditions and constant shooting, the group agreed that the safari-tested field guns proved dependable and well-balanced, surpassing everyone's expectations.

Jeff Johnston, Brand Editor, *Field*

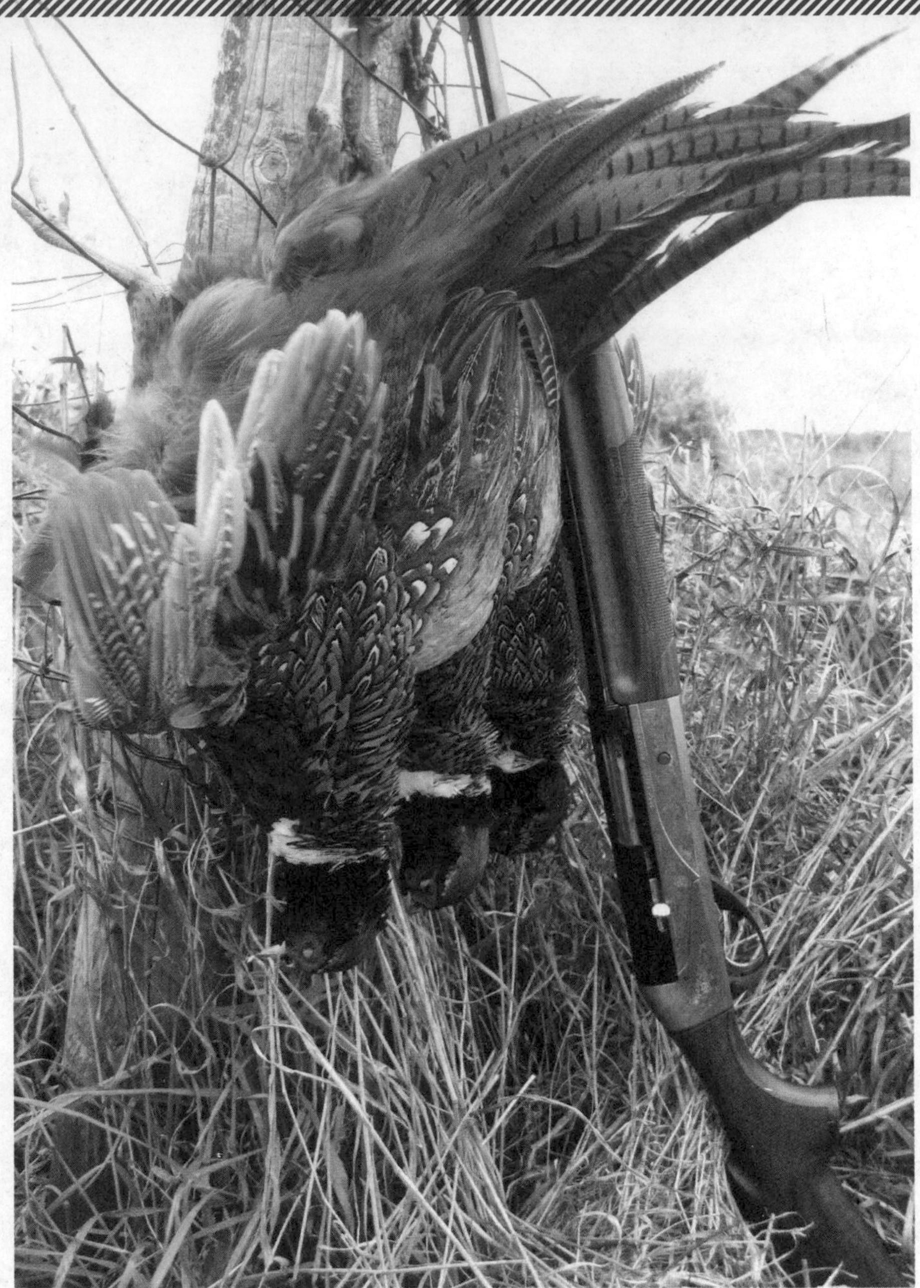
The Benelli Legacy 28 gauge.

Ethos, summed up his experience.

"Is halfway around the world a long way to go for a few birds, you ask? Where else can you run down vulturine guinea fowl, shoot waves of sandgrouse in the shadow of Mount Kilimanjaro, hunt doves near the treacherous Galana River with Joe Coogan in the exact same place he took his first elephant, stand on the Tsavo railway bridge where two man-eating lions stymied the British Empire, and wrestle Masai warriors after a glorious day of hunting crested francolin and yellow-necked spurfowl? Fact is, you can't do these things in South Dakota, Texas, Argentina or even New Zealand," he explained. *"Is Kenya a long way to go for a few birds? It seemed awful short to me."*

A SPECIAL SUPERPOSED

One of my most treasured shotguns comes from my Africa days — a Browning Superposed 20 gauge over/under that initially belonged to Harry Selby, one of Africa's most-respected professional hunters. Harry was featured in Robert Ruark's best-selling book, *Horn of the Hunter,* and later in his novels, *Something of Value* and *Uhuru,* about Kenya's Mau Mau uprising during the early 1950s.

"From my earliest days in the safari business," Harry had explained, "clients often brought Browning over & under shotguns on their hunts. And from my first experience with the Superposed shotgun, I was so impressed with them, I knew one day I would own one."

In the late 1960s, Harry visited a local gun dealer in Durban, South Africa. He spotted a Belgium-made 20-gauge Browning Superposed and immediately liked the little shotgun. The "long-tang, round-knob" gun was clearly a standout in a long row of shotguns.

"I asked to see the gun," Harry said, "and when I held the little Browning in my hands and brought it to my shoulder, I quickly asked, how much?"

The Superposed was a Grade I over & under, which was cut to satisfy the design preferences of the European market. The 26-inch, fixed-choke barrels were topped with an integral solid rib and a brass front sight bead. The gun was embellished with subtle engraving and featured a slim Prince-of-Wales pistol grip with an extended triggerguard tang and slender forearm, all of which combined to impart an elegant, understated look.

Harry was pleased with the gun's fit and feel, and his pride in shooting it well showed in his smile whenever he handled it. His safari clients watched birds fold to the bang of Harry's little 20 gauge, often shouting "good shot" or "well done." Whether it was knocking down high-flying driven guinea fowl, folding a flushing francolin or dropping numerous sandgrouse and doves coming to waterholes, in Harry's hands, the Superposed's impressive performance contributed to many a delicious meal enjoyed around safari campfires.

During the next 40 years, the little Browning saw plenty of action tackling the wing shooting challenges of Botswana's abundant game bird population and became one of Harry's favorite personal guns. Harry's daughter, Gail, also found the little Browning to her liking. In addition to being a crack shot on sandgrouse and doves, Gail was particularly adept at dispatching the odd spitting cobra or mamba that slithered into the Selby's home gardens in Maun.

By early 2000, Harry Selby had cut way

Benelli's Super Black Eagle III and M2 Field are available with rifled slug barrels and iron sights, while turkey models are offered in Realtree and Mossy Oak camo patterns and feature pistol-gripped stocks. The author and Craig Boddington (right) with a Barbary wild boar taken with Benelli's Super Black Eagle II slug gun in Tunisia — only slug guns are allowed for hunting wild boar there.

back on his safari schedule and realized the hard truth that nobody likes to face — he had too many guns, certainly more than he was using with any regularity. Sadly, this included the little 20-gauge Superposed shotgun.

Knowing how much I admired his Superposed, Harry unexpectedly suggested I might like to have the gun to take back to the States. He knew my interest in bird shooting would ensure that it continued to be used in the manner for which it was built. I, of course, was literally speechless at his sudden suggestion. Words failed me as I regarded the honor of Harry entrusting his favorite bird gun to my care.

"I know this Browning will have an excellent home in America," Harry said as he handed me the gun. "I have to say, this neat little shotgun has given me a lot of pleasure, and I hope you enjoy it in the future as much as Gail and I have during its years in Botswana."

In keeping with Harry's wishes, I have done my best to fulfill his expectations by "exercising" his beloved Superposed wherever doves, quail, or pheasants congregate. And having done so whenever the opportunity arose, from Kentucky to Texas to Florida, I can confirm that this timeless, well-traveled, citizen-of-the-world shotgun is truly at home on any continent and in any field or patch of the bush where game birds might hide, flush or fly.

Shotguns developed around the turn of the 20th century are still great guns. That's true of those currently produced that embody many of the same time-proven features. For those of us old enough to remember hunting ducks with lead shot, steel shot requirements ushered in the end of an era for the duck guns with names like Winchester Model 12 pump and Model 21 double, Parker double, Ithaca Featherweight and Browning Superposed over & under and Model A-5 semi-auto — guns that are always described with the words "classy" or "elegant."

Much of the development in current shotguns, especially for waterfowlers, can be credited to the necessity of steel-shot-compatible guns capable of digesting steady diets of magnum loads in 3- and 3 ½-inch shells. Whether you shoot an old gun or a new one, it will always be a gun to treasure if the design is correct and the quality reliable. GD

The Forgotten .33 Winchester

SHANE JAHN

WINCHESTER
.33 CALIBER RIFLES
The Winchester Model 1886 .33 Caliber is the highest-powered rifle made in take-down style. It is popular with big-game hunters on account of the take-down feature and hard-hitting qualities of the cartridge. The latter is loaded with smokeless powder and a 200-grain, soft point, metal patched bullet, which has special mushrooming qualities, owing to its size and high velocity. It is a particularly desirable rifle for hunting big game generally shot at fairly long range.
Winchester Guns and Ammunition Are Sold Everywhere
WINCHESTER REPEATING ARMS CO.
NEW HAVEN, CONN.

An old .33 WCF advertisement.

In the present age of long-range shooting and extended-range hunting, specialty cartridges designed and groomed for those applications, cell phone ballistic apps, and turreted scopes rivaling the ocular strength of the Hubble telescope, we've forgotten something. Peruse various reloading manuals from recent decades, and you won't find it. Scrutinize volumes of books dedicated to guns and cartridges; it's not there. Heck, some books detail wildcat cartridge designs that only a select group of shooters have heard of — with nary a mention of this old classic. Indeed, the .33 Winchester has been almost forgotten.

I've been lucky to have assembled a decent "gun book" library over the years. Very few of the titles in my collection give any detail about the .33 Winchester. However, the cartridge is mentioned in the "Obsolete American Rifle Cartridges" section of Cartridges of the World. As best as I can tell, the old cartridge was the first commercially offered round in the

The .33 Winchester is a hunter's round.

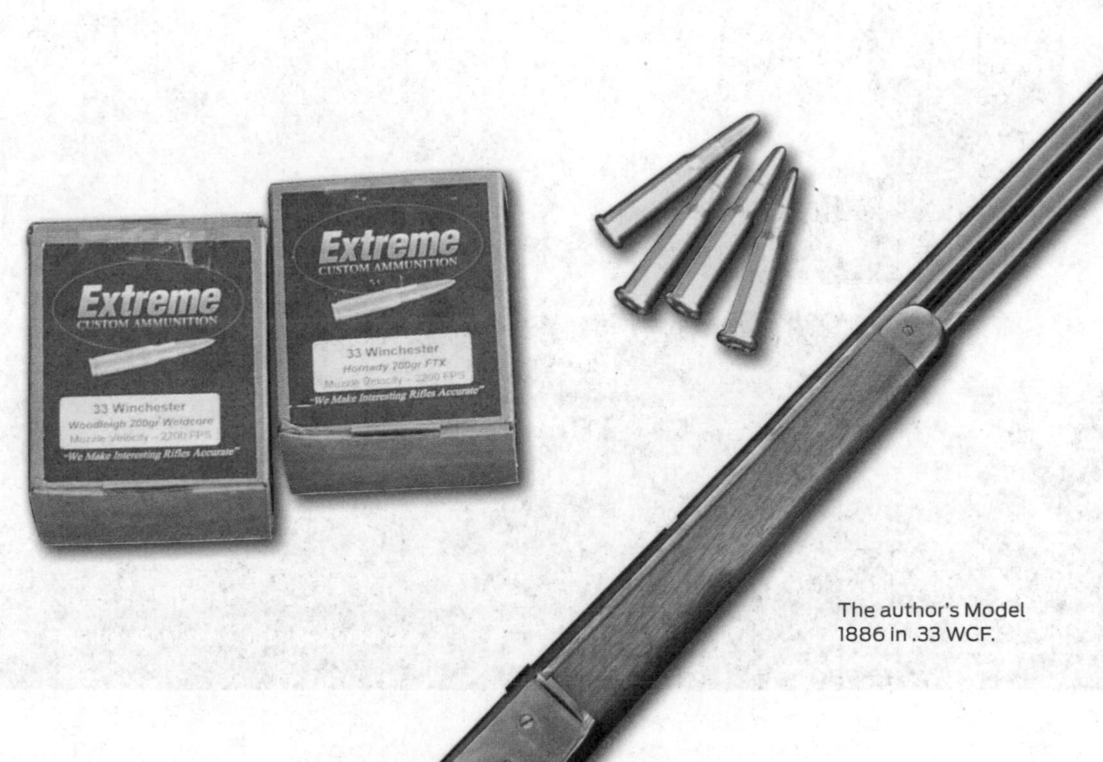

The author's Model 1886 in .33 WCF.

United States that seated a .338-caliber bullet in a factory case. Announced in 1902, the new .33 Winchester (aka .33 WCF) was chambered in Winchester's rugged 1886 lever-action rifle. It was also the only round introduced as a smokeless powder cartridge in the Model 1886. It is simply a .45-70 Government necked down to .338 caliber.

The .33 Winchester enabled shooters to sling the new-fangled smokeless round at 2,000 fps when other widely used lever-action cartridges were lagging by several hundred feet per second. We are told it became a reliable killer at responsible ranges for pronghorn, deer, black bear and even elk. My limited experience with it would make me agree with those claims. The .33 WCF held good popularity among savvy hunters and was even acclaimed by the legendary Ben Lilly, who hunted bears and mountain lions across the rugged southwestern United States.

Its 200-grain-2,000 fps fame was relatively short-lived in terms of cartridge longevity. With almost 160,000 Model 86s manufactured from 1886 to 1935 chambered in at least 10 different cartridges, the Model 1886 was turned to pasture for the new and improved Model 71 chambered in the .348 Winchester. That new round pushed a 200-grain bullet toward 2,500 fps. Most folks like a little more velocity, whether they really need it, so the .33 WCF fell by the wayside. Would a deer know the difference if shot with a .33 or .348 Winchester of equal bullet weight?

MY .33 WINCHESTER

I had the great pleasure of knowing legendary Charlie Pirtle. Charlie was a man's man and earned the valued (and much deserved) reputation of being one of the best sign-cutters and trackers in the U.S. Border Patrol. He was also a member of the agency's elite pistol team. Charlie was an accomplished hunter and a connoisseur of fine firearms from the

Skinner Sights' low-profile peep sight.

Old West, namely Colt's fine Single Action Army revolvers and classic Winchester lever actions.

The first 86 Winchesters I ever handled were Charlie's: a rifle version in .45-70 with a heavy, octagonal barrel and a lightweight version with shotgun butt, round barrel and partial-length magazine tube chambered in .33 WCF. I wanted an 86 of my own, and Charlie kept a sharp eye peeled for one that would fit my budget. Not surprisingly, he came through and notified me of a neatly re-blued Model 86 he had tracked down. He reported that the lever gun was clean, the action tight, and chambered in .33 WCF. I didn't hesitate and purchased the old gun. The Winchester 1886 Short Rifle was made in 1908. It has a 24-inch round barrel, a full-length magazine tube that holds eight rounds and a steel crescent buttplate. The front sight is a white bead measuring 0.06 inch in diameter. The trigger on my gun breaks at a crisp 4 pounds.

I like receiver-mounted ghost ring sights on my lever actions, and Skinner Sights makes some of the best. Machined from solid bar stock, they are tough. The solidly built, low-profile sight is adjustable for windage and elevation and made in beautiful Montana, USA. Skinners offer a variety of sturdy sights for many rifle styles; it even has a scope should you prefer one. I had my friend Curtis Janke install the sight at Gunsmoke Outfitters in Alpine, Texas. Curtis's focus is custom hunting rifles, but he has a soft spot for old guns.

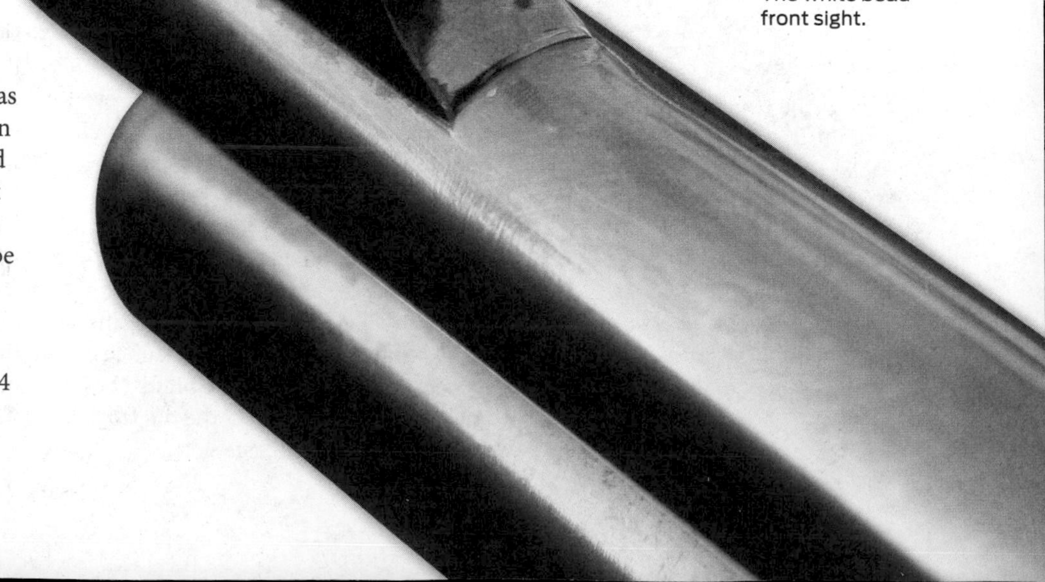

The white bead front sight.

The classic .45-70 flanked by .33 Winchesters.

GUNS CHAMBERED FOR .33 WCF

Winchester also chambered its 1885 single-shot in .33 Winchester and Marlin offered the Model 1895 in the cartridge. I have not found any Winchester 85s or Marlin 95s in .33 WCF for sale as of late, but you can find 1886s all day long. As I am writing this article, there are no fewer than 19 Winchester 86s chambered in .33 WCF listed on Gunbroker.com. Obviously, many of these old guns are still around; the lack of factory ammunition is the problem.

ORIGINAL AMMO

The original Winchester loading had a 200-grain soft-point metal-patched bullet upwards of 2,200 fps. If I could find any at a reasonable price, which isn't likely to happen, I would like to run a few over the chronograph to see what that old ammo will do.

CURRENT SPECIALTY AMMUNITION

Hendershot's Sporting Goods, Inc. of Hancock, Maryland, provides two good loads for the .33 WCF through its high-quality "Extreme" custom ammunition. Hendershots carefully loads each cartridge one at a time by hand on benchrest-quality equipment.

One load is topped with the Woodleigh 200-grain Weldcore bullet, while the other uses Hornady's 200-grain FTX. Both loads are rated at 2,200 fps. The Hendershot FTX load provided the best group in my rifle at 50 yards measuring 1.33 inches. The average group size with that load was 2.74 inches and averaged 2,115 fps. My rifle doesn't shoot the Weldcore load quite as well but remained respectable with an average of 3.65 inches at 50 yards and 2,149 fps.

Additional specialty-loaded ammunition can be found on the Buffalo Arms Co. website, which offers two .33 WCF loads. As with so many components and cartridges these days, both were out of stock at this writing in late January 2022. The company assures me they will be available for purchase soon. One load uses the 200-grain Hornady FTX bullet and the other a 200-grain Jacketed FN bullet. I had a few rounds of the Buffalo Arms FTX load on hand that I purchased in the past. Groups fired with that ammo averaged 2.47 inches and 2,005 fps.

BRASS FOR HANDLOADING

There are a few places that offer .33 WCF at times. Of course, these days, availability is more limited than usual. Some are marked "33 Win," while others carry the .45-70 Govt label.

Another option is to purchase resizing dies yourself and neck down .45-70 brass. I had been warned that resizing fired brass is more difficult, and it very well could be. I can't say for sure as I do not have any new .45-70 brass on hand and have not been able to find any. Having never done it before, I bought a Redding Form #1 die and necked down some once-fired .45-70 cases and didn't run into any issues resizing them. My friend Colby Brandon resizes new .40-65 cases for his .33 WCF and tells me this is a much easier undertaking.

Mike Venturino suggests resizing .45-70 cases in stages in his book *Shooting Lever Guns of the Old West*. First resize to .40-65, then to .38-56, and down to .33 WCF. He also mentions action-cycling problems with his .33 WCF when using handloads and fast-burning powders. I have had the same thing happen. Venturino's solution was to switch to a slower-burning powder, namely Hodgdon H4350. This advice is good information to know should you experience hard-cycling in your lever gun.

Besides old loading manuals, reloading info for the .33 WCF is scarce. This is where places like LoadData.com become especially handy. While gathering information for this article, I found a photocopy from an old *Hornady Handbook* tucked away in one of the loading books that Charlie Pirtle sent me years ago with loads for the .33 Winchester. Similarly, stashed LoadData.com printouts I had long forgotten about also offered a variety of recipes for the old relic.

HANDLOADS FOR TESTING

My buddy Jase Harkins is a consummate perfectionist for long-range rifle shooting and custom ammunition loading. That probably explains why he is one of the best rifle shots I have ever seen.

I found a handful of long out-of-production Hornady 200-grain flat-point bullets on the Internet and quickly bought them for testing. I have long been intrigued by the Lee Precision powder dippers from the company's Powder Measure Kit (you can buy a set for under $15 online). The kit contains multiple numbered dippers (my old kit has 15) and a sliding scale chart for various powders. The chart depicts a particular powder with each numbered dipper and the coinciding grains of that powder for each dipper.

Those familiar with Lee Precision already know it supplies a dipper with some reloading dies and a load chart. When I broke out the 2,8cc dipper and declared a careful scoop of IMR 3031 would be one of my loads, Harkins thought I had lost my mind. "There's no way that can be accurate!" he decried. I uniformly dipped a couple of charges and weighed them individually, showing they were pretty accurate. They are exceptionally accurate for an open-sighted lever action that was made when Teddy Roosevelt held office at 1600 Pennsylvania Avenue! That load, by the way, produced a 1.88-inch group at 50 yards. The load data provided with the dies indicate that the 2,8cc dipper of IMR 3031 should provide 2,000 fps with 180- to 200-grain bullets. Mine averaged 1,966 fps.

While we're on the subject, I've loaded lots of handgun ammo with the dipper method and Lee Breech Lock Hand Press. It's simple, relaxing and good for the soul.

My next load was brewed with IMR 4350. I didn't have my dipper kit handy, so this load was weighed out on the scale. It averaged 2,059 fps and a 2.25-inch group.

It's still possible to load your own ammo for the .33 WCF.

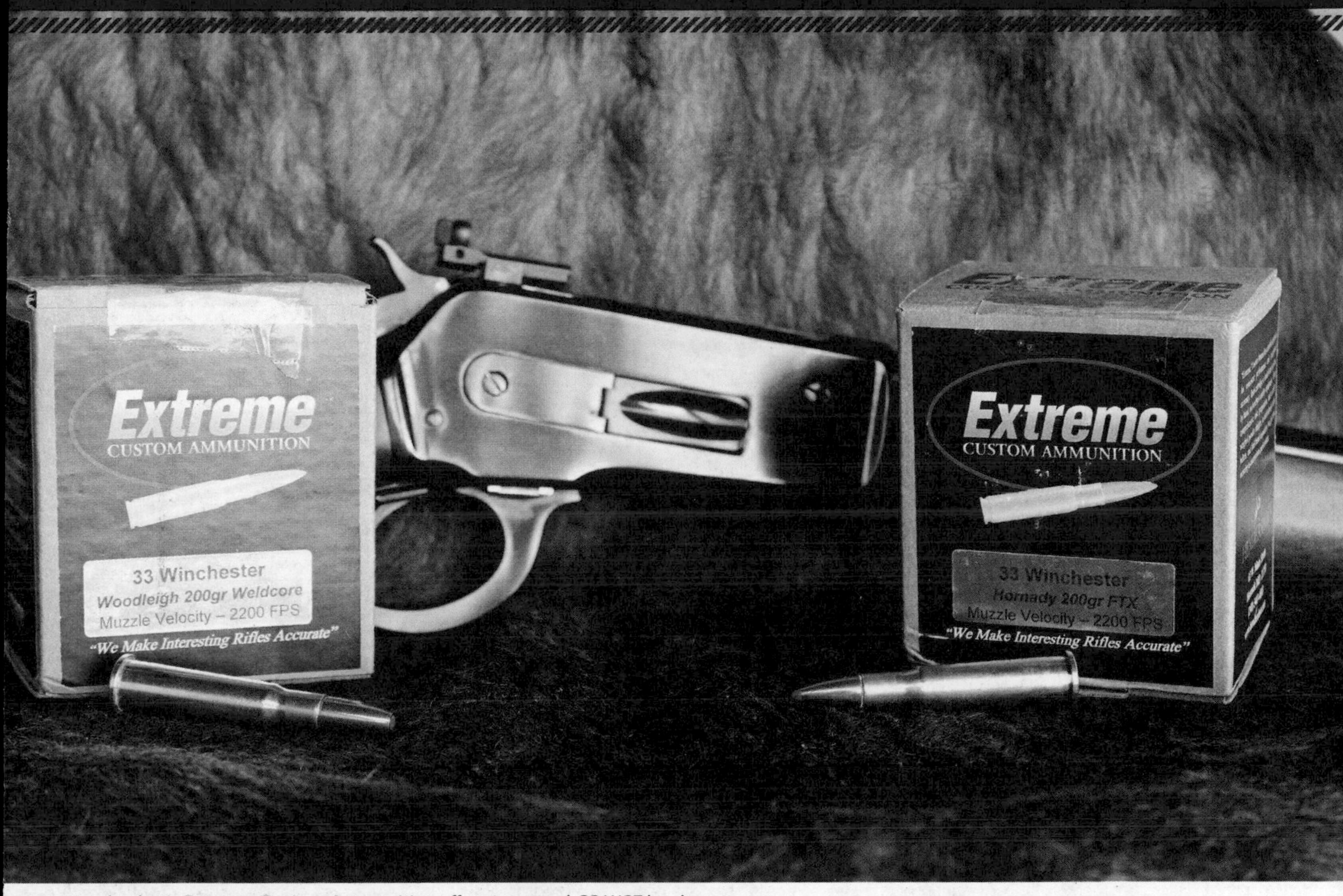

Hendershot's Extreme Custom Ammunition offers two good .33 WCF loads.

RANGE PERFORMANCE

I shot my groups from a rest at 50 yards to eliminate as much human error as possible and thwart less than precision aiming that might occur while shooting for groups farther out at 100 yards. Groups from five different loadings (two Hendershot's Extreme, one Buffalo Arms and two handloads) ranged from 1.33 to 4.14 inches. For the most part, they fell somewhere in between with an occasional flyer that increased overall group size. I feel these patterns are entirely acceptable for hunting accuracy from a 114-year-old rifle. Muzzle velocities for the five loads were from 1,928 fps on the low side to 2,261 fps on the upper.

I had no trouble slapping a steel silhouette (roughly 12x15 inches) at 100 yards, even while shooting in the flag-straightening winds of far west Texas. If you're going to hunt or shoot in the Big Bend Region, you will deal with wind.

THE ULTIMATE TEST

I took the .33 to one of my favorite places, the Harkins Ranch north of Sanderson, Texas. Over 50 square miles of rough, sprawling Trans-Pecos country is represented by sotol-studded limestone hills, almost every type of cactus the Chihuahuan Desert offers and brush-choked draws teaming with whitetail deer. Up early, I made myself a burrito, doused it with spicy *salsa verde* and washed it down with a hot cup of strong, black coffee. Stepping outside for an official weather report, it appeared to be a fine day, so I gathered up my gear, a handful of Hendershot's ammo and set out for the morning hunt.

After several unproductive days, a fresh norther sent down a stiff, frigid wind. It was one of those mornings when you didn't mind hunting from a box blind. I worried the gusts might be a bit much and could keep the deer in their brushy beds. Heavy westerly winds the previous afternoon had put a damper on deer movement. Fortunately, my concerns were for naught. As soon as the dust-laden sky gathered light, I could see the dark forms of deer emerging from the tall, yellow grass and prickly pear flats. Several old does were present, so I decided to take one if an opportunity came. A big-bodied deer walked out of the cedars and slowly headed in my direction. It was an old, tight-racked buck — a perfect candidate for the .33 WCF. Its short tines lacked mass; a hunter who obsesses over "score" would not look twice at this deer. But to me, the buck had the true trophy characteristic I look for first: advanced age. Its belly sagged, hip bones stuck out, hide appeared loose. The buck was past its prime, and its teeth were later aged by a biologist to have survived more than six years of droughts, fights with other bucks, predators, diseases and a hellacious cold storm last year that was detrimental to livestock and wildlife. A true trophy.

Winchester's Model 86 in .33 WCF is a solid choice in a lever gun. Photo: Katy Jahn

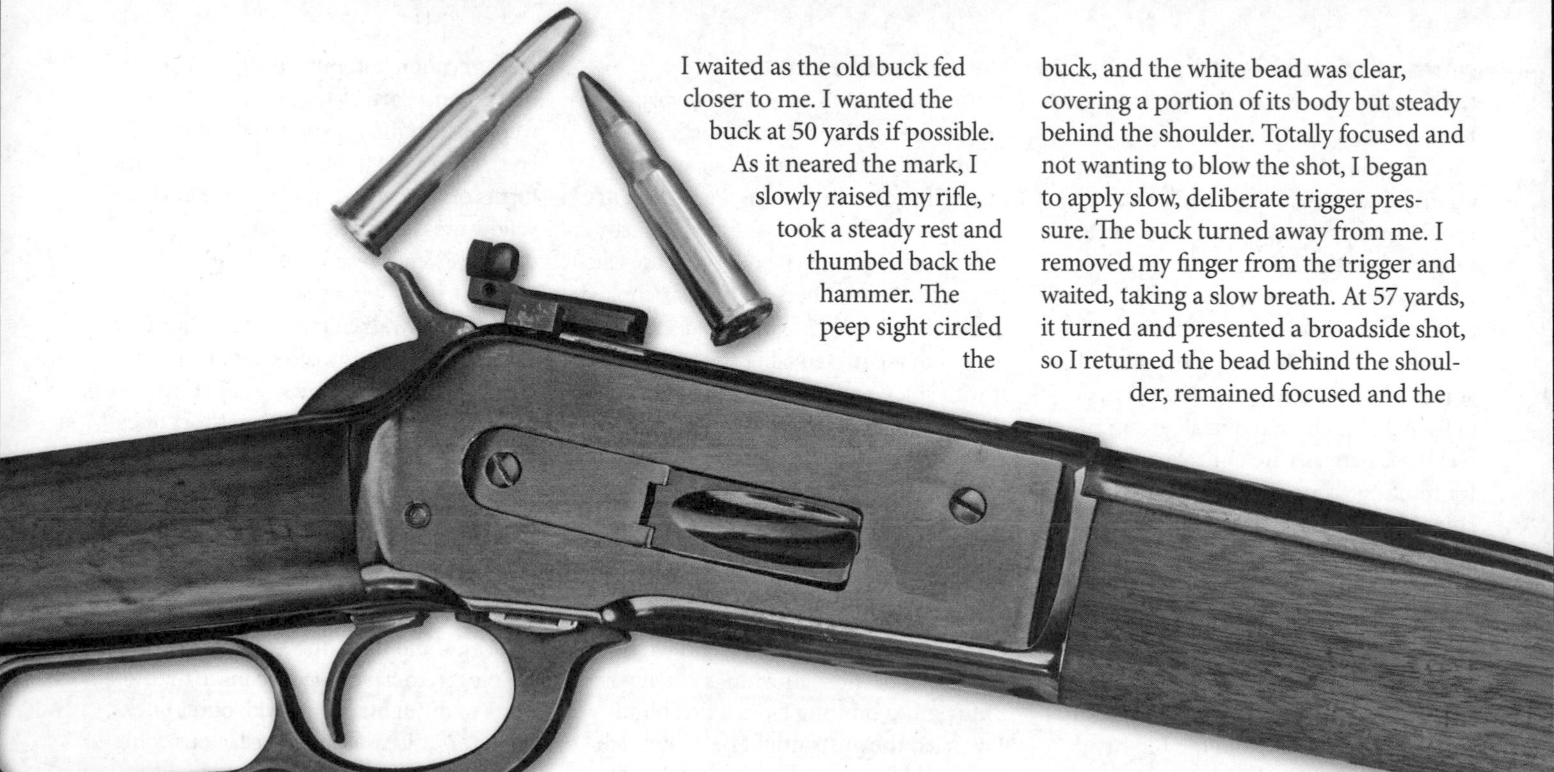

I waited as the old buck fed closer to me. I wanted the buck at 50 yards if possible. As it neared the mark, I slowly raised my rifle, took a steady rest and thumbed back the hammer. The peep sight circled the buck, and the white bead was clear, covering a portion of its body but steady behind the shoulder. Totally focused and not wanting to blow the shot, I began to apply slow, deliberate trigger pressure. The buck turned away from me. I removed my finger from the trigger and waited, taking a slow breath. At 57 yards, it turned and presented a broadside shot, so I returned the bead behind the shoulder, remained focused and the

Ol' .33 barked with pleasant recoil. The buck hit the ground at the shot, sending up a cloud of dry caliche dust. Hendershot's 200-grain Hornady Flex-Tip load performed beautifully and knocked the buck smooth off its feet.

Thankfully, companies like Hendershot's and Buffalo Arms still offer ammunition in America's first commercially loaded .338-caliber cartridge. With enough interest from shooters and hunters, other manufacturers might see fit to bring back the old round, at least in limited runs. It isn't a super-fast long-range cartridge meant for ringing steel on yonder hillsides. It is a hunter's cartridge meant for killing game with authority at moderate ranges. Do yourself a favor. Pick up a rifle chambered in .33 WCF, give Hendershot's and Buffalo Arms a call or mix up some homemade loads on the press. Then take the nostalgic rifle and cartridge to the field. The old .33 Winchester is just too good to be forgotten. GD

RESOURCES

- Hendershot's Sporting Goods, Inc. hendershots.net
- Skinner Sights skinnersights.com
- Gunsmoke Outfitters, Curtis Jahnke, Custom Gun Builder, 701-238-3680, gunsmoke@casselton.net
- Buffalo Arms buffaloarms.com
- Lee Precision leeprecision.com

An old whitetail buck and Winchester's Model 1886 in .33 WCF, three classic trophies! Photo: Austin Stolte

Federal Premium's Centennial Anniversary

Celebrating over 100 years of premium ammunition and countless adventures!

› PHIL MASSARO

It was 1988, the opening day of our New York deer season — a family holiday and one held in reverence to this day — and my dad and I were each in our favorite spots. I was eager to prove my worth as a deer hunter (especially to my father), and my Winchester 94 and I were absolutely ready to work. It hadn't been daylight for an hour when I heard the familiar report of Ol' Grumpy Pants' Mossberg .308 Winchester. Knowing a single shot meant 'meat,' I stayed on the stand, figuring he could hog-dress the buck, and I'd help him drag it later. Fifteen minutes had hardly gone by, and I heard him shoot again. That was puzzling because G.P. didn't miss. Perhaps a half-hour after the second, a third shot had me wondering just what was going on 300 yards to the east because I'd seen only a doe and her fawn the entire morning.

Soon I saw G.P.'s orange stocking cap bobbing down the logging road; he also wore a big grin.

"You'll have to come help me drag them."

Them? Whaddya mean *them*?

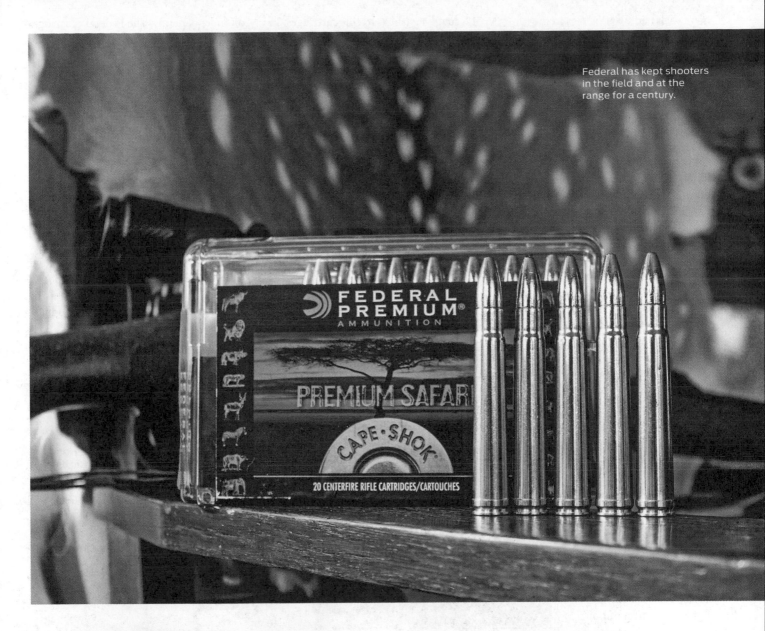

Federal has kept shooters in the field and at the range for a century.

In celebration of Federal Ammunition's 100-year anniversary and rich history of shotshell manufacturing, the company is releasing four commemorative shotshell packages. In Federal's early years, shotshells were the heart of the lineup. Target loads went by many names and had many looks over the decades, from Hi-Power and Monark to Reliable and Champion, and many more. There are four different retro packaging designs to be released throughout 2022. These shells are offered in 12 gauge, shot size No. 8 in 25-count boxes.

We each had two doe tags in the pocket and the buck tag we were allotted, but in that era, you could use a doe tag for a buck, but I knew he wouldn't be shooting does for at least a week.

"How many is *them*?" I inquired.

He just laughed and tapped the half-empty plastic cartridge holder on his belt, included in every box of Federal ammo.

The first one was a nice big eight-pointer, then there was the forkhorn that followed in its tracks, and the third was a spike buck with a brow tine, which stopped in the wrong place. Opening morning saw G.P. up by a score of 3 to 0, and the rest of my day was spent dragging deer. He and that inexpensive .308 have accounted for a great number of deer, and it was with that rifle I first experienced the benefits of Federal Premium ammunition.

You're not wrong if you sense a blend of reverence and competition with my father in my writings. We're 21 years apart in age, have worked together since I was 11 years old and have done all sorts of stuff together. He taught me most of what I know about hunting and ballistics, though I feel confident that I've taken things a bit further. But it was G.P. who showed me the benefits of premium ammunition, and I've never looked back. His choice of Federal Premium ammunition — loaded with the 165-grain Sierra boattail spitzer bullet — showed me what accuracy was all about, and I'd look down at my little .30-30 carbine and wonder why I wasn't getting the 1-MOA accuracy he got;. However, there was more to the equation. I was amazed at the accuracy of that rifle/ammo combination. Three-plus decades later, that rifle still shoots well, and while we've all come to expect sub-MOA groups from every rifle we pick up, that wasn't the case when I was a younger man.

Federal Premium: the name evoked a superior product, and I used its products as often as possible. From .410-bore and 12-gauge shotshells to rifle cartridges, I appreciated the consistency of the ammo and have used Federal ammo whenever I could get it. Chatting with my dad about rifle cartridges and their attributes, he explained that Federal was the only source of factory-loaded Sierra bullets (at that time) and that the performance of that load in his rifle allowed him to 'thread the needle' in the thick deer woods of New York. Embracing the projectiles of another company was a unique move for Federal, and it showed its level of dedication to bringing the best product possible to the masses.

The company was born from an idea hatched by the Sherman brothers, who had experience with the Western Cartridge Company and wanted to branch off independently. The Federal Cartridge and Machine Company officially saw the light of day in 1916 in a factory in Anoka, Minnesota. Louis and Harry Sherman had barely gotten their fledgling company off the ground when it fizzled out; by 1920, the Anoka factory was dark and idle.

On April 17, 1922, the Federal Cartridge Company was saved from obscurity by one Mr. Charles L. Horn and became the company we know today. Born in Iowa in 1888, Horn graduated from the University of Minnesota's Law program in 1912. Shortly after finishing law school, Horn became president of the American Ball Company, manufacturing steel ball bearings, which led to his involvement with the Shermans and his

Left: Charles L. Horn, the man who established the Federal Cartridge Company in 1922. He was the head of Federal from 1922 until he stepped down in 1974.

Below: An early photograph of the Federal Cartridge Corporation facility in Anoka, Minnesota.

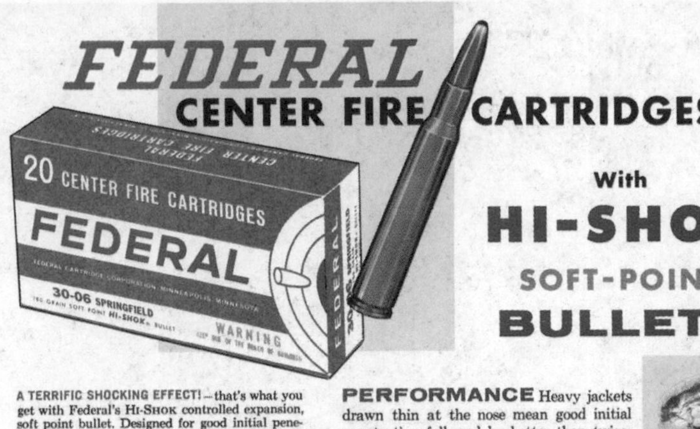

A TERRIFIC SHOCKING EFFECT!—that's what you get with Federal's HI-SHOK controlled expansion, soft point bullet. Designed for good initial penetration followed by mushrooming expansion to over twice the original bullet diameter. Lead weight loss by bullet fragmentation is kept to a minimum, intensifying the shock.

NOTHING BEATS a soft point bullet for all-around, reliable performance. Federal's HI-SHOK hunting bullet combines the traditional advantages of the soft point style with design improvements and careful manufacturing that make it outstanding!

PERFORMANCE Heavy jackets drawn thin at the nose mean good initial penetration followed by better than twice-diameter expansion with minimum bullet weight loss through fragmentation.

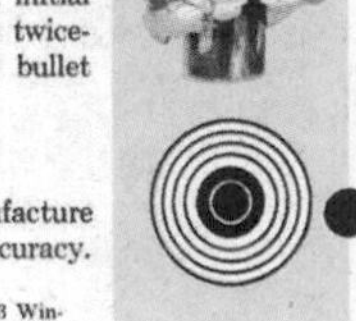

ACCURACY Careful manufacture and loading make Federals excel in accuracy.

HI-SHOK bullets are used on all Federals except caliber 222 Remington, 50 grain, and 243 Winchester, 80 grain. These two use the fast shattering soft points that varmint hunters prefer for safety.

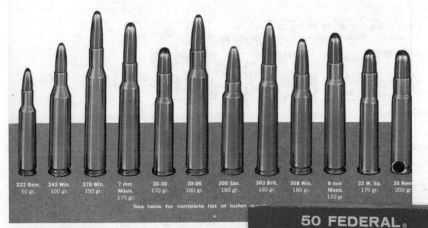

222 Rem. 50 gr. · 243 Win. 100 gr. · 270 Win. 150 gr. · 7 mm Maus. 175 gr. · 30-30 170 gr. · 30-06 180 gr. · 300 Sav. 180 gr. · 303 Brit. 180 gr. · 308 Win. 180 gr. · 8 mm Maus. 170 gr. · 32 W. Sp. 170 gr. · 35 Rem 200 gr

See table for complete list of bullet we...

50 FEDERAL®
38 special MATCH
MONARK®
MID RANGE CARTRIDGES
148 GRAIN LEAD WAD CUTTER BULLET
WARNING KEEP OUT OF THE REACH OF CHILDREN
PERFORATION
TWIST FIRMLY
FEDERAL
38 SPECIAL MATCH

FEDERAL introduces
color-coded shells!

16 GAUGE · 20 GAUGE · 12 GAUGE

...in colors, by gauge, for your safety and convenience

You can tell a shotgun shell's gauge by its *color*. How? By reaching for the new color-coded *plastic* shells from Federal. *Red* means 12-gauge, *purple* means 16-gauge, and *yellow* means 20-gauge. So you *know* you have the right gauge—there's no chance of error with Federals.

But what really counts is Federals' performance. To give you the hardest hitting shotgun shells possible, we've become meticulous about the makings.

The ingredients: super-igniting primer, the finest and most uniform propellent powder, and our exclusive Altite® gas-harnessing wad column.

In plastic Hi-Power shells we add Federal's famous extra hard-shot enclosed in a polyethylene shot cup—the perfect combination for long range performance.

The best in the world and we mean it. *You* can prove it!

FEDERAL

Top: An early Federal centerfire rifle ammunition advert. (ca. 1963), showcasing the Hi-Shok bullets.

Inset: Early Federal handgun ammunition: Monark .38 Special wadcutters.

Left: Federal began color-coding its shotshells in 1966; that helps avoid confusion, leading to injury or worse.

purchase of the Federal Cartridge and Machine Company. A sharp businessman, he soon had a distribution plan, which put his Federal products in the most common points of sale: gas stations, barbershops and grocery stores.

Horn was the type of business owner who was unafraid to help out and get his hands dirty. (Though John Haller, whom Horn brought over from the Sherman era, asked him to stop 'helping' as the machines were being broken due to his efforts.) Soon, Federal was a thriving business. The year 1924 saw Federal .22 Long Rifle ammunition on the market, and by 1926 shotshells were available in 12, 16, and 20 gauge and .410 bore.

In a somewhat ironic move, Franklin Olin, head of the Western Cartridge Company, became one of Federal's principal stockholders in 1925 and was the company's owner by 1932, having also purchased Winchester Repeating Arms Corporation a year prior. Olin kept Charles Horn on as President of Federal, and by 1935 Horn had secured a government contract for a serious amount of ammunition, resulting in the 1941 construction of the Twin Cities Ordnance Plant in nearby New Brighton, Minnesota. By the contract's end in 1945, over 5 *billion* rounds of ammunition were produced from that plant, which employed more than 25,000 people. The plant was reactivated for the Korean War in 1950 and 1965 for the Vietnam War.

In 1963, Federal would add rifle and pistol ammunition to its catalog (a game-changer in years to come) and two years later would introduce the plastic shotshell hull. Then in 1966, it would begin the color-coding scheme of shotshells that we all know so well. Federal's proprietary Hi-Shok soft-point bullet was a flat-base cup-and-core bullet, advertized to have a thick copper jacket, drawn thinner at the nose for a combination of deep penetration and expansion better than twice the original diameter. The Hi-Shok was offered in the standard cartridges of the day, including .300

Savage, .270 Winchester, 7mm Mauser, 8mm Mauser, .30-'06 Springfield, .308 Winchester, .30-30 Winchester, .32 Winchester Special, .35 Remington and .303 British; a fast-expanding varmint bullet was offered in the .222 Remington and .243 Winchester. Federal would use its experience making military cartridges as an advertising point for the new rifle ammunition. While I haven't personally used the Hi-Shok bullet, those older than me remember it fondly. Throughout the 1950s and '60s, Federal primers and other reloading components were a staple among the reloading community.

Charles Horn was the President of Federal from 1922 until he stepped down in 1974; there's no denying the man's influence over the company as it grew from fledgling to behemoth. The ever-diligent Horn would stay on as Chairman of the Board until the end of 1977, when he would officially retire — with his son William Horn taking over the role of president. Instrumental in the passing of the Pittman-Robertson Federal Aid in Wildlife Restoration Act, which would put an 11-percent tax on ammunition to aid in the restoration of wildlife and habitat and raise billions of dollars, Charles would pass away just a year later. Still, his son William would radically expand the company until its sale in 1985.

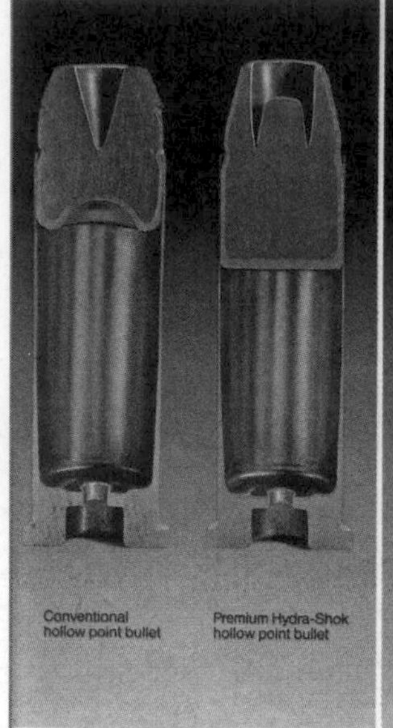

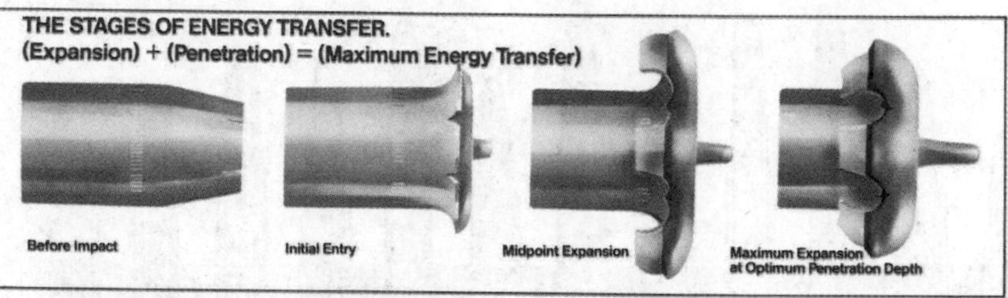

Premium Pistol and Revolver Ballistics (Approximate)

Federal Load No.	Caliber	Bullet Wgt. in Grains	Bullet Wgt. in Grams	Bullet Style	Factory Primer No.	Velocity in Feet Per Second Muzzle	25 yds.	50 yds.	Energy in Foot/Pounds Muzzle	25 yds.	50 yds.	Mid-Range Trajectory 25 yds.	50 yds.	Test Barrel Length Inches
P9HS1	9mm Luger (9x19mm Parabellum)	124	8.03	Hydra-Shok HP	100	1120	1070	1030	345	315	290	0.2	0.9	4
P9HS3	9mm Luger (9x19mm) (+P+)	124	8.03	Hydra-Shok HP	100	1220	1150	1090	410	360	325	0.2	0.8	4
P9HS2	9mm Luger (9x19mm Parabellum)	147	9.52	Hydra-Shok HP	100	1050	1010	980	360	335	310	0.3	1.1	4
P45HS1	45 Auto	230	14.90	Hydra-Shok HP	150	850	830	810	370	350	335	0.4	1.6	5
P38HS1	38 Special (High Velocity +P)	129	8.36	Hydra-Shok HP	100	945	930	910	255	245	235	0.3	1.3	4-V
P357HS1	357 Magnum	158	10.23	Hydra-Shok HP	100	1235	1160	1104	535	475	428	0.2	0.8	4-V

+P+ and +P ammunition is loaded to a higher pressure. Use only in firearms so recommended by the gun manufacturer. In addition, +P+ ammunition is available for law enforcement and government sales only. "V" indicates vented barrel to simulate service conditions.

Above: Released in 1989, the Federal Hydra-Shok bullet was most definitely a game-changer.

Charles Horn would still be in charge when, in 1973, Federal was at the forefront of the movement to keep lead shot out of our waterways by loading steel shot for testing. It would be almost two decades, but in 1991 we would see the complete ban of lead shot for waterfowling. William would be at the helm when Federal released its Premium line in 1977, the first instance of a major ammunition company using components from other manufacturers.

NEW
FEDERAL
.416
Rigby
Solid
Premium
SAFARI
20 CENTER FIRE RIFLE CARTRIDGES 20 CARTOUCHES A PERCUSSION CENTRAL

Left: In 1989, Federal helped revive the classic .416 Rigby and .470 Nitro Express cartridges by producing readily available ammunition in the Premium Safari line.

My dad preferred the Sierra soft points for his deer hunting — and still does — though Federal also offered the excellent Nosler Partition. This period marked a sea-change in the ammunition industry. Most major manufacturers would adopt the policy; Remington, Winchester, Norma, and many smaller companies would offer those projectiles previously only available as a reloading component. This move would be the first in many innovative measures on the part of Federal over the next few decades, despite some shuffling of ownership.

Tax reform laws passed at the end of the 1960s gave 20 years for foundations to relinquish the primary ownership of any publicly traded company, so the Olin Foundation was forced to sell Federal. In 1985, Federal-Hoffman, Inc. took possession of the Federal Cartridge Company, turning ownership over to the 2,900

Left: Federal's Big Game Animals of North America poster, with centerfire ammunition in the red, white and blue box.

Lower Left: A 1982 magazine ad for the Federal Hi-Power rifle ammunition.

Below: A 1978 advert announcing the introduction of the Federal Premium line of shotshells and rifle ammunition.

Accuracy that's right "on the mark."

Accuracy plus power. Precision manufacturing is the key to the consistent high performance of Federal centerfire ammunition.

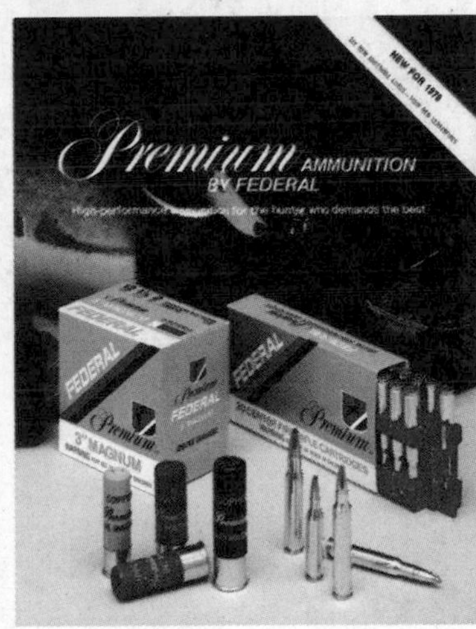

employees who would earn dividends and wages. The Federal of the mid-1980s is the one I became immediately familiar with as I began my hunting career, and I watched the company step up to the plate with several game-changing products.

Pentair, Inc. purchased Federal in 1988 and named Ron Mason as President of the new company, and it wasted no time. Pairing with Mossberg, Federal would play an integral role in the development and 1988 release of the 3 ½-inch 12-gauge shotshell, which would become the darling of turkey hunters and waterfowlers alike. Rivaling the performance of the mighty 10 gauge, the 3 ½-inch shells would be offered in the Mossberg 835 Ulti-Mag shotgun and would become an instant hit.

The following year was a landmark year for Federal, as it released innovative products that some folks might take for granted, but in that era were monumental. The first was born from an FBI shootout in Miami, Florida, three years before, where a pair of armed bank robbers forced the bureau to rethink its choice of handguns and cartridges. The now-standard FBI protocol tests were developed. As Federal had long provided ammunition to the government and its various agencies, it developed what would become a law enforcement staple: the Hydra-Shok.

The brainchild of ballistic engineer Tom Burczynski, the Hydra-Shok was explicitly developed to better the terminal ballistics of a standard cup-and-core jacketed bullet design, and it did precisely that. With a deep hollow cavity and its signature center post initiating expansion, the Hydra-Shok used a skived copper jacket to create a large wound channel and give deep penetration in many different shooting situations, including all FBI obstacles. The Hydra-Shok has traditionally given weight retentions in the 90 percent range, holding together very well in several mediums. It would become the benchmark bullet for both law enforcement and civilians alike.

Being interested in big game (the bigger, the better, as far as I'm concerned), I vividly remember reading about Federal's announcement of the Premium Safari line of ammunition in 1989. That's when it brought back ammo for the near-obsolete .416 Rigby and .470 Nitro Express cartridges and the ever-popular .375 H&H Magnum and .458 Winchester Magnum and other calibers better suited for plains game species. The release of the first pair offered quality factory ammo for those classics for the first time in decades. Using what many consider to be the best bullets available in that era — including Jack Carter's Trophy Bonded Bear Claw soft point and Sledgehammer solids, Australia's Woodleigh Weldcore soft point, and the classic Nosler Partition — the Premium Safari line was a welcome addition for those of us whose hearts reside on the Dark Continent.

Ron Mason's goal would be to see his

The HST line of pistol bullets might be considered the next evolution of the Hydra-Shok and is the author's favorite defensive bullet.

Federal's Gold Medal Match .22 LR ammunition can produce one ragged hole on your target.

Avoiding the need for polymer hulls, Federal once again offers Gold Medal target loads with paper hulls.

company's ammunition win an Olympic medal, and he would see that goal come to fruition. In 1992, Federal's Gold Medal UltraMatch .22 LR ammunition would bring home both gold and silver in the hands of the U.S. Shooting Team at Barcelona, Spain. That same year, Federal and bullet designer Jack Carter agreed to have Federal manufacture the Trophy Bonded Bear Claw and Trophy Bonded Sledgehammer projectiles under the Federal brand. While the Federal variety differed from Carter's original design, it was a great design. As you will see shortly, the revamp of Carter's brainchild would lead to an entire line of fantastic rifle projectiles, many of which have been with me on some of my favorite hunting adventures.

The Ron Mason era would see many new releases, and by the late 1990s, Mason would relate that one-quarter of the company's revenue came from newly released products. In 1997, Blount Industries would purchase Federal, making it one of many outdoor/shooting brands under that umbrella; Speer, CCI, Outers and others would be a part of that group when Blount put the conglomerate up for sale just two years later. Lehman Brothers bought the lot and held onto it for just two years. In 2001, Minnesota-based ATK would buy Federal — in addition to Speer, RCBS, CCI, Champion and many more brands — and would usher in what I consider the most significant era of development in the company's history. Under ATK, Federal released its first branded cartridges: the .338 Federal developed with Sako and the .327 Federal Magnum developed with Smith & Wesson.

The Black Cloud shotshell, featuring the FLITESTOPPER pellet (with a ring reminiscent of the planet Saturn), Prairie Storm upland shells and 3rd Degree turkey shotshells were revolutionary. Federal expanded the lineup of rifle projectiles available in its Premium lineup to include the Nosler Ballistic Tip, Nosler AccuBond, Barnes X, Berger Hybrid OTM, Swift A-Frame, Swift Scirocco and more. The proprietary lineup of Federal bullets was also expanded to include the Trophy Copper and Trophy Bonded Tip bullets, the first child of the Trophy Bonded Bear

A modern aerial view of the vast Federal facility in Anoka, Minnesota. Charles Horn would undoubtedly be proud.

Claw, featuring a boattail and polymer tip. Handgun bullets like the HST, Guard Dog and the revised Hydra-Shok made the effectiveness of our classic handgun cartridges even more effective. Syntech ammunition, featuring a polymer-coated lead projectile, would allow affordable practice while keeping bore fouling and lead vapors to a minimum.

ATK would split internally in 2015, allowing the newly formed Vista Outdoor to handle the sporting brands, while ATK would cover the governmental end of things. Federal would be Vista's flagship brand, and the innovation didn't slow down.

While it doesn't bear the Federal name, the .224 Valkyrie revolutionized the potential of the AR-15 platform, giving the shooter a new level of performance from a .22-caliber centerfire. I distinctly remember watching the vapor trail of my bullet rip air just an instant before the 90-grain slug made a splatter on the steel target 900 yards away. Flat trajectory, high Ballistic Coefficient (BC), and minimal recoil are all characteristics of the Valkyrie, and it remains a fantastic cartridge, staying supersonic out to 1,300 yards under proper conditions.

Remember that family of projectiles based on the Trophy Bonded Bear Claw

For its 90th anniversary, Federal issued ammunition in special packaging; the centennial is celebrated by throwback boxes.

Designed for thick-skinned dangerous game, the Federal Trophy Bonded SledgeHammer solids offer excellent penetration.

The author used the Federal Trophy Bonded SledgeHammer solid in his Heym .470 double rifle to take this Cape buffalo bull in Zimbabwe.

I mentioned earlier? The Trophy Bonded Tip was just the first of the line; the 2019 release of the Edge TLR would see the third iteration of Carter's brainchild. Using the shortened lead core and a copper-alloy jacket and base, the Edge TLR used the Slipstream polymer tip and the AccuGroove channel to reduce fouling and bearing surface. The Edge TLR was an exceptionally accurate bullet, decked out in a black oxide finish. I say 'was' because Federal quickly morphed it into the latest design, the Terminal Ascent.

If you appreciate the benefits of a bullet with a high BC, giving both a flat trajectory and minimal wind deflection, having the ability to expand at low velocities (read that as longer distances, where the bullet has slowed down) yet which can handle the high-velocity impacts of magnum cartridges at close ranges, look to the Federal Terminal Ascent. High weight retention — a product of that long copper-alloy base — and expansion approaching twice that of caliber dimension — a result of the Slipstream polymer tip and the forward-located lead core — are typical of the Terminal Ascent. Available in factory-loaded ammunition and as a component to handloaders, Terminal Ascent is among the latest and greatest projectile designs.

Federal's innovations in muzzleloading rifles have been nothing shy of amazing. The Trophy Copper B.O.R. Lock muzzleloader bullet, which uses a lead-free design with a polymer tip and a polymer cup at the base that doesn't require a sabot, is an excellent design. It retains energy well and has a flat trajectory to make it a viable candidate for 200-yard shots. As if this bullet weren't exciting enough, 2020 saw Federal pair with Traditions (maker of muzzleloading rifles) to develop the FireStick system. That system uses a polymer capsule filled with a 100- or 120-grain charge of Hodgdon Triple 8 powder to deliver the most consistent results I've ever seen from an inline muzzleloader. You simply load the bullet from the muzzle to the small shelf at the base of the barrel, then load a 209 primer at the base of the FireStick polymer charge and insert the combination into the breech.

My rifle prints three Trophy Copper B.O.R. Lock MZ bullets into a 1-MOA group. Considering that most traditional muzzleloaders run at four to five times that figure, the FireStick system (though not legal in all states for muzzleloading seasons) is the most consistent and accurate inline I've ever seen.

With the popularity of long-range target shooting, Federal's Gold Medal Match line of ammo, now loaded with Sierra MatchKing and Berger Hybrid projectiles, is more revered

A descendant of the Trophy Bonded Bear Claw, Federal's Trophy Bonded Tip uses a short lead core, a long copper shank at the rear and a polymer tip. The lead core is chemically bonded to the jacket to slow expansion.

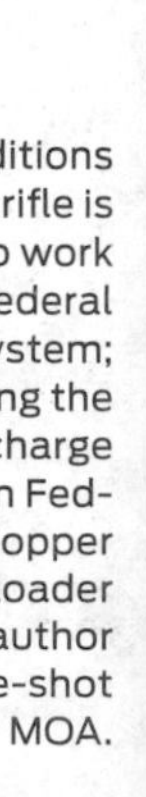

The Traditions NitroFire rifle is designed to work with the Federal FireStick system; when using the 100-grain charge and 270-grain Federal Trophy Copper Muzzleloader bullet, the author printed three-shot groups of 1 MOA.

Massaro used the Federal B.O.R. Lock Trophy Copper bullet and the 100-grain FireStick charge, sparked by Federal 209 Muzzleloading Primers, to take this Kentucky whitetail.

Federal TSS turkey shotshells use tungsten shot to deliver unprecedented killing power, routinely dropping toms at greater distances.

than ever and has earned a reputation for excellent accuracy.

2019 saw the release of the Federal Custom Shop, which offers a bespoke experience; each cartridge is handloaded to ensure the most consistent product possible. While the cartridge selection is limited and consists primarily of popular rounds, you can choose the bullet style from Federal's menu. The Custom Shop will also make you a custom shotshell, where you pick the gauge/length/shot size from several options.

Federal has made ammunition specialized for the lever actions (HammerDown), unique buckshot loads built around segmenting copper-plated pellets (Force X2), expanded its defensive handgun line (Punch) for value, and has most recently released the latest handgun cartridge: the .30 Super Carry. Designed to better the ballistics of the .380 Auto in a configuration where you can fit more in the magazine than a 9mm Luger, the .30 Super Carry may be met with skepticism initially. Still, Federal has done its homework on this one, and it'll prove a winner.

The loaded ammunition is not all Federal produces; I've relied on Federal's primers, cases and component bullets for my reloading. The Gold Medal Match series of primers have long been my favorite, as I feel they are the most consistent available, and they've been taken around the globe in my handloads. Federal cases are an excellent platform for building an accurate handload. Its component bullets include the Trophy Bonded Bear Claw, Sledgehammer solid, Trophy Bonded Tip, Terminal Ascent, Fusion Hydra-Shok, and Syntech — all mainstays at my reloading bench.

One hundred years after its conception, Federal is still in Anoka, Minnesota, and maintains close ties to the community. In fact, in the 1950s, Federal helped to finance the Anoka City Hall. Looking at the building from the air, one could easily make out the outline of an autoloading handgun. Coincidence? Perhaps, but I prefer to think it was planned.

If Charles L. Horn could have seen what his company would become a century after his initial investment, I'm confident his business acumen would cause an involuntary smile. Federal has become an international success, with a reputation for excellence and innovation. Horn's marketing skills have most certainly blossomed into a global presence. His son's idea of utilizing the projectiles of other companies worked out just fine, creating a network of companies interested in cross-promoting its products, bringing everyone involved upward. Having the privilege of touring the Federal facility, I got the sense of family among the employees, young and old. Everyone took their job seriously, and the result showed. When I break the seal on a box of Federal ammunition, I know I'm using one of the best ammunition products on the market.

From the Monark handgun loads of my grandfather's era to the earliest Federal Premium ammo of my father's time to the Hi-Power loads of my own youth and the Terminal Ascent loads of my adulthood, Federal has been a consistent part of my family's hunting and shooting experiences. I look forward to Federal's continued efforts in the rimfire, shotshell, handgun and centerfire rifle markets and its fantastic reloading components. I'm sure my grandchildren will rely on Federal products as generations before — no matter the type of shooting or outdoor adventure they enjoy. GD

SAVAGE
NOMAD
ADJUSTABLE ACCUTRIGGER
AccuStock

Five Blue-Collar Deer Guns

Rifles, muzzleloaders and scopes to hunt whitetails on a budget, wherever they live.

›WILL BRANTLEY

Taking aim with a Savage 110 Storm on a hunt for chamois in New Zealand. The gun worked there, and it'll work in the deer woods.

I wish Generation X would claim me, but the truth is, I was born in 1983, and that makes me a Millennial. I'd as soon wander the land blind and naked as to pull on a pair of skinny jeans and horn-rimmed glasses, but I accept the title, kicking and screaming the whole way because, hey, kicking and screaming is what my generation does when we don't get our way.

But it's not all bad, being a child of the past 40 years. Even the most grizzled gun nuts must admit that when it comes to advances in hunting equipment, the 21st century has been special. We've gotten the trail camera and the ThermaCell, laser rangefinders that'll fit in a shirt pocket, tungsten super shot and custom scope turrets. There are smartphone apps that'll show you the property boundaries in any state and others that'll pair with your smart scope and make ballistic calculations for you right in the field.

But maybe best of all, we've been flooded with inexpensive deer rifles that'll really shoot. In fact, these days, sub-MOA accuracy is the expectation for any off-the-shelf bolt action, even if it costs $400. And that's what this list of rifles is all about. Blue-collar. Working-class. Affordable. Hell, call them cheap if you want, since some of life's best perks are

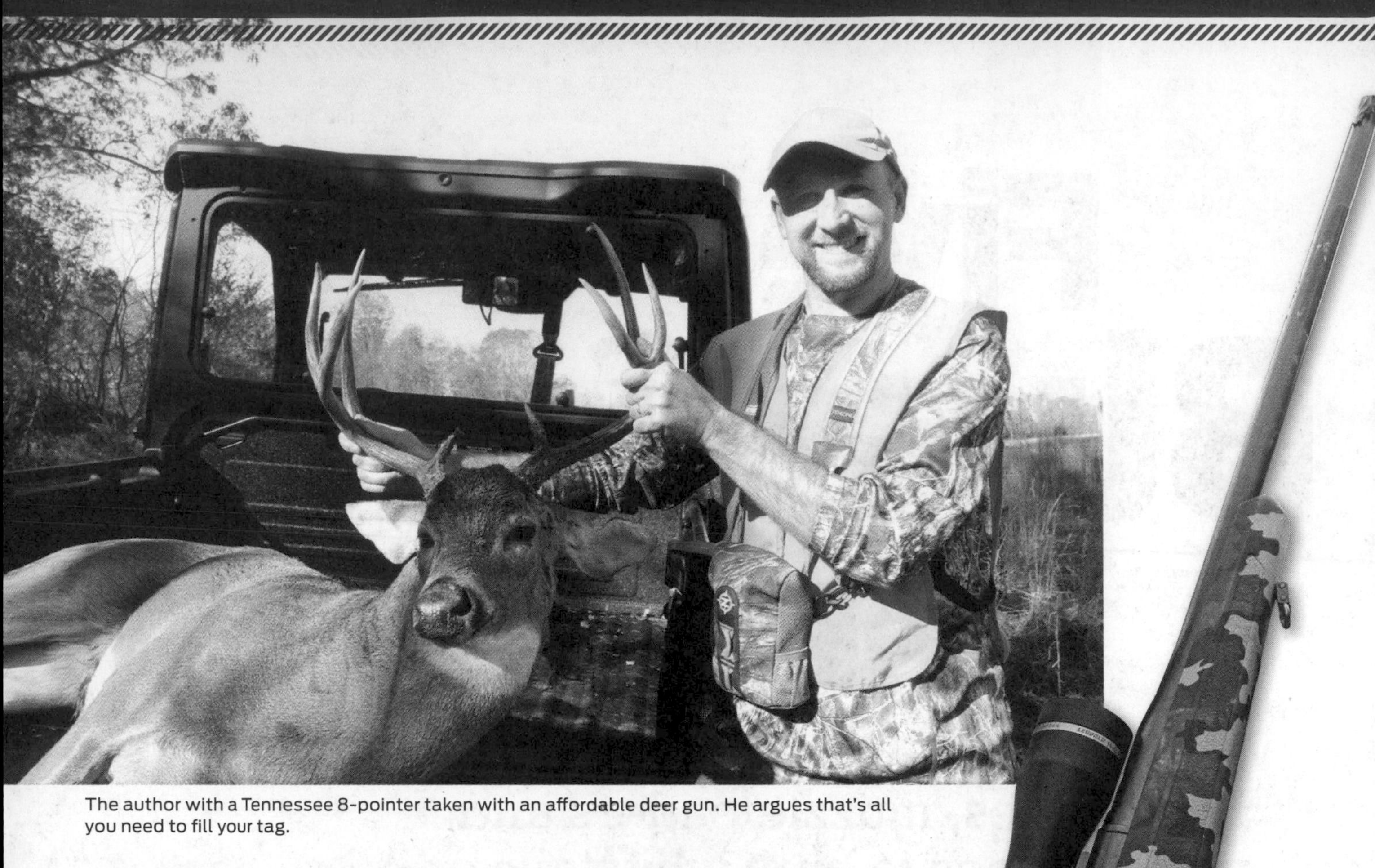

The author with a Tennessee 8-pointer taken with an affordable deer gun. He argues that's all you need to fill your tag.

cheap. These guns will give you a lifetime of hunting service without costing much money. I've personally hunted and killed something with every gun on this list, and though they're not all pretty (or perfect), they do all *shoot.* Above all, that's what a deer hunter needs.

CALIBERS AND ACTIONS

These rifles can be pressed into use for various big game animals. I've used some in adventures abroad for good-sized critters. But here, I'm explicitly talking about whitetail guns. For all the critters and adventures you might read about in this book, whitetails are the world's most ubiquitous game animal and the species hunted above all others, especially here in the states. I've hunted them for 30 years and in various states, and I make part of my annual income outfitting for them in Kentucky. A mature whitetail buck, common as it is, is a challenging critter to kill.

Since whitetails live in various habitats — and in states with diverse regulations — what you'd need for sitting in a box blind in South Texas is slightly different from what you'd need in the Appalachian foothills of southern Ohio. Still, I don't get too hung up on caliber choice. I don't like .22 centerfires because the tiny hole —particularly just one tiny hole — doesn't leak much blood. For that matter, I'm not a big fan of the .243 Winchester, even though I killed my first buck with one as a kid.

But the 6.5 Creedmoor? Well, any Millennial worth his man bun will vouch for that. I'd put it at about the ballistic threshold at which serious deer cartridges begin. It is a mysteriously good whitetail killer and easy to shoot.

Though I own two Creeds and use them often, my personal go-to deer gun is still a boring old .30-06. Classics like that, as well as the .270 and .308 Winchester, are tough to beat. So are the 7mm Remington Mag. and .300 Win. Mag., if you don't mind the extra shoulder slap. The bolt actions on this list are available in all the above, so take your pick. A few can be had in short-action magnum calibers, including .300 WSM and 6.5 PRC. Both are good rounds, and so is the up-and-coming 6.8 Western, which isn't available in any of these rifles at press time that I know of

The T/C Compass II is an excellent example of a functional, accurate deer rifle that doesn't cost much money.

but will be soon and is intriguing.

As for bullets, I like to err on heavy and just this side of explosive. Whitetails are easy to penetrate but have a reputation of being pound-for-pound tough. More than that, I think, wounded whitetails tend to dive into thickets, where finding blood and getting follow-up shots is difficult. Over-gunning them a bit doesn't hurt. Classic soft points in the 130- to 180-grain range such as the Winchester Powerpoint, Remington Core-Lokt and Federal Power Shock aren't exciting to write about, but they're effective. I love .30-caliber Nosler Ballistic Tips, too.

Of course, those cartridges are illegal in some of the best whitetail states, where hunters are limited to shotgun slugs, muzzleloaders or straight-wall cartridges. Many straight-walls make up for lack of speed with big bullets, and they're lethal deer killers at close range. For example, I've killed several whitetails with a .357 Magnum lever gun and never had one take more than a few steps.

But Winchester's .350 Legend is a better choice all the way around, both ballistically and because of the number of rifles chambered for it. The Legend was explicitly designed to meet the legal rifle cartridge requirements for deer hunting in states like Ohio and Iowa. Hunting bullet weights of 150 to 180 grains traveling 2,100 to 2,300 fps didn't excite any benchrest nerds but offered real in-the-field advantages to hunters accustomed to being stuck with shotguns and slugs. The .350 Legend flattens whitetails to 200 yards with far better accuracy than any slug gun I've tried, and it does it with a fraction of the recoil. It's rapidly becoming one of the most popular deer cartridges available for certain Midwestern states.

NOTES ON SCOPES

There is the potential for a more extended shot in some good whitetail places. The prairies of western Nebraska and Kansas come to mind, as do the sprawling beanfields and green fields of the Deep South. Still, most whitetail country has more thickets than fields, and property lines are rarely far away. At the risk of sounding preachy, I've not seen many 300-yard-plus shots at whitetails end well. Most of them are killed within 100 yards, and many are shot within 50.

With that in mind, you don't need 16x magnification, a Christmas tree reticle, ballistic app pairing, side parallax adjustment or an adjustable turret on your scope. Really, all you need is a scope that'll hold zero, which is impervious to moisture and will provide low-light visibility. Just about every decent scope these days will do all the above. I don't mind paying a little extra for good glass, but it's hard to stomach topping a $450 rifle with a $600 scope.

A 3-9x40 with a 1-inch tube works just fine. It doesn't hurt to have a little more — or even a little less — magnification (I've got a 30mm, 2-10x50 on one of my favorite deer rifles, and a 2-7x30 on another). A 50mm objective bell might help you eek another minute or two of legal light out of the day, and that's never a bad thing on a whitetail gun. You just have to buy mounts and/or rings to ensure the scope clears the rifle's barrel.

What brand should you get? I think Leupold's VX-Freedom series is pretty damn solid for the money. The basic 3-9x40 comes with the Custom Dial System or CDS (which you don't need for whitetails but is handy for double-duty western big game) and starts at about $300. It's at the top of this price list.

The Burris Fullfield E1 is another solid "ham-n-beans" 3x9 that offers a few ballistic reticle options, none of which are too complicated. I've hunted with these scopes and favor the basic Ballistic Plex reticle. Figure out the corresponding ranges for your rifle and the hash marks on the crosshair, and you're good to go, akin to sighting in the static pins of a compound bow.

The Bushnell Engage series is another good lineup with a few perfect configurations for whitetails. The standard 3-9x40

The author with a South Texas buck he took with the Franchi Momentum in .308.

doesn't have an adjustable turret, but you can get one for less than $200. I've got a couple of these scopes on various guns and have never had a minute's trouble.

No talk of blue-collar scopes would be complete without mentioning Vortex. I've used the Crossfire II only a little myself. Still, I have several close hunting buddies who've outfitted their primary hunting rifles with one version or another of that scope. They love it, mainly because of Vortex's VIP Warranty and repair guarantee.

My general takeaway on scopes and calibers is that shooting whitetails is not that hard, though hunting them can be. I err on the side of simple and proven with my gear, more than trendy and expensive. That's why I like all these guns, too.

WINCHESTER XPR

I've used the XPR more than any rifle on this list, including on two bucket-list big game hunts in Canada. I killed an Alberta bull moose with an XPR in .300 WSM and a British Columbia black bear with another one in .300 Win. Mag. The rifle is an accurate shooter and cycles smoothly, part of which I credit to its simple, single-stack magazine. The XPR has a good trigger, called the M.O.A. System, and Winchester claims it has zero take-up, creep or overtravel. I can attest that it is crisp, though the XPR in my safe breaks a tad heavy at 5 pounds, 8 ounces. The rifle has a standard two-position safety and a bolt release button to load or unload the rifle without manipulating the safety.

Speaking of loading the rifle, when working the bolt of the XPR, you'll notice that it seems large enough to serve as a front porch pillar. It's built from chrome-moly steel bar stock with three locking lugs and has a short, 60-degree throw that certainly helps when cycling the rifle in a hurry (like, when a moose you're pretty sure is hit hard is turning to walk back into the North Woods amongst the wolves). I wouldn't say the bolt is entirely without play, but it's close enough.

The XPR is available in 16 calibers, ranging from .223 to .338 Win. Mag. and .325 WSM. Here at home in Kentucky, I've used it on a few whitetails, and one of my favorite versions of it was chambered in .350 Legend. If I were looking to buy a serious straight-wall deer gun to use in the timber, an XPR Compact, with a slightly shorter length of pull (never a bad thing when you're in a treestand with six layers of clothing) and 20-inch barrel chambered in the .350 Legend would be atop my list.

FRANCHI MOMENTUM

The Momentum has excellent ergonomics and, to my mind, is both the best-handling and best-looking gun on this list. It costs a few dollars more than the XPR but is still well within the blue-collar budget. Suppose you feel like splurging a bit to class up this cheap date. You could get the Momentum Elite, which substitutes a hinged floorplate for a box magazine, adds a Cerakote finish to the barrel and hardware, a camo finish to the stock, and a muzzle brake, Picatinny rail, and optional 6.5 PRC chambering (the standard Momentum is available in 6.5 Creedmoor, .350 Legend, .308 Win., and .300 Win. Mag.).

Franchi is an Italian brand (under the umbrella of Beretta, Benelli, and Stoeger) long known for quality shotguns. The

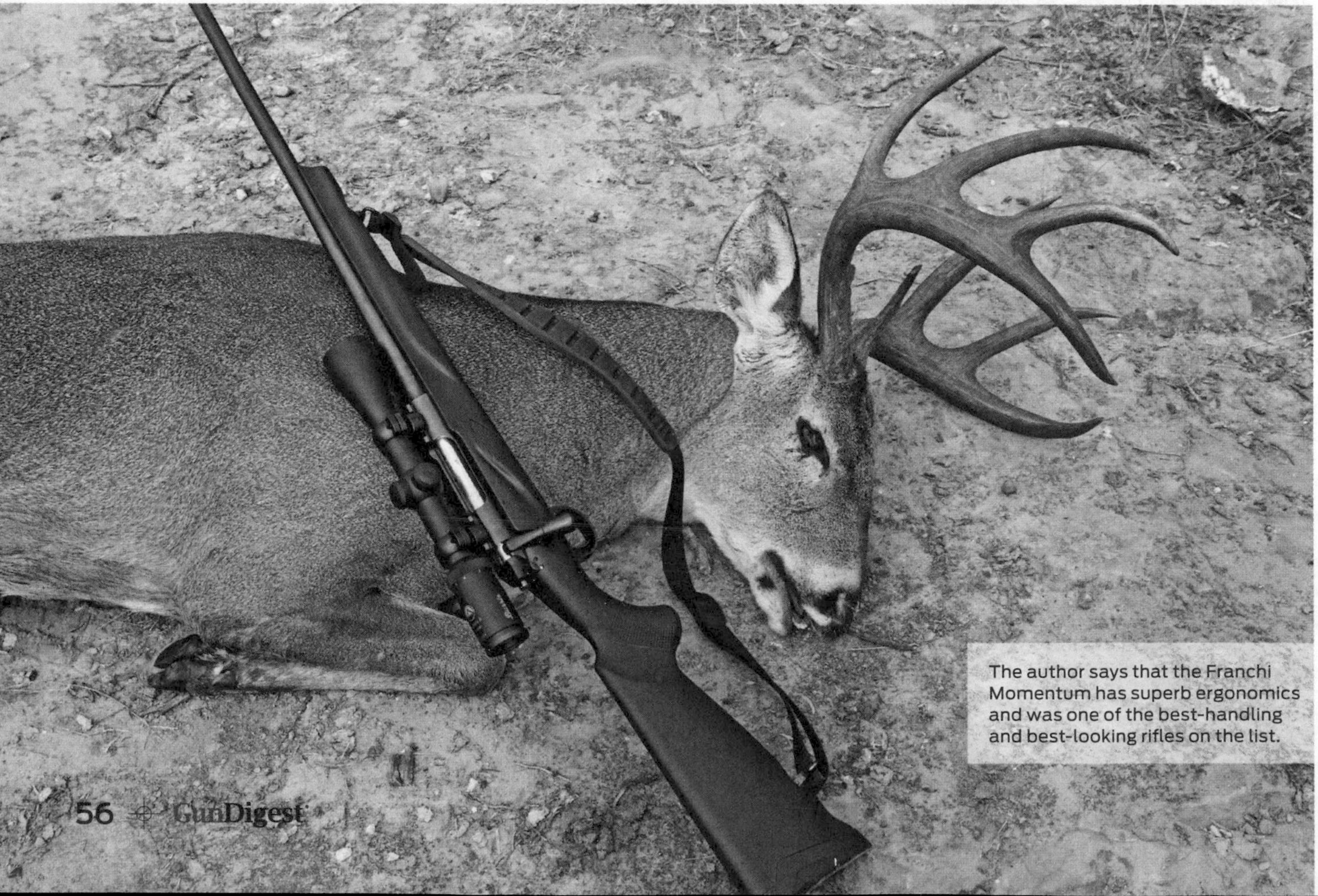

The author says that the Franchi Momentum has superb ergonomics and was one of the best-handling and best-looking rifles on the list.

The Winchester XPR is the author's favorite budget bolt action.

Momentum was Franchi's initial foray into the rifle world, and I got a chance to use a prototype paired with a Burris Fullfield for a week in South Texas when it was introduced in 2018. If I make it to Heaven, I expect at least part of it will look like Texas brush country and be teeming with critters. My test rifle that week was a .308, and I shot a couple of pigs, javelina, some whitetail does, and a 9-year-old 160-class buck with signature chocolate Texas antlers — one of my best whitetails to date.

The Momentum is accurate (with a 1 MOA guarantee), nimble, and lightweight with a threaded, free-floating barrel. It also has Franchi's signature TSA recoil pad built-in, a system that works well with its hard-kicking turkey guns and makes the Momentum a milquetoast kicker indeed, particularly in the Creed or Legend. The Momentum is available with a 24-inch barrel in 6.5 Creedmoor, .300 Win. Mag., or .350 Legend, but if I were buying, I'd go for the 22-inch version in .308. Such a configuration is perfect for hunting whitetails on an oak ridge, where shots might happen quickly and close, or in a Texas *sendero,* where they can average 200 yards. This gun will excel in either place.

THOMPSON/CENTER COMPASS II

I own two 6.5 Creedmoor guns, as mentioned above. One is a higher-end rifle that cost me about a thousand bucks, and the other is a T/C Compass II that cost about a third of that. The Compass II is not a pretty rifle, nor does it always feed perfectly. But it'll shoot neat little quarter-sized groups with just about any ammo I put through it. I've antelope hunted with it in Wyoming and have shot a pickup truck full of hogs with it in Texas. Most of the time, it's a truck gun, but a deer rifle come November.

I didn't have any experience with the Compass — T/C's original budget bolt gun — but word on the street was that the trigger wasn't great. If that's so, the upgraded Generation 2 trigger fixes the problem. The trigger on my rifle breaks at 2 pounds, 9 ounces, and there's nothing wrong with it. The three-lug bolt has a 60-degree throw, but the action is where I see the most significant difference in this rifle compared to, say, the Winchester XPR. The Compass II is a little rough, and the cartridges can be a little sticky when feeding out of the box magazine. The rifle's specs claim the magazine will hold five rounds, but if you can mash more than four rounds, you've figured out a trick that I have not.

Still, those are minor complaints because, at just over $400 MSRP, the Compass II is an incredible value, far and away the blue-collar-friendliest in this list of blue-collar guns. It has a free-floated, threaded barrel that's just shy of 22 inches long in calibers ranging from .223 to .30-06 and 24 inches in 7mm Rem. Mag. and .300 Win. Mag. It's difficult for me to poor-mouth the 6.5 Creedmoor version, but if you absolutely cannot sleep at night for fear of your buddies finding out that you hunt with such a metrosexual round, then the .308, .270 or .30-06 versions of the Compass II should work just fine.

Hunters can expect minute-of-deer-heart accuracy from many modern muzzleloaders, and the CVA Optima is among the best bargains.

SAVAGE 110 STORM

If any rifle changed the preconception that an accurate bolt action had to be expensive, it was the Savage 110. Today's 110s have undergone some pretty significant changes, but the lineup is more robust than any platform on this list. You can get a 20-inch "Hog Hunter" version with iron sights and an oversized bolt handle, or on the other end of the spectrum, the 110 Long Range Hunter in .338 Lapua. There are left- and right-handed guns available. The rifle's hallmark is the user-adjustable AccuTrigger — an excellent system upon which many other modern triggers are based — and a detachable box magazine and sliding tang-style safety.

In the context of this discussion, the 110 Apex Hunter, which comes from the factory with an optional Vortex Crossfire II scope — one of the optics mentioned above — probably makes the most sense. It'll be mounted and bore-sighted, but you'll want to fine-tune things before hunting. It would seem a shame to buy an American package like that in anything other than .30-06. Still, it's available in 20 calibers from .204 Ruger to .450 Bushmaster, including all the classics in between.

However, suppose you've gotten a nice bonus this year and want to spend just a bit more. The 110 Storm is a nicer rifle with stainless steel hardware and Savage's excellent AccuFit stock that allows you to customize the rifle to your exact length of pull and preferred comb height. I carried that rifle in .30-06 for a week in New Zealand, hunting weird critters, none of which were immune to the Springfield. It's a touch heavy in the mountains but would be ideal for sitting in a box blind.

CVA OPTIMA V2

Just about every state in the country has additional hunting opportunities for muzzleloader shooters, and some of the best big-buck chances happen during muzzleloader-only seasons. For example, Kansas has a unique early September hunt, where muzzleloader hunters get a chance to hunt whitetails in late-summer patterns and maybe even a velvet buck. Meanwhile, the former world-record non-typical was taken during Tennessee's early November muzzleloader season in 2016. Some truly giant whitetails fall every January in Ohio and Iowa during the late muzzleloader seasons.

Some states require loose powder, open sights, and even flintlock ignition — but most modern whitetail hunters tote a scoped inline. Loaded with two or three pelletized, 50-grain powder charges behind a saboted bullet, and you've got a gun that'll reliably kill a buck to 200 yards. The break-action style, popularized by the Thompson/Center Encore, is now the standard, and guns like the CVA Optima V2 are tough to beat for the money. I've got a couple of them, with synthetic stocks and stainless hardware. It comes with open sights or a one-piece scope mount, a breech lever on the trigger guard and a breech plug that's easily removable (by hand, if you keep it clean and lubricated).

The guns are rated to 150 grains of blackpowder or equivalent and rely on 209 shotshell primer ignition. I get the best muzzleloader groups (with this and other inlines) with 100 to 110 grains of loose Blackhorn 209 powder and a 270-grain Federal BOR Lock Trophy Copper bullet. Still, you'll want to replace the factory breech plug with a Blackhorn QR plug to ensure reliable ignition (it's a sub-$40 upgrade via Amazon). A pair of 50-grain Triple-7 or Pyrodex pellets with the bullet of your choice usually works just fine to get 2-inch groups +/- at 100 yards. That's minute-of-deer-heart, as they say, and you can't ask for much more from a bargain-priced muzzleloader that'll last you forever so long as you keep it clean.

Buy that and two of the rifles above — one in .350 Legend and another in something with a little more range — and you'll be set to hunt whitetails just about anywhere in the country, with money to spare for your processor's best venison sausage. GD

Rethinking Rifling

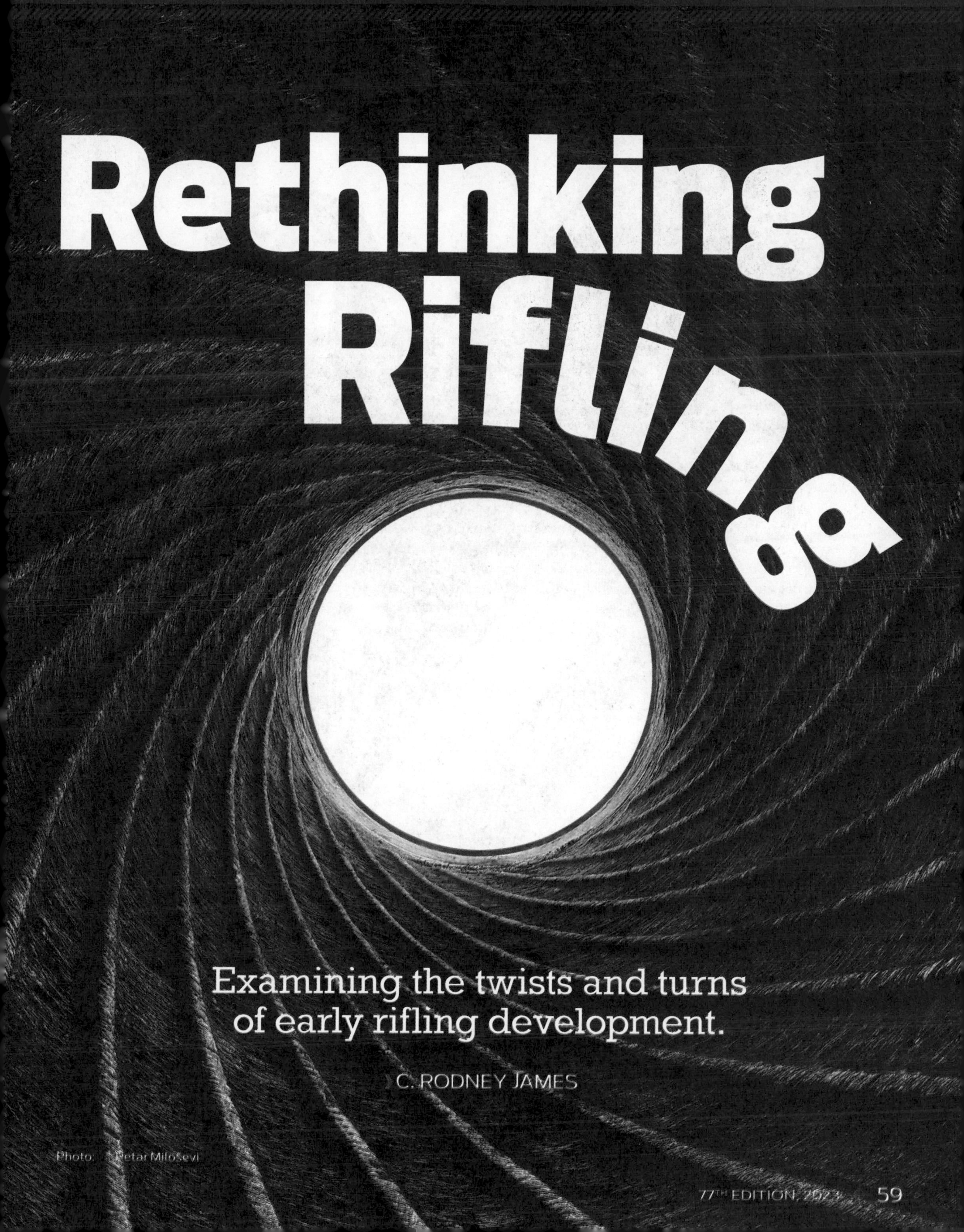

Examining the twists and turns of early rifling development.

C. RODNEY JAMES

Photo: Petar Miloševi

Italian gunmaker Davide Pedersoli produces a reproduction Whitworth rifle in .451 caliber with genuine hexagonal Whitworth rifling. Photo: Pedersoli

In the 1500s, spiral grooves cut into gun bores were used to spin-stabilize bullets fired through them. While the method of creating these grooves has changed, this system has remained the same and is considered "best" by nearly all barrel makers.

Attempts to improve land-and-groove rifling included choke boring, free boring, gain twist, deep and shallow grooves, few and many grooves, and odd and even numbers. No one system demonstrated significant superiority over another. About 1850, the first alternatives to land and groove (L&G) rifling made their appearance.

Charles Lancaster was considered the first to produce a rifled barrel using a spiral bore in England. Referred to as oval or elliptical boring, the oval interior was turned as though a straight oval tube was twisted, causing a bullet fired through it to be swaged into a slightly oval shape and spun as it traveled down the bore. The idea (in part) was to create a barrel that would perform equally well with a solid bullet or a charge of shot, but that goal did not succeed if experiments firing shot loads through rifled shotgun barrels are any indication. Nevertheless, the system worked with solid bullets. The success was tempered, for blackpowder fouling presented a more significant problem than a deep-groove rifled barrel.

The Civil War saw the Greene Oval Bore Rifle, an early bolt action wherein two bullets were loaded, with the second bullet with its powder charge acting as a gas check behind the charge of the first load. When the action fouled, the rifle had to be used as a muzzleloader. They were made in America with machinery bought from Lancaster. Recovered bullets from Antietam indicate some use.

A similar spiral-bore effort used polygonal rifling. While it is unknown who produced the first such barrel, the best-known effort was by Sir Joseph Whitworth in England in 1853. While the hexagonal-bore Whitworth could be fired with a cylindrical bullet, it was soon found that the best accuracy was obtained only with a six-sided bullet contoured to a mechanical fit. Semi-military Whitworth rifles, equipped with telescopic sights, were used by Confederate sharpshooters to pick off several Union officers. Major General John Sedgwick was the most famous who was killed by a single bullet at more than 500 yards. The system was also successfully used in artillery pieces, two of which were employed by Confederates at Gettysburg.

Sir Joseph Whitworth (December 21, 1803–January 22, 1887) was an English engineer, entrepreneur, inventor and philanthropist. He devised the Whitworth rifle, often called the "sharpshooter" because of its accuracy, considered one of the earliest examples of a sniper rifle.

Charles Ingram English Volunteer Pattern Percussion Rifle in .45 Whitworth. Photo: Jim Supica *The Illustrated History of Firearms, 2nd Edition*

The last rifling innovation of the 19th century came in 1871, the work of William E. Metford, a British engineer. Metford's system utilized shallow rifling with rounded lands, which reduced the bullet's drag and deformation. Accuracy was excellent, and the design was used in the British military rifle designed by James Paris Lee in 1888.

Unfortunately, highly erosive smokeless powders and corrosive primers soon degraded the accuracy of the soft-steel barrels of the day. A similar system was used in Japanese Arisaka rifles, which benefitted from better steel and maintained accuracy better than conventional L&G barrels. Barrels made in America by Charles Newton also used this system, utilizing five rounded lands and grooves.

In 1901, the first head-to-head tests of an oval-boring system versus conventional rifling began at the Springfield Armory. The details are fully documented in the *Annual Reports of the WAR DEPARTMENT for the Fiscal year ended June 30,1902, Volume VII, Reports of the Chief of Ordnance and Board of Ordnance and Fortification, Appendix XII.*

The project began July 16, 1901, with the following letter to the Chief of Ordnance:

"Dear Sir: I have invented a gun with an elliptical bore of .30 caliber, suitable to take the ordinary fixed ammunition of this caliber. I desire to have a thorough Government test, such as will demonstrate the quality of the gun for service. I desire to have the test made at the earliest convenience in order that I may be present.

Very Respectfully,

W.F. Cole M.D."

The Chief of Ordnance was Brigadier-General A.R. Buffington, inventor of the Buffington "wind gauge" sight — the most sophisticated military type of its day — used on the M-1884 and M-1888 Springfield rifles and carbines. General Buffington ordered, "test without delay the gun presented by Dr. Cole" and invited Cole to attend the tests.

Two days later, Dr. Cole met with the Board to test his rifle, which had the same 30-inch barrel as the Krag and used the same ammunition. "The cross-section of the bore is an ellipse the short diameter being .30", the long diameter .31", and having a twist of one turn in 7.29."[1]

The rifle was tested against the Krag at 1,000 yards. Three five-shot groups for each rifle averaged 25.11 inches for the Krag and 13.72 inches for the Cole rifle (extreme spread). The next day, a 300-yard test was conducted with a different Krag with better results. Velocity tests for the Krag (at 53 feet) were 1,991.55 fps, and for the Cole, 2,058.66 fps. On July 23 and 26, three five-shot groups were fired at 1,000 yards. Results were 18.96 inches (Krag) and 17.46 inches (Cole.) The test on the 26th had the Krag set up with a different stock and fittings. Results: 15.71 inches (Krag), 17.68 inches (Cole). On

William Ellis Metford (October 4, 1824–October 14, 1899) was a British engineer best known for designing the Metford rifling in .303 caliber Lee-Metford and Martini-Metford service rifles in the late 19th century.

October 1, firings were done at 1,200 and 1,500 yards. At 1,200: 28.6 inches (Krag), 23.5 inches (Cole) and 23.1 inches (new model Springfield rifle 2,300 fps velocity). At 1,500 yards, the results were 40.3 inches (Krag), 37.0 inches (Cole) and 26.9 inches (Springfield).

At this point, the Board in charge of testing sought to conduct further tests to determine the effects of different twist rates and the type of rifling with "an exhaustive series of firings with a barrel rifled according to Dr. Cole's plan."

On June 14, 1902, the Board met to consider test results comparing a new Cole barrel with an 8-inch twist to the new Springfield barrel with 8-, 9- and 10-inch twists.

Through March and April, 80 five-shot groups were fired in the above three twist rates at 500 yards with a group average of 4.4 inches for the four-groove Springfield barrel. The same number was fired through a Cole barrel rifled with an 8-inch twist for a group average of 3.9 inches. 80 groups were shot through the Springfield at 500 yards from May through June using 8- and 9-inch twists for a group average of 4.07 inches. Through the same period, 72 groups were fired through the Cole, and the group average was 3.8 inches. From February through June, 46 groups were fired at 1,000 yards through the Springfield for a group average of 11.33 inches. Simultaneously, 38 groups were fired through the Cole for group averages of 10.33 inches. Pressure measurements for the Cole and Springfield rifles were virtually the same.

The Board recommended that Cole system barrels be made for the first 500 Springfield magazine rifles produced for field and armory testing.

By this time, Buffington, who had served as interim Chief of Ordnance, had been replaced by William Crozier. Crozier raised the issue that the superiority of Cole's system may have resulted from gas escape in the four-groove barrel and recommended cupping the base of the bullet. Frankford Arsenal produced 3,000 rounds of this ammunition.

The bolt-action Lee–Metford was a British army service rifle that used James Paris Lee's rear-locking bolt system, detachable magazine, and an innovative seven-groove rifled barrel designed by William Ellis Metford. Photo: Armémuseum

Beginning July 26, 1902, 20 barrels of each type were produced for further testing with a 1-10-inch twist. The results for 500-yard tests (one five-shot group per barrel) yielded an average of 5.6 inches for the Cole and 5.9 for the Springfield. At 1,000 yards, the results were 15.6 for the Cole and 22.3 for the Springfield. Considering the terrible results of the Springfield 1-10 twist, two additional barrels with a 1-8-inch twist were produced of each type. At 500 yards, the Cole averaged 4.6 inches and the Springfield 5.4 inches for five groups, and at 1,000 yards, the results were Cole 7.5 inches, Springfield, 10.0. In terms of velocity, at 1,000 yards, the Cole had an advantage.

At the request of Captain Lissak, the above two rifles were sent to the Seagirt, New Jersey range, where the National matches were being held. There, opportunities were offered to various and sundry to try them out. The reported results for 200, 600 and 1,000 yards rated both rifles equally accurate, with opinions favoring the Springfield rifling.

In its September 23, 1902 report, the Board recommended two other rifles be produced with the 1-8 twist, one with each type of rifling for analysis of accuracy plus endurance. To this end, the production of 10,000 cartridges was requested for a 5,000-round test for each rifle. The Board's report garnered the following reply:

"OFFICE OF THE CHIEF OF ORDNANCE

Washington, September 29, 1902

Respectfully returned to the com-

The Springfield Armory's experimental shop (Building 28), circa 1923.

manding officer, Springfield Armory. The experiments with the elliptical-groove system (Cole's) should be discontinued. Dr. Cole has been informed that the Department does not consider that it possesses sufficient advantages over present system to warrant further experiments.

William Crozier

Brigadier-General, Chief of Ordnance"

The ANNUAL REPORT offers no further comments from Board members or any expert shooters at the Springfield Armory, including Freeman Bull and Richard Hare!

In the January 13, 1910 *Arms and the Man* (which predated *American Rifleman*), gun-designer Charles Newton excoriated the Crozier decision. "In conclusion we have failed to find any point in which the land and groove system is proven or even claimed to be superior to the oval bore in a smokeless-powder rifle and the latter is conclusively shown by the Ordnance Department's experiments above cited to be more accurate and it will hardly be questioned that it is more durable, more easily cleaned and delivers its bullets in more perfect condition than the land-and-groove type."[2]

To this day, barrels of every U.S. military small arm have been rifled with the land and groove system.

The next phase in alternative rifling came in the late 1930s with the German application of hammer forging to barrel making. This method was first applied to

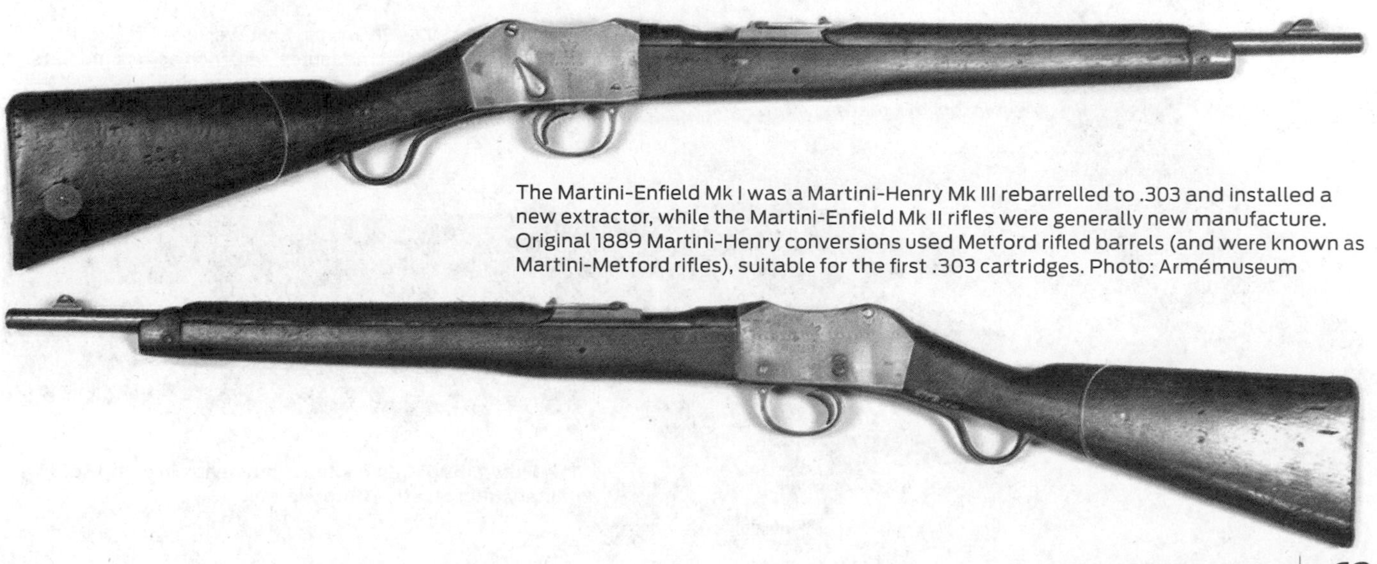

The Martini-Enfield Mk I was a Martini-Henry Mk III rebarrelled to .303 and installed a new extractor, while the Martini-Enfield Mk II rifles were generally new manufacture. Original 1889 Martini-Henry conversions used Metford rifled barrels (and were known as Martini-Metford rifles), suitable for the first .303 cartridges. Photo: Armémuseum the MG42 machine gun, where the barrel was hammered into shape over a mandrel placed in the bore of a barrel blank, shaping, rifling and chambering in one step. Hammer forging requires expensive machinery.

In the Post-War era, this technique is mainly used to produce what is now termed "polygonal rifling." For clarity's sake, the only actual polygonal rifling was that in Whitworth-pattern barrels with flat sides and angled corners. Current "polygonal" bores have sloping sides and rounded corners. This term also encompasses Metford rifling and oval boring.

In the 1960s, Heckler & Koch (HK) began marketing a line of rifles and handguns with polygonal rifling. While the details of HK's testing are proprietary, its conclusion is as follows: "Compared to conventional land-and-groove profile barrels, bullets fired through polygonal barrels have a higher muzzle velocity, as there is little gas leakage. This increases the amount of energy acting on the base of the bullet. There is no chance of the propellant gases "overtaking" the bullet and adversely affecting its flight properties and directional stability.

A polygonal profiled barrel does not have any sharp internal edges. This virtually eliminates the deposit of residues. A polygonal barrel is easily cleaned, reflects heat more efficiently and has a high resistance to erosion. With no sharp edges as with land and groove barrels, the notching effect on bullets is also avoided. The net effect is increased barrel service life plus no need to finish machine the barrel or chrome plate it. Manufactured with HK's famous cold hammer-forged barrel process, these polygonal barrels are made of HK proprietary cannon grade steel."[3]

Given the advantages of longer barrel life, virtually all current polygonal barrels are used on semi-automatic and automatic guns (both rifles and handguns), which see far more shooting than other actions.

Additional advantages of polygonal bores: they can be produced through buttoning and cutting. There is controversy over the use of lead-alloy bullets, particularly in semi-auto handguns where lead buildup just forward of the chamber can cause excessive pressures. Careful inspection and cleaning are the rule and heeding warnings issued by the manufacturer.

Currently, polygonal rifling is used by HK, CZ, Kahr, Glock, Magnum Research and Tanfoglio. The only American company to enter this market is La Rue Tactical, which produces high-end uppers for M-16 platform rifles and its own competition/sniper models.

Will polygonal rifling become the new standard? Significant changes may soon follow with the U.S. Army's adoption of the HK M110A1 Squad Designated Marksman Rifle, Cal 7.62x51 (.308). A modified version, the G28 Compact Semi-Automatic Sniper System (CSASS), is the latest.

The reader may well wonder at the abrupt and apparently nonsensical decision to abandon oval boring on the part of William Crozier. The politics within the American military bureaucracy gives

The U.S. Springfield Model 1896 Krag-Jorgensen bolt-action in .30-40 Krag. Photo: Jim Supica *The Illustrated History of Firearms, 2nd Edition*

The 560-grain Civil War-era Whitworth bullet measures .450 inch across the flats. The design may have inspired the .45-70-500 gr. "long-range" bullet developed for the M-1884 and M-1888 Springfield rifles.

The Model 1896 Krag figured prominently in early U.S. military rifling tests. Photo: Hmaag

The Heckler & Koch rifling system features rounded corners and sloping sides.

new meaning to the word "byzantine." This dynamic is documented in the 1994 book *MISFIRE: The History of How America's Small Arms Have Failed Our Military* by William H. Hallahan. Though this work has been criticized for specific technical errors, in terms of analyzing the personality quirks of those in charge of small arms development, it appears dead on.

A.R. Buffington was required to retire at age 64. Crozier (then a captain) was a popular and highly respected inventor in the Ordnance Department. His work on an improved Krag had little resemblance to the 96 Krag. Crozier was on good terms with Teddy Roosevelt and his Secretary of War, Elihu Root. When Root appointed Crozier Chief, the latter jumped over thirty officers his senior and rank to brigadier general. The old guard fought the appointment in Congress, but Root won in his shake-up of the military. Roosevelt and Root pressured Crozier to deliver a rifle equivalent to the Mausers Roosevelt had faced in Cuba.

It would seem understandable that Crozier had little interest in *any* modifications that might delay the delivery of the new rifle. The M-1903 Springfield was indeed an equivalent to the 98 Mauser. In fact, it bore enough similarities that the government paid Mauser $200,000 to avoid a patent-infringement lawsuit. Crozier later tangled with Isaac Newton Lewis over his machine gun. After a Senate investigation, Crozier was fired. GD

The Pedersoli Whitworth reproduction allows you to try a unique hexagonal-rifled gun like those used during the Civil War, which equipped the sharpshooters of the Confederate Army, hence the name "Whitworth sharpshooters."

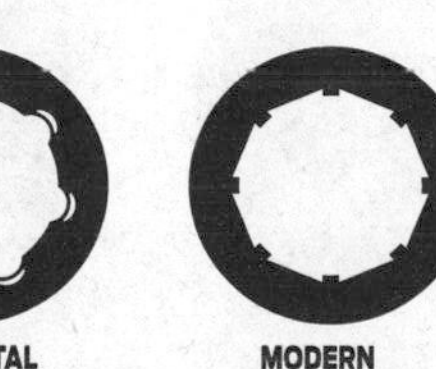

Rifling systems (*Our Rifles*, Charles Sawyer, p. 330). While this chart doesn't cover everything, it hits the high points. The main issue in the 1850s was the odd-versus-even land and groove numbers, the theory being that with an even number, the pressure of two opposed lands created more bullet distortion than when each land was opposed by a groove. What became the standard Springfield rifle resulted from extensive testing at Springfield and Harper's Ferry, published by the authority of the Secretary of War in 1856. After 1855, rifles and carbines from the Springfield Armory (until the Krag was adopted) featured three grooves of approximately equal width. The Krag had four. The idea of gain-twist rifling never demonstrated any improvement over a fixed system.

ENDNOTES

1 In the original text, inch marks (") were in front of numbers. These have been placed in back for today's reader.

2 Arms and the Man, Volume XLVII. No 15 January 13, 1910. "Oval Bore Rifles" By Charles Newton, pp 295,6.

3 Personal communication from Steve Galloway: Director of Creative Services. Heckler & Koch.

.500 Jeffery, Ultimate GAME STOPPER

At One Time the Most Powerful Sporting Cartridge Ever Produced

›TOM TABOR

When you compare the .30-06 and the big .500 Jeffery Rimless, the difference in power seems obvious.

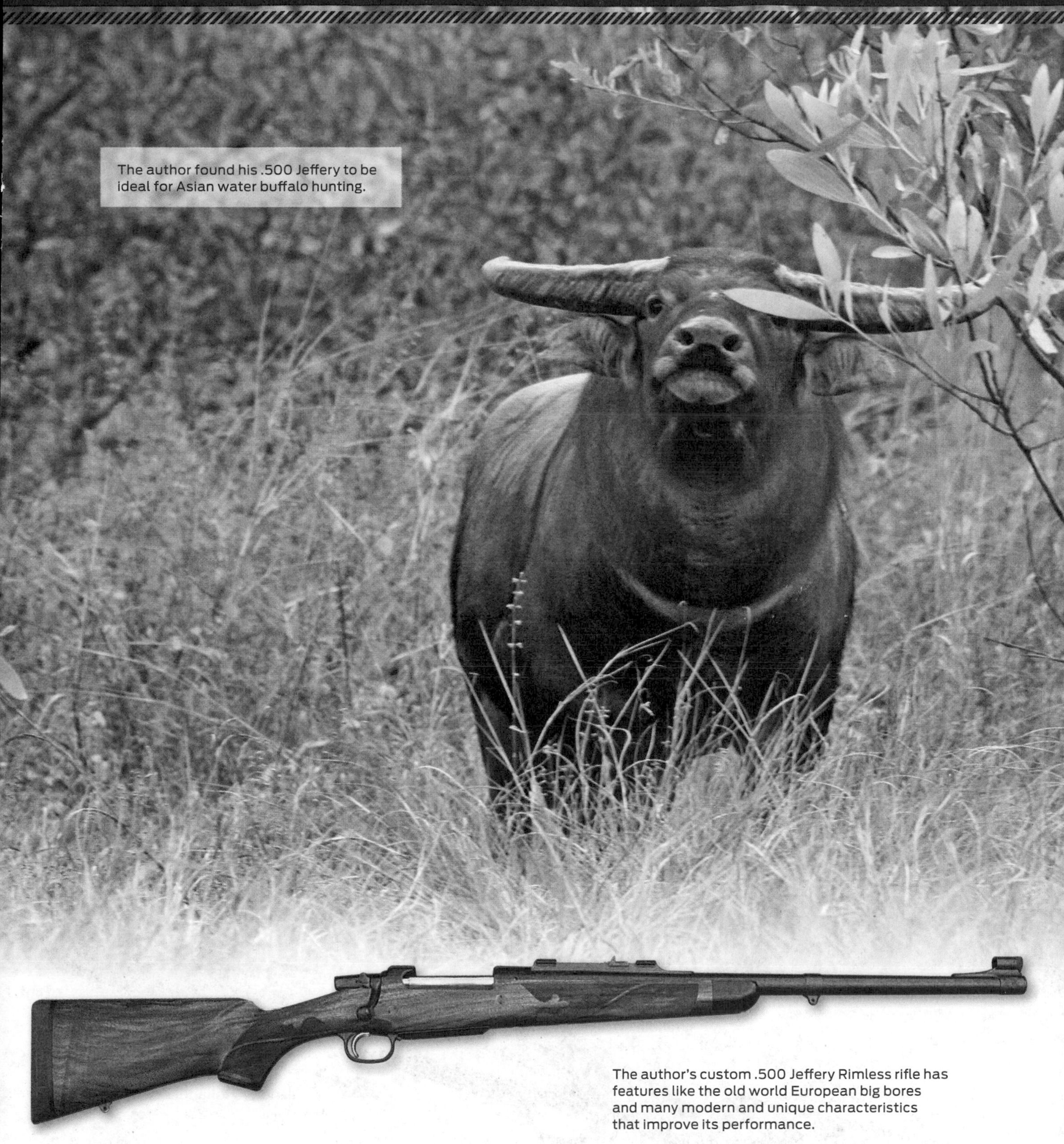

The author found his .500 Jeffery to be ideal for Asian water buffalo hunting.

The author's custom .500 Jeffery Rimless rifle has features like the old world European big bores and many modern and unique characteristics that improve its performance.

I have had a lifelong attraction to big-bore rifles. As a result, I've devoured virtually everything I could lay my hands on about that subject. And understandably, that eventually evolved into the ownership of many big bores chambered for a variety of different cartridges. But while each of these rifles came with its desirable features, none seemed to fit what I viewed to be the perfect big bore. That was until I finally decided to have a custom rifle explicitly built around my own desired characteristics and chambered in what I finally decided to be the ultimate big-bore cartridge — the .500 Jeffery Rimless.

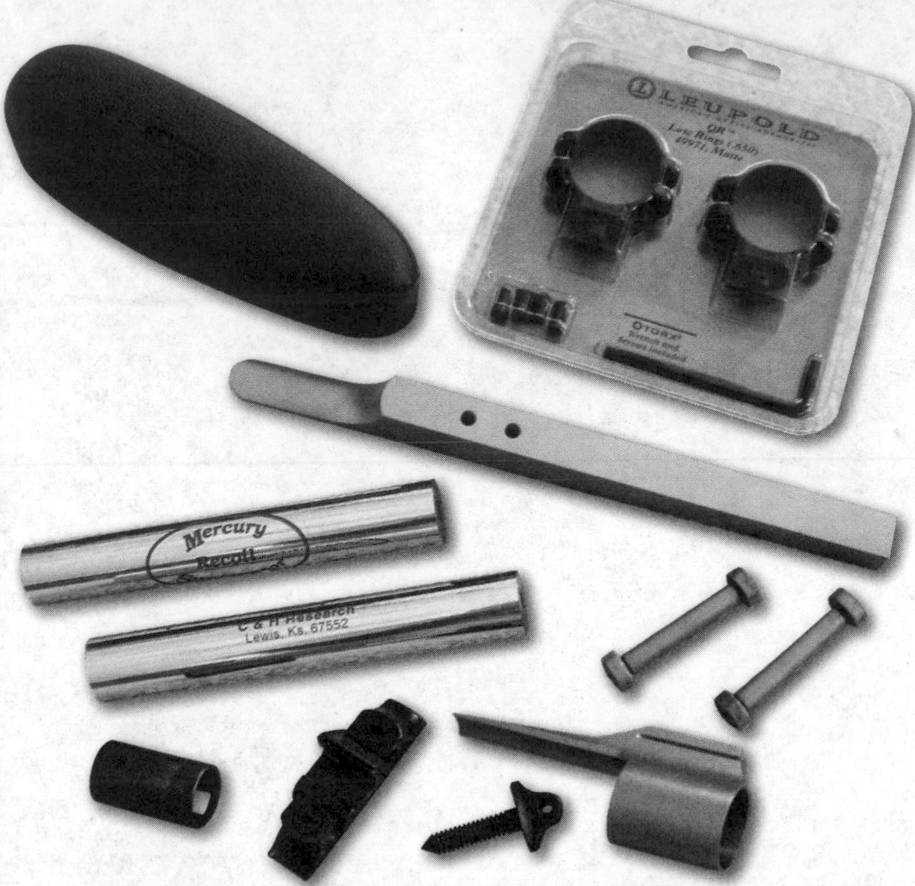

When building a custom big-bore rifle, give considerable thought to selecting the best parts.

Many experts have recognized the .500 Jeffery as the most powerful shoulder-fired sporting rifle cartridge ever produced. It only relinquished that noteworthy title when, in 1959, Weatherby came out with its .460 Weatherby Magnum. But 29 years later, Jim Bell and William Feldstein developed an even more powerful cartridge. Having been turned down by Holland & Holland to produce a safari rifle chambered in .600 Nitro Express, they vowed to retaliate. The result was the monstrous .700 Nitro Express.

Settling on the .500 Jeffery as the perfect big-bore caliber wasn't an easy decision, one I made after pawing over every historical and modern piece of ballistics and performance data I could find. I considered wildcat versions from famous cartridge experimenters like Mashburn and Ackley and many modern-day varieties from Lott, A-Square, Dakota, and Ruger. But my passion was with the legendary historic cartridges that often were a part of the exciting adventures of the Ivory Trail and carried names such as Rigby, Holland & Holland, and of course, Jeffery.

A BIT OF .500 JEFFERY HISTORY

The name of this cartridge is a bit of a misnomer as British manufacturer W.J. Jeffery did not initially design it. Instead, it was the brainchild of August Schuler, who originally called the cartridge the 12.5x70mm Schuler when he

Once finished and blued, the author's custom quarter rib turned out to be a work of gunsmithing art.

developed it in Germany in the 1920s.

After World War I concluded in 1918, German rifle production suffered greatly due to the Versailles Treaty and the economic woes and strife. Because newly produced rifle actions had become difficult to get, it forced the rifle manufacturers to take advantage of any actions they could find. Since military Mauser Model 98s were quite plentiful and available at the time, Schuler acquired some and developed a big-bore cartridge that was short enough to function in those actions yet powerful enough to fulfill the needs of the elephant hunter. Schuler designed the new cartridge with considerable girth, a shortened neck, and a sharper shoulder angle than many of its competitors to compensate for that shorter overall length and the reduction in powder capacity. The result was a cartridge that functioned perfectly in the typically less expensive bolt-action rifles and was fully capable of effectively killing any critter that roamed the earth.

Seeing the effectiveness of Schuler's design, a few years later, around 1925, the premier London rifle builder W.J. Jeffery adopted that same general design and gave it his English moniker, calling it the .500 Jeffery Rimless. But while many consider these two cartridges identical, they are not. Very slight variations are present, preventing interchangeability.

As the most powerful hunting round of that era, the .500 Jeffery's reputation grew with the ivory hunters. The famous Rhodesian hunter, C. Fletcher Jamieson, and John 'Pondoro' Taylor frequently sang its praises and wrote about it in their books. Jamieson's own .500 Jeffery was a special order rifle directly from W.J. Jeffery, which weighed close to 13 pounds and was reportedly responsible for killing over 300 elephants during a single decade.

During the early years, the cartridge was usually loaded with 535-grain bullets, backed by 90 grains of Cordite powder. But that load fell short of tapping into the full potential of the cartridge. Today, with the diverse variety of improved and heavier bullets —and far superior smokeless powders — the .500 reaches even new heights in performance and killing abilities.

WHY THE .500 JEFFERY RIMLESS?

If you intend to face the most dangerous beasts on earth, which may very well be planning to stomp, gore, or eat you, packing something like the .500

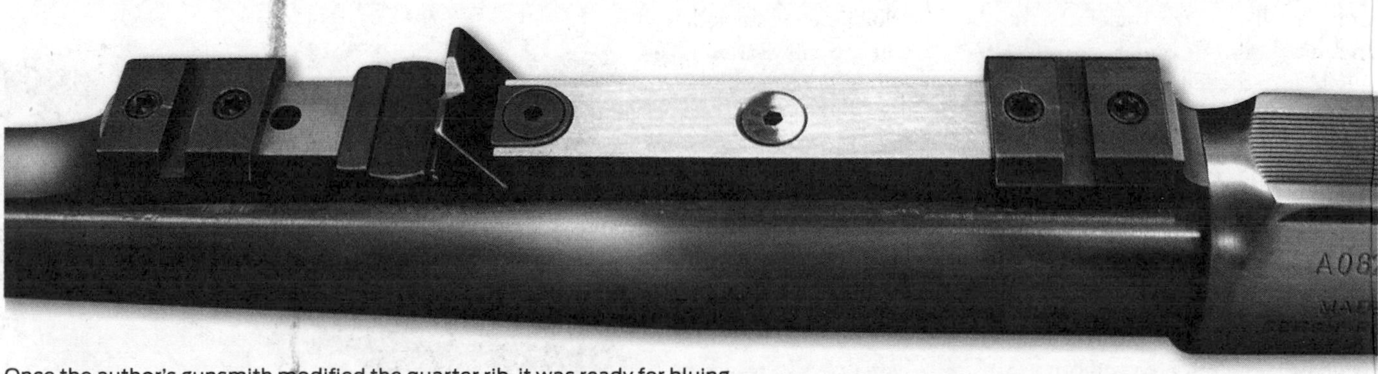

Once the author's gunsmith modified the quarter rib, it was ready for bluing.

Jeffery provides you with a distinct level of confidence. Just knowing you will be sending a slug comparable in weight to a 1-1/3 ounce fishing sinker delivering up to about 3-1/2 tons of energy on impact has to be a comforting thought to most dangerous game hunters. But the downside of such performance comes in the form of the .500's heavy recoil. While a standard .30-06 may generate around 15 ft-lbs of felt recoil, a rifle chambered in .500 Jeffery can dole out nearly 100 ft-lbs of shoulder-jarring abuse, which only gives credence to the old saying, "it kills at both ends." However, the good news is there are ways to tame and offset some of that secondary energy.

If you're contemplating having a custom rifle built, there are more recoil-softening measures available to you. However, even when purchasing an over-the-counter rifle, you can still take advantage of some of those same modifications. Either way, a rifle possessing a straight-styled stock certainly helps to direct the recoil to your shoulder rather than directly into your more vulnerable head and face, and, of course, rifle weight absorbs some of that energy. I installed two 1-pound mercury recoil reducers inside the buttstock, and you can do the same with a production-built rifle. A side benefit of doing so shifts the center of weight away from the muzzle, encouraging quicker pointing ability. I purposely built my stock heavy, kept the barrel contour large, and installed a well-designed recoil pad, all to keep the abusive recoil at bay. My finished rifle tipped the scales at just slightly less than 12 pounds (unloaded).

I desired to keep the gun's appearance like the historic safari rifles, so I chose not to install a muzzle brake. On the other hand, muzzle brakes can substantially reduce the felt recoil, and a good gunsmith can add one to most rifles.

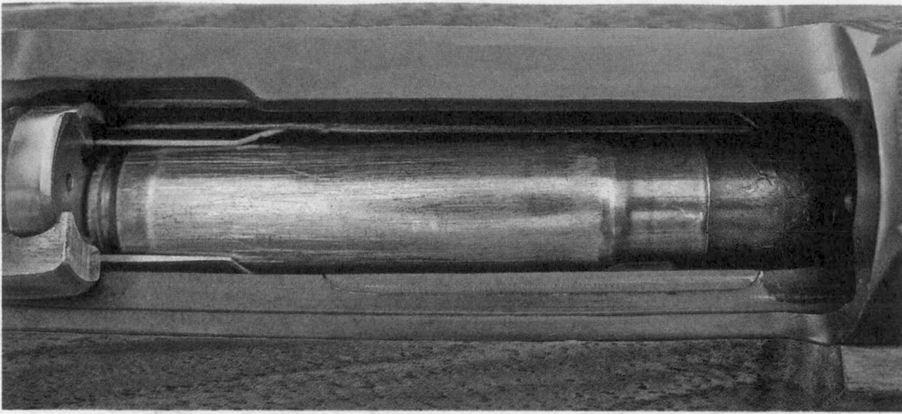

Because of the immense overall size of the .500 Jeffery cartridge, the gunsmith converted the magazine to a single-stack feed.

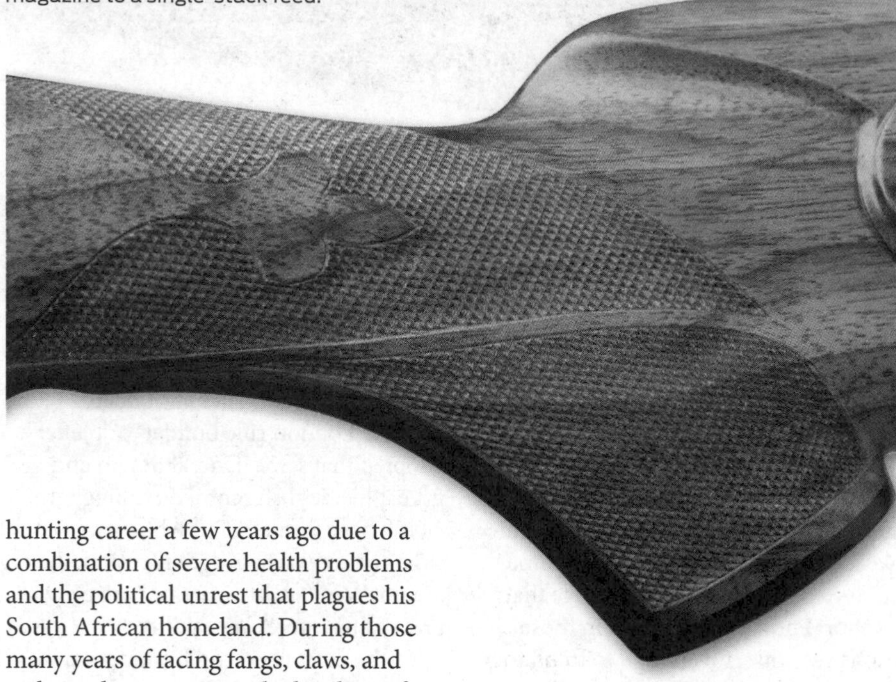

Nothing adds classy looks to a stock like *fleur-de-lis* checkering.

CUSTOM RIFLE MOVES FORWARD

Down through the years, I've acquired a great deal of advice from many experts in the field of big bores, including much from my friend and African Professional Hunter Carl Labuschagne. After decades of pursuing the Big Five and other dangerous game, Carl ended his professional hunting career a few years ago due to a combination of severe health problems and the political unrest that plagues his South African homeland. During those many years of facing fangs, claws, and tusks under sometimes the harshest of African conditions, Carl compiled an extensive background of knowledge that he often shared with me.

One of the recommendations he stressed was to equip the rifle with a low-powered scope mounted with a reliable set of quick detachable mounts. Rather than mounting the scope above the action, he mounted a long eye relief optic on the barrel. This style encourages you to shoot with both eyes open for quicker pointing, faster target acquisition, and better peripheral vision. But even more critical,

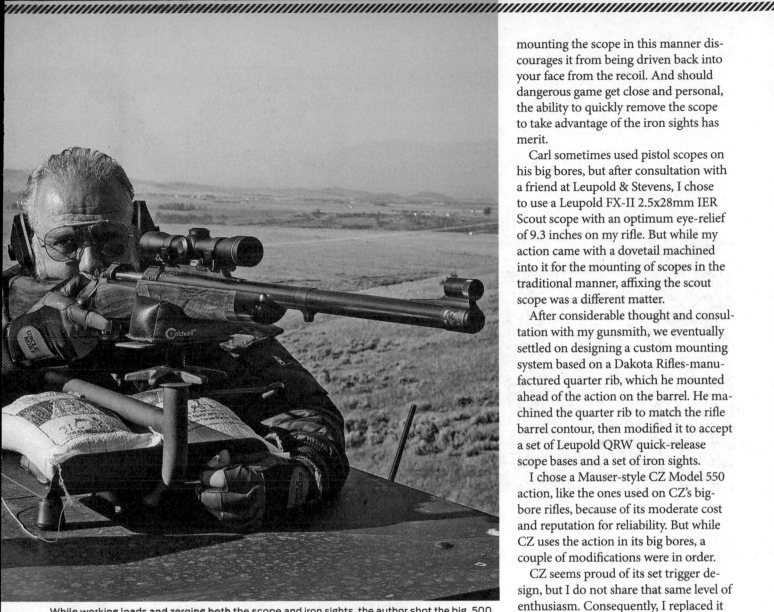

While working loads and zeroing both the scope and iron sights, the author shot the big .500 off the bench using a lead-sled loaded down with extra weight to soften the recoil.

mounting the scope in this manner discourages it from being driven back into your face from the recoil. And should dangerous game get close and personal, the ability to quickly remove the scope to take advantage of the iron sights has merit.

Carl sometimes used pistol scopes on his big bores, but after consultation with a friend at Leupold & Stevens, I chose to use a Leupold FX-II 2.5x28mm IER Scout scope with an optimum eye-relief of 9.3 inches on my rifle. But while my action came with a dovetail machined into it for the mounting of scopes in the traditional manner, affixing the scout scope was a different matter.

After considerable thought and consultation with my gunsmith, we eventually settled on designing a custom mounting system based on a Dakota Rifles-manufactured quarter rib, which he mounted ahead of the action on the barrel. He machined the quarter rib to match the rifle barrel contour, then modified it to accept a set of Leupold QRW quick-release scope bases and a set of iron sights.

I chose a Mauser-style CZ Model 550 action, like the ones used on CZ's big-bore rifles, because of its moderate cost and reputation for reliability. But while CZ uses the action in its big bores, a couple of modifications were in order.

CZ seems proud of its set trigger design, but I do not share that same level of enthusiasm. Consequently, I replaced it with a custom trigger that my gunsmith had designed himself. He converted the magazine to a single-stack feed design for more reliable feeding of the massive, nose-heavy .50-caliber cartridges. He then installed a heavier magazine spring to facilitate proper cartridge feeding in the chamber. Such modifications underscore the importance of a good gunsmith with knowledge and experience in gunsmithing big bores.

Sometimes called a "scout mount," an extended eye relief scope mounted in this manner eliminates the possibility of getting the rim of the scope driven back into the shooter's face.

A PROBLEM FOR ALL .500 JEFFERY SHOOTERS

From the beginning, many of the

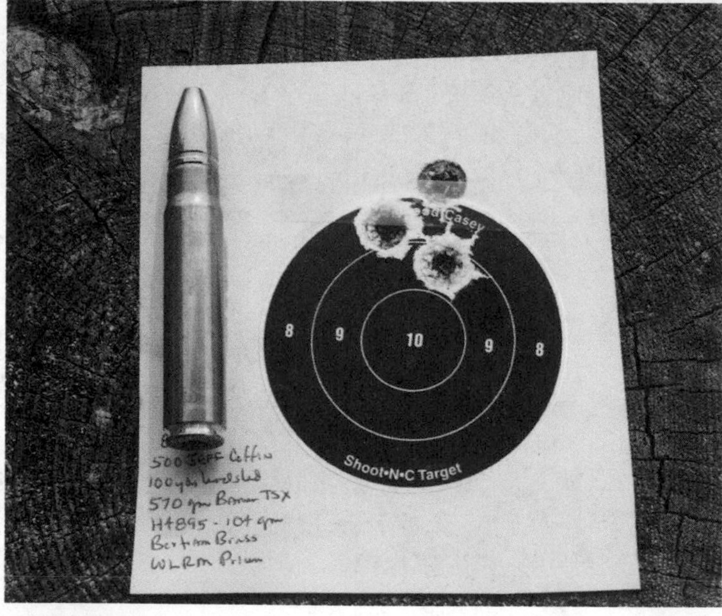

The potential accuracy of the .500 Jeffery takes a back seat to few other rifles.

premier rifle manufacturers in Europe offered the .500 Jeffery. But it wasn't until around the turn of this century that the U.S. manufacturers such as Dakota and CZ-USA began offering it. And, of course, as those new rifles started hitting the market, there was a need for commercially produced ammunition to feed them, a challenge several of the top cartridge manufacturers accepted. Unfortunately, some of these companies failed to realize that the .500 Jeffery Rimless is not a standardized cartridge design. As such, there are several slight dimensional variations of it floating around. While minor in most respects, these differences eventually showed up in the form of chambering issues, something that hasn't been good for the cartridge's overall reputation. Rather than facing the problem head-on, ammo makers chose to drop the production of the .500 from their lines.

Custom building a rifle comes with the advantage of avoiding such dimensional issues. A knowledgeable gunsmith will cut your chamber with enough tolerance to accommodate all of the currently available commercial ammunition. To do so, your gunsmith should work closely with the chamber reamer manufacturer and, if you are planning on handloading ammunition, consult with the die manufacturer.

Because of the price of the factory-loaded ammunition, many big-bore shooters prefer to handload. Several companies offer reloading dies for the .500 Jeffery Rimless, and I chose a set of custom dies Hornady made on the

1-inch stock rather than the standard 7/8 inch. The people at Hornady were highly knowledgeable and great to work with throughout the process. Knowing that there were dimensional variations around the .500 Jeffery, they suggested that I send them a couple of spent cases to match the dimensions to the resizing die. I explained that that would not be possible because I hadn't built the rifle yet.

Once the Hornady folks fully understood my situation, they said they would be happy to work with the chamber reamer manufacturer: Dave Kiff of Pacific Tool & Gauge. That way, the chamber, and the reloading die specifications would match perfectly. I couldn't have been happier with both Dave Kiff and Hornady for the cooperation they provided me. They worked excellently together, and it was a fine example of old-fashioned customer service that is often lacking today. Eventually, I had the properly sized reamer, a perfectly matched set of reloading dies, and the assurance that my chamber would properly accept my handloads and all the currently available commercial ammunition.

THE JEFFERY DOWN UNDER

My first outing with the new rifle was an Asian water buffalo hunt in the Northern Territory of Australia. While the water buffalo isn't as dangerous as its African counterpart, the Cape buffalo, it is nevertheless a formidable, hard-to-kill beast that can tip the scales close to a ton in weight. And under certain situations, it can become quite a dangerous adversary, particularly when wounded.

While arranging for the hunt, word somehow got out that an American gun writer was coming to the area, creating a once-in-a-lifetime offer. A game ranger working for the Aborigine Territory contacted me and asked if I could layover for a few days to accompany him on a buffalo culling operation. In some areas, the non-indigenous buffalo were causing a significant amount of erosion. In some instances, that resulted in threatening the stability of the historic Aborigine rock paintings and other ancestral artifacts. As a result, they were interested in reducing the number of buffalo in specific locales and considered a commercial hunting concession in the Territory. As such, they were asking me to help in their culling project and provide them with any insight and advice I might have on the establishment of a commercial hunting operation. I quickly agreed, and soon I was on my way, headed Down Under.

Between the trophy hunt and the culling operation, my .500 Jeffery was responsible for a little over a dozen buffalo kills. In most cases, these were one-shot kills with handloaded ammunition using 570-grain Barnes Triple-Shock X bullets. Most shots were to the lung area, which resulted in dispatching the animals quickly and humanely. In one case, the bullet entered broadside just behind the shoulder, taking out both lungs and a couple of ribs. After penetrating close to three feet of muscle mass and bones, we found the bullet lodged just under the skin on the opposite side. The TSX mushroomed perfectly and retained a full 100 percent of its original weight. It had brought the big buff down within seconds after the hit.

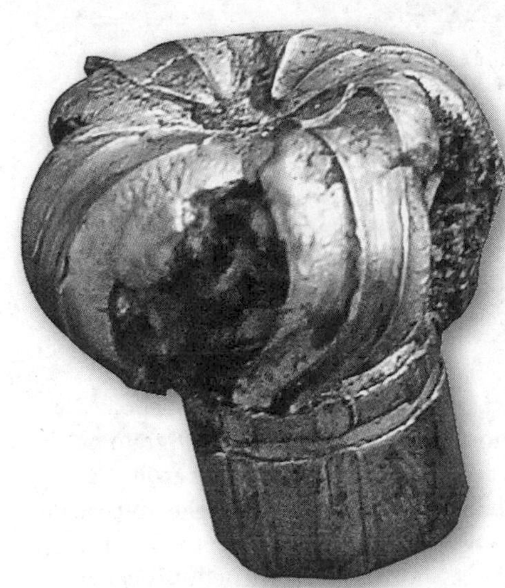

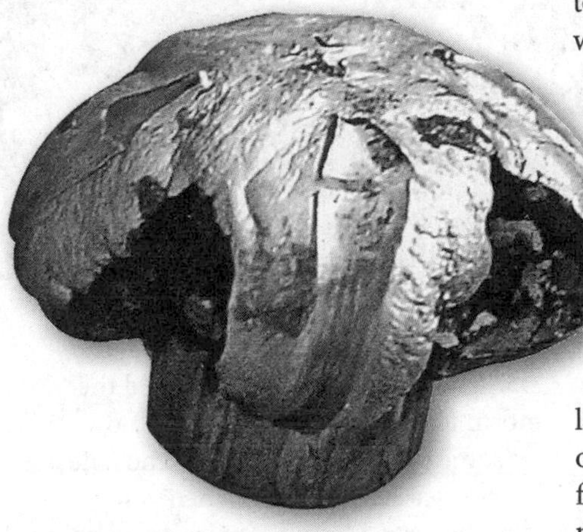

The author recovered these Barnes Triple-Shock 570-grain bullets from the water buffalo. They show perfect mushroom performance and 100 percent weight retention.

AMMO VERSATILITY

Understandably, the .500 Jeffery Rimless is best suited for hunting the largest, toughest, and most deadly game on earth. And as such, it is well-designed for that purpose. I believe every cartridge performs best within a narrow range of bullet weights. For example, the .270 Winchester prefers 130-grain bullets; the .22-250 likely will shoot the 55-grain bul-

This extra tough ol' Northern Territory water buff absorbed two perfectly placed 570-grain slugs from the author's .500 Jeffery before succumbing.

lets best; all of my .300 Win. Mag. rifles like the 180-grain weight bullets, which ballistically outperform both the heavier and lighter weight choices in virtually all situations; and when it comes to the .500 Jeffery, I believe a high-quality 570-grain bullet provides the ultimate in performance.

In the early years on the Dark Continent, when Cordite powder ruled, the 535-grain bullets were considered the norm for the .500 Jeffery, and I know of some professional hunters who still prefer that weight bullet when going after big cats. I know of at least one bullet manufacturer that offers a big 600-grain option on the other end of the spectrum. But even though these bullet weights are available in .50 caliber, the best choice for most applications lies in a 570-grain bullet of high quality. And as far as the best choice of bullets in that weight, you can't go wrong with the solid copper Barnes Triple Shock X. It can penetrate deeply through bone and tissue like a solid yet hold together and still produce extensive tissue damage.

The .500 Thwarts a Lion Attack

Before the construction of my .500, I was on a plains game hunt in Africa when I noticed my professional hunter was sometimes packing a very fine-looking English-made safari rifle. When I inquired about the caliber, I was pleasantly surprised to find he chambered it in .500 Jeffery Rimless, which led to many interesting discussions, including a hair-raising tale about a lion hunt he had recently undertaken.

A few months earlier, he was guiding a bowhunter, which unbeknownst to him at the time of the booking, apparently possessed little in the way of any experience or even a rudimentary amount of bowhunting knowledge. After verbally explaining how that hunt had escalated into a perilous situation and only saved by using his .500 Jeffery, he promised upon returning to camp to show me the entire account, which they captured on video.

The situation began when they spotted a lion, and the hunter decided to take the shot at about 35 yards. But even though the shot appeared to be easy for an experienced archer, the arrow made an impact but failed to strike any of the lion's vitals. The lion disappeared into a dense patch of chest-high grass. That evening, while watching the scene play out on the video and listening to almost constant roars of the injured lion, I felt chills run up and down my spine. Knowing full well how dangerous the situation had become, the PH sent someone to fetch the vehicle and use it to penetrate the cover where the lion had holed up.

Once someone retrieved the truck, the PH and the bowhunter climbed into the truck's open bed and made their way back to the scene. Before long, the lion came into view at moderate range. The hunter drew back his bow but refused to take the shot, fearing a bad angle. They repositioned the vehicle several times before the hunter finally launched two more arrows at his target, with the first arrow missing completely. The second arrow hit, dropping the lion. Lying on its side and appearing to be mortally wounded and taking its last breaths, the truck inched forward until next to the lion. The hunt seemed to be over. The PH remained on alert with his big .500 fully at the ready. And, it was a good thing he did.

In a blink of the eye, the beast sprung to life and propelled itself airborne directly toward the open truck bed and its offending pursuers. The quick-thinking PH brought his .500 up but, because of the unnatural angle, the only shot he had on the airborne lion was by holding his rifle high over his head on extended arms. He shot; instantly, the bullet ripped into the body of the charging beast knocking it lifelessly to the ground just outside of the vehicle.

Having fired my own .500 many times and knowing full well how much recoil it produces, I am amazed that such a shot didn't break the PH's arm or shoulder. Fortunately, all ended well, though, and I believe it is fair to say the hunter and PH learned a few lessons. In this case, possibly none was more important than for a hunter to understand their limitations and don't take on a hunt like this if you cannot properly handle it. And for the PH, I'm sure he won't be booking another dangerous game hunt without fully understanding how knowledgeable and capable the hunter.

My question is, if the PH had been shooting a lesser-caliber rifle, would the result have been the same? We will never know, but it makes me feel that Elmer Keith's belief that there is no such thing as too much firepower applied in this situation.

If you decide to shoot different bullet weights, expect a change in the bullet's impact point. I found my 535-grain handloads impacted about 2-1/4 inches higher than my 570-grain loads at 100-yards.

THE WAY I SEE IT

Many big-bore cartridges are the rimmed type, making them more suitable for break open-style rifles, like the traditional safari side-by-side doubles. On the other hand, rimless cartridges like the .500 Jeffery perform best in bolt actions. A significant advantage of the bolt guns is that they are easier to produce and consequently less expensive. And that results in many more gun enthusiasts being able to afford the purchase of a big bore.

Big-bore rifles chambering thumpers like the .500 Jeffery Rimless are not everyone's cup of tea. Without a doubt, they come with some inherent disadvantages. For one thing, the rifles are heavier than your dad's ol' aught-six he might have used for deer hunting; the recoil can be stout enough to bruise your shoulder

TABLE 1 — .500 JEFFERY RIMLESS RELOADING DATA

BULLET (TYPE/ GRAINS)	CASE	POWDER (TYPE)	POWDER (GRAINS)	PRIMER	MUZZLE VELOCITY (FPS)	MUZZLE ENERGY (FT-LBS)
Barnes Banded Solid 570	Bertram	IMR 4895	103	Federal GM215M	2,288	6,627
Barnes Banded Solid 570	Bertram	IMR 4895	105	Federal GM215M	2,359	7,044
Barnes Banded Solid 570	Bertram	H4895	102	Federal 215	2,223	6,256
Barnes Banded Solid 570	Bertram	H4895	104	Federal 215	2,311	6,761
Barnes Triple Shock 570	Bertram	H4895	102	Federal 215	2,228	6,284
Barnes Triple Shock 570	Bertram	H4895	104	Federal 215	2,277	6,563

Note: All loads shot to the same point in the author's test rifle at 100-yards. The author noted no signs of pressure, and all rounds functioned flawlessly.

Starting point references: 1) http://www.accuratereloading.com/500jef.html, 2) A-Square Reloading Manual.

Warning: Even though these loads were safe in the author's firearm, always start 5-10 percent lower than any reputable published data and work up to a maximum safe level for your firearm. The author and this publication take no responsibility for any result stemming from the use of this data.

TABLE 2 — BIG-BORE VELOCITY AND ENERGY COMPARISON

CARTRIDGE	BULLET WEIGHT (GRAINS)	MUZZLE VELOCITY (FPS)	MUZZLE ENERGY (FT-LBS)	100-YARD VELOCITY (FPS)	100-YARD ENERGY (FT-LBS)
.375 H&H Mag.	350	2,300	4,112	2,062	3,306
.404 Jeffery	450	2,150	4,620	1,949	3,795
.416 Riby	450	2,150	4,620	1,933	3,715
.416 Rem. Mag.	450	2,150	4,620	1,933	3,715
.458 Win. Mag.	500	2,150	4,897	1,868	3,874
.470 Nitro Exp.	500	2,100	4,897	1,906	4,035
.500 Nitro Exp.	500	2,100	5,583	1,903	4,585
.500 Jeff. Rimless*	570	2,200	6,127	1,997	5,050
.505 Gibbs	600	2,100	5,877	1,899	4,805

* Ballistics can vary between ammo manufacturers and handloads. The author's handloaded .500 Jeffery Rimless cartridges produce an average measured velocity of 2,387 fps pushing a Barnes Triple-Shock X bullet weighing 570 grains.

TABLE 3 — .500 JEFFERY RIMLESS (100-YARD 3-SHOT GROUPS). BRASS: BERTRAM; PRIMER: FEDERAL 215 & CCI 250; POWDER: IMR 4895

BULLET (TYPE/ GRAINS)	POWDER (TYPE)	POWDER CHARGE (GRAINS)	MUZZLE VELOCITY (FPS)	SMALLEST GROUP (INCHES)	AVERAGE GROUP (INCHES)	LARGEST GROUP (INCHES)
Barnes Banded Solid 570	IMR 4895	103	2,280	2.5	2.5	2.5
Barnes TSX 570	IMR 4895	104	2,228	.875	1.875	2.875
Barnes Banded Solid 570	IMR 4895	105	2,359	.875	1.375	1.625
Woodleigh 535	IMR 4350	104	2,430	1.75	1.75	1.75

Note: When the author zeroed the rifle to shoot dead-on at 100-yards with the other loads, the Woodleigh 535-grain load impacted 2.250 inches high at that distance.

The .500 Jeffery's competition (left to right): .600 N.E., .505 Gibbs, .500 Jeffrey Rimless, .416 Rigby, .450-400, and .375 H&H.

and to jar a tooth filling loose; the ammunition and reloading components are more expensive. Even so, while a good bolt-action big bore will generally cost considerably less than a side-by-side in a comparable caliber, in my mind, the pleasures of owning and shooting one of these rifles far outweigh those somewhat minor hindrances.

It took me many years of research to determine which big-bore caliber I would prefer. Finally, having settled on the .500 Jeffery, I am confident I made the right decision. Ballistically, it is superior and outperforms all its competition. Nevertheless, over the years, other big bores have found their way into my hands.

Some of those I only owned a short time before becoming disillusioned and sending them off to take up residency in someone else's gun safe. Others, however, still reside with me, one of which I built to match the outward appearance of the .500 but scaled down in size and chambered for .416 Rigby. But no matter how many big bores I shoot, the .500 Jeffery will always be considered my pride and joy. It may very well be the best dangerous game cartridge man has ever developed. GD

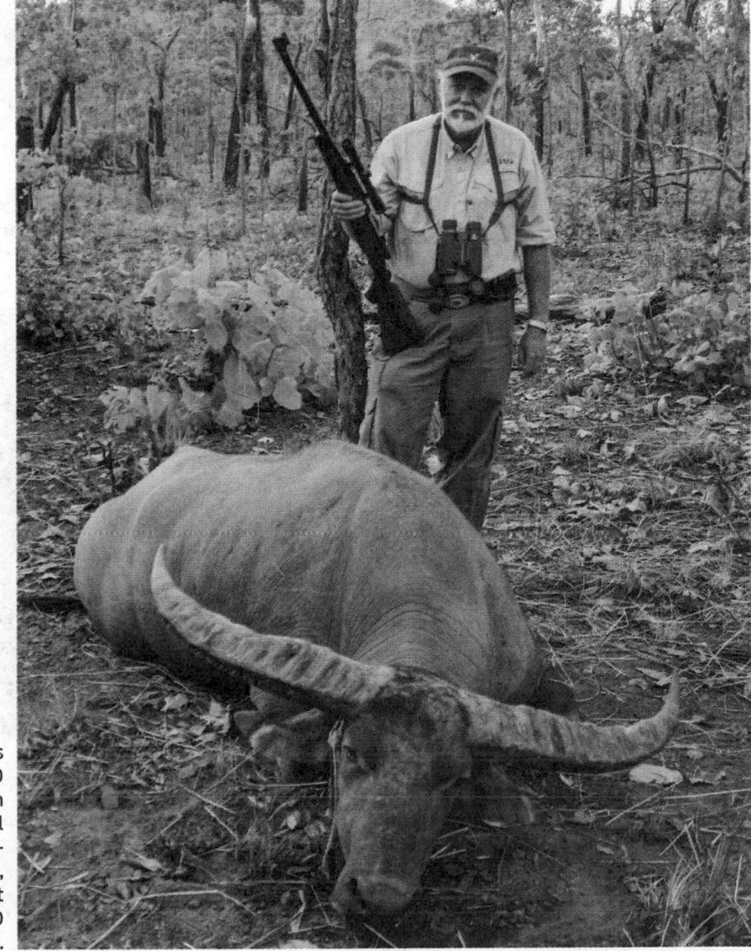

The author's best .500 Jeffery Asian buffalo bull had a 48-inch spread, scored just under 100 points.

On Custom Guns

Were the 'Good Old Days' *Really* Better?

›TOM TURPIN

All photos by author unless noted

Invariably, when discussing custom guns with interested aficionados, one topic will come up. Are today's custom guns better than the infamous good old days? Answering that question to everyone's satisfaction is not simple and is likely impossible.

With the help of ample photos, I'll make a stab at coming up with an answer. However, what follows is but one fan's opinion — mine! I believe my opinion is educated and not a hipshot in all humility. It's based on over a half-century of owning, using, discussing, writing about, and even building a couple of custom rifles. Still, it is but an opinion. My thoughts on the subject are worth only such credence as you, the reader, assign to them — no more and no less.

I have had the opportunity to visit the shops of many of our finest (and a few not so fine) custom gunmakers and observed as they created their magic.

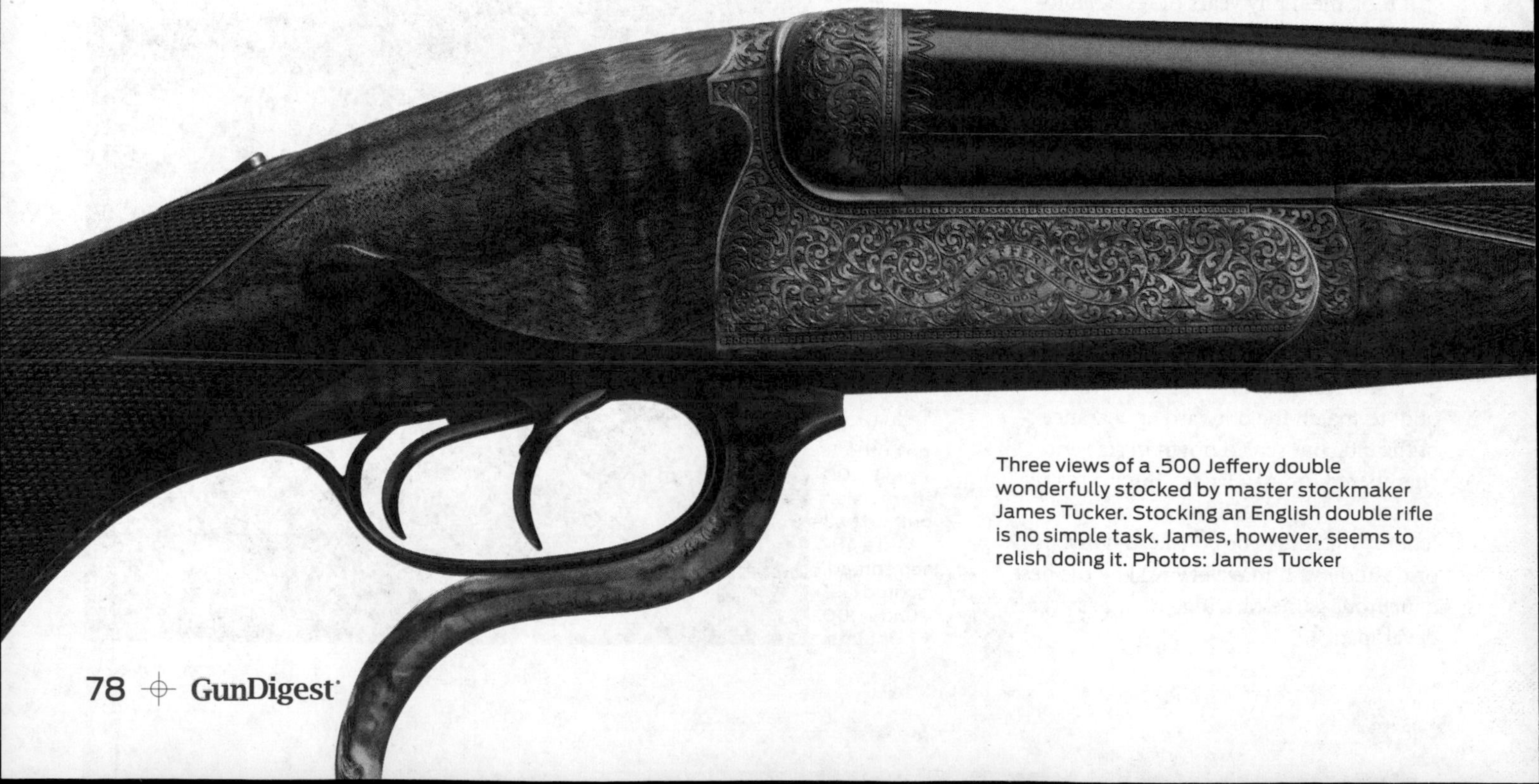

Three views of a .500 Jeffery double wonderfully stocked by master stockmaker James Tucker. Stocking an English double rifle is no simple task. James, however, seems to relish doing it. Photos: James Tucker

Most welcomed me into their shops and devoted some of their valuable time to show me what they do and how. Thankfully, only very few seemed to look upon my visit with all the enthusiasm of undergoing a root canal without Novocain! At least, I cannot recall ever being barred or asked to leave a maker's shop prematurely.

I do, however, remember having a well-known English gunmaker cover much of his work with a cloth doing my visit. I have no idea why. Perhaps he had something going on that he didn't want me to see. Possibly he thought me a spy, out to steal his secrets.

Custom guns run the gamut from the maker obtaining a factory-barreled action, slicking it up a bit, sticking it into a glass bedded synthetic stock, checking it to ensure it goes bang when it's supposed to and sending it down the road. A few I've met, thankfully very few, didn't even do that much.

On the other hand, others I've met practically remanufacture the factory-made parts used in their projects. Some spend many, many hours honing parts and fittings to the precision of a Swiss watch. They also spend many more hours at the range and reloading bench, tailoring effective loads for their creations. Yet others, I have heard, never leave their shops.

Some maker's shops are models of efficiency, with every tool in a dedicated storage place or in use. Others spend much, if not most, of their valuable time looking for things. Usually, I've found a maker's shop organization indicative of most everything else in the maker's life, but not always. There are exceptions. One person I knew was a world-class metalsmith. He could do almost everything involving metal and did it superbly — none better. His shop, though, was an unmitigated disaster. Sadly, he passed away a few years back, and I suspect his heirs are still looking for stuff.

I know another exceptionally talented maker who

This rifle represents the efforts of Fred Wells, his wife Rachel and his son Rube. Fred and Rube built the rifle, and Rachel engraved it. The Wells machined the Magnum Mauser action from a steel block in their shop, chambered for the Wells-designed .510 Wells cartridge. Fred was a big man who liked big rifles.

Noted Arizona maker W.A. Sukalle worked at various times in Tucson and Phoenix. He did a lot of work for another Arizonan, Jack O'Connor. This .270 is considerably more ornate than most of his work. The scope and mounts are early Bausch & Lomb models, and sight adjustments were made in the mounts and not the scope.

can do all aspects of riflemaking exceptionally well, ranking right up there among the very best. He can find anything in his well-equipped shop in less than five minutes, usually considerably less. Every item has a designated location, and the tool is either in that spot or being used, with no exceptions. He is exceptionally anal about enforcing this shop rule. Like his shop organization, his work is fantastic and very expensive. Nothing is left to chance, including tools, parts or rifles.

Many of the early makers I did not know and never visited. Tom Shelhamer, Al Linden, W.A. Sukalle, and several others died before I came on the scene. In those cases, I have judged their work from completed examples that I have seen. Fortunately, a few collector friends of mine have examples of work from the most well-known makers of the era. Thankfully, they allow me access to evaluate and photograph their collections when needed.

Finally, one critical factor in fairly evaluating a maker's work is directly related to pricing. This factor is in play on most items, particularly expensive non-essential ones, including custom guns. Having the skills to craft a world-class custom gun is one thing. Having the talent to sell the item for a profit is quite another. Both skills are necessary for success.

I once knew an extremely gifted maker whose rifles were spectacular, second to none, and equaled by very few. It pains me to report that he could make them, but he couldn't sell a hot dog at the World Series! He tried to make a go of it, but his shop was closed last I heard, and he was painting barns for a living. I've also known a few others whose skills were not quite so exceptional as the barn painter but outstanding. Another was as skilled as my painter friend but had a nasty habit of quitting before finishing the project. While not turning out equal quality rifles to my painter pal, the makers involved were excellent salesmen. They were able to survive nicely. Go figure.

Most custom makers are one-person shops. In addition to turning out superb custom guns, they are usually the salesman, bookkeeper, janitor, and the purveyor of other chief, cook, and bottle washer chores. All those chores are necessary, but crafting and selling are, of course, critical. Frankly, most would agree that crafting is the most important, but I admit a strong case can be logically made that sales take the Oscar. This has always been the case, good old days or today. I doubt that it will ever change. I believe that the 'smiths of yore had a much more difficult time equaling their modern counterparts and for many reasons.

Most importantly, I suspect that the raw talents of the old makers and those of today are similar. Automation in its many forms was not available to the old artisans, giving today's crop a significant advantage. Today's tooling and machinery are also superior to those in the old days. Of course, I agree that in the hands of a skilled operator, a good set of files can do most tasks superbly. However, consider how long it takes to do it manually and the resulting labor costs.

I also believe that the clientele these days are somewhat more numerous and more willing and able to commission custom gun projects than in the old days. They are still not plentiful, but more so than in earlier times. I recall a chat I had with Ken Warner many moons ago. He said he believed the number of serious custom gun clients was about 1,500. Ken wrote a book on custom guns and was an editor and publisher of several magazines over the years, including the annual *Gun Digest*. I thought the number was higher than his estimate, yet not so many as commonly thought. GD

The 40th Anniversary of the American Custom Gun Makers Guild

› PHIL MASSARO

JERRY FISHER GOLD
Three views of the work of three fabulous artisans on a magnificent rifle. Tom Burgess did the metalwork, Jerry Fisher the stock and Eric Gold the engraving. Probably a fourth master, Marvin Huey, crafted the oak and leather-style case.Photos: Steve Heilmann

"Custom gun." Those two words just have a ring to them, and to an aficionado of fine firearms ignite the possibilities of something beyond the ordinary. Having a custom gun built will invariably involve the talents of a gunsmith capable of handling one or more of the aspects of making a bespoke firearm. The craftsman's efforts stand out in a world of cookie-cutter, mass-produced goods, which is easily seen in firearms.

In centuries past, firearms were crafted by hand, and those entering the profession went through a long and arduous apprenticeship. The art was handed down from generation to generation. Sadly, throughout the last half of the 20th century, the hands-on work in the firearms industry quickly diminished, and the number of bespoke firearms continually declined. John T. Amber — longtime editor of this fine publication and *Handloader's Digest* — saw the wisdom of creating an organization to keep the traditions of gunmaking alive and was instrumental in developing the American Custom Gunmakers Guild.

The goal of the guild, officially formed in Phoenix, Arizona, on May 5, 1983, was listed as follows: "*The specific and primary purpose of the guild is to form an association of craftsmen who are actively engaged in the art of custom stockmaking and custom metalsmithing to the end that such craftsmen may exchange ideas concerning their craft, promote public awareness of custom gunmakers and their work and promote the betterment of custom gunmaking. In so doing the guild will sponsor a newsletter, publish articles of interest to custom gunmakers, and encourage education of new gunmakers.*"

There were 76 members when the guild was founded, with Don Allen (the founder of Dakota Firearms) serving as the first President.

Amber would, in the first issue of the ACGG Newsletter in July 1983, define the state of the art of custom gunmaking

AL BIESEN .280 — THE LAST O'CONNOR RIFLE
This outstanding example was the final rifle crafted by Al Biesen for Jack O'Connor. Surprisingly, it is not a .270 but rather a .280 Remington. O'Connor never saw the rifle as he passed away before it was completed.

AL BIESEN .270 PAIR
This pair of rifles is well known to Jack O'Connor's fans, and they were well used by him. They didn't start out as a pair, though. Jack ordered a single rifle from Al Biesen using a standard Winchester Model 70. Biesen trimmed the barreled action down to featherweight specs, and custom stocked it. O'Connor was so pleased with the rifle and its accuracy that he was concerned that he'd shoot the barrel out too quickly, so he ordered a second one like the first. His intent was to do most of his shooting with the second rifle saving the first for hunting only. As it turned out, the second rifle shot even better than the first. Number two became his all-time favorite.

STEVE HEILMANN .22
One of our best artisans working at the bench is Steve Heilmann. His work is impeccable, whether in wood or metal. He farmed out the engraving but did everything else in-house. Photo: Steve Heilmann

as such: *"I think a fair definition of this now-much-used phrase--hardly heard of a decade or so ago--would be something like this: That product, service, or work of art made or created in the context of its time in history in the best possible manner known to the worker, using his skills, and knowledge to the very utmost. Or, put another way, if a craftsman, artist, or atrizan (artisan) has put his heart and soul into a project, exercising to the fullest extent his mannual (sic) and mental abilities, he has at least approached a state of the art plateau. He may, indeed, have achieved that desirable, laudable goal."*

Amber was very proud of the organization, as he should have been. The world was already deviating from handmade goods — especially in the firearms industry — by the time the ACGG was founded, the craftsman becoming a rarity. Indeed, the efforts to preserve the discipline of crafting a firearm are respectable.

Forty years later, the ACGG still survives as a testament to that faction of the market that appreciates the efforts, talents and products of those dedicated to bespoke firearms. There are eight categories within the ACGG: Metalsmith, Engraver, Stockmaker, Checkering Specialist, Metal Finisher, Barrelmaker, Toolmaker and Casemaker. Some members have qualified in multiple categories, but many people stick to a particular discipline. I reached out to several of the members to ask for an idea of the state of their art.

"Traditional metal finishing almost became a lost art. The original craftsmen of the 1800s held onto methods and materials very tightly. And as time went on, modern metals and mass production meant that new ways of finishing were required. Fast-forward many decades and to the days when Turnbull Restoration was first starting out. Through our early restoration work, we re-discovered the old ways of finishing metal. The process of figuring out traditional finishes was long and sometimes painstaking. We worked closely with collectors to help us know

FISHER .22 SPRINGFIELD
A very unusual rifle by two of our finest artisans. Tom Burgess did the metalwork, and Jerry Fisher the stock. Marvin Huey possibly crafted the leather case. Fantastic work.

STEVE HEILMANN .375 H&H
A magnum Mauser .375 H&H from the Heilmann shop, the epitome of what a magnum Mauser should look and feel like. This rifle has everything it needs and nothing it doesn't. Superb. Photo: Steve Heilmann

WELLS .300 H&H
A pretty standard custom Mauser from Fred Wells' Prescott, Arizona shop. In addition to building fine rifles, Fred had a world-class collection of Mauser factory rifles.

when we got it right. And thankfully they were always honest when we didn't get it right. That's how we learned. As members of the American Custom Gunmakers Guild, we're proud to provide our restoration customers with authentic finishes using ways that were essentially rescued from extinction. And like our fellow Guild members, we're able to assure our customers that their job is done the right way."

– Doug Turnbull, Founder & CEO, Turnbull Restoration Co.

• • •

"Stock making is what sets American custom gunmaking apart from the rest of the world. Here we obsess over a perfectly filled stock finish and inletting with no gaps showing between the wood and metal, like nowhere else. Additionally, the hand checkering of a gun stock done in the United States is second to no one else in the world. A gunstock is the most visually dominating part of a custom made firearm, so much so that unaltered factory metal work, which has been fitted with a finely crafted custom stock, is generally considered a custom rifle. The most commonly used material for fine guns made by hand is thin-shelled English walnut, which has names like California English, French, Turkish, Australian, New Zealand but it is all essentially the same tree; the difference in the personality depending on the mineral content in the ground and the growing conditions where the tree grew. Most stocks are precision duplicated with a pantograph from a pattern that was made by the stockmaker. The stock is then hand inletted, the outside is final shaped, sanded, finished and finally checkered all by hand. Some stocks are still made from the blank entirely by hand, usually roughed in on a vertical mill. It is a requirement of the guild that a stockmaker must have made of their project guns from the block by hand. The level of custom stockmaking done today is better than has ever been done in the past. Great Ameri-

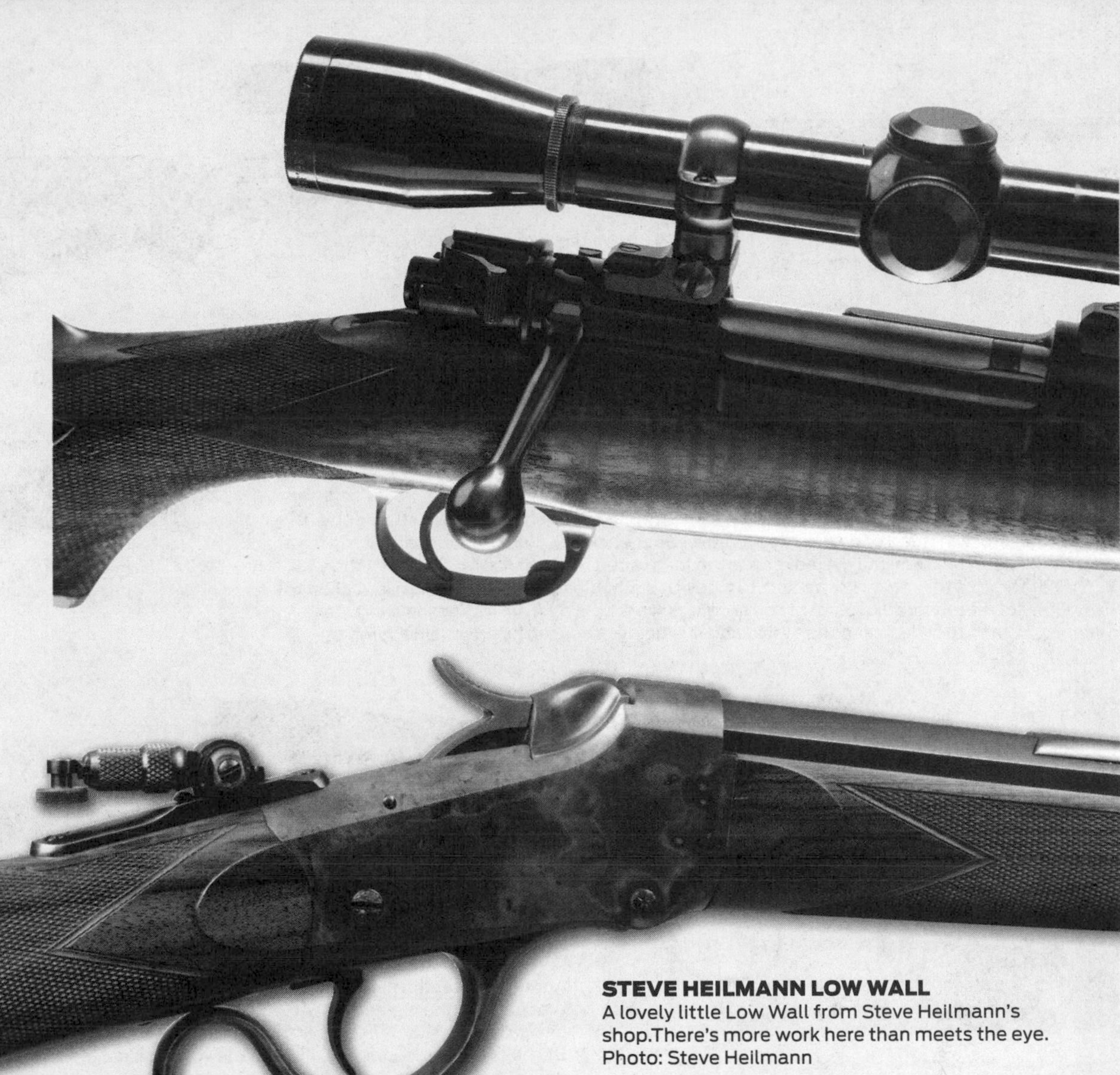

TOM BURGESS CUSTOM
This lovely rifle came from the shop of Tom Burgess. Tom did the metalwork, and the carved stock was likely Jerry Fisher.

STEVE HEILMANN LOW WALL
A lovely little Low Wall from Steve Heilmann's shop.There's more work here than meets the eye. Photo: Steve Heilmann

can gunmakers of the past such as Jerry Fisher, Dale Goens, and Al Biesen to name a few, set the standard that the current generation learned from and works to further perfect. The purchasers of custom guns continue to set the bar higher and higher toward perfection, which bodes well for the future of high quality gunmaking. There also seems to be no diminishing for demand of finely crafted firearms in today's market, as all of the best gunmakers have a several year backlog of commissions on the books to be delivered."

– Jeff Tapp, Stockmaker.

• • •

"This is the Golden Age of metalsmithing. The quality of the tools and materials available to the small shop is unprecedented. However, while modern tools and metallurgy enable us to create a superior firearm, the quality still comes from the details. Precision machining and hours of careful, detailed hand work are, and always will be, what makes a fine firearm."

– Glenn Fewless, Metalsmith

• • •

"The American Custom Gunmakers Guild represents an almost four-decade long commitment to the art of hand crafted custom firearms. It was started by a group of professional gunmakers who wished to see the craft promoted as a whole. They also wished to create an organization that would be identified by the quality of its members. To this end, in order to obtain Professional Member status a gunmaker must submit examples of their work to be viewed and voted on by existing members. The guild also demands high ethical standards from its members. The guild sponsors aspiring gunmakers through various educational efforts, including scholarships and seminars. Professional Members are encouraged to visit the various Gunsmithing schools to help pass on their knowledge. We are working to establish a 501c3 foundation to help raise money to further our educational efforts. Plans for the future include a Guild

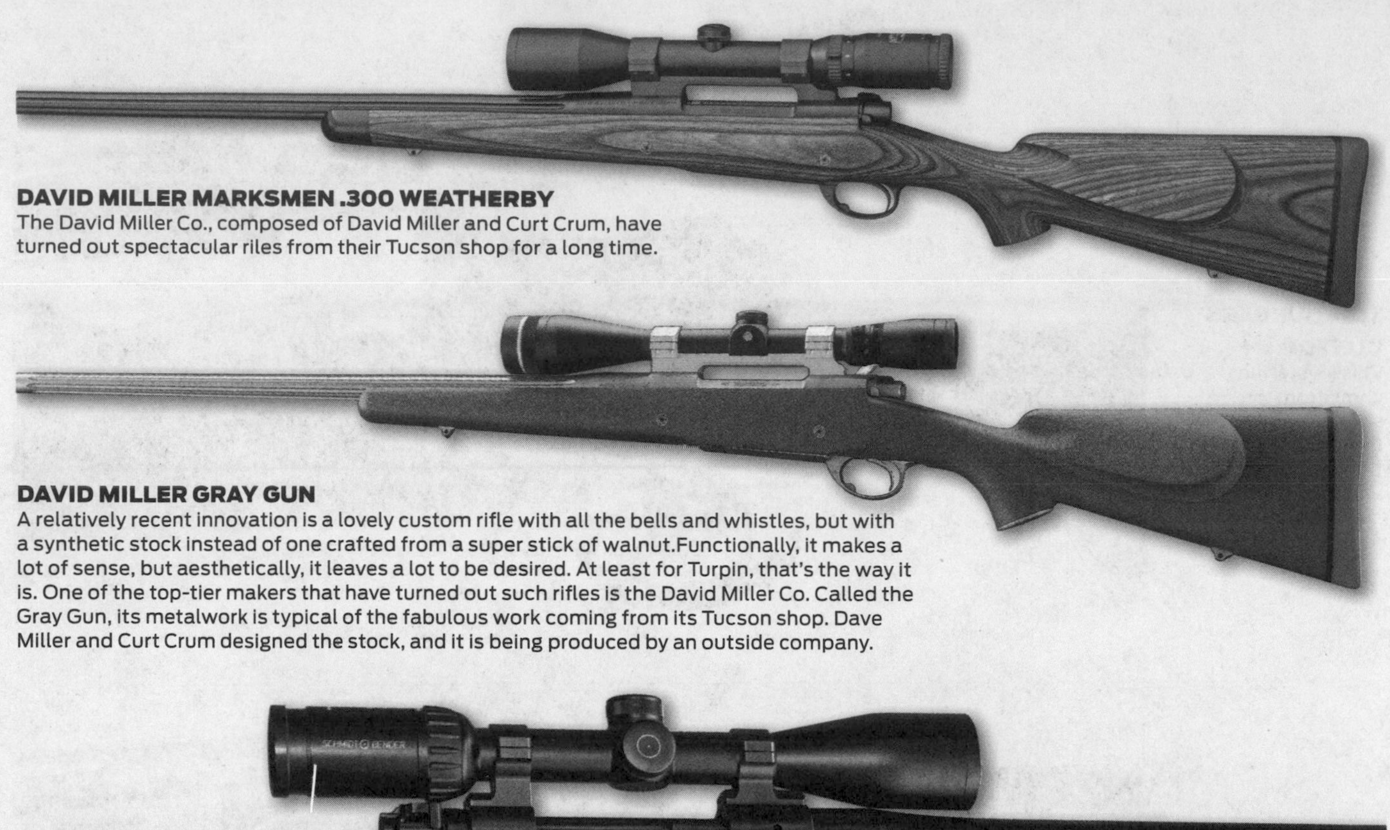

DAVID MILLER MARKSMEN .300 WEATHERBY
The David Miller Co., composed of David Miller and Curt Crum, have turned out spectacular riles from their Tucson shop for a long time.

DAVID MILLER GRAY GUN
A relatively recent innovation is a lovely custom rifle with all the bells and whistles, but with a synthetic stock instead of one crafted from a super stick of walnut.Functionally, it makes a lot of sense, but aesthetically, it leaves a lot to be desired. At least for Turpin, that's the way it is. One of the top-tier makers that have turned out such rifles is the David Miller Co. Called the Gray Gun, its metalwork is typical of the fabulous work coming from its Tucson shop. Dave Miller and Curt Crum designed the stock, and it is being produced by an outside company.

D'ARCY ECHOLS LEGEND
Another fantastic maker that has developed a synthetic-stocked custom rifle that he calls the Legend is D'Arcy Echols. The Legend stock is made for him to his design by McMillan. His classic rifles are second to none, and the Legend is one of the best synthetic-stocked rifles. Made with unexcelled performance as a goal, it delivers. D'Arcy has developed his own action and is having them manufactured in Utah. It is what a pre-'64 Model should have been and then some.

presence at different venues around the country to supplement our annual show in Dallas (Editor's note: the ACGG has a display each year at the Dallas Safari Club convention). *An increased presence on several social media platforms is also in the works."*

– Eric Dehn, Executive Director, ACGG

• • •

Tom Turpin handles our cherished Custom and Engraved Guns section each year and has had an extensive relationship with the guild, and I thought it only fitting that he weighs in on this anniversary. Tom had the following to add:

"Most of what I know came from a dinner at one of the trade shows, most likely SHOT. That would have been around 1980 or 81, I believe. At that time, John T. Amber and Gun Digest was about the only USA published source pushing anything remotely European, particularly related to guns and hunting. The dinner attendee's were JTA, Peter Bang, the Managing Direction of Heym GmbH in Germany, and me. I was in with Heym as I was a consultant to them to re-establish the company in the US marketplace. I was also doing an occasional yarn for John and Gun Digest, usually dealing with European subjects.

JTA was very familiar with the European hunting and firearms scene and we had a very long session on those topics over fine steaks and a few tongue-loosening drinks. As I recall the conversation, lo these many years later, it centered around the custom gun trade in the US, and the luxury sporting trade factory products from top European manufacturers.

John was well aware of many of the shortcomings in the custom gun trade and he felt strongly that the trade needed a governing body to police the members, if and when the situation dictated. He felt that self policing, although desirable, was sometimes not enough. He felt that if only one or two members strayed, it would affect the entire trade, not just the transgressors. He felt very strongly that a governing body with authority to correct issues was essential. He felt so strongly on this issue that he told us that he would endow such an organization with a substantial sum, which he did. That money, coupled with

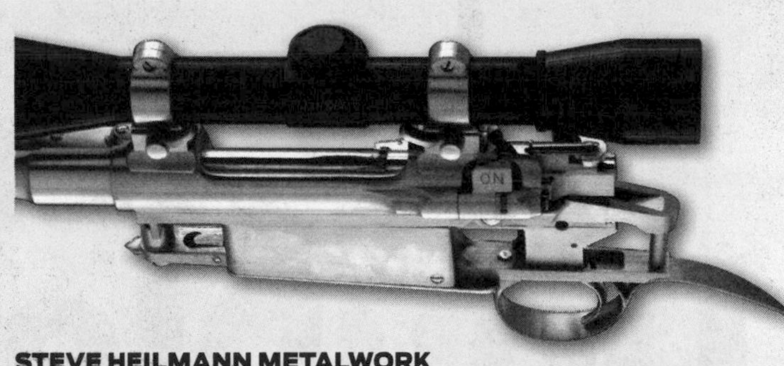

STEVE HEILMANN METALWORK
You can't make a silk purse out of a sow's ear, is an old saying that is true in most cases. Unless that is, your name is Steve Heilmann. Shown here is photographic proof that it can be done. Photo: Steve Heilmann

JESSE KAUFMAN MOD 32
Jesse Kaufman is a multi-talented gunmaker. He spent most of his early career with Dakota Arms, mostly doing stock work and checkering. Later, when Dakota changed owners a couple times, Jesse decided to learn to engrave. He has done remarkably well. He has been on his own, engraving full time, for several years now, continuing his engraving education as time and availability permit.This Remington O/U is his most ambitious project to date. The client requested that his dad's well-used bird gun be restored to its original condition and fully engraved. Jesse is doing much of the restoration and all the engraving. Great work. Photos: Jesse Kaufman

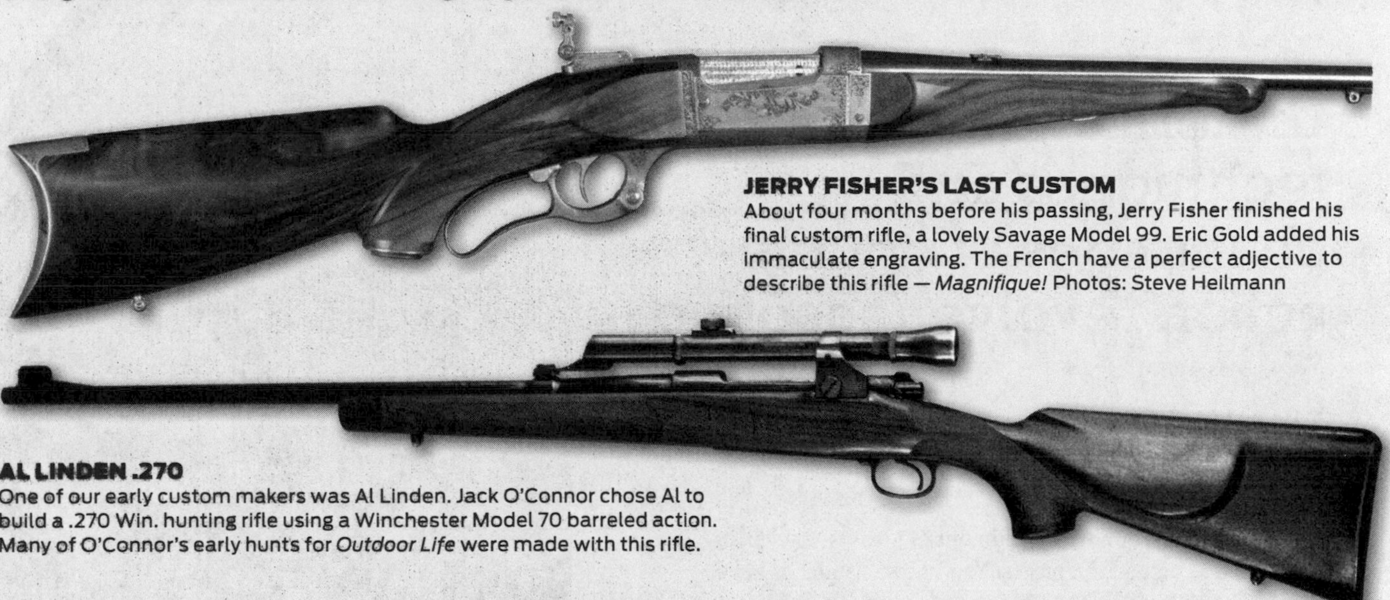

JERRY FISHER'S LAST CUSTOM
About four months before his passing, Jerry Fisher finished his final custom rifle, a lovely Savage Model 99. Eric Gold added his immaculate engraving. The French have a perfect adjective to describe this rifle — *Magnifique!* Photos: Steve Heilmann

AL LINDEN .270
One of our early custom makers was Al Linden. Jack O'Connor chose Al to build a .270 Win. hunting rifle using a Winchester Model 70 barreled action. Many of O'Connor's early hunts for *Outdoor Life* were made with this rifle.

a hundred dollar bill from each founding member, got the guild up and running. Now, forty years later, it still runs strong.

It has had its ups and downs of course. But I'm convinced that without Amber's influence and financial backing, it would have failed, or more likely, never gotten off the ground."

The allure of a custom gun — one you have had a part in planning, if not in the execution — is as unique as the individual purchasing it. I have but one 'custom' gun, and though the .318 Westley Richards may be a simple rebarrel of a classic Gewehr 98 Mauser with a modified Sears & Roebuck walnut stock, I really enjoyed the entire process. I enjoyed taking that classic cartridge on safari to Zimbabwe and using it for hunting both a zebra stallion and an old, heavy-horned kudu bull. That rifle was the topic of conversation on a subsequent safari to Zimbabwe, where I found myself sharing camp with ACGG Professional Members Jim Bisio and Jeff Tapp. Each had brought their own creations across the pond, Jeff taking his first Cape buffalo bull and Jim connecting on a fine tom leopard at the eleventh hour. Our conversation around the campfire showed their passion for their chosen profession and was the impetus for this article.

Even though the firearms hall at the Dallas Safari Club annual convention has some of the biggest names in the industry (including John Rigby & Co., Westley Richards, Heym, William Evans and more), I always enjoy my annual stroll through the ACGG display, chatting with the highly talented gunmakers, and catching up with good folks like Doug Turnbull, Dan Rossiter, and others who I am honored to call friends. There is a changing of the guard at ACGG, with the sitting Executive Director Eric Dehn handing the reins of power over to Amanda Rutherford, a talented young lady who — I am certain — will bring a new perspective and fresh energy to the guild. Keep up the excellent work, friends, and here's to another 40 years of custom guns!

Mastering the Double-Action Revolver

Understanding the techniques and challenges of double-action revolver shooting.

› JIM WILSON

Sometimes, gun writers run out of ideas, so they like to do comparison pieces. You know, "Which is better, the .270 or the .30/06?" I remember one time when Bill Jordan and Charlie Askins teamed up to argue autos vs. revolvers. Askins took the side that the revolver was horribly old-fashioned, and the auto was simply the only way to go. I found that particularly interesting because Askins had done all his fighting with revolvers in the Border Patrol and World War II. At any rate, I don't recall that this debate was very informative or entertaining; perhaps *amusing* would be a better description.

Double-action (DA) revolvers are still around after all these years because they work and meet the needs of defensive shooters. In fact, it's interesting to note that there is a bit of a resurgence in revolver popularity among those interested in personal defense. And a bunch of us who are still kicking continue to have a warm spot in our hearts for the wheelguns, and regularly rely on them. It is not about debating. It is all about understanding that we are blessed with many guns that will give good service in protecting our hides, revolvers and autos included.

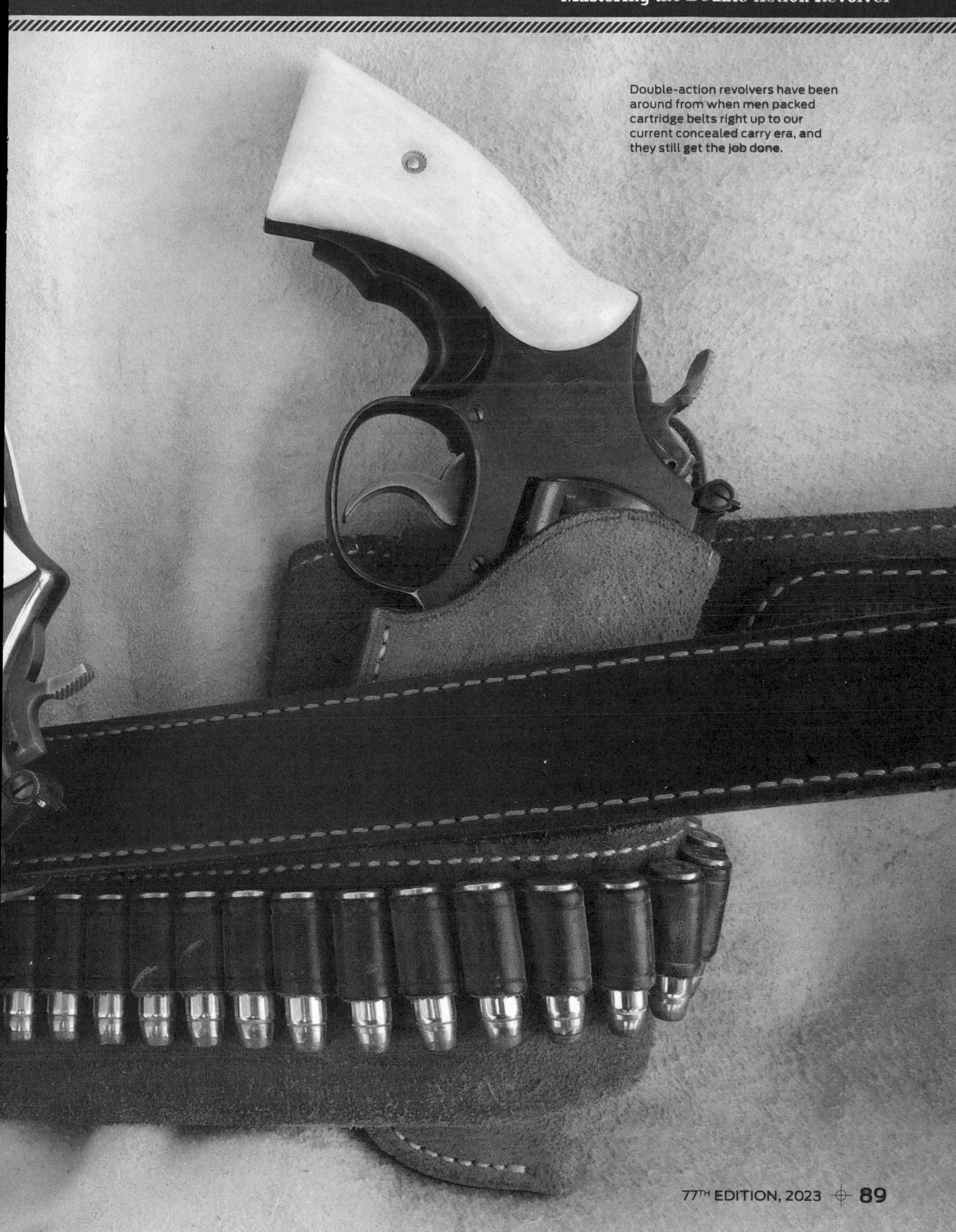

Double-action revolvers have been around from when men packed cartridge belts right up to our current concealed carry era, and they still get the job done.

Shooters should avoid this low grip because it makes fast, accurate double-action shooting difficult.

A high grip on the revolver is the only way for fast, accurate DA shooting.

The revolver should fit the shooter's hand, so there is a straight line from the muzzle through the forearm, which aids in managing recoil and a proper trigger press.

Nowadays, many folks concerned about personal defense buy their first defensive handgun, and quite a few of them will find that a quality revolver is appealing. Since I've been shooting the darned things since JFK was president, I thought I'd share some of the double-action revolver tricks and techniques that had proven themselves over the years when lives were on the line.

DOUBLE-ACTION GRIP AND TRIGGER

To begin with, the key to mastering the DA revolver is to conquer the double-action trigger pull. However, there is more to it than just manipulating the trigger. Simply put, the revolver must fit the shooter's hand. The shooter should be able to grip the gun to center it in the web of the shooting hand between the thumb and trigger finger. There should be a straight line from the gun muzzle, through the shooting grip, and down the forearm when properly gripped. When the fist is pointed at the target, the gun muzzle points at the target and the shooter uses the sights to fine-tune the alignment for a center hit.

At the same time, the trigger finger should engage the trigger at the joint between the first and second segments of the finger. This method is different from those who shoot single-action autos and rifles since they use the pad of the first segment of the finger to engage the trigger. Double-action shooters get more fingers on the trigger to have greater control of that heavy DA trigger pull.

Now, this works for some folks better than it does for others. My hands are too small to do this with the large-frame revolvers. By the same token, I tend to stick too much finger into the trigger guard on the small-frame guns if I'm not careful, pulling my shots off. However, the medium-frame revolver is just about right for me, and it is no surprise that I do my best work with medium-sized guns.

The shooter's hand should be as high on the grip frame as possible so long as it doesn't interfere with the cycling of the DA hammer. You will see photos and videos of shooters using a much lower grip. However, such a grip impedes the ability to control recoil and manage the gun, especially when shooting fast. I suspect they do it because it reduces the felt recoil, and they simply don't know any better.

A solution is that quality revolvers can be found in many different sizes. You might get along best with a Colt Cobra; I do my best work with a Smith & Wesson K-frame, and the next person might handle a Ruger Redhawk best of all. A new shooter should try out many different revolvers, and if they stay with quality guns, they can't go wrong.

Once the shooter has found a gun that passes the straight-line and trigger-finger tests, they might fine-tune things by finding a set of stocks that really fit. And the first thought that occurs is that there are so many different kinds that it is confusing. There are synthetic stocks, some soft and some hard, some cover the gun's backstrap, and some don't. And there are various kinds of wood stocks, some smooth and some checkered, others that have a filler behind the trigger guard and many that don't. And then there are the revolver stocks made of ivory, pearl, bison horn, stag, and other exotics, which aren't any better than the rest, but they look pretty.

I wish I could look at a particular shooter and tell them which stocks will suit them best. I can get close, but, unfortunately, the shooter will have to work out the final fit for themselves. The proof is that most of us who are life-long revolver shooters will happily show you the box in our gun room that holds all the revolver stocks we've tried and rejected.

In my case, K-frame Smiths tend to be stocked with either smooth wood or smooth ivory. If the stock set doesn't have a filler behind the trigger guard, I'll install a grip adapter that fills the space between the grip frame and trigger guard.

All this business of selecting the proper gun size and figuring out what kind of stocks work for you may seem frustrating. While many of today's autos are a one-size-fits-all, take-it-or-leave-it proposition, revolvers can be customized to fit

Managing the trigger press is the key to success with the DA revolver.

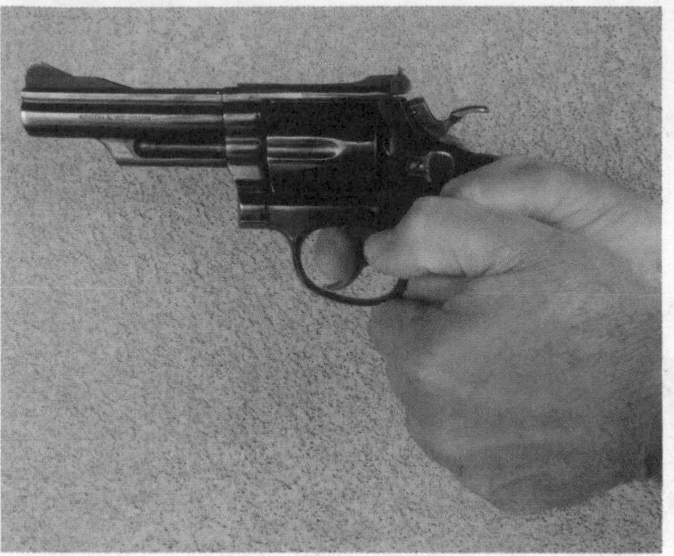

A two-handed grip for DA revolvers. Notice that the thumbs are curled down for added strength in managing recoil and quickly getting back on the target.

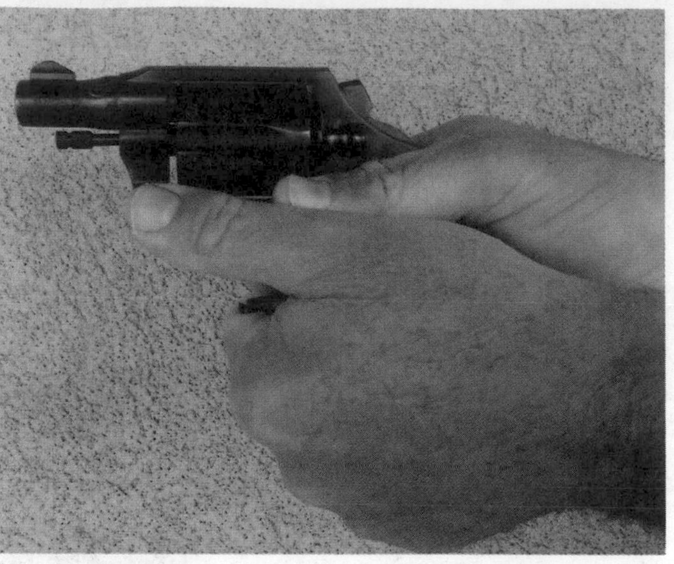

Popular with auto shooters, the thumbs-forward grip can result in a nasty burn from gases escaping from the cylinder gap.

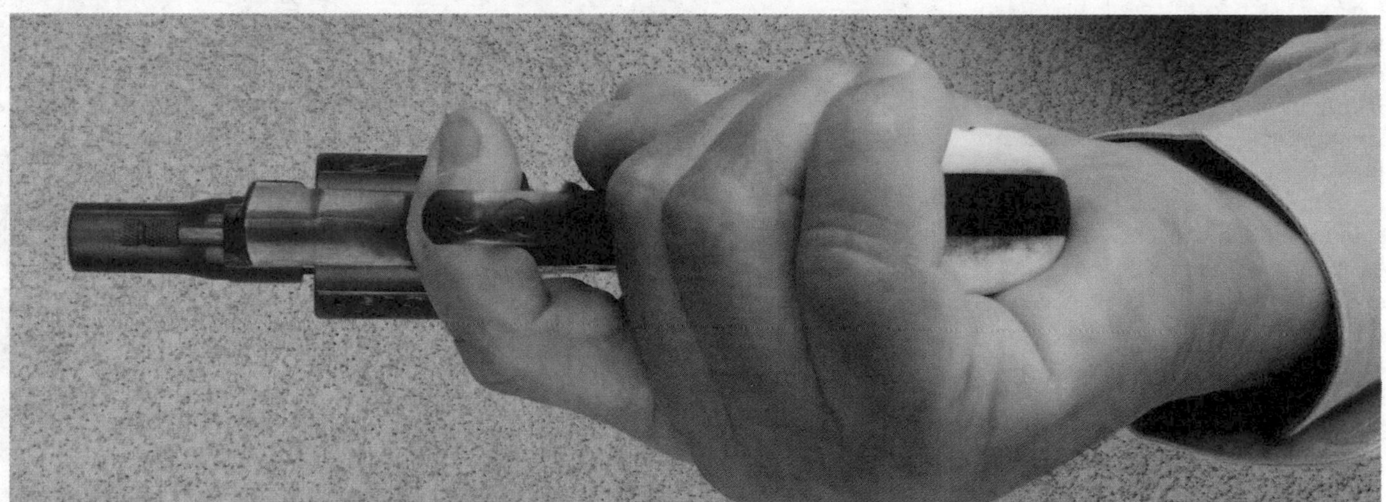

Note that the first joint of the trigger finger is engaging the trigger for maximum control during DA firing.

Like this one from Bianchi, a speed strip is handy for reloading, especially when only a few shots have been fired.

the individual. The better the revolver fits you, the better you'll be able to control and master the DA trigger pull.

Thanks to the lawyers and bean counters, most of today's firearms come with lousy trigger pulls, and revolvers are no exception. Let's face it; no one is going to do their best work with a 25- to 35-ounce gun with a 12-pound trigger pull.

If I plan to carry a particular gun for personal defense, I want it to be worked over by a competent pistolsmith. Now, I'm not talking about "Charlie the neighborhood gun butcher" — I'm talking about a trained, professional gunsmith. I generally ask the gunsmith to simply

Here are just some of the various stocks available to revolver shooters. (Clockwise from the top.) Factory wood, soft synthetic with filler behind the triggerguard, classic shape ivory with BK grip adapter, and hard synthetic with filler behind the triggerguard.

smooth up the internal working parts and remove any burrs or sloppy action. I don't think it is ever a good idea to weaken or cut any of the springs. Regardless of who has worked on the revolver, the next step is to make sure that the gun positively fires the ammunition to be used for personal defense. Not all ammo makers use the same make of primers; some are harder than others. So, ensure the revolver's mainspring is strong enough to forcefully ignite that primer, and do that while firing the revolver in double-action mode since the DA hammer stroke is shorter and less powerful than the single-action stroke.

PRACTICE, OF COURSE!

Once the shooter has a revolver that fits their hand, it's time to get busy and practice. Of course, this is true with any defensive handgun, but especially so with the DA revolver. The more a person practices in the DA mode, the stronger the shooting hand and trigger finger become and the more likely the shots will be center hits.

I am also a firm believer in dry-fire practice. Dry practice is simply cycling and snapping the gun on targets while the gun is empty. Various companies even sell dummy rounds specifically for this sort of drill. The key is to be safe. Unload the gun — I know you already did that, but recheck it — and move the live ammo well away from your practice area. Work for smoothness in the draw stroke, getting on target (whatever the target might be), and pressing the trigger all the way through until the hammer cycles and falls. The idea is to run the gun in the double-action mode so smoothly that the sights stay on target throughout the drill.

The best two-hand hold is with the shooting thumb curled down on the stocks and the support thumb overlapping, as this allows for a firm grip that will help manage recoil. Lately, a target shooter's grip has become popular, with both thumbs pointed forward. The problem with this grip style for revolvers is that the thumb tips get too close to the gap between the cylinder and the barrel, depending on the shooter's hand size and the gun size. The shooter is reminded that an awful lot of hot gas leaves the revolver from this location and can cause painful injury to the shooter's thumbs. However, it's a self-correcting mistake, and one seldom must be cautioned about repeating it.

As with any defensive handgun, you should carry extra ammunition for the revolver. Carry at least one speed loader for when the gun is shot dry. But also carry at least one speed strip for reloading when some (but not all) cartridges are fired. During the warm months of the year, I'll also carry another speed strip that holds snake shot here in the Southwest. And, of course, the speed loader and strips can carry ammunition of different power levels to deal with two-footed and four-footed predators.

RELOADING TECHNIQUES

There are several reloading techniques that the defensive shooter should be aware of. An empty gun being of little use, it's always a good idea to practice quick, smooth reloads.

The gun stays in the shooter's right hand in the first technique. Use your right thumb to depress the cylinder

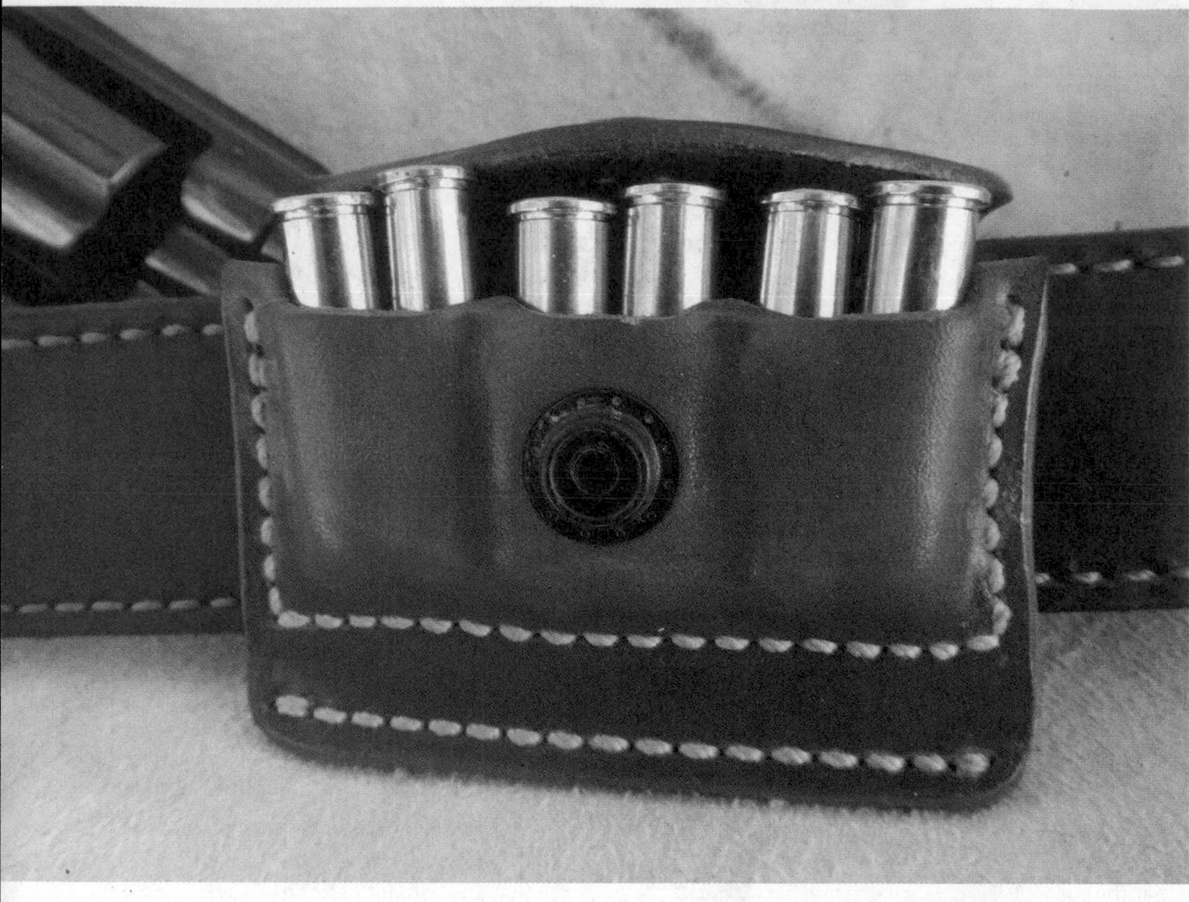

Like this one from Galco International, a good ammo pouch is another handy way for the DA shooter to carry spare ammunition.

release and your index finger to push the cylinder out. Pointing the muzzle straight up, hit the ejector rod with your left hand and dump the empties. Turning the muzzle straight down, reload the cylinder with your left hand. Advocates of this technique like it because the revolver never leaves the shooting hand.

My preferred method is to place the gun in the palm of the left hand, using the right thumb to depress the cylinder release. The index finger and little finger of the left hand stay on the right side of the frame while the two middle fingers push the cylinder open and, along with the left thumb, hold the cylinder. The muzzle is then turned up, and the right hand smacks the ejector rod and ejects empties. Then, with the muzzle pointed down, the right hand reloads. I like this method because it gives me a more secure hold on the gun should I fall or get knocked down.

Left-handed shooters can use their trigger finger to depress the cylinder release with the right index finger to push the cylinder out. The right thumb and index finger then hold the gun by the front of the frame while the left hand is used to dump empties and reload.

Regardless of which technique is used, smack the ejector rod with the palm of the hand instead of just using the thumb. Use some force here to ensure the empties are entirely driven out of the gun with a single stroke; a gunfight is no place to be picking empties out with one's fingers. Let gravity work for you during this process; turn the muzzle straight up while dumping empties and straight down while reloading.

A speedloader is handy when the revolver has been shot dry, and a quick reload is needed. This HKS speedloader is just one of many styles available.

Hold the gun as high as possible while unloading and reloading — about shirt pocket high would be about right. This is to maintain peripheral vision during the reload and see what the bad guys are doing. And, of course, when reloading during a gunfight, always do so behind cover.

MALFUNCTIONS

Malfunctions are not nearly as common with DA revolvers as with autos, but they still happen. One malfunction occurs when a cartridge slips under the cylinder star at the back of the cylinder. This jam usually occurs when the chambers have not been adequately cleaned, the ejector rod is not smacked with proper authority, or the gun muzzle is not pointed straight-up to take advantage of gravity.

Another problem occurs when the ejector rod unscrews itself and backs out enough to tie the gun up and keep the cylinder from opening. Always check the ejector rod to see if it unscrews easily during cleaning. If so, a bit of nail polish or Lok-Tite on the ejector rod threads will solve the problem.

Finally, a raised primer can tie up a revolver. The solution is what every defensive shooter should do, whether they carry a revolver or auto: physically and visually inspect every cartridge loaded into the gun and every loading device. Our ammunition companies do an excellent job checking out their ammo before shipping. Still, over the years, I have found quality ammo with the loaded bullet upside down, damaged cases, high primers, or primers loaded upside down. It doesn't happen often, but in a gunfight, once is enough.

It has been said that the double-action revolver is easy to shoot but difficult to shoot well. Its real value is that, given quality guns, no other handgun is more accurate or reliable. You do not have to go to the trouble to find a gun that fits best — nor wade through the vast selection of available stocks. And you certainly don't have to go to the expense of having a pistolsmith tune your weapon. On the other hand, these steps and a lot of practice will put you on the fast track to being genuinely proficient with the double-action revolver. The revolver has saved lives and will continue to save lives in the hands of dedicated handgunners. I wouldn't keep house without a good double-action revolver nearby. GD

For further study, I suggest the following books. All of them are available through local bookstores or various online services.

No Second Place Winner by Bill Jordan

Protect Yourself With Your Snubnose Revolver by Grant Cunningham

The Snubby Revolver by Ed Lovette

The Modern Technique of the Pistol by Gregory Boyce Morrison

When ejecting empties, gravity is your friend. Turn that muzzle up and smack the ejector rod with the palm of the hand. Don't be dainty; just get those empties out and reload that gun.

Gravity is your friend when reloading a double-action revolver. Pointing the muzzle down when reloading will quickly and positively drop the rounds into the chambers.

This elephant bull is curious, not threatening; there's little real danger, and the "no shoot" decision has been made. Even so, a big double is comforting. For elephant, a big-bore double is easily the best choice.

Double or Nothing?

For dangerous game — and everything else — the age-old debate between double rifles and mag-fed bolt guns continues.

› CRAIG BODDINGTON

Made in 1895, this H&H Royal in .303, though regulated with 215-grain bullets, has responded well to handloads with modern bullets. These are three pairs from each barrel, excellent regulation, with elevation adjusted using the flip-up aperture sight.

A century ago, the debate among advocates of magazine-fed bolt guns or double rifles was a hot topic. The British gun trade took heavy losses in World War I, but in the 1920s, dozens of houses, large and small, still churned out double rifles … and newfangled bolt actions.

Fifty years later, the subject was silly. World War II followed the worldwide depression. After the war, Great Britain's colonial empire shrank rapidly. Partitioning of India and Pakistan came early, in 1948. This timeline is essential to our story because more British doubles went to India than ever went "out to Africa." Partition thus killed a primary market. Tanganyika gained independence in 1961, Kenya in 1963, but the British double rifle was an anachronism.

In part, the British gun trade did it to itself through the "proprietary system," whereby the larger firms had their own cartridges and were the primary source for rifles so chambered and their ammunition. There were too many similar big-bore Nitro Express cartridges plus a host of mostly forgotten proprietary "flanged" cartridges.

In coastal Mozambique, Boddington is about to take a buffalo with a scoped Rigby Big Game rifle in .416 Rigby. This would be the longest shot he has ever taken on a buffalo, about 160 yards, possible with a scoped rifle, but unwise with iron sights. Just one shot was needed.

Kynoch was the primary producer of the myriad and confusing British cartridges. In the mid-1950s, Kynoch started discontinuing the least popular numbers, and by the early 1960s, there was no fresh ammo for any of the big Nitro Expresses. In 1970, Kynoch's parent, Imperial Chemical Industries (ICI), ceased manufacturing all sporting ammunition.

Timing is everything. I doubt Winchester saw this coming when it introduced the .458 Winchester Magnum in 1956, but it reaped the benefit. Rifles and ammo were cheap and available. American handloaders kept the Nitro Express cartridges alive, but this did little for hunters in the field because handloading is illegal in many countries. Few doubles were made in the postwar years with diminished demand, and many doubles in use were abandoned for lack of ammo.

I began my African odyssey in 1977. My professional hunter (PH), Willem van Dyk, had a .475 double but had given it up (no ammo) and carried an over/under .458, which failed when we needed it. Because of inherently weak extraction, double rifles need rimmed cartridges for absolute reliability.

Over the next dozen years, most of the PHs I encountered carried bolt-action .458s or were "making do" with .375s. Double rifles were respected, but few African hunters still used them. Exceptions: An Austrian over/under .470 carried by Bill Illingsworth in Zambia in 1983 and a .475 No. 2 carried by Ian MacFarlane in Botswana in 1985. Otherwise, until the 1990s, the only double rifles I encountered in Africa were my own: a Wilkes .470 and a C.W. Andrews .470 I used for a decade. Otherwise, bolt guns ruled.

RETURN OF THE DOUBLE

Today, "double versus magazine" is again a valid argument. Thanks mainly to dies from Fred Huntington and bullets from Barnes, the double rifle refused to die. When I got my first .470, Jack Lott showed me how to remove and seat unfamiliar Berdan primers using hoarded Kynoch brass. In the early '80s, Jim Bell's Brass Extrusion Laboratories Ltd (BELL) offered new Boxer-primed cases.

Vintage doubles were still cheap (compared to today), but there were few new double rifles. Heym's Model 88B, initially in .470, was probably the first "new" large-caliber double marketed in the U.S. I took a rhino with an early Heym .470 in 1986 and used another in .500-3" in Mozambique in 1989.

It's an overstatement to say that Heym opened the floodgates, but there was an obvious market. Using shotgun actions, American Butch Searcy was building double rifles apace. Rival German firms Krieghoff and Merkel soon followed Heym into the double rifle market, joined by Austrian, Belgian, French and Italian makers. With rifles came ammo: BELL and A-Square, then Federal's .470 load (1989). Eventually came offerings from Hornady, Norma, David Little's new Kynoch and smaller companies. Fresh, rimmed Nitro Express ammo was no longer a problem.

FAMILIARITY

In the "double versus magazine" argument, it must appear that I come down solidly on the side of the "two-pipe." Not exactly! The double rifle is a different platform from a repeating action. About 1968, I bought a Spanish side-by-side 12 gauge. It took a while to get used to the wide sighting plane and master the double triggers, but I came to love that shotgun.

I read too much Ruark and J.A. Hunter when I was a kid; I always wanted a big-bore double. Thanks to that Spanish bird gun, there was no learning curve when I sprung for my first .470. The feel was familiar, and the second trigger was natural.

However, not everyone makes the transition. Dad was as good with a shotgun as anyone I've ever seen. He loved the feel of my double shotgun and tried to use it. In his hands, it might as well have been a single shot; he could never remember the rear trigger.

Single-trigger double rifles exist but are rare. To some extent, they go against the theory of the double gun: Two complete actions, full redundancy in case of a mechanical failure. However, a lot of shooters have trouble finding the second trigger.

Properly, as with two-trigger shotguns, one fires the front trigger first, then rear — less finger/hand movement, so faster. With big bores, some shooters inadvertently hit the second (rear) trigger during recoil. That's most unpleasant and can hurt you. Do it once, and you'll pay attention. If it happens again, the quick cure is to reverse the firing order: Rear trigger first, then the front. Not as "proper" and milliseconds slower, but doubling is unlikely.

As with any unfamiliar firearm, confidence is mostly a matter of practice. This past July, son-in-law Brad Jannenga and I were hunting in Zambia with PH

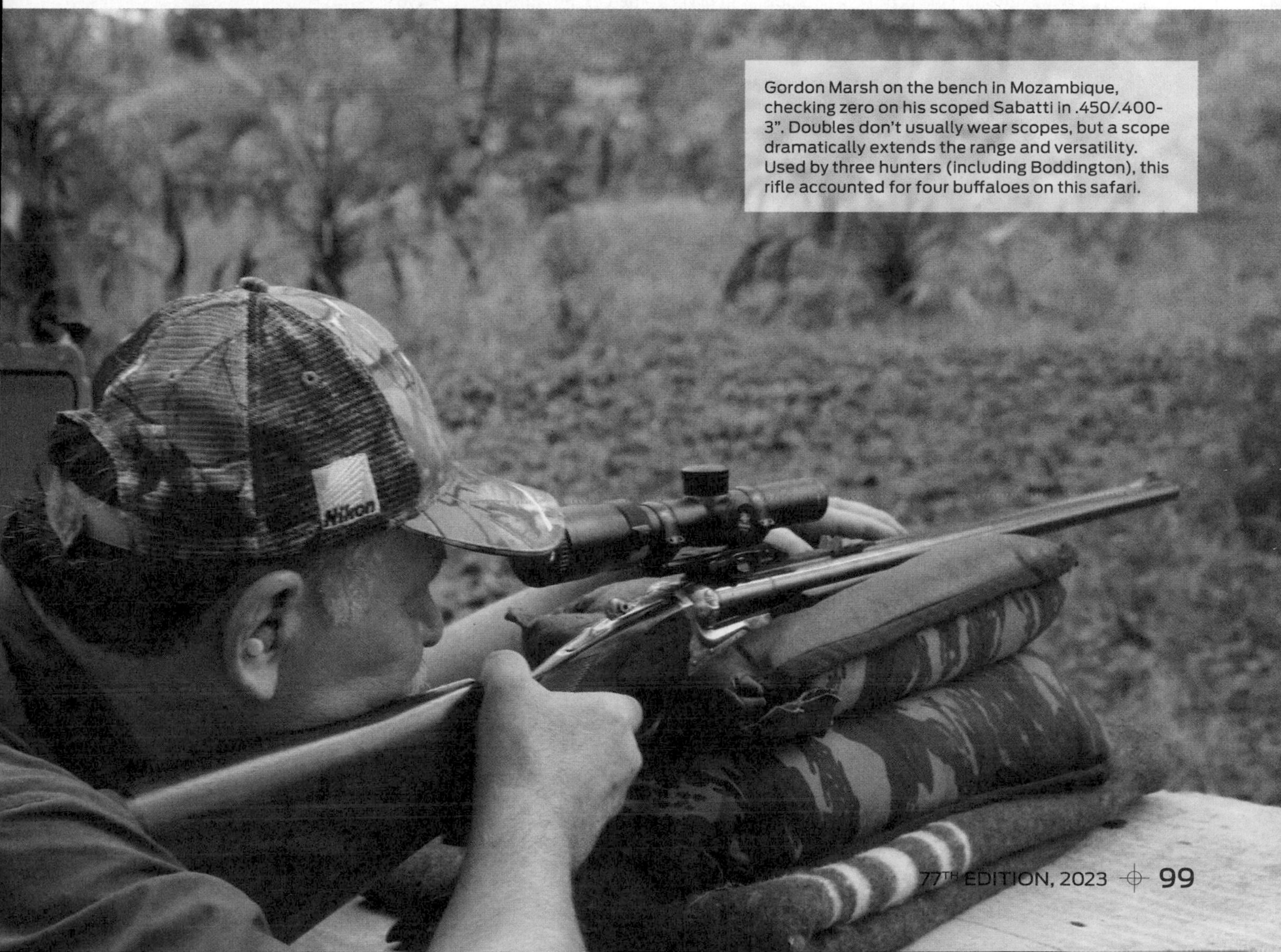

Gordon Marsh on the bench in Mozambique, checking zero on his scoped Sabatti in .450/.400-3". Doubles don't usually wear scopes, but a scope dramatically extends the range and versatility. Used by three hunters (including Boddington), this rifle accounted for four buffaloes on this safari.

Davon Goldstone, carrying a gorgeous new Verney-Carron double .500. He handled it like an old friend, but it was his first double, a significant upgrade from a bolt-action .458. He told me he'd put 200 rounds through it before the season. That's a significant investment in ammo, but probably minimal if you're starting out cold with a double.

Today, with the greater availability of rifles and more ammo sources, most African PHs who hunt dangerous game have gravitated back to the big-bore double. These days I don't see a lot of older rifles in the field; they're too valuable to beat up, plus most English rifles were made before 1939 and getting old. (My William Evans .470 was made in 1906. I'm using it, but I'm not a PH who carries a rifle daily.) Goldstone's Verney-Carron is an excellent rifle; I especially like its round-bottom action. But I see more Heym, Krieghoff and Merkel rifles — probably due to cost and availability.

Acceptance of the double rifle is not universal; some never get the hang of it and choose not to force it. My old friend Michel Mantheakis, hunting in Tanzania, tried a double and returned to a bolt action, now carrying a .450 Dakota Magnum. Similarly, hunting across Southern Africa and Uganda, Jumbo Moore carries a bolt-action .500 Jeffery. Richard Harland, who culled elephant for Rhodesia Parks and Wildlife, carries a rare George Gibbs .505. All three have swapped firepower and horsepower for the double's almost certain second shot.

OTHER ACTIONS

In Africa, a repeating rifle is almost universally a bolt action or "magazine rifle." All the action types are suitable for a variety of game, but if we include dangerous game, then doubles, bolt actions and single shots are the most likely to be chambered to suitable cartridges.

Semi-autos are illegal in most African jurisdictions and are seldom built for large cartridges. Slide-action rifles remain popular in parts of the U.S. but rarely chambered to dangerous game cartridges. Lever actions are possible. With the proper loads in modern actions, the .45-70 is adequate at least up to buffalo, likewise the old .405 Winchester.

In North America, we still love our lever actions. Big lever guns are popular with bear hunters, including grizzly and Alaskan brown bears, which certainly qualify as "large and dangerous." A big lever action's power and fast operation cannot be discounted, but elsewhere they are uncommon. The only lever actions I've personally seen in Africa were rifles I carried: Savage 99 and Winchester 88 in plains game cartridges and a Winchester 1886 in .475 Turnbull, plenty of gun for buffalo, and proven on elephant.

Since the blackpowder era, single shots have been chambered to the most powerful cartridges. Modern single shots like the Ruger No. 1, Dakota Model 10, and the Thompson/Center still are.

Frederick Selous was famous for his preference for falling-block single shots. We assume Selous was adept at the fast reload, but few experienced hunters

With PH Mark Haldane coaching, Boddington is ready to take a buffalo with a scoped Sabatti double in .450/.400-3". The 100-yard shot would have been tough with an iron-sighted double; the scope made it simple.

The herd is stopped in short-grass savanna in coastal Mozambique, with no cover to get closer. This is not double rifle country; a scoped rifle is almost essential.

Boddington put an Aimpoint optic on his Sabatti .450-3 ¼" double. Red-dot sights are lighter and less bulky than scopes, a good compromise on double rifles for dangerous game.

recommend singles for dangerous game. Mind you, I use them; I've taken a lot of buffalo with Rugers and Dakotas. However, I rarely hunt dangerous game alone; an experienced PH is usually nearby with a suitable rifle — a big-bore double or bolt action. The single shot is excellent for plains game, OK to take on safari for dangerous game in suitable chamberings, but questionable for a PH — and foolish for hunters who might be alone.

DANGEROUS GAME

The most likely choices are thus double rifles or bolt guns. The double has three limitations: Cost, accuracy and sights. A few words about each.

Top, a scoped Ruger No. 1 single shot. Bottom, a Heym, both in .450/.400-3". An accurate single shot is fine for safari hunters but a risky choice for PHs or resident hunters who might pursue dangerous game alone.

High-grade custom bolt actions often cost more than basic, modern double rifles. However, if you compare apples to apples, one can obtain a serviceable bolt action in .375 (H&H or Ruger), .416 (Ruger or Remington), or .458 (Lott or Win. Mag.), for possibly $1,000. In similarly powerful chamberings, the least costly double will be ten times more. Understanding this, I am continually surprised at how many *young* PHs today have gone to double rifles. Many with families consider the cost an insurance premium. They want that instantaneous, reliable second chance.

Accuracy is a severe limitation because of the impossibility of regulating a double so that both barrels group together at long distances. Most doubles are regulated at 50 meters or 60 yards. Ideally, shots from the two barrels are more or less parallel at the regulation distance. Eventually, the strikes drift apart, or the paths will cross and spread farther apart. Today, we hunger for accuracy at longer ranges. The double rifle cannot deliver. Most elephant are shot within 30 yards; the average on buffalo is perhaps 75 yards. A double with average regulation will be OK and probably acceptable to 150 yards.

No double is suitable for mountain sheep or floodplain waterbuck. The African PH who carries a double doesn't care, nor do Alaskan guides who carry doubles on brown bear hunts. The job is to protect the party in a charge or prevent the escape of a wounded animal. In the first case, the PH wants that quick second shot, which only the double provides. The second case is often in the hip or up the bum after an animal has been hit. Such a shot might be well past 100 yards, so more accuracy could be useful. However, the target is large, and the double rifle should be accurate enough.

The third limitation, sights, is a problem for all shots that require precision. The most common configuration for a double rifle is open express sights, but they are not mandatory. Most new doubles can be fitted with a detachable scope or red-dot sight. However, most PHs carry rifles with open sights. Their reasoning is simple: Fewer things to go wrong, less weight to carry, less projection to snag on brush. And, after all, the most likely use is up close and serious!

It's unavoidable that we safari hunters develop hero worship for our PHs. They give us some of our fondest memories, and we want to emulate them. So, we pony up and bring an open-sighted big-bore double on a subsequent safari. We must understand that our purposes are different. Our job is to take the animal cleanly, so the PH doesn't need to shoot. The PH's job is to never shoot … *unless things go wrong.*

On elephant, the double rifle is superior because the fast second shot is often needed, and distances are so close that open sights are no handicap. Much the same for the rhino hunting still done. Hippo can go either way. On land, charges are likely; a double can save the day. In water, hippos are sniped with precise brain shots; a magnifying scope is almost essential. For cats, the light-gathering capability of a scope is mandatory.

Buffalo can also go either way. We all hope for a shot at a big bull at 50 yards. When that happens, an open-sighted double works, but you can't always get that close. The average 75-yard shot is practical with open sights, but that pushes it, especially for those of us with older eyes or little experience with iron sights. Nobody takes long shots at buffalo. However, sometimes the bull you want presents at 150 yards in open country or in a herd, take it or leave it. That is too far and risky for most of us using open sights.

To a "gun guy," the rifle is integral to the hunt. If you have a big double that you're itching to use, fine, but understand you limit acceptable shots. Zimbabwe PH Andrew Dawson, who carries a lovely William Evans .470, put a number on it: "If a hunter insists on carrying an open-sighted rifle for buffalo, he's probably giving up 60 percent of his shots."

I've said this many times: You and I, as hunting clients, are best-served with scoped bolt actions chambered with appropriate cartridges. On buffalo, year in and year out, we will take more and better bulls with a low-power scope.

OPTICS ON DOUBLES

Magnifying scopes and reflex (red-dot) sights are non-traditional on double rifles and, to my eye, look like hell. But: They change the game. As he got older, experienced African hunter Joe Greenfield modified his H&H double to take a red-dot sight. The thought makes me cringe, but it allowed him to use his pet double on several more safaris. Greenfield's longtime PH Joey O'Bannon did the same on his double .500.

We gun guys get stubborn. I won't modify my William Evans to mount an optical sight, and I accept that the open sights restrict its use more with each passing year. Not a huge problem. I doubt I'll hunt elephant again, and I've shot my share of buffalo; I can live with passing a shot.

This excellent Uganda buffalo was taken with a 1906 Wm. Evans .470, so far as is known, the rifle's first return to Africa since 1910. The author admits to trouble resolving open sights today, but this shot was just 40 yards, perfect.

For you, on your long-dreamed-of safari, give it some thought. I put an Aimpoint on my Sabatti .450-3 ¼" double, expanding range and utility, and I have a 1-4x scope on my 9.3x74R double, which is also a Sabatti. Friends Gordon Marsh and John Stucker have Sabatti doubles in .450/.400-3", both wearing scopes in the Italian detachable Contessa mount.

I've used their rifles to take buffalo in coastal Mozambique, also my own with both scope and Aimpoint. This is an area of big herds and, sometimes, open ground. Unusually, I'd say the average shot there is closer to 100 yards. That's chancy with open sights, and, between glare and shifting buffalo, it's not easy to pick out a bull with a red-dot sight. Here

Boddington's Wm. Evans .470, made in 1906, responded well to handloads with 500-grain bullets at the standard 2,150 fps velocity.

Below: A gorgeous nyala, taken in Mozambique with an old H&H double in .303 British.

A Sabatti in.450-3 ¼" accounted for this excellent Mozambique bull, taken with an Aimpoint red-dot sight. At about 100 yards, this would have been a difficult shot with express sights.

a low-magnification scope is superior, and a scoped double is perfect.

OTHER HUNTING

The double rifle is not a versatile tool because of its limited range and typical sighting equipment. In fact, other than on dangerous game, using a double rifle is an eccentric act of ego. However, if you have one, you probably want to use it, and there are many situations where doubles are effective. Europeans often use them for close, fast shooting on driven hunts. I do a lot of pig hunting with my doubles. No big deal if I can't get close enough or run out of light.

The big-bore double is overpowered for most game. European doubles are still made in milder, more versatile cartridges such as 7x57R, 7x65R, and 8x57R, all rare over here. Son-in-law Brad has a well-regulated Krieghoff .30-06 side-by-side, great fun. He shoots it well, and we use it often for Texas game.

My shot distance with open sights is more limited than his; I must be careful. The 9.3x74R is a European standard, needlessly powerful for deer-sized game, but, with my scoped rifle, it's effective and regulated well enough for 200-yard shooting. Despite scarcity and eccentricity, I always thought a light-caliber double would be fun. Recently I acquired a nice, old side-by-side in .303 British. Well-regulated, it responded well to handloads. No, I'm not going to scope it, but this one has a pop-up tang aperture sight, much better than open express sights.

The range is still limited, but there are times and places where it shines. So far, I've used it for hog hunting, and in September '21, I used it in Mozambique. It accounted for a variety of game, including bushbuck, nyala and warthog. Performance was perfect; I just knew I had to get close. No matter the game, that's part of the deal with a double rifle. GD

"A Gentleman's Right ..."

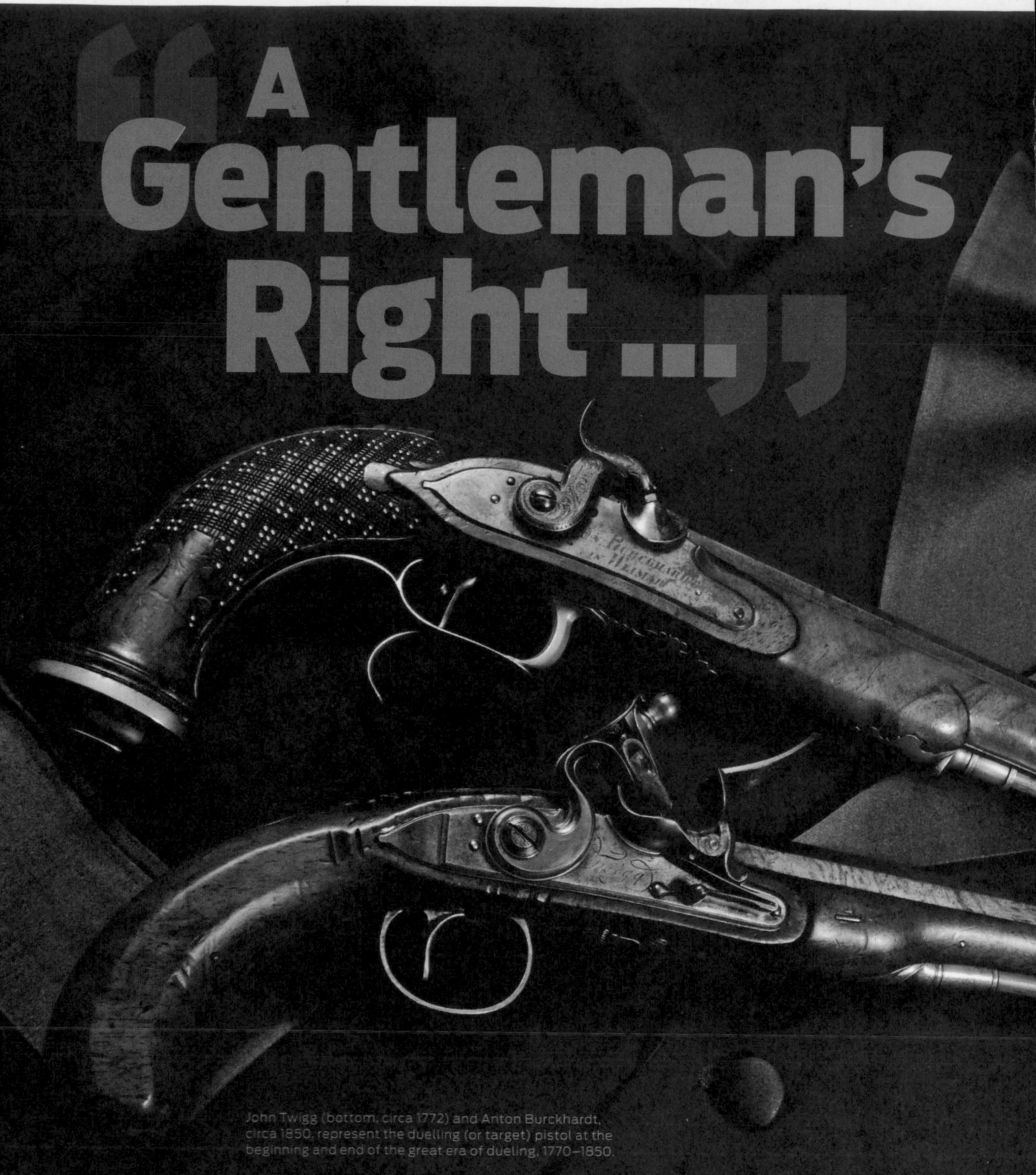

John Twigg (bottom, circa 1772) and Anton Burckhardt, circa 1850, represent the duelling (or target) pistol at the beginning and end of the great era of dueling, 1770–1850.

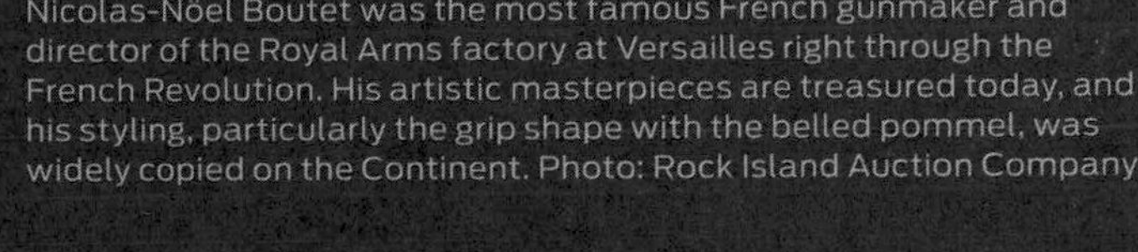

Nicolas-Nöel Boutet was the most famous French gunmaker and director of the Royal Arms factory at Versailles right through the French Revolution. His artistic masterpieces are treasured today, and his styling, particularly the grip shape with the belled pommel, was widely copied on the Continent. Photo: Rock Island Auction Company

The duelling pistol in cult and culture.

TERRY WIELAND

Many years after Waterloo, the Duke of Wellington was asked about the battle. He replied that it was as impossible to tell the story of a battle as it was to tell the story of a ball. It consists of constant motion — of many things happening at once, involving many different people. No one can see it as a whole, and everyone sees his own part out of proportion to the rest.

The same is true of the British duelling pistol. During an 80-year span, it was established as a recognizable type, underwent many technological improvements and aesthetic changes, made a few men rich and many men dead. Its story is one of contradictions, dramas large and small, a fair share of tragedy and occasional comedy. By an odd coincidence, its life span — 1770–1850 — was almost that of the Iron Duke himself (1769–1852).

Although duelling pistols were made in different parts of Europe and even in the United States, their development is centered in London, with the London gunmakers. These craftsmen made significant inventions, set the styles, and established a standard of excellence in manufacturing others tried to emulate.

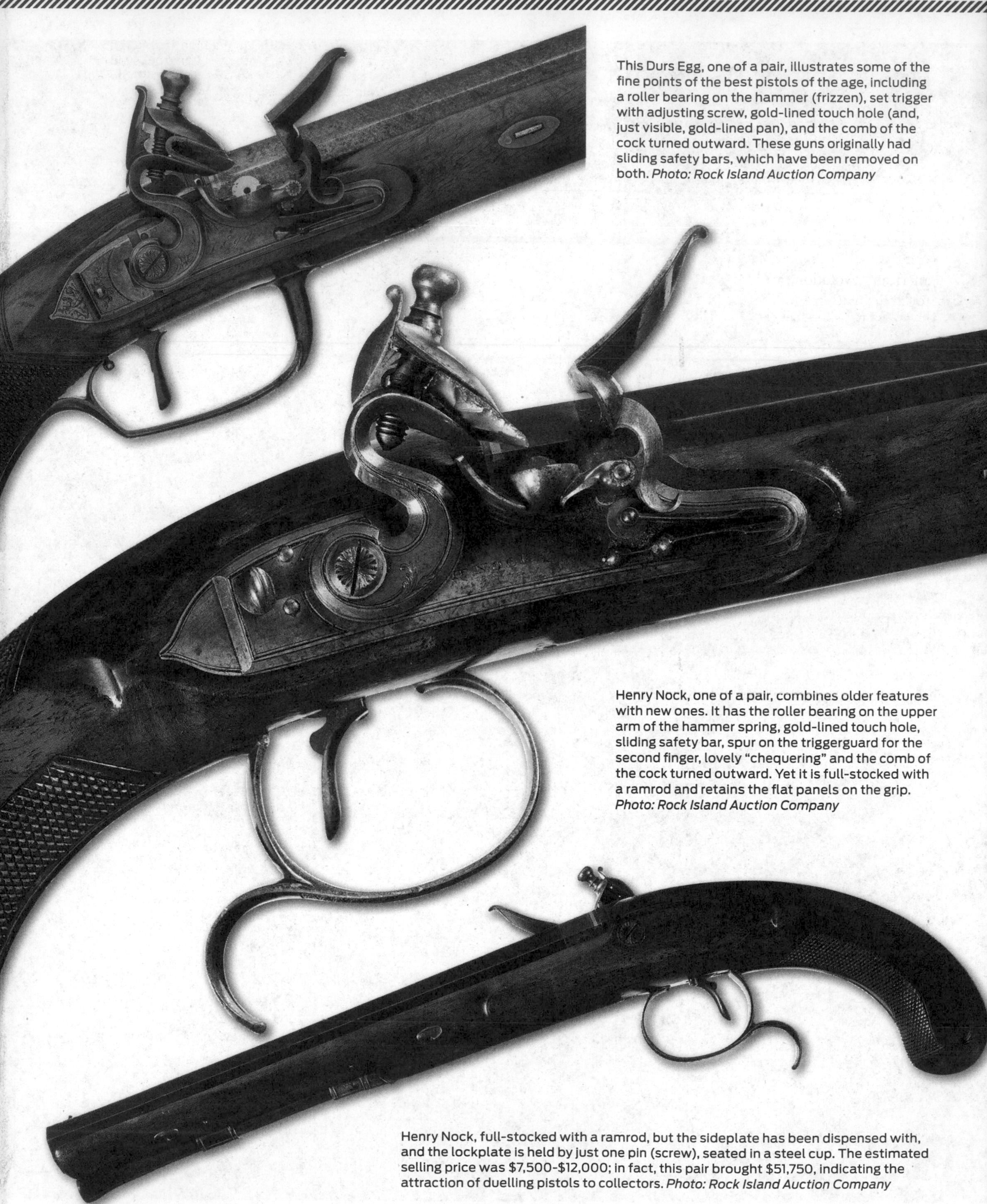

This Durs Egg, one of a pair, illustrates some of the fine points of the best pistols of the age, including a roller bearing on the hammer (frizzen), set trigger with adjusting screw, gold-lined touch hole (and, just visible, gold-lined pan), and the comb of the cock turned outward. These guns originally had sliding safety bars, which have been removed on both. *Photo: Rock Island Auction Company*

Henry Nock, one of a pair, combines older features with new ones. It has the roller bearing on the upper arm of the hammer spring, gold-lined touch hole, sliding safety bar, spur on the triggerguard for the second finger, lovely "chequering" and the comb of the cock turned outward. Yet it is full-stocked with a ramrod and retains the flat panels on the grip. *Photo: Rock Island Auction Company*

Henry Nock, full-stocked with a ramrod, but the sideplate has been dispensed with, and the lockplate is held by just one pin (screw), seated in a steel cup. The estimated selling price was $7,500-$12,000; in fact, this pair brought $51,750, indicating the attraction of duelling pistols to collectors. *Photo: Rock Island Auction Company*

The "saw-handle" grip came into fashion around 1805. Combined with the triggerguard spur, some believed it gave the firmest and most natural hold. *Photo: Rock Island Auction Company*

This period began just before the American Revolution, spanned the French Revolution and Napoleonic Wars, and ended in the Crimea. It was the time of Beau Brummell, Lord Byron and the Regency. When it began, men were wearing pea-green coats and powdered wigs; when it ended, they were dressed in Brummell's form-fitting black. It's a play with an extraordinary cast of characters, some of whom delivered one memorable line and retired from the stage. Essentially, the same is true of the pistols themselves. However, to understand the pistols, it's necessary to understand something about the practice of dueling.

Let us begin with an anomaly. The word "dueling" was initially spelled with two "lls." Gradually, the second was dropped, except when used as a modifier for "pistol." That remained duelling. Why? No one knows. But it illustrates the quirks and eccentricities that pervade the dueling world, which in its heyday amounted to a culture in itself and constituted, as John Atkinson describes in *The British Duelling Pistol* (1978), "almost a national sport."

The practice of two men agreeing to meet in a private spot to settle their differences with weapons began with the dawn of humanity and continues to this day, but formal dueling? Atkinson describes it as a "300-year red scar" running through British history.

Of course, men fought duels with pistols before 1770 and after 1850. Its significance lies in the fact that in the 1760s, English gunmakers began refining existing pistols into specialized dealers of death. Eighty years later, every good pistol made anywhere incorporated refinements previously found only in duelling pistols — and primarily because of them.

As well, the influence of the duelling pistol extended far beyond the realm of man-to-man combat. Duelling pistols led, most famously through John and Joseph Manton, to the great age of the English shotgun and an era in which firearms ceased to be crude tools and became master-

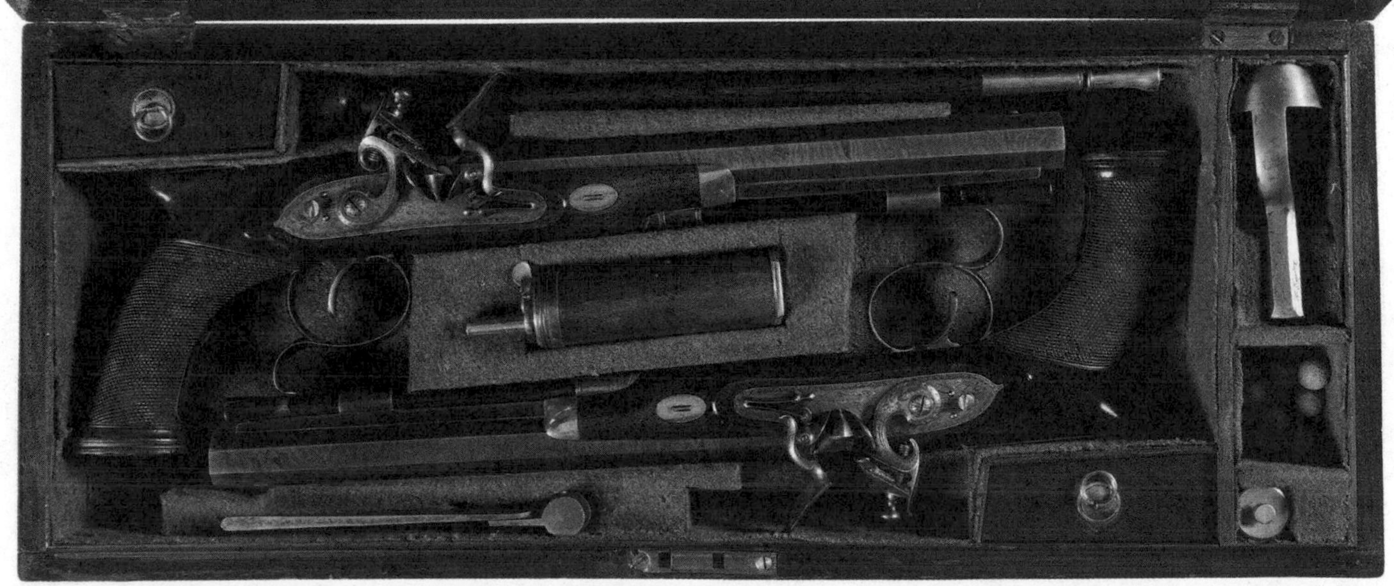

This pair of H.W. Mortimer pistols from about 1810 is cutting-edge for their time, particularly in stock design. Note half stocks and deep priming pan, an aid to reliable combustion. *Photo: Rock Island Auction Company*

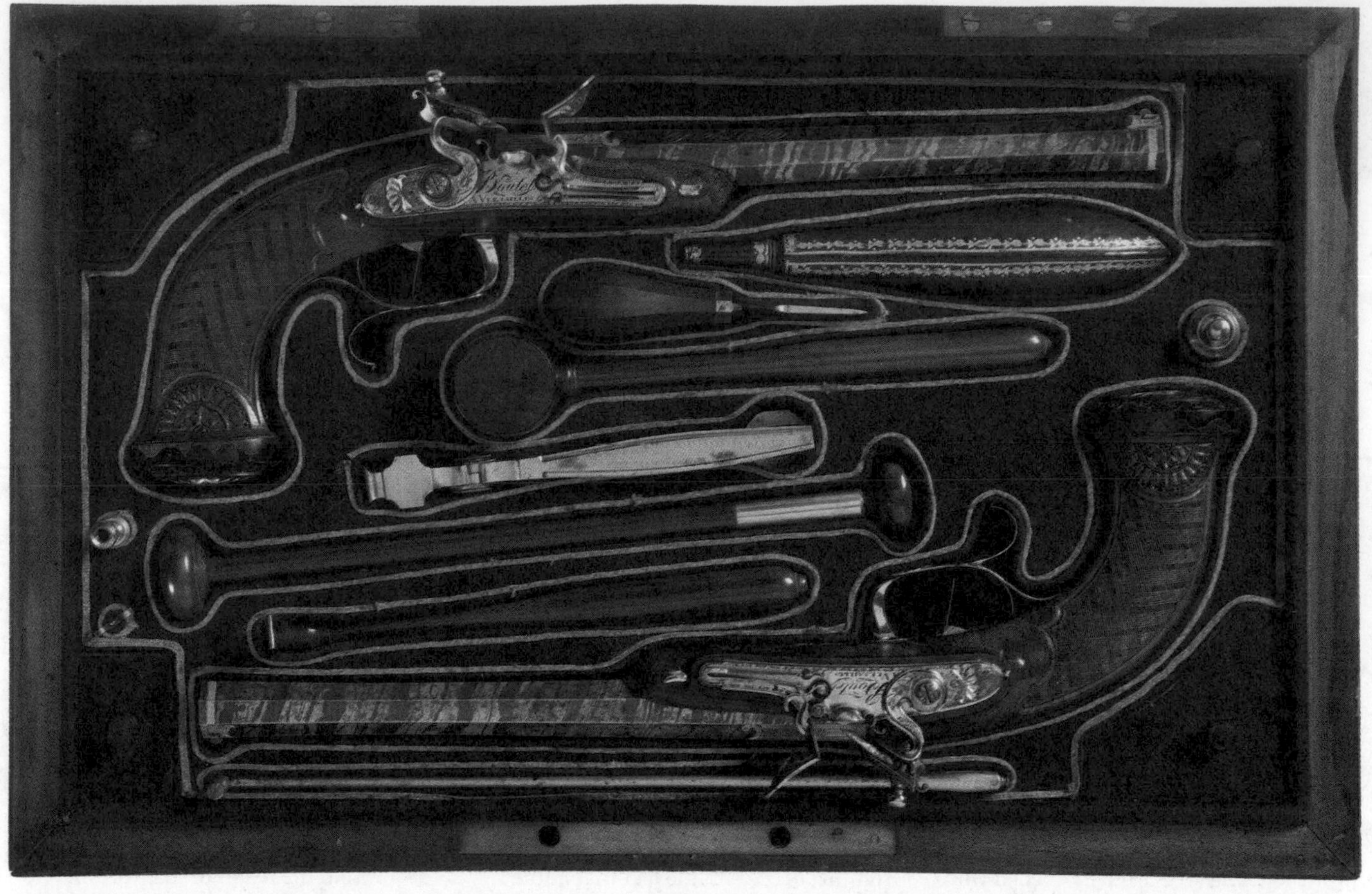

Gorgeous pair by Nicolas-Nöel Boutet, circa 1800. Boutet retained sideplates long after they'd gone out of fashion in London, probably because they afforded more scope for decoration. Skip-line checkering predates "California styling" by 150 years. Also, note the case — the origin of "French fitting." This pair sold at Rock Island Auctions, in 2020, for $74,750. *Photo: Rock Island Auction Company*

pieces of design and workmanship.

In 1900, one author estimated that some 200 books were written about dueling, and there have been more since. There have also been countless magazine articles. Given this fact, it's no wonder so many myths surround the practice, primarily propagated by movies and television.

To begin with, the notorious "Code Duello" did exist, but it was neither law nor even universally accepted practice. It was instituted in Ireland at the 1777 assizes and contained provisions as to how things should be done and with what, but it barely extended beyond Ireland's shores. (The Anglo-Irish gentry were enthusiastic duelers, and Irish gunmakers established a reputation as crafters of duelling pistols, including the original John Rigby of Dublin.)

Anyway, laws could hardly be passed to regulate dueling since it was outlawed, legally if not in practice, in many jurisdictions and generally frowned upon everywhere else. It would be like prohibiting bank robbery, then setting rules for how it must be done.

At this point, we should mention that while dueling occurred almost everywhere, England led the way not just in practice but in pistol development. Continental gunmakers generally followed London's lead. Liège (Belgium) and Paris were two major European centers for duelling pistol manufacture. They were also made in Vienna, the German states and as far east as Tula in Russia.

Other erroneous but widely held beliefs are that combatants would stand back to back, pistols pointed in the air at shoulder level, pace off the distance, then turn and fire. In fact, the distance agreed upon was measured off, and the men took up their positions, pistols pointed at the ground and waited for the order to fire.

Duelling pistols commonly came to be made in pairs, but not so the combatants would have identical guns. Participants used their own pistols, inspected by the seconds to ensure they complied with the agreed terms. Enthusiasts bought, practiced with, and fought duels with their own guns. Matched pairs ensured that your backup gun felt and shot precisely the same as the other if you needed to resort to it. This led, a century later, to matched pairs of shotguns.

Anyone who has tried to use an unfamiliar gun, especially where you have one shot on which your life might depend, often equipped with an ultra-sensitive hair-trigger, will appreciate the absurdity of agreeing to use someone else's pistol. From 1770 on, pistols became ever more carefully custom-fitted to the hand of the man who ordered them, much in the manner of a shotgun stock today.

Choice of weapons was supposedly left to the aggrieved party, but this becomes a gray area. Is this the offended party who then issued the challenge? Or is it the one who was challenged? Which one is "aggrieved?" Explanations vary.

The duel rules were simply conditions agreed upon by both parties from first to last. This included distance separating them; 12 paces were standard but gradually lengthened to 20 or even 30 as pistols became more accurate and the shooting more deliberate. But it could be any distance, from arm's length to the property line.

Then there is the practice of "deloping," or deliberately missing by firing into the air or ground. This happens more in movies than in practice, where it was frowned upon. Ireland's Code Duello actually forbade it for safety reasons. Actual instances of deloping were rare, although one famous one in 1829 inspired its popularity as a device among novelists.

The custom of dueling with pistols became common as wearing a short sword in everyday dress passed out of fashion after about 1750. The great advantage of pistols was leveling the playing field. With a sword, one man might have an insuperable advantage in skill or agility; with pistols, almost anyone could become proficient with instruction and practice.

Before 1770, pistols came in many forms, from horse or "holster" pistols (carried in holsters attached to the saddle) to carriage pistols, to pocket pistols for personal defense. Their form was dictated by considerations other than accuracy, ergonomics and sheer deadliness in each case. Horse pistols were heavy; a carriage pistol often had two barrels, while a pocket pistol was small and compact.

Since our eight-decade span was a period of almost constant warfare for the British somewhere in the world, many men saw military service. There was a steady demand for military pistols, usually described in auction catalogs as "officer's pistols." Many of these incorporated features of duelling pistols, although heavier and more robust. They often replicated the man's own dueling pair.

As dueling with pistols gained acceptance, London gunmakers realized that a dedicated duelling pistol would confer an advantage. Gunmaker Joseph Griffin is credited with being the first to make such guns, refining the existing form of holster pistols into a more ergonomic and deadly form. This refinement included increasing attention to weight, balance, shape and size of the grip, trigger sensitivity and speed and reliability of ignition. John Atkinson considered Griffin the "father" of the British duelling pistol. By the time he died in 1783, it had assumed its modern form and was being produced, in fierce competition, by many fine gunmakers.

The first duelling pistols were shaped by the first dueling customs. A typical duel in 1775 involved two men facing one another 12 paces apart, pistols down at their sides, cocked and ready. At the signal to fire (rarely a dropped handkerchief, photogenic though it be), they would raise their pistols at arm's length and fire what amounted to a snapshot with no hesitation. Taking careful aim was considered ungentlemanly, so early pistols had rudimentary sights at most. Nor were the barrels rifled for the same reason.

The ideal pistol for dueling was an instinctive weapon, and the fit and balance were essential for the same reasons.

This did not mean they were inaccurate. Some early smoothbore flintlocks are astonishingly precise — capable of perforating a playing card with a dozen shots. But accuracy was only part of the equation.

A horse pistol had a grip shaped roughly like a hockey stick, broadening out into a pommel with a heavy bronze

John Twigg, one of the greatest English gunmakers, was influential in terms of both style and function. He originated the use of flat grip panels and the slim, full octagonal barrel. Twigg was an early proponent of fitted cases. This pair was converted to percussion, then reconverted to flint and professionally restored. *Photo: Rock Island Auction Company*

Napoleon Bonaparte was noted for giving (and receiving) Boutet weapons as gifts. Still, for his personal use, he preferred guns by Le Page, a private company dating from 1717 that lasted through the Revolution, the Napoleonic period, and into the Bourbon Restoration. This pair sold for $10,350 in 2020. *Photo: Rock Island Auction Company*

or iron grip cap (for use as a club) and trigger pulls to match. Only someone with large hands could really use them comfortably. Gunmakers realized that a slimmer, radiused grip, in the shape of a 'J,' fit the typical man's hand and pointed more naturally. One of the greatest British gunmakers, John Twigg, originated the practice of taking a round grip in cross-section and filing flat panels on the sides. Eventually, they measured a man's hand to ensure the grip fit him properly, just as they might measure for gloves. The goal was a pistol that came up quickly, pointed naturally like an extension of your arm and delivered the ball exactly where you were looking.

Over the years, gunmakers fiddled with this feature, making the panels wider, then thinner, then almost eliminating them altogether as cross-hatching became popular. Its rough surface afforded a more secure grip, and this gradually evolved into checkering as we know it today.

Broadly speaking, we can say that the duelling pistol began as an increasingly refined flintlock horse pistol and, over 80 years evolved into the sophisticated percussion target pistol of 1850. This evolution included aesthetic, stylistic and technological changes. Still, aesthetics was never allowed to interfere with the duelling pistol's primary purpose: It was a deadly weapon — first, foremost and always.

Gradually, "snap shooting" gave way to careful aiming, and the pistols reflected this. They became heavier (1.5 pounds was typical in 1775, 2.5 pounds in 1850), the barrels longer and the guns more muzzle-heavy; better sights were fitted, bores were rifled and set triggers became more common.

*****

Many factors affected the design and evolution of duelling pistols. Advances in gun powder, barrel steel, flintlock mechanism design, and finally — the most influential — the transition, after 1820, from flint to percussion.

There is a broader question relating to supply and demand. By the 1790s, many makers were producing duelling pistols — almost three dozen craftsmen in London alone, according to one directory — and they were in intense competition in terms of workmanship and technology. This market could not have existed without serious demand from people with money. Yet, if dueling was illegal (or officially frowned upon), how could such demand exist? First, and probably foremost, there was the military.

The British army's "Articles of War," which governed officers' conduct in peace and war, was frankly contradictory. On the one hand, it forbade dueling; on the other, it stated that if an officer allowed himself to be insulted and did *not* challenge the other party, he had disgraced himself and his regiment and could be drummed out of the service.

In 1789, a famous duel occurred between the Duke of York (brother of

King George III) and Colonel Lennox of the Coldstream Guards. The Duke said Colonel Lennox had heard things about him in his club that no gentleman should tolerate. He was, in other words, a coward. He challenged the Duke, they met on Wimbledon Common, and Lennox came close to killing him. Colonel Lennox used a pair by Robert Wogdon, the most celebrated of all makers of duelling pistols. This contradiction was not resolved until 1844 when the Articles were amended.

Then there was the civilian element. Young men of wealth and position had little to do except seeking amusement and defend their honor, and this they did. They gambled, raced horses and gigs, frequented the less admirable parts of London and fought duels. Dueling became so common that Atkinson referred to it as "almost a national sport" and quotes surprising statistics about the number of duels fought in a region during one period. The Anglo-Irish nobility was particularly combative. When a young man began paying court to a young lady who might become his wife, a common question was, "Has he blazed?" meaning had he faced another man in a duel and acquitted himself well?

This, then, was the market for duelling pistols that encouraged Joseph Griffin, John Twigg, Wogdon, Durs Egg, Henry Nock, H.W. Mortimer, John Manton, Joseph Manton, John Rigby, and ultimately James Purdey, among many others, to compete ferociously with one another. It's why they designed better mechanisms, perfected construction and built durable businesses on their reputations.

One can trace the evolution of pistols by their makers, who worked for whom, or by their features or styling. Leave us begin with the makers because these were the men who refined the mechanisms, invented improvements, and catered to the wishes of their clients, many of whom had a great experience in dueling and were worth listening to and trying to accommodate.

Joseph Griffin is generally acknowledged as the father of the duelling pistol, experimenting with weight, balance and other refinements through the 1760s. One of the giants of English gun making, John Twigg, began in business around 1760 and made several significant contributions through the 1770s. When John Manton completed his apprenticeship in Grantham and came to London, he went to work for Twigg, eventually becoming a shop foreman. In 1781, Manton set up on his own in Dover Street. His brother Joseph, 15 years younger, also apprenticed in the country before coming to London to work for his brother. Joseph went out on his own in 1789 and later took on James Purdey, who eventually became his head stocker, before starting his own firm. Other great names who worked for Joseph Manton included Charles Lancaster, Thomas Boss and

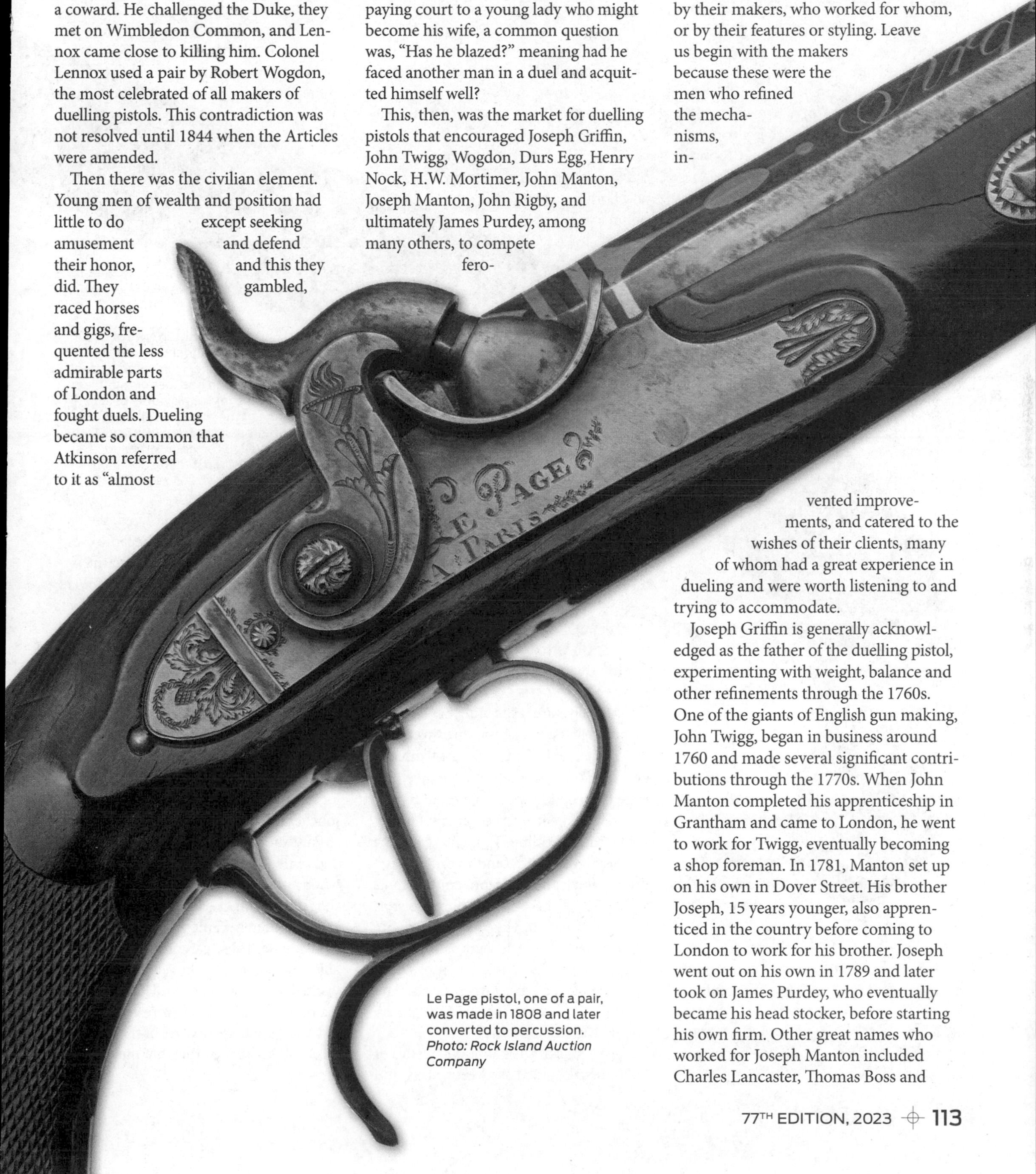

Le Page pistol, one of a pair, was made in 1808 and later converted to percussion. *Photo: Rock Island Auction Company*

William Greener. Two centuries later, James Purdey & Sons is still in London, still in business in South Audley Street and still making "best" guns.

We have looked at a typical duelling pistol circa 1770. What changes did John Twigg initiate, other than flat panels on the grip?

The main one was the barrel. In the 1760s, "Spanish form" barrels were standard. These had an octagonal section forward from the breech, giving way to round and a heavy, cannonesque look. Twigg made barrels octagonal to the muzzle but slim and graceful. Octagonal barrels on duelling pistols — twist or Damascus — were standard for decades, although round barrels were also popular. Robert Wogdon, especially, favored round ones.

Twigg introduced fitted wooden cases to hold the pistol, and later pairs of pistols with flints, powder, wads and necessary tools. Storing a ramrod in the case allowed gunmakers to dispense with one under the barrel, affording both better balance and a smarter appearance. John Manton followed Twigg's preferences in case design, which was later adapted to shotgun cases and is reflected in virtually every fine gun case to this day.

If pistols became more accurate, reliable, and deadly, those enthusiasts using them realized that practice was essential to becoming proficient. This imperative gave rise to the establishment of shooting galleries, usually connected with a gunmaker's premises. Joseph Manton's gallery in London became famous in part because Lord Byron was a frequent visitor. One time, after an outstanding performance, Byron proclaimed himself the "finest shot in London." Manton coolly replied, "not the best, my lord, but you shot respectably today," and Lord Byron stormed out in a temper.

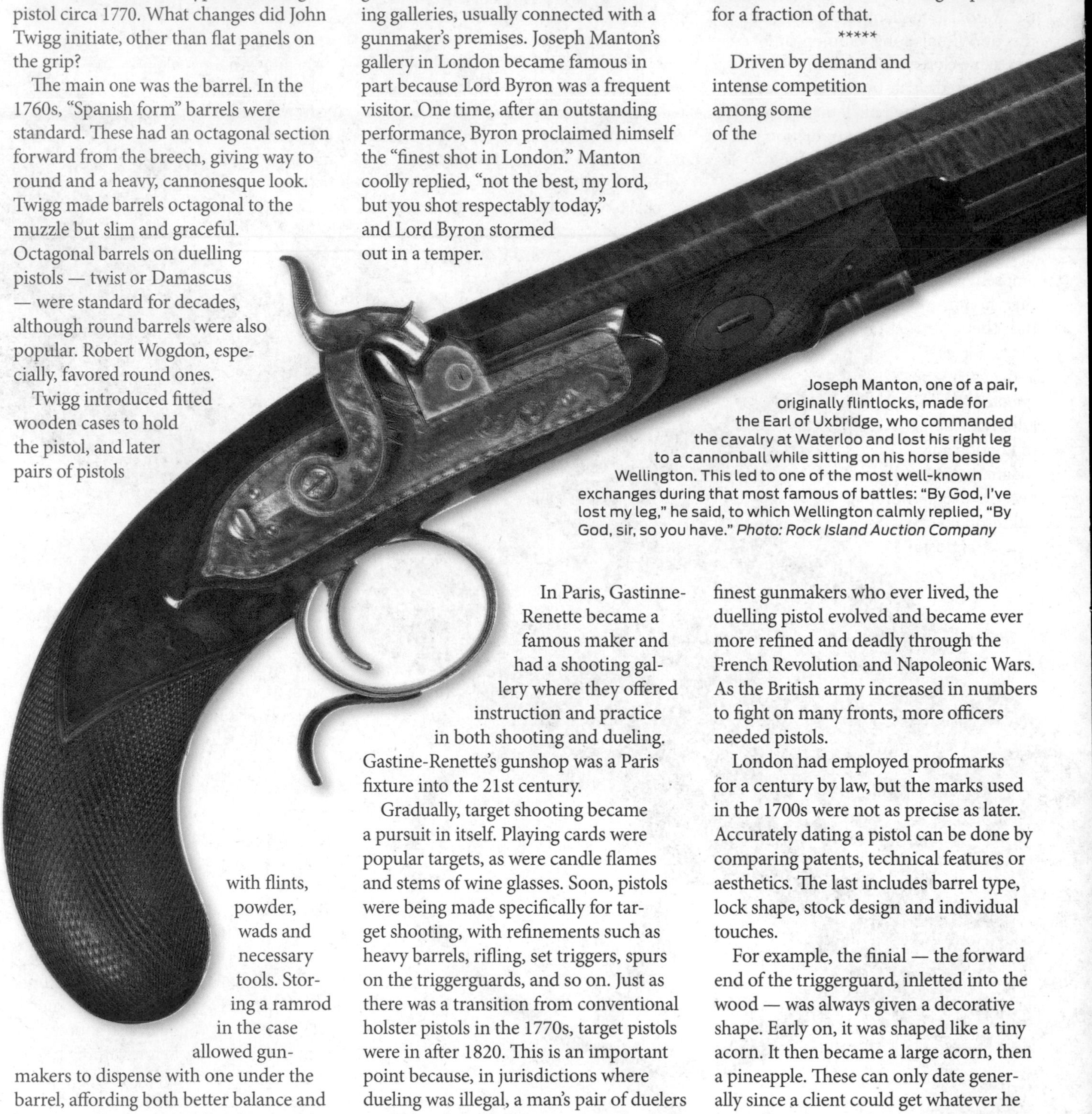

Joseph Manton, one of a pair, originally flintlocks, made for the Earl of Uxbridge, who commanded the cavalry at Waterloo and lost his right leg to a cannonball while sitting on his horse beside Wellington. This led to one of the most well-known exchanges during that most famous of battles: "By God, I've lost my leg," he said, to which Wellington calmly replied, "By God, sir, so you have." *Photo: Rock Island Auction Company*

In Paris, Gastinne-Renette became a famous maker and had a shooting gallery where they offered instruction and practice in both shooting and dueling. Gastine-Renette's gunshop was a Paris fixture into the 21st century.

Gradually, target shooting became a pursuit in itself. Playing cards were popular targets, as were candle flames and stems of wine glasses. Soon, pistols were being made specifically for target shooting, with refinements such as heavy barrels, rifling, set triggers, spurs on the triggerguards, and so on. Just as there was a transition from conventional holster pistols in the 1770s, target pistols were in after 1820. This is an important point because, in jurisdictions where dueling was illegal, a man's pair of duelers could be passed off as target pistols. And, of course, a pistol of appropriate caliber could be used for both.

Today, we see sets of antique pistols offered for sale, billed as target pistols, and often bringing a lower price. Collectors who yearn for a set of duelling pistols but don't have $25,000 for a pair of Joseph Mantons might get a beautiful pair of Kuchenreuter (German) "target" pistols for a fraction of that.

*****

Driven by demand and intense competition among some of the finest gunmakers who ever lived, the duelling pistol evolved and became ever more refined and deadly through the French Revolution and Napoleonic Wars. As the British army increased in numbers to fight on many fronts, more officers needed pistols.

London had employed proofmarks for a century by law, but the marks used in the 1700s were not as precise as later. Accurately dating a pistol can be done by comparing patents, technical features or aesthetics. The last includes barrel type, lock shape, stock design and individual touches.

For example, the finial — the forward end of the triggerguard, inletted into the wood — was always given a decorative shape. Early on, it was shaped like a tiny acorn. It then became a large acorn, then a pineapple. These can only date generally since a client could get whatever he wanted, and many demanded standard features even after they were considered old-fashioned. This is one of the many facets of duelling pistols that make them so fascinating.

Dating a pistol requires considering the way the maker lettered his name on the barrel or lock, the patent dates for a particular feature, and so on. Usually, you come up with a conclusion such as "This could not have been made before such and such a date" and gradually narrow it down.

A significant point to consider is that many pistols began as flintlocks and were converted to percussion, and then a few were even converted back. Often, this work is so well done it can fool an expert. The Joseph Mantons shown here that belonged to the Earl of Uxbridge began as flintlocks, probably around 1808, but were converted after 1820. On the other hand, the John Twigg pair was converted, then reconverted to flintlock.

The primary area of innovation and refining was the lock. Gunmakers realized early that the two critical factors with flint were reliability and ignition speed. (A note on terminology: What Americans call the hammer, the British called the cock, and what we call the frizzen, they called the hammer. Here, we'll use British terminology, as most books do.) A major innovation was to install a tiny steel roller bearing on the tail of the hammer so it would slide more easily on the hammer spring and snap back smartly. Later, the roller was moved to the tip of the spring itself. This progression — no roller, roller on the hammer, roller on the spring — helps date flintlocks.

Again, Robert Wogdon was an exception, believing the best way to ensure a quick, smooth response was to tune the hammer spring carefully. Wogdon was building pistols into the 1790s, still without the roller bearing, long after it had become standard.

Locks evolved aesthetically as well. The side plate on the left side, which seated

The Kuchenreuter family of Regensburg, Bavaria, were the most noted of the German makers of duelling pistols. This percussion pair could be billed as target pistols, cased with elaborate (and beautifully made) accoutrements. Their overall line follows the French pattern of Boutet and Le Page. The carved dog's head in place of a forend tip is a typical German touch on firearms. *Photo: Rock Island Auction Company*

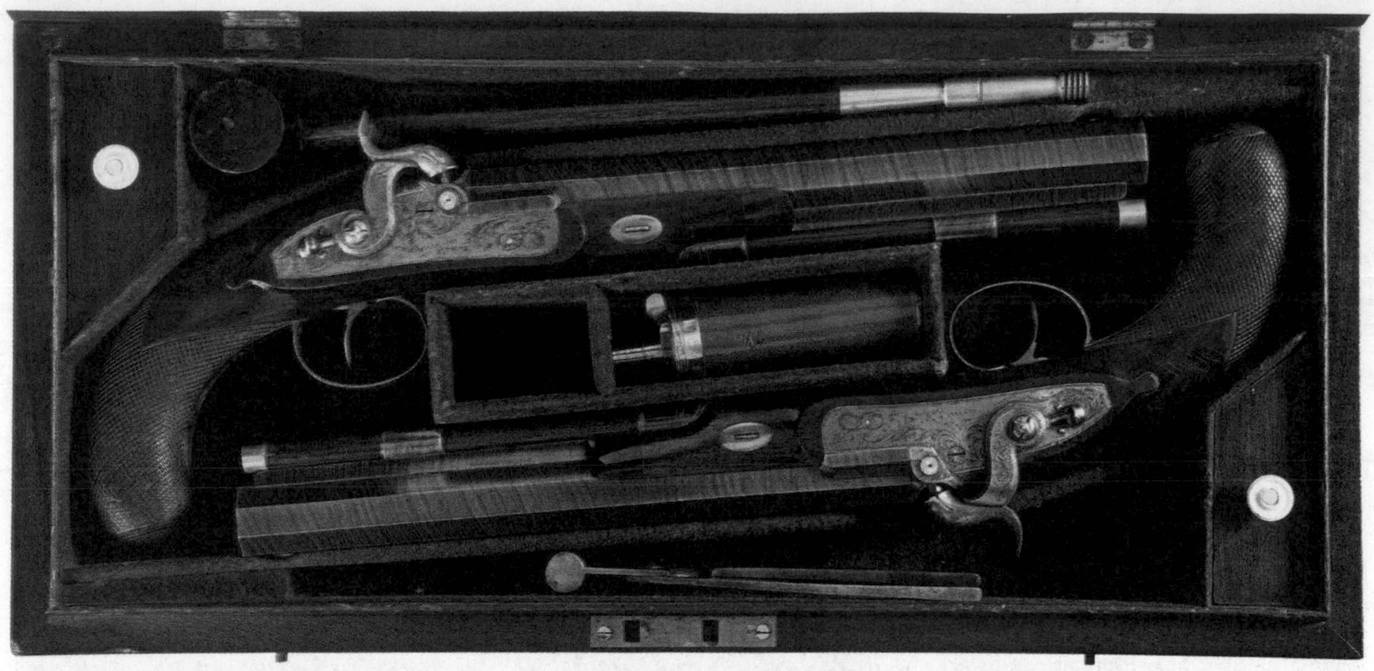

Pair of John Manton percussion pistols. Manton followed Twigg's pattern for his cases — not surprising since he worked for Twigg when he came to London, rose to shop foreman, went out on his own in 1781, and bought the business after Twigg's death. John was more conservative than his brother, Joseph, sticking with flint until the percussion system was established. *Photo: Rock Island Auction Company*

the pins holding the lock, gradually disappeared, replaced first by two metal cups to hold the pins, then only one, with the front pin replaced by a hook on the lock plate. At first, the comb of the cock was turned in toward the flint, then later turned out. Finally, the shape of the lock plate itself at the rear — initially knifepoint, then a vertical flat and finally radiused in the percussion era.

All this effort to improve locks enhanced the reputation of English flintlocks throughout Europe. Many commented that they had an "oily" feel that no other locks quite matched. Joseph Manton was noted for taking special pains with his locks.

Other innovations include Henry Nock's patent breech, with its improved combustion chamber, variations in pans (including "waterproof" ones) by John Manton, and Wogdon's efforts to make barrels "shoot true" at 12 paces, the usual distance for dueling.

As well as favoring round barrels and eschewing roller bearings, Robert Wogdon (in business c.1765–1800) was influential in other ways. Early in his career, he favored beautiful silver fittings on his pistols but gradually made them plainer and more austere while emphasizing superb workmanship. A typical late Wogdon is "dark and deadly." He also clung to full-length stocks long after half stocks had become widespread.

Both W. Keith Neal and John Atkinson consider Robert Wogdon the gun maker whose reputation rested primarily on his duelling pistols. A dispute between gentlemen that could only be settled with pistols became known as a "Wogdon case." He is particularly famous in America because Aaron Burr killed Alexander Hamilton with a Wogdon. Robert Wogdon built a small fortune on the strength of his duelling pistols and retired in comfort.

Gradually, the trend to "Quaker-like chasteness of taste" that Wogdon initiated seeped into other areas of gun manufacture — notably the fowling-pieces of the Mantons and, later, James Purdey and Thomas Boss. While European makers clung to ornate decoration, British makers as a class became renowned for their restraint. Part of this trend can be attributed to Beau Brummell and the revolution in men's attire he inspired between 1800 and 1835.

The gradual transition to dual-purpose "target" pistols brought with it an emphasis on accuracy. Rifling, heretofore considered "ungentlemanly," slowly gained acceptance. At first, it was in the form of "scratch" rifling — grooves so tiny they appeared to be merely scratches and sometimes confined to a few inches forward of the breech, where it could not be spotted by punctilious seconds. These sufficed to stabilize the ball and impart better accuracy, for one shot at least.

Similarly, set triggers gained popularity. Some were adjustable by the user, others by the gunmaker to sensitivity he considered appropriate.

Finally, tastes in stock shape evolved. Full stocks were replaced by half stocks (Wogdon excepted), and "saw-handle" stocks were introduced around 1805. These never supplanted the sleek radiused grip, but they could be superb. Keith Neal wrote that a Purdey duelling pistol made in the 1820s, with a 7-inch barrel and saw-handle grip, was "by far the finest duelling pistol (he) ever handled." And Neal handled a great many.

"So perfectly is this weapon designed to fit the hand," he wrote, "that one has only to look at the target and bring the weapon up to find the sights correctly aligned. It is equally good for snap shooting or slow accurate target work."

Early Robert Wogdon is as dark and deadly as Wogdon's reputation. He was one of the first London gunmakers to minimize decoration — a practice that grew into the "Quaker-like chasteness of taste" for which Purdey et al. are noted to this day. Disputes that could only be resolved by a duel became known as "Wogdon cases." Flat panels on grip, the comb of cock turned in, and acorn finial (just visible) denote an early (1770s) gun. *Photo: Rock Island Auction Company*

The Purdey had a trigger guard spur for the second finger, significantly improving stability. This feature became increasingly popular until, by 1850, it was unusual to see a fine target or duelling pistol without one.

Other refinements and features that were introduced, some invented by one gunmaker or another, include Henry Nock's patent breech, gold-lined touch holes and pans, set triggers, better sights and rifling.

Nock's breech (1787) was a significant step forward. It allowed for a chamber smaller than the bore diameter for the powder in the breech piece that screwed into the barrel. This allowed the exact seating of the ball and kept the powder from being compressed, which improved combustion.

Gold-lined touch holes had been in use for some time, intended to protect the steel from the corrosive effects of blackpowder. Although the latter's usefulness was questionable, they were widely adopted, along with gold-lined pans. In time, gold was replaced by platinum, which was more durable. Joseph Manton claimed credit for this, but the evidence says otherwise.

However, the most significant change was introducing and perfecting percussion ignition. Invented by the Rev. Alexander Forsyth, gunmakers took more than a decade to

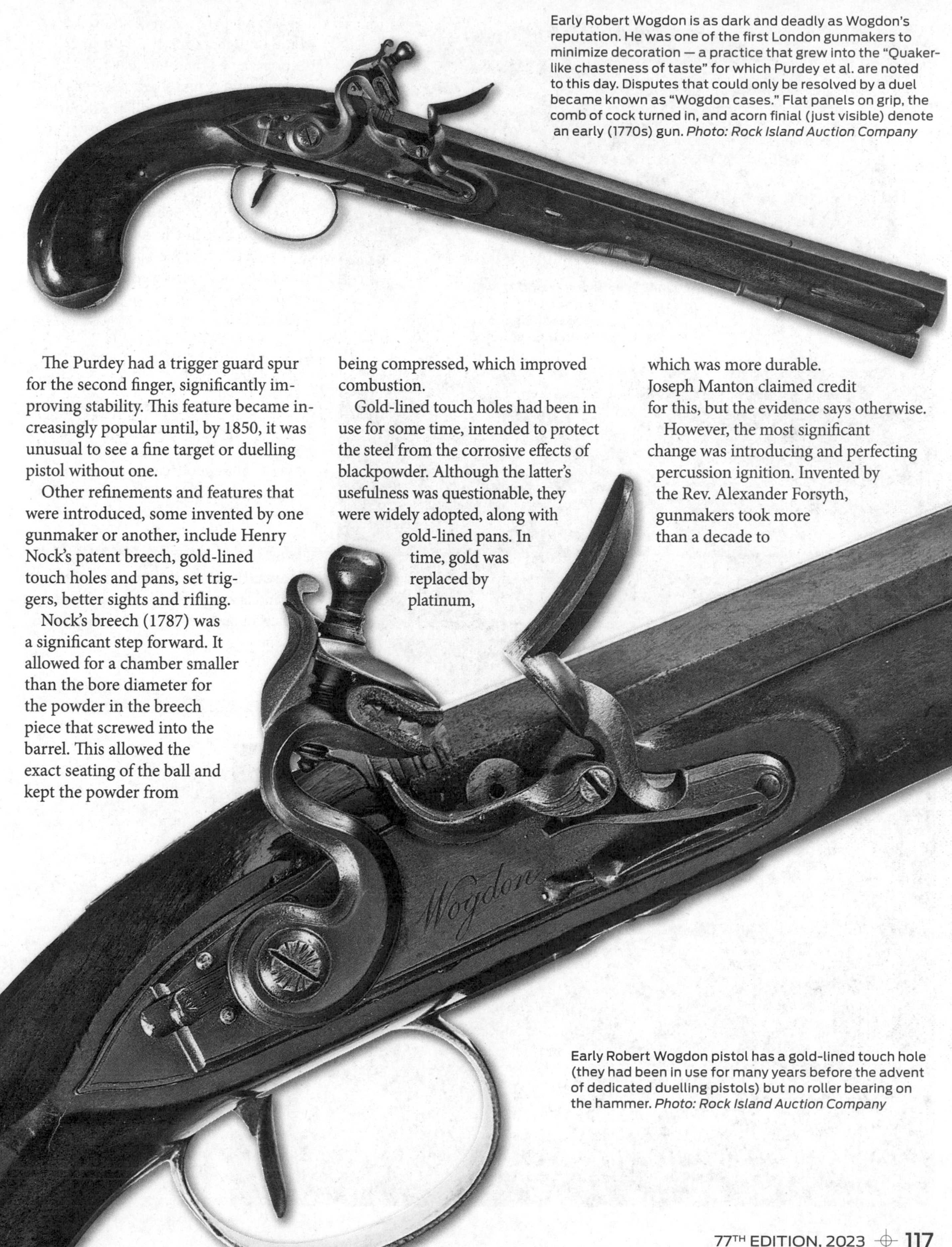

Early Robert Wogdon pistol has a gold-lined touch hole (they had been in use for many years before the advent of dedicated duelling pistols) but no roller bearing on the hammer. *Photo: Rock Island Auction Company*

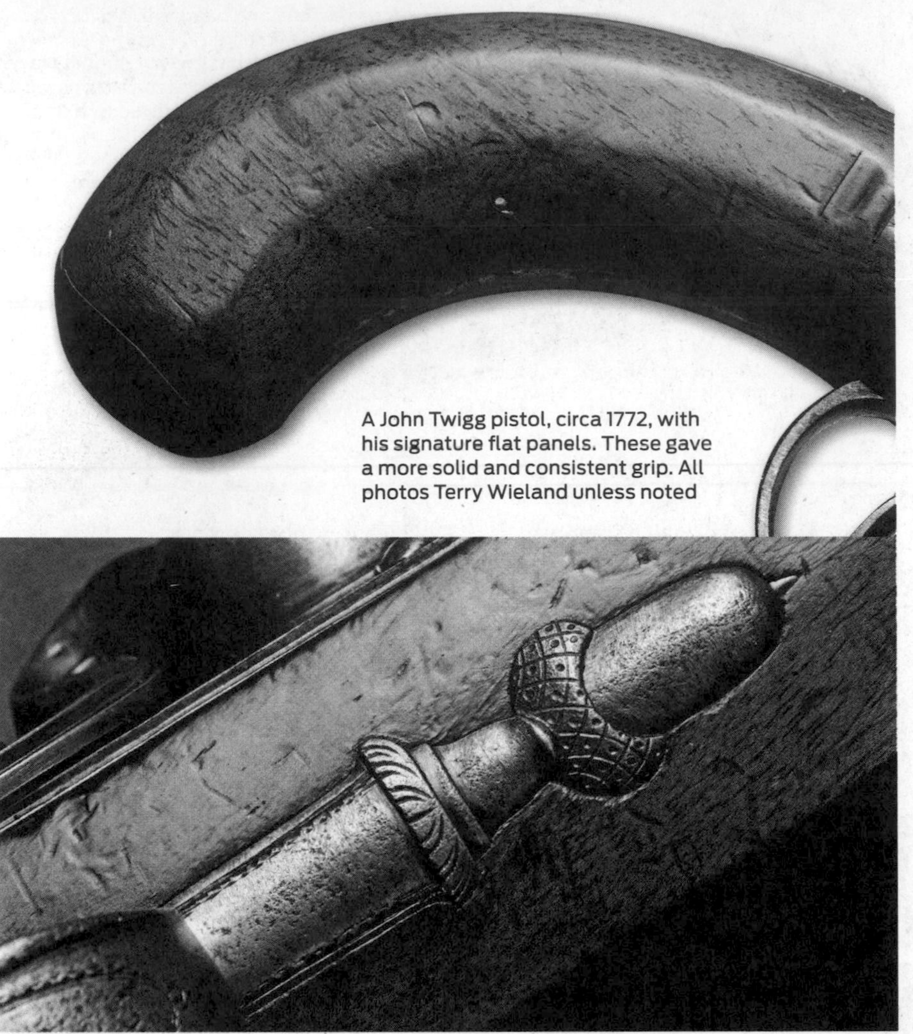

A John Twigg pistol, circa 1772, with his signature flat panels. These gave a more solid and consistent grip. All photos Terry Wieland unless noted

Twigg again, sporting the early small-acorn finial. Later, a larger acorn was used, and finally, a pineapple. The shape of the finial is a rough way of dating a gun.

arrive at the percussion cap as we know it, and until that time, most duelling pistols retained their flintlocks. No maker would compromise reliability, nor would their clients want it. The flintlock had been perfected to such a stage that many refused to give it up. John Manton was especially stubborn in this regard, continuing to make flintlocks even after the percussion cap became predominant. Many especially fine flintlocks were converted to percussion because their owners did not want to give up their extraordinary handling and shooting qualities.

This brings us back to the Duke of Wellington and his one and only duel.

In 1829, Wellington was Prime Minister and endeavored to pass the Catholic Emancipation Act, which would allow Roman Catholics many previously limited political rights. That move was highly controversial, and the Duke was coming under vicious attack. The Earl of Winchilsea, an "Ultra"-Protestant, published a letter where he impugned Wellington's motives. The Duke demanded a retraction and apology; when these were not forthcoming, he challenged Winchilsea to a duel.

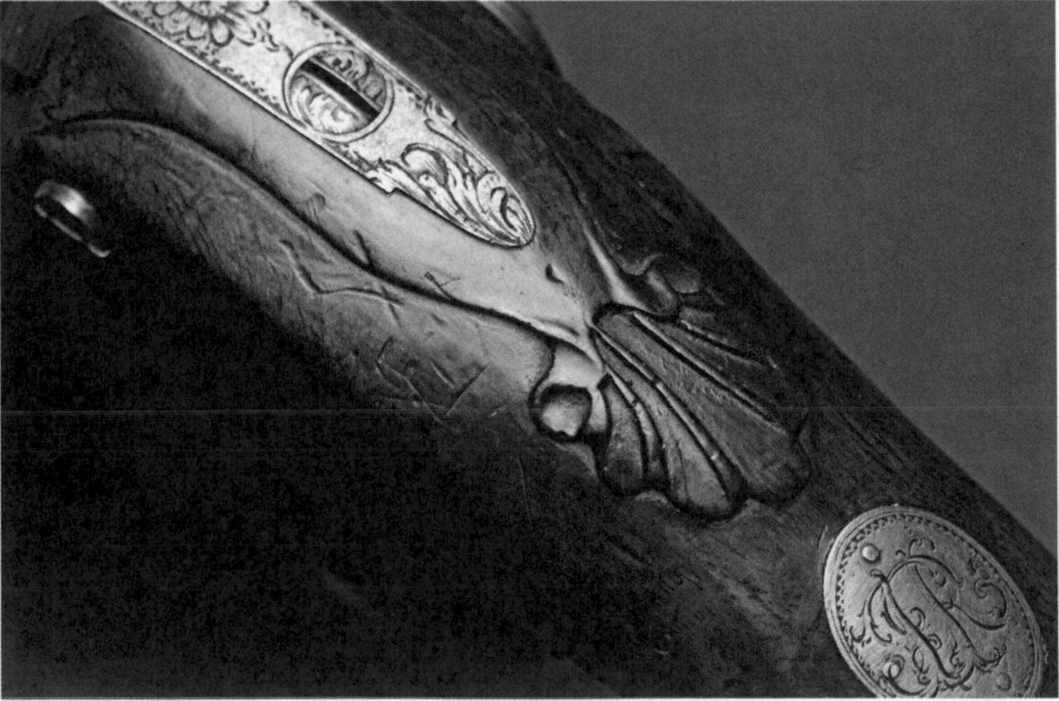

A Twigg aesthetic touch: In his early years, he carved a clamshell behind the topstrap, and many other makers followed his lead. The practice died out by the 1790s.

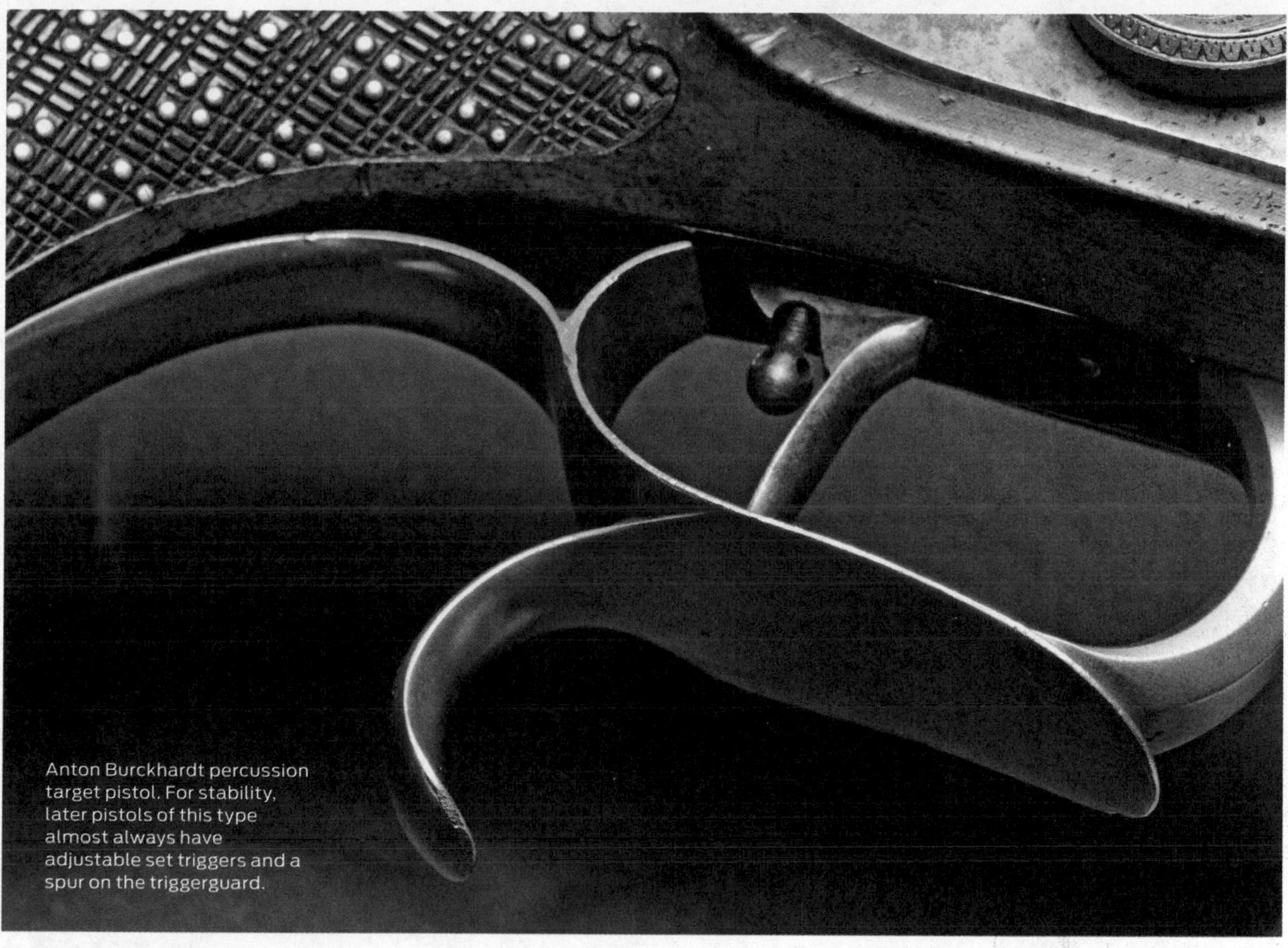
Anton Burckhardt percussion target pistol. For stability, later pistols of this type almost always have adjustable set triggers and a spur on the triggerguard.

Throughout his career in the army, Wellington had opposed dueling. Early on, while stationed in India, a close friend was killed in one. The Duke forbade dueling, on pain of death, in every command he held. So why now? As he explained it, the letter was not just an insult to himself but to the cabinet he led and His Majesty's government and could not be allowed to go unchallenged. He demanded, "... that satisfaction for your conduct a gentleman has a right to require, and which a gentleman never refuses to give."

The Duke owned a pair of very fine flintlock duelling pistols, made by C.A. Jones of London — a gift from the East India Company to honor his victory at Waterloo. They had every technical wrinkle one could ask for, but they were flintlocks, and it was 1829. Wellington asked his second, Sir Henry Hardinge, to request his doctor, J.H. Hume, to meet them at Battersea, where the duel was to take place and bring his percussion pistols.

Attempts to extract an apology failing yet again, Hardinge stepped off 12 paces, marked the positions, and the antagonists took their places with pistols down at their sides. Sir Henry asked if they were ready, then gave the order to fire. Wellington had intended only to wound Winchelsea in the leg but seeing his opponent did not raise his pistol, Wellington deliberately fired off to one side. At that, Winchilsea smiled and fired his pistol into the air. He then apologized for the libel.

The result was to make the Duke of Wellington a public hero for having faced death in defense of the government's good name. The Catholic emancipation bill passed with a considerable majority.

History does not record any details about Dr. Hume's duelling pistols, nor those of the Earl of Winchilsea, but the Duke of Wellington's pair are now in the London Museum.

By 1844, dueling was severely frowned upon by civilians. The contradictions in the Articles of War had even come to the attention of Queen Victoria. She asked her then-prime minister, Sir Robert Peel, to reword them to eliminate the clause that, to all intents, forced officers to fight duels. This he did, and the great age of English dueling ended.

Its legacy, however, lived on in the form of great gunmakers such as James Purdey and John Rigby and their magnificent rifles and fowling pieces — masterpieces that could trace their style and technical excellence directly back to the duelling pistol. Today, fine pairs bearing names such as Wogdon, Egg, Nock, Mortimer, Twigg, and the Mantons are highly prized by collectors and change hands for massive amounts. GD

A Tribute to Bob Dunlap

A 1911 to Shoot or Admire, by Two of His Revering Students

› LENÉE LANDIS

1911 Tribute photos courtesy of Brion Lincoln, all others courtesy Bob Dunlap

Master Gunsmith Bob Dunlap embodied a kaleidoscope of interests that revolved around people, places, and things, mainly of the bang variety. He was a man who made a memorable imprint on many a student gunsmith who represented a good chunk of his life's work. He was born in June 1938 and left this good earth in December 2019.

I ran, tripped, and fell into the firearms world and met Bob, who would be one of the generous and spirited people I came to know and love — a bigger than life man, born in an era where people made, made do, and figured it out, powered by curiosity and action. At some point, I realized the wealth of information in people of a certain age. With the idea of crystallizing this for readers, I grabbed the trusty digital recorder and spent hours chronicling their lessons, logic and exploits to be compiled as the project grew. Bob was one of these wise people.

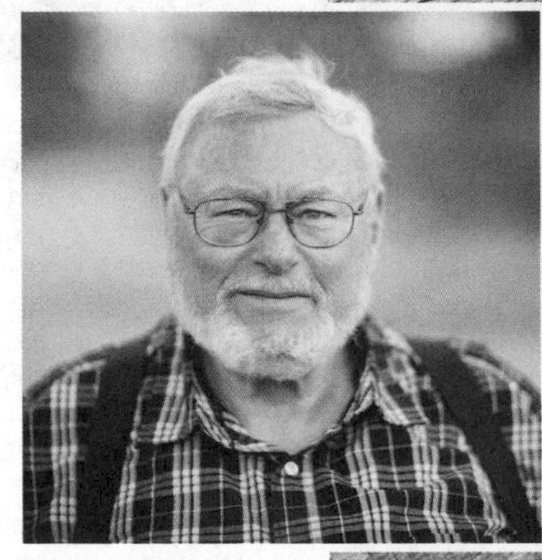

Legendary Master Gunsmith Bob Dunlap.

It is humbling now as I celebrate his life through two of his students who felt compelled to make a tribute 1911 with the idea it would be auctioned off and proceeds contributed to a deserving charity. Fred Zeglin and Ken Brooks, both students of Bob's through the Lassen Community College Gunsmithing Program, graduated

The end result of a tribute collaboration to Bob Dunlap.

in 1984 and 1991, respectively. They later met through Bob and while attending the SHOT Show.

BOB DUNLAP'S PATH TO GUNSMITHING

Bob was industrious, even as a youngster. Around the age of seven, during WWII, his grandfather showed him how to pick up English and black walnuts and dry and shell them. He recalled the black walnut trees seemed to grow wild at the side of the road, where he would collect the bounty. No one ever stopped him. Dunlap would diligently pound them with a hammer to crack them and pick the walnut meat out to store it in a jar. Bob's job was to open black walnuts because the hard shells made it more time-consuming; you had to be motivated. His grandpa took care of processing the English walnuts, selling and delivering them to a bakery each morning. He then paid Bob.

Dunlap and Ken Brooks at Tisas.

This was in the town of Gridley, California, a town a bit over two square miles, about 50 miles north of Sacramento. At age 12, Bob lived with his mother and new stepfather on a leased rice farm in the same town. His stepdad made use of Bob's willingness to work.

The factory original Tisas M1911 Regent as found in Bob Dunlap's personal collection.

During planting season, bags of seed were soaked until they started to germinate, the fields were flooded, and then the bi-plane was loaded and flew back and forth, dropping sprouted seed. Bob would go up the rows and back to flag the end of the row for the pilot's visual, mud sucking the bottom of his shoes and getting pelted with falling seeds when the plane sometimes overshot the mark. He checked and adjusted the water level in the dikes and, during harvest, ran the dryer. His stepdad always paid him for his work. The money he made financed the beginning of a lifetime of collecting guns, starting with a cap gun and escalating quickly. He also held on to a principle: if you wanted something, you worked. It was a principle he taught through his attitude, students learning by osmosis.

It was a toss-up whether Bob wanted to be a mechanic or a gunsmith. Teaching was not in the mix at that point, though it turned out to be something he would come to love. He initially took mechanical engineering at Yuba College in Marysville, California.

One of the incidents that funneled him to gunsmithing happened while working under his MG TD sports car in a tight fit on a cement pad. With a tie rod above his head, glasses off because he "didn't need them," oil dripped in his eye. He decided right then and there: nope, gunsmith it is. The second incident sealed this trajectory: he transferred to Chico State from Yuba College to take additional mechanical engineering classes, noticed the guys standing around to sign up and thought, "they're all geeks; I don't want to work with a bunch of geeks all my life." He jumped in his car.

He left Chico and drove to Lassen College, where class signups were also in progress, got in line, and signed up for the gunsmithing program. He admitted now he was a geek; I mentioned he hadn't realized the panache geeks can have. He acknowledged that the 2 ½ years of mechanical engineering experience helped him immensely in gunsmithing.

In 1959, Bob completed the Lassen program after a year and a half of study. In 1970, 11 years later, he returned to the gunsmithing program as an instructor, where he stayed for the next 25 years, retiring as the senior instructor. In the meantime, in 1974, Bob opened his

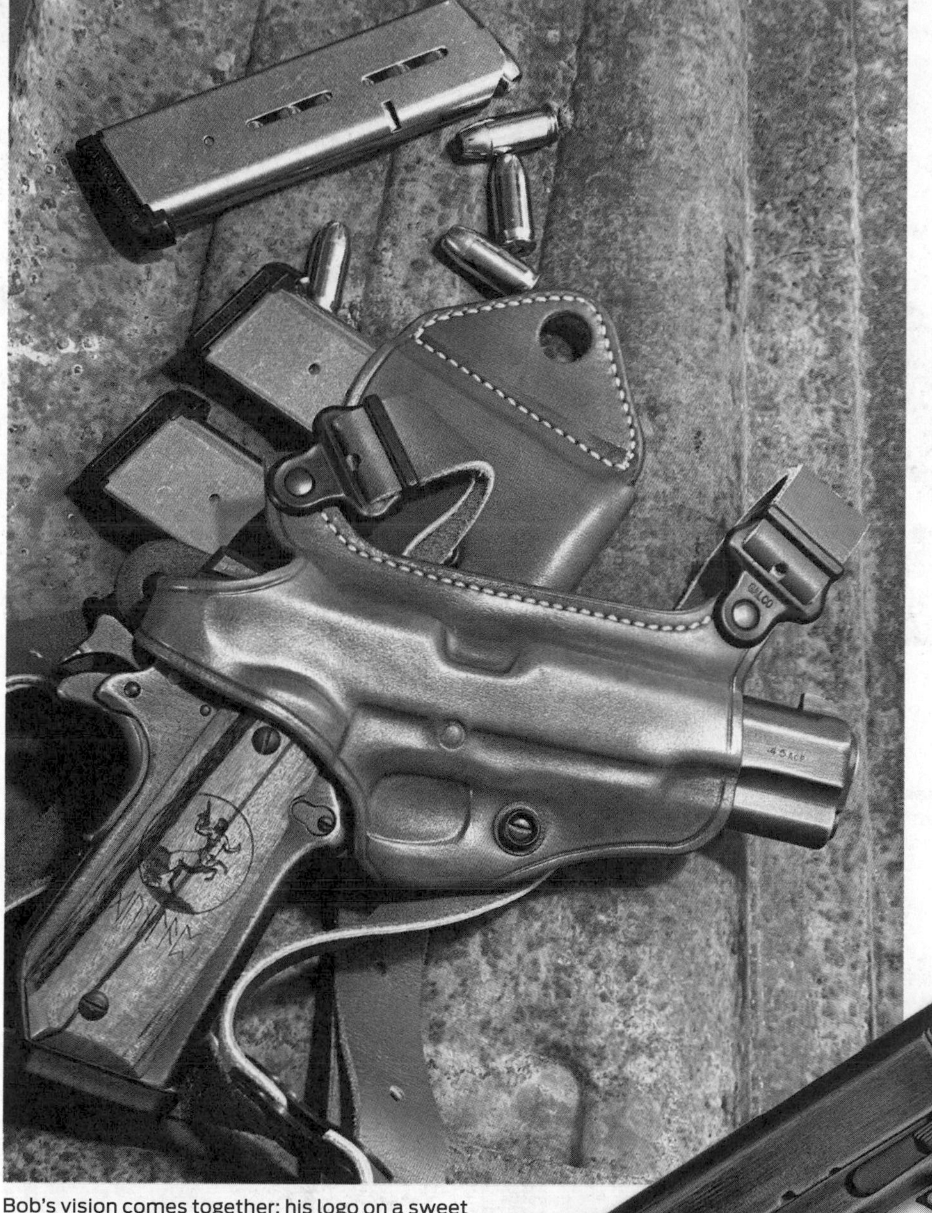

Bob's vision comes together: his logo on a sweet 1911 ready for concealed carry.

shop, Pacific International Service Co. or PISCO, which did warranty work for just about every gunmaker you can name while keeping nine gunsmiths busy. After he retired from Lassen, Bob moved the shop to Coquille, Oregon, where it continues today, Ken Brooks taking over ownership around 2014.

THE TEACHING YEARS

Between graduating and returning to Lassen as an instructor, Bob worked for about four years at General Motors' Delco Defense Research Laboratory in the hypervelocity gun lab in Goleta. He got the job because of his engineering background and gunsmithing ability. You could still hear the marvel in his voice when he said, "Ooh, that taught me a lot."

In one such example, they'd shoot a two-stage pump gun with a high-pressure tapered section on the muzzle and an 8-inch projectile at a mind-blowing five-figure fps, which Bob said: "makes a .220 Swift look like a piker." They would shoot in a flight range where they pumped down the air to less than a micron and added whatever gases were needed to simulate the atmosphere at a particular altitude in space. In most cases, they put the projectile — what looked like a faux spaceship — into a sabot and launched it. The sabot caught, the projectile went through a 2 ¼-inch valve, which went from closed to fully open to closed in 1.4/10,000 of a second, a short window for the projectile to pass through. As it went downrange, radar and Schlieren cameras, which can photograph a shockwave, chronicled the state of that attempt.

The ultimate objective varied, and they experimented and learned how to knock out an incoming warhead, destroy an incoming missile or tank that's bulletproofed, and what it takes to penetrate the protective coating on a missile or tank. Dunlap changed the backstop after every shot because they didn't want it going through the 10-foot diameter, 6-inch-thick door, rounded so it wouldn't cave in. One day, he opened it to replace the backstop after just one shot; they had fired a different kind of projectile, studying something else. He found that the door's condition had significantly changed, an *aha* moment. Since his clearance was top but not of the ultra-double shiny golden clearance variety, he was informed he wasn't allowed to open the door anymore.

Bob would have loved how every corner of the gun is melted.

We laughed; he knew what was happening at the time because of his understanding of physics. My grasp now of the situation came from common sense. My synopsis/question was: did this mean they had accidentally found a way to penetrate a certain kind of mate-

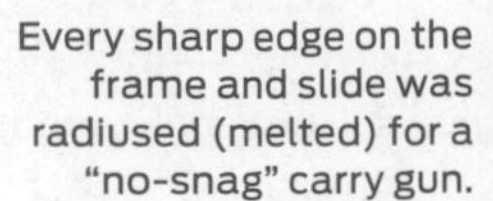

Every sharp edge on the frame and slide was radiused (melted) for a "no-snag" carry gun.

Tisas original cast hammer and hand-cut checkering.

Slide with all the corners "melted."

Low-profile sight roughed in. Notice on the finished gun how all the lines are blended.

Bobtail mainspring housing fully fit and blended into the frame.

Machining for the low-profile rear sight.

Fred used a fixture in the mill vise to cut the bevels on the magazine well.

Compare the factory lines of the 1911 before it was melted.

Filing in the corners of the magazine well bevel.

The factory magazine well.

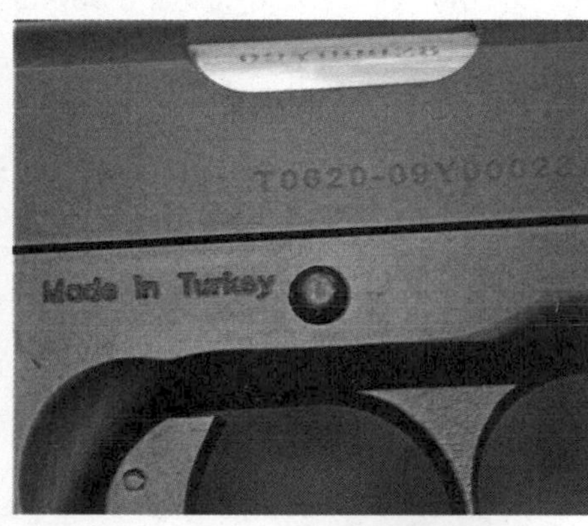

Import markings and the factory ejection port.

Using a fixture to drill the new Bobtail mainspring housing retaining pin.

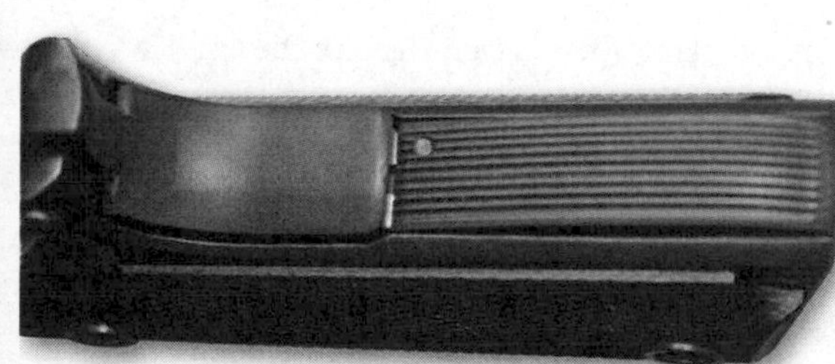

The factory mainspring housing.

The original rear sight.

rial based on what they were using that launched another industry far away that none of us are cleared for, and someone would make a lot of money? He laughed and agreed.

He returned to real-world gunsmithing full-time, first in Sacramento and then a Lassen as an instructor. A few years into it, Bob reworked the program into his "design, function and repair" approach as the ability to earn a living for most gunsmiths was in repairing guns rather than custom stock making and similar work. Bob enjoyed the program's growth, with 105 students enrolled at its fullest. Many more than that who graduated stayed in the industry. Some worked for manufacturers, became head gunsmiths and found success.

Bob did have a practical joker side. Ken thought that had died down by the time he went through the program, but Fred remembered. "If a student left a gun unattended on their bench, it would often be fully disassembled when they returned — or Bob would use his knowledge of guns to make them fail when you were turning them in for grades." He only played jokes on the students he liked, and there was some method to the madness — sometimes you need a break from metal on metal; it keeps you engaged.

So, class time was not entirely nose-to-the-grindstone, but you could have fooled John Allchin. It's fair to say that John, now the owner of Allchin Gun Parts in Santa Margarita, California, will never forget being alone in the middle of a stunt instigated by Fred Zeglin. It was Finals week, and there was a ton of work due from each student. Fred explains the moment: "I got all the students in one class to share the cost of a cheesecake and renting a copy of Star Wars (Bob was a big fan). I called the AV department at the college and had a TV and VCR delivered to the classroom. When Bob came down the hall, we had the lights out, and the opening credits were running. He said, "Nice try," then walked to the front of the room and saw the cheesecake, "Oh crap." Anyone who wanted to leave did so, while some stayed and watched the movie with Bob. I was gone."

John remembers clearly because he was the only guy who opted to do the assignment for the test. He had to write the complete cycle of operations for a gun of Bob's choosing. "John said everything that could go wrong with that gun did; he can't recall how many days he spent on the assignment, but he remembers the rest of us skated."

Notice the uniform surface through the rear sight, no protrusions, and the cocobolo grip detail.

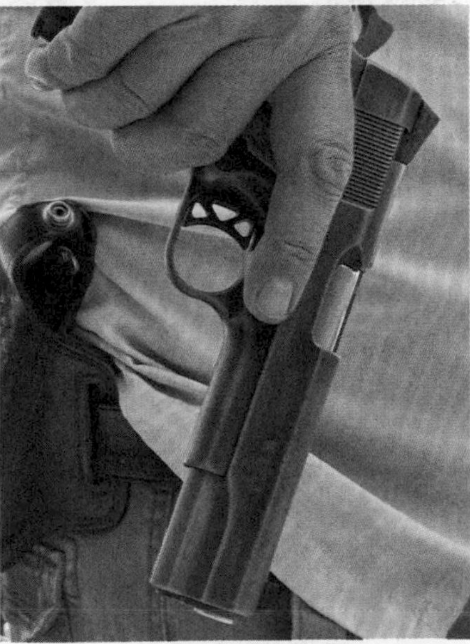

Reliability and function were Bob's priorities with a carry gun.

Ken recalled some practical jokes by the students: a group of pranksters stole Bob's knife, which they suspended in the middle of an epoxy block and displayed. Bob was shocked but began to see the humor, even more so when he realized they had actually borrowed his knife and bought a new one to enshrine just to put one over on him.

Another group moved all the benches out, parked Bob's vehicle in the middle of the shop, and then put the benches back in their rightful place, effectively trapping his mode of transportation as a centerpiece, which Bob found when he went to go home that day. Respect is one thing,

The Cerakote battle finish from Stealth Hydrographics is sublime.

Novak ghost sight for a no-snag sight picture and quick aiming.

but when you add in the bravado it took to prank Bob, it said something about you and him.

GUNS AND OTHER TOYS

Bob's outside interests expanded to include vehicles that interested him. His crown jewel was likely the 1957 Armstrong Siddeley limo, a British motorcar with elegant lines, which he used to transport kids to proms, dances and wedding receptions in Susanville. He didn't charge. After moving to Coquille, Dunlap advertised the service for a low cost, noting if he said it was free, he would probably work all the time, but he had no intent to charge. It was the first car he had collected. "Marion reluctantly went along with it. It's fun, very pretty, and draws a lot of attention. It's noisy; it's hard to drive." It was a project. "The electrical was terrible; there weren't any brakes. The only electrical things that worked were the ignition, the starter, and the headlights. And the headlights stopped working the second day I had it." I asked if it was hard to get parts. "You make them."

Another vehicle he added to the collection was a black 1938 Citroen, made in late 1937 and sold in June 1938, the month he was born. He said he "had to have it." There were many such vehicles. During the after-Thanksgiving sitdown, I learned he had whittled his collection down, including a 24x48-foot tent. "Oh, I forgot about that," he said. It held three or four Mark 2 and 3 Jaguars, a Hudson, a Triumph Herald sport convertible, a Rover, a .53 Singer and a Sunbeam Talbot convertible. He had no intention of ever becoming a collector. "It just sort of happened," he grinned. The same thing "sort of" happened too with cartridges, books, signs, information, whatever else interested him.

In the center of all this was his main concern, his family. Bob met Marion when he was about 28 years old at church, married her, and was blessed with a daughter who later married a young man Bob thought highly of and soon had another title: Grandpa, which he reveled in.

Bob served as an expert witness on behalf of firearm companies and became involved in many projects in his spare time. Regardless of whether it was a paid arrangement, he continued to teach because that was his nature. He was captured on video for the American Gunsmithing Institute's Pro Course by another of his graduated students, Gene Kelly, and hours of other gun-related topics. That project started when Gene talked him into doing a video on the 1911. Bob often attended SHOT Show in the AGI booth, where a stream of fans and students, past and present, stopped by to see him. Bob tirelessly answered questions and brightened upon picking up any firearm, unable to contain his natural inclination to discover the state of the gun, expound further and render his opinion.

He also traveled to China several times, to Rizhao on the Yellow Sea to work out the bugs on another firearm, a pump shotgun, bought by Savage.

Another project in the quest to improve firearm accuracy, reliability, and

The "melted" aspects of the 1911 are clearly visible.

Author Lenee Landis and the late Bob Dunlap hamming it up at SHOT Show.

Ken's improvements aren't visible here, but most of Fred's are, including the bobtail, bevels, melted edges, K-hole trigger, finish and the Cocobolo grips with the original PISCO logo.

safety was traveling to Turkey to help Tisas fine-tune its 1911. That's when Interstate Arms, the American importer at that time, requested his expertise for some warranty work. Bob went for about a week and returned later with Ken, with the engineers tweaking changes in the production line as they were suggested in real-time to improve the manufacturing process.

They ultimately took 10 guns, running 100 rounds of ammo through each and noting the serial numbers to see what came in for warranty work after that and determine whether the tolerances were holding. Bob wound up with some of the guns they replaced. One of these would eventually become the firearm Fred and Ken chose to customize in this 1911 tribute to Bob.

Though Fred and Ken were students under Bob, they treated him like a second dad or a beloved uncle you needed to keep an eye on. Both would likely say they didn't necessarily feel warm fuzziness when they first attended Bob's class all those years ago. Dunlap quickly established his reputation, having an innate ability to call on a student for something they thought they might skate by on that day. Bob's expectations and requirements engendered more than respect in the long run. Ultimately, he appealed to those who naturally anticipated becoming top-notch in their field and possessed the wherewithal to buckle down, get it handled and appreciate the trip.

In December 2019, Bob had surgery, was released from the hospital, was on the mend and was quite cheery on the phone when I last spoke to him. He said he would be at SHOT Show the following month and then jokingly, "Marion doesn't think so." I figured he would not be ready for the whirlwind a month later. A few days later, he was back in the hospital and passed. It shocked everyone close to him. The shock has worn off but not the inclination to call him or think, "I can always ask Bob."

THE TRIBUTE PROJECT BEGINS

The 1911 Tribute grew organically over time. Zeglin described the parameters he and Brooks outlined as they embarked on the project. "We wanted to build a gun that Bob would like. He was not about bells and whistles. He wanted a basic carry gun that would not print or snag. That makes it tough for a custom maker to create something that turns heads. Ken and I spoke at length about what we could do that fell within the narrow window that Bob liked."

Ken examined the selected 1911 from Bob's trove of guns to make it function as it should. He shaped, polished and tensioned the extractor; chamfered the chamber mouth; polished the chamber, the frame ramp, chamber mouth and the breech face as needed; adjusted and polished the ejection port; adjusted the sear-disconnector-hammer for correct operation and crisp pull weight; removed the loose breech; adjusted the lockup as needed and ensured all safeties operated correctly. That took care of the run factor, and then Fred took it over to enhance the appeal.

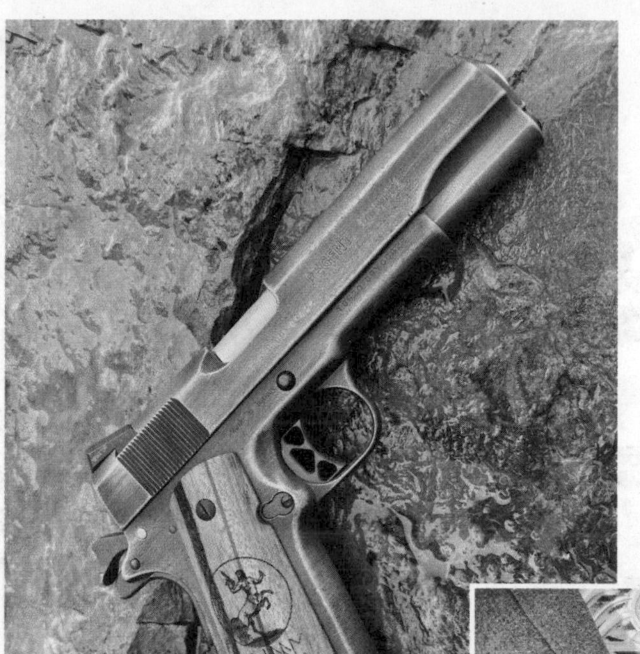

As comfortable in nature as concealed under a garment, the tribute 1911's battle-worn finish fits in wherever you go.

Dress it up or dress it down. The functional 1911 turned out to be a first-class looker, appropriate for any occasion.

Fred Zeglin writes, designs cartridges, channels P.O. Ackley, works as a gunsmith, teaches and owns 4-D Reamer Rentals and Z Hat Custom. He continued the 1911 transformation, "melting" all the exposed parts, including the frame and slide, with no sharp edges. Fred mated the back of the slide and extractor to the frame to create one smooth line. He bobtailed the frame, installed a bobtail mainspring housing, lowered and fluted the ejection port, beveled the magazine well, and cut bevels on the slide stop takedown hole and the magazine release for improved functionality.

Zeglin installed a low-profile "Ghost" rear sight and matching front (two-dot system) to improve the sight picture and a Fusion Firearms K-Hole Trigger just to dress it up. He hand-cut checkering on the hammer and mainspring plug. The "Battle Worn" Cerakote finish is by Stealth Hydrographics of Kalispell, Montana.

The custom Cocobolo grips have PISCO's original logo with DUNLAP spelled out below in what appears to be Viking runes (a hat tip to Fred's son for deciphering that). How did Bob come up with that? What was the thought process … aren't centaurs Greek? I looked it up, and there's this from the website thijsporck.com; the post is titled *Half-assed humanoids: Centaurs in early medieval England.*

"According to the anonymous author of the *Encomium Emmae Regina* (1041–1042), for instance, centaurs could be seen on the Viking longboats used by Swein Forkbeard when he invaded England in the year 1013."

I imagine seeing Bob's humor when he decided to use the centaur and runes in the logo years ago, but I do not know. It does make me smile, though.

The next stop for this gun will be at an auction, with proceeds going to a deserving non-profit. The ultimate resting place for this work of dedication from Fred and Ken will be with a person who appreciates 1911s, loves Bob, is enamored with something different, or plain enjoys shooting a gun that runs like the wind and feels natural in hand — with an appearance that just makes you want to touch it.

These two students are far from the only ones who will continue to think of Bob now and again as they pore over metal or do the gunsmith crawl hunting for a spring that popped free. One of the many will be yours truly. For me, it started from a simple gesture of encouraging my late husband, Jack Landis, to attend the NRA Gunsmithing classes in Susanville one summer years ago. That moment was the springboard that brought about the first I knew of Bob. "How'd it go?" Jack was wound up and told me what was going on, and some of the incidents in class sounded to me like Bob was mildly terrifying.

Jack went on to say he didn't have a certain reamer and neither did anyone in town, which would deep-six his project. So, he mentioned to the guys he would ask Bob if he could borrow his. They all shook their heads. *That'll never happen.* Bob did not loan tools to students. Jack was not deterred — the exact details are faded, but part of it was he would give Bob a cash deposit which would cover a new one should he somehow spoil the integrity of the tool. They were both of German stock, and the stubborn factor was a solid 10, but, of course, after considering the offer, Bob handed it over. Hence, the project was saved. I asked Jack how he had been so confident it would happen. "There was no downside for him."

There was no downside for me either: I had no inkling that urging Jack to pursue what he wanted would mushroom into a firearms life and bring lifetime friends, vacations in Susanville (of all places), and a plethora of solid, decent, entertaining people along with it. But that's another story, and I can hear them both: "Time's a-wasting, girl, get back to work."

What John Moses Browning was to the design of guns, Robert Hale Dunlap was to the molding of gunsmiths. Job well done, Mr. Bob. You'd be proud of these guys for the thought that went into this and the execution, and I know you'd appreciate the result. This 1911 tribute serves as a gentle reminder to appreciate those who have gone before us. And to leave something for those who follow. GD

The Case for Single-Shot Handguns

A Personal Journey with Rifle-Chambered Hand Cannons

› LARRY WEISHUHN

"And pray tell, what are you going to do with *that* thing?" questioned the grizzled guide when I pulled a scoped 14-inch barreled Thompson/ Center Contender out of my rifle case. I smiled, did not reply, simply sat down at the bench, loaded a .309 JDJ cartridge, cocked the hammer, got steady and gently tugged the trigger. The bullet took out the "X" of the bullseye at the 100-yard target. I extracted the spent case and loaded another round without saying a word. The second shot only slightly enlarged the first hole. Smiling, but only inwardly, I shot a third time and again barely enlarged the group to a .4-inch hole. My single-shot handgun group was considerably smaller than groups rifle hunters in camp were shooting. I was not surprised.

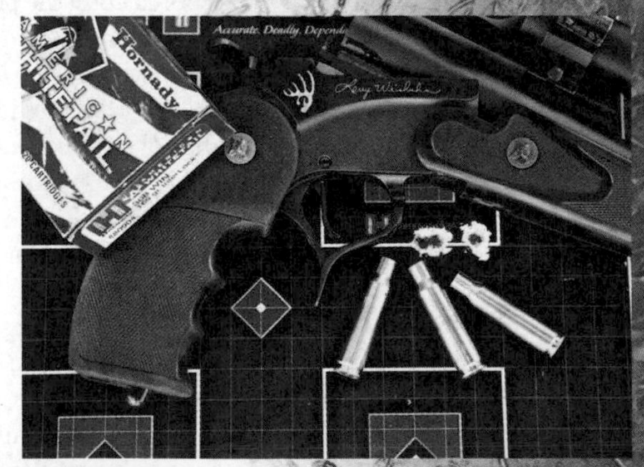

Honored by T/C back in the early 2000s, Larry Weishuhn Signature Encore Hunter, using Hornady's American Whitetail 165-grain InterLock shoots accurately! All photos Larry Weishuhn Outdoors unless noted.

Weishuhn and his Alaskan moose were taken in the Brooks Range's northern extremes with the T/C Encore in .30-06, using Hornady 180-grain soft-point ammo.

"Mmm!" I heard the outfitter say, followed by, "Maybe … I misjudged that short-barreled gun!"

Indeed, he had. Later that same trip from a solid rest on shooting sticks, I shot a dandy brush country whitetail with my .309 JDJ Contender pistol.

A year earlier, after shooting a T/C Contender .30-30 Win. for a few years, I had received my .309 JDJ Contender barrel from J.D. Jones' SSK Industries, creator of the JDJ line of wildcat handgun cartridges, often referred to as "hand cannons." With my .30-30, I had learned with the single-shot break-open handgun that I could handload spitzer-style bullets, thus making such rounds as the .30-30 Win. much more accurate and efficient downrange than if using blunt-nose-style bullets, which needed to be used in a traditional lever action. This was back in the mid-1970s.

Thompson/Center had introduced its "Contender" handgun in 1967. Designer Warren Center had gotten together with the K.W. Thompson Tool Company to produce the innovative break-open action handgun using a frame, allowing interchanging barrels. Changing barrels involved removing the forend and the hinge pin which held the barrel to the frame, changing the barrel, and again putting the hinge pin in place and screwing the forend to the barrel. Changing barrels was that simple.

The early Contenders were chambered for everything from .22 rimfire to the powerful .45-70 Government, centerfire rifle rounds with lesser pressure. To accommodate the rimfire cartridge, a selector switch on the hammer for either rimfire or centerfire directed the firing pin to strike the appropriate place.

My first Contender was produced early in the handgun's life. I have two barrels, one chambered for the .30-30 Winchester and the second for .410 shotshell and .45 Long Colt. Unfortunately, I "lost" that handgun for several years during a move to our present home. I recently found it, albeit complete with some slight rusting but thankfully none in the barrel. I used that .30-30 barrel for whitetails, javelinas, and occasionally hogs and predators. I used the .410/.45 Long Colt barrel as a shotgun for rabbits and squirrels and on rare occasions bobwhite quail.

Once the Contender was introduced, it did not take long for J. D. Jones with SSK Industries to start producing his line of wildcat cartridges. Those included the .309 JDJ (akin to the .308 Win.), 6.5 JDJ, .338 Woodstalker, the true powerhouse .375 JDJ (based on the .444 Marlin case) and numerous other calibers and rounds. For a while, Thompson/Center Arms through Hornady commercially produced .375 JDJ ammunition using Hornady's 220-grain Flat Point Interlock bullet. It was an excellent load for many big game species; unfortunately, that was then, and this is now. Today, JDJ rounds require handloading and often fire-forming brass as well.

In 1984, J.D. Jones took his .375 JDJ creation to Africa and shot numerous

Mark Hampton has hunted the world with single-shot handguns, here with a mountain nyala taken with a customized Remington XP-100. Photo: Mark Hampton

A comparison of early Contenders, a .410/.45 Colt acquired in the early 1970s, and the T/C Encore — one of the early production guns produced after Weishuhn introduced the T/C Encore in 1996, chambered in .30-06, which he hunted with extensively for many years.

elephants, proving that the round was sufficient for even the biggest dangerous game. About the same time, Jones started producing wildcat-chambered barrels for the Contender. Larry Kelly at Magnaport began porting barrels, leaving Jones' hand cannon creations "a hand full," but not totally unpleasant to shoot and hunt with. Jones' and Kelly's writing and promotion of handgun hunting were further fueled by fellow Texan Hal Swiggett and long-time friends and outdoor writers J. Wayne Fears and Bob Milek. Jointly, they and several others spurred great interest in hunting with single-shot handguns.

Remington entered the handgun hunting market in 1961, with its single-shot bolt-action XP100 handgun, chambered originally for the .221 Fireball and 6x45mm designed primarily for metallic silhouette competition. It was advertised as "The World's Hottest Handgun." Later, Remington added the .35 Remington and other rounds to the XP100 lineup. I hunted with a .35 Remington XP100 for a while. It was accurate and fun to shoot. I used it to take several very nice whitetails and big wild hogs. In time, the design changed to a "repeater" when a magazine was added to accommodate multiple rounds. That version was manufactured until about 1998. Both single-shot and box-fed magazine versions are available through used or secondary markets.

For several years, I hunted with and shot a wide variety of caliber and rounds using SSK Industries and standard-issue barrels from Thompson/Center and its custom shop on my Contender frames.

In late summer 1995, I got a phone call from Ken French, who headed up all things at Thompson/Center Arms. "We've got a Maine moose tag for you and J. Wayne Fears. The hunt is set up. Do not bring a gun. We've got something new for you to hunt with!" At the time, I had been shooting and hunting with many different T/C muzzleloaders, so I naturally thought the company was coming out with another muzzleloader.

When Fears and I arrived at French's

A comparison of two of the author's favorite single-shot handgun rounds. .375 JDJ on the left, .30-06 on the right. He used both to hunt big game throughout the U.S., including Alaska.

"Quitchabitchin Camp" near the K.I. area of central Maine, Ken handed J. Wayne an elongated wrapped package and me a much shorter box. We opened them at the same time. J. Wayne's gun looked somewhat like a beefed-up Contender Carbine. Mine looked like a much "beefier" Contender; mine had a large frame and a 15-inch barrel. Stamped on the barrel was .308 Win. as was the rifle. I loved how the handgun felt.

"It's brand new, both the pistol and the rifle version. We finished the pistol two days ago. We've only shot it a few times to prove it. We'll need to go to our range and sight them in. You both need to shoot your guns several times to get used to them before we start hunting moose two days from now." I could hardly wait!

At the range, I loaded the then yet-to-be-named handgun with Hornady's 180-grain Soft Point, got a solid rest on a sandbag and shot at the 50-yard target, the bullet striking just above the bullseye. The following two formed a cloverleaf with the first. After letting the barrel cool, I moved to the 100-yard target and put three shots within a less than one-inch group, an inch above the center of the target. I looked over at French and Fears. They nodded approvingly. Yes, there was a little recoil, but manageable. Fun to shoot and truly accurate!

I had not previously had the opportunity to hunt moose and now truly yearned to take a bull with the new T/C handgun. Later, using that Encore, I was able to take moose in Maine and Colorado, Wyoming and Alaska with a handgun.

The night before the hunt, I learned the new T/C handgun was to be called the "Encore," appropriately named, following the success of the Contender. The following morning, we found a 50-inch wide, nicely antlered bull with double drop-tines, one Ken French had seen earlier that fall and hoped we could find when the hunt started.

My first shot at a hundred yards, from a solid rest, hit the mature bull squarely in its slightly quartering-to onside shoulder. The Hornady bullet penetrated heavy bone, then

Some of Weishuhn's single-shot T/C handguns, from left to right, his original Contender in .410/45 LC, an early model in .30-30 Win., a G2 Contender in .375 JDJ and his first Encore in .30-06. The Contender and G2 Contender barrels are interchangeable, but not with the Encore barrel, only used on Encores.

This whitetail fell to Weishuhn's shot on the Perlitz Ranch in south Texas. The hand cannon: A Remington XP-100 single shot chambered in .35 Remington.

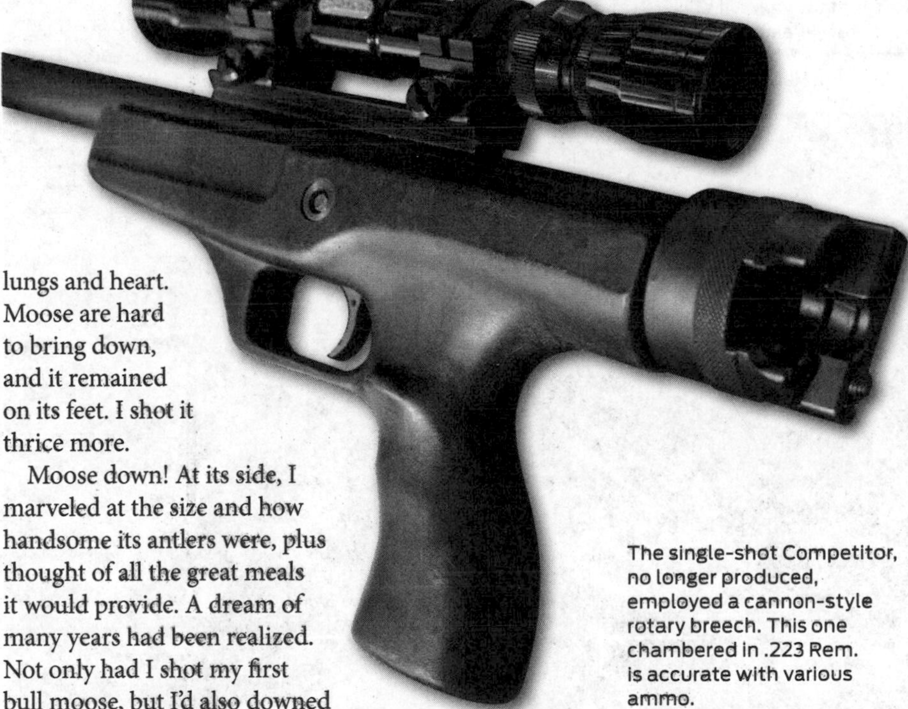

The single-shot Competitor, no longer produced, employed a cannon-style rotary breech. This one chambered in .223 Rem. is accurate with various ammo.

T/C Contenders have a selector switch to accommodate rimfire and centerfire rounds, "C" for centerfire and "R" for rimfire. When positioned in the center, the firing pin cannot be struck.

lungs and heart. Moose are hard to bring down, and it remained on its feet. I shot it thrice more.

Moose down! At its side, I marveled at the size and how handsome its antlers were, plus thought of all the great meals it would provide. A dream of many years had been realized. Not only had I shot my first bull moose, but I'd also downed the first animal ever taken with the new T/C Encore. Three days later, J. Wayne shot his moose with the rifle version of the Encore.

A few weeks later, I shot a Shiras moose in Colorado while hunting with my old friend Jim Zumbo (both of us having drawn tags in adjoining units). I used the same handgun/scope/ammo combination. I returned to Colorado two weeks later to hunt elk with the new .308 Win. T/C Encore handgun, taking an extremely nice 6x6 bull at 125 yards. That one dropped in its tracks.

After taking two moose and an elk with the new handgun, I got a call from Ken French. "Larry, you have to return the handgun as soon as possible!" I argued as best I could. I did not want to send it back to T/C.

"You don't understand," French said. "We cannot start production on the gun until we get back the original and get certain specs!"

I reluctantly agreed, but with the understanding that I would get one of the very first production guns. I introduced the new T/C Encore in the April

1996 issue of *Shooting Times*, where I served as the hunting editor. Interest in the new hunting handgun was nothing short of phenomenal — requests for it greatly exceeded even T/C's most hopeful expectations.

Thankfully, T/C quickly sent me an Encore, chambered in .30-06. With a 15-inch barrel, it was like the .308 Win. in a rifle in terms of ballistics and downrange energy. With that gun, I took a lot of different big game species, including Alaskan and Wyoming moose, numerous elk, caribou, black bears, pronghorns, mule and whitetail deer, javelinas, even prairie dogs. I also used the handgun on a few other species abroad. Using a variety of Hornady bullets and loads, that gun would shoot sub-one-inch, three-shot groups at 100 yards if I did my part. It still does today, wearing a Nikon Encore 2.5-8x Long Eye Relief scope. I've never done any modifications to it, and it still is as it came from the factory, although now showing considerable wear from many days afield.

J.D. Jones' .375 JDJ is a single-shot handgun cartridge ideal for any worldwide hunting adventure. Thompson/Center Arms through Hornady produced a commercially available 220-grain Flat Nose Interlock ammo line for a short time.

Weishuhn's long-favored T/C Encore single shot, which he recently shot after pulling it out from the back of his safe after many years. It still shoots accurately, especially with Hornady's 178-grain ELD-X Precision Hunter.

During the late 1990s and early 2000s, I worked with Thompson/Center Arms in marketing and media while also writing, hosting, co-hosting or producing numerous outdoor television shows. Doing so gave me the opportunities to hunt a considerable amount with the T/C Encore handgun. In the 2000s, Thompson/Center honored the work I had done for T/C with a "Larry Weishuhn Signature Encore Hunter" pistol, chambered in .308 Win., including lovely wood and my signature and brand on the frame. Shortly after T/C was bought by Smith & Wesson, I left the company.

The T/C Encore handgun barrels were chambered in a wide variety of rifle rounds. Between factory barrels from T/C and those produced by Bullberry Barrels (bullberrylegacy.com) and SSK Industries (sskfirearms.com) and others, more than 200 different rounds are likely chambered for the Encore. The chamberings range from .17 to the .45 and .50

Mark Hampton, one of the world's best-known handgun hunters and user of single-shot handguns with a forest buffalo taken with a customized T/C Encore in .375 JDJ. Photo: Mark Hampton

(.500 S&W Mag) calibers and many in between. Ken French once let me shoot a 20-gauge handgun Encore barrel from the T/C Custom Shop.

I have not mentioned to this point the T/C G2 Contender. If you cocked the hammer on the original Contender and decided not to shoot, you could return the hammer to a "safe" position by hanging on to the hammer while pulling the trigger, so the firing pin doesn't hit the primer when you pull the trigger. But before cocking it again, you had to break open the action. Then you could cock the hammer again. With the G2 Contender, if you cocked the hammer and did not shoot, thus returning it to a safe position as just described, you could again cock the hammer without opening the action. There were obviously some other slight internal changes, but that, in a nutshell, is the advantage of a G2 over an original Contender. Barrels for Contenders and G2 Contenders are interchangeable. But barrels for Contenders and Encores are not interchangeable.

I'm a hunter and not a competition shooter, so my experience with handguns comes from hunting with them. But I have shot many rounds on the bench practicing and hunting with handguns. Over the years, I've hunted with a fair number of different calibers and rounds in the Contender, G2 Contender and Encore. I can state without question I loved all of them and have had different favorites over the years. My favorite will always be my .30-06, which I hunted with a tremendous amount, followed by the .375 JDJ. I confess that for a while, I hunted with a stainless steel version of the T/C Encore, known as the "Pro Hunter," chambered in .460 S&W Mag. The beauty of that chambering is that it also accepts and accurately shoots .454 Casull and .45 Long Colt equally well. With it, I took some impressive whitetails at ranges from near to nearly 200 yards.

Of course, there have been other single-shots. The "Competitor" is a rotary-style breech employed in most cannons. The one I have is chambered in .223 and shoots great. It has not been produced in years. Undoubtedly, there were numerous others, including some modern-day muzzleloading handguns used for hunting.

As I write this, Thompson/Center Arms, now part of Smith & Wesson, is for sale. No T/C handguns are currently in production.

Shooting and hunting with a single-shot handgun to me is something I thoroughly enjoy. Albeit somewhat of a misnomer, a "single-shot pistol" can undoubtedly be shot more than one time. When I regularly hunted with singles, I could shoot, extract the spent case and shove in another round quickly. However, knowing you must make that first shot count — which should be your goal regardless of the style or type of handgun or any other gun one uses — makes you concentrate all the more on getting a proper rest, breathing, trigger pull and precise shot placement.

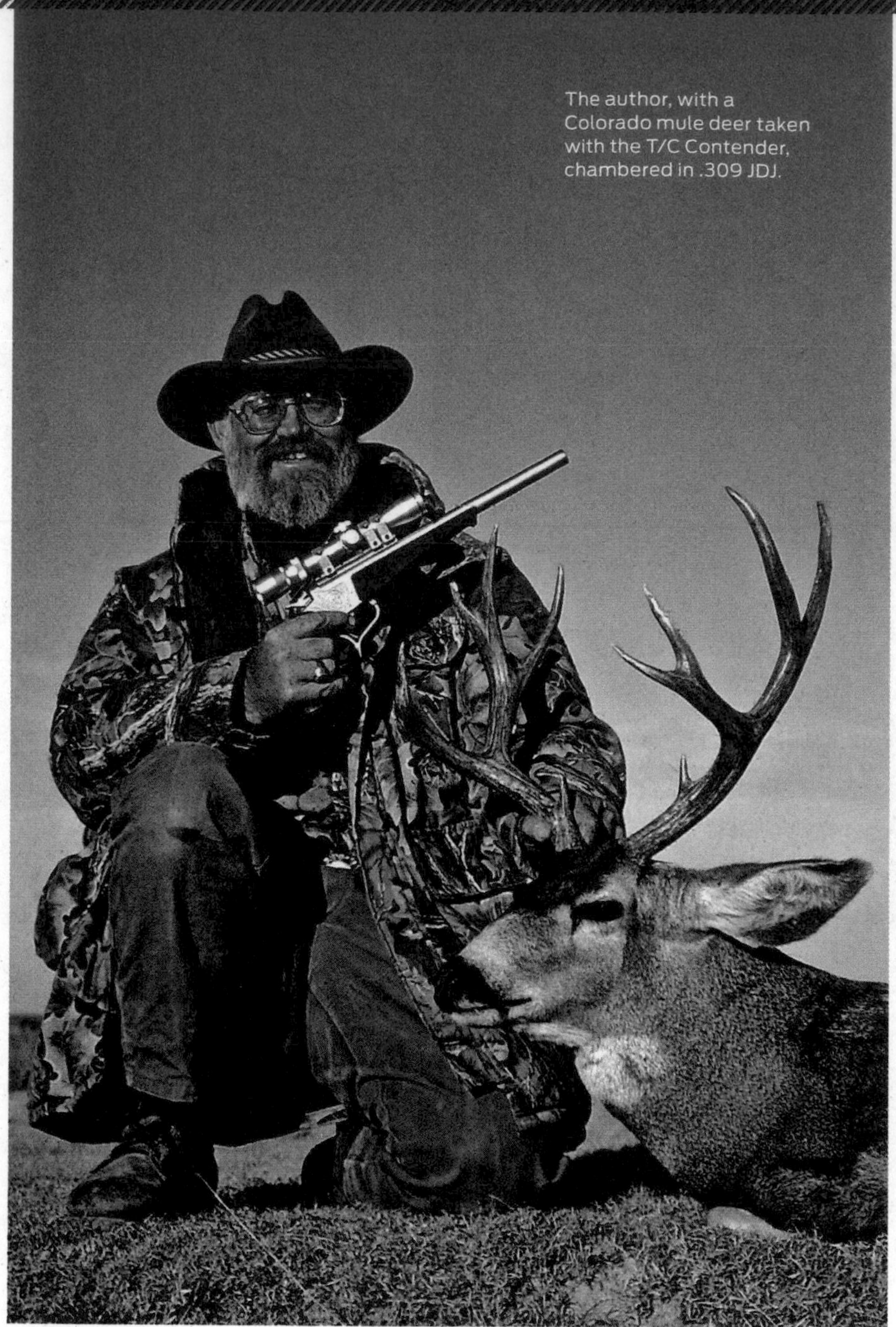
The author, with a Colorado mule deer taken with the T/C Contender, chambered in .309 JDJ.

Recently, I pulled some Contenders and Encores out of the back of my gun safes. I set up a target at the 100-yard marker and shot a three-round group with my old favorite .30-06 Encore and my signature model .308 Win. Encore. Using Hornady's Precision Hunter 178-grain ELD-X in the .30-06, I cloverleafed three shots in a smaller than .75-inch group, although about 1 ½-inches below the dead center of the bullseye. Obviously, with that combination, the handgun was still sighted in. Switching to the .308 Win., I loaded a Hornady 165-grain InterLock American Whitetail round. My first two shots touched, and the third was about a half-inch to the left, but still a one-inch group, outside to outside. Interestingly, it had been a few years since I had last shot either gun.

The following day, I returned to my place after going through a storage shed to find some .375 JDJ ammo. I found three 220-grain Flat Point InterLock T/C-Hornady commercially produced loads. Using one of my older Contenders frames, I switched the existing .309 JDJ barrel to a stainless steel .375 JDJ. The barrel is scoped with one of the best long eye-relief scopes I have ever used, an old Simmons 1.5-4x28. When last I shot the combination, I used the 220-grain load, sighted dead-on at 100 yards.

I pulled the trigger on the combination three times from a good rest. All three shots were easily within a .75-inch group. Did I happen to say the single-shot rifle cartridge handguns were accurate, often as accurate, or more accurate than rifles chambered in the same rounds? Seeing how well these three handguns shot, I think it is high time I do another hunt with them and the several other Contenders and Encores I own.

Over the years, I've had numerous single-shot pistol heroes. One that has long been a friend is Missouri's Mark Hampton. Appropriately, he was recently nominated for the highly prestigious Weatherby Award. Mark has hunted throughout the world with single-shot handguns. In closing, I would like to quote him: "After hunting with single-shot handguns for over 40 years, I've learned a thing or two about the platform. First, when set up properly, single shots are extremely accurate. In most hunting opportunities, the first shot you get is going to be the best shot you're going to get … and a magazine full of ammo doesn't trump a first well-placed shot. Accuracy is paramount, and the single-shot delivers it in spades. Single-shot handguns, for me personally, are user-friendly, easy to shoot accurately, painless to load and unload. Over the years, I've been fortunate to take a shipload of game with single-shot handguns, including Africa's Big Five, all the buffalo species in Africa, Australia and South America. With my single-shot handguns, I have taken big Alaskan brown bear, grizzly along with a wide variety of mountain game in North America, Europe and Asia. This experience with single-shot handguns has touched six continents and leaves me with unshakeable confidence. For serious large and dangerous game, the .375 JDJ is my all-time favorite. It has never let me down. The single-shot handgun provides a solid choice for hunting any game, anywhere on this planet."

Enough said!

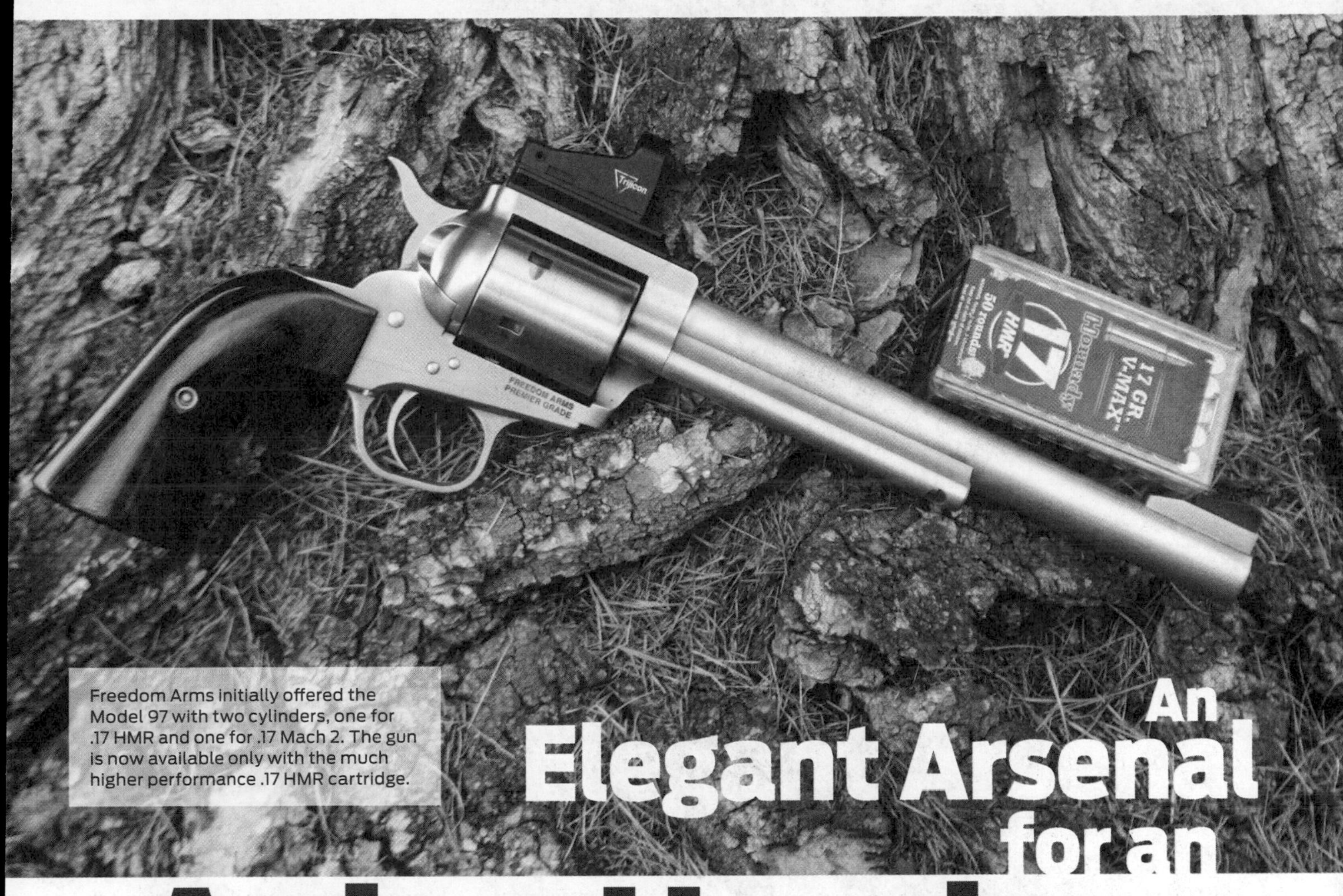

Freedom Arms initially offered the Model 97 with two cylinders, one for .17 HMR and one for .17 Mach 2. The gun is now available only with the much higher performance .17 HMR cartridge.

An Elegant Arsenal for an Aging Handgun Hunter

Functional artistry has kept these wheelguns in the author's gun safe.

›DICK WILLIAMS

I've concluded that every living thing on this planet is a hunter. In the animal world, it begins with a simple premise, from Bugs Bunny raiding your backyard garden plot for carrots and fresh lettuce to a pride of lions trying to take down a Cape buffalo. To eat, you must hunt for food. In today's civilized world, it's easy. You can stalk the aisles of your local supermarket and simply put the items of your choice in your cart.

My first hunting memories go back to when I was eight years old. In most of the places where I grew up, concrete was much less prevalent than open land and trees. I didn't hunt for food because I was hungry; I just had an urge to hunt. My arsenal began with slingshots and worked up through BB guns and pellet rifles to the mighty .22 LR. At 16, I got my first handgun, a Ruger Single Six with fixed sights, and everything fell into focus. I was born to be a handgun hunter!

Equipped with a Trijicon red-dot scope and Magnaport's muzzle brake, this Freedom Arms .454 is ready to hunt anything on the planet with minimal punishment inflicted on the shooter.

The author racked up three decades of handgun hunting experience before finally taking a good bull elk with a handgun, here the Freedom Arms .454 Casull. Moments like this make it all worthwhile.

Calibers got larger as I hunted larger game. Some satisfying custom alterations were made to Ruger .357 and .44 Magnums, but handguns came and went whenever I saw something new I just had to have. When I started writing about guns, specifically ones worked on by artistic gunsmiths, I realized it would be smart and satisfying to keep the models that combined beauty with functional modifications and accessories. I can't remember the exact acquisition sequence, so I'll start at the highest power level and work down.

FREEDOM ARMS .454 CASULL

Around the late 1980s to early '90s, Freedom Arms (FA) revolvers dominated the revolver class of long-range metallic silhouette shooting. If you wanted to make the shoot-offs, or more specifically, *win the shoot-offs*, you needed a Freedom Arms. While the Model 84 in .357 Magnum was the choice of most silhouette shooters, I had learned that all Freedom Arms calibers were capable of 1- to 3-inch groups at 100 yards depending on who was behind the trigger. And at that time, Freedom's .454 Casull had the title of "Most powerful handgun in the world." There didn't seem to be a better factory-produced hunting handgun for big game. For medium game like Wyoming antelope, the .454's higher velocities flattened trajectories that allowed hold-on shots at longer ranges.

When I got a writing assignment utilizing a Freedom Arms .454, Ken Kelly at Magnaport offered to "touch it up." Following that work, the most noticeable improvement was the muzzle brake that dramatically tamed the muzzle flip and reduced felt recoil when firing 1,600 to 1,800 fps jacketed bullets. The fit of the threaded port to the barrel was so good it's almost impossible to see where the two come together. He did an action job by jeweling the hammer and trigger, polishing the frame pins, ejector rod button, cylinder pin, and externally visible screw heads. Finally, he installed sling studs under the barrel and the grip frame, giving me the option of carrying the 10-inch barreled beauty with a short sling.

I've since exchanged the pistol scope initially on the gun for a Trijicon red-dot optic, which is handier to manipulate and

On one of those rare occasions in life, the author bagged two javelina with one shot from his Magnaported Ruger in Texas. Fortunately, his Texas hunting license allowed two pigs per season.

Ignore the pink gun case and brightly polished parts of the Ruger. It's a .44 Magnum that will not back down from any mission.

The Wiegand Hunter, built on a large-frame Model 629, will handle a wide variety of magnum ammunition for critters ranging in size from javelina to moose.

much easier to acquire targets through the short window as opposed to a 6-inch scope tube. This Magnaported Freedom hunting handgun is the envy of every revolver in my gun vault!

RUGER .44 MAGNUM

The .44 Magnum has been my "go-to" caliber for big game hunting for decades. On most occasions, there is usually a 4- to 5-inch Ruger riding on my right hip. Perhaps it deserves special consideration when you put that much faith into something over an extended period. Once again, Ken Kelly of Magnaport stepped up with some thoughts. For a base gun, he selected a Ruger New Model Super Blackhawk with a 4.625-inch barrel and Magnaported it with his 4-pattern trapezoidal slots. He replaced the front sight blade with a green plastic blade the same size as the original, and the rear sight blade received a white outline around the square notch. These changes enhanced the visibility of the sights at the beginning and end of daylight hunting hours. There's a dished-out muzzle crown to protect the rifling from any nicks and bumps sometimes inflicted by clumsy or overzealous hunters.

The barrel, cylinder and frame all have a brushed satin finish, which has worn well over the years. There are a couple of rub marks on the cylinder, but these are the kind of things that guns acquire when they are loved enough to join their owner on special outings. The .44 has the same Magnaport trademark polished pins, screws, hammer, trigger and ejector rod button that Ken installed on the Freedom Arms .454 but with the addition of two evenly spaced polished bands near the front of the cylinder. As far as I'm concerned, those polished bands are striking and announce to the world that this is my special .44 Magnum belt gun.

It's hard to remember since I've had the gun for 30 years, but I believe that I added the faux staghorn grips after Magnaport had finished. The Ruger certainly deserves some extra unique grip panels, but I'm not about to change anything after all the quality time we've spent together.

WIEGAND SMITH & WESSON .44 MAG. HUNTER

This Smith was more of a "purpose-built" hunting handgun. I don't usually hunt with pistol scopes; while they magnify the target, they also magnify my wobble. In addition, finding a target looking through the scope tube can be difficult if I'm shooting offhand. But when you're taking a stand or hunting from a blind, things get easier. You have time to prepare, and if you've done a little planning, you'll be able to shoot from a reasonably steady rest. Starting with an older 6.5-inch-barrel Model 629, Jack Wiegand installed a 10-hole porting system near the muzzle and a 1.5-4x variable power Simmons extended eye-relief pistol scope on a slotted base mount above the cylinder. The optics added some light-gathering capabilities, while the 4-power setting allowed for longer shots with a solid rest. Frame and barrel received a brushed, satin finish and a wide, smooth combat-style trigger with the front surface highly polished. All the screws in the frame were also highly polished. A beautiful set of wood grips with finger grooves was installed on the rounded grip frame.

The grips filled in the space behind the triggerguard but still maintained a hint of the rounded shape. The result fitted my hand perfectly. My longest shot with the S&W was 80 yards, and the pig went down for the count on the first shot.

SMITH & WESSON MODEL 27 W/8 3/8-INCH BARREL

I don't do much big game hunting with the N-frame .357 Magnum for two reasons. First, the cylinder is too short to take full advantage of the heavier bullets needed for large critters. Second, I succumbed early in life to the siren call of the .44 Magnum, a far superior caliber for big game. That said, a debt is owed to the .357 by all ardent handgun hunters for getting the ball rolling when it was introduced as the first "Magnum" handgun in the 1930s and proceeded to generate thrilling big game hunting stories in magazines.

This handgun is one of only two factory models that made my list and the last one to be acquired. Like most things of great inherent beauty, the Model 27 needs no makeup. The black Patridge front sight blade and adjustable rear sight remain as they were when they left the factory in the blue box and are still as effective as they were for Major Wesson.

A friend of mine agreed to part with the Model 27 when varmint hunting with SPUR Outfitters in Wyoming a few years ago. It had been used but not abused, and we spent an afternoon shooting all his ammo before we struck a deal. Although I've never thought of the .357 as a proper caliber for big beasts, the revolver seemed perfect for the smaller whitetail deer I hunt in Texas.

For example, on one deer hunt, it was just before dusk when a doe walked to within 45 yards of my favorite blind and became some of my favorite meals in 2019. I'm not sure we'll hunt together again, but this long-barreled beauty is a great companion for an elegant afternoon of shooting with friends.

GARY REEDER RUGER SINGLE SIX .22 MAGNUM

Destiny arranged the first meeting between this artfully decorated Ruger and me. I'd stopped at the Pistol Parlor in Flagstaff, Arizona, visiting with proprietor and pistolsmith Gary Reeder. Gary is an avid handgun hunter and makes custom revolvers and single shots, including some chambered for his family of proprietary cartridges. Sitting in his display case was this prototype Black Widow, a .22 Magnum Ruger Single Six in which he had installed an 8-shot cylinder. He had also installed a rear sight blade with a white outline around the notch, crowned the muzzle, widened the hammer spur, reshaped the hammer to more of a Bisley look, rounded the grip frame to the "Gunfighter" shape, fitted black Micarta grip panels to the frame and applied his bright blue-black finish to the highly polished surfaces of the entire gun.

A "gold" spider graces the left side of the frame and barrel plus on both sides of the cylinder. Our relationship began as a writing project with the gun just being on loan. Still, the Reeder Ruger's incredible performance on our

The elegant, long-barreled Model 27 is a classic beauty that has withstood the test of time and still excites envy among shooters at the range.

first ground squirrel hunt at Tejon Ranch made it impossible for me to return. It has become my favorite companion for strolls through rodent country.

FREEDOM ARMS .17 HMR

The smallest caliber in my dream collection takes us back to Freedom Arms and is the second gun that has no aftermarket custom work. Bob Baker of Freedom Arms and I were both varmint hunting with .17 HMRs together on the SPUR, me with a Winchester Model 9417 and Bob with one of his Model 97 single actions, which had a 7.5-inch barrel and a Trijicon red dot mounted on the topstrap. Two things make Bob a great salesman for his revolvers: He loves to hunt with them — and uses them to deadly effect. It was a factory Freedom gun except for the red dot, which he'd been using for about a year on his varmint outings. Being the astute reader you are, you've already deduced that his gun went home with me. As I get older, am less mobile, and more recoil intolerant, the Freedom .17 HMR has become my favorite hunting handgun, and varmint hunting has become my favorite handgun sport. GD

Dave Sturm of SPUR Outfitters utilized the Freedom Arms .17 HMR's accuracy to head shoot this badger at 60 yards in Wyoming.

With a gunfighter's grip and the bite of a venomous spider, the little Gary Reeder Ruger .22 Mag. is the perfect companion for a wilderness stroll.

The Interrupted Trajectory of the M704 CRF Action

A look at an unusual controlled-round-feed hybrid rifle action.

› RON SPOMER

A .416 Rigby Mauser circa 1935 exemplifies the M98 controlled-round-feed action.

The Mauser M98 was the original CRF bolt action that has inspired copies and imitations. This one holds a .416 Rigby cartridge.

Alaska Master Guide and bear whisperer Phil Shoemaker introduced me to the M704 controlled-round-feed bolt action. It was not in Alaska, more's the pity, nor anywhere near a brown bear, unless you count the spectacularly mounted specimens on the Safari Club Convention floor.

"Now, this is something different!" Phil insisted, handing me a nondescript, black bolt-action sporting rifle.

"Why?" I wondered aloud. "Looks like just another push feed in a synthetic stock."

"Look again."

I looked.

"At the bolt face."

I looked more closely.

"Lower bolt face."

"Hey, there's a gap. About a third of the recess ring is missing."

"We have a winner!" Phil was too polite to say that, but I suspect he wanted to. And he was right: This was something different. It was pistolsmith Ed Brown's M704 controlled-round push-feed hybrid action. Brown, famous for his slick 1911 pistols, created the M704 action early in the 21st century. In 2006, he began building and selling finished rifles based on this unusual, controlled-round push feed.

THE MAUSER INFLUENCE

To appreciate that amalgam, one must understand both the controlled-round-feed and push-feed actions. Credit Paul Mauser with the former. Probably a Frenchman in the 1880s, or someone else might have hatched the basic idea. Still, as far as I know, Mauser blessed the shooting world with the first wildly successful controlled-round-feed (CRF) action via his Model 1898 Mauser, the bolt-action repeater perfected. The M98 was so perfectly engineered that it is still produced in its original form or very minimally refined. And CRF was a significant contributor to that longevity.

Mauser strapped a leaf spring to the outside of his rifle's bolt. A right-angle hook on its front reached over the edge of the bolt face with just enough face-to-claw clearance to admit the rim of an 8x57 or 7x57 Mauser cartridge. That rim slipped or, more accurately, sprang under the claw from the rifle's vertical-stack magazine when a forward push of the bolt caught the upper edge of the cartridge rim and pushed the round forward until it leaped clear of the action's feed lips. The rim then popped between claw and bolt face to find itself captured and controlled. It was held in place, nose first, neatly aligned for a straight, scrape-free ride into the chamber, after which a sharp downturn of the bolt handle locked it in place ahead of two massive lugs of steel.

While Mauser's CRF prevented bullet tips from suffering scratches and gouges from ramping up into the chamber, its real advantage was preventing chambering and extraction failures. If an excited shooter, thinking more about incoming fire or elephant than rifle operations, pulled back the bolt to chamber another round before fully closing the bolt to fire the round already on the bolt face, they would not suffer a highly undesirable double feed. Actually, that's a misnomer because it's a non-feed, the bolt trying to shove two rounds into one hole.

Instead of this major faux pas, the claw-bolt-cartridge connection ensured the first round stayed home until and unless the bolt was pulled back sufficiently to slide over the ejector blade in the rear receiver ring. This blade would then push against the left-bottom rim of the cartridge, throwing it right, up and out of the loading port. Only then would room be made for the bolt face to nudge from the magazine a fresh round on its subsequent slide forward.

So brilliantly engineered was this CRF bolt action that the U.S. military essentially copied it to make the Springfield Model 1903, which entered WWI chambered in .30-06. Winchester later drew heavily upon the Springfield and Mauser to engineer what would be celebrated as the Rifleman's Rifle, the Winchester Model 70. Controlled-round feeds one and all. Modern CRFs with the classic Mauser leaf spring extractor include the M70 and Mauser 98 "replicas" from various brands/manufacturers, Ruger M77 Hawk-

Original Mauser M98 bolthead. Note the groove around the head in which the leaf spring extractor blade swivels, beveled extractor face for sliding over top-fed cartridges (dropped atop magazine follower rather than pushed into the magazine), ejector slot in the left-side locking bolt, as well as the bolt head and gas escape ports.

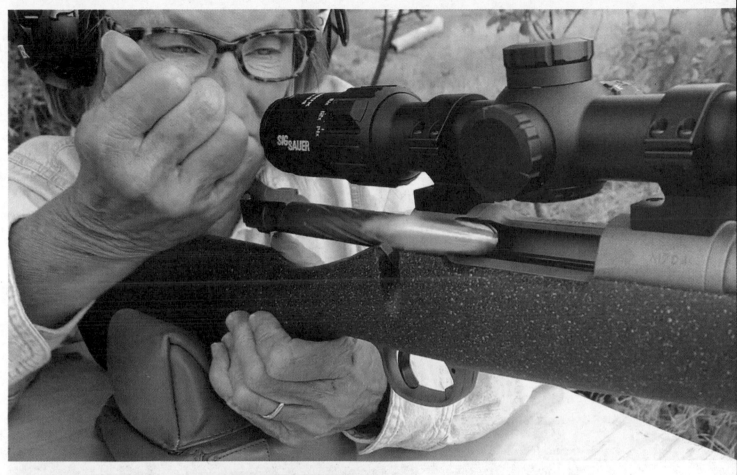

The M704 ejects brass as soft or hard as the operator determines by the pull of the bolt.

The difference between push feed (left) and CRF bolt faces.

eye, all Kimber bolt-action centerfires and the new Parkwest SD-76. The CZ M550 bolt actions were a solid Mauser-style CRF but were recently discontinued.

At the other goal line is the push-feed type, perhaps best known through the Remington Models 721, 722, 600, 700, Seven and variations thereof. You'll find them on Savage 110s, Mossberg Patriots, Browning X-Bolts, Weatherbys, New Ultra Light Arms, Howa 1500s, etc. The push feeds usually feature a recessed bolt face surrounding the cartridge head. This design has been touted as a full Ring of Steel surrounding and strengthening the cartridge head, preventing ruptures, explosions and shrapnel. The lower lip of this bolt rim hits the cartridge rim protruding slightly above the magazine and shoves it forward until it springs free of the mag. It then remains "free" to rattle and ramp its way up and into the chamber — so long as the bolt is pushed forward. When said cartridge hits its headspacing stop within the chamber, a spring-loaded extractor hook (typically inset in the bolt head) snaps over the rim to grab the extraction groove.

Getting rid of this cartridge, fired or not, requires the shooter to lift and pull back the bolt. When the cartridge is no longer impeded by the barrel breech or receiver ring, pressure from a plunger-style ejector inset in the bolt face pushes it up and right, out of the loading port. Some push feeds use the same type of

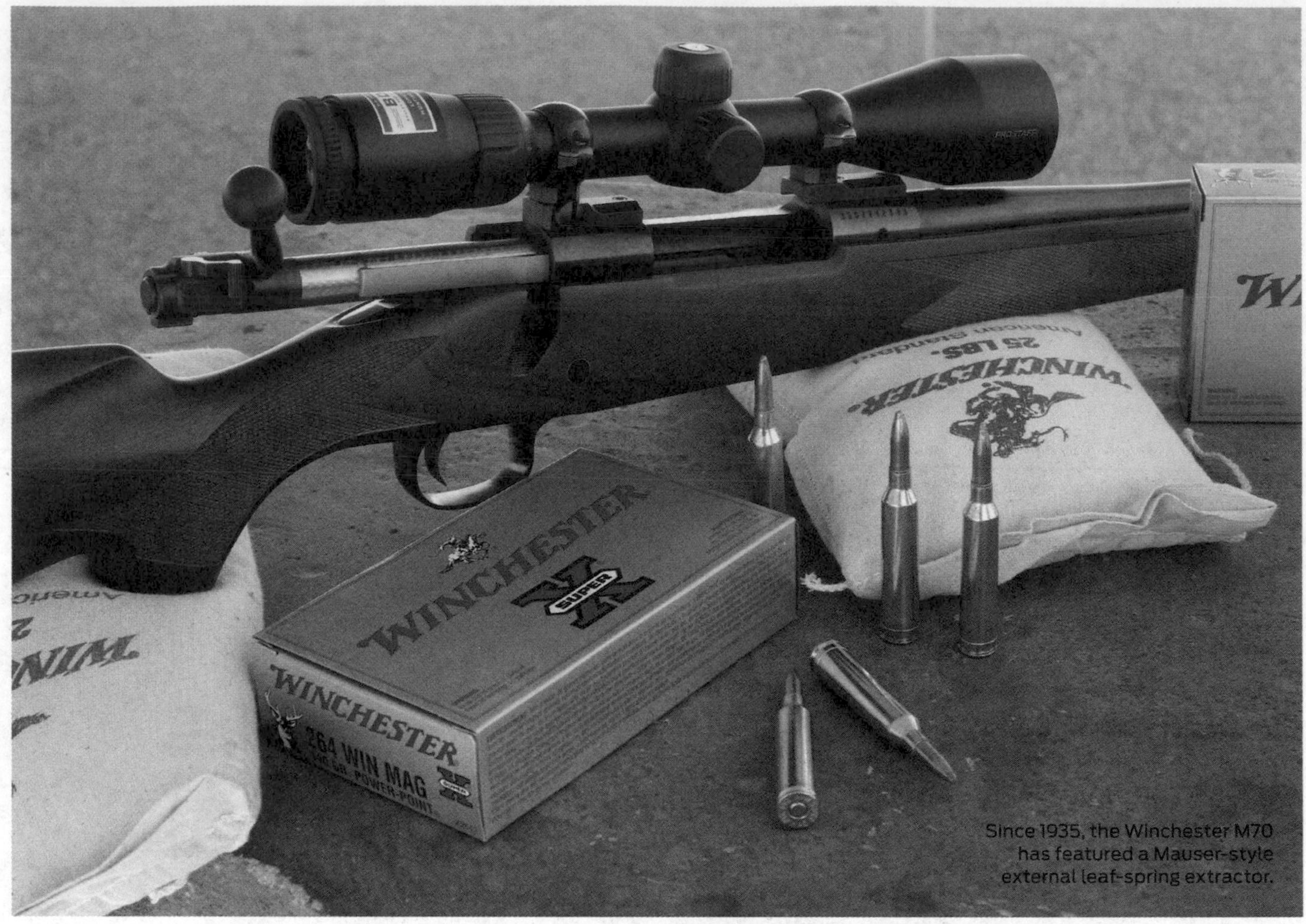

Since 1935, the Winchester M70 has featured a Mauser-style external leaf-spring extractor.

rear ejector blade as the Mauser/M70 style to shove the case off the bolt face.

ADVANTAGES AND DISADVANTAGES

The downsides to push feeds, according to conventional wisdom, are several. 1. Because the cartridge isn't controlled, it can roll out of the action if the gun is operated unconventionally (tipped sideways or upside down, the standard operating procedure for most hunters — kidding.) 2. The uncontrolled cartridge can fail to ramp up smoothly, bullets snagging and deforming, sometimes even failing to enter the chamber. 3. The inset extractor hook doesn't provide a significant gripping surface for extracting "sticky" cartridges. 4. The extractor hook is fragile and often breaks. 5. The extractor spring (housed within the bolt head) can weaken or break.

6. (And this is the Big One) If an excited shooter fails to push the bolt fully forward to snap the extractor over the cartridge rim and then pulls back to pick up the next round from the magazine, that round will be shoved against the previous round still in the chamber. 7. Plunger ejectors can weaken or break, and they always kick out empties with the same power and velocities. This can make finding empties challenging.

The advantages to push feeds are lower manufacturing costs and (claimed) better accuracy. The accuracy claim may have more to do with the barrels and careful manufacturing of specific popular push-feed actions than any inherent accuracy within the system. Most push feeds have certainly been more straightforward and less expensive to mass manufacture. But they've also

A Winchester M70 bolt (top) securely holds a .30-06 round against the bolt face while the three-lug push feed at the bottom demonstrates how cartridges are not controlled.

been easier to customize, leading to the construction of many hyper-accurate push-feed custom rifles.

CRF downsides include 1. More mass/ weight than push feeds. 2. Need to load rounds from the magazine, not single-fed through the port. 3. A clunky-looking, debris-catching leaf spring along the outside length of the bolt body.

We've already mentioned CRF's major advantages.1. Complete control of the cartridge means it stays on the bolt face and in line with the chamber regardless of the rifle's position. 2. Huge extractor hook edge for removing recalcitrant cases. 3. Prevention of double feeding or leaving an unfired cartridge in the magazine during incomplete operation by the shooter.

The M704 bolt shows a gas escape port in the body, extractor hook left-side (bottom) locking lugs and ejector blade slot.

NOT REALLY

Most of these pluses and minuses are more theory than reality. You can single-load most modern CRF rifles because a beveled claw extractor face will pop over the rim. You can operate most push feeds upside down without losing the round because most cartridges are well into the chamber before they spring free from the magazine. Some push-feed extractors provide more rim contact than CRFs. And some — perhaps most — CRFs can pick up a subsequent round without kicking the first one off the bolt face! I've done it with M70s, one Mauser M98 and an M704 action rifle. Preventing double feeding depends on how well each model was designed and put together (timed) and how effectively they are operated. Some bullets snag or scrape into the chamber in poorly designed or assembled push feeds, but these are rare and can be fixed. But there is one potentially serious issue with push feeds: they leave rounds in the chamber if you don't slam the bolt forward hard enough to snap the extractor hook over the rim. You do not want this to happen with a buffalo inbound, but neither would you welcome it with a 6x6 bull elk about to step into the trees.

The M704 striker assembly twists out quickly and easily with a 1/4 turn thanks to ingenious miniature locking lugs. The firing pin and spring can be easily dried and cleaned.

An M704 bolt holds a .308 Winchester cartridge securely. The gap in the top locking lug was milled to fit the extractor hook. The action rail rides in the longitudinal groove to eliminate binding.

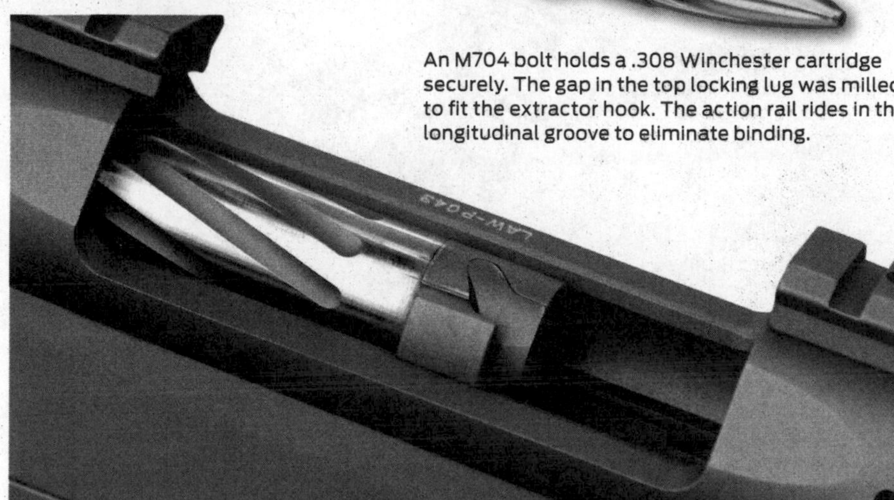

The right-side locking lug rides the action rail. Note the large extractor hook.

THE M704 ALTERNATIVE

Regardless of the potential problems with either the classic CRF or push-feed actions, the M704 hybrid seems a solution. As Phil made me see, a quick look at the M704 bolt face reveals the trick. Here is a recessed bolt face with the bottom third of the rim removed. A fourth of the "ring" is really a massive extractor hook, the M16-style. By my measurement, it contacts .260 inch of a .473-inch cartridge rim (.30-06/.308/6.5 CM

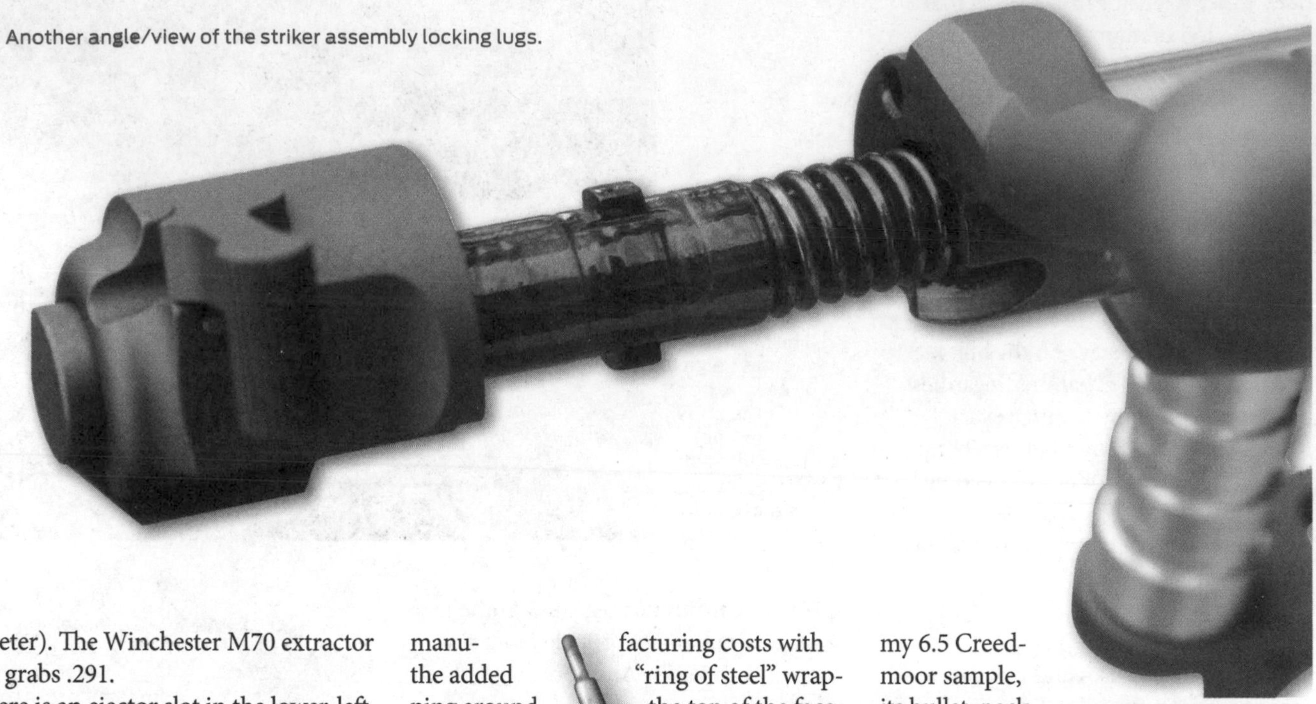

Another angle/view of the striker assembly locking lugs.

diameter). The Winchester M70 extractor hook grabs .291.

There is an ejector slot in the lower-left face of the bolt, just like in the M70 and Mauser bolts. The right locking lug is carved out to accept the extractor. There is a raceway cut through it (as on the M70) to serve as a guide to keep the bolt riding straight and smoothly along the right receiver rail. In essence, the M704 bolt is the Mauser or M70 Winchester bolt minus the long exterior extractor leaf spring and the rather complicated collar needed to keep it attached. This simplifies manufacturing costs with the added "ring of steel" wrapping around the top of the face.

In practice, the M704 does just what the M70 does. Push the bolt forward, and it catches the top rim of the top cartridge in the rifle's magazine. Keep pushing, and when the round clears the feed lips, it pops up. But by then, at least on my 6.5 Creedmoor sample, its bullet, neck and a bit of body behind the shoulder are already in the rear of the chamber. It has slid up a broad, smooth ramp in the bottom of the front receiver ring before springing high enough to be captured against the bolt face.

Some may say this is not a true CRF because the cartridge wasn't captured and fed straight into the chamber, the bullet never riding a ramp. But my Winchester M70 in .30-06 does the same thing. The bullet and neck slide up the

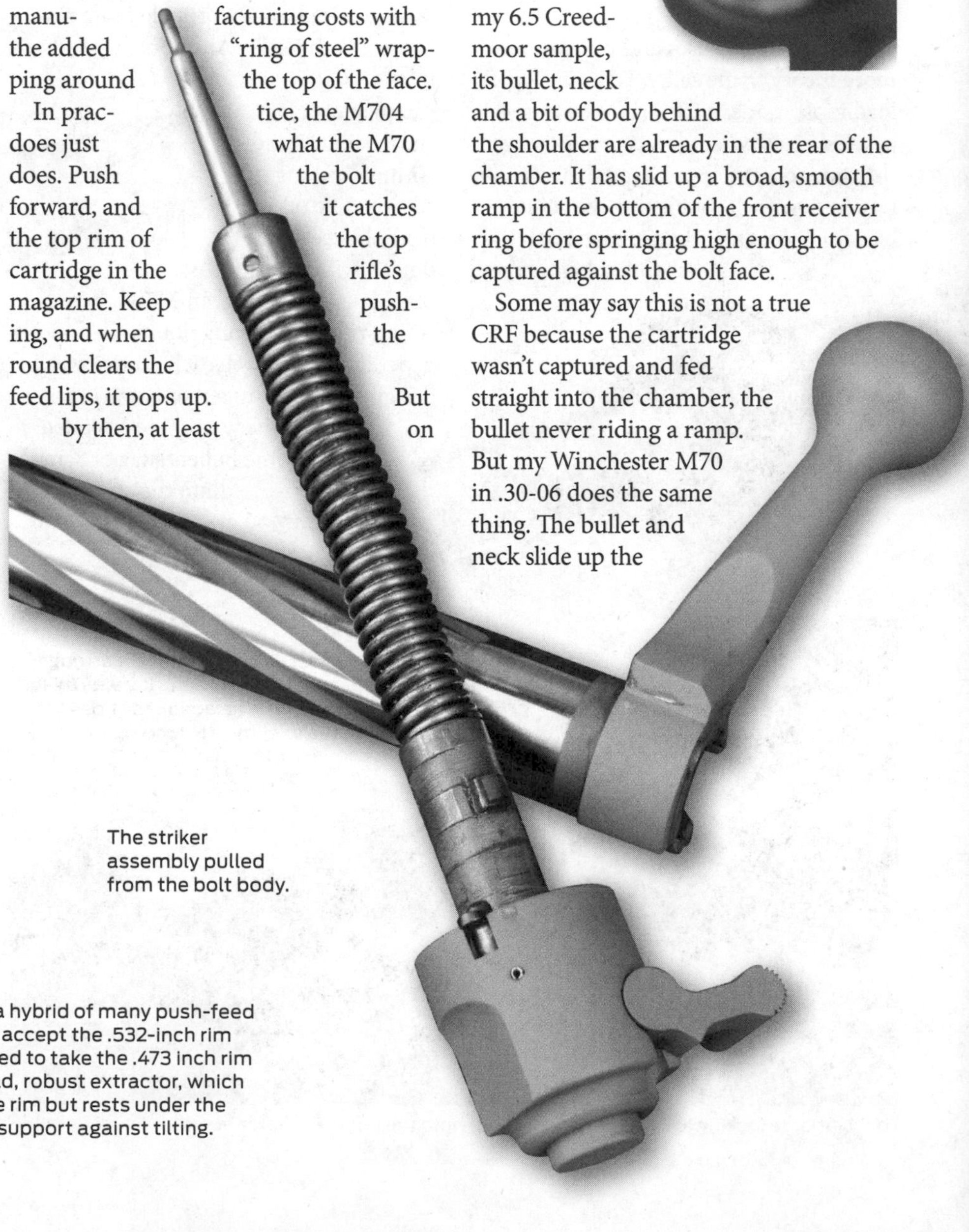

The bolt face of the M704 action clearly shows a hybrid of many push-feed and CRF actions. The top bolt is wide enough to accept the .532-inch rim of the 6.5 PRC cartridge. The bottom is configured to take the .473 inch rim of the 6.5 Creedmoor and friends. Note the broad, robust extractor, which not only provides a hefty grasp of each cartridge rim but rests under the cartridge when it is locked into battery, giving it support against tilting.

The striker assembly pulled from the bolt body.

The LAW Professional features a reverse follower, so the first round nestles on the left side

receiver ramp and enter the chamber before the rim snaps under the claw.

Regardless of how you feel about the "legitimacy" of these as CRF actions, the reality is that they both control the cartridge before it is fully or even halfway in the chamber. Your first cartridge will be extracted if you fail to push completely forward and come back for a second round. Come back far enough to smack the ejector blade, and your first (still live) round will be ejected, leaving the bolt face free to pick up your second round and slam it into battery. Let's hope that you're completing your part of the job by this juncture. (Don't baby the bolt!)

CRF WITH BENEFITS

In addition to that positive extraction, the M704 supports a cartridge in battery. Once the locking lugs are turned in, the wide extractor hook rests beneath the cartridge rim, supporting it by gravity. Should the chamber be reamed toward the looser end of SAAMI tolerances, this support might help hold the case in better alignment with the bore, which you also get with most fully recessed push-feed bolt heads.

A bonus with the M704 is its easily removed and reinstalled firing pin. Pull back a small, spring-loaded lever atop the bolt shroud, turn the shroud clockwise an eighth turn, and pull back. Two small locking lugs align with grooves in the rear bolt tube, so the fire control system easily slides out. Makes cleaning the firing pin and spring a quick and easy affair even in the field.

The M704 includes a classic, M70-style 3-position wing safety, unlike many

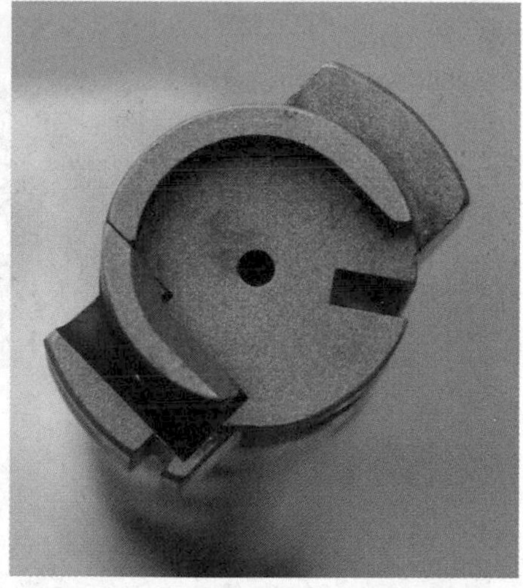

The striker assembly pulled from the bolt body.

The open, flat face of the M704 bolt head contacts cartridges in the magazine to push them forward. They slide under the extractor hook on the bolt's right side when they clear the action rails and pop up. Note the right locking lug riding on the action rail.

Spomer readies to bench test a LAW Professional II rifle in 6.5 PRC based on the M704 action. It shot sub-MOA with Hornady Match ammo.

Legendary Arms Works Professional in 6.5 Creedmoor built around the M704 action.

The M704 CRF bolt holds a 6.5 PRC cartridge.

push-feed actions. Fully back, it blocks the firing pin and locks down the bolt. No chance a stray limb will knock open your bolt and kick a cartridge into the snow. Push the safety forward one notch, and the bolt is released, but the firing pin is still blocked to facilitate safer unloading. Pushed fully forward, the rifle is ready to fire.

MOVING ON

Ed Brown sold a variety of rifles on the M704 action from 2006 to 2010, models Savanna, Damara, and Varmint, all with McMillan synthetic stocks and Shilen triggers. I test drove a Savanna in .308

Winchester back then, finding it smooth, perfectly functional, and sub-MOA accurate with several factory loads. But either Mr. Brown was too busy building and selling his excellent pistols to continue rifle production, or sales didn't warrant it. The M704 action was in danger of becoming a collector's item.

Legendary Arms Works (LAW), featuring custom gunmaker Mark Bansner, didn't let that happen. It bought the M704 in 2014 and began building Legendary Arms Works rifles on the M704 action. LAW mated them with Wilson match barrels, Timney triggers, and High Tech synthetic stocks (with aluminum bedding blocks), and they came in three styles: the standard-weight Closer, lightweight Professional and heavyweight Big Five. These were a superior build and a top performer by all reviews and assessments. Thus LAW rifles gained favorable press, some significant Rifle of the Year awards and a flurry of orders. And that became a problem.

Legendary Arms Works was not a custom rifle building operation, but neither was it a high-volume, mass-marketing rifle manufacturer. The sudden demand couldn't be met without major upsizing. That required significant outside capital that came with demands for quick, if not immediate, profits. With insufficient time to hire and train additional craftsmen and machinists, LAW fell behind, chits were called in, and investors pulled the rug out.

New investors tried again in 2019, putting out the Legendary Arms Works Professional II with minimal changes and upgrades but at a more realistic price set to keep the brand profitable with manageable output. But the new LAW rather quickly fell through due to market conditions.

LIKE MYTHICAL PHOENIX

Fortunately for bolt-action aficionados, the round-bottom M704 is like the mythical Phoenix bird that rises from the ashes again and again. As of this writing, it is being CNC manufactured in short and long actions and sold to gunmakers as the Legendary Action Works M704. Bolt bodies are spiral-fluted for self-cleaning. The bolt and handle are machined from one bar of steel. Timney trigger, magazine box, reverse follower, bottom metal, heavy-duty recoil lug and similar accessories are available, suggesting a custom build with one's favorite barrel. GD

The M704 isn't the only CRF/push-feed hybrid in history. Sako's M85 (2006 release) is similar but with three locking lugs. The Fierce three-lug CRF action is nearly identical. For a short time in the early 2000s, Winchester offered a CRF/push hybrid, mainly in the short-lived WSSM chamberings and on some lower-priced M70 models like the Super Shadow and Coyote Outback. Ruger's original M77 is a push feed with a Mauser-style claw extractor that doesn't quite capture the cartridge until it has progressed rather deeply into the chamber. The M77 also has a plunger ejector in the bolt face.

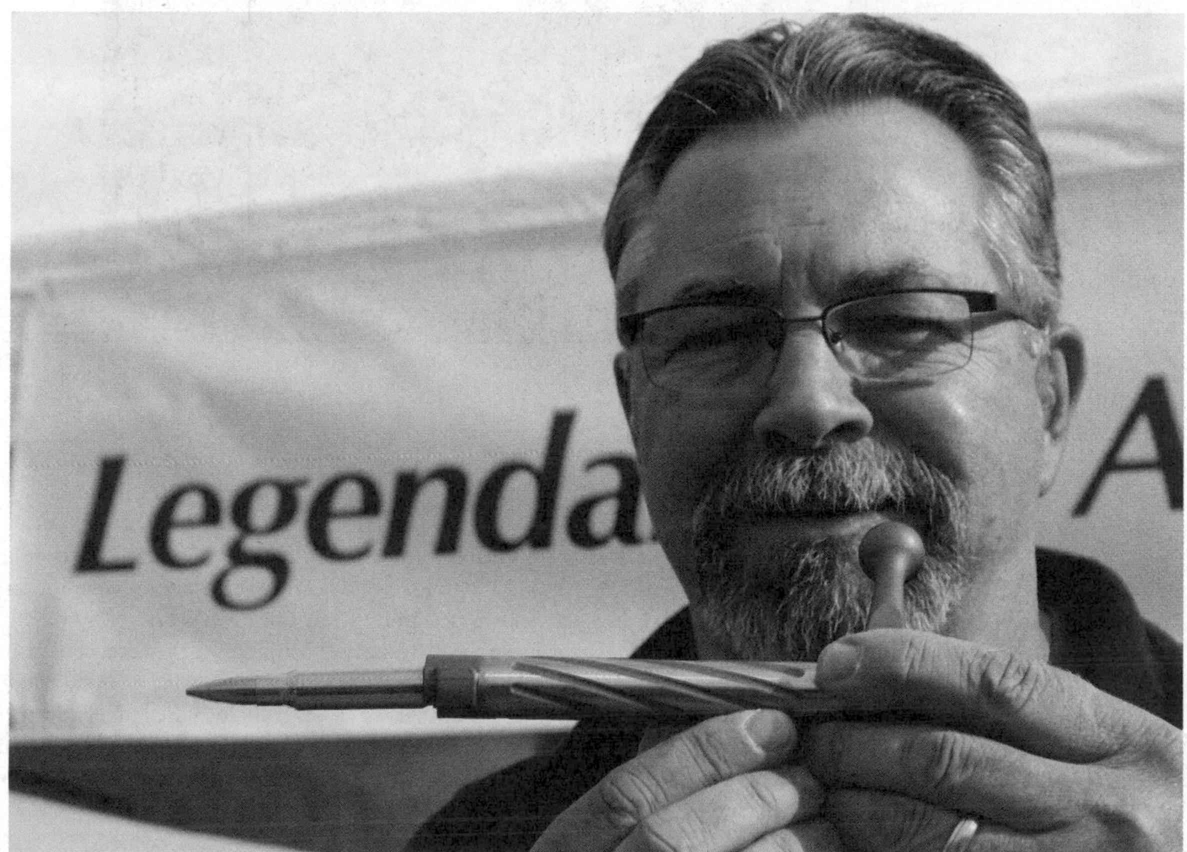

Mark Bansner demonstrates the cartridge-gripping feature of the M704 bolt.

Bolt-Action Sporting Rifles of the Early 20th Century

By 1900, American hunters witnessed rapid and astonishing changes in rifle development.

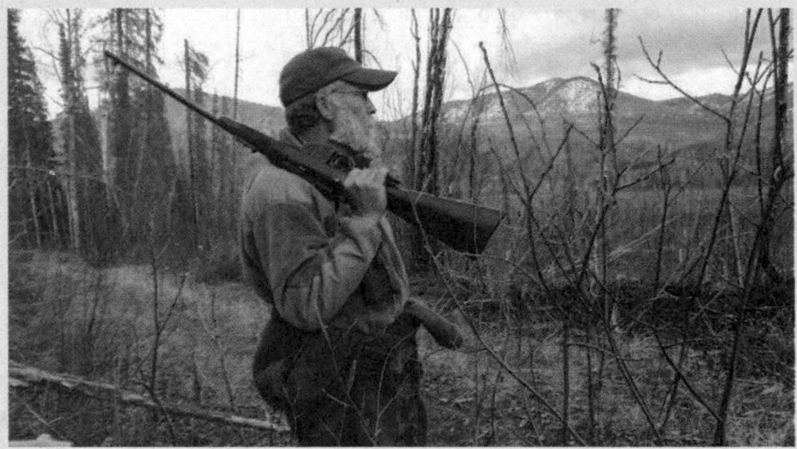

The author used a BSA-made Lee-Speed .303 during a spring black bear hunt along the Yukon River.

› PHIL SHOEMAKER

Although Winchester, Savage and Marlin lever-action rifles were ubiquitous and a favorite of hunters, numerous new bolt-action designs were being introduced and closely examined by the world's militaries at the close of the 19th century. The simple design of using a protruding bolt handle to load and secure a rifle action was not an entirely new concept as it preceded the lever-action design by a few hundred years.

During the mid-16th century, Peter Peck, a clever, well-respected Munich watchmaker and gunsmith, designed and built a breechloading matchlock musket that fired a pre-loaded steel cartridge. A bolt handle held the cartridge and secured it in the chamber when inserted into the barrel and turned down into a recess. An indentation on top of the bolt served as the ignition pan for the lighted match. Almost three centuries later, the Prussian army adopted the 1840 Dreyse "needle gun," and the world began to seriously consider the bolt action.

Wars have always been incubators for new weapon designs, and the American Civil War in the mid-1800s was no exception. It marked the change from single-shot muzzleloading rifles and muskets to repeating rifles firing self-contained cartridges. In 1857, U.S Army Lt. Col. J. Durrell Greene patented a breechloading bolt-action design that saw limited use during the war. By war's end in 1865, 1,000 Palmer single-shot, bolt-action carbines were accepted for U.S. issuance, and the French adopted the tactically innovative Chassepot bolt-action rifle.

During the following three decades, various branches of the U.S. military began testing bolt-action designs procured from around the globe. Offerings came from Brown Manufacturing Company, John Henry Blake, Chaffee-Reece, Colt, Hotchkiss, Keene, James Paris Lee and Ward-Burton. Samuel Norris, an employee of Remington Arms, had been sent to Germany to work with brothers Paul and Wilhelm Mauser, and in 1868 he received U.S. Patent No 78,603 for the Mauser model 67/69 bolt action.

Trials in the United States continued with varying degrees of success. In 1871, Springfield Armory produced nearly a thousand Ward-Burton .50-caliber bolt-action rifles. They were not well-received by troops. It wasn't until November 4, 1879, that James Paris Lee, a Scottish-born American citizen and one of the most prolific and influential firearm designers, received a patent for what was to evolve into one of the world's greatest magazine-fed, bolt-action battle rifles.

At the time, Remington was busy building 1874 Keene bolt-action single shots, and Lee was working for the Sharps rifle company. In 1881, Sharps declared bankruptcy, and Remington acquired all of Sharp's assets, including the fixtures and machinery needed to build Lee's new design. Remington also hired Lee, who continued working on and improving his design until the U.S. Navy purchased 1,500 of his Remington-Lee 1884 guns for trials. Chambered in

Three of the author's turn-of-the-century bolt guns. Left to right: 1903 Springfield sporterized by Adolph Wundhammer, 1903 vintage Rigby 7x57 and 1903 Mannlicher Schoenauer.

Mannlicher (Haenel) Repeating Rifles.

8 M-M or .315 Caliber.

No. 1 SPORTING RIFLE.

Extra Finish, Raised Matted Rib, Half Octagon Barrel; Lengths, 24, 26 or 28 inches; with Sling, Swivels, Hair Trigger; Checkered Pistol Grip, Double Reversible Front Sight; Weight, 7 lbs. $40 00
40 grains Walsrode powder; weight of bullet, 236 grains. Cartridges, per 100 .... 5.00
Point Blank Range, 300 yards; Muzzle Velocity, 2000 feet per second; Penetration, 50 inches of pine.

New Model, 9 M-M or .354 Caliber.

Extra Finish; Raised Matted Rib; Half Octagon Barrel; Lengths, 26 or 28 inches; Sling Swivels; Hair Trigger; Checkered Pistol Grip; all Bright Parts Matted; Weight, 7½ lbs. $50.00
Extra charge for any but regular finish.
Cartridges, per 100 .... 3 50
Point Blank Range, 300 yards; Velocity, 2000 feet per second; 44 grains Smokeless Powder; Bullet weighing 280 grains.

System G. Roth. 8 M-M or .315 Caliber.

THE HAENEL AUTOMATIC RIFLE.

First and Only High Power Automatic Rifle on the market. Handsomely finished, weight 7½ pounds $150.00
Special Cartridges, per 100 .... 3.50

SEND FOR CATALOGUE.

Sole Agent, A. H. FUNKE, 325 Broadway, New York.

PACIFIC HARDWARE AND STEEL CO., Coast Agent, San Francisco, Cal.

An early Mannlicher-Haenel advertisement.

.45/70, the Navy used the rifles for the next 20 years.

The U.S. Army trials of the same period rejected Lee's design, favoring the Norwegian-designed Krag-Jorgensen. Great Britain, however, recognized its value and adopted the Lee design in 1888, christening it the .303 Lee-Medford Magazine Rifle Mark I. In 1892, with the switch from blackpowder to smokeless cordite, the Brits changed the rifling pattern from the segmental Medford style to the more durable Enfield pattern. The resulting Lee-Enfield evolved into one of the best, most rugged and longest-serving bolt-action military rifles in history and served England well from 1889 until 1959.

Harry Staser hunting meat for railroad construction crews on Alaska's Kenai Peninsula, circa 1915–16 using what appears to be a Wundhammer sporterized 1903 Springfield.

Most new rifle designs were intended for military use, but a tiny handful of the Remington-Keene and the Remington-Lee models 1879, 1882 and 1885 were produced as sporting rifles. Remington eventually produced approximately 7,000 of the Remington-Lee 1899 model until ending production in 1906. The rifles were accurate, rugged, reliable and available in an astounding array of military and civilian calibers of the era.

Except for the handful of 1899 Remington-Lee sporting rifles and a smattering of Birmingham Small Arms (BSA) and London Small Arms (LSA) manufactured "Lee Speed" rifles, the designs of James Paris Lee were seldom built into proper sporters. (Although a few 1899 Remington-Lee and Lee Speed sporting rifles made it to the Alaskan territory.)

I acquired a slim, accurate sporting version of the 1899 Remington-Lee during my wanderings around Alaska. It's chambered for the old .32/40, the favored cartridge of serious riflemen of the day due to its intrinsic accuracy. Using its bolt-mounted peep sight and pushing .32-caliber, 170-grain Speer Hot-Cor bullets over 28 grains of 3031 powder, that rifle still possesses excellent accuracy and proved ideal for hunting the small blacktail deer on Kodiak Island.

The Remington-Lee was built with a unique half-cock feature as an early, transition-era bolt action. There is an upright protrusion on the rear of the striker, and when the rifle is cocked by the regular operation of the bolt, you can lower it to a half-cocked position just as you would with a hammer gun. The bolt is locked closed in that position, and the rifle is safe. Pull the striker back with your thumb just as you would a hammer to fire it. It is intuitive and straightforward to operate. I also appreciate the slim javelin forearm with the Schnabel forend and the curved steel buttplate. The rifle does yeoman duty as a handy walking staff in steep and uneven terrain. The Schnabel forend makes for a perfect handhold, and the curved steel buttplate bites into slick, uneven terrain.

I have also owned and hunted with a BSA version of the "Lee Speed" in .303 British. It is considerably more powerful than the .32/40, and I used it for hunting black bears along the Yukon River in interior Alaska. While a useful feature on a military weapon, the protruding box magazine initially caused a slight annoyance when carrying it. However, it and the Remington-Lee balanced well, and after a few days of carrying them, I quickly became accustomed to the feel. They were no worse to carry than the popular 1895 Winchester lever-action carbines.

Another design from the fertile mind of James Paris Lee was the unique straight-pull 6mm 1895 Lee-Navy. It was Lee's final design, and obviously his favorite as it is the rifle carved on his gravestone. It was the first clip-loading magazine rifle officially adopted by the U.S military. Winchester received the government contract and produced 20,000 rifles for the Navy. Once the military contract was complete in 1897, Winchester assembled an additional 1,700 sporting versions. They were lightweight, quick-firing with a slim 24-inch nickel-steel barrel and trim sporting stock. With a jacketed 112-grain bullet and a muzzle velocity of 2,550 fps, it was the most advanced and flattest-shooting rifle of its day. However, the steep list price of $32 made it the most expensive rifle in the Winchester line. It could not compete with the popular lever actions and was discontinued in 1902. But the advantages of modern bolt-action rifles, utilizing small-bore, high-velocity ammunition, did not go unnoticed by serious Alaskan hunters.

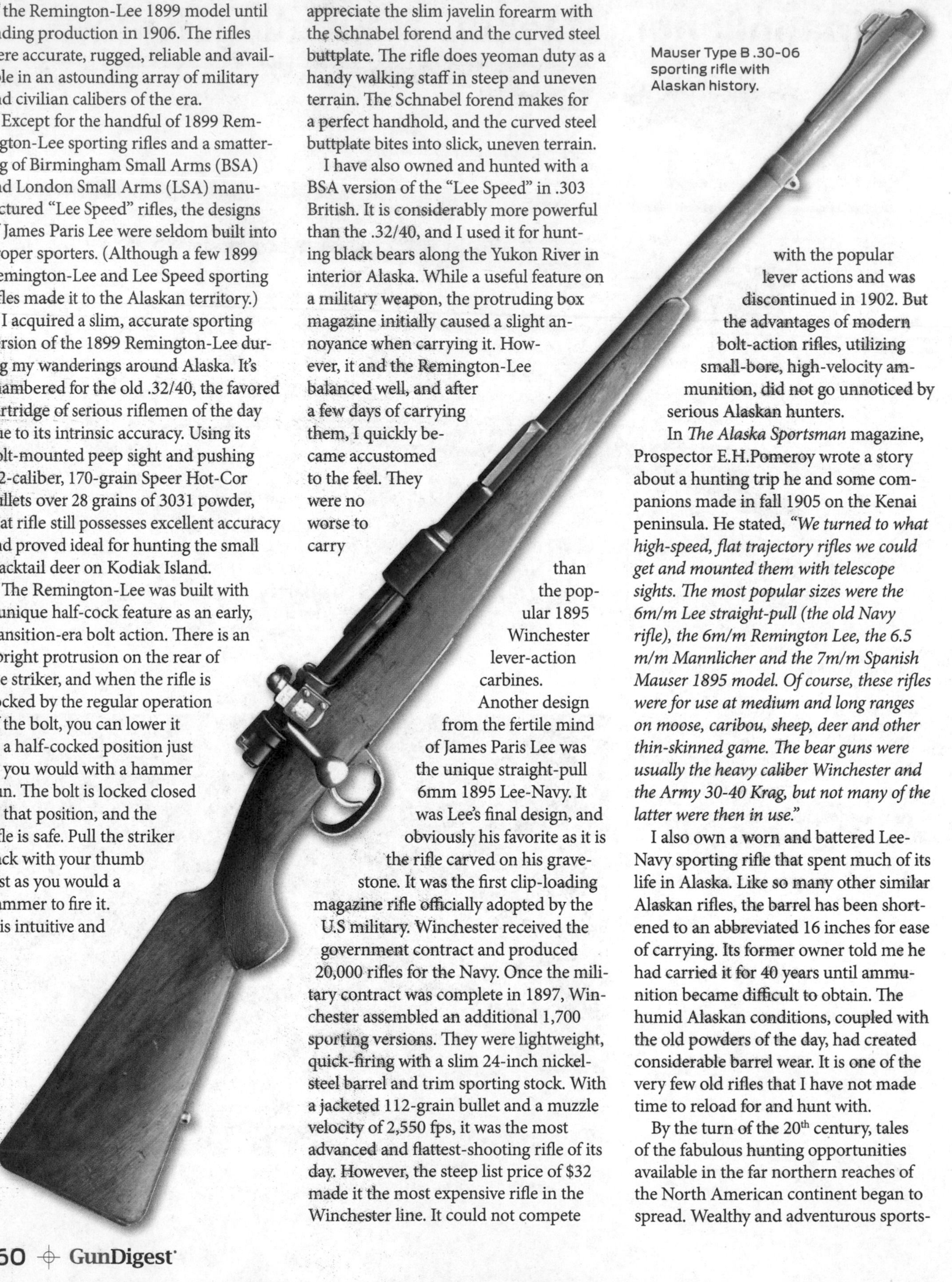

Mauser Type B .30-06 sporting rifle with Alaskan history.

In *The Alaska Sportsman* magazine, Prospector E.H.Pomeroy wrote a story about a hunting trip he and some companions made in fall 1905 on the Kenai peninsula. He stated, "*We turned to what high-speed, flat trajectory rifles we could get and mounted them with telescope sights. The most popular sizes were the 6m/m Lee straight-pull (the old Navy rifle), the 6m/m Remington Lee, the 6.5 m/m Mannlicher and the 7m/m Spanish Mauser 1895 model. Of course, these rifles were for use at medium and long ranges on moose, caribou, sheep, deer and other thin-skinned game. The bear guns were usually the heavy caliber Winchester and the Army 30-40 Krag, but not many of the latter were then in use.*"

I also own a worn and battered Lee-Navy sporting rifle that spent much of its life in Alaska. Like so many other similar Alaskan rifles, the barrel has been shortened to an abbreviated 16 inches for ease of carrying. Its former owner told me he had carried it for 40 years until ammunition became difficult to obtain. The humid Alaskan conditions, coupled with the old powders of the day, had created considerable barrel wear. It is one of the very few old rifles that I have not made time to reload for and hunt with.

By the turn of the 20th century, tales of the fabulous hunting opportunities available in the far northern reaches of the North American continent began to spread. Wealthy and adventurous sportsmen from around the globe arrived in the Alaskan territory. In 1903, Captain C.R.E. Radclyffe, an English gentleman-hunter, visited Alaska with a permit from the British Museum to collect Dall sheep, brown bears and moose. Like most visiting hunters of the era, he carried the most up-to-date armament, including an 8x57 bolt-action sporter built by C.G. Haenel on the German M-88 commission action.

In 1906, a wealthy Yale-educated hunter-naturalist, Charles Sheldon, also journeyed into the Ogilvie Mountains dividing the Alaskan territory from the Yukon. Sheldon was accompanied by Wilfred H. Osgood of the U.S. Biological Survey, famed wildlife artist Carl Rungius, and a soon-to-become-iconic African hunter-naturalist, Frederick Courteney Selous. Selous carried a pair of his beloved Farquharson single-shot rifles and wrote, *"... personally I have found a .303 and a .375 bore rifles* [the early 2 1/2" flanged nitro express cartridge with a 270-gr. bullet @ 2,000 fps, rather than the .375 H&H belted nitro express that wasn't introduced until 1912] *both by Holland, very effective weapons against moose and caribou, whilst several of my friends believe that the .256 Mannlicher is the best of all the small bores."* One of the friends Selous was referring to was Sheldon, who, in his extensive writings, claimed that *"... for large game my Mannlicher .256 caliber is the only rifle I have ever used in the North."*

Sheldon's .256 Mannlicher was the British designation for 1903 Mannlicher Schoenauer 6.5x54. The design, a corroborative effort between Ferdinand Ritter von Mannlicher and Otto Schoenauer, was a direct, derivative descendant of the Dreyse, Chassepot and German 1888 Commission rifles. It was finalized in Steyr's Austria factory in 1900 and adopted by the militaries of Portugal and Greece. It offered nothing remarkable as a military weapon but made a wonderful little sporting rifle.

The rifle received enthusiastic receptions and endorsements wherever it was used. Slim, trim, lightweight and reliable, it offered unheard-of velocity and flat trajectory for the time. It simplified longer shots, and its heavy-for-caliber bullets gave astonishing penetration. It became a universal favorite of Arctic explorers and African safaris.

My little 1903 Mannlicher Schoenauer carbine was purchased from a friend on Kodiak Island and has become a favorite carrying rifle when hunting the Emerald Isle. Like many full-stock carbines, a previous owner had removed the constricting steel nose cap and shortened the forend six inches to improve accuracy. With its Lyman No. 36 peep sight and 140-grain Nosler Accubond bullets loaded ahead of 36.5 gr of IMR 4064, the little carbine still clusters three-shot groups within an inch at 100 yards. It's no surprise it became a worldwide hunting icon.

In contrast with the American, British and French designs, Austrian and German bolt actions fared better as sporting rifles; in fact, from their very inception, sporting rifles were produced alongside military rifles. In 1895, New Jersey dealer Oscar Hesse imported high-grade German-pattern 88 bolt-action sporters made by C.G. Haenel. Shortly after that, H. Tauscher, a dealer from New York, and P. Von Franrzius, a dealer from Chicago, began offering Oberndorf Mauser sporting rifles. In the 1900 Christmas Is-

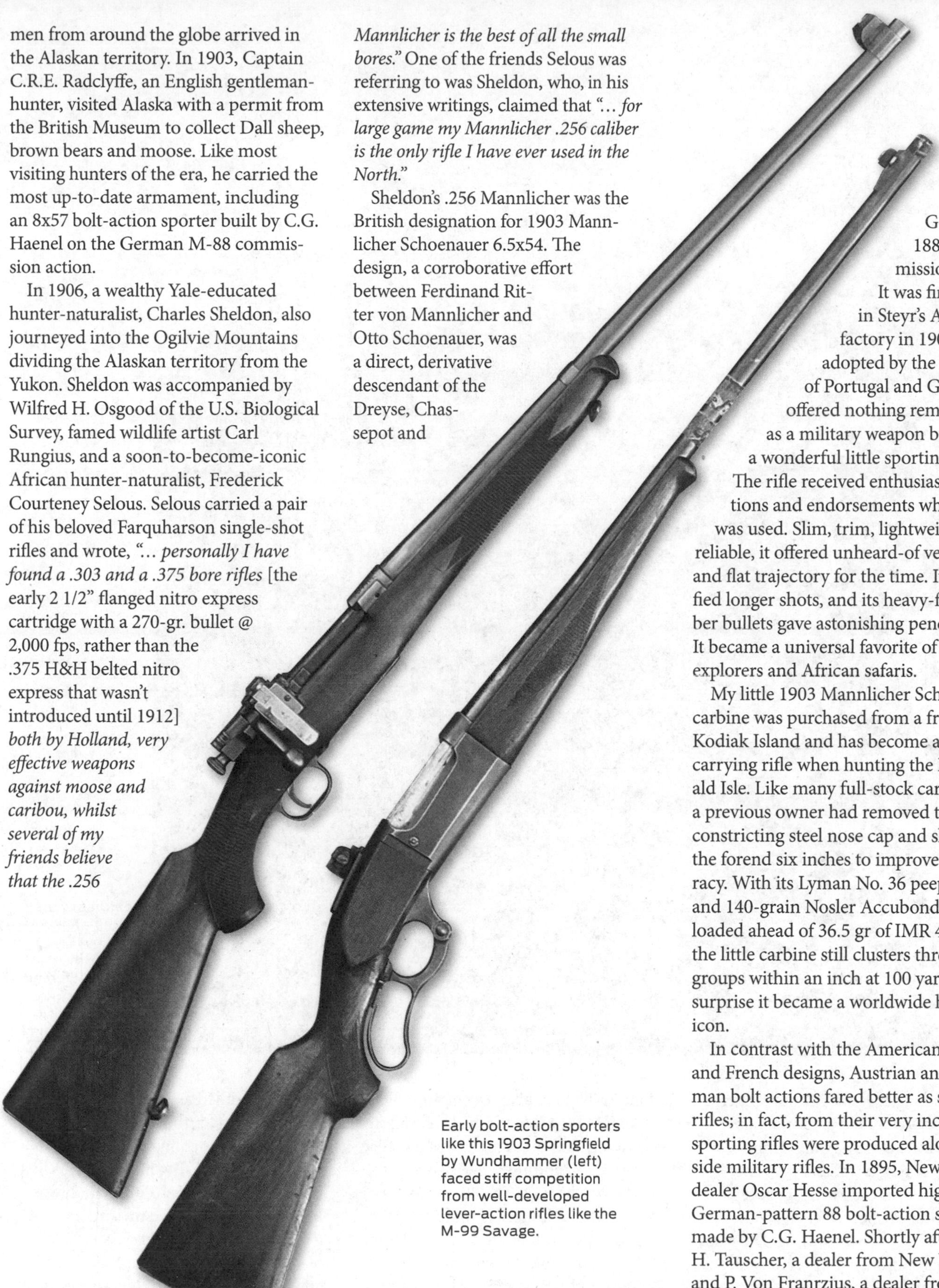

Early bolt-action sporters like this 1903 Springfield by Wundhammer (left) faced stiff competition from well-developed lever-action rifles like the M-99 Savage.

Features of the author's Remington-Lee .32-40, such as the thin Schnabel forend and curved steel butt, proved valuable assets in rough terrain.

sue of *Shooting & Fishing,* Von Lengerke & Detmold advertised genuine Mauser sporting rifles. By 1902 other importers like A.H. Funke and Schoverling, Daly & Gales were advertising bolt guns made by Mannlicher-Haenel, Haenel and Schilling. In 1910, Schoverling, Daly and Gales began importing J.P. Sauer-built Mauser sporters in the new American .30-06 caliber.

The novelty and obviously high quality of imported European rifles made them attractive but, when the average wage for a working man in America was less than $2 per day, spending $12 for a Winchester M-94 .30-30 or $30 or a Winchester M-95 .30-06 was more appealing than the $50 required to order a Mauser. But along the gold-bearing streams of the Alaskan and Yukon territories, fortunes were being made. During the long winter evenings, miners, trappers and meat hunters huddled around blazing wood stoves and under the glare of kerosene lanterns, scrutinizing the most recent catalogs and sporting magazines. When the year's monetary accumulation was tallied, many scribbled out orders to be mailed off with the next passing dog team. It is not all that unusual to run across old, high-grade rifles in the most isolated areas of the state.

I have owned several early Mauser

The early 1899 Remington-Lee design utilized a half-cocked feature in place of a safety.

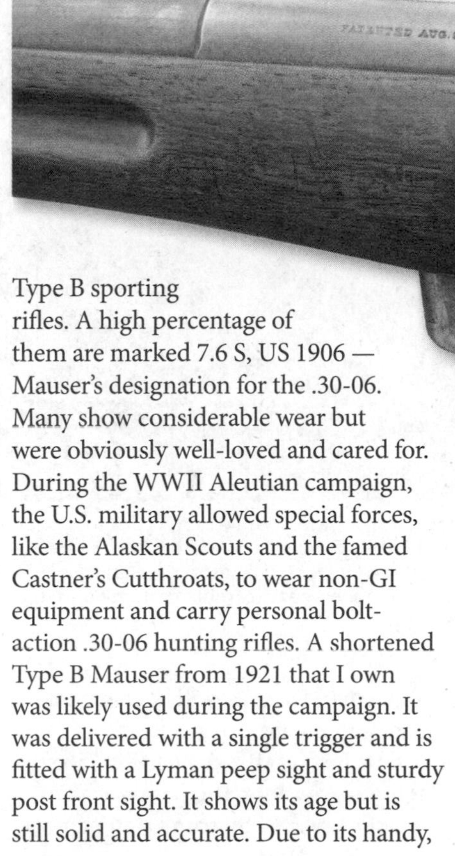

Type B sporting rifles. A high percentage of them are marked 7.6 S, US 1906 — Mauser's designation for the .30-06. Many show considerable wear but were obviously well-loved and cared for. During the WWII Aleutian campaign, the U.S. military allowed special forces, like the Alaskan Scouts and the famed Castner's Cutthroats, to wear non-GI equipment and carry personal bolt-action .30-06 hunting rifles. A shortened Type B Mauser from 1921 that I own was likely used during the campaign. It was delivered with a single trigger and is fitted with a Lyman peep sight and sturdy post front sight. It shows its age but is still solid and accurate. Due to its handy, abbreviated length, it's one of my favorite everyday carrying carbines.

My son Taj acquired another interesting rifle on Kodiak. At the risk of offending Anglophiles, it is basically just another Mauser sporter, only imported by the English firm of John Rigby. Delivered in 1903, it was fitted with one of Rigby's classic stocks and marketed as the Rigby No. 1, 7x57. It's sighted for use with the wonderfully effective 175-grain soft and solid bullets and quickly earned icon status in British East Africa. So far, Taj has used it on Kodiak blacktails, and I've carried it on a moose hunt on the Alaskan Peninsula.

My latest acquisition is an early German M88 Commission sporting rifle built by the famous Otto Bock. Like many high-quality rifles of the era, it has a quarter octagonal to round barrel with full integral rib, double set triggers, a crystal clear claw-mounted Weku/Braunfels scope with a German 3 plex reticle. It is bedded in a beautifully executed, ultra-slim, Teutonic-styled stock. Chambered in the rimless 6.5x52, I'm looking forward to using it this coming deer season, loaded with 100-grain .25-caliber Swift A-Frame bullets over 26 grains of Varget.

The choice of what constituted a proper hunting rifle has always elicited debate. During the early part of the 20th century, debates raged in the pages of sporting publications like *Outers'*, *Outdoor Life*, *Field & Stream* and *Arms and Man at Arms* about the attributes of lever actions versus the new bolt guns. As is usual in discussions of this type, more smoke and heat were generated than light. Lever actions remained a popular choice among hunters. It was not until the doughboys came home after WWI that American hunters noticed and adapted the advantages of the bolt action. At the close of that conflict, hundreds of thousands of GIs returned home to resume their lives. Many new trappers, miners and hunters moving into the Alaskan territory had served in the military and were familiar with bolt actions' power, long-range accuracy and rugged reliability.

The rifle and cartridge combination that Americans came to cherish in the decades following WWI was the accurate, smooth-feeding 1903 Springfield .30-06. While unimaginable today, the 1903 Springfield was the most up-to-date military battle rifle. It was made available for purchase by civilians in March 1905 by U.S. Public Law No.149. Theodore Roosevelt, the wildly popular president who was also an avid outdoorsman and hunter, championed it. In 1903, when a new Springfield rifle was introduced, Roosevelt ordered a customized sporting version directly from the U.S. Springfield armory. In 1910, shortly after publishing *African Game Trails*, his book extolling the virtues of the 1903 Springfield, a Bavarian-trained gunsmith working in Los Angles, Ludwig (Louis) Wundhammer, recognized the potential of the new rifle.

Louis Wundhammer is credited with crafting the first and finest-handling bolt guns built on the 1903 Springfield action. Each rifle incorporated first-class craftsmanship, including turned-down barrels and artistically tapered receiver ring and tang. He needed no Baroque architectural features, with convoluted flutings, moldings and shadow lines to illustrate his woodworking skills. Like the English master John Rigby, Wundhammer's rifles were slim, trim hunting tools

One of the first LX-1 rifles from D'Arcy Echols, being used on safari. While of new production, the rifle has many features suggestive of turn-of-the-century quality (see sidebar). The buffalo was taken in Mozambique, yes it was shot with the very first LX-1Prototype, Serial No. 0001, Caliber .375 H&H. The rifle went on this Safari and then one to Zambia a month and a half later. It has accounted for quite a bit of game to date.

D'Arcy Echols' New LX-1

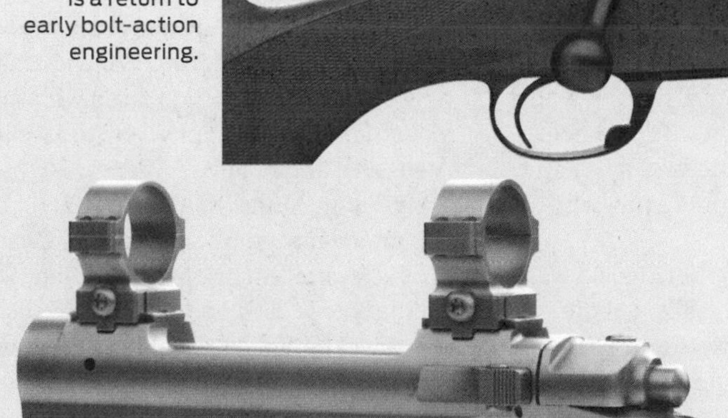

The LX-1 from D'Arcy Echols is a return to early bolt-action engineering.

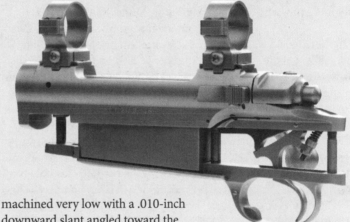

The LX-1's receiver is like the Winchester Model 70's, as is the trigger.

Having spent the last four decades revamping, modifying and morphing pre-existing receivers into highly reliable actions for big game hunting, I finally had to admit I'd become very tired of repairing and repainting the same old fence.

The new LX-1 from D'Arcy Echols is a return to early bolt-action engineering. The rifle combines the best features from various receivers made in the past blended into a modern-manufactured receiver. That's all thanks to computer numerical controlled (CNC) machining, modern materials and advanced heat treatment.

The end goal was to produce a receiver and bolt that did not require blueprinting or rebuilding the trigger, safety and fire control system. It also needed a correctly set up feeding mechanism and a bullet-proof scope mounting system right out of the box.

LX-1 OLD-SCHOOL FEATURES

1 The receiver is like the Winchester Model 70's, made from 416 stainless and available in right- and left-handed models. The sides are radial in cross-section and tapered under the stock line to allow ease in bedding.

2 The bolt body and most remaining parts are chrome-moly steel. This steel composition allows the C/M bolt to operate or run with less friction when manipulated.

3 The simple bolt stop is robust and fits flat against the receiver, and will take the impact of the bolt being manipulated under stress. The flange also acts as a gas block within the bolt raceway.

4 Scope bases are integrally machined into the receiver with dovetails machined very low with a .010-inch downward slant angled toward the muzzle.

5 The trigger is a direct copy of the original Model 70, although machined to closer tolerances. The advantage of this design is the brilliance of so few moving parts.

6 The claw extractor system is made from appropriate machined steel and fits the OD groove diameter of the cartridge case.

7 The bolt shroud, with a three-position wing safety, is machined, timed and fit to prevent the shroud, firing pin and safety from rising away from the sear pad and affecting the pull weight. A flange on the shroud's leading edge acts as a directional gas shield.

8 The floorplate and trigger bow assembly are made in a three-piece design. The magazine boxes and followers are cartridge-specific and made from heat-treated steel. Currently, there are three separate magazine boxes available: One type for the .25-06 through .35 Whelen, another for the standard belted magnums, such as .264 Winchester through .416 Remington and .458 Lott, and the last for the .300 H&H and .375 H&H Magnum.

9 Scope rings are made from heat-treated 4130 chrome-moly steel and are available in 1-inch and 30mm diameters. These rings can be rapidly detached in seconds. A recoil stop is machined integrally into the clamp jaw of each ring and prevents any forward or rearward movement of the scope during recoil.

10 Scope rings, floorplate and trigger bow assemblies are also available in 7075 aluminum for those who wish to reduce weight.

devoid of plethoric excesses. The impeccably balanced stocks with cast-off and a subtle bulge through the pistol grip (now known as the Wundhammer swell) made his rifles coveted hunting companions.

Astute Alaskans who carried rifles daily, like guides Andrew Berg, Slim Moore, Jay Williams, Charlie Madsen and territorial hunter and warden Hosea Sarber, quickly recognized the benefits of 1903 Springfield sporters. They used them regularly on everything from sheep and caribou to grizzlies and brown bears. In his book *Alaskan Adventure,* Williams writes, *"My little Springfield sporter, fashioned by Ludwig Wundhammer, was picked up in the morning as regularly as my hat."* It was his daily companion for thirty years until eventually lost in a boat fire. He soon replaced it with another Springfield sporter, restocked by Alvin Linden, in the slightly more powerful .35 Whelen.

The popularity of the Springfield was such that the best rifle makers of the time — Fred Adolph, Seymour Griffin, Barney Worthen and Adolf Minar — immediately began to build sporters using Springfield-barreled actions. The Philadelphia firm of R.F. Sedgley was one of the largest and most widely known. Even today, their rifles can still be found in the hands of Alaskan hunters.

I've owned and used many classic sporterized 1903 Springfields. Still, my favorite is a Wundhammer that once belonged to the late Michael Petrov, an Alaskan collector and expert on Springfield sporting rifles. With its long-slide Lyman M48 peep sight and Black Hills ammunition loaded with 180-grain TSX bullets, it consistently groups well under 1 MOA and was the rifle I chose for a month-long float hunting expedition along the Coleville River in northern Alaska.

Two years after the "The Great War," Savage Arms became the first major American company to produce a viable commercial bolt-action centerfire sporting rifle. Referred to as the model 1920, it had the misfortune to be in direct competition with Savage's immensely popular, slim and flat-shooting .250-300 Model 99 lever action. With the same barrel contour and stock shape as the M-99 lever action, the Model 1920 bolt action was presciently innovative. Weighing less than 6 pounds, it featured a simple receiver milled from round stock with a separate recoil lug sandwiched between the barrel and the receiver. The receiver was of correct proportions for the short .250/3000 and .300 Savage cartridges, and the magazine box had patented shoulders to securely hold rounds and keep them from becoming battered. The Savage 1920 also had a simple rugged ejector, much like the 1903 Springfield, a tang-mounted safety and a striker-mounted peep sight. Despite its modern features and being chambered for top-rated cartridges, the newly introduced Savage faced the same conundrum Winchester's 1884 Hotchkiss bolt action faced with the Model 1886. Lever actions were too well-established and popular.

My Savage Model 1920 .250/3000 presents an intriguing conundrum. Overall, it is in excellent original condition, but the bore is dark, and the twist rate is best suited for lighter-weight bullets than I prefer. I am still working on a compromise load for Alaskan deer, caribou, goats and black bears. I've discussed reboring it with Arizona barrel maker Danny Peterson. He assures me that a rebore and rechamber for the currently fashionable 6.5 Creedmoor will clean up the old barrel and give the rifle a new lease on life. Decisions, decisions.

Newly introduced bolt-action sporting rifles had to compete with America's affection for lever guns. They also had the misfortune to compete with a massive surplus of military rifles and carbines leftover from WWI. They were ordered inexpensively by mail from the Sears, Roebuck & Co. catalog. Surplus .30-40 Krag rifles were highly popular in the Alaska territory. Inexpensive, rugged and powerful, they were highly regarded for their smoothness, reliability and effectiveness. The round-nosed 220-grain bullet at 2,200 fps was as solid a killer on large Alaskan game back then as it is now.

Missouri-born Bill Pinnell, who eventually would earn fame as one of Kodiak's premier brown bear guides, arrived on Kodiak in 1938 with an inexpensive, surplus 8x57 German Model 88 carbine. It would seem an unlikely choice for hunting brown bears by today's standards, but Bill used it for a quarter of a century as he and his partner Morris Tallifson hunted, trapped, and mined on the island. A section near the muzzle end of the full-length stock was whittled out to act as a handhold when using the little carbine as a climbing staff while traversing the steep Kodiak terrain. The one advantage of the bolt action was becoming apparent to hunters: it was easier to obtain a powerful, flat-shooting cartridge in a lighter weight carbine than was available in a lever action.

In 1919, the 1,538-mile border between the Alaskan and Yukon territories was porous and ill-defined, and it was not unusual, nor illegal, for hunters and guides to work both sides of the border. Jean and Louis, the famed Jacquot brothers from Kluane Lake in the Yukon territory, met wealthy American hunters, G.O Young, Dr. A.H. Evans and J.C. Snider, near the Kennicott mine region in Alaska. They hunted the White River drainage of the Wrangle mountains back into the Yukon.

Like most guides, Louis and Jean used readily accessible armament. Jean liked his Savage M-99 in .250/3000, but Louis preferred his more powerful 1903 Springfield .30-06 sporter. Like today, their wealthy clients chose the newest, most up-to-date rifles — Snider a .256 Newton, Young a .280 Ross and Dr. Evans a pump-action Remington Model 14 .35 Auto and Winchester Model 95 .30-40.

In the late 1920s, John Eddy was another sportsman of that era who chose to hunt with a custom Griffin & Howe Springfield chambered for the .35 Whelen. He hunted brown bears on the lower Alaskan Peninsula with guide Andy Simons. His two companions, Edward Garrett and Joshua Green chose similar rifles chambered in .30-06.

Left with a large stock of military 1917 Enfield parts after WWI, Remington began re-working the surplus parts into sporting rifles. In 1921, a year after Savage introduced its Model 1920 bolt action, Remington decided to introduce the Model 30. It was an unusual mixture of components. The action retained the military cock-on-closing striker, and it had finger grooves along a javelin slim,

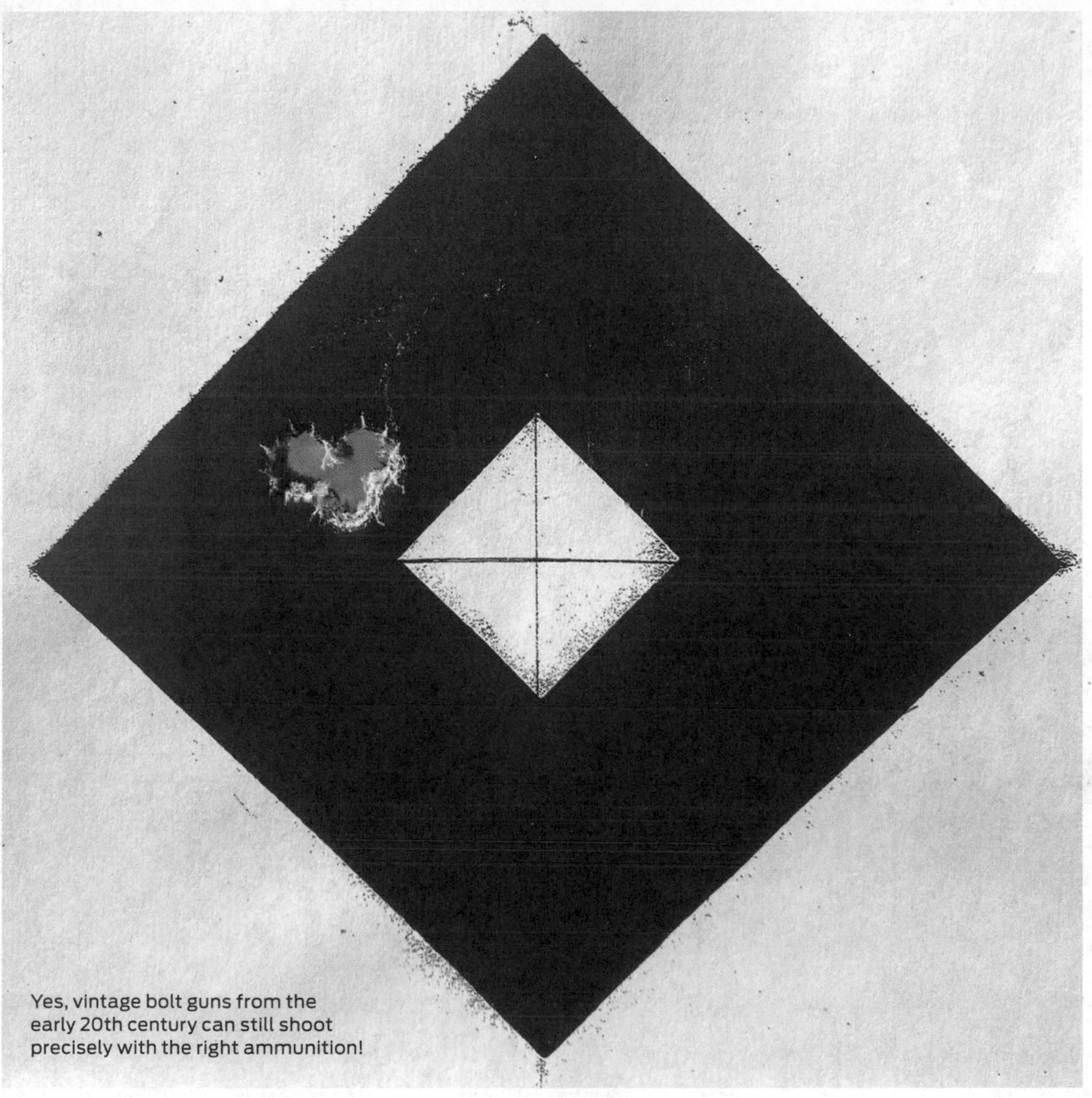
Yes, vintage bolt guns from the early 20th century can still shoot precisely with the right ammunition!

I purchased an M-54 .30-06 over 50 years ago, and it remains a lively hunting companion. I also own a short .30 WCF M54 carbine that is relatively rare as it couldn't compete with Winchester's iconic 1894 lever action.

When Winchester decided to refine the M54 in the 1930s, the firm sought input from knowledgeable Alaskan riflemen like guide Jay Williams and his close friend, Alaskan game commissioner Frank Dufresne. Winchester also solicited advice from Townsend Whelen and Elmer Keith, both popular gun writers of the era. The resulting Winchester Model 70 became known as "The Rifleman's Rifle" and owes much of its existence to the early Mauser and Springfield sporters.

short forend and a curved steel buttplate reminiscent of the early lever actions. Chambering the .30-06 was natural, but it was also offered in the same under-powered .25, .30, .32 and .35 Remington chambering as the Model 8 autoloaders.

I owned one of the early M-30s, and it was an ill-balanced, bulky, under-powdered, uncomfortable and unappealing little rifle. With advice from the firearms authorities and writers of the time (who were primarily target shooters), Remington updated the cock-on-closing feature and the stock design. Using the "N.R.A." style target stock with a higher, straighter comb, tighter grip and more extended, fuller forearm, it became the forerunner of the current "American" stock style. Referred to as the Model 30 S, it was and remains a solid and reliable rifle.

Four years later, Winchester introduced its newly designed Model 54 sporting rifle. It adopted the Springfield's coned breech and the slim, lithe stock features, including the Schnabel forend tip of many custom Springfield sporters. The M-54 was reasonably well-received, but it needed some improvements. It utilized its sear as a bolt stop, had a less than attractive stamped triggerguard, and neither the safety nor bolt handle was contoured for mounting a scope. In addition, the gun writers of the time were primarily target shooters who were preaching the virtues of thicker, heavier stocks.

My journey of discovery with sporting rifles remains an ongoing endeavor. It has been a traverse from flintlock jaegers and colonial American long rifles to sporters of the present. I have learned that every design has strengths and weaknesses and that military design parameters are not required, nor necessarily beneficial, for sportsmen. I think that is something that the modern marketers currently promoting heavy, blocky, chassis-style rifles and observatory-sized optics have yet to learn. Despite new, improved bolt-action designs being introduced, I don't think the well-executed bolt actions of yesteryear will be replaced soon. GD

The author's custom 9.3x62mm Mauser is built on a rescued Brno ZG-47 action. It is a plain-Jane rifle for rugged work with a semi-octagonal 24-inch barrel, full-length rib and three-leaf rear sight. The front sight bead is ivory.

Chronology of Czech Bolt-Action Hunting Rifles

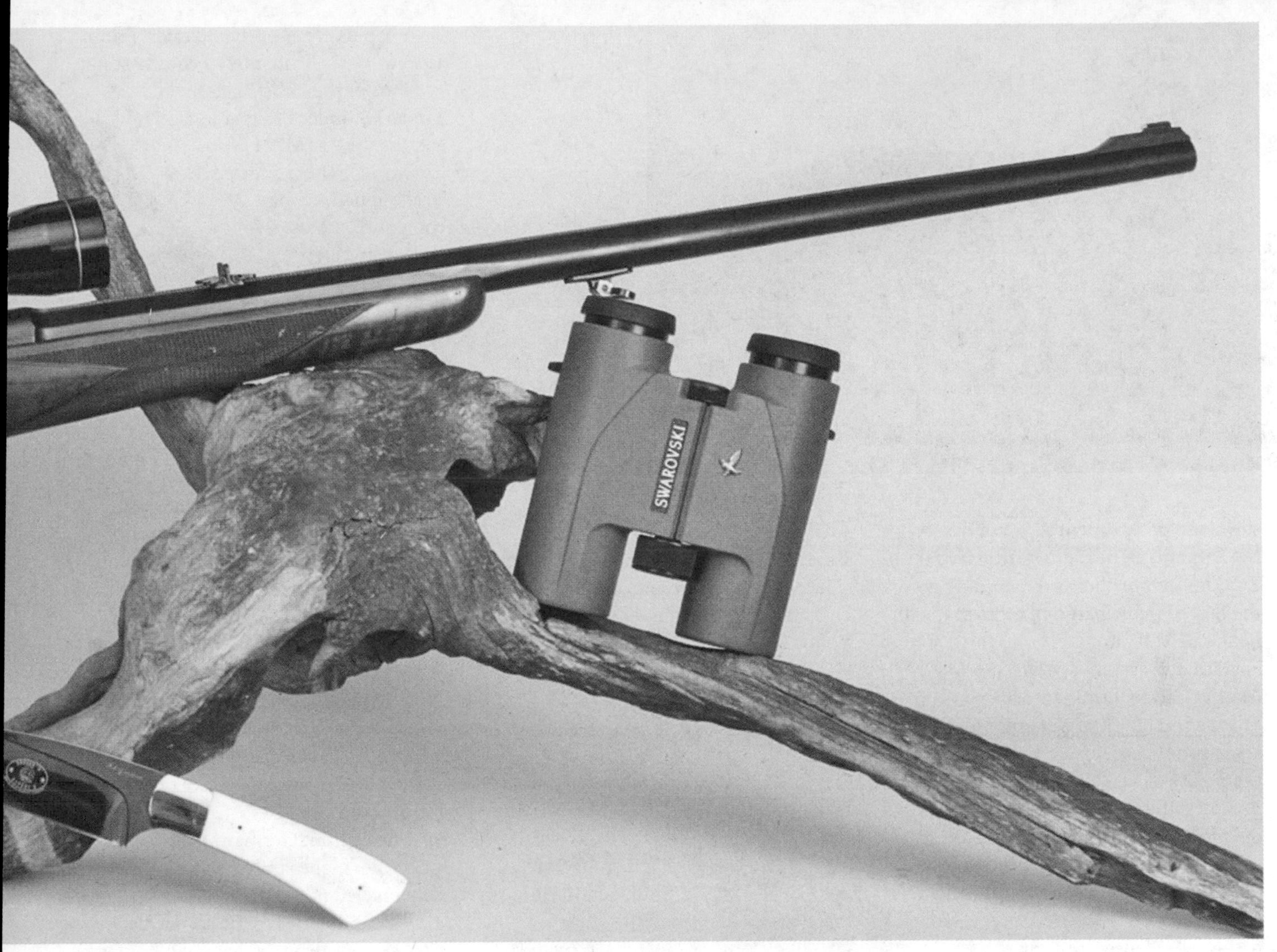

A clear-eyed look at the history of CZ and Brno development.

›PIERRE VAN DER WALT

The fascinating history of Czech big game bolt-action rifles dates to the Austro-Hungarian Empire, followed by the secretive years of communist rule over Czechoslovakia. All the details will probably never be uncovered, but I've condensed as many known facts as possible into the prevailing space constraints. Essentially, it entails the activities of two companies: *Zbrojovka Brno* (*Zbrojovka* meaning arms factory) and *Ceská zbrojovka-Uherský Brod*. To simplify the "plot," they will be referred to as "Brno" (pronounced *Bir-noh*, phonetically bɜːrnoʊ) and "CZ-UB" despite a plethora of unpronounceable names over the decades in question.

BRNO MAUSER ERA (1914–1936)

One part of the story begins in the city of Brno in 1914. That year a workshop to repair carriages of the Austro-Hungarian Empire's Škoda M85 field gun was established in the city. Two years later, the facility became the Moravian branch of that empire's Imperial and Royal Armoury, the latter headquartered in Vienna. In 1916, the Imperial and Royal Armoury also established an arms manufacturing plant near the carriage workshop, but in the Zábrdovice suburb between the Svitava river and the railway line. After WWI, several countries in the region broke away from the Hapsburg's collapsed Austro-Hungarian Empire. Czechoslovakia, which included the Moravia region, came into being because of this fragmentation. In 1919, the new Czecho-

The deserted Brno head office next to the main plant entrance photographed in October 2021 presents a sad reminder of a once glorious company. Photo: Adam Kostrunek

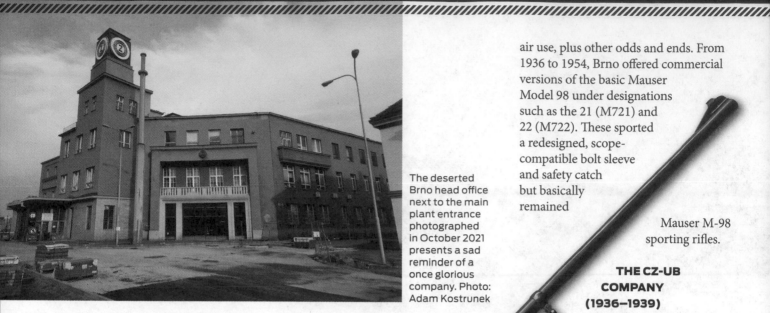

slovakian government took control of the Brno plant, headquartering it in the Zábrdovice precinct and renaming it — the first of many name changes that will not be delved into.

Germany and thus *Waffenfabrik Mauser* had to terminate arms production after the war and sell its arms-producing infrastructure under the Treaty of Versailles. This mandate provided the Czechoslovak Ministry of Defence the opportunity to acquire a complete Mauser M-98 production line comprising 1,500 machines and matching tooling from Mauser. The first M-98 Mauser military rifles rolled off Brno's production line in 1922 and were sold worldwide. By 1924, the Vz.24 Czech version of the Mauser, inspired by Brno engineer Joseph Jelen, became the predominant Czechoslovak military rifle. Brno soon expanded to 30,000 employees, and the Brno brand acquired strong international recognition.

By then, the general policy for the Czechoslovak arms industry had crystalized: Brno would manufacture bolt-action rifles and the other company, CZ, would manufacture pistols, and machine guns for land and air use, plus other odds and ends. From 1936 to 1954, Brno offered commercial versions of the basic Mauser Model 98 under designations such as the 21 (M721) and 22 (M722). These sported a redesigned, scope-compatible bolt sleeve and safety catch but basically remained Mauser M-98 sporting rifles.

Brno Model 21/22 rifles were all built on small-ring Mauser dimensions. Rifles with serial numbers below 23,000 had round-top receiver rings decorated with fine checkering around a centralized Brno logo. After that, Brno introduced the trademark flat top, which remained part of its rifles until the CZ550's 2021 demise.

THE CZ-UB COMPANY (1936–1939)

CZ-UB is the other company of interest. It considers 1936 its birth year, but there is more to the story. CZ-UB evolved from several older companies, namely *Jihoceská zbrojovka* (JZ) of Plzen, which started in 1919, relocated to Strakonice in 1921, and one more — the Hubertus company, which JZ had acquired in 1922 and then renamed to *Ceská zbrojovka* (CZ).

The Czechoslovakian cities of Plzen and Strakonice are less than 50km from then-belligerent Germany — too close for comfort. The strategic vulnerability of Bohemia led to the decision to relocate strategic industries to the somewhat more distant Brno, which is 220km from Germany as the crow flies. A new company, which served as a satellite plant for

The Brno Model 21 and 22 rifles were also marketed as Models 721/722, as can be seen on one of the few surviving product brochures. Photo: Casey Lewis

CZ Strakonice, was established in Brno in 1936. The new CZ satellite plant was one of the most modern and capable globally. It devoted itself to the highly demanding production of aircraft and other machine guns as dictated by policy. This satellite plant is the company we know as CZ-UB today; hence CZ-UB had 1936 as its year of establishment.

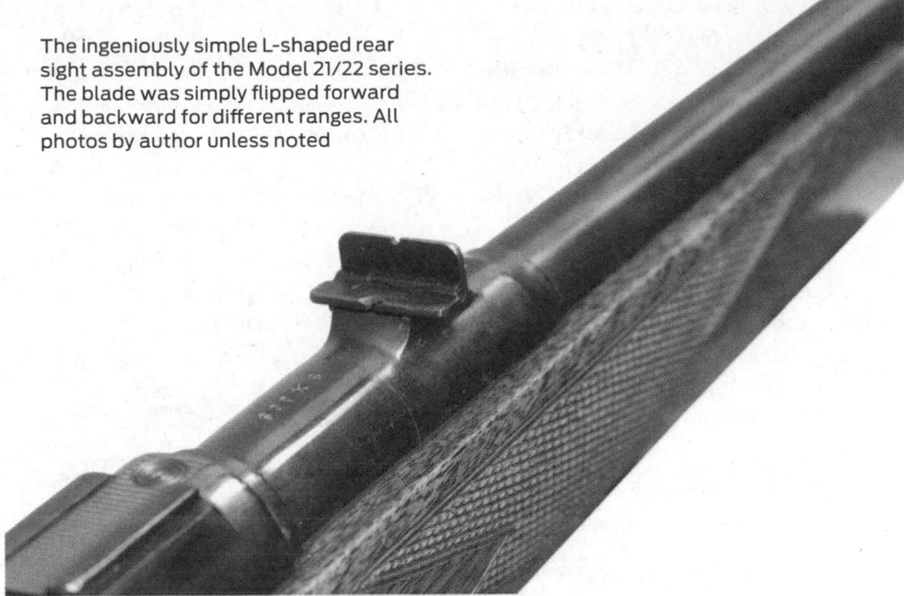

The ingeniously simple L-shaped rear sight assembly of the Model 21/22 series. The blade was simply flipped forward and backward for different ranges. All photos by author unless noted

BRNO MAUSER M-98 (1936–1945)

Having manufactured more than 775,600 Vz.24 military versions of the Mauser M-98 from 1926, Brno began offering sporters in 1936. The first sporters were designated Model A (halfstock) and Model B (fullstock) — the main difference between the sporter and military actions was the omission of the clip-loader notch from the front face of the bridge.

All the relocation was in vain, though, because in March 1939, the Nazis marched into Czechoslovakia and declared Bohemia and Moravia protectorates of the Third Reich. Since Brno was the bolt-action rifle manufacturer, our first focus must be on Brno rather than CZ-UB.

Critical Brno documents and funds were shipped to England, India and Iran to prevent the Nazis from laying their hands on everything. Technicians were also evacuated — about 150 Brno

The bolt shroud on Model 21/22 rifles exhibited a reasonably elegant and smooth geometry and was equipped with low-lift flag safeties that were riflescope compatible.

MAUSER DESIGNS PRODUCED BY BRNO

	BRNO A	BRNO B	BRNO M(7)21	BRNO M(7)22	TRANSITION
Introduced	1936	1936	~1941	~1941	
Terminated	~1940	~1940	1955	1955	
Produced					
Chamberings	6.5x57	6.5x57	6.5x57	6.5x57	6.5x57
	7x57	7x57	7x57	7x57	7x57
	7x64	7x64	7x64	7x64	7x64
	8x60S	8x60S	8x60S	8x60S	8x60S
	8x64S	8x64S	8x64S	8x64S	8x64S
Magazine	4	4	4	4	4
Barrel length (in.)	23.5	20.5	23.5	20.5	20.5
Stock Styles	Halfstock	Fullstock	Halfstock	Fullstock	Fullstock
Overall Length (in.)		41.75		41.75	41.75
Designer	Mauser	Mauser	Mauser	Mauser	Mauser
Receiver Top	Round	Round	Rnd & Flat	Rnd & Flat	Rnd & Flat
Size	Small Ring	Small Ring	Small Ring	Small Ring	Small Ring

technicians to Great Britain alone. Less than six months later, WWII broke out, with the city of Brno and the two companies already firmly in German hands.

The Nazis placed Brno under the control of the *Reichswerke Herman Göring* military-industrial conglomerate in Berlin. It was renamed *Waffen-Union Škoda Brün* and compelled to manufacture those weapons of war that the German *Oberkommando der Wehrmacht* (OKW - Supreme Command of the Armed Forces) dictated.

The A and B models were superseded in 1941 by the Model 721 (halfstock) and 722 (fullstock) with 20.5- and 23.5-inch barrel lengths, respectively. During the German occupation, the Model 721/2 was marked as manufactured by *Waffen Werke A.G. Brünn*. These models differed from the military design in that:

- There was no thumb-cut in the left receiver wall.
- A redesigned bolt shroud with scope-compatible low-swing safety was fitted.
- The bolt handle was in butterknife style, but examples with a ball exist.
- The bolt shaft lacked the longitudinal guide rib.
- The receiver ring was graced by fine checkering and the logo.
- They were equipped with double-set triggers. Single-trigger versions mostly are Canadian conversions.

From about serial number 23,000, Brno modified the bridge and ring tops to a flat-topped configuration. These 19mm-wide flat tops (double square bridge style) contained integral scope mounting slots, which has remained a feature of Czech big game bolt actions until recently. Brno also added a bolt guide rib to the bolt shaft. These Brno "Mausers" were chambered in 6.5x57mm, 7x57mm, 7x64mm, 8x57JS and 8x60JS.

After WWII, the complete nationalization and reorganization of the entire Czechoslovak arms industry followed the installation of a Soviet-backed communist regime in the country. A central state planning agency controlled all production of arms, ammunition and related materials consistent with Stalin's collectivist production model.

THE BRNO ZG-47 (1947)

Most Brno technicians working in England returned to Czechoslovakia to resume their former positions during the war. As the communist grip tightened over Czechoslovakia, product type and production instructions were imposed on Brno. The repatriated Brno employees nevertheless got down to the firearm business and did exceedingly well regardless. The remaining inventory of Mauser K-98 parts was used to assemble and sell military rifles designated the Vz.98N. The business became good again for Brno.

During the German occupation, the German Army Weapons Office (*Heereswaffenamt*) had ordered Brno to design a .22 LR-caliber training rifle with a military-style Mauser K-98 fullstock. Brno obviously complied, and a rimfire rifle designated the ZKM451 was duly designed by a team consisting of Josef Koucký (1904–1989). He was assisted by his brother František (1907–1994). The "M" in the designation stands for *Malorážka* (rimfire); hence the ZKM (*Zbrojovka, Koucký, Malorážka*) prefix. Brno realized the commercial potential of the ZKM451. After the war, it introduced a civilian version known as the Brno Model 1.

The company also identified an opportunity in the

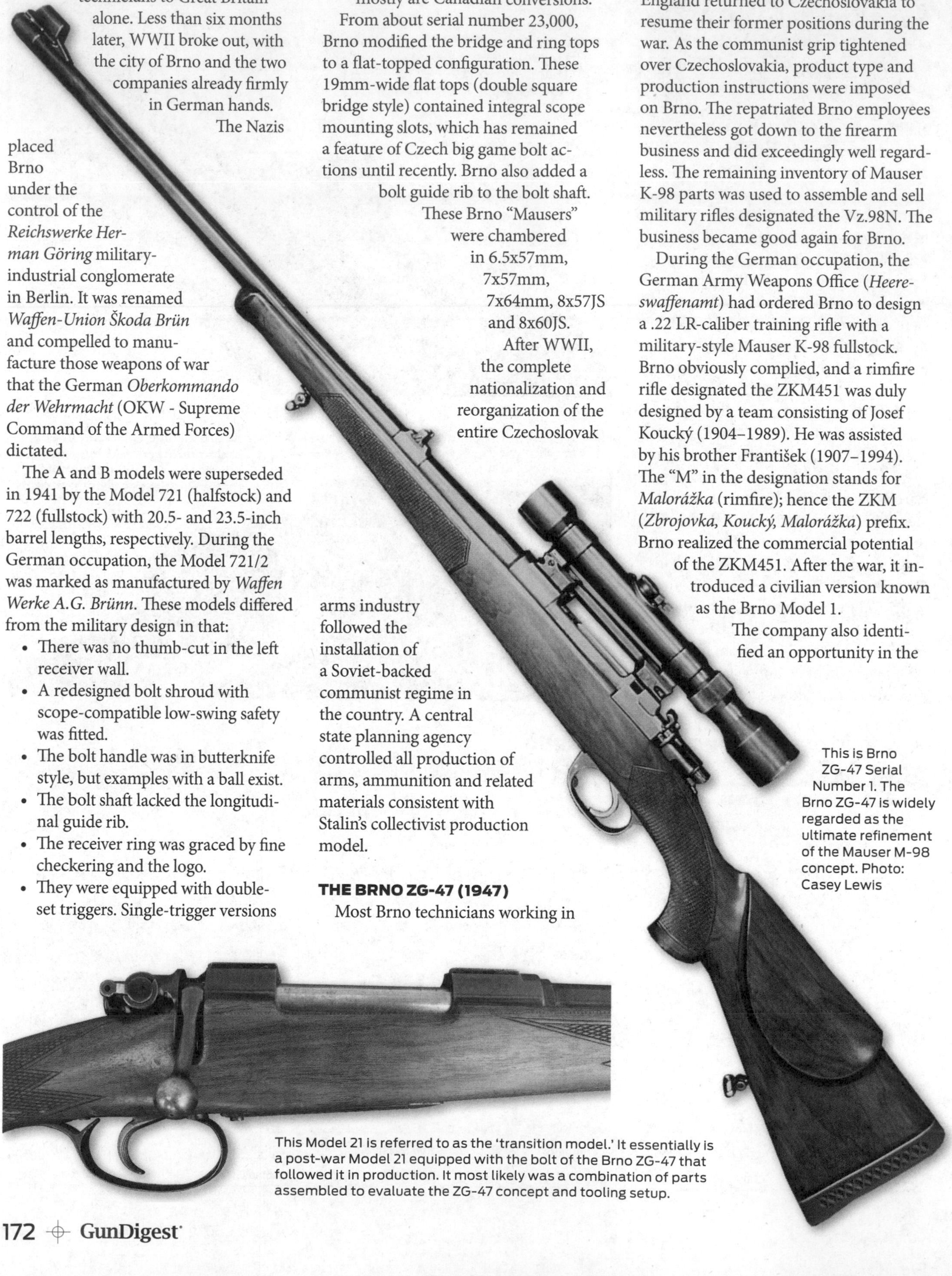

This is Brno ZG-47 Serial Number 1. The Brno ZG-47 is widely regarded as the ultimate refinement of the Mauser M-98 concept. Photo: Casey Lewis

This Model 21 is referred to as the 'transition model.' It essentially is a post-war Model 21 equipped with the bolt of the Brno ZG-47 that followed it in production. It most likely was a combination of parts assembled to evaluate the ZG-47 concept and tooling setup.

Brno factory publication cover-dated 1958. The man holding the rifle is Otakar Galas, to whom the Brno ZG-47 design is attributed. Photos: Arthur Nutbey

Otakar Galas is in his prime on the left.

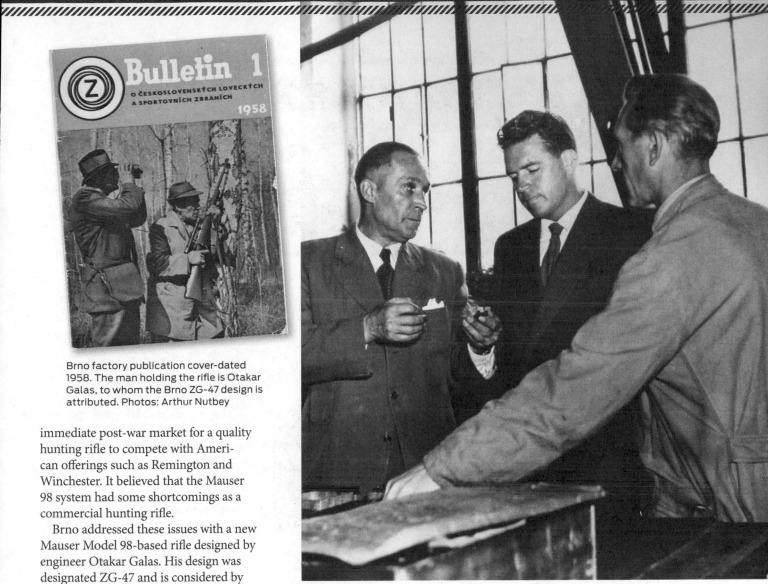

immediate post-war market for a quality hunting rifle to compete with American offerings such as Remington and Winchester. It believed that the Mauser 98 system had some shortcomings as a commercial hunting rifle.

Brno addressed these issues with a new Mauser Model 98-based rifle designed by engineer Otakar Galas. His design was designated ZG-47 and is considered by many to be the utmost refinement of the

This Model 21 is referred to as the 'transition model.' It essentially is a post-war Model 21 equipped with the bolt of the Brno ZG-47 that followed it in production. It most likely was a combination of parts assembled to evaluate the ZG-47 concept and tooling setup.

A Brno ZG-47 showing the detail of a factory-fitted riflescope and the bridge-style bases used at the time. Photo: Gary Przbilla.

Cutaway showing aspects of the Brno ZG-47 trigger mechanism. The ZG-47 has one of the most conveniently shaped triggers ever produced. However, the design had one drawback: it was held in place by a cross-pin at the front but no attachment system at the rear. The trigger rear was simply pinched between the receiver tang and the stock. The sear engagement was dependent on stock integrity. Photo: Adam Kostrunek.

Mauser M-98. Very little is known about most Czechoslovakians who worked in the arms industry at the time. Otakar Galas is sometimes also identified as Otakara (Otogara) Galaše. He was born in 1904 in Syrovice and graduated from the State Technical University in 1927 as an engineer, after which he began working at Brno. He oversaw the modifications that turned the Vz.24 into the Brno Model 721/M22 sporters. Galas also was one of the Brno technicians temporarily evacuated to England for the duration of WWII.

The Czech government interfered just as the ZG-47 was poised to storm the market. In 1950, Joseph Stalin gave a direct order to Czechoslovakia to prepare for the invasion of Europe. The then Czech Minister of Defence, Alexei Čepička, immediately suspended sporting arms production, which disrupted ZG-47 manufacturing until 1955.

The ZG-47 was an evolution of the Model 721/2 series but essentially remained a Mauser M-98. It had the double square bridge receiver tops of the late models 721/2, a brand-new so-called 'Blitz' (lightning) override trigger design and a completely reconfigured bolt sleeve and safety catch. The barrel was given a smooth contour rather than the preceding models' stepped military-type configuration. The magazine box and trigger were changed from the one-piece M-98 design and replaced by a heavy sheet metal box that could be changed for different cartridges.

Obviously, BRNO fitted sporting stocks to the ZG-47. These came in two styles, namely the standard and the deluxe, the latter offered in three formats. The additional two optional styles were variations on the deluxe formats.

- Standard. A classic-style stock with a Schnabel forend and no check piece. The buttplate was made of an artificial horn, and the grip lacked a cap. Checkering was not standard on this version.
- Deluxe A. The deluxe models were sold with riflescopes fitted and sported butts with Monte Carlo combs and pancake-style cheekpieces that curved into the comb nose. The A format had a rounded contrasting black forend tip and grip cap.
- Deluxe B. Same as the A version, but it had a Schnabel forend without tip.
- Deluxe C. The C models had a classic stock with an egg-shaped cheekpiece and Schnabel forend.
- Fullstock. A full-length forend was added to any one of the deluxe formats.
- Super Deluxe. Semi-custom rifles where the customer had considerable input: including initials inlaid in gold. High-grade wood, engraving and carvings could be in the factory or personal style.

All the above ex-factory stock options were brochure-listed in three versions that related to barrel configuration, namely heavy or light barrel:

- The Basic version had a medium-heavy forend and barrel channel for the heavy barrel.
- The Relieved version was intended for identical barrels but had a more streamlined forend.
- The Light version was intended for the light barrel configuration with a forend comparable to the Relieved version.

Basic specifications, chamberings and production details of the ZG-47 are contained in the enclosed table. The ZG-47 could also be had on special order in 10.75x68 and 5.6x61 Vom Hofe or any other rimless cartridge whose overall length did not exceed 3.33 inches (85mm). A friend owns a ZG-47 chambered for the 8x68mmS. It was specially made for the Polish ambassador to South Africa, and I've seen a 6.5x57 advertised once.

CZ-UB (1946–1950)

From 1946 to 1950, the nationalized CZ-UB still operated as a satellite of CZ Strakonice and primarily manufactured machine guns. From 1946 to 1992, CZ-UB was reorganized or restructured no less than six times to conform with the CSSR economic plan! During its 1950 restructuring, CZ-UB finally became a fully independent concern reporting to a central administrative unit. However, it remained a military-orientated production facility still of no importance to civilian bolt-action rifle users.

BRNO: END OF AN ERA (1950–1965)

When the production of the ZG-47 recommenced in 1950, the international market had changed. Germany and Scandinavian rifle producers had entered the fray. Many new cartridges from as small as the .222 Remington to as big as thc .416 Rigby configured outside the standard Mauser M-98 dimensional parameters entered the scene. The Mauser M-98 Brno ZG-47 could not cover this cartridge spectrum. Brno had missed the boat, and a new bolt-action hunting rifle was required. ZG-47 production was terminated in 1958. The final assembly from spares in stock ended in 1963 after production of about 22,647 units.

Otokar Galas had by then retired and, in 1960, the task to design a replacement for the ZG-47 fell on Brno's brilliant brothers Koucký. They completed the design in 1963. Only one prototype of their design was manufactured at Brno. This new rifle was the first original Czech, from-the-ground-up, big game, bolt-action sporter to have seen the light of day.

BRNO DESIGNS PRODUCED BY CZ-UB

	ZKK600	ZKK601	ZKK602
Introduced	1966	1966-68	1967-77
Terminated	1997	1970-96	79-80/82-99
Produced	112,252	64,203	26,662
Chamberings	.270 Win.	.222 Rem.	7mm Rem. Mag.
	7x57	.222 Rem. Mag.	.300 Win. Mag.
	7x64	.243 Win.	.358 Norma Mag.
	.30-06	.308 Win.	.375 H&H
	8x57S		.458 Win. Mag.
	8x64S		
	9.3x62		
	10.75x68		
Magazine	4 & 5	5 & 6	5
Barrel length (in.)	23.6	23.6	25.4
Av. Weight (lb.)	7.16	6.83	9.26
Stock Styles	3	3	3
Overall Length (in.)	43.3	43.1	45.3
Designer	F & J Koucký	F & J Koucký	F & J Koucký
Receiver Top	Flat	Flat	Flat
Size	Large Ring	Large Ring	Large Ring

Photo showing details of the highly complex Brno ZG-47 bolt shroud and safety assembly. The safety is convenient, except that it requires more force than is usually associated with safety catches.

Although CZ-UB and Brno were physically different manufacturing facilities, each was a part of the National Enterprise. A decline in demand for civilian firearms resulted from virtually all Brno arms production being moved to CZ-UB (named *Přesné strojírenství* at the time) from 1963 on. By 1965, the transfer process had been completed. This included the production of the Koucký design. Firearm production at Brno was turned into a secondary activity. It only continued to produce shotguns and combination shotgun/rifles, but its focus changed to manufacturing Zetor tractors and diesel engines, Zeta typewriters and office equipment.

The central planners realized Brno still had greater name recognition outside Czechoslovakia than any Czech firearm brand. Therefore, the Ministry of Foreign Trade and the Czechoslovak Proof Authority decided that all firearms exported from Czechoslovakia would bear Brno markings, regardless of the actual manufacturing concern.

CZ-UB RESTRUCTURED YET AGAIN (1950–1965)

The most significant development after CZ-UB's 1950 restructuring was the closing of the Strakonice and Prague firearm manufacturing plants in 1954. In 1958, all Czechoslovak industries were restructured into VHJs (Productive Economic Units), part of a single umbrella company reporting to the relevant Ministry. The government also decided to allocate handgun production at CZ-UB.

BRNO COMPANY HISTORY (1966–2020)

Too many things have been left in the air about the Czech sporting arms industry. So, let us for once wrap that company's history up.

After the Velvet Revolution, Brno fell into difficult times because the owners were not prepared to invest in keeping it competitive. It was also the subject of massive financial crime by role players such as the infamous judge, Jiri Berka, who was sentenced to eight years and six months imprisonment in 2018 for his part in the scheme. Brno was placed under curatorship or administration and traded until it was finally liquidated in 2006. Before liquidation, Brno's massive collection of rival firearm designs and Brno prototypes had disappeared and remain missing to this day.

The Brno logo and trademark were purchased at auction by CZ-UB on November 6, 2007 — a sad day in the history of a once-illustrious company. CZ-UB registered a new company called Brno Rifles (since renamed *Zbrojovka Brno*), which only produces shotguns and top-break rifles.

CZ-UB: A NEW ERA (1966–2020)

The 1965 transfer of ZKK production from Brno to CZ-UB was just one of several positive changes for the company.

The first and very important was that it became part of the National Enterprise when Brno was made a tractor manufacturer and ZKK production moved to CZ-UB. Since CZ-UB had traditionally dominated the military market and Brno the European civilian market, CZ-UB had no practical experience in the civilian export market and the range of competing foreign products. That explains the Brno brand being used for CZ-UB product exports. Closer affiliation with Brno opened many doors for CZ-UB and led to CZ-UB staff accompanying Brno staff on several business trips to Western Europe in the late 1960s. That presented excellent insights to CZ-UB staff and proved a great learning curve.

ZKK600 MASTERPIECE (1966–1996)

CZ-UB's production of the new Koucký-designed Brno bolt-action rifle commenced in 1966. It was designated the ZKK600 series. As an aside, Brno had used a model designation system of the 'Z' followed by the first letter of the designer's surname plus the year the project

The classic-stocked no-frills standard version of the ZKK600 series of hunting rifles.

The Brno ZKK retained most of the receiver features of its ZG-47 predecessor. Early models contained a pop-up ghost ring sight recessed in the bridge, but this was later omitted. The bolt sleeve and safety were changed with the safety moved to the tang. The safety operates in reverse when compared to the Remington M-700.

commenced; hence designations like the ZG-47. That was deviated from slightly with the rimfire ZKM451 model when the '1' was added to represent the first version/model. When the second model was introduced nine years later (1954), it became the ZKM452 as version two of the 1945 project.

The ZKK model designation does not fully conform to Brno or CZ-UB model designation systems. **The 'Z' obviously stood for** *Zbrojovka*. The first 'K' represents Koucký, and the second stands for *Kulovnice* (centrefire) and not for the second Koucký brother, as has often been incorrectly stated in print. However, the '60' clearly refers to the year the project was launched (1960). The second '0' cannot refer to the Brno method of model designation as the first version would need '1' as a designation. I speculate that this methodology change is probably a consequence of production at CZ-UB and relates to the action length rather than the version, especially since version designations were not changed when the pop-up peep sight was later scrapped (~1978). The ZKK came in three action lengths:

- ZKK600 – for cartridges measuring between 75-85mm in length, such as the .30-06 Springfield.
- ZKK601 – for cartridges shorter than 72mm, such as the .308 Winchester.
- ZKK602 – for all belted cartridges up to 95mm length, such as the .375 H&H Magnum.

ZKK Rifle Series

If you are the type of hunter who prefers the accuracy and dependability of a bolt action rifle, then this is the firearm you should be shooting.

Where you usually pay a small fortune for optional features on other makes of guns these same options are often standard on the ZKK. Standard features include:

1) Front and rear sights
2) Pop-up peep sight
3) Supplied with 2 triggers
   a) simple single stage grooved trigger
   b) set trigger with stretcher
4) Mounted sling swivels and many others (see specs)

The ZKK rifle series is available in eight popular calibres from .243 Win. to .458 Win. Magnum.

The different stock style options of the Brno ZKK series. Not included in this brochure is the Schnabel forend version. Photo: Alf Smith

There was more to the ZKK series than having been the original Czech bolt-action sporter. Its production was technologically advanced; the receiver and the bolt were forgings. That preceded Bill Ruger's investment casting of hunting rifle actions in the USA by two years. It is testimony to the innovation and leadership of Czech arms design that stretches back over a century — even despite communist handicapping, which was an uneasy yoke to wear for many Czechs. The ZKK600 series and the CZ 75 pistol, the latter of which was then also produced at CZ-UB, ensuring the company's 18 years of unprecedented success.

The ZKKs had the following features:

- Three action lengths for cartridges from .222 Rem. to the .458 Lott. It could be modified to handle the massive .416 Rigby and .460 Weatherby Mag cartridges.
- Flat-topped receiver with integral scope rails.
- Custom-level features include barrel-banded front and rear sight units, adjustable fold-down rear sight blades and two trigger options.
- Cartridge-specific heavy sheet metal magazine box.
- Dovetailed anti-bind cocking piece channel in tang with matching cocking piece tail profile.
- Unique bridge-mounted pop-up ghost ring.
- Controlled feeding.
- Minimized lock-time.
- All screws were of standard dimen-

The front sight assembly of the Brno ZKK was essentially a continuation of the Brno ZG-47 front sight assembly with the bead in an axial slot and retained by a spring-loaded plunger. As with the earlier ZG-47 and later CZ550 series rifles, it included a barrel band. Photos: Riflechair

The brilliant brothers Koucký were the primary designers of the Brno ZKK series. They began their careers at Brno and ended them at CZ. Their influence is visible in numerous Brno and CZ designs. Photo: Brno

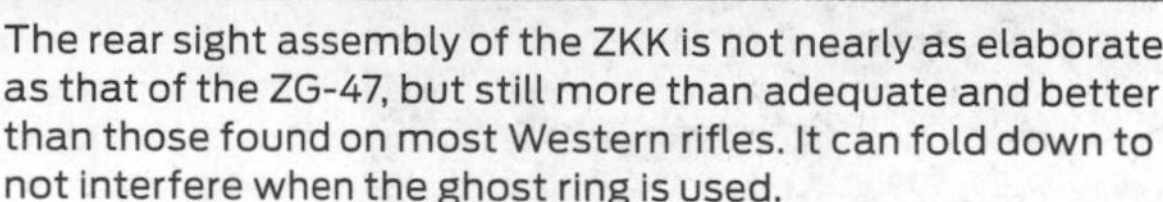

The rear sight assembly of the ZKK is not nearly as elaborate as that of the ZG-47, but still more than adequate and better than those found on most Western rifles. It can fold down to not interfere when the ghost ring is used.

Left-hand detail of a CZ537 rifle. Note bolt sleeve design clearly paved the way for what later became the CZ550 bolt sleeve after further development.

sions and thread.

- There are three stock styles; Weatherby-style Monte Carlo, English Classic, and Euro Classic with Schnabel.

There was no other bolt-action sporter on the market with all these features, and the ZKK was priced lower than Mausers, Winchesters and Remingtons. Not to even mention Steyrs, Sauers and British rifles.

Many top-class gunsmiths over the decades have named the ZKK the closest-to-perfect bolt-action design to work on. The ZKK was not without fault, though. The main criticisms have been:

- The action exterior had a sandblasted appearance.
- The side-mounted tang safety function was noisy and reversed function to that of the Remington M-700.
- The sheet metal magazine box suffered criticism from hunters used to the machined steel boxes in its early years. The ZKK approach has, however, been well-vindicated since.
- The bolt shroud did not block the raceways against escaping gasses in the event of ruptured cases.
- Units produced in the aftermath of the 1968 Warsaw Pact invasion of Czechoslovakia were particularly poorly finished. Of course, the offensive tool marks could be removed with some tender loving care, but that rightfully was not something Western (mainly American) buyers appreciated.

The inferior surface finish on ZKKs reflects on the manufacture and not the design, and the other criticisms are consequences of preferences rather than any flaw. The ZKK has stood the test of time as one of the top bolt-action sporter designs. It is incredibly robust and reliable, yet elegant. It is Africa-proof, and that says a lot!

During the 1980s, ZKK series tooling had become increasingly tired. CZ-UB had to decide on a course of action. The Velvet Revolution had finally resulted in the scrapping of the centralized collective trust management system, but this had little effect on the company's day-to-day operations. As the communist system and Agrozet collapsed, CZ-UB regained some of its independence. This offered dramatic opportunities for marketing, export and modernization, and, as the preeminent arms manufacturer in the country, CZ-UB prepared for this by commencing experimentation with new

The most significant aspect of this photo of a CZ537 is the inverted T shape of the cocking piece. It is an anti-binding and stabilizing feature found on several Brno and CZ hunting rifle designs.

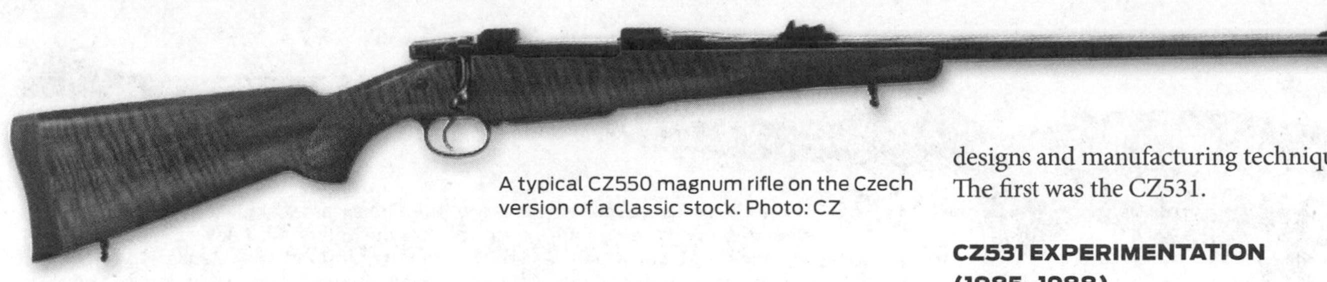

A typical CZ550 magnum rifle on the Czech version of a classic stock. Photo: CZ

The oversized bolt sleeve introduced on the CZ550 was not the most elegant. Still, the CZ550 has proven itself on the Dark Continent, though it is not as revered as the Brno ZKK600 series. The magnum version of the action permitted the building of dangerous game rifles chambered for cartridges popular for African dangerous game hunting — thereby contributing to its popularity.

A CZ550 bolt sleeve shows one of the modifications to the CZ537 bolt sleeve.

CZ equipped its CZ550 magnums with an express-type three-leaf sight calibrated for 100, 200 and 300 yards mounted on a saddle integral to the barrel. It is a very sturdy design.

designs and manufacturing techniques. The first was the CZ531.

CZ531 EXPERIMENTATION (1985–1988)

CZ-UB's initial deviation from the proven ZKK controlled-feed design was the CZ531. The first prototypes of this rifle, apparently designed by engineer J. Pitner, were completed in 1985. By 1988, precisely 766 model CZ531 rifles had been manufactured, but no serial production of the CZ531 ever occurred. The CZ531 was a round-top design, drilled and tapped for riflescope installation with Monte Carlo and Bavaria stock styles that contained a fixed, integral magazine. It employed a push-feed bolt with a plunger ejector recessed in the bolt face. The CZ531 also sported a shotgun-style tang-mounted safety. The bolt sleeve was bulky and plain ugly, and it was only available with a double-set trigger system. No chamberings other than .308 Winchester and .30-06 Springfield have surfaced.

CZ537 TRANSITION (1989–1995)

CZ-UB also began using CNC manufacturing on bolt-action rifles. Growing sophistication in marketing, coupled with frustrations with earlier importers, led to CZ-UB establishing an international holding company (CZ-USA) in 1991 as its importer and distributor in the United States. The CZ531 was soon (1989) replaced by another Pitner design, the CZ537.

The CZ537, CZ-UB's first CNC-dominant sporting rifle, visually reverted to several proven and appreciated ZKK features. It once again employed a flat-top, integral telescope dovetail system. The bolt reverted to the controlled feed with an external extractor design, but the bolt sleeve was new; it was a more streamlined version of the CZ531 design but still bulky. The safety catch was once again positioned on the right side of the receiver tang, but unlike the ZKK's, its directional operation duplicated the Remington M-700's. The new trigger also reverted to the single

The new CZ600 is a modern design without an external Mauser-style extractor. The extractor and ejector are integrated into the bolt head. It nevertheless remains a controlled feed rather than a push-feed design. The cost of manufacturing Mauser-style external extractor designs has become exorbitant. Although African hunters cling to its benefits, they represent too small a market for major manufacturers to continue producing. Photo: CZ

set-trigger system reminiscent of the ZKK. The rifle could be had in removable or fixed magazine options. Barrels were initially made by combining a push-and-pull button system but later changed to cold hammer forging.

The unpopular CZ537 was short-lived, with only 15,000 rifles manufactured. Production terminated in 1995 with the introduction of the CZ550 design, and surplus part assembly ended in 1999.

CZ550 MODERNIZATION (1995–2020)

In the early 1990s, CZ-UB gradually moved away from the intricate and expensive Mauser M-98 design for cost and production reasons. It instructed its designer, Vítěslav Guryča, to commence working on modular, push-feed, multiple rear-lug designs. He completed what is known as the CZ538/CZ700 by 1995, but CZ-UB then went through financial hardship and could not afford to invest in the tooling needed for the project. That saved the external extractor concept, and it introduced a redesigned ZKK as the CZ550 in 1995.

The CZ550 not only became the CZ flagship but also its most successful centerfire hunting rifle design to date. The CZ550 and CZ550 Magnum rifles were produced in the widest variety of chamberings from the .22-250 Remington to the massive .500 Jeffery. By 2010, 178,000 of these rifles had already been produced. I have been unable to obtain exact production numbers, but from 1995 to 2020, when production was terminated, more than 300,000 must have been produced.

The CZ550 followed the external features of the CZ537 with a flat-top dovetailed receiver, the basic but aesthetically improved bolt shroud on a Mauser-style bolt, with dual opposed locking lugs at the front. The bolt face rim is opened at the bottom for controlled feed in conjunction with the external claw extractor and Winchester pre' 64-style static ejector in the receiver bridge. It also employs a redesigned, fully adjustable single-set trigger. The safety remained on the right side of the tang, and both two- and three-position versions exist.

Pushing the safety forward disengages both versions. The integral sheet metal box magazine is the most common version, but some models were available with removable mags. Literally, dozens of barrel and stock options were offered over its quarter-century in production, but this model's tooling was becoming fatigued and outdated. Termination of production was the only economically sound option. And so, the era of the external extractor, static ejector, controlled-feed CZ550 with its reputation as a totally reliable, indestructible, affordable workhorse, second only to the ZKK, ended in 2020.

CZ-UB THE COMPANY SINCE

Production carried on at CZ-UB during the production of the CZ550, but the company and its rifles continued to evolve. It foresaw the eventual demise of the CZ550, realizing that the era of affordable bolt-action rifle designs requiring considerable manual input was quickly becoming impossible in the competitive modern market. The first evolutionary step was the introduction of the CZ555.

CZ555 PREPARING FOR THE INEVITABLE (2004–2012)

Following its 1990s design philosophy and in anticipation of the eventual demise of the CZ550, CZ-UB introduced the CZ555 in 2004. The primary differences between the two designs were that the latter was equipped with a push-feed bolt that housed an integral extractor and plunger ejector in the fully rimmed bolt face; it also sported a removable 3-shot magazine and was offered in a limited range of chamberings. The CZ555 could not fairly compete with the flagship CZ550 at the top end, but neither was it sufficiently evolved to compete with budget-priced push-feed alternatives from the U.S. and Western Europe from a production perspective. The CZ555 soon faltered, but CZ-UB had learned much about market trends and consumer preferences.

The American hunting rifle market is the preeminent global market, and CZ-UB had to position itself accordingly. In 1998, CZ-USA, initially located in Oakhurst, California, was moved to its current location in Kansas City, Kansas. By focusing on North America, the company established a solid footprint and has turned the U.S. into the primary customer for CZ-UB products.

In 2005, it acquired Dan Wesson Firearms via CZ-USA. Dan Wesson originated as a revolver company in 1968, founded by the great-grandson of the famous Daniel B. Wesson. Still, Dan Wesson Firearms soon became one of the most recognized manufacturers of modern 1911 pistol clones under Czech-American leadership.

CZ-UB positioned itself for a drastic change in 2006 with the appointment of Lubomír Kovařík as the new CEO and Ladislav Britaňák as sales director. The new management immediately engaged in extensive modernization and "from-ground-up-development" of new weapon designs. These included assault rifles, submachine guns and grenade launchers. Success followed, and, in 2011, it received the contract to re-arm the Czech

Republic military. That gave CZ-UB a massive injection, and it could accelerate its product renovation process.

CZ557 AFFORDABLE OPTION (2012–2020)

The CZ555 obviously was a quality stopgap measure, and CZ-UB used it to obtain consumer feedback. This feedback enabled the company to plot its sporting arms portfolio direction and, in 2009, the design specifications for a replacement of the CZ555. These developments sounded the death knell for designs that still required extensive manual operations. And they necessitated the introduction of cost-effective, CNC-friendly designs.

The company employed an experienced young gunsmith, Víťa Sedlák, in 2007. Sedlák already had a decade of high-performance gunsmithing experience and had fine-tuned the rifles of the successful Czech-Moravian Hunting Union shooting team. He was also tasked to design the CZ557, the rifle to replace the CZ555. Sedlák turned out a thoroughly modern and accurate design in the budget rifle market sector and quickly achieved excellent market acceptance.

GLOBAL RESTRUCTURING (2018)

CZ was restructured in 2018 into an international holding company known as the CZ Group (CZG), with CZ-UB, *Zbrojovka Brno* (ZB), CZ-USA and Dan Wesson as subsidiaries. CZG also owned tactical equipment manufacturing companies and purchased the Colt Holding Company, LLC with its subsidiaries for U.S. $220 million in 2021. In 2020, CZ-UB employed 1,450 workers and manufactured 1,577 firearms per day, while CZ Group revenue for 2020 amounted to U.S. $310,000,000.

CZ600 NEW DIRECTION

In November 2021, CZG announced that a new bolt action, the CZ600, would replace all its existing big game bolt-action designs. It was both a sad and exciting moment. Sadly, CZ-UB will never again produce a "traditional" bolt-action sporter, but it's exciting that it has finally embraced everything that technology offers the hunter. The CZ600 story must, however, wait for another day. GD

MODELS DESIGNED AND PRODUCED BY CZ-UB

	CZ531	CZ537	CZ550	CZ550M	CZ550SC	CZ555	CZ557
Introduced	1985	1989	1995			2004	2012
Terminated	1988	1995	2020	2020	2020	2012	2020
Produced	766	15,000					
Chamberings	.308 Win.	.243 Win.	.22-250	.375 H&H	.270 Win.	7x64	.243 Win.
	.30-06	6.5x55	.243 Win.	.416 Rigby	.30-06	.308 Win.	6.5x55
		.270 Win.	6.5x55	.458 Win. Mag.	.300 H&H	.30-06	.270 Win.
	.243 Win	7x57	.270 Win	.458 Lott	.300 RUM		7x64
	.270 Win	7x64	7x57		.338 Win. Mag.		.308 Win.
	7x64	.308 Win.	7x64		.338 Lapua		.30-06
	8x57S	.30-06	7mm Rem. Mag.		9.3x62		8x57JS
	8x60S		.308 Win.		.375 Ruger		
	8x64S		.30-06		.416 Taylor		
	8x68S		.300 Win. Mag.		.416 Ruger		
			8x57S		.416 Rem. Mag.		
			8x68S		.416 Rigby		
			.338 Win. Mag.		.404 Jeffery		
			9.3x62		.458 Lott		
					.450 Rigby		
					.505 Gibbs		
					.500 Jef		
Magazine	4 & 5	4 & 5	3, 4 & 5	3 & 5	3, 4 & 5	3	
Barrel length (in.)	23.6	18.1	23.6	25	20-24	23.6	20.5
Av. Weight (lb.)	7.28	7.28	7.3	9.3	9.3	7.28	6.8
Stock Styles	1	2	10+	4	Custom	Halfstock	Halfstock
Overall Length (in.)	44.5	44.7	44.7	46	42.5-46.5	4.7	41-42.1
Designer	J Pitner*	J Pitner*					Víťa Sedlák
Receiver Top	Round	Flat	Flat	Flat	Flat	Flat	Flat
Size	Large Ring	Large Ring	Large Ring	Large Ring	Large Ring	Large Ring	Large Ring

A Potpourri of Varmint Wildcats

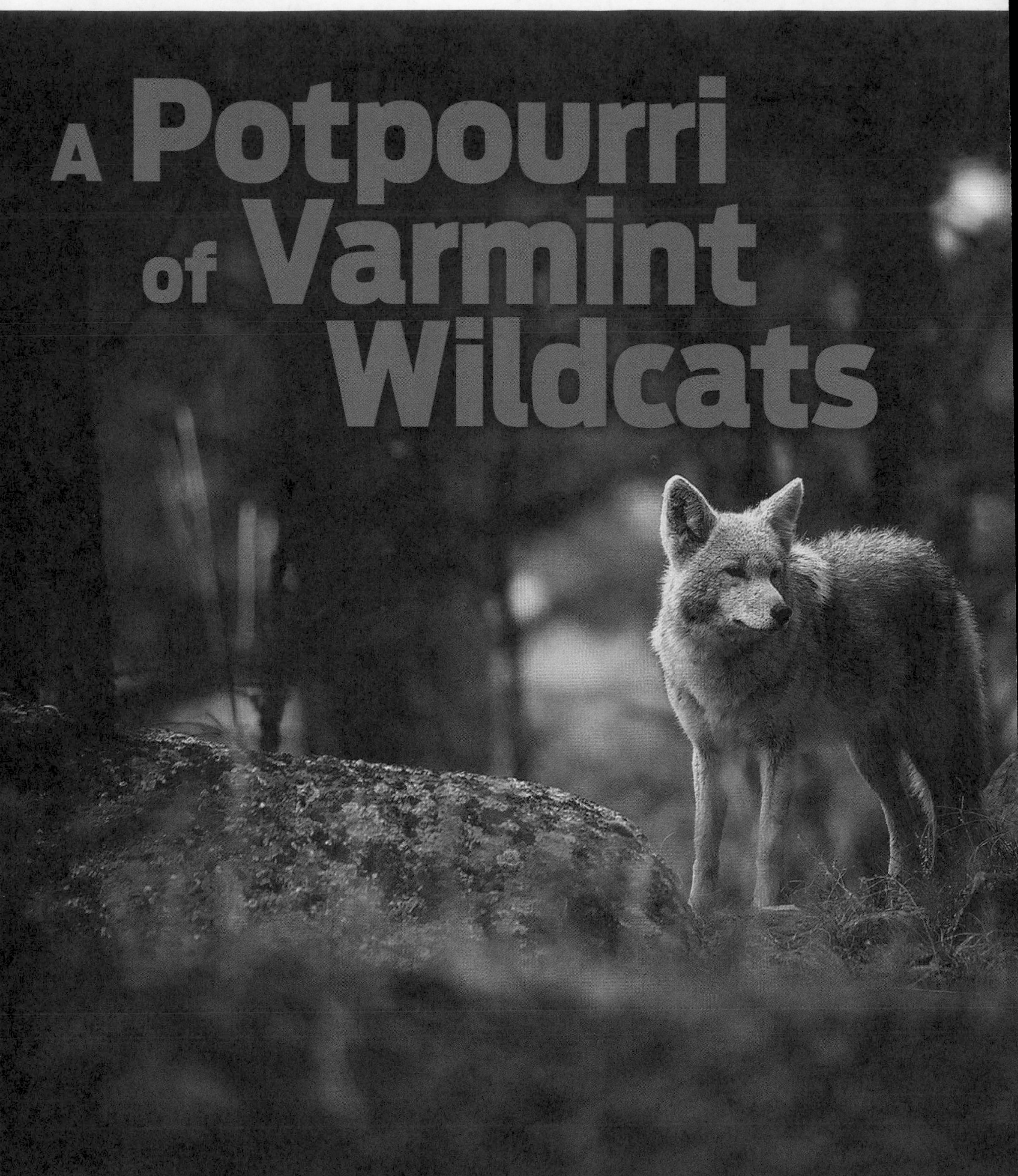

A baker's dozen of the author's favorite improved and wildcat cartridges.

› STAN TRZONIEC

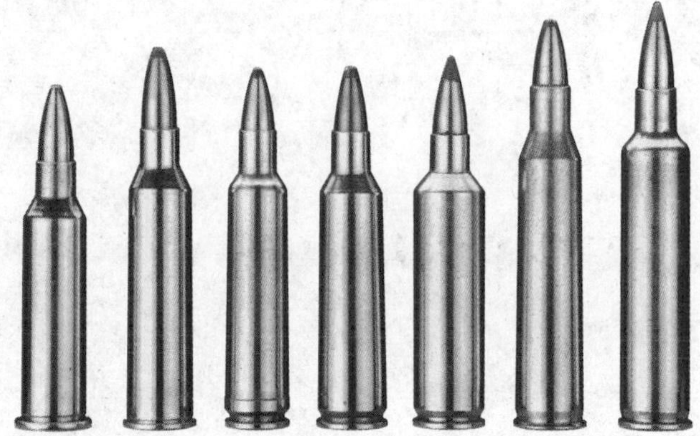

Popular .22-caliber varmint cartridges the author has used in addition to his work with the wildcats. Shown left to right include such notables as the .219 Donaldson Wasp, .225 Winchester, .224 Weatherby Magnum, .22/250 Remington, .22/250 Remington Ackley Improved, .220 Swift and the .220 Weatherby Rocket.

Occasionally, I like to take a rifle I had not used for a while to the range to renew old acquaintances with both it and the cartridge. While that's not a big deal, this time, I had some looks from the shooter beside me as the thumbhole-stocked Thompson Center rifle caught his attention. One thing led to another, and when he asked what the gun was chambered for, I replied the .22 K-Hornet, a wildcat of some significance in the shooting world.

Looking down at me on the bench, then the gun, and picking up a cartridge from my loading block, he casually asked, "why bother?" as he tempted my knowledge by saying that the good ol' .22 Hornet would do just fine. Maybe yes, maybe no, but pushing the conversation, he told me he never wanted to get into wildcatting cartridges. As I explained to him that it was one of the easier wildcats I had worked with, I could see the wheels turning as he mulled it over; I may have had a convert to trying his hand at wildcatting.

Custom rifle from E. R. Shaw chambered in the .22/6mm TTH.

I've worked with and shot over two dozen wildcats, most of which circled the .22 caliber and below. While I have worked with others, being a small game and 'chuck hunter, the .17 or .22 calibers suited me perfectly. Converting to this caliber was easy, less expensive than fooling with necking down heavy-duty rifle cartridges or rifles — and furthermore, it was fun. Now add in some researching time, finding a gunsmith who would take on a project with a new rifle, and there you have it!

Even in this age of high-tech cartridges, wildcats still have a niche in our sport. Granted, you're only looking at a 10 to 15 percent velocity and energy gain from an 8 to 10 percent powder increase. That's not much, you say, but looking at our .22 K-Hornet and dealing with the case and its internal volume, which goes from 2,545 fps (with Remington factory 45-grain ammunition) to 2,932 fps with a Speer 45-grain spitzer over 11.5 grains of Alliant 2400 powder is enough to make this shooter happy.

How can you begin wildcatting? If you go with cartridges like the .22 PPC or .22 Remington BR, the brass is out there, and little effort is needed to go from loading at the bench to final sighting in and field shooting. On the other hand, .22 K-Hornet, .223 Ackley Improved, or .220 Weatherby Rocket brass is fireformed by shooting .22 Hornet, .223 Remington or .220 Swift ammo, respectively, in the improved or wildcat-chambered rifle. For those who like to work the brass through various steps in sizing or trim dies to get the finished product (read .219 Donaldson Wasp), various companies such as RCBS or Redding are there to help. Nothing changes in bullets, primers or powders, with up-to-date loading manuals, online information or past literature to take you to the shooting range in no time.

Naturally, there are (with a few exceptions) many rifles chambered off the shelf for wildcat cartridges. The few would include the .22 PPC, where Sako and Ruger had it listed in their catalogs or the .17 Mach IV and .218 Mashburn Bee, which were staples from Cooper Arms for a long time in various models. Other than that, E.R. Shaw has helped me with the .20 VarTarg, .22 Remington BR and .22 Texas Trophy Hunter (TTH) by re-chambering a few of my lesser-used rifles to accommodate these wildcats, starting them on a new life.

At one time, when Thompson Center was still going full bore in New Hampshire before the buyout, it had a list of over three-dozen standard, magnum and wildcat cartridges that fit handily into its single-shot pistols. While T/C no longer has a Custom Shop, you still can find barrels at gun shows. Additionally, checking on the web, at shows or from other enthusiasts, custom rifle makers will help with your requests, and that is how I had a Ruger No. 1 single-shot rifle chambered for the .219 Donaldson Wasp — one of my all-time favorite cartridges.

To help you along the wildcat path, I've detailed a baker's dozen of both .17- and .22-caliber wildcats. Some are what I call "easy": all you do is fireform them in a rifle chamber, neck size, load and off you go. Others are born from factory brass, while some require time to get right. Naturally, you can design your own wildcat, but be warned when fooling around with the unknowns of case capacity, having dies custom made, working with a Powley Computer or software and dealing with sometimes hidden ballistics.

For the record, all groups were three shots at 100 yards.

.17 MACH IV

While most of our wildcats are formed in the rifle chamber, the .17 Mach IV must go through preliminary steps to prepare it for loading and shooting, with either RCBS or Redding die sets and an extended shellholder. Designed by Vern O' Brian in 1962 and starting with .221 Fireball cases, you run the brass through the first trim die to bring the neck down to .20 caliber. The case goes into another die to reduce it to around .178 inch, then

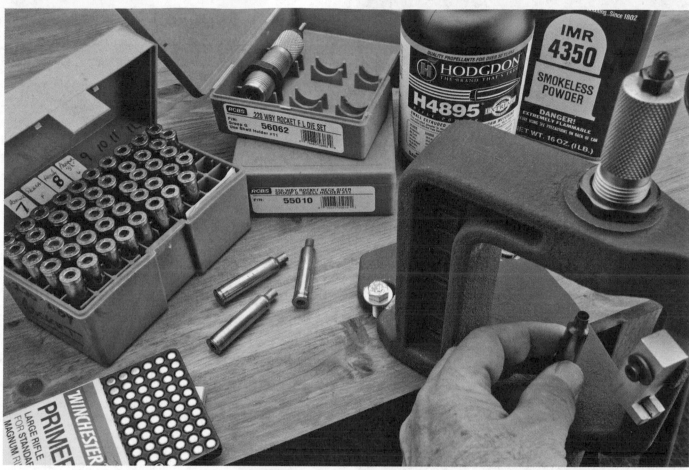

A loading bench set up for the .220 Weatherby Rocket with dies, powder, press, brass, and primers is everything you need to load your favorite varmint wildcat.

full-length sized to clean up the neck and shoulder until the initial loading and fireforming. After that, neck size for subsequent loadings.

In the past, .17-caliber bullets were hard to get and make. Today, there is a wide choice of bullets, including Berger, Hornady, Nosler, and more, to suit your needs. No matter your choice, I found them all accurate and when teamed with a 25-grain bullet and H4198, H322 or AA2520, sub-minute groups were possible without much effort.

The other challenge is the rifle. Years past, Cooper and Kimber had rifles for the .17 Mach IV cartridge but have since discontinued them, though a check on the secondary market shows they are still available. My rifle is the trim Cooper Model 21, complete with high-grade wood, excellent checkering and a Schnabel forend. Checking in around

The transition from the standard .22 Hornet on the left to the "improved" version on the right is easily formed in the rifle chamber, then neck-sized before loading.

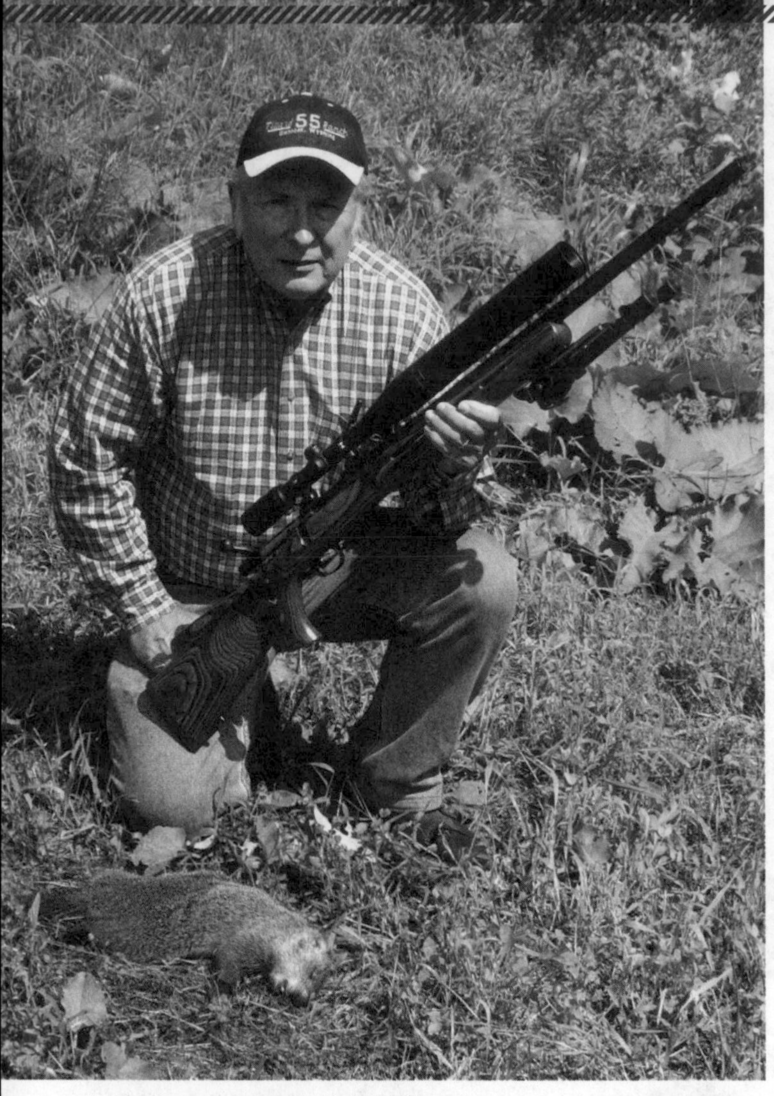

When it came to the .20 VarTarg, Trzoniec went with a Remington XR-100 rifle and a new barrel from Shaws.

The .17 Mach IV is one of those cartridges that might scratch the itch to have something different in your varmint rifle collection. It's accurate, but rifles are hard to find, and the .17 Remington Fireball might be a better choice since the specs are nearly the same and the rifles are in production.

six pounds with a Leupold scope, it's an excellent gun, what many call a walking varminter.

However, the .17 Mach IV has been upstaged by the .17 Remington Fireball. With factory brass available, it's a more convenient way to utilize the assets of the .17 caliber, but don't give up yet on it. If you want braggin' rights at the range, this is the one!

Best Load: Remington cases, Remington 7½ Benchrest-type primers. Hornady 25-grain bullet, 18.5 grains of H322 powder, .500-inch groups, 3,502 fps.

.20 VARTARG

Memory fails on how I was hooked on the .20 VarTarg. I believe it was the Remington XR-100 rifle that first got my attention, then the VarTarg — stands for VARmint/TARGet — as a new addition to my varmint rifle collection. Since the rifle had the same bolt face as the .222 or .223 Remington and the .20 VarTarg was born from the .221 Remington Fireball, a match was made. So, while I was waiting for the die sets from RCBS and Redding to arrive, the rifle went to E.R. Shaw for a barrel (Dakota made a rifle for it if

Trzoniec lists the .218 Mashburn as an "easy" wildcat. With the parent case on the left, the new case on the right shows the difference in added powder capacity by fireforming the case in the rifle chamber.

you wanted one off the shelf) along with a reamer from Dave Manson of Grand Blanc, Michigan to finish the project.

Like the Mach II, the .20 VarTarg takes some time to get from raw brass to the finished project. First, the cases are necked down to .20 caliber and then neck-turned on a Sinclair Neck Turning tool to remove .002 inch from each case to allow a snug fit in the chamber. The turning takes a little practice for first-timers since when you trim a neck, you only want to cut down to the neck/shoulder area and no more. Precision is the byword here.

To keep everything within close limits, I sent a fired case to the RCBS Custom Shop so it could get the neck just right after fireforming. After the range session, the cases grew to about 1.410 inches, but still within the limits of 1.415 inches, then trimmed back to 1.405.

The .20 VarTarg is an easy cartridge to load. I was not disappointed with powders such as VV-N120, H4198, H4198 and H335. All produced groups under that magical minute of angle.

The .20 VarTarg is a true wildcat, and while you must go through a few different stages of preparation, it's a fun round to have.

Best Load: Remington .221 Fireball cases, CCI BR-4 small rifle primers. Hornady 40-grain V-Max bullet, 20.5 grains of H335 powder, .500-inch groups, 3,318 fps.

One of the author's favorites, the .219 Donaldson is accurate and can be chambered in several rifles today (his being the Ruger No. 1). He uses .30-30 Winchester brass, which, once formed, goes a long way without any troubles from stretching or splitting.

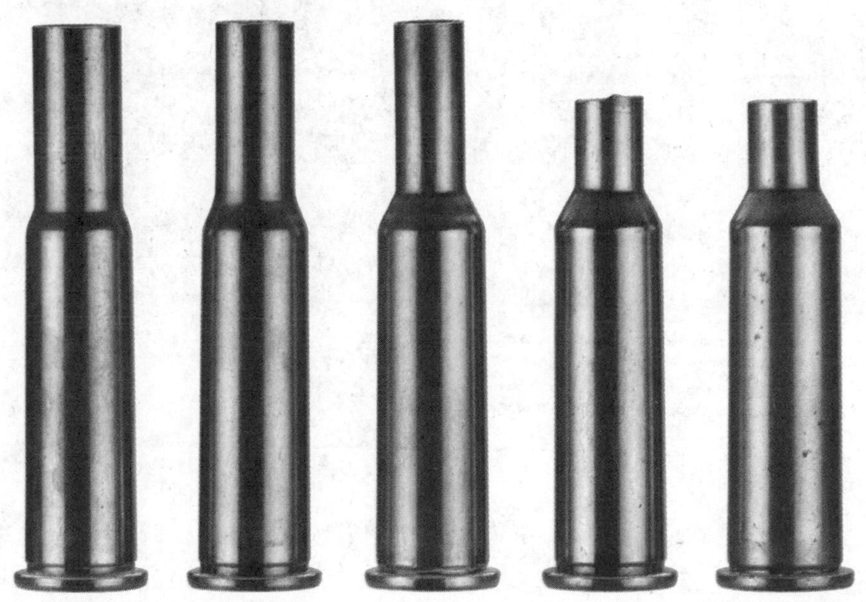
Case forming the .219 Donaldson is a matter of working the brass neck down to .22 caliber, trimming, and it's ready to go.

.218 MASHBURN BEE

Like some of our other varmint cartridge picks, the .218 Mashburn Bee owes its life to its parent, the .218 Bee. It was born during the "golden age" of cartridges in the 1930s. With advancements in powders and rifles, the Mashburn grew from the likes of the Gibson and Ackley Improved, evolving into this more up-to-date version.

To create this wildcat, first have a rifle chambered for the Mashburn cartridge, insert standard .218 Bee ammunition, and *voilà!* you have the improved version with the flick of the trigger. However, I did find that since the cartridge's shoulder is significantly relocated, there's a very slight amount of case splitting due to the stretching in fireforming. Not to fret, however, as I believe that my total was only about 2 percent of the total rounds fired on the first go around.

The gun was another Cooper rifle made on the Model 38 action as the Varminter. The Mashburn is not listed in the Cooper catalog, though there are some for sale online, and since the regular Bee is so easy to convert to the Mashburn version, I don't think you'll have any trouble finding a competent gunsmith to take on the job. Specifications on this rifle include a stock equally at home on the bench or field. It sports an AA-grade stock finely finished to include an oil-type finish and checkered on the pistol grip, and the forearm is flared to a beavertail configuration and equipped with a 26-inch stainless barrel.

Nothing gives me more pleasure than loading and working with a wildcat cartridge like the Mashburn. Powders

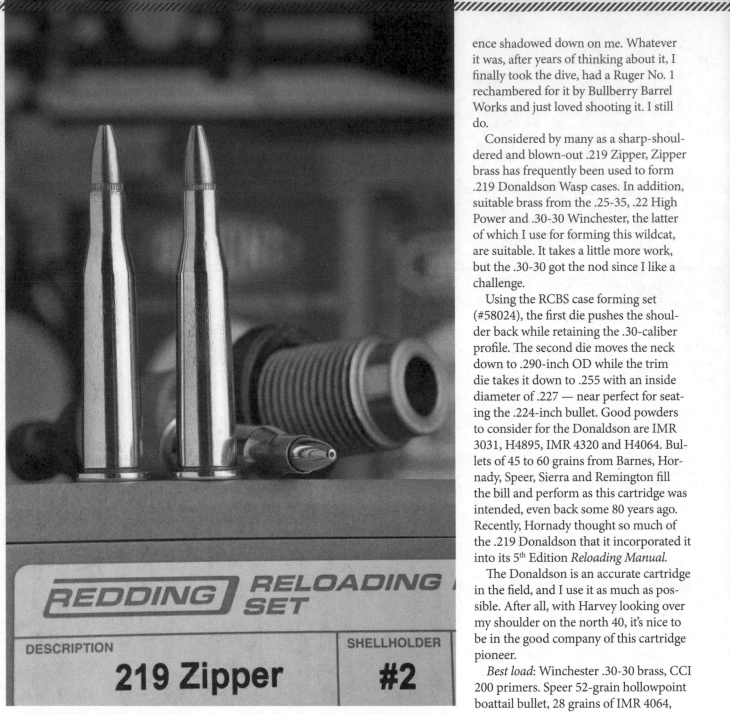

Long a forgotten cartridge, the .219 Zipper can still be loaded using dies from Redding and a barrel (if you can find one) from Thompson/Center.

such as Alliant 2400, H4198 or IMR 4227 make the most of the small case in velocity and accuracy. Dies from the RCBS Custom Shop (special order), Remington brass and bullets from Nosler, plus Winchester and Hornady components, made it easy to safely attain velocities up to 3,233 fps with under minute-of-angle groups.

Best load: Remington cases, Remington Benchrest primers. Hornady 50-grain V-Max bullet, 17.5 grains of H4198 powder, .185-inch groups, 2,950 fps.

.219 DONALDSON WASP

For some reason, I've always been attracted to the .219 Donaldson Wasp. Perhaps it was because ol' Harvey Donaldson had a place only 43 miles northwest of where I did some serious woodchucking on my uncle's farm near Cooperstown, New York, and his influence shadowed down on me. Whatever it was, after years of thinking about it, I finally took the dive, had a Ruger No. 1 rechambered for it by Bullberry Barrel Works and just loved shooting it. I still do.

Considered by many as a sharp-shouldered and blown-out .219 Zipper, Zipper brass has frequently been used to form .219 Donaldson Wasp cases. In addition, suitable brass from the .25-35, .22 High Power and .30-30 Winchester, the latter of which I use for forming this wildcat, are suitable. It takes a little more work, but the .30-30 got the nod since I like a challenge.

Using the RCBS case forming set (#58024), the first die pushes the shoulder back while retaining the .30-caliber profile. The second die moves the neck down to .290-inch OD while the trim die takes it down to .255 with an inside diameter of .227 — near perfect for seating the .224-inch bullet. Good powders to consider for the Donaldson are IMR 3031, H4895, IMR 4320 and H4064. Bullets of 45 to 60 grains from Barnes, Hornady, Speer, Sierra and Remington fill the bill and perform as this cartridge was intended, even back some 80 years ago. Recently, Hornady thought so much of the .219 Donaldson that it incorporated it into its 5th Edition *Reloading Manual.*

The Donaldson is an accurate cartridge in the field, and I use it as much as possible. After all, with Harvey looking over my shoulder on the north 40, it's nice to be in the good company of this cartridge pioneer.

Best load: Winchester .30-30 brass, CCI 200 primers. Speer 52-grain hollowpoint boattail bullet, 28 grains of IMR 4064, .75-inch groups, 3,160 fps.

.219 ZIPPER

Look no further than the .219 Zipper if you want a real challenge. First, if you can find a Winchester Model 64 chambered for the Zipper, good luck! I found one, but the innards were such a complete mess that I gave up until, as luck would have it, I located a 24-inch custom barrel in the cartridge, and, since I had a T/C receiver and stock, I was ready to go. (The Thompson/Center Custom Shop would turn out nearly anything you wanted in a

Forming the .219 Zipper can take some time, but the final product (right) is ready to go — all from standard .30-30 brass!

wildcat or standard cartridge.)

The Zipper can be formed from .25-35 brass if you can get it from Winchester or Hornady. I had some .30-30 brass leftover from the Donaldson Wasp project, so with a bit of help in the die department from Redding — it took four dies to get it going — and fireforming, I had perfectly formed .219 Zipper brass to work in my T/C barrel.

Like the Donaldson, I had somewhat of the same problem with the Zipper in the first die: that of pushing the neck back too far, causing dents in the shoulder. Annealing helped somewhat, but not entirely. The solution was to place a bit of lube around the case mouth with two fingers, and when entering the die, most of the lube was expended on the neck before it reached the shoulder junction of the case. Again, patience is needed. Later, a mild load of 24.0 grains of BL-C2 under any 50-grain bullet will smooth things out.

The Zipper is easy to work with using H4895, IMR 4320 or IMR 3031 powders, and 50- to 55-grain bullets from any manufacturer will give you small groups downrange with velocities over 3,200 fps.

Best load: Remington .30-30 cases, Federal 210 primers. Nosler 55-grain Spitzer, 29.0 grains of H4895 powder, 1-inch groups, 3,298 fps.

.22 K-HORNET

One of my favorite "improved" varmint cartridges is the .22 K-Hornet. An offshoot of the parent .22 Hornet introduced by Winchester in 1930 and modified by Lysle Kilbourn for more velocity and improved performance, simply place the .22 Hornet case into the chamber of the K-Hornet, and you're ready to go.

Having been taught never to place a cartridge in a gun not so marked for it, the feeling was unnerving as I placed case after case of .22 Hornet ammunition into the chamber of my new T/C Custom Shop Contender to form the improved version. Using Winchester factory ammunition with the 45-grain bullet, all but one (split case) of over 200 cases came out clean and well-defined. When I returned home, the RCBS die set (#26201) had arrived, and I was ready for some serious loading and subsequent range testing.

Starting the process, I "smoke" the formed cases with the soot of a candle, then run them up and into the die until the die base just kisses the top of the shoulder. As the black soot disappears, keep advancing the case up and into the die. This method is an easy way to track the progress of resizing only the neck of the case. A variety of powders was employed, with the best group going to Winchester 296, 680 and Accurate Arms 1680. These groups were all under an inch, perfect for small varmints and within safe operating limits.

Interestingly, because of its inherent accuracy, small (read economical) powder charges and some difficulty in getting a custom rifle made, the K-Hornet continues to be a popular choice for wildcat shooters.

Best load: Winchester cases, CCI 400 primers. Hornady 45-grain "Hornet" bullet, 12.5 grains of Olin 680 powder, .375-inch groups, 2,725 fps.

.22 PPC

This one got away, and I didn't realize it until it was gone! I had the Sako rifle in my hands for testing and enjoyed both the rifle and the .22 PPC cartridge, figuring both would be around for a while. The rifle went back to Stoeger — much to my regret later. In any event, I did have time to work with both and was duly impressed with the pair.

The rifle was Sako's Vixen model, all decked out with attractive wood and fine craftsmanship capable of delivering great accuracy, especially with a Bushnell 6-18x40mm scope. Along with the rifle, Stoeger sent a quantity of factory ammunition in the new .22 PPC and brass for handloading chores.

Around 1974, when varmint shooters were clamoring for something new, Dr. Louis Palmisano and Ferris Pindell came up with a wildcat based on the .220 Russian for benchrest use. In 1987, the case went "public," and the .22 PPC was born, with Ruger and Sako producing rifles. The cartridge soon developed a reputation for fine accuracy in rifles easily obtained on the market.

With brass on hand, fireformed and neck-sized only with dies from RCBS, the best powders were H322, AA2520, H4895, and Winchester 748. Bullets ranged from 45 to 55 grains in spitzer, hollowpoint and match designs. For the most part, all velocities were above the 3,000 fps mark. Factory ammo from Sako proved its mettle with 3/4-inch groups hitting 3,223 fps. The .22 PPC proved such an easy wildcat to work with that both men developed the 6MM PPC with almost equal success. Darn, I should have kept that rifle.

Best load: Sako USA cases, Remington 7 ½ Bench Rest primers. Remington 55-grain hollowpoint bullet, 28.5 grains of Accurate 2520 powder, .375-inch groups, 3,202 fps.

.22 REMINGTON JET

Developed in late 1961 by Remington and Smith & Wesson, the .22 Remington Jet was designed as a sporting cartridge in the Model 53 revolver. The case — known for its unusually long and tapered neck — is made from the typical .357 Magnum necked down to .22 caliber through a set of dies. While it was popular at the onset of its introduction, trouble was brewing with the tapered case backing out of the cylinder after firing, causing problems.

The Smith Model 53 remained the only gun chambered for the round a decade later, although Marlin planned a lever

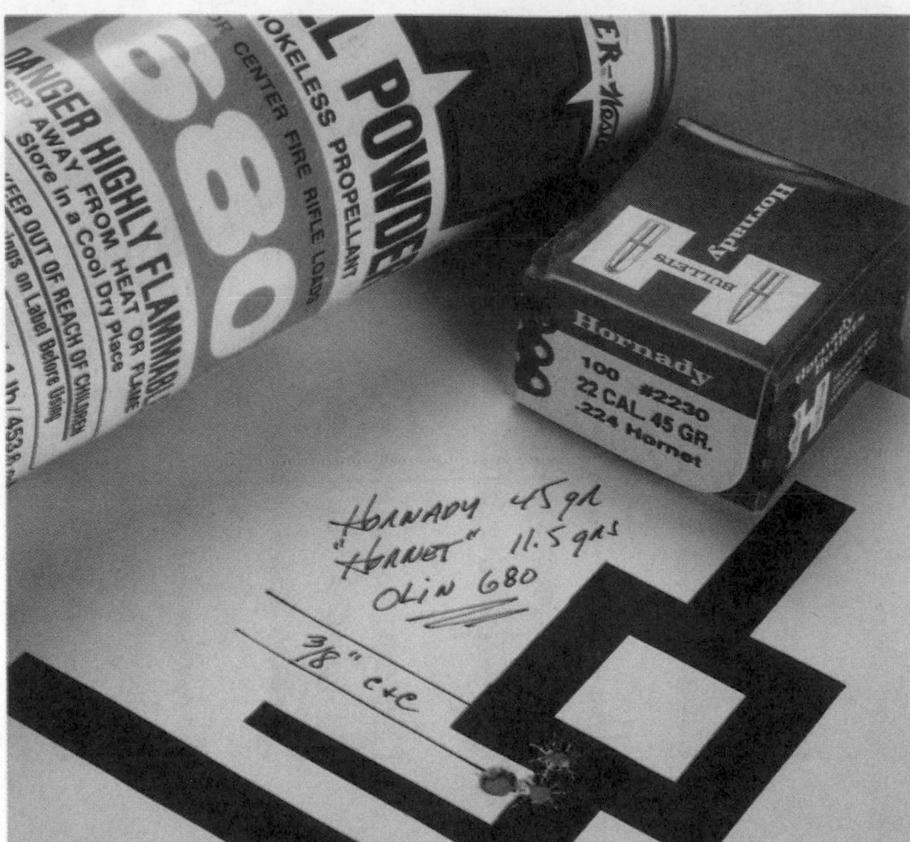

The .22 K-Hornet is an accurate and easy cartridge to form, load and shoot. This 3/8-inch group is proof of the pudding.

Most reloading tool makers offer a die set for the .22 PPC. Once fired, neck sizing is the best way to accuracy.

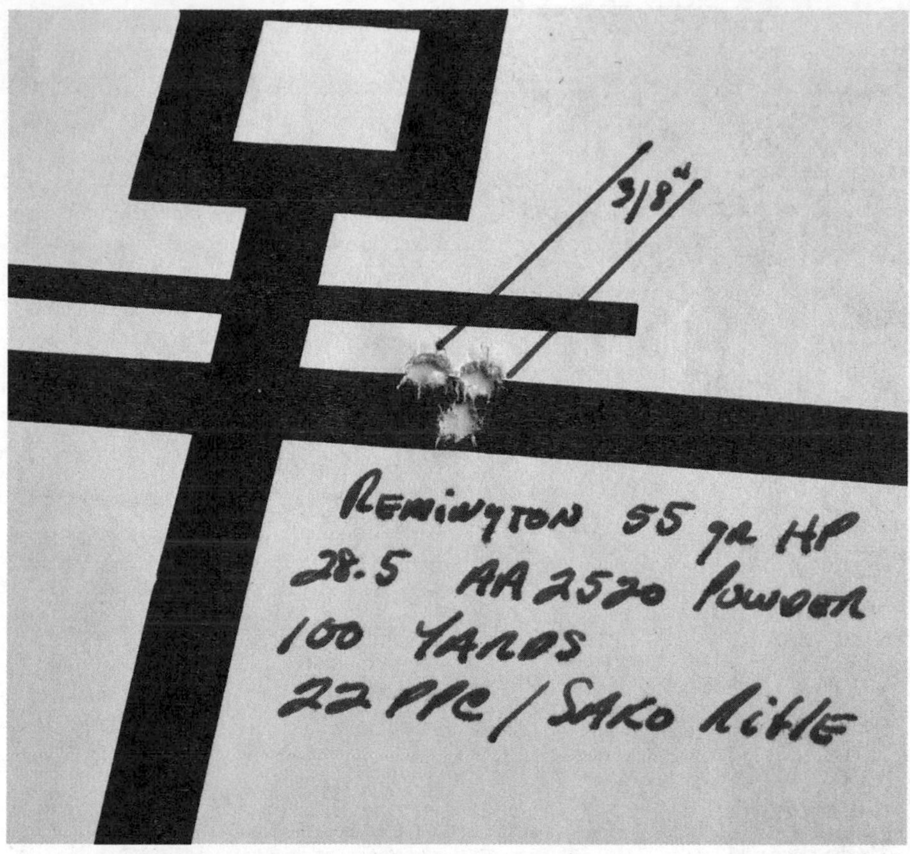

With the Remington 55-grain bullet and AA2520 powder, Trzoniec could work the .22 PPC-chambered Sako to some small groups at 100 yards.

The .22 Jet takes some time to get to the final product, and the trim die is part of the package. This wildcat cartridge is accurate and economical on powder.

Easily formed from standard .357 magnum brass, the .22 Jet is a likable candidate for those looking for something unique. Once chambered in the S&W Model 53 revolver, it is now an orphan, only to be found in T/C barrels.

gun, which never materialized. The only viable alternative was a Custom Shop Thompson/Center Contender. I had one made and was thoroughly pleased with the gun, but because the cartridge was no longer made, it takes almost a half-dozen steps to get to the loading and firing stage.

Using a die and form set from Redding, I used fresh .357 brass from Remington, marching through the steps outlined by Redding until I had about 60 pieces in my cache. Since the forming is rather severe, annealing is the best way to prevent split or cracked cases. The first forming die will bring the neck down to .336 inch, the next die to .255, then it is into the trim die to be filed down to 1.278.

Being a proprietary "pistol" case, I turned to a couple of powders I was familiar with from the .357 — notably, Hodgdon H110 and Winchester W296. Holding roughly 19.0 grains of water, I combined powder charges with bullets from Hornady (its special "Jet" bullet), Sierra, and Speer in weights from 40 to 45 grains. With the right combination, velocities ran from a low of 2,919 fps to a high of 3,278 fps. I purchased a box of Remington 40-grain Jet ammunition at a show and, running it through the Contender, came up with a mean of 2,864 fps with 1-inch groups.

While the T/C barrel can be found online or at shows, the S&W Model 53 demands serious collector prices and is seemingly out of reach for many shooters. If you can find the Contender barrel, go for it.

Best load: Remington cases, CCI 550 primers. Speer 40-grain soft-point bullet, 14.9 grains of W296 powder, .75-inch groups, 3,248 fps.

.22 REMINGTON BR

Since I was looking at the hard and expensive road to getting a .22 PPC rifle, I started exploring elsewhere for a substitute. Doing some research, I came across the .22 Remington Bench Rest (BR), which closely matched the size, ballistics and accuracy of the PPC. Moreover, I could build a rifle to my likes and hunting style.

I ordered a Remington Model 700 in

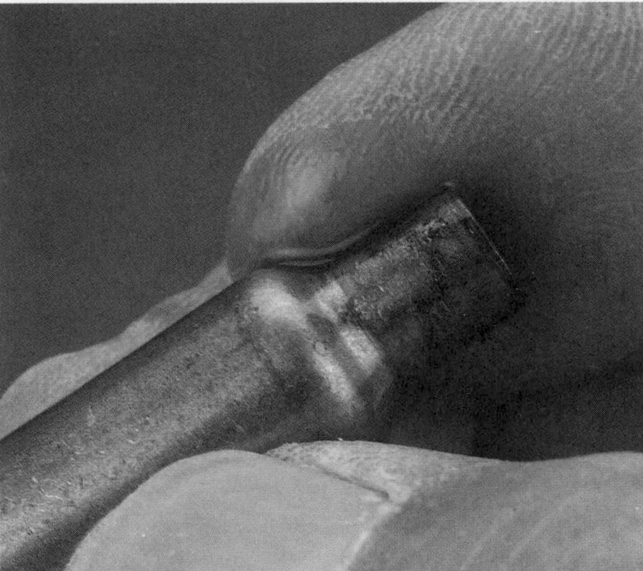

The .22 Remington BR fits easily into the Model 700 short action. E.R. Shaw of Pennsylvania took care of the barreling in this caliber.

When working with neck-sizing only, avoid case dents or neck splits on .22-caliber brass by placing a tiny bit of lube on the neck before placing the case into the die.

.22/250 and sent the barreled action to E.R. Shaw's for a new barrel in the BR version. Shaw can match the barrel contour, install and headspace it all, so it fits right back into the factory stock perfectly. I added a recoil pad to keep the gun from slipping while I closed the gates in the north 40.

While I came full circle getting to the .22 Remington BR, I finally purchased 6mm BR brass from Blue Star Cartridge of Searcy, Arkansas. The transition was easy: simply run it through the .22 BR die with just a bit of case trimming from 1.560 to 1.510 inches. Neck thickness does not change with this minor forming, and with the addition of CCI benchrest primers, powders are next.

With a case holding around 34.0 grains of water, H335, H322 and BLC-2 powders fill the bill with better-than-average velocities close to 4,000 fps using the lighter 40- to 45-grain bullets. Regarding bullets, I tried to use as much variety as possible from Nosler, Speer, Remington, Sierra, Hornady and Barnes, with similar results.

The .22 Remington Bench Rest is an easy-to-work-with .22-caliber cartridge deserving more recognition from small game hunters. The parent company should take the hint and chamber it in the Model 700 Varmint rifle. Now that would be one hell'va field rifle.

Best load: Remington cases, CCI 400 BR primers. Speer 45-grain spitzer bullet, 33.0 grains of H335 powder, .375-inch groups, 3,964 fps.

.22 TEXAS TROPHY HUNTER

I can't recall where I picked up the idea of necking down a 6mm Remington to .22 caliber. Looking back and digging into my data banks, I believe it was at a Remington bash talking to my good friend, the late Ralph Lermayer. He developed it for low recoil in various bullet weights from light to heavy, ensuring clean kills on larger animals.

Simple enough, I thought, and it was. First, I needed a rifle, and E.R. Shaw took care of that quickly. Equipped with a 24-inch barrel, walnut stock, and a trigger that broke like the proverbial glass rod, I added a Leupold Long Range 30mm scope. I ordered 6mm brass from Winchester and a die set from Redding. These completed the "parts" needed to convert from a neck size of .243 to .224 inch — all with only one case out of a hundred showing cracks at the neck — while retaining the 26-degree shoulder.

My goal was to use 55-grain .224-inch bullets — a weight that has proved to be the best compromise in a .224-inch bore for stabilization, accuracy and velocities to 4,000 fps. Again, bullets from Hornady, Remington, Sierra, Nosler and Winchester fill out the list. My choice of powders was narrowed down to RL-15, VV N150 and IMR 4350. The 4350 was the best choice, with lighter bullets in some of the largest-cased cartridges. Whereas the nearest competition might be the Swift, it overshadows or exceeds this classic with all bullet weights while using standard rifle actions and magazines. While not chambered in current production rifles, there are custom makers that will take your money and deliver the goods for shooting this hot and fun-filled cartridge!

Best load: Winchester cases, Federal #210 primers. Sierra spitzer bullet, 46.2 grains of IMR 4350 powder, .625-inch groups, 3,954 fps.

.22/250 ACKLEY IMPROVED

I've always wanted to tinker with the Ackley Improved version of the famous

For reaching out to distant small game, it's hard to beat the .22 Texas Trophy Hunter for velocity and accuracy. Shaw made the complete rifle with polished stainless steel action and a walnut stock.

The .22/250 Improved is still another entry in the improved class of cartridges. The author found this wildcat an excellent addition to his varmint battery.

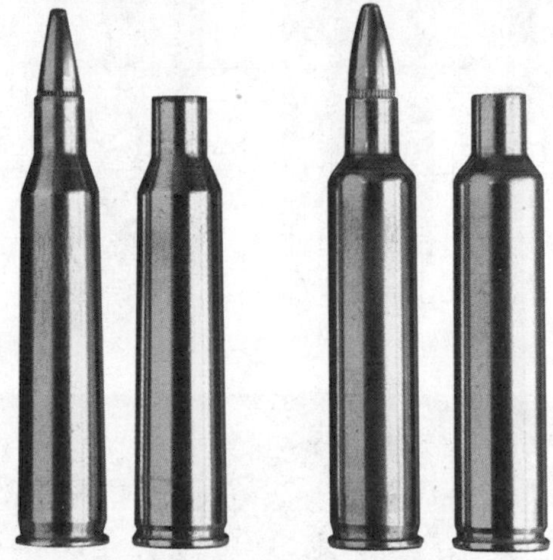

Considered an "easy wildcat," the .220 Weatherby Rocket is formed in the chamber of the host rifle. Parent Swift on the left, new Rocket on the right.

.22/250 Remington cartridge. So, when the opportunity came with a complete rifle from Shaws, I couldn't wait to start the loading and shooting process.

While the original, unimproved .22/250 case holds 45.0 grains of water, Ackley's Improved brass tops out at 48.5 grains, an improvement of around 8 percent, which will give (over the chronograph) about a 5 to 6 percent velocity boost. While this version can use upwards of 70-grain bullets, my interest is in bullet weights from 40 to 55 grains

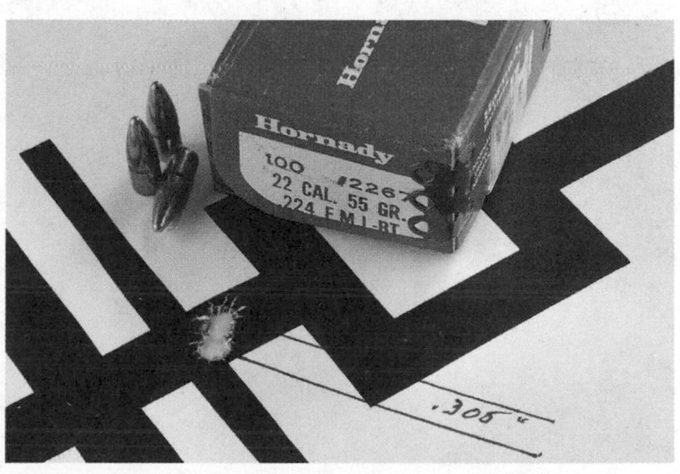

Roy Weatherby would be proud of this almost one-hole group of .305 inch at 100 yards. The .220 Rocket is still a superb cartridge and a worthy addition to your rifle battery.

with decent velocities I can live with. Like other wildcats, .22/250 AI dies are available from most makers, so Redding was my choice. My practice is to neck size all fired cases and rub a small amount of lube on the neck to size without the fear of case dents or neck splits.

Forming cases via the rifle — fire-forming — versus running them up and down in a die allows you to take the gun to the range and sight in without wasting valuable time later with carefully weighed handloads. For powders, I would start out with IMR 4064, IMR 3031 and trusty Varget when moving on to the heavier weight bullets. For bullets, Hornady, Speer or Nosler gave the best groups, but running 15 loads through the gun in various weights from 40 to 55 grains, the average of all groups was 1.14 inches. Not all that great, but as time wears on, they will get better. Besides, where else can you have a new rifle and cartridge to fool around with that gives you velocities to nearly 4,100 fps with little or no effort?

Best load: Remington .22/250 cases, Remington 9 ½ primers. Hornady 40-grain V-Max bullet, 40 grains of IMR 4064 powder, .750-inch groups, 4298 fps.

P.O. Ackley took the parent .223 Remington and turned it into another one of his improved cartridges, as shown on the right. It's a fun cartridge, slightly boosting velocity and accuracy.

.220 WEATHERBY ROCKET

Nothing pleases me more than to shoot a cartridge with the Weatherby name on it — especially when it's one of Roy Weatherby's first efforts from the beginning of his shooting career. Such is the case with the .220 Weatherby Rocket. Developed in 1943 and entered commercially in 1945, in simple terms, it is nothing more than a blown-out .220 Swift case.

Sacrificing a new Ruger M77 Target rifle chambered for the Swift, I sent it to High Tech Customs for a refit to the Weatherby Rocket. I added a Leupold 6.5-20x scope, and when the RCBS neck-sizing die arrived, I went to work. You can fireform .220 Swift factory loads or new Swift brass, load them up with a mild charge of 40 grains of H380 and fire away. You may lose a few to sidewall cracks, but that's it. Mark a case neck with the soot of a candle and run it up and into the die until the die just kisses the shoulder of the case, indicating the neck has been fully-sized back to .22-caliber dimensions.

The cases will show a slightly reduced body taper out of the rifle, which is a good thing as this always eases extraction. Clean and chamfer the inside and outside of the neck, prime with large rifle benchrest primers one at a time, which leads to uniformity from the first to last case. Interesting to note

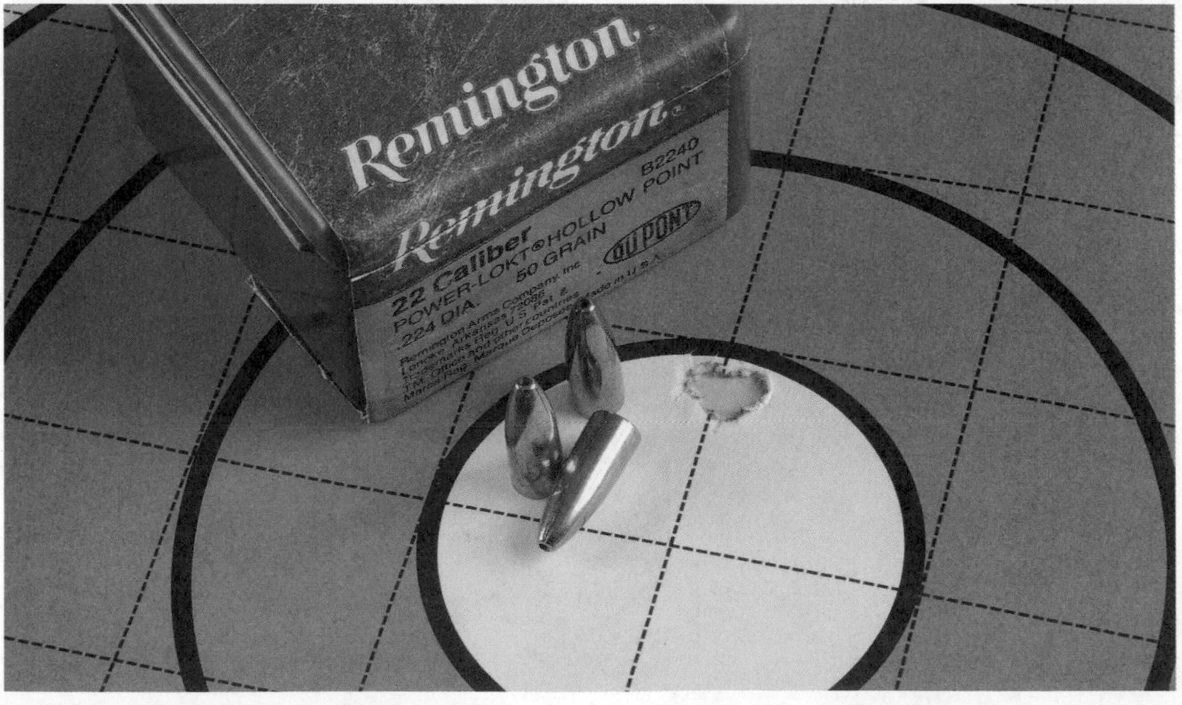

Looking at the photo, it's hard to believe this group from the .223 AI is three shots! It came in at a very tight .205 inch at 100 yards with a Remington bullet.

The Thompson Center Contender has been a test rifle for many of Trzoniec's wildcat cartridges. With a thumbhole stock and a semi-beavertail forearm, this one was set up for the .223 Remington Ackley Improved.

is that in my library, copies of the past *Weatherby Guide* used a 55-grain bullet over 45 grains of IMR 4064. Taking that as gospel, my results showed some extraction problems, blown primers and velocities hitting almost 4,200 fps! That's too hot for sure, and I later throttled it down to a lesser charge of the same powder for half-inch groups or less, around 4,005 fps — much better.

I love to hunt with the .220 Rocket Ruger as I feel both Bill Ruger and Roy Weatherby are right there in the field with me when I zero in on that 'chuck downrange.

Best load: Remington cases, CCI BR2 primers. Hornady 55-grain FMJ-BT bullet, 42.0 grains of IMR 4064 powder, .300-inch groups, 4,005 fps.

.223 ACKLEY IMPROVED

Looking for different avenues to take, I came across a new barrel chambered for the .223 Ackley Improved. Again, this came from the T/C Custom Shop and was the perfect addition to my collection of Contender barrels.

Credit must be given to P.O. Ackley for his work with "improved" cartridges, and the .223 Ackley Improved is undoubtedly one of them. And while the .223 Remington has really done nothing for me, the .223 Improved was something else. It's easy to make. Just put a lightly loaded .223 Remington round into the .223 Improved barrel, and bingo! — you have a new cartridge with a side benefit of extra velocity and enhanced accuracy downrange.

Bullets tend to be a personal choice based on what was the best in your gun before trying the Ackley Improved chamber. Like others in its ilk, this cartridge likes bullets from 40 to 55 grains and heavier depending on your needs. I've used Sierra, Hornady, Nosler and Berger, but that doesn't mean they're the best; they are the best for me. Small rifle primers are needed, as is IMR 8208 XBR, Power Pro Varmint, or Benchmark powders.

For a varmint round, the .223 Remington AI is easy to load, pleasant to shoot, and above all, very accurate with a wide range of bullets. Keep in mind that for subsequent loadings, all fireformed cases were neck-sized only. Setting up the neck-sizing die is easy. Smoke the neck/shoulder area with the soot from a candle (or other marking methods) to monitor die movement down the neck to not touch the shoulder. Secure the sizing die, finish all the cases, clean them and prime. Charge the cases with powder and seat the bullet to the overall length stated on the chart.

If you can find the right barrel or have a rifle rechambered for this Improved version, go for it — and some fantastic groups might just reward you.

Best load: Federal .223 Remington brass, CCI Benchrest primers. 50-grain Remington hollowpoint bullet, 28.0 grains of IMR 8208 XBR powder, .205-inch group, 3,520 fps. GD

The Nepalese Gehendra Rifle

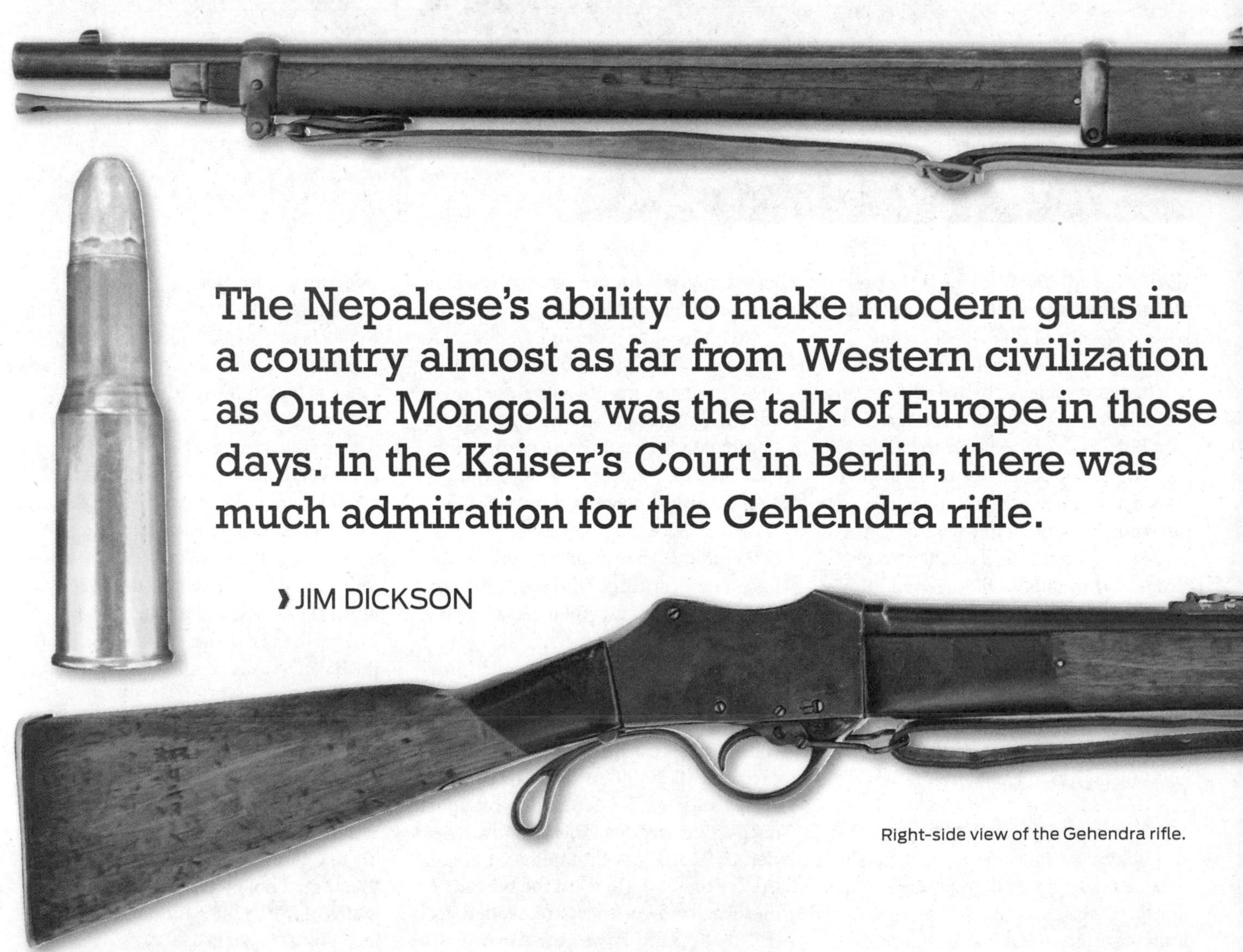

The Nepalese's ability to make modern guns in a country almost as far from Western civilization as Outer Mongolia was the talk of Europe in those days. In the Kaiser's Court in Berlin, there was much admiration for the Gehendra rifle.

› JIM DICKSON

Right-side view of the Gehendra rifle.

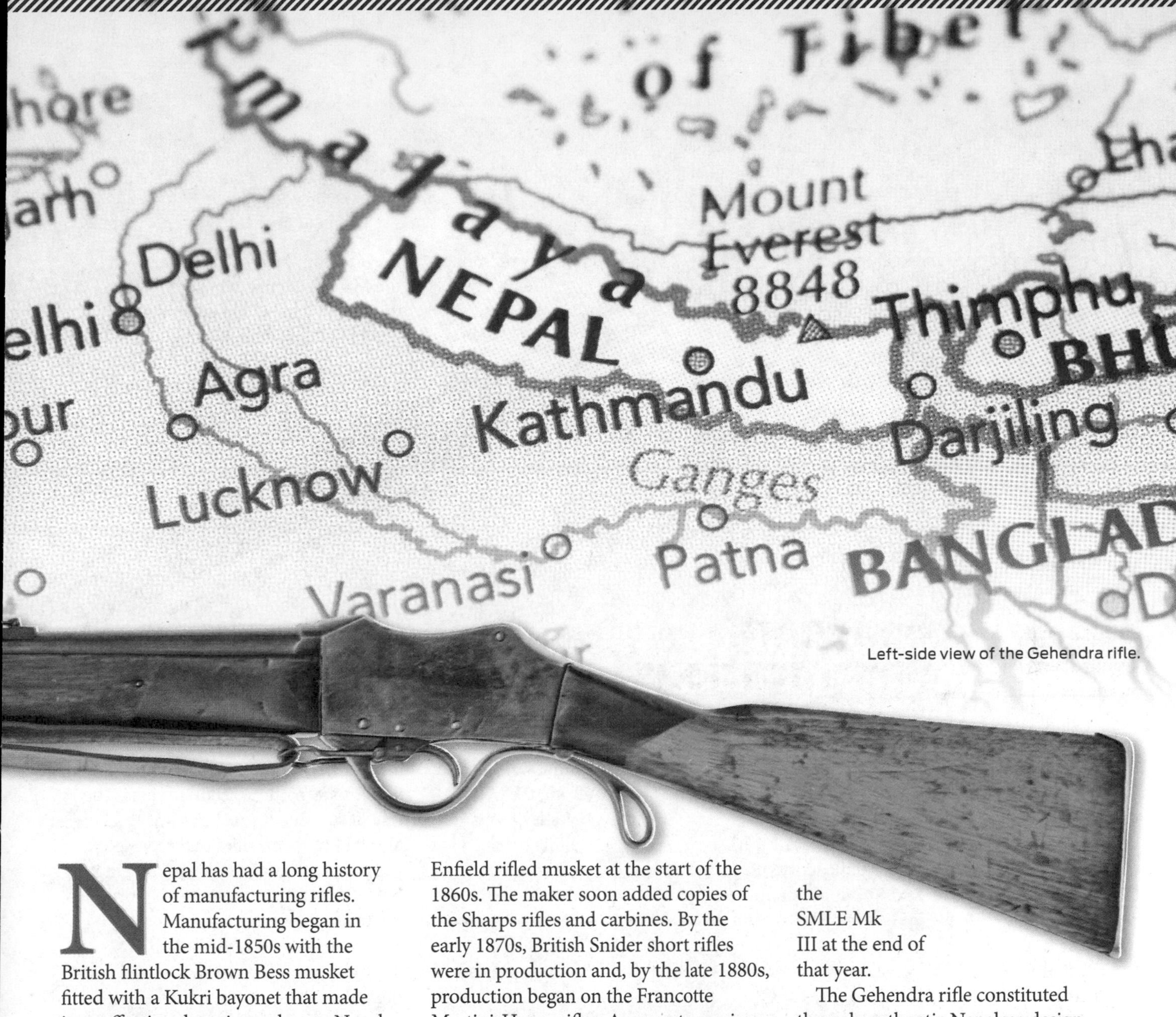

Left-side view of the Gehendra rifle.

Nepal has had a long history of manufacturing rifles. Manufacturing began in the mid-1850s with the British flintlock Brown Bess musket fitted with a Kukri bayonet that made it an effective chopping polearm. Nepal started making the British Brunswick rifle as a smoothbore just a couple of years later. The British did not deem the extra accuracy as worth the slower, more difficult loading with the belted ball projectile.

By the late 1850s, the East India Company was producing its Pattern F musket initially, and later the Pattern 53 Enfield rifled musket at the start of the 1860s. The maker soon added copies of the Sharps rifles and carbines. By the early 1870s, British Snider short rifles were in production and, by the late 1880s, production began on the Francotte Martini-Henry rifles. A separate receiver distinguishes these within the receiver so you can easily remove the entire inner works of the gun for cleaning — a feature of the best value in the days of blackpowder. By the mid-1890s, other makers manufactured copies of the British Martini-Henry. Then in 1895–96, Gehendra produced its rifle. It would remain in production until 1913, when the British began making copies of the SMLE Mk III at the end of that year.

The Gehendra rifle constituted the only authentic Nepalese design and is, therefore, worthy of special attention. It was the product of Gehendra Shumsher, who was like the Thomas Edison of Nepal. Born in 1871, he was Bir Shumsher's son and later became prime minister of Nepal. At age 14, Gehendra was appointed head of the ammunition department for Nepal's army. He had a lifelong love for arms and ammunition. He was also the first man to produce electricity in Nepal using hydroelectric generation. He built a 7-boiler rice mill and also a windmill to pump water. In Balaju, he built a leather tanning factory. Determined to make arms locally using local iron and coal, he built factories at Jamal (Seto Durbar), Balaju, Sundarijal, and Megchan (Bhojpur).

Gehendra modernized Nepal's army. He also designed and made his double-barreled machine gun based on the Gardiner gun. He named this the Bira gun after his father. His new cannon design was named the Dhir-Gun in honor of his grandfather, Dhir Shumshir. He also served as Nepal's spy chief and the head of its police for a time.

Like Edison, Gehendra was a tinkerer who always believed he could make any design better. He took the M1869 Westley Richards falling block design and modified it to produce the Gehendra.

Like many geniuses, some competitors perceived him as a threat. Nepal's prime ministers thought nothing of killing any siblings or relatives that they perceived as potential rivals. When Chandra Shumsher became prime minister, he was scared of Gehendra's political and military influence, so he publicly humiliated him by stripping him of his power and gun factory. In 1906, Shumsher poisoned Gehendra, and Nepal lost its most extraordinary mind. Indeed, without Gehendra, its modernization faced a significant setback. At that time, Gehendra had been preparing to build and fly the first airplane ever made in Asia.

The Gehendra rifle (also known as the Ge-rifle for short) was the British Martini-Henry's equal. The gun it was derived from, the M1869 Westley Richards falling block, was considered superior to the foreign-designed Martini-Henry by many in England's gun trade. In truth, these were all effectively equals. The Gehendra's advantage for Nepal was that it utilized a leaf spring instead of the Martini-Henry coil spring, which had proved challenging to manufacture in Nepal. Plus, it was a Nepalese design. The value of this to a county's pride can be seen in every country's prejudice toward its innovations in firearms throughout history.

The effectiveness of these three designs is evident in the most-produced one, the Martini-Henry, which sees action in the Far East wars. The average gun was capable of 2- to 3-inch groups at 100 yards, but the inverted-V front sight and V-notch rear sight were not well-suited for target use. Where they excelled was as fast-acquisition combat sights. The average soldier could put all his shots in 3 to 4 inches at 50 yards and inside one foot at 100 yards. Such marksmanship was better than the average 21st Century soldier could do with modern, more accurate rifles. The rate of sustained aimed fire was the same as the bolt-action rifles that replaced it, the advantage of the bolt action being better economy of movement in producing that rate of fire.

The cartridge was the British .577-450, which was the old .577 Snider case necked down to .450 and loaded with a 480-grain lead bullet backed by 85 grains of blackpowder for 1,400 fps velocity. Before you label this an obsolete cartridge, note that the Afghans found this gun and cartridge perfect for damaging the tail rotor of Soviet Hind helicopters so effectively that they shot down several of the multi-million dollar attack helicopters. It outperformed the modern standard-issue infantryman's cartridges for such work.

Sportsmen used the British .577-450 extensively for hunting. They killed many elephants by angling the shot from behind the shoulder to reach the heart between the elephant's shoulders. The U.S. Army tested it in the 1870s and said it kicked too much. Actual felt recoil is comparable to a .450-400 Nitro Express,

Gehendra Specifications

Weight: 10 lbs.
Weight with Bayonet: 10 3/4 lbs.
Overall length: 49 3/4 in.
Length with 13 in. blade bayonet: 63 in.
Length of pull: 14 1/2 in.
Trigger pull: 12 lbs.
Maximum bore diameter: .445
Sights: V-notch rear and inverted V front
Rear sight: Set at 100 yards adjustable to 1,300 yards
Barrel length: 33 1/4 in. well-crowned, made from one piece of solid drawn material
Buttplate: 1 3/4 X 4 1/2 in.
Trigger: grooved
Rifling: Henry type, 7 grooves, right-hand twist
Stock: Painted black on each side of the action for protection. Clean blackpowder with hot soapy water
Ramrod: Shorter than the barrel and threaded for an extension

which is not intolerable.

All three rifles handle a ruptured case or pierced primer perfectly. Nothing will get in your face, but you will have to clean the fouling out of the breechblock when you clean the gun as the fouling goes in the firing pin hole with a pierced primer.

To clean the gun, take out the breechblock by removing the split pin at the upper rear of the Martini-Henry rifle or the screw in the Gehendra and open the lever. Press down on the front of the breechblock, and it will pop out. Now pour a gallon of boiling water through a funnel down the barrel's breech end to clear out the blackpowder fouling. Since you must use water to clean the breechblock and action, follow up with a mixture of 25 percent Ballistol oil and 75 percent water on all metal parts. You can put this mixture in a pump spray bottle for easy use. Dry and then oil with pure Ballistol. Ballistol was the German army's oil from 1904 to 1945, and it forms an emulsion with water that remains, preventing rust after the water evaporates. It sure makes life easier for blackpowder shooters. It works equally well on metal, wood, and leather, just as Ballistol designed it. Heavy machinery under a tarp stored outside is prone to rust, but I have used Ballistol to prevent it on a 1,200-pound Little Giant Power Hammer. When moisture forms, it mixes into a harmless emulsion with the Ballistol. (Available from Ballistol USA, P.O. Box 900, Kitty Hawk, N.C., 27949, 1-800-253-2460.)

Gehendra Shumsher JBR, the first scientist of Nepal, with his wife. Shumsher was an innovator and based the Gehendra rifle on the M1869 Westley Richards falling block. Photo: Ashim nep

I had a fine arsenal-rebuilt Gehendra on loan from Hunter's Lodge in Ethridge, Tennessee, for test firing. Hunter's Lodge has the last of Interarm's Ye Old Hunter's inventory of surplus guns from surplus imports' glory days in the 1960s. Its Gehendras were imported many years ago and are in far better condition than the more recent imports. Hunter's Lodge acquired the last ones that the Nepalese considered suitable for reissue to the troops. Bob Stahl of Colorado Custom Cartridge made the ammo. This gun had a maximum bore diameter of .445 inch between the grooves. (The British Proof

Gehendra rifle with bayonet attached.

Close-up of the action.

House specifications call for a minimum of .4645 inch between the grooves.)

Wayne Massey at the Birmingham, England Proof House thought this was enough difference to blow up a barrel with standard ammo, so someone had to make .445-inch diameter bullets for the gun. For owners of these rifles with undersize bores, this is not necessarily a bad thing. You can send the firearm to someone who makes muzzleloading rifle barrels and have it "freshened out" by removing just enough metal to bring it up to a .4645-inch groove diameter. This work will make your old barrel like new and enable you to use standard .577-450 ammo in the gun. If you wish to retain the barrel in its original condition, it is a good idea to do a chamber and bore cast and tailor the ammo for your gun as the Nepalese guns have much more variation in dimensions than the English ones ever did.

It appears that the Nepalese took their bore size from a Webley .455 revolver as they have a .441-inch bore size. Since it purports to be a .455 caliber, it would seem logical that this was the British way of doing things and should be correct for the rifle. It wasn't.

Brass makers used 24-gauge brass shotgun cases, as rifle brass in this caliber was not available. The first loads turned out to be squibs that did not have enough velocity to stabilize the bullet. The bullets tumbled and hit the target sideways. After going through both sides of the thin cardboard box, they would fall to the ground a few feet behind the box. I went back and asked for something that would shoot to the sights. The next box came loaded with Trail Boss, a popular smokeless powder for blackpowder rifles today. The case head sheared off on the first shot, and escaping gas blew a chip

Action open.

out of the fore-end. A quick call to an English gunmaker confirmed that the 24-gauge shotgun brass was to blame, as the .577-450 develops four times the pressure of the 24-gauge shotgun. At this point, I was out of time and discontinued attempts to shoot this gun. I cleaned the bore with Shooter's Choice bore cleaner and oiled it with FP-10 before sending it back to Hunter's Lodge.

With good ammo, I would not hesitate to take this gun hunting today. If hunting dangerous game like wild boar, I would also not hesitate to take its bayonet — as this is a single-shot, not a semi-auto! They don't call the old bayonets "pig stickers" for nothing.

The gun is lively in the hands and steady on target. A long barrel's weight at the muzzle end acts as a lever, giving you more steadying weight without having to carry extra pounds. The sights are readily visible and align almost automatically. They are fast and excellent for combat or hunting.

Several specifications are worth noting. The length of pull (LOP) is a proper 14-1/2 inches, which is slightly longer than the British MkII Martini-Henry rifles and a definite improvement. The longer you extend, the more accurately you can point. I am 6' 2" and use a 15-9/16-inch LOP on guns stocked to fit me. The M1903 Springfield has a 12-1/2-inch LOP, and the M1 carbine has a 13-inch LOP. In the British gun trade, custom makers fit the 12-1/2 and 13-inch LOP guns to short 4-1/2 to 5-foot tall women.

The bayonet is shorter than the British issue as befitting the smaller stature of the Nepalese soldiers. The Nepalese individually fitted these bayonets to the individual guns. Bayonet formation

The case head completely separated from the case body on firing, proving you cannot make .577-450 rifle cases safely out of 24-gauge shotgun brass because the .577-450 rifle pressures are four times that of a 24-gauge shotgun.

fighting was a reality in the 19th Century. At Rorke's Drift, the Zulus were so afraid of the British bayonets that they pulled their charge up short, hesitating at the bayonets with fatal consequences. Their fear was well-founded. The Zulu shield is an oversized clumsy buckler held in the fist instead of slung on the arm as a shield. Soldiers held the rifle and bayonet in both hands. To fight a Zulu with a British Martini-Henry and bayonet, you raised the barrel at a 45-degree angle and brought it down against the cowhide shield, knocking it past the Zulu's body and against his spear hand. As the bayonet's point passed the Zulu's chest, you thrust hard — killing the Zulu. It was simple and effective. If your enemy attempted to push against his shield with his spear hand, and you couldn't force his shield aside, you raised the gun's butt as you pivoted the barrel against the shield — angling into where you could thrust with your bayonet.

The rear sight works like a tangent sight set at 100 yards when down and elevates to 200, 300, and 400 yards by sliding the rear sight forward. You can raise the rear sight to 1,300 yards in 100-yard increments. Accurate fire at long range by snipers continues with this type of rifle today in the Far East, and volley fire at long range by the soldiers was a highly effective means of hitting enemy formations at a far distance.

This gun came with an original sling in very sound condition. To be safe, I rubbed in Blackrock Leather' N' Rich wax as this is the standard among collectors for preserving antique leather. The stock was dry, so I rubbed in multiple coats of artist-quality linseed oil. The Gehendra is a beautiful gun that makes you want to care for it properly. Artist-quality linseed oil is very thin, which is good for penetrating wood but bad for a quick finish build-up. I then finished up with Birchwood Casey Tru-Oil gunstock finish.

Like all Gehendras, the maker profusely marked it in Nepalese script. Being quite illiterate when it comes to reading Nepalese, I turned to Professor Prem Sing Basnyat, Ph.D., ex-Brigadier

The Gehendra rear sight markings.

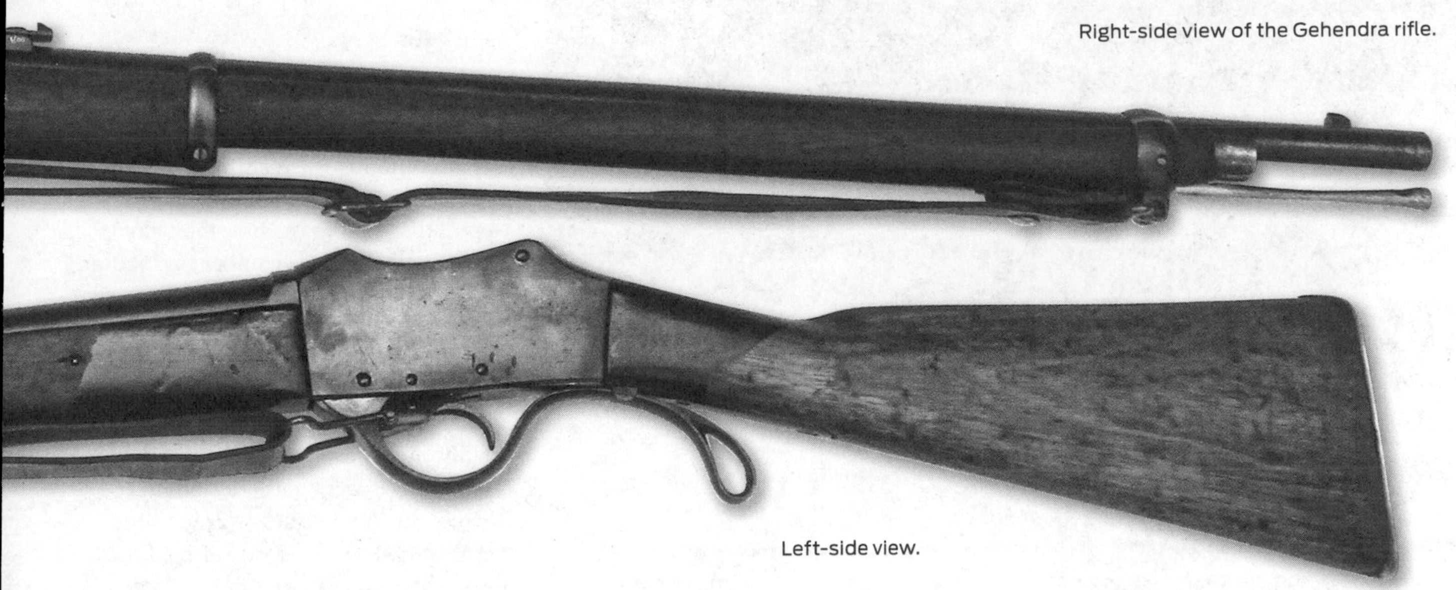

Right-side view of the Gehendra rifle.

Left-side view.

General, and a British Chevening Scholar who kindly translated it for me. General Basnyat is also responsible for preserving the remaining machinery for making the Gehendra rifles at the Nepal Army Museum. General Basnyat bought most of them in Birmingham, England, but some were Nepalese. The English-made machines were ordered from Greenwood & Batley Ltd. of Leeds and delivered in 1896 when the manufacture of both the Gehendra rifle and the twin-barrel Bira manually operated machine gun began.

The rear of the receiver is marked:

- Shree 3 Chandra Samseer Jang (Shree shree shree (Mr.) king Chander samser Rana) At that time, Nepal had two types of kings: His majesty the king Shree five, and Shree three king, the prime minister.
- Sam. 1964 (Nepali Date Bikram sambat 1964): Date of manufacturing. The Nepalese calendar is 57 years ahead of the A.D. calendar used in the West, so the manufacture date translates to 1907 A.D.
- Nam. 93 (Serial number of the rifle was 93)

On the bottom of the cocking lever, you find the marking Sundari Rifle (the rifle maker's name was Sundari). Later, Sundari Jal Arsenal manufactured the Gehendra, far from Katmandu Valley, and the rifles made there were called Sundari Rifles. Jamal Arsenal originally produced the Gehendra at Katmandu inside the Gehendra Palace.

While Gehendra utilized the basic design of the M1869 Westley Richards rifle, he also made improvements. The Westley Richards V-type mainspring and the leaf trigger spring were moved behind the trigger, allowing the use of the Francotte-Martini forearm. These are the only two springs in the rifle, and they are both mounted on the trigger plate. Gehendra altered the hammer to the same axis as the breech lever pin.

While similar in appearance to the Martini-Henry, you can quickly discern that its receiver tapers to the rear, while the Martini-Henry tapers to the front. Plus, the Gehendra lacks the checkered

Escaping gas from the case head separation blew this chip out of the forearm, where it abuts the action.

The markings on the rear of the receiver.

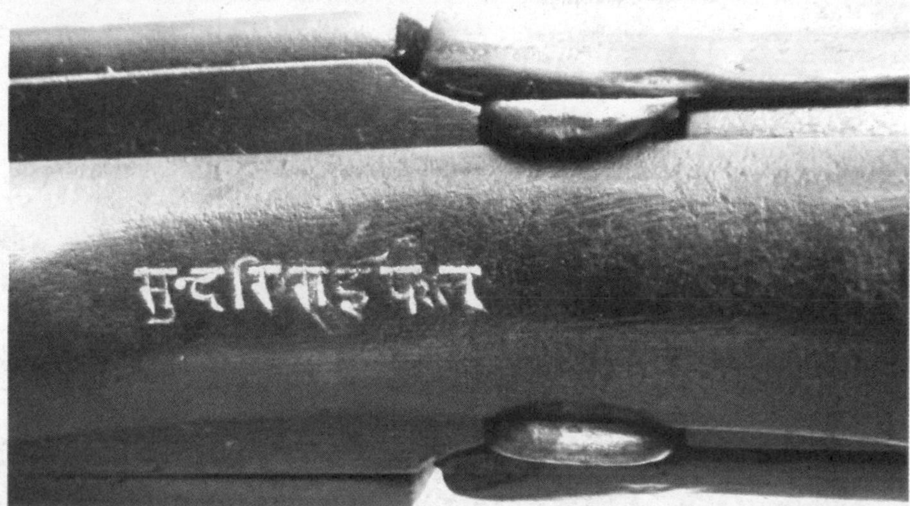

The markings on the cocking lever.

thumb rest and cocking indicator of the Martini-Henry. The distinctive stirrup-like rear sling swivel is peculiar to the Gehendra.

Two arms of a single piece of spring steel formed into a U shape and fixed to the trigger plate hold the loading lever in place. Pulling the loading lever down causes the shoulders of the loading lever to pull the front of the breechblock down, exposing the chamber for loading and forcing the extractor to remove any case in the chamber. The hammer is pushed back and caught on the trigger. Insert a fresh cartridge, close the lever, and you are ready to fire — simple and deadly effective.

Gehendras were battle-tested first in 1897 during the short war between Tibet and Nepal. There are also a few short-barreled carbines made for the king's bodyguard cavalry. These are 37.9 inches long with 21.4-inch barrels, and their leaf sights go only to 1,000 yards.

The year 1911 saw the final form of the Gehendra. The improved rifle had the separate mainspring and trigger spring combined into one V-spring sliding into a finger-like retainer on the trigger plate's rear (you can identify these guns by the position of the rearmost lower traversing screw). Early Gehendras have this feature over the trigger, and the improved versions have it at the rear of the receiver. The number of guns that exist with only one spring is unknown.

This brilliant piece was the brainchild of Captain Bhakta Bahadur Basnyat (no relation to General Basnyat). He was one of eight students sent to Japan in April 1902 for technical and scientific education to help modernize Nepal. Captain Basnyat returned to Nepal in September 1905, where he developed a breechloading 3-pounder gun and improved the Gehendra design.

Today, the Gehendra is a rare collector's item. However, should any still be in the Far East's battle areas, they will undoubtedly serve alongside their British counterpart, the Martini-Henry. These guns will still be soldiering on at Armageddon. GD

The Emergency Gun

In uncertain times, a simple approach to personal protection firearms is best.

›BOB CAMPBELL

This Galco shoulder holster is among the best options in a load-bearing system. It distributes your handgun's weight and frees up your hands to work on other preparedness tasks, an advantage over lugging around a long gun.

For most of my life, I've owned and used emergency guns; that includes the handgun I carried every day. I've carried a shotgun or rifle in the cruiser trunk, and later both, and when they were deployed, it was something serious that I had a minute's warning concerning. Even if I had little warning, the handgun would be a formidable firearm. The pistol is the handiest of tools. It is light but reliable and practical. You can use it to take control of a situation and save lives.

By the same token, handguns are far less capable than long guns. About half of the firearms I see carried daily and ending up in CWP training classes are practically worthless as emergency guns. Compact pistols under .38 caliber don't match my criteria. Owning an emergency gun is like having a spare tire, jack and lug wrench in the trunk: we hope we don't need it, but we need it badly if we do.

Some people have guns on hand that are well-suited for emergency use. Others purchase specialty firearms such as a long-slide 9mm or AR-15 rifle specifically for emergency use. But they have not fired them extensively. Training is minimal. This puts these individuals in the position of being armed with a deadly weapon but unable to defend themselves effectively. You must maintain a higher skill level, or the emergency gun isn't worthwhile.

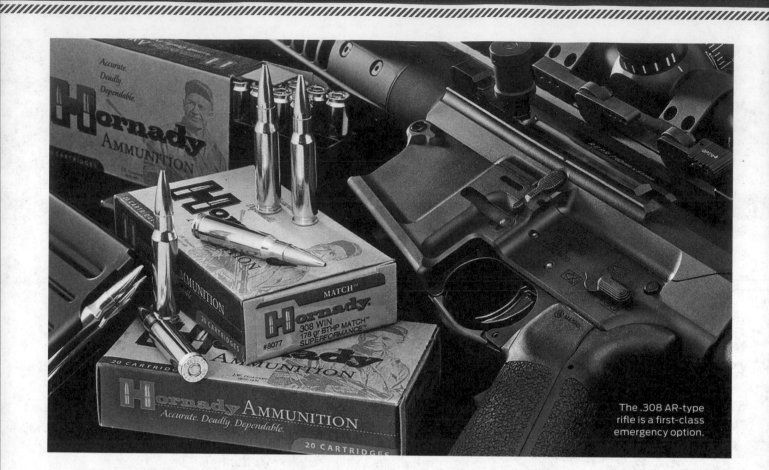

The .308 AR-type rifle is a first-class emergency option.

You are far better served with simple workman-like firearms you've mastered than overly complicated ones you haven't. A man who knows his .357 Magnum lever-action rifle, as an example, is well-armed indeed. I would never discount a quality double-action revolver. A firearm you've grown up with and use often may be the best emergency gun. I have quite a few firearms intended primarily for personal defense and others for hunting. A few are purely recreational. There is some overlap in purpose.

A quality .45 auto pistol will take game. In fact, I've taken two deer with a 1911 .45, and, in each case, the range was less than 35 yards. By the same token, the Bergara Special Purpose .308 deer rifle would serve well in many critical scenarios. Experience indicates the emergency gun must be a reliable, robust and handy firearm that takes a standard cartridge and is easy to maintain. The firearm is one of many emergency tools. A first aid kit and entrenching tool, as well as emergency food supply, should be at the top of the list. Arming your spouse, partner, and family members is a consideration. If they're interested shooters, then they have their own ideas. The commonality

A Remington 870 shotgun, Wilson Combat CQB pistol and the Bergara Special-Purpose rifle cover just about any preparedness challenge you can imagine.

A quality AR-15 rifle or carbine is among the finest of emergency rifles. Low recoil and large ammo capacity make it suitable for use by trained family members.

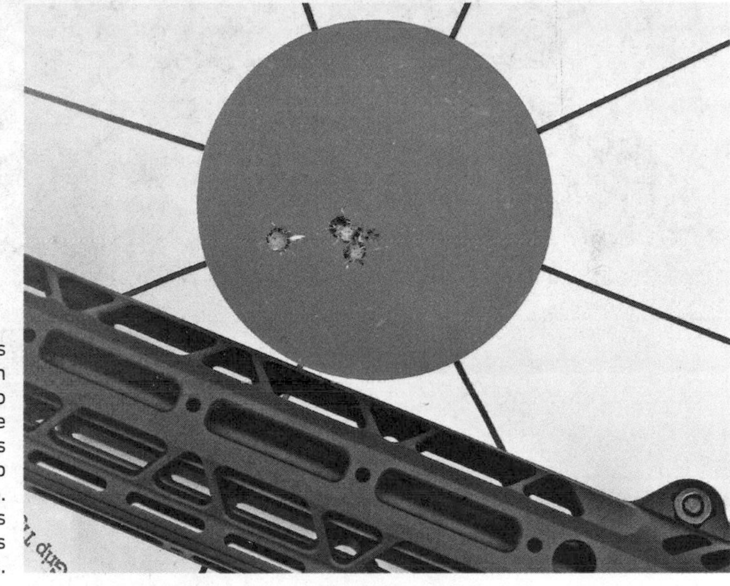
Black Hills Ammunition and a TruGlo Omnia scope produced this 100-yard group with a PSA rifle. The flyer rests on the author's shoulders.

of ammunition and magazines may be beneficial.

Having two AR rifles is an excellent idea. However, if the other folks are not interested in shooting and training, an extra gun could become a liability. If you're reading this report, then you are a gun enthusiast and may own quite a few firearms … or just a couple. Your life has accommodated firearms, and your job may require you to use them. You may be a bird hunter and only equipped with shotguns but have been thinking about something in the safe just in case of an emergency. As for me, firearms are an essential part of my life and have been for about as long as I have been out of three-cornered britches. Just the same, practical choices are most beneficial for emergency guns. But no matter how humble the emergency gun is, it can be a lifesaver if used well.

If the buying public and the millions of new gun owners have learned anything, it's that even in a highly industrialized and organized nation, demand can outstrip supply. You need to procure your emergency guns now, not later. For more years than I have been alive, it has been standard policy among homeowners to purchase a firearm, learn how to shoot it and throw the thing in a drawer "just in case." Fortunately, that has worked well for many. For others, not so well. Folks have been killed in their home by their own gun because it wasn't secured properly. Gun safety and safe storage are crucial subjects worth a report all its own. Having the gun readily available in case of an emergency is equally vital. Balance speed of access with security.

While it is OK to accumulate as many guns as your lifestyle will support, you don't need that many for emergency use. You may not hole up in your castle during an emergency; you may need to get out of Dodge during a natural event such as a storm. Weather-related emergencies are more likely than widespread civil unrest, although nothing seems out of the question. Some of us may need mobility.

A standard setup modeled after 3-Gun competition is ideal. That's right, 3-Gun shooting competition as a model is the way to go, which means a good rifle, pistol and shotgun. You need to decide which of the three is the primary firearm — the gun you will depend on for most of your personal defense needs. It isn't always simple to choose. The handgun was the most important when I worked as a peace officer. It was the piece that was always with me. The shotgun was the backup in the trunk of the cruiser. The rifle was seldom seen in my early years, and later it was a special-purpose 'arm rather than backup. The shotgun is the most crucial firearm for home defense for many of us.

A rifle is a primary firearm and the most useful for those living in wide-open spaces. The sidearm should be as light as possible if you will be carrying a long gun slung on your shoulder. On the other hand, if you're backpacking, a more capable long-barreled handgun may be needed if it's your only firearm. Let's look at some of the better choices.

An advantage of stainless steel revolvers is that they resist rusting and pitting.

One note: Some of my friends who have been in dire straits across the world find the pistol primarily helpful in defending against feral dogs. Some of our home-bred attack dogs are formidable and will be loose and hungry during emergencies. My rescue animal was saved during some terrible storms about five years ago. She is a wonderful, sweet animal that the grandchildren love. An animal mistreated and then left to fend for itself will not be friendly to humans. The threat profile should be studied. A feral man is at the top of the danger list. Feral dogs next. Wild animals are the least likely threat, but then bears and big cats take a toll on humans every year. Feeding yourself by hunting with a firearm should be part of the plan. Develop your skills before the ball goes up.

REVOLVERS

If you could have only one firearm to do everything — and you are skilled or willing to invest the time to build the skills — a quality 4-inch-barrel .357 Magnum is a good choice. A medium-frame revolver such as the Smith & Wesson 686 or Colt Python is perfect. The vault-tough Ruger GP 100 is another. These revolvers will take game with the proper load and a marksman behind the sights, and the .357 Magnum is among the most-effective anti-personnel cartridges. A general-purpose load such as the Remington 125-grain JHP, Hornady Critical Duty, or Winchester Silvertip should be stored. Concealing this firearm is more complicated than some. Be sure to choose a high-riding holster that rides close to your body and won't interfere with your long gun.

If you're leery of .357 Magnum recoil, a good .38 Special revolver is a reasonable alternative. (You can also load .38 Special in your magnum revolver.) The Smith & Wesson Combat Masterpiece is

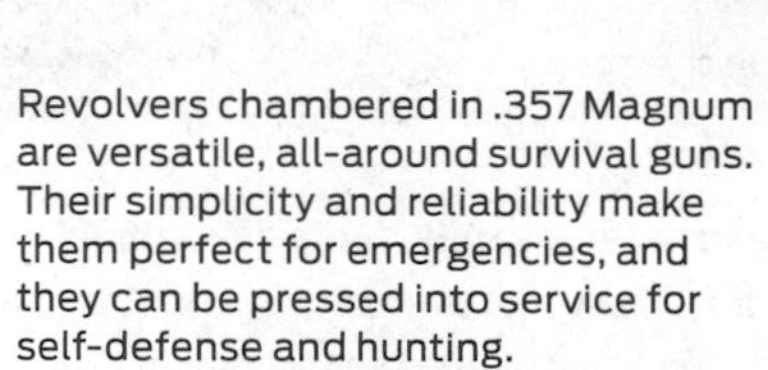

Revolvers chambered in .357 Magnum are versatile, all-around survival guns. Their simplicity and reliability make them perfect for emergencies, and they can be pressed into service for self-defense and hunting.

among the finest, best-fitted and most accurate revolvers of all time. Quality defense loads such as the Federal Punch are widely available. If the .38 Special is deployed in the wild, use a heavy Buffalo Bore Outdoorsman load. You might consider purchasing a .38 Special snubnose as a backup or hideout gun.

The Springfield TRP is among the best 1911s for rugged use.

SELF-LOADERS

The polymer-frame striker-fired pistol has several advantages. Among these are reliability and affordability. The Glock is a baseline for reliability. If the pistol costs less than a Glock, corners have been cut. If it costs more, be sure you get your money's worth. The 9mm offers enough power for personal defense with quality defensive ammo. The Hornady XTP, Federal HST, Winchester Silvertip, and Remington Golden Saber are a few of these. The 9mm pistol should have self-luminous iron sights (night sights) and a light rail. With a reserve of 15 to 18 cartridges, the autoloader will allow you to take on long odds if you can shoot well. Magazines are plentiful. For concealed carry, the Shadow Systems MR20 is an ideal choice.

For those who may find themselves in floodwater, the Glock Mariner is an excellent option. No, you won't be shooting underwater, but the Mariner features special striker cups that enhance the pistol's reliability after immersion. A standard Glock is easily converted. A 5-inch barrel 9mm such as the Smith & Wesson Performance Center Military & Police 2.0 is a credible choice that gives a trained shooter every advantage.

Clockwise left to right: Citadel, Colt and Guncrafter 1911 types. A lot of skillful work building and gunsmithing must go into these handguns.

This Del-Ton .308 is equipped with a variable power scope. A setup like this covers you for close-range trouble and mid-range hunting opportunities.

SAO AND DA FIRST-SHOT GUNS

Aluminum-frame handguns strike a balance between fit, feel, weight and durability. They are lighter than steel-frame guns but heavier than polymer-frame ones. Among the best choices are the SIG single-action only (SAO) types. The SIG Legend P226 9mm is by far my favorite 9mm. Magazines are plentiful. The pistol features night sights, an accessory rail and legendary reliability. The SIG P220 SAO offers a hard-hitting .45 ACP cartridge without the drawbacks of the 1911 for many shooters. The Beretta 92 and SIG series double-action (DA) first-shot pistols have the appeal of being safe to leave laying on the ground, on the chest over a sleeping bag, or beside the bed but instantly ready to get into action. The double-action first shot is more challenging to master, while the single-action shot is wonderfully crisp and accurate.

1911

The 1911 is an excellent handgun — but don't get a cheap one. Quality 1911s include the Ruger SR 1911, Springfield Ronin and SIG 1911 — all top performers. Colt 1911s are good pistols overall but are somewhat outclassed by modern developments. If you can afford a Dan Wesson, Wilson Combat, or Nighthawk, you will have a firearm built to close tolerances and more accurate than some rifles. The .45 ACP cartridge has excellent wound potential and practical accuracy.

Advantages of the 1911 include a straight-to-the-rear trigger compression, a low-bore axis that limits muzzle flip and excellent speed to an accurate first shot. Be sure you learn to handle .45 ACP's recoil.

RIFLES

We always wish we had more power from our handguns, while the rifle may have more potency than needed. We worry about adequate penetration with a handgun. We use an expanding bullet to limit penetration and cause more damage with the rifle. When it comes to an emergency rifle, among the first choices is the AR-15. Even inexpensive AR-15 rifles and carbines are reliable and accurate, at least in the short term. A quality AR such as the Colt, Springfield SAINT, or Ruger are good options. These rifles offer ample ammunition reserve, are easy to use well, and the better versions are very accurate.

America's Rifle — aka the AR-15 — is capable of a wide range of chores. The .223/5.56mm chambering is preferred. Some calibers may not be widely available in times of shortage. You can carry a lot of ammunition in a few magazines. The .223 is the finest defense rifle available based on power, low recoil and terminal effects. Stock up on 60- to 73-grain JSP loads. In the .223, even FMJ loads are effective for personal defense. For some, the hard-hitting AR-10 .308 is a counterpoint. Powerful and as accurate as all but the most precise bolt-action rifles, the AR-10 has a lot going for it.

There is nothing quite like the lever-action rifle for those who prefer a manually operated rifle. The lever gun shoots flat, is fast-handling, easy to operate and gives you many advantages. A pistol-caliber carbine has more leverage, and you can fire it more quickly than the .30-30 type. The .357 Magnum lever-action rifle should be considered — even if you don't own a revolver in that chambering. If you need more punch and greater range, consider a .30-30 rifle. Several companies, including Henry, offer 'black rifle' versions of the lever-action. They are well worth your time considering high-visibility sights and excellent handling.

CZ's 527 is a brilliantly accurate and lightweight little rifle. CZ chambers it in the mid-range 7.62x39mm cartridge.

BOLT-ACTION RIFLES

The bolt-action rifle for personal defense is sometimes called the Scout Rifle. These are formidable firearms with a 16- to 18-inch barrel and a 10-shot magazine. The Savage Scout in .308 is among my favorites. The balance of value for price and overall handling is superb. The scout should feature quality aperture sights for fast work. A .308 rifle is effective on 200-pound game to 200 yards. If the range is close, you could stretch that weight rule and take larger game, and a .308 may be accurate well past 200 yards if quality optics are fitted. A 10-round mag offers plenty of firepower for most situations. The .308 is for the person who sees taking game as an essential part of the picture. In a worst-case scenario, the .308 will shoot through two or three car doors — something the .223 won't do — and it's more effective against vehicle glass and light cover.

The carbine-type bolt-action rifle with a 3-9x optic is a typical deer gun. But it may be more versatile than most would

The Benelli M4 is expensive, but performance cannot be faulted. The U.S. military fields these hardworking and reliable shotguns.

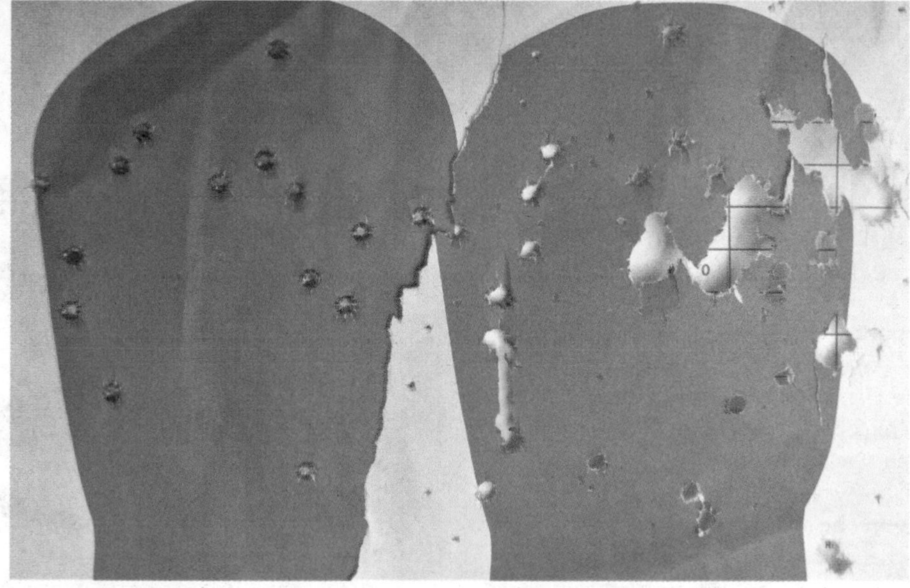

A barrage of 9mm at the left, fired from 25 yards, compared to shotgun buckshot and slugs, right. There is no comparison in effect!

think. With the elevation cranked down, it's fast on target at moderate ranges, yet it gives a trained shooter an edge well past 200 yards. I don't think I would be poorly armed with this rifle in many situations. The CZ 527 is a compact bolt gun in 7.62x39mm that just may be the best buy in a light rifle on the market. The CZ features a set trigger making offhand accuracy easy.

SHOTGUNS

The shotgun is probably the most misunderstood and underutilized of emergency guns. It is easily the most effective and the most likely of all firearms to put a threat down with one shot. Not long ago, I viewed a video of a wildlife agent in Asia hunting a man-eating crocodile that had killed a villager. The agent tracked the croc in a boat, closed in, and fired a single shotgun blast at perhaps five yards. The colossal crocodile turned over in the water and died. Marine shotguns are kept on hand to kill sharks taken on board with the commercial catch. Buckshot is deadly effective but won't destroy the deck, they say. Shotguns can be light and lovely upland field guns designed to take small game birds or relatively heavy tactical guns configured for house-to-house fighting. The best breed is versatile and will take game and save your life.

There are many loads available. For defense use, you need only two — buckshot and slugs. Birdshot is sometimes recommended for home defense by those who must not have done research or have no experience in the subject. Birdshot is made to kill a small game bird you could hold in your hand humanely. Penetration is less than six inches of gelatin or water. Birdshot could be stopped in a heavy coat at a few yards' distance! The payload is essential, and some buckshot loads maintain a cohesive pattern across 25 yards. Landing five or six of the eight or nine pellets into the target is vital to ensure good effect. Hornady Black and Federal Flite Wad are better choices for the extended ranges, Remington Managed Recoil is another.

For home defense, any buckshot load is fine with a cohesive pattern to 7 yards. Don't neglect slugs, as they are effective, even in open choke shotguns, to at least 50 yards, and in a dedicated rifled-bore shotgun, past 100 yards. Solid slugs have good penetration and offer outstanding wound potential.

As for specific shotgun models, if it's intended as a projectile launcher, then the exact choice isn't as crucial as other firearms. You can purchase a Turkish-made pump-action shotgun for three-hundred dollars, perhaps a little less, or a used Remington or Mossberg for about the same. The shotgun may not be as smooth

This Black Aces 12 gauge is remarkably compact but easy to use well.

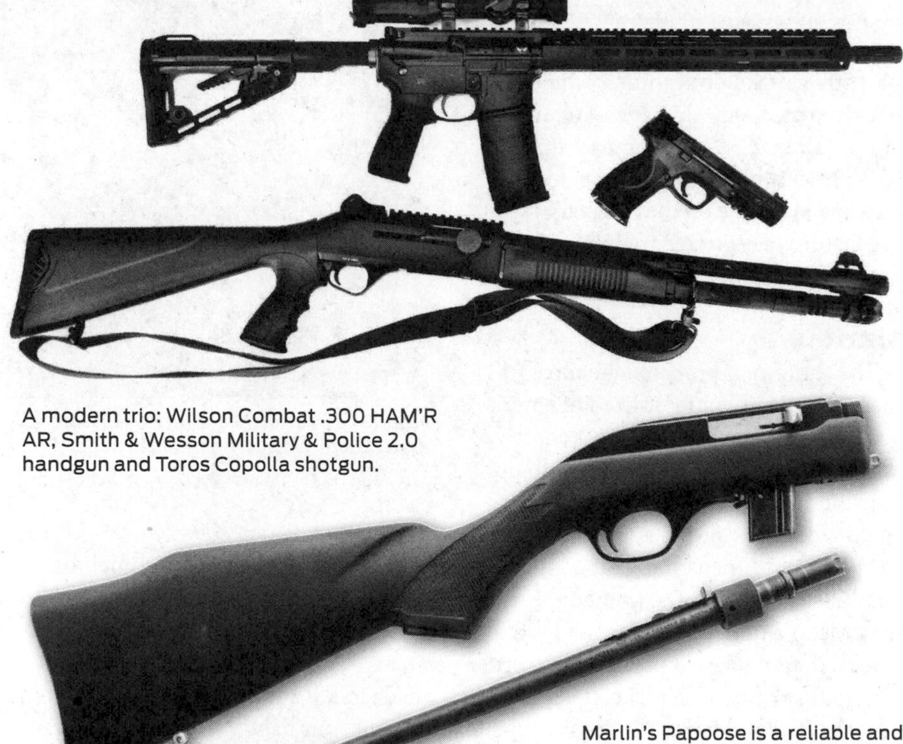

A modern trio: Wilson Combat .300 HAM'R AR, Smith & Wesson Military & Police 2.0 handgun and Toros Copolla shotgun.

Marlin's Papoose is a reliable and lightweight .22 you can break down and stuff into a bug-out bag.

as some or have the specialized features, but it will work every time you shuck the action. The pump action is the most practical type of emergency shotgun. It uses a trouble-free tubular magazine, and shells are loaded one at a time by sliding the forend forward and rearward (thus, they're always known as slide-action). During a battle, you can top off the gun one load at a time. You can quickly change between buckshot and slugs.

I do not care for the new breed of magazine-fed pump-action shotguns. The shotgun handles mainly by feel and balance, and a magazine destroys this balance. Likewise, the AK- and AR-type shotguns don't strike me as viable, either. They simply don't handle quickly, and a shotgun isn't a rifle. The pump-action shotgun is the best choice.

For example, the Ithaca Deerslayer is something of a legendary slug gun. The bottom ejecting shotgun is well-made of the finest material. With a tight chamber and rifle sights, this shotgun is used in places not allowing rifles due to range restrictions. You could even use the Deerslayer as a sporting gun simply by changing barrels. Go bird or rabbit hunting one day, then change the barrel for deer.

For most uses, a dedicated personal-defense shotgun needs to have only a bead front sight. A Remington 870 Express is perhaps the most trouble-free shotgun on the planet. It is the gold standard for pumps for fast handling, reliability and simplicity to use. But some folks prefer a self-loading shotgun. The self-loader is less versatile as it will not take light loads and continue to function reliably. It will function consistently only with full-power loads. That said, a quality self-loading shotgun is a formidable firearm if you have a dependable load dialed in.

Load-bearing gear is critical! Don't go cheap and carefully consider the gear. Blackhawk! is a good source. On the far left is the Adaptive Tactical 10/22 magazine holder.

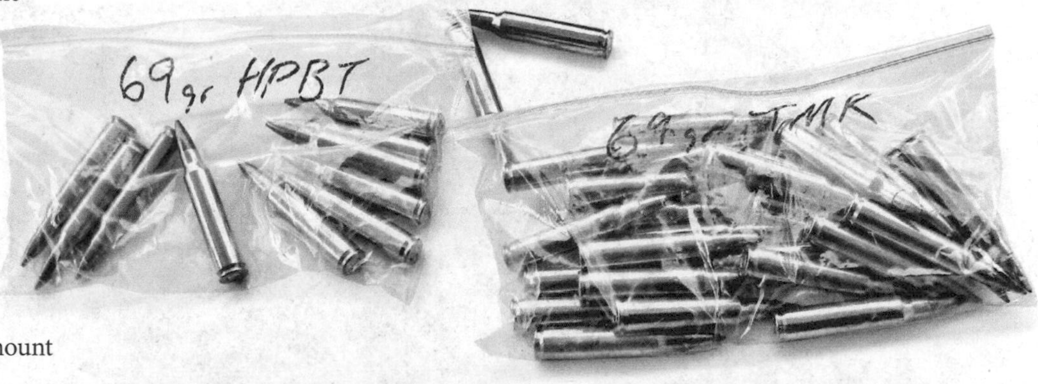

It's OK to store handloads in bags for range work, but this would never work for long-term storage.

Storing factory ammunition in original packaging is an acceptable means of preserving it.

Among the very best of modern shotguns is the Remington Versa Max Tactical. With the proven Versa Max action and a generous magazine capacity of six to eight shells depending on the model, the Versa Max gets my vote. The Versa Max features enlarged controls for positive manipulation and XS sights. Another legendary shotgun useful for emergency duty is the Benelli M4, proven on battlefields worldwide. However, while I appreciate the M4, its price severely cuts into the budget for other firearms.

The Toros Copolla T4 is comparable in every way to the M4. In fact, the Toros is kind of a wonder gun. The trigger action is improved over the Benelli, and the triggerguard is improved by enlarging the opening for gloved hand use. Every part is interchangeable with the Benelli. An advantage of this shotgun is that it's fitted with choke tubes. While it isn't a conventional hunting shotgun, it could venture into the hunting class using choke tubes. The T4 features excellent sights and plenty of real estate to mount optics.

RIMFIRE OPTIONS

Quite a few folks own rimfire firearms and nothing else. By default, these are their emergency guns. Quite a few of my liberal friends own one firearm — a lightweight .22 kit gun they carry while hiking the Appalachian Trail. Despite this, I find the history of the .22 caliber handgun in personal defense dismal. The .22 rifle is another matter. Good shot placement, a fast backup shot, and adequate penetration sometimes allow the .22 to take on tasks well out of its weight class. A good-quality .22 rifle is a reasonable choice if you can shoot straight. The affordability and availability of the Ruger 10/22 put it at the top of the list. A quality .22 lever-action rifle such as the Browning, Henry or Rossi are worthy alternatives. They are light, accurate, reliable and capable of taking small edible game.

LOAD-BEARING GEAR

The worst-case scenario should be met with planning. Load-bearing gear is essential. It would be a disaster to grab a rifle and start stuffing ammunition into your pants pockets. You should have a ready bag — Blackhawk! is a personal favorite of mine — with first aid supplies such as Quik Klot, burn and bite treatment, bandaids, dressing, water, a camp knife and a hatchet. The backpack should be strong, durable and rugged. Long guns must have a sling (I look to Galco for affordable slings). The sling should be wider on the shoulder and naturally carry the firearm. A sling also aids in offhand accuracy.

Ammunition should never be stored loose. An airtight container is best; factory packaging works in most circumstances. Carry spare ammo in a magazine carrier on your belt. Four spare magazines are plenty. Adaptive Tactical offers one of the finest carriers for the Ruger X rimfire mag. A shotgun-style bandolier holding about 20 shotshells is a good investment.

For handguns, there are plenty of magazine carriers from Galco. Carrying the handgun should take some thought. A cheap holster will be a chafing nuisance. A quality shoulder holster will keep the handgun out of the way during camp chores or when repairing the house and keep it from bumping into the long gun during movement. You will be carrying life-saving gear on your back, so take as much time to consider the backpack and load-bearing system as choosing a firearm. Don't go cheap!

We should prepare, train, equip and pray for the best. If the worst-case scenario comes, be ready with carefully chosen gear. In the end, the man or woman behind the tool matters most. GD

With its Cerakote-protected stainless steel receiver and barrel, the X-Bolt Mountain Pro is a true go-anywhere rifle designed to withstand the elements.

Browning X-Bolt Rifles: Evolving TOWARD PERFECTION

›MIKE DICKERSON

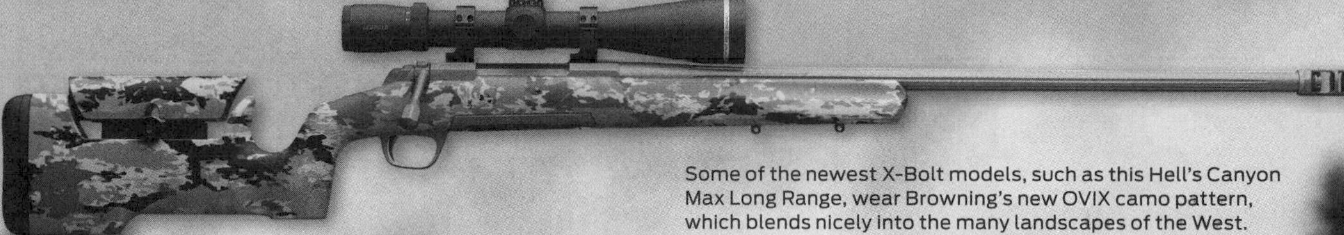

Some of the newest X-Bolt models, such as this Hell's Canyon Max Long Range, wear Browning's new OVIX camo pattern, which blends nicely into the many landscapes of the West.

If you're like me, when you pick up a new hunting rifle, you run your hands over the lines of the stock and examine its fit and finish. You work the bolt several times to see how smoothly it cycles and check how the rifle balances in your hands. You work the safety, throw the rifle to your shoulder and dry fire the gun several times to get a feel for the trigger. Sometimes, you may be unimpressed and question some of the decisions made by the manufacturer. But occasionally, the initial examination makes you smile, and a little voice inside your head whispers, "This one's a shooter."

That has been my reaction every time I've examined a new Browning X-Bolt rifle, and in every case, that little voice has been correct. Each X-Bolt model I've tested has proven unfailingly accurate and a joy to shoot.

To the uninformed, one bolt-action rifle might seem much like any other — they all function in basically the same manner, and there are only so many ways they can be improved. Some insist that an inexpensive rifle will do the job of a more expensive one. Maybe it will, but maybe it won't. Cheap rifles may not have the consistent accuracy needed for shooting game at longer distances. They may not be built to withstand bad weather, and they may not be light enough for hunting in the remote high country. With rifles, as with most things, the difference between a good design and a great one is careful attention to the details, and in the case of X-Bolt rifles, Browning engineers got the details right. X-Bolts exude quality

With its long, high-BC, heavy-for-caliber bullets, the new 6.8 Western cartridge from Winchester and Browning has quickly become one of the best-selling chamberings in X-Bolt rifles. Photo: Mike Dickerson

in ways that elude many other factory rifles, and that's no accident. Just about everyone at Browning is a hunter or shooter, and every detail of each X-Bolt rifle has been designed from the perspective of avid hunters and shooters.

TAKING THINGS A STEP FURTHER

Browning unveiled the X-Bolt to the public in 2008, and those first rifles incorporated numerous features common to all X-Bolts. These included a crisp, three-lever Feather Trigger system, adjustable from 3 to 5 lbs., shooter-friendly tang-mounted safety, and a bolt unlock button atop the bolt handle that allows you to safely cycle rounds through the action with the safety engaged. The rifles were equipped with a new Inflex recoil pad that directs recoil energy in a downward deflection to reduce perceived recoil and muzzle climb. The guns utilized a detachable rotary magazine designed to feed cartridges directly in-line with the bolt instead of feeding from an offset position like traditional leaf-spring magazines. Those first models introduced the unique and rock-solid X-Lock scope base mounting system. Bolts had a short, 60-degree lift to speed up cycling and provide ample scope clearance. Barrels were free-floated, and receivers were bedded fore and aft for stability.

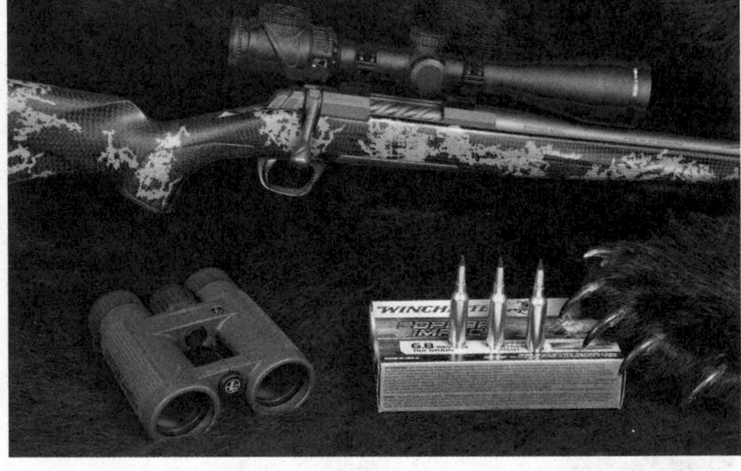

The new carbon-fiber-stocked X-Bolt Mountain Pro rifle weighs just 6 lbs., 2 oz., and is, in the author's opinion, the finest X-Bolt rifle made to date. Photo: Mike Dickerson

The X-Bolt design began four years before the rifle's introduction. The design didn't happen because one person had a better idea. The rifle had its genesis when Browning's marketing team told its engineers that it needed a new rifle. The A-Bolt rifle was, at that time, Browning's flagship bolt action. The A-Bolt was a good gun, but the design was getting a little long in the tooth and wasn't without its flaws. There was room for improvement. Long-range shooting became increasingly popular, and Browning wanted a rifle with a better trigger, tightened accuracy and improved long-range performance incorporating modern features.

The engineering team considered all the features that the marketing team wanted. Still, it took things a step further, according to Marcus Heath, Browning's director of research and development. Heath was a quality manager and one of the first engineers to work on the X-Bolt. "We thought we could improve the receiver and add rigidity and improve accuracy," he says. "The A-Bolt has one of its locking lugs in the six o'clock position. We went away from that to make everything more compact and minimize the height of the action. With the X-Bolt, one lug is in the twelve o'clock position, so that limited the amount of material above to drill and tap for scope mounting. Instead of two screws in the center (for each set of rings), we went to four outboard."

The result was the X-Bolt's iconic X-Lock scope mounting system, with its total of eight mounting screw holes, which is about as solid as things get in mounting scopes to rifles. Changing the position of the locking lugs also allowed Browning to ditch a hinged floorplate in favor of a flush-fitting, detachable rotary magazine. This feature enabled Browning to add more material to the bottom of the receiver, enhancing rigidity and accuracy. Designers used a small-diameter bolt with three locking lugs to save weight and retain strength. They wanted to retain the A-Bolt's 60-degree bolt lift, but to do so in a compact receiver meant they had to re-engineer the design to ensure that undue force wasn't required to lift the bolt.

One underappreciated aspect of the X-Bolt's design is the detachable rotary magazine, which played a critical role in allowing designers to do what they wanted with the receiver. The heavy-duty polymer magazine is more robust than it looks and is made to withstand abuse. It retains cartridges by the case shoulder rather than allowing rounds to ride freely within the magazine. This prevents bullet noses from slamming into the front wall of the magazine under recoil. That eliminates the possibility of changing the tip shape and BC of every bullet. It's a critical feature for consistent accuracy in long-range shooting, and the magazine design was patented under Marcus Heath's name.

The first group fired while the author zeroed a new X-Bolt Mountain Pro for a hunt. Subsequent groups shot even tighter. Photo: Mike Dickerson

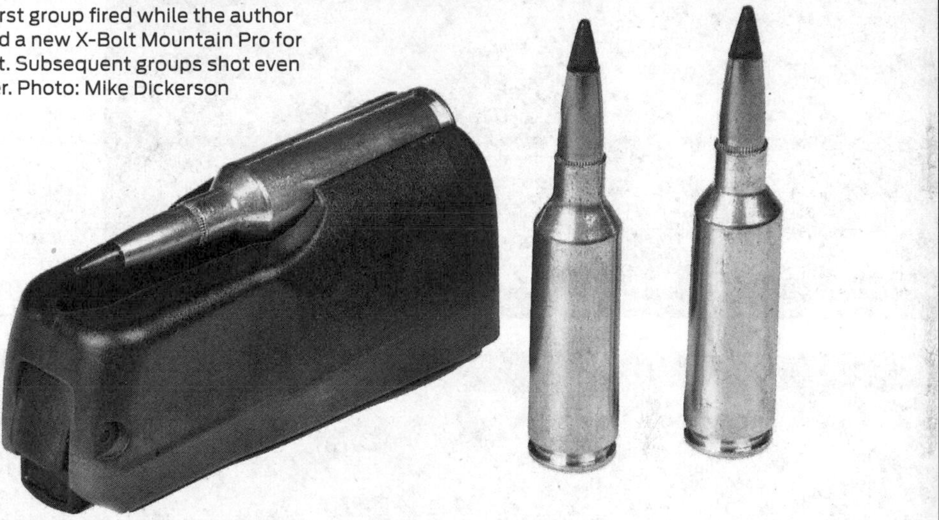

In designing the X-Bolt, Browning ditched a hinged-floorplate magazine for a flush-fitting detachable magazine for a streamlined, compact receiver with more material added at the bottom for greater rigidity and accuracy. Photo: Mike Dickerson

CONSISTENTLY ACCURATE

Of course, any rifle is only as good as its barrel, and Browning is justifiably proud of X-Bolt barrels, which are button-rifled and made by Miroku in Japan. "It's the best production barrel out there," says Aaron Cummins, senior product manager. "I have no problem saying that. Most barrels have a hole

Browning's new Recoil Hawg muzzle brake used on some X-Bolt models reduces perceived recoil by 77 percent. Photo: Mike Dickerson

drilled and are reamed and go straight to rifling. Miroku reams our barrels in three separate steps, and then there's a separate honing process before rifling to give the barrel the smoothest surface before the button is pulled through the barrel. The quality control and inspection process at the factory are very detailed."

The quality of the barrels has been amply demonstrated to me by several different X-Bolt models I've tested in recent years. Each rifle produced excellent accuracy without exception, turning in sub-MOA groups with the ammo they liked. Two rifles in non-magnum chamberings consistently shot ½-MOA groups or better, with many groups measuring just ⅓-MOA, with factory ammo. That's an impressive performance for any rifle and a testament to the quality of the barrels.

X-Bolt designers left no stone unturned in their efforts to build a superior rifle. It wasn't just a mechanical upgrade to the A-Bolt. It was a completely new design with an aesthetically pleasing appearance characterized by trim, sleek lines and stocks with more rounded bottoms and tapered forends. At the time X-Bolts were introduced, the look was a bit unorthodox. The updated styling is today considered more mainstream.

The X-Bolt was initially offered in Hunter and Medallion models with wood stocks; Stalker and Stainless Stalker models wore composite stocks. Initial chamberings ranged from .243 Win. to .375 H&H Mag. Not content to stop there, Browning has constantly introduced new X-Bolt models while discontinuing others. That's partly because Browning often produces limited editions that are only available for a specific period. Sometimes, Browning makes a significant modification, as it did with the stock of the Stalker, so the old model was replaced with a new one. Some models are also discontinued because camo patterns age, mature and fall out of favor.

X-Bolt rifles have a short, 60-degree bolt throw, providing ample scope clearance.

CONTINUOUS IMPROVEMENT

Browning has remained committed to continuously improving the X-Bolt as the rifle has evolved. That process was abundantly evident — and well-received — when Browning introduced the

The author took this big-bodied seven-point Oklahoma whitetail with a perfectly placed heart shot at 200 yards. The X-Bolt Mountain Pro rifle has accuracy in spades despite its light weight. Photo: Mike Dickerson

Rafe Nielsen, director of marketing and communications for Browning, took this Columbian whitetail in Oregon with an X-Bolt Mountain Pro rifle.

The X-Bolt Max Long Range rifle is tailored for long-range accuracy. The stock has an adjustable comb, spacers to adjust the length of pull and a vertical pistol grip.

Hell's Canyon Speed in 2016. "The Hell's Canyon Speed rifle has been the most popular X-Bolt," says Cummins. "It gave the line a huge boost and opened the collective eyes of those who hadn't looked at an X-Bolt before."

The Hell's Canyon Speed made an impressive debut thanks to its well-conceived combination of features and that it looked as good as it shot. It had fluted barrels threaded for muzzle brakes, a stock covered with A-TACS AU (Arid/Urban) camouflage and metalwork covered in a protective burnt bronze Cerakote finish. "I was a little worried doing that color," says Cummins. "But it worked well with the camo."

As of this writing, Browning offers a dizzying array of X-Bolt models in configurations ranging from rifles designed for everyday hunting to specialized ones for specific applications. Happily, for southpaws, many popular models come in left-hand versions. Depending on the model, prices range from about $1,000 to a little more than $3,000. The line still includes the more affordable Hunter and Stalker models and Western Hunter models with adjustable comb systems that come in several variations. Several Medallion models have a classic and refined appearance with high-grade, gloss-finished walnut stocks with spacers and rosewood forend tips for those who prefer their rifles with the refined traditional wood stock look.

Several Micro Midas models are sized for smaller shooters. There's a Predator Hunter model and an Eclipse version with a thumbhole stock and a target gun with a McMillan stock. A wide range is available, including standard and long-range guns with Browning composite or McMillan stocks and various camo patterns and Cerakote finishes. X-Bolt Max rifles are also designed to help varmint and target shooters go the distance.

The newest X-Bolt models include

In country where long shots are the norm, the inherent accuracy of X-Bolt rifles gives hunters an edge.

the X-Bolt Speed OVIX and Speed Long Range OVIX, which dropped "Hell's Canyon" from their name and now wear Browning's versatile and attractive OVIX camo pattern on their stocks. Other X-Bolts getting the OVIX camo treatment include the Western Hunter Long Range, Hell's Canyon Long Range McMillan and Hell's Canyon Max Long Range.

Browning currently lists 28 different chamberings spread across the X-Bolt line ranging from .204 Ruger to .375 H&H Mag, with many interesting stops in between. Browning says the top-selling chambering in X-Bolt rifles for many years has been the 6.5 Creedmoor, followed by the .300 Win. Mag., .308 Win, 6.5 PRC and 6.8 Western.

Much of the X-Bolt's evolution has been driven by the popularity of long-range shooting. That has been a factor in the X-Bolt's success, and it speaks to the rifle's inherent accuracy, but the primary driver in hunting rifles is still deer hunting.

We like accuracy and shooting long distances as riflemen, but people buy hunting rifles to shoot deer. Many people have less time to hunt these days, and hunting seasons in some places are getting shorter, so many want to buy rifles that deliver superior quality and reliability. All X-bolt rifles do precisely that, but there's one in the lineup that stands above the rest.

A newer X-Bolt model that's sure to gain a following is the Speed Long Range OVIX. It's optimized for long-range shooting and features a stock with an adjustable comb and OVIX camo pattern, a heavy fluted sporter barrel and an extended bolt handle.

BEST OF THE BEST

Sitting atop the pinnacle of the X-Bolt line are the new carbon-fiber-stocked X-Bolt Pro rifles. Browning calls these guns, which weigh less than previous carbon-fiber-stocked models, "semi-custom" rifles. The one most recently sent to me for testing, which quickly convinced me that it needed to find a home in my gun safe, is the Mountain Pro Burnt Bronze model, chambered for the new 6.8 Western cartridge from Winchester and Browning. It's a marriage made in heaven.

I instantly became a fan of the cartridge when I first tested it and used it in a Winchester rifle to take a 10-point Texas whitetail with a tricky quartering-on shot. I followed that up by shooting a big-bodied seven-point Oklahoma buck using the Mountain Pro and Browning's 170-grain Long Range Pro Hunter load. The buck fell to a perfectly placed heart shot at 200 yards. That takes an accurate rifle, and the X-Bolt Mountain Pro has accuracy in spades, consistently producing ⅓- to ½-MOA groups with the two loads I've tested.

In addition to all the standard X-Bolt features, this rifle has a carbon-fiber stock, a spiral-fluted bolt and a spiral-fluted, stainless steel 24-inch barrel. Combined with the X-Bolt's streamlined stainless receiver, these features bring the rifle's weight to a svelte 6 lbs., 2 oz. Its weight is even more impressive considering that the barrel comes with a sizeable installed Recoil Hawg muzzle brake, which Browning says can reduce recoil by 77 percent. Based on my own experiences shooting the rifle, that claim is legit. Interestingly, Browning even built a special bench just for testing muzzle brakes before settling on the final design of the Recoil Hawg, and the reduction is immediately evident when shooting the gun. Despite its light weight, this is one rifle you can shoot all day.

Browning's semi-custom treatment includes subjecting the rifle's barrel to a proprietary lapping process to minimize the need for break-in, improving accuracy and reducing cleaning time. The twist rate is a zippy 1:7.5 to stabilize the long, high-BC, heavy-for-caliber bullets used in 6.8 Western ammo.

Except for the gold-plated trigger, all exterior metal has a burnt bronze Cerakote finish that goes nicely with the two-tone accent patterns on the stock, filled with a noise-dampening foam. To my eye, the overall look is quite pleasing, and the rifle tends to turn heads at the range. Swivel studs are included, as is a removable short Picatinny accessory rail beneath the stock's forend.

The Mountain Pro is also offered in Long Range variants and versions with tungsten Cerakote finishes. In addition to 6.8 Western, you can get the rifle in 6.5 Creedmoor, 6.5 PRC, .300 WSM, .30-06 Springfield, 7mm Rem. Mag., 28 Nosler, .300 Win. Mag. and .300 PRC. The Mountain Pro Long Range rifle comes with 26-inch barrels and is offered in most of the same chamberings plus 30 Nosler and .300 RUM.

The X-Bolt Mountain Pro isn't cheap, with an MSRP of about $2,500. The best seldom is, but the X-Bolt Mountain Pro fits the bill if you want a light, superbly accurate rifle that can go anywhere and take the worst that nature can dish out. I'd call it Browning's best in a line of outstanding rifles. GD

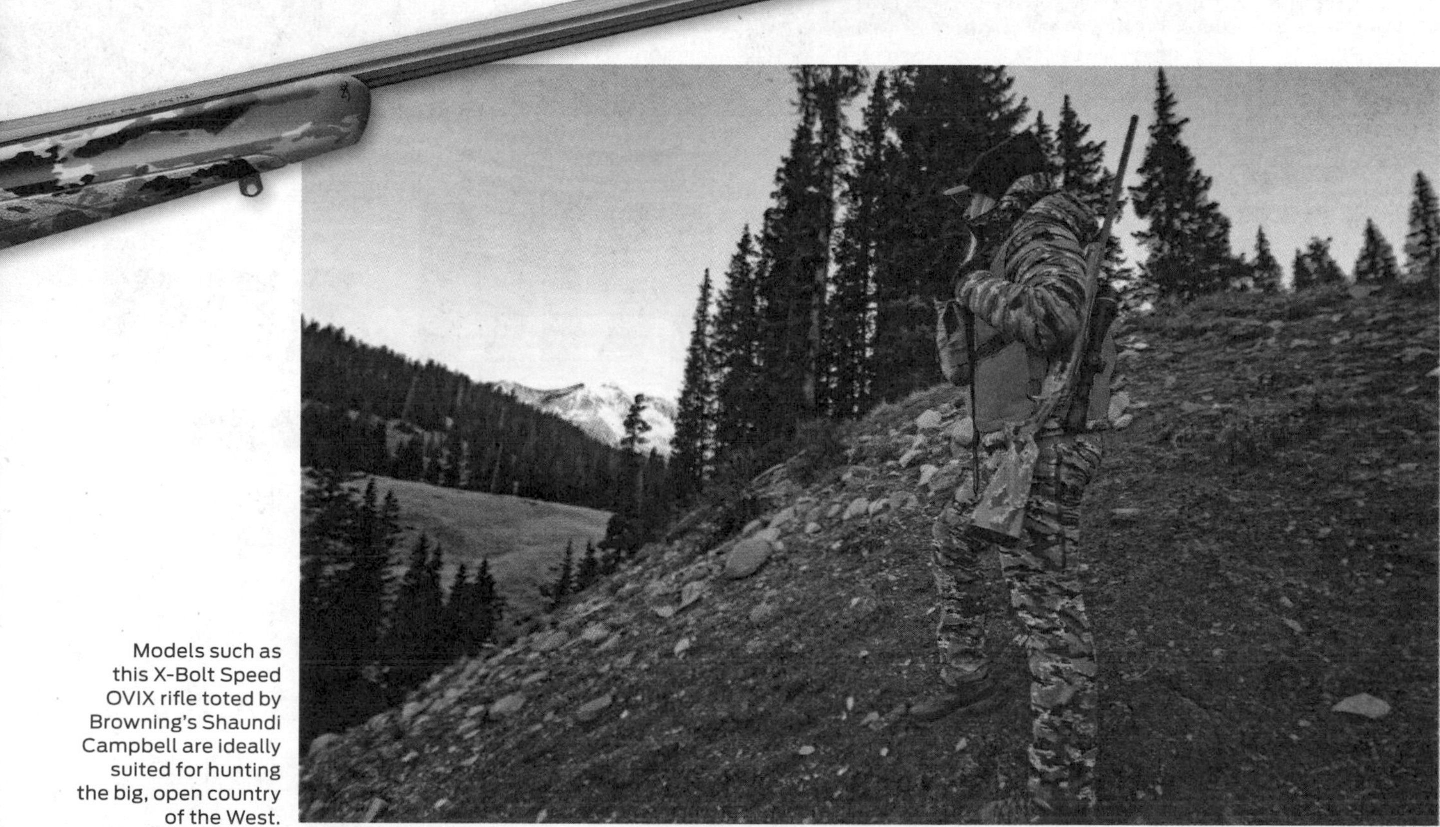

Models such as this X-Bolt Speed OVIX rifle toted by Browning's Shaundi Campbell are ideally suited for hunting the big, open country of the West.

THE STORM and THE TEMPEST

Developed during World War II, the Sturmgewehr 44, a.k.a. *StG-44*, revolutionized tactical infantry combat.

› MIKE HASKEW

Photos: Rock Island Auction Company rockislandauction.com

Perhaps the most significant blunder Adolf Hitler committed during World War II was turning his war machine, the *Wehrmacht*, eastward in summer 1941 and invading the Soviet Union. After tremendous initial successes, the German Army got caught in the grip of the resurgent Red Army, and an avalanche of well-armed enemy troops and modern armor, artillery, and automatic rifles brought the conflict to a catastrophic climax on the doorstep of the Nazi capital of Berlin. As the military situation eroded in the East, Hitler gathered with his generals and bluntly asked what they needed to bring about a reversal of fortune.

One of his generals quickly replied that many more of the new rifles issued in recent months would undoubtedly help the situation. But the volume of deliveries would never materialize, and the request surprised Hitler, who was supposedly unaware that a "new" rifle even existed. Although it had been a potential war winner, the Sturmgewehr 44, literally the "Storm Rifle," came in too few numbers and too late to alter the course of World War II in Europe.

Nevertheless, the impact of the Sturmgewehr 44, the world's first widely produced and issued assault rifle, was far-reaching.

Since the mid-20th Century, the ubiquitous assault rifle — as evidenced by the proliferation of the Soviet-made AK-47 and the American M-16 — has come to symbolize modern warfare on land. The AK-47 is emblematic of the Third World's rise, the favored gun of the armed insurgency, and the Cold War-era Warsaw Pact armies' standard issue. Today, whatever its origin or country of manufacture, from the FN FAL to the M4, the assault rifle traces its lineage to the German Sturmgewehr 44.

MP44 (Sturmgewehr 44), Germany. Caliber 8x33mm Kurz. From the collection of the Armémuseum (Swedish Army Museum), Stockholm.

The development of the modern assault rifle began about a century ago, as armies were locked in the holocaust of World War I. The first operational ones came about a generation later. That's when senior German commanders realized that the common infantryman, armed with the reliable Mauser Karabiner 98k (K98k) bolt-action rifle, needed a select-fire gun that could provide semi-automatic or automatic fire as the situation required.

The German military had long understood the need for increased firepower at the squad level. At the same time, the K98k, an updated version of the standard-issue Gewehr 98 infantry rifle of World War I, remained the German soldier's primary shoulder arm after its formal adoption in 1935. The Karabiner was dependable, accurate, and certainly deserving of its place among the great rifles of the 20th Century. However, it was too bulky to function efficiently for combat troops, particularly armored infantrymen (*panzergrenadiers*) who needed to quickly move in and out of vehicles or support personnel such as anti-aircraft or supply units.

The experience of World War I revealed that most infantry battles had occurred at distances greater than 800 yards, and while the K98k was a fine bolt gun, the soldier rarely singled out a target and fired effectively at that distance. Artillery had been the primary killer of enemy soldiers at that range. With its high rate of fire, the machine gun was also an effective anti-personnel choice at more extended range. During the Great War, however, when opposing infantrymen did manage to close the distance between them and engage in close combat, automatic rifles proved devastating. The lethality of the submachine gun became a given. The German MP-18 (*Maschinenpistole 18*), designed by the famed firearms magnate Hugo Schmeisser, became the first of its kind used in combat.

During the interwar years, the major powers continued their development of submachine guns. German designer Heinrich Vollmer revised earlier such types to develop the well-known MP-38 and MP-40 machine pistols that became famous during World War II. During the conflict, Allied troops commonly called these "*Schmeissers*." Although Hugo Schmeisser took virtually no active role in developing the MP-38 or MP-40, he maintained a patent on its straight magazines.

These machine pistols were indeed effective in close combat. But their low muzzle velocity of about 1,300 fps and the limited effective range — only slightly more than 100 yards — was inadequate for infantry operations during standard combat maneuvers. The German machine pistols fired the 9x19mm Parabellum cartridge, while the K98k and the primary infantry machine guns of the day, the MG-34 and MG-42, fired the standard 7.92x57mm infantry rifle cartridge. The former was inadequate for midrange action, while the latter was too powerful.

The German military establishment recognized the need for a select-fire rifle that an individual soldier could carry to provide increased firepower with some modicum of accuracy in semi-automatic mode and an adequate suppressive fire rate in full-auto. Some believed the new rifle could replace the K98k, existing submachine guns, and light machine guns altogether in practice. However, the primary concern with such a firearm was the infantrymen's ability to control it during automatic fire. The recoil of the powerful 7.92x57mm cartridge would cause the muzzle to steadily "climb," rendering it less than effective.

Interestingly, by the early months of

World War II, a potential solution to the problem of control was already available. Since the mid-1930s, German arms manufacturers had been developing intermediate-range cartridges. Much of their research centered on 7mm and 7.75mm options, somewhat smaller than the standard 7.92mm cartridge common among the armed forces and German industry. The *Heereswaffenamt*, or Army Weapons Office (HwaA), chose to maintain the existing caliber of 7.92mm to reduce expenses associated with retooling that would otherwise involve new factory equipment to produce smaller cartridges and replacement barrels for small arms.

Photo: German Federal Archives

In 1938, the Polte Werke Company of Magdeburg introduced the innovative 7.92x33mm Kurz Patrone or short cartridge. While it maintained the same caliber as the larger round, the Kurz was substantially shorter and less powerful. It propelled a 125-grain bullet at 2,231 fps, while the standard 7.92x57mm cartridge exhibited a muzzle velocity of 2,493 fps.

As the Kurz Patrone cartridge seemed equal to the intermediate round's envisioned task, the objective became a carbine design that could accommodate the cartridge while delivering the other prerequisites of mobility and relative ease of production. In 1939, the HwaA issued specifications for a new rifle chambered for the Kurz round. The directive stated that the gun had to conform to existing production standards, such as the 7.92mm specification. It had to be cost-effective and straightforward for a wartime economy to produce, especially amid continuing high-grade steel shortages. Therefore, stamping of components was preferable to the need for machining of parts. The rifle was to be select-fire and perform optimally at a range up to 440 yards, aligning with the post-World War I doctrine that most future infantry combat would occur at distances of less than 330 yards.

Both arms manufacturers C.G. Haenel Waffen und Fahrradbrik and Walther Waffenfabrik AG responded with similar designs under the project labeled *Maschinenkarabiner 1942*, or Machine Carbine MKb-42. Since the competing models were similar, they added the letters "H" and "W" to distinguish one from another. In preliminary tests during 1942, the Haenel design team, headed by none other than Hugo Schmeisser himself, produced the superior arm and won the contract.

Both companies had developed a select-fire rifle operated with a gas piston

The Gerät 06(H) Prototype.

The Haenel MKb 42(H) rifle of 1942.

The 1942 Mkb 42W (Walther).

Collecting the StG-44

This extremely rare German (StG) Sturmgewehr was manufactured with an early designed sheet metal sniper mount, which was fitted with a matching "prototype" ZF4 sniper scope. It appeared in Rock Island Auction Company's December 2018 auction with an estimated value of $70,000 to $90,000. Photo: Rock Island Auction Company rockislandauction.com

Original examples of the StG-44 are scarce and command high prices at auction or in private sales. At the low end of the scale, originals that have been rendered non-working have sold for just under $4,000. However, working examples are absolute showstoppers. Such StG-44s often meet or exceed anticipated prices. Several have sold for more than $30,000, and in an October 2018 release, the Rock Island Auction Company listed two StG-44s among its "Top 10 Machine Guns with Sale Prices." An example of the curve-barreled Krummerlauf sold in September 2014 for $63,250, while an example of the standard assault rifle sold for an identical price in September 2016. RIA described it as "…one of the best, all original, matching late war MP44 [StG-44] assault rifles we have ever offered."

Rock Island also presented an StG-44 equipped with an early prototype ZF4 scope with a serial number matching that of the rifle at $70,000 to $90,000 in its December 2018 catalog.

Interestingly, original examples of the StG-44 have surfaced in somewhat unlikely places. In 2012, a Hartford, Connecticut woman responded to a local police firearms buyback event by turning in an StG-44 that her father, a World War II veteran, had brought home as a souvenir. The officers who received the assault rifle

system, a departure from the blowback systems prevalent in automatic small arms. The earlier blowback system had relied on the cartridge's firing to drive the bolt back and expel the spent cartridge at the same time. It then picked up a new cartridge while moving forward and pushed the fixed firing pin into it. The gas piston system was like that of the U.S. semi-automatic M1 Garand infantry rifle. It captured the fired cartridge's energy in the barrel and used it to force the piston rearward. During this process, the carrier engaged the bolt and extracted the fired cartridge, then rechambered a new round during the return.

In the early MKb-42, both prototypes retained an inherent weakness. In combat, to keep the gun ready to fire, the bolt remained in the open position, exposing it to the elements and furthering the wear and tear of continuing operations. Field testing in November 1942 brought this shortcoming to the attention of the HwaA, which addressed it. Nevertheless, the MKb-42 received German soldiers' praise, and Haenel manufactured 11,833

The receiver's front-left side is stamped with the standard markings of: "1552 aj/45" with the "StG44" marks on the receiver's upper-rear section. The underside of the forward portion of the receiver is marked "fxo." There is a small importer's stamping on the upper-front left side of the receiver. The stock is the correct laminated version. Photo: Rock Island Auction Company rockislandauction.com

were stunned, and a historian who evaluated it pronounced that it was in excellent condition and worth up to $40,000.

In April 2009, the Chesapeake, Virginia, police department seized a working StG-44 from a vehicle during an arrest. It remained in storage for a decade before it was rediscovered and recognized as a historic find. That StG-44, valued at more than $30,000, was not returned to the owner, who was convicted on several charges. However, the individual, who no longer lives in the area, was contacted in 2018 and explained that his father, an Army veteran of World War II, had mailed it to his home while still in Europe.

"I'm not proud of how it was confiscated," the man said, "But I'm proud of him." The previous owner also remembered playing with it as a boy and leaving it outside in the rain a few times.

The Chesapeake City Council subsequently voted unanimously to donate the StG-44, valued at approximately $30,000, to the Naval History and Heritage Command in Washington, D.C.

The optic is the real rarity in that it is a purpose-built ZF4 sniper scope that has been calibrated precisely for the 7.92x33mm Kurz round. The scope was also explicitly numbered, matching this rifle, indicating that it was probably Mauser's attempt to manufacture a dedicated StG44 Sniper Rifle using a ZF4 scope. The left-rear side of the optic is correctly marked with: "Gw ZF4/71576/ddx (Voigtlander & Sohns)" next to a blue triangle, then the left front is stamped with the additional information in large bold markings of: "P. Kurz Patr./Nr. 1552," clearly indicating that it was calibrated for use with only the 7.92x33mm Kurz ammunition and not the 7.92mm used in the K98 rifle. Photo: Rock Island Auction Company rockislandauction.com

examples for further testing in 1943.

When HwaA evaluated the test results, it asked Haenel to develop a closed bolt, hammer firing system to improve the firearm's accuracy in semi-automatic mode. Schmeisser went to work on a redesign that incorporated elements of the hammer system initially seen in the Walther prototype. When completed, the redesign permitted firing from the closed bolt position. The spring-driven striker integral to the hammer system eliminated the bolt's need to rely on forward energy to engage the firing pin with the chambered cartridge. It added a spring-loaded ejector port for spent cartridges, opening and closing during the firing process, and the bolt remained closed at all times except for actual firing.

The classic Sturmgewehr 44 was a revolutionary rifle. Neither infantry rifle nor submachine gun, it was a deadly combination of both, and its descendants would radically change the face of combat operations. The firearm was comparatively short at 37 inches overall with a barrel length of 16.5 inches and heavy at 11.5 pounds fully

A StG-44 on display at the Parachute Regiment exhibition of the Imperial War Museum in Duxford. Photo: Rama

Photo: German Federal Archives

loaded. Its V-notch rear and hooded post front sights were adjustable, it fired the 7.92x33mm Kurz cartridge from a distinctive curved and detachable 30-round box magazine, and its rate of fire was a respectable 550-600 rounds per minute.

The receiver and forward section of the Sturmgewehr 44 were constructed from stamped steel and welded into a single unit. The butt was hewn from wood and pinned to the rear of the receiver. The operating spring was housed within the wooden butt and vulnerable to damage since a crack or shattering of the butt would render it inoperable. Designers fashioned the bolt to tip and lock into a steel pivot point pinned to the receiver. The trigger mechanism housing pivoted on a hinge to open downward to facilitate cleaning.

The cocking handle was positioned to the left of the receiver and locked directly into the bolt carrier. The safety sat to the right, and the cross-bolted change lever was just above it. In semi-automatic mode, you pushed the switch to the right. For fully automatic firing, you engaged it to the left. Originally, designers incorporated a bayonet lug into the muzzle. Still, they soon discarded it, viewing it as time-consuming and essentially irrelevant because of its actual concept as an intermediate-range small arm. Makers equipped a few MKb-42s with rails for sniper scopes but abandoned that with the MP-43 update.

The evolution of the Sturmgewehr perhaps met its sternest test when confronted with the Nazi bureaucracy. Due to materials shortages and political infighting, just as Haenel was perfecting the new closed-bolt firing system, Hitler suspended the development of any new small arms in the Third Reich on at least two occasions. A veteran of the trench warfare of World War I, Hitler inherently favored the time-tested Mauser rifles, the Gewehr 98 and K98k. He was also keenly aware of the need to maintain standardization in production and was concerned that a new gun might reach the front in too few numbers. In this respect, he was correct. There were about 12 million K98k bolt-action rifles in service with the German armed forces.

However, those close to the project realized its magnitude and proceeded undeterred, employing subterfuge in the process. Rather than continuing with the MKb-42 project as a distinct and "new" initiative, HWaA renamed it the MP-43 (*Maschinenpistole 1943*) and authorized continuing work under the guise of a modification of the existing machine pistol types.

In February 1943, manufacturers

churned out a limited production total of 1,217 MP-43s as Walther and other contractors pitched in with stamped metal parts and finished guns. The earliest combat deployment of the MP-43 occurred on the Eastern Front that spring as grenadiers of the 5th SS Panzer Division "*Wiking*" fought the surging Red Army in Ukraine around Kharkov. In the autumn of that year, the army's 93rd Infantry Division also received the new rifles. The Western Allies met the StG-44 during the Italian Campaign of 1943–1945. Many were stunned by the firepower they faced during the Battle of the Bulge from December 1944 to January 1945.

The individual German soldier offered stellar reviews of the new military rifle and, as enthusiastic reports from the front poured in, factories made slight tweaks to the MP-43. These included bases for the front sight and a grenade launcher feature, resulting in sub-designations such as the MP-43/1 and MP-43/2. Not only did it prove tough and effective, but unlike other German military equipment, it continued to perform in the extreme cold of the Russian winter that incapacitated much of Wehrmacht's equipment and mechanized weapons on the Eastern Front. In action, the StG-44 did supplant the light machine gun as a small arm of choice in providing covering fire. It was more mobile since single soldiers carried it and did not require the same time as a machine gun team to displace and set up. It was also surprisingly accurate in fully automatic mode, partially due to its rate of fire being considerably lower than the MG-34 or MG-42.

Hitler learned of the deception during the famed meeting in July 1944. The Führer had already reviewed the results of some field testing and shown an interest. However, he had not come to the full realization that the MP-43 was an entirely new rifle. After observing test firing, he gave the rifle his support and is said to have personally christened it the Sturmgewehr, or "Storm Rifle," a compelling moniker that was ideal for propaganda purposes. Soon, the rifle was known as the MP-44 or Sturmgewehr 44 (StG-44). It was virtually the same firearm the military had previously called the MP-43.

The urgency of the general's outburst during the 1944 meeting stemmed from the concern that the Russians on the Eastern Front had outgunned German soldiers at the squad level. The Soviet soldier was well-armed with the SVT-38 and SVT-40 automatic rifles and the PPS and PPsh-41 submachine guns. The Germans had experimented with an automatic rifle of their own, the Gewehr 41, but its performance was disappointing. Meanwhile, the Soviet submachine guns were particularly troublesome. The PPS and PPsh-41 were cheap to manufacture, mainly from stamped metal parts, and they fired the 7.62x25mm Tokarev rimless pistol cartridge from a 71-round drum or 35-round box magazine. Although the range was more limited than the K98k,

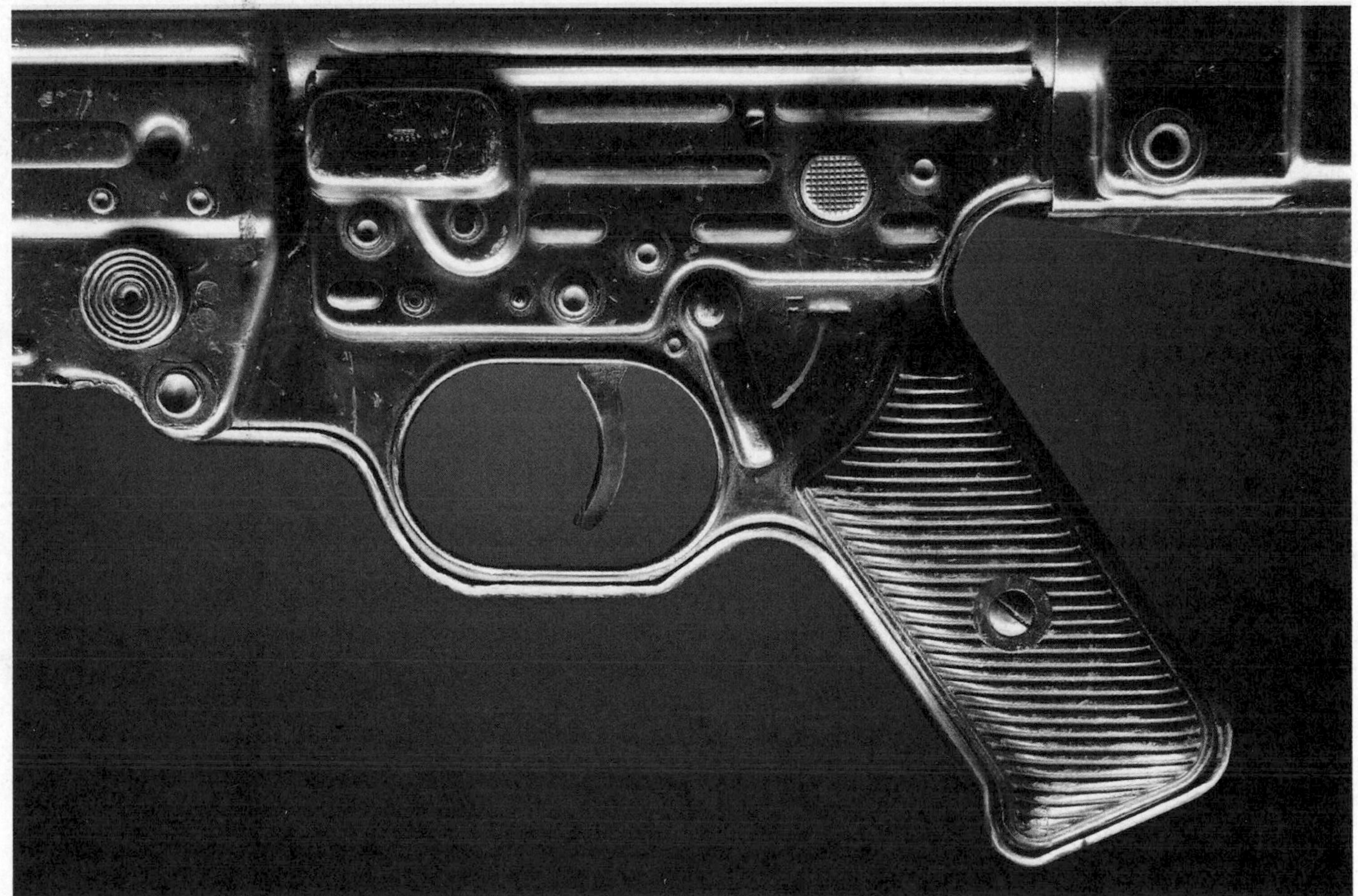

The Sturm's stamped metal construction was a design spec the Germans required for wartime production. Photo: Rama

STURMGEWEHR 44 Reproductions

The mystique of the Sturmgewehr 44 looms large among collectors, reenactors, and those who appreciate the iconic military rifle's place in history. Existing firearms laws restrict automatic firearms sales and ownership in many jurisdictions around the world. However, realistic and true-to-original non-firing reproductions are available. At the same time, working models chambered for various cartridges, largely .22 caliber, fulfill a sense of the past and pride of ownership among enthusiasts of both classic firearms and the history of modern warfare.

The HMG reproduction StG-44 is chambered in four options, .300 BLK, 5.56X45, 7.62X39, and 7.92X33.

Located in the Atlanta suburb of Alpharetta, Georgia, Hill & Mac Gunworks (HMG) announced at the 2016 SHOT Show that it would begin producing a replica StG-44. Production delays have resulted in long wait times, but the reproduction remains available via the company website with a price tag of $1,799.99 and an alert that relates **SHIPPING SOON**. The replica is strikingly representative in the look and feel of the original and chambered in four options, .300 BLK, 5.56X45, 7.62X39, and 7.92X33. Its specifications are like the original with a length of 37.5 inches, weight 11 pounds, 10 ounces unloaded, and beechwood grip and stock. Short versions are also available.

The Spanish-made DENIX is a non-firing Sturmgewehr replica with working action and correct dimensions.

German Sport Guns, established in the city of Ense in 2002, has since 2012 offered a single-action StG-44 reproduction chambered for rimfire .22 LR. It is slightly shorter than 37 inches in length though it looks and feels authentic. It weighs only 9.5 pounds unloaded. The GSG reproduction is complete with wooden stock and grip, a California-compliant 10-round magazine (or a 25-round mag), and the metal parts are either in blued or black finish. Most details are non-functioning; however, the safety, magazine release, and bolt handle are workable as if someone had wrapped the StG-44 exterior around a .22-caliber rifle. It ships in an authentic box, retail prices range from $400 to $600. The box itself is collectible, but some recipients have struggled to remove the hard foam packing material that prevents damage during shipping. American Tactical Imports (ATI) exclusively imports the GSG StG-44 to the United States.

Since 1966, the Spanish firm DENIX has been building remarkable reproductions of historic guns. The company produces a non-firing StG-44 in full size and weight as the original with a working metal body and action. The wooden stock is well-formed and complements the overall appearance of the replica assault rifle. DENIX carefully crafts the StG-44 replica to prevent modification into a working firearm, and many examples appear in motion pictures, television, and with reenactor groups. Examples for such uses are often complete with worn or aged finishes, while new models sport a black finish. The DENIX reproduction has received praise for its likeness to the original and is available in the United States. The replica is 36.5 inches long and features a detachable magazine. Retail pricing is between $200 and $300.

Distributor Atlantic Firearms touts a non-firing StG-44 replica as the best on the market with proper length and weight to the original and constructed in all-metal and wood rather than plastic or resin. The bolt and trigger are operational with an authentic snap, and the magazine is detachable. The company also offers the GSG and HMG .22-caliber rifles in working models.

An active aftermarket for StG-44 replicas has seen some appreciation in values, at times as much as double the original MSRP. Of course, resale value is heavily dependent on condition.

the PPS and PPsh-41 were superior to the German bolt-action rifle in close combat.

Once Hitler was thoroughly convinced of the Sturmgewehr 44's capabilities, he was committed to mass production and deployment in large numbers. By the end of World War II, Haenel, Walther, Steyr-Daimler-Puch AG, Sauer & Sohn, and Erma facilities manufactured 425,977 in all variants, at roughly 15 percent of the small arms produced in Germany during the war years and a fraction of the 1.5 million originally ordered and the 4 million planned for eventual delivery. Relatively few, therefore, reached the front lines, and these were routinely plagued with ammunition shortages as the demand for the Kurz cartridge far exceeded the supply. German industry could not keep up. Consequently, German brass ordered soldiers armed with the StG-44 to keep it in semi-automatic mode as much as possible to conserve ammunition.

A pair of innovations associated with the Sturmgewehr 44 are worthy of note. The British War Office identified an infrared sighting unit that was attached to a few of the guns. Codenamed *Vampir* (Vampire), the *Zielgerät 1229* apparatus gave the German soldier some degree of night vision. It had a hood to hide muzzle flash and prevent blinding. The British noted, "The image given is of great brilliance and good contrast. Men standing can be discerned up to a distance of 80 yards, especially when moving about."

According to the British assessment, the Vampir system included a 35-watt transmitter lamp, a 30-pound battery pack that supplied up to five hours of power, and a telescopic unit for magnification. However, other sources reference a battery life of only 15 minutes. Vampir made its appearance late in the war, and only about 300 StG-44s used it. However, it is the progenitor of later infrared systems that enhanced the combat infantryman's operational effectiveness in darkness.

A handful of Sturmgewehr 44s sported the *Krummerlauf*, literally "bent barrel," which allowed soldiers to fire around corners or for tank crewmen (without exposing themselves to enemy fire) to shoot through hatches and ports. Intended for short-range engagements only, the Krummerlauf utilized a barrel bent to a 30- or 90-degree angle! A periscope allowed the shooter to aim. As the bullet traveled through the curved barrel, its velocity slowed, and it became somewhat deformed, curtailing the device's effectiveness. Only the 30-degree version entered limited production.

Despite its positive attributes, some criticism of the Sturmgewehr 44 emerged, particularly among the Allies, as they examined captured examples. Allied small arms development had concentrated on improving the infantry rifle's utility, producing the M1 Garand, M1 Carbine, and the Lee-Enfield No. 4 Mk 1, all outstanding rifles. However, this trend probably tainted Allied objectivity to a degree.

A U.S. intelligence report on the StG-44 published in Spring 1945 observed, "…In their attempts to produce a light, accurate weapon having considerable fire power by mass production methods, however, the Germans encountered difficulties which have seriously limited the effectiveness of the Sturmgewehr. Because it is largely constructed of cheap stampings, it dents easily and therefore is subject to jamming. Although provision is made for both full automatic and semi-automatic fire, it is incapable of sustained firing … and its general construction is such that it may have been intended as an expendable weapon … All things considered, the Sturmgewehr remains a bulky, unhandy weapon, comparatively heavy and without the balance and reliability of the U.S. M1 carbine…."

The report concluded, "Its design appears to be dictated by production rather than by military considerations. Though far from a satisfactory weapon, it is apparent that Germany's unfavorable military situation makes necessary the mass production of this weapon, rather than of a machine carbine of a more satisfactory pattern."

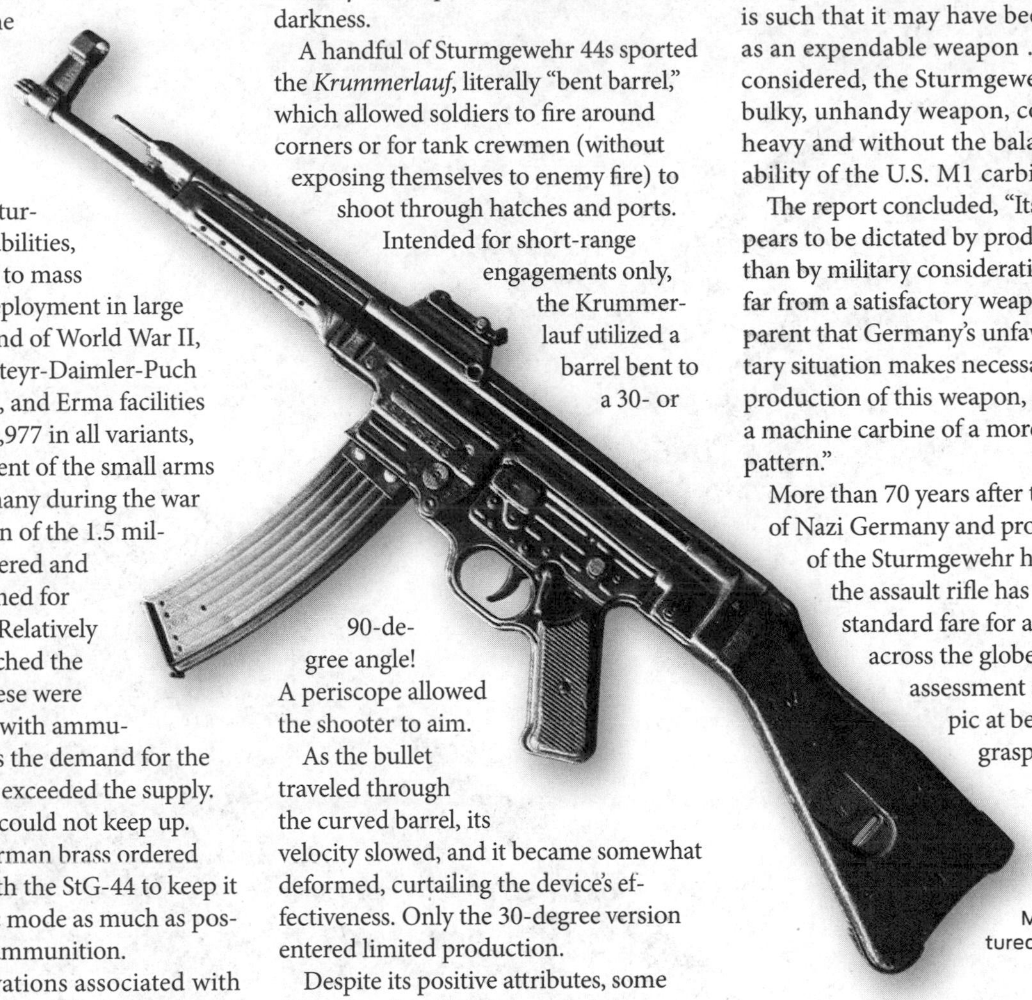

More than 70 years after the defeat of Nazi Germany and production of the Sturmgewehr has ceased, the assault rifle has emerged as standard fare for armed forces across the globe. The 1945 assessment appears myopic at best, failing to grasp the evolution of combat in the post-World War II era and beyond.

MP 44 manufactured in 1945. Photo: DCB Shooting

After World War II, the Sturmgewehr 44 remained in service with police forces in East Germany and with the armies of communist Czechoslovakia and Yugoslavia. Historians differ as to whether Hugo Schmeisser had any direct involvement with Mikhail Kalashnikov in developing the iconic AK-47. However, the lineage and influence of the German Storm Rifle are undeniable.

The StG-44 has more recently appeared in the hands of the Palestinian Liberation Organization, Hezbollah, and Hamas. More recently, StG-44s have appeared among guerrilla forces in Iraq, and American soldiers have captured several serviceable examples.

The Sturmgewehr 44 revolutionized the concept of modern warfare decades ago and continues to cast a long shadow across the modern battlefield. GD

One of the most obscure submachine guns issued behind the Iron Curtain was the Polish PM 63 "Rak." Pioneer Arms of Radom, Poland, recently redesigned it using original surplus components, transforming it into a legal-to-own, semi-automatic pistol, marketed as the PM 63C. Imported into the United States in 2020, the highly unique 9mm Makarov caliber arm has instantly become a "must-have" on the Com Bloc collector's wishlist. Aside from its re-engineered semi-auto fire control system, it fires from a closed bolt, the telescoping buttstock is welded inoperable, and its vertical forearm is locked in place. The original right slide flat is dated 1970, along with the Warsaw Pact-era "Factory 11" logo (manufactured from 1967 to 1977). As shown, the original fully automatic PM 63 fired from an open bolt/slide.

Pioneer Arms Polish PM 63C "Rak"

Return of A Practically Unknown Com Bloc Favorite

›GEORGE LAYMAN

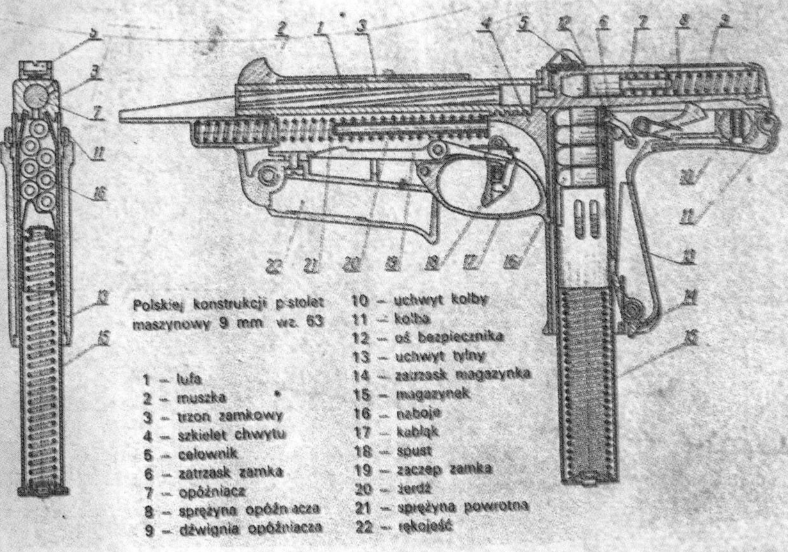

For the shooter and collector of Warsaw Pact military guns, Pioneer Arms has introduced and transformed an internally redesigned, but nearly unseen, Cold War-era submachine gun into an exciting, legal-to-own semi-automatic pistol.

Yes, it was worth the wait as Pioneer Arms Corporation (PAC) of Radom, Poland, had something special on the drawing board for some years. In 2019, it had finally become a reality.

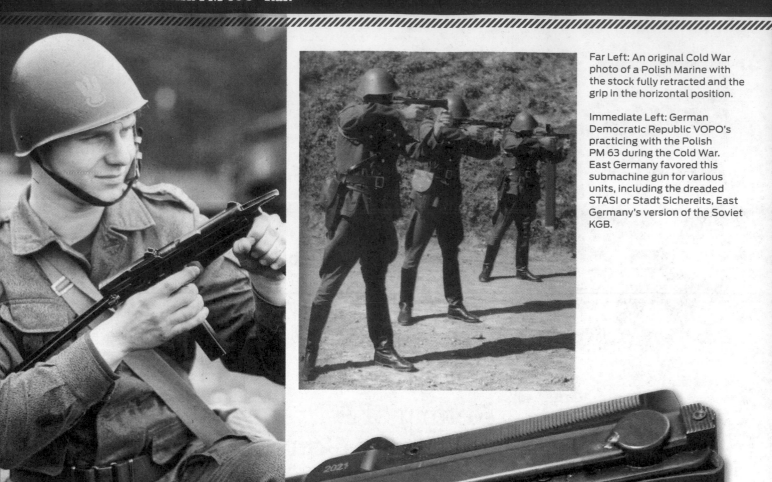

Far Left: An original Cold War photo of a Polish Marine with the stock fully retracted and the grip in the horizontal position.

Immediate Left: German Democratic Republic VOPO's practicing with the Polish PM 63 during the Cold War. East Germany favored this submachine gun for various units, including the dreaded STASI or Stadt Sichereits, East Germany's version of the Soviet KGB.

The original PM 63 thigh holster is available from several surplus dealers online. Due to the spoon-like protrusion, the holster's leather retaining strap will only engage the stud if the slide is fully retracted to the rear per the original weapon. Using an empty magazine, and racking the slide back to its stop point, will lock it in the open position. If wishing to carry a loaded 15-round magazine in this condition, the safety lever must be placed at the three o'clock position to securely carry the pistol. When readying to fire, the lever is rotated down to the six o'clock position as shown, which automatically releases the slide home to chamber the first cartridge. Photos: Dianna Kelly

PAC founder Michael Michalzuk planned to introduce the once little-known PM 63 submachine gun, transformed into a fully legal, semi-automatic variation. Adding to its line of AKs and the well-established PPS 43c semi-auto pistol, the first batch of Pioneer's PM 63C pistols had a little over two and a half years ago hit the U.S. arms market. Imported through Pioneer's U.S.-based facility in Port Orange, Florida, this Iron Curtain legend was ingeniously reconfigured from a fully automatic arm initially fired from an open bolt/slide combination into a conventional, closed bolt system.

Historically speaking, full production began in 1967, when it was introduced as the *Pistolet Masznowy 63* or PM 63 "Rak" in 9mm Makarov. It combined the Czech 23/25 and the Israeli Uzi and a host of indigenous Polish ideas. The brainchild of Piotr Wilniewczyc, the development of the PM 63 began in the late 1950s. It was a time when the People's Army of Poland was searching for a versatile, fully automatic personal defense weapon to arm paratroopers, armored vehicle personnel, machine gun crews and special operations units. It had to be something very compact to fit several specified roles; thus, nothing the Soviets offered at the time met such a need.

According to my Polish colleague and good friend, Leszek Erenfeicht, Deputy Chief Editor of the Polish firearms magazine, *STRZAL.pl*, the PM 63 was among the most expensive and high-quality submachine guns ever developed by a former member of the Warsaw Pact — not to mention the most unique configuration ever to surface. It was perhaps the second Polish design of its type to surface in decades.

But first, let's back up about forty-five years. It should be kept in mind that during Poland's Second Republic (1918–1939), the country would again soon have a working arms industry (initially established in the early 1920s), which included a pool of well-educated engineers and weapons designers. Quality-wise, Polish arms design was on par with Germany when introducing specific, indigenous armament patterns and excellent workmanship, equaling the best. Unlike Russia, the Poles could produce arms with near-complete originality, a dexterity the Russians lacked.

After the defeat of the Bolsheviks in the 1919–1920 period, Poland acquired massive quantities of Russian Mosin-Nagant rifles in 7.62x54mm, and one of its first large arms projects was the conversion of some 76,000 to 78,000 — the rifles were reworked and re-chambered to the 8x57mm or 8mm Mauser cartridge. Using a combination of Model 98 Mauser parts, which saw the creation of the wz.91/98/23, the 91/98/25 and 91/98/26 carbines were cleverly refurbished to use the German service cartridge, along with many thousand spare Mauser parts. The barrel lengths were reduced to 24 inches, and the carbines were used primarily by border guards until the German invasion of 1939.

To classical military handgun collectors, perhaps one of the finest Polish-designed small arms was the prewar VIS 1935 or P-35 Radom pistol as it is often coined. Its prefix VIS stems from the initials of the last names of its designers, Vilniewczyz and Skrzpinski. This superbly designed semi-automatic borrowed some features from John Browning's Model 1911 and was chambered for

The left-rear slide flat of the author's example is marked 2021, indicating the year of the conversion. Much like the double-action Polish P-64 9x18 Makarov pistol, the PM 63 was not an inexpensive firearm to manufacture. Unlike many former Communist Bloc submachine guns made in the Soviet Union and elsewhere, the PM 63C required several precision machining steps. Behind the Pioneer Arms Corporation's U.S. import address at the rear-top of the slide remains the Pioneer Arms Factory 11 cartouche of the "Archer" or Lucznik symbol of Radom, Poland, a logo representing many high-quality arms manufactured in the heart of the Polish arms-making industry.

To obtain accurate shot placement, a two-hand hold is almost a necessity in the absence of the sliding stock. Single-handed shooting is possible, but precise accuracy is dubious unless placing the free hand beneath the magazine well at the bottom of the grip. Quick, rapid-fire shooting is possible if desired. The PM 63C has a very manageable, 6-pound trigger pull and fast sear recovery. In the author's initial test at 15 yards using Sellier & Bellot 9x18 fodder, rapid-fire produced nearly all printing throughout the six ring, aside from seven flyers. Unless using lacquered steel cases, brass-cased ammo functioned without issue, compared to standard steel-cased 9mm Makarov cartridges.

the 9mm Parabellum cartridge. Unlike the Browning 1911, it was not cammed by a link but used a ledge-type arrangement by which the barrel was forced down on its rearward travel with the slide using recoil force. Its cosmetics differed noticeably from the M1911, with a fit and finish equaling or surpassing many other handguns of the time.

Following Poland's takeover by the Nazi occupation, the quality of the VIS 35 suffered as the war continued due to production shortcuts. Poland was forced to march in lockstep with the Soviet Union and standardized its weapons production accordingly at the war's end. The late 1950s and 1960s saw Poland given the leeway to manufacture its own designs. Under that freedom, it introduced both the 9mm Makarov PM 63 submachine gun and the P-64 CZAK semi-automatic pistol. The Polish designs were costlier than most other Warsaw Pact members had budgeted for domestic or licensed arms production.

Though not often – if ever – seen outside the communist world during its heyday, the PM 63 submachine gun was so well received that even East Germany's People's Police or *Volkspolizei*, and several special DDR units issued it in the years following domestic adoption by the Polish armed forces. However, on the other side of the Berlin Wall, several PM 63 submachine guns inadvertently slipped out of the Eastern Zone. They became a favorite with numerous terrorist groups, most notably the West German-based, radical Red Army Faction, or *Rote Armee Fraction,* commonly coined in period media as the *Baeder-Meinhof* gang. The gang used the PM 63 in several attacks in West Germany during the 1970s and 80s.

An unknown quantity was also distributed throughout the Middle East in the hands of the PLO, terrorist groups and non-state actors. A 1970s photo of PLO leader Yassir Arafat has been viewed with a PM 63 close at hand. Used in the 2003 Iraq war and 2014 Ukrainian troubles, the PM 63 was also acquired by North Korea in the 1980s, but in unknown numbers.

The nickname "Rak" can have a two-fold meaning: it can be translated as both crayfish or cancer in Polish. Its original designer, Pioter Wilniewczyc, while in the middle of his project, tragically succumbed to the latter in December 1960. In another sense, the design of the PM 63, with its stock unfolded, and front vertical handguard, could be reminiscent of a crayfish to a degree. Those viewing it for the first time with its front grip and stock deployed sometimes had problems distinguishing the front and rear of the weapon. When Wilniewczyc passed away, three colleagues, Gregorz Czubak, Marian Wakalski and Tadeusz Bednarski took over the project.

Following extensive development and several military trials, 1963 saw the *Pistolet Masznowy Wzor 1963* officially accepted into Polish army service. Firing with an open blowback slide/bolt with the flimsy stock extended, it can come very close to one's face and compel the shooter to remain attentive to this somewhat unorthodox arrangement. Otherwise, the results could lead to broken eyeglasses or worse. Some undoubtedly lost a few teeth. The selective-fire PM 63 could be used in either mode with its two-stage trigger, which, when pulled lightly to the first stage, could be used as a semi-automatic. And when pulled entirely to the rear, it produced fully automatic fire, an ingenious arrangement, sans the need for a selector switch.

The newly redesigned Pioneer Arms version has been designed solely as a semi-automatic pistol, firing from a more conventional closed bolt with the installation of an internal hammer within the fire control group. In compliance with ATF directives, the original but lightly constructed, flat, telescoping folding stock, butt plate, and vertical foregrip were permanently pinned or welded, making them non-functional. On the upside, the locked-in-place horizontal foregrip can help stabilize the 4-pound pistol when firing with both hands, which is the most conducive method for accuracy.

Aside from omitting certain parts (such as the unnecessary rate reducer) and reworked internal components, the Pioneer PM 63C uses surplus parts from the original and is as close to the real deal as legally possible. The oval "Luczik" or Archer cartouche marked 11 at the base appears as a nostalgic leftover symbol of communist times on the rear, upper slide, giving it a genuine flavor of a time in history, now long gone. The basic design utilizes a unique feature, unseen on its ilk's other, more conventional firearms. A protruding, trough-shaped spoon-like compensator that served three functions. In addition to keeping the original version from climbing during fully automatic fire, it also protected the shooter's hand on the somewhat wobbly vertical foregrip if inadvertently slipping upward to the front of the muzzle when used in the full-auto mode. And lastly, instead of pulling the slide rearward with the second hand, you merely pushed the "spoon's" nose against a solid surface like a wall or

These close-up views of the muzzle area show the "ready to fire" position of both the original PM 63 and the new Pioneer semi-automatic. With its slide retracted in the ready mode, the original's protruding compensator is nearly flush with its chrome-plated barrel, whereas the PM 63C has it some 2-3/8 inches ahead of the muzzle. The author prefers Pioneer's semi-auto conversion and considers the closed-bolt configuration a plus due to a practical center-of-gravity that contributes to a conducive center of balance and uses the "spoon" against a solid surface for one-handed chambering. Additionally, the rearward locked slide exposes the open breech to dirt or foreign matter that could impede the gun's function if used in the field during a real-world scenario. Photos: Jude Steele floor of a vehicle to cock the gun and ready it for firing.

In the new Pioneer PM 63C, the "spoon" performs an identical function with a loaded magazine when the slide is forward, but the slide returns to the forward position, all with one hand.

The adjustable L-type flip-up sight is calibrated for 75 and 150 meters. Supplied with a 15- and 25-round magazine, the grip's center doubles as the magazine well — like handling an Uzi, but much lighter in weight. The 9mm Makarov cartridge has very manageable recoil during rapid-fire, especially with a two-hand hold, and surprisingly the accuracy of this pistol at 20 yards is spot on.

Regarding ammunition, the Rak functioned flawlessly with brass-cased ammunition, whereas steel-cased cartridges saw some stovepipes, extraction and failure-to-feed issues. Also, the rear of the slide needs a boost to close with steel cases. My choice of ammunition was both the Polish-produced Red Army Standard with 93-grain full metal jacketed hardball and 95-grain Czech Sellier & Bellot. The exception to the feeding issues was that lacquered steel-cased ammo ran smoothly without interruption.

In the not-too-distant past, I was an ardent fan of the Czech Vz 61 Skorpion in Com Bloc PDW submachine gun/machine pistol reworks. Following four 300-round range sessions with the new Pioneer offering, despite the all too real ammo shortages, I've switched personal preference to the 9x18mm Makarov, PM 63C. It has been learned through experience that many open bolt submachine guns converted to a closed bolt configuration have more than once harbored a

The Pioneer PM 63C is supplied with an instruction manual, a 15- and 25-round magazine, a cleaning kit and an original Polish solvent/lubricant container. Up to this point, the author has found it to be one of the most reliable closed-bolt conversions of an original open-bolt submachine gun converted to semi-automatic.

host of problems with reliability — be it design or ammunition issues. Aside from two instances where the slide had to be given a nudge forward, returning it to battery — a very minor shortcoming — the PM 63C ran reliably.

Regarding the steel-cased ammunition feeding problem, it may be worth noting the use of worn surplus magazines with bent followers can be another culprit. This issue must be evaluated on a per gun/per magazine basis. In addition to supplying two mags, Pioneer's PM 63C includes a detailed instruction manual, surplus Polish military oil/solvent can, and an original PM 63 cleaning kit, with a rod, brush, jag and oiler accompanying each new pistol. Other accessories such as the thigh-length web holster and magazine pouches can be obtained from various surplus suppliers. Note that the original surplus PM 63 holster's fastening strap will only reach the retaining stud with the pistol's slide locked to the rear due to the length of the "spoon" compensator. With a loaded magazine and the safety latch on, the slide solidly remains rearward until the safety is switched to the fire position at nine o'clock, automatically releasing it and chambering the first cartridge.

In a nutshell, the PM 63C is a superbly constructed new addition to the Com Bloc aficionado's arsenal. Coupled up with the efficient 9mm Makarov cartridge, it makes a perfect combination of an almost unknown submachine gun of the past, transformed into a new semi-automatic pistol. This conversion of a once well-received personal defensive arm from the Warsaw Pact blends an aura of the past still fresh in the memory of those who remember the looming threat of intercontinental nuclear missiles and Soviet M-4 "Bison" long-range bombers reaching our shores during a very tense Cold War. It is not yet completely erased. However, back in the day, few in the West knew much about the PM 63 Rak — a very lethal Polish crayfish! GD

The PM 63C with the first Polish 9mm Makarov-caliber service pistol, the P-64 CZAK, the last four initials taken from its designers. Both were used in the same period, and one can see closely that they are exceedingly well made and were not low-cost firearms to produce. They displayed precise machining, precision cuts and radiuses and were likely among the most expensive guns produced within the Warsaw Pact sphere.

Author's note: Those who submit the proper documentation to the ATF can reconvert this pistol to reactivate the sliding flat steel buttstock and vertical foregrip to SBR status, of which a gunsmith should be consulted. I wish to thank Michael Michalzuk of Pioneer Arms, Radom, Poland, and Ancel Roberts of PAC USA, Port Orange Florida, and a special "Dziekuje Ci" to my colleague Leszek Erenfeicht, Deputy Chief Editor, of STRZAL.pl magazine, in Warsaw, Poland.

This early .577 Black Powder Express double rifle took big beasts with blunt bullets at modest speeds.

Are Bullets Too Sharp?

Like cheetahs, fast bullets look the part. But speed alone doesn't kill. And reach unused is pointless.

›WAYNE VAN ZWOLL

In case he comes: A heavy round- or square-nose solid bullet of high sectional density. Then another.

I shed my pack, slid my arm through the sling and crawled ahead. Only tines showed. The weeds were noisy. Each advancing inch carried risk. Belly to earth, I settled the crosswire above the antler. This close in, with dead air, my scent would reach him soon. "Hey, buck," I said softly. An ear tip twitched. Again, and its head swiveled. I raised my foot, gently let it fall. The reticle quivered. The buck rose fluidly, one heartbeat from gone, collapsing at the report. On the treeless prairie, whose bleached grass bled to sagging November skies, my bullet had traveled perhaps a dozen steps.

"The last desert ram I shot was not over 30 yards away," wrote Jack O'Connor, "and the best Dall I have ever taken was maybe about 40 yards from the muzzle…." He allowed that most of the sheep he'd shot probably fell inside 150 yards. Like mid-continent's prairie, northern sheep country yields much to the hunter's glass. That killing shots would come close in such environs might seem odd. But long pokes are seldom needed. On my first Alaskan sheep hunt, I carried an iron-sighted Springfield, downing a Dall's ram at 70 yards on bald shale. Even for sharp-eyed pronghorns on featureless flats, I've found lever rifles with aperture sights adequate. The utility of such rifles in eastern whitetail cover is obvious.

Still, the focus of cartridge and bullet design now is on flatter flight and more precise hits at long range. Powerful optics make accurate aim possible beyond the practical reach of traditional "deer rifles," with their blunt bullets at modest speeds. Sounds like progress.

But wait a minute.

Indeed, the 19th-century shift from patched round balls to conical bullets was a step forward for hunters using muzzle-loaders. The ratio of weight to frontal area was higher for conicals, so they fought drag better. They packed more momentum and penetrated deeper.

The march of breechloading rifles into the 1860s, and the advent of smokeless powder 30 years later, had little effect on bullet shape. Primitive optical sights weren't reliable enough for hunters. Lethal reach was primarily determined by how well hunters and soldiers could aim with iron sights. But smokeless fuel forced changes in bullet *construction*, as it sent naked lead bullets so fast they stripped in the rifling and left lead smears in the bore. The U.S. Army tried tin plating but found it could "cold solder" to the case mouth, bumping pressures. One bullet left wearing the neck! Cupro-nickel jackets (60/40 copper/nickel) were better. By 1922, Western Cartridge had a jacket alloy of 90 percent copper, 8 percent zinc, 2 percent tin. Called Lubaloy, this "gilding metal" blessed Western's Palma Match cartridges that year. Now, most bullet makers use jackets comprising 95

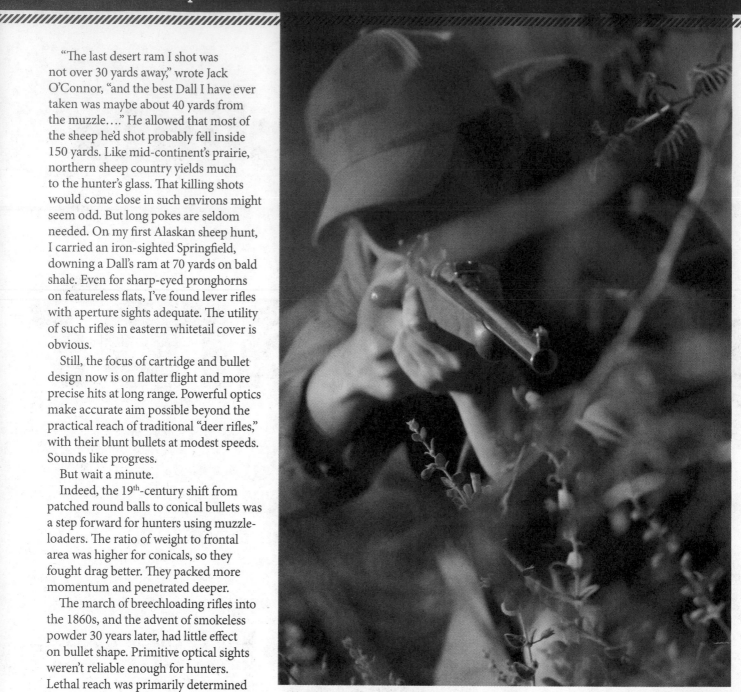

In the African bush, pointed bullets are pointless. This 9.3x62 hurls 286-grain round-nose bullets, SD .305.

"Softs and solids," 260 to 350 grains, make the .375 versatile. Use heaviest bullets for big game close.

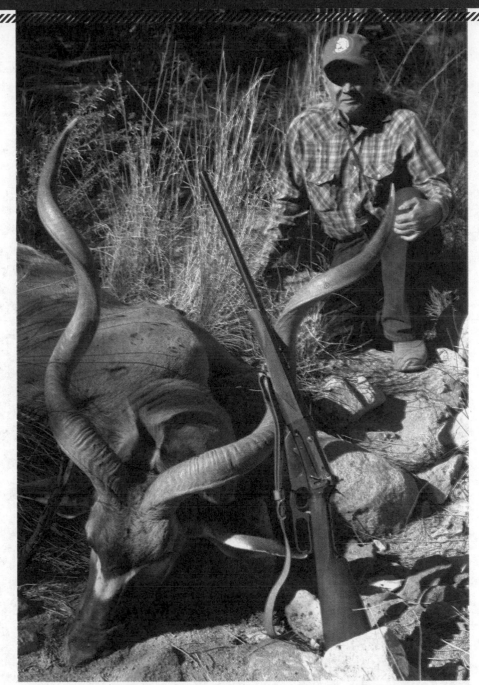

Like T.R., Barry Fisher took an iron-sighted Winchester '95 on safari. He killed this kudu at 45 yards.

Flat-nose bullets in "deer cartridges" for tube-fed lever rifles help prevent recoil-induced detonation.

percent copper and 5 percent zinc.

Improved propellants and more dependable optical sights with jackets that endured greater bore friction pushed the development of frothy cartridges than bullets that *held* their velocity better at a distance. The first cartridge in 1898 Mausers was a smokeless 8mm for the 1888 Commission rifle, which had little Mauser influence. Officially, the 7.9x57 or 7.9x57J (correctly, I; in German, these letters can interchange) sent a 227-grain .318 bullet at 2,100 fps. Germany soon had a more potent round for the stronger 1898. The 8x57, with a 154-grain pointed .323 bullet at 2,870 fps, appeared in 1905. Designated 7.9x57IS and 8x57IS, the 8x57 would see Germany through WWII. A Lange Visier rear sight could be set for dead-on aim to 2,000 yards. This 8mm inspired the U.S. Army to swap a blunt bullet for a spitzer in the .30-06.

Round- and flat-nose bullets remained standard in cartridges for tube-fed Winchester and Marlin lever rifles, as primers resting on pointed bullets in the magazine could detonate when the rifle recoiled.

***

For soldiers firing full-jacket bullets, the shift to spitzers dramatically increased effective range. But hunters also had to consider how an expanding bullet behaved after winning its battle with air. On a 1946 moose hunt, John Nosler famously failed to drop a mud-spackled bull with his .300 H&H. When at last the bull succumbed, Nosler found his first bullet had fragmented on entry. With machine-shop savvy from re-building automobile engines, he designed a two-part bullet with a web of jacket material between nose and heel. The heel powered on as a solid if the nose failed, ensuring penetration. Next season, John and his pal Clarence Purdie handily killed moose with this homemade bullet. The Nosler Partition Bullet Company was soon birthed in Ashland, Oregon. (Incidentally, in 1915, Charles Newton had designed a partitioned bullet. Poor timing doomed it and Newton's other worthy projects.)

Also, to improve bullet performance in tough game, Bill Steiger soldered a thick, ductile copper jacket to a lead core. In 1964, he founded Bitterroot Bonded Core

Bullets in Lewiston, Idaho — where he also wrote Speer's first five loading manuals. Years later, IBM executive Jack Carter was drawn to bonded bullets when, in Africa, a Cape buffalo absorbed several shots from his .375. He designed a bullet with a thick copper heel and a bonded nose. Its center of gravity lay farther forward than that of a pointed lead-core bullet. He sold his Trophy Bonded Bear Claw bullet to Federal, which began loading it in 1992. Next year, Federal brought production in-house, changing jacket material from copper to 90/10 gilding metal, which Nosler had used for Partition bullets turned on screw machines until 1970.

Geoff McDonald's rural Australia shop chugs out Woodleigh Weldcore bullets, bonding 90/10 jackets to lead cores. His are big-bore bullets, solid and softnose, for traditional dangerous-game rounds. In the early 1980s, Lee Reed improved Nosler's Partition by bonding its front section. Swift's A-Frame resulted. Since then, all major ammunition makers have cataloged bonded-bullet loads (Federal, Norma and Kynoch have featured Woodleighs). Their common purpose: deep penetration and dependable upset in tough game, with at least 90 percent weight retention.

None of these bullets had Pinocchio noses. Nobody at the time seemed to care.

The Era of the Sharp Polymer Tip followed a pre-occupation with long-range hits, first on paper and steel targets, then on game. Not to say testing the reach of rifles, ammunition and shooters is new: In 1874, Remington's L.L. Hepburn designed a Rolling Block rifle to beat the Irish champs in a long-range match. Each

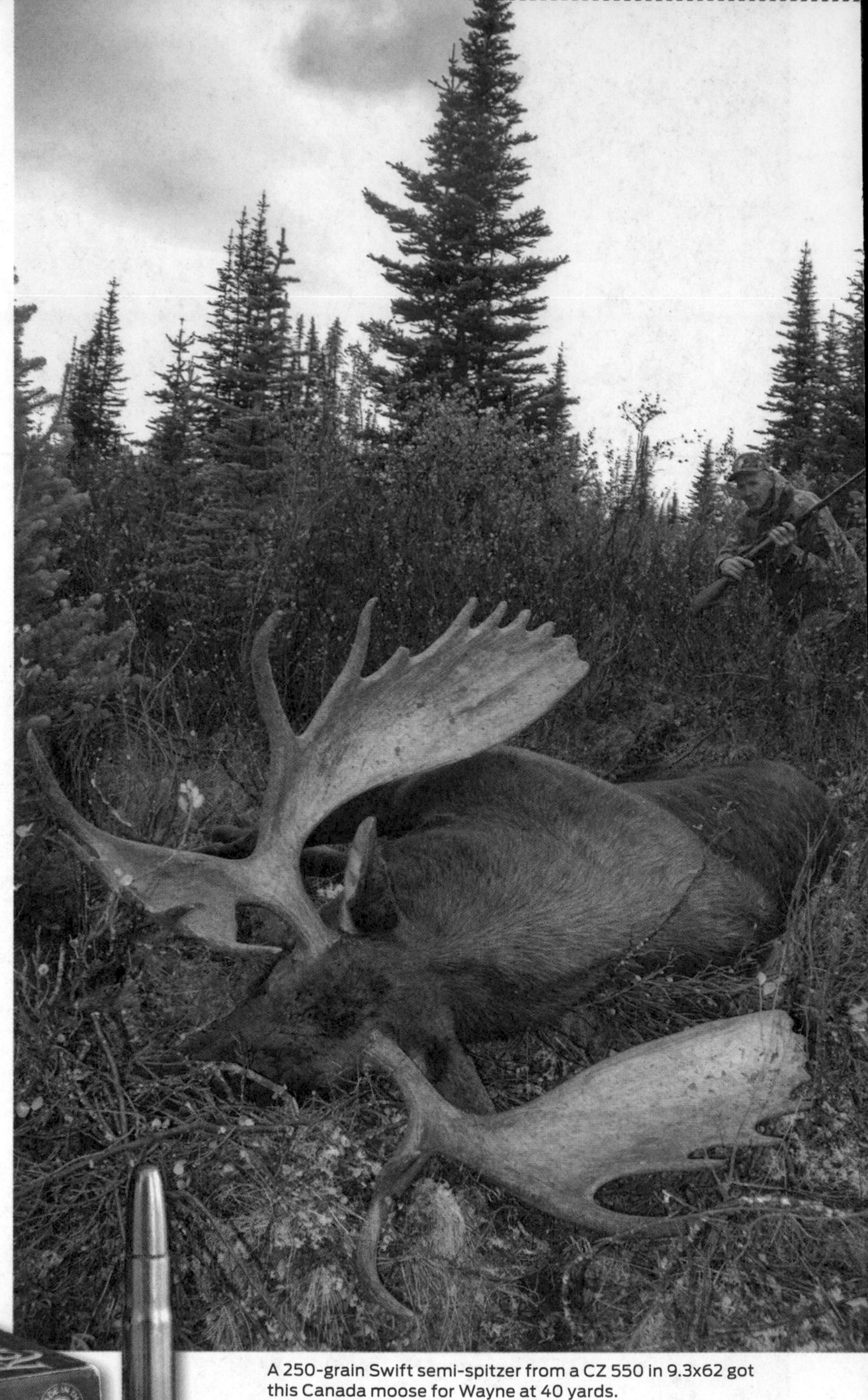

A 250-grain Swift semi-spitzer from a CZ 550 in 9.3x62 got this Canada moose for Wayne at 40 yards.

The .35 Whelen, loaded with the classic 250-grain round nose Core-Lokt.

Heavy blunt bullets may outperform speedy spitzers in thickets, but no bullet reliably "busts brush."

What About Brush?

As missile-shaped bullets look eager for long pokes, the linebacker profile of blunt bullets sets them up as brush-busters. Sadly, while round- or flat-nose bullets of high SD may stay on course in light brush better than pointed ones (especially long ones marginally stable), no bullet is deflection-proof.

Francis Sell, who used a 6.5x55 for his hunts in western Oregon blacktail cover, conducted trials to determine the effect of bullet shape and speed on deflection in screens of huckleberry and heavier alder and hazel. Blunt bullets at 2,500 to 2,700 fps deflected least: less than lighter, faster spitzers, but also less than 500-grain bullets clocking 1,450 fps from a .45-70.

The results of my deflection trials with sagebrush screens are much the same. Even 12-bore shotgun slugs yielded to small sagebrush branches. Targets as close as 6 feet behind the brush screen showed bent bullet tracks and some keyholing. To hit the point of aim, savvy hunters shoot *between* branches!

team would comprise six men, shooting three rounds at 800, 900 and 1,000 yards, 15 shots per round. A young National Rifle Association, with the cities of New York and Brooklyn, each put up $5,000 for a venue on Long Island's Creed's Farm, provided by the State of New York. In September, the Irish team lost to the Americans firing 550-grain bullets from their .44-90s. Sharps dropping-block rifles contributed to the winning score: 934 to 931, with one Irish crossfire. No sharp bullets.

A century and a half later, shooters prop heavy-barreled bolt-actions on bipods and read mirage through riflescopes the diameter of truck axles, with magnifications once reserved for spotting scopes. Once a rare stunt, hitting generous targets at a mile (1,700 yards) has become the first step toward a two-mile attempt. Such efforts have given rise to long-range bullets with high ballistic coefficients (BCs).

BC is a number representing a bullet's ability to cleave the air. It incorporates bullet weight, shape and diameter. Change any of these variables, and you change the BC. Long, sleek aerodynamic bullets have high BCs. Hornady's 143-grain 6.5mm ELD-X is .623. A corresponding 7mm bullet (162 grains) comes in at .631. Most traditional pointed soft-nose game bullets hover in the .380 to .490 range. These are "G1" figures, computed using a "standard bullet" (for comparisons) of a century ago. Ballisticians have since adopted a standard bullet better resembling the sleek, long-nose boattails popular now. Result: the "G7" BC. A bullet's G7 BC is lower than its G1 BC. The values are equally useful. Think

TABLE 1

BULLET DIAMETER/ WEIGHT	SECTIONAL DENSITY SD (M/D2)
.264 (6.5mm): 160 gr.	.328
.284 (7mm): 175 gr.	.310
.308: 200 gr.	.301
.308: 220 gr.	.331
.311 (.303 British): 215 gr.	.316
.323 (8mm): 220 gr.	.301
.338: 250 gr.	.313
.338: 275 gr.	.348
.358: 275 gr.	.306
.366 (9.3mm): 286 gr.	.305
.366 (9.3mm): 300 gr.	.320
.375: 300 gr.	.305
.416: 400 gr.	.330
.458: 500 gr.	.341

of any object that can be measured in inches or centimeters. Comparisons are valid if the units are the same.

Lost in this race to higher BCs and hits at more extended ranges is bullet performance on game.

***

The soft-nose struck audibly. With a bellow, the buffalo spun toward me. Through the dust, I sent a solid. The bull absorbed it, lunged off course, then crashed to earth as another solid broke its neck.

The three 9.3x62 bullets ending my Namibian hunt had round noses. For much of the world's big game hunting, blunt is still best. A blunt bullet is heavier than a pointed bullet of the same length, as nose taper exacts a cost in material. The only way to add weight to a pointed bullet is to make it longer, bringing challenges from the rifle's action, magazine and rifling twist.

Bullets heavy for their diameter have a high sectional density (SD). In a number, SD is the bullet's mass (weight) divided by its diameter squared: M/D^2. Alternatively, it is mass divided by cross-sectional area: M/R^2 x pi. (Yes, the results differ, but by a constant ratio).

For any given weight, the slimmer a bullet, the higher its SD. The longer a bullet, the higher its SD, if the nose shape is the same for any given diameter.

What is a "high" SD? My arbitrary threshold is .300. These bullets meet it (see Table 1).

While even round-nose and semi-spitzer bullets fly flatter and carry energy more efficiently than missiles shaped like soup cans, a tapered nose isn't necessary. Before vehicles entered Kenya's Serengeti Plain, a Dutchman named Fourrie guided John A. Hunter's safari toward Ngorongoro Crater. Fourrie was a resourceful fellow. When hunters in the party rashly shot their way out of solid bullets, Fourrie reversed soft points in their cases. These flat-nose "solids" drove deep and broke big bones in heavy game.

Skeptics sneer that as soon as round- or flat-nose bullets leave the muzzle, they "head for dirt." In fact, many blunt bullets with SDs of .300 fly flat enough for 200-yard zeros. For some, point-blank range (farthest at which a bullet stays within 3 vertical inches of sightline) exceeds 240 yards. These examples are from an old B&L list (See Table 2).

Early in the 20th century, the 6.5x45 M-S, 7x57 Mauser and .303 British served famous explorers and hunters like Charles Sheldon, F.C. Selous, Jim Corbett and W.D.M. Bell on dangerous game. While speedy bullets with high BCs can kill at eye-popping distances, heavy round-noses or semi-spitzers excel at the ranges most game is killed — especially where quartering shots are typical. The average shot distance for the dozen deer,

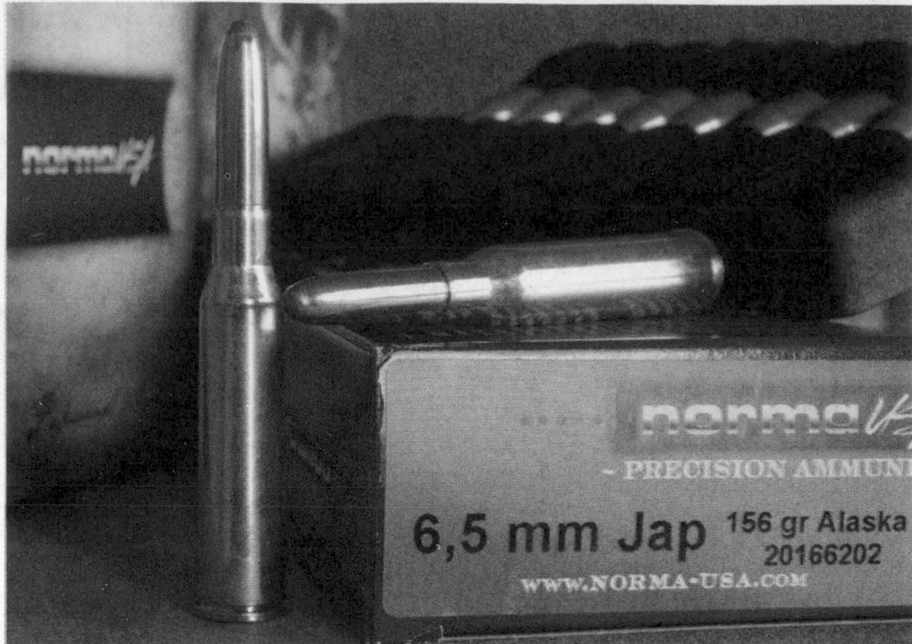

Norma's soft-point load for the 6.5 Japanese Arisaka features long, blunt bullets, SD .320. Effective!

TABLE 2

CARTRIDGE/ WEIGHT	ZERO RANGE (YDS.)	MAXIMUM POINT-BLANK RANGE (YDS.)
6.5x54 M-S, 156 gr.	206	242
6.5x55 Swedish, 156 gr.	209	245
7x57 Mauser, 175 gr.	201	235
.280 Remington, 165 gr.	228	266
.30-40 Krag, 220 gr.	185	217
.300 Savage, 180 gr.	190	222
.308 Winchester, 200 gr.	203	238
.30-06, 220 gr.	197	230
.300 H&H Mag., 220 gr.	217	254
.303 British, 215 gr.	182	213
.338 Win. Mag., 250 gr.	221	259
.348 Winchester, 250 gr.	186	216
.358 Winchester, 250 gr.	187	219
.375 H&H Mag., 300 gr.	226	264

Left: Round-nose bullets need not be seated as deeply as pointed (note cannelures). More space for powder.

elk and African plains animals I've shot most recently: 103 yards. Seldom is an animal so far or a sneak so difficult that I can't get close enough to aim dead-on with a semi-spitzer. In fact, I recall fewer than a dozen shots *in 50 years* that all but mandated a pointed bullet.

More often, I've been pleased there was a *heavy* bullet in the barrel.

Not long ago, bellying through thin grass on loose sand toward a blue wildebeest in a thorn patch, I could see only a suggestion of the bull in its bed. At about 50 yards, I stopped and snugged the sling. The bull rose side-to but moved only to thorn's hem before quartering steeply off. A blunt 196-grain 8mm soft-nose from my iron-sighted 8x57 drove through rear ribs, paunch and vitals toward the off-shoulder. The tough animal galloped away but nosed in under a cloud of dust about 80 yards on. The bullet's momentum and high SD made that shot lethal.

***

Blunt bullets are best for short shots at durable beasts, where SD trumps BC, and in tube magazines to nix primer detonation. But are they as versatile as pointed bullets? Long bullet noses (o-gives) and sharp poly tips sell well because they flatten bullet arcs and reduce the rate of velocity loss for easier hits and more punch at distance — ostensibly at no cost in killing effect up close.

Actually, there *is* a cost. Long, slender noses limit options for making bullets upset and penetrate predictably. Jacket thickness and the cavity size of hollow-points are constrained near the tip. So, too, the shape and amount of exposed lead of soft points. While clever engineers have designed pointed bullets to open at impact speeds as low as 1,600 fps *and* retain their integrity to drive deep, I'm told that task isn't easy. Small bullet diameters and nose cavities make it more difficult. Federal's Jared Kutney says the new Terminal Ascent bullet will upset at about 1,500 fps; Swift CEO Bill Hober insists the Scirocco opens at 1,440. Jeremy Millard at Hornady tells me it's hard to make slim *copper* noses peel at low speeds without "shaving BC and inviting disintegration at 3,000 fps."

Long bullets can crowd rifle actions, throats and magazines. Deep seating in the case eats powder space. Recent "long-range" cartridges like the .224 Valkyrie, 6.5 Creedmoor, 6.5 PRC and .300 PRC are short from base to shoulder to give the neck full grip on long bullet shanks without exceeding specified cartridge overall length.

Pinocchio noses threaten flight stability unless the long bullet gets a faster spin. Until recently, standard rifling twists worked for any bullet because the heaviest ones were blunt. Fast-twist rifling is most offered in .223 rifles. Early cartridges featured 55-grain spitzers. Sisk 70-grain semi-spitzer hunting bullets were about the same length. But current match bullets, as heavy as 80 grains, are much longer and beg sharper twists than the original 1:14. As lead-free bullets are longer for their weight than jacketed lead, twist rates for the LF become critical at a lighter threshold. An accurate 1960s rifle I fed solid-copper 55-grain bullets wouldn't keep them inside a cabbage at

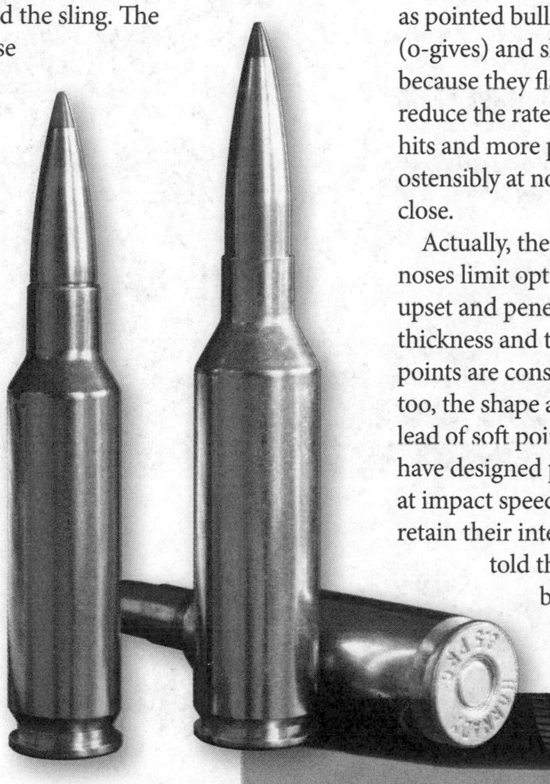

New "long-range" rounds have shoulders set back, so the neck gets a full grip on the shanks of sleek bullets.

Ballistic champs, long noses can be hard to design for reliable upset across a range of impact speeds.

The author used an iron-sighted 1899 Savage in .303 Savage, with bullets like this, to take an elk last year.

In whitetail cover, 100 yards is a long shot. This buck was killed at 20 feet. No need for sharp bullets.

The Truth About Drop

Blunt bullets from modern hunting cartridges do not exit "lookin' for dirt." Consider these 7mms, round-nose and pointed, each with an SD of .310, fired from a 7mm Remington Magnum rifle:

TABLE 3

LOAD		MUZZLE	100 YDS.	200 YDS.	300 YDS.	400 YDS.
Hornady 175-gr. Roundnose, BC .285	Velocity (fps)	2,900	2,579	2,279	2,000	1,742
	Energy (ft-lbs)	3,267	2,583	2,018	1,554	1,180
	Arc (ins.)	0.0	+1.9	0.0	-8.6	-26.0

TABLE 4

LOAD		MUZZLE	100 YDS.	200 YDS.	300 YDS.	400 YDS.
Hornady 175-gr. Spire Point, BC .462	Velocity (fps)	2,900	2,699	2,507	2,322	2,146
	Energy (ft-lbs)	3,267	2,830	2,441	2,096	1,789
	Arc (ins.)	0.0	+1.6	0.0	-7.2	-20.8

Not until the bullets pass 300 yards is a significant difference in drop from a 200-yard zero. That's much farther than many hunters will ever fire at game.

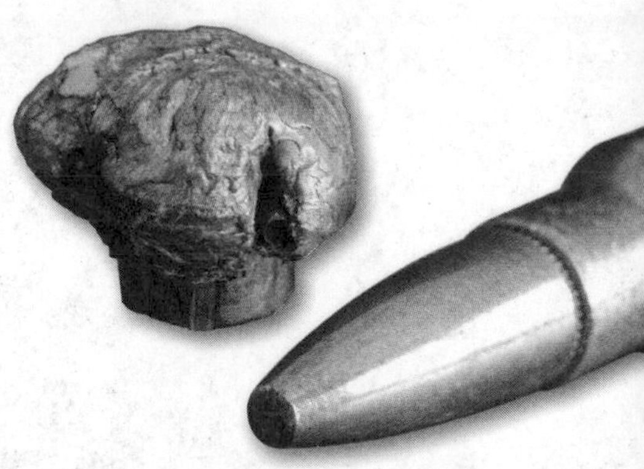

This Core-Lokt bullet, from a .308, upset beautifully in game. It's a spitzer bullet — but not a needle-nose.

A 1950s-vintage .300 Savage and a round-nose Core-Lokt bullet downed this fine bull at 130 yards.

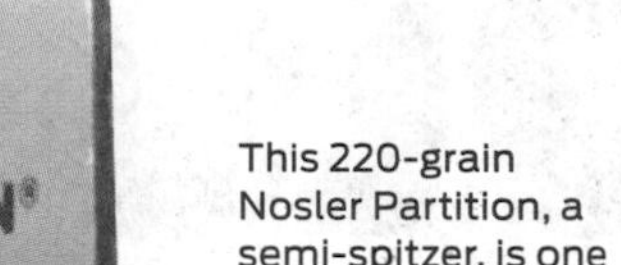

This 220-grain Nosler Partition, a semi-spitzer, is one of the deadliest .30-bore bullets for tough game.

100 yards. Now, .223 barrels come with a twist as fast as 1:7.5. Insufficient spin can cause bullets to enter targets sideways (keyhole).

The stability of a bullet *after* the hit matters, too. Ivory hunters favored heavy, blunt bullets not just for their penetration but also because they stayed on course in tough going better than pointed bullets. That's still true. Bullets with *flat* noses are said to drive more reliably straight than either — the reason Woodleigh and Swift solids for heavy game now feature them. Of course, soft points change shape as they penetrate. Proper spin for stability in the air isn't always adequate in a denser medium. A 300-grain .375 bullet from 1:14 rifling is stabilized at a rate of 2,229 rotations per second through air. Entering water, it must turn 66,870 rps to maintain stability! As animal muscles, bones and organs aren't of uniform consistency, the ideal spin rate changes as a bullet penetrates. But bullets become shorter as they expand, reducing the spin needed for stability. A pointed bullet barely stable in the air can have a tough time staying stable after impact.

In sum, bullets with long sharp noses aren't beneficial at ordinary shot ranges. Their niche is The Long Poke. Their lofty BCs trace shallow arcs, defy wind and maintain speed and energy well. When you needn't kill a township away — arguably a hard sell anytime — blunt bullet noses can deliver the result you want. GD

Rimfire Revolution

Modern Rimfire Ammunition from .22 Short to .17 HMR

› MICHAEL SHEA

Going long with a V-22 in a JP APAC topped with an Athlon BTR optic. Photo: Cosmo Genova

Precision and accuracy are not the same things. *Precision* is the spread of individual shots. When you measure group size, you measure precision or how well the shots cluster together — also called "dispersion." *Accuracy* is a measure of how centered those shots are on a specific target. A bullseye hit is an accurate shot. The bullet went where you aimed. Likewise, five shots spaced around a bullseye at the same distance is an accurate group. A tight cluster of shots in the bullseye, or the "one ragged hole" we all chase, is both precise and accurate.

Precision is inherent to a rifle system. For our purposes, a rifle system is a combination of rifle, optic, mounts, ammunition, and the shooter. You derive precision from the quality of components. As we've learned, match ammunition is more precise because of primer, powder, bullet, and brass quality and how manufacturers assemble them. Likewise, you can make a rifle more or less precise through gunsmithing or by adding higher-quality components. For example, when you swap a factory sporter 10/22 barrel for a premium hand-lapped drop-in, you hope it shrinks your groups. You can adjust accuracy through more straightforward means. By spinning the elevation or windage turrets in a riflescope, you can change the point of aim, thereby making the system more accurate — or more likely to hit the target. When those shots cluster tightly in the bullseye, the system is both precise and accurate. You may have gotten this far and wondered, *Why so few target photos in this book?* After all, it is commonplace for gun writers to test a rifle and show off the teeny tiny groups they've inflicted on paper. The assumption is that if Joe Gun Writer can lay down ¼-inch groups with Rifle ABC, then Rifle ABC is a quarter-minute gun, and you, the reader, should buy it. Frankly, this is malarkey. I'm guilty of it myself, reviewing rifles and publishing show-stopper groups, then generalizing on the precision and accuracy of some new rifle. Why is this problematic? Because it is a sample size of one. The reviewer may have had a gem or a lemon. It may have been a prototype, or the tester happened to shoot the rifle with the one lot of ammunition that sang in that barrel.

Furthermore, the shooter is an integral part of a rifle system. Am I a better shooter than you? Was I shooting off a bipod in the desert with a 20 mile per hour crosswind? Was I shooting indoors? In a tunnel? Off a machine rest? I used to think if I shot several hundred rounds with various ammunition in 5-shot groups and measured and averaged them all, I could get to some general accuracy conclusion about that rifle. With a well-tuned, sophisticated rifle, I also believed that I could shoot and measure different ammunition and make broad claims about which manufacturers have more or less accurate offerings. The deeper down the rabbit hole I've gone, the less I believe either of these things is true.

As you'll see later in this chapter, I took four very nice rifles to the Lapua Rimfire Performance Center in Marengo, Ohio. At this 100-meter test tunnel, I tested eight lots of Center-X and eight lots of Midas+ ammo in all four rifles, with the guns in a vise and the test center manager on the trigger — a four-time NCAA All-American rimfire shooter. One rifle, a CZ 457 with an aftermarket 20-inch PROOF carbon-fiber barrel, stood out. Adjusting from millimeters to inches and meters to yards (more on that later), the CZ laid down the equivalent of a 10-shot 100-yard group just .825-inch center-to-center. That's ten shots at 100 yards! With a different lot of the same Center-X ammo, it also put down a 3.5-inch group — the worst of all rifles and lots tested by a factor of two. No other rifle or ammo combination was even half that bad.

IS THE CZ A SUB-MOA BARN BURNER OR A DUD?

The average group size of the CZ at the (adjusted) 100 yards of all ammo shot that day was 1.438 inches. The median group size was 1.035 inches. Cal Zant of the Precision Rifle Blog has an excellent series on statistics for shooters. In it, he describes the difference between average and median group sets, quoting *Naked Statistics* by Charles Wheelan:

"10 guys are sitting in a middle-class bar in Seattle, and each of them earns $35,000 a year. That means the average annual income for the group is $35,000. Bill Gates then walks into the bar, and let's say his annual income is $1 billion. When Bill sits down on the 11th stool, the average income rises to around $91 million. The original ten drinkers aren't any richer. If we described this bar's patrons as having an average annual income of $91 million, that statement would be statistically correct and grossly misleading. That isn't a bar where multimillionaires hang out; it's a bar where guys with relatively low incomes happen to be sitting next to Bill Gates."

Averages are powerfully affected by outliers. A median is the number that divides a data set in half, so in the Bill Gates example, the drinkers' median income is $35,000. As Zant concludes, "If you had to bet $100 on what the income was of the very next guy who walked in the door, would $35,000 or $91 million be more likely? When we're talking about what is most likely to happen in the

Tiny groups on paper targets make good photos but don't provide much information outside that specific rifle system.

This 50-yard group was shot with CCI Standard in a Savage B22 Precision.

future, the median can often be a better choice than the average."

That much should be clear. By testing ammo and measuring groups, you're trying to predict the future or know with certainty how that rifle and ammo will behave in the future to make a successful winning shot on a target in a match or a critter in the woods.

Now, let's go back to my CZ. In lot testing rimfire ammo, *we were looking for outliers*. I wanted to find the lot of ammo that shot the smallest groups. Lots are production runs of ammunition. So, if the loading machines at Lapua, or ELEY, or CCI, are loaded with ammo components, the lot starts when the operators turn on the loading machines and end when they turn them off. That can be as little as 15,000 total rounds for match ammunition but is more typically 20,000 to 30,000. (At CCI, Federal, Winchester, it may be a lot of 100,000 to 250,000 rounds.) One of the quirks of rimfire is that every ammo lot — always made of the same primer, powder, bullet, brass, and on the same machines — tests *vastly different* from one another, even within the same rifle. When pressed, accuracy-obsessed rimfire shooters will tell you it's impossible even to say this rifle likes Brand X ammunition best. A gun may seem to prefer Brand X ammunition but could shoot one lot very poorly and set world records with the next. The poor lot of Brand X may also shoot worse than an average lot of Brand Y.

If your head is spinning, welcome to rimfire.

By testing lots, you're matching ammunition to the rifle and barrel. By testing lots of lots, we obtained an average and median figure of how well my CZ generally shot Center-X, but this is meaningless, too. If I plan to buy cases (or the entire lot) of the ammunition that shot the best, the average or mean performer of many lots isn't helpful. Lot 23 proved the best in the CZ during my time at Lapua, so I wanted to focus on that. We got 100-yard equivalents of 1.142, 1.145, and another fish-stank 3.511-inch group — taken with 0.825 inch that gave us a lot average of 1.656 inches and a median of 1.144 inches. Why is this rifle throwing the occasional flyer that was ruining my numbers? That could be an issue with the ammo, or it could — more likely, I think — be a mechanical issue in the fire control system. Still, Lot 23 proved the best in the CZ and one of my Vudoos. At this point, knowing the mean of that lot can be very helpful in predicting future outcomes. You might be thinking you should find Lot 23 of Lapua Center-X. Well, you can't. I bought the whole lot.

That is what's interesting, maddening, exciting, and futile with publishing rimfire targets and generalizing those conclusions:

The accuracy data only speak to a particular rifle system at one moment in time, and;

It's not helpful to anyone other than that rifle's owner because if he or she discovers a magic lot, it's sold out before any reader ever hears about it, and;

Even if you managed to get a case of that lot, there's no promise it will perform the same way in your rifle.

So, to maximize precision and accuracy in a rifle, you must test lots of lots of ammunition. But how does this help someone looking to buy a new rimfire rifle? Can we make any generalizations about precision and accuracy over a design or factory run of guns?

What I took away from my time at Lapua was discovering a single lot of ammunition that performed best across a

The test tunnel at Lapua is a must-stop for rimfire accuracy freaks.

The author tested two Vudoos, in addition to a RimX and a CZ 457, with 16 total ammo lots.

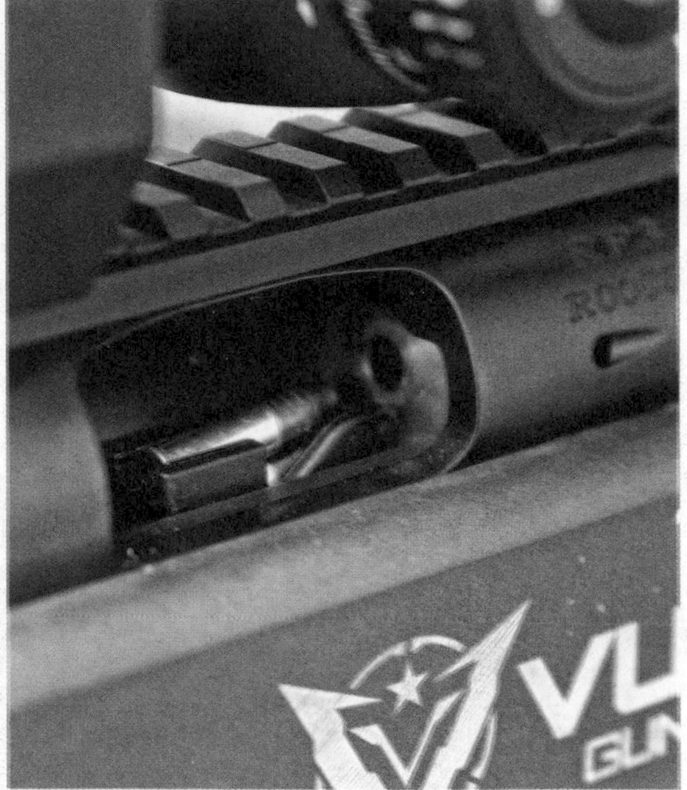

A RimX action in a Remington 700 footprint fixture made for Lapua by Vudoo Gun Works.

few of my rifles and a potential mechanical issue to dig into on my CZ. For me, the big takeaway was a belief that the rifles I tested and the ammunition I found will make a good foundation of a rifle system I want to develop further for NRL- and ELR-style shooting. If my accuracy goals were competitive benchrest shooting, I would have left Ohio underwhelmed. That said, to say my rifle shoots 10-shot .825-inch groups at 100 yards is not false, but it is misleading. It did that once. If it did that with every 10-shot group, I reckon it would be a benchrest contender.

For this book, I've highlighted rifles that I've shot firsthand or seen shot that, like my CZ, are worth working with further. The rifles covered in the earlier chapters can all make the foundation of an accurate, tactical, precision rifle system. That means that they can shoot ½-inch 5-shot groups at 50 yards easily with match ammunition. (Most of them can shoot much better than that.) That is not one group. I shoot at least ten 5-shot groups, measure the outside group diameter, subtract .224 (the diameter of a .22 LR bullet), then compute the average and the median. When those figures are below a ½-inch, I tend to relax. That said, there are many other ways to measure groups that may be better than this. More critical to group size, in my thinking, is understanding how a rifle action works. Focusing on the action opens the door to improvements, so for example, when my CZ throws flyers, I'm not too concerned because I'm confident I can break down the system, work on it, and improve the overall precision.

It's also worth noting that precision in rifles generally — unfortunately — tracks to price. As Dan Killough of Killough Shooting Sports in Winter Park, Texas, who runs ELEY USA's test tunnel, told me, "Mechanical accuracy can be bought." More expensive rifles generally use higher-quality materials and more hands-on care of assembly. That is not to say CZs or Rugers or Savages don't exist that can outshoot the Vudoos and Anschützes of the world, but on the whole, you are much less likely to find a barn-burning $500 rifle than you are to find one in the $2,000 category. How much is that expensive rifle compared to a less expensive one? Again, no easy answers. As Killough put it:

"Say you spend $500 on a baseline CZ 457 rifle or Tikka T1x. Very accurate, very nice rifles. Can we get you something better? Yes. But now we're talking another $700 to step up to an Anschütz if we're considering factory rifles. So that means the price has more than doubled. But that does not mean the accuracy has doubled … say you're at a ½ inch, and you spend that $1,200 on a new rifle, you may go from .500 inch to .400 inch. Then, say you jump up to custom action, custom barrel, custom everything. You spend $3,500, and you went from .400 to .350. Yes, you're more accurate, but each tenth of an inch gets increasingly expensive as you get smaller and smaller."

It's possible to find a 457 or T1x that shoots in the .400s and get an Anschütz

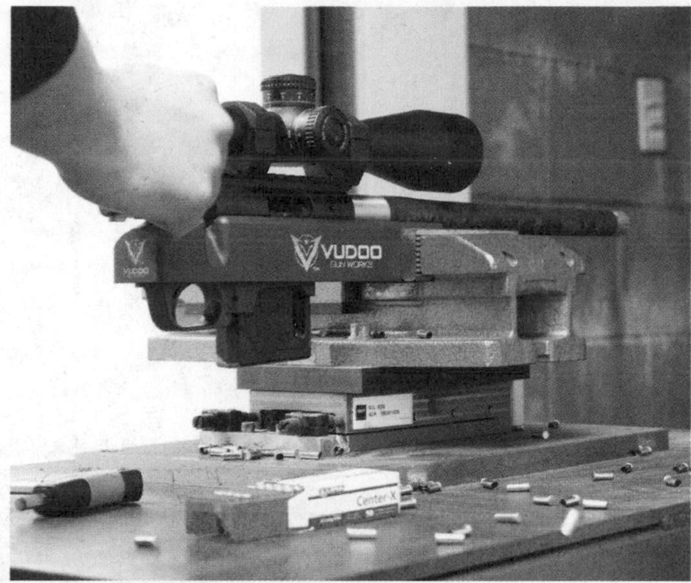

Test protocol: one 10-shot group. If that shows promise, test two or three more 10-shot groups of that ammo lot.

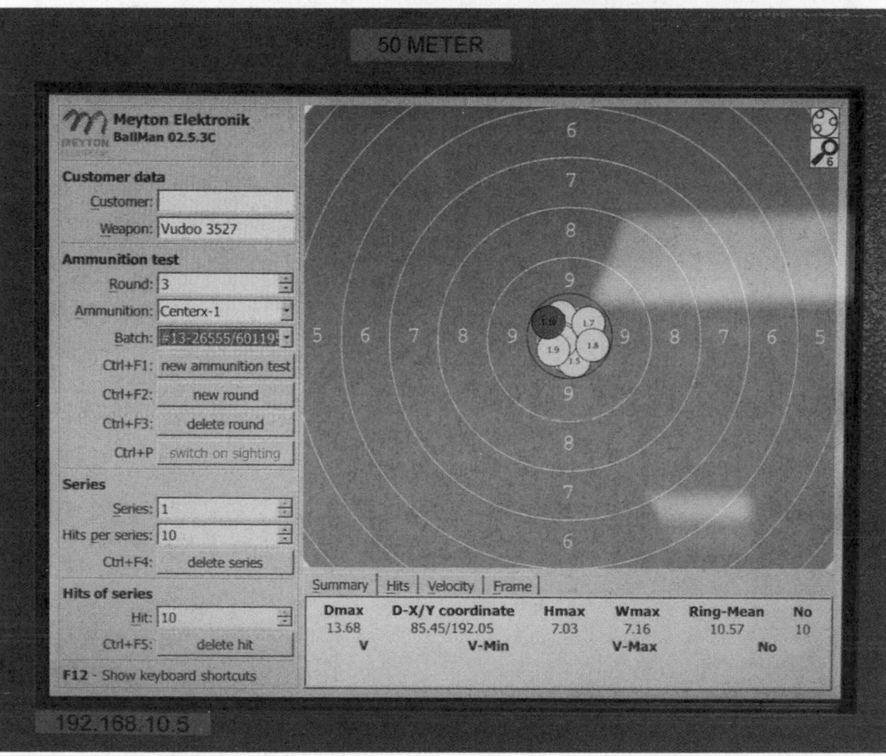

The Meyton Elektronik range system provides live results shot-to-shot on two computer screens.

This is the kind of 50-yard group all shooters seek, as shown in this promotional image from Vudoo.

that tops out at .500s to use Killough's numbers. There are few guarantees. In part, you see something of a division in the precision rimfire online forums. You have shooters who buy inexpensive guns and work on them relentlessly to get them to shoot. You have another group that buys and tests every new rifle, prospecting. Then you have the "buy once, cry once" group that puts out for a very high-end rifle and is done with it.

These factors lead me to believe budget and shooter personality are the best criteria for selecting a new rifle — not precision, not accuracy. If you have $500 and like to tinker, it's hard to beat a CZ with the wide world of aftermarket parts and the online brain trust of CZ shooters who know how to make them precise. (See the CZ Forum on rimfirecentral.com.) If you don't like to tinker and have the same $500 to spend, the Tikka, to my mind, is very hard to beat. If you have $1,200, or $2,000 to $4,000, that recommendation changes.

When shopping, it's also essential to consider the optic, mounts, and ammunition. In NRL22-style shooting, where targets are inside 100 yards, *the optic is more important than the rifle.* I repeat: *The optic is more important than the rifle.* That means most factory rifles, even the inexpensive ones, are accurate enough to connect on the typically 2 MOA targets inside 100 yards. Cheap scopes, not so much. With a cheap, blurry scope, it's difficult to see a ¼-inch target at 25 yards. As a general rule, spend equally for optics and rifle — and half that for ammunition. If you plan to spend $500 on a rifle, drop another $500 for the scope and mounts and $250 more to buy ammo. Every real competitor out there would take a Tikka with a mid-tier Vortex shooting Center-X over a Vudoo with a Tasco shooting bulk pack. When it comes to precise and accurate rimfire shooting, optics and ammunition are equally important — if not more important — than the rifle itself. When considering precision and accuracy, you must think about the total rifle system, not just the bare rifle on the gun shop wall.

UNIVERSAL RIFLE SETUP

Suppose you've read this far, grew inspired, and bought a new rimfire rifle, optic, and mounts. To set it up correctly is not difficult. It requires a torque wrench (like a set of Fix It Sticks), some bubble levels, a basic rifle cleaning kit, and a cradle or vise. In a pinch, it's possible to level a rifle on bags. Then:

Clean the rifle. Rifles do not come clean from the factory. There is often left-over compound in the bore from the manufacturing process. To remove it, run an oiled patch down the barrel with a cleaning rod, then follow with dry patches until they come out clean.

Remove the barreled action from the stock. Often there's grit and other manufacturing grime you can wipe off the action's underside and in the stock. Inspect and assess the quality of the bedding during this process.

Check the recommended torque for the action screws, which you'll typically find in the owner's manual. If not, you can find it easily online. Re-install the barreled action to the recommended torque. With some rimfire rifles, group size will change based on the torque, so it's good to know your starting torque value. If the recommended torque is a range, say 35 to 45 in-lbs, I tend to start on the high end and work backward if needed.

Level the rifle at the receiver in a cradle or vise. There are scope leveling kits widely available for this job, but a two-pack of inexpensive bubble levels works just as well in most cases.

If you bought a Picatinny rail or another base, install it to the leveled receiver with a drop of Loctite 242 (blue) in the screw holes. Torque it down to what the rail manufacturer recommends or 25 in-lbs. Give it a little time to dry.

Loosely attach the rings to the scope, if vertical rings like Warnes, or the bottom half of the horizontal rings to the Pic rail. The scope rings should be snugged forward on the Pic rail or base while tightening down in both cases. (The recoil impulse of a rifle pushes the action and optic forward, not backward.)

Tighten the rings to the base or rail to the recommended torque, and the scope rings to the scope just enough to hold it in place.

Confirm proper eye relief by shouldering the rifle with the scope at its highest power. You should be able to comfortably see through the scope without excessive shading or moving your head out of its most natural position.

Put the rifle back in the cradle or vise, level the receiver, then level the scope by resting a bubble level on the elevation turret. Turn the scope in the rings until the scope level matches the receiver level.

Alternate tightening the screws in a crisscross pattern, i.e., bottom left screw, top right, etc., and don't tighten them down in one go. Snug them all hand tight and ensure the gaps in the rings are similar on all sides. Continue to tighten them in this crisscross pattern until you hit the recommended torque. For scope rings, that's usually between 15 and 25 in-lbs but always follow the scope manufacturer guidelines.

Now you're ready to sight in the rifle. Most NRL22 shooters zero at 50 yards, as that equates to a dead-center hold on targets between 25 and 55 or 60 yards with match ammunition. Others advocate for 25 to 35 yards as that zeros the optic at the peak of the bullet's trajectory. There are pros and cons to each method. I zero all my .22 LRs at 50 yards, .17 Mach 2s at 30 yards, and magnum rimfires at 100 yards.

With a bolt gun and a normal-sized target, it's easy to get on paper. Remove the bolt and secure the rifle in a cradle or on bags. Look through and center the bore on the target. While looking through the scope, carefully turn the elevation and windage turrets until you center the reticle on the target. This procedure almost always gets you on paper. You can then zero the rifle at your desired yardage.

The Lilja BREAK-IN PROCEDURE for Centerfire and Jacketed Rimfire Barrels

"We are concerned with two types of fouling: copper fouling from bullet jacket material in the bore and powder fouling. During the first few rounds, substantial copper fouling will coat the barrel. Remove this fouling thoroughly after each shot to help prevent a build-up later on. Powder fouling is ongoing but easy to remove. Do not use moly-coated bullets during the break-in procedure.

"For an effective break-in, you should clean the bore after every shot for the first 10-12 rounds or until copper fouling stops. Our procedure is to push a cotton patch that is wet with solvent through the barrel. This process will remove much of the powder fouling and wet the inside of the barrel with solvent. Next, wet a **bronze brush** (not a nylon brush) with solvent and stroke the barrel 5-10 times. Follow this by another wet patch and then one dry patch. Now soak the barrel with a strong copper-removing solvent, removing the blue mess from the barrel. The copper fouling will be heavy for a few rounds and then taper off quickly in just one or two shots. Once it has stopped or diminished significantly, it is time to start shooting 5-shot groups, cleaning after each one. After 25-30 rounds, clean at a regular interval of 10-25 rounds. Your barrel is now broken-in."

RIMFIRE BARREL BREAK-IN

Breaking in a rifle barrel through a routine of shooting, then cleaning, then shooting some more is either a required step for a precision rimfire rifle system or not necessary at all, depending with whom you talk.

The more accurate answer to rimfire barrel break-in is, "it depends."

First, consider the caliber. A .22 LR shooting lead bullets may require a different process than a .17 HMR or .22 WMR that shoots jacketed bullets. Lilja Rifles, Inc., no stranger to precision shooting, says, "Rimfire rifle barrels are different from centerfire barrels in that they require minimal cleaning and essentially no break-in procedure." Then they go on to state, "The .22 WMR and .17 HMR cartridges are rimfires, but they fire a jacketed bullet and therefore centerfire cleaning, and break-in instructions apply." (See sidebar.)

An important note here, Lilja barrels — and Shilen, Muller, Bartlein, and other premium makers — are hand-lapped to a mirror polish. That means they remove any tooling marks left in the bore from the barrel-making process. That is not the case with factory barrels. With a borescope, you can see plain as day little ridges and nicks in many factory bar-

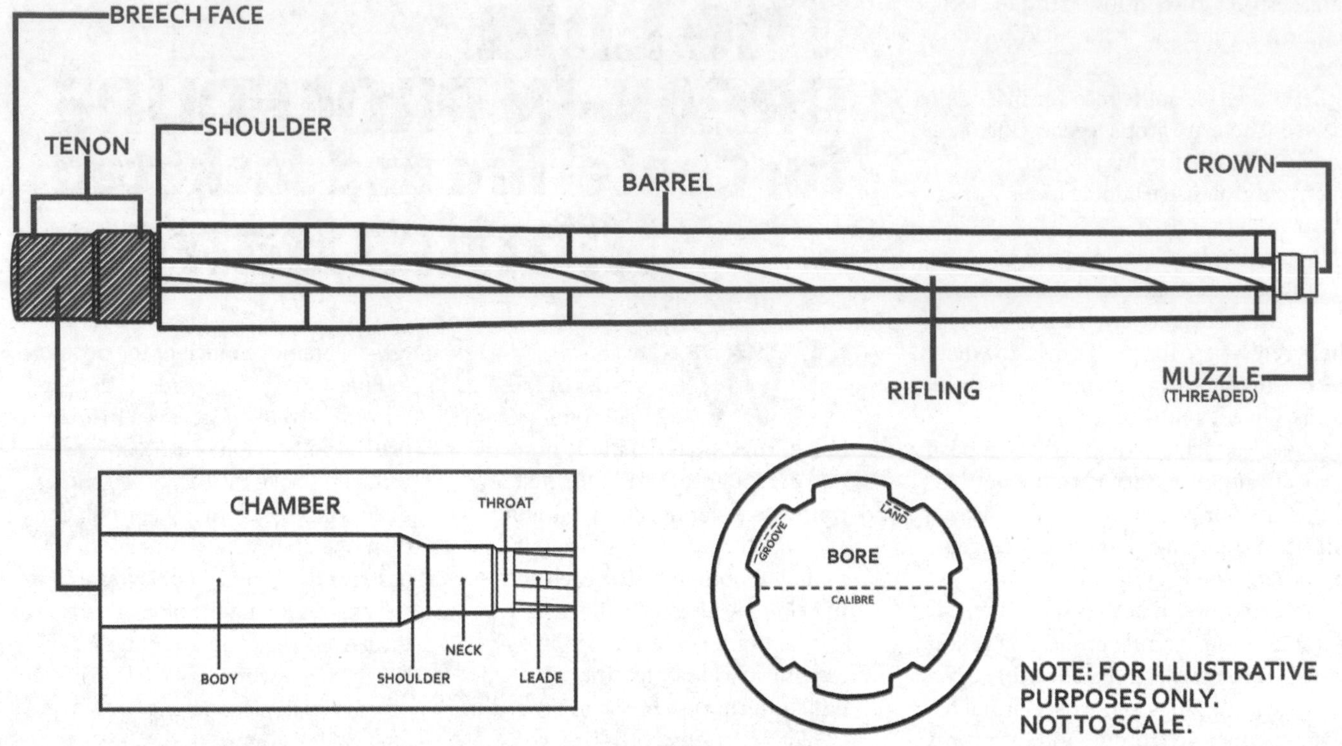

rels. Those imperfections can be made smoother after shooting lead .22 LRs down the bore, as imperfections fill in with lead and lube, which slicks up the bore and makes for better groups. That is why so many factory rimfires seem to shoot better after many hundreds of rounds and why so many rimfire shooters seem allergic to ever cleaning their bores. However, there are downsides to an always dirty barrel — as we'll see in the chapter on cleaning.

It seems a factory or rough barrel can be broken in by shooting it a lot, whereas a hand-lapped barrel does not require this. Likewise, a hand-lapped premium barrel can be kept cleaner for longevity's sake, as it only takes half a box of ammo or less to "re-foul" the bore and for accurate shooting. In both cases, it is not as necessary to shoot, clean, shoot, clean using some prescribed protocol as it is for barrels that send copper-jacketed bullets downrange.

BOX TESTING

As a rule of thumb, a good thing to do while breaking in or fouling a rimfire barrel is box testing the riflescope. The weak link in most rifle systems is the optic. More specifically, the way the elevation and windage adjustments in the scope track as they're changed. In other words, that 0.1-MIL click adjustment at 100 yards may be closer to 0.125 or 0.75 MILs in a poorly made or defective scope. These errors may not make a huge difference when shooting close, but they can compound and make shots way off at farther yardages.

Frank Galli of snipershide.com, who has forgotten more about precision shooting than most of us will ever know, has written that "It's typical to see a 2 percent error factor in scopes at or below [the $1,500] price point, and that has a cascading effect on accuracy results. If you're using any ballistic software, this is your most significant point of failure when the ballistic curve does not line up with your rig." [Editor's note: Galli is the author of *Precision Rifle Marksmanship: The Fundamentals – A Marine Sniper's Guide to Long Range Shooting*, available at GunDigestStore.com.]

A box test requires a 24- to 36-inch target at 100 yards. Lock down the rifle scope, either in a jig or with the rifle strapped into a heavy cradle. For rimfires, I do a watered-down live-fire version of this on my 50-yard home range. I sight in at 50 yards. Then I hang a tall sheet of paper downrange with a bullseye on the paper's bottom edge. I take a shot at 50, then spin up 1 MIL or 1 MOA of elevation (depending on the scope) and shoot another round. I do this until I run out of paper, which is typically 8 or 9 MILs. I then spin the elevation back to zero, pick a bullet hole in the middle of the target, do the same thing with windage, add 1 MIL, shoot a shot, etc., moving both left and right while maintaining the hold on that center bullet hole. When at the extreme left and right edge of the paper, I track the elevation again.

The result is a big cross on the paper downrange with one to four small boxes. If there are no issues, I can see the bullet holes line up with the hash marks in my scope reticle. That is, the 2-MIL bullet hole lines up with the 2-MIL hash mark when I hold to that point of aim. This method is not as accurate as a test that runs through the entire usable range of the optic, but it lets me quickly know if something significant is off in the scope.

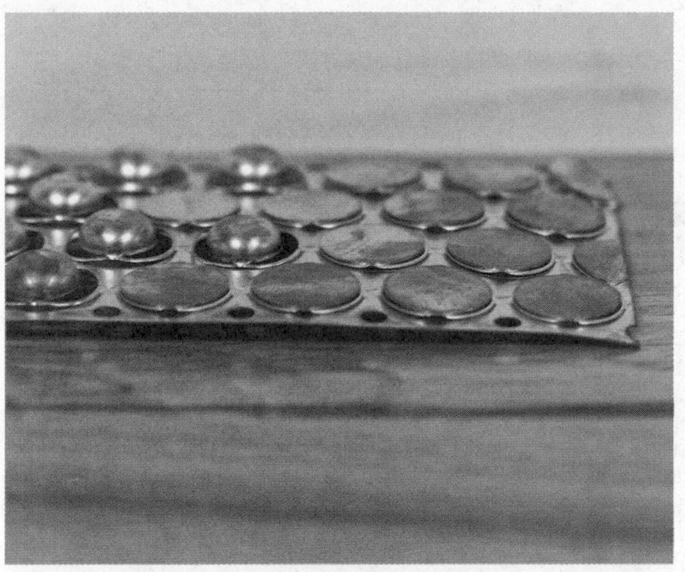

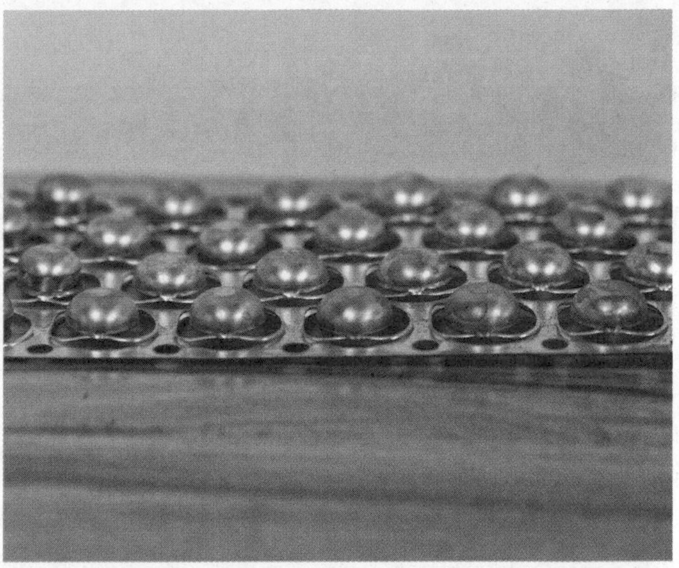

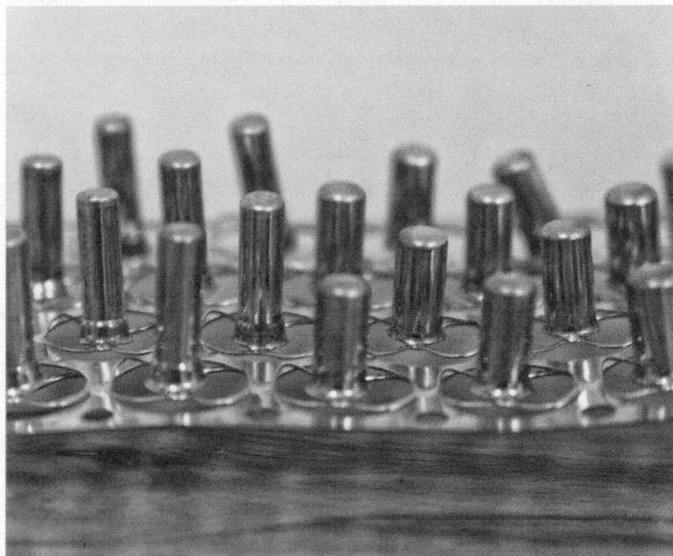

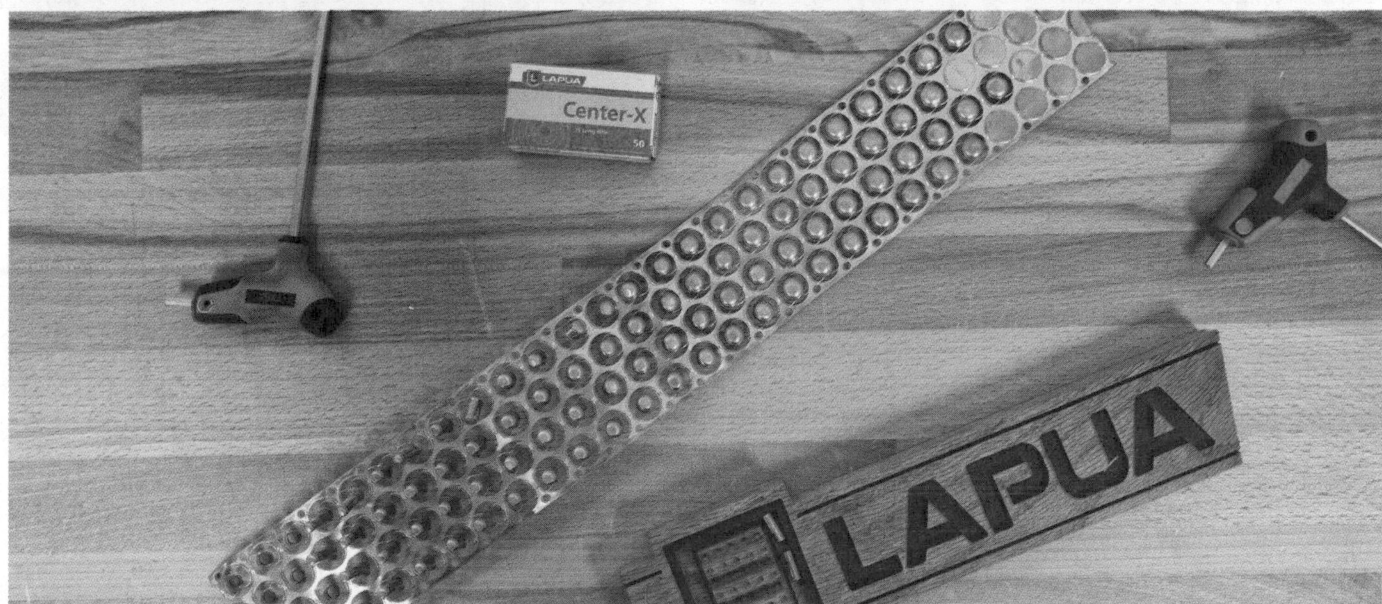

The steps by which ammo makers change brass sheeting into brass .22 LR cases.

Common .22 Chamber SPECIFICATIONS

Pacific Tool & Gauge publishes a list of specs for the wide variety of chamber reamers it sells. You can find other specs online, and more still are considered propriety and closely held secrets. Combining all available sources, this is the best list I could come up with for .22 LR chamber specs. If anything, this list demonstrates how wide the variance in chambers can be.

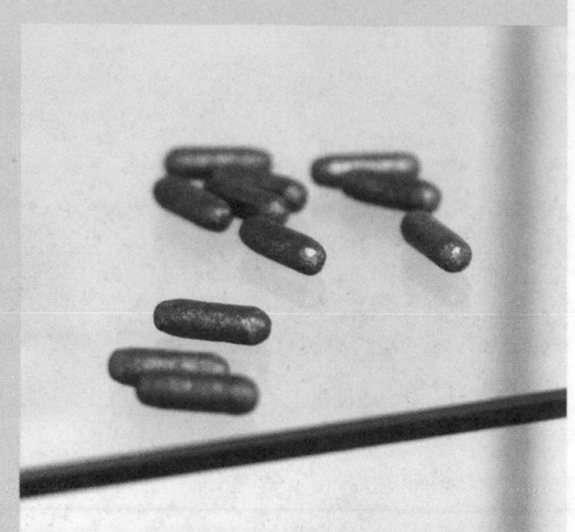

Lead slugs that are swage formed into shaped .22 LR bullets.

BARRELS

A survey of rifle precision and accuracy would be incomplete without a look at barrels. A rifle action's mechanical repeatability, lock time speed, trigger, and bedding quality, contribute to a precision rifle system. Still, no one variable is more important than the quality of the barrel.

Rimfire barrels are most often made of type 416 stainless steel or type 4140 chrome-moly steel. Chrome-moly is easier to machine, requires less lubrication, as it is less susceptible to galling. Stainless steel is better at resisting oxidation but contains carbon and will rust in bad conditions or left filthy in a moist environment. Barrels are rifled one of four ways:

- Cut or single-point cut rifling, cutting one groove at a time;
- Broached rifling, or cutting all the grooves at the same time, an uncommon practice these days;
- Hammer forging, or pounding the barrel over a tungsten carbide mandrel with the reverse image of the rifling;
- Button rifling, or pressing the grooves into the steel with a short carbide "button" with the rifling's reverse image pulled down the barrel's length with immense force.

Most barrel makers do one method or the other. There is a fierce debate over which approach makes the "most accurate" or "most precise" barrel. In the world of competitive rimfire benchrest, only two barrel makers are routinely winning these days, and both use a button rifling process — Shilen and Muller Works. Other close contenders, Benchmark, Broughton, and Douglas, are buttoned. Vudoo Gun Works uses single-point cut Ace Barrels, and Mike Bush has been vocal in his belief that the accuracy potential is every bit as good as the super-premium button-rifled barrels. He likens the dominance of button-rifled barrels in benchrest to their much wider use within that sport, sort of like why red sports cars get more speeding tickets — because there are more red cars on the road. As Vudoo's new single-shot benchrest action with Ace barrel sees time on the firing line at national-level benchrest matches, we will learn more.

Of the barrel makers popular with precision shooters, Bartlein, PROOF Research, and IBI use the cut method. Krieger offers both cut and buttoned barrels. Lilja, Hart, and Lothar Walther are buttoned. Anschütz, Bergara, and Savage button rifle their barrels. CZ, Ruger, and Sako/Tikka cold hammer forge.

Drawbacks: Some believe hammer-forged barrels are less precise, yet they're much less expensive to manufacture. Cut rifling is slow and costly and not conducive to mass production — as anyone who's tried to order a custom cut-rifled barrel quickly will tell you. Button-rifled barrels are accurate, cost-effective, and mass-produce quickly but *must* be appropriately heat-treated to relieve the stress induced by the rifling process. If not, the bore's internal dimensions can warp when the barrel is contoured or when you thread the muzzle for a brake.

Whatever the rifling process, they all ultimately do the same thing: Cut, press, or forge in the spiral lands and grooves inside the barrel. How much that spiral spins is called "twist rate," and for the longest time, the twist rate for .22 LR has been 1:16 or one full rotation over 16 inches of barrel. Some barrel makers tweak that up to 1:17 and down to 1:15. No one has any idea which is best. Generally, faster twists are better for longer, heavier bullets. Yet this is moot in a .22 LR landscape where 99 percent of precision shooters are shooting 40-grain match loads. The advent of cooper-solid extreme long-range rimfire ammunition may change that. The .17-caliber rimfires run almost exclusively with a 1:9 or 1:10 twist.

The number of lands and grooves — and the shape of the lands — can vary from maker to maker. For centuries, standard rifling was square with sharp corners. Rimfire specialists changed some of their rifling patterning over time, tapering the shape of the lands. The Shilen Ratchet is the most famous example of this. The 5R profile is another. As to an ideal number of lands and grooves, it pays to look at the world of benchrest.

The Shilen Ratchet is a four-groove. It also offers a standard eight-groove. Muller Works offers a 5R in four- or eight-groove. Douglas and Broughton, two other highly respected barrel manufacturers, use a four-groove rifle pattern. Benchmark has a two- and three-groove, and Lilja offers three-, four-, and six-groove depending on twist rate. The lands and grooves' internal dimensions also vary by manufacturer, but in all cases, they're appreciably tighter than the soft lead .224-diameter .22 LR bullet. Lilja, for example, writes on its website: "Our standard dimensions are a

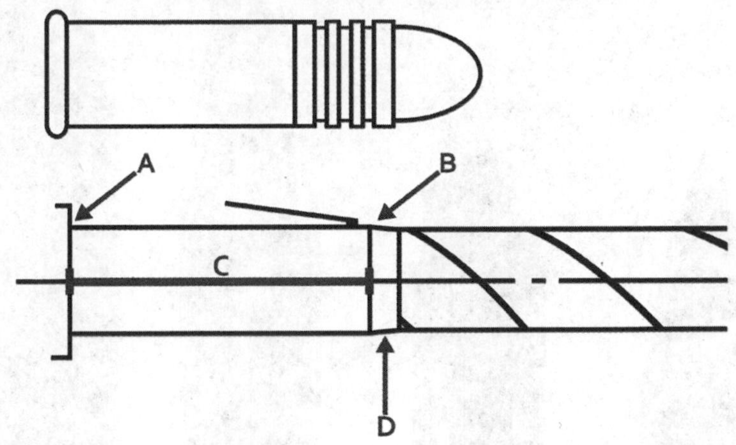

.22 LR CHAMBER SPECIFICATIONS

DESCRIPTION	A DIAMETER	B DIAMETER	C LENGTH	D ANGLE
.22 Bentz	.2278	.2264	.6787	1°35'
.22 Browning	.228	.226	.670	2°
.22 Butler Creek	.228	.225	.750	2°
.22 Chipmunk	.228	.226	.670	2°
.22 ELEY EPS Target	.2254	.2252	.617	1°30'
.22 ELEY Match	.2252	.2252	.590	1°
.22 ELEY SA Match	.2255	.2255	.595	1°30'
.22 Freeland MG	.2242	.224	.600	2°
.22 Lakefield	.229	.227	.700	2°
.22 Lilja	.2267	.224	.630	2°
.22 Meyers	.225	.2248	.600	1°30'
.22 PPG Match	.2269	.2256	.630	1°30'
.22 Rogue	.2225	.2242	.620	1°30'
.22 Stinger	.2275	.226	.735	1°30'
.22 Straight I	.225	.225	.600	2° or 2°30'
.22 Straight II	.2255	.2255	.600	2° or 2°30'
.22 Straight III	.2260	.226	.600	2° or 2°30'
.22 Time	.2262	.2248	.610	1°
.22 Ultimate EPS	.2252	.2252	.600	2° or 2°30'
.22 LR 547	.2261	.2251	.600	2°
.22 LR Anschütz	.2255	.2248	.619	1/2°
.22 LR Match	.2267	.2248	.600	5°
.22 LR Sporting	.2307	.227	.775	5°
Calfee I	.2255	.2255	.600	1°30'
Calfee II	.2255	.225	.600	2°
Win 52D Match	.2278	.225	.580	2°
.22 Short	.2291	.227	.431	5°
.22 Long	.2306	.227	.775	5°
.22 LR Shot	.2284	.2236	.871	30°

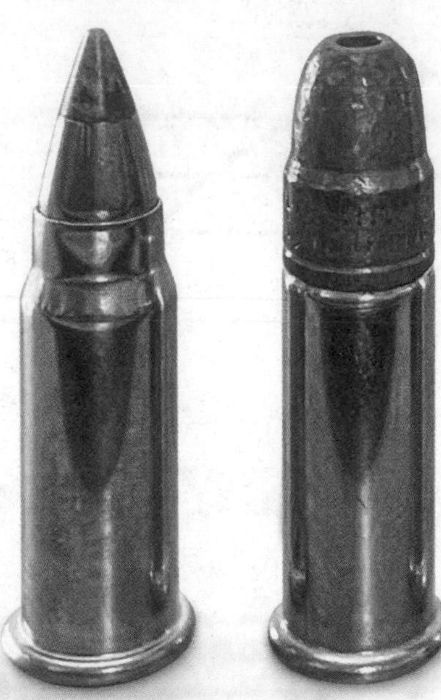
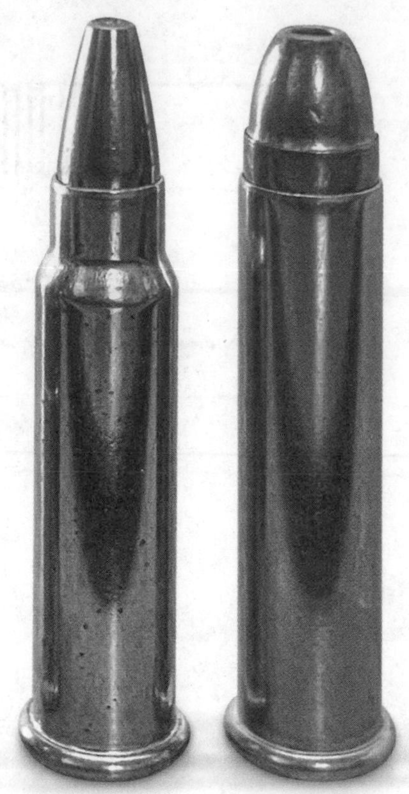

The big four (left to right): .17 HM2, .22 LR, .17 HMR, .22 WMR. These are the most common rimfire rounds.

.2215-inch diameter groove and a .217-inch diameter bore. The 'tight' barrels are .2200- by .215-inch diameters." Bore tightness affects squeezing or molding the soft lead bullet to the lands, which shapes each bullet more uniform, thereby more consistent and accurate — or so the thinking goes.

The best barrels are hand-lapped or hand-polished. No factory barrels are hand-lapped. It's a labor-intensive process, which is why custom barrels cost so much more. In the lapping process, you make a lead slug to the bore's internal dimensions for an exact fit. You then coat the lap with a gritty lapping compound and oil. It's pushed and pulled through the barrel many hundreds or thousands of times by hand. Lapping is a skill, and when the person on the lap "feels" they've completed the job, they stop. They then check the finish with a borescope and measure the lands, grooves, and bore diameter.

Traditionally, an "accurate" bore has the same diameter to 0.0001 of an inch from chamber to muzzle. Some manufactures grade their barrels with the most premium blanks running a uniform 0.0002 to 0.0001 inch the full length of the barrel. For some perspective, consider a sheet of paper. A piece of paper is around 0.002-inch thick, so hand lappers take these barrels to a tolerance of 20th of that! The benchrest shooter, gunsmith, and writer Bill Calfee pioneered the idea of lapping and cutting barrel blanks for "choke" or at a tight spot in a barrel. Calfee found tight areas in barrel blanks by pushing a lead slug down a blank and feeling where it hung up. He then cut the blank at that tight spot so the muzzle, or last point of contact between bullet and barrel, was a fraction tighter than the rest of the bore. This method, he believed, released the bullet at its best harmonic node. Calfee hung blanks and taped them like wind chimes to hear how they rang, homing in on these tight spots and their harmonic differences. His ideas are controversial in benchrest circles, but no one will argue his impact on the discussion of super accuracy in rimfire rifles. His book, *The Art of Rimfire Accuracy,* is well worth a read for those who want to wade deep into the weeds. The last essay in the book, *A Rifle's Tale* by Wallace Smallwood is the best thing I've ever read on how a custom rifle gets made.

Rimfire barrel lengths typically run from 16 to 24 inches for rimfires, and .22 LR bullet velocities tend to run consistently in good barrels from 16 to 20 inches. After that, in most cases, the barrel imparts "drag" on the bullet, slowing it down. For accurate shooting and tiny groups, this is a good or bad thing, depending on who you consult. Contours or shapes can be straight and heavy, like a bull or MTU. They can be spaghetti thin like a sporter or pencil contour. There is no definitive guide for length or contour related to the accuracy, but many have theories. It's worth noting that precision barrels tend to be heavier and longer. Tuners or devices that clamp to a barrel muzzle and adjust to tweak barrel harmonics generally work better on thinner, less heavy premium barrels. Tuners click to different lengths and move weight toward or away from the shooter, thereby changing the barrel harmonics. The general theory with tuners, and the entire process of matching ammunition to a barrel, arrives at the most repeatable, consistent harmonics, which translates — so the thinking goes — to the most consistent groups. GD

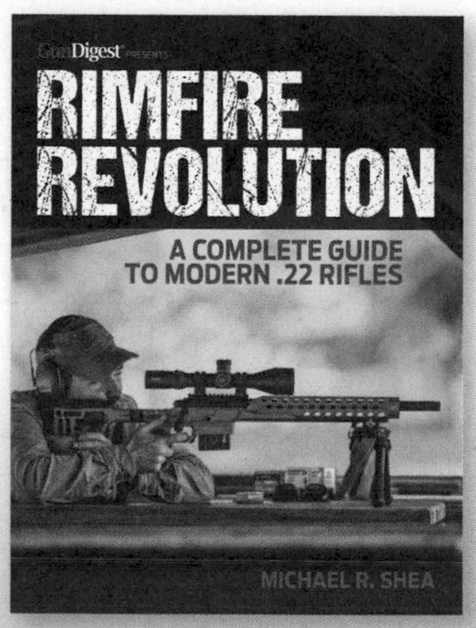

This article is an excerpt from the book Rimfire Revolution: A Complete Guide to Modern .22 Rifles *by Michael Shea, available at GunDigestStore.com.*

Handloading Economics

What's the real cost and savings of reloading your own ammo?

PHIL MASSARO

I got into reloading for a couple of reasons: first, it was something I wanted to do with my Dad, as it kept us shooting together in the offseason; second, it allowed me to build premium ammunition at a lower cost than I could buy it. I'm not sure that is true any longer, but it warrants taking a detailed look at the cost breakdown of what it takes to make a box of cartridges compared to what it would cost to buy factory loaded stuff. And, never forget, your time is worth something, even if you spend it performing a labor of love.

Factory ammunition for a standard chambering such as the .30-06 Springfield is generally available and affordable, but once you experience the freedom of handloading, you may never look back.

Brands such as American Eagle offer an incredible value. When you consider the cost of the investment in reloading tools and components, plus your valuable time, bulk factory ammo may be the better value (only if you can get it).

The volume of ammo you expend will affect the numbers game, as you'll need to purchase the same tools to make one box of ammunition as you'll need to load twenty. And it'll also depend on the cartridge you're shooting; the cost ratio of reloading to factory ammo is going to be much different for the 9mm Luger, .45 ACP, .223 Remington, and .30-06 Springfield than it will be for the .455 Webley, .318 Westley Richards, .333 Jeffery, and .350 Rigby Magnum. Then there is the ability to load for rifles and pistols that have no factory ammunition option. You can then only place the value on the ability to shoot that gun, making the cost of reloading irrelevant as it's the only option you've got.

Couple these ideas with the ammunition drought of 2013–2014 and the incredible increase in sales of both firearms and ammunition in the madness that began in 2020, and you'd have to add some value to having the ability to reload when there is almost nothing available on store shelves. No matter what the usual market price of your favorite factory ammo, when it's unavailable, you'll pay a premium. The value of handloads increases accordingly.

The author reloads at his reloading station getting ready for his next hunt.

WHAT'S THE REAL COST?

Let's use the universal and popular .30-06 Springfield as an example for cost analysis, assuming you're a new reloader and starting with no more gear other than a heaping pile of once-fired brass you've saved in a shoebox over the years. Looking at the big picture, at a bare minimum, you'll need a reloading press, a set of dies, a scale, trimming capabilities, measuring tools, case lube, reloading manual, and other accouterments. Let's say you jump into the pool with one of the reloading kits, such as the Rock Chucker Supreme Master Reloading Kit, which has a street price of $400. I'd add to that a trimmer, say an RCBS for $135, and a set of standard dies at $40. Before you buy a single component, you're now $475 in the hole. You'll need a pound of powder for roughly $30 and a box of 100 large rifle primers for $4. Let's use a standard deer hunting bullet such as the Sierra GameKing 165-grain spitzer boattail at $30 per box of 100. You've invested $539 and have the capability of loading five boxes of ammo. That works out to $107.80 per box of 20, but that's not realistic because you can use the tools for decades.

Suppose you take care of your reloading tools, and they last you a lifetime. Further, to simplify the analysis, let's remove the equipment's initial cost from the equation. To be conservative, let's throw in 100 brass cases from Federal at $62/100. Our components for 100 newly loaded .30-06 rounds would come to about $126, or $1.26/round. By comparison, a 20-round box of Federal Premium with that same Sierra 165-grain

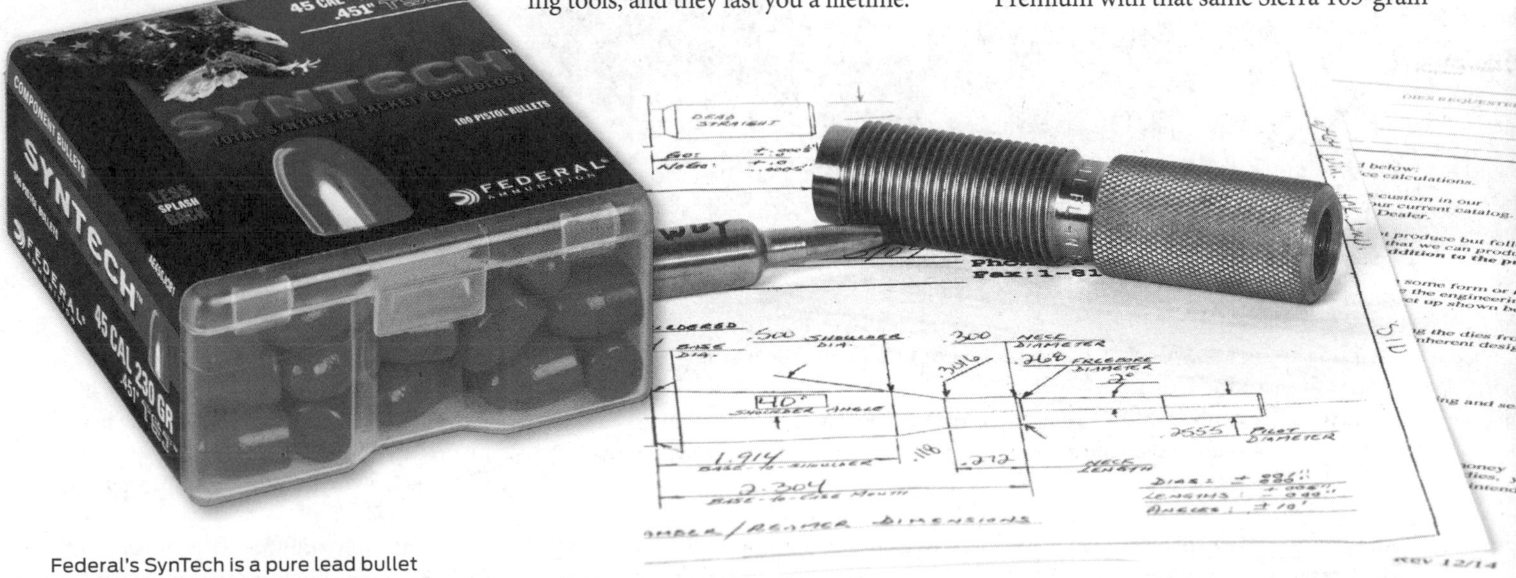

Federal's SynTech is a pure lead bullet encapsulated in a polymer coating. It's ideal for indoor ranges.

Redding offers a custom die service, which can be a considerable aid to the wildcatter.

The Weatherby Magnum factory-loaded cartridges can be expensive, and you'll see the financial benefits of reloading these proprietary cartridges.

GameKing bullet fetches $30-$37 — or $1.50-$1.85/round. So, yes, you can handload these rounds for a $.24-$.59 cent per round savings. Not only that, as I write this, there is a run on ammo, and you can't find that Federal factory load in stock. If you have the components on hand, you can always load some up.

If you're a one-deer-a-year consumer who generally confirms zero on Ol' Besty and heads afield, perhaps the factory ammunition is the way for you to go. But if you enjoy recreational shooting and the benefits of routine practice with your big game rifle, you can see how the investment in reloading tools can pay for itself in a short amount of time. If you get a couple of buddies together to share the tools' cost, you can see a return on your investment even sooner.

Compare this idea to a cartridge such as the .300 Weatherby Magnum, where factory ammunition runs from $40 to $90 per box. Suddenly, your investment in tools seems much more worthwhile. Should you shoot multiple calibers — both rifle and pistol — you will see how reloading gear can quickly provide a return on your money. I've also experienced the frustration of finding a factory load that a rifle loves, only to have the factory change the recipe (whether intentional or not, I cannot answer), resulting in ruined accuracy and me scratching my head wondering what happened to the rifle. What's more, experimenting with different factory loads can be a hefty investment, especially if you're shooting a rare and costly cartridge. The initial investment of the reloading tools, and the cost of components, coupled with the time spent developing a load, are all well worth it to me. I can grab primer X, charge the case with my known charge of powder Y, and seat bullet Z on top to arrive at the load that will serve for the rifle's life.

I gave the example of purchasing a reloading kit, and that is certainly a sound idea, but you could also buy your tools individually. Depending on your budget, you can make the tool list as expensive or inexpensive as you choose. One benefit of reloading: dies and presses are interchangeable — should you choose a Redding press, you could easily use a Hornady resizing die, an RCBS seating die and a Lee crimp die, or just about any combination. You can buy as you go, keeping your eyes open for specials and deals on reloading gear to keep costs to a minimum.

Online shopping has become popular, and that applies to reloading as well. But primers and powder require a Hazardous Materials fee on shipping. This fee can add a considerable amount of money to your components' cost, so keep that in mind and try and order in bulk, even if you have to combine orders with a friend or two. I recommend combining primers and powder on the same order under the same HazMat fee.

For the high-volume handgun shooter, there are many quality, inexpensive projectiles available that will keep the cost of ammunition down. Federal's SynTech is a great example. It's a synthetic-coated lead bullet, perfect for the indoor ranges, which cost between $23 and $27 per box of 100, or roughly 2/3rds the cost of Federal's premium handgun bullets. It runs clean and is accurate for practice. If you don't mind scrubbing lead from your bore, companies such as Meister Bullets offer hardcast lead bullets in bulk that can be as cheap as $0.07 per bullet for the classic 230-grain round-nose .45 ACP bullet if you buy them by the 1,000 count. Berry's Bullets offers plated projectiles for both rifles and pistols at an affordable rate; they are accurate, and you can use them in an indoor range.

AVAILABILITY IS PRICELESS

Whether or not you intend to handload for hunting, target shooting, self-defense, or competition, reloading can make the difference between having any ammo or none at all. At the risk of sounding like an alarmist, 2020 has shown that the ammunition shelves can go bare in less than a fortnight. If you've purchased this book, and especially if you've read to this point, you possess a desire to reload. Let me say this: just as you've learned how to safely store, handle and shoot a firearm, learning how to reload may save someone's life, especially when there is a shortage of factory-loaded ammo.

Whether it's hunting for meat to fill the freezer for the winter or defending your loved ones from a riotous mob, a firearm

Reloading gives the advantage of availability and economy, provided you have components onhand.

The .300 Holland & Holland Magnum on safari. The author handloaded 180-grain Federal Trophy Bonded Tip bullets to impressive effect.

Between dies from RCBS, cases from Bertram and Roberson Cartridge Company, and bullets from Woodleigh and Peregrine, handloading keeps the .318 Westley Richards alive.

without ammunition is no more effective than a club. The components need to be on hand, and the primers are the one part that cannot be reused or created, and therefore must be purchased. In a pinch, you can make crude blackpowder, and you can cast bullets from lead, but you must stockpile the primers.

Lead has become more difficult to source in recent years, though you can still hit the junkyards to procure material for pouring bullets. Working as a surveyor, I've picked up wheel weights on the side of the road, but there are too many varieties of metals in wheel weights these days to bother with them. Linotype alloy ingots can be purchased from the reloading supply shops and mixed with lead to achieve appropriate hardness. RCBS has long made a line of bullet molds for both rifle and pistol, and though sales are assuredly down, there is a small but enthusiastic group of cast bullet fans who keep the flame alight.

KEEPING THE CLASSICS ALIVE

A group of us, cartridge nerds, enjoy shooting and hunting with cartridges that are less-than-popular. We recognize, and use, some of the more common ones such as the .30-06 Springfield, 7mm-08 Remington, .300 Winchester Magnum, .22-250 Remington, 6.5 Creedmoor, and .375 H&H Magnum, yet also enjoy the early 20th-century British safari cartridges including the .318 Westley Richards, .300 H&H Magnum, .350 Rigby Magnum, .350 Remington Magnum and more. Many tragically overlook these latter-mentioned rarities to one degree or another, and components, cases, and bullets may present unique challenges to the shooter who is enamored with them. Factory ammunition is most prevalent for the .350 Remington Magnum and .300 H&H Magnum but is limited at best. The other two are limited to the odd run of Kynoch ammunition (which, in my honest opinion, is equally overpriced and overrated, with the bullets giving an erratic terminal performance and the cost running as much as $10 per round), and that stuff has seen better days. My best option for all of these cartridges is to handload them and keep them running with the limited list of components and tools available. RCBS once made dies for both the .318 Westley Richards and .350 Rigby Magnum, but the Huntington Dies Specialties custom die shop was closed in 2019. Even so, there are alternate custom die options. Also, you can form the .318 Westley Richards case from ultra-common .30-06 Springfield brass. But the .350 Rigby Magnum — which predates its more popular and larger sibling, the .416 Rigby, by a few years — is a unique design, and you can't fashion its cases from any other cartridge.

To handload the .350 Rigby Magnum, you'll either have to source some of the Kynoch spent cases or rely on a custom cartridge company to make some new brass for you. When I was building a .350 Rigby Magnum rifle, I relied on component cases from Roberson Cartridge Company in Texas to produce new brass for me. Were their cases inexpensive? No, but you get what you pay for, and the Roberson stuff is uber-consistent and lasts considerably longer than the cheaper stuff. Roberson cuts its brass instead of drawing it, and the molecular structure is both unique and unparalleled. Bottom line, you're going to have to handload for the latter two cartridges if you want reliable ammo. The .350 Rigby Magnum uses the lineup of .358-inch-diameter bullets common to the .35 Whelen, .358 Winchester, .358 STA, and .358 Norma — as does the .350 Remington Magnum — so there is no lack of component bullets. My rifle likes the 250-grain Nosler Partition and Hornady Interlock. At the same time, Dave deMoulpied's Remington 700 Classic in .350 Remington Magnum prefers the shorter bullets, such as the 220-grain Speer Hot-Cor, 200-grain Hornady InterLock, and 200-grain North Fork. GD

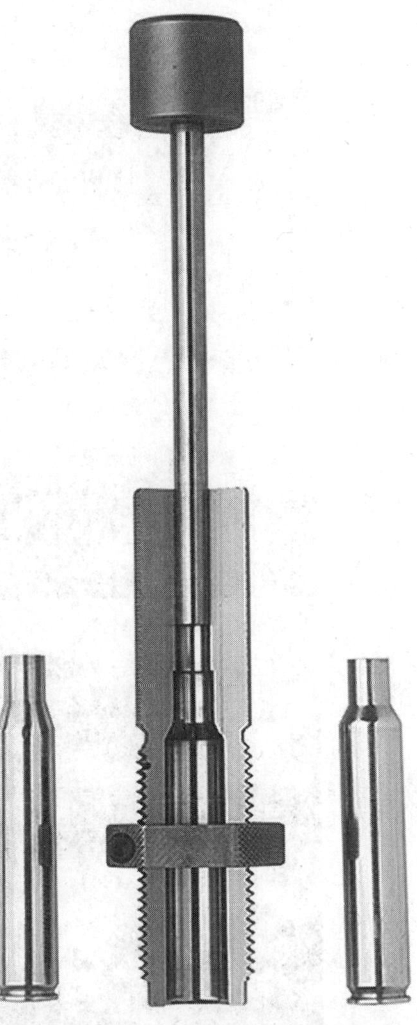

Hornady's hydraulic die-forming system.

The .350 Remington Magnum works best with shorter bullets, like these Hornady InterLock round-nose projectiles.

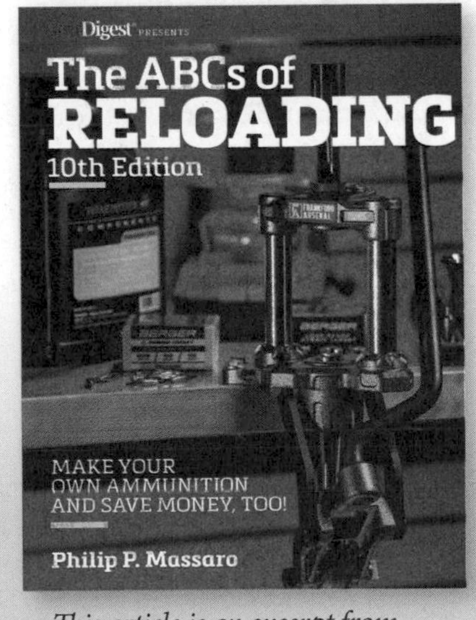

This article is an excerpt from ABCs of Reloading, 10th Edition *available at GunDigestStore.com.*

The Age of Chassis Rifle Systems

Move Over Traditional Rifle Stock, Chassis Are Here to Stay

›THOMAS GOMEZ

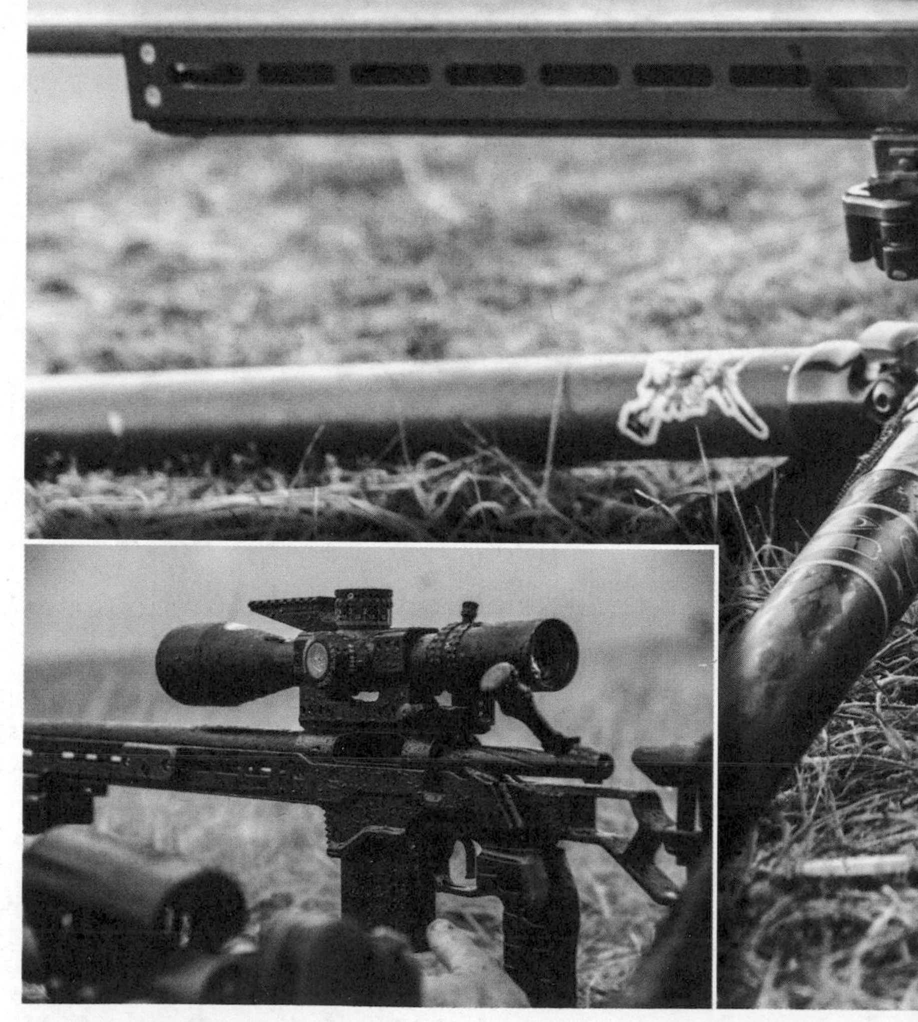

Chassis rifle systems have grown in popularity over the last decade, with most major rifle manufacturers offering chassis rifles and dozens of companies making aftermarket systems. Chassis rifle systems were originally purpose-built for military and law enforcement but have quickly found their way into competitions, hunting and general shooting.

The modularity and adaptability of chassis systems cannot be understated. Photo: Modular Driven Technologies

Accuracy International L96A1: One of the first chassis rifle systems.

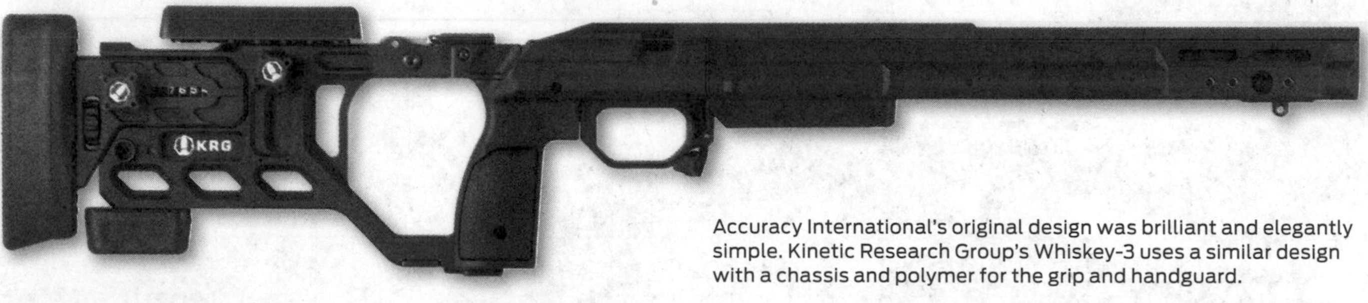

Accuracy International's original design was brilliant and elegantly simple. Kinetic Research Group's Whiskey-3 uses a similar design with a chassis and polymer for the grip and handguard.

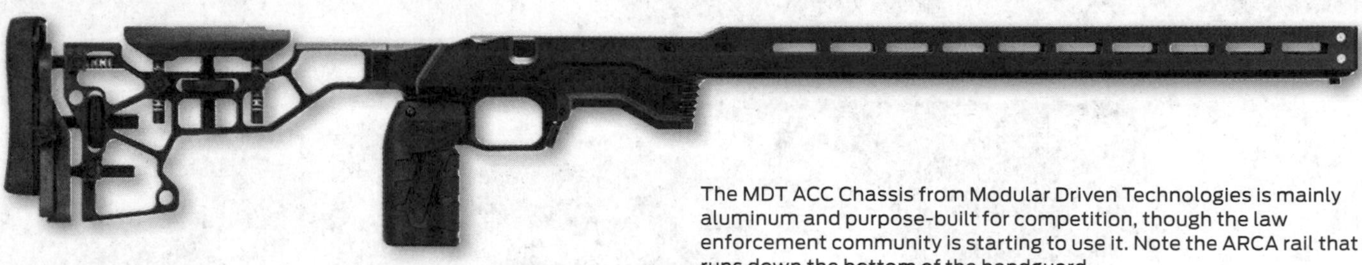

The MDT ACC Chassis from Modular Driven Technologies is mainly aluminum and purpose-built for competition, though the law enforcement community is starting to use it. Note the ARCA rail that runs down the bottom of the handguard.

What is a rifle chassis system, and what distinguishes it from a traditional rifle stock? A traditional rifle stock can be made from wood, polymer, or carbon fiber and mates the receiver or action to the stock via action screws that secure the bottom metal. A chassis system is usually a solid piece of aluminum that incorporates the buttstock, triggerguard and magazine well into one unit. Installing a barreled action into a chassis requires the end-user to simply mate the action to the chassis, tighten the action screws to a specific torque setting, and the rifle system is good to go.

Chassis systems utilize polymer for grips, side panels, or stocks, but the system's core is an aluminum block mated to the action. Traditional rifle stocks can benefit from bedding the action to increase accuracy; chassis do not require bedding and can feature either a V-block or a precise bedding block for the receiver.

DEVELOPMENT AND EVOLUTION

One of the first was the Accuracy International PM rifle developed in the United Kingdom in the early 1980s for the British army. This rifle system was designated the L96A1 and, after further development at the request of the Swedish military, the L118A1/L118A2. The AI PM was unique because it featured the Accuracy International Chassis System, an aluminum chassis that ran the rifle's length from the handguard to the buttpad. Polymer side panels were attached to the chassis that made up the grip, comb and handguard. Accuracy International also developed the detachable steel box magazine, which has become the standard in the industry and has been copied by companies like Magpul and Accurate Mag and further refined by Modular Driven Technologies.

By 2012, Kinetic Research Group, XLR Industries, Modular Driven Technologies, Cadex Defense and McRees Precision were on the scene, refining the chassis system and making some excellent products. The systems became lighter and more skeletonized and started showing features on the AR-15/M16/M4/

An AICS-style magazine manufactured by Modular Driven Technologies. Remington 700 mated to an MDT XRS Chassis System.

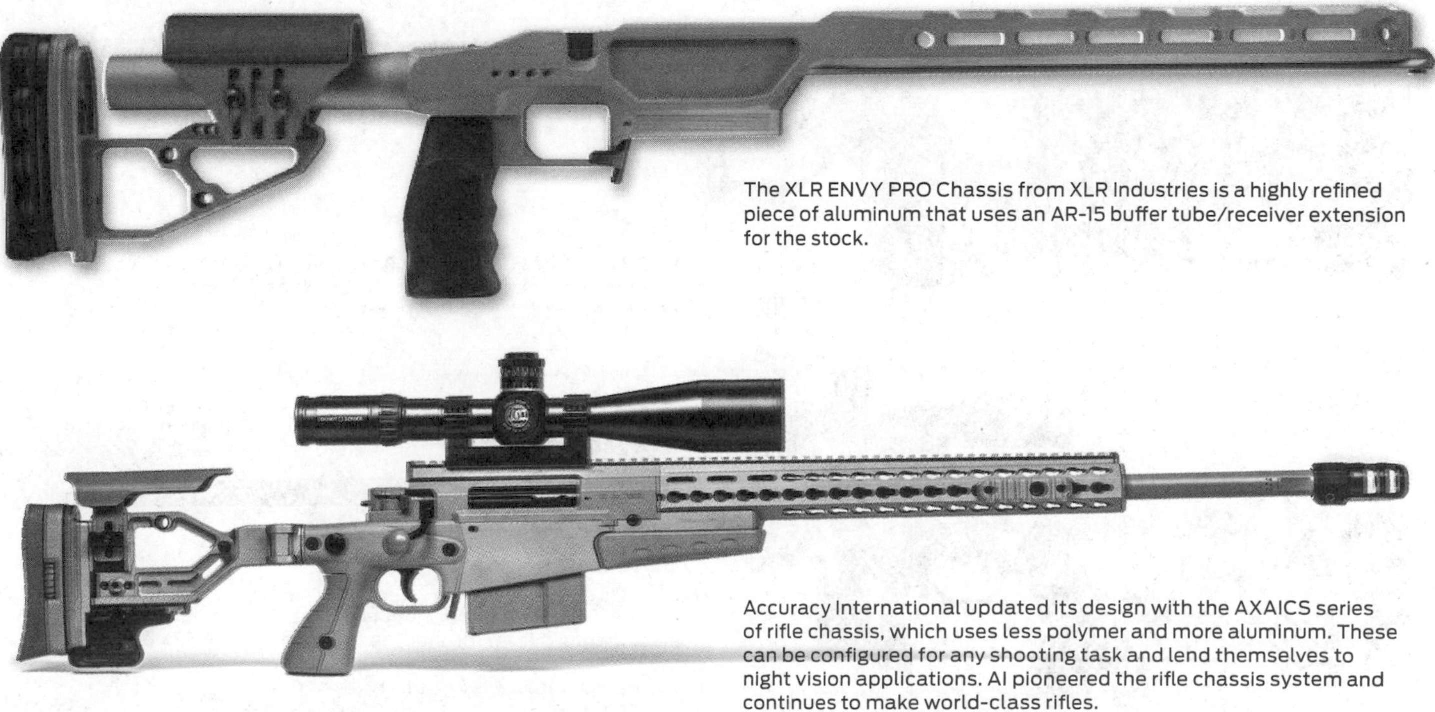

The XLR ENVY PRO Chassis from XLR Industries is a highly refined piece of aluminum that uses an AR-15 buffer tube/receiver extension for the stock.

Accuracy International updated its design with the AXAICS series of rifle chassis, which uses less polymer and more aluminum. These can be configured for any shooting task and lend themselves to night vision applications. AI pioneered the rifle chassis system and continues to make world-class rifles.

Mk18 family of weapons, such as M-LOK interfaces, AR-15 grips, MIL-STD 1913/ Picatinny rails and AR-15-style buttstocks.

Fast-forward to 2022, and the chassis market comprises more than a dozen companies producing quality products in a competitive environment. Specialization is inevitable when markets get saturated. Highly sophisticated systems are available for specific disciplines such as hunting, competition, law enforcement and military applications. Let's look at the form factor of the most common chassis systems.

FORM FOLLOWS FUNCTION

Chassis have evolved into three dominant form factors. The first represents the original design pioneered by Accuracy International, a chassis augmented with polymer panels or sides. The second is a highly machined piece of aluminum that accepts an AR-15-style grip, AR-15 stock via a buffer tube/receiver extension or proprietary stock. The third represents the traditional rifle stock with an aluminum chassis core and polymer or wood panels. Any chassis system can be used for any discipline. However, evolution has preserved certain form factors better at specific tasks, including competition, hunting, or leveraging technology for law enforcement, military or night vision applications.

Chassis can be heavy compared to traditional wood, polymer or carbon-fiber counterparts. With a growing customer base that has become accustomed to the features a chassis system affords, end-users may be hesitant to carry a chassis rifle into the woods or high desert due to the weight. However, the industry has responded with some ultra-light chassis options for hunters who want to build a lightweight rifle.

CHASSIS RIFLE SYSTEM ANALYSIS

I've used rifle chassis systems for at least a decade on my ranch rifle, long-range rifles, competitions rifles, and a fleet of class rifles that I maintain for Quiet Professional Defense in Albuquerque, New Mexico. Let's look at what makes these systems unique.

Chassis systems are inherently accurate. Since the action is bolted to a V-block or a bedding block, and the barrel is free-floated, there are fewer variables, particularly those causing harmonics issues. Aluminum is temperature stable and near impervious to the elements — making chassis rifle systems less sensitive to changes in the atmosphere. They are designed to be "plug and play" where an end-user simply drops in their action, torques it down and is ready to go. The overall rigidity makes them less prone to flexion from aggressively wrapping into a sling or loading into a bipod, thus maintaining accuracy.

Chassis allow the end-user to easily adjust comb height and length-of-pull, allowing one to tailor a rifle to one's morphology or body type. Being comfortable behind a rifle and quickly establishing a clear sight picture are two signs that an individual's rifle stock is appropriately set up. If a shooter is not fighting with their rifle system, they can focus energy on executing the fundamentals of marksmanship. Proper rifle fitment ultimately leads to a better shooting experience.

Chassis rifles are great for families or couples sharing a gun since each user preference can be noted, and the chassis system tailored to the individual shooter. For example, with a few turns of an adjustment knob, a 6-ft., 240-lb. father can share his custom hunting rifle with his

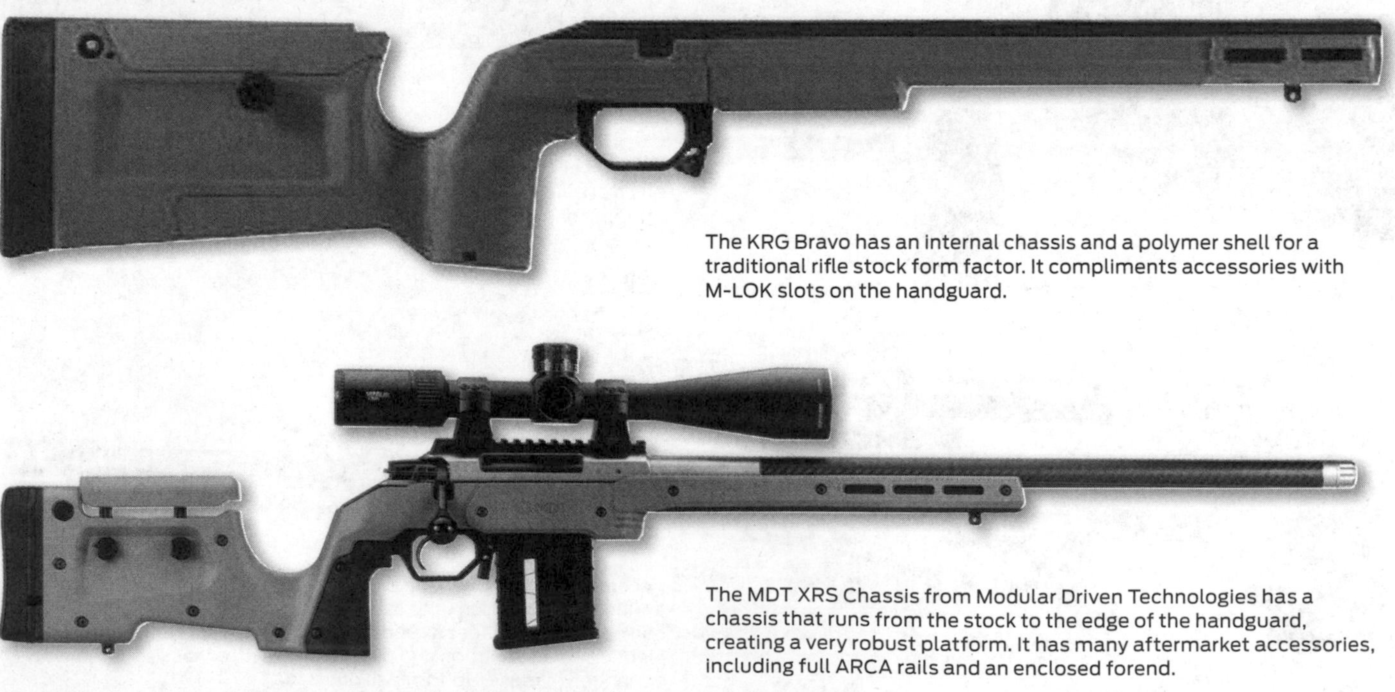

The KRG Bravo has an internal chassis and a polymer shell for a traditional rifle stock form factor. It compliments accessories with M-LOK slots on the handguard.

The MDT XRS Chassis from Modular Driven Technologies has a chassis that runs from the stock to the edge of the handguard, creating a very robust platform. It has many aftermarket accessories, including full ARCA rails and an enclosed forend.

Custom Tikka made by 782 Custom Gunworks LTD chambered in 6.5 PRC attached to a KRG Bravo Chassis. Note the 20 MIL Prism in front of the riflescope. This rifle was set up for shots beyond 1,800 yards.

5-ft, 110-lb. daughter. Chassis systems are also great for young shooters because as the shooter grows and develops, the chassis can be continually adjusted accordingly or tailored for specific disciplines.

These systems are modular and can be easily customized or tailored to meet the needs of specific uses, such as competition, night vision application or extreme long-range shooting. They leverage M-LOK and MIL-STD 1913/Picatinny rails that allow shooters to add barrier stops, hand stops, ARCA rails, additional Picatinny rails, lights, lasers, weights, bipods, tripods, cardholders and monopods. Setting up your rifle for a Precision Rifle Series or PRS-style competition in the morning, then re-configuring without changing the zero for a night vision hog hunt in the evening, is feasible and easily accomplished.

I predominately own chassis systems from Kinetic Research Group and Modular Driven Technologies. These companies make excellent products, and I recommend both. Other great brands include Magpul, XLR Industries, Oryx, JP Rifles, JAE Chassis, Cadex Defence, MPA, GRS and Accuracy International. Save for some family heirlooms or beautiful wood-stocked Mannlicher-style hunting rifles, I do all my testing, training and hunting with chassis rifles. They maximize the accuracy potential of my rifles, allow me to customize sling attachment points and ARCA rails for my tripods and bipods, and generally fit my large frame better than traditional stocks.

I can also quickly adjust my rifle for other shooters should the need arise. For years, the only downside to chassis was weight, but that has become a moot point with the rise of carbon-fiber parts, carbon-fiber-wrapped barrels and purpose-built ultra-light chassis systems.

Do you need a chassis? It would be hard for me to go back to a regular stock now that I'm used to a chassis system's modularity and custom fit. I recently shot long-range with friends, mainly firing from the prone position. After our "serious" shooting was done for the day, zeroing, testing scopes, and gathering data, we broke out the fun guns for some plinking. A friend handed me a non-chassis rifle with a traditional stock and told me to take a few shots. I could

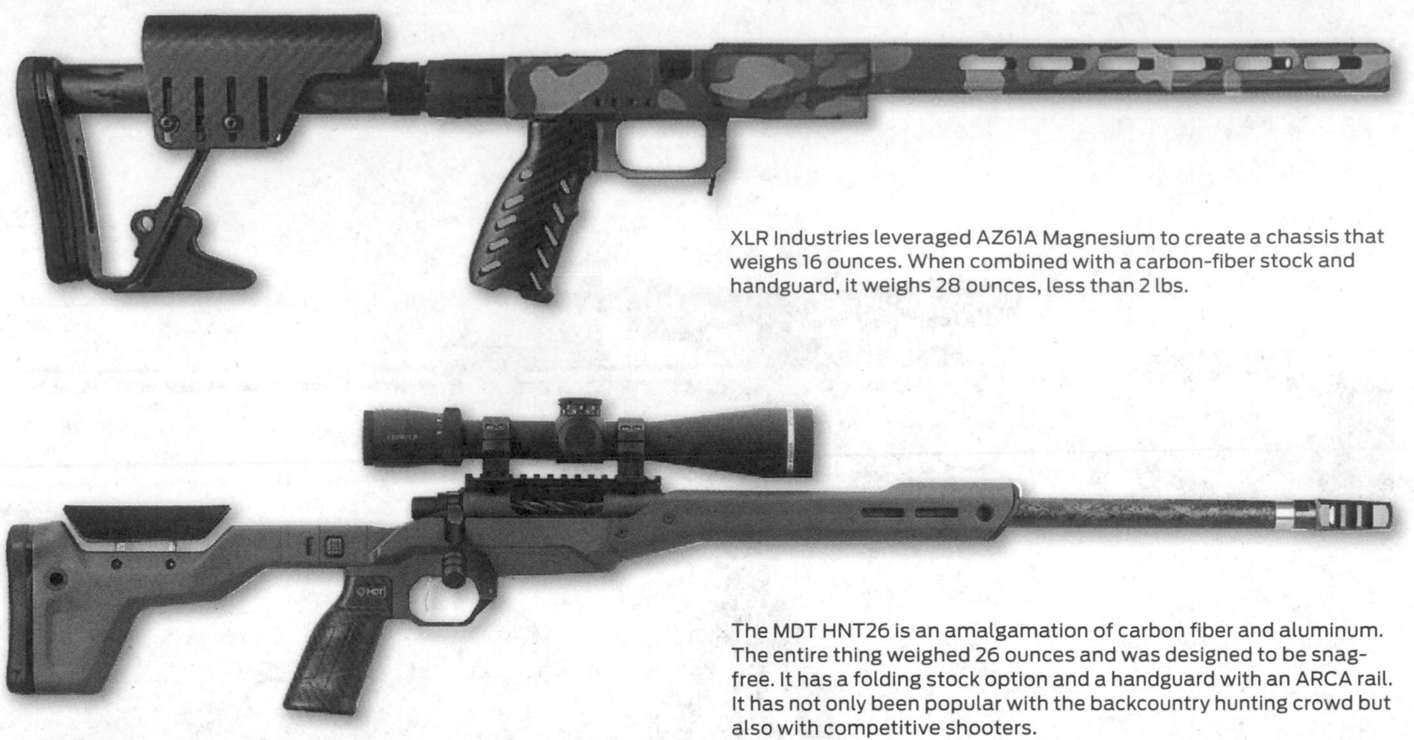

XLR Industries leveraged AZ61A Magnesium to create a chassis that weighs 16 ounces. When combined with a carbon-fiber stock and handguard, it weighs 28 ounces, less than 2 lbs.

The MDT HNT26 is an amalgamation of carbon fiber and aluminum. The entire thing weighed 26 ounces and was designed to be snag-free. It has a folding stock option and a handguard with an ARCA rail. It has not only been popular with the backcountry hunting crowd but also with competitive shooters.

The author's goddaughter getting ready to harvest an antelope at 556 yards in the high plains of New Mexico. Her rifle is a Howa 1500 chambered in 6.5 Creedmoor mated to a KRG Whiskey chassis.

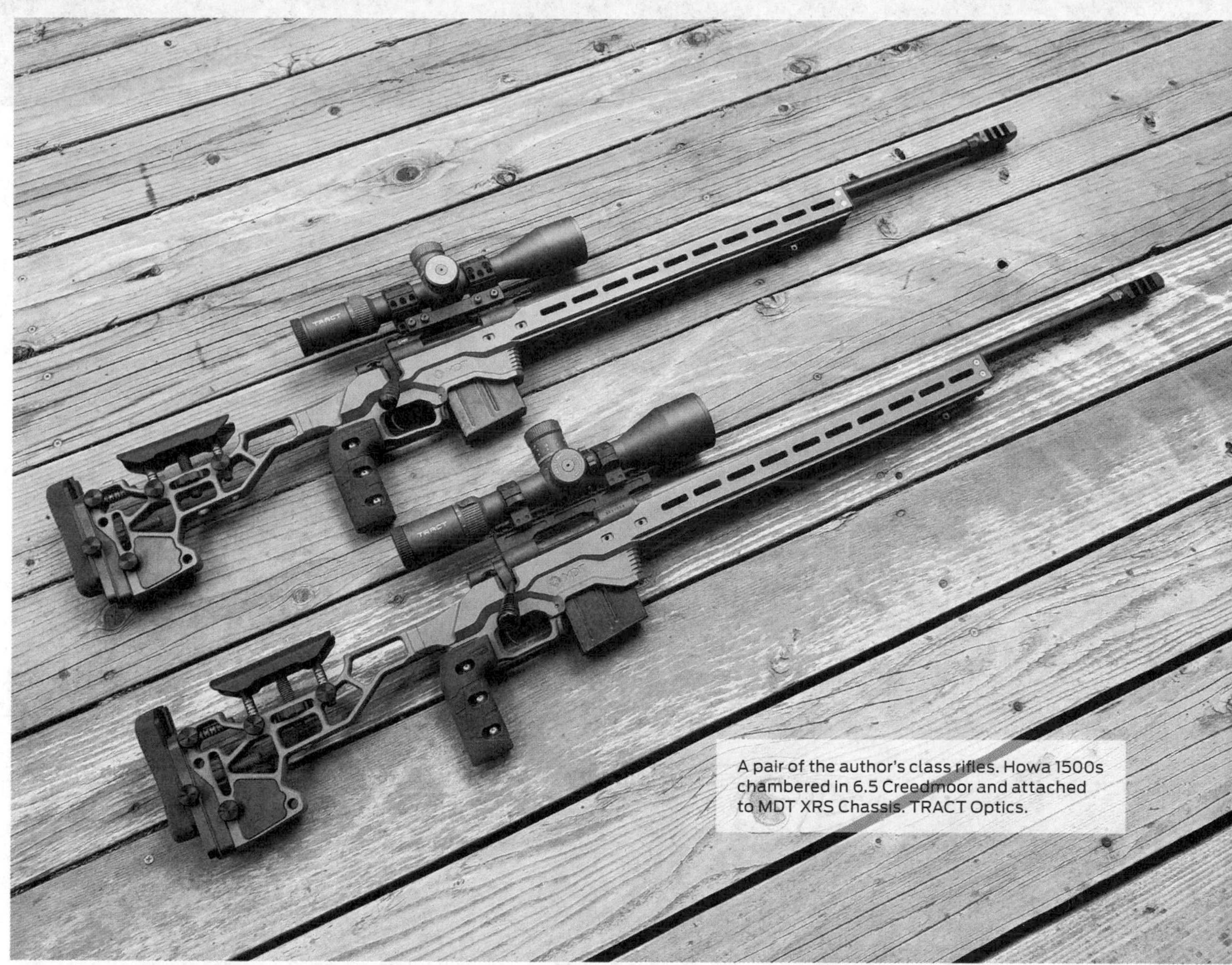

A pair of the author's class rifles. Howa 1500s chambered in 6.5 Creedmoor and attached to MDT XRS Chassis. TRACT Optics.

not get comfortable behind the rifle, nor could I get a proper cheek weld, eye relief or sight picture from the prone position. After a minute of trying to get settled, I unloaded the rifle, complimented him on his setup and handed it back without firing a shot.

There was no reason to waste ammunition if I was not entirely confident in my ability to achieve a perfect shot. Had the rifle had a chassis, I could have made minor adjustments and been good to go.

CLOSING THOUGHTS

Chassis systems used to be expensive, but with the industry maturing, decent ones such as the Oryx or Trybe Defense R.O.C.S. can be purchased for around $400. Chassis systems do not require a gunsmith for installation and typically come with a set of action screws. Most companies have robust customer support. There are dozens of forums and user groups online that discuss them and will be quick to help should you need advice.

My goddaughter learned the fundamentals of precision marksmanship on a Howa Mini rifle, chambered in 7.62x39, which was mated to an LSSXL chassis from Modular Driven Technologies. Her primary hunting rifle is a Howa 1500 chambered in 6.5 Creedmoor mated to an old KRG Whiskey Chassis. She used that rifle for an elk hunt in the Valles Caldera National Preserve, where she shot an elk clean through the heart at 450 yards. Last Fall, we tweaked her rifle for tripod use, and she harvested a pronghorn antelope at 556 yards. Watching her grow as a shooter has been a fun and positive experience, and the fact that she had a chassis rifle system certainly made the entire process easier. My two daughters are a few years out from starting their shooting careers, but both will fire their first shots from a chassis-equipped rifle.

The chassis market has reached its apex with options available for every discipline. Due to the highly modular nature of these systems, I expect the next generation of rifles to be built on them, represent the latest in materials science and even have an electronic component. I'm excited to see what happens in the coming years. GD

The GUN DIGEST

6th EDITION 1952

COMPLETE INFORMATION & PRICES

- Domestic & Foreign Firearms
- Shotguns & Rifles
- Pistols & Revolvers
- Scope & Iron Sights

SPECIAL FEATURES

- Weapons of Soviet Russia
- Whitney Arms Catalog, 1878
- How to Shoot the M1
- Gun Engraving
- Shooting the Muzzle Loaders
- British Double & Single Rifles
- Winchester's "Forgotten" Cartridges, 1860-1900
- Collecting Single Shot Rifles
- A Selected List of Gun Books

Edited by John T. Amber

It Ain't So, Mac!

› WARREN PAGE

Editor's Note: It's always fun to look back at our historical pieces and see how the gun writers of yesteryear wrestled with the myths of their day. Here, from the 1952 Gun Digest, 6th Edition, *legendary shooter Warren Page tackles some of the ideas that were floating around during his era.*

Will one shotgun shoot the same shell harder than another one? Is the autoloader less "powerful" than the bolt action? Do you hold over or under when the target is up on a hill? Down in a canyon? Do duck loads shoot harder straight up, or on the flat? Does this rifle of mine shoot just as fast as the ballistics tables say it does? Does the 12 gauge kill birds farther or more easily because it spreads the shot more widely? Will bullets glance away from a tree trunk they almost but not quite hit? How far does a high-velocity bullet travel from the gun muzzle before it begins to fall?

Questions like these are cause for puzzlement and mighty strenuous argufying even among pretty smart shooters. These and forty-'leven others, the old wives' tales of gunnery, have had shooters fooled for years — and have kept more hot-stove sessions going through more midnights than any other questions of gun facts. I know, because in my job I answer stacks of letters on 'em, and settle some red-faced disagreements on the facts. Facts? Certainly. Who wants to referee a set-to that's a matter solely of personal opinion? The common fallacies and misunderstandings referred to in that opening paragraph, and a score more like them, are matters of proven fact, or at least they can be.

If a chap wants to know whether the grouse is a better game bird than the quail, or the 270 a better all-round caliber than the 30-06, it's easy to offer an opinion, and probably not too hard to make it stand up, whichever side of the fence we're on — but we can't *prove* absolutely that we're right. The answer in either case depends on what we expect of a bird or a rifle, or the circumstances under which we shoot either one.

MORE POWER FROM SEMI-AUTO OR BOLT ACTION?

But if the point at issue is whether a blowback 22, for example, develops as much or less "power" than a bolt action 22 of similar barrel dimensions using the same cartridges — and there are thousands of shooters who are tripped up on that one — on such a question we can dig up some hard facts.

You won't dig 'em up in your back yard; at least I was never able to arrive at anything significant from shooting into chunks of timber and measuring penetration. Few of us have the laboratory chronograph equipment which is the only way of getting exact checks on velocity, hence on "power." So, being fortunate in knowing the ballisticians who toil in the ranges under Winchester's New Haven plant, and also Dr. C. (for Chuck) Cummings, who has charge of all those fancy gadgets in the Remington lab, I spent some time and some loading-company money finding out. The answer is: Stop worrying; there isn't any difference in any practical sense.

Let's look at some facts. Up at Remington, they took one of their Model 550 22 semi-autos (the rifle that has a little "kicker" or sliding inner chamber so that its blowback action will function with either shorts, longs, or long rifles) and two boxes of long rifle fodder from the same carton. The first box of 50 was fired with the gun operating normally; the second with the action blocked up, so that the gun was performing just like a locked-breech bolt action. Several thousand dollars' worth of Potter electronic counter chronograph revealed a difference of 12 f.p.s. instrumental speed in favor of the action *when it blew back normally!* Then Doc Cummings tried it with a Colt Woodsman, a 4½-inch-barreled model. Another 50 with the action opening normally, followed by as many more shots with it blocked up, tallied an average 12 f.p.s. higher from the locked breech. Ah-HAH! says the proponent of the bolt or locked-breech action. But that differential is of absolutely no significance in any practical shooting sense, since if the loading companies could turn out 22 long rifle fodder that would deliver the same speed every shot, plus or minus *twice* 12 f.p.s., they'd be very happy indeed. The difference is probably not even significant to a hair-splitting laboratory technician, guns and ammunition being what they inevitably are.

Just to put the clincher on, I got the dope on experiments the Winchester people had run with one of their Model 74 semi-auto 22 rifles. They fired 20-round strings, standard production ammunition from the same box. When the action was permitted to blow back as designed, the average 15-foot instrumental velocity for that fodder was 1,226 f.p.s. With the action jimmied so that it could not blow open, the speed averaged 1,219 f.p.s., 7 f.p.s. *slower.* Again the difference, imperceptible even had it been the other way around, is no more than a variation normal to all ammunition.

In all common sense, there is no particular reason to expect a blowback 22 to be less powerful than a similar bolt, lever, or trombone type. True, the breechblock is free to move backward, save for its own inertia and the light thrust of the counter-recoil spring, when the powder goes off and the bullet starts on its way. But, since the bullet weighs 40 grains, and the breechblock many times as much — the Colt Woodsman slide weighs about 6½ ounces or 2,844 grains, 70 times more than the bullet — it starts back mighty slowly in comparison. Furthermore, the cartridge case itself is held tightly to the chamber walls for an instant by pressure. The bullet, therefore, is beyond the muzzle, or at least way beyond the point of pressure and velocity build-up, before the back door opens, so to speak, to cause any velocity loss.

Figuring that an autoloading shotgun is puny as compared to a pump, with the same loads and barrel length, is equally wrong — and for even stronger reasons, since in the typical Browning-designed action the barrel and the breechblock are firmly tied together until they have moved nearly all the way back into the receiver, where they are separated by a tripping action so that the barrel can go back into battery, the spent shell be kicked out, and the breechblock come forward later to pick up a fresh round. Clearly the inertia of barrel plus chunk of breechblock is so vastly greater than that of the accelerating shot that the pellets will be gone before there's any speed loss

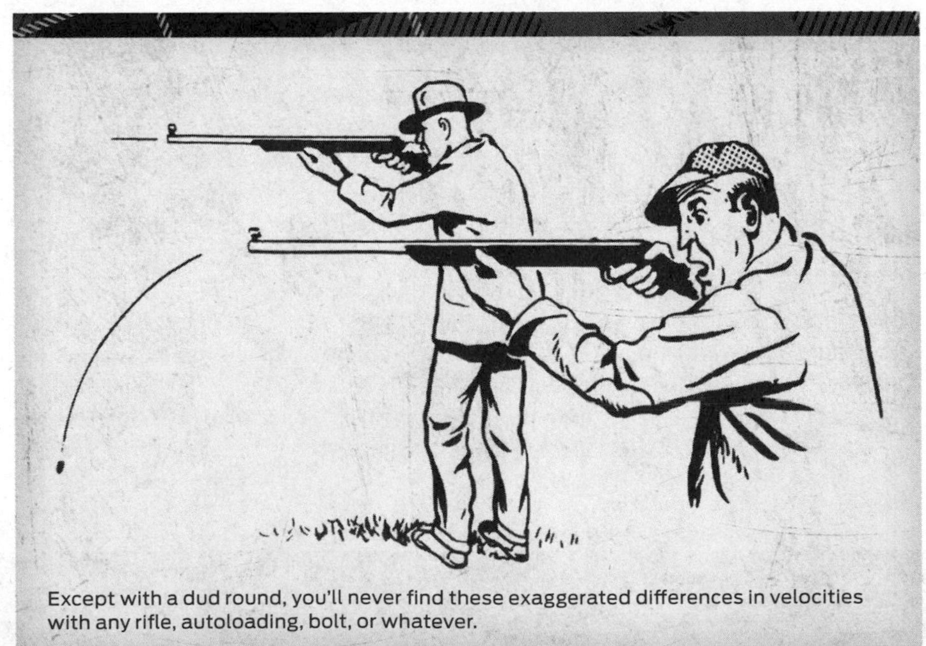

Except with a dud round, you'll never find these exaggerated differences in velocities with any rifle, autoloading, bolt, or whatever.

because of the breech opening. Taking shot velocities with absolute accuracy is a tough job — but it's a cinch that if we fired a Browning type autoloader both locked and unlocked, any difference would come within the speed variation limits natural to shot shells.

Now there may be certain peculiar actions, and individual loads, where the flat statement that there is no sensible "power" differential doesn't hold water. Winchester found that the Garand gained some 28 f.p.s. when the action was locked shut, for example; so the situation in gas-operated guns, where pressure is tapped off behind the slug, well ahead of the chamber, may be different. But for the 22's and shotguns, which are the pieces whose "power" people worry about, there's no meaningful difference.

Rifle shooters are pretty hard to get along with on occasion, but if you rib a smoothbore artist about the hard-shooting qualities of his pet shot-squirter, there's apt to be blood on the floor. Most riflemen will grudgingly admit that their game rifle doesn't shoot any harder than the next guy's in the same caliber — just straighter — but the shotgunner is plumb hardheaded about his long-range killer.

Ballistics tables are reliable — to a point — but you'll know more about YOUR rifle by shooting it.

DO RIFLE VELOCITIES AGREE WITH BALLISTICS TABLES?

The rifleman, however, is likely to be a slave to the ballistics tables, to accept their figures for his own rifle without question, assuming that it has a barrel of standard length. That's not, as a matter of absolute truth, quite correct, although for purposes of doping trajectory, sighting in rifles, or comparing loads, it's good enough in a practical sense.

A couple of years ago I carted up to the Remington ballistics labs three rifles in 270 caliber, plus a batch of factory ammunition of a lot which had given me excellent accuracy, hence must have been uniform in delivered velocity. I was primarily interested in the relationship between barrel length and speed; consequently the three guns were picked for their 24, 22, and 19-inch lengths. All were apparently standard save that the 22-incher was cut with a 1-in-12 twist.

When the smoke had cleared away and the figures were averaged up, it appeared that identical factory ammunition fired from the standard length 24-incher gave a 60-foot instrumental speed of 2,980 f.p.s.; the 22-inch sporter, 3,031 f.p.s.; and the stubby 19-inch barrel, 2,793 f.p.s. Note these points. First, the barrel of 24 inches, the standard length used in all the ballistics tables for 270 caliber, could not by any stretch of the slide rule deliver the 3,140 f.p.s. calculated muzzle speed published for the load. Second, the barrel 2 inches shorter gave higher speeds with the same load!

Now you can draw any conclusions you want to about the barrel-length vs. velocity business, but this little incident points up what Phil Sharpe's extended experiments have developed more fully — that the inevitable variations in the inside dimensions of rifle barrels, of chamber, throat, and bore, are productive of very considerable pressure and speed differences with the same loads, sometimes even greater differences than those caused by a couple of inches of barrel length, which latter variations or losses are usually less important than we think anyway. In practice, of course, if rifle A starts its slug 50 feet faster than rifle B, the buck doesn't much care which slug misses him, and he won't know the difference if both hit him, not out at a couple of hundred yards. Those ballistic table figures are evolved from tests with precisely made laboratory barrels — not with smokesticks bored and reamed to ordinary production tolerances — so treat the figures with the merest pinch of salt.

While the matter of barrel length and velocity in center fire rifles is an engrossing subject, and one on which many shooters are either confused or full of opinionated beans, it would take a whole article to skim around its edges. Let's save it, and say that the old rule of thumb for so-called "high-power" cartridges, which calls for a velocity loss of 25 f.p.s. per inch of barrel removed, in terms of ordinary sporter lengths, is only the roughest kind of approximation. With the extremely hot loads using high pressures clear out to a standard length muzzle, this figure is usually too low; with the 35,000 to 45,000-pound loads, it's usually too high. Exact chronograph checks often reveal that other factors in a barrel's innards or in the load — inside dimensions all the way out, bullet type and diameter, ignition, the burning qualities of the specific powder — are more important than a couple of inches of muzzle end. In common-sense terms, we are not going to skimp too much on the velocity delivered *at the animal* if we make our barrel for the 270 to 30-06 type of cartridge 22 inches long; for the Magnums, 24 inches; for the 30-30, 32 Special, 35 Rem, even the 300 Savage with the heavier bullets, a handy 20 inches. A lot more noise when we cut 'em back from standard, but not a catastrophic speed loss.

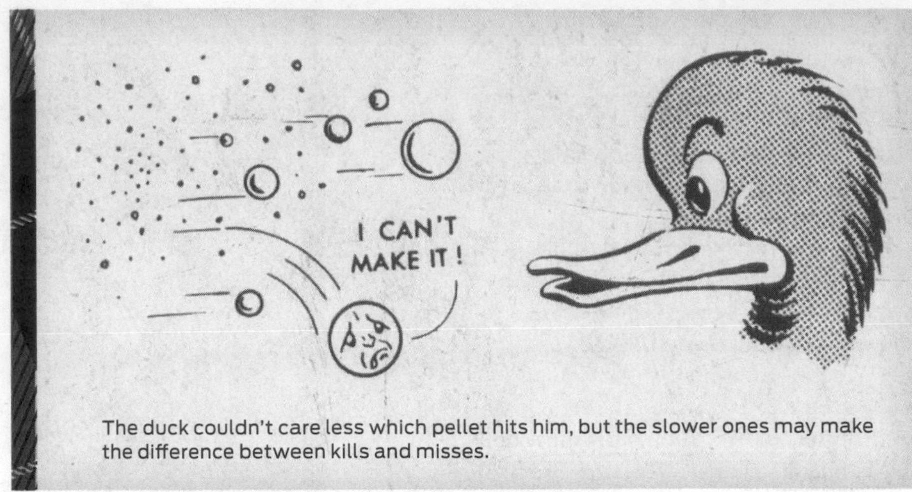

The duck couldn't care less which pellet hits him, but the slower ones may make the difference between kills and misses.

DOES ONE SHOTGUN SHOOT HARDER THAN ANOTHER?

Now that character with the hard-shooting shotgun is itching to get in his two-bits' worth. The heck of it is, in a laboratory sense, if not in a practical sense, he has some right on his side. For example, I have data showing average shot velocities delivered over 40 yards, same loads of course, by a couple of shotguns with identical barrel lengths and almost exactly the same amount of choke constriction. One gun shot 38 f.p.s. faster than the other. Why? Perhaps because the cylindrical section of its barrel was 9/1,000 of an inch smaller. Or maybe it was a difference back at the forcing cone. No telling. BUT, when the loading companies can put out shot shells which will constantly stay within a 25 f.p.s. velocity tolerance, there'll be dancing on the green. It isn't practical.

As a matter of fact, since the difference in speed between the fastest and the slowest pellets in any one shot shell is fully 25 f.p.s., and since the loads themselves vary more than that out of the same box, and since 1/1,000 of an inch of choke constriction (in a tight-bored gun there may be nearly 40/1,000) means one added foot per second of average speed over 40 yards, and since temperature and humidity affect speed almost as much as some of the individual gun measurements, it is quite possible that from one combination of guns and conditions we could get from 50 to 100 f.p.s. of difference in speed. That would show nicely on laboratory equipment, but it would be pretty tough to measure it by shooting at either telephone books or high-flying ducks. This velocity business, then, is apt to be rather academic, even if it is rather nice to know that from two barrels absolutely identical save that one is 26 inches, the other 30, the average shot speeds over 40 yards will be between 25 and 30 f.p.s. less for the shorter barrel. But it is not yet established what even this means to a duck of average intelligence and sensitiveness to chilled shot.

There is actually a very great difference in how hard individual shotguns will shoot, even though seemingly much alike. Velocity is not the only element in shotgun power if we assume the same shot size and charge; delivered pattern density is a much more important one. Counting patterns is an easy way to go nuts, but I have many times observed that certain of my guns patterned certain shot shells much closer than others marked as having the same choke. Up in New Haven not long ago they counted 200 patterns from eight different "full-choke" guns of assorted makes, all pump guns as I remember it, and found that with the same duck load of No. 6 shot the 40-yard, 30-inch patterning circles were perforated by anything from 66 percent to 75 percent averages from the different guns. Now the 66-percenter would put 185 shot into the circle; the 75-percenter, 211. Those extra 25 or so pellets *might* be just the ones to kill the duck! Shotguns *do* have individually hard-shooting qualities sometimes, even in standard factory borings, depending on just how the fickle fowling pieces will throw their, patterns.

DOES THE 12 THROW A BIGGER SPREAD THAN THE 20?

And that brings us to a question on which there is a very wide range of misunderstanding — the width of the spreads thrown by 12, 16, and 20-gauge guns which are of the same degree of choke, when fired with comparable loads. This is a real whing-ding. Ask any confirmed 12-bore shooter and he will swear that his full-choke gun will spread its shot over more of the barn door — or more of the covey of quail, chukars, or what have you — than a full-choked 20 gauge. He may even want to fight about it. In a practical sense, he's completely wrong. The man who holds coats during fist-fights just stepped out, so wait a minute, friends, let's see what the figures say. Cold-turkey data from the ballistics labs will prove more than any casual one- or two-shot guesstimates.

Winchester was inquisitive on this point, among others, and fired both Super-X and Ranger loads, No. 6 shot, from full-choked 12's, 16's, and 20's, Model 12 pump guns. With the heavy loads, all three gauges put from 72% to 74% into 30 inches at 40 yards; with the lighter loads, 69% to 70%. If we count 90% of all the shot holes on the pattern board — no sense in looking at *all* the shot holes, since in any charge there are some deformed shot that go flying off south-southeast — maximum diameters would range between 46 and 50 inches with the easy load, 48 to 50 inches with the duck load, *regardless of the gauge fired.*

When I put the proposition up to Cummings at Remington, he burned up a lot of green shells to arrive at virtually identical results. He drew 40-inch circles on the papers bearing the patterns, (25 from each gauge) shot with a fully choked 20 gauge handling an ounce of 6's, a 12-gauge choke-bore firing duck loads, 1¼ ounces of the same shot, and the same 12 gauge firing a one-ounce dose of 6's at a speed identical to the 20-gauge setup. Inside those 40-inch circles *all* three guns put from 81% to 86% of their shot, and the averages were even closer on 10, 20, and 30-inch inner circles. Obviously, except for odd stray pellets, the guns were throwing the same overall spread.

The bigger hole in the 12 bore therefore does not, assuming the same choke, throw any wider slather of shot than the smaller bores — but it does throw more shot into the same area, for a denser pattern that will hold together further out. Consequently, choke for choke, it will have greater killing power. To put it another way, at a given range we can use roughly one degree less choke with the bigger bore and get similar pattern density with larger overall, spread. Catch on?

DO SHOTGUNS SHOOT HARDER STRAIGHT UP, OR ON THE LEVEL?

Now one more common question about shotgun performance. This is one you can figure out yourself. Why is it that a load of 4's or 6's seems to hit a duck less hard when he's crossing straight overhead than when he's at the same range out over the decoys? The answer is, it doesn't.

The argument that shotgun shells somehow have less "oomph," their shot less striking velocity, when fired straight up than they do when fired on the level or up at a shallow angle, is an old-timer — wrong as can be, but popping up perennially. The reason why it crops up, particularly after some half-frozen duck-shooter has had a very tough day in the blind, is one of the reasons for his tough day — faulty range estimation. When a bird is up over us, where there are no ground points or known objects against which to judge his apparent size, it's a lot easier to figure the 70-yard cloud-splitter at a shootable 50 yards than when he is nearer the water. There we have our decoys, the next point, possibly trees, to go by and can guess his distance that much more accurately. A shot charge doesn't slow noticeably faster than normal just because we shoot it straight up.

There can't be any difference save that exerted by the force of gravity, which on a straight-up shot does help slow the pellets. A maximum load of 6's is in flight .167 seconds, or thereabouts, in traveling 50 yards. The downward acceleration of gravity, at the accepted rate of 32 feet per second per second, would therefore slow the straight-up pellets so that they'd smack the duck approximately 5 f.p.s. slower than they would if he were on the level in front of the blind. That speed difference is *not* going to be the difference between two teal and a full limit of black ducks, however, not when human eyes are judging the range!

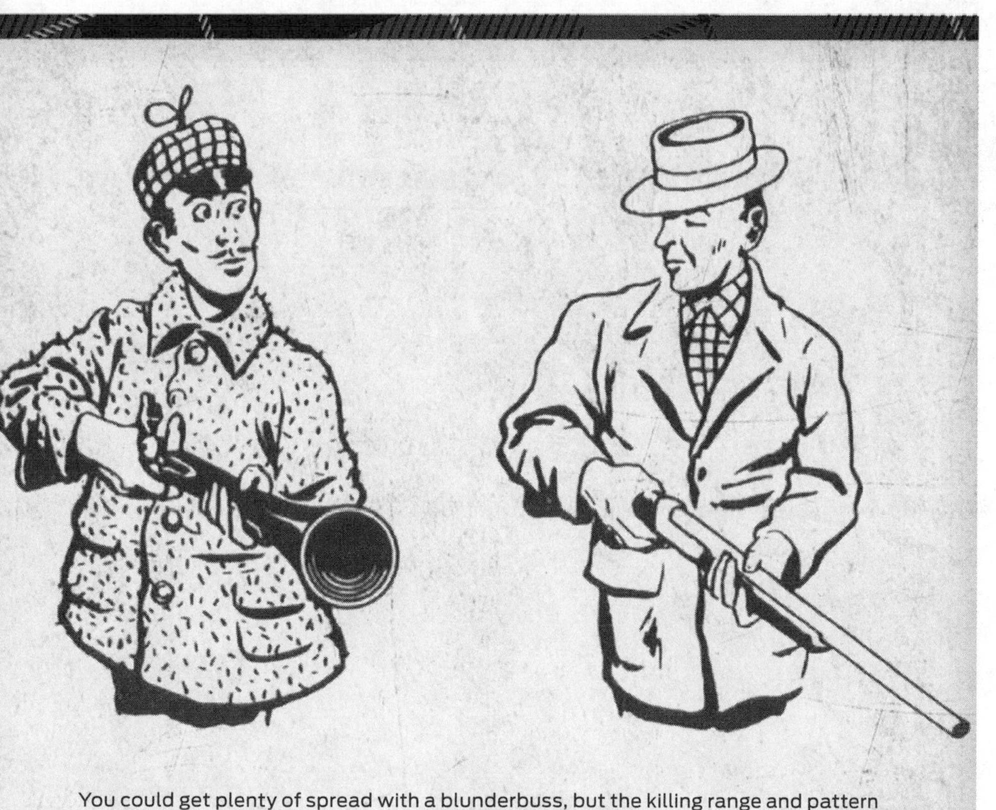

You could get plenty of spread with a blunderbuss, but the killing range and pattern density would be lousy.

WHERE SHOULD WE AIM ON UPHILL OR DOWNHILL SHOTS?

Gravity does play some rather odd tricks in respect to rifle trajectory. Not only does it continue to pull every bullet downward, at a rate of acceleration remarkably constant regardless of bullet weight, from the very instant it leaves the muzzle; but it also, in this constant pull, can lead us to some long-range misses even with carefully sighted and held rifles. Probably such misses, although they are uncommon with high-velocity, flat-trajectory cartridges, give rise to the common questions regarding the proper point of aim on uphill or downhill shots at long range. The mathematics of these questions is tough, the logic a bit easier.

Those who remember trigonometry well enough can not only prove that for large angles of elevation or depression (greater than 10°) the slant hitting range of a rifle sighted in on the horizontal is greater than the hitting range of that same rifle on a horizontal, flat-country shot, but he can also rough out the error. The ordinary guy, who relies on trigger-nometry rather than trigonometry, can also grasp the idea this way.

Assume our rifle to be zeroed in at 200 yards. In that distance the bullet has risen above our line of sight, by virtue of the original sight correction for the effect of gravity, and has just come back down to it again. Hence on a 300-yard target, straight out on the flat, we'd have to hold over to allow for the continuing effect of gravity — in the case of the scope-sighted 30-06 with 180-grain bullet, about 11 inches. Now if our 300-yard target, a sheep for example, is perched up on a shale slide above us by some 45°, the pull of gravity, still straight down, is working in reference not to a roughly horizontal line through the center of our rifle bore, but to a line tipped up slightly more than 45°. Hence its effect on the bullet in relation to that line is not as great, and we won't have quite as much drop to worry about on that 300-yard sheep. That is, the slant hitting range is increased. Matter of fact, instead of needing to hold over by

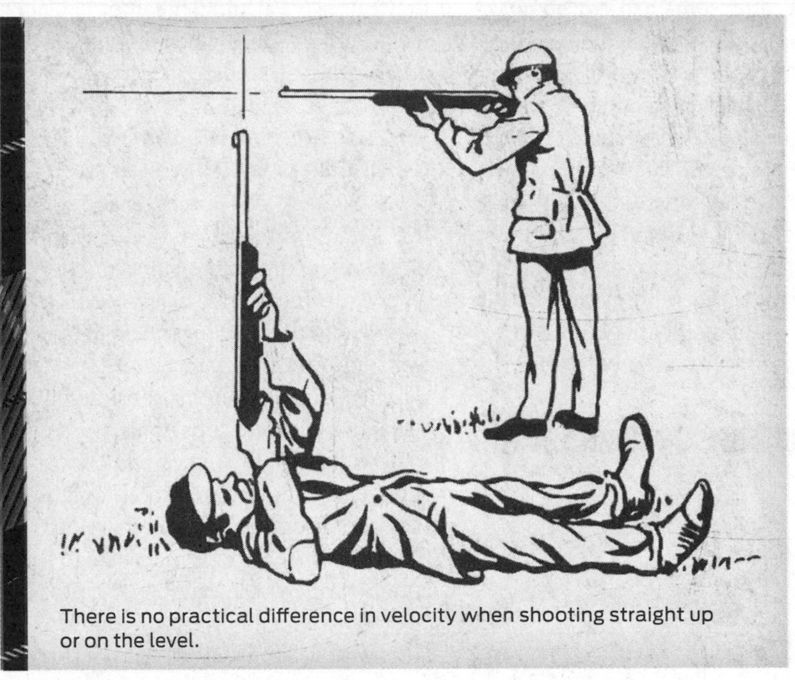
There is no practical difference in velocity when shooting straight up or on the level.

11 inches, under the simple conditions outlined we'd need to figure as if we were shooting on the flat at 213 yards, and hence would need only a couple of inches of hold-over, which in a practical shooting sense is nothing at all. The conclusion we have arrived at here is that on shots sharply uphill or downhill we should hold *under* the point of aim we would think correct for that range on the flat.

To estimate the effective range over which we are shooting, as distinct from the actual distance from our own case of buck fever out to the trophy sheep, try to imagine how far it would be from you on the horizontal to a point straight into the hill under the sheep up there, and figure your hold accordingly. Too tough? Well, with modern cartridges like the 270, 30-06, 257, 300 Magnum, and so forth, when the rifles are properly sighted in for the big and rough country where such problems are likely, just forget the whole deal and hold a little low.

But if you're the type of character who carries a pad and pencil up the mountain, or can do rapid calculation, you can arrive at your effective range (the one according to which you should sight or hold) in terms of a formula in an informative book by ballistician C. S. Cummings, entitled *Everyday Ballistics*, published by Stackpole & Heck:

EFFECT OF SLOPE ANGLE ON EFFECTIVE RANGE

ANGLE OF SLOPE (UP OR DOWN)	DIVIDE ESTIMATED RANGE BY
15°	1.04
20°	1.06
25°	1.10
30°	1.15
35°	1.22
40°	1.31
45°	1.41

EFFECT OF SLOPE ANGLE ON EFFECTIVE RANGE

In actual hunting, any such mathematics may go with the wind, either literally or figuratively. Your dope may also be upset by the different sling tension put on your rifle by the peculiar way the rocks make you belly down; or you may make a bum guess — and this is a very important point — as to just where on that odd-looking critter way up or down there the bullet should hit to drive into his boiler room. Try looking at a mule deer from 45° above him sometime, and you'll discover that the bull's-eye isn't painted on him in the same place it usually is! The ideal hitting point for a heart shot — how would it shift under those conditions?

CAN BULLETS BOUNCE FROM TREES THEY DON'T HIT?

While that last line is being stewed

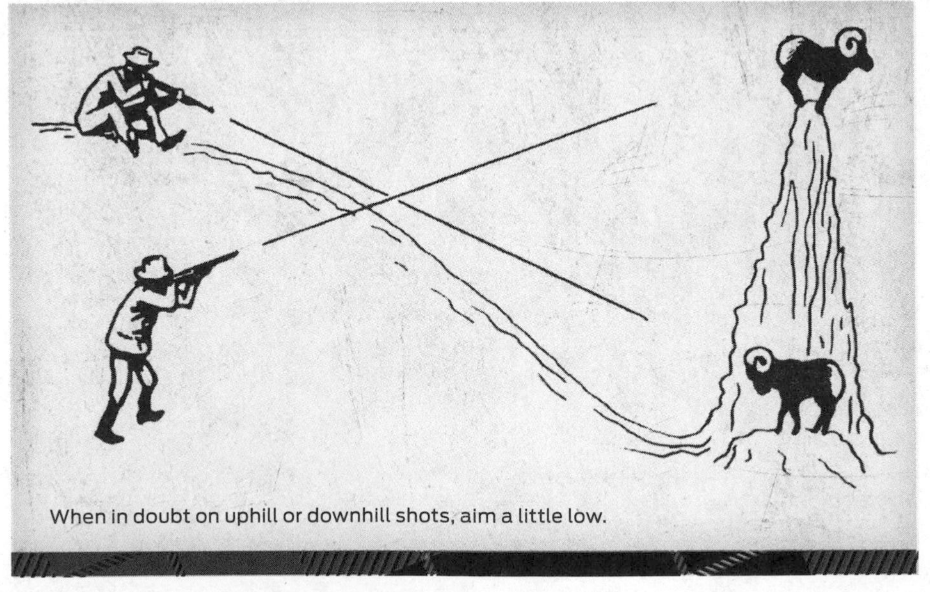
When in doubt on uphill or downhill shots, aim a little low.

over, let's move to another subject for hot-stove-league arguments. Is a bullet deflected off course away from a tree or a rock or a fence post between you and the target, when it comes whisker-close to that tree but doesn't actually tick it?

It is often argued, with plenty of convincing table-thumping, that in passing very close to an object, the bullet in flight compresses a thin pad of air between it and the object and so is bounced a bit off line. Or maybe the shock wave tearing along with the bullet has something to do with it. At any rate, the chap who is banging the table is convinced that some such mysterious effect caused him to miss the trophy shot of a lifetime. Not so.

If the slug even just barely touched the branch, it was probably deflected some, perhaps a lot. Long and heavy bullets with round noses plow through the shrubbery better than light, short, or pointed ones; ultra-fast projectiles may be completely broken up even by light impact. But if it didn't actually touch — bullet weight, speed, or shape has nothing to do with the case — the bullet will keep on as straight as it ever did.

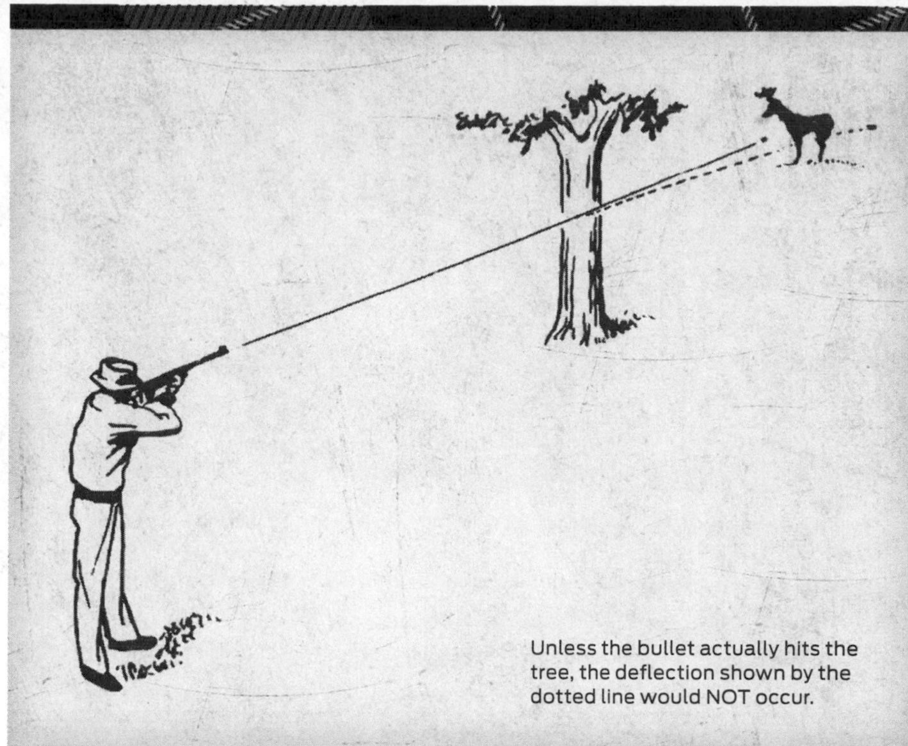

Unless the bullet actually hits the tree, the deflection shown by the dotted line would NOT occur.

To check on this, I did what has already been done before. I set up a target at 100 yards, locating it so that the bark of an 8-inch rock maple 60 yards out was a-a-a-lmost exactly in line with it and my rifle on the sandbags. The rifle (a supremely accurate 220 Wilson Arrow, whose Pfeifer target-weight barrel and FN action had been put together and chambered up by L. E. Wilson himself, the stock beautifully inletted and designed for sandbag work in bullet testing by Bill Humphrey of Virginia) had earlier been targeted against another marker on the same board and had made three 5-shot groups from 6/16" to 11/16" extreme spread. These groups centered 1¾" above the aiming point, a strong ¼" right of center.

Then I fired ten shots at the marker, which was located so that all ten must just squeeze by the tree. But two didn't. They *hit* the bark, one flying off into the butts somewhere, the other keyholing into the target about 5 inches out of the group. The other eight, which did not hit the rock maple, but must have come within an inch or less of it, printed up a nice group only ⅝" across, centering 1¾" high, perhaps ⅜" right. The tree was on the right side. Was any bullet in the least deflected which did not actually contact the tree? Was either the accuracy of the rifle or its point of impact altered when the bullets skimmed the mid-range obstacle? The answer is *No* in both cases, and there's every reason to feel that it would be *No* in other similar ones, regardless of bullet weight, shape, speed, or even proximity to the obstacle, so long as there is no actual contact.

However, it must be admitted that the great ballistics experimenter, F. W. Mann, working with cast bullets at velocities under 2,000 f.p.s. (slow by today's standards), turned up some evidence of bullet deflection in his plank-shooting tests. His bullets shifted impact away from or toward the plank according to whether their distance from it was greater or less than half an inch. But his bullets were fired to pass alongside flat planks *4 to 16 feet long;* they were not zipping past tree branches. Even Mann noted no deflection when his "plank" was a 4" block. Hence his experiments do not controvert but rather support those made with modern high-speed loads.

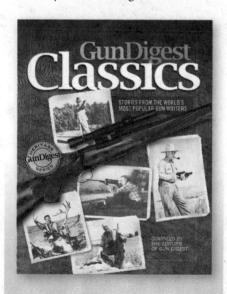

Every batch of mail that shooters send to gun editors, and every session of chin-music among shooters either amateur or expert, will turn up more of these odd questions. When they are matters of opinion, let it be every man to his own, and long may we shooters rave — but when the debate hinges on matters of fact, let's turn either to the professional ballistician's gadgets or to the back-yard laboratory to find the right answer. GD

STEVENS MODEL 301 TURKEY GUN

› STEVE GASH

The M-301, a dot sight, and Federal TSS ammo make a deadly combination for turkey hunting.

"Hey, Steve, come take a look at this!" a voice bellowed as I cruised the aisles of guns at the SHOT Show. I saw a waving arm beckoning me to a booth with new guns from Savage/Stevens.

The object of the adulation was a cute little single-shot break-action .410 shotgun. Okay, so what? This neat little gem had a spiffy camouflage finish, a scope mount base on its receiver, and a curious-looking choke tube protruding from the muzzle. "What's this," I sniffed insouciantly, "a .410 turkey gun?" The booth representative from Stevens was not amused and, with considerable restraint, replied that yes, it was indeed a ".410 turkey gun." Somewhat chagrinned, I tried to look interested. "This is the perfect gun for the beginning turkey hunter or someone who's recoil adverse," the booth master intoned, stringing his words along like cantaloupes on a vine.

"The new gun is the Stevens Model 301 Turkey," he said as he thrust it into my hands. As I looked it over, I had to admit that it was an appealing little gun, light and handy and downright attractive. After his presentation, I knew I had to have one, and I received one for testing. The M-301 is an elegant synergy of design, execution and specialized ammo. Collectively, it was quite a revelation. Let me tell you about it and its ultimate application.

The Stevens Model 301 is a unique break-action single-shot .410 built for turkey hunting.

First, the M-301 is light, at a mere 5 pounds, 4 ounces, and is only 42 inches long. The slender barrel is 26 inches long and has a 3-inch chamber and a brass bead front sight. What is a bit unusual is the Weaver-style scope base on the receiver. Many shotguns wear optic sights these days, but the M-301 is optics-ready right out of the box, at no additional cost. The metal has a non-glare matte black finish. The Stevens press release says that the barrel and choke tube I mentioned earlier is "optimized" for Federal's new .410 turkey load (more on this fantastic new product later).

The M-301 has a host of innovative features. The gun is ultra-safe, as it has an exposed hammer, and there's a two-position safety at the left-rear of the receiver that blocks the hammer. Cocking the hammer makes a distinct "click," but disengaging it is noiseless, so it won't scare off an approaching bird.

The stock and forend are made of a rigid synthetic material finished in Mossy Oak Obsession like my test gun or Mossy Oak Bottomland camo. The length of pull is 14¼ inches, sling swivel studs are installed on both ends, and there is a nice, soft 1-inch recoil pad. A recoil pad on a .410, you ask? Yes, and it works great with the superload especially made for the gun.

Many — okay, most — shotguns have yucky triggers, but the one on my M-301 test gun was pretty darn good, breaking at a neat 3 pounds, 14.1 ounces, as measured with my Wheeler Digital Trigger gauge, and reasonably crisp.

The M-301 arrived a few days before the Missouri spring turkey season, and Federal Premium forwarded a supply of its new .410 Heavyweight Tungsten Super Shot (TSS) ammo. These shells are pretty amazing. The load has a rated velocity of 1,100 fps and is packed with 13/16 ounces of #9 TSS shot. That's .81 ounces, which is more than the standard 28-gauge load of ¾ oz. I've shot several turkeys with Federal 12-gauge ammo loaded with #9 and #7 TSS shot (albeit not in .410 bore), and it is the deadliest turkey load I've ever used in 50 years of gobbler pursuit.

(left) The M-301 comes with an extended extra-full choke turkey tube.

For testing, I mounted a new TRUGLO "Gobble-Stopper" dual-color dot sight on the M-301. The supplied mounting base made mounting a snap. The sight comes in anodized black or Realtree APG camo. The reticle can be displayed in red or green, with five brightness levels and an "off" setting in between each level. The supplied CR-2023 battery powers the sight, and there is a storage compartment in the rheostat turret for an extra battery (supplied). Zeroing the sight is easy, and the elevation and windage turrets have retention lanyards.

As I say with rifles and handguns, holes in paper don't lie, so I got out my rangefinder, put up some Champion

20 yards.

25 yards, with ammo.

35 yards.

turkey targets, and headed to my range with a couple of boxes of the .410 TSS ammo. I fired the load at 20, 25, and 35 yards, and the results are readily apparent in the photos. The bottom line is that any turkey within 35 yards has a one-way ticket punched to Thanksgiving dinner as the guest of honor. In fact, this load patterns so tightly that you must be careful when shooting at closer-range turkeys, as a miss at 15 yards would be easy. This is where the utility of a dot sight comes in.

I've saved the best and (depending on your point of view) the worst for last. The good news is that the M-301 retails for $199; the street price is less. Talk about a bargain.

The "worst?" Well, the little gun is made in China. Some may recoil in horror at this revelation, but it is what it is: a solid, well-made gun built for a specific purpose and target market. I like it, and I bet you will, too.

The M-301 was made to hunt turkeys, so hunt with it I did. I did not get a turkey, but I later learned that a much more significant event occurred after the M-301 ended up where it belonged all along — in the hands of a fledgling turkey hunter. Here is the rest of the story.

I had bought the M-301 from Stevens, and when my FFL dealer, a serious gun crank, took a shine to it, I sold it to him. Crafty merchandiser that he is, he had a plan to see that the gun found its rightful home.

A good customer named Chet Parker has two fine youngsters, and both are already hunters. Chet's daughter can take turkey hunting or leave it and would rather hunt whitetails. His son, appropriately named Jake, is a turkey hunter, as is his mom.

The Missouri Department of Conservation has a "youth" season for spring turkeys scheduled before the regular season. It gives young hunters an edge and is a great learning experience. The requirements of the youth season are straightforward and well structured. A "youth" hunter must be at least six years old and no older than 15; Jake was seven at the time. Youths with hunter certification may hunt alone, but those without certification must hunt with a mentor aged 18 or older. A youth permit is $8.50 for residents and non-residents. The mentor does not need a permit.

The spring youth turkey season in 2021 opened on April 10 as Jake, and his mom and dad were hunting. The weather didn't cooperate, and they had to take frequent breaks to get out of the drenching rain. Jake had practiced shooting with "regular" .410 ammo in the M-301 in the backyard and was well-schooled. (The box of the pricey Federal #9 TSS .410 turkey loads that went with the sale to my dealer ended up with Jake, who used them in the M-301 for hunting.)

Opening day jitters can plague hunters of any age now and then, and while Chet called in some gobblers, Jake missed the first three he shot at. But after another rain delay, the intrepid camo-clad duo was back in the field, eyeing the decoy, and Chet was calling.

Jake was sitting in dad's lap, ready. A bearded hen appeared and slowly sauntered in the hunters' direction. (Any bearded turkey is legal in the Missouri spring season.) When the hen got within range, Chet told Jake that he could shoot whenever he was ready.

At 17 paces, the .410 *boomed* — success! It was a fitting start to a new hunter's career and the perfect application of a well-designed tool for precisely this task. I think the photo of the happy hunters tells the story. As Festus would say, "Don't that just plant your 'taters?" GD

A happy seven-year-old Jake Parker and dad Chet with the turkey Jake took with the Stevens M-301 .410. Photo: Connie Parker

STEVENS MODEL 301 TURKEY GUN

MANUFACTURER:	Sun city Machinery Co., Ltd., People's Republic of China
TYPE:	Break-action single shot
CALIBER:	.410 bore.
CAPACITY:	1
BARREL:	26 inches, 3-inch chamber
CHOKE:	Extra-full choke tube provided (Win. choke pattern)
OVERALL LENGTH:	42 inches
WEIGHT, EMPTY:	5 pounds 4 ounces; (gun only); 5 pounds, 11 ounces with Truglo Gobbler-Stopper optical sight (as tested)
STOCK AND FOREND:	Synthetic, with Mossy Oak Obsession (tested) or Mossy Oak Bottom Land camouflage, one-inch recoil pad and sling swivel studs installed.
LENGTH OF PULL:	14¼ inches
FINISH:	Matte black on barrel and receiver
SIGHTS:	Brass bead front, Weaver-type base on receiver, tested with TruGlo Gobbler Stopper optical dot sight
TRIGGER:	Weight of pull 3 pounds, 14.1 ounces (as tested)
SAFETY:	Manual hammer-blocking two-position at the left rear of the receiver
WARRANTY:	1 year
IMPORTER:	Savage Arms, Inc., Westfield, MA
MSRP:	$199.00

RUGER PRECISION

CUSTOM SHOP SPECIAL

Big country, long-range. Stretching out the new Ruger Custom Shop Precision Rifle in 6.5 Creedmoor.

A BLUEPRINTED MASTERPIECE OF CHASSIS GUN BUILDING ART FROM MUZZLE TO BUTTSTOCK.

› L.P. BREZNY

In 2010, I got ahold of Remington's newest U.S. Army sniper rifle to test for my third book on long-range shooting. The rifle was chambered in .300 Win. Mag., the replacement for the 7.62 NATO round. The rifle came in a massive hard-cased drag bag system, housed a suppressor and field tools for on-the-fly barrel changes or whatever was the day's problem. I installed a bipod, and when a round was chambered, the military-grade scope (no name) with 100-yard zero sent very accurate rounds to 1,500 yards with ease. The price tag for this Model 2010 Chassis sniper rifle? About $24,000 and change.

Several years after that introduction to chassis rifles, which were a bit new to the shooting public, Ruger came along with its idea of a very workable and priced-right chassis rifle. I was issued one of the early models that rolled off the production line. I had drilled several hundred rounds of factory and handloaded fodder into steel targets that ranged from 600 to 1,200 yards. That test rifle was chambered in 6.5 Creedmoor, that round being the hot item, and still is. The first series Gen

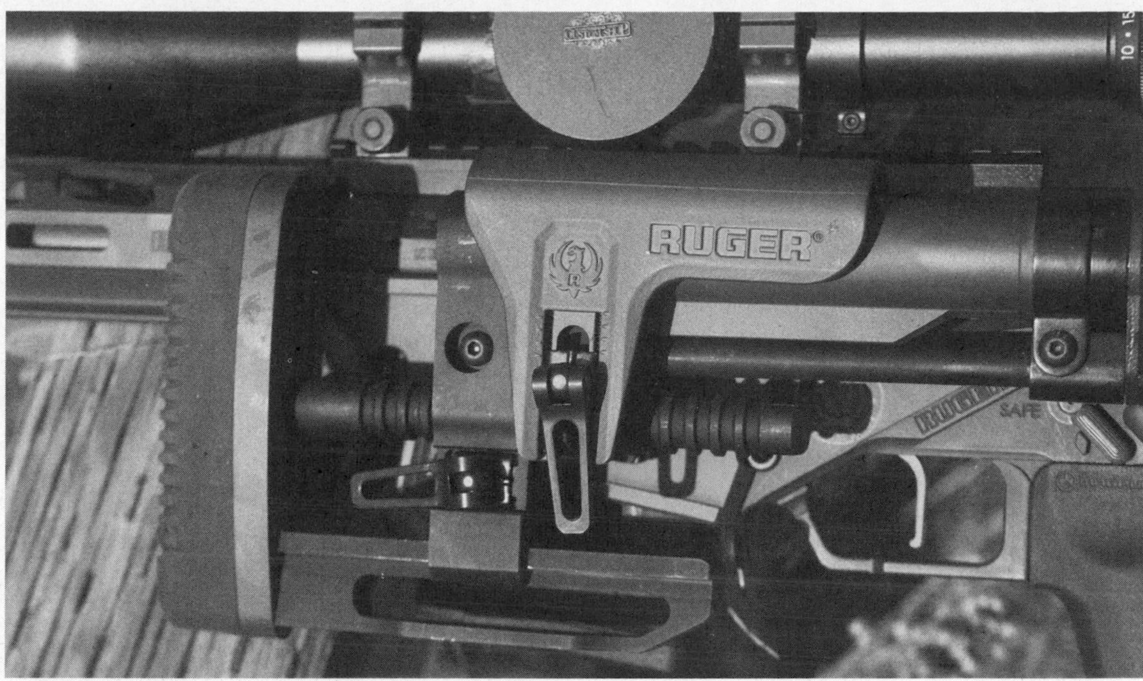

Attention to detail is exemplified by Ruger's fully adjustable buttstock, and it is a folder for carrying and cleaning ease.

I Ruger Precision Rifle (RPR) was shorter and lighter than many current Gen III models. Otherwise, there was not much design difference between them.

Ruger took the lead in building a very close copy of the Remington 2010 sniper rifle — both retain the folding left-sider stock, fully adjustable comb and length of pull to fit any shooter regardless of body size or optics deployed. The Ruger had a removable muzzle brake to install a suppressed system, allowed cleaning by a simple withdrawing of the bolt out the back door of the receiver, and utilized AR grips with left-side safety controls. The first rifles shot very well indeed. Never a complaint about accuracy by way of the Russian-designed 5-R five-groove rifling in a very-well machined bore.

With that background information, the question is, What's the big deal with the new Ruger Precision as a Gen III design built inside Ruger's Custom Shop?

That was my thinking exactly when the rifle first arrived. What was going to be so special save for a few elements like red paint on controls and a special handgrip just forward of the receiver designed for competitive match shooting? The Gen III target rifle had a slightly different cant to the bolt assembly that was also oversized for ease of finding it under the pressure of timed match fire. Still, it was not until I actually tied down a scope and hauled the rifle onto the range did I get more answers to my questions.

Regarding ammunition selected for testing, Hornady offered a case of the outstanding 6.5 Creedmoor 140-grain ELD MATCH target loads. With some time on the computer and using the Hornady ballistic program, I quickly doped out my firing solutions to the last yard, printed out the results to fill in my database as a hands-on reference open field folder, and headed for the rifle range.

Shooting off the benchrest and sandbagged, the 100-yard zero three-shot group measured .595 inch. I moved to the 600-yard steel targets and turned up the elevation 13.1 MOA with the top scope turret. At the shot, I put the first round downrange into the torso center of the A/T heavy steel target. With the trigger as smooth as soft silk, the let-off was 2.5 pounds with a clean and crisp break. The action and overall feel of the rifle were spot-on perfect. The rifle performed much like the costly Remington 2010 I had tested previously. In fact, I found myself comparing the new Ruger Precision to

The author approved of the Ruger Custom Shop Precision Rifle's clean lines, accessible controls and overall construction quality.

(left) M-LOK system in place on the forearm. (belowThe author tested the new Custom Shop Ruger Precision in the hills of South Dakota to 1,300 yards. The rifle measured up to guns he's evaluated that cost several thousands of dollars more.

the military sniper rifle.

Group shooting to 600 yards put five shots into a rough-cut circle the size of a soup can top. Satisfied with those results, I picked up my gear, loaded up the 4X4, and headed for Dead Horse Ridge, which put me about 100 feet above the valley floor. I had command of my 1,000- through 1,500-yard steel targets from this ridge. In terms of that first day's trials, the rifle would see work to 1,000 yards if the early morning Dakota winds held off.

Setting up on a portable benchrest and using 25-lb. sandbags at the forend, the old Tasco Custom Shop sniper/target (1970s vintage) scope was cranked to just about her maximum elevation in MOAs with 28.7 clicks. I added a slight pull into a soft morning breeze of 3 to 5 MPH.

At the shot, the 140-grain ELD Match bullet was sent out over the valley, dropping about 11 1/2 feet below the ridge's sight angle.

In what seemed like three seconds (forever), the bullet slapped the A/T hardened steel, bringing a smile to my face. It's always nice to get that first-round hit, and to be quite honest, that is not always the case in the long-range shooting game. Five more rounds downrange resulted in at least three more confirmed steel target hits. Checking targets up close was not possible due to field conditions downrange. No rain for a month and fire everyplace in the mountains in West River, South Dakota, meant no driving was possible beyond the 600-yard heavily used two-track road. I knew that the rifle, ammunition and glass were spot-on. Now it was time to wait out the scorching summer drought.

FREELANCE GUNNING FOR PERFORMANCE EFFECT

To showcase the rifle's accuracy, I turned the monster loose on the buffalo grass and backcountry badlands near my home by shooting the tops of mud buttes. I'd blast big white limestone rocks on mountainsides, which would offer little white rocks to also shoot at as secondary targets.

This was no small rifle with a dry weight of 12.8 lbs, and with glass and a loaded magazine, it was an easy 15-lb. cannon when hauled into the field. Static gun came to mind the first day I laid eyes on the rifle, as this was no flyweight in long-range equipment. This rifle was designed for the target shooting bench and prone position match shooters. Hunters would own the whole valley when gunning long-range warm targets like varmints.

Sighting on an 800-yard dry bend waterhole from about 90 feet in elevation above the target, I chambered a round of Match Hornady 140-grain ELD, dropped behind the scope and with an almost full rotation MOA spun the elevation knob. Then, I dropped off half a breath and stroked the crisp "TriggerTech" trigger. With the massive heavy-contour (.850 inch at the muzzle) barrel, and .264-bore muzzle brake to control barrel whip and vibration, round one went downrange. After a long lag time, a high geyser of heavy mud — with the bullet impacting the target's six, just under the edge of the bolder.

After a second check for elevation using the scope's turret and ranging a drainage cut at 1,100 yards, again the process was repeated with a slight wind drift left, the elevation correctly computed. Chambering a second round from the Accuracy International-style box magazine, the bullet cut into the right edge of another boulder.

The Ruger-designed "barrier stop" directly in front of the magazine well produced additional support for maintaining a steady hold. Accuracy and fire control were not an issue with my 25-pound sandbag rest set on the portable bench.

Magpul MOE K2 grips with molded rubber for traction aided in controlling

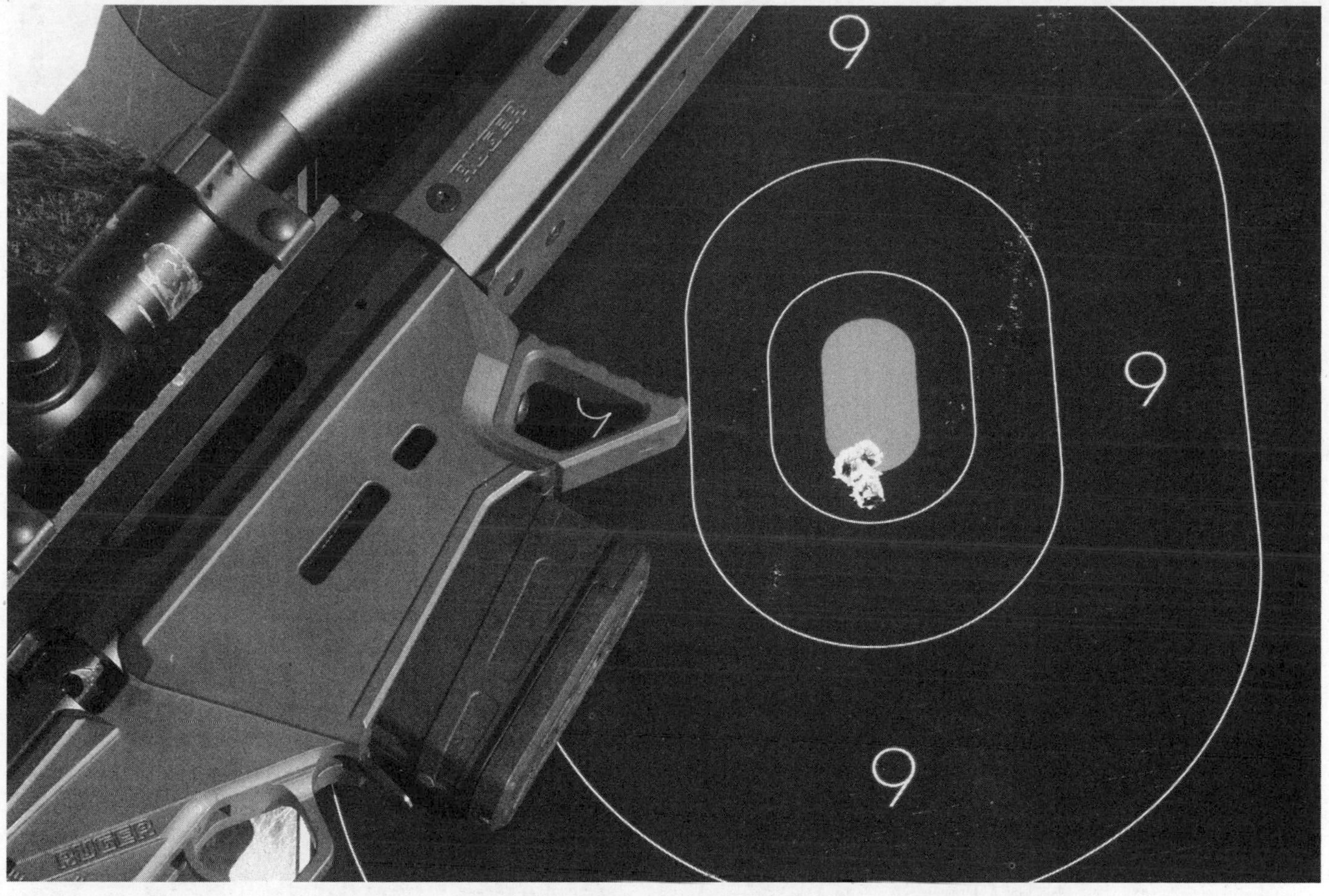
Accuracy using Hornady 140-gr. Match ammo was not to be questioned. The RPR's 5-R rifling was spot-on.

the rifle, and the flat-shaped handguard with full-length M-LOK accessory points also kept the rifle stable. It was not a swing and shoot sporter, to be sure, but when using tripods, bags or bipods, the gunning system would be rock solid.

Even recoil from the 6.5 Creedmoor was not much more than a .243 Winchester in a heavy rifle. At times, I shot the rifle with my weak-side arm draped over the handguard loosely and my strong-side trigger hand folded under the triggerguard. I could have shot the rifle all day, lacking any recoil and fatigue whatsoever.

Over four months, I hauled the Custom Shop RPR across western South Dakota and almost into the Wyoming Rocky Mountains to the west of my place. The longest shot I took was 1,300 yards, which stretched the glass I was using to its maximum limit even with halving my sights from sub-tensions to turret settings. The old Tasco had the advantage of its maximum 50x power setting, which saved miles of walking to see precisely what and where I hit.

What are you getting with the new Custom Shop Ruger Precision Rifle?

The receiver is CNC machined, and surface treatments use the Cerakote process. The receiver steel is pre-hardened 4140 chrome-moly, with a cold hammer-forged stainless steel barrel with 5-R rifling. The rifle bolt is one-piece CNC machined, nitride-treated for corrosion resistance. The bolt has a 70-degree throw and features duel-cocking cams. Control surfaces are AR-style for grip and safety. The folding buttstock is outstanding and simplifies cleaning and bore sighting. The hardware will accept AR-style buttstocks if the shooter wants to make a switch.

The 6.5 Creedmoor is designed as a 1,000-yard target round, fitting for the rifle. Pushing this bullet even in the well-designed Hornady ELD 140 grain means transonic performance at sea level soon after crossing the 1,000-yard mark. I know everyone and his brother are shooting one mile with everything now that will push a bullet. Talking accuracy and performance on the Internet is one thing, but the real-world ballistics of most rounds is a totally different kettle of fish.

With a price tag of about $2,000, the Custom Shop RPR is a massively good buy considering how much rifle you're getting for the money. While I've tested rifles worth $24k, with many from $4,000 to $8,000, none have done more than this high-performance chassis target rifle. Currently, I am running the Ruger Precision Rifle in a pair of 6.5 Creedmoor guns and in .300 PRC, .300 Win. Mag. and .338 Lapua Mag. — and I'm doing so for less money total than some individual rifles I have tested previously. GD

MARLIN 1895 SBL .45-70

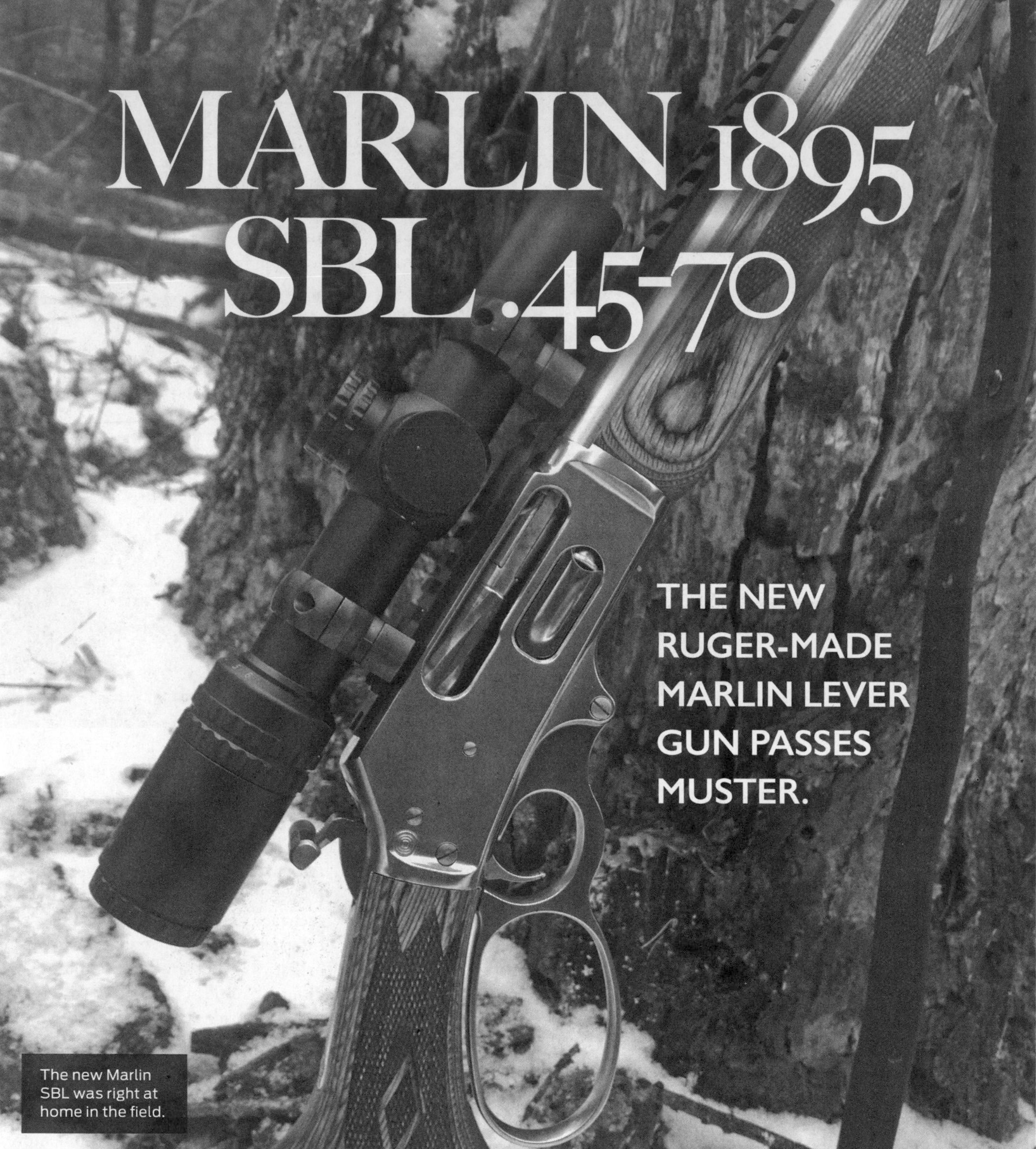

THE NEW RUGER-MADE MARLIN LEVER GUN PASSES MUSTER.

The new Marlin SBL was right at home in the field.

› ANDY LARSSON

The snow crunched as we slipped through the frozen woods. We had crossed the track of a foot-dragging whitetail buck in full rut mode. The timber was semi-open with some scattered spruce thickets. We trailed along with the wind in our face, hoping to get a glimpse before it spotted us. Too late, the doe spooked, and exited stage left — taking the buck along. As they fled, the rifle in my hands instinctively came to shoulder, cheek down on the stock, as the 1x scope gave crisp clarity to the departure but no clear shot.

The rifle was brand new. I'd received it a couple days before, taken a few shots to sight it in and since it was late fall deer

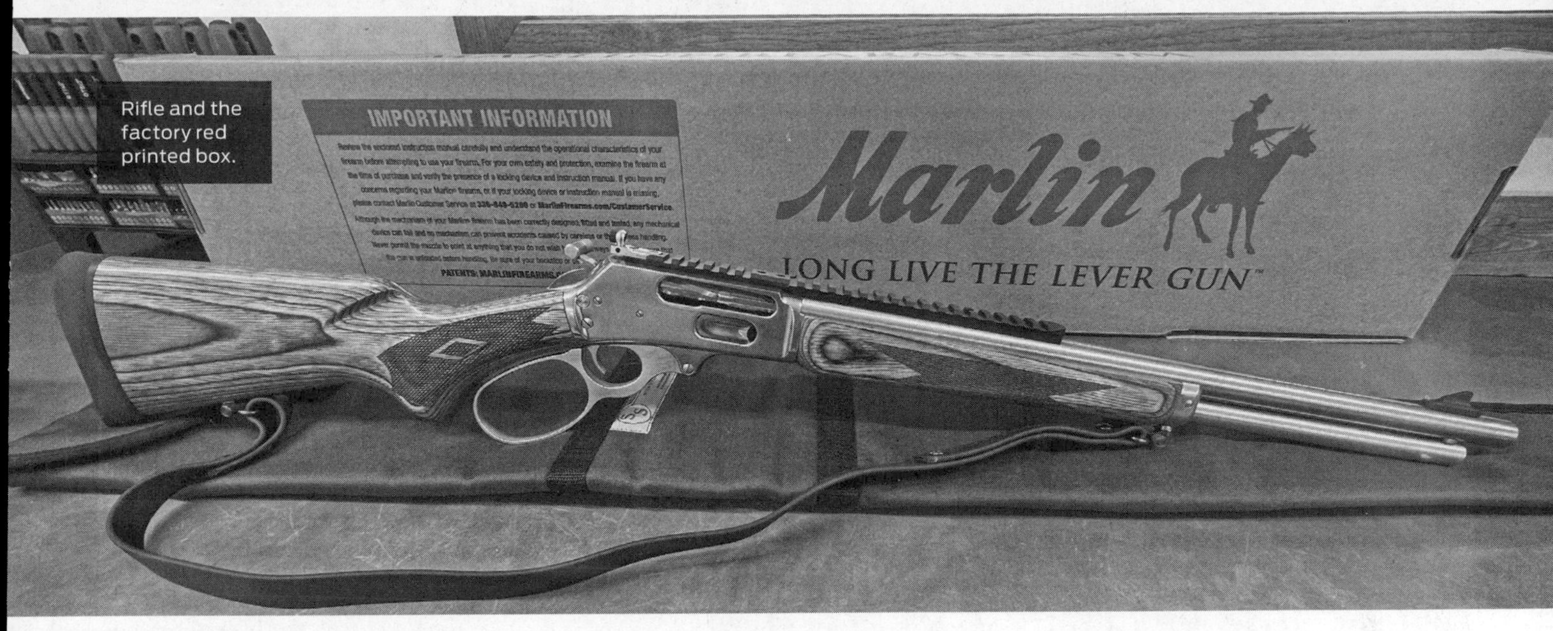

Rifle and the factory red printed box.

season where I live in Montana, I couldn't wait to take it into my favorite hunting grounds looking for a buck. That's a bit risky by some standards, taking a new rifle to the woods. However, the rifle was one of the first of its kind produced by the manufacturer, and it was, by design, already an old friend — one of the first production Marlin 1895 SBL (Stainless Big Loop) .45-70 rifles produced by Ruger!

Since I've been shooting Marlins and Rugers all my life, this was a marriage made in heaven for me. Sturm, Ruger & Company is one of the largest firearms manufacturers in North America. After purchasing the Marlin Firearms Company through a 2020 bankruptcy sale that liquidated Remington Arms Co. and its various sub-companies, Ruger spent almost a year bringing this first Marlin back to the market.

What did it do in that year? Besides relocating the equipment, machines, and some of the best talents from Ilion, New York, to Mayodan, North Carolina, Ruger also went over every detail of the Marlin construction to re-engineer and perfect the manufacturing process. Though the Ruger company had produced a couple lever-action rifles (Models 96/44 and 96/22, now discontinued), the manufacturing behemoth is best known for its timeless semi-auto .22 pistols, the 10-22 rifle, single- and double-action revolvers, bolt-action rifles, exquisite No. 1 single shots, some fantastic Old World-quality shotguns, and more recently a wide range of polymer injection-molded striker-fired handguns, and more. Taking on this new line of traditional lever-action rifles would challenge the best engineers and production managers at Ruger, who pledged to not release any Marlins until quality and performance were perfect.

The importance of this detail is in the back story. When the almost 150-year-old Marlin Firearms Corporation was purchased by Remington in 2007, then moved to Ilion, the next several years floundered as quality and function suffered to the point of flat-out rejection by hunters and shooters worldwide. About 2010, Remington formed a team to evaluate and repair the damage done to the brand. Team Marlin brought back quality and function to what we remembered, loved and expected. "Blue" brand loyalty was created inside the "Green Machine," and slowly but steadily, Marlin began to take its place on the

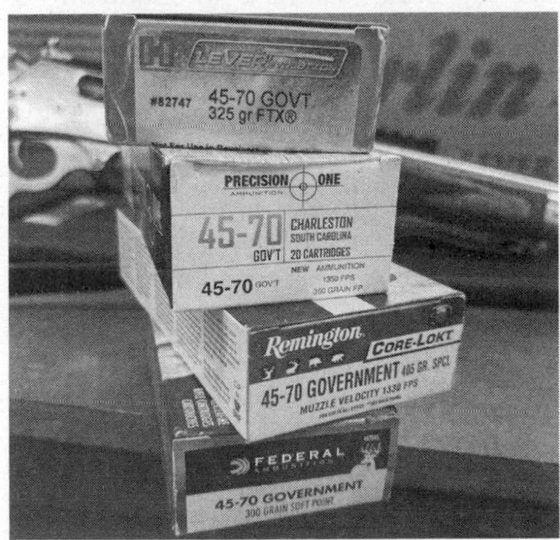

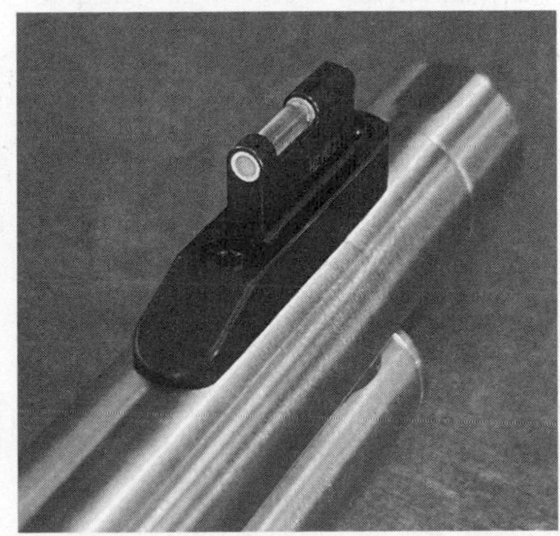

(above left) Assorted ammo used in testing. (above center) Factory Marlin front sight Tritium-illuminated fiber optic. (above right) New Ruger "RP" proof mark on the left side of the barrel just forward of the receiver.

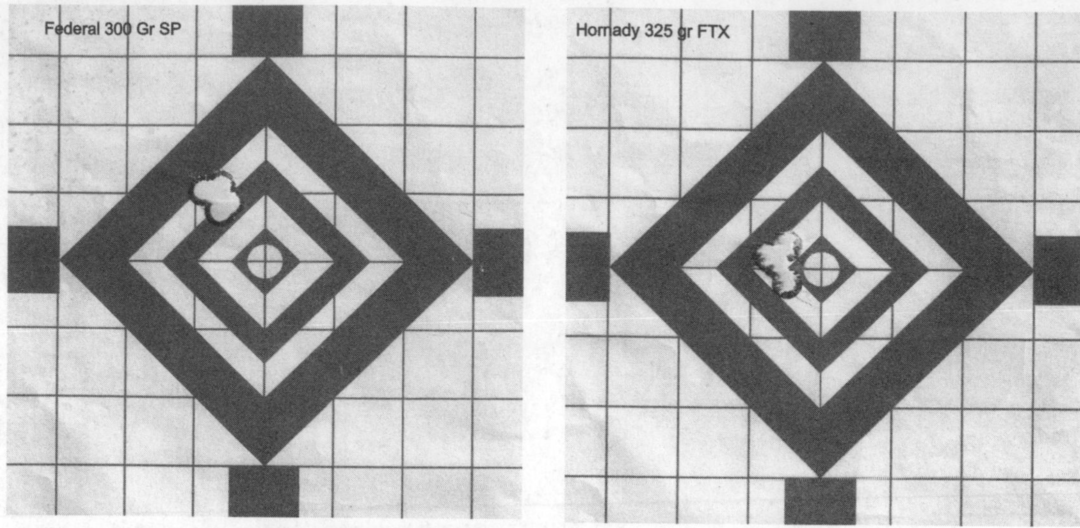

(above left) Five-shot 50-yard target shot out the pickup window off the Montana Bench Rest. Although all makes were excellent, Federal 300-gr. SP was the most accurate of all ammo tested for this rifle. (above right) Five-shot 50-yard target shot with Hornady 325-gr. FTX.

world lever-gun stage again.

Unfortunately, friction between engineers, production, marketing, and bean counters continued at Remington, and after a brief brush with bankruptcy in 2018, Remington went under in 2020, taking Marlin with it. At the time of the Remington demise, the Marlin portion of the company had come back to life and was turning a good profit, which had not gone unnoticed by Ruger. In fact, the value of Marlin was worth almost twice as much as the older and larger Remington Arms Co. At auction, Ruger purchased Marlin for $30 million. (Interestingly, the larger Remington Arms Co. sold for about half that at $18 million.) Ruger's acquisition of Marlin is what we call a "best-case scenario" and heralded by the shooting world as "hope for the future!"

As a sight maker for rifles and owner of Skinner Sights (skinnersights.com), I've worked closely with lever-gun manufacturers, establishing close ties and relationships. I was happy to oblige when given a chance to do a hands-on evaluation of the new Marlin SBL.

The rifle arrived in the first part of November 2021, along with several boxes of assorted ammunition with varying bullet weights. A moment much of the gun world was waiting for with bated breath was here, sitting on my bench.

The first thing I noticed was how much care had gone into the packaging — no flimsy cardboard inner support to fight with during unboxing. A ridged foam cutout protected the firearm and was durable for re-use.

The gray laminated stocks fit very well. The buttstock-to-receiver fit wasn't custom quality, but for a production gun, was excellent. The more I handled the gun, the better the fit looked. Ruger said to be brutal, so I looked with a critical eye. The forend was slimmer than older Marlins, a subtle but welcome change. The medium line checkering on the grip and forend is crisp, clean and sharp. The butt has a generous recoil pad that should tame even the heaviest Buffalo Bore loads. A nice Marlin horse and rider logo has been lasered into the grip cap, and the traditional Marlin bullseye was retained with one change. The black center is now red (red and black have been used symbolically by Ruger, which is a tribute to the brand's new relationship). The length of pull – at 13 ½ inches – is industry standard for a lever gun. On a dangerous game gun, slightly shorter is better than slightly long. The sling swivel studs are standard and perform as expected.

Measuring 19 inches long (1/2 inch longer than earlier SBLs), the barrel's muzzle is threaded 11/16x24 for mounting a suppressor or muzzle brake (a barrel polished matching thread protector is included). The barrel and magazine finish is brushed, non-reflective stainless, while the forged/machined receiver is polished bright. The barrel markings are crisp and clear. At first, I was a little surprised that the Ruger brand name is not found on the gun. Thinking about it, this is a good choice on Ruger's part. These are Marlin rifles carrying forward John Marlin's 150-year legacy in the shooting and sporting world. In place of the famous JM proof stamp on the barrel, look for a crisp Ruger proof mark to identify manufacturing approval.

Due to the clean, precision machining throughout, the action cycles smoothly. I've worked on Marlin lever guns for over 40 years, and the machine work on this rifle is the best I've ever seen. Spiral flats on the bolt are a nice touch which, along with looking "cool," should be somewhat

TABLE A. MARLIN 1895 SBL .45-70

Load	Velocity (fps)	Group Size (in.)
Federal 300-gr. SP	1,850	.387
Hornady 325-gr. FTX	2,000	.517
Precision One 350-gr. FMJ Flat Point	1,350	.582
Remington 405-gr. SPCL	1,330	.622

Ruger-Marlin 1895 SBL 2021. Ammo tested at 50 yards. Five-shot groups. Factory-published velocities. Average .527 inch.

self-cleaning and make cycling the action smoother. The ejector looks good, and the ejector raceway in the bolt is smooth, another contributor to the reliable and easy functioning of the action. Timing on the carrier/lifter is very good, with the radius on the lever that contacts the lifter slightly redesigned to maintain tolerances longer and prevent the occasional "Marlin jam." The surface and radius on the bottom of the lifter seem to be a bit more robust and function well.

The sighting system is an 11-inch Picatinny rail with a Ruger-built ghost ring sight in the rear. The non-threaded inner hole of the ring is .222 inch, and the sight has approximately 20 MOA windage and 16 MOA elevation adjustment. The front sight is a .155-inch wide blade featuring a green fiber optic enclosed in a .125-inch white ring powered by tritium for nighttime illumination. Under the rail is a standard 3/8-inch dovetail should you wish to remove the rail and use a traditional notch/buckhorn-type sight. The receiver mounting holes are like prior Marlins dating back to the mid-1950s, allowing you to mount any sights or optics you desire. For example, I prefer a non-rail lever gun fit with the Skinner Express peep sight. This rifle accommodates everyone's sight preferences.

I mounted a Skinner Sights Optic 1-6X24 LPVO on the factory rail for testing. Using medium height rings, the rear sight needed to be removed to clear the scope. An offset hammer spur was included with the rifle, making cocking and de-cocking safer and easier. Ruger retained the crossbolt safety and a hammer half-cock notch traditional safety. I understand the issues with the crossbolt but must admit I found it helpful when cycling loaded rounds out of the gun back at the vehicle or cabin. The crossbolt safety is here to stay, so we learn to adapt, appreciate its benefits and deal with its shortcomings.

The author harvested a Montana whitetail with the new Marlin SBL and a Remington 300-gr. HP load.

RANGE REPORT

This rifle performed flawlessly at the range (in my case, the local gravel pit shooting off the Montana Bench Rest, aka my pickup). I shot four different factory loadings with impressive results. Shooting at the 50-yard maximum distance, the five-shot group size varied from .387 to .622 inch center-to-center with an average of .507 inch, essentially 1 MOA. That's pretty impressive for any rifle shooting a variety of factory ammo — let alone a lever-action big-bore throwing 300 to 400 grains of copper and lead at various velocities. The barrel twist rate is 1:20 with six right-hand Ballard-type hammer-forged grooves. This twist rate should handle any standard .45-70 bullet weights and even some of the more uncommon. I have been shooting these guns all my life, and this rifle surpassed my expectations.

One of the secrets to accuracy is a crisp, clean trigger break. Breaking at about 4 1/2 pounds, I could detect a slight amount of creep when addressed like a benchrest trigger; however, as a hunting trigger, it was nearly perfect.

I am not a fan of the big loop as it's slower to cycle the action requiring more movement. Standard loops work fine with gloves, but there's a perception that they're needed in the cold country. They look good and sell well, so big loops work from a marketing perspective, and the customer is happy. Eventually, I will want to swap the lever out for a standard loop if they become available. Loop style is a personal preference with no reflection on the quality of the build of this rifle. Besides, then it wouldn't be an SBL!

Overall, Ruger has knocked it out of the park. The time and attention the Ruger Team put into fine-tuning the manufacturing process and every minute detail has paid off.

I'm sure these rifles and subsequent models will only improve as Ruger becomes more familiar with the Marlin design. Hats off for keeping Marlin as Marlin. Let the legacy continue!

A few days later, back in the woods, I found that buck again. It came home with me and my old friend — the new Ruger-made Marlin. GD

MODEL 70478

Caliber:	.45-70 Govt.
Capacity:	6+1
Stock:	Gray Laminate
Material:	Stainless Steel
Finish:	Polished Stainless
Front Sight:	High Visibility Tritium Fiber Optic
Rear Sight:	Adjustable Ghost Ring
Weight:	7.3 lbs.
Overall Length:	37.25 in.
Length of Pull:	13.38 in.
Barrel Length:	19 in.
Thread Pattern:	11/16 x 24
Thread Cap:	Match-Polished
Barrel:	Cold Hammer-Forged Stainless Steel
Twist:	1:20 RH
Grooves:	6
Suggested Retail:	$1,399.00

HERITAGE BARKEEP

The standard Heritage Barkeep comes with full-sized grips, but bird's head grips are a popular aftermarket option.

THERE'S A NEW COWBOY GUN IN TOWN, AND THIS ONE MIGHT JUST BE YOUR HUCKLEBERRY.

› AL DOYLE

Can a firearms manufacturer take its basic product — the single-action rimfire revolver — and tweak it to make something with broader appeal? The Heritage Barkeep in .22 LR and .22 Magnum exemplifies how creativity can lead to a fast-selling product.

In this case, less is more. Unlike other Heritage single actions, the Barkeep lacks an ejector rod due to the barrels' short length (2.68 inches and 3.6 inches, respectively). A wood-handled punch is provided to remove brass. A "Boot" version with a 1.68-inch barrel and bird's head grips minus the front sight debuted shortly after the 2022 SHOT show.

The Barkeep concept is based on modified single-action Colt wheelguns of the late 1800s and on the firm's Sheriff's and Storekeeper's models produced sporadically from 1960 to 2010. Shortened barrels turned holstered weapons into late-19th century concealed guns. Heritage's marketing plays on the old-school vibe, as a derby-hatted gambler is shown drawing a Barkeep — perhaps on someone dealing from a marked deck — during a poker game.

Mention "single-action revolver" in gun circles, and the Old West immediately comes to mind. The Barkeep's ancestors also resided near cash registers and other hidey holes all over America. These were among the guns in rough-and-tumble saloons near the Chicago stockyards and Pittsburgh steel mills.

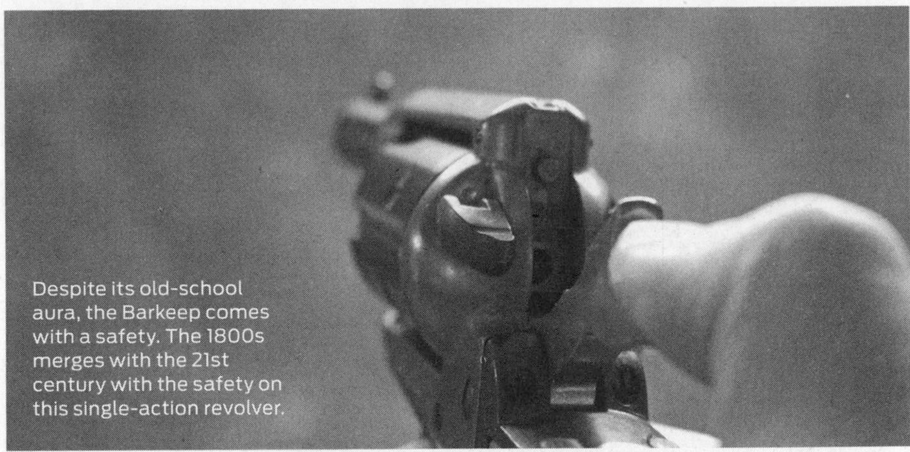
Despite its old-school aura, the Barkeep comes with a safety. The 1800s merges with the 21st century with the safety on this single-action revolver.

First impressions are vital, and the Barkeep succeeds in that department. The bluing displays some glossiness. The Barkeep with simulated case hardening and laser-engraved wood grips is pleasing to the eye. Revolvers with a plastic "gray pearl" finish and American flag grips are also available. The Heritage website offers an assortment of other grips for those who want to customize their six-shooters. A .22 Magnum cylinder can be ordered, and a coupon that comes in the box provides free shipping.

The standard-sized grips are one detail that generates some online discussion. Why aren't bird's head grips provided? Remember that Colts in .44-40 and .45 Colt were the inspiration for the Barkeep, and those calibers require something more substantial for sure handling. The Heritage website (heritagemfg.com) offers everything needed to make the conversion to the bird's head style.

A pair of good deals on Gunbroker.com and a loaner from a friend (the 2.68-inch Barkeep with bird's head grips) provided me with a trio of rimfire snubbies for testing. Striving for historical accuracy, Heritage dispenses with a rear sight and opts for the notch found on the old Colts combined with a blued front sight. I like old-school authenticity, so that setup seemed fine. Add in 63-year-old eyes that require thick bifocals, and it became a different story with standard black paper targets.

Putting two or three shots within an inch or less at seven yards was easy enough, but there was always a flyer or two. The Barkeep's sights are the polar opposite of the neon-style ones found on the Smith & Wesson Victory, the .22 pistol I typically shoot. In this case, the flaw is not with the gun but with the person holding it. Those with younger eyes and who don't have nearsightedness should be able to adjust to the Barkeep's setup.

Was there another way to test the Heritage on paper? Neon and pastel 3x5 index cards proved an easy and low-cost choice. This may sound like heresy to traditionalists, but my Barkeeps may be getting a dab of orange paint on the front sights. Unlike many other low-priced firearms, the Barkeep comes through in the ergonomics department. Both the 2.68-inch (26 ounces) and 3.6-inch (27 ounces) versions point well and are nicely balanced.

There is one area where the Barkeep takes the 21st-century path: A single-action revolver with a safety knob on the back of the cylinder frame? Say it ain't so!

Newcomers will grasp that concept quickly since there are no old habits to break, but those with plenty of trigger time on single actions will drop the hammer when the safety is on. I did it a dozen times while testing, with no rounds going down the barrel. The safety clearly does its job. Flip the safety knob, and a red dot appears.

Several indoor (this was during a Wisconsin winter) sessions at the state-of-the-art Trigger Action Sports range in Little Chute, Wisconsin, spotlighted the difference between shooting the Barkeep compared to semi-auto .22 rifles and revolvers. Other customers often fired their weapons at a rapid clip. It's a different story with a single-action six-shooter. With the Heritage, pull the hammer back two clicks and open the loading gate to allow the cylinder to rotate and load the bullets. Although a single action can be fired quickly, the necessity of pulling the hammer back before each

(above left) Modern packaging for a product inspired by handguns from 125 years ago. (above right) This is just a sample of the different types of ammunition that can be fired from the Barkeep.

(left) Despite its low cost, the Barkeep comes in three different barrel lengths and a choice of finishes and grips.
(above) Everyone from new shooters to old-timers can handle the Barkeep. Low recoil makes shooting it a pleasant experience.

shot tends to slow down the pace.

Repeat the process to reload but have the punch ready to empty the chambers before replacing the spent brass. This is a relaxing and pleasant exercise in shooting. You soon realize that pouring the most lead downrange isn't the only way to have a good time.

Another advantage to a .22 revolver is the ability to shoot various rounds. The eight ammo types tested included Aguila 29-grain .22 Short Super Extra, American Eagle 45-grain Suppressor made for legally quieted (as in a Class 3 license) semi-autos, Winchester Super-X, CCI Stingers and Aguila's 60-grain SSS, which features a long, heavy bullet stuffed into .22 Short brass.

Results are listed below.

Although a .22 is less than ideal for self-defense, a Barkeep with the right load (don't skimp on ammo here!) is better than a stick or frantically shouting "Stop!" at a thug.

My time with the Barkeep brought back memories of another .22 revolver that sold for modest prices. The Harrington & Richardson 622 was a double action, but the solid frame meant the cylinder had to be removed for reloading. With the H&R, the cylinder pin doubled as a punch to knock out the old brass. Thankfully, the Second Amendment has no income test, and those who make affordable guns provide a vital service to tens of millions of Americans.

I could not obtain first-year sales figures for the Barkeep, but circumstantial evidence points to a successful launch for Heritage. While the Rough Rider series of .22 single actions is often discounted to $129 to $149 in weekly sales flyers at local retailers, no such promotions have been run by those same stores on the Barkeep.

Heritage offered a $20 rebate on Rough Riders during the first three months of 2022, but Barkeep buyers didn't get the same break. The sheer volume of YouTube videos and other reviews means the Barkeep has quickly developed a broad and enthusiastic market.

How can a gun that retails for $200 or less fill several roles? The Barkeep is perfect for serving as what used to be known as a "tackle box gun" or a handy knockabout piece that is always close at hand. Since shooting is supposed to be fun, here is a low-cost path to plinking enjoyment. The compact Heritage is an excellent gift (where legal) to introduce novices to the world of firearms ownership.

If money is tight, Heritage's Barkeep might be right for you. GD

TABLE A. 3.6-INCH HERITAGE BARKEEP VELOCITIES (FPS)

Load	Average	High	Low
Federal 36-grain hollowpoint bulk pack	752	794	683
CCI standard velocity 40 grain	774	815	741
Armscor 36-grain hollowpoint	859	889	818
CCI Stinger 32-grain hollowpoint	952	1,056	903
Aguila 60-grain SSS (sniper subsonic)	661	680	648
Winchester Super-X 40-grain	961	981	936
American Eagle 45-grain Suppressor	804	841	775
Aguila 29-grain Short Super Extra	866	886	838

TABLE B. 2.68-INCH HERITAGE BARKEEP VELOCITIES (FPS)

Load	Average	High	Low
Federal 36-grain hollowpoint bulk pack	704	736	668
CCI standard velocity 40 grain	743	835	663
Armscor 36-grain hollowpoint	854	903	829
CCI Stinger 32-grain hollowpoint	916	976	879
Aguila 60-grain SSS (sniper subsonic)	653	709	641
Winchester Super-X 40-grain	963	999	922
American Eagle 45-grain Suppressor	807	842	771
Aguila 29-grain Short Super Extra	857	890	834

All photos by Safari Classics Productions.

A Few Good Guns

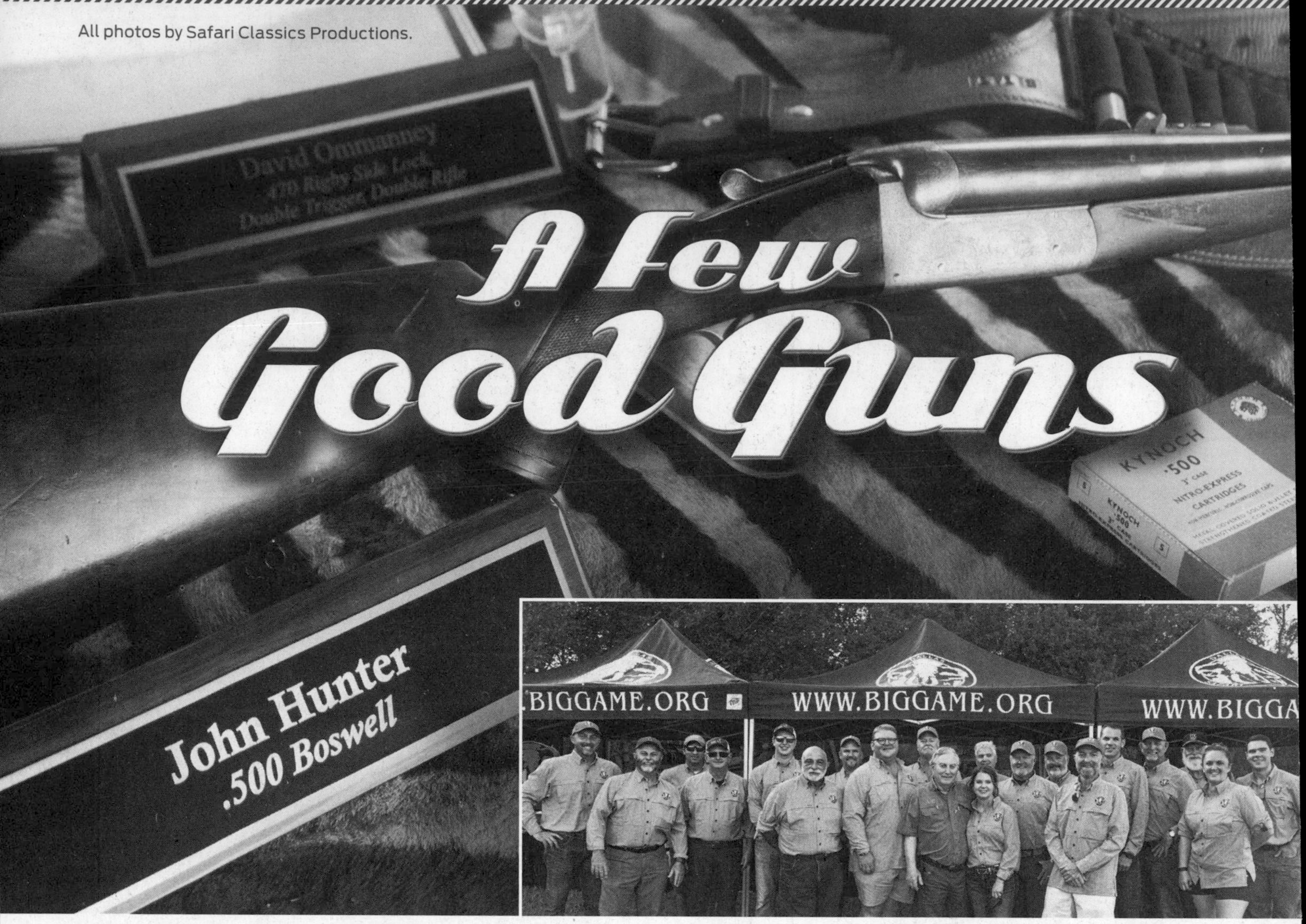

Hunter's .500 NE double was responsible for taking over 1,000 rhinos along the Mombasa railroad. (above right) The inaugural gathering of the Dallas Safari Club's Historic Rifle Society.

›PHIL MASSARO

In October 2021, I was invited to Dallas, Texas, to participate in one of the most extraordinary shooting events ever planned: the Dallas Safari Club's Historic Rifle Society. If you could imagine having the opportunity to take a lap in your favorite race car or to take batting practice with Mickey Mantle's bat, this was precisely the sentiment. To raise funds for the Advocacy tenant of the DSC Mission, the distinguished collection of Mr. Bill Jones would be made available for the participants to not only handle but to shoot. We'd gather at the Omni Hotel at the Kay Bailey Hutchinson Convention Center in Dallas for a presentation, then be chartered to the nearby private rifle range of Chris Sells, President of Heym USA.

To say that Bill Jones has an impressive rifle collection is, quite possibly, the understatement of this century. Indeed, he has amassed a collection of fine rifles with the proper pedigree, but the rifles we'd be handling and shooting this day weren't just high-quality guns, they were famous. Through diligent tracing, tracking and bidding, Bill has acquired an unparalleled collection of rifles used by some of the most famous hunters ever; these were some of the rifles I've been reading about since my youth. The guns of Hemingway, Roosevelt, Selous, Hunter, Sanchez-Ariño, Corbett and more were represented in this lot; we're talking about rifles that had sometimes done the unimaginable in the hands of authors who have inspired us for generations. Some rifles were used briefly by their famous owner, some were responsible for taking incredible numbers of game animals, and others were carried on larger-than-life adventures. Each had a story to tell, and handling and shooting them resulted in different emotions. How often does someone hand you President Theodore Roosevelt's Winchester 1886 and a cartridge to send downrange? It was better than Christmas morning.

There were just ten of us attending this inaugural event, plus the good folks

from Dallas Safari Club, and everyone got to shoot each of the rifles except for the pair of guns that belonged to Selous (the ammunition for these is so rare that it couldn't be procured in enough quantity for everyone). I'd like to share the list of rifles I was able to shoot that fine October afternoon, touching on their history and some thoughts on each. Oh, and lest I forget to mention, Bill Jones doesn't just collect these rifles. He hunts with them as well. That's correct. He's taken elephant with Hemingway's double, buffalo with Selous's falling block, etc. These guns aren't relegated to a safe or museum; they continue to see the hunting fields in Bill's hands.

So here are some of my favorites from the day, in no particular order representing the best of what I would contend is the greatest rifle collection on earth.

Ernest Hemingway's Westley Richards .577 NE. Papa's impact on the African safari was indelible; his *Green Hills of Africa, The Short Happy Life of Francis Macomber* and *The Snows of Kilimanjaro* all inspired hunters to journey to the Dark Continent. His most famous rifle — a Griffin & Howe sporterized Springfield in .30-'06 — has been lost to time, but his big double was used on his second safari in 1953, where back-to-back plane crashes nearly claimed his life. Shooting this amazing boxlock completed a strange circle for me; when visiting Key West in 2009, the staff at Hemingway's house told me there was "some sort of elephant gun of his" at a museum a few blocks away.

I forced march to enter the building five minutes before closing and pressed my nose against the Plexiglas box that housed the rifle. When Tim Danklef (of Safari Classics Productions) handed me the rifle and one of the massive, rimmed .577 cartridges, I couldn't help but imagine the conversations this rifle heard between Papa and Philip Percival, his Professional Hunter. The rifle probably weighed 13 pounds, which helped to mitigate the recoil of the big stopping round, and I felt it wasn't hard on the shoulder at all. Ordered by a British soldier just before the First World War, he was killed early on. The rifle would find its way to Hemingway through a friend and accompany him on the Pilar, the fishing boat he used to hunt Nazi submarines in the Caribbean. Though it sports a few honestly earned dings and scratches, it is an iconic rifle.

J.A. Hunter's Boswell .500 NE. John Alexander Hunter emigrated from

(top) Papa Hemingway's famous .577 NE Westley Richards double rifle. (above) The inimitable Ernest Hemingway with a Cape buffalo bull taken with his .577 in Tanganyika.

Scotland to Kenya in the early 1900s and proved to be a very talented hunter. He would do animal control work for the Kenyan government and the Uganda railroad and would take over 1,000 rhinos while helping to prepare land for the resettlement of native Africans. This Boswell boxlock rifle had a surprisingly short length of pull but shot very well for a .500 NE; while I own and love a Heym .470 NE, I think the recoil of the .500 is a bit slower and smoother. If you haven't read any of Hunter's books, I recommend *Hunter and Hunter's Tracks*. He was a well-respected Professional Hunter and personal friend of Denys Finch Hatton; Hunter was present when Finch Hatton's plane crashed at Voi and was first on the scene. Probably, this rifle was there for that tragic event. Holding Hunter's double rifle evoked a sense of truly wild Africa, and feeling the well-worn stock told just how much this gun was relied upon.

C. Fletcher Jamieson's .500 Jeffery. If you've spent any time reading John' Pondoro' Taylor's *African Rifles and Cartridges*, you probably noticed how he praises his friend C. Fletcher Jamieson, the hunter from Southern Rhodesia, now Zimbabwe. Jamieson was a prolific ivory hunter and stood about 6'6" though a childhood injury left his left arm slightly disabled, so holding a double rifle was a problem. Jamicson ordered a rifle from W.J. Jeffery chambered in the .500 Jeffery cartridge; it was the most powerful centerfire round made at the time. With a long length-of-pull and a 26-inch barrel, this would be one of only 24 rifles made by Jeffery; specifically, this rifle is No. 20. And while the .500 Jeffery can be a brutal cartridge to shoot, the dimensions and balance of this rifle were spot-on.

The rebated rim of the .500 Jeff can be a problem if the magazine follower isn't perfect, the last cartridge in the magazine often sits slightly nose up, and the bolt face will ride over the cartridge base. Fletcher's rifle had no issue feeding a single cartridge, nor did it show any issues with extraction. C. Fletcher Jamieson died in a tragic accident at home, being electrocuted while working on a well pump. But his amazing rifle stands as a testament to the life of a hunter.

Col. Jim Corbett's Jeffery .450-400 3" NE. Edward James Corbett was born in 1875 in Nainital, India, and would attain the rank of Colonel in the British army. He devoted his spare time to hunting and eradicating man-eating tigers and leopards in northern India. In the first decade of the 20th century, Corbett would obtain a Jeffery boxlock in the excellent .450-400 3" Nitro Express, also known as the .400 Jeffery. Corbett would use this rifle to end the career of the Mohan ManEater, the Chuka ManEater and other deadly tigers and leopards.

(top) J.A. Hunter's famous .500 NE Boswell double rifle. (above left) Crawford Fletcher Jamieson's .500 Jeffery rifle was made famous in John Taylor's *African Rifles and Cartridges*. (above right) Bill Jones now owns Jamieson's .500 Jeffery and still takes it to Africa to hunt. (bottom right)Massaro holding a piece of African hunting history: C. Fletcher Jamieson's .500 Jeffery, a rare specimen built by W.J. Jeffery & Co.

(left) The author shooting Col. Jim Corbett's .450/400 NE double rifle. (right)The group had difficulty getting Col. Corbett's rifle out of Dave Fulson's hands; note the custom tiger targets on the board.

This rifle is so iconic that Elmer Keith would own it for some time, and I have to say that I was enamored most with it among this incredible lot. The right chamber might have been used a bit more than the left, as the spent brass would crack at the mouth, but just to have the honor of bringing Col. Corbett's rifle to shoulder was terrific. The rifle hit precisely where I aimed it, and as a neat little addition to the day, Dave Fulson (also of Safari Classic Productions) had a bunch of custom tiger targets made just for the event. The rifle seems to have its own energy — if that is possible — and I can only imagine the emotions Corbett went through while in the presence of those tigers.

Corbett would retire to Kenya, working at Tree Tops hotel in the early 1950s. In fact, he hosted then Princess Elizabeth when she toured the colony, and her father passed away in his sleep. Corbett related, *"For the first time in the history of the world, a young girl climbed into a tree one day a Princess, and after having what she described as her most thrilling experience, she climbed down from the tree the next day a Queen — God bless her."*

President Theodore Roosevelt's Winchester 1886. TR has long been one of my hunting heroes, and his chronicles of hunts from the Adirondacks to the Dakotas to his famous African safari of 1909–1910 have made for great reading. Teddy was a visionary, seeing the wanton destruction of fauna and flora in my home state of New York and playing an integral role in implementing hunting seasons, national parks and the conservation model we've all come to follow.

Bill Jones owns Roosevelt's lever-action Winchester Model 1886, chambered in .45-90, engraved "Africa 1909." However, Jones is the first to admit that there is absolutely no evidence that the rifle went along on that safari. I am a massive fan of any 1886, let alone one that was Teddy Roosevelt's, and shooting this rifle was an amazing experience. The 1886 has a steel crescent buttplate and was built for a smaller frame than I have. I've spent quite a bit of time with my father's Browning 1886 in .45-70, which can really poke you in the shoulder, but TR's .45-90 was no worse than the modern rifle. Perhaps the fact that I was shooting a Presidential rifle played a part.

Elmer Keith's Westley Richards .476 NE double rifle. Of the old regime of gun writers — pioneers who were a blend of writer, hunter, explorer and gun nut — Elmer Keith is one of my favorites. The man was curt, honest and rugged and had a penchant for large African game. Elmer loved his double rifles (who doesn't?) and owned quite a few in his day, including the Corbett rifle mentioned above.

His Westley Richards boxlock double was chambered in the rare .476 Nitro Express, aka .476 Westley Richards. This rifle was one of the nicest vintage doubles I've ever handled, coming quickly to the

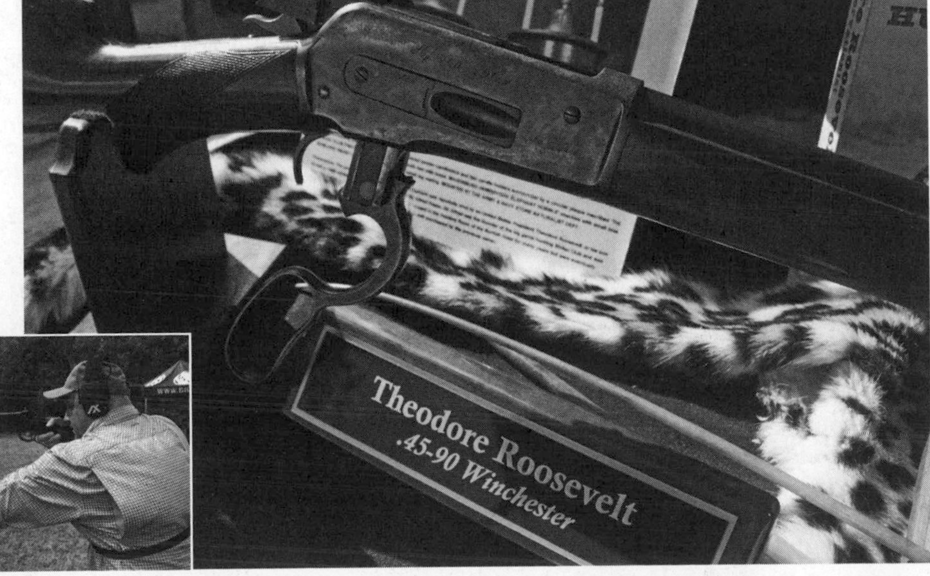

(right) Massaro took aim with President Roosevelt's Winchester 1886 in .45-90. (far right)President Theodore Roosevelt's .45-90; despite the markings, there is no proof of TR taking the rifle to Africa.

(top) Keith's .476 Westley Richards double is still a fine rifle. (left)The custom inlays of Elmer Keith's Westley Richards .476 NE. (right) Elmer Keith with an elephant bull taken with his .476 Nitro Express.

shoulder, having the dimensions that fit my frame perfectly, and smooth recoil. The .476 NE is one of the cartridges designed to take the place of the .450 NE when that bore diameter was banned in India and Sudan, driving a 520-grain bullet of nominal diameter at a muzzle velocity of 2,100 fps. I enjoyed this rifle, and I'm sure Elmer Keith did too; I know Bill Jones is particularly fond of it.

There were many other rifles shot that day, including Jack O'Connor's Model 70 .458 Winchester Magnum, built by the famous Al Biesen, David Ommanney's Rigby .470 NE sidelock (remember Winchester's Man in Africa?), Philip Percival's Rigby boxlock in .470 NE, Tony Sanchez-Ariño's .500 Jeffery Improved (a fantastic rifle), John Kingsley-Heath's custom Winchester 70 in .458 Winchester Magnum with its extended box magazine and the Rigby double rifle belonging to the Maharaja of Surguja, which began life as a double .416 Rigby. Still, the Maharaja shot the barrels out on tigers, taking over 1,500 of the big cats, and is now a .470 double. The pair of falling block rifles belonging to the famous Frederick Courteney Selous was fantastic just to hold, even if we couldn't fire them, as the history of that fabled hunter is, or should be, known by anyone who appreciates the era of African exploration.

My shooting day concluded with Bill Jones offering the opportunity to shoot one of his two J. & L. Wilkins & Co. double rifles in .700 Nitro Express. 'Curiosity killed the cat,' or so the old saying goes, but I couldn't resist the opportunity. The rifle weighed somewhere near 23 pounds, and the cartridge sends a 1,000-grain bullet of nominal diameter at a muzzle velocity of 2,000 fps for 9,000 ft-lbs of energy. It's the only rifle that has ever lifted my left foot off the ground from recoil, and though I'm thrilled I chose to fire the beast, I think I'll stick to my .470 NE and .404 Jeffery for hunting. Bill concluded our range time by firing his 8-bore hammer double, and the resulting flame from the muzzle would impress a dragon. Kudos to you, Bill, for handling that level of recoil!

Our grinning shooters gathered for dinner to discuss the merits of the cause we'd gathered to support and share the emotions we all felt as we were handed each of these famous rifles. Everyone felt like a dream had come true. While most of us hunters are guilty of hero-worship, the occupants of that room were well versed in the characters who'd owned these guns. We were grateful to Bill Jones for his generosity in sharing his prized collection. I'd like to thank the Dallas Safari Club, Chris Sells from Heym USA, and Mr. Jones for making what wasn't even a possibility in my mind an absolute reality. I'm confident that DSC will hold subsequent events, so please inquire if you'd like to participate in an event of this magnitude.

The CEO of both DSC and the DSC Foundation, Corey Mason, was integral in the organizing of this event, as well as putting the organization's best foot forward on the legal end of things.

The .700 Club, weighing 23 lbs, still had impressive recoil.

Corey himself summed the day up best: *"Through the generosity of Mr. Bill Jones, DSC has been able to fulfill its strategic vision of increasing our presence in Washington, D.C. to better face threats to legal, regulated hunting and sustainable use. The Historic Rifle Society events have raised critical funds, while allowing participants the incredible opportunity to hold and shoot the most iconic sporting rifles in existence. Rifles owned and taken to the field by notables like Ernest Hemingway, President Theodore Roosevelt, F.C. Selous, Jim Corbett, and many more is truly a once in a lifetime opportunity. We are grateful to Bill for his amazing support of DSC through these events. Through his generosity to DSC, we are increasing our advocacy presence with the hiring of a Government Affairs Director to purposefully work with Members of Congress, Committees, and staff with the USFWS and DOI to support legal, regulated hunting and oppose the attacks brought by the anti-hunting community."* GD

The Benelli 828U Field 20 Gauge is at home in the grouse woods. At 6 pounds, it points fast, while its streamlined receiver makes it a joy to carry through the tightest October Aspen tangle.

Benelli 828U Trim Twenty!

A streamlined 20-gauge over/under shotgun marries innovative design with traditional class in a package that upland hunters love.

›COREY GRAFF

With age comes an appreciation for the finer things in life — an uppity bird dog eagerly launching into the brush, a lightweight shotgun that doesn't dislocate your shoulder, and those rare episodes during which you don't forget your name or which day it is. And, if you're lucky, somewhere in between bouts of fleeting consciousness, you find the time to hunt some birds. It was during such reprieves that the Benelli 828U Field 20-Gauge proved itself a fine little shotgun for securing a crockpot of tasty upland game and got my vote for One Good Gun.

Introduced in January 2020, the 20-gauge version of Benelli's 828U line was practically destined for success, given its 12-gauge version's popularity among competitors and hunters. And even a muddy-brained amateur shotgunner like me can see why: Benelli's steel locking system snaps shut tighter than Fort Knox. Benelli engineers locked the steel breech block to a monoblock, containing all pressures from the shotshell and preventing energy transfer to the receiver and hinge pins. The result? Less wear and tear on the break-action, making the 828U a firearm that won't wear out. Also, the 20-gauge receiver is scaled down to the smaller shell; Benelli didn't just downsize the tubes, so it's a trimmer, sleeker design to boot. Not only that, but the design allowed engineers to use steel where strength was needed while keeping the lightweight receiver aluminum.

The 828U's trigger resets when you unlock the top lever, which opens the action smoothly while the ejector is entirely contained in the barrels, reducing the number of linkages. It all adds up to a streamlined action with Italian race car lines (no surprise there, Benelli Armi SpA of Urbino, Italy used to make motorcycles). The Crio (cryogenically treated) over/under barrels — my test gun had the 28-inchers; a 26-inch version is available in 20 — are joined near the muzzle, and an air space between them reduces wind push when you're chasing pheasants on the open prairie. A low-profile carbon-fiber rib graces the top barrel.

Of course, with a retail MSRP of $3,199, there are other refinements — eye-popping AA-grade satin walnut stocks, engraved nickel-plated receiver, gloss-blued barrels and laser-cut fish scale checkering make a shotgun lover squeal with delight. In addition, Benelli tucks its Progressive Comfort System into the stock, which uses polymer buffers that compress to absorb recoil energy. Adjustable spacers allow you to customize the drop and cast to optimize pointability and achieve a bespoke-like fit. I used it as-is from the box, and it hit what I looked at like a natural extension of my hand-eye coordination.

The whole enchilada includes choke tubes and stock spacers in a plastic plaid-lined case that is functional and classy-looking.

But what makes the 828U truly one good gun is its handiness in the field. At six pounds, the lightweight 828U is designed to chase grouse and other speedy upland birds through the thick and thorny tangles.

Now, I admit to never fully grasping the intricacies of daily bird movements or what on God's green earth is going on in their tiny bird brains, but even I can manage to stumble into a bevy of grouse if I walk enough miles. In fact, the handy little Benelli accompanied me while working on perfecting my bird hunting technique, which you could describe as random walking patterns to confuse the grouse. The basic idea is to hunt the birds where no sane individual would ever expect them to be and walk in disjointed patterns that, coincidentally, resemble a confused middle-aged man walking in disjointed patterns. Sometimes, a bird will get up, and the little Benelli barks without you ever realizing you brought it to shoulder or swung

No amount of evasive flight maneuvering by woodcocks (aka Timberdoodles) is enough to escape the agile-pointing characteristics of the 828U 20 gauge.

Locking the steel breech block to a monoblock completely contains all pressures from the shotshell, preventing energy transfer to the receiver and hinge pins. The result? Less wear and tear on the break-action, making the 828U a firearm that won't wear out.

A streamlined aluminum receiver keeps the 828U 20 Gauge lightweight, making it a joy to carry around all day in upland bird country.

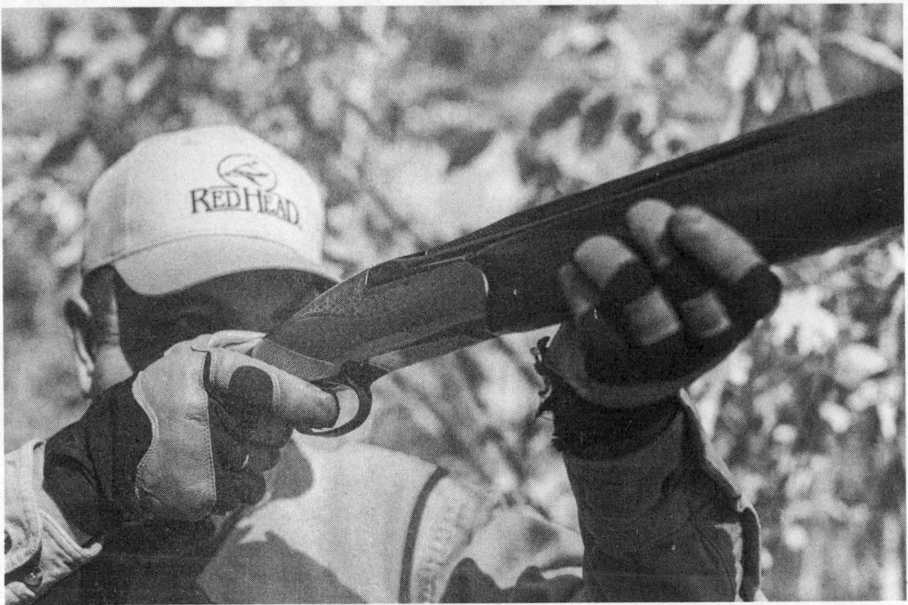

(top left) The Benelli 828U 20 Gauge is quick to the shoulder in thick brush thanks to its trim aluminum receiver. An innovative enclosed steel monoblock and re-designed ejector system contained in the barrels makes it possible. (left) The 828U in 20 gauge proved the ideal upland shotgun for grouse and woodcock during the author's northern Wisconsin hunts. A good gun dog like Birdie, pictured here, makes it all the more enjoyable.

through the bird.

A good shotgun is like that. It's neutral, so your mind can complete the trajectory calculations required to magically connect shot load with fleeing bird. "Empty your mind, be formless," said Bruce Lee, who exhorts us to be "Shapeless, like water." Musicians say the same thing. A properly set up musical instrument is neutral; you don't have to fight it. It gets out of the way, so the art flows through it. That's what the Benelli 828U is all about — everything from its lines and ergonomics to its smooth function gives you a blank canvas upon which you paint your ideas. The grouse, of course, have a different opinion of it.

Good guns are exquisite to look at and are easy to use. You can carry the 828U 20 gauge all day and not worry about fatigue, rotator cuff damage or your dentures launching into the ionosphere at high velocity. The gun's impulse-driven ejection system launches spent hulls with gusto and keeps unfired shells at the receiver for easy plucking. I bumbled into a few situations where woodcocks would launch one after another as if taking off in fighter formation. It was nice having the fast-pointing twenty to secure those shifty little timberdoodles as they dodged and weaved through the sky.

On the sporting clays course, the 828U is right at home. You can powder clays until the fat lady sings and not be the worse for wear. Despite its lack of mass, this sweet twenty won't pulverize your shoulder and leave you twitching with anxiety from sharp recoil.

Benelli even designed the 828U to be easy to disassemble and clean. You can quickly remove the self-contained trigger module using the included tool. The barrels slide back into the receiver like glass, thanks to precision-ground surfaces and thoughtful design features.

On the one hand, the 20-gauge 828U over/under shotgun sports complex, innovative design features that redefine break-action tradition. On the other, Benelli kept the functioning stuff under the hood, so you don't have to be a mechanical engineer to figure out how to use it or to appreciate its features. So many new guns come on the market rehashing what's already been done, propped up with careful marketing. However, Benelli delivered true innovation with its 828U line. The 20-gauge model is a no-brainer. It modernizes the break-action shotgun with the kind of quality you'd expect out of an old-school builder's shop. GD

BENELLI 828U FIELD 20 GAUGE

Gauge:	20
Barrel Length:	26 and 28 in.
Weight:	5.9 and 6.0 lbs.
Stock/Finish:	AA-Grade satin walnut with engraved nickel receiver
Crio Chokes:	C, IC, M, IM, F
Sights:	Fiber-optic front sight with red insert
Length-of-Pull:	14 3/8 in.
Drop at Heel:	2 1/8 in.
Drop at Comb:	1½ in.
MSRP:	$3,199

benelliusa.com

THE GREAT .450 ACKLEY

A PERFECT BOLT-ACTION DANGEROUS GAME RIFLE.

› TERRY WIELAND

The rifle is fitted with claw mounts low over the receiver. German gunsmiths prefer to fit them high to allow unfettered access to the magazine; the author prefers them low for better sighting with his cheek firmly on the stock. Siegfried was right about most things, but this was one argument Wieland won.

It would be rash indeed to call any rifle perfect, but I will say this about my .450 Ackley, built 30 years ago on a much-traveled FN Supreme action: There is not a single thing about it I would change, and I cannot say that of many other guns.

The .450 Ackley began taking shape in my mind during a safari in Tanzania, hunting Cape buffalo. On that trip, I was shooting a then-new .416 Weatherby. Jack Carter, the developer of the Trophy Bonded bullet, was shooting a custom pre-'64 in .450 Ackley. I had problems with the Weatherby and returned home determined to have a rifle built that would be like Jack's.

At the time, money was in short supply, but I had two assets: First, a .375 H&H built on an FN Supreme action that was an amateur custom job and, as such, expendable; second, I knew a superb old-time German gunmaker by the name of Siegfried Trillus. As it turned out, that was all I needed to begin. The money situation was rectified later.

The .375 had come my way through a trade with a self-styled rifle expert who had restocked it himself and replaced the tacky original alloy Browning bottom metal with steel from an English Mauser-action Whitworth. It was a decent rifle, but I had to start somewhere and did not have the cash to pursue my ideal route, which would have been buying a Dakota 76 action from Brownells and starting from scratch.

I delivered the rifle to Siegfried and outlined my desires: Caliber, .450 Ackley; replace the bolt shroud with one having a Model 70-style three-position safety; 22-inch barrel; scope mounted in a German claw mount, low over the action. I had a 26mm steel-tube Swarovski Habicht fixed-power 1.5x in my possession, which would do fine.

In 1991, when Siegfried began work, not all the necessary parts were readily available. The aftermarket shroud, for example, was an expensive semi-custom item then, and there was a waiting list. Claw mounts and rings came from Germany, as did a suitable rear barrel sight; the ramp front sight with a shroud was the easiest thing to find. Siegfried liked Douglas barrels, so that's what we got.

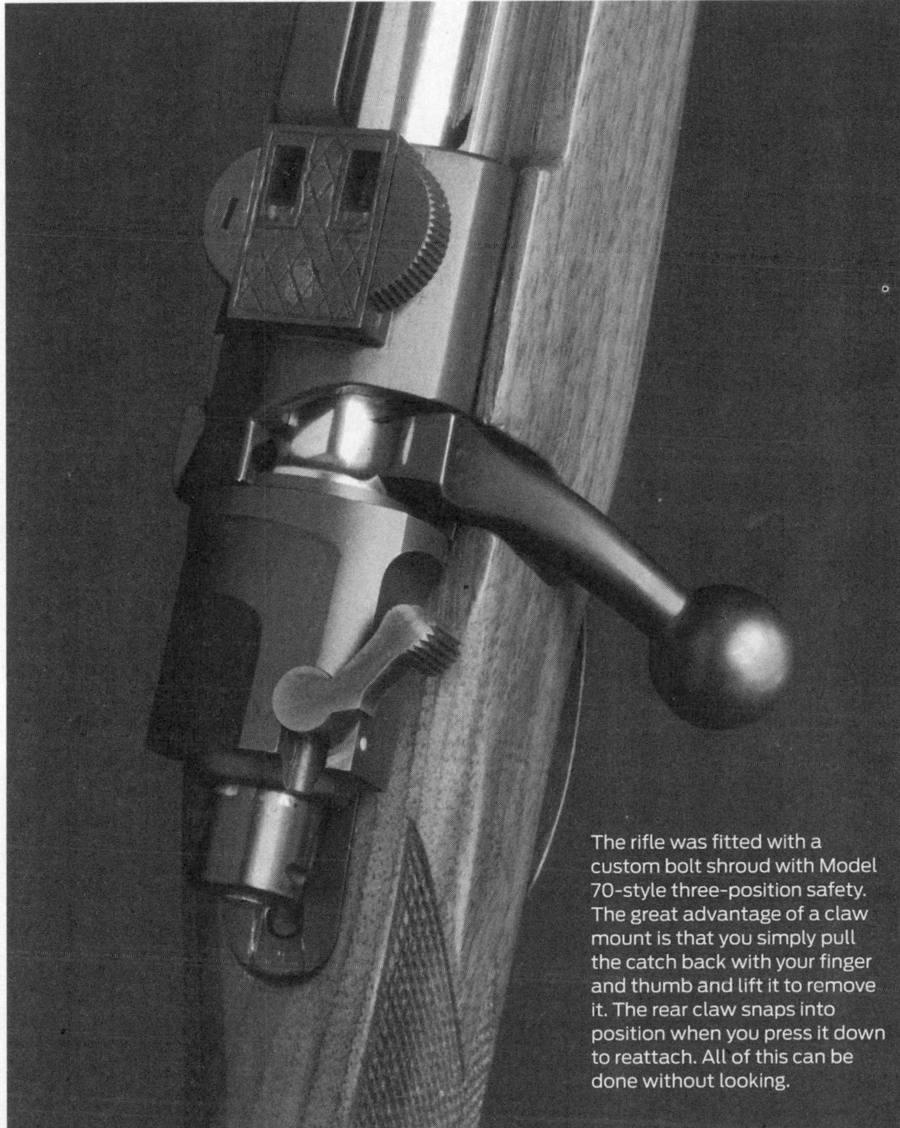

The rifle was fitted with a custom bolt shroud with Model 70-style three-position safety. The great advantage of a claw mount is that you simply pull the catch back with your finger and thumb and lift it to remove it. The rear claw snaps into position when you press it down to reattach. All of this can be done without looking.

With the barrel almost finished, I did something I would not do today, but nor would I change what I have: I sent it to Mag-Na-Port to mill a moderate (repeat: *moderate*) muzzle brake. I stipulated that it should *only* reduce muzzle jump and not increase muzzle blast, and it accomplished those two things reasonably well. Having it has somewhat

(below) To ensure the floorplate never opens under recoil, the rifle was fitted with a pin through the triggerguard. The floorplate release was ground to a minimum to prevent it from accidentally opening.

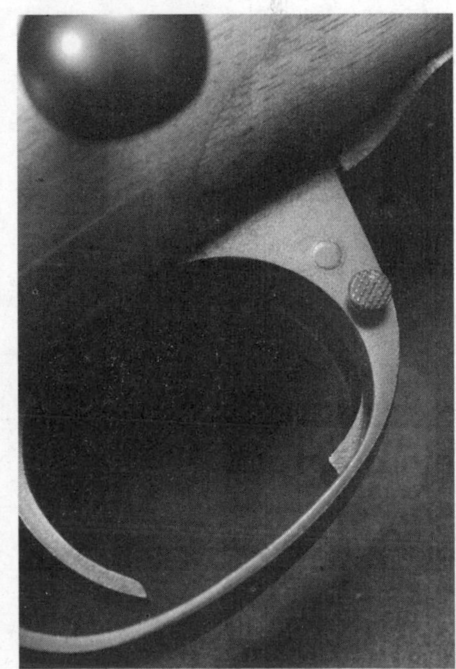

The forend in cross-section is a horizontal oval and checkered around to give the best possible grip.

compromised my position in later rantings about muzzle brakes, but I can do nothing about that.

One of the difficulties I encountered with the .416 Weatherby in Tanzania and Botswana in 1990 was a deafening muzzle blast and a drastic shift in point of impact when the brake was removed. I was determined not to repeat this.

My cartridge choice was a bit eccentric; Jack Carter recommended the .458 Lott instead of the Ackley. The Lott had come along after his rifle was built, and he thought it was more practical. However, the Lott was not yet a factory cartridge, so I would be handloading either way. I would explain why I decided on the Ackley, but I can't remember. I'm sure there was a good reason. You can shoot factory .458 Lott ammunition in the Ackley, a lucky accident, although I have never had to do it. You can also use factory .458 Winchester, good insurance when roaming around Africa. Ballistically, the Lott and the Ackley are identical.

The other major decision was the stock, and I was entirely in Siegfried's hands. Being a German gunmaker of the old school, he was equally good with wood and metal. Years earlier, he cut down an American black walnut tree, sawing it into stock blanks, and stacked the blanks to season naturally. The stack was sitting out behind his shop. He started going through it to find one that had precisely the correct grain to withstand the punishment from the big .450. He called me to approve it, which I did, and he set to work with a spokeshave and wood chisels to turn it into a rifle stock.

Under Jack Carter's influence, I argued in favor of the style that was known as "American classic." That was more or less what I got, but with Siegfried's personal preferences and a few Teutonic touches. He glass bedded the action for strength and made the butt larger than usual to accommodate an oversized recoil pad; this helped tame the beast. He also made the pistol grip radius more pronounced for the same reason: One can really get a grip on it. The forend is challenging to describe, other than to say it's perfect for the purpose, and I don't understand why more stockmakers don't do it that way. In cross-section, it's a horizontal oval or, as Jack O'Connor and Al Biesen described it, almost pear-shaped. It's slim and streamlined, viewed from the side, but your fingers wrap up around it rather than forcing your fingertips into the checkering like grim death to keep it under control.

Most modern stockmakers couldn't do it if they wanted to because it's now common to save a lot of time and effort by having the blank shaped on a pantograph or duplicating machine. The overall shape is decided for them, and the most common forend pattern is a deep vertical oval. They prefer this for two reasons: It's easier to checker, and it affords them a generous "canvas" on which to display their checkering virtuosity. Usability be damned: They want the world to see how talented they are. Anyway, fewer and fewer so-called stockmakers can fashion a stock from scratch, from a raw blank, the way Siegfried did.

My other request was a London oil

The action is an FN Supreme from a Browning High Power with steel bottom metal from an English Whitworth and a custom bolt shroud and safety. The scope is a 26mm steel-tube Swarovski Habicht 1.5x20, fitted in a German claw mount. The stock is American black walnut, carved by Siegfried Trillus from a tree he cut down, sawed into blanks and seasoned himself.

finish, but this Siegfried flatly refused to do. Instead, he applied a finish that I refer to as Varathane, although what the stuff was, I don't know. He wanted the wood to resist moisture and assured me he could make it non-reflective but with a warm glow like oil, and he did. As for tough, well, it's undoubtedly tough, and it has been around. I have never been troubled with a change in point of impact.

In 2006, I hunted with it during the rainy season in Tanzania. Through days of continuous downpour, it didn't alter an inch when I could literally wring water out of its leather sling. I killed two bulls with it in about five minutes on that trip.

I didn't want a grip cap or forend tip, but Siegfried did for moisture resistance, so the rifle was given ebony fittings. And quite handsome they are. The stock has a cheekpiece but no Monte Carlo. Finally, he gave the stock some cast-off (a slight bend to the right, for right-handed shooters), and the rifle comes to my shoulder naturally, like a fine shotgun, with the sights aligned.

We ran into another little difficulty with the claw mounts. Because of recoil, Siegfried insisted the bases be attached with both screws and silver solder. Other gunsmiths were horrified, insisting that heat from silver soldering would soften the action.

"Not if you know how to use a heat sink," Siegfried growled, and that was that.

Some wondered at the expensive claw mount when Talley mounts were all the rage on custom rifles and a hell of a lot cheaper. First, a detachable mount is essential on a dangerous game rifle, and the claw is, without a doubt and with no room for argument, the best such system ever devised. Properly installed and regulated, it's as close to foolproof as you can get. The scope can be removed with one quick movement of one hand without needing to look, which means you can take the scope off and tuck it in your pocket without taking your eyes off the spot where the buffalo disappeared into the brush. And if the buff reappears on the other side, you can reattach the scope the same way, just by feel. Nothing needs to be tightened, and there is no danger of losing any parts. This is not true of any other system. Claw mounts are certainly expensive, but not on a rifle that may save your life.

One minor hitch: I wanted the scope mounted as low as possible, which is not the German way. That required ordering a second (lower) set of rings from Germany, but this was one argument I won. As with any rifle, there was a running-in period. I found the German open rear sight did not like recoil, and I was down on my hands and knees searching for the moveable

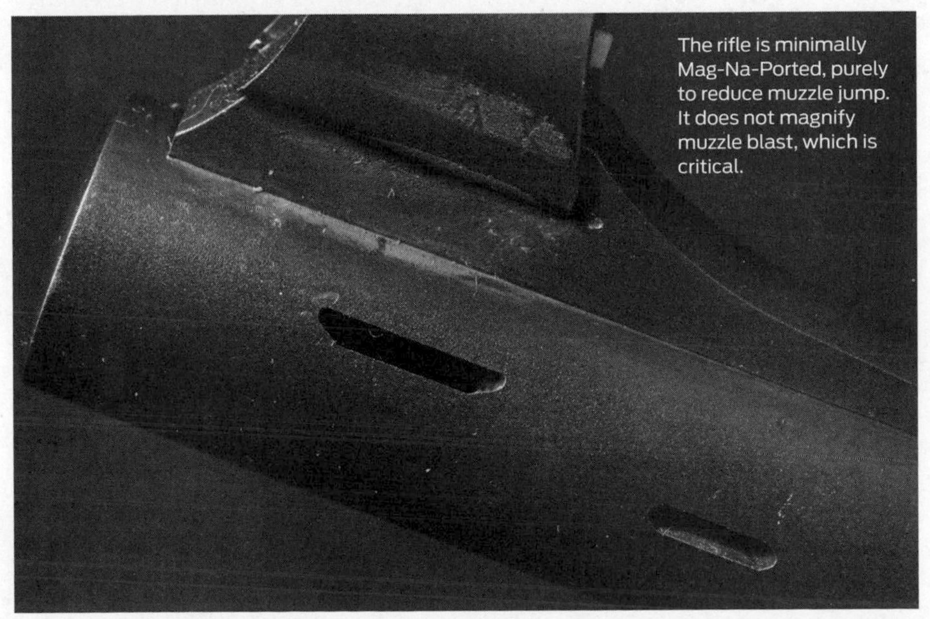

The rifle is minimally Mag-Na-Ported, purely to reduce muzzle jump. It does not magnify muzzle blast, which is critical.

(above) Wieland with a Cape buffalo in the Rift Valley. This was the rifle's second bull of the afternoon. There is nothing like a safely dead Cape buffalo to make everyone in the crew happy and breathe easy. From the left, they are Lekina Sandeti, Abedi Shimba and Momella Torongoi. (right) The second bull is safely dead. A decent set of horns, given that the rifle is 42 inches long.

slide in the grass a couple of times. Eventually, after Siegfried's untimely death, his friend and acolyte, Edwin von Atzigen, fitted a hefty additional set screw to lock it down.

Another problem was of my own making. I tried a different powder with 500-grain bullets — one not recommended by the manufacturer. With the first shot, the floorplate slammed open; unwisely, I tried the next in the series. The floorplate slammed open, the primer blew, and the wire reticle in the scope popped loose and curled up like a singed hair. The scope was returned to Swarovski for repairs, while the triggerguard was fitted with a removable pin to keep the floorplate release from moving in an unscheduled manner. (This was a problem I'd had in Africa with the Weatherby — solved temporarily with a matchstick and some electrician's tape. Hence my concern.)

We later found the rifle had developed excessive headspace, which required turning the barrel one revolution and rechambering. It now has a 21 3/4-inch barrel.

The Trillus rifle made its first trip to Africa in 1994, where I killed a zebra — a contract killing for a friend who wanted a rug. It returned in 1999 and stayed in Africa for two years; during that time, I took a gemsbok and a greater kudu in the Okavango. None of these were the rifle's intended prey, but it was what I had at the time, and it acquitted itself well. I found that a .458 with light bullets — say, 300 to 450 grains — when loaded right, becomes very versatile, especially in those parts of Africa where ranges are not long.

In 2006, it finally got its chance to shine on Cape buffalo in Tanzania. I had tags for two bulls, and we'd been climbing, tracking, and stalking — mostly in pouring rain — for the better part of a week. Then, the sky cleared one day, and we came upon a herd in the mixed brush on a mountainside. I unlimbered the rifle and anchored one bull at about a hundred yards. I was finishing the bull off when my Masai tracker, Lekina Sandeti, came running up to tell me another bunch was heading down a donga, and there was an old bull among them. We raced to the edge, set up the sticks, and I took that bull, too, as the herd stampeded.

Two Cape buffalo inside five minutes, with a lot of adrenalin but no tense moments. At this point, I figure the rifle has nothing left to prove. GD

The Underappreciated .356 Winchester

Compact, potent, and elegant, the .356 Winchester Model 94 is a superb tool for hunters.

›JIM HOUSE

Many hunting and shooting products have been produced that did not make it in the marketplace. The list includes several cartridges introduced with considerable fanfare and favorable words in print. I even have a few favorite ones on that list. Even though there is a fetish at this time for long-range shooting, the fact remains that most medium game is taken at ranges less than 200 yards and much within half that distance. So, a cartridge that delivers excellent performance to 200 yards should be the answer to the wishes of many hunters.

Perhaps the most recognizable centerfire rifle is the Winchester Model 94, introduced in 1894 with its most popular

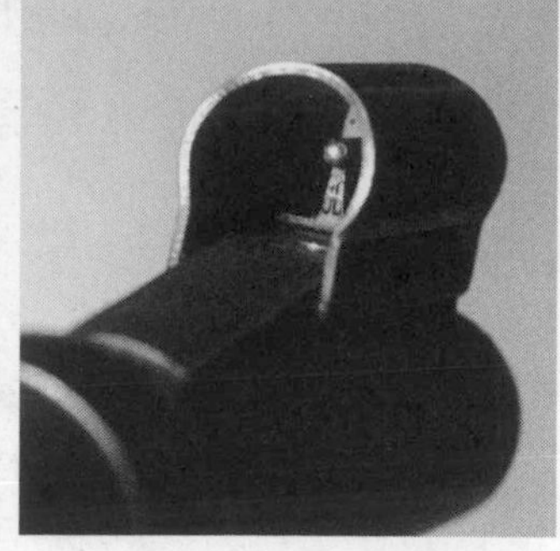

(left) Winchester Big Bore rifles made in 1994 were marked to denote a century of production of the Model 94. (center) A fully adjustable folding rear sight is used on the .356 Big Bore. (right) The front sight utilizes a hooded bead on a ramp.

.30-30 Winchester chambering. The .30-30 was initially loaded with a 160-grain bullet pushed by smokeless powder to 1,900 fps. Modern loadings include a 150-grain bullet with a nominal muzzle velocity of 2,390 fps or a 170-grain bullet at 2,200 fps. With approximately 7 million Model 94s produced, the rifle's popularity is undeniable. For most of its production life, one problem with the Model 94 was that empty cases were ejected upward from the action, so it was not convenient to mount a scope on the rifle except by using an awkward side mount.

By modern standards, .30-30 ballistics are modest but adequate for taking medium-sized game when the range is less than 175 to 200 yards. Therefore, a new caliber that would give ballistics greatly exceeding the .30-30 in a rifle as popular as the Model 94 Winchester would produce a winning combination, right? Not so fast. In 1978, Winchester brought out a strengthened version of the Model 94 known as the Big Bore chambered for the .375 Winchester cartridge. The maximum pressure for the new cartridge was in the range of 50,000–52,000 psi. The two factory loads featured a 200-grain bullet with a velocity of 2,200 fps and a 250-grain bullet at 1,900 fps.

In 1982, Winchester altered the Model 94 so that ejection was at an angle out the side of the action, making it possible to add a top-mounted scope. Subsequently, the Angle Eject was offered in .30-30, and the new Big Bore models came in the new .307 Winchester and .356 Winchester calibers having bullet diameters of .308 and .358 inch, respectively. These rifles featured highly polished, deeply blued metal and beautifully checkered walnut stocks and forearms. Cases for the new cartridges were based on the .308 Winchester case with a slight rim for reliable extraction. As a result, the newer cartridges have performance characteristics very similar to the .308 and .358 Winchester. However, they are not precisely equivalent because of internal differences in the cases. Of course, the .307 and .356 utilize flat-point bullets in tubular magazines, to avoid the possibility of magazine detonation.

Eventually, Marlin offered the Model 336 in .356 Winchester, designated as the Extended Range (ER) model. I once saw one at a very low price, but I already had a Model 94 in .356, so I did

Only two factory loads were produced by Winchester: 200- and 250-grain Power-Points. These cartridges are (left to right): 200-grain .356 Winchester, 180-grain .308 Winchester (the parent case for the .356), and a 250-grain .356 Winchester.

The safety button rests in a recess on the right-hand side of the receiver. The safety is off when pushed to the left, and a red band appears on the shaft. A block makes it impossible for the hammer to strike the firing pin when the safety is on.

not think I needed multiples. That was a mistake.

Early versions of the .307 and .356 Winchester 94s featured a stock with a raised comb to facilitate shooting the rifles with scopes attached. My first .356 was one of those, but when I added a later model, I sold my first one to my brother for what I paid for it. That was another mistake because I had initially bought it cheap on clearance, and I have since seen such rifles with price tags of over $1,000.

So, what's great about the .356 Winchester? First, there is the fact that the velocity, especially with the 200-grain bullet, is high enough to make it a 225- to 250-yard cartridge. For example, the Winchester data show that with a sight-in distance of 175 yards, the bullet strikes 2.3 inches high at 100 yards and about 7 inches low at 250 yards. When zeroed at 200 yards, the point of impact is about 3.2 inches high at 100 yards and only about 5 inches low at 250 yards. Most hunting for medium game takes place well within that range limit.

The .356 Winchester is a versatile cartridge for those who handload their own ammunition. Not only can the .356 be loaded with 200-grain flat- or round-nose bullets, it can be used with the 200-grain FTX bullet from Hornady. This bullet has a spitzer shape, but the point consists of a polymer insert that can deform under pressure. Therefore, such cartridges can be safely loaded in a tubular magazine where the point of one bullet rests against the primer in the cartridge in front. The Hornady FTX bullet has a ballistic coefficient of .300 compared to approximately .250 for a flat point of the same weight. Using a bullet having a higher ballistic coefficient at a given velocity can give a somewhat flatter trajectory and higher remaining energy at longer ranges.

Bullet choices in .358-inch diameter are not nearly as numerous as for diameters such as .308 inch. In addition to the 200-grain FTX, Hornady also produces a 200-grain round-nose bullet suitable for loading in tubular magazines. Speer offers two flat-pointed bullets with weights of 180 and 220 grains, and Sierra markets a 200-grain round nose. Several manufacturers produce cast and plated bullets that can be used successfully in a .356 lever action.

With a case of modest capacity that holds a large diameter bullet, propellants having medium-burn rates work best. These include Winchester 748, Hodgdon

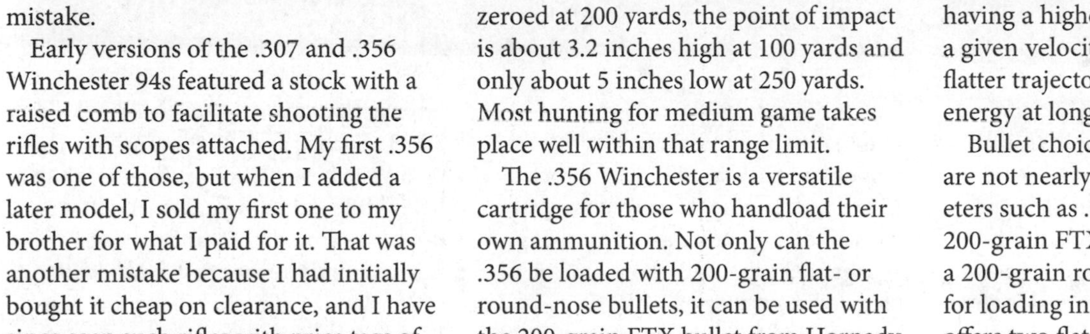

Handloads can be prepared for the .356 Winchester with 110- to 220-grain bullets.

With this Weaver K2.5 scope attached, the .356 Winchester Big Bore is an ideal rifle for the hunter who stalks game rather than taking long-range shots.

Varget, H335, BL-C(2) and H322. Some IMR powders that work well in the .356 are 4895, 4320, and my favorite, 4064. There are others, such as AA 2015 and Viht. N133, but I have not personally used these. However, *do not* use load data for the .358 Winchester for loading the .356 Winchester.

For tinkerers and reloaders, .356 Winchester cases can be loaded with bullets intended for use in handguns such as the .38 Special and .357 Magnum. Such bullets ranging in weights from 110 to 180 grains are not typically loaded in full-power cartridges, but they make a .356 Winchester into a deadly varmint rifle even at modest velocities. Cast bullets can also be used to produce loads suitable for varmints or animals up to the size of deer.

There may be an issue when it comes to finding .356 Winchester cases, especially as this is written in early 2022. I found brass cases available in the past, but none are currently in stock from the usual suppliers of reloading items. However, I laid in a supply of .356 cases when I got my rifle long ago, and Hornady produces .307 Winchester brass (and loaded ammunition). It is simple to open the neck of .307 cases with a .358 expander plug. However, it may be easier to do in two steps by first using an expander plug of .338 or some other intermediate diameter.

About .356 Winchester, a great deal of praise is in order. Reports that I have read indicate that accuracy is perfectly acceptable for the intended use, and mine is no exception. With that out of the way, one should be aware that a relatively short, light rifle that shoots heavy bullets generates considerable recoil. Under hunting conditions, this is not a problem. However, bullets of .35 caliber that expand well hit with much authority, as many hunters have found out. The performance of the .356 Winchester dramatically exceeds that of the .35 Remington.

A great deal of the desirability of a Model 94 in .356 Winchester caliber is that such a rifle is of convenient size and weight and has the handling qualities of a short, flat, lever action. Moreover, the power capability greatly exceeds lever-action favorites such as the .30-30, .32 Special and .35 Remington. The .356 Winchester Big Bore is more than a "deer" rifle. It is a big game rifle that can double as a predator hunting tool.

If one finds a Winchester Model 94 or Marlin 336 chambered for the .356 Winchester, expect an asking price of 50 percent or more of the same rifle in standard calibers. The same is true for rifles in calibers such as .358 Winchester and others. The short production span and number of units produced dictate the price. What I don't understand is, with that market demand, why wouldn't manufacturers make a run of rifles in some of the more unusual calibers for both users and collectors. Surely the supply and demand keeps the prices of existing models high, so why wouldn't consumers buy sufficient quantities to justify new production? Well, I can't say, but my .356 Winchester Model 94 Big Bore is not going to be for sale or trade. It is truly one good gun and would be about the last item I'd ever part with out of the safe. GD

The well-traveled Browning Double Automatic Twentyweight with gun club patches of various places where it spent time. The small badge on the left (the stag head) is for all U.S. military rod and gun clubs in Europe. The little gold-colored round lapel button on the right (with a pheasant head, which unfortunately does not show in the photo) is for Zenryo, the All Japan Hunting Club.

A Well-Traveled Shotgun

If only this Browning Double Automatic "Twentyweight" 12-gauge could talk!

›NICK HAHN

"If only this gun could talk!" We've all heard the comment or seen this in print referring to a particular gun with some history. Many such hunting guns have fascinating tales to tell. Classic rifles with a rich history of African or other exotic big game hunting or side-by-side shotguns, usually the so-called "Best Guns," were used for driven-game shooting. Then again, there are guns with not-so-illustrious pedigrees, but with just as interesting background and history as the London Best or other fine arms that belonged to the wealthy and privileged.

This Browning Double Automatic "Twentyweight" shotgun has had a curious and fascinating history. Made in 1957, one of the first Twentyweight models produced at the FN factory in Liege, Belgium, was shipped to a U.S. Army rod and gun club in Bamberg, Germany. It was purchased by a person stationed at Bamberg in late 1957, but the purchaser's identity is not very

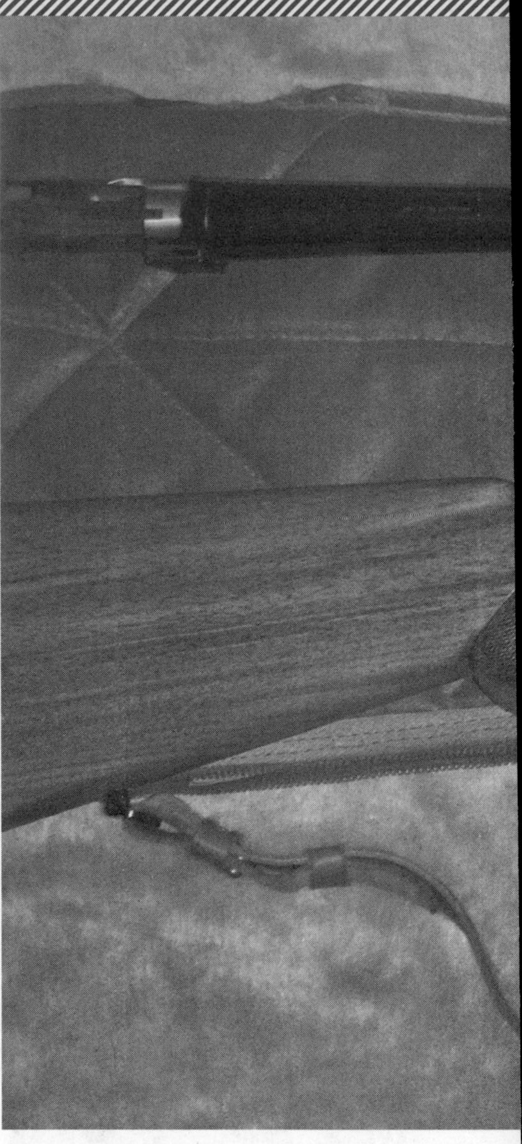

(above) The long-tailed yamadori (Japanese copper pheasant) is perhaps Japan's most-prized upland game bird. The gun's first owner belonged to Camp Zama Sportsman's Club, represented by the triangular patch on the left. The magazine in the center is called *Zenryo*, the All Japan Hunting Club publication of the same name to which the Japanese owner of the gun belonged. The last American gun owner in Japan belonged to the Kanto Plains Sportsman's Club, the round patch on the right. (right) The Twentyweight with a vintage Boyt takedown case covered with brown, leather-like vinyl material, unlike the more recent cases covered in cotton canvas. This case dates to the 1950s and '60s, possibly even the '70s, so it could have been purchased with the gun. Such cases were very inexpensive, usually sold for under $10.

clear. The gun retailed for $147.00 plus tax in the U.S. at the time of purchase, but at the military exchanges and rod and gun clubs overseas (tax-free and discounted), it sold for much less at $112.00. It was not cheap when considering that the very popular Remington Model 11-48 autoloader cost $117.00 stateside and sold for around $75.00 at the same club where the Browning Double Automatic was purchased.

In the late 1950s, from Germany, the gun traveled with its owner, who was reassigned to Camp Zama, Japan, located 28 miles southwest of Tokyo. In the early 1960s, before he departed from Japan, the American owner sold the gun. The new Japanese owner paid all the necessary taxes, fees and the purchase price, which brought the total amount to a little more than what the gun cost new stateside! He then took it to his local police station for registration, at which time he produced his purchase receipt and the original receipt from Bamberg Rod and Gun Club, which was provided by the seller. The police noted this information, the gun was measured and weighed, and all the particulars, such as the gun's condition, etc., were meticulously recorded in the little registration booklet. However, the previous owner's name was not listed anywhere despite all the other detailed information. Whatever the case, Japanese gun laws were designed to discourage gun ownership, even back in those days.

The Japanese owner took excellent care of the gun. He must have really cherished this lightweight shotgun, which made for a perfect upland gun in Japan, where much walking is done in very rugged and challenging terrain. He also had the modified choke in the barrel opened to weak modified or Winchester Skeet 2. This change was recorded in the registration booklet. According to an American gunsmith who examined the barrel, the honing of the bore was done by hand, judiciously and very carefully.

The gun apparently remained in his possession from the early 1960s until it was sold to a gun shop called Fujikoshi in Aoyama, Tokyo, which sold it at a mass sale held at Camp Zama Sportsman's Club in the late 1970s. According to the sales representative from Fujikoshi, it bought the gun from the widow of the Japanese owner, a well-known, long-time customer of the gun shop. The salesman said that the late owner was an avid pheasant and partridge hunter and past president of the All Japan Hunting Club, Japan's version of NRA/DU.

These special gun sales are held to benefit U.S. military personnel, although they are open to the general public. Usually, a group of Japanese gun shops participates. Basically, they use the opportunity to unload their used gun inventory sitting in their racks. The guns are heavily discounted for a quick sale, and some are great bargains. Such was the case for this Browning Double Automatic. The new owner, a member of the U.S. Air Force stationed at Yokota Air Force Base, heard about the sale through the Kanto Plains Sportsman's Club at Yokota. There was a notice on the club bulletin board about a special gun sale at Camp Zama, so he decided to go there and see what was available. The Browning Double Automatic caught his eye right away, and he bought it.

After a whirlwind military tour in pos-

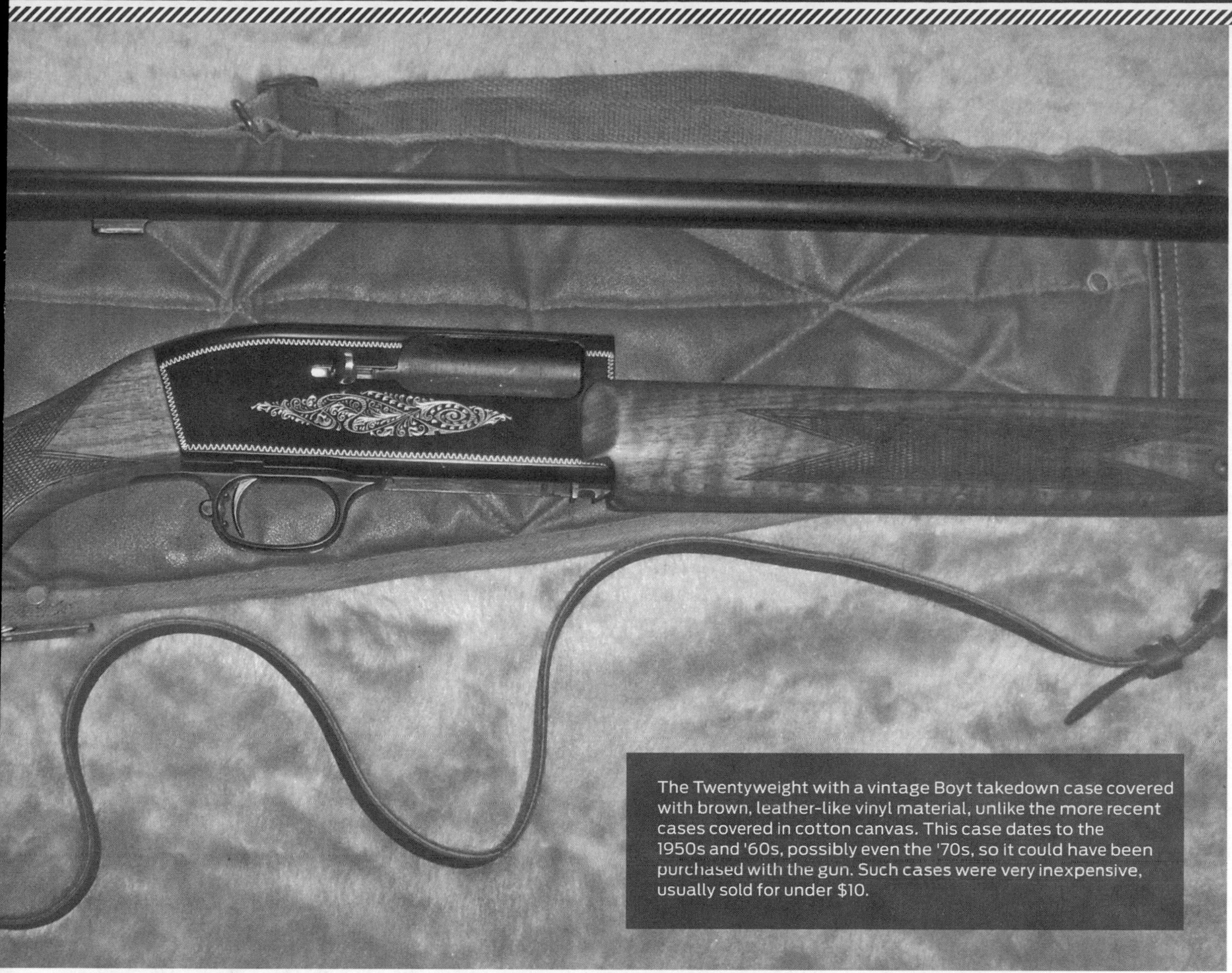

The Twentyweight with a vintage Boyt takedown case covered with brown, leather-like vinyl material, unlike the more recent cases covered in cotton canvas. This case dates to the 1950s and '60s, possibly even the '70s, so it could have been purchased with the gun. Such cases were very inexpensive, usually sold for under $10.

session of the shotgun, he retired from the U.S. Air Force in Arizona, near Luke Air Force Base, in the early 1990s. That's when he decided to sell the Browning, and its history was passed on orally. Everything was by word of mouth, and, by this time, there was no documentary proof.

It might have bagged some of the local game birds in Germany, including waldschnepfe (Eurasian woodcock), and even the fabled Auerhahn (Capercaille), the giant forest grouse. Then in Japan, where it spent the most time, it no doubt was used to hunt kojiuke (bamboo partridge), as well as kiji (Japanese green pheasant) and the prized yamadori (Japanese copper pheasant), as well as other Japanese game birds. The U.S. Air Force officer who bought the gun in Japan did not have a chance to use it in the field; he just shot some skeet at Yokota Air Force Base. But according to him, in Greece, he shot perlikez (red-legged partridge) and bekazza (Eurasian woodcock), two very popular game birds. In Florida, he shot snipes and doves. He shot a few Mariana fruit doves and the Guam rail in Guam, but he mostly used the gun to shoot skeet. He said that it shot beautifully at skeet and handled well and balanced for him perfectly. He shot some doves and desert quail in Arizona before he sold it. I had the gun checked out by my gunsmith friend, who measured the choking and examined the bore. I have shot a few doves with it, and it still functions perfectly and handles like a dream, a proper upland gun.

The shotgun is nothing special, just a typical Browning Double Automatic, an early version of the Twentyweight model. It has a thin 26 ½-inch plain-matted top barrel marked modified to reduce weight. It is a very light gun for a 12 gauge, weighing a mere 6 pounds 2 ounces. (If it had a ventilated rib, it would have weighed more. The ventilated rib on a Browning autoloader usually adds about 4 ounces, depending on the length of the barrel. But with a plain barrel, it is genuinely lightweight.) According to Browning's official listing, the Twentyweight was offered only in two colors, black and brown. This one has the most common color, the so-called "Dragon Black" receiver.

The Twentyweight's brown receiver was made only from 1957 until 1959, while the black receiver was made until the gun was discontinued in 1971. However, I have heard unsubstantiated reports of Twentyweight Double Automatics in the "Forest Green" and "Velvet Gray." Supposedly, these guns were not aftermarket re-coloring but rather very early models made in the first year, around 1957. Thus far, I haven't seen any other factory original colors for the Twentyweight other than black and brown, but that certainly doesn't rule out the possibility that other colors exist.

Despite its age and apparent use, this gun is in remarkably good shape, and the anodizing on the receiver is only lightly scratched in some spots. The bluing on the barrel is excellent. Only the wood was heavily scratched and dinged, and the original lacquer finish was badly worn off, flaking in spots, so the wood was refinished. Like most Browning shotguns made before the mid-1960s, this one has a bone buttplate rather than plastic, and the wood was finished in lacquer, not the glossy, glass-like polyurethane finish used today.

The only difference from factory standard is its 3/4-inch European sling swivels. The European market guns, i.e., those sold as FN guns and Browning Arms, come with swivels unless ordered. However, this gun is a Browning Arms shotgun meant for the U.S. market, which was not supplied with swivels, unless special ordered. Also, Browning's factory-installed swivels were usually ⅞, not ¾ inch. Of course, there are exceptions. However, the swivels on this gun were likely installed in Germany or Japan, where they are standard on shotguns. Sling swivels on shotguns

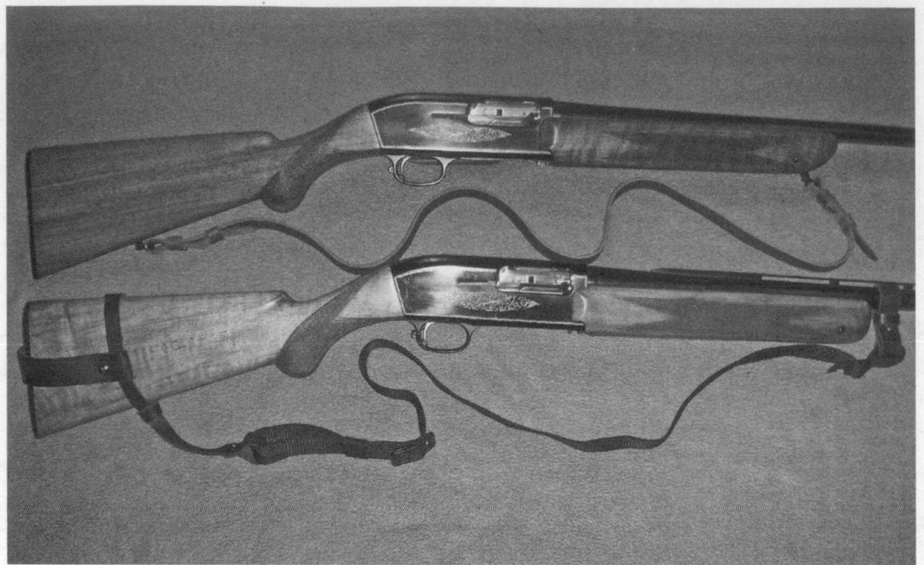

(top right) At the top is the 1957 vintage Twentyweight with 3/4-inch European swivels and a lightweight leather sling. Below is the 1963 vintage Twentyweight (note the difference in the shape of the forearm tip) with a ventilated rib and a slip-on, swivel-less sling. The 1957 vintage gun, with a plain barrel, weighs 6 pounds, 2 ounces, while the 1963 vintage shotgun with a ribbed barrel weighs 6 pounds, 7 ounces — 5 ounces more.

(right) The Twentyweight at 6 pounds, 2 ounces, surrounded by a classic 12-gauge Dumoulin side-by-side sidelock round body at 6 pounds, 10 ounces on the left, and CSMC's 20-gauge "Inverness" round body over/under at 6 pounds, 4 ounces on the right. The Dumoulin is chambered for the 2 3/4-inch shells and, therefore, is of proper weight but on the light side. Side-by-sides chambered for 2 1/2-inch shells typically weigh around 6 1/2 pounds, but those for 2 3/4 inches usually tip the scale at 6 pounds, 12 ounces to 7 pounds or more. The "Inverness" at 6 pounds, 4 ounces is of proper weight for an over/under 20 gauge. Guns on the lighter side tend to have unpleasant recoil, while a heavier 6 1/2-pound 20 gauge is really in the 16- or light 12-gauge category. The Twentyweight is lighter than either gun, yet the felt recoil (using 1 1/8-ounce loads) is much less than the heavier Dumoulin side-by-side.

were never popular in America, except for slug guns. Until around the mid-1980s, sling swivels were rarely seen on shotguns, not even waterfowl guns, as they are more commonly found today.

I have always been partial to the Browning Double Automatic. As a kid in the 1950s, I drooled over the guns displayed in stores when they made their first appearance. I find this gun to be unique, wonderfully balanced, and for me, two shots are more than enough. As an upland gun, the Double Automatic has few equals among repeaters. The Twentyweight and the slightly heavier "Twelvette" make for excellent upland guns with proper choking. The Twelvette also makes for a great duck gun over decoys. Of course, you would have to use Bismuth or other softer shot than steel or have steel shot choke tubes installed, which is not an expensive or difficult modification.

Some claim the Twentyweight is unpleasant to shoot and recoils too much because of its light weight. I find it quite the contrary, and its recoil is barely noticeable for a lightweight gun. Val Browning's short recoil system does a remarkable job of absorbing recoil, much better than the long recoil arrangement of the more popular A-5 "Humpback," which produces the "double shuffle" effect that many dislike. Of course, the Twentyweight will recoil more if you stuff heavy loads into it. But with normal field loads for which it was built, it is enjoyable to shoot with remarkably light recoil. As Browning advertised, the Twentyweight will handle all loads, but it was designed to be used with lighter ones.

Val Browning designed the Double Automatic to be durable and dependable. It was initially designed as a Live Pigeon gun at the request of Val's pigeon shooting friends. Rumors about the Double Automatic's lack of durability and dependability are totally unfounded. They are just that, rumors, usually generated by self-acknowledged gun experts. These unfounded rumors probably did more damage to the reputation of the Double Automatic and dissuaded prospective purchasers more than anything else. The critics never considered why Browning would make the Twelvette and the Twentyweight in target versions for skeet and trap if they were not dependable and durable shotguns. Browning would have never produced target versions if the guns did not hold up.

In 1971, the Double Automatic was made in trap, skeet and field models to the final days of production. There were more Twelvettes produced than Twentyweights. But still, it is not unusual to find Twentyweight skeet guns. These are not simply Twentyweights with a Twelvette skeet barrel attached; the Twentyweight skeet models were made with their own 26 1/2" barrel while the "Twelvette" had a 25 1/2-inch barrel. So, if the Twentyweight recoiled too much or was not durable, why would Browning make it as a skeet gun?

Twentyweight skeet guns have gone through thousands of rounds of skeet and are still functioning perfectly. I believe that, for the most part, those who complained about the recoil of the Twentyweight were using heavy loads that would kick hard in

the gun that
dares to be different
BROWNING
DOUBLE AUTOMATIC
12 gauge
It's *different* from any shotgun ever produced! *Different* . . . to make your shooting more effective — your hunt in field or marsh more enjoyable — and you less tired at the end of the day. The Browning Double Automatic was designed to be *different* . . . with a purpose.
. . . **One pound less to carry** — you have 12 gauge performance with a gun that's light as a 20.
. . . **A balance that intensifies its lightness** — it carries, points and swings as if it were part of you.
. . . **The comfort of cushioned recoil** — pleasant to shoot whatever your size and weight.
. . . **Split-second loading** — you'll load it faster and easier, even with gloves, right or left hand.
. . . **Shoots all loads without adjustment** — all 2¾ inch shells in any combination without adjustment of any kind.
Heft it — Load it — Swing it — Shoot it
You'll distinguish the difference!
YOUR BROWNING DEALER
A 12 gauge as light as a 20 gauge
The perfect balance good shooting requires
ghtweight model $139.50
Prices subject to change without notice.
GUNS BROWNING
Write for "GUNS BY BROWNING," a 28-page catalog showing all Browning guns in color, plus special chapters on shooting — practical information for gun enthusiasts. Browning Arms Co., Dept. 3T, St. Louis 3, Mo.

A full-page ad from the 1950s touted "the gun that dares to be different" and the exceptional light weight of the Double Automatic, which has "12 gauge performance with a gun that's as light as a 20."

After leaving the factory in 1957 and covering more than 45,000 miles during its worldwide odyssey, this gun undoubtedly bagged more than its share of game. After all that time, it is still quite capable of doing what it was built to do more than half a century ago if the person behind it does their part.

any gun. But, for the most part, they were simply rumors. It also didn't help that even some recognized gun authorities, such as the late Don Zutz, said negative things about the Twentyweight. Zutz stated in his discussion of the Browning Double Automatic that the Twentyweight tended to "jump" forward when a shot was fired due to the heavy recoil spring returning to battery. I am puzzled by that statement. I have never experienced or felt this "jump" forward sensation when shooting it, which I have shot a lot! Besides, the recoil spring on a Double Automatic is relatively small compared to recoil springs on long-recoil shotguns like the A-5. To his credit, Zutz did not say that he personally experienced this but rather that he was told by others who claimed that the Twentyweight "jumped" forward when fired.

For me, as a 12-gauge repeater for upland birds, the Browning Double Automatic Twentyweight has no equal. It is a pity that more shotgunners didn't take to it. I think that as a so-called "Prairie Gun," which most believe should be a 12 gauge with at least a modified bore, the Twentyweight is hard to beat with its superb balance and light weight that you can carry all day for long miles. You'd be hard-pressed to find a 12-gauge autoloader that is as light. (A lightweight repeater such as a Franchi 48 AL or a Benelli is almost as light but will not have that "between the hands" feel and handle. They just cannot attain the Double Automatic's feel and balance.)

All repeaters, owing to the nature of their design with the magazine tube, have a weight-forward feel that is very difficult to negate. The exception was the Winchester Model 50, but that gun was the opposite — butt heavy! The Franchi and the Benelli could be like the Double Automatic in handling and feel, but you would have to go down to a 20 gauge.

I own and shoot all types of shotguns. But if I had to confine my choice to one gun for the uplands, especially if it had to be a 12-gauge repeater, I'd pick the Browning Double Automatic Twentyweight without hesitation. I would also elect to have sling swivels attached with a sling. I've used slings on my shotguns through the years, especially repeaters. All my waterfowl guns had slings going back to when they were rarely seen in the duck blinds of America. I have also used slings on my upland guns, which I find very useful on those long treks or climbing up and down steep terrain after game like chukar. I use slip-on, swivel-less slings for some of my guns if they are not equipped with swivels; others are equipped with swivels to use regular slings.

This Browning Double Automatic Twentyweight is ideal for upland use. It is lighter than most 20 gauges, yet it is a 12 gauge allowing a wide variety of loads, anything from 1 to 1 1/4 ounces. It is like the 16 gauge, often advertised as "shoots like a 12, carries like a 20," except the Twentyweight is really "a 12 that carries like a 20!" It can handle everything in the uplands, from the smallish dove and quail to the larger pheasant and turkey, and if need be, will serve well in a duck blind with proper loads. Set up as it is with a sling, it can be carried anywhere and, when slung on the shoulder, allows the use of both hands for other needs. Yes, this Browning Double Automatic is an ideal repeater for upland birds. To borrow Winchester's famous advertising slogan for its legendary Model 12 pump gun, this well-traveled shotgun is "a perfect repeater!" GD

- REPORTS - from the Field RIFLES

WAYNE VAN ZWOLL

Oddly enough, the German-made Sauer Pantera was the first to chamber the 6.5 PRC, now in many rifles.

With production pressed to meet the demand for existing models, does the industry need new ones?

Brisk demand fueled by record numbers of new shooters and fears of further firearms restrictions continues to buoy rifle production. Cosmetic tweaks and new chamberings define much of what's new in bolt rifles as manufacturers keep production lines humming. But 2022 rosters include some fresh models and useful changes to proven designs. Attrition in traditional walnut-stocked lever actions is mitigated by worthy Italian reproductions for U.S. importers like Cimarron and Taylor's. The Dakota brand shelved by Remington's dissolution has been replaced as Dakota's talented crew continues to fill existing rifle orders in a nearby shop under the ParkWest shingle. Strong sales of long-range rifles inspire semi-custom work from small shops; factory models bear more palatable prices.

While ammunition shortages continue to plague shooters, rifle enthusiasts should find plenty of reasons to buy in 2022!

ANSCHUTZ

The 1700 series of Anschutz sporting rifles has welcomed the Model 1712. With a Monte Carlo comb, its top-shelf Match 54 barreled action is stocked in checkered walnut. It has an adjustable two-stage trigger and a five-shot detachable magazine. Anschutz recently added a sliding safety on the receiver's right-hand side. It blocks the sear and trigger. The 1761 sporter in .22 LR, .22 WMR and .17 HMR are among the most accurate available. Anschutz small-bore centerfires, perfectly proportioned for the chamberings, include the 1771 in .17 Hornet, .22 Hornet, .204, .222 and .223. The 1780 and 1782 come in chamberings from .243 to 9.3x62. *anschutznorthamerica.com*

A classy new .22, the Anschutz 1712 uses the German company's top-tier Match 54 action.

BENELLI

Trotted out in 2020, Benelli's Lupo bolt-action centerfire rifle was notable for its rakish, futuristic guard bow and angular stock. Forthcoming accounts gave it good marks for function and accuracy.

Benelli's rakish Lupo, here a standard model, offers a new high-gloss metal finish and a walnut stock.

In '22, the Lupo comes in a new limited-edition form, with a high-gloss metal finish so effective in preventing rust and corrosion that it comes with a 25-year warranty. The standard model's synthetic stock gives way on the new rifle to satin-finished checkered walnut, "AA grade." Butt spacers adjust the stock length from 13.8 to 14.8 inches. The threaded barrel is chambered in 6.5 Creedmoor and .300 Win. Mag. This limited-edition Lupo has its forebear's three-lug bolt for a low 60-degree lift. Trigger pull adjusts from 2.2 to 4.4 pounds. List price: $2,199. *benelli.com*

BERETTA

The BRX1, new for 2022, is the first Beretta straight-pull rifle and the first of that type ever produced in Italy. It's also the first bolt-action rifle marketed under the Beretta name (though Beretta Holdings also controls Sako, Tikka and Victrix Armaments and has blessed the introductions of Franchi and Benelli bolt rifles). The BRX1 has a rotating bolt head, with eight locking lugs for standard cartridges and 16 for the magnums. The bolt locks into a barrel extension; you need only swap barrel, bolt head, and magazine to switch chamberings. The three-position tang safety serves right- and left-handed shooters. The charging handle can be placed on either side of the action, and the bolt head can be rotated to eject hulls right or left. Any small-tipped tool can remove the trigger group, including a bullet tip. Trigger pull adjusts from 2 to 3.3 pounds. The BRX1 can be fitted with a Picatinny rail, a Tikka-style 17mm dovetail or Beretta's new proprietary scope mount. The black polymer stock has dual-texture contact surfaces, interchangeable palm swells and buttpads to adjust grip diameter and length of pull. A detachable, flush-fit, orange polymer box carries five rounds in 6.5 Creedmoor, .308 and .30-06. The BRX1 is also available in .300 Win. Mag. Muzzle-threaded barrels come in lengths of 20, 22 and 24 inches. *beretta.com*

BERGARA

Known for its barrels, which bless CVA muzzleloaders, the Bergara brand borrows the name of the Spanish town where, in 1999, a factory was making ri-

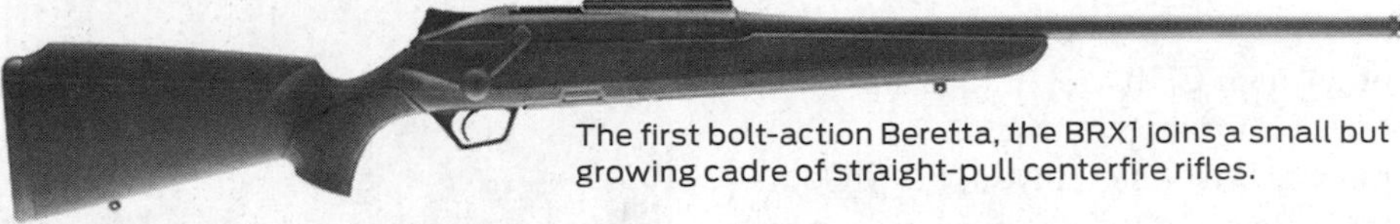

The first bolt-action Beretta, the BRX1 joins a small but growing cadre of straight-pull centerfire rifles.

Bergara's Divide has its Premier action, an AG Composites stock designed for long-range shooting.

fle barrels for BPI Outdoors. Soon that factory was furnishing OEM barrels for several gunmakers. Bergara bolt-action rifles followed — the Premier and more affordable B-14 series. Chrome-moly barrels for both are button-rifled, stress-relieved and true to .0002 inch. The stainless Ridgeback ($2,100) and Highlander ($1,800) feature Palma mid-weight and fluted sporter barrels, respectively, each on a Cerakoted Premier action with a cone-shaped bolt head and a TriggerTech trigger. The Ridgeback has a prone stock and a detachable box; the Highlander has a hunting-style stock and an internal magazine.

New for '22, the Divide sports a carbon-fiber barrel on a Premier action in an AG Composites stock. With elements of both tactical and sporting rifles, it weighs 7.2 to 7.4 pounds in 6.5 Creedmoor, 6.5 PRC, .308, and .300 Win. Mag. Price: $2,499. Bergara has also unveiled the B-14 Wilderness Series in Sniper Grey Cerakote. In 6.5 Creedmoor to .28 Nosler and .300 Win. Mag, the Hunter and Ridge models have internal magazines, SoftTouch stock finish. This year, there's a new Bergara Canyon on the Premier action, with an AG Composites carbon-fiber stock and AICS magazine. Its 20- or 22-inch barrels are bored for cartridges from 6.5 Creedmoor to .375 H&H. The Canyon weighs 6.2 to 6.5 pounds, lists for $2,149. Its new sibling is Bergara's MG Lite, also with an AICS box. A long-range "precision rifle," it has a 22- or 24-inch CF barrel in four flat-shooting chamberings and scales just 6.8 pounds. Like the Canyon, the MG Lite takes Remington 700 scope bases with 8-40 screws. It retails for $2,999. Bergara is one of five BPI brands; it shares marketing with PowerBelt, DuraSite, Quake and CVA. *bergarausa.com*

BIGHORN ARMORY

Incorporating elements of John Browning-designed Winchester '86 and '92 rifles, the Bighorn Armory Model 89 has the vertical locking lugs of the single shot that brought Browning's genius to Winchester's attention. The 89 boasts modern steels and machining to handle the breech pressures of the .500 Smith & Wesson and now .500 Linebaugh cartridges. The encore: Bighorn's Model 90, .460 S&W. In handguns, the recoil of full-house loads can bring tears to your eyes. But Bighorn rifles — 7.5 to 8.1 pounds with 16-, 18- and 22-inch barrels and 1-inch recoil pads — make them manageable. These powerful rifles are built of 17-4 stainless steel, in brushed stainless or Hunter Black finish. Case-colored receivers are an option. Stocks of American walnut or brown or gray laminates include a buttstock swivel stud and an integral stud in the forend cap. The magazine is dovetailed to the barrel. Bolt-mounted aperture sights complement flat gold beads on the Model 89 and 90 rifles I've fired, but a blade front sight is listed. The lever is generous enough for a gloved hand. Trigger break is clean, cycling hitch-free, extraction and top

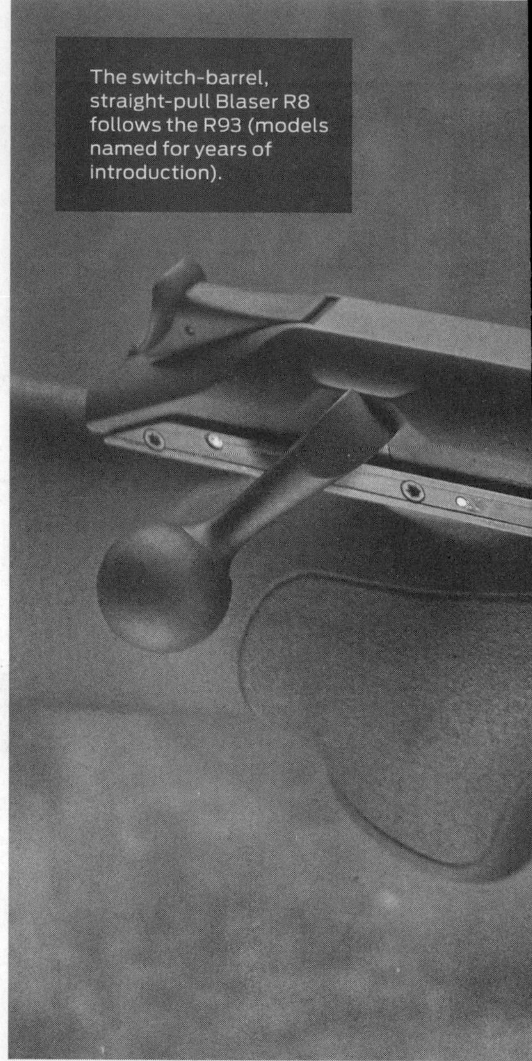
The switch-barrel, straight-pull Blaser R8 follows the R93 (models named for years of introduction).

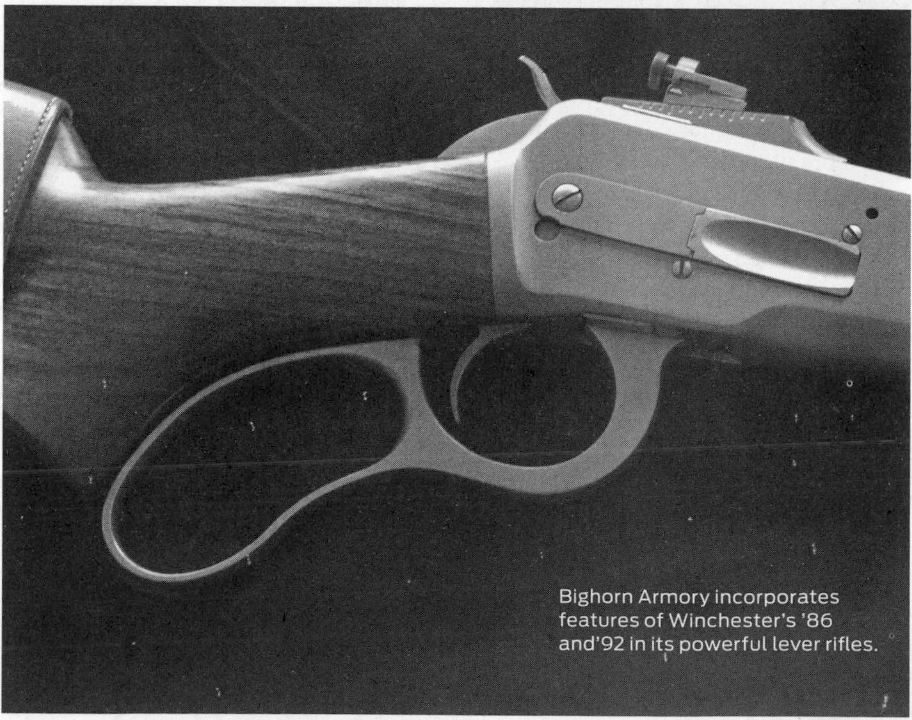
Bighorn Armory incorporates features of Winchester's '86 and'92 in its powerful lever rifles.

ejection smooth and reliable. Base price: $3,700. *bighornarmory.com*

BLASER

Last year, Blaser announced a .22 rimfire barrel for its straight-pull R8 rifle. The R8's radial-head telescoping bolt with expanding collet and direct-to-barrel lock-up doesn't make it easier. But Blaser's talented crew in Isny, Germany, persevered. With quick swaps of the barrel, bolt head and magazine innards, the R8 adds the .22 LR to 47 switch-barrel centerfire options.

While you will save money on ammo practicing with a .22, Blaser's rimfire conversion isn't cheap. A more reasonable rationale: you can practice where a centerfire is verboten or impractical. Avoiding flinch-inducing recoil and using the same rifle you'll carry on a hunt have apparent advantages. Besides its new .22 barrel option, the R8 has many assets. It's stout enough to brook 120,000 psi. Its tang-mounted thumbpiece is not a safety but a cocking switch; the rifle can be carried safely with a loaded chamber. Plasma nitriding on hammer-forged barrels makes the surface very hard, so Blaser QD scope rings cinch securely into topside dimples. A feather-light, aramid-reinforced magazine snuggles in its detachable trigger group. A sliding tab inside the box locks it in the rifle, but you can topload it. R8 stocks come in fine European walnut and synthetic versions in several profiles.

Blaser also makes a single-shot rifle, the K95. With elegant and traditional European form, it is now chambered for a new cartridge: the 8.5x55 Blaser. Its 8.5mm (.338) bullet fills a "caliber gap," identified by shooters who lust for a new rifle, between European favorites in 7mm and 9.3mm. The slightly rebated case suggests .404 Jeffery heritage. The 8.5x55 should serve well in the short barrels wearing suppressors. Norma loads ammunition: 230-grain bullets at 2,960 fps, for 3,696 ft-lbs of energy. A new K95 Ultimate Carbon has a sleek leather-accented stock per the R8's Professional Success Leather. *blaser-usa.com*

Blaser's newest R8 wizardry: interchangeable barrel/bolt head to convert centerfires to .22 rimfire.

Browning's new X-Bolt Speed rifles include this prone-stocked model with Recoil Hawg brake.

BROWNING

The X-Bolt centerfire bolt rifle has grown from a family to a clan. Browning lists 13 new X-Bolt versions for 2022, differing primarily in details and finishes. The X-Bolt Western Hunter Long Range that appeared in 2021 with a 26-inch barrel in nine frothy chamberings, 6.5 Creedmoor to .300 PRC, 30 Nosler and .300 Ultra Mag, satisfied shooters' long-range lust for $1,100. A Max Long Range Hunter added an adjustable stock, heavy, fluted barrel and Recoil Hawg brake.

This year, Browning offers these and other X-Bolts in Smoked Bronze Cerakoting, OVIX camo stock finish. All boast the model's smooth-running three-lug bolt with a 60-degree bolt lift, a flush rotary magazine and a bolt unlock button for cycling "on safe." A new Speed "mountain rifle" features fluted 22-, 23-, 24- and 26-inch barrels with Browning's radial brake in 16 chamberings, .243 to .300 RUM. Weights: from 6.4 pounds. Price: $1,340. The Speed LR, bored for 11 cartridges, 6.5 Creedmoor to .28 Nosler and .300 Win. Mag. wears 26-inch barrels, weighs just over 7 pounds and costs $1,360. The Hell's Canyon McMillan, with that company's Game Scout stock, is similar, in seven long-range chamberings with a heavy sporter barrel and a Recoil Hawg brake. It starts at $2,400. The Mountain Pro Long Range with carbon-fiber stock trims 10 ounces off that rifle's weight at 6.8 pounds with barrels of similar contour in nine chamberings, 6.5C to .300 RUM. A Tungsten version does not have tungsten components, but Tungsten Cerakoting on its 26-inch stainless barrels to .300 PRC. Price: $2,520. The Max LR, with adjustable prone stock, weighs 8 pounds and retails from $1,540.

The "what's new" roster includes autoloaders, too. An autoloading .22 on the slim bottom-ejecting Browning action has a thick 16.2-inch barrel and a high comb over the buttstock magazine for $960. A new BAR Mk 3 Speed in eight chamberings — .243 to .300 Win. Mag. — has a synthetic stock. Average weight: 6.6 pounds. It costs $1,720. *browning.com*

CHRISTENSEN ARMS

Christensen Arms uses Remington 700-pattern actions, CNC machined to tight tolerances. The recoil lugs are surface-ground, bolt bodies spiral-fluted and black nitride-treated. Magnum actions have dual ejectors. Receivers are pillar-bedded to prone-style stocks adjustable at comb and butt. Newest on the Christensen roster: the Ridgeline Scout. Compact but in powerful chamberings, it has a detachable box and a receiver-mounted. It weighs just 5.9 pounds and lists for $2,200. *christensenarms.com*

CVA

CVA's first bolt-action centerfire rifle, the Cascade, appeared in 2020. Like many products new that year, it's had limited exposure. Just $499 at its debut for the blued version, the Cascade has a smooth-running three-lug bolt with a 70-degree lift. The threaded 22-inch Bergara barrel is chambered in 6.5 Creedmoor, 7mm-08, .308 and .350 Legend. The gray synthetic stock, with SoftTouch finish, is handsome and practical in profile. New for 2022, the SB (Short Barrel) Cascade has a 16.5- or 18-inch barrel with Graphite Black Cerakoting. The fiberglass-reinforced stock in Veil Tac Black is adjustable for length and fitted with dual front swivel studs. In 6.5 Creedmoor, .300 Blackout and .308, with a flush, detachable magazine, it lists for $670. *cva.com*

CZ

Recently, CZ's stable of rimfire rifles changed again. The Model 457 supplanted the 455, which had replaced the 452. The 457 has a shorter receiver than the 455 (both boast interchangeable barrels). Its cleanly profiled walnut stock is as handsome as it is accurate. Other CZ rimfires, .22 LR, .22 WMR and .17 HMR, include a 457 Royal sporter in figured walnut with a 20.5-inch threaded barrel. The 457 Premium is a deluxe rifle of European profile in walnut, with a 24.5-inch barrel; the beech-stocked 457 Jaguar has a 28.5-inch threaded barrel. Both these rifles wear adjustable iron sights. The new Varmint Precision Chassis has an alloy chassis, an adjustable AR-type stock and a threaded muzzle.

CZ's big news in 2022 is sad news for hunters enamored of the 550 action with its non-rotating Mauser extractor. Once the company's flagship, it was replaced in all but Magnum and Safari rifles a few years ago by the similar but push-feed 557. I like the 557, too, and have bought two. These traditional CZs — and the lithe, small-action 527 — have been supplanted by a new 600 series of centerfires. The first four 600s to arrive cover many

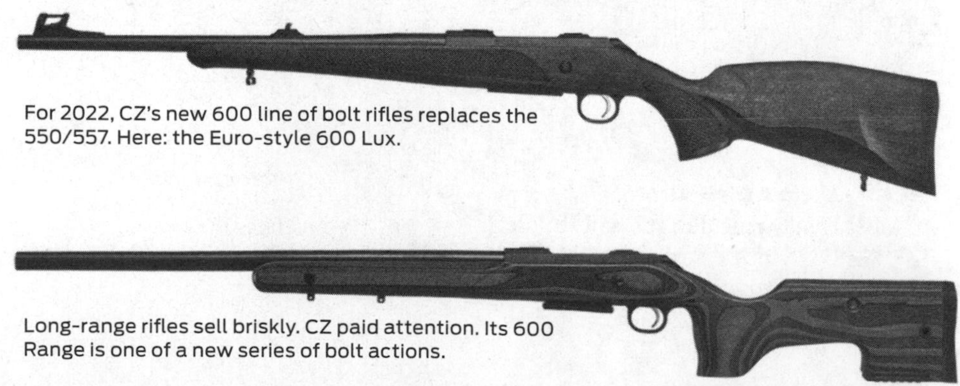

For 2022, CZ's new 600 line of bolt rifles replaces the 550/557. Here: the Euro-style 600 Lux.

Long-range rifles sell briskly. CZ paid attention. Its 600 Range is one of a new series of bolt actions.

Henry's Long Ranger has a multiple-lug rotating bolt and bottles pressures from the .223 and 6.5 Creedmoor.

New for '22: Howa's 4.5-pound Super Lite, with trued action, flush magazine.

uses. The synthetic-stocked Alpha is an all-around sporter, suitable too for long-range shooting. The Lux serves hunters who like its walnut and European profile. The Range is a laminate-stocked "precision rifle." CZ plays to modern tastes with its Trail, a lightweight model on an alloy chassis with a 16-inch barrel and AR-style stock. Priced from $749 to $1,199, all versions feature a lockable magazine and interchangeable barrels. *cz-usa.com*

FRANCHI

A couple of years after introducing its first bolt rifle, The Momentum, Franchi has followed up with an Elite version. Despite the name, this is not a fancy rifle. Nor, at $899, is it expensive. Its chamberings and finishes differ from the base model in .308 and .30-06. The Elite comes in 6.5 Creedmoor and .350 Legend. Both feature Cerakoted metal. The 6.5's stock has Optifade's Elevated II camo pattern. The .350 wears True Timber Strata on the same synthetic stock. Barrel lengths differ: 24 inches for the 6.5 and 22 for the .350. The 6.5 has a brake. Scaling just over 7.5 pounds, both share the mechanical innards of the lighter, less costly standard model. A three-lug bolt feeds from an internal box over a hinged floorplate (hooray!). I like the palm-friendly bolt knob — not so much the stock's fixed, molded sling swivel tabs. The textured grip surfaces and cushy recoil pad are functional. The Momentum balances well. *franchiusa.com*

HENRY REPEATING ARMS

Most Henry rifle designs hail from the 1990s when Anthony Imperato founded the company on an inexpensive lever-action .22 rifle built in the U.S. "It's still a top seller," he said, five years after he'd sold a million of them!

Imperato's ambition and vision have taken the company far. Now it manufactures centerfire lever rifles. Henry Big Boy short-action rifles from under $875 show up at Cowboy Action shoots. My .45-70, on a longer frame, cycles smoothly, punches tight groups and is kinder in recoil than were its forebears. The box-fed Long Ranger has a rotating six-lug bolt head to handle high-velocity rounds like the .223, .243, 6.5 Creedmoor and .308. Ever aware of shifts in the market, Imperato added a side-loading gate to rifles whose magazines first fed from the front. "Both options are popular; we've kept both." Shooters applauded with their checkbooks. Henrys for '22 include synthetic-stocked rifles of traditional profile but with fiber-optic sights, M-LOK slots and forend rail. "Many customers are young, with contemporary tastes," said Imperato. *henryrifles.com*

HOWA

For '22, there's the Howa Super Lite, a 4.5-pound rifle with a "trued" action, a flush, detachable magazine and a slender 20-inch barrel in 6.5 Creedmoor and .308. It has a rail and a featherweight synthetic stock in Kryptek camo. Price: $1,399. *legacysports.com*

MARLIN

Marlin was the sole member of Remington's firearms family not approved for sale to Roundhill Group, LLC by a U.S. bankruptcy court in September 2020. Having just marked its 150th birthday, Marlin would go to Sturm, Ruger two months later. A company spokesman added: "We hope to begin production of Marlin firearms sometime in the second half of 2021."

Well-finished Marlin 1895 rifles from the Ruger shop started showing up in January 2022, pretty much on schedule. I snared one soon after that

Marlin's '95, revived in stainless/laminate form, died with Remington Arms. Ruger has resurrected it.

and am impressed. Clearly, a descendant of Marlins built before the turn of the last century and of follow-ups barely a decade ago, this .45-70 has equally visible departures. The action is essentially the same; the stainless steel and gray-laminate stock are 21st-century.

Ruger has paired the adjustable Skinner aperture sight with a fiber-optic, tritium-assisted front bead and topped the rifle with a new rail for scope mounts. The bolt is fluted and nickel-plated. A slimmer forend and crisp stock detailing (lost during Remington's production) are enhanced by a better stock finish. The receiver was polished more evenly and to a higher gloss. Ruger laser-engraved Marlin's horse-and-rider logo on the grip heel, changed the traditional black and white stock-belly bullseye to red and white, added an "RM" prefix to the serial number and "Mayodan, NC" as the place of manufacture on the threaded 19-inch barrel. Its 1-in-20 rifling is hammer forged now. Like Custom Shop Marlins produced at the Dakota shop in Sturgis, South Dakota, the new 1895 shows careful fitting and has an oversize lever, a practical feature for shooters wearing gloves. Price: $1,399. *marlinfirearms.com*

MOSSBERG

The growing Patriot line of Mossberg bolt rifles now chambers the .350 Legend for deer hunters in states permitting straight-walled cartridges in what were once shotgun-only counties. Fresh walnut- and synthetic-stocked models have 24-inch threaded barrels in 7mm, .300 and .338 Magnum. These appear in Combo scope-and-rifle pairings as well. The MVP Scout, Patrol, Predator and Light Chassis rifles feature AR-style detachable magazines, while the MVP LR has a prone-style stock with an adjustable comb.

New for '22: the MVP .300 Blackout

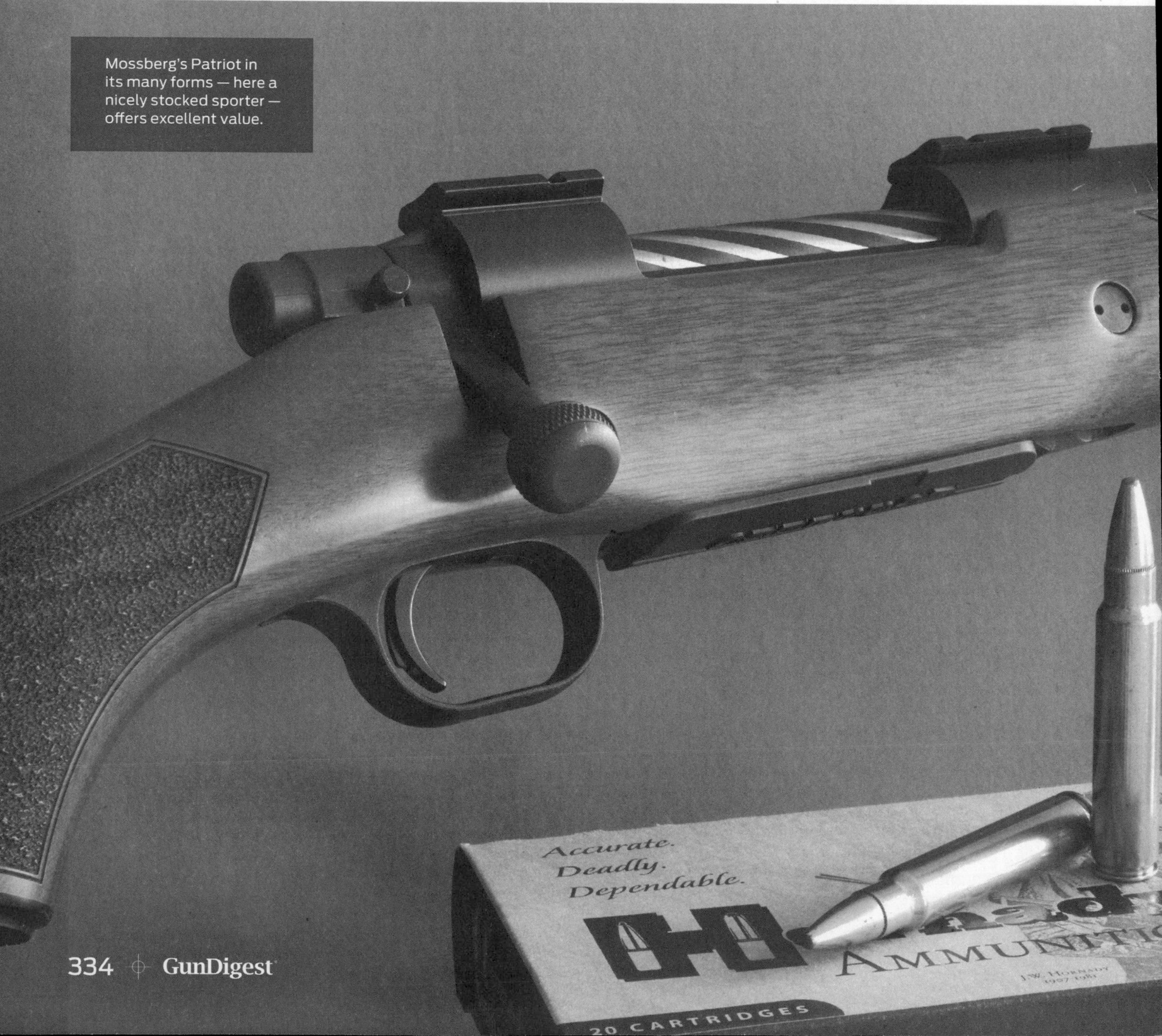

Mossberg's Patriot in its many forms — here a nicely stocked sporter — offers excellent value.

Nosler has added a new Model 21 bolt rifle to its Model 48 series. It comes in 12 chamberings.

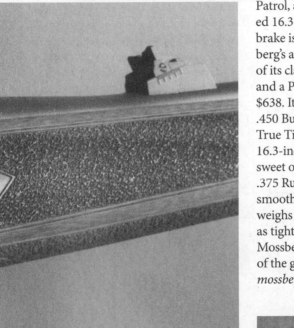

Patrol, a 6.5-pound carbine with a threaded 16.3-inch barrel. An A2-type muzzle brake is included. This model has Mossberg's adjustable LBA trigger like others of its clan. Bolt fluting, a fiber-optic sight and a Picatinny rail are standard. Price: $638. It's similar to the Patriot Predator in .450 Bushmaster, in Flat Dark Earth and True Timber Strata camo, with a threaded 16.3-inch barrel under iron sights. I'm sweet on my walnut-stocked Patriot in .375 Ruger. It balances well, functions smoothly, wears useful iron sights and weighs just 6.5 pounds. It has shot groups as tight as .7 inch. Priced from $396, Mossberg's Patriot series seems to be one of the great bargains in hunting rifles. *mossberg.com*

NOSLER

New from Nosler for '22: the Model 21 rifle. It "blends the best of the Mack Brothers' EVO action" with Nosler features. Its receiver is wire-EDM-machined. It has a fluted one-piece bolt, a TriggerTech trigger and a Picatinny rail. Shilen's match-grade barrel comes in 12 chamberings, 6.5 Creedmoor to .375 H&H. The gray-Cerakoted barreled action snugs into a McMillan carbon-fiber stock. Price: $2,795. *nosler.com*

RUGER

After the company bought everything Marlin during the dissolution of Remington, headline news from Ruger is the re-introduction of Marlin's 1895

In .308 and (here) .450 Bushmaster, the Ruger Scout is now available in .350 Legend.

rifle. It's covered here under the "Marlin" heading.

An insatiable demand for striker-fired pistols has held Ruger's focus, albeit its rifles are selling briskly.

Seven sub-models of the American bolt action come in chamberings from .223 to .300 Winchester. The Hunter features a Magpul stock and muzzle brake. More traditional Americans start at just $489. The growing list of chamberings now includes the straight-walled .350 Legend and .450 Bushmaster, also the 6.5 PRC and .25-06. Five rimfire Americans, in .22 LR, .22 WMR and .17 HMR, include a Long Range Target version.

Long shooting continues to drive rifle design and sales. The Ruger Precision Rifle (RPR) is now available in magnum chamberings and 6mm Creedmoor. A Long-Range Hunter, the progeny of the Long-Range Target, but with a 22-inch sporting-weight barrel, has joined the Hawkeye series. Picatinny rails with 20 minutes of gain ensure plenty of vertical adjustment for long zeros. Hawkeyes have non-rotating Mauser extractors, fixed ejectors, and three-position safeties. Unlike early M77s, feeding is truly controlled, follower to chamber. New 77-Series rifles come in .17 WSM and .17 and .22 Hornet, and in .357 and .44 Magnum, the latter two with iron sights on 18 ½-inch barrels. Ruger's Scout rifle and its AR-556 are now bored to .350 Legend (the AR-556 also to .300 BLK and .450 Bushmaster, at $799). Ruger's No. 1 rifle is available in limited numbers annually, in one chambering, save for "distributor specials." *ruger.com*

SAVAGE

New from Savage for '22 is the 110 Magpul Hunter in 6.5 Creedmoor and .308. It pairs a stiff 18-inch barrel with a blueprinted 110 action and a Magpul stock adjustable for length and comb height. The forend has M-LOK slots, the receiver a Picatinny rail. Fed by an AICS magazine, the bore features fast-twist rifling for long bullets. This new 9-pound rifle costs $1,049. *savagearms.com*

SIG SAUER

A new bolt-action rifle from handgun giant Sig Sauer was designed for hunters and Precision Rifle Series (PRS) shooters. The 6.5-pound Cross has a one-piece alloy receiver, a removable Picatinny rail, and a detachable magazine. Its skeletal folding stock adjusts for length and comb height. An AR-style handguard has M-LOK slots. The 18-inch stainless threaded barrel in 6.5 Creedmoor (or 16-inch barrel in .308 or SIG's .277 Fury) puts collapsed length at 27 (or 25) inches. A two-stage match trigger helps you wring all the accuracy from the Cross. It comes in a black anodized finish at $1,600 and Lite Cipher Armorkote at $1,800. What's the .277 Fury? It is essentially a .270 based on the .308 case and has a unique two-part hull whose steel head is designed to bottle very high pressures. At 80,000 psi, the .277 Fury flings 140-grain bullets at 3,000 fps from a 16-inch barrel. Cases are costly but, of course, reloadable. *sigsauer.com*

VOLQUARTSEN

Specializing in super-accurate self-loading rimfire rifles, Volquartsen welcomed 2022 with a new switch-barrel rifle in .22 WMR and .17 HMR. The VT2 has an alloy receiver, a slender 16.5-inch barrel, and a Magpul stock with M-LOK slots. The clever button-and-lever mechanism makes a barrel change a snap — "no tools, twists or tightening." Push the button, pull the lever, and slip the barrel from the receiver. Re-install that barrel or insert another, then bring the lever back up! The VT2 costs $2,352 with one barrel or $2,871 with both. A lot of money for a rimfire? Volquartsen's in .22 LR, .17 Mach 2, .22 WMR and .17 HMR — and now .17 WSM — have match-rifle refinements, deliver one-hole accuracy. CNC and EDM machining ensures precise fit of tungsten alloy bolts to stainless and alloy receivers. Counterweighted bolts for the WMR ensure fault-free cycling. Rotary magazines feed silkily. Compensators are available on stainless and carbon-fiber barrels. Volquartsen's TG2000 trigger adjusts to 2.3 pounds and breaks like thin ice. Stocks of synthetics and laminates include thumbhole profiles. *volquartsen.com*

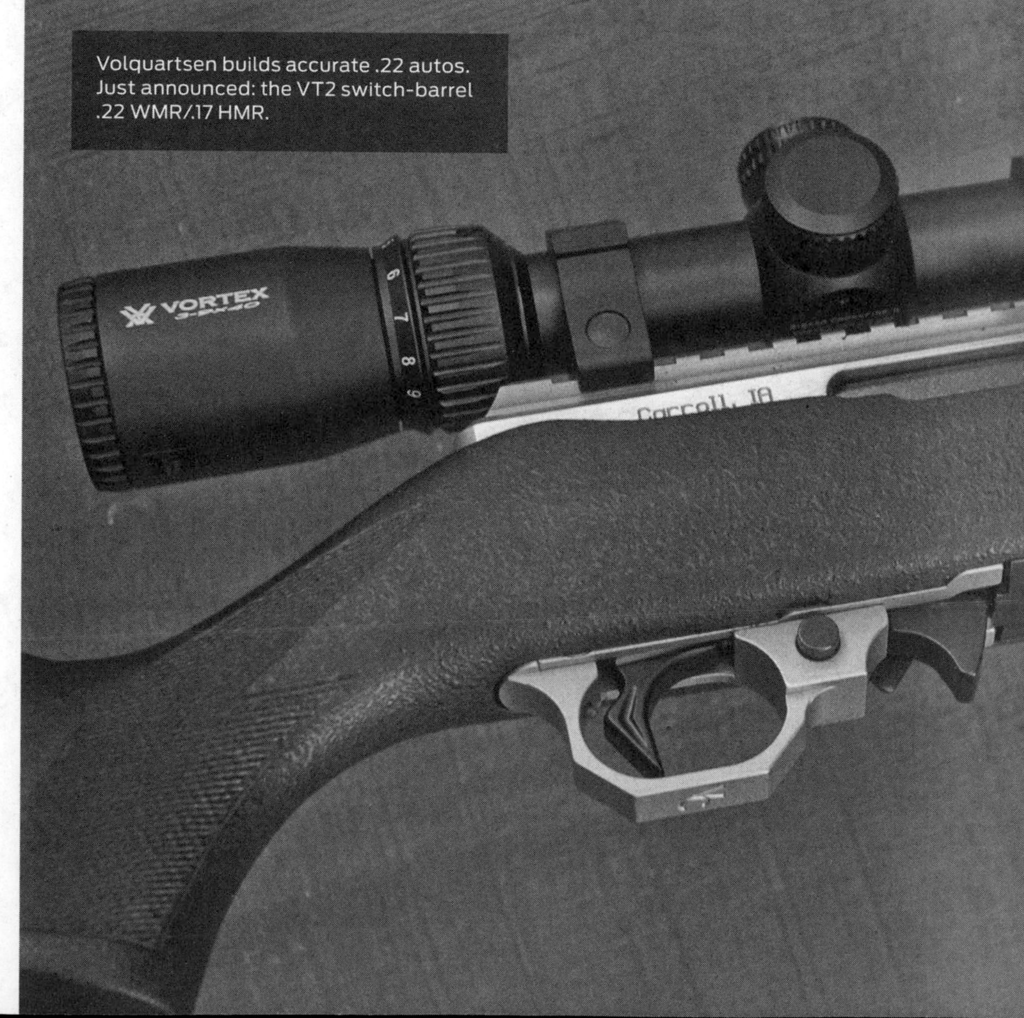

Volquartsen builds accurate .22 autos. Just announced: the VT2 switch-barrel .22 WMR/.17 HMR.

The push-feed Winchester XPR, now in several forms, has Winchester's excellent M.O.A. trigger.

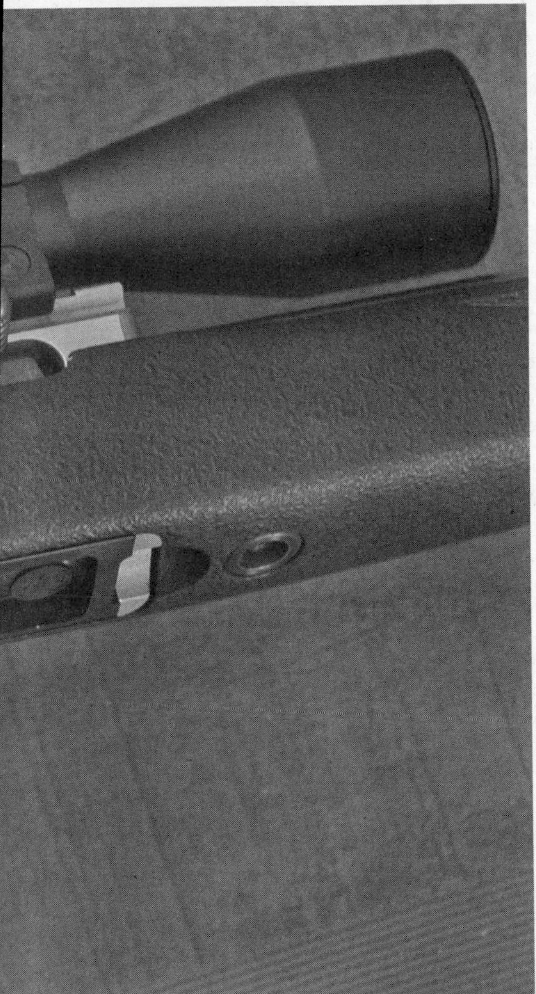

WINCHESTER

Model 70 bolt rifles include the Extreme Weather SS (stainless steel, synthetic stock) in 14 chamberings, at $1,339 for standard cartridges and $1,379 for magnums. The Extreme Weather MB and Long Range MB ("MB" for "muzzle brake") arrived in 2021 from $1,560. The Extreme Midnight MB is new for '22. Winchester's Super Grade Model 70 now comes in 13 chamberings, the same as the 70 Featherweight. Both wear walnut. Super grades get figured wood and high metal polish and list for $1,550. Featherweight and Featherweight Compact rifles come in at $1,090. Walnut-stocked Safari Express 70s in .375 H&H, .416 Rem. Mag. and .458 Win. Mag. retail for $1,680. Alaskan rifles, .30-06 to .375, start at $1,490. All Model 70s now have the original non-rotating extractor for controlled feed. The push-feed XPR is now a clan of 18 variations, each with a full-diameter, three-lug bolt, nickel Teflon-coated for slick travel in a receiver machined from bar stock. Cartridges strip from a single-stack detachable box you can feed from the top! A two-position safety blocks Winchester's excellent M.O.A trigger.

The Sporter is in walnut. Like the Compact, the 6.8-pound Hunter Strata True Timber ($750), Hunter Mossy Oak DNA ($650) and Extreme Hunter ($770) wear synthetic stocks. They've recently added the .350 Legend to their lists of more than a dozen chamberings, from .223. The Thumbhole Varmint is bored for nine cartridges, .223 to .30-06, weighs 8 pounds and retails for $860. The Renegade Long Range SR, with a prone stock, oversize bolt knob, and the stiff, threaded barrel, comes in at 8.5 pounds in six short-action chamberings, .243 to .300 WSM. Price: $1,090. *winchesterguns.com* GD

- REPORTS - from the Field AR-STYLE RIFLES

› TODD WOODARD

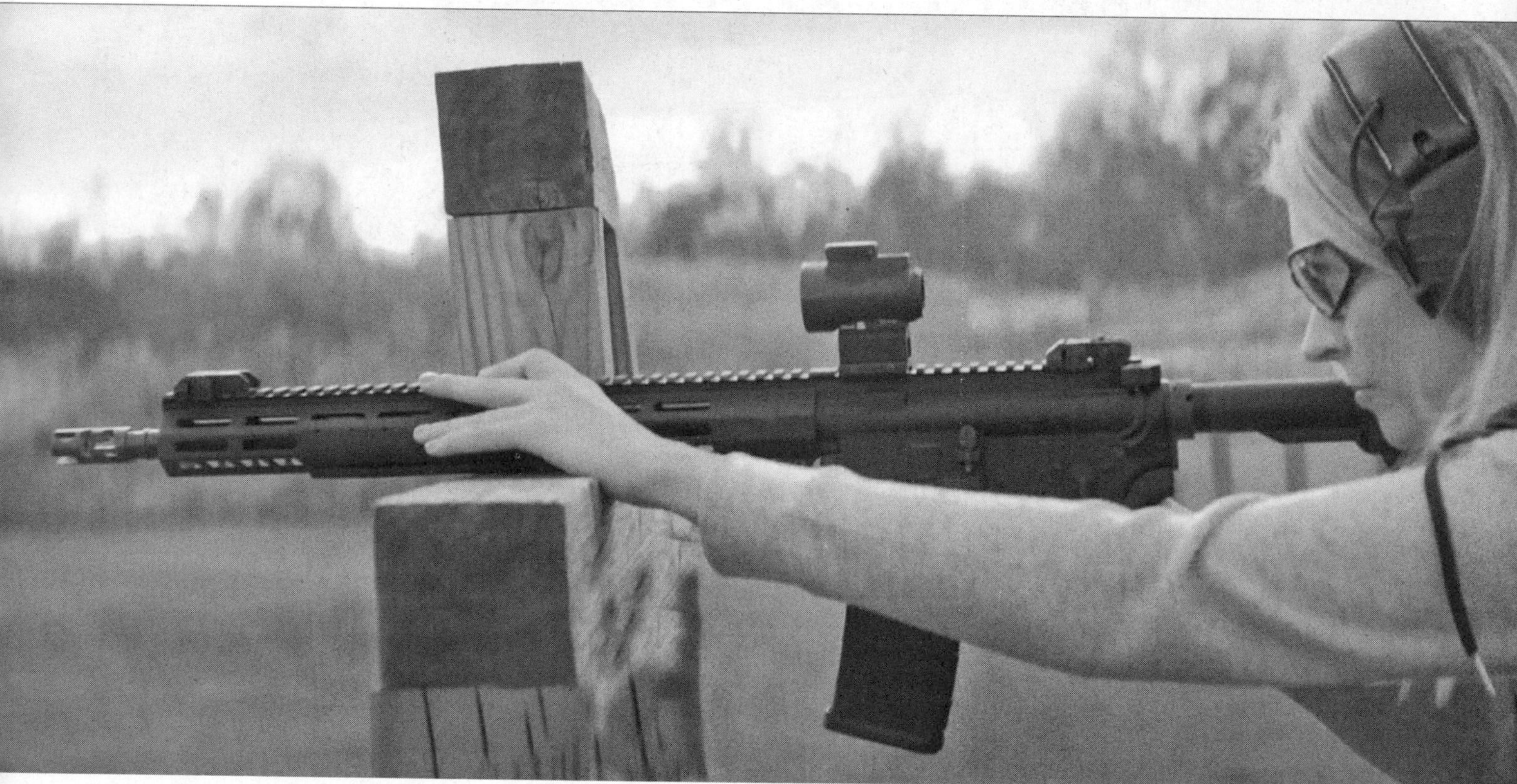

What a difference a year makes. President Joe Biden has been in power for two years now, and he hasn't made a move yet to take away our AR-15s. Amazing, but his term is young.

Those of us who own and enjoy ARs wonder what such ban fusses are all about. The rifles are simply lightweight, customizable shooting tools that are accurate and easy to maintain — my Daniel Defense rifle more so than others. I've never cleaned her, and she ticks along just fine with thousands of rounds under her belt. Yes, I'm ashamed to admit that — I used to clean my Walther every 40 shots — but now it's a point of honor for Double-D .223. Someday the Daniel Defense will hiccup, and I'll break down and do the takedown she so richly deserves. "Just not today," as Lieutenant Alex Hopper observes in *Battleship*.

Shortages for all firearms in 2020 seem to have eased considerably in 2021 and 2022, and supply has caught up. Here are a few ARs you might want to check out.

2A Armament Xanthos Lite XLR-20 rifle.

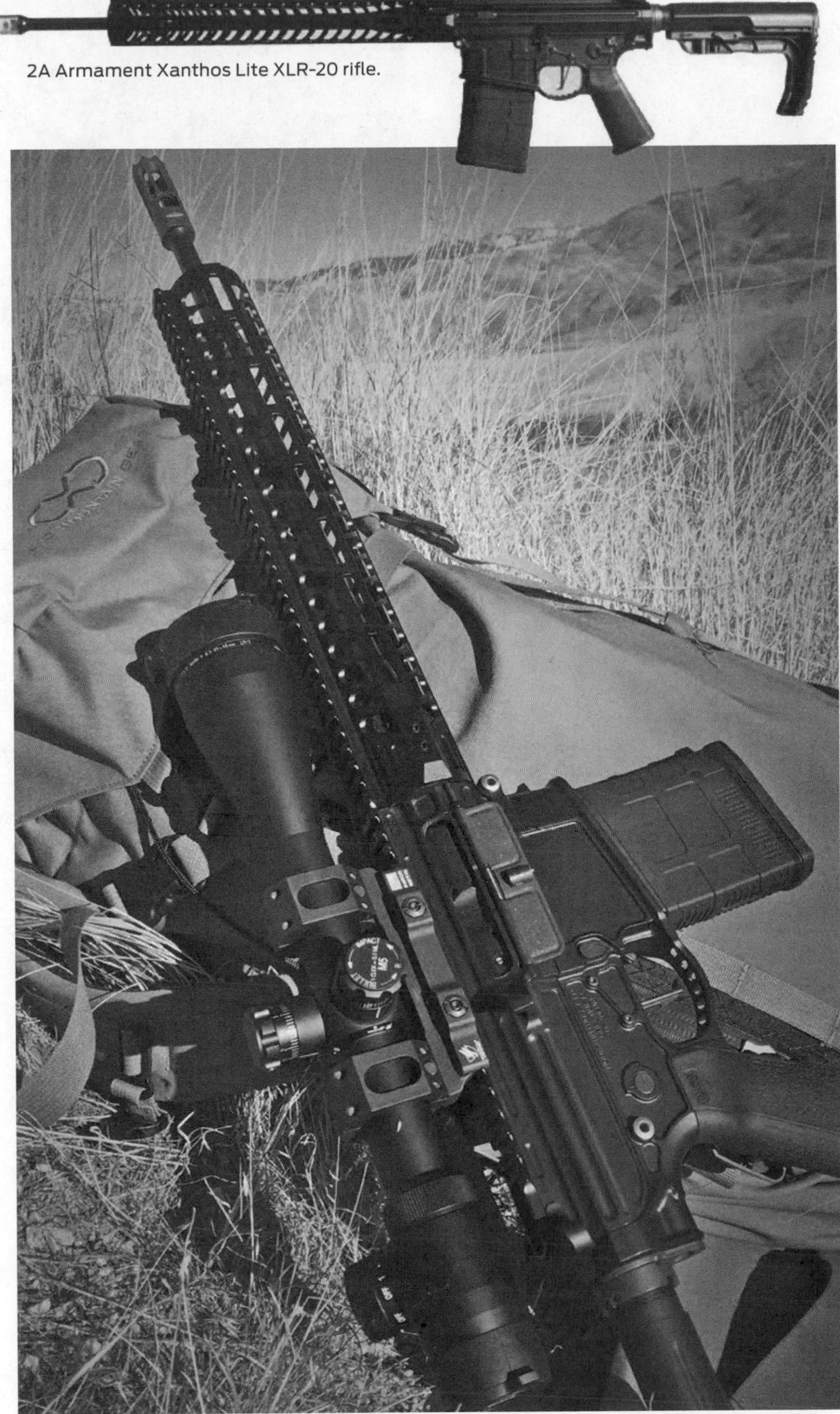

The Adams Arms P3.

2A ARMAMENT

Based in Boise, 2A Armament is an advanced machine shop for the aerospace, medical, prosthetic, motorsports, semiconductor and outdoor recreation markets. One of its innovative long arms is the Xanthos Lite XLR-20 chambered in 6.5mm Creedmoor. This fully assembled rifle weighs in at only 6.85 pounds, lighter than many AR-15s. It loses weight because of a straight-cut Xanthos Lite Rail and several titanium parts, including the gas block, takedown pins, and the X4 brake. The machined billet lower receiver has a flared magwell, and the upper has a "slick side" design, retained port door rod, M4-style feed ramps, and machined T numbers in its Picatinny rail. The 20-inch light-contour barrel has a rifle-length gas system, a 6.5mm Creedmoor SAAMI chamber for widespread ammo acceptance, and a 1:8 twist. The giggle switch is a Timney two-stage flat trigger that can be set down to 2 pounds. MSRP, $2,724. *2A-arms.com*

ADAMS ARMS

The Adams Arms Retro-Fit Piston Drive System uses a gas port on the barrel to work the action of an inverted piston. Instead of directing the gases into the receiver, they go into a gas plug and drive a rod sleeve Adams Arms invented. The gases are contained inside the drive rod sleeve and push the bolt carrier rearward, using the gas pressure to cycle the action. Thus, the Adams Arms proprietary gas-piston operating system mechanically actuates the bolt carrier outside the receiver. This keeps the internal receiver and all the critical moving parts clean and free from heat and carbon build-up.

The Adams Arms P3 is the performance, match-grade model in the P-Series lineup. The .224 Valkyrie FGAA-00434-R has a 20-inch Proof Research carbon-fiber-wrapped barrel, a jet comp, an ergonomic free-float rail, and a P-Series Low Profile Adjustable Piston System. There's also an ambidextrous safety selector, an ambidextrous charging handle, a flat-faced CMC trigger, an Ergo grip, and an adjustable LUTH-AR stock with a cheek riser. MSRP is $2,800. *adamsarms.net*

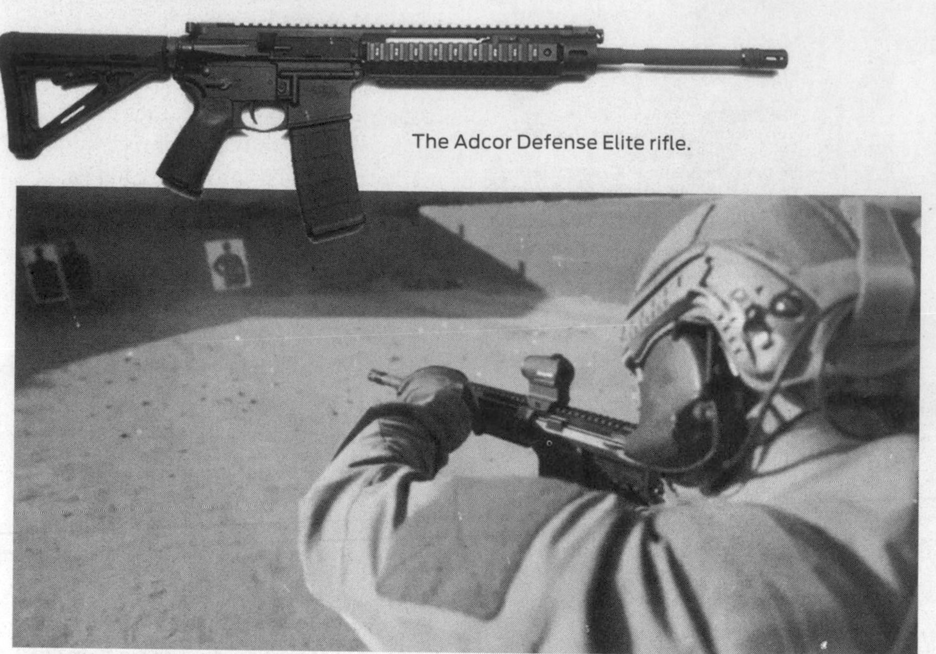
The Adcor Defense Elite rifle.

American Tactical Milsport .410 semi-auto shotgun.

ADCOR DEFENSE

Adcor Defense, Inc. of Baltimore, Maryland, is a national defense contractor for the Trident missile system, radar system components for the F-16 fighter, and other components for the U.S. military small arms industrial base. The Adcor Elite rifle has a revolutionary gas-piston system differing from other M4-type ARs. The gas-driven piston is incorporated into the upper half of the forward rail system. That allows shooters to keep their strong hand on the firearm and use the other hand to clear the rifle. The ambidextrous charging handle detaches easily without special tools and returns to a locked position once used. It folds forward, recessed, and easily swings back in a single motion. The handle is non-reciprocating and only engages when the operator charges or clears the rifle. MSRP: $2,300. *adcordefense.com*

ALEX PRO FIREARMS

Alex Pro Firearms makes several unusual long-action rifles chambered for the MLR (Magnum Long Rifle) line, such as 26 Nosler, 28 Nosler, 30 Nosler, 33 Nosler, 7mm Rem. Mag, and .300 Win. Mag. Building a semi-auto AR platform for a powerful long-distance round like the 7mm Remington Magnum is not easy. The MLR is a lightweight semi-auto platform that offers high-quality craftsmanship, pinpoint precision, and modern options. It comes in at 9.8 pounds with a 22-inch barrel and includes a CMC 3.5 Flatblade Trigger, a Luth-AR MBA-2 fixed stock, and a 15.5-inch MLOK handguard. As far as accessories, the MLR includes a rollable hard case and four APF five-round magazines. MSRP: $3,000. *apfarmory.com*

AMERICAN TACTICAL, INC.

Summerville, SC-based American Tactical, Inc. manufactures and imports firearms. What caught my eye in its lineup was the Milsport 410 semi-auto shotgun, which has a patented .410-gauge modular upper receiver and is chambered for 2 ½-inch .410-gauge shells. Featuring an 18.5-inch barrel with a custom 13-inch Keymod rail, the Milsport .410 runs on a gas-operated short-stroke balanced piston system. Each Milsport 410 comes with one five-round American Tactical polymer magazine. (It will only operate with the patent-pending American Tactical polymer .410 magazine. Okay. Down with that.) Also, every Milsport .410 can be converted to 5.56 or .300 BLK by changing the upper receiver, which is built to standard AR specs and can be installed on most mil-spec lowers. $800.00 MSRP. *americantactical.us*

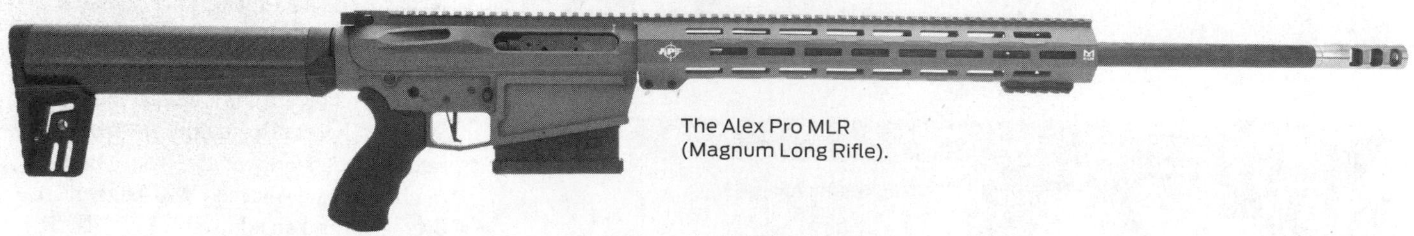
The Alex Pro MLR (Magnum Long Rifle).

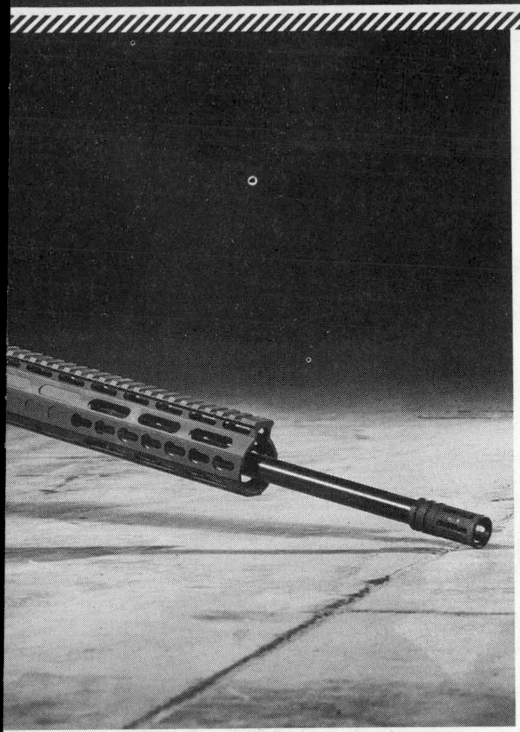

Armalite M-15 Competition Rifle.

Bravo Company BCM MK12, based on the US Navy MK12 Mod 0 Special Purpose Rifle (SPR).

Anderson Manufacturing AM-15.

ANDERSON MANUFACTURING

Anderson Manufacturing AM-15.

You likely didn't know that Anderson Manufacturing was ranked number one in Miscellaneous Firearms Production in 2019 with 342,271 firearms, frames or receivers, etc., that are not identified as particular firearms. Anderson is so successful in this segment because it offers a lot of choices for the handy rifle builder, everything from an assembled A2 lower ($421) to an AM-15 assembled lower receiver minus buffer system, no logo lower receiver ($112). It also sells stripped lowers, 80-percent lowers, and lower receiver parts. But I have my eye on the AM-15 assembled M4 lower receiver, FDE Magpul MOE furniture, $233. *andersonmanufacturing.com*

ARMALITE

Among the well-appointed rifles in the Armalite lineup is the M-15 Competition Rifle, built for 3-Gun and practical rifle competition in either 13.5- or 18-inch barrels. This rifle is highly customizable, with an adjustable gas block and tunable muzzle brake to allow the rifle to be easily modified for specific purposes or ammunition. The lightweight MBA-1 buttstock features an adjustable cheekpiece and length-of-pull. A Timney 4-pound single-stage trigger and Ergo wide grip come standard. $1,450. *armalite.com*

BARRETT

Barrett's REC10 Carbine echoes design cues from the REC7 5.56 rifles, but this is a well-thought-out AR-10-style gun, not just an upsized AR-15. The barrel is a chrome-lined button-rifled 16-inch version to save a little weight on this 8-pound shooter. The handguard, an M-LOK design, is lightweight while providing plenty of room for lights, laser aiming devices, or other accessories. For a tight fit, the upper and lower receivers are machined from billet 7075-T6 aluminum. The REC10 also uses a DLC-treated bolt-carrier group and a chrome-lined chamber. The twist rate is 1:10 to stabilize the .308 Win., and the rifle measures 37.75 inches OAL. The colors are black, FDE, and gray Cerakote. *barrett.net*

BRAVO COMPANY MFG.

One of the often-overlooked products in BCM's stable is the MK12, a heavily modified designated marksman-type rifle designed to extend the effective range of the M4 carbine without having to use a 20-inch barrel. Based on the US Navy MK12 Mod 0 Special Purpose Rifle (SPR), the BCM MK12 features a hand-lapped 1:8 twist rate, button-rifled 18-inch barrel with M4 feed ramp barrel extensions. The barrel sits inside a PRI Gen III 12-inch handguard constructed of lightweight, high-strength carbon fiber and aluminum that reduces heat transfer from rapid or high-volume fire. A steel top rail matches the height of a standard flat top receiver for an optimized combination of weight and strength. $2,550. *bravocompanyusa.com*

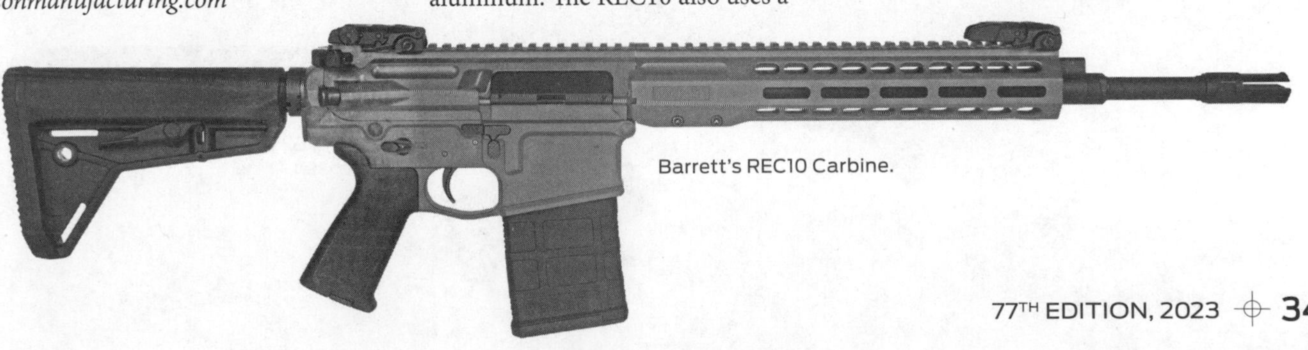

Barrett's REC10 Carbine.

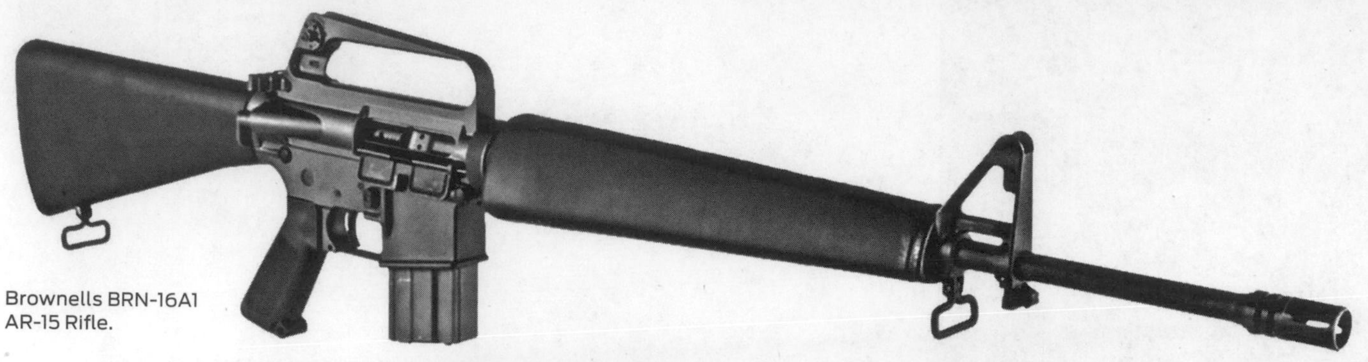

Brownells BRN-16A1 AR-15 Rifle.

BROWNELLS

The Brownells BRN-16A1 AR-15 Rifle pays tribute to the classic arm that filled the hands of thousands of U.S. military members during the war in Vietnam, providing modern-day enthusiasts with a faithful reproduction of the classic M16A1 design. Available as a kit starting in 2022, the Brownells BRN-16A1 AR-15 Rifle is a near-exact reproduction of the completed M16A1 introduced in 1967 and used well into the 1980s as the standard rifle of the U.S. Armed Forces. The rifle is constructed from all-new parts, not relying on any surplus components, and features the magazine fence, chromed bore and chamber, and an A1-style flash hider. The Brownells BRN-16A Rifle also features the mil-spec phosphate bolt-carrier group and a 1:12-inch rate of twist and gray-Cerakote receiver. Chambered in 5.56 NATO. Length: 40 inches. Weight: 6.8 lbs. $1,300. *brownells.com*

CMMG 350 Legend.

CHRISTENSEN ARMS

Based in Gunnison, Utah, Christensen Arms developed the first carbon-fiber rifle barrel, so its barrels are of particular interest. One, the $1,700 CA5five6 build, has a .223 Wylde chamber in a Christensen Arms carbon-fiber-wrapped 16-inch 1:8-twist stainless barrel. Set in a carbon-aluminum hybrid handguard, it only weighs 6.3 pounds. But wait, there's less: The CA-15 G2 is a custom-built AR-style rifle with a matched receiver set, contour-matching carbon-fiber handguard, and carbon-fiber barrel that weighs 5.8 pounds. $1,800. *christensenarms.com*

CMMG

For the deer hunter who is limited to straight-wall cartridges, CMMG has a rifle solution chambered in .350 Legend. The .350 Legend was developed to meet straight-wall case hunting regulations in states that do not allow bottleneck centerfire cartridges. The .350 Legend is the fastest SAAMI-approved, straight-walled cartridge. The increased velocity flattens trajectory, and it features

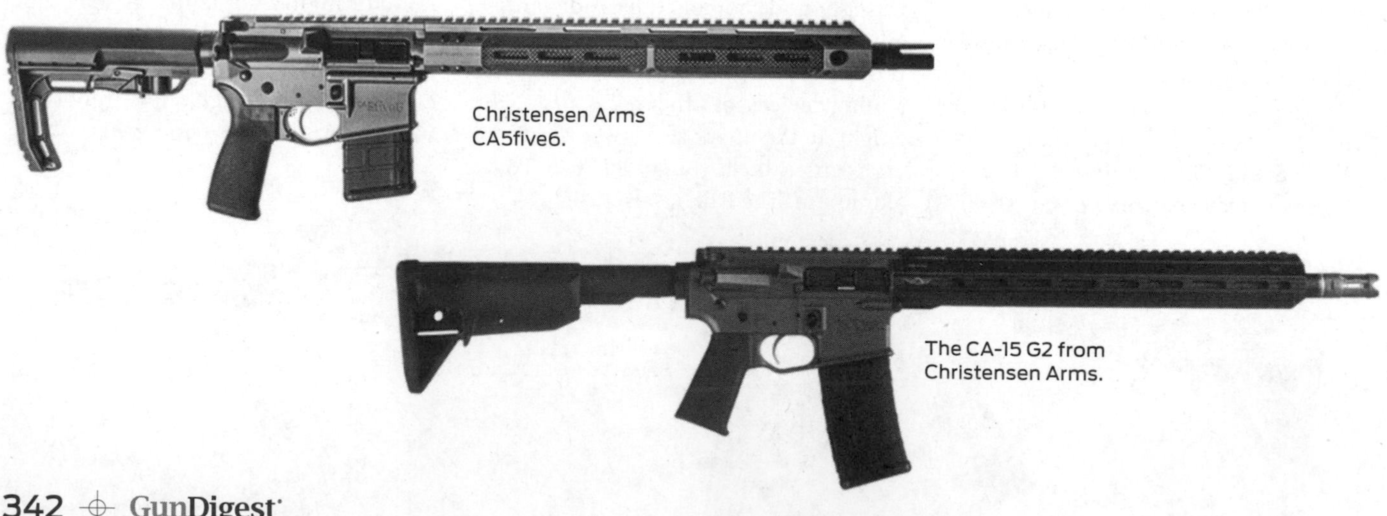

Christensen Arms CA5five6.

The CA-15 G2 from Christensen Arms.

Daniel Defense FDE M4A1.

more energy than the .30-30, .300 BLK and .223 with less recoil than the .450 Bushmaster, .30-30 and .243 Win. CMMG .350 Legend-chambered rifles are found in the Resolute platform, with three series options available. Also, fitted with a charging handle and bolt carrier groups, .350 Legend upper receiver groups are offered, with three series options. For those building their own AR from scratch, 16.1-inch barrels can be had. Finally, for any .350 Legend owner, CMMG has 5-, 10-, or 20-round magazines available. *cmmg.com*

DANIEL DEFENSE

As mentioned, I own an older DD rifle and wouldn't mind replacing it. I'm currently considering a new one in either the M4A1, MK12, or MK18 denominations, and all three are part of Daniel Defense's DDM4 line and chambered in 5.56mm NATO. They feature Picatinny rails, cold hammer-forged barrels, Daniel Defense's rubber overmolded pistol grip and buttstock, and an ambidextrous safety selector. I'm leaning toward the FDE M4A1, which has an M4 profile 14.5-inch barrel with a permanent pinned and welded extended flash hider that extends the overall barrel length to 16 inches, so it is not an SBR. Its gas system is carbine-length, and the RIS II Rail System is exceptionally robust. The bolt-up system in the back of the rifle features six connection points that allow the rail to free-float and not interfere with barrel harmonics. With an overall length of 31.5 to 34.75 inches and a weight of 6.74 pounds, this is a well-rounded rifle suitable for the uses I need most. Yes, at $2,128, it's spendy, but DD offers financing to spread that out. *danieldefense.com*

RUGER

Sturm, Ruger has made an exciting upgrade to its AR-556 line by chambering the .300 Blackout round in its free-float-handguard rifle lineup. I enjoy shooting the .300 BLK in light rifles because the round doesn't pound the shoulder like other larger chamberings above the 5.56.

Beyond the chambering, the rifle free floats inside the 11-inch aluminum handguard, which has Magpul M-LOK accessory attachment slots along the 3-, 6- and 9-o'clock positions and additional slots on the angled faces near the muzzle. Also helpful is the flattop upper receiver with a full Picatinny top rail for easy attachment of magnified optic, red dot, or open sights. Inside, the 9310-steel bolt is shot-peened and proof-tested, and the bolt carrier is made of 8620 steel. The inside diameter of the carrier and gas key are chrome plated, and the key is staked for longevity. The heavy-contour, cold hammer-forged 4140 chrome-moly steel barrel should provide exceptional accuracy with the .300 Blackout. It comes with one 30-round metal magazine. Price: $1,009. *ruger.com*

Ruger AR-556 in .300 BLK.

The Smith & Wesson Volunteer XV Pro 16.

SMITH & WESSON

A new lineup of Smith & Wesson Modern Sporting Rifles has launched, and the company's M&P Volunteer line of rifles pays homage to S&W's soon-to-be new home state of Tennessee, the Volunteer State. There are four groups of rifles: Volunteer XV, Volunteer XV OR, Volunteer XV PRO, and Volunteer XV DMR. At launch, there are 11 models across the families. Currently, each is chambered in 5.56mm NATO/.223 Rem. with 1:8 twist, 5R rifling in the tubes. I'm interested in the Volunteer XV Pro rifles equipped with a mid-length gas system and a 15-inch free-floated handguard equipped with M-LOK slots. The XV Pro also has a B5 pistol grip and includes a B5 Sopmod stock. *smith-wesson.com*

SPRINGFIELD ARMORY

Springfield Armory's new Saint Edge rifles with .223 Wylde chambers are a departure for ARs. First, these are chassis rifles; in fact, the ATC stands for "Accurized Tactical Chassis." Springfield is confident enough to guarantee sub-MOA accuracy for three shots with match-grade ammunition. Of course, the shooter has to do their part. The chassis system comprises a one-piece monolithic lower machined from 6061 T6 aluminum. The free-floated design ensures that the barrel, barrel nut, and gas system don't touch the lower chassis. There's also an Accu-Tite Plus tensioning system — an adjustable set of conical set screws in the lower — eliminating any play between the upper receiver and lower chassis.

The Saint Edge ATC Elite Coyote Brown variant features a LaRue two-stage trigger and collapsible B5 Systems Precision Stock, B5 Systems Type 23 P-Grip and 20-round Magpul PMAG. Both ATC models' barrels are 18 inches and are manufactured by Ballistic Advantage. They have a 1:7 rate of twist to stabilize longer bullets and a Melonite coating. The .223 Wylde chamber can fire .223 and 5.56 NATO, but with a chamber throat that is tight enough to wring the most performance out of match-grade ammunition. The Saint Edge ATC Elite comes in at an MSRP of $1,899. *springfield-armory.com* GD

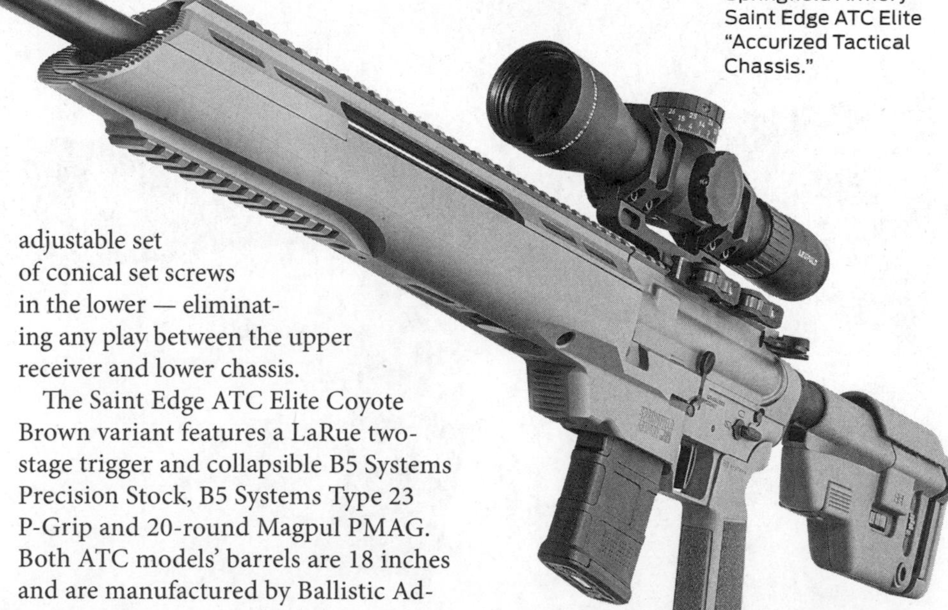

Springfield Armory Saint Edge ATC Elite "Accurized Tactical Chassis."

- REPORTS - from the Field SEMI-AUTO PISTOLS

›ROBERT SADOWSKI

There are plenty of new semi-auto pistols available this year, including this gold-accented Canik Rival.

The CZ TS 2 in racing green color.

We had just finished mourning the loss of the Browning Hi-Power when Springfield Armory decided to introduce a new clone of the iconic pistol. Then, FN, the original manufacturer of the Hi-Power, did the classic pistol one better with a reworked design. I've run the SA-35 and can on-ly say I am smitten. The only question is: Do we call it a Hi-Power or High Power?

There were other new semi-auto pistol happenings: Look for micro nines that are red-dot ready from H&K, Taurus, Mossberg, SCCY, SIG and others. These compact pistols are excellent for concealed carry. Kimber and Springfield Armory continue to evolve the 1911 platform with new releases. The Kimber Rapide series is a beautiful yet highly functional line. The Emissary from Springfield Armory brings near-custom gun quality direct from the factory. Brands like CZ, Browning and Canik are pushing the envelope on competition pistols. What's new in semi-automatic pistols? Read on.

BROWNING

Get your rimfire competition on with the new Buck Mark Plus Vision Americana Suppressor Ready (MSRP $799.99). It features an anodized blue receiver with white stars and cutout stripes revealing a red barrel. Includes a Picatinny optics rail, suppressor-ready threaded barrel, muzzle brake, UFX overmolded grips, fiber-optic front sight and adjustable rear sight with white outline. The Buck Mark Plus Vision Black/Gold Suppressor Ready (MSRP $749.99) has all the features of the Americana but with a matte black frame and barrel sleeve with diamond shape cutouts that reveal a gold barrel. *browning.com*

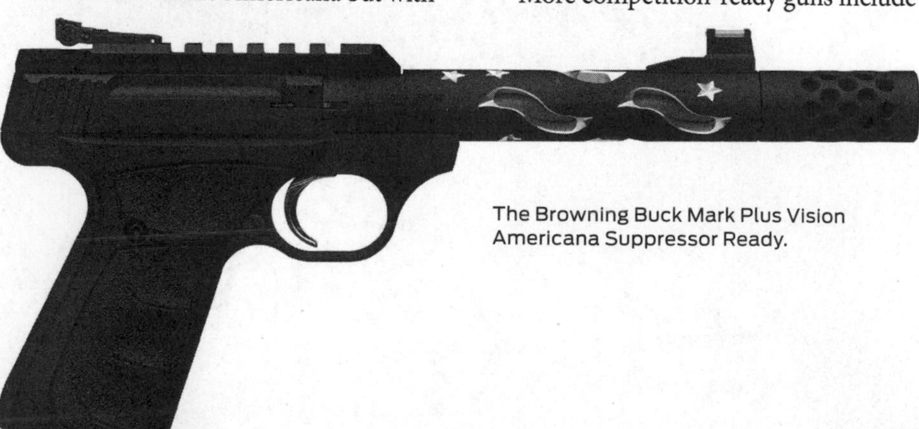

The Browning Buck Mark Plus Vision Americana Suppressor Ready.

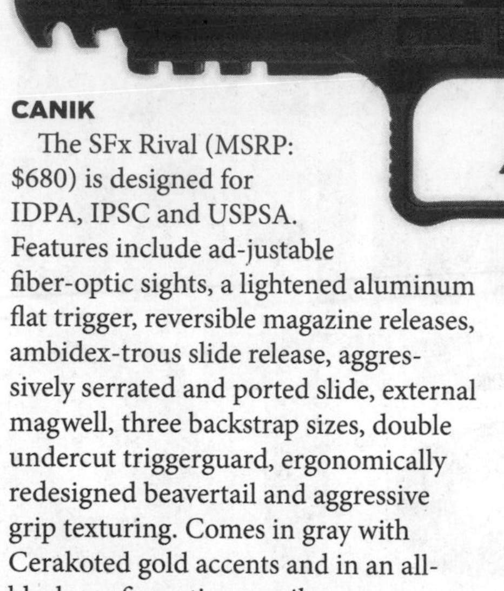

The Canik Rival.

CANIK

The SFx Rival (MSRP: $680) is designed for IDPA, IPSC and USPSA. Features include ad-justable fiber-optic sights, a lightened aluminum flat trigger, reversible magazine releases, ambidex-trous slide release, aggressively serrated and ported slide, external magwell, three backstrap sizes, double undercut triggerguard, ergonomically redesigned beavertail and aggressive grip texturing. Comes in gray with Cerakoted gold accents and in an all-black configuration. *canikusa.com*

CZ-USA

The P-10 F Competition-Ready (MSRP: $1,009) is built for speed and accuracy. This 9mm is built on a full-size P-10 F frame with a half-inch longer barrel and slide for an extended sight radi-us. Features include fiber-optic front sight and fixed serrated rear sight, optics ready, Apex Tactical extended magazine catch, extended slide stop, and HB Industries trigger. Comes with a matte black finish and gold accents on the barrel, slide cover and trigger. Ships three magazines equipped with aluminum Henning Group bases.

CZ P10 F Competition-Ready.

More competition-ready guns include an updated CZ TS 2 (MSRP: $1,695) built on the clas-sic but highly modified CZ 75 frame. This racer features a slide profile like the Shadow 2, so recip-rocating weight is focused as low as possible. Chambered in 9mm and 40 S&W. The CZ TS 2 Racing Green (MSRP: $2,055) is an evolution of the new TS2, bringing in some critical features like thin green anodized aluminum grips, magazines with green anodized bases, height-adjustable rear sight, extended left-side safety, thumb rest, flat side stop and adjustable green magazine re-lease. Also new to the P-10 series is the P-10 M (MSRP: $505), a concealed carry 9mm with an internal slide stop. No controls or levers are on either side of the gun other than the magazine re-lease. This helps prevent any part of the pistol from snagging on clothing during the draw. *cz-usa.com*

Heckler & Koch VP9-SK.

HECKLER & KOCH

HK's new VP9-SK (MSRP: $899-$999) is now optics-ready and is compatible with virtually any red-dot optic. Two variants are offered, one with night sights and three magazines (two 13-round and one 10-round) and the second with two mags (one 13-round and one 10-round). *heckler-koch.com*

FN

The High Power legend is reborn. FN — the original manufacturer of the famed High Power 9mm — has introduced a modern update to one of the world's most-trusted single-action combat pistols. The new High Power (MSRP: $1,269–$1,369) has improved ergonomics and controls and a more straightforward take-down design. It comes with steel sights, two sets of G10 grips and two 17-round magazines, and you can get it in stainless steel, blued or FDE.

Want some low-cost rimfire fun? The new 502 Tactical (MSRP: $519.00) is FN's first .22 LR pistol, and it comes tricked out with tactical features. The slide is optics-ready with co-witness iron sights, 15-round magazine, front slide serrations, accessory rail and threaded barrel. The hammer-fired 502 has a similar weight to its 9mm big brother, the 509, so while having fun, you can also train with the 502. Comes in FDE and black with 10- and 15-round magazines. *fnamerica.com*

Kel-Tec P15.

KEL-TEC

There's a new 9mm striker-fire in town called the P15 (MSRP: $425). Kel Tec's new compact pistol has a 15+1 capacity; the flush-fit magazine holds 12 rounds. Sights consist of tritium and fiber-optic front with a fully adjustable, tritium, two-dot rear. *keltecweapons.com*

MOSSBERG

The MC2 series of compact striker-fired 9mms now has two new models. The MC2sc (MSRP: $556.00) features 3-dot sights and is optics-ready. It also has a 10-round flush-fit maga-zine and a 14-round extended magazine. The MC2sc TruGlo (MSRP: $662) is set up with TruG-loc Tritium Pro Night sights and is also optics-ready. *mossberg.com*

Mossberg MC2sc.

Kimber Micro 9 Rapide in black.

KIMBER

Kimber's entrant into the world of high-capacity micro nines is the R7 Mako O.R (MSRP: $599.00) with TruGlo night sights and the R7 Mako O.I. (MSRP: $799.00) that comes with a Crimson Trace CTS-1500 red dot co-witnessed with TruGlo night sights. Both striker-fired pistols feature polymer frames, 11-round flush-fit magazines and 13-round extended magazines. Kimber's Performance Carry Trigger also features a smooth, consistent pull and clean break. Kimber gives the O.I. treatment to both the Micro 9 Black OI (MSRP: $905) and Micro 9 Stainless OI (MSRP: $904); these micro 9mm pistols are factory-fitted with a Swampfox Sentinel Optic red dot.

Other new Micro 9 models include the Rapide treatment of stepped cocking serrations and slide lightening cuts to four Micro 9 models. The Micro 9 Rapide (Black Ice) (MSRP: $986) has a Black KimPro finish, TiN-coated barrel and flush-fitting magwell; the Micro 9 Rapide (MSRP: $986) has a black finish with gold accents; the Micro 9 Rapide Dawn (MSRP: $986) wears a strik-ing two-tone KimPro finish and TIN gold-coated barrel; the Micro 9 Rapide Scorpius (MSRP: $986) has the Kimpro II black finish on the frame, and the slide wears brushed stainless sides. The Micro 9 ESV Two Tone (MC)(TP) (MSRP: $976) features a mini-compensator to reduce muzzle flip and felt recoil. The ESV slide is topped with TruGlo Tritium Pro

Kimber R7 Mako.

SIG Sauer P320 AXG Pro.

SCCY DVG-1.

Savage Stance.

night sights. It wears Hogue black rubber wraparound grips.

For the 1911 platform, Kimber also extends the Rapide treatment. The Rapide (Dawn) (MSRP: $1,733) has the Kimpro Silver finish with brush-polished flats and a gold TiN finish bar-rel. The Rapide (Scorpius) (MSRP: $1,733) has a Kimpro Black with brush-polished flats with a black DLC barrel. Both Rapide 1911s are full-size and chambered in 9mm. *kimberamerica.com*

SAVAGE

Savage has returned to its roots with a new micro-compact 9mm called the Stance (MSRP: $479). This pistol is designed for shooting comfort and EDC. Unique is the chassis system, which is the serialized component of the pistol, giving users the flexibility to use a wide variety of grip frames. Features include two 18-degree interchangeable grip modules to adjust grip size, ambidex-trous magazine release and slide catch, and a short, crisp trigger with a short reset. Magazine op-tions run from 7-, 8- and 10-round capacities. *savagearms.com*

SCCY

The popular and affordable striker-fired DVG-1 is available in a red-dot-ready configuration (MSRP: $469). This lightweight offers a 10+1 capacity and is available in various colors — from lime green and pink to black and purple. *sccy.com*

SIG SAUER

SIG continues to evolve the P320 design with two new variants: The P320 AXG Pro (MSRP: $1,199.00) and P320 AXG Classic. The 9mm pistols use the AXG alloy frame, as far from a pol-ymer frame as possible. The AXG frames offer more weight for better recoil management. I've been running a P320 AXG Pro, and I am impressed. I like the grip angle and flat-face trigger. Man, did I reduce my split time with this factory pistol! The slide has SIG's Pro-Cut treatment, so it looks like a CNC programmer was given free rein. The slide looks racy, and it has a soft recoil pulse. It's also cut for a red dot and outfitted for fast reloads with a gaping alloy mag well and 17-round magazines with Henning Group aluminum base pads.

The P320 Classic is a retro take on the P320 design. This pistol uses the P320 trigger module assembly in the metal frame, and you'd swear it looks like an old-school SIG. The Hogue walnut grips give it a classic look. Also new to the P320 line is the P320 AXG Equinox (MSRP: $1,200), which should look familiar to SIG fans. The AXG alloy frame and slide have the Equinox treat-ment consisting of a two-tone polished slide and nickel-plated con-

SIG P365XL Spectre Comp.

Spring Armory SA-35.

trols. This pistol will only be available for a limited time.

The P365 line also has a new variant with the P365XL Spectre Comp (MSRP: $1,299). As the name implies, this version of the P365 XL has an integrated compensator to reduce muzzle flip and recoil. It features a laser-stippled grip module, optics-ready slide, titanium nitride gold barrel and XSeries flat trigger. *sigsauer.com*

SPRINGFIELD ARMORY

If you haven't heard, Springfield Armory introduced its version of the iconic Hi-Power pistol, called the SA-35 (MSRP: $699). At first glance, it might seem to be just another Hi-Power clone, but it's not. SA made subtle design changes like a forged frame and slide, recontoured hammer (so there is no hammer bite), oversized thumb safety, and big, bold modern sights. Springfield also ditched the magazine disconnect, so the mag drops free, and you can fire the pistol without a magazine inserted.

The 1911 Garrison series are heirloom-quality 1911s chambered in .45 Auto in either classic hot salt blue finish (MSRP: $849) or stainless steel (MSRP: $899). Features include thin line wood grips, low-profile 3-dot sights, extended thumb safety, skeletonized hammer and extended beavertail. Need a 1911 outfitted with duty-grade tactical features? Check out the 1911 Operator .45 ACP (MSRP: $1,159). This 1911 has Tactical Rack rear/tritium front sights, G10 grips, ambi-dextrous safety, two 8-round magazines with bumper pads, forward-cocking serrations and a match-grade barrel. The 1911 Emissary (MSRP: $1.349) chambered in .45 Auto is as close as you can get to a custom gun without paying custom gun prices. It features a trip top-slide to diffuse light and U-Dot sights for clean target acquisition. It has a unique squared-off triggerguard with a flat trigger, an accessory rail, and thin G10 grips with

The Smith & Wesson M&P Shield Plus.

Smith & Wesson CSX.

M&P M2.0 in 10mm.

SMITH & WESSON

How's this for ignoring the striker-fire trend? The new CSX (MSRP: $609.00) is a hammer-fired subcompact 9mm build on an aluminum alloy frame. It has interchangeable polymer grip in-serts, ambidextrous slide stops, and thumb safety. Comes with 10- and 12-round magazines. It weighs only 19.5 ounces unloaded and is just 6.1 inches in length. S&W is chambering the M&P Shield Plus (MSRP: $595) in 9mm and the all-new .30 Super Carry cartridge. With 9mm, you get a 13+1 round capacity; with .30 Super Carry, you get a whopping 15+1 rounds. Both models fea-ture a flat-face trigger, slide cut for optics, tritium sights, and that comfortable 18-degree angle the M&P line is known for. S&W has also gotten back in the 10mm game by introducing the M&P M2.0 (MSRP: $665.00) in 10mm. This big-bore, full-size M&P has all the M&P M2.0 features, including a flat-face trigger, a slide cut for red dots, four interchangeable palm swell grip inserts, etc. *smith-wesson.com*

Springfield Armory Emissary 1911 in .45 ACP.

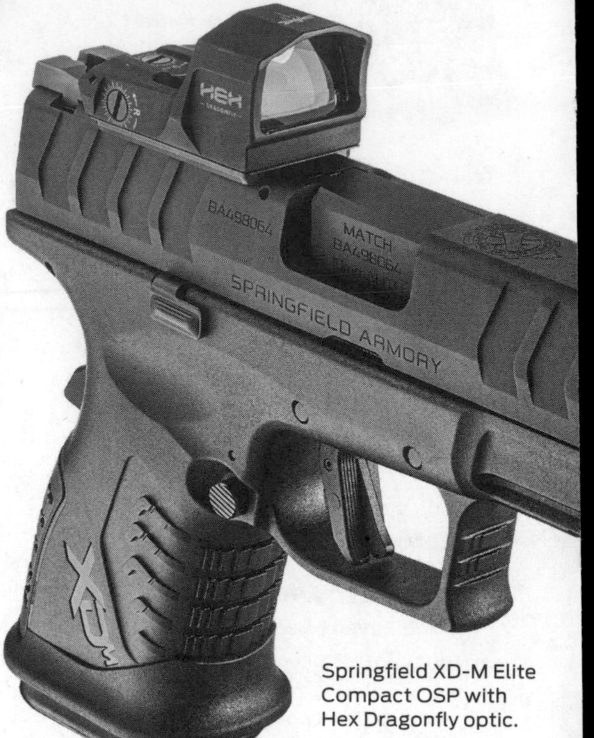

Springfield XD-M Elite Compact OSP with Hex Dragonfly optic.

grenade texture. New to the Ronin 1911 se-ries is a commander-size model chambered in 9mm or .45 Auto (MSRP: $899). There are two new 9mm Ronin EMP (MSRP: $899) models — one with a 3-inch barrel, the other with a 4-inch bar-rel.

New to the XD-M series is the XD-M Elite Compact OSP (MSRP: $653) with a 3.8-inch match barrel and chambered in big-bore calibers like .45 Auto and 10mm. These compact pistols have 10-round magazines and come optics-ready. The XD-M Elite Compact OSP with Hex Dragonfly optic (MSRP: $837) comes with a factory-installed red dot. The single-stack XD-S (MSRP: $465) 3.3 and 4 (MSRP: $465) feature a 3.3- or 4-inch barrel and a compact grip. They are also available with a factory-mounted red-dot sight (MSRP: $568).

Finally, the Hellcat gets a bit of the Roland Special treatment in the Hellcat RDP 3.8 inch (MSRP: $962) with a self-indexing compensator and Hex Wasp red-dot sight. This 9mm comes with 11-round flush-mount magazines and a 13-round extended magazine. *springfield-armory.com*

Hellcat RDP 3.8 inch with Hex Wasp red-dot sight.

The Stoeger STR-9C.

STOEGER

Stoeger has added three new models to the STR-9 striker-fire 9mm pistol line. The STR-9F is full size (MSRP: $329) with a 4.6-inch barrel, 17+1 capacity and modular backstrap. A 3.8-inch barrel is featured on the STR-9C compact (MSRP: $399) with a 13+1 capacity, and it comes op-tics-ready. The STR-9SC subcompact (MSRP: $329-$399) has a 3.5-inch barrel, 10+1 capacity, medium backstrap and one variant is optics-ready. *stoegerindustries.com*

WALTHER

New to the Walther PDP line is the PDP PRO SD Full-Size (MSRP: $829) with a 5.1-inch threaded barrel, Dynamic Performance trigger, aluminum magwell, and comes with three 18-round magazines with aluminum base pads. A compact version, PDP PRO SD (MSRP: $829), has the same features as the full size except for a 4.6-inch threaded barrel and 15-round magazines. *waltherarms.com* GD

Taurus TX22 Competition SCR.

TAURUS

Taurus has added the new GX4 T.O.R.O. (MSRP: $468.00) to the GX4 line. This model fea-tures the T.O.R.O. (Taurus Optic Ready Option) mounting system for attaching a red dot. The G3 series now includes a G3X (MSRP: $342.00) — a compact 9mm with a full-size grip, manual thumb safety and a redesigned 6-pound trigger. The TX22 Competition SCR (MSRP: $589.00) is the next iteration of Taurus' TX22 platform. SCR stands for Steel Challenge Ready and features Tandem-Kross Game Changer PRO squared compensator for added weight and a custom bull bar-rel for enhanced accuracy. *taurususa.com*

- REPORTS - from the Field REVOLVERS & OTHERS

› SHANE JAHN

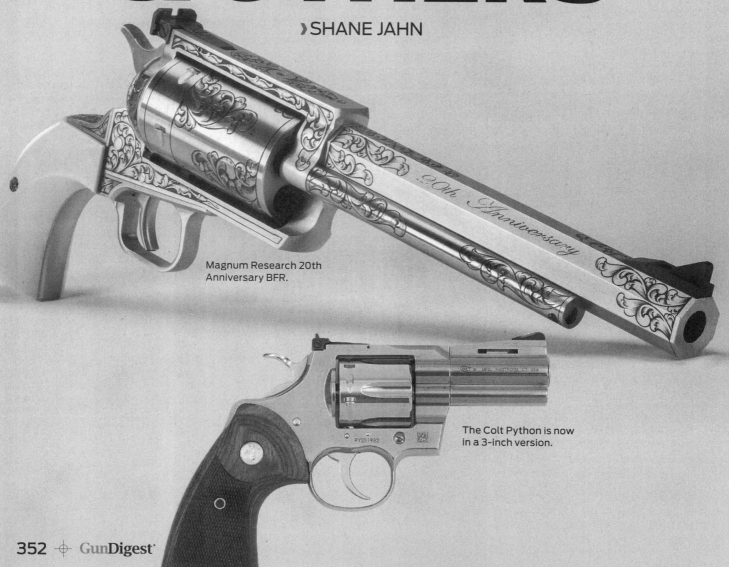

Magnum Research 20th Anniversary BFR.

The Colt Python is now in a 3-inch version.

My plan was to get my hands on as many of the "new for 2022" handguns as I could to provide information gained from handling and shooting them. This was easier said than done as many manufacturers are still backlogged with orders, and it is tough, even for a gun writer, to get some firearms quickly. Few companies could come through before my deadline, and I am incredibly grateful for those who did and those who tried.

The Bond Arms Stinger.

BOND ARMS

There are times when wearing a full-size handgun might not be optimal, like going for a jog or an afternoon walk or just kicking back at the house and enjoying the sunset from the front porch. Still, it's never a bad idea to be prepared to defend yourself and your loved ones. On the other hand, maybe you want two guns and prefer one to be a smaller but potent backup. Bond Arms has just the prescription to fit these needs with its new, slim Stinger derringers. Bond Arms sent me two guns for evaluation, one in .380 ACP and its twin in 9mm. These guns measure 5 inches from grip to muzzle and just 3/4 of an inch in width. They're perfect in a pocket holster for discreet carry; I've been carrying them so in my front pants pocket. With their minimal but adequate size and featherweight, you hardly know they are there. These shooters are perfect for dropping in a vest or coat pocket.

Mr. Bond said he was sending the .380 because it is fun to shoot. He was right! At 3 and 7 yards — what I would call realistic derringer distances — this little gun is surprisingly accurate, with the top barrel hitting where I aimed. The 9mm Stinger is snappier but still very manageable. I tried a CCI snake shot load to see how it performed in such a short barrel. At 3 yards, you could smoke a coiled rattler, no problem. The triggers are heavy, at 7 and 8 pounds, but crisp, making them easier to shoot. Those heavy triggers will be the least of your worries in a bad close-up situation. These little guns are intended for added security at short ranges. As long as you ask of them their intended purpose, I think you will be pretty pleased with their performance. *bondarms.com*

Chiappa Rhino 30DS Nebula .357 Magnum.

CHIAPPA

Italian manufacturer Chiappa has added additions to its Rhino revolver in the 30DS Nebula .357 Magnum with a 3-inch barrel; there is also the new "California Legal" 30SAR model. Unlike traditional revolvers, these unconventional-looking wheelguns fire from the bottom of the cylinder instead of the top, thus lowering the bore axis to reduce muzzle rise and felt recoil. *chiappafirearms.com*

COLT

Colt finally got back into the DA revolver market a few years ago by resurrecting the "Snake Guns." The classic stainless steel Python returned with 4.25- and 6-inch barrels in 2020. Now, in 2022 Colt offers this fine gun in an easy-packing 3-inch barrel. Our local gun store had a couple 4.25-inchers in the showcase I was able to handle. The county sheriff, who owns the establishment, would have frowned upon me running rounds through his NIB sixguns, so I have not yet fired one, but they have a good feel, and the 3-inch barreled revolver ought to make a great-packing gun. If you're a Colt aficionado, I predict this short-barreled Python will definitely be one you'll want. *colt.com*

Colt Python.

The Diamondback Sidekick.

DIAMONDBACK FIREARMS

Diamondback Firearms brought us an interesting .22 revolver in the Sidekick. The single-action-looking revolver is actually a double-action 9-shooter available with .22 LR and .22 WMR swing-out cylinders. With its 4.5-inch barrel, fixed-blade front sight and rear notch, the black Cerakote finished revolver is a perfect candidate for a handy woods gun. *diamondbackfirearms.com*

HERITAGE MANUFACTURING

With last year's unveiling of the 2- and 3-inch Barkeep, a handy little single-action revolver in .22 LR/.22 WMR, the folks at Heritage Manufacturing one-up'd (well, actually one-down'd) the "pint-sized revolver with an Old West flair" this year by offering it with a shorter, 1-inch barrel sans front sight. The six-shooter is dubbed the Barkeep Boot, and why, you might ask, would anyone want a .22 LR revolver with a thumb-width-length barrel and no sights? Well, at less than $200 bucks, why not? I live in rattlesnake country, and this sightless shooter filled with CCI shotshells might be pretty handy when those venomous reptiles trespass in our yard's immediate area, endangering kids and pets.

Heritage's new Rough Rider Tactical Cowboy is a modern twist on its SA revolver, complete with Picatinny rail, fiber-optic sight and threaded 6.5-inch barrel. I mean, if you're gonna be tactical, be cowboy tactical! *heritagemfg.com*

MAGNUM RESEARCH BFR

I started paying attention to the BFRs (that's Biggest Finest Revolver, by the way. Not what some of you thought that stood for, was it?) after reading articles about them. I couldn't wait to handle a BFR as they looked like one rugged revolver. Well, they are. So far, I've only played around with the Long-Cylinder Model in .30-30 Winchester. These guns are built plenty stout and are reasonably priced. If you want to go all-out on a big-bore revolver this year, the 20th Anniversary BFR might be the hogleg you're looking for. Complete with an octagonal barrel, white polymer grips and elegant scrollwork by artists at Tyler Gun Works, this big five-shooter is chambered in .45-70 Government. As you would expect, this highly customized gun isn't cheap at around $7,000, but with only 20 being made, it's likely a worthwhile investment. You can tell your wife (with an honest face) that it will increase in value over time! And if she says no to that one, their regular models will feel like a steal at only a grand and a half. *magnumresearch.com*

Magnum Research's 20th Anniversary BFR in .45-70.

Savage Model 110 PCS.

PIETTA/EMF

The Italian manufacturer Pietta is offering another classy-looking revolver labeled the GWII Posse II. This .357 Magnum SA sports a 3.5-inch octagonal barrel, color-cased frame, brass triggerguard, and smooth, finely finished walnut stocks, giving it a handsome custom look. I have a couple 3.5-inch SAAs and find them very handy and easy to wear in a belt holster. *piettausa.com*

RUGER

Ruger has always offered its tough revolvers at a reasonable price. Look no further if you're in the market for a good, rugged sixgun. Want a solid platform to build a custom or semi-custom revolver? Same deal; get a Ruger. They are just fine out of the box or are great candidates to explore customized handgun creativity. I own several, and this is the advice I give when asked by a novice, "what kind of revolver should I get?" A couple years ago, Ruger brought out the budget-priced Wrangler .22 that can be had for around $200. I bought one and like it. I had Doc Barranti build one of his good holsters for it, slapped on a set of synthetic aged-ivory grips and figured it would make a handy plinker and a good finishing gun to have along hunting to administer the *coup de grace* when needed.

Every year I struggle with what gun to wear when rounding up livestock on the Harkins Ranch. We don't use horses; they prefer ATVs to gather their numerous goats and cattle. It's rough, dusty work. If I wear a holstered gun, I remove it when we start the pen work as it will take a beating in the corrals. Often, I have a snub-nosed .38 revolver in a pocket holster of my jeans. Ruger might have just provided me with the perfect roundup gun with its Wrangler Birdshead. The little .22 LR has a 3.75-inch barrel and rounded grip, making it low profile yet effectively handy. And let's be realistic: it's cheap, so I won't be worried about dings, dust, and scratches, but I have no doubt the tough little Ruger will hold up. One of Barranti's cross-draw holsters will be just the ticket to carry this revolver during roundups, and, being left-handed, it's quickly removed from my belt once all the critters are penned. Ruger also has some neat distributor exclusives, so keep an eye out for them. *ruger.com*

The Ruger Wrangler Birdshead.

SAVAGE ARMS

Firearms and hunting trends are like fashion. OK, I'm the first to admit I know nothing of fashion. Some hugely popular things 20 to 30 years ago faded away, only to be rediscovered by new generations of shooters and hunters. Back in the day, gun and hunting magazines were chocked full of articles on "hand rifles" like XP-100s and Contenders with great yarns woven by men like Milek, Jones, Hampton, Grennell, Swiggett and many others.

Enter Savage's Model 110 PCS. Not your grandaddy's bolt-action handgun. This one is modern and a bit tactical in appearance. It has a left-handed bolt with right-side ejection, adjustable AccuTrigger, one-piece aluminum chassis, a detachable box magazine, and it accepts most AR-style grips. See, I told you it was a little tacticool in looks! I own a savage rifle that is a shooter, and I expect this handgun is as well. Want to add a little challenge to your hunting? Taking a handgun like this to the field might be what you are looking for without limiting your shots to revolver ranges.

The 110 PCS comes with a 10.5-inch threaded barrel and is chambered in .223 Rem, .300AAC Blackout, .308 Win and .350 Legend. *savagearms.com*

Taylor's & Company Gunfighter Defender.

TAYLOR'S & COMPANY

Taylor's & Company continues to offer a raft of single-action revolvers. The Gunfighter Defender looks to be a handy addition to its extensive line. The 1860-style grip frame allows for a full grip on the gun; like gripping a Ruger Bisley, there's no need to drop your pinky under the grip frame like most of us do on the traditional SAA. The more time I spend shooting my custom Ruger Number Five, Ruger Bisleys, and Freedom Arms revolvers, the more I appreciate the full grip, especially when recoil is involved. I am anxiously (and patiently) awaiting the arrival of the Gunfighter Defender for a full review. This revolver is offered in .45 Colt or .357 Magnum with 4.75- or 5.5-inch barrels, lowered Runnin' Iron hammer spur, and optional Taylor Tuned action job, including hand-polished parts and custom springs.

A Texas Game Warden friend of mine who is an accomplished pistolero has a Taylor Tuned revolver he bought a few months ago and tells me it's a heck of a shooter. I expect this one will be as well. *taylorsfirearms.com*

TAURUS

I helped Sheriff Jim Wilson with a torture test on a Taurus revolver many years ago. We ran several-thousand rounds through that gun with no major issues other than a couple screws understandably backing out over time, which was quickly remedied with a dab of Loctite. I even killed a whitetail with that .357 Magnum. Taurus is still going strong and offering new versions of its sturdy revolvers.

One is the Model 327, offered in .327 Federal Magnum. When the .327 Mag. first came about, I paid little attention. It turns out that the .327 Federal is a smokin' cartridge fully capable as a defensive round and deer-sized game hunting round. Not only that, but it's incredibly versatile for target practice and small game, allowing you to shoot .32 S&W Long and .32 H&R Magnum

Taurus 327.

cartridges. Available with 2- or 3-inch barrels, this should be a good-packing revolver.

Taurus' 605 Defender in a 5-shot .357 Magnum is another good carry gun option in a well-balanced 3-inch barrel model with an Ameriglo front sight that makes a lot of sense on this breed of gun. Some versions have VZ's G10 grips; I have a set on one of my DA revolvers and find they are some of the best aftermarket stocks for my medium-sized hands. VZ Grips are one of the very few that are thin enough for me, ensuring a good, correct grip on a DA revolver. *taurususa.com*

The Uberti 1873 Cattleman Brass Dual Cylinder 9mm/.357 Magnum.

UBERTI

A couple years ago, I reviewed Uberti's Dalton revolver in .45 Colt. It shot so well that I bought it. This year, Uberti chamber the El Patron in 9mm and offers the 1873 Single-Action Cattleman Brass in 9mm and .357 Magnum with a cylinder chambered for each. If you only want the Cattleman Brass in 9mm, you can have that, too. I must admit I like this idea of the 9mm sixgun for a few reasons. It's one of the few popular rounds one seems to be able to find in this ammo drought.

The 9mm is plenty stout to take care of business with good ammunition but can also be had in lighter loads for plinking or teaching folks how to shoot without adding unnecessary recoil. On top of that, the light-recoiling nine should be a blast to shoot in a traditional SAA-style revolver. The 1873 Cattleman Brass Dual Cylinder 9mm/.357 Magnum offers shooters a revolver that can handle most handgunning chores and creates a three-in-one gun, 9mm Luger, .38 Special and .357 Magnum. *uberti-usa.com*

In our modern world, it's pleasing to see that time-proven revolvers and "others" are still getting the job done, and quite well. The new models available from the manufacturers listed above offer excellent variations and new additions to their fine guns. The classic and graceful wheelgun remains popular among savvy shooters for self-defense, hunting, and enjoyable days at the range. At the same time, additional action platforms like tough, double-barreled derringers, break-open single shots, and bolt-action handguns offer an expanded range of options for our shooting and hunting pleasure. We are truly living in extraordinary times with all these solid options! GD

- REPORTS - from the Field SHOTGUNS

›KRISTIN ALBERTS

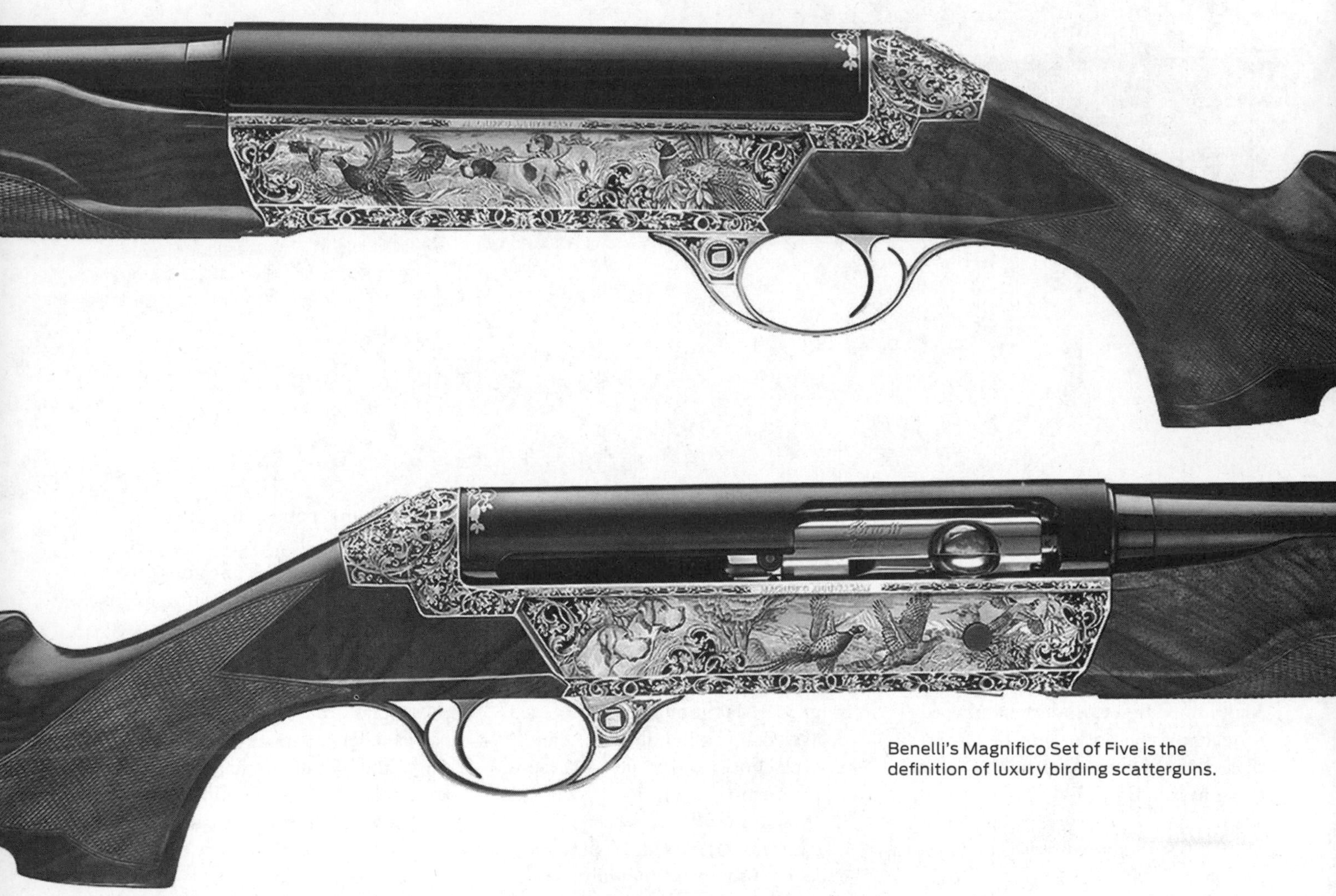

Benelli's Magnifico Set of Five is the definition of luxury birding scatterguns.

As this edition hits your hands, ammunition and firearms continue to see unprecedented demand and frustrating shortages. Shotguns are not immune, be they hunting, defensive or even sporting. That isn't bad news for manufacturers that are, in many cases, working around the clock not only to ante up production but to innovate fresh models for every demographic and shooting style. We're even looking at you, oft-forgotten left-handers. This year more than ever, shotgun builders are tailoring southpaw-specific variants on some of the most desirable models.

If double shotguns have you thinking stuffy European manufacture, guess again. While there will always be a place for stunning luxury guns and finely crafted sporting arms, this is, in fact, an ever-changing modern era. Ever heard of crowd-sourcing shotguns? Yeah, neither had we until CZ-USA partnered with Project Upland to allow hardcore hunters to tell the gun maker precisely what they wanted in both O/U and SxS models. Then, CZ produced the darned doubles, and they're both beautiful and practical.

One thing is sure. While many of us struggle to negotiate these unusual times, firearms manufacture and sales — shotguns included — are more relevant and stronger than ever.

BENELLI

Hunters are sure to be pleased with the expanded and enhanced offerings from Benelli.

The meteoric rise in sub-gauge popularity continues, and with it comes a growing interest in 3-inch "magnum" 28-gauge shells and the shotguns tailored for them. Benelli capitalizes on that movement with a Super Black Eagle III (SBE3) model developed specifically for that round. Not only does the newbie feature slimmer lines and a gauge-specific frame, but it packs a harder hitting, and denser-patterning 28, with the quality that hunters have to come to expect from the inertia-driven SBE3 parentage.

Fans of the larger bores on the SBE3 weren't left in the cold, either. The year sees added options for existing models — a dressing in either Gore Optifade Timber or Marsh patterns mated with coordinating Cerakote metalwork.

Perhaps the grandest unveiling from Benelli is also the most unobtainable, unless, of course, you're a much higher roller than I and all my hunting buddies combined. Benelli's Magnifico Set of Five is the pure definition of luxury birding scatterguns. The company sought out Italy's finest modern craftspeople, which is apparent in the inertia-driven guns replete with master engraving, gold accents, exceptional Walnut and tipped with buffalo horn buttplates. The set comprises a pair of 12s and 20s, along with a sleek 28. From the handmade leather case to the multitude of extras, the Magnifico stands as an exaltation of firearms as artwork.

Following an invitation-only debut at Safari Club International's annual show, the set goes on tour before being sold to the highest bidder. Benelli will donate a healthy sum to conservation and humanitarian causes. *benelli.com*

The Benelli Magnifico Set of Five features master engraving with gold accents and tipped with buffalo horn buttplates.

The Beretta Ultraleggero over/under tips the scales just over 6 pounds.

BERETTA

Lugging a hefty, albeit well-built, shotgun afield all day can quickly turn joy to misery. Backed by its extensive history in gun building, Beretta aims to change that with what it's touting as "the lightest steel shotgun in the field." Meet the Ultraleggero, an O/U based on the 690 series offering the strength benefits of steel with the lightness of aluminum. It's based on what is essentially a skeletonized receiver that includes only those structural elements necessary for "resistance and performance." The milled-out areas are filled with what the company calls Techno-polymer inserts, showing off unique and lovely floral motifs. The most svelte model with 24-inch barrels tips the scales just over 6 pounds. Though the receiver is steel, Ultraleggero's triggerguard is aluminum, as is the forend system. Lightweight does not mean less capable. In fact, the Ultraleggero uses 3-inch chambers and is rated for magnum cartridges up to 56 grams of lead or steel shot. Though we've yet to see them, the Ultraleggero is reported to be available in 12 gauge with four different barrel lengths from 24 to 30 inches.

The Ultraleggero joins Beretta's full contingent of other sporting and hunting shotguns, including the A300, A400, 686, and 690, just to name a few of the most popular current production shotgun families. *beretta.com*

BROWNING

The Buckmark brand rolls into another year with a full contingent of scattergun upgrades, additions and ample 16-gauge love.

Fans of the old Sweet Sixteen Auto-5 long-strokes from decades ago will welcome this year's additions to the revamped A5 family. The Sweet Sixteen Upland shows a brushed nickel receiver and oil-finished Walnut. A Mossy Oak Shadow Grass Habitat version is dressed with full camouflage coverage for the hunt. The Lightning Sweet Sixteen partners a lightweight black anodized receiver with gloss Turkish Walnut and a rounded pistol grip. While there will never be a replacement for the early original Belgian-made, round-knob gems showing the patina of age, it sure is a pleasure to see many choices back on the block.

Even if 16s aren't your forte, other A5s join the already well-fed stable. A pair of throwback camo variants have been launched. The A5 Vintage Tan and A5 Wicked Wing — both in that same retro pattern of abstract tan, brown, and cream blotches — are reminiscent of 1950s-era duck hunts.

Last but not least are upgrades to Browning's respected over/unders, revered amongst sporting shooters since the Superposed days of yore. The Cynergy family gets duded up for the hunt. The sleek Wicked Wing gets Vintage Tan furniture. Meanwhile, the Ultimate Turkey shows off complete Mossy

The Browning A5 Sweet Sixteen.

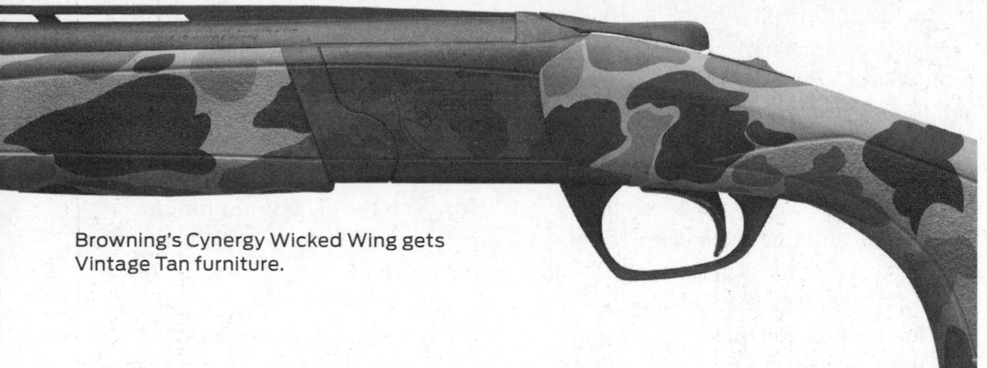

Browning's Cynergy Wicked Wing gets Vintage Tan furniture.

Oak Bottomland coverage, a Marbles Arms bullseye rear and fiber-optic front sight, and a Picatinny rail. *browning.com*

CZ-USA

The most creative move of the shotgunning year goes to CZ, taking the contemporary avenue of crowd-sourcing to produce the latest pair of O/U and SxS design upgrades. Consumers often wonder if their favored gun builder is in tune with their needs and desires. CZ answered that call.

"Get any group of wingshooters around a campfire or dinner table, and the conversation inevitably turns to shotguns and the features they like," said Daniel Holder of CZ-USA. "Letting the online community design their ideal upland shotgun, these fine side-by-side and over/under builds were created by popular vote, with each and every aspect determined by the many followers of Project Upland."

The result of that crowd-sourcing project is Project Upland variants on CZ's Bobwhite G2 and Redhead Premier platforms. CZ's Bobwhite G2 side-by-side has been a hit for years. This upgraded variant is offered in 12, 20, and 28 gauge with a color case finish, decorative side plates, hand engraving, 28-inch barrels and double triggers. A move to high-grade Turkish Walnut is a nice touch, with the models we've seen showing exceptional grain patterns. There's a splinter forend design and straight-style English buttstock, true to the Bobwhite's original design.

Likewise, the Redhead Premier, recognized by CZ as its flagship O/U, formed the basis for building Project Upland's stacked barrel masterpiece. The same one-piece CNC'ed ejector action, single trigger, pistol grip, solid mid-rib, vented top rib, silver chrome receiver and black chrome barrels remain. Enhancements are multiple, with aesthetic ones immediately grabbing the eye. Select Grade Turkish Walnut stocks show killer grain figure. The forend is now described as "upland-style," with a shape reminiscent of the older Drake models, along with attractive checkering fore and aft.

In addition to a brass front bead, ventilated recoil pad, and set of five chokes, the Project Upland O/U's hidden feature is perhaps its most interesting. Debuted last year on limited All-Terrain model variants, the patent-pending magnetic chamber was much-desired by the voting masses. That feature allows the shotgun to be opened with the barrel held vertically, keeping the shells from dropping out. Such a facet could come in handy when a hunter with an open chamber bends to grab a bird, tend a dog or any other unplanned field ventures. With retail prices from $1,429.00, the Project Upland-ers may be purpose-built for the birding fields, but they're sure to be seen on clay courses. *cz-usa.com*

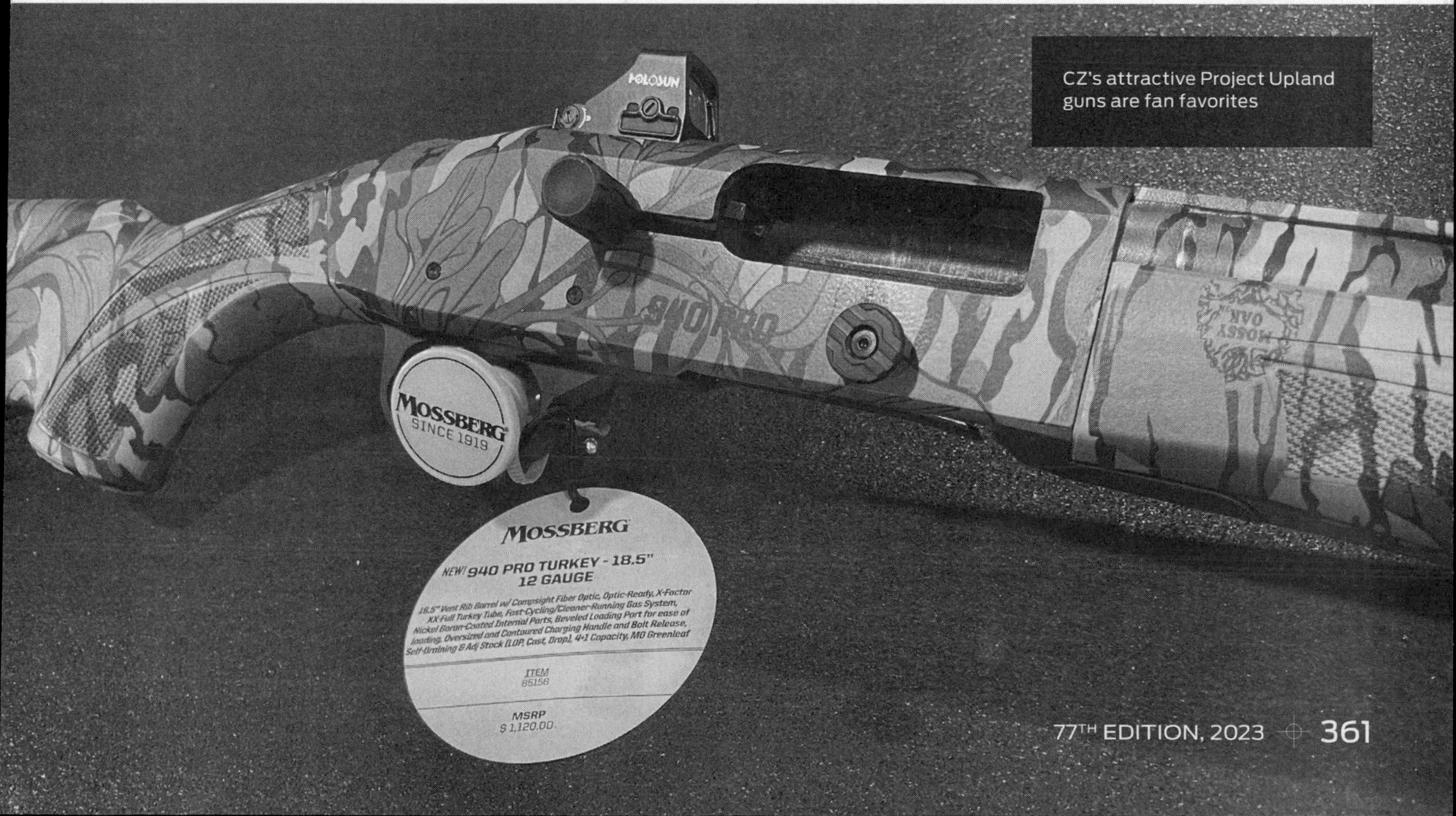

CZ's attractive Project Upland guns are fan favorites

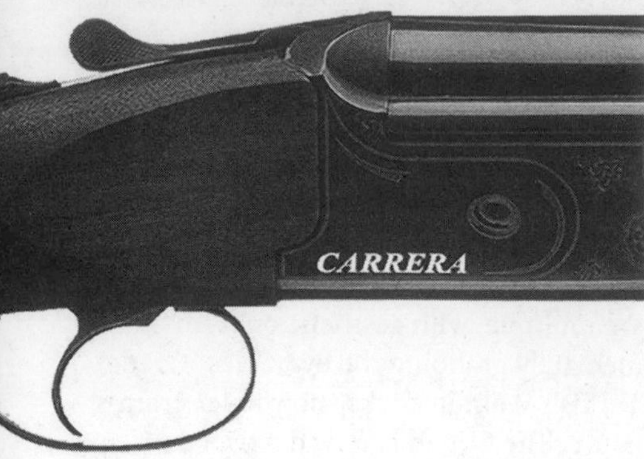

The Italian-made FAIR Carrera One sports 30-inch barrels, Select European Walnut adjustable XR-stock.

F.A.I.R.

For those unfamiliar, FAIR is the trade name of *Fabbrica Armi Isidoro Rizzini*, established in 1971 to manufacture functional and reliable sporting and hunting shotguns. The Italian-built scatterguns are imported to the States as part of the Italian Firearms Group (IFG) and other big-name brands, including Pedersoli, Sabatti and Tanfoglio.

Though we've met precious few casual shooters who've had the pleasure of firing FAIR over/unders or side-by-sides, its guns are worth knowing. The most recent addition that is being imported is the Carrera One.

FAIR's Carrera One over/under 12 gauges are built primarily as sporting guns with 30-inch barrels, Select European Walnut adjustable XR-stock design and the company's TechniChoke system. Looks are on point, with triple-depth laser engraving, a bright black action showing golden clay pigeons, model name detail and fine-pitch checkering. Engineered with oversized cross-locking bolt-on double lugs, the Carrera also uses long-stroke auto ejectors, a single selective trigger and a manual tang safety. FAIR also offers a Carrera One HR with a similar build but adding a taller 15mm high ventilated rib and Monte Carlo-style XR-Stock. The Carrera One retails from $1,988.00, while the HR starts $200.00 higher. *fair.it*

FRANCHI

The company whose tagline is "feels right" is now, more than ever, catering to southpaw shooters. Left-handed versions of the Affinity 3 autoloaders were recently announced in 20-gauge chamberings. They join 12-gauge, reverse-built repeaters, giving lefties even more serious choices in sporting and hunting shotguns.

In addition to those Affinity 3 supplements, Franchi is also throwing in some clean finish options with a host of camo-and-Cerakote hunting companions. Choices of Realtree or Mossy Oak are matched with accenting Patriot Brown or Midnight Bronze Cerakote for a practical blend of hunting stealth and durability.

However, the biggest headline is the launch of the company's first-ever Sideplate model double gun. The Instinct Sideplate is a looker and a shooter. In addition to the color casehardened steel receiver, engraving, and gold inlay, there's AA-grade Walnut and lovely Schnabel forend paired with a Prince of Wales stock. While driven by the golden age of gun building, Franchi brings updated engineering, a red fiber-optic front sight, five interchangeable chokes, automatic safety and a slender rubber recoil pad. The Instinct Sideplate will be available in 12 or 20 gauge with 28-inch gloss blued barrels, and retail pricing starting at $2,229.00. *franchiusa.com*

Lovely engraving on the Franchi Instinct Sideplate double accent a fine gun.

HENRY REPEATING ARMS

Though known for building buttery-smooth-running lever-action rifles, the company revered for wearing patriotism on its sleeves with a Made-in-America-or-Not-Made-At-All guarantee has not forgotten shotgunners. Over the last few years, Henry's expanded its catalog to include more than a dozen scatterguns. There are multiple lever-driven, side-loading gate .410 bores in polished brass, traditional wood-and-blued-steel, and modernized, blacked-out X-Model.

Believe it or not, 'tis not all levers at Henry. In fact, the company's single-shot lineup has been receiving attention for its blend of simplicity, affordability, and reliability — all geared toward hunters. Gobbler chasers can bag beards with the Single Shot Turkey Camo. There's full Mossy Oak Obsession coverage over American Walnut, fiber-optic irons and a magnum 3.5-inch chamber. Likewise, deer and bear hunters have appreciated the Single Shot Slug with its 24-inch rifled slug barrel, blued steel, American Walnut, fiber optics and stout recoil pad.

The company offers brass and steel one-shooters in 12, 20 and .410 bores for more do-all scatterguns. There's even a Youth Single Shot in 20 gauge with a shorter LOP that works just as well for

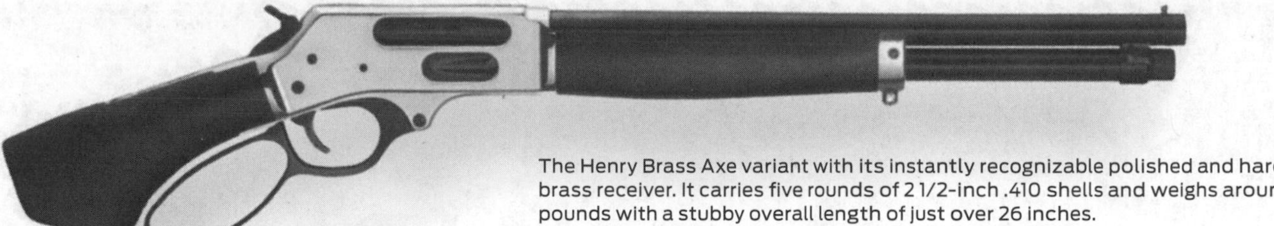

The Henry Brass Axe variant with its instantly recognizable polished and hardened brass receiver. It carries five rounds of 2 1/2-inch .410 shells and weighs around 5.75 pounds with a stubby overall length of just over 26 inches.

smaller-framed shooters. Lefties take note: the single shots are southpaw friendly.

The latest additions to Henry's shotshell launchers may have an identity crisis. Are they shotguns, handguns or something else entirely? No matter how defined, the result is unbridled enjoyment. Henry first launched the Axe, a handheld, ax-handled, 15-inch-barreled sub-gauge. The most recent addition is a Brass Axe variant with its instantly recognizable polished and hardened brass receiver. Both carry five rounds of 2 1/2-inch .410 shells and weigh in around 5.75 pounds with a stubby overall length of just over 26 inches. The pint-sized shotties, attracting much of the same crowd as Mossberg's half-sized pump Shockwave, are threaded for Invector-style chokes. Per the BATFE, Henry's lever-run Axe falls into the same non-Class 3/NFA "firearm" category as the Shockwave, meaning buyers need neither special paperwork nor tax stamp. *henryusa.com*

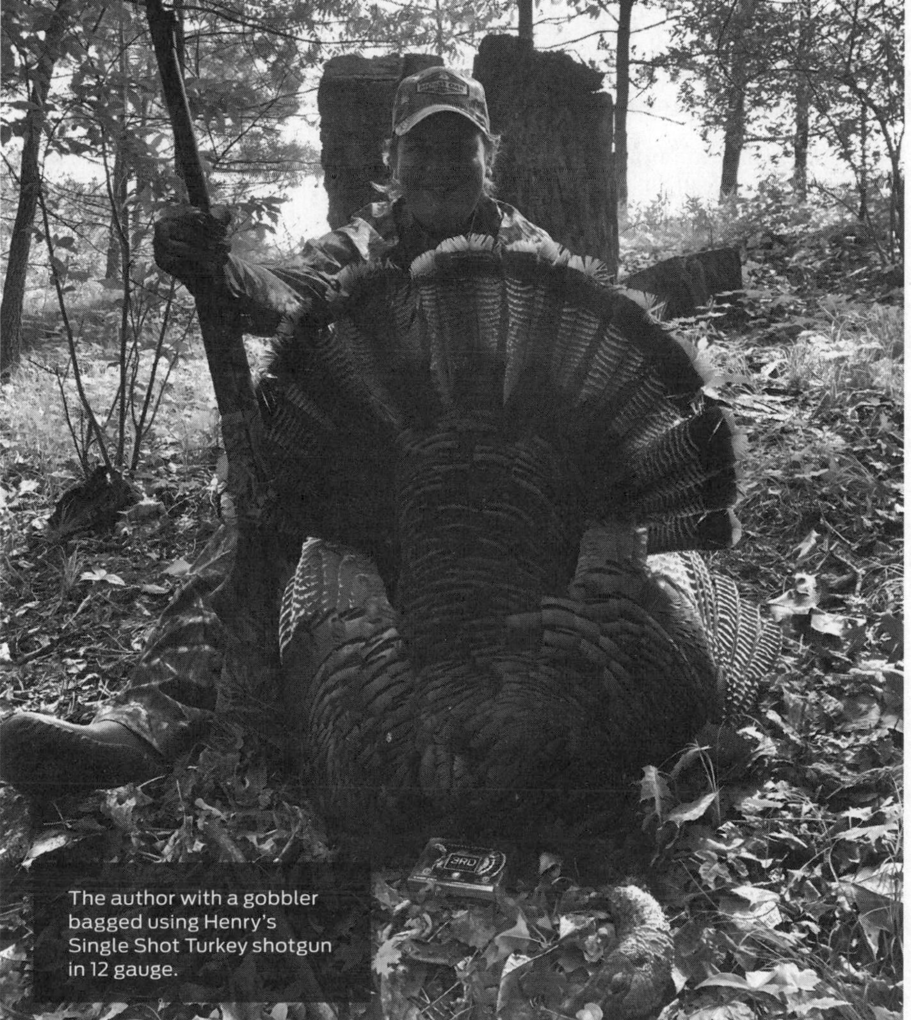

The author with a gobbler bagged using Henry's Single Shot Turkey shotgun in 12 gauge.

MOSSBERG

Sitting two miles off the Maine coast in mid-December, praying for Eider Sea ducks to fly, I also hoped the new Mossberg 940 Pro Waterfowl was up to this arduous task. What do you get when you mix below-zero weather with freezing saltwater spray? A nightmare for many autoloaders, that's what. While the ducks didn't decoy as well as planned, the Mossbergs were remarkable. Since that trip, we've run hundreds of rounds through that shotgun, and whether wet, frozen, or gritty, it hasn't missed a beat. Notably, it survived rust-free the mistreatment of East coast hunting without a cleaning.

The 940 Pro Waterfowl is now one among many in the company's burgeoning lineup of 940 Pro gas-driven semi-autos. Joining the initial competition-geared 940 JM Pro, Field, and Waterfowl this year is a duo of gobbler-specific variants called the 940 Pro Turkey.

(below) The Mossberg 940 Pro Turkey is the stuff of nightmares for gobblers across the land. It wears a quality HiViz CompSight green front fiber optic sight.

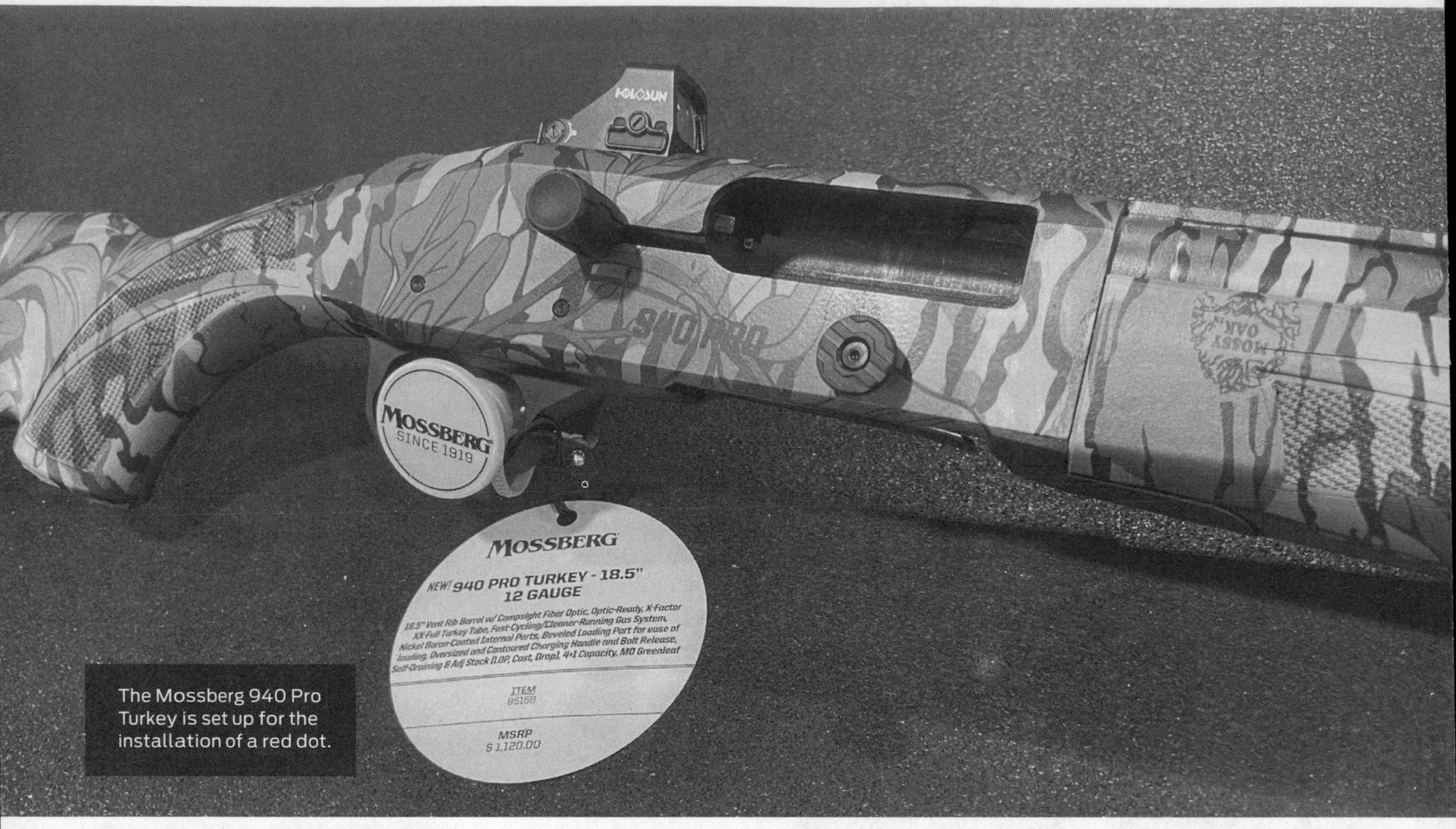

The Mossberg 940 Pro Turkey is set up for the installation of a red dot.

Along with the same in-house torture-tested action, these young'uns feature full Mossy Oak Greenleaf coverage, an adjustable LOP, and a mean extended XX-Full choke tube dead set on hammering birds. In a forward-thinking move, the receiver comes machined for low-profile optics like microdots and a filler plate drilled and tapped for standard bases. And for those like us who often forgo fancy, the 940 Pro Turkeys still wear a quality HiViz CompSight green front fiber optic.

The first has a 24-inch vent rib barrel, while the other that really grabs our attention sports an 18.5-inch, ultra-wieldy one. Holding it at SHOT Show, all I could think was how handy that would be in the thick brush of Spring turkey woodlots. Both Turkey Pros retail for the same $1,120.00.

While 940 Pros steal Mossberg's thunder in shotgun announcement, other introductions are cruising below the radar. One of the company's proven offerings, as evidenced by its continual appearance on best-seller lists at retailers across the web, is some version of the Shockwave. This time around, it's the 590S Shockwave available in two barrel lengths — 18.5 or 14.375 inches, both with a Raptor grip and Corn-Cob forend with hand-strap. Those shoot-from-the hip guns remain as much fun on the range blasting pumpkins as they do for more heavy-duty defending the home. *mossberg.com*

SAVAGE ARMS

Powering the continued success of the Renegauge is its unique engineering and design elements. There's the industry-first and patented dual-valve self-regulating DRIV gas system, developed to cycle high-power hunting and low-power target loads with ease and cut down on felt recoil. In addition, the Melonite-treated fluted barrel, adjustable LOP and comb height, one-piece chrome-plated bolt carrier, and oversized controls all point to hardcore outdoor performance and creature comforts.

The Renegauge Security boasts an 18.5-inch barrel with an extended 6+1 capacity magazine tube that runs the entire length of the barrel. In a nod toward strength and detail, the company adds a dual-point clamp connecting the barrel to the mag tube, and that piece is machined with an M-LOK slot for attaching accessories. Adjustable ghost ring sights offer quick target acquisition and rapid shots in defensive situations, while the one-piece rail makes for easy optics mounting. The Security comes packed with three chokes in a hard case.

As all the above are 12 gauge, 3-inch only, the shooting world continues to await 20-gauge offerings, which are sure to come. While naysayers will continue to crow about the lack of a 3.5-inch magnum chambered model, we never once felt slighted by the 3-incher, especially given the wide range of premium hunting shotshells and specialty shot now dominating the market.

We've had the opportunity to shoot clays and hunt gobblers with one of the early Renegauge iterations, and we enjoyed every minute. The guns are light-recoiling. The inclusion of the AccuStock popularized on the 110 rifles means Renegauge shooters can tailor both comb height and LOP for a custom-feel-

The Smith & Wesson M&P-12 looks and feels bullpup, is optics-ready and packs 14 rounds.

ing fit. While on an out-of-state hunting trip, two very differently sized shooters can swap the included gel comb inserts and buttpads in only minutes, sharing one quality shotgun with stellar results. *savagearms.com*

SMITH & WESSON

Not since the high-gloss sporting Models 1000 and 3000 of the 1970s and '80s have Smith & Wesson seriously put its name on a shotgun. The M&P-12 goes an entirely different direction, chasing a more tactical market instead and marking S&W's entry into an alternative product category.

With a 19-inch barrel, twin magazine tubes and an overall length of only 27.8 inches, the pump-action M&P 12 gauge looks and feels bullpup, building on the popularity of double-tube guns like those from Standard Manufacturing and Kel Tec. It is optics ready, has an ambidextrous safety, and ships with four interchangeable palm-swell inserts ala the company's semi-automatic pistols.

Though the initial launch was rocky with a safety recall, S&W took care of business, and the bullpups are better than ever. Buyers can rest — and shoot — easily knowing the M&P-12 is backed with a full lifetime service warranty. The Made-in-America bullpup has found a ready audience. When the need arises for a reliable pump action packing up to 14 rounds, the M&P-12 will be ready. *smith-wesson.com*

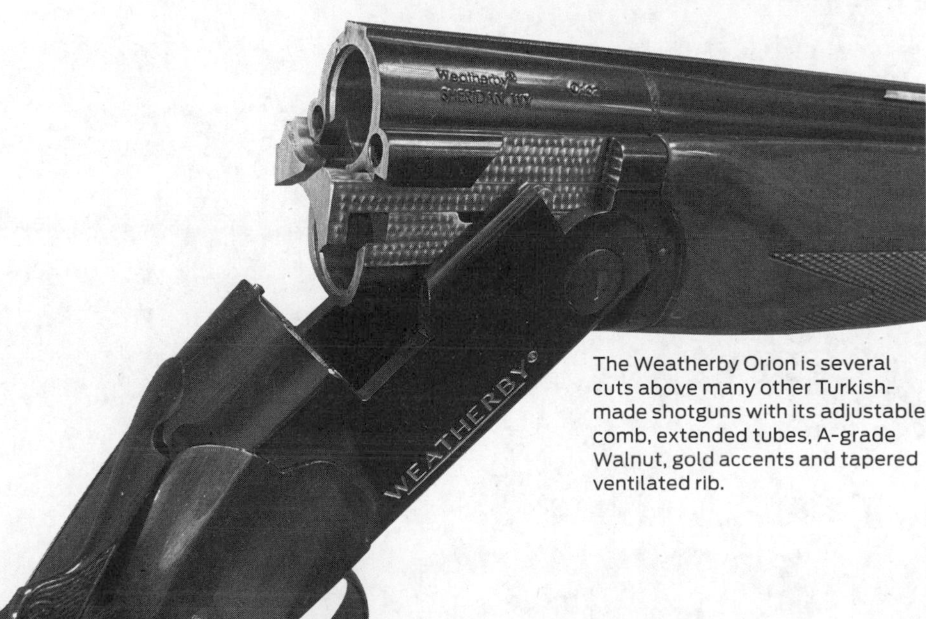

The Weatherby Orion is several cuts above many other Turkish-made shotguns with its adjustable comb, extended tubes, A-grade Walnut, gold accents and tapered ventilated rib.

WEATHERBY

While Weatherby's primary renown will remain its rock-solid Mark V rifle platforms and proprietary chamberings, the company's upgraded line of shotguns is not to be overlooked. With the move to firearms-friendly Wyoming in the rear-view mirror, Weatherby feels revitalized. Besides, that Sheridan, WY roll mark on the shotguns is pretty darn sweet. The latest scattergun additions are our favorites to date, all centered around the over/under Orion family.

We recently had a chance to run some rounds through the Orion Sporting, and the results were impressive. Not only does it shoulder and balance well, but it shows keen attention to detail. The fit-and-finish is superior to that found on other Turkish-made guns. The adjustable comb, extended tubes, A-grade Walnut, gold accents, and tapered ventilated rib add to one fine-looking O/U and more busted clays.

In addition to the Orion, Weatherby continues producing other shotgun lines, including the inertia-driven 18i and Element. The gas-operated autoloader SA-08 is still listed in the company catalog, though with few offerings. However, the pump-action PA family has been axed, with no replacement slide guns announced to take its more affordable place. *weatherby.com* GD

- REPORTS - from the Field MUZZLELOADERS

BOB CAMPBELL

A 209 primer in the base of the Firestick.

The CVA Paramount Pro.

The CVA Paramount HTR, another smoking-fast .40-cal. frontstuffer.

The muzzleloader is more challenging to use well than most modern cartridge guns. It can be difficult to load, ignition isn't as reliable as most firearms, it is dirty, and slow to reload. Yet, we keep enjoying these smokepoles. And that is the bottom line: Muzzleloaders are enjoyable. And while some chose the more difficult route of muzzleloaders for hunting simply to enjoy blackpowder hunting seasons, makers have produced models that are easier to use for the past decade or more. Quite a few are triumphs of technology. Some stretch the definition. Let's look at what's new.

CVA

The CVA Paramount Pro .40 is a neglected caliber in muzzleloading rifles. With a new emphasis on long-range ballistics, CVA offers a .40 version of the Paramount. The Paramount is a popular rifle with plenty of smash and a good reputation. But it left something to be desired for those hunting areas demanding longer range, especially in the mountains. The Paramount Pro is simply the Paramount with enhanced features. I like the modern Cerakote finish, which is ideal for woods use, but the significant change is the .40 caliber and superior ballistics.

The Paramount Pro features a Grayboe Terrain-pattern polymer stock specially designed to complement the optics on the rifle. There are built-in swivel studs as well. This configuration works well for both sling and bipod use. Unlike most rifles, this one offers a Picatinny rail — that is almost a future shock for this writer. If you like other sling mounts, no sweat: the stock has flush cup attachments. I'm familiar with centerfire Bergara barrels and was pleased that CVA uses a 26-inch Nitride-treated one in the Paramount Pro. The barrel is Cerakote covered but underneath the coat is 416 stainless steel.

So, what's the advantage of the .40? First, CVA tested the Powerbelt ELR bullet, landing on a 1-in-20 inch twist. Accuracy is exceptional. Of course, Bergara cuts the muzzle to guide the bullet into the barrel and uses exterior fluting for heat dispersion. A muzzle brake is also used since the .40 high-velocity loading introduces something into muzzleloaders not previously experienced by many of us — sharp recoil. An adjustable trigger gives you a range of adjustment guaranteed from 1.5 to 3.5 pounds. CVA went past the standard 209 primer and designed VariFlame ignition into the Paramount Pro. The VariFlame is needed when igniting 150 grains by powder volume — driving a 280-grain bullet to 2,200 fps! Some experiments have sent a 225-grain bullet to 2,800 fps. Ballistics like that should make for an excellent long-range mountain rifle.

The package is built around the CVA bolt. The self-headspacing bolt is spring-loaded, making for the tight seal needed with the combination of VariFlame and huge powder charges. There is no blowback with this type of lockup. CVA wisely chose to design the rifle to take standard Remington 700 scope mounts. When you purchase this rifle, you get 15 PowerBelt ELR projectiles, 10 VariFlame adapters, a re-priming tool, a breech wrench, a ramrod (there is no ramrod under the barrel, which is free-floated) and a flush cup mount Quake sling. The muzzle brake must be purchased separately.

This rifle and its polymer-tipped bullets will positively impact the hunting field during the next few years. I'm looking forward to seeing it in the hands of hardy souls, mountain hunting with the muzzleloader.

Another new smoking-fast .40-caliber offering from CVA is the Paramount HTR.

"Recently, I fired CVA's new Paramount long-range muzzleloading HTR .40," writes Gun Digest contributor Wayne van Zwoll. "Like the earlier .45 and .50 Paramounts, this bolt-action muzzleloader is designed to fire Power Belt conical ELR bullets — in this case, 220-grain missiles. Boosted by burly charges of Blackhorn 209, they clock 2,740 fps and fly flat enough that I routinely hit 8-inch gongs at 300 yards. The Paramount's VariFlame firing cap snugs into a capsule you slip into the breech. The synthetic stock, adjustable at the comb, has shims to change length. A 26-inch Bergara barrel is rifled 1-in-20. The chassis is alloy, so also is one of two supplied ramrods." *cva.com*

TRADITIONS

Two of my most trusted companies, Federal Ammunition and Traditions, have teamed up on this one. The firms created the NitroFire and Firestick. I think that the term innovation is apt, and arguably the NitroFire and Firestick have changed the game, if not the face of blackpowder hunting.

The problem with hunting is always the same. Time, and not enough of it, and not enough opportunity. Most hunters who take up traditional firearms also invest in gear for the blackpowder season. They may not be real smokepole enthusiasts, but they do the best they can. Just the same, a traditional shooter handling the NitroFire may find that they are swayed by the fascinating technology.

I am calling the NitroFire a blackpowder rifle, though it stretches the definition of the muzzleloader. Actually, the rifle is part muzzleloader and part breechloader. I am confident that it fits the definition of a primitive weapon in my state but be sure to check your regulations. The rifle is one of the popular traditional break-open types. The concept is simple and rugged: The NitroFire is part breechloader as the FireStick is loaded in the breech end. However, the projectile is rammed into the barrel in the literal sense of a muzzleloader. (By the way, the Bureau of Alcohol, Tobacco and Firearms has ruled the NitroFire a modern firearm requiring paperwork to purchase, unlike most other blackpowder firearms. No big deal, and perhaps the BATF will change the ruling later. Traditions found it easier to get the rifle to the end-user, hoping for a different ruling soon. So, you can use the rifle during the muzzleloading season in many states.)

The Traditions NitroFire rifle is a nice-looking gun. The system keeps the shooter and the rifle cleaner, but some powder residue is left when firing. The FireStick system keeps the components in one shell as neatly as possible, save for the projectile itself. The FireStick is designed in two types, one with 100 grains of Hodgdon Triple Eight and another with 120 grains of Triple Eight. Ignition comes from the standard 209 muzzleloader/shotshell-type primer. While primers are sometimes tricky to find, so are percussion caps. I have located 209 primers in

NitroFire/FireStick gear is neatly packaged. The FireStick contains a powder charge and is reusable. Ramming the projectile home is simple enough. This is the only traditional aspect of the NitroFire.

The Traditions NitroFire is one of the significant innovations of the decade.

While not traditional in some ways, the new NitroFire is a neat trick that simplifies blackpowder shooting.

stock within easy driving distance. And the fact is, blackpowder shooters don't use that many primers. A hundred 209 primers will do a long, long time.

For safety's sake, seat the projectile first. Once this is accomplished, simply open the breech and insert the shell holding the powder charge. The FireStick is as simple to use as a single-shot shotgun. The safety features are evident. You never should climb a treestand with a loaded rifle. Simply break the action open and remove the FireStick charge. The FireStick can be used for multiple firings. Simply reload the powder charge yourself. When firing the NitroFire, the best results come with a lubricated sabot. I've had good luck with Traditions and Hornady. I don't need many of these for blackpowder practice, and these two makers have filled my needs. While the system is the biggest news, the NitroFire rifle is a neat trick. It's delivered with a bore-sighted scope installed. Unlike most blackpowder rifles, checking if the barrel has a bullet loaded is straightforward. Open the action and look! It is loaded if you cannot see the light through the barrel.

(top) The NitroFire is a simple break-open design. (center) It is safe to load the primer in the field after inserting the FireStick. (below) Firing the NitroFire is a pleasure to shoot. And accurate!

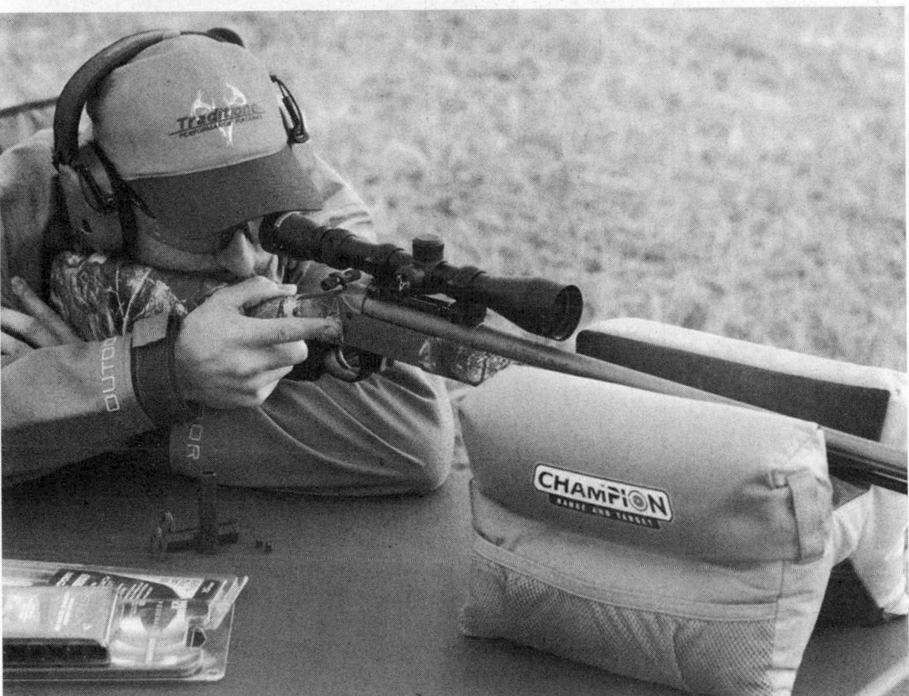

Be sure to seat the bullet to the correct depth (I could hear the bullet seat). There is a bullet stop just before the chamber. The bullet ram is carried under the barrel just like any old-fashioned musket. Once the bullet is seated, you're ready to charge the rifle. This is where the procedure departs from prior experience. The FireStick isn't supplied with a primer. To begin, press the primer into place in the base of the FireStick. Next, break open the NitroFire rifle and insert the FireStick into the action. It slips in nicely. Close the NitroFire action, and you are loaded.

The rifle is capable of excellent accuracy potential, and the new system makes for very consistent shots. The powder charge is exactly the same as specified in every FireStick. You can fire 10 to 12 shots before fouling becomes a problem. Shooters report that the FireStick charge doesn't have the offensive smell of some blackpowder.

Accuracy and ease of loading are a given. But what about power? The rifle will quickly push a 250-grain bullet to 2,000 fps or a tad more. That is plenty of energy for thin-skinned name. The consistency of the FireStrick/Nitrofire combination is impressive. The muzzleloader is quite an accomplishment, with accuracy and power similar to my .45-70 rifle. It's the type of rifle that a conventional shooter, using centerfire cartridges, will find friendly for their forays during primitive weapon hunting seasons. Another significant advantage: it is remarkably easy to clean. The blackpowder doesn't seem to find its way into the action but remains in the barrel.

The rifle may not be a traditional blackpowder choice some shooters desire, and that's fine. But it's an incredible innovation for the occasional shooter or hunter wishing to get into the blackpowder world as simply as possible. *traditionsfirearms.com* GD

- REPORTS - from the Field OPTICS

›JOE ARTERBURN

The Frontier 34 FFP from Hawke can be had in 3-18x50 and 5-30x56, with calibrated reticles based on scope magnification. It's ideal for extreme long-range shooting.

Vortex's new Viper HD 3000 laser rangefinder has a 3,000-yard max range (up to 2,000 on deer and game) and four target modes (normal, first, last, and ELR) with two ranging modes for either horizontal line-of-sight or angle-compensated rangefinding.

Technology, it appears, is immune to coronavirus. While some aspects of ordinary life, including manufacturing, were slowed or shut down the last couple of years by the COVID-19 pandemic, the optics industry ran full steam ahead through it all. New and new-and-improved products have come regularly off the design table and out of manufacturing facilities.

Technology is the keyword. As technological advancements continue, optics continue to evolve, adapting new concepts and capabilities in a race to produce quality optics, many with multi-functional capabilities to meet increasing demands and expectations of end-users.

That race or competition to outpace the pack produces innovative, cutting-edge products. We'd say this is the Golden Age of Optics, but we see no sign of the optics industry slowing down. That's good news for all of us.

AIMPOINT ACRO P-2 RED-DOT SIGHT

Aimpoint's new Acro P-2 red-dot sight, which features an improved LED emitter and higher-capacity battery, is designed to endure G-force pounding of semi-autos and, adding to the reliability quotient, you can expect up to five years (50,000 hours) battery life even with constant use. The crisp 3.5 MOA dot provides fast target acquisition. An adjustable digital intensity keypad, placed next to the battery compartment to help prevent unintentional changes, provides a tactile feel for adjusting dot brightness. Essentially, Aimpoint managed to triple the battery life by fitting a larger CR2032 battery in the same compact footprint of the predecessor Acro P-1. Primarily designed for handguns, expect to see them on shotguns, carbines and rifles — and used as backup sights on magnified scopes and thermal imagers. MSRP: $667 *aimpoint.us*

The Aimpoint Acro P2 red-dot optic features an improved 5-year (50,000 hours) battery life.

A rangefinding binocular with an MSRP of $700? Indeed, the 10x42 Bushnell Fusion X pulled it off.

BUSHNELL

Bushnell's Fusion X Rangefinding binoculars can range reflective targets at a full mile with 1-yard plus/minus accuracy. A cool feature is the new ACTIVSYNC display that morphs from black to red, depending on lighting conditions, so you can see readings equally well from before dawn through changing lighting conditions throughout the day all the way to dusk, let's say dark. These are full-size 10x42 binos with Bushnell's quality glass and easy-to-use ergonomics. Push the ranging button to power up and activate either the single range or scan mode. A second button allows the selection of multiple modes. Near/far-ranging modes home in on targets while ignoring objects in the foreground and background. Meanwhile, bow and rifle ballistics modes provide data to help assure a good shot. And it has a height mode to calculate the height of an object, like a tree. MSRP: $699.99; *bushnell.com*

GERMAN PRECISION OPTICS (GPO)

The small size and light weight of GPO's new Rangeguide laser rangefinding binoculars belie the quality optics and powerful rangefinding engine that can accurately measure to 3,062 yards, with inclination/declination compensation. The extreme distance is on highly reflective targets, but it will reliably range a tree to 1,093 yards and a deer to 766. These compact units are only 5.4 inches tall and weigh 24.3 ounces (thanks to the armor-coated magnesium frame). They also measure ambient temperature, humidity and air pressure to help with shot placement on long-range shots. They feature 32mm objective lenses with GPObright high-transmission lens coatings to maximize brightness, sharpness and resolution. Two models: 8x32, $1,099.99; and 10x32, $1,149.99.

GPO also upgraded and reintroduced its GPOTAC 8Xi 1-824i first-focal plane riflescope, built on a 34mm machined aircraft aluminum main tube and an upgraded mil-spec horseshoe reticle. The

The compact GPO RangeGuide 8x32 binos can accurately range targets to 3,000 yards.

Long-range shooters should check out the GPOTAC 4.5-27x50i from German Precision Optics (GPO). It's a first-focal plane optic loaded with features professionals expect.

upgrade included high-quality lenses and a brighter, larger reticle, especially nice for those who rely on a 1x reticle in bright daylight. The iControl illuminated reticle has an automatic on/off feature to save battery power when not in use but turns on instantly when needed. MSRP: $1,899.99 *gpo-usa.com*

HAWKE

Hawke Optics makes no bones about its new Vantage 8x42 and 10x42 binoculars, saying it set out to produce quality entry-level binoculars that are downright affordable. It hit the mark, incorporating the crisp, clear System H2 Optics into a dependable, water- and fog-proof package. As Hawke will tell you upfront, these are for hunters, birders, sports enthusiasts and others looking for their first binos or as a backup or secondary pair in the truck or boat. Both models weigh just over 19 ounces. MSRP is $159 for the 8x42; $169 for the 10x42.

Designed for extreme long-range shooting, Hawke's new addition to the premier Frontier riflescope line — the Frontier 34 FFP — is available in two magnification models, 3-18x50 and 5-30x56, each with illuminated reticle options, the Mil Pro Ext and MOA Pro EXT calibrated to the scope's magnification and specifically designed for extreme long-range shooting. These first-focal plane scopes have 34mm tubes, side focus adjustment and Zero, Lock' n Stop turrets that are resettable, lockable and have a return-to-zero feature. MSRP: 3-18x50,

The Phenom UHD 20-60x85 spotting scope will feature fixed-power reticle eyepieces for making wind calls, something long-range shooters will want to make a note of.

UHD is designed with tight tolerances and high optical quality, which encompasses a lot of factors. Still, the result is sharp images, high resolution and color fidelity, which means comfortable viewing even if you're glassing for hours. *hawkeoptics.com*

KAHLES

Kahles introduced the K525i DLR (Dynamic Long Range) 5-25x56 first-focal plane riflescope, focusing on tactical use and long-distance shooting. Improvements include 100-click-per-rotation turret adjustment, with 10 mils of adjustment per rotation, and an 8-percent increase in the field of view for faster target acquisition with the illuminated reticle. Operation is easily and comfortably accomplished without reaching over the scope or moving out of the shooting position. The patented parallax correction is located on top of the 34mm tube. MSRP: $3,549. *swarovskioptik.com*

KONUS

Konus' new Flame-R Thermal Riflescope combines an enhanced electro-optical sensor with an advanced image-processing technology to produce clear thermal images in viewing, photo or video formats. There's a 16GB built-in memory for storage, and it's connectable to your phone via Wi-Fi (built-in rechargeable battery). It's versatile enough to work as a riflescope or handheld monocular. This unit has a 2.5-20x magnification range and five selectable digital reticles in three colors. Thermal imaging is available in four palettes, and it includes a universal mounting system for Picatinny rails, so it fits right in with hunting or tactical firearms. MSRP: $3,129.99

Competitive shooters looking for an enormous magnification range (5 to 40x) and clarity and sharpness of fine ED glass will find it in the Konus Ab-

The new Konus Flame-R Thermal Riflescope has a 2.5-20x magnification range and five selectable digital reticles in three colors.

The new Kahles K525i DLR (Dynamic Long Range) 5-25x56 first-focal plane riflescope offers a 100-click-per-rotation turret adjustment (10 mils per turn).

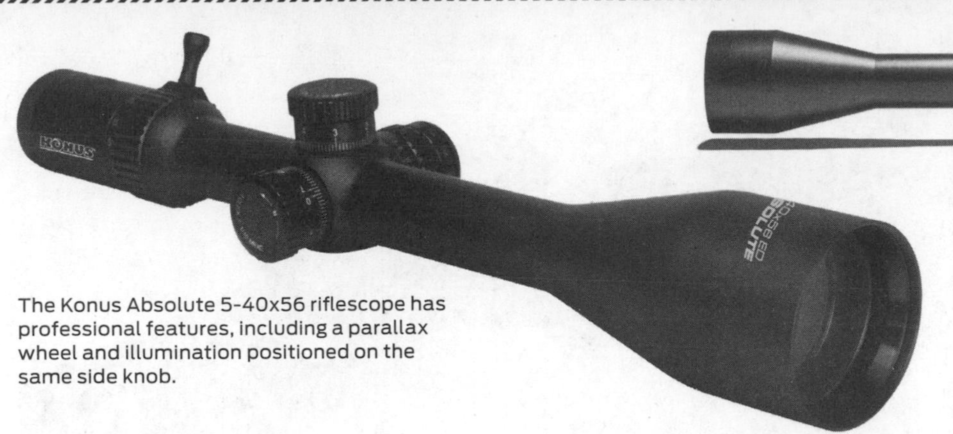

The Konus Absolute 5-40x56 riflescope has professional features, including a parallax wheel and illumination positioned on the same side knob.

The all-purpose Maven CRS.1 (3-12x40) is for hunters wanting more reach in their magnification range.

solute 5-40x56 riflescope. It's equipped with professional features, including a parallax wheel and illumination positioned on the same side knob, removable zoom lever, 30mm tube and newly designed erector tube that can handle heavy recoil. The Konus-exclusive dual-illuminated, laser-etched reticle is a variation of the Half Mil-Dot with additional aiming points. MSRP is $1,186.99. *konusscopes.com*

LEICA

Leica rocked the binocular world when it introduced the original Geovid rangefinder binoculars, and it's making waves again with the new compact, lightweight Geovid Pro 32. Available in 8x32 or 10x32 models, they measure precisely to 2,500 yards, even on non-reflective targets. Slim and ergonomic in design, the Geovid Pro 32 uses enhanced Bluetooth connectivity with the Leica Hunting App to deliver data to your phone. It also combines onboard atmospheric sensors with new Applied Ballistics technology and has advanced GPS tracking to guide you to the target. It's the first to feature GPS mapping integration through BaseMaps, Google Maps and Garmin. And the ProTrack feature aids in in-field tracking, surveying and game recovery. MSRP: $2,899. *leica-sportoptics.com*

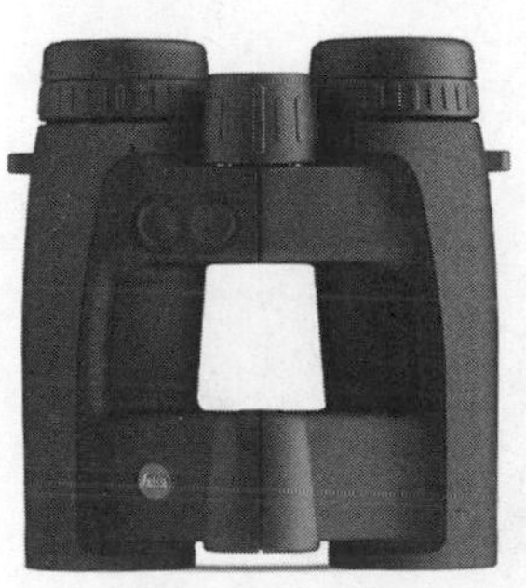

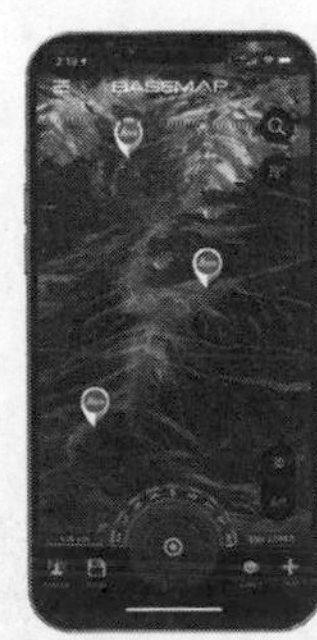

Leica's new compact, lightweight Geovid Pro 32 is available in 8x32 or 10x32 models. They measure precisely to 2,500 yards, even on non-reflective targets.

The Leupold Mark 3HD 3-9x40 tactical scope with MIL-based adjustments and high-definition lenses.

LEUPOLD

Leupold's new RX1500i TBR/W laser rangefinder features ½-yard accuracy, 6x magnification and True Ballistic Range/Wind technology, which uses ballistically calculated ranges to keep you on target, even on uphill or downhill shots. It'll range to 1,500 yards on reflective targets; 1,200 on soft targets, all in a compact unit. There's also a bow mode that'll generate an arrow drop to 175 yards. Price: $299.99

The Mark 3HD is Leupold's new tactical scope line with MIL-based adjustments, high-definition lenses, exposed elevation adjustment dial and low-profile power selector ring, just the type of features tactical and competitive shooters want. Expect excellent dawn-to-dusk light transmission from all nine models in the line, and choose from up to six reticles, depending on the model. Price: $499.99 to $699.99. *leupold.com*

MAVEN

Maven's new CRS Series of riflescopes, built with its proprietary award-winning glass and a unique version of its popular Simplified Holdover Reticle, include the all-purpose CRS.1 (3-12x40) and for hunters wanting more reach in their magnification range, the CRS.2 (4-16x44). Maven's C Series glass provides clear, bright and high-contrast images and color fidelity. Both models are a second-focal plane configuration, keeping the reticle crisp and clear at all magnifications. The CRS.2 adds side parallax adjustment too. A direct-to-customer operation, Maven developed the CRS line based on customer requests. MSRP: CRS.1, $450; CRS.2, $550. *mavenoptics.com*

MEOPTA

Meopta's new MeoPro HD Plus binocular is a completely redesigned version of its award-winning MeoPro bino line. These binos deliver sharper, brighter images with better contrast and resolution than the first-generation binos. The focus wheel is redesigned for smoother, faster and more precise focusing, and the rubber-armored exterior provides improved grip. Edge-to-

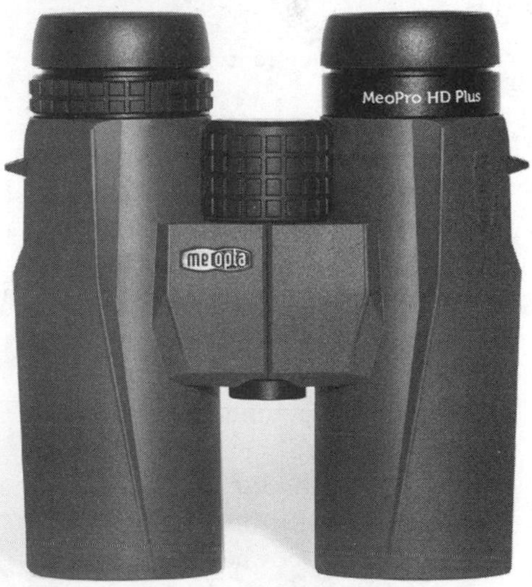

Meopta's new MeoPro HD Plus binocular comes in 10x42 and 8x56, MSRPs from $499 to $749.

edge clarity, wide field of view and low-light performance are plusses. Meopta's lens coatings enhance imaging, plus there's MeoShield anti-abrasion coating and MeoDrop hydrophobic coating to help protect the glass. Two models: 10x42, $499; 8x56, $749. *meoptasportsoptics.com*

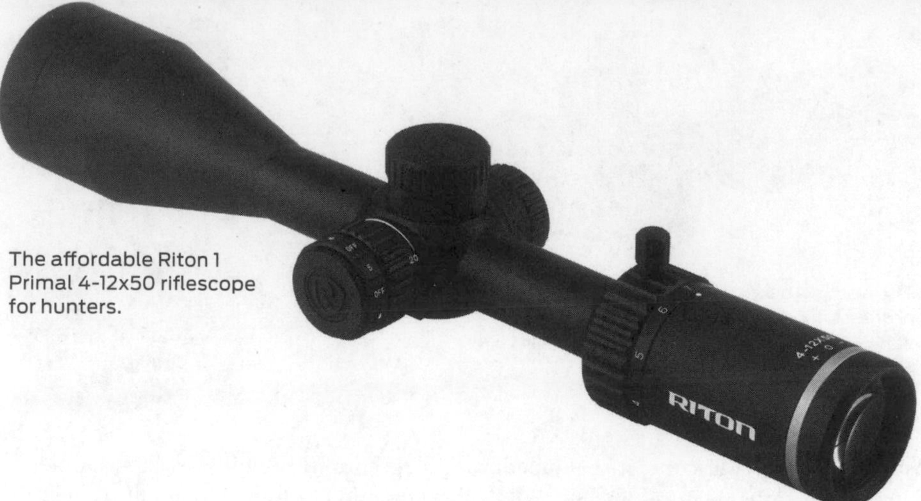

The affordable Riton 1 Primal 4-12x50 riflescope for hunters.

PRIMARY ARMS

Primary Arms' PLx 1-8x24 First Focal Plane Compact Riflescope measures 9.28 inches. It weighs 16.95 ounces with batteries, making it compatible with rifles for hunting and tactical situations. It boasts a large field of view and edge-to-edge sight picture due to mechanical construction that virtually eliminates perception of the ocular ring during sighting. AutoLive reticle illumination turns on and off via a motion sensor, so it's ready when you need it and saves battery power when you don't. MSRP: $1,499.99

The Primary Arms SLx 1x Micro-Prism Scope, with a handy motion sensor to save on the juice.

Primary Arms also has two new micro-prism scopes, one in 1x and the other 3x. The SLx 1x Micro-Prism Scope (MSRP: $249.99) features quality ED glass and the same technology that produces the edge-to-edge sight picture and large field of view while virtually eliminating notice of the ocular ring. A motion sensor turns it off and on. The SLx 3x version adds 3x magnification and 13 settings, including three night-vision settings. The aluminum alloy main body has a hard-coat anodized finish. There are eight mounting height options from 1.1 to 2.075 inches. MSRP: $299.99; *primaryarms.com*

RITON

Riton unveiled its first angled spotting scope, the 5 Primal 15-45x60, a relatively compact unit that packs a lot of spotting power in a package measuring only 12.75 inches and weighing 2.75 lbs. Riton says it is its most-requested item. The fast-focus eyepiece, and HD/ED fully multi-coated glass, provides sharp, clear imaging and low-light enhancement. MSRP: $1,099.99

Riton's 1 Primal 4-12x50 riflescope is designed to provide hunters crystal-clear optics and necessary bells and whistles at a decent value. Features include high-definition glass, fully multi-coated lenses, parallax adjustment, 1-inch main tube, capped zero-resettable turrets and an integrated throw lever. MSRP: $369.99 *ritonoptics.com*

SIG SAUER

The Electro-Optics ROMEO2 is Sig's latest version of its miniature reflex sight for full-width frame handguns, rifles or PCCs. The high-efficiency point source LED emitter and aspheric glass lens combined with special coatings and reticle settings provide sharp viewing and make it compatible with Gen3 night-vision devices. It has 15 brightness settings and either 3- or 6-MOA red dot for rapid target engagement with both eyes open for situational awareness. The MOTAC motion-activated illumination system and Sig's new Magnetac magnetic activation technology (used in conjunction with special Romeo2 holsters) automatically powers up when unholstered; it powers down when holstered. MSRP: $779.99

The KILO K-Series is Sig's next-generation laser rangefinder, featuring the LightWave DSP Gen II rangefinding engine with extended-range XR technology, BaseMap integration, onboard Applied Ballistics capability and configurability with all Sig Electro-Optics BDX devices. KILO5K 7x25 will range reflective targets to 5,000 yards, trees to 2,500 yards and deer to 2,000 yards. And you can range a target

The Sig Sauer ROMEO2 reflex sight uses Magnetac magnetic activation technology (in conjunction with special Romeo2 holsters) to automatically power up when unholstered.

Sig Sauer's new KILO 5K Rangefinder 7x25 will range reflective targets to 5,000 yards, trees to 2,500 yards and deer to 2,000 yards. And you can range a target and instantly drop waypoints into the BaseMap app to help navigate to that target.

and instantly drop waypoints into the BaseMap app to help navigate to that target. A vivid red segmented OLED display provides the range to the target, elevation holdover, and wind holds. MSRP: $779.99 *sigsauer.com*

MSRP: 8x42, $3,999; 10x42, $4,110

Swarovski's new tM35 is a thermal imaging clip-on device you simply clip onto your Swarovski riflescope, turning the scope into a night-vision optic for hunting in the dark, no re-sighting required. Compatible with Z8i, Z6(i), Z5(i) and Z3 series riflescopes, the tM35 attaches with an optional tMA Thermal Monocular Adapter ($254). The SWAROLIGHT automatic on/off switch saves juice by activating when picked up and deactivating when the firearm is set down. The automatic brightness adjustment adapts to ambient light conditions. Reacting to thermal radiation, both white-hot and black-hot modes identify more details depending on the environment. MSRP: $5,554. *swarovskioptik.com*

The Swarovski tM35 Thermal Imaging device is compatible with Z8i, Z6(i), Z5(i) and Z3 series riflescopes with the optional tMA Thermal Monocular Adapter.

SWAROVSKI

Swarovski's redesigned EL Range binocular now features Tracking Assistant, which helps narrow down the location of the last place ranged, so theoretically the location of your target animal. They also allow you to transfer your own ballistics data. And using the built-in Bluetooth interface, three different ballistics curves can be loaded, though configuring ballistics requires the EL Range with Tracking Assistant Configurator App. These will range from 10.9 to 2,200 yards. Angle, temperature and air pressure are automatically measured in the calculations. Available in two models.

TRACT

Tract came out with the first TORIC Ultra High Definition Spotting Scope, specifically designed for shooters to spot bullet impacts and hunters to spot game under demanding conditions. The 27-55x80 angled scope features Tract's Schott High Transmission glass and Extra-Low Dispersion lens for sharp, bright imaging and edge-to-edge clarity. The fully multi-coated lenses and prisms maximize light transmission; phase correction coating provides better contrast, color reproduction and sharper resolution. MSRP: $1,394 *tractoptics.com*

Tract's TORIC 27-55x80 Spotting Scope uses Schott High Transmission glass and Extra-Low Dispersion lens for sharp, bright imaging and edge-to-edge clarity.

Functionally identical to the current U.S. Marines Corp Squad Common Optic, Trijicon's SCO VCOG 1-8x28 has only minor cosmetic differences.

TRIJICON

Trijicon is making its Variable Combat Optical Gunsight (VCOG) 1-8x28 Squad Common Optic available to the public for the first time. Functionally identical to the current U.S. Marines Corp Squad Common Optic, the VCOG has only minor cosmetic changes. With a magnification range suitable from close-quarters to long-range applications, it's an all-purpose, rigorous-duty scope tested to deliver a nearly indestructible sighting system. Features include tethered turret covers, Tenebraex flip caps, integrated base and a LaRue Tactical LT799 mount that provides rock-solid quick-detach mounting while maintaining zero. The first focal plane reticle allows rapid range estimation and correct hold throughout the magnification range. Illuminated red segmented circle MRAD tree reticle, with nine day and two night-vision settings, and 35 MRAD total travel in windage and elevation. MSRP: $3,150. *trijicon.com*

VORTEX OPTICS

Vortex's hot-off-the-line Strike Eagle 1-8x24 riflescope answers requests for a first-focal-plane version of its popular second-focal-plane Strike Eagle scope. The illuminated EBR-8 reticle provides red dot-like performance at 1x for close-quarters target acquisition and accurate holdovers to 600 yards at higher settings. It has nine daylight and two night-vision settings to match light conditions. A throw lever allows rapid magnification changes for quick adaptation of changing target distances. MSRP: $599.99

Long-range hunters and others who like to dial long distances are going to want to look at Vortex's new Diamondback HD 2000 and Viper HD 3000 laser rangefinders. Here's why.

The Diamondback will provide accurate readings in .1-yard increments to 2,000 yards on the top end; up to 1,400 on game. With 7x magnification and high-def optics, you'll be able to pick apart the landscape and pinpoint your target. It has a red OLED display for use in any light condition and two target modes, normal and last, and two ranging modes (horizontal line of sight and angle compensation). It's tripod adaptable, so you can keep it steady and on long-range targets. Think Midwestern and Western bow and rifle hunting. MSRP: $449.99

The Viper HD 3000, as the name suggests, has a 3,000-yard max range (up to 2,000 on deer and game) and four target modes (normal, first, last and ELR) with two ranging modes for either horizontal line-of-sight or angle-compensated rangefinding. The ELR mode is for ranging extreme distance, which requires a slightly longer response time, so a tripod is recommended. It sports a red OLED display and high-def optics with 7x magnification. Think open country and tall timber. MSRP: $599.99. *vortexoptics.com*

Yes, you can now get a first-focal plane Strike Eagle from Vortex.

ZEISS

Zeiss announced its new LRP S5 first-focal plane riflescopes. Built with 34mm tubes, these are designed to withstand massive 1,500 G-force recoil. The 3-18x50 and 5-25x56 models have two new FFP reticle options (MOA or MRAD).

Zeiss announced its new LRP S5 first-focal plane riflescopes. Built with 34mm tubes, these are designed to withstand massive 1,500 G-force recoil. The 3-18x50 and 5-25x56 models have two new FFP reticle options (MOA or MRAD).

When Zeiss announced its new LRP S5 first-focal plane riflescopes, long-range shooters noticed. Compact, heavy-duty and made with Zeiss quality optics, they feature digitally controlled illuminated reticles (visible in the daytime), precise, repeatable, tactile turrets (with solid Ballistic Stop return to zero) and best-in-class total elevation travel. Built with 34mm tubes, they're designed to withstand massive 1,500 G-force recoil. The 3-18x50 and 5-25x56 models have two new FFP reticle options (MOA or MRAD), each with distinct, easy-to-understand reference marks along horizontal and vertical lines, as well as windage hold-offs, fine-line subtensions and floating center dots. MSRP: 3-18x50, $3,299.99; 5-25x56, $3,599.99 *zeiss.com*

- REPORTS - from the Field AIRGUNS

›JIM HOUSE

Although modest in price, the Umarex Gauntlet 2 is an excellent entry-level PCP rifle.

As with so many types of equipment, the term 'airgun' embraces a broad spectrum of products. On the one hand, there are the low-powered BB guns of the Daisy Red Ryder genre, and on the other are the high-powered behemoth models of .45 or .50 caliber.

The term airgun also applies to models that launch BBs or pellets utilizing expanding carbon dioxide. Although BB guns that shoot by cocking to compress air and then release it to send the projectile still exist, the airgun industry has grown to include rifles for hunting medium game. There is an airgun for any taste. In this survey, it's impossible

Daisy's Red Ryder is the most recognizable airgun in history.

to discuss the many available models, so the interested reader should consult the catalog section to see more products.

AIR POWER

Power to propel projectiles by non-combustion means is most often supplied by compressed air. Still, guns powered by compressed carbon dioxide escaping from a pressurized cylinder also fall under the general heading of airguns. Compressed air is held in a reservoir filled by one of several means. First, low-powered models are powered by a single cocking stroke operated by a lever like traditional BB guns. Second, some airguns have a lever that functions as a pump handle, operated repetitively to compress air in a reservoir. These are the multi-pump models typified by the single shots of Benjamin, Daisy, and Sheridan that empty the reservoir when fired. Some models of this type are sufficiently powerful for hunting small species. An important advantage of a multi-pump is that nothing else is needed because the rifle has a self-contained pump.

Third, some guns' barrels (or a rod below or alongside the barrel) function as the cocking lever. These are the so-called break-barrel models. The cocking stroke compresses a strong spring (spring-piston models) or gas behind a piston in a cylinder (gas-ram models). The piston is driven forward to provide compressed air behind the projectile when the gun is fired. Some guns of this type are high-powered models suitable for hunting small game and pests.

A fourth and somewhat different power source is employed in the pre-charged pneumatic (PCP) guns. For these, a cylinder is filled with compressed air using an external pump, a scuba tank or a special air compressor. The cylinder is filled to 3,000 psi (higher in some models), and part of the air is released at firing. Generally, the cylinder holds enough air to power several shots. These are the real powerhouses of the air rifle models.

WHERE ARE WE HEADED?

I once showed a .45 Auto firearm and a BB-firing replica to a conservation officer and asked him, without looking at the muzzles, which was the BB pistol? He could not tell the difference without handling them. With Glocks being so popular, it is not surprising that a BB-firing Glock is available. The Smith & Wesson Model 29 in .44 Magnum caliber is one of the most recognizable revolvers. A very realistic BB imitation is available.

Second, models that fire BBs in full-auto (BB machine guns) are becoming popular for recreational shooting. Some mimic actual machine guns, and many are designed to resemble centerfire handguns. Such models illustrate a significant direction of the airgun industry, giving shooters airguns that exhibit a high degree of realism. A third direction of the industry is to produce airguns that are sufficiently powerful to hunt medium game. These are generally of at least .35 caliber and almost always use a pre-charged cylinder as a power source. It's not uncommon for such rifles to cost as much as $1,000, but in some cases, they allow the hunter to pursue their sport in areas where firearms are prohibited.

The Glock 17 displays the realism of some BB pistols.

The Gamo Swarm Maxxim is s break-action of moderate price and power.

FUN AND PURSUIT OF SMALL PREY

Airguns have been used to dispatch pests and harvest small game for many years. My brother hunted squirrels with a .22-caliber Benjamin multi-pump as a youngster. When I contacted a conservation officer about using airguns for small game hunting, he responded that they were considered the same as any other legal type of rifle. He said that he had hunted with his air rifle for years. If a break action or multi-pump is to be used this way, it's preferable to select one of the .20- or .22-caliber models because the heavier pellets of larger diameter hit harder. There are dozens of break-action models available with the general characteristic of an advertised velocity of 1,000 fps in .177 caliber. Typical of this genre is the Gamo Swarm Maxxim, which is also a 10-shot repeater.

However, the PCP models offer the advantages of higher power and quicker repeated shots. As PCPs became more popular, larger reservoirs became more common, as did the ability to launch larger projectiles. Some models that shoot .357, .457, or larger projectiles have become popular. The projectiles are sometimes called pellets, but they resemble cast bullets used in firearm ammunition. Moreover, new rifle designs include some that depart from the early single shots by functioning as repeaters. With the ability to launch such large projectiles at velocities as high as 1,000 fps, such air rifles can dispatch even game as large as deer or hogs. Thus, hunting with airguns has expanded to a new dimension, as reflected by the inclusion of regular feature articles that deal with their use in hunting in publications such as Airgun Hobbyist and Predator Xtreme. Hunting with airguns has expanded vastly from the past days of hunting squirrels or rabbits with a Benjamin or Sheridan multi-pump.

Rifles that utilize PCP power sources are available from numerous manufacturers and retailers. Crosman Corporation, a division of Velocity Outdoors, produces models that range from the Benjamin Maximus single shot in .177 and .22 calibers to the Bulldog .457. The Maximus and its predecessor, the Benjamin Discovery, are single-shot models that operate with a reservoir that can be pressurized to 2,000 psi. Although the Maximus is not an extremely high-powered airgun, .22 pellet velocity can be up to 850 fps (up to 1,000 fps in .177 caliber) with up to 30 shots from a filled cylinder. Unlike many high-powered guns, it comes with sights. The Maximus is well-suited for hunting small species.

MULTI-PUMPS PERSIST

As a fan of multi-pump airguns, one of the products of interest to me is the Crosman C362, a .22-caliber model. With an MSPR of only $109.99 and pellet velocities advertised to be up to 875

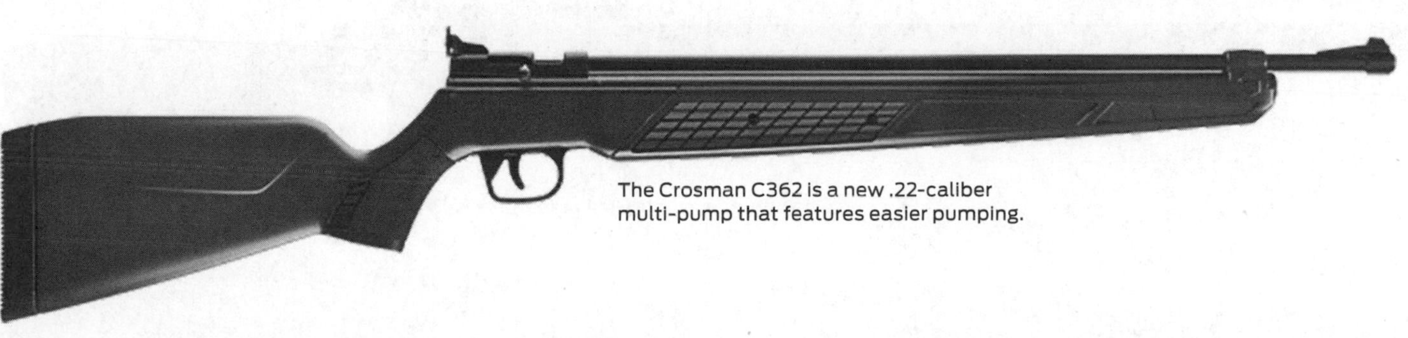

The Crosman C362 is a new .22-caliber multi-pump that features easier pumping.

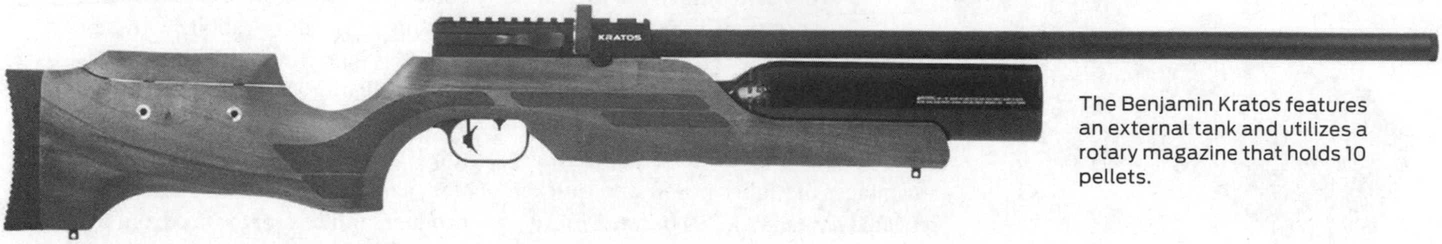

The Benjamin Kratos features an external tank and utilizes a rotary magazine that holds 10 pellets.

fps, this could be a bargain — although the stock and pump handle are made of black polymer.

Multi-pump rifles get rather hard to pump after several strokes. One of the unique features of the C392 is the redesigned pump handle and linkage, which provide greater leverage to reduce pumping effort. A weak point in the C392 design is the rear sight design. It's located at the receiver's rear, which places a square notch so close to the eye that the front sight occupies very little space in the notch. This design makes accurate sight alignment impossible. Inverting the blade also provides a tiny hole that is supposed to serve as a peep sight, but the aperture is much too small. Because it is a rather powerful model, the C392 would be a good choice for pest removal or hunting small game. The traditional Benjamin multi-pump is also available as the .177-caliber Model 397 and .22-caliber Model 392.

Although the multi-pump .20-caliber Sheridan Blue and Silver Streaks and Crosman Classic 2200 in .22 caliber are gone, the Crosman 2100 Classic .177 caliber can still be had. This handsome rifle can be used as a single shot, firing pellets, or as a repeater, firing BBs. I recommend against using steel BBs because I have examined the bores of such rifles that show the tops of rifling lands worn off by them. With pellet velocities of up to 800 fps and the choice of appropriate pellets, the 2100 is an efficient pest eradicator. The Remington 77 Airmaster is essentially the same rifle except for cosmetic changes.

PURSUIT OF LARGER PREY

Crosman continues to offer the Benjamin Marauder in .22 and .25 calibers. This rifle gives up to 1,000 fps in .22 caliber and 900 fps in .25 caliber, making it a good choice for use on larger pests and small game. Also marketed by Crosman is the Benjamin Kratos, which

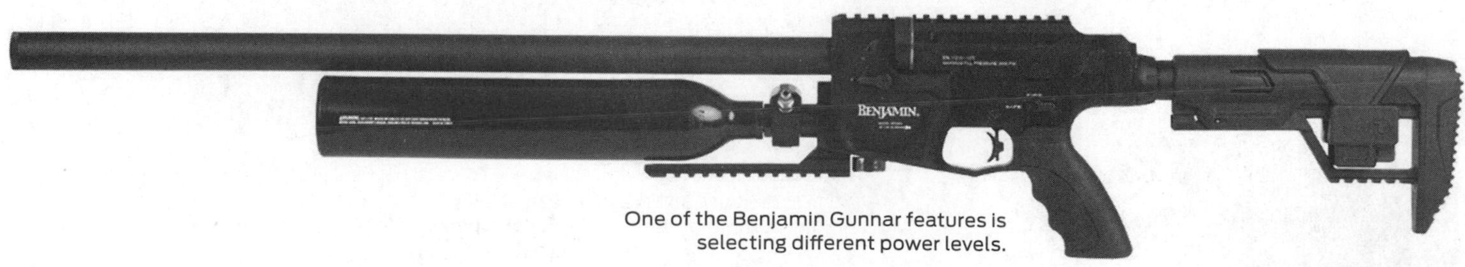

One of the Benjamin Gunnar features is selecting different power levels.

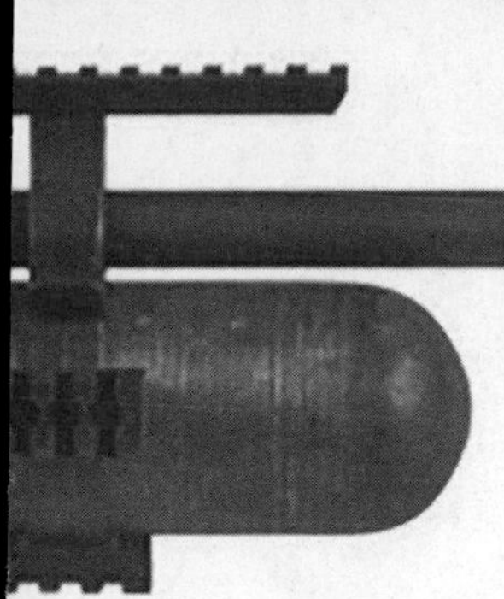

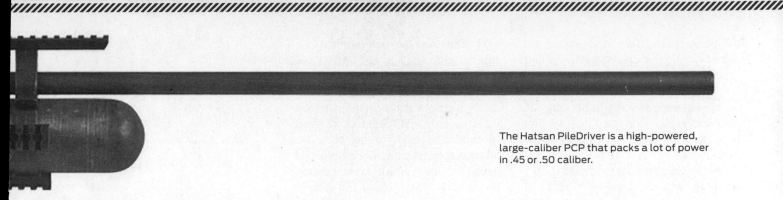

The Hatsan PileDriver is a high-powered, large-caliber PCP that packs a lot of power in .45 or .50 caliber.

utilizes a 10-shot rotary magazine. Velocities produced are like those from the Marauder, and a reservoir with air at 3,000 psi can provide up to 60 shots. The Kratos features a side lever for cocking and a rotating magazine for repeat shots. It also has a Turkish walnut stock, the comb of which can be adjusted for height. The MSRP of the Kratos is $664.

One of the newest .457-caliber air rifles is the Benjamin Bulldog 457 (MSRP $1,099). This big-bore bullpup sends pellets to 760 fps, but pellet weight is not specified. When charged to 3,000 psi, up to three shots can be fired before refilling. It's also available in .357 caliber (MSRP $949.99), gives up to 10 shots per filled reservoir and has velocities of 800 fps.

The Benjamin Gunnar is a new PCP model available in .22 and .25 calibers. Velocities obtained from a full tank at 3,000 psi are up to 1,000 fps for the .22 and 900 fps for the .25. A handy feature of the Gunnar is that it has adjustable power levels with five settings, so, depending on the use, lower power can be selected if appropriate.

Most .457-caliber pellets weigh 200-300 grains, although some are lighter and heavier. A pellet of such weight traveling at 700 to 800 fps packs power approximately equal to a .45 Auto or .45 Colt handgun. Carefully placed, such projectiles would be effective on relatively large animals. The behemoth of airguns is represented by the .50-caliber Umarex Hammer. It can drive a 200-grain projectile at over 1,000 fps or a 550-grain pellet at 760 fps. The corresponding energies are 485 and 705 ft-lbs, respectively. Projectiles between these extremes of weight can be given intermediate velocities and energies. The Airforce Texan produces similar ballistics, and it has an MSRP of $1,214.95.

Another PCP from Umarex is the Gauntlet 2, available in .22 and .25 calibers with advertised velocities of up to 1,100 and 980 fps, respectively. Corresponding energies are approximately 33 and 51 ft-lbs, respectively. These models are priced at $429.99 and $439.99 for the .22- and .25-caliber models. An even more economical model is the Origin .22, which has an MSRP of $329.99. It features an efficient pumping system with an external pump available as an accessory.

Hatsan produces a potent PCP model known as the PileDriver, available in .45 and .50 calibers. In the .45 caliber, the velocity is specified as up to 900 fps, and in .50, the velocity may be up to 850 fps. Such power has its price, and the PileDriver is 46.5 inches in length and weighs 10 pounds. It has an MSRP of $1,299.99. Numerous other models are also offered by Hatsan.

Pellets in .357 or .457 caliber generally cost from $.50-$1.00 each, so shooting a large-caliber airgun is not cheap. However, as a hunting tool, such an expense pales compared to other costs. Large-caliber airguns are not the usual tools for rolling pop cans or plinking pinecones. The use of airguns for hunting specific species varies by state, and many states do not allow their use for hunting deer. Generally, those who do specify a lower-caliber limit of .30 or .35 and PCP power. A very convenient reference can be found at pyramydair.com/airgun-map/, which shows a U.S. map.

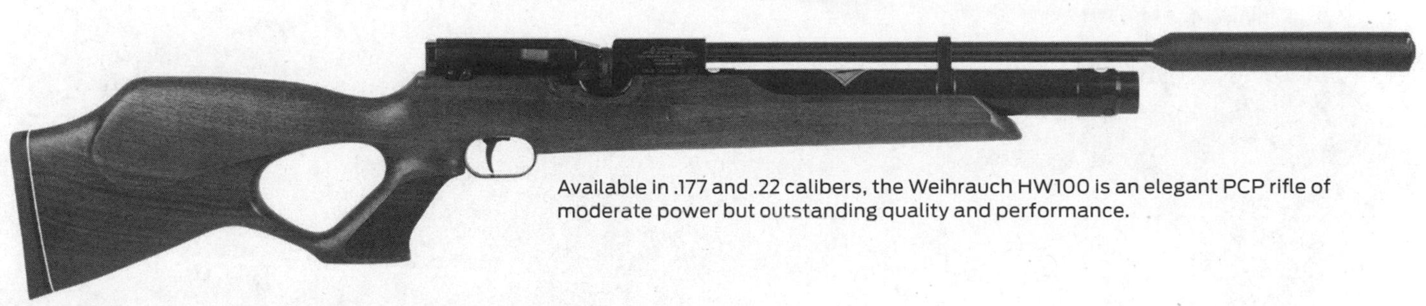

Available in .177 and .22 calibers, the Weihrauch HW100 is an elegant PCP rifle of moderate power but outstanding quality and performance.

Clicking a particular state brings up a list of species that can be legally hunted there with airguns.

Not all PCP rifles are high-powered models intended for use in hunting medium game. An elegant PCP 14-shot repeater from Weihrauch is the HW100, available in .177 and .22 calibers. From a full tank pressurized to 2,900 psi, 40 shots are on deck in .177 or 35 in .22 caliber. Velocities are 1,035 fps in .177 caliber or 870 fps in .22 caliber. The rifle wears a beautiful walnut thumbhole stock. With an MSRP of $1,499.99, this is a high-quality airgun for the serious competitor or small game hunter.

Airguns of Arizona offers several PCP models, one of which is the 10-shot Brocock Sniper XR Magnum in .22 caliber. It delivers energy up to 46 ft-lbs, making it a good choice for smaller pests or predator species up to the size of foxes or coyotes. Another superb model is the American Air Arms EVOL .30 Magnum, measuring only 37 inches and weighing 6.0 pounds, making it an excellent air rifle for hunting. At $2,695.00, it is a tool for the dedicated airgunner.

The American Air Arms EVOL in .22 caliber can deliver energies up to 60 ft-lbs, roughly equivalent to a .22 Short. In addition to these, Airguns of Arizona offers numerous other models produced by American Air Arms, Beeman, Brocock, Daystate, Hatsan and other manufacturers.

There can be no doubt that the airgun market is alive and well. However, with the current arms and ammo situation, there are shortages. Checking dealers' websites reveals the message "out of stock" frequently. The availability of airguns suitable for almost any purpose has caused many firearms users to gravitate toward this exciting and useful field. GD

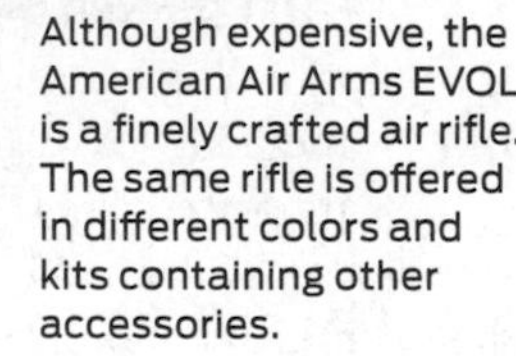

Although expensive, the American Air Arms EVOL is a finely crafted air rifle. The same rifle is offered in different colors and kits containing other accessories.

- REPORTS - from the Field AMMUNITION

›PHILIP MASSARO

Norma's EVOSTRIKE is a highly frangible, lead-free bullet suitable for varmints, furbearers and small to medium game.

(right) Federal's new .30 Super Carry promises to shake up the personal defense handgun ammo market. It uses a 100-grain .312-inch-diameter bullet at a muzzle velocity of 1,250 fps to deliver a cartridge optimal for concealed carry.

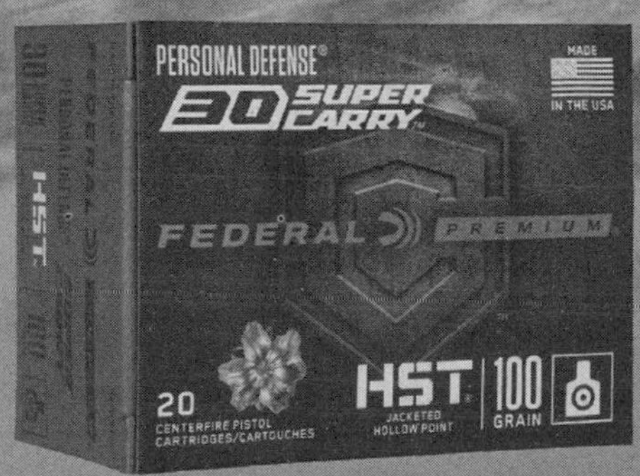

Ammunition and its availability, or lack thereof, has been a hot topic over the last couple of years. Happily, I can report that, slowly, ammunition is finding its way back onto the shelves, though perhaps not in the volume we all would like. Still, this is a good sign, and I hope things will have returned to normal the next time we chat. And even though the production of existing ammunition lines has been the focus of the ammunition companies, the research and development teams have not exactly been idle. There are some exciting product line extensions, a couple new cartridges, and some centennial commemorative ammo releases. Let's dive right in and see what's new.

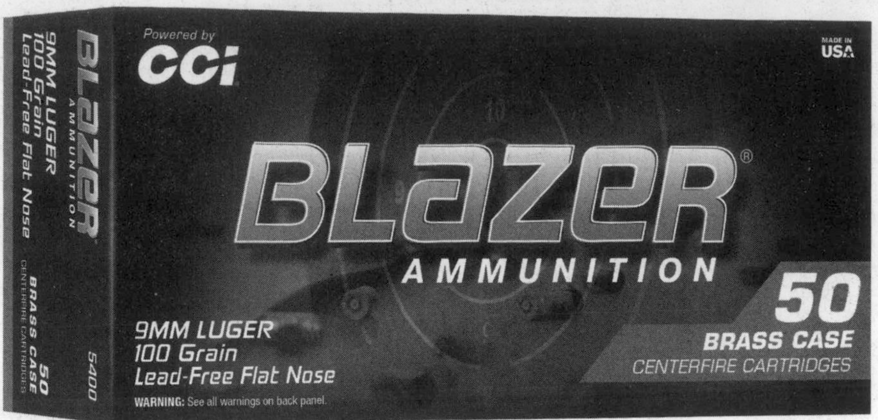

CCI BLAZER

The Blazer line has been extended to include the new .30 Super Carry (see below), using brass cases and a 115-grain full metal jacket bullet. Sold in 50-count boxes. *cci-ammunition.com*

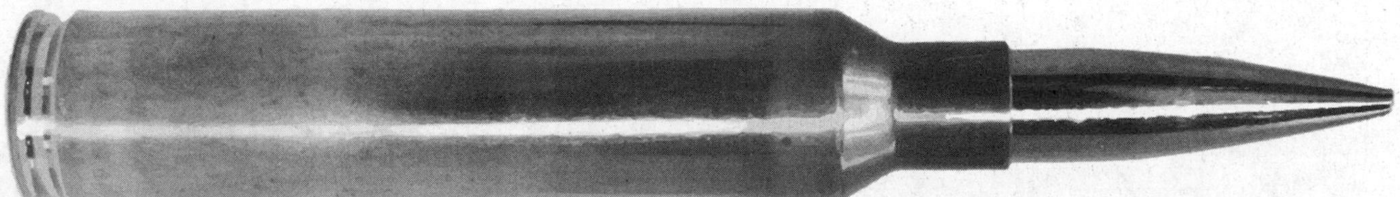

BERGER

For 2022, Berger has extended its loaded ammunition line to include the 6.5 PRC and .300 PRC, using its Elite Hunter projectiles. The 6.5 PRC load uses a 156-grain Elite Hunter bullet, with a G1 B.C. of .679, at a muzzle velocity of 2,960 fps, and the .300 PRC ammo uses a 205-grain Elite Hunter bullet at 2,985 fps. Berger has chosen a temperature-stable powder and loads it in premium cartridge cases. Sold in 20-count boxes. *bergerbullets.com*

BROWNING

Browning's Pro22 rimfire ammunition uses a 40-grain round-nose lead bullet at a subsonic velocity of 1,085 fps. The goal is to avoid the accuracy issues attributed to a rimfire bullet going through the transonic phase; there's no transonic window if it never goes supersonic. Browning has also used a precision target crimp for the optimum bullet alignment into the barrel's throat. Sold in boxes of 100 rounds. *browningammo.com*

FEDERAL

This year is the 100th anniversary of Federal ammunition, which is celebrated with some Limited Edition ammunition and product line extensions and a brand-new handgun cartridge.

Starting with the latter, the .30 Super Carry cartridge uses a 100-grain .312-inch-diameter bullet at a muzzle velocity of 1,250 fps to deliver a cartridge optimal for concealed carry. Giving better penetration depth and energy figures than the .380 Auto in a cartridge body small enough to best the 9mm Luger on magazine capacity, the .30 Super Carry has the potential to become a serious contender in the defensive handgun market. Available in the Federal Personal Defense line, it's loaded with the excellent HST hollowpoint bullet for self-defense. The American Eagle line has a full metal jacket bullet, great for economical practice.

The Personal Defense HST line has been extended to include the .327 Federal Magnum with a 104-grain HST bullet and the .357 Magnum with a 154-grain HST; this gives fans of those cartridges the excellent performance of the HST, which I consider to be the finest defensive handgun bullet on the market. The Punch handgun ammo line has been extended to include the .44 S&W Special, with a 180-grain jacketed hollowpoint, making an excellent choice for a defensive round for recoil-sensitive shooters or those who wish to use their .44 Magnum handguns at a lesser recoil level.

Federal is offering a trio of throwback boxes of ammunition to celebrate its 100th anniversary. The original Federal Blue Box in .30-30 Winchester, the vintage Monark box is available in .45 ACP. The old pattern of Hi-Power trap loads rounds out the trio of anniversary ammo. Federal's HammerDown line has been extended for lever-gun fans in .35 Remington with 220-grain hollowpoint bullets and the .444 Marlin with 270-grain hollowpoints; I can hear the Marlin fans rejoicing already.

Federal has introduced the High Over All competition target shotshells; these premium loads are designed to give you the best performance from your shotgun. With a

Federal has several new offerings in 6.5 PRC, including these from the Fusion line.

wide variety of 12-gauge loads built around 7.5, 8, 8.5, and 9 shot using the new PODIUM shot wad and loads in 20 gauge, 28 gauge and .410 bore to choose from, the new High Over All line comes with a tapered plastic hull and brass head for ease of reloading. A target shotshell primer gives uniform ignition, and an eight-segment crimp keeps the shot column in place.

Finally, Federal offers a 109-grain Berger Long Range Hybrid with a 6mm Creedmoor bullet at a muzzle velocity of 2,975 fps for long-range target shooters. With a G1 B.C. of .568, this load will give a flat trajectory and resist wind deflection. Sold in 20-count boxes. *federalpremium.com*

FIOCCHI

New for 2022, Fiocchi enters the world of turkey hunting with the new Golden Turkey TSS shotshells. Using Tungsten Super Shot weighing 18 grams per cubic centimeter, Fiocchi delivers the tight patterns that turkey hunters love. Because the shot is so dense, smaller pellet sizes can be employed, giving a dense pattern to quickly put that tom on the ground.

When I started hunting turkeys in the mid-1980s, heavy loads of large shot were the norm, and if my grandfather had lived long enough to see hunters using a .410-bore shotgun loaded with No. 9 shot for toms at 50 yards, I don't think he'd have believed his eyes. Fiocchi offers the Golden Turkey TSS in five packs, in 12-gauge 3-inch 1-5/8 oz. of No. 7 or No. 9 at 1,200 fps, 20-gauge 3-inch 1-3/8 oz. of No. 9 at 1,225 fps, and .410 bore 13/16 oz. of No. 9 at 1,100 fps. *fiocchiusa.com*

HORNADY

The big news from Hornady for 2022 is the new CX copper-alloy bullet, which is now featured in the Outfitter ammunition line. The CX (Copper alloy eXpanding) bullet is a new twist on the concepts embraced in the Hornady GMX (Gilding Metal eXpanding), with increased performance.

The CX bullet uses the same Heat Shield polymer tip of the ELD-X and ELD Match bullets, which resists deformation from the friction of atmospheric drag. This tip keeps a uniform Ballistic Coefficient for the best downrange consistency. Hornady engineers have revised the geometry of the grooves cut into the bullet's shank to further optimize the bullet's flight. Like the GMX, the CX offers high weight retention and reliable expansion and is compliant with lead-free areas. Hornady's Outfitter ammo uses nickel-plated cases to resist corrosion and a primer sealant to keep your powder dry.

Available in .243 Winchester 80 gr., .257 Weatherby Magnum 90 gr., 6.5 Creedmoor 120 gr., 6.5 PRC 130 gr., .270 WSM 130 gr., 7mm Remington Magnum 150 gr., 7mm WSM 150 gr., .308 Winchester 165 gr., .30-'06 Springfield 180 gr., .300 WSM 180 gr., .300 Winchester Magnum 180 gr., .300 Weatherby Magnum 180 gr., .300 PRC 190 gr., .300 Remington Ultra Magnum 180 gr., .338 Winchester Magnum 225 gr., .375 Ruger 250 gr., .375 H&H Magnum 250 gr., all in 20-count boxes. *hornady.com*

NOSLER

Nosler introduces its ASP (Assured Stopping Power) Handgun ammo, featuring the proprietary ASP hollowpoint bullet. When it comes to ammunition for your carry gun — the one upon which you may need to save the lives of yourself and/or loved ones — feeding, expansion, penetration and accuracy are paramount.

Nosler's ASP has a nicely curved ogive to ensure smooth feeding each time and a deeply skived copper jacket for consistent expansion upon impact at varying velocities. The ASP line extends the Nosler Match Grade ammo line and is loaded in brass cases with the Nosler headstamp. Coming in 20- or 50-count boxes, the new Nosler ASP ammo is available in 9mm Luger, with 115-, 124- and 147-grain bullets, the .40 S&W with 150- and 180-grain bullets, 10mm Auto with 180-grain bullets and .45 ACP with 185- and 230-grain bullets. *nosler.com*

NORMA

Fourth in the Strike series of ammunition, Norma has released its new EVOSTRIKE ammunition. This new hunting projectile and ammo line is the answer for those seeking a highly frangible yet lead-free bullet suitable for varmints, furbearers and small to medium game species. The EVOSTRIKE uses dual cores of tin. The front core is pre-fragmented for rapid expansion, and the rear core is designed to remain solid — at caliber dimension — to give the necessary penetration. A polymer tip is seated over a hollow cavity at the nose to initiate rapid expansion and maintain the meplat's shape. Norma uses a thin jacket and its proprietary 'tin-lock' to keep the cores in place, and the bullet features a nickel-coating to extend the life of your barrel. Rounding things out, Norma employs a boattail to increase the Ballistic Coefficient, keeping the trajectory as flat as possible and resisting wind deflection.

Now, we have become accustomed to the fact that copper is lighter than lead, and comparatively, the copper bullet will be longer than its lead counterpart, but tin is even lighter than copper. It would be challenging to get a tin bullet in many of the standard bullet weights to stabilize, so the EVOSTRIKE series features bullet weights on the shorter side of the spectrum. The EVOSTRIKE line includes the 6.5 Creedmoor and 6.5x55SE with a 93-grain bullet, .270 Winchester with a 96-grain bullet, 7mm Remington Magnum with a 127-grain bullet, .308 Winchester, .30-'06 Springfield and .300 Winchester Magnum with a 139-grain bullet, 8x57mm with a 139-grain bullet and 9.3x62 with a 184-grain bullet, all in 20-count boxes. *norma-ammunition.com*

REMINGTON

Remington's ammunition is back, though now under the umbrella of Vista Outdoor, and has some interesting new products for 2022. The famous Core-Lokt bullet has received a face-lift with the addition of the Big Green polymer tip, which has become so common of late, initiating expansion and maintaining the bullet's profile. However, the flat base of the original Core-Lokt has been retained. The copper jacket is still mechanically locked to the lead core. Available in 20-count boxes in .243 Winchester with a 95-grain bullet, 6.5 Creedmoor with 129-grain bullet, .270 Winchester with 130-grain bullet, 7mm Remington Magnum with 140-grain bullet, .308 Winchester and .30-'06 Springfield with 150-, 165-, and 180-grain bullets, .300 WSM with 150-grain bullet and .300 Winchester Magnum with 180-grain bullet.

Remington's Premier Match line is loaded with Berger and Sierra Match bullets and will deliver the pinpoint accuracy target shooters desire. The lineup includes the .223 Remington with 62-, 69-, and 77-grain Sierra MatchKing bullets, .224 Valkyrie with 90-grain MatchKings, 6mm Creedmoor with 107-grain MatchKings, 6.5 Grendel with 130-grain Berger bullets, 6.5 Creedmoor with 140-grain MatchKing bullets, 6.8 SPC with 115-grain Sierra MatchKings, .300 AAC Blackout with 125-grain Sierra MatchKing and .308 Winchester with

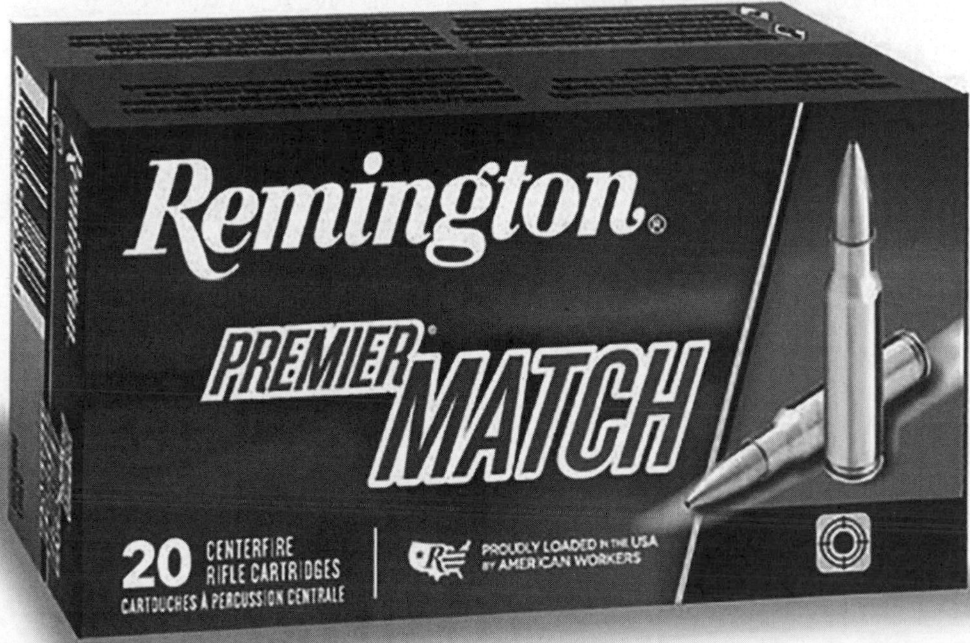

Weatherby's new .338 RPM, a heavy cartridge built for lightweight rifles.

168- and 175-grain Sierras.

The Peter's Premier Blue Paper Shotshells are back for a limited time this year, giving the retro feel of paper hulls with modern powders, primers and wads. These paper hulls reduce felt recoil, allowing for a better shooting experience for extended periods. Available in 12-gauge 2 ¾-inch in shot sizes of 7.5 and 8, with 1 oz. and 1 1/8 oz. loads.

Remington will offer two loads for the new .30 Super Carry cartridge, one in the High Terminal Performance line with a jacketed hollowpoint bullet, another in the UMC Range Ready line featuring a full metal jacket bullet that will minimize the exposure to lead vapors.

Remington has also reintroduced its rimfire ammo line and, for this year, will offer three loads for the .22 WMR and one for the .17 HMR, each in 50-count boxes. The .22 WMR will be loaded with a pointed soft-point bullet and a jacketed hollowpoint bullet, each at 40 grains and a 33-grain AccuTip-V bullet. The .17 HMR load uses a 17-grain AccuTip-V bullet. *remington.com*

SPEER

The .30 Super Carry is now loaded with the 100-grain Gold Dot hollowpoint, offering proven performance in the new concealed carry cartridge. With its uniform jacket bonded to the pressure-formed lead core, the Gold Dot is the choice of law enforcement and defensive handgunners alike, and the 100-grain Gold Dot leaves the muzzle at 1,150 fps from a 4-inch test barrel. Sold in 20-count boxes, in nickel-plated cases to resist corrosion and feed smoothly every time. *speer.com*

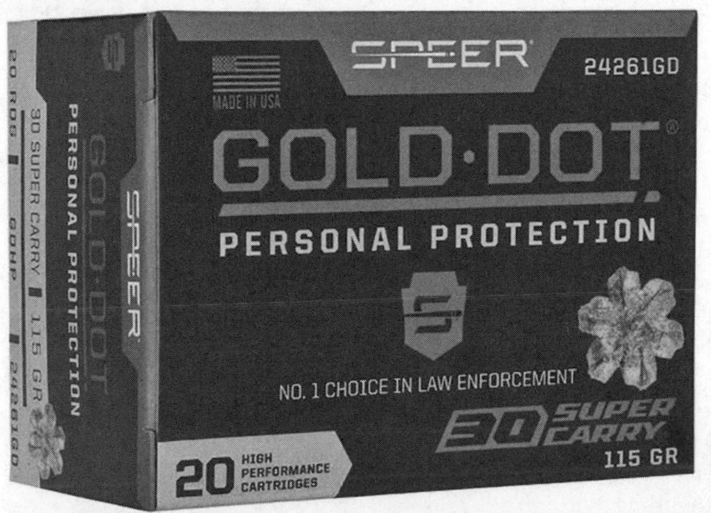

Winchester's 6.8 Western in now available with the lead-free Copper Impact bullet.

WEATHERBY

Building on the success of the 6.5 Weatherby RPM (Rebated Precision Magnum), Weatherby introduces the .338 Weatherby RPM. It is the 16th cartridge to achieve SAAMI approval and the second to feature an angular shoulder instead of the double-radius shoulder that is the Weatherby signature.

The 6.5 RPM was an elongated 6.5-284 Norma, and the .338 Weatherby RPM is simply the 6.5 RPM necked up to hold .338-inch-diameter bullets, retaining the rebated rim and larger body diameter. The concept is to give more killing power than the 6.5 RPM in a cartridge suited to the lighter Weatherby Backcountry rifles. The .338 Weatherby RPM uses a 225-grain bullet at a muzzle velocity of more than 2,800 fps and will cleanly take the largest North American species. If you like a light rifle with plenty of striking power, keep your eye on the .338 Weatherby RPM. *weatherby.com*

WINCHESTER

In the hot new 6.8 Western cartridge, Winchester uses a 162-grain Copper Extreme Point bullet.

Winchester has some interesting new products for the rifleman, bird hunter and varmint hunter alike. Starting with the rifle ammo, the 6.8 Western (of which I am an unabashed fan) gets a line extension with the addition of the 162-grain Copper Impact load, featuring the Copper Extreme Point bullet. I had the chance to hunt with this ammo last fall in Colorado, and while I didn't have the opportunity to use it on a warm target, I did take it out to 500 yards (at 100-yard increments) at the target range. It is wonderfully accurate, and the terminal performance demonstrated by my hunting partners showed that it is incredibly effective. Leaving the muzzle at 2,875 fps, it has a flat trajectory and will retain a significant portion of its weight.

Winchester also brings the 170-grain Power Point cup-and-core bullet to the 6.8 Western family, leaving the muzzle at 2,920 fps and giving the terminal performance of that classic design. Sold in 20-count boxes.

Winchester's Super X brand celebrates its 100th anniversary this year, and there are commemorative boxes of centerfire and rimfire ammo, plus shotshells to mark the occasion. Rifle ammo is loaded with the Power Point soft-point bullet, available in .243 Winchester, .270 Winchester, .30-30 Winchester and .308 Winchester. Shotshells include a heavy-game load and a buckshot load, both in 12 gauge, and the rimfire offering is the .22 LR with a 40-grain Power Point jacketed hollowpoint. The Super Pheasant Diamond Grade is built around charges of antimony-rich No. 5 shot, featuring two 12-gauge loads — a 2 ¾-inch shell with 1 3/8 oz. of shot and a 3-inch shell with 1 5/8 oz. of shot at 1,300 and 1,350 fps respectively, and a 2 ¾-inch 20-gauge load using a 1-oz. payload at a velocity of 1,300 fps. Sold in 25-count boxes, the Diamond Grade shotshells will give the roosters cause for panic.

The Blind Side 2 waterfowl shotshells feature the proprietary Hex shot, rounded on the edges but offer the geometrical advantage of staking nice and neat in the shot column. The shotshell's head is nickel-plated to resist the effects of the weather that waterfowl and waterfowlers alike adore, but their ammunition does not. Furthermore, the Drylock wad keeps the shot column tight yet prevents moisture from reaching the powder charge while using a conformation that interacts positively with varying chokes. Sold in 25-count boxes. *winchester.com* GD

- REPORTS - from the Field RELOADING

›PHILIP MASSARO

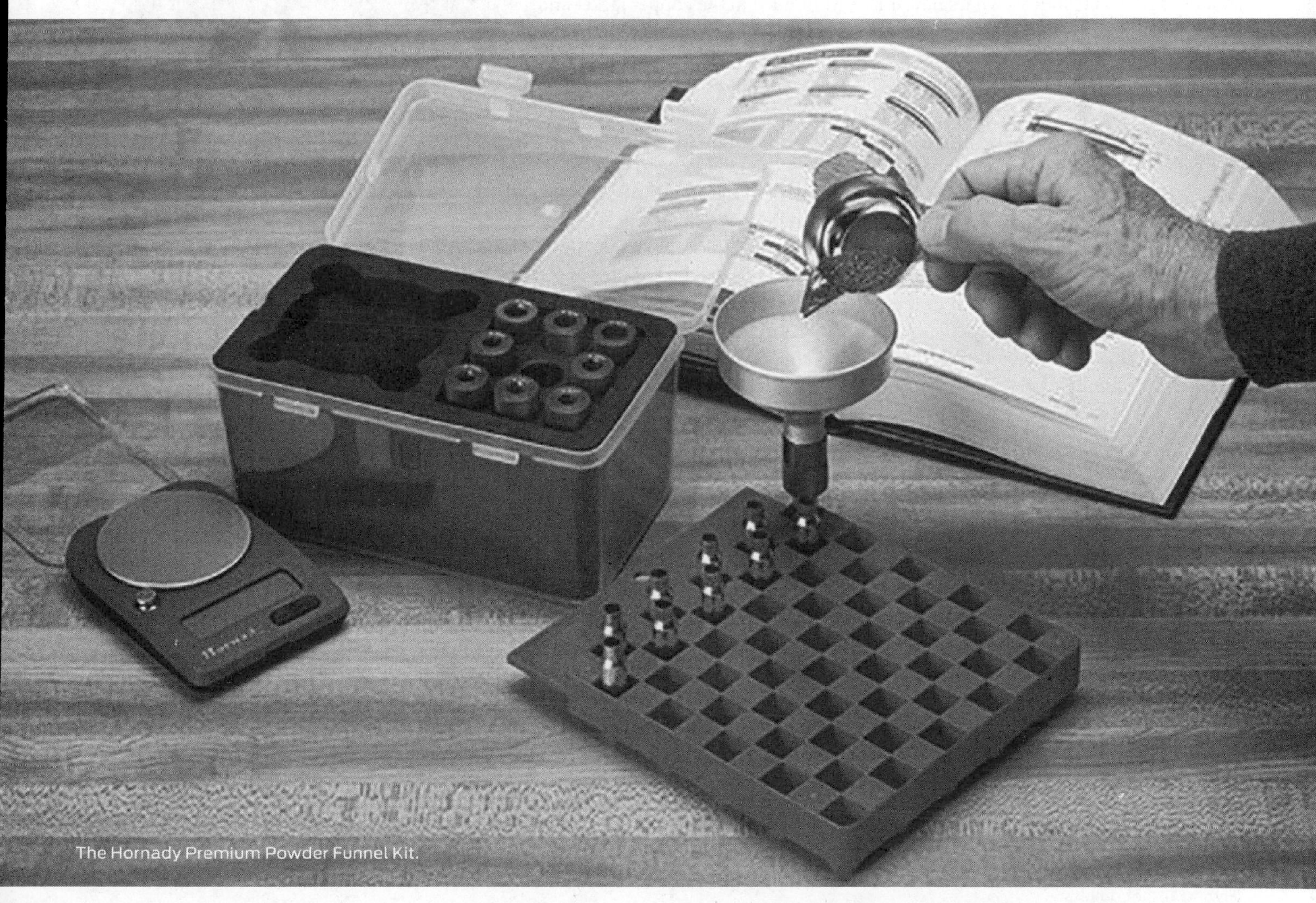
The Hornady Premium Powder Funnel Kit.

With the ammunition crunch slowly — very slowly — beginning to end, shooters are now faced with the terrible truth that ammunition costs are higher than ever, and with the state of our current economy, there isn't much chance of that changing anytime soon. As a result, I've seen a renewed interest in reloading, though many of those prospective loaders will meet a similar crunch when it comes to reloading components. Powder seems to be trickling back into supply, and bullets are much more readily available than they were when last we spoke, but it's the primers that are posing the biggest issue now. With fingers crossed, we'll see some primers at reasonable prices sooner rather than later.

All the crunch stuff aside, the reloading tools/component bullet companies have not been idle. Let's look at what's new for this year.

BERGER

Berger's new .30-cal. 245-grain Long-Range Hybrid Target bullets.

Leaders in the development of new bullet technology, Berger announced the release of the 245-grain .30-caliber Long Range Hybrid Target bullet. As Berger has demonstrated, the long-range shooter's best friend is a bullet with the lowest variation in Ballistic Coefficient, not necessarily the bullet with the highest stated B.C. value.

Berger's latest has less than 1 percent variation (verified by Doppler Radar) and at 245 grains will certainly retain enough energy and velocity to give consistent results beyond the one-mile mark. The LRHT uses the same hybrid tangent-to-secant ogive that allows the bullet to best 'jump' into the lands yet maintain that high B.C. value. This bullet has a stunning G1 B.C. value of 0.846 and a G7 B.C. value of 0.433. It is a sound choice for loading in cartridges such as the .300 PRC, .300 Norma Magnum and .300 Remington Ultra Magnum. Berger Meplat Reduction Technology enhances B.C. uniformity, and the J4 jacket has long proven its worth. *berger.com*

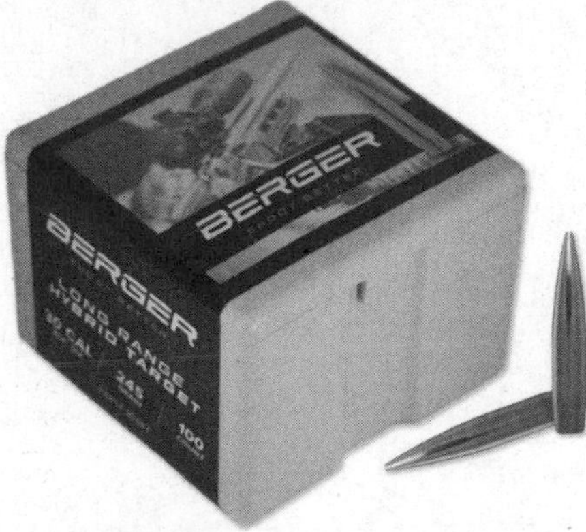

Berger's new .30-cal. 245-grain Long-Range Hybrid Target bullets.

FEDERAL

For 2022, Federal extends the Terminal Ascent component bullet line to include some heavier weights in .277, 7mm, and .308 calibers. Terminal Ascent is the latest in the family of Trophy Bonded Bear Claw designs with the highest B.C. of any family member. The short lead core is bonded to the copper jacket and thick copper base at the bullet's rear, and Federal's SlipStream polymer tip resists deformation in flight and initiates expansion. To minimize the effects of atmospheric drag, as well as reduce bearing pressures, Federal utilizes the AccuChannel grooves on the bullet shank. The popular line will include 155-grain .277 inch, 175-grain .284-inch (7mm) and 215-grain .308-diameter offerings. *federalpremium.com*

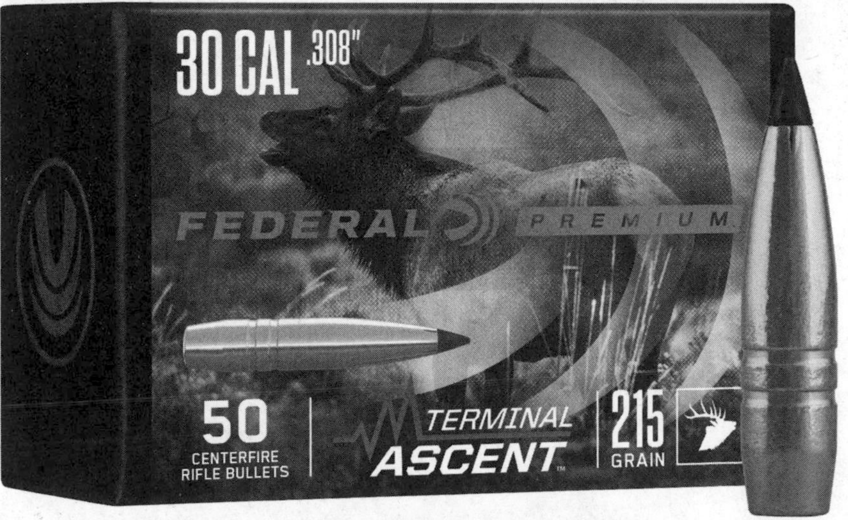

Federal's Terminal Ascent bullet.

FORSTER

Famous for its Co-Ax reloading press, which allows the reloading die to be snapped into a recess rather than be threaded into place, Forster announces a pair of useful tools. First up is the Accu-Ring Die Lock Ring, which is

Forster Neck Tension Gauge.

The Forster Accu-Ring Die Lock Ring.

graduated radially to give .001-inch adjustment per graduation when used with the Co-Ax press. Quite obviously, this will greatly aid in the precise adjustment of resizing, crimping and seating dies.

Second is the Forster Neck Tension Gauge, an ingenious yet simple tool designed to help the reloader sort their brass based on neck tension. Each caliber-specific tool — which looks like a rod with a screwdriver handle — has four different stepped-diameter areas, allowing the user to feel exactly how much tension their brass is giving (based on inside neck diameter), and to check to see if a 'donut' of brass has formed at the neck-shoulder junction. Consistency is key when it comes to precision shooting and keeping your neck tension uniform will improve your rifle's performance. Available in .223, .243, .264, .284, and .308, either individually or as a kit with all five gauges. *forsterproducts.com*

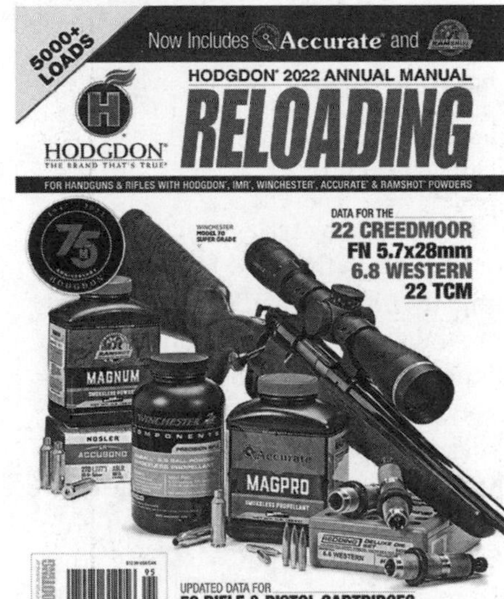

Hodgdon Powder Company's 75th Anniversary 2022 Annual Reloading Manual.

HODGDON

To celebrate the 75th Anniversary of Hodgdon Powder, the company's *2022 Annual Reloading Manual* is thicker than ever with more than 5,000 loads and has been updated to include Accurate and Ramshot powders. At 192 pages, it's stocked with good stuff, including eight feature pieces and new data for the .22 Creedmoor, .22 TCM, FN 5.7x28mm, and (one of my favorites) the 6.8 Western. While I always look forward to the annual release of the Hodgdon manual, this year's anniversary edition is a special one, and will have a place on the reloading library shelf. *hodgdon.com*

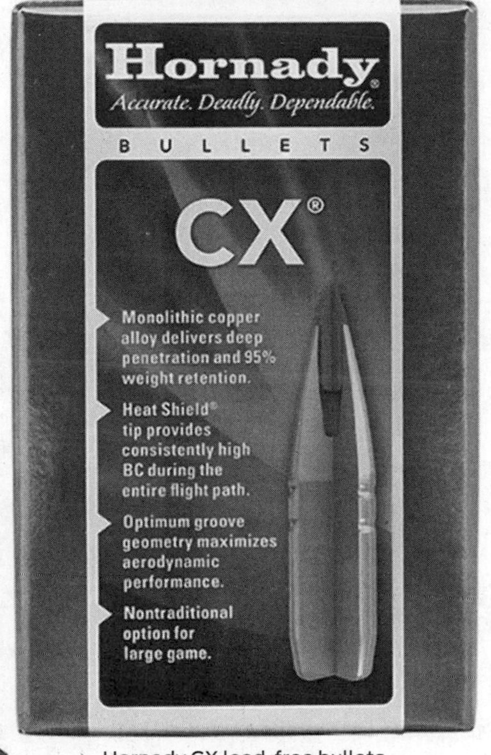

Hornady CX lead-free bullets.

HORNADY

The Big Red H has a new bullet line for 2022: the CX (Copper alloy eXpanding) lead-free, polymer-tip projectile. Replacing the Hornady GMX bullet, the new CX design features the same Heat Shield Tip Hornady uses for the ELD-X and ELD Match bullets. Hornady has also revised the groove geometry on the bullet's shank to give better downrange performance. The bullet is compliant in the lead-free zones, and like the GMX, weight retention is high, expansion reliable, and penetration deep. Available in 6mm (80 and 90 grains), .257 (90 grains), 6.5mm (120 and 130 grains), .277 (100 and 130 grains), 7mm (139 and 150 grains), .308 (165, 180 and 190 grains), .338 (185 and 225 grains) and .375 (250 grains).

Hornady has also announced the release of the Premium Powder Funnel Kit: a set of caliber-specific high-capacity funnels that are static free, and keep your powder where it belongs: in the case, and not all over the bench. There are nine different caliber funnels in the kit: .224, .243/6mm, .257, .264/6.5mm, .277, .284/7mm, .308, .338, and .375. *hornady.com*

LEE PRECISION

Lee Precision offers new Pacesetter dies sets for the 6.5 Weatherby RPM and 6.8 Western — and the excellent Factory Crimp die for both cartridges. These dies sets feature the Lee Ultimate Lock Rings. Also new is a 4 Die Set for the new .30 Super Carry, which includes the

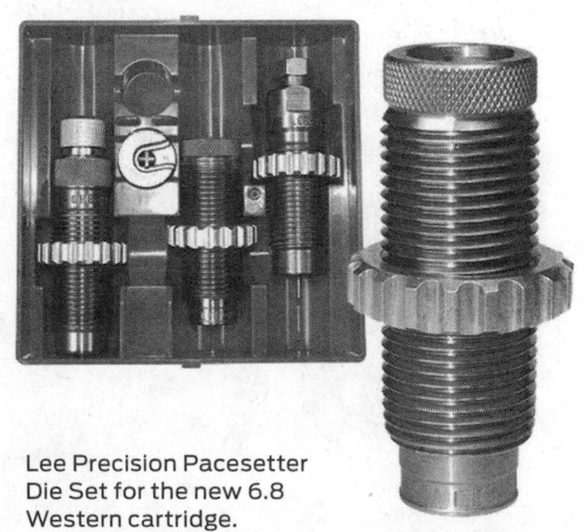

Lee Precision Pacesetter Die Set for the new 6.8 Western cartridge.

Full Length Sizing Die, Bullet Seating Die, Powder Through Expanding Die and Carbide Factory Crimp die. Like all Lee die sets, it includes a Universal Shell Holder, polymer powder dipper and load data sheet. *leeprecision.com*

North Fork 6.5 hunting bullets.

NORTH FORK

Though there may not be any newly announced products from North Fork, I felt it worthy to include it here for no other reason that its products are in the hands of reloaders once again. After closing its doors, and being sold to a Swedish company, there were rumors of going back into production, but there were no bullets on the shelves. Happily, that has changed, and these excellent hunting bullets are once again a viable option for those headed to the hunting fields. *northforkbullets.com*

NOSLER

Though Nosler may be famous for its rifle bullets — and rightfully so — this year it has introduced a new handgun bullet: the Assured Stopping Power or ASP jacketed hollowpoint. The idea behind the ASP is to give the accuracy of the Nosler Sporting Handgun bullet, but with a skived jacket to provide immediate expansion for defensive applications. Nosler's engineers have created a bullet which will give the penetration needed to stop the threat, yet that skived jacket will expand enough to minimize the chances of over-penetration. Nosler offers this bullet in loaded ammunition, as well as in component form for the reloader. Available in 9mm (115, 124 and 147 grains), 10mm (135, 150,180 and 200 grains) and .45 (230 grains), in 250-count boxes. *nosler.com*

Nosler Assured Stopping Power (ASP) jacketed hollowpoint.

RCBS ChargeMaster Link.

RCBS ChargeMaster Supreme.

RCBS

RCBS introduces two new electronic powder dispensers in its ChargeMaster series. The ChargeMaster Link is based on the load cell of the Chargemaster Lite, has an LCD touchscreen, 2,000-grain capacity and can be run via Bluetooth, using the free RCBS app. With .1-grain accuracy, the ChargeMaster Link runs off the included power supply or an external battery pack, for those who wish to bring it along to the range for load development or competition.

The ChargeMaster Supreme is similar, but with a few more features that might appeal to certain customers. The 1,500-grain capacity will handle the largest of powder loads, and like the Link, accuracy is good to .1 grain. The Supreme can store 50 of your favorite loads, is Bluetooth-enabled and can run on the wall power supply or an external battery pack. Perhaps best of all, it comes with a powder drain alarm, and if (like me) you've ever dumped a half-pound of powder into the dispenser, only to have it drain all over the bench, you'll appreciate this feature. Both units have an audible beep, which can be silenced if you so choose, and a flashing overcharge warning. *rcbs.com*

Redding NXGen Carbide Sizing Dies for straightwall cases.

REDDING

There is a new series of sizing dies for 2022 from the good folks at Redding: the NXGen Carbide Sizing Dies for straightwall cases. Redding was a pioneer in the use of titanium carbide, evolving into the introduction of the Dual Ring Carbide Sizing Dies. Redding's new sizing dies address the entire case, not just the forward portion holding the projectile. "NXGen Carbide sizing dies leverage the latest advances in materials science, specifically as related to Carbide, creating new and innovative designs to increase ease of use and improved dimensional accuracy in straight-walled cases," Redding notes.

"These NXGen designs create cases with profiles which do not exhibit the Wasp Waist often found with use of a traditional single ring carbide. NXGen uses a greater carbide contact surface giving these dies the ability to better compensate for a variety of wall thicknesses without over sizing the case body." *redding-reloading.com* GD

AUTO-ORDNANCE 1927A-1 THOMPSON
Caliber: .45 ACP. Barrel: 16.5 in. Weight: 13 lbs. Length: About 41 in. overall (Deluxe). Stock: Walnut stock and vertical fore-end. Sights: Blade front, open rear adjustable for windage. Features: Recreation of Thompson Model 1927. Semi-auto only. Deluxe model has finned barrel, adjustable rear sight and compensator; Standard model has plain barrel and military sight. Available with 100-round drum or 30-round stick magazine. Made in USA by Auto-Ordnance Corp., a division of Kahr Arms.
Price: Deluxe w/stick magazine **$1,551.00**
Price: Deluxe w/drum magazine **$2,583.00**
Price: Lightweight model w/stick mag **$1,403.00**

AUTO-ORDNANCE CASE HARDENED THOMPSON
Calibers: 45 ACP. Capacity: 20-round stick magazine. Barrel: 18-in. finned. Weight: 13 lbs. Length: 41 in. Stock: Walnut, fixed buttstock with vertical foregrip. Sights: Blade front with open, adjustable rear. Features: Hand-machined semi-automatic example of the original Thomson submachine gun, using blued steel and hard wood stocks. The Case Hardened line of Tommy Guns are meant to be a work of art built around a 1927 pattern Thompson. American made.
Price: **$1,872.00**

AUTO-ORDNANCE 1927 A-1 COMMANDO
Similar to the 1927 A-1 except has Parkerized finish, black-finish wood butt, pistol grip, horizontal fore-end. Comes with black nylon sling. Introduced 1998. Made in USA by Auto-Ordnance Corp., a division of Kahr Arms.
Price: T1-C **$1,479.00**

AUTO ORDNANCE M1 CARBINE
Caliber: .30 Carbine (15-shot magazine). Barrel: 18 in. Weight: 5.4 to 5.8 lbs. Length: 36.5 in. Stock: Wood or polymer. Sights: Blade front, flip-style rear. Features: A faithful recreation of the military carbine.
Price: **$1,036.00**
Price: Folding stock **$1,137.00**

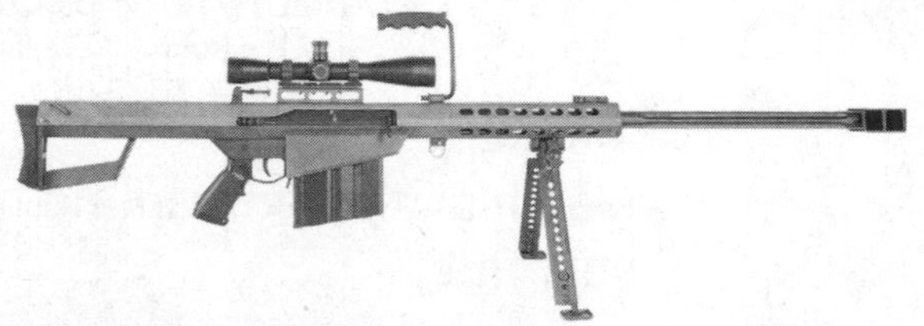

BARRETT MODEL 82A-1 SEMI-AUTOMATIC
Calibers: .416 Barret, 50 BMG. Capacity: 10-shot detachable box magazine. Barrel: 29 in. Weight: 28.5 lbs. Length: 57 in. overall. Stock: Composition with energy-absorbing recoil pad. Sights: Scope optional. Features: Semiautomatic, recoil operated with recoiling barrel. Three-lug locking bolt; muzzle brake. Adjustable bipod. Introduced 1985. Made in USA by Barrett Firearms.
Price: **$9,119.00**

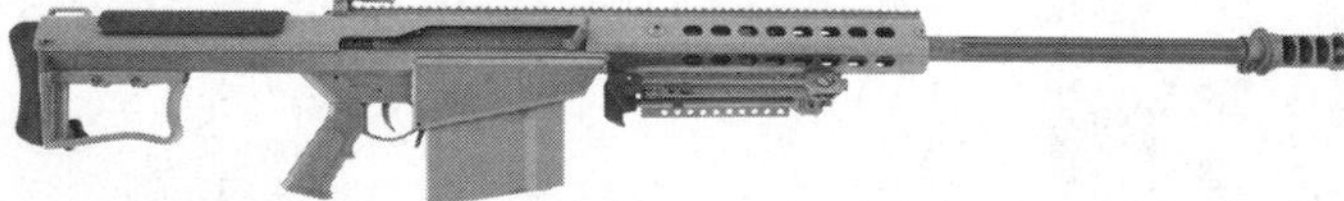

BARRETT M107A1
Caliber: 50 BMG. Capacity: 10-round detachable magazine. Barrels: 20 or 29 in. Sights: 27-in. optics rail with flip-up iron sights. Weight: 30.9 lbs. Finish: Flat Dark Earth. Features: Four-port cylindrical muzzle brake. Quick-detachable Barrett QDL Suppressor. Adjustable bipod and monopod.
Price: **$12,281.00**

BERETTA CX4 STORM CARBINE
Calibers: 9mm, 40 S&W, .45 ACP. Barrel: 16.6 in. Stock: Black synthetic with thumbhole. Sights: Ghost ring. Features: Blowback single action, ambidextrous controls, Picatinny quad rail system. Reintroduced in 2017.
Price: **$700.00**

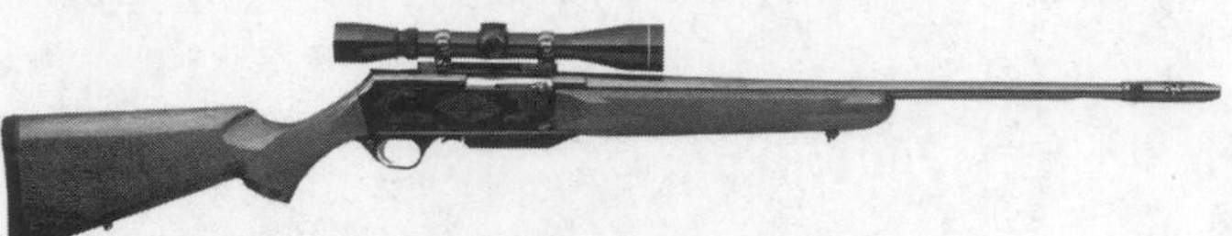

BROWNING BAR SAFARI AND SAFARI W/BOSS SEMI-AUTO
Calibers: Safari: .25-06 Rem., .270 Win., 7mm Rem. Mag., .30-06, .308 Win., .300 Win. Mag., .338 Win. Mag. Safari w/BOSS: .270 Win., 7mm Rem. Mag., .30-06 Spfl., .300 Win. Mag., .338 Win. Mag. Barrels: 22–24 in. round tapered. Weights: 7.4–8.2 lbs. Lengths: 43–45 in. overall. Stock: French walnut pistol grip stock and fore-end, hand checkered. Sights: No sights. Features: Has new bolt release lever; removable trigger assembly with larger trigger guard; redesigned gas and buffer systems. Detachable 4-round box magazine. Scroll-engraved receiver is tapped for scope mounting. BOSS barrel vibration modulator and muzzle brake system available. Mark II Safari introduced 1993. Made in Belgium.
Price: BAR MK II Safari **$1,230.00**
Price: BAR Safari w/BOSS **$1,400.00**

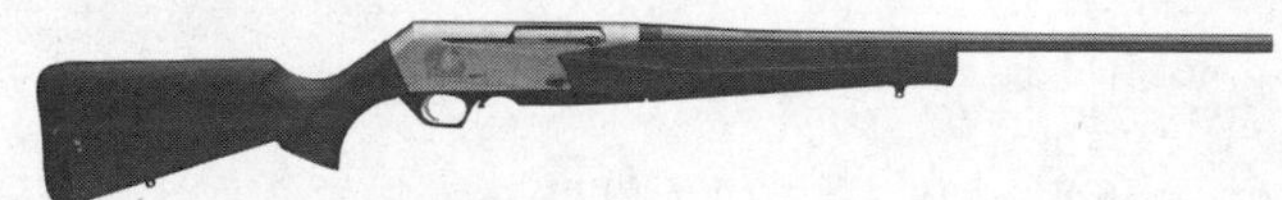

BROWNING BAR MK III SERIES
Calibers: .243 Win., 7mm-08, .270 Win., .270 WSM, 7mm Rem., .308 Win, .30-06, .300 Win. Mag., .300 WSM. Capacities: Detachable 4 or 5-shot magazine. Barrel: 22, 23 or 24 in.es. Stock: Grade II checkered walnut, shim adjustable. Camo stock with composite gripping surfaces available. Stalker model has composite stock. Weight: 7.5 lbs. Features: Satin nickel alloy with high relief engraving, stylized fore-end.
Price: .... **$1,340.00–$1,440.00**
Price: Left Hand .... **$1,380.00–$1,480.00**
Price: Camo **$1,380.00**
Price: Stalker .... **$1,340.00–$1,440.00**
Price: Left-hand BAR MK3 Stalker .... **$1,380.00–$1,480.00**
Price: Smoked Bronze Cerakote and OVIX camo .... **$1,719.00–$1,829.00**

BROWNING BAR MK 3 DBM SERIES
Caliber: 308 Win. Capacity: 10-round "detachable box magazine," so named for the DBM series. Barrel: 18-in. fluted blued. Length: 40-1/8 in. Weight: 7 lbs. 6 oz. Stock: Choice of two model variants. DBM Wood uses Grade II Turkish Walnut with oil finish. DBM Stalker uses black synthetic. Features: Picatinny top rail for optics mounting. Other features comparable to standard BAR Mk 3.
Price: BAR MK3 DBM Wood **$1,590.00**
Price: BAR MK3 DBM Stalker **$1,560.00**
Price: Left-hand BAR MK3 DBM Wood **$1,570.00**
Price: Left-hand BAR MK3 DBM Stalker **$1,540.00**

CENTURY INTERNATIONAL AES-10 HI-CAP
Caliber: 7.62x39mm. Capacity: 30-shot magazine. Barrel: 23.2 in. Weight: NA. Length: 41.5 in. overall. Stock: Wood grip, fore-end. Sights: Fixed notch rear, windage-adjustable post front. Features: RPK-style, accepts standard double-stack AK-type mags. Side-mounted scope mount, integral carry handle, bipod. Imported by Century Arms Int'l.
Price: AES-10, From **$450.00**

Prices given are believed to be accurate at time of publication however, many factors affect retail pricing so exact prices are not possible.

CENTURY INTERNATIONAL M70AB2 SPORTER
Caliber: 7.62x39mm. Capacity: 30-shot magazine. Barrel: 16.25 in. Weight: 7.5 lbs. Length: 34.25 in. overall. Stocks: Metal grip, wood fore-end. Sights: Fixed notch rear, windage-adjustable post front. Features: Two 30-rd. double-stack magazine, cleaning kit, compensator, bayonet lug and bayonet. Paratrooper-style Kalashnikov with under-folding stock. Imported by Century Arms Int'l.
Price: M70AB2, From **$480.00**

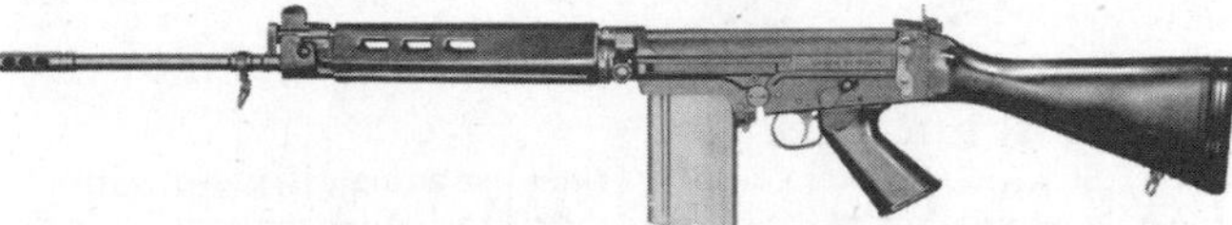

DSA SA58 STANDARD
Caliber: .308 Win. Barrel: 21 in. bipod cut w/threaded flash hider. Weight: 8.75 lbs. Length: 43 in. Stock: Synthetic, X-Series or optional folding para stock. Sights: Elevation-adjustable post front, windage-adjustable rear peep. Features: Fully adjustable short gas system, high-grade steel or 416 stainless upper receiver. Many variants available. Made in USA by DSA, Inc.
Price: From **$1,700.00**

DSA SA58 CARBINE
Caliber: .308 Win. Barrel: 16.25 in. bipod cut w/threaded flash hider. Features: Carbine variation of FAL-style rifle. Other features identical to SA58 Standard model. Made in USA by DSA, Inc.
Price: **$1,700.00**

EXCEL ARMS X-SERIES
Caliber: .22 LR, 5.7x28mm (10 or 25-round); .30 Carbine (10 or 20-round magazine). 9mm (10 or 17 rounds). Barrel: 18 in. Weight: 6.25 lbs. Length: 34 to 38 in. Features: Available with or without adjustable iron sights. Blow-back action (5.57x28) or delayed blow-back (.30 Carbine).
Price: .22 LR **$504.00**
Price: 5.7x28 or 9mm .... **$795.00–$916.00**

FNH FNAR COMPETITION
Caliber: .308 Win. Capacity: 10-shot magazine. Barrel: 20 in. fluted. Weight: 8.9 lbs. Length: 41.25 in. overall. Sights: None furnished. Optical rail atop receiver, three accessory rails on fore-end. Stock: Adjustable for comb height, length of pull, cast-on and cast-off. Blue/gray laminate. Based on BAR design.
Price: **$1,767.00**

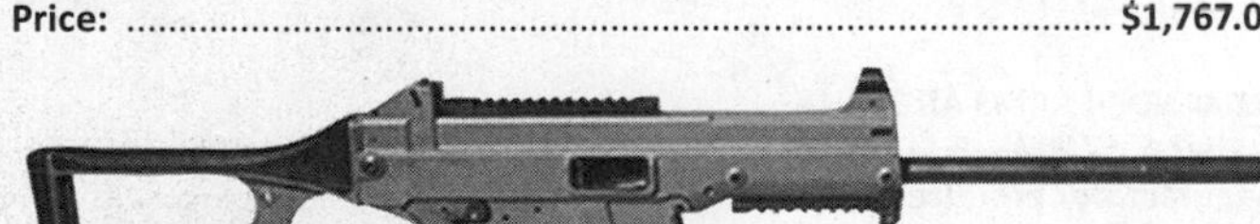

HECKLER & KOCH MODEL USC
Caliber: .45 ACP. Capacity: 10-round magazine. Barrel: 16 in. Weight: 6.13 lbs. Length: 35.4 in. Features: Polymer construction, adjustable rear sight, ambidextrous safety/selector, optional Picatinny rail. Civilian version of HK UMP submachine gun.
Price: **$1,499.00**

INLAND M1 1945 CARBINE
Caliber: .30 Carbine. Capacity: 15 rounds. Barrel: 18 in. Weight: 5 lbs. 3 oz. Features: A faithful reproduction of the last model that Inland manufactured in 1945, featuring a type 3 bayonet lug/barrel band, adjustable rear sight, push button safety, and walnut stock. Scout Model has 16.5-in. barrel, flash hider, synthetic stock with accessory rail. Made in the USA.
Price: **$1,299.00**
Price: Scout Model **$1,449.00**

KALASHNIKOV USA
Caliber: 7.62x39mm. Capacity: 30-round magazine. AK-47 series made in the USA in several variants and styles. Barrel: 16.25 in. Weight: 7.52 lbs.
Price: KR-9 Side-folding stock **$1,249.00**
Price: US132S Synthetic stock **$799.00**
Price: US132W Wood carbine **$836.00**

RUGER PC CARBINE
Calibers: 9mm or 40 S&W. Capacity: 17 (9mm), 15 (40 S&W) pistol magazines.10-round state-compliant versions available. Barrel: 16-in. cold-hammer forged, threaded, fluted. Sights: Standard model with iron sights; chassis models with Picatinny optics rail. Length: 32.25–35.5 in. Weight: 7.3 lbs. Stock: Choice of synthetic, fixed, or adjustable aluminum chassis furniture. Features: Aluminum alloy receiver, hardcoat anodized. Utilizes 10/22 trigger components with light, crisp pull. Ergonomic pistol grip with extended trigger reach for precise control. Interchangeable magazine wells for use with common Ruger and Glock magazines.
Price: **$649.00**
Price: With handguard **$729.00**
Price: Adjustable Chassis **$799.00**
Price: State Compliant **$799.00**
Price: Distributor Exclusives .... **$779.00–$899.00**

RUGER MINI-14 RANCH RIFLE
Calibers: .223 Rem., .300 Blackout (Tactical Rifle). Capacity: 5-shot or 20-shot detachable box magazine. Barrel: 18.5 in. Rifling twist 1:9 in. Weights: 6.75–7 lbs. Length: 37.25 in. overall. Stocks: American hardwood, steel reinforced, or synthetic. Sights: Protected blade front, fully adjustable Ghost Ring rear. Features: Fixed piston gas-operated, positive primary extraction. New buffer system, redesigned ejector system. Ruger S100RM scope rings included on Ranch Rifle. Heavier barrels added in 2008, 20-round magazine added in 2009.
Price: Mini-14/5, Ranch Rifle, blued, wood stock **$999.00**
Price: K-Mini-14/5, Ranch Rifle, stainless, scope rings **$1,069.00**
Price: Mini-14 Tactical Rifle: Similar to Mini-14 but with 16.12 in. barrel with flash hider, black synthetic stock, adjustable sights **$1,019.00**

SIG-SAUER MPX PCC
Caliber: 9mm. 30-round capacity. Barrel: 16 in. Features: M-LOK handguard, 5-position folding telescoping stock. Weight: 6.6 lbs. Sights: none.
Price: From **$2,016.00**

SPRINGFIELD ARMORY M1A
Caliber: 7.62mm NATO (.308). Capacities: 5- or 10-shot box magazine. Barrel: 25.062 in. with flash suppressor, 22 in. without suppressor. Weight: 9.75 lbs. Length: 44.25 in. overall. Stock: American walnut with walnut-colored heat-resistant fiberglass handguard. Matching walnut handguard available. Also available with fiberglass stock. Sights: Military, square blade front, full click-adjustable aperture rear. Features: Commercial equivalent of the U.S. M-14 service rifle with no provision for automatic firing. From Springfield Armory.
Price: SOCOM 16 .... **$1,987.00**
Price: Scout Squad, From **$1,850.00**
Price: Standard M1A, From **$1,685.00**
Price: Loaded Standard, From **$1,847.00**
Price: National Match, From **$2,434.00**
Price: Super Match (heavy premium barrel) about **$2,965.00**
Price: Tactical, From .... **$3,619.00–$4,046.00**

2A ARMAMENT BLR-16 RIFLES

Calibers: 5.56 NATO/.223 Rem., 16-in. barrels. 2A Armament is a subsidiary of 2A Machine, a CNC, ISO 9001 and AS 9100 certified advanced-manufacturing machining shop for the aerospace, medical, prosthetic, motorsports, semiconductor and outdoor recreation markets. Established 2009. Based in Boise, Idaho. BLR-16 Gen 2 is company's lightest rifle at 5.0 lbs. No magazine included. BLR Gen 2 Carbon has Proof Research carbon-fiber barrel, Timney 2-stage trigger, MAGPUL CTR stock, and "2A-GRAY" Cerakote finish. Palouse-Lite Rifle has forged U/L receiver. Weight: 5.3 lbs.

Price: BLR-16 GEN 2 Rifle **$2,100.00**
Price: BLR-16 Kuiu Vias 2.0 .... **$2,600.00**
Price: BLR-16 GEN 2 Carbon Rifle **$3,675.00**

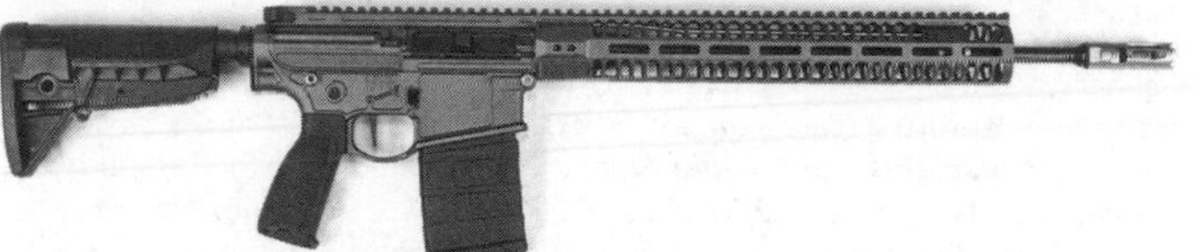

2A ARMAMENT XLR-18 RIFLES

Calibers: .308 Win. Barrels: 18 in. Xanthos Lite fully assembled rifle is Cerakoted in Cobalt Grey and weighs in at 6.75 lbs. Introduced 2020. Key features include Straight Cut Xanthos Lite rail, tension lock design for attachment with an M-LOK mounting solution. Titanium parts include gas block, takedown pins, and X4 brake. Lower receiver is CNC machined 7075-T6 billet with flared mag-well, type III class 2 anodized finish, rear tensioning screw, rear takedown spring retainer, and screw-in bolt catch pin. Upper receiver has retained port door rod, M4-style feed ramps, machined T numbers in Picatinny rail. Bolt and carrier (full mass) are 8620 machined body with QPQ process, 9310 machined bolt, cryogenically treated, MPT, QPQ process. Barrel is a lightweight contour .308 profile, 4150 gun barrel steel with QPQ Nitride, black oxide extension, rifle-length gas system, .308 Match chamber, 1 in 10 twist. Other features: .750 diameter titanium gas block; titanium .308 X4 brake; BCM MOD 0 grip, BCM SOPMOD stock; Timney 2-stage, flat trigger; through-drilled titanium takedown pins.

Price: **$2,650.00**

2A ARMAMENT XLR-20 RIFLES

Calibers: 6.5 Creedmoor. Barrels: 20 in. Similar configuration to XLR-18 rifles. Xanthos Lite XLR-20 weight, 6.85 lbs. Barrel is 2A contour lightweight profile, 4150 barrel steel with QPQ Nitride, black oxide extension, rifle-length gas system, 6.5mm Creedmoor SAAMI Chamber, 1:8 twist.

Price: **$2,725.00**
Price: w/Kuiu Vias camo Cerakote finish **$3,225.00**

ADAMS ARMS P-SERIES RIFLES

Adams Arms' proprietary gas-piston operating systems mechanically actuate the bolt carrier external of the receiver. P1 model features ergonomic mid-length handguards, standard Picatinny adjustable block piston system, tactical stock and grip with QD mounts, enhanced triggerguard. Barrel lengths and chamberings: 16 in. (5.56). P2 model includes ergonomic free float rail, P-Series Micro Block piston system. P2 barrel lengths and chamberings: 16 in. (5.56); 16 in. (300 BLK). P3 line features Proof Research carbon-fiber-wrapped barrel, jet comp, ergonomic free float rail, and P-Series Micro Block piston system. Other features include CMC Flat Bow trigger, a rubber ergonomic grip, adjustable stock with cheek riser. P3 barrel lengths and chamberings: 16 in. (.223 Wylde), 20 in. (.224 Valkyrie).

Price: P1 Rifle 16 in. **$1,000.00**
Price: P2 Rifle 16 in. **$1,375.00**
Price: P3 Rifle .223 Wylde 16 in. **$2,250.00**
Price: P3 Rifle .224 Valkyrie 20 in. **$2,550.00**

ADCOR DEFENSE ELITE RIFLES

Caliber: 5.56 NATO/.223 Rem. ADCOR's rifles use a ringless, gas-driven piston built into the top of the forward rail system. Adjustable cyclic rate, no carrier tilt, and a free-floating barrel. Forward ambi charging handle is non-reciprocating. Based in Baltimore, Maryland. Barrel lengths: 10.5, 14.5, 16 in. for 5.56. Rifle-length gas-system barrel lengths of 18 and 20 in. 1:7 twist chrome-lined barrels. Weight: 7 lbs.

Price: **$2,300.00**

ALEX PRO FIREARMS

Alexandria, Minnesota-based Alex Pro Firearms (APF) was established in May 2013. Firearms come in several lines, including Carbines, DMR Rifles, Varmint, Target, Hunter, and MLR (Magnum Long Rifle). Specializes in making nickel-boron bolt-carrier group and hunting-caliber AR-style rifles in both AR-15 and AR-10 sizes. Carbine chamberings: 5.56 NATO/.223 Rem., 223 Wylde, 300 Blackout, .308 Win., 9mm Luger, 450 Bushmaster. DMR chamberings: 22 Nosler, 6mm ARC, .223 Wylde, 6.5 Grendel. Varmint chamberings: .204 Ruger, 22 Nosler, .22-250 Rem., 223 Wylde, .243 Win. Target chamberings: .204 Ruger, 223 Wylde, .22-250 Rem., .243 Win., 6.5 CM, .308 Win. Hunter chamberings: 6.5 CM, 6.8 SPC, .308 Win., 450 Bushmaster. MLR chamberings: 26 Nosler, 28 Nosler, 30 Nosler, 33 Nosler, 7mm Rem. Mag, .300 Win. Mag.

Price: APF Carbine Slim Tactical 5.56 .... **$975.00**
Price: APF Carbine Alpha 5.56 No Optic **$750.00**
Price: APF Carbine Sidecharging 9mm **$1,500.00**
Price: APF DMR 6ARC Carbon Fiber Proof Research Barrel **$2,000.00**
Price: APF DMR Rifle 223 Wylde **$2,000.00**
Price: APF Varmint Sniper Green 22 Nosler **$1,400.00**
Price: APF Target Gray .243 Win. **$1,875.00**
Price: APF Hunter Texas Edition 6.8 SPC **$2,000.00**
Price: APF Hunter .308 Win. **$1,375.00**
Price: APF MLR 33 Nosler **$3,000.00**

ALEXANDER ARMS AR SERIES

Calibers: .17 HMR, 5.56 NATO, 6.5 Grendel, .300 AAC, .50 Beowulf. This manufacturer produces a wide range of AR-15 type rifles and carbines. Barrels: 16, 18, 20 or 24 in. Models are available for consumer, law enforcement and military markets. Depending on the specific model, features include forged flattop receiver with Picatinny rail, button-rifled stainless-steel barrels, composite free-floating handguard, A2 flash hider, M4 collapsible stock, gas-piston operating system.

Price: .17 HMR From **$1,150.00**
Price: .17 HMR Tactical **$1,740.00**
Price: 6.5 Grendel Hunter 18 in. **$1,560.00**
Price: .300 AAC **$1,400.00**
Price: .50 Beowulf Classic Laminate **$1,500.00**

Prices given are believed to be accurate at time of publication however, many factors affect retail pricing so exact prices are not possible.

AMERICAN TACTICAL, INC. OMNI SERIES

Calibers: 5.56/.223 Rem.; .22 LR, .300 BLK, 9mm Luger. American Tactical, Inc. is a firearms manufacturer and importer based out of Summerville, SC. Built on forged aluminum Mil-Sport upper and polymer hybrid Omni lower receiver. Barrels: M4 profile, 1:7 button-cut rifling, black-nitride coated. Carbine-length gas system with rail-height Picatinny-topped gas block, six-position adjustable Roger's Superstock, and A2-style compensator. AR-15 pattern, Mil-Spec lower parts kit. Maxx line comes with high-strength-fiberglass composite polymer upper and lower receiver with strengthened metal inserts and one magazine. Mil-Sport AR-15 pattern rifle is built on an M16A3 pattern forged aluminum upper and AR-15 Mil-Sport pattern lower receiver. 9mm Milsport Carbines feature a billet aluminum receiver, 31-round ETS Glock-style magazines. Limited Lifetime Warranty.

Price: ATI Omni Hybrid Quad Rail 16 in. 5.56 .... **$449.00**
Price: ATI Omni Hybrid Maxx KeyMod 16 in. 5.56 .... **$479.00**
Price: ATI Mil-Sport OD CERAKOTE 16 in. 5.56 .... **$669.00**
Price: ATI Mil-Sport 16 in. 9mm **$969.00**
Price: ATI Mil-Sport 9mm Carbine **$899.00**

ANDERSON MANUFACTURING AM-15 RIFLES

Calibers: 5.56 NATO, 6.5 Grendel, .300 BLK, 7.62x39. This manufacturer, based in Hebron, Kentucky, produces a range of AR-15 type rifles and carbines. Barrels: 16, 18, 24 in. Builds include CNC-machined 7075 T6 aluminum forgings for uppers and lowers, machined to military specifications and marked "Multi-Cal" to be used with multiple calibers on the AR-15 platform. Proprietary RF85 metal treatment on some rifles is billed as needing "zero lubrication."

Price: AM-15 M4 Optic Ready 5.56, 16 in. **$559.00**
Price: AM-15 M4 Optic Ready 5.56, RF85, 16 in. **$775.00**
Price: AM-15 M-LOK, Magpul MOE Grip 5.56 .... **$700.00**
Price: AM-15 M4 Optic Ready 6.5 Grendel **$600.00**
Price: AM-15 M4 Optic Ready 7.62x39 .... **$790.00**
Price: AM-15 M-LOK, RF85, 300 BLK. 16 in. **$1,000.00**
Price: AM-15 Sniper M-LOK, 5.56, 24 in. barrel **$1,655.00**
Price: AM-15 Sniper M-LOK, 5.56, 24 in. RF85 .... **$1,700.00**

ANDERSON MANUFACTURING AM-10 RIFLES

Calibers: .308 Win., Barrels: 16, 18, 24 in.

Price: AM-10 M-LOK .308 Win., 18 in. **$1,200.00**
Price: AM-10 Hunter .308 Win., 18 in. **$1,500.00**
Price: AM-10 Sniper M-LOK .308 Win. 24 in. **$2,000.00**

ANDERSON MANUFACTURING AM-9 RIFLES

Price: AM-9 M-LOK 9mm 16 in. **$800.00**

ARMALITE M-15 AND AR-10 COMPETITION RIFLES

Caliber: .223 Wylde or .308 Win. chambers. Built for 3-Gun and practical rifle competition. Timney 4-lb. single-stage trigger, Ergo wide grip MBA-1 buttstock with adjustable cheek piece and length-of-pull. Factory ambidextrous safety and Raptor charging handle, adjustable gasblock. On 13.5 in. model, tunable proprietary Armalite muzzle brake is pinned and welded to create an overall length of 16 inches.

Price: M-15 Competition Rifle, 13.5 or 18 in. barrel **$1,725.00**
Price: AR-10 Competition Rifle, 13.5 or 18 in. barrel **$2,231.00**

ARMALITE M-15 AND AR-10 TACTICAL RIFLES

Caliber: 5.56 NATO/.223 Rem., .308 Win. Slim handguard with octagonal profile, full-length MIL-STD 1913 12 o'clock rail. Adjustable gas block, Magpul MBUS flip-up sights. Non-NFA models come in barrel lengths of 14.5, 16, 18, and 20 in.

Price: M-15 Tactical Rifle 5.56, 14.5 and 16 in. barrel **$1,620.00**
Price: M-15 Tactical Rifle 5.56, 18 in. barrel **$1,725.00**
Price: AR-10 Tactical Rifle .308 Win., 16 in. barrel **$2,050.00**
Price: AR-10 Tactical Rifle .308 Win., 18 in. and 20 in. barrel **$2,130.00**

ARMALITE M-15 AND AR-10 DEFENSIVE SPORTING RIFLES

Caliber: 5.56 NATO or .308 Win. Weight: 6.1 lbs. Forged flat-top receiver with MIL-STD 1913 rail. Optics-ready and pinned Mil-Spec A2 front sight base models.

Price: M-15 Defensive Sporting Rifle 5.56 16 in. **$817.00**
Price: AR-10 Defensive Sporting Rifle .308 Win. 16 in. **$1,125.00**

ARMALITE M-15 LIGHT TACTICAL CARBINE

Caliber: 5.56 NATO. Armalite free-floating tactical M-LOK handguard, low-profile gas block. Weight: 6 lbs.

Price: M-15 Light Tactical Carbine (LTC) M15LTC16 5.56, 16 in. **$1,015.00**

BARRETT REC7 DI DMR

Caliber: 5.56 NATO. Capacity: 20. DMR line has 18 in. 1:7.7-in. barrel. Overall length: 35.3 in. Weight: 7.9 lbs. Colors include Black Cerakote, FDE Cerakote, Tungsten Grey.

Price: REC7 DI DMR **$1,700.00**

BARRETT REC10

Caliber: .308 Win. Capacity: 20. Direct impingement gas system. DMR model has 16 in. barrel, 1:10 twist. Overall length: 34.5 in. Weight: 9.0 lbs. LR model has 20 in. barrel, 1:10 twist. Overall length: 41.5 in. Weight: 11.1 lbs.

Price: REC10 DMR **$2,800.00**

BRAVO COMPANY MFG. BCM M4 CARBINES

Caliber: 5.56mm NATO. Capacity: 30 rounds. Barrel: 16 in., standard government profile, 1:7 twist, M4 feed ramp barrel extension. USGI chrome-lined bore and chamber. Mil-Spec 11595E barrel steel, manganese phosphate finish. Stock: BCM Gunfighter. Sights: Flat-top rail, post front. Weight: 6.3 lbs. Overall Length: 32.5 to 35.5 in. MOD 0 has BCM PKMR Handguard. 6.3 pounds. MOD 2 has BCM QRF Handguard. 6.5 lbs.

Price: MOD 0 .... **$985.00**
Price: MOD 2 .... **$1,700.00**

BRAVO COMPANY MFG. BCM RECCE CARBINES

Caliber: 5.56mm NATO. Capacity: 30 rounds. Barrels: 14.5 in., 16 in. 1:7 Twist, M4 feed ramp barrel extension. USGI chrome-lined bore and chamber. MIL-SPEC 11595E barrel steel, manganese phosphate finish. Stock: BCM. Sights: M4 feed ramp flat top with laser T-markings. Mid-length gas systems. Five models in RECCE-14 line: KMR-A and KMR-A LW, MCMR and MCMR LW, and QRF. Four additional models in RECCE-16 line: KMR-A Precision, MCMR Precision, and 300 BLK KMR-A and 300 BLK MCMR.

Price: Bravo Co. RECCE-14 KMR-A 5.56, 6 lbs. **$1,500.00**
Price: Bravo Co. RECCE-16 KMR-A 5.56, 6.1 lbs. **$1,500.00**

BRAVO COMPANY MFG. BCM MID16 RIFLES

Caliber: 5.56mm NATO. Mid-length gas systems. MOD 0 has PKMR handguard. MOD 2 has QRF Handguard.

Price: BCM MID16 MOD 0 .... **$1,130.00**

BRAVO COMPANY MFG. MARKSMAN RIFLES

Caliber: 5.56mm NATO. Based on the US Navy MK12 Mod 0 Special Purpose Rifle (SPR), the BCM MK12 is a heavily modified DMR-type weapon. 18 in. barrels, various contours. Also includes RECCE-18 rifles. Weights: 7-9 lbs.

Price: Bravo Co. MK12 MOD 0 .... **$4,500.00**

BROWNELLS "WHAT WOULD STONER DO" 2020 RIFLE

Caliber: 5.56 NATO or .223 Rem (.223 Wylde chamber). Capacity: 30-round Magpul P-Mag. Barrel: 14.5 in., with titanium flash hider for OAL of 16 in., 1/2-28 tpi muzzle threads. Twist rate: 1:8, Nitride finish. Upper/Lower Receivers: KE Arms MK3 polymer receiver. Weight: 4 lbs. Trigger: SLT-1 Sear Link Technology. Overall Length: 42. The What Would Stoner Do carbine was the brainchild of YouTubers Ian McCollum and Karl Kasarda, who wondered what a modern AR-15 would feel like if built by Eugene Stoner. Features: One-piece polymer lower with an improved mag well that's been optimized for use with Magpul P-Mags and D-60 drum mags. Ambidextrous selector, ambi mag release, ambidextrous charging handle, PDQ lever, JP Silent Capture Spring System, carbon-fiber handguard. The Mk3 lower

will also be available separately either stripped or with Mil-Spec internals. Manufactured by KE Arms of Phoenix, Arizona.
Price: $1,700.00

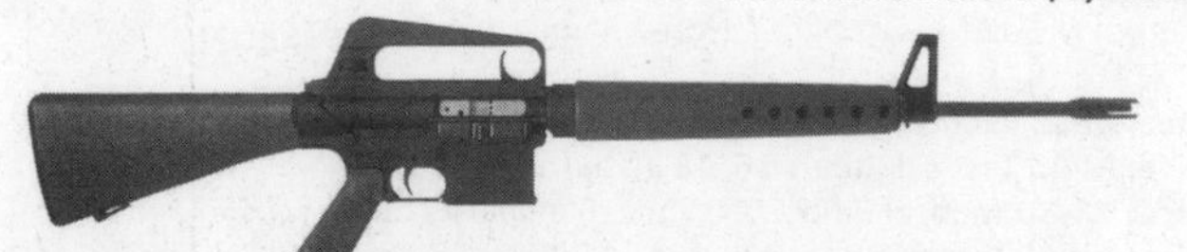

BROWNELLS BRN-10 RETRO RIFLE
Caliber: .308 Winchester. Capacity: (1) supplied 20-round Brownells aluminum magazine. Compatible with metal DPMS/SR-25 magazines. Barrel: 20 in. 1:10 RH twist, 5/8x24 tpi muzzle threads. QPQ Nitride finish. 3-prong Dutch-style flash hider. .750 in. diameter at the gas block. Direct impingement. Upper/Lower Receivers: Machined from 7075 T6 aluminum billet. Weight: 8.6 lbs. Overall Length: 40.5 in. Recreation of Eugene Stoner's original lightweight .308 caliber battle rifle, Armalite AR-10. Many components are compatible with modern DPMS/SR-25 parts or AR-15 parts. The BRN-10B is inspired by later export rifles and has a closed-prong, Portuguese-type flash hider, later-style black furniture, and a lightweight barrel. Weight: 7.8 lbs. Length: 40.75 in. As of 2022, only available as a build kit, not as a complete rifle.
Price: BRN-10A $1,260.00
Price: BRN-10B $1,186.00

BROWNELLS BRN-PROTO 5.56
Caliber: 5.56 NATO. Faithful replica of the Eugene Stoner's very first AR-15 prototype. Features: Trigger-like charging handle under the carry handle, "slick-side" upper receiver, and stock, handguard, and pistol grip of brown reinforced polymer that replicates the look of original fiberglass furniture. Round cross-section handguard, matte-gray, anodized receiver, skinny A1-profile barrel, three-prong "duckbill" flash suppressor. Capacity: (1) 25-round steel bodied magazine replica. Barrel, 20 in. with 1:12 rifling. Rifle-length gas tube. Internal dimensions conform to modern "mil-spec" standards. As of 2022, only available as a build kit, not as a complete rifle.
Price: BRN-PROTO $1,600.00

CHRISTENSEN ARMS MODERN SPORTING RIFLES
Christensen Arms, based in Gunnison, was founded in Utah in 1995. Christensen Arms developed the first carbon-fiber rifle barrel. The company focuses on using aerospace materials and processes to make lightweight, precise, and accurate firearms. Chamber: .223 Wylde. The CA5five6 build features a forged aluminum receiver set and a black nitride-finished BCG matched with a Christensen Arms carbon-fiber-wrapped 16 in. 1:8-twist stainless barrel and a carbon-aluminum hybrid handguard. Weight: 6.3 lbs. CA-15 G2 is a custom built AR-style rifle optimized for weight and accuracy. Features: Matched receiver set with contour-matching carbon-fiber handguard, black nitride-finished BCG, single stage match-grade trigger assembly. Stainless-steel or carbon-fiber barrels. Weight: 5.8 lbs. CA-10 G2 in .308 Win. (18 in. barrel, 1:10 twist) and 6.5 CM (20 in. barrel 1:8 twist) is designed for larger calibers and longer shots. Features: Aerospace-grade carbon-fiber free-floating handguard, billet aluminum receiver set, M-Lok or KeyMod fitments. Similar barrel finishes and triggers to CA-15 G2. Weight: 7.2 lbs. CA-10 DMR is a long-range rifle with an aluminum receiver set, proprietary barrel nut, and aerospace-grade carbon fiber handguard assembly. Comes with Christensen Arms carbon-fiber-wrapped barrel options in 6.5 CM (20 and 22 in., 1:8 twist) and .308 Win. (18 and 20 in., 1:10 twist). Titanium side baffle brake, ⅝×24 threaded muzzle. Weight: 7.8 lbs.
Price: CA5five6 black anodized 5.56........ $1,700.00
Price: CA-15 G2 5.56 .... $1,800.00
Price: CA-10 G2 .308 Win., 6.5 CM........ $3,200.00
Price: CA-10 DMR .308 Win., 6.5 CM, ... $3,400.00

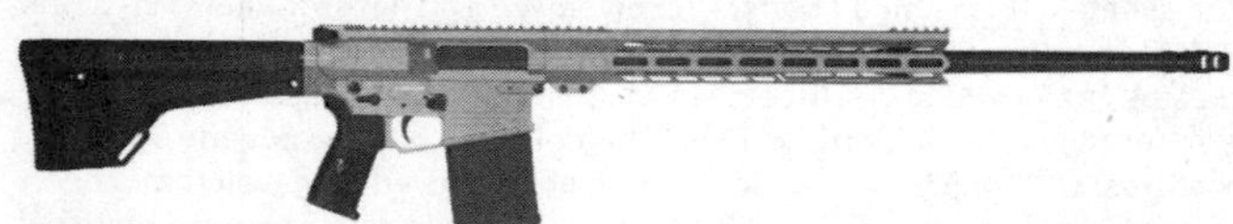

CMMG ENDEAVOR RIFLES
Calibers: 5.56x45mm, 6.5 Creedmoor, .308 Win. Longer and heavier (18, 20, 24 in.) stainless barrels compared to Resolute line. Platforms: Mk3, Mk4. Weight: 7 lbs. Length: 37.8 in. depending on barrel length.
Price: Endeavor MK4 5.56x45mm NATO, 18 in. $1,400.00
Price: Endeavor MK3 6.5 CM, 20 in. $2,000.00
Price: Endeavor MK3 .308 Win., 24 in. $2,050.00

COLT LE6920 M4 CARBINE
Caliber: 5.56 NATO. Barrel: 16.1-in. chrome lined. Sights: Adjustable. Based on military M4. Direct gas/locking bolt operating system. Magpul MOE handguard, carbine stock, pistol grip, vertical grip.
Price: M4 Carbine........ $1,099.00
Price: M4 Carbine Magpul........ $1,199.00

COLT M16A1 RETRO REISSUE
Caliber: 5.56 NATO. Classic design, unique triangular handguard, 20-inch pencil-profile chrome-lined barrel with a 1:12-inch twist, and recognizable carrying handle.
Price: $2,500.00

COLT XM177E2 RETRO CARBINE
Caliber: 5.56 NATO. Built to the Original Colt Model 629 specifications from the 1960s. 11.5-in. barrel with extended flash hider, vinyl-acetate coated aluminum buttstock reproduction, and U.S. Property-marked rollmarks.
Price: CRXM177E2........ $2,000.00

DANIEL DEFENSE DD5 RIFLES
Calibers: 6.5 CM, .260 Rem., 7.62x51mm/.308 Win. Capacity: 20-round Magpul PMAG. Barrel: 16, 18, 20 in. 5⁄8×24 tpi muzzle thread, S2W barrel profile, 1:11 twist. Stock: Daniel Defense Buttstock. Sights: Full length top rail. Trigger: Daniel Defense Mil-Spec. Handguard: Daniel Defense DD5 Rail 15.0, 6061-T6 aluminum, M-LOK. Weight: ~8.3 lbs. Overall Length: 33.375 to 37 in. Features: Intermediate gas system, two-position adjustable gas block, DLC-coated bolt carrier group, cold hammer chrome-lined forged barrel, Mil-Spec heavy phosphate coated. 4-Bolt Connection System, ambidextrous controls (bolt catch, magazine release, safety selector, furniture, GRIP-N-RIP charging handle). Daniel Defense Superior Suppression Device, 6-position Mil-Spec 7075-T6 aluminum receiver extension. Daniel Defense Pistol Grip, accepts all SR-25 magazines.
Price: DD5V3 (.308 Win., 16 in.)........ $2,599.00
Price: DD5V4 (6.5 CM, .308 Win. 18 in.)........ $2,599.00
Price: DD5V5 (6.5 CM, .260 Rem. 20 in.)........ $2,599.00

DANIEL DEFENSE AR-15 RIFLES
Caliber: 5.56 NATO/.223., 6.8 SPC, .300 BLK. Non-NFA Barrels: 14.5, 16 or 18 in. Weight: 7.4 lbs. Lengths: 34.75 to 37.85 in. overall. Stock: Glass-filled polymer with SoftTouch overmolding. Sights: None. Features: Lower receiver is Mil-Spec with enhanced and flared magazine well, QD swivel attachment point. Upper receiver has M4 feed ramps. Lower and upper CNC machined of 7075-T6 aluminum, hard coat anodized. Shown is MK12, one of many AR variants. Made in the USA.
Price: DDM4V7 .... $1,870.00
Price: DDM4V7 Pro........ $2,162.00
Price: DDM4 Hunter 6.8........ $1,946.00
Price: DDM4ISR .300 Blackout $3,390.00
Price: DDM4V9........ $1,975.00
Price: MK12 .... $2,350.00
Price: M4A1 .... $2,130.00

DEL-TON INC. AR-15 RIFLES
Chamberings: 5.56 NATO, .223 Wylde, 7.62x39. Del-Ton offers a complete line of AR-15 style modern sporting rifles. Hundreds of variations and options are available. Based in Elizabethtown, North Carolina.
Price: 5.56 models, 16, 20 in. barrels .... $675.00–$915.00
Price: DTI Sierra 3G, .223 Wylde, 16 in. barrel $1,320.00

Prices given are believed to be accurate at time of publication however, many factors affect retail pricing so exact prices are not possible.

DEL-TON INC. AR-10 RIFLES
Chambering: .308 Win. Echo optics-ready and Alpha sighted models. Upper and lower receivers: Forged 7075 T6 aluminum, integral triggerguard, 18" CMV 1x10 barrel, Magpul M-LOK standard length handguard, ERGO Sure Ambi grip, Magpul 20-round P-Mag.
Price: Alpha 308 M-LOK Rifle, .308 Win., 18" **$1,100.00**

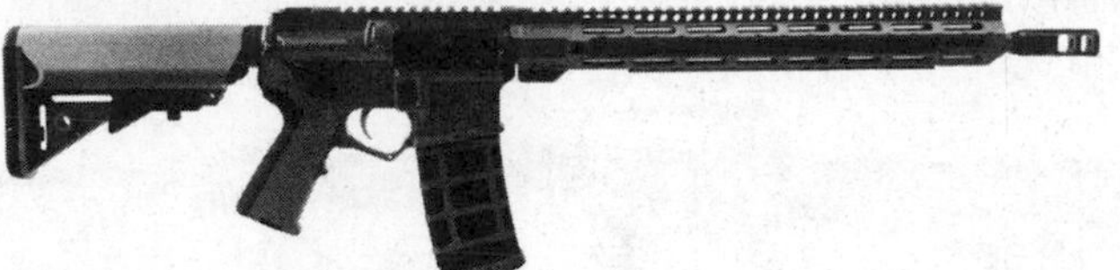

DSARMS AR15 ZM4 5.56 RIFLES
Caliber: 5.56 NATO. D.S. Arms was founded 1987, manufacturer of FN FAL 7.62mm rifles in the United States. In addition, DSA manufactures M16/M4 series rifles, parts and accessories. Based in Lake Barrington, Illinois. Capacity: Magpul Custom G2 MOE 30-round magazine, black with flat dark earth ribs. Barrel: 14.7, 16, 18 and 20 in., lightweight mid-length. 1:8 twist, M4 feed ramps on both barrel extension and upper receiver. Stock: B5 Systems Custom SOPMOD Stock, flat dark earth, B5 Systems QD end plate. Sights: Full length top rail. Weight: 6.9 lbs. Trigger: ALG Defense Advanced Combat Trigger. Overall Length: 33 to 35 in. Features: Premium match barrel machined from either 416-R stainless steel or 4150-11595 Mil-Spec material, 5.56 match chamber. Enhanced A3M4 upper receiver, upgraded fire control group, ambidextrous selector switch and WarZ triggerguard, bolt catch and charging handle. Low-Mass sand cut bolt carrier group with nitride finish. DuraCoat finish in flat dark earth over the hardcoat anodized lower receiver, upper receiver and handguard. 4140-steel MK12-style low profile set screw gas block, stainless steel mid-length gas tube. Midwest Industries 15 in. Combat Series M-LOK free float handguard. Magpul Custom MIAD Modular Pistol Grip, flat dark earth with black two tone. DSArms Enhanced FDE alloy triggerguard, SureFire Pro Comp (1/2x28 tpi).
Price: Combat Companion **$870.00**
Price: A3 M4 Flat Top Carbine **$800.00**
Price: FDE **$1,150.00**
Price: Titanium **$1,150.00**

F-1 FIREARMS BDRX-15 SKELETONIZED RIFLE
Caliber: .223 Wylde chamber for 5.56 NATO or .223 Rem., .224 Valkyrie, .300 AAC, 7.62x39mm. Capacity: 30-round magazines standard. Barrel: 16 in. (standard) or 18 in., light, medium, fluted contours, 1:8 twist. 1:10 twist on 7.62x39mm, stainless and black-nitride finishes. Upper/Lower Receivers: 7075-T6511 BDRx-15 billet receiver matched set, skeletonized. Black Type III hard anodizing. Stock: Magpul MOE standard. Handguard: C7K 12.75-in., 7-series aluminum lightweight free-float rail system, scalloped partial top rail. Weight: 8 lbs. Trigger: Hiperfire EDT Heavy Gunner standard. Velocity and Geissele brands available as options. Length: 33–37.5 in. Features: Introduced 2019. Modular build; user selects options on almost all components. 60-degree beveled mag well.
Price: **$2,000.00**

F-1 FIREARMS FU KING F15 FORGED RIFLE
Caliber: 5.56 NATO. FU KING F15 forged receiver set, 13-in. M-LOK free-float handguard, 16-in. 1:8 twist stainless barrel. Black nitride bolt-carrier group, MIL-SPEC stock, grip, and charging handle. A2 flash hider.
Price: **$850.00**

F-1 FIREARMS PATRIOT FDR-15 RIFLES
Caliber: 5.56 NATO. Mil-Spec base model rifle with enhanced tolerances. 7075-T6511 lower, upper, and handrail with a match-grade barrel together capable of sub MOA. Barrel: 16 in. medium contour, 1:8 twist.
Price: **$1,170.00**

F-1 FIREARMS BDRX-10 SKELETONIZED RIFLE
Calibers: .308 Win., 6.5 Creedmoor. Capacity: 20-round magazines. Barrels: 16, 18, 20 in., 1:10 twist, medium contour (.308, 416 stainless steel), 22 in. Criterion (6.5 CM). Proof Research carbine-fiber barrels offered as upgrades (+$500). Upper/Lower Receivers: 7075-T6511 BDRx-15 billet receiver matched set, skeletonized. Large-frame DPMS High-Profile-style comparable, 60-degree beveled mag well. Black Type III hard anodizing. Stock: Magpul MOE standard. Handguard: C7K 14-in., 7-series aluminum lightweight free-float rail system. Sights: None, scalloped partial top rail. Weight: 8.4 lbs. Trigger: Hiperfire EDT Heavy Gunner standard. Length: 33–37.5 in. Features: Accepts all Mil-Spec (DPMS) patterned parts as well as SR25-pattern mags.
Price: **$2,450.00**

FN 15 SERIES
Caliber: 5.56x45. Capacity: 20 or 30 rounds. Barrels: 16 in., 18 in., 20 in. Features: AR-style rifle/carbine series with most standard features and options.
Price: TAC3 Duty 16 in. **$1,600.00**
Price: TAC3 16 in. **$1,800.00**
Price: SRP G2 5.56 ....**$1,460.00**
Price: Military Collector M4 and M16 ....**$1,840.00**

FN 15 TACTICAL CARBINE FDA P-LOK
Caliber: 5.56x45mm. Capacity: 30-shot PMAG. Barrel: 16-in. free-floating and chrome-lined with FN 3-prong flash hider. Stock: B5 Systems buttstock and grip. Weight: 7.2 lbs. Finish: Flat Dark Earth. Features: P-LOK handguard, M-LOK accessory mounting system, hard anodized aluminum flat-top receiver with Picatinny rail, forward assist.
Price: **$1,499.00**

FNH SCAR 16S
Caliber: 5.56mm/.223. Capacities: 10 or 30 rounds. Barrel: 16.25 in. Weight: 7.25 lbs. Lengths: 27.5–37.5 in. (extended stock). Stock: Telescoping, side-folding polymer. Adjustable cheekpiece, A2 style pistol grip. Sights: Adjustable folding front and rear. Features: Hard anodized aluminum receiver with four accessory rails. Ambidextrous safety and mag release. Charging handle can be mounted on right or left side. Semi-auto version of newest service rifle of U.S. Special Forces.
Price: **$2,899.00**

FNH SCAR 17S
Caliber: 7.62x51 NATO/.308. Capacities: 10 or 30 rounds. Barrel: 16.25 in. Weight: 8 lbs. Lengths: 28.5–38.5 in. (extended stock). Features: Other features the same as SCAR 16S.
Price: **$3,499.00**

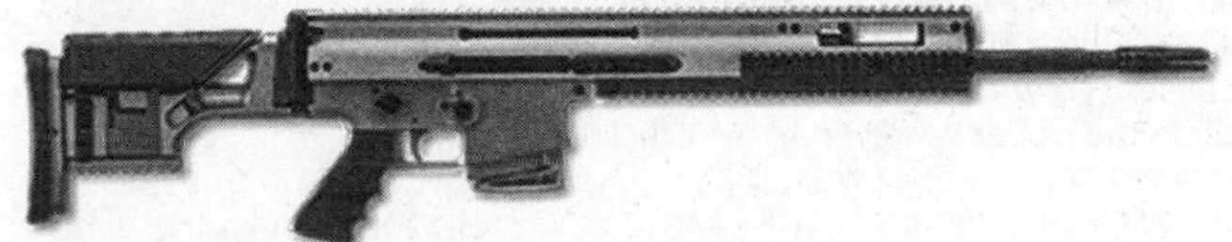

FNH SCAR 20S
Caliber: 7.62x51mm. Capacities: 10. Barrel: 20 in. Weight: 11.2 lbs.

Lengths: 40.6-42.5 in. (extended stock). Stock: Precision adjustable for LOP, adjustable cheek piece, Hogue rubber pistol grip with finger grooves. Features: Hard anodized aluminum receiver with four accessory rails, two-stage match trigger, Semi-auto version of newest service rifle of U.S. Special Forces.

Price: **$3,999.00**

FRANKLIN ARMORY F17-X

Similar to other F17-Series models. Barrel: 16-in. M4 Contour. Sights: Fixed front & MBUS. Lower Receiver: FAI. Handguard/Upper: Magpul MOE SL M-Lok Gray. Stock: Magpul SL. Grip: Magpul K2. Stock: A2. Grip: A2. Weight: 6.7 lbs.

Price: **$1,550.00**

FRANKLIN ARMORY BFSIII M4

Caliber: 5.56mm/.223. Capacities: 30 rounds. AR-type rifles and carbines offered with the BFSIII Binary Trigger. Barrel: 16 in., LTW Contour, 1:7 RH twist, A2 muzzle device. Stock: M4. Sights: Optics ready, 12 o'clock full-length Picatinny rail. Weight: NA. Trigger: BFSIII Binary Trigger. Overall Length: 32.5 to 35.5 in. Features: Standard charging handle, low-profile gas block, 15-in. FST Handguard/Upper, salt bath nitride bolt carrier, A2 Grip. FAI-15 lower.

Price: **$1,100**

FRANKLIN ARMORY LIBERTAS-L 16

Calibers: 5.56 NATO. Similar to other Franklin Armory offerings but with billet lower. Incorporates integrated ambidextrous, anti-rotational Quick Detach sling mounts. Textured Memory Index Point, enlarged and beveled magazine well, integral over-sized triggerguard. Front of the magazine well is also textured so it can be used as a grip for forward support. Carbine length, 6-position collapsible stock. Barrel: 16 in. M4 Contour 1:7 RH twist. Handguard: 15 in. FSR. Sights: Magpul MBUS. Mid-length gas system. Stock: Magpul CTR. Grip: Ergo Ambi Sure.

Price: **$1,700**

FULTON ARMORY FAR-15 LEGACY RIFLE

Caliber: 5.56 NATO or .223 Rem. Several builds make up the Fulton Armory AR lineup, six with fixed stocks, and five with front sight posts. Legacy specs include the Upper Receiver: M16 Slick Side, with new A1 rear sight (forged, machined, anodized). Retro 601 charging handle. Parts: GI & True Mil Spec, GI Chrome M16/AR15 HPT/MPI Bolt with HD extractor spring, early slip ring. Barrel: 20 in. 1x12, "pencil" profile, match quality, chrome lined, .223/5.56 NATO hybrid match chamber. Handguard: New M16, triangular. Gas Block/Front Sight: Forged, with bayonet lug, taper pinned. Front Sight Post: A1, round. Muzzle Device: 3-prong flash suppressor. Lower Receiver: FA, with Accu-wedge (forged, machined, anodized, & Teflon coated per mil spec). Butt Stock: Fixed, A1 with A1 butt plate. Grip: A1. Trigger: Standard military, single-stage. Included accessories: FA 10-round magazine, OD cotton web sling, and owner's manual. Precision Guarantee: 1.5 MOA with Federal Gold Medal Match Ammunition. Weight: 6.75 lbs. Length: 39 in.

Price: **$1,500.00**

FULTON ARMORY FAR-15 A2 AND A4 SERVICE RIFLES

Similar to FAR-15 Legacy rifle, but with 20 in. barrel, 1x7, A2 Government Profile, match quality, chrome lined, .223/5.56 NATO Hybrid Match Chamber and 12 in. round A2 handguard with heat shields. A2 weight: 8.05 lbs. A4 lacks carrying handle and has a top receiver Picatinny rail.

Price: FAR-15 A2 .... **$1,350.00**

Price: FAR-15 A4 .... **$1,275.00**

FULTON ARMORY FAR-15 PEERLESS NM A4 SERVICE RIFLE

Similar to FAR-15 Legacy rifle, but with 20 in. 1x8 barrel, HBAR profile, match quality, stainless steel, .223/5.56 NATO hybrid match chamber. Handguard: 12 in., round A2, modified for float tube.

Price: **$1,500.00**

GEISSELE AUTOMATICS SUPER DUTY RIFLE 16 INCH

Chamberings: 5.56 NATO. Features a Nanoweapon-coated Surefire Closed-Tine Warcomp mounted to a 16-in. mag phosphated cold hammer forged, chrome-lined Geissele barrel. Twist: 1:7 in. Gas system: Geissele Length, with Geissele Super Compact Gas Block. Trigger: SSA-E X with Lightning Bow trigger, a nanocoated, two-stage unit. BCG: Machined from mil-spec 8620 steel, properly torqued and staked chrome-lined gas key. Lower: Machined from 7075-T6 aluminum with Geissele's Ultra Duty Lower Parts Kit. Ambidextrous Super Configurable safety and Ultra Precision triggerguard. Mil-spec Geissele Buffer Tube with Super-42 in H2 buffer ensures this rifle is properly tuned out of the box. 15 MK16 Super Modular Rail mates to Super Duty Upper Receiver via a center aligning tab. Sights: None. Grips: Geissele Rifle Grip. Rails: 15 in. MK16 Super Modular. Stock: B5 Enhanced Sopmod. No magazine. Colors: Luna Black, DDC (Desert Dirt Color), ODG (OD Green).

Price: **$1,975.00**

HECKLER & KOCH MODEL MR556A1

Caliber: .223 Remington/5.56 NATO. Capacity: 10+1. Barrel: 16.5 in. Weight: 8.9 lbs. Lengths: 33.9 to 37.68 in. Stock: Black synthetic adjustable. Features: Uses the gas piston system found on the HK 416 and G26, which does not introduce propellant gases and carbon fouling into the rifle's interior.

Price: **$3,200.00**

HECKLER & KOCH MODEL MR762A1
Caliber: 7.62x51mm/.308 Win. Otherwise, similar to Model MR556A1. Weight: 10 lbs. w/empty magazine. Lengths: 36 to 39.5 in. Features: Variety of optional sights are available. Stock has five adjustable positions.
Price: **$4,130.00**

HK-USA MR762A1 LONG RIFLE PACKAGE II
Caliber: 7.62x51mm. Capacity: 10- or 20-round magazines. Barrel: 16.5 in., four lands and grooves, right twist, 1:11. Stock: Fully adjustable G28 buttstock. Sights: Leupold 3-9VX-R Patrol 3-9x40 mm scope, base, mounts. Weight: 10.42 lbs. Trigger: Two stage. Overall Length: 36.5 to 40.5 in. Features: MR762 semi-auto rifle with LaRue/Harris bipod, new long 14.7 in. Modular Rail System (MRS) handguard, Blue Force Gear sling and sling mount, one 10-round and one 20-round magazine, OTIS cleaning kit, HK multi-tool, and Pelican Model 1720 case.
Price: **$7,250.00**

JP ENTERPRISES LRP-07
Calibers: .308 Win, .260 Rem., 6.5 Creedmoor, 6mm Creedmoor. Barrels: 16–22 in., polished stainless with compensator. Buttstock: A2, ACE ARFX, Tactical Tactical Intent Carbine, Magpul MOE. Grip: Hogue Pistol Grip. Features: Machined upper and lower receivers with left-side charging system. MKIII Hand Guard. Adjustable gas system.
Price: **$3,550.00**

JP ENTERPRISES JP-15
Calibers: .223, .204 Ruger, 6.5 Grendel, .300 Blackout, .22 LR. Barrels: 18 or 24 in. Buttstock: Synthetic modified thumbhole or laminate thumbhole. Grip: Hogue Pistol grip. Basic AR-type general-purpose rifle with numerous options.
Price: Professional Rifle **$2,110.00**

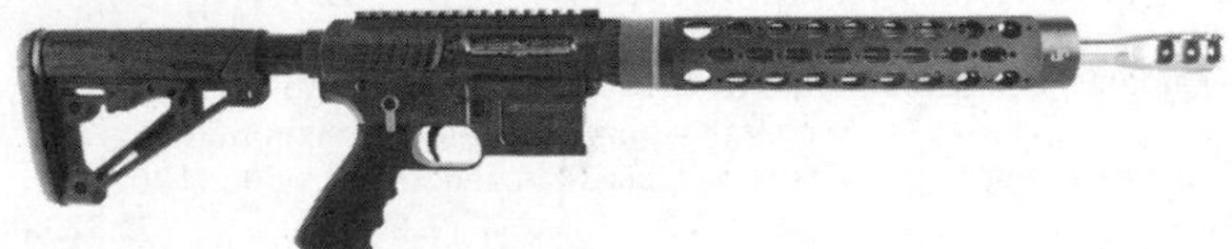

JP ENTERPRISES SCR-11 RIFLE
Calibers: .223, 6.5 Grendel, .224 Valkyrie, .22 LR. Capacity: Magazines vary by chambering. Receiver: Machined from billet 7075-T6 upper/lower receiver set with left-side charging system on upper receiver. Matte black hardcoat anodizing on aluminum components. Barrel: JP Supermatch 416R air-gauged, button-rifled, cryogenically treated barrel Thermo-Fit to receiver, polished stainless, JP Compensator. Stock: Hogue OverMolded, Magpul MOE, Magpul CTR, LUTH-AR "Skullaton," or Mission First Tactical BATTLELINK. Handguard: JP MK III system. Grip: Hogue pistol grip. Sights: Optics ready top rail. Trigger: JP Fire Control Package available in weights of 3.0 to 4.5 lbs. Overall Length: NA. Features: Scaled-down version of the LRP-07 available with the same caliber, barrel, handguard, metal finishing and stock options as the CTR-02. Exaggerated bevel on the magazine well. JP adjustable gas system; choice of JP Low Mass Operating System or JP Full Mass Operating System.
Price: **$2,700.00**

JP ENTERPRISES LRI-20 SEMI-MONOLITHIC LONG RANGE PRECISION RIFLE
Calibers: 6mm and 6.5 Creedmoor, .260 Rem. and .308 Win. Capacity: Magazines vary by chambering. Receiver: Machined from billet 7075-T6 upper/lower receiver set with left-side charging system on upper receiver. Matte-black hardcoat anodizing on aluminum components. Barrel: JP Supermatch 416R air-gauged, button-rifled, cryogenically treated barrel Thermo-Fit to receiver, polished stainless, JP Compensator. Stock: Hogue OverMolded, Magpul MOE, Magpul CTR, LUTH-AR "Skullaton," or Mission First Tactical BATTLELINK. Handguard: JP MK III system (Signature or Rapid configuration). Grip: Hogue pistol grip. Sights: Optics ready top rail. Weight: NA. Trigger: JP Fire Control Package available in weights of 3.5 to 4.5 lbs. Features: Scaled-down version of the LRP-07 available with the same caliber, barrel, handguard, metal finishing and stock options as the CTR-02. Exaggerated bevel on the magazine well. New integral handguard nut stabilizes the barrel mount and front pivot-pin joint. MicroFit Takedown Pins, lightened military-style upper design, dust cover and forward assist paired with dedicated side-charging handle. Thermo-Fit installation. LRI-20 upper assemblies pair with any existing LRP-07 side-charge lower. JP adjustable gas system; JP .308 Low Mass Operating System with JP High-Pressure Enhanced Bolt.
Price: **$3,500.00**

KEL-TEC SU-16 SERIES
Caliber: 5.56 NATO/.223. Capacity: 10-round magazine. Barrels: 16 or 18.5 in. Weights: 4.5–5 lbs. Features: Offered in several rifle and carbine variations.
Price: **$575.00**

KNIGHTS ARMAMENT CO. SR-15 CARBINE
Caliber: 5.56mm NATO. Barrel: 14.5 in. Chrome-lined mil-spec, proprietary mid-length gas system. Free-floated, hammer forged, 1:7 twist. E3 round-lug bolt design; ambidextrous bolt release, selector, and magazine release. Drop-in two-stage trigger. 3-Prong Flash Eliminator. Weight: 6.3 lbs. Length: 32 to 35 in.
Price: **$2,475.00**

KNIGHTS ARMAMENT CO. SR-25 COMBAT CARBINE
Caliber: 7.62mm NATO/.308 Win. Ambidextrous bolt release, selector, and magazine release. Drop-in 2-stage trigger, 7.62 QDC flash suppressor. Barrel: 16 in., hammer forged, chrome lined, 1:10 twist. Weight: 8.4 lbs. Length: 35.75 to 39.5 in.
Price: **$4,900.00**

LARUE TACTICAL OBR
Calibers: 5.56 NATO/.223, 7.62 NATO/.308 Win. Barrels: 16.1, 18, or 20 in. Weights: 7.5–9.25 lbs. Features: Manufacturer of several models of AR-style rifles and carbines. Optimized Battle Rifle (OBR) series is made in both NATO calibers. Many AR-type options available. Made in the USA.
Price: OBR 5.56 .... **$2,750.00**
Price: OBR 7.62 .... **$4,125.00**

LEWIS MACHINE & TOOL RIFLES
Calibers: 5.56 NATO/.223, 7.62 NATO/.308 Win. Barrels: 16.1, 18, or 20 in. Weights: 7.5–9.25 lbs. Features: Manufactures wide range of AR-style carbines with many options. SOPMOD stock, gas piston operating system, monolithic rail platform, tactical sights. Modular Ambidextrous Rifle System (MARS) rifles are fully ambidextrous systems. Made in the USA by Lewis Machine & Tool.
Price: Standard 16 5.56 .... **$1,949.00**
Price: DEFENDER-L 5.56 .... **$2,149.00**
Price: DEFENDER-H 7.62 .... **$2,799.00**

Price: MARS-L 5.56 .... **$2,529.00**
Price: MARS-H 7.62 .... **$3,459.00**
Price: MARS-H 6.5 DMR **$3,759.00**

LWRC INTERNATIONAL IC-PSD
Caliber: 5.56 NATO. Barrel: 8.5 in. Capacity: Magpul PMAG 30-round magazine. Stock: LWRC adjustable compact stock. Sights: Low-profile, flip-up Skirmish Sights. Weight: 5.9 lbs. Trigger: LWRC Enhanced Fire Control Group. Overall Length: 25-28 in. Features: Part of the Individual Carbine series of rifles. NFA item. LWRCI Monoforge upper receiver with modular 7-in. rail system. Nickel-boron coated bolt carrier, LWRCI High Efficiency 4-Prong Flash Hider.
Price: **$2,400.00**

LWRC INTERNATIONAL REPR MKII
Caliber: 6.5 Creedmoor, 7.62 NATO. Rapid Engagement Precision Rifle. Capacity: Magpul 20 Round PMAG. Barrel: 12.7, 16.1, 20, and 22 in. stainless steel. 1:8 RH twist, 5/8x24 muzzle threads. Stock: Magpul PRS. Grip: Magpul MOE+. Sights: Low-profile flip-up Skirmish Sights. Weight: 10.5 lbs. Trigger: Geissele SSA-E 2-Stage Precision. Overall Length: 43.5 in. Non-reciprocating side charging handle, 20-position tunable gas block, short-stroke gas piston system, Monoforge upper receiver with integrated rail-base, removable top rail design, removable barrel, fully ambidextrous lower receiver controls include bolt catch and release, magazine release, and safety selector. LWRCI Advanced Triggerguard, Skirmish Back-Up Iron Sights, Enhanced 4-port Ultra Static muzzle brake.
Price: REPR MKII....... **$4,225.00**

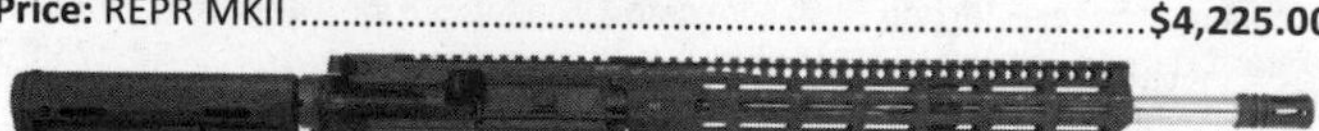

MIDWEST INDUSTRIES COMBAT RIFLES
Caliber: 5.56 NATO/.223 Rem., .223 Wylde. Barrels: 16, 18, 20 in. Upper receiver: Forged 7075 T6 aluminum, M16/M4 specs, M4 feed ramps, hardcoat anodized Mil 8625 Type-3 Class-2 Finish, .250 takedown pins. MI M16 bolt carrier group, MI-CRM12.625 Combat series handguard, M-LOK compatible. Criterion barrels, mid-Length hybrid profile, 1:8 twist, .223 Wylde chamber, chrome-lined, .625 diameter. A2 flash hider. Lower receiver: Receiver rear takedown pin detent hole threaded for a 4-40 set screw, Mil-Spec-diameter buffer tube. Magpul CTR buttstock, MOE grip, MOE triggerguard. Heavy-duty quick-detach end plate.
Price: MI-FH16CRM12, 16 in. **$1,400.00**
Price: MI-FLW18CRM15, 18 in. **$1,400.00**
Price: MI-FC20-CRM15, 20 in. **$1,500.00**

MIDWEST INDUSTRIES MI .308 RIFLES
Caliber: .308 Win. Capacity: (1) Magpul 10 round; accepts SR-25 pattern magazines. Barrel: 16, 18 in.; Criterion 1:10 twist, stainless-nitride finish. Upper/Lower Receivers: Forged 7075 aluminum. Stock: Magpul Gen 3 PRS buttstock. Grip: Magpul MOE. Sights: Optics ready top rail. Weight: 8.2 lbs. for MI-10F-16M. Features: Midwest Industries 308 Bolt carrier group, 12-in. M-LOK handguard, two chamber enhanced muzzle brake, mid-length gas system .750-in. gas block, MI-HDEP heavy-duty quick-detach end plate.
Price: MI-10F-16M, 16 in. **$1,700**
Price: MI-10F-18M, 18 in. **$1,750**

MIDWEST INDUSTRIES MI TACTICAL RESPONSE RIFLE
Caliber: 5.56 NATO/.223 Rem. Weight: 6.25 lbs. Outfitted with Magpul CTR Stock, MOE grip, MOE triggerguard, heavy duty quick detach end plate MI-HDEP, and has Custom Tactical Response logo laser engraved on receiver. Barrel: 16 in., 1:8 twist. Weight: 6.5 lbs.
Price: **$1,500.00**

NOVESKE RIFLEWORKS GEN 4 N4 PDW
Caliber: 5.56 NATO/.223 Rem. Barrel: 16 in., stainless steel hammer forged, muzzle thread pitch 1/2×28. Twist: 1:7. Low-profile adjustable gas block, direct impingement. PDW-style collapsible stock. M-LOK free-float handguard, Magpul MBUS PRO folding sights, and a Geissele Super Badass charging handle. Full-length Picatinny rail, ambidextrous safety selector.
Price: **$2,785.00**

PALMETTO STATE ARMORY AR-15 RIFLE
Chamber: 5.56 NATO. Barrel: 16 in. 4150V Chrome Moly Vanadium Steel, Nitride finish. Barrel Profile: A2 Style, Twist Rate: 1:7 in. M4 extension. Mid-length gas system, Low profile .750-in. gas block. Upper Receiver Style: M4 flat top with feed ramps. Handguard: PSA 13.5 in. Lightweight M-Lok Free Float Rail. Bolt Steel: Carpenter 158. Bolt Carrier Steel: 8620. Staked gas key. PSA AR-15 Enhanced Polished Trigger (EPT). Mil-Spec buffer tube. Magpul MOE Carbine 6-position collapsible stock. (1) 30-round magazine (where available by law). Backup Sights: Magpul MBUS. Length: 32 in.
Price: **$600.00**

PATRIOT ORDNANCE FACTORY MINUTEMAN RIFLE
Caliber: 5.56 NATO. Direct Impingement. Nitride heat-treated barrel, 16.5 in. Features: Rear QD ambidextrous sling swivel plate, anti-tilt buffer tube, ambidextrous Strike Eagle charging handle. 3.5-lbs. straight match-grade trigger. Mid-length gas system. 6.2 lbs. 34 in. length. Introduced 2022.
Price: **$1,525.00**

PATRIOT ORDNANCE FACTORY PRESCOTT
Caliber: 6.5 Creedmoor. Built on Rogue platform. Weight: 7 lbs. Barrel: 20 in. Collapsed length: 41
Price: **$1,950.00**

PATRIOT ORDNANCE FACTORY REVOLUTION DI
Caliber: 7.62x51mm NATO (.308 Win.) or 6.5 Creedmoor. Introduced 2019. Similar to PD Revolution, but with direct-impingement operation, 9-position adjustable Dictator gas block and Renegade rail. Weight: 6.8 lbs. Barrel: 16.5 in. for .308 Win., 20 in. for 6.5 CM.
Price: .308 Win. or 6.5 CM **$2,700.00**

PATRIOT ORDNANCE FACTORY WONDER RIFLE
Caliber: 5.56 NATO. Direct impingement. Barrel: 16.5 in. Match-grade Nitride heat-treated Puritan barrel, 1:8 twist, 1/2x28 barrel threads. Lightweight carbine with some upgrades. Ambidextrous rear sling mount, Renegade Rail with heat sink barrel nut, DI bolt carrier group with Roller Cam Pin, single-stage straight match grade trigger, Strike Eagle Ambi

Charging Handle, Micro B single-port muzzle brake. Weight: 6.18 lbs. Length: 3 in. Introduced 2022.
Price: $1,700.00

ROCK RIVER ARMS LAR SERIES
Chamberings in .350 Legend were added in 2020, initially in RRAGE 3G Rifles. Chambering was changed to CAR line in 2022. Calibers: 204 Ruger, .223/5.56, .223 Wylde chamber, .243 Win., 6.5 Creedmoor, 6.8 SPC, .300 AAC Blackout, 7.62x39mm, .308/7.62, 338 Lapua, .450 Bushmaster, .458 SOCOM, 9mm and .40 S&W. Rifles and carbines available with a wide range of options, including left-hand versions.
Price: ....$840.00–$2,200.00

RUGER AR-556 STANDARD
Caliber: 5.56 NATO. Capacity: 30-round magazine. 16.1 in. barrel, 1:8-in. RH twist, 1/2x28 muzzle thread pattern. Features: Basic AR M4-style Modern Sporting Rifle with direct impingement operation, forged aluminum upper and lower receivers, and cold hammer-forged chrome-moly steel barrel with M4 feed ramp cuts. Other features include Ruger Rapid Deploy folding rear sight, milled F-height gas block with post front sight, telescoping 6-position stock and one 30-round Magpul magazine. Weight: 6.5 lb. Overall Length: 32.25 to 35.50 in. Introduced in 2015.
Price: $990.00

RUGER AR-556 MPR (Multi Purpose Rifle)
Caliber: 5.56 NATO, .350 Legend, .450 Bushmaster. MPR model has 16.1, 18, 18.38, and 18.63 in. barrels with muzzle brake, flat-top upper, 15-in. free-floating handguard with Magpul M-LOK accessory slots, Magpul MOE SL collapsible buttstock and MOE grip.
Price: 5.56 ....$1,089.00
Price: 350 Legend, .450 Bushmaster...$1,269.00

RUGER AR-556 FREE-FLOAT HANDGUARD
Caliber: 5.56 NATO, .300 BLK. 16.1-in. barrel. Similar to MPR model, with 11-in. aluminum free-floated handguard. Magpul M-LOK accessory attachment slots at the 3, 6, and 9 o'clock positions with additional slots on the angled faces near the muzzle.
Price: $1,009.00

SAVAGE MSR 15 RECON 2.0
Calibers: 5.56 NATO/223 Rem. Barrel: 16.125 in., 1:8 5R rifling; Melonite QPQ finish. Direct-impingement operation. Nickel-boron coated trigger, free-float handguard, Magpul adjustable buttstock and pistol grip. Recon 1.0 introduced 2017. Recon 2.0 introduced 2021. 7.3 lbs. Length: 33.5 to 36.75 in.
Price: $1,150.00

SAVAGE MSR 10 LONG RANGE
Similar to MSR 10 Hunter, but with 20-in. carbon-steel barrel. Built on compact frame with a non-reciprocating side-charging handle.
Price: $2,659.00

SAVAGE MSR 10 PRECISION
Similar to MSR 10 Hunter, but with 22.5-in. stainless-steel heavy barrel. 18-in. Arca handguard, Magpul PRS stock, TangoDown Battlegrip Flip Grip, +2 gas system. 44 in. long, 11.4 lbs.
Price: $2,829.00

SEEKINS PRECISION SP15
Chamber: .223 Wylde/5.56 NATO. Glen Seekins founded Seekins Precision in 2004. Seekins now offers a full line-up of AR accessories and AR gun platforms, from small-frame AR pistols to large-frame AR gassers. The company is based in Lewiston, Idaho. The SP15 rifles are the company's entry level-platform. Barrel: 16 in. 1:7 twist 5R chromoly. Muzzle device: Seekins NEST Flash Hider 1/2x28. Receivers: SP15 7075-T6 billet upper/lower receiver set. Handguard: 15 in. SP15 M-LOK. Gas Block: Seekins Low Profile Adjustable Gas Block. Trigger: Mil-Spec. Stock: 6-position adjustable carbine stock. Weight: 7 lbs.
Price: $925.00

SEEKINS PRECISION SP15 DMR
Chamber: .223 Wylde/5.56 NATO. Similar to SP15, but with Seekins 10X stock.
Price: $925.00

SEEKINS PRECISION NX15
Chamber: .223 Wylde/5.56 NATO. Similar to SP15, but with higher-level components, including an upgraded Timney trigger, NX15 skeletonized upper/lower receiver set and NOX handguard, ambidextrous controls. Barrel: 16 in. 1:8 twist 5R 416 stainless steel. Weight: 7 lbs.
Price: $1,650.00

SIG SAUER 716i TREAD
Caliber: .308 Win. Capacity: one 20-round magazine, compatible with SR-25 magazines. Barrel: 16 in., 1:10 RH twist, stainless steel. Upper/Lower Receivers: Forged aluminum, hardcoat anodized finish. Stock: Magpul SL-K 6-position telescoping stock. Sights: None, optics ready. Weight: 8.5 lbs. Trigger: Two-stage match. Overall Length: 33.8 to 37 in. Features: Direct-impingement operating system, integral QD mount, ambi safety selector, charging handle, free-floating 15-in. M-LOK handguard.
Price: $1,900.00

SIG 516 PATROL
Caliber: 5.56 NATO. Features: AR-style rifle with included 30-round magazine, 16-in. chrome-lined barrel with muzzle brake; free-floating, aluminum quad Picatinny rail, Magpul MOE adjustable stock, black anodized or Flat Dark Earth finish, various configurations available.
Price: $1,700.00

SIG SAUER SIG716G2 DMR
Caliber: 7.62 NATO. Barrel: 16 in. 1:8 twist, carbon steel, with 5/8x24 threads. Capacity: 20-round magazine, compatible with SR-25 magazines. Overall Length: 35.8 in. M-LOK handguard. Weight: 8.8 lbs.
Price: **$2,625.00**

SMITH & WESSON M&P15
Caliber: 5.56mm NATO/.223. Capacity: 30-shot steel magazine. Barrel: 16 in., 1:9 in. twist. Weight: 6.74 lbs., w/o magazine. Lengths: 32–35 in. overall. Stock: Black synthetic. Sights: Adjustable post front sight, adjustable dual aperture rear sight. Features: 6-position telescopic stock, thermo-set M4 handguard. 14.75 in. sight radius. 7-lbs. (approx.) trigger pull. 7075 T6 aluminum upper, 4140 steel barrel. Chromed barrel bore, gas key, bolt carrier. Hard-coat black-anodized receiver and barrel finish. OR (Optics Ready) model has no sights. TS model has Magpul stock and folding sights. Made in USA by Smith & Wesson.
Price: Sport Model **$739.00**
Price: OR Model **$1,069.00**
Price: TS model **$1,569.00**

SMITH & WESSON M&P15 SPORT II SERIES
Caliber: 5.56mm NATO/.223. Capacity: 30-shot steel magazine. Barrel: 16 in., 1:9-in. twist. Weight: 6.74 lbs., w/o magazine. Lengths: 32 to 35 in. overall. Stock: Black synthetic. Sights: Adjustable post front sight, adjustable dual aperture rear sight. Features: 6-position telescopic stock, thermo-set M4 handguard. 14.75 in. sight radius. 7-lb. (approx.) trigger pull. 7075 T6 aluminum upper, 4140 steel barrel. OR (Optics Ready) model has Crimson Trace CTS-103 Red/Green Dot Electronic Sight. Hardcoat black-anodized receiver and barrel finish. Made in USA.
Price: Sport II **$812.00**
Price: Sport II OR **$831.00**

SMITH & WESSON M&P15 VOLUNTEER XV OPTICS READY
Caliber: 5.56mm NATO/.223. Similar to Volunteer XV except has gas block with integral Picatinny-style rail. Weight: 9 lbs. Length: 36.25 in. No. 13510. Introduced 2022.
Price: **$1,049.00**

SMITH & WESSON M&P15 VOLUNTEER XV SERIES
Caliber: 5.56mm NATO/.223. Capacity: 30-shot steel magazine. Barrel: 16-in. 4140 steel, 1:8 twist. Flat-faced trigger. BCM Gunfighter forend with M-LOK attachments. Gas block with integral Picatinny-style rail. B5 Systems Bravo Stock and P-Grip 23 pistol grip. Chromed firing pin. Forward assist. A2 flash suppressor. Adjustable A2 front sight post. Forged integral triggerguard. Armornite finish on barrel (internal and external). Weight: 8.8 lbs. Length: 36.25 in. No. 13507. Introduced 2022.
Price: **$1,049.00**

SMITH & WESSON M&P15 VOLUNTEER XV PRO
Caliber: 5.56mm NATO/.223. Similar to Volunteer XV except has gas block with integral Picatinny-style rail, B5 SOPMOD stock, and upright B5 grip. Mid-length gas system, 15-in. aluminum S&W M-LOK forend. Primary Weapons Systems muzzle brake, and 5R rifling. Sights: WGS Tactical Folding Sight front and rear. 16-in. target crowned, threaded barrel (No. 13515) or 14.5 in. (No. 13516), the latter with a with a pinned flash hider. Weight: 6.8 lbs. Length: 36.75 in. Introduced 2022.
Price: **$1,569.00**

SMITH & WESSON M&P10
Caliber: .308 Win., 6.5 Creedmoor. Capacity: 10 rounds. Barrel: 18 to 20 in. Weight: 7.7 pounds. Features: Magpul MOE stock with MOE Plus grip, 15-in. free-float Troy M-LOK handguard, black hard anodized finish. Camo-finish hunting model available w/5-round magazine.
Price: M&P10 OR .308 Win. **$1,679.00**
Price: M&P10 6.5 Creedmoor **$2095.00**

SPRINGFIELD ARMORY SAINT AR-15 RIFLES
Caliber: 5.56 NATO. Introduced 2016. Springfield Armory's first entry into AR category. Capacity: 30-round magazine. Barrel: 16 in., 1:8 twist. Weight: 6 lbs., 11 oz. Sights: A2-style fixed post front or gas block with Pic rail, flip-up aperture rear. Features: Mid-length gas system, BCM 6-position stock, Mod 3 grip PMT KeyMod handguard 7075 T6 aluminum receivers. In 2020, several models with M-LOK handguards were added. The Bravo Company handguards have an internal aluminum heat shield.
Price: **$1,023.00**

SPRINGFIELD ARMORY SAINT EDGE ATC STANDARD
Chamber: .223 Wylde. Introduced December 2021. Accurized Tactical Chassis rifles comes with guaranteed sub-MOA accuracy for three shots with match-grade ammunition and a skilled shooter. Features: Chassis system of a one-piece monolithic lower machined from 6061 T6 aluminum. Free-floated design keeps the barrel, barrel nut, and gas system from contacting the lower chassis. Also includes Accu-Tite Plus tensioning system, conical set screws in the lower that eliminate play between the upper receiver and lower chassis. Barrel: 18-in. Ballistic Advantage, 1:7-in. rate of twist, Melonite coating. Comes with B5 Systems Enhanced SOPMOD collapsible stock, flat modular match trigger, B5 Systems Type 23 P-Grip, 20-round Magpul PMAG. Weight: 9.5 lbs. Length: 35.5 to 38.25 in. Model No. STA918223B.
Price: **$1,549.00**

SPRINGFIELD ARMORY SAINT EDGE ATC ELITE
Chamber: .223 Wylde. Introduced December 2021. Similar to Standard model. Elite variant features LaRue 2-stage trigger and collapsible B5 Systems Precision Stock. Weight: 10.1 lbs. Length: 36.5 to 39.75 in. Model No. STAE918223CB.
Price: **$1,899.00**

Prices given are believed to be accurate at time of publication however, many factors affect retail pricing so exact prices are not possible.

STAG ARMS STAG 15 RIFLES

Calibers: 5.56 NATO/.223, 6mm ARC, 6.8 SPC II. Capacities: 20- or 30-round magazine. Features: This manufacturer offers many AR-style rifles or carbines with many optional features including barrel length and configurations, stocks, sights, rail systems and both direct-impingement and gas-piston operating systems. Left-hand models are available on some products.

Price: Stag 15 Tactical 16 .... $1,150.00
Price: Stag 15 M4 .... $1,100.00
Price: Stag 15 Retro $1,150.00
Price: Stag 15 Super Varminter (6.8) $1,350.00
Price: Stag 15 LEO $1,150.00
Price: Stag 15 Tactical SBR 10.5 .... $1,050.00
Price: Stag 15 3Gun Elite $1,600.00

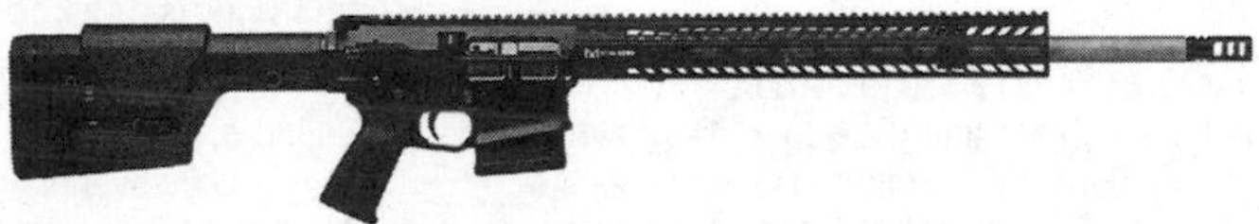

STAG ARMS AR-10 STYLE RIFLES

Similar to AR-15 models, but chambered in .308 Win. or 6.5 Creedmoor.

Price: Stag 10 Tactical 16 in. $1,770.00
Price: Stag 10 Classic 18 in. $1,550.00
Price: Stag 10 Classic 20 in. $1,600.00
Price: Stag 10 Marksman 18 in. LH $1,850.00
Price: Stag 10 Long Range 20 in. $2,120.00
Price: Stag 10 Long Range 24 in. $2,300.00

STONER TACTICAL ORDNANCE SR-15 MOD 2 RIFLE

Caliber: 5.56mm NATO. Capacity: 30-round magazine. Barrel: 14.5 in. 1:7 twist, free-floated inside M-LOK URX handguard. Weight: 6.3 lbs. Length: 32 to 35 in. overall. Stock: Mag-Pul MOE. Sights: Post front, fully adjustable rear (300-meter sight). Features: URX-4 upper receiver; two-stage trigger, 30-round magazine. Black finish. Made in USA by Knight's Armament Co.

Price: $2,450.00

STONER TACTICAL ORDNANCE LPR MOD 2

Caliber: .223. Capacity: 30-round magazine. Barrel: 18 in., free-floated inside M-LOK URSx handguard. Weight: 7.6 lbs. Length: 38 in. overall. Stock: Mag-Pul MOE. Sights: Post front, fully adjustable rear (300-meter sight). Features: URX-4 upper receiver; two-stage trigger, 30-round magazine. Black finish. Made in USA by Knight's Armament Co.

Price: $2,720.00

STONER TACTICAL ORDNANCE SR-25 APC

Caliber: 7.62 NATO. Capacity: 10- or 20-shot steel magazine. Barrel: 16 in. with flash hider. Weight: 8.5 lbs. Carbine features: Shortened, non-slip handguard; drop-in two-stage match trigger, removable carrying handle, ambidextrous controls, matte-black finish. Made in USA by Knight's Armament Co.

Price: $4,900.00

STONER TACTICAL ORDNANCE SR-25 APR

Caliber: 7.62 NATO. Similar to APC, but Rifle length. 20-in. heavy barrel.

Price: $4,900.00

WILSON COMBAT AR-15 RIFLES

Caliber: .204 Ruger, 5.56mm NATO, .223 Wylde, .22 Nosler, .224 Valkyrie, 6.5 Grendel, 6.8 SPC, .300 Blackout, .300 Ham'r, .350 Legend, .375 SOCOM, .458 SOCOM, .450 Bushmaster. Capacity: Accepts all M-16/AR-15 Style Magazines, includes one 20-round magazine. Barrel: 16.25", 1:9-in. twist, match-grade fluted. Weight: 6.9 lbs. Length: 36.25 in. overall. Stock: Fixed or collapsible. Features: Free-float ventilated aluminum quad-rail handguard, Mil-Spec Parkerized barrel and steel components, anodized receiver, precision CNC-machined upper and lower receivers, 7075 T6 aluminum forgings. Single-stage JP Trigger/Hammer Group, Wilson Combat Tactical muzzle brake, nylon tactical rifle case. Made in USA by Wilson Combat.

Price: Ranger $2,500.00
Price: Ultralight Ranger $2,600.00
Price: Recon Tactical $2,450.00
Price: Protector $2,100.00
Price: Super Sniper $2,475.00
Price: Urban Super Sniper $2,450.00

WILSON COMBAT AR-10 RIFLES

Caliber: .243 Win., .260 Rem., 6.5 Creedmoor, 7mm-08 Rem., .308 Win., .338 Federal, .358 Win. Large format BILLet-AR rifles with precision-machined match-grade barrels, M-LOK handguard rail, Tactical Trigger Units. Barrels: 14.7" barrel with pinned muzzle device on Recon Tactical. Also, 16, 18, and 20 in. fluted or standard Medium Recon profile barrels. Receivers accept metal or polymer SR-25-pattern magazines.

Price: Recon Tactical $3,285.00
Price: Super Sniper $3,235.00
Price: Tactical Hunter $3,335.00
Price: Ranger $3,285.00
Price: Ultralight Ranger $3,400.00

WINDHAM WEAPONRY 20 VARMINT

Caliber: .223 Rem./5.56mm NATO. Capacity: 5+1, ships with one 5-round magazine (accepts all standard AR-15 sizes). Barrel: 20 in., 1:8 RH twist, fluted 416R stainless steel, matte finish. Upper/Lower Receivers: A4-type flattop upper receiver, forged 7075 T6 aircraft aluminum with aluminum triggerguard. Electroless nickel-plated finish. Forend: 15 in. Windham Weaponry Aluminum M-LOK Free Float. Pistol Grip: Hogue OverMolded rubber pistol grip. Sights: None, optics ready, Picatinny top rail. Weight: 8.4 lbs. Length: 38.1 in. Features: Gas-impingement system, Carpenter 158 steel bolt. Compass Lake chamber specification with matched bolt. LUTH MBA-1 stock. Comes with hard-plastic gun case with black web sling.

Price: $1,500.00

WINDHAM WEAPONRY A1 GOVERNMENT

Caliber: .223 Rem./5.56mm NATO. Capacity: 30+1, ships with one 30-round magazine (accepts all standard AR-15 sizes). Barrel: 20 in., A2 profile, chrome-lined with A1 flash suppressor, 4150 chrome-moly-vanadium 11595E steel with M4 feed ramps. Rifling: 1:7 RH twist. Receivers: A1 upper with brass deflector and teardrop forward assist. Forend: Rifle-length triangular handguard with A1 Delta Ring. Pistol Grip: A1 Black Plastic Grip. Rear Sight: A1 dual aperture rear sight. Front Sight: Adjustable-height square post in A2 standard base. Trigger: Standard Mil-Spec Trigger. Stock: A2 Solid Stock with Trapdoor Storage Compartment. Weight: 7.45 lbs. Length: 39.5 in.

Price: $1,325.00

WINDHAM WEAPONRY SRC-308

Caliber: .308 Win. Capacity: 20+1, ships with one 20-round Magpul PMag magazine. Barrel: 16.5-in., medium profile, chrome lined with A2 flash suppressor; 4150M chrome-moly-vanadium 11595E steel; 1:10 right-hand-twist rifling, 6 lands and grooves. Upper/Lower Receivers: A4-type flattop upper receiver, forged 7075 T6 aircraft aluminum with aluminum triggerguard. Forend: Mid-length tapered shielded handguards. Pistol Grip: Hogue OverMolded rubber pistol grip. Sights: None, optics ready, Picatinny top rail. Weight: 7.55 lbs. Length: 34.188 to 38 in. Features: Gas-impingement system, Carpenter 158 steel bolt. Compass Lake chamber specification with matched bolt. Six-position telescoping buttstock. Comes with hard-plastic gun case with black web sling.

Price: $1,400.00

Prices given are believed to be accurate at time of publication however, many factors affect retail pricing so exact prices are not possible.

BIGHORN ARMORY MODEL 89 BLACK THUNDER
Calibers: .500 S&W Magnum. Capacity: 6-round tubular magazine. Barrel: 16.25 in. steel. Weight: 7 lbs. 6 oz. Length: 36 in. Stock: Black laminate with M-LOK rail on the front of the forend. Sights: Skinner iron sights and factory-installed scout rail. Features: Expansion of the Model 89 lever-action line built as a carbine with a shorter barrel, ideal for hunting, home defense, and survival. Robust stainless steel construction, heat-treated, and coated with a black nitride finish. Bighorn Armory rifles built in Cody, WY.
Price: **$1,235.00**

BIG HORN ARMORY MODEL 89 RIFLE AND CARBINE
Caliber: .500 S&W Mag. Capacities: 5- or 7-round magazine. Features: Lever-action rifle or carbine chambered for .500 S&W Magnum. 22- or 18-in. barrel; walnut or maple stocks with pistol grip; aperture rear and blade front sights; recoil pad; sling swivels; enlarged lever loop; magazine capacity 5 (rifle) or 7 (carbine) rounds.
Price: **$2,424.00**

BIG HORN ARMORY MODEL 90 SERIES
Calibers: .460 S&W, .454 Casull. Features similar to Model 89. Several wood and finish upgrades available.
Price: .460 S&W **$2,849.00**
Price: .454 Casull, .45 Colt **$3,049.00**
Price: .500 Linebaugh **$3,699.00**

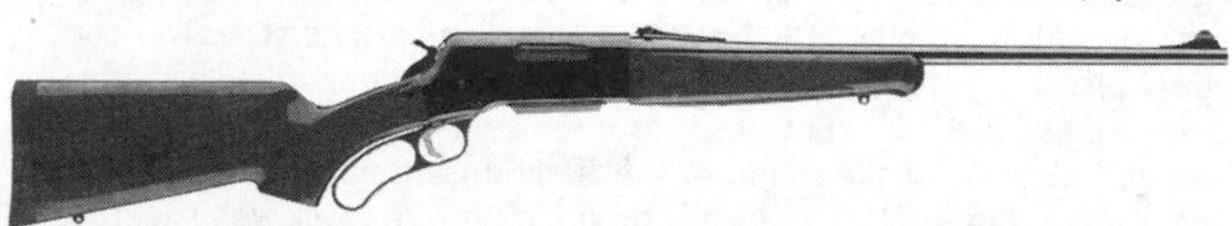

BROWNING BLR
Features: Lever action with rotating bolt head, multiple-lug breech bolt with recessed bolt face, side ejection. Rack-and-pinion lever. Flush-mounted detachable magazines, with 4+1 capacity for magnum cartridges, 5+1 for standard rounds. Barrel: Button-rifled chrome-moly steel with crowned muzzle. Stock: Buttstocks and fore-ends are American walnut with grip and forend checkering. Recoil pad installed. Trigger: Wide-groove design, trigger travels with lever. Half-cock hammer safety; fold-down hammer. Sights: Gold bead on ramp front; low-profile square-notch adjustable rear. Features: Blued barrel and receiver, high-gloss wood finish. Receivers are drilled and tapped for scope mounts, swivel studs included. Action lock provided. Introduced 1996. Imported from Japan by Browning.

BROWNING BLR GOLD MEDALLION
Calibers: .243 Win., 6.5 Creedmoor, .308 Win., .270 Win., .30-06 Spfld., .300 Win. Mag. Capacity: 3–5 round magazine, depending on caliber. Barrel: 20, 22, or 24 in. Length: 40–45 in. Weight: 6 lbs. 8 oz.–7 lbs. 4 oz. Stock: Grade III/IV Walnut stock with Schnabel forearm and brass spacers and rosewood caps. Features: High Grade lever action centerfire limited edition. Gloss finish engraved receiver built of lightweight aluminum. Gloss blued barrel drilled and tapped for optic mounts. Detachable box magazine. Iron sights. Pachmayr Decelerator recoil pad. Gold-plated trigger and gold inlay receiver branding.
Price: Short actions **$1,540.00**
Price: Long actions **$1,630.00**

CHIAPPA MODEL 1892 RIFLE
Calibers: .38 Special/357 Magnum, .38-40, .44-40, .44 Mag., .45 Colt. Barrels: 16 in. (Trapper), 20 in. round and 24 in. octagonal (Takedown). Weight: 7.7 lbs. Stock: Walnut. Sights: Blade front, buckhorn. Trapper model has interchangeable front sight blades. Features: Finishes are blue/case colored. Magazine capacity is 12 rounds with 24 in. bbl.; 10 rounds with 20 in. barrel; 9 rounds in 16 in. barrel. Mare's Leg models have 4-shot magazine, 9- or 12-in. barrel.
Price: **$1,329.00**
Price: Takedown **$1,435.00**
Price: Trapper **$1,329.00**
Price: Mare's Leg **$1,288.00**

CHIAPPA MODEL 1886
Caliber: .45-70. Barrels: 16, 18.5, 22, 26 in. Replica of famous Winchester model offered in several variants.
Price: Rifle **$1,709.00**
Price: Carbine **$1,629.00**

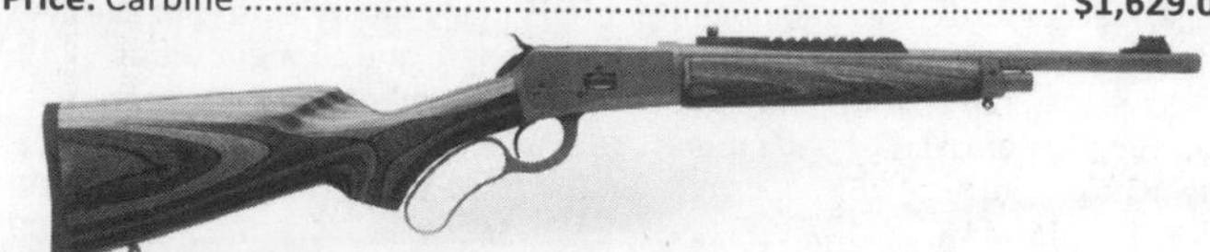

CHIAPPA 1892 LEVER-ACTION WILDLANDS
Caliber: .44 Mag. Capacity: 5. Barrel: 16.5 in., stainless steel, Cerakote dark gray or color case finish, heavy. Stock: Wood laminate or hand-oiled walnut. Sights: Fixed fiber-optic front, Skinner peep rear. Weight: 6.3 lbs. Features: Takedown and solid-frame configurations, mag tube fed.
Price: .... **$1,434.00-$1,689.00**

CIMARRON 1873 SHORT RIFLE
Calibers: .357 Magnum, .38 Special, .32 WCF, .38 WCF, .44 Special, .44 WCF, .45 Colt. Barrel: 20 in. tapered octagon. Weight: 7.5 lbs. Length: 39 in. overall. Stock: Walnut. Sights: Bead front, adjustable semi-buckhorn rear. Features: Has half "button" magazine. Original-type markings, including caliber, on barrel and elevator and "Kings" patent. Trapper Carbine (.357 Mag., .44 WCF, .45 Colt). From Cimarron F.A. Co.
Price: **$1,299.00**
Price: Trapper Carbine 16-in. bbl. **$1,352.00**

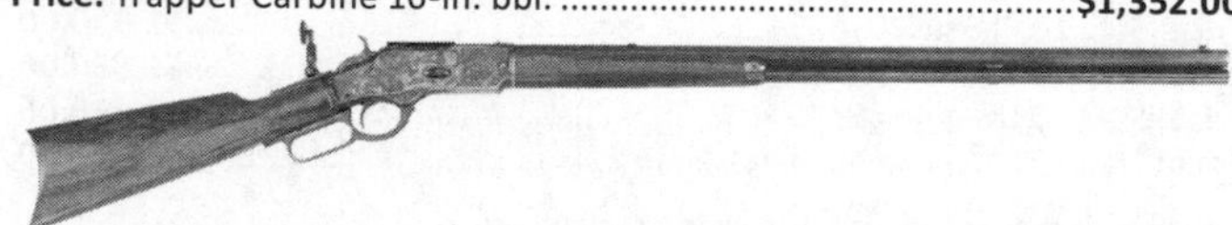

CIMARRON 1873 DELUXE SPORTING
Similar to the 1873 Short Rifle except has 24-in. barrel with half-magazine.
Price: **$1,485.00**

CIMARRON 1873 LONG RANGE SPORTING
Calibers: .44 WCF, .45 Colt. Barrel: 30 in., octagonal. Weight: 8.5 lbs. Length: 48 in. overall. Stock: Walnut. Sights: Blade front, semi-buckhorn ramp rear. Tang sight optional. Features: Color casehardened frame; choice of modern blued-black or charcoal blued for other parts. Barrel marked "Kings Improvement." From Cimarron F.A. Co.
Price: **$1,385.00**

EMF 1866 YELLOWBOY LEVER ACTIONS
Calibers: .38 Special, .44-40, .45 LC. Barrels: 19 in. (carbine), 24 in. (rifle). Weight: 9 lbs. Length: 43 in. overall (rifle). Stock: European walnut. Sights: Bead front, open adjustable rear. Features: Solid brass frame, blued barrel, lever, hammer, buttplate. Imported from Italy by EMF.
Price: Rifle **$1,175.00**

EMF MODEL 1873 LEVER-ACTION
Calibers: .32/20, .357 Magnum, .38/40, .44-40, .45 Colt. Barrels: 18 in., 20 in., 24 in., 30 in. Weight: 8 lbs. Length: 43.25 in. overall. Stock: European walnut. Sights: Bead front, rear adjustable for windage and elevation. Features: Color casehardened frame (blued on carbine). Imported by EMF.
Price: **$1,250.00**

HENRY NEW ORIGINAL RIFLE
Calibers: .44-40 Win, .45 Colt. Capacity: 13-round tubular magazine. Barrel: 24-in. octagonal blued steel. Weight: 9 lbs. Length: 43 in. Stock: Fancy-grade American Walnut with straight-grip buttstock. Sights: Folding ladder rear with blade front. Features: Hardened brass receiver finished in high polish. Essentially identical to the 1860 original, except for caliber. Serial numbers begin with "BTH" prefix in honor of Benjamin Tyler Henry, inventor of the lever action repeating rifle that went on to become the most legendary firearm in American history.

Prices given are believed to be accurate at time of publication however, many factors affect retail pricing so exact prices are not possible.

Made in the USA. Only this standard model New Original is available in the .45 Colt chambering; all other New Original Models below are .44-40 Win. only.
Price: $2,590.00
Price: New Original Deluxe Engraved $3,810.00
Price: New Original B.T. Henry 200th Anniv. Edition $4,286.00
Price: New Original Rare Carbine $2,590.00
Price: New Original Iron Framed $3,023.00
Price: New Original Silver Deluxe Engraved $4,078.00

HENRY SIDE GATE MODELS
Beginning in 2020, Henry began building the centerfire lever actions listed below with a side loading gate in addition to the tubular magazine charging port. These are not to be confused with the specific Henry Side Gate Model H024. NOTE: All previous Henry centerfire models without the side gate are now discontinued and considered "Legacy" models with slightly lower value at time of publication.
Price: Big Boy Color Case Hardened Side Gate $1,141.00
Price: Big Boy Steel Side Gate, Carbine or Rifle $969.00
Price: Big Boy Steel Side Gate, Large Loop $986.00
Price: Color Case Hardened Side Gate .30-30 and .45-70 .... $1,141.00
Price: Steel .30-30 Side Gate $969.00
Price: Steel .30-30 Side Gate Large Loop $986.00
Price: Steel .45-70 Side Gate $969.00
Price: Steel Wildlife Edition Side Gate $1,618.00

HENRY MODEL H024 SIDE GATE LEVER ACTION
Calibers: .38-55 Win., .30-30 Win., .45-70 Govt, .35 Rem. Capacity: 4 or 5-round tubular magazine. Barrel: 20-in. round blued steel. Weight: 7.5 lbs. Length: 38.3 in. Stock: American Walnut straight style with special deep checkering including floral scroll and Henry logo wood detail not found on any other models. Sights: Fully adjustable semi-buckhorn diamond-insert rear. Front ramp with 0.62-in. ivory bead. Drilled and tapped. Features: This H024 is the debut model using Henry's side loading gate design in addition to the standard tubular loading port. These hardened brass receiver centerfires are instantly recognizable with the special engraved and checkered stocks. Polished brass buttplate, barrel band, and swivel stud. Standard-size lever loop. Transfer bar safety.
Price: $1,100.00

HENRY BIG BOY X MODEL
Calibers: .45 Colt, .357/.38 Spl, .44 Mag/.44 Spl. Capacity: 7. Barrel: 17.4 in., round blue steel. Stock: Synthetic. Sights: Fiber optic. Weight: 7.3 lbs. Features: Robust and versatile, solid rubber buttpad, M-LOK Picatinny rail optional.
Price: $970.00

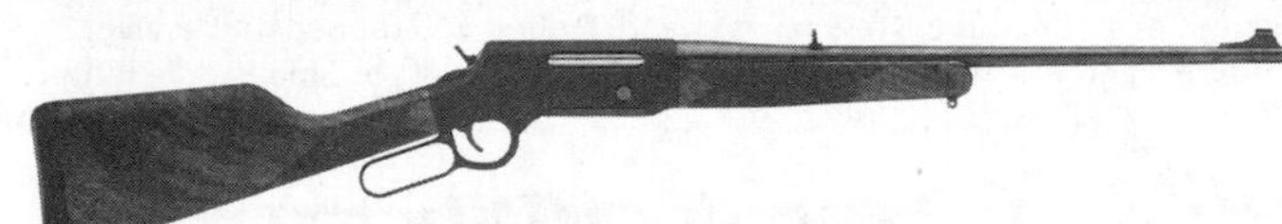

HENRY LONG RANGER
Calibers: .223 Rem., .243 Win., 6.5 Creedmoor, .308 Win. Capacity: 4 (.243, 6.5CM, .308) or 5 (.223) box magazine. Barrel: 20 or 22 in. (6.5 Creedmoor) round blued steel. Weight: 7 lbs. Length: 40.5–42.5 in. Stock: Straight-grip, checkered, oil-finished American Walnut. Sights: Two models, one sighted with folding fully adjustable rear and ramp ivory bead front. The other does not have iron sights but includes scope bases and hammer extension instead. Both are drilled and tapped. Features: Geared action with side ejection port. Chromed steel bolt with six lugs. Flush-fit box magazine with side push-button release. Sling studs, rubber recoil pad. Transfer bar safety.
Price: $1,138.00
Price: Long Ranger Wildlife Editions $1,973.00
Price: Long Ranger Deluxe Engraved $1,973.00

HENRY LONG RANGER EXPRESS
Calibers: .223 Rem/5.56 NATO. Capacity: 5-round steel box magazine. Barrel: 16.5-in. threaded round blued steel. Weight: 7 lbs. Length: 37 in. Stock: Birch laminate in black/gray. Sights: Top Picatinny rail. No iron sights. Features: Expansion of the Long Ranger line, this one a more compact platform. Same geared action with side ejection port. Chromed steel bolt with six lugs. Flush fit dropbox magazine with side push-button release. Sling studs, rubber recoil pad. Transfer bar safety. Hammer extension included. Barrel threaded at 5/8x24.
Price: $1,235.00

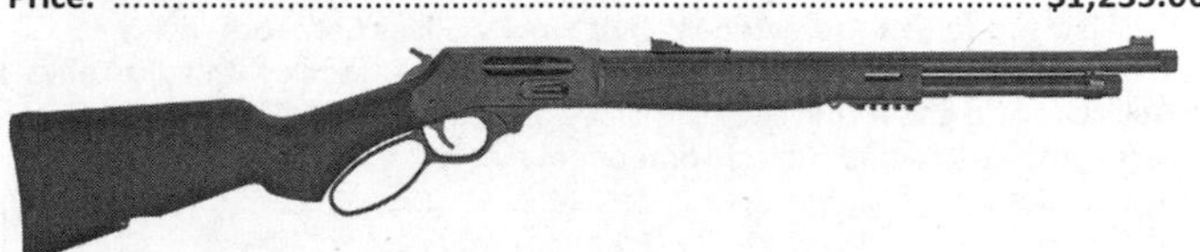

HENRY X-MODELS
Calibers: .30-30 Win., .45-70 Govt., .45 Colt, .44 Mag., .38 Spl./.357 Mag. Capacity: 4 (.45-70), 5 (.30-30), or 7 (Big Boys) tubular magazine Barrel: 17.4-, 19.8-, 21.375-in. round blued steel. Weight: 7.3–8.07 lbs. Length: 36.3–40.375 in. Stock: Black synthetic with M-LOK attachment points and lower Picatinny rail. Sights: Fully adjustable fiber-optic front and rear. Also drilled and tapped for Weaver 63B base. Features: Blacked-out lever actions built around several of Henry's existing family lines of long guns. Large loop lever. Barrel threaded at 5/8x24 for easy suppressor or brake attachment. Transfer bar safety. Solid rubber recoil pad. Sling studs. Matte blued steel metalwork.
Price: Big Boy X-Model $1,000.00
Price: X-Model .30-30 .... $1,019.00
Price: X-Model .45-70 .... $1,000.00

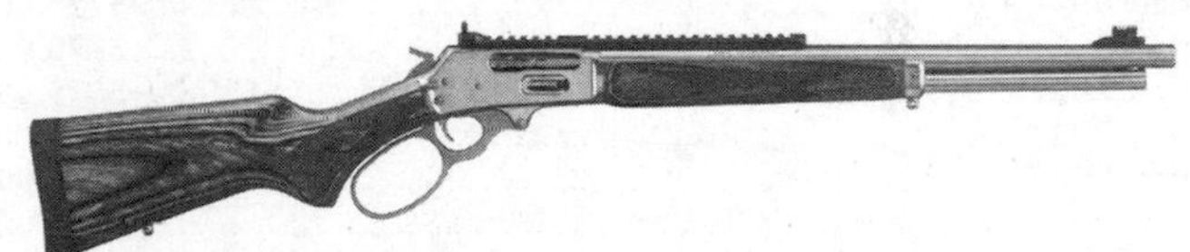

MARLIN 1895 SBL
Calibers: .45-70 Govt. Capacity: 6+1-round tubular magazine. Barrel: 19 in. threaded, cold-hammer-forged stainless steel. Weight: 7.3 lbs. Length: 37.25 in. Stock: Gray laminate with checkering. Sights: Adjustable Ghost ring rear, Tritium fiber-optic front. Picatinny rail. Features: The much-anticipated lever gun launch under Ruger ownership of the Marlin brand. Polished stainless metalwork. Nickel-plated, spiral fluted bolt. Barrel threaded at 11/16x24. Rubber buttpad. Push-button, cross-bolt manual safety and half-cock hammer. Oversized lever loop and slimmed-down forend. Includes swivel studs and offset hammer spur. Marlin horse-and-rider logo laser engraved on the grip. Made in Mayodan, NC. Ruger-made Marlin rifles begin with the serial prefix "RM." Traditional Marlin stock bullseye is now red/white.
Price: $1,399.00

NAVY ARMS 1873 RIFLE
Calibers: .357 Magnum, .45 Colt. Capacity: 12-round magazine. Barrels: 20 in., 24.25 in., full octagonal. Stock: Deluxe checkered American walnut. Sights: Gold bead front, semi-buckhorn rear. Features: Turnbull color case-hardened frame, rest blued. Full-octagon barrel. Available exclusively from Navy Arms. Made by Winchester.
Price: $2,500.00

NAVY ARMS 1892 SHORT RIFLE
Calibers: .45 Colt, .44 Magnum. Capacity: 10-round magazine. Barrel: 20 in. full octagon. Stock: Checkered Grade 1 American walnut. Sights: Marble's Semi-Buckhorn rear and gold bead front. Finish: Color casehardened.
Price: $2,300.00

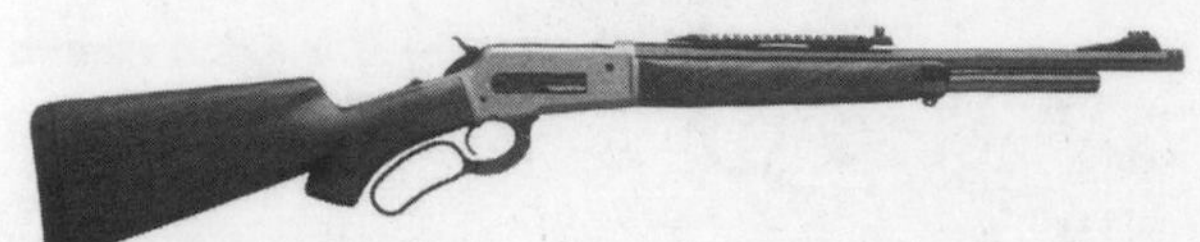

PEDERSOLI 86/71 BOARBUSTER

Calibers: .45-70 Govt. Capacity: 5-round tubular magazine. Barrel: 19-in. round. Weight: 7.93–8.25 lbs. Length: 37-7/16 in. Stock: Varied by model. Sights: Scout-style Picatinny rail and fiber-optic iron sights. Receiver drilled and tapped for side scope mounts. Features: Big-bore lever action based on the 1886. Several models use two-piece, interchangeable loop loading lever on several models. Pedersoli's Boarbuster line is comprised of five model variants. Mark II wears coated black Walnut with Silicon grip film adjustable cheek piece and Bronze Cerakote metal finish. HV-1 wears orange and black HV-1 camo stocks with Silicon grip film and black Cerakote. Evolution is a classic model with selected Walnut stocks, Silver Cerakote receiver, and blued barrel. Shadow uses gray techno-polymer stock with adjustable cheek riser and ghost ring sights in place of Picatinny rail. Guidemaster wears camo stocks and fully chromed metalwork.

Price: **$1,792.00**

ROSSI R92 LEVER-ACTION CARBINE

Calibers: .38 Special/.357 Magnum, .44 Magnum., .44-40 Win., .45 Colt. Barrels: 16or 20 in. with round barrel, 20 or 24 in. with octagon barrel. Weight: 4.8–7 lbs. Length: 34–41.5 in. Features: Blued or stainless finish. Various options available in selected chamberings (large lever loop, fiber-optic sights, cheekpiece).

Price: R92 Blued Rifle **$730.00**
Price: R92 Stainless Rifle **$770.00**
Price: R92 Carbine **$725.00**
Price: R92 Stainless Carbine **$770.00**
Price: R92 Octagonal Barrel ...... **$830.00–$875.00**
Price: R92 Gold **$810.00**
Price: R92 Triple Black **$925.00**
Price: R92 .454 Casull **$950.00**

UBERTI 1873 SPORTING RIFLE

Calibers: .357 Magnum, .44-40, .45 Colt. Barrels: 16.1 in. round, 19 in. round or 20 in., 24.25 in. octagonal. Weight: Up to 8.2 lbs. Length: Up to 43.3 in. overall. Stock: Walnut, straight grip and pistol grip. Sights: Blade front adjustable for windage, open rear adjustable for elevation. Features: Color casehardened frame, blued barrel, hammer, lever, buttplate, brass elevator. Imported by Stoeger Industries.

Price: Carbine 19-in. bbl. **$1,309.00**
Price: Trapper 16.1-in. bbl. **$1,329.00**
Price: Carbine 18-in. half oct. bbl. **$1,379.00**
Price: Short Rifle 20-in. bbl. **$1,339.00**
Price: Sporting Rifle, 24.25-in. bbl. **$1,339.00**
Price: Special Sporting Rifle, A-grade walnut **$1,449.00**

UBERTI 1860 HENRY

Calibers: .44-40, .45 Colt. Barrel: 24.25 in. half-octagon. Weight: 9.2 lbs. Length: 43.75 in. overall. Stock: American walnut. Sights: Blade front, rear adjustable for elevation. Imported by Stoeger Industries.

Price: 1860 Henry Trapper, 18.5-in. barrel, brass frame **$1,499.00**
Price: 1860 Henry Rifle Iron Frame, 24.25-in. barrel **$1,499.00**

WINCHESTER MODEL 94 SHORT RIFLE

Calibers: .30-30, .38-55, .32 Special. Barrel: 20 in. Weight: 6.75 lbs. Sights: Semi-buckhorn rear, gold bead front. Stock: Walnut with straight grip. Fore-end has black grip cap. Also available in Trail's End takedown design in .450 Marlin or .30-30.

Price: **$1,230.00**
Price: (Takedown) **$1,460.00**

WINCHESTER MODEL 94 SPORTER

Calibers: .30-30, .38-55. Barrel: 24 in. Weight: 7.5 lbs. Features: Same features of Model 94 Short Rifle except for crescent butt and steel buttplate, 24 in. half-round, half-octagon barrel, checkered stock.

Price: **$1,400.00**
Price: Deluxe Sporting 24 in. .30-30 Win., .38-55 Win. **$2,169.00**

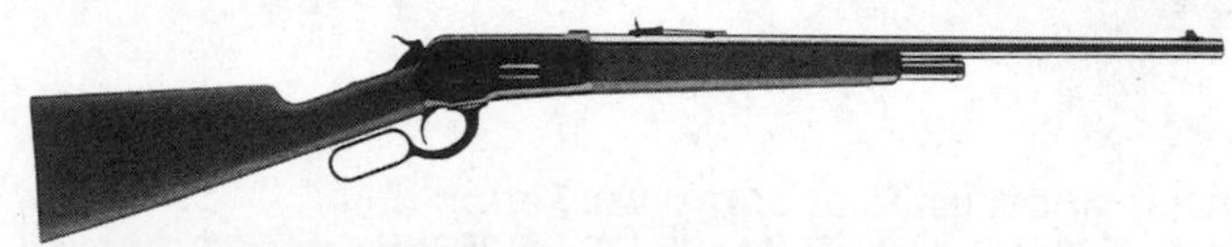

WINCHESTER 1873 SHORT RIFLE

Calibers: .357 Magnum, .44-40, .45 Colt. Capacities: Tubular magazine holds 10 rounds (.44-40, .45 Colt), 11 rounds (.38 Special). Barrel: 20 in. Weight: 7.25 lbs. Sights: Marble semi-buckhorn rear, gold bead front. Tang is drilled and tapped for optional peep sight. Stock: Satin finished, straight-grip walnut with steel crescent buttplate and steel fore-end cap. Tang safety. A modern version of the "Gun That Won the West."

Price: **$1,300.00**
Price: Deluxe Sporting Rifle **$1,800.00**
Price: Competition Carbine High Grade 20 in..45 Colt or .357 Mag.... **$1,839.00**
Price: Deluxe Sporting 24 in. .44-40 Win. **$2,119.00**

WINCHESTER MODEL 1886 SADDLE RING CARBINE

Calibers: .45-70 Govt, .45-90 Win. Capacity: 7-round tubular magazine. Barrel: 22-in. round polished blued steel. Weight: 8 lbs. Length: 41 in. Stock: Grade I Black Walnut with straight grip and carbine-style forearm, oil finished. Sights: Carbine ladder-style rear and blade front. Features: Full-length magazine tube, steel barrel band. Drilled and tapped for receiver mount sight. Brushed polish receiver finish. Tang safety. Side Saddle Ring.

Price: **$1,549.00**

WINCHESTER MODEL 1895

Calibers: .30-06 Spfld., .405 Win. Capacity: 4-round internal magazine. Barrel: 24-in. gloss blued steel, button rifled. Weight: 8 lbs. Length: 42 in. Stock: Grade I Black Walnut, straight grip with traditional cut checkering. Sights: Drilled and tapped receiver for side mount sight; Marble Arms gold bead front and Buckhorn rear. Features: Throwback lever gun reminiscent of Teddy Roosevelt's "Big Medicine." Grade I Model 1895 lever action with scalloped receiver, two-piece lever, and Schnabel forend.

Price: ...... **$1,369.00–$1,439.00**
Price: Grade III/IV Black Walnut .30-40 Krag **$1,699.00–1,769.00**

ARMALITE AR-50A1
Caliber: .50 BMG, .416 Barrett. Capacity: Bolt-action single-shot. Barrel: 30 in. with muzzle brake. National Match model (shown) has 33-in. fluted barrel. Weight: 34.1 lbs. Stock: Three-section. Extruded fore-end, machined vertical grip, forged and machined buttstock that is vertically adjustable. National Match model (.50 BMG only) has V-block patented bedding system, Armalite Skid System to ensure straight-back recoil.
Price: **$3,359.00**

ANSCHUTZ 1782
Calibers: .243 Win., 6.5 Creedmoor, .308 Win., .30-06, 8x57, 9.3x62. Capacity: 3. Barrel: 20.5 to 23.8 in., blued, threaded. Stock: Walnut. Sights: Integrated Picatinny rail. Weight: 8 lbs. Features: Solid-steel milled action, 60-degree bolt lift, sliding safety catch.
Price: **$2,795.00**

BENELLI LUPO
Calibers: .243 Win., 6mm Creedmoor, 6.5 Creedmoor, .308 Win., 6.5 PRC, .30-06 Spfld., .270 Win, 7mm Rem. Mag., .300 Win. Mag. Capacity: 4–5-round box magazine. Barrel: 22 and 24 in. Crio-treated, free-floating, threaded barrel with thread cover. Length: 44.25–46.62 in. Stock: Black Synthetic. Sights: None. Includes two piece Picatinny rail. Weight: 6.9–7.1 lbs. Features: Shims allow stock adjustment. Matte blued metalwork. Progressive comfort recoil reduction system. Sub-MOA guarantee. CombTech cheek pad. Ambidextrous safety. Integral swivel mounts.
Price: **$1,699.00**
Price: B.E.S.T. CAMO, Elevated II or Open Country camo **$1,899.00**

BENELLI LUPO WOOD B.E.S.T.
Calibers: 6.5 Creedmoor, .308 Win., .300 Win. Mag. Capacity: 4–5 round box magazine. Barrel: 22- and 24-in. Crio-treated, free-floating, threaded barrel with thread cover. Length: 44.225–46.625 in. Stock: AA-grade satin Walnut. Sights: Two-piece Picatinny bases. No iron sights. Weight: 7.1 lbs. Features: The new model Lupo replaces synthetic furniture with Walnut but keeps most other features. Also adds B.E.S.T. surface treatment to metal surfaces for added durability. Trigger reach spacers. Ambidextrous safety. Progressive comfort recoil reduction system. Sub-MOA guarantee.
Price: .... **$1,899.00–$2,199.00**

BARRETT FIELDCRAFT HUNTING RIFLE
Calibers: .22-250 Rem., .243 Win., 6mm Creedmoor, .25-06, 6.5 Creedmoor, 6.5x55, 7mm-08 Rem., .308 Win. .270 Win., .30-06. Capacity: 4-round magazine. Barrel: 18 (threaded), 21 or 24 inches. Weight: 5.2-5.6 lbs. Features: Two-position safety, Timney trigger. Receiver, barrels and bolts are scaled for specific calibers. Barrels and action are made from 416 stainless steel and are full-length hand bedded.
Price: .... **$1,879.00-$1,929.00**

BARRETT MRAD
Calibers: .260 Rem., 6.5 Creedmoor, .308 Win., .300 Win. Mag., .338 Lapua Magnum. Capacity: 10-round magazine. Barrels: 20 in., 24 in. or 26 in. fluted or heavy. Features: User-interchangeable barrel system, folding stock, adjustable cheekpiece, 5-position length of pull adjustment button, match-grade trigger, 22-in. optics rail.
Price: .... **$5,850.00–$6,000.00**

BERGARA B-14 SERIES
Calibers: 6.5 Creedmoor, .270 Win., 7mm Rem. Mag., .308 Win., .30-06, .300 Win. Mag. Barrels: 22 or 24 in. Weight: 7 lbs. Features: Synthetic with Soft touch finish, recoil pad, swivel studs, adjustable trigger, choice of detachable mag or hinged floorplate. Made in Spain.
Price: **$825.00**
Price: Walnut Stock (Shown, Top) **$945.00**
Price: Premier Series **$2,190.00**
Price: Hunting and Match Rifle (HMR)(Shown, Bottom).......... **$1,150.00**

BERGARA PREMIER CANYON
Calibers: 6.5 Creedmoor, 6.5 PRC, .308 Win., 28 Nosler, .300 Win. Mag., 300 PRC, .375 H&H. Capacity: AICS-style detachable 3-round mag. provided, 5-round long action. 375 uses hinged floorplate with 3-round capacity. Barrel: 20–22 in. No. 4 taper, fluted stainless steel. Weight: 6.2–6.5 lbs. Length: 41–44 in. Stock: AG Composite 100% carbon fiber. Sights: Drilled and tapped for Remington 700 bases with 8-40 screws. Features: Classic style hunting rifle. Bolt uses a non-rotating gas shield, coned bolt nose, and sliding plate extractor. TriggerTech frictionless release trigger with two-position safety. Threaded muzzle with Omni Muzzle Brake. Sniper Grey Cerakote. Guaranteed MOA accuracy.
Price: .... **$2,379.00–$2,429.00**

BERGARA PREMIER DIVIDE
Calibers: 6.5 Creedmoor, 6.5 PRC, .308 Win., .300 Win. Mag. Capacity: AICS-style detachable, 5 standard, 3 magnum. Barrel: 22 in., 24 in. No. 6 CURE carbon fiber. Weight: 7.2–7.4 lbs. Length: 43–46 in. Stock: AG Composite 100% carbon fiber. Sights: Drilled and tapped for Remington 700 bases with 8-40 screws. Features: Built to bridge the divide between tactical and hunting rifles. Bolt uses a non-rotating gas shield, coned bolt nose, and sliding plate extractor. TriggerTech frictionless release trigger with two-position safety. Threaded muzzle with Omni Muzzle Brake. Patriot Brown Cerakote finish. Guaranteed MOA accuracy.
Price: .... **$2,749.00–$2,799.00**

BERGARA PREMIER MG LITE
Calibers: 6.5 Creedmoor, 6.5 PRC, .308 Win., .300 Win Mag. Capacity: 5 standard, 3 magnum. Barrel: 22 in. or 24 in. fully free-floated, proprietary CURE carbon fiber. Weight: 6.7–6.8 lbs. Length: 43–45 in. Stock: Ultra-lightweight XLR Element 4.0 magnesium chassis with folding buttstock. Sights: Drilled and tapped for Remington 700 bases with 8-40 screws. Features: Precision bolt-action hunting rifle with a non-rotating gas shield, coned bolt nose, and sliding plate extractor. TriggerTech frictionless release trigger with two-position safety. Threaded muzzle with Omni Muzzle Brake. Graphite Black Cerakote. Guaranteed MOA accuracy.
Price: .... **$3,229.00–$3,349.00**

BLASER R-8 SERIES
Calibers: Available in virtually all standard and metric calibers from .204 Ruger to .500 Jeffery. Straight-pull bolt action. Barrels: 20.5, 23, or 25.75

in. Weights: 6.375–8.375 lbs. Lengths: 40 in. overall (22 in. barrel). Stocks: Synthetic or Turkish walnut. Sights: None furnished; drilled and tapped for scope mounting. Features: Thumb-activated safety slide/cocking mechanism; interchangeable barrels and bolt heads. Many optional features. Imported from Germany by Blaser USA. *Note, Blaser R8 bolt action series adds a .22 LR rimfire conversion system.*
Price: **$3,787.00**

BLASER R8 ULTIMATE CARBON
Calibers: Available in wide range of calibers from .22 LR to .500 Jeffery, now including 6.5 Creedmoor and 6.5 PRC. Barrel: 20.5, 23, or 25.75 in. Stock: Hand-laid 100% carbon fiber thumbhole stock with Elastomer grip inserts. An Ultimate Carbon Leather variant is available with dark brown weather-proof leather inserts. Sights: Drilled and tapped. Features: Straight-pull bolt-action hunting rifle with interchangeable barrels and bolt heads. Ultimate Carbon variant designed for max performance and minimum weight. Blaser Precision trigger. Thumb-activated safety slide/cocking mechanism. Optional upgrades include an adjustable comb and recoil absorption system or adjustable recoil pad. Imported from Germany by Blaser Group.
Price: **$11,500.00**

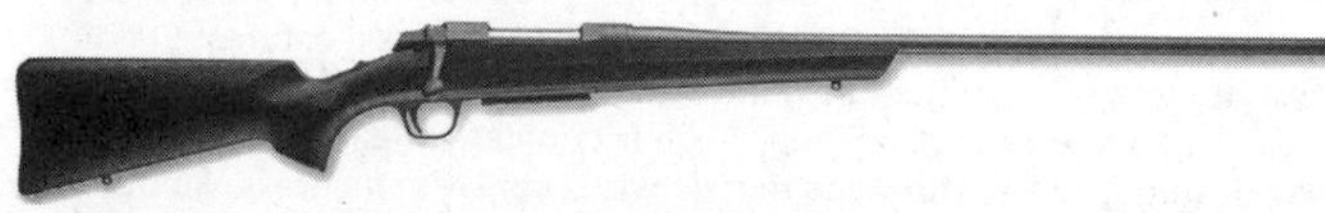

BROWNING AB3 COMPOSITE STALKER
Calibers: .243, 6.5 Creedmoor, .270 Win., .270 WSM, 7mm-08, 7mm Rem. Mag., .30-06, .300 Win. Mag., .300 WSM or .308 Win. Barrels: 22 in, 26 in. for magnums. Weights: 6.8–7.4 lbs. Stock: Matte black synthetic. Sights: None. Picatinny rail scope mount included.
Price: **$600.00**
Price: Micro Stalker **$600.00**
Price: Hunter.. **$670.00**

BROWNING X-BOLT HUNTER
Calibers: .223, .22-250, .243 Win., 6mm Creedmoor, 6.5 Creedmoor, .25-06 Rem., .270 Win., .270 WSM, .280 Rem., 7mm Rem. Mag., 7mm WSM, 7mm-08 Rem., .308 Win., .30-06, .300 Win. Mag., .300 WSM, .325 WSM, .338 Win. Mag., .375 H&H Mag, 6.8 Western. Barrels: 22 in., 23 in., 24 in., 26 in., varies by model. Matte blued or stainless free-floated barrel, recessed muzzle crown. Weights: 6.3–7 lbs. Stocks: Hunter and Medallion models have black walnut stocks; Composite Stalker and Stainless Stalker models have composite stocks. Inflex Technology recoil pad. Sights: None, drilled and tapped receiver, X-Lock scope mounts. Features: Adjustable three-lever Feather Trigger system, polished hard-chromed steel components, factory pre-set at 3.5 lbs., alloy trigger housing. Bolt unlock button, detachable rotary magazine, 60-degree bolt lift, three locking lugs, top-tang safety, sling swivel studs. Introduced 2008.
Price: Standard calibers **$900.00**
Price: Magnum calibers **$950.00**
Price: Left-hand models.. **$940.00–$980.00**

BROWNING X-BOLT WESTERN HUNTER LONG RANGE
Calibers: 6.5 Creedmoor, 6.5 PRC, 7mm Rem. Mag., 28 Nosler, .280 Ackley Improved, .300 Win. Mag., 30 Nosler, .300 Rem. Ultra Mag., .300 PRC, 6.8 Western. Capacity: 3 or 4-round removeable rotary magazine Barrel: 26-in. heavy sporter contour with removeable muzzle brake. Length: 46–46.75 in. Weight: 7 lbs. 7 oz.–7 lbs. 12 oz. Stock: Composite with new adjustable comb system, A-TACS AU camo finish, and textured grip panels. Features: Top tang thumb safety. Extended bolt handle. Feather Trigger, InFlex recoil pad. X-Lock scope mount system. Gold-plated trigger. Sling studs.
Price: .... **$1,099.00–$1,219.00**

BROWNING X-BOLT HUNTER LONG RANGE
Calibers: 6.5 Creedmoor, 6.5 PRC, .308 Win., .270 Win., .30-06, 7MM Rem. Mag., .300 Win. Mag., 6.8 Western. Capacity: 3 to 4. Barrel: 22 to 26 in., blued sporter, heavy. Stock: Satin finish checkered walnut. Sights: None, drilled and tapped. Weight: 7.6 to 8 lbs. Features: Ambidextrous adjustable comb, muzzle brake with suppressor threads.
Price: **$1,300.00**

BROWNING X-BOLT MAX LONG RANGE
Calibers: 6mm Creedmoor, 6.5 Creedmoor, .308 Win., .300 WSM, 7MM Rem. Mag., 28 Nosler, .300 Win.Mag, .300 RUM, 6.5 PRC, 30 Nosler, .300 PRC, 6.8 Western. Capacity: 3 to 4. Barrel: 26 in., satin gray stainless steel sporter, heavy. Stock: Composite black, gray splatter. Sights: None, drilled and tapped. Weight: 8.2 to 8.6 lbs. Features: Adjustable comb, extended bolt handle, three swivel studs for sling and bipod use.
Price: .... **$1,300.00-$1,340.00**

BROWNING X-BOLT MEDALLION
Calibers: Most popular calibers from .223 Rem. to .375 H&H, 6.8 Western. Barrels: 22, 24 or 26 in. free-floated. Features: Engraved receiver with polished blue finish, gloss finished and checkered walnut stock with rosewood grip and fore-end caps, detachable rotary magazine. Medallion Maple model has AAA-grade maple stock.
Price: **$1,040.00**
Price: Medallion Maple **$1,070.00**

BROWNING X-BOLT HELL'S CANYON
Calibers: .22 Nosler, 6mm Creedmoor, .243 Win., 26 Nosler, 6.5 Creedmoor, .270 Win., .270 WSM, 7mm-08 Rem., 7mm Rem. Mag., .308 Win., .30-06, .300 Win. Mag., .300 WSM, 6.8 Western. Barrels: 22–26-in. fluted and free-floating with muzzle brake or thread protector. Stock: A-TACS AU Camo composite with checkered grip panels. Features: Detachable rotary magazine, adjustable trigger, Cerakote Burnt Bronze finish on receiver and barrel.
Price: .... **$1,260.00–$1,320.00**

BROWNING X-BOLT HELLS CANYON MAX LONG RANGE
Calibers: 6.5 Creed, 6.5 PRC, 7mm Rem. Mag., 28 Nosler, .280 Ackley Improved, .300 Win. Mag., 30 Nosler, .300 Rem. Ultra Mag., .300 PRC, 6.8 Western. Capacity: 3- or 4-round box magazine. Barrel: 26-in. heavy sporter. Weight: 8–8 lbs. 7oz. Length: 46-3/4 in. Stock: Composite Max in either A-TACS AU or OVIX camo with adjustable comb, LOP spacers, and vertical pistol grip. Features: Long-range bolt-action platform with steel receiver. Cerakote Burnt Bronze finish. Removeable Browning Recoil Hawg muzzle brake. Top tang thumb safety. Extended bolt handle. Three swivel studs. FeatherTrigger, InFlex recoil pad. Gold-plated trigger and branding detail.
Price: .... **$1,539.00–$1,619.00**

BROWNING X-BOLT MOUNTAIN PRO
Caliber: 6.5 Creedmoor, 6.5 PRC, 6.8 Western, .300 WSM, .30-06 Spfld., 7mm Rem. Mag., 28 Nosler, .300 Win. Mag., 30 Nosler, .300 PRC, .300 Rem. UM. Capacity: 3- or 4-round box magazine. Barrel: 22, 23, 24, or 26 in. sporter weight, threaded, with Recoil Hawg muzzle brake. Length: 42–46.75 in. Weight: 5 lbs. 14 oz.–6 lbs. 6 oz. Stock: Carbon fiber filled with noise-dampening foam and finished with accent graphics. Features: Choice of

Prices given are believed to be accurate at time of publication however, many factors affect retail pricing so exact prices are not possible.

either Burnt Bronze or Tungsten models. Big game bolt-action semi-custom hunting rifle. New proprietary lapping process for easier bore cleaning and avoiding break-in. Cerakote finish on stainless steel barrel and action. Spiral fluted bolt and barrel. Quarter-pound weight reduction over previous models. Removeable Picatinny accessory rail. Swivel studs. Feather trigger. X-Lock optics mounting system. InFlex recoil pad. Gold-plated trigger and brand detail. Thread protector included.

Price: .... $2,479.00–$2,539.00
Price: MOUNTAIN PRO LR 26 in. heavy contour .... $2,469.00–$2,579.00

BROWNING X-BOLT PRO SERIES

Calibers: 6mm Creedmoor, 6.5 Creedmoor, 26 Nosler, 28 Nosler, .270 Win., 7mm Rem. Mag., .308 Win., .30-06., .300 Win.Mag, 6.8 Western. Detachable rotary magazine. Barrels: 22–26 in. Stainless steel, fluted with threaded/removable muzzle brake. Weights: 6–7.5 lbs. Finish: Cerakote Burnt Bronze. Stock: Second generation carbon fiber with palm swell, textured gripping surfaces. Adjustable trigger, top tang safety, sling swivel studs. Long Range has heavy sporter-contour barrel, proprietary lapping process.

Price: X-Bolt Pro .... $2,070.00–$2,130.00
Price: X-Bolt Pro Long Range .... $2,100.00–$2,180.00
Price: X-Bolt Pro Tungsten .... $2,070.00–$2,130.00
Price: PRO LONG RANGE 26-in. heavy barrel, carbon-fiber stock. .... $2,239.00–$2,269.00

CADEX DEFENCE CDX-R7 CRBN SERIES

Calibers: 6.5 Creedmoor, 6.5 PRC, .308 Win., .300 WSM, .300 PRC, .338 Lapua Mag. Capacity: Varies by box magazine. Barrel: 24 or 26 in. Proof Research carbon fiber threaded. Weight: 8.2–8.3 lbs. Length: 45.25–48.06 in. Stock: Lightweight Tundra Strike chassis with aluminum bedding blocks available in 14 color combinations. Cadex recoil pad, neoprene cheek pad, and rubberized grip panel. Sights: None. 0 MOA Picatinny rail standard, 20 or 30 MOA rails available. Features: Bolt-action rifle designed with backcountry hunters in mind. Hunting style muzzle brake and bolt knob. Spiral fluted bolt. Cerakote metalwork. DX2 Evo single-/two-stage selectable trigger. Oversized triggerguard and mag release. Hard case included.

Price: $3,359.00

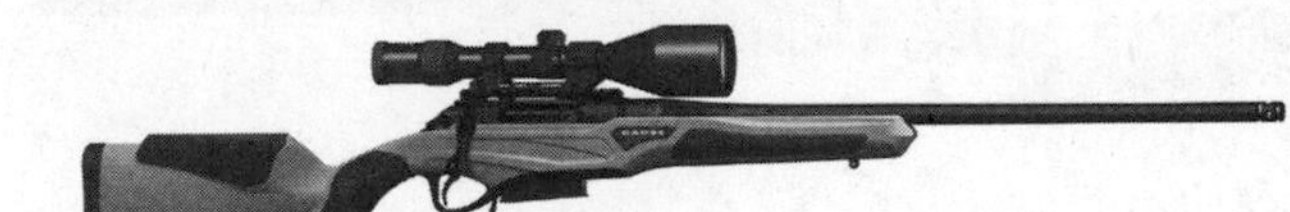

CADEX DEFENCE CDX-R7 SPTR SERIES

Calibers: 6.5 Creedmoor, 6.5 PRC, .308 Win., .300 WSM, .300 PRC, 338 Lapua Mag. Capacity: varies by box magazine. Barrel: 24 or 26 in. sporter profile stainless, fluted and threaded. Weight: 8.2–8.5 lbs. Length: 45.25–48.06 in. Stock: Lightweight Tundra Strike chassis with aluminum bedding blocks available in 14 color combinations. Cadex recoil pad, neoprene cheek pad, and rubberized grip panel. Sights: None. 0 MOA Picatinny rail standard, 20 or 30 MOA rails available. Features: Bolt-action rifle similar to the CRBN series, but without the carbon-fiber barrel. Hunting-style muzzle brake and bolt knob. Spiral fluted bolt. DX2 Evo single-/two-stage selectable trigger. Oversized triggerguard and mag release. Hard case included.

Price: $2,769.00

CHEYTAC M-200

Calibers: .357 CheyTac, .408 CheyTac. Capacity: 7-round magazine. Barrel: 30 in. Length: 55 in. stock extended. Weight: 27 lbs. (steel barrel); 24 lbs. (carbon-fiber barrel). Stock: Retractable. Sights: None, scope rail provided. Features: CNC-machined receiver, attachable Picatinny rail M-1913, detachable barrel, integral bipod, 3.5-lb. trigger pull, muzzle brake. Made in USA by CheyTac, LLC.

Price: $11,700.00

CHRISTENSEN ARMS RIDGELINE FFT

Calibers: .450 Bushmaster, .22-250 Rem., .243 Rem, 6.5 Creed, 6.5 PRC, 6.5-284, 26 Nosler, .270 Win., 7mm-08, .280 Ackley, 28 Nosler, 7mm Rem. Mag., .308 Win., .30-06, 30 Nosler, .300 WSM, .300 Win. Mag., .300 PRC, .300 RUM. Capacity: FFT hinged floor plate with internal magazine. 4-round standard, 3-round magnum. Barrel: 20 or 22-in. carbon-fiber wrapped stainless, button-rifled, hand-lapped, free-floating. Weight: From 5.3 lbs. Stock: Proprietary Flash Forged Technology (FFT) carbon-fiber sporter style with stainless steel bedding pillars. Choice of black with gray webbing, green with black and tan webbing, Sitka Subalpine camo, or Sitka Elevated II camo. Sights: No iron sights. Drilled and tapped at 6-48 for Remington 700 bases. Features: Upgraded version of the Ridgeline uses the latest in carbon-fiber technology to build the rifle a full pound lighter. New side-baffle brake and stylish paint scheme distinguish the upgraded model. Choice of natural stainless or Burnt Bronze Cerakote metalwork. Enlarged ejection port. Billet aluminum bottom metal. Sub-MOA guarantee, excluding .450 Bushmaster. Multiple calibers available in a left-hand rifle.

Price: $2,399.00

CHRISTENSEN ARMS RIDGELINE SCOUT

Calibers: .223 Rem, 6mm ARC, 6.5 Creed, .308 Win., .300 Blackout. Capacity: 10-round AICS box magazine. Barrel: 16-in. carbon-fiber wrapped stainless, button rifled, free-floating. Weight: From 5.9 lbs. Stock: Carbon-fiber composite, sporter style with stainless steel bedding pillars. Tan with black webbing. Sights: No iron sights. 0 MOA rail. Features: Compact, scout-rifle version of the Ridgeline bolt-action hunting rifle. Black nitride-coated action. Flat-shoe TriggerTech trigger. Match chamber. Three-prong flash hider removes for easy suppressor use. Forward mount lower rail with barricade stop. MOA guarantee.

Price: $2,199.00

CHRISTENSEN ARMS RIDGELINE TITANIUM EDITION

Calibers: 6.5 Creedmoor, 6.5 PRC, .308 Win., .300 Win. Mag. Capacity: 3 to 4. Barrel: 22 to 24 in., 416R stainless steel, carbon-fiber wrapped. Stock: Carbon-fiber composite, sporter style. Sights: Picatinny rail. Weight: 5.8 lbs. Features: Titanium radial brake, M16-style extractor, LimbSaver recoil pad.

Price: $2,495.00

COOPER MODEL 21

Calibers: Virtually any factory or wildcat chambering in the .223 Rem. family is available including: .17 Rem., .19-223, Tactical 20, .204 Ruger, .222 Rem, .222 Rem. Mag., .223 Rem, .223 Rem AI, 6x45, 6x47. Single shot. Barrels: 22–24 in. for Classic configurations, 24–26 in. for Varminter configurations. Weights: 6.5–8.0 lbs., depending on type. Stock: AA-AAA select claro walnut, 20 LPI checkering. Sights: None furnished. Features: Three front locking-lug, bolt-action, single-shot. Action: 7.75 in. long, Sako extractor. Button ejector. Fully adjustable single-stage trigger. Options include wood upgrades, case-color metalwork, barrel fluting, custom LOP, and many others.

Price: Classic $2,495.00
Price: Custom Classic. $2,995.00
Price: Western Classic. $3,795.00
Price: Varminter $2,495.00
Price: Mannlicher $4,395.000

COOPER MODEL 52

Calibers: .30-06, .270 Win., .280 Rem, .25-06, .284 Win., .257 Weatherby Mag., .264 Win. Mag., .270 Weatherby Mag., 7mm Remington Mag., 7mm Weatherby Mag., 7mm Shooting Times Westerner, .300 Holland & Holland,

.300 Win. Mag., .300 Weatherby Mag., .308 Norma Mag., 8mm Rem. Mag., .338 Win. Mag., .340 Weatherby V. Three-shot magazine. Barrels: 22 in. or 24 in. in Classic configurations, 24 in. or 26 in. in Varminter configurations. Weight: 7.75–8 lbs. depending on type. Stock: AA-AAA select claro walnut, 20 LPI checkering. Sights: None furnished. Features: Three front locking-lug bolt-action single shot. Action: 7 in. long, Sako style extractor. Button ejector. Fully adjustable single-stage trigger. Options include wood upgrades, case-color metalwork, barrel fluting, custom LOP, and many others.
Price: Classic. **$2,495.00**
Price: Custom Classic. **$3,335.00**
Price: Western Classic. **$3,995.00**
Price: Jackson Game **$2,595.00**
Price: Jackson Hunter **$2,595.00**
Price: Excalibur. **$2,595.00**
Price: Mannlicher **$4,755.00**
Price: Open Country Long Range **$3,795.00-4,155.00**
Price: Timberline, Synthetic Stock **$2,595.00**
Price: Raptor, Synthetic tactical stock **$2,755.00**

CVA CASCADE
Calibers: .243 Win., 6.5 Creedmoor, 7mm-08 Rem., .308 Win., .350 Legend, .450 Bushmaster, .22-250 Rem., 6.5 PRC, 7mm Rem. Mag., .300 Win. Mag. Capacity: 3 or 4-round flush-fit detachable magazine Barrel: 22-in. 4140 carbon steel in either matte blue or Cerakote FDE. Weight: 6.85–7.25 lbs. Length: 42.5–45.5 in. Stock: Synthetic, fiber-glass reinforced with SoftTouch finish. Available in either charcoal gray or Veil Wideland camo. Sights: Drilled and tapped for Savage 110 mounts; aftermarket CVA 20-MOA one-piece base available. Features: Bolt designed with 70-degree throw. Two-position safety. Threaded muzzle. Dual front swivel studs. Buttstock has adjustable LOP with removeable spacer. MOA guarantee.
Price: .... **$567.00–$658.00**
Price: Cascade SB (Short Barrel) Series **$670.00**

CZ 600 ALPHA
Calibers: .223 Rem, .224 Valkyrie, 6mm Creed, 6.5 Creed, .308 Win., 6.5 PRC, 7.62x39, .30-06, .300 Win. Mag. Capacity: 3 or 5 rounds depending on caliber, detachable locking magazine. Barrel: 18-, 20-, or 22-in. semi-heavy, cold hammer forged. Weight: 6.6–7.5 lbs. Length: 40.7–43.1 in. Stock: Black polymer with serrated grip zones. Sights: No iron sights. Integral, two-piece bases. Features: CZ's new 600 family of bolt-action rifles. The Alpha is essentially the base model. Threaded, suppressor ready. Adjustable, single-stage trigger. Sling studs. Sub-MOA guarantee.
Price: **$749.00**

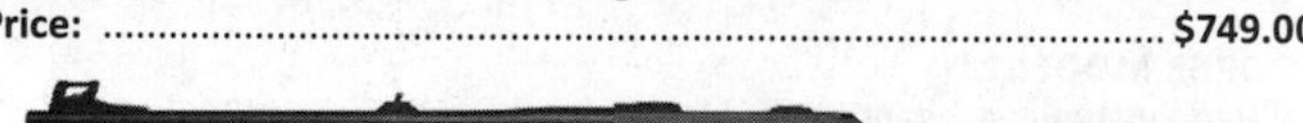

CZ 600 LUX
Calibers: .223 Rem, .308 Win., .30-06, .300 Win. Mag. Capacity: 3 or 5 rounds depending on caliber, detachable locking magazine. Barrel: 20 or 24 in. light cold-hammer forged, threaded. Weight: 6.8–8.6 lbs. Length: 41–44 in. Stock: Oil-finished, select-grade Walnut, Bavarian-style with fish-scale checkering. Sights: Rear adjustable iron sights with fiber-optic front. Drilled and tapped for Remington 700 mounts. Features: CZ's new 600 family of bolt-action rifles. The Lux fits a steel receiver to a European-style Walnut stock. Matching wooden bolt knob. Adjustable, single-stage trigger. Vertical, two-position tang safety. Sling studs. Sub-MOA guarantee.
Price: **$849.00**

CZ 600 RANGE
Calibers: 6mm Creedmoor, .308 Win. Capacity: 5-round detachable magazine. Barrel: 24 in. heavy, cold hammer forged, threaded. Weight: 10 lbs. Length: 44.9 in. Stock: Laminate Precision with tool-less adjustable comb. Sights: None. Drilled and tapped for Remington 700 mounts. Features: CZ's new 600 family of bolt-action rifles. The Range is designed as the precision shooting and varmint hunting model. Adjustable, single-stage trigger. Vertical two-position safety. Suppressor ready. Dual forend sling studs. QD studs beneath the forend and sockets on each side. Five-shot Sub-3/4 MOA guarantee at 100 meters.
Price: **$1,199.00**

CZ 600 TRAIL
Calibers: .223 Rem, 7.62x39. Capacity: 10-round detachable magazine. The .223 Rem. uses AR-style mags; 7.62 uses CZ Bren 2 mags. Barrel: 16.2-in. semi-heavy, cold hammer forged, threaded. Weight: 6.1 lbs. Length: Adjustable from 27.2–35 in. Stock: Polymer black PDW-style, four-position adjustable; Aluminum forend with M-LOK slots. Sights: None. Picatinny rail. Features: CZ's new 600 family of bolt-action rifles. The Trail is designed as a light, compact that will feel familiar to those accustomed to AR-platforms. Built on an aluminum action with a polymer chassis. Adjustable, two-stage trigger. Suppressor ready. Ambidextrous mag release and AR-style safety.
Price: **$1,199.00**

FIERCE FIREARMS CARBON FURY
Calibers: .300 PRC, 6.5 Creedmoor, 6.5 PRC, 7MM Rem. Mag, .300 Win. Mag, .300 RUM, .300 WSM, 28 Nosler. Capacity: 4 to 5. Barrel: 24 to 26 in., stainless steel liner, carbon-fiber overlay. Stock: Carbon-fiber Monte Carlo. Sights: None, drilled and tapped. Weight: 6.6 lbs. Features: Guaranteed half-inch three-shot group at 100 yards; target crown for accuracy.
Price: **$2,740.00**

FIERCE FIREARMS RIVAL
Calibers: 6.5 Creedmoor, 6.5 PRC, 7mm Rem., 28 Nosler, .300 Win., .300 PRC, .300 RUM. Capacity: 4 to 5. Barrel: 20 to 26 in., spiral-fluted, match-grade stainless steel or carbon fiber. Stock: Fierce Tech C3 carbon fiber. Sights: None, drilled and tapped. Weight: 6.4 to 7 lbs. Features: Cerakote finish, Trigger Tech trigger, built-in bipod rail.
Price: .... **$2,295.00-$2,795.00**

FRANCHI MOMENTUM
Calibers: .243 Win., 6.5 Creedmoor, .270 Win., .308 Win., .30-06, .300 Win. Mag. Barrels: 22 or 24 in. Weights: 6.5–7.5 lbs. Stock: Black synthetic with checkered gripping surface, recessed sling swivel studs, TSA recoil pad. Sights: None. Features: Available with Burris Fullfield II 3-9X40mm scope.
Price: Varminter **$609.00**
Price: With Burris 3-9X scope **$729.00**

FRANCHI MOMENTUM ELITE
Calibers: .223 Rem., 6.5 Creedmoor, 6.5 PRC, .308 Win., .300 Win. Mag., .350 Legend. Capacity: 3 or 4-round box magazine. Barrel: 22- or 24-in. free floating, cold hammer forged with threaded muzzle brake. Weight: 7.1–7.5 lbs. Stock: Synthetic in True Timber Strata, Realtree Excape, and now also available with Sitka Optifade Elevation II camouflage. Sights: Picatinny rail. Features: TSA recoil pad absorbs up to 50 percent of felt recoil. Sling attachment points recessed into stock. One-piece spiral fluted bolt with three locking lugs and 60-degree throw. Two-position safety. RELIA trigger adjustable from 2 to 4 pounds. Cobalt Cerakote metalwork on the Sitka camo models.
Price: **$899.00**

FRANCHI MOMENTUM ELITE VARMINT
Calibers: .223 Rem., .22-250 Rem., .224 Valkyrie, 6.5 Creedmoor, .308 Win. Capacity: 3–4-round flush magazines or 7–8-round extended magazines. Barrel: 24-in. free-floating, heavy, spiral-fluted, threaded. Weight: 9.0–9.4 lbs. Length: 46.75 in. Stock: Evolved EGONOM-X synthetic with removeable cheek rest and checkered-polymer grip, finished in Sitka OptiFade Subalpine camo. Sights: One-piece Picatinny rail. Features: Varmint addition to the Momentum Elite family gets caliber additions for 2022. Stock designed specifically for varmint hunting. Midnight Bronze Cerakote metalwork. RELIA-Trigger adjustable from 2–4 pounds. MOA accuracy guarantee. DEPENDA bolt with three locking lugs and 60-degree throw.
Price: **$999.00**

GUNWERKS CLYMR
Calibers: 7 LRM, .22-250, 6mm Creed, 6.5 Creed, 6.5-284 Norma, 6.5 PRC, 28 Nosler, 7mm Rem. Mag., 7 SAUM, .300 Win. Mag., 30 Nosler, 300 PRC. Capacity: 3-round capacity in the internal mag. Option to upgrade to dropbox mags. Barrel: Carbon wrapped, threaded, 20- or 22-in. barrel come standard. Upgrade to 18 in. available. Weight: Varies by options selected. Stock: Carbon fiber in choice of ten paint finishes with negative comb and flat toe line. Sights: No sights. Drilled and tapped. Choice of multiple base, scope ring, and scope options direct from the factory. Features: Lightweight, semi-custom, bolt-action hunting rifle built for mountain hunting and available as a user-built rifle system with multiple options. Choice of standard GLR SS action or Titanium action upgrade. Add $150 for Left-hand action. Eleven metal finish colors available, as well as option of directional muzzle brake or thread cap. LOP of 13.5 in. Prices increase significantly as options are added for custom factory builds.
Price: **$5,245.00**

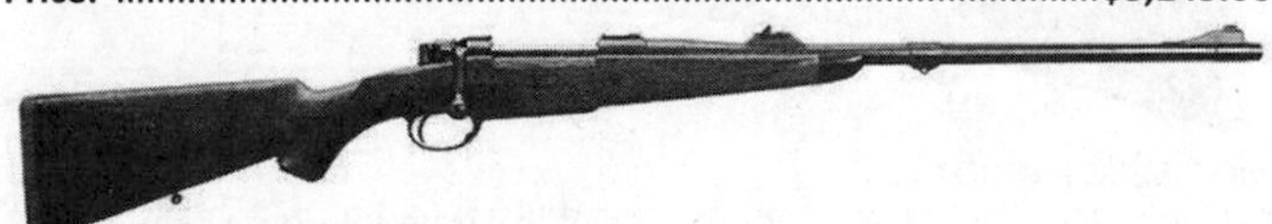

HEYM EXPRESS BOLT-ACTION RIFLE
Calibers: .375 H&H Mag., .416 Rigby, .404 Jeffery, .458 Lott, .450 Rigby. Capacity: 5. Barrel: 24 in., Krupp steel, hammer-forged. Stock: Custom select European walnut. Sights: Iron, barrel-banded front. Weight: 9 to 10.5 lbs. Features: Caliber-specific action and magazine box, classic English sporting rifle, three-position safety.
Price: **$12,000.00**

HOWA MINI ACTION FULL DIP
Calibers: .223 Rem., 6.5 Grendel, 7.62x39. Capacity: 5. Barrel: 20 in., threaded, heavy. Stock: Hogue pillar-bedded. Sights: 3.5-10x44 scope. Weight: 10 lbs. Features: Full-dipped camo, forged, one-piece bolt with locking lugs.
Price: **$769.00**

HOWA HS CARBON FIBER
Caliber: 6.5 Creedmoor. Capacity: 4. Barrel: 24 in., carbon-fiber wrapped. Stock: Synthetic, CNC-machined aluminum bedding block. Sights: None, drilled and tapped. Weight: 7.8 lbs. Features: Lightweight, hand-finished stock, scope optional.
Price: **$1,819.00**

HOWA CARBON ELEVATE
Calibers: .6.5 Grendel, 6.5 Creedmoor, .308 Win., 6.5 PRC. Capacity: Varies by caliber and depending on flush mount or extended magazine. Barrel: 24-in. heavy threaded barrel. Weight: from 4 lbs. 13 oz. Stock: Stocky's Custom carbon-fiber super lightweight design available in natural carbon fiber or Kryptek Altitude. Sights: No sights. Drilled and tapped. Features: Ultra-lightweight bolt-action hunting rifle with AccuBlock lug bed. Three-position safety. Sub-MOA accuracy assurance. HACT two-stage trigger. LimbSaver buttpad. Suppressor-ready. Sub-MOA guarantee. Manufacturer Lifetime Warranty.
Price: **$1,528.00**

J.P. SAUER & SOHN 404 SYNCHRO XTC
Calibers: .243 Win., .270 Win., 6.5 Creedmoor, 6.5x55, .308 Win., .30-06 Spfld., 7x64, 8x57IS, 9.3x62, 7mm Rem. Mag., .300 Win. Mag., .338 Win. Mag., .404 Jeffery, 10.3x60R. Barrel: 22-in. fluted, cold-hammer forged. Sights: Integral scope bases. Length: 42 in. Weight: 6.1 lbs. Stock: Carbon-fiber XTC thumbhole style with Green/Black/Grey carbon-fiber camo and adjustable comb. Features: Fully modular concept rifle. Adjustable trigger blade and trigger pull, from 1.2–2.7 lbs. Manual cocking. Threaded muzzle. MagLock magazine safety. Matte black hard anodized aluminum receiver. Engineered for changing bolt heads and barrels. SUS combination tool integrated into front sling swivel. Miniature universal tool integrated into rear sling swivel.
Price: **$8,199.00**

KENNY JARRETT RIFLES
Calibers: Custom built in virtually any chambering including .223 Rem., .243 Improved, .243 Catbird, 7mm-08 Improved, .280 Remington, .280 Ackley Improved, 7mm Rem. Mag., .284 Jarrett, .30-06 Springfield, .300 Win. Mag., .300 Jarrett, .323 Jarrett, .338 Jarrett, .375 H&H, .416 Rem., .450 Rigby, other modern cartridges. Numerous options regarding barrel type and weight, stock styles and material. Features: Tri-Lock receiver. Talley rings and bases. Accuracy guarantees and custom loaded ammunition. Newest series is the Shikar featuring 28-year aged American Black walnut hand-checkered stock with Jarrett-designed stabilizing aluminum chassis. Accuracy guaranteed to be .5 MOA with standard calibers, .75 MOA with magnums.
Price: Shikar Series **$10,320.00**
Price: Signature Series **$8,320.00**
Price: Long Ranger Series **$8,320.00**
Price: Ridge Walker Series **$8,320.00**
Price: Wind Walker **$8,320.00**
Price: Original Beanfield (customer's receiver) **$6,050.00**
Price: Professional Hunter **$11,070.00**
Price: SA/Custom **$7,000.00**

KIMBER HUNTER PRO
Calibers: 6.5 Creedmoor, .308 Win., .280 Ackley Improved. Capacity:

Prices given are believed to be accurate at time of publication however, many factors affect retail pricing so exact prices are not possible.

3-round box magazine. Barrel: 22 or 24 in. sporter with satin finish and muzzle brake. Weight: 5 lbs. 7oz.–5 lbs. 12 oz. Length: 41.25 in. Stock: Fiber-reinforced polymer in Desolve Blak pattern with pillar bedding. Sights: No iron sights. Drilled and tapped. Features: Full stainless build based on 84M action with Mauser claw extraction. Three-position wing safety. Sling studs. One-inch rubber recoil pad. Match-grade chamber. Factory adjustable trigger set at 3.5–4 lbs. Sub-MOA guarantee.
Price: **$1,006.00**

KIMBER MODEL 8400
Calibers: .25-06 Rem., .270 Win., 7mm, .30-06, .300 Win. Mag., .338 Win. Mag., or .325 WSM. Capacity: 4. Barrel: 24 in. Weights: 6 lbs., 3 oz.–6 lbs., 10 oz. Length: 43.25 in. Stocks: Claro walnut or Kevlar-reinforced fiberglass. Sights: None; drilled and tapped for bases. Features: Mauser claw extractor, two-position wing safety, action bedded on aluminum pillars and fiberglass, free-floated barrel, match-grade adjustable trigger set at 4 lbs., matte or polished blue or matte stainless finish. Introduced 2003. Sonora model (2008) has brown laminated stock, hand-rubbed oil finish, chambered in .25-06 Rem., .30-06, and .300 Win. Mag. Weighs 8.5 lbs., measures 44.50 in. overall length. Front swivel stud only for bipod. Stainless steel bull barrel, 24 in. satin stainless steel finish. Made in USA by Kimber Mfg. Inc.
Price: Classic **$1,223.00**
Price: Classic Select Grade, French walnut stock (2008) **$1,427.00**
Price: SuperAmerica, AAA walnut stock **$2,240.00**
Price: Patrol Tactical **$2,447.00**
Price: Montana **$1,427.00**

KIMBER ADVANCED TACTICAL SOC/SRC II
Calibers: 6.5 Creedmoor, .308 Win. SRC chambered only in .308. Capacity: 5-round magazine. Barrel: 22-in. (SOC) stainless steel, (18 in. (SRC) with threaded muzzle. Stock: Side-folding aluminum with adjustable comb. Features: Stainless steel action, matte black or Flat Dark Earth finish. 3-position Model 70-type safety.
Price: **$2,449.00**

KIMBER OPEN RANGE PRO CARBON
Calibers: 6.5 Creedmoor, .308 Win. Capacity: 4. Barrel: 24 in., carbon-fiber wrapped, Proof Research. Stock: Carbon fiber. Sights: None, drilled and tapped. Weight: 6 lbs. Features: Sub-MOA accuracy, 84M stainless controlled-round-feed action, three-position safety.
Price: **$3,099.00**

MAUSER M-12 PURE
Calibers: .22-250, .243, 6.5x55SE, .270 Win., 7x64mm, 7mm Rem. Mag., .308 Win., .30-06, .300 Win Mag., 8x57mm IS, .338 Win. Mag. 9.3x62mm. Capacity: 5-round magazine. Barrel: 22 in. Sights: Adjustable rear, blade front. Stock: Walnut with ebony fore-end tip.
Price: **$1,971.00**

MAUSER M-18
Calibers: .223 Rem., .243 Win., 6.5x55, 6.5 PRC, 6.5 Creedmoor, .270 Win., .308 Win., .30-06 Spfld., 8x57IS, 9.3x62, 7mm Rem. Mag., .300 Win. Mag. Capacity: 5-round box magazine. Barrel: 21.75 or 24.5 in. Weight: 6.5–6.8 lbs. Length: 41.7–44.0 in. Stock: Polymer with softgrip inlays. Sights: No iron sights. Drilled and tapped. Features: Adjustable trigger. Three-position safety. Removeable recoil pad section with interior buttstock storage. Budget-priced option tagged "The People's Rifle."
Price: **$699.00**

MAUSER M18 SAVANNA
Calibers: .223 Rem., .243 Win., 6.5 PRC, 6.5 Creedmoor, .270 Win., .308 Win., .30-06 Spfld., 7mm Rem. Mag., .300 Win. Mag. Capacity: 5-round magazine standard; 10-rounders available. Barrel: 21.75 or 24.5-in. cold-hammer forged, German-steel, threaded. Weight: 6.5–6.8 lbs. Length: 41.7–44.0 in. Stock: Savanna Tan Polymer with grip inserts. Sights: No iron sights. Drilled and tapped. Features: Adjustable trigger. Sixty-degree oversized bolt. Three-position safety. Removeable recoil pad section with Interior buttstock storage. Sub-MOA guarantee and 10-year warranty.
Price: **$799.00**

MOSSBERG MVP PATROL
.300 AAC Blackout. 16.25-in. barrel. 6.5-lb. weight. 36.5-in. length. 10+1-round capacity
Price: **$638.00**

MOSSBERG MVP SERIES
Caliber: .223/5.56 NATO. Capacity: 10-round AR-style magazines. Barrels: 16.25-in. medium bull, 20-in. fluted sporter. Weight: 6.5–7 lbs. Stock: Classic black textured polymer. Sights: Adjustable folding rear, adjustable blade front. Features: Available with factory mounted 3-9x32 scope, (4-16x50 on Varmint model). FLEX model has 20-in. fluted sporter barrel, FLEX AR-style 6-position adjustable stock. Varmint model has laminated stock, 24-in. barrel. Thunder Ranch model has 18-in. bull barrel, OD Green synthetic stock.
Price: Patrol Model **$732.00**
Price: Patrol Model w/scope **$863.00**
Price: FLEX Model **$764.00**
Price: FLEX Model w/scope **$897.00**
Price: Thunder Ranch Model **$755.00**
Price: Predator Model **$732.00**
Price: Predator Model w/scope **$872.00**
Price: Varmint Model **$753.00**
Price: Varmint Model w/scope **$912.00**
Price: Long Range Rifle (LR) **$974.00**

MOSSBERG PATRIOT
Calibers: .22-250, .243 Win., .25-06, .270 Win., 7mm-08, .7mm Rem., .308 Win., .30-06, .300 Win. Mag., .38 Win. Mag., .375 Ruger, 350 Legend. Capacities: 4- or 5-round magazine. Barrels: 22-in. sporter or fluted. Stock: Walnut, laminate, camo or synthetic black. Weights: 7.5–8 lbs. Finish: Matte blued. Sights: Adjustable or none. Some models available with 3-9x40 scope. Other features include patented Lightning Bolt Action Trigger adjustable from 2 to 7 pounds, spiral-fluted bolt. Not all variants available in all calibers. Introduced in 2015.
Price: Walnut stock **$559.00**
Price: Walnut with premium Vortex Crossfire scope **$649.00**
Price: Synthetic stock **$396.00**
Price: Synthetic stock with standard scope **$436.00**
Price: Laminate stock w/iron sights **$584.00**
Price: Deer THUG w/Mossy Oak Infinity Camo stock **$500.00**
Price: Bantam **$396.00**

NESIKA SPORTER RIFLE

Calibers: .260 Rem., 6.5x284, 7mm-08, .280 Rem., 7mm Rem. Mag., 308 Win., .30-06, .300 Win. Mag. Barrels: 24 or 26 in. Douglas air-gauged stainless. Stock: Composite with aluminum bedding block. Sights: None, Leupold QRW bases. Weight: 8 lbs. Features: Timney trigger set at 3 pounds, receiver made from 15-5 stainless steel, one-piece bolt from 4340 CM steel. Guaranteed accuracy at 100 yards.

Price: **$3,499.00**
Price: Long Range w/heavy bbl., varmint stock **$3,999.00**
Price: Tactical w/28î bbl., muzzle brake, adj. stock **$4,499.00**

NEW ULTRA LIGHT ARMS

Calibers: Custom made in virtually every current chambering. Barrel: Douglas, length to order. Weights: 4.75–7.5 lbs. Length: Varies. Stock: Kevlar graphite composite, variety of finishes. Sights: None furnished; drilled and tapped for scope mounts. Features: Timney trigger, hand-lapped action, button-rifled barrel, hand-bedded action, recoil pad, sling-swivel studs, optional Jewell trigger. Made in USA by New Ultra Light Arms.

Price: Model 20 Ultimate Mountain Rifle **$3,500.00**
Price: Model 20 Ultimate Varmint Rifle **$3,500.00**
Price: Model 24 Ultimate Plains Rifle **$3,600.00**
Price: Model 28 Ultimate Alaskan Rifle **$3,900.00**
Price: Model 40 Ultimate African Rifle **$3,900.00**

NOSLER M48 MOUNTAIN CARBON

Calibers: 6mm Creedmoor, 6.5 Creedmoor, 6.5 PRC, 26 Nosler, 27 Nosler, .280 Ackley Improved, 28 Nosler, .300 Win. Mag., 30 Nosler, 33 Nosler. Capacity: 3 or 4-round hinged aluminum floorplate. Barrel: 24-in. light Sendero contour, carbon-fiber wrapped with cut rifling. Sights: No iron sights; contoured to accept any standard two-piece scope base that would otherwise fit a Remington 700. Weight: 6.0 lbs. Length: 44.4–45 in. Stock: Carbon fiber Mountain Hunter stock in either Granite Green or Shale Gray with textured finish. Features: Built around a Model 48 action. Match-grade, cut-rifled, carbon-wrapped, fully free-floating barrel with guaranteed sub-MOA accuracy. Glass and aluminum pillar bedded into ultra-light Mountain Hunter stock. Steel surfaces coated in Tungsten Grey Cerakote for weather resistance. Timney trigger with two-position safety. Threaded muzzle with knurled thread protector. *Note, Nosler has discontinued all rifles except the Mountain Carbon and Long Range Carbon. Liberty and Heritage are no longer in current production.*

Price: **$3,140.00**

NOSLER LONG RANGE CARBON

Calibers: 6.5 Creedmoor, 6.5 PRC, 26 Nosler, 27 Nosler, 28 Nosler, .300 Win. Mag., 30 Nosler, 33 Nosler. Capacity: 3 or 4 rounds with hinged floorplate. Barrel: 26-in. PROOF, light Sendero contour, carbon-fiber wrapped, fully free-floating. Weight: 7.0 lbs. Length: 48 in. Stock: Manners MCS-T Elite Tac 100 percent carbon-fiber stock in Elite Midnight Camo with textured finish. Sights: No iron sights; contoured to accept any standard two-piece scope base that would otherwise fit a Remington 700. Features: Custom Nosler Model 48 action. Timney trigger with two-position safety. Threaded muzzle with knurled thread protector. Glass and aluminum pillar bedding. Action and bottom metal Cerakoted in Sniper Grey. Dual fore-end sling swivels. Guaranteed MOA accuracy. *Note, Nosler has discontinued all rifles except the Mountain Carbon and Long Range Carbon. Liberty and Heritage are no longer in current production.*

Price: **$3,190.00**

NOSLER MODEL 21

Calibers: 22 Nosler, 6.5 Creedmoor, 6.5 PRC, 26 Nosler, 27 Nosler, .280 Ackley Improved, 28 Nosler, .308 Win., .300 Win. Mag., 30 Nosler, 33 Nosler, .375 H&H Magnum. Capacity: 3 or 4 rounds depending on caliber. Barrel: 22- or 24-in. Shilen match-grade stainless Weight: 6.8–7.1 lbs. Length: 41.625–44.5 in. Stock: McMillian Hunters Edge Sporter 100% carbon fiber painted in all-weather epoxy-style finish. Sights: No iron sights; contoured to accept any standard two-piece scope base that would otherwise fit a Remington 700. Features: Nosler's new rifle design for 2022 with a blueprinted action, wire EDM machined receiver, spriral-fluted, one-piece, nitride coated bolt. TriggerTech Frictionless Release trigger. M16-style extractor and fire control group feature tool-less takedown. LOP of 13.5-in. with one-inch recoil pad. Threaded barrel with knurled cover.

Price: **$2,795.00**

RUGER GUIDE GUN

Calibers: .30-06, .300 Win. Mag., .338 Win. Mag., .375 Ruger, .416 Ruger. Capacities: 3 or 4 rounds. Barrel: 20 in. with barrel band sling swivel and removable muzzle brake. Weights: 8–8.12 pounds. Stock: Green Mountain laminate. Finish: Hawkeye matte stainless. Sights: Adjustable rear, bead front. Introduced 2013.

Price: **$1,269.00**

RUGER HAWKEYE

Calibers: .204 Ruger, .223 Rem., .243 Win., .270 Win., 6.5 PRC, 6.5 Creedmoor, 7mm/08, 7mm Rem. Mag., .308 Win., .30-06, .300 Win. Mag., .338 Win. Mag., .375 Ruger, .416 Ruger. Capacities: 4-round magazine, except 3-round magazine for magnums; 5-round magazine for .204 Ruger and .223 Rem. Barrels: 22 in., 24 in. Weight: 6.75–8.25 lbs. Length: 42–44.4 in. overall. Stock: American walnut, laminate or synthetic. FTW has camo stock, muzzle brake. Long Range Target has adjustable target stock, heavy barrel. Sights: None furnished. Receiver has Ruger integral scope mount base, Ruger 1 in. rings. Features: Includes Ruger LC6 trigger, new red rubber recoil pad, Mauser-type controlled feeding, claw extractor, 3-position safety, hammer-forged steel barrels, Ruger scope rings. Walnut stocks have wrap-around cut checkering on the forearm, and more rounded contours on stock and top of pistol grips. Matte stainless all-weather version features synthetic stock. Hawkeye African chambered in .375 Ruger, .416 Ruger and has 23-in. blued barrel, checkered walnut stock, windage-adjustable shallow V-notch rear sight, white bead front sight. Introduced 2007. *(Note: VT Varmint Target and Compact Magnum are no longer currently produced)*

Price: Standard, right- and left-hand **$939.00**
Price: Compact **$939.00**
Price: Laminate Compact **$999.00**
Price: Compact Magnum **$969.00**
Price: Hawkeye Hunter **$1,099.00**
Price: VT Varmint Target **$1,139.00**
Price: Predator **$1,139.00**
Price: Alaskan **$1,279.00**
Price: Long Range Hunter **$1,279.00**
Price: African with muzzle brake **$1,279.00**
Price: FTW Hunter **$1,279.00**
Price: Long Range Target **$1,279.00**

SAKO TRG-22 TACTICAL RIFLE

Calibers: 6.5 Creedmoor, .308 Winchester (TRG-22). For TRG-22A1 add .260 Rem. TRG-42 only available in .300 Win. Mag., or .338 Lapua. Features: Target-grade Cr-Mo or stainless barrels with muzzle brake; three locking lugs; 60-degree bolt throw; adjustable two-stage target trigger; adjustable or folding synthetic stock; receiver-mounted integral 17mm axial optics rails with recoil stop-slots; tactical scope mount for modern three-turret tactical scopes (30 and 34 mm tube diameter); optional bipod. 22A1 has folding stock with two-hinge design, M-LOK fore-end, full aluminum middle chassis.

Price: TRG-22 .... **$3,495.00**
Price: TRG-22A1 .... **$6,725.00**
Price: TRG-42 .... **$4,550.00**

SAKO MODEL 85

Calibers: .22-250 Rem., .243 Win., .25-06 Rem., .260 Rem., 6.5x55mm, .270 Win., .270 WSM, 7mm-08 Rem., 7x64, .308 Win., .30-06; 7mm WSM, .300 WSM, .338 Federal, 8x57IS, 9.3x62. Barrels: 22.4 in., 22.9 in., 24.4 in. Weight: 7.75 lbs. Length: NA. Stock: Polymer, laminated or high-grade walnut, straight comb, shadow-line cheekpiece. Sights: None furnished. Features: Controlled-round feeding, adjustable trigger, matte stainless or nonreflective satin blue. Offered in a wide range of variations and models. Introduced 2006. Imported from Finland by Beretta USA.

Price: Grey Wolf **$1,725.00**
Price: Black Bear **$1,850.00**
Price: Kodiak **$1,950.00**
Price: Varmint Laminated **$2,025.00**
Price: Classic **$2,275.00**
Price: Bavarian .... **$2,200.00–$2,300.00**
Price: Bavarian carbine, Full-length stock **$2,400.00**
Price: Brown Bear **$2,175.00**

SAKO S20

Calibers: .243 Win., 6.5 Creedmoor, 6.5 PRC, .270 Win., .308 Win., .30-06 Spfld., 7mm Rem. Mag., .300 Win. Mag. Capacity: 5 (3 Magnum), and 10 (7 magnum) double-stacked magazines, glass-reinforced composite. Barrel: 20- to 24-in. cold-hammer forged, fluted, threaded. Weight: 7.3–8.8 lbs. Length: 42.9–46.9 in. Stock: Choice of two interchangeable injection-molded synthetic stock types — tactical precision or ergonomic hunting thumbhole. Sights: Picatinny rail integral to receiver. Features: Designed as a hybrid rifle for both hunters and precision shooters. Full aluminum rifle chassis. Takedown-style stock design allows user configuration. Adjustable recoil pad for LOP and adjustable cheek piece. QD sling attachments. Two-stage multi-adjustable trigger. Five-shot sub MOA guarantee.

Price: **$1,598.00**

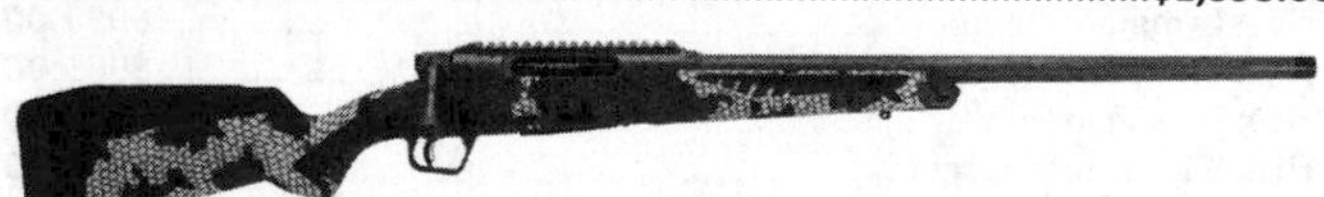

SAVAGE IMPULSE BIG GAME

Calibers: .243 Win., .308 Win., 6.5 Creedmoor, .308 Win., .300 Win. Mag., .300 WSM. Capacity: 2, 3, or 4-round flush-fit detachable box magazine. Barrel: 22- or 24-in. medium contour, carbon steel, fluted, and threaded. Sights: Single piece 20 MOA rail machined into receiver. Length: 43.5–45.5 in. Weight: 8.8–8.9 lbs. Stock: Sporter-style AccuStock with AccuFit user-adjustable system and Kuiu Verde 2.0 camouflage finish. Features: New straight-pull bolt action uses HexLock bolt system. Ambidextrous rotary bolt handle. Tang safety. Free-floating, tool-free, interchangeable bolt head. Four-bolt barrel clamp system. Adjustable AccuTrigger. Hazel Green Cerakote aluminum receiver. Removeable and user-adjustable round bolt knob handle.

Price: **$1,449.00**

SAVAGE IMPULSE HOG HUNTER

Calibers: 6.5 Creedmoor, .308 Win., .30-06 Spfld., .300 Win. Mag. Capacity: 3- or 4-round flush-fit detachable box magazine. Barrel: 18-, 20-, or 24-in. medium contour, carbon steel, threaded. Sights: Single piece 20 MOA rail machined into receiver. Length: 39.25–44.25 in. Weight: 8.41–9.1 lbs. Stock: OD Green Sporter-style AccuStock with AccuFit user-adjustable system. Features: New straight pull bolt action uses HexLock bolt system. Ambidextrous rotary bolt handle. Tang safety. Free-floating, tool-free, interchangeable bolt head. Four-bolt barrel clamp system. Adjustable AccuTrigger. Matte black aluminum receiver. Removeable and user adjustable round bolt knob handle.

Price: **$1,379.00**

SAVAGE IMPULSE PREDATOR

Calibers: .22-250 Rem., .243 Win., 6.5 Creedmoor, .308 Win. Capacity: 10-round AICS-style magazine with ambidextrous release. Barrel: 20-in. medium contour, threaded. Sights: Single piece 20 MOA rail machined into receiver. Length: 41.25 in. Weight: 8.75 lbs. Stock: Mossy Oak Terra Gila camouflage AccuStock with AccuFit user-adjustable system. Features: New straight-pull bolt action uses HexLock bolt system. Ambidextrous rotary bolt handle. Tang safety. Free-floating, tool-free, interchangeable bolt head. Four-bolt barrel clamp system. Adjustable AccuTrigger. Matte black aluminum receiver. Removeable and user adjustable round bolt knob handle.

Price: **$1,379.00**

SAVAGE 110 CARBON TACTICAL

Calibers: 6.5 Creedmoor, .308 Win., 6.5 PRC. Capacity: 10-round AICS magazine. Barrel: 22-in. Proof Research stainless steel, carbon-fiber wrapped, threaded. Length: 42 in. Weight: 7.65 lbs. Stock: Synthetic AccuFit with included interchangeable LOP spacers and comb risers. Features: Factory blueprinted Model 110 bolt action. User-adjustable AccuTrigger. Tactical knurled bolt handle. One-piece 20MOA rail. Beavertail forend with three sling studs.

Price: **$1,789.00**

SAVAGE MODEL 110 PRECISION

Calibers: .308 Win., .300 Win. Mag, .338 Lapua, 6.5 Creedmoor. Capacity: 5, 8/10. Barrel: 20 to 24 in., carbon steel, heavy, threaded. Stock: Aluminum chassis. Sights: Picatinny rail. Weight: 8.9 lbs. Features: BA muzzle brake, skeletonized stock with adjustable comb height and LOP.

Price: **$1,499.00**

SAVAGE AXIS II PRECISION

Calibers: .243 Win., .223 Rem, .270 Win., .30-06, .308 Win., 6.5 Creedmoor. Capacity: 5 to 10. Barrel: 22 in., carbon steel, button-rifled heavy, threaded

Prices given are believed to be accurate at time of publication however, many factors affect retail pricing so exact prices are not possible.

w/cap. Stock: Aluminum MDT chassis. Sights: Picatinny rail. Weight: 9.9 lbs. Features: AccuTrigger, adjustable comb height and LOP spacers, AICS magazine.
Price: $949.00

SAVAGE CLASSIC SERIES MODEL 14/114
Calibers: .243 Win., 7mm-08 Rem., .308 Win., .270 Win., 7mm Rem. Mag., .30-06, .300 Win. Mag. Capacities: 3- or 4-round magazine. Barrels: 22 in. or 24 in. Weight: 7–7.5 lbs. Length: 41.75–43.75 in. overall (Model 14 short action); 43.25–45.25 in. overall (Model 114 long action). Stock: Satin lacquer American walnut with ebony fore-end, wraparound checkering, Monte Carlo comb and cheekpiece. Sights: None furnished. Receiver drilled and tapped for scope mounting. Features: AccuTrigger, matte blued barrel and action, hinged floorplate.
Price: $979.00

SAVAGE MODEL 12 VARMINT/TARGET SERIES
Calibers: .204 Ruger, .223 Rem., .22-250 Rem. Capacity: 4-shot magazine. Barrel: 26 in. stainless barreled action, heavy fluted, free-floating and button-rifled barrel. Weight: 10 lbs. Length: 46.25 in. overall. Stock: Dual pillar bedded, low profile, black synthetic or laminated stock with extra-wide beavertail fore-end. Sights: None furnished; drilled and tapped for scope mounting. Features: Recessed target-style muzzle. AccuTrigger, oversized bolt handle, detachable box magazine, swivel studs. Model 112BVSS has heavy target-style prone laminated stock with high comb, Wundhammer palm swell, internal box magazine. Model 12VLP DBM has black synthetic stock, detachable magazine, and additional chamberings in .243, .308 Win., .300 Win. Mag. Model 12FV has blued receiver. Model 12BTCSS has brown laminate vented thumbhole stock. Made in USA by Savage Arms, Inc.
Price: 12 FCV $780.00
Price: 12 BVSS $1,146.00
Price: 12 Varminter Low Profile (VLP) $1,181.00
Price: 12 Long Range Precision $1,288.00
Price: 12 BTCSS Thumbhole stock $1,293.00
Price: 12 Long Range Precision Varminter $1,554.00
Price: 12 F Class $1,648.00
Price: 12 Palma $2,147.00

SAVAGE MODEL 110 PREDATOR
Calibers: .204 Ruger. .223, .22-250, .243, .260 Rem., 6.5 Creedmoor. Capacity: 4-round magazine. Barrels: 22 or 24 in. threaded heavy contour. Weight: 8.5 lbs. Stock: AccuStock with Mossy Oak Max-1 camo finish, soft grip surfaces, adjustable length of pull.
Price: $899.00

SAVAGE MODEL 110 TACTICAL
Caliber: .308 Win. Capacity: 10-round magazine. Barrels: 20 or 24 in. threaded and fluted heavy contour. Weight: 8.65 lbs. Stock: AccuStock with soft-grip surfaces, AccuFit system. Features: Top Picatinny rail, right- or left-hand operation.
Price: $784.00
Price: Tactical Desert (6mm, 6.5 Creedmoor, FDE finish $769.00

SAVAGE MODEL 12 PRECISION TARGET SERIES BENCHREST
Calibers: .308 Win., 6.5x284 Norma, 6mm Norma BR. Barrel: 29-in. ultra-heavy. Weight: 12.75 lbs. Length: 50 in. overall. Stock: Gray laminate. Features: New Left-Load, Right-Eject target action, Target AccuTrigger adjustable from approx. 6 oz. to 2.5 lbs. oversized bolt handle, stainless extra-heavy free-floating and button-rifled barrel.
Price: $1,629.00

SAVAGE MODEL 12 PRECISION TARGET PALMA
Similar to Model 12 Benchrest but in .308 Win. only, 30-in. barrel, multi-adjustable stock, weighs 13.3 lbs.
Price: $2,147.00

SAVAGE MODEL 12 F/TR TARGET RIFLE
Similar to Model 12 Benchrest but in .308 Win. only, 30-in. barrel, weighs 12.65 lbs.
Price: $1,538.00

SAVAGE MODEL 112 MAGNUM TARGET
Caliber: .338 Lapua Magnum. Single shot. Barrel: 26-in. heavy with muzzle brake. Stock: Wood laminate. Features: AccuTrigger, matte black finish, oversized bolt handle, pillar bedding.
Price: $1,177.00

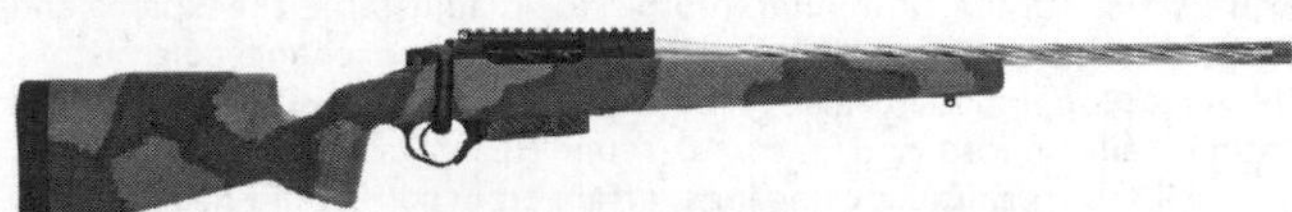

SEEKINS PRECISION HAVAK ELEMENT
Calibers: 28 Nosler, 6mm Creedmoor, 6.5 Creedmoor, .308 Win., 6.5 PRC, .300 Win. Mag., .300 PRC. Capacity: 3 or 5-round detachable Magpul PMAG or carbon-fiber magazine, depending on caliber. Barrel: 21- or 22-in. Mountain Hunter spiral fluted, built of 5R 416 stainless steel. Sights: 20 MOA rail. Weight: 5.5 lbs. short actions; long actions at 6.0 lbs. Stock: Element camouflage Carbon Composition stock. Features: Drawing on years of precision AR-rifle experience comes the bolt action, hybrid, ultra-lightweight Havak Element. Aerospace-grade 7075 aluminum encases stainless steel on a Mountain Hunter barrel. Four locking lugs on 90-degree bolt with removable head. ATC muzzle brake on long actions. M-16-style extractor. Muzzle threaded at 5/8x24. Integrated recoil lug, and bubble level.
Price: $2,795.00

SEEKINS PRECISION HAVAK PRO HUNTER PH2
Calibers: 6mm Creedmoor, 6.5 Creedmoor, 6.5 PRC, .308 Win., 28 Nosler, 7mm Rem. Mag., .300 Win. Mag., 300 PRC, .338 Win. Mag. Capacity: 5, short action; 3, long action detachable magazine. Barrel: 24 in. short action; 26 in. long action built of 5R 416 stainless steel. Weight: 6.9–7.2 lbs. Stock: Seekins carbon composite in Charcoal Gray. Sights: 20 MOA Picatinny rail with 8-32 screws. Features: Timney Elite Hunter trigger set at 2.5 lbs. Bead-blasted barreled action. Threaded muzzle. Integrated recoil lug and M16-style extractor. Bolt with four locking lugs and 90-degree throw. Removeable bolt head. Extended cartridge overall length with Seekins carbon-fiber magazines.
Price: $1,895.00

SPRINGFIELD ARMORY 2020 WAYPOINT
Calibers: 6mm Creedmoor, 6.5 Creedmoor, .308 Win., 6.5 PRC. Capacity: 3 or 5-round AICS-pattern magazine. Barrel: 20, 22, or 24 in. Option of steel or carbon fiber. Weight: 6 lbs. 10 oz.–7 lbs. 6 oz. Length: 41.5–45.5 in. Stock: Choice of two stock configurations, premium AG Composites carbon fiber with custom camo in Evergreen or Ridgeline. Features: Stainless steel receiver. Dual locking lugs on a fluted bolt. Picatinny rail. 90-degree bolt handle with removeable knob. Enlarged ejection port and sliding extractor. Hybrid dual-plane feed ramp. Adjustable Trigger Tech trigger. Five QD stock mounts. SA Radial muzzle brake. Cerakote metalwork in Desert Verde or Mil-Spec Green. Pachmayr Decelerator recoil pad. Available in two stock configurations, one with three-axis adjustable cheek comb and two barrel choices. Accuracy guarantee of .75 MOA.
Price: Steel barrel, standard stock $1,699.00
Price: Steel barrel, adjustable stock $1,825.00
Price: Carbon-fiber barrel, standard stock $2,275.00
Price: Carbon-fiber barrel, adjustable stock $2,399.00

Prices given are believed to be accurate at time of publication however, many factors affect retail pricing so exact prices are not possible.

STEYR PRO HUNTER II

Calibers: .223 Rem., 7mm-08 Rem., 6.5 Creedmoor, .308 Win. Capacity: 4 to 5. Barrel: 20 in., hammer-forged stainless steel. Stock: Wood laminate, Boyds. Sights: None, drilled and tapped. Weight: 7 lbs. Features: Three-position safety, crisp 3-lb. trigger.

Price: **$1,199.00**

STEYR SSG08

Calibers: .243 Win., 7.62x51 NATO (.308Win), 7.62x63B (.300 Win Mag)., .338 Lapua Mag. Capacity: 10-round magazine. Barrels: 20, 23.6 or 25.6 in. Stock: Dural aluminum folding stock black with .280 mm long UIT-rail and various Picatinny rails. Sights: Front post sight and rear adjustable. Features: High-grade aluminum folding stock, adjustable cheekpiece and buttplate with height marking, and an ergonomical exchangeable pistol grip. Versa-Pod, muzzle brake, Picatinny rail, UIT rail on stock and various Picatinny rails on fore-end, and a 10-round HC-magazine. SBS rotary bolt action with four frontal locking lugs, arranged in pairs. Cold-hammer-forged barrels are available in standard or compact lengths.

Price: **$5,899.00**

STEYR SM 12

Calibers: .243, 6.5x55SE, .270 Win., 7mm-08 Rem., .308 Win., .30-06, .300 Win. Mag, .300 WSM, 9.3x62mm. Barrels: 20-in. blue or 25-in. stainless. Stock: Walnut with checkered grip and fore-end. Available in half or full-length configurations. Sights: Adjustable rear, ramp front with bead. Stainless barrel has no sights. Features: Sling swivels, Bavarian cheekpiece, hand-cocking system operated by thumb manually cocks firing mechanism.

Price: Standard-length stock.. **$2,545.00**
Price: Full length (Mannlicher) **$2,750.00**

STRASSER RS 14 EVOLUTION STANDARD

Calibers: .222 Rem., .223 Rem., .300 AAC Blackout, .22-250 Rem., .243 Win., 6 XC, 6.5 Creedmoor, .284 Norma, 6.5x55SE, 6.5x65RWS, .270 Win., 7x64, 7mm-08 Rem, .308 Win., .30-06, 8x57 IS, 8.5x63, 9.3x62, 9.3x57, 7mm Rem. Mag., .300 Win. Mag., .375 Ruger, .338 Win. Mag., .458 Win. Mag., 10.3x68. Capacity: 3 to 7. Barrel: 22 to 24 in., blued. Stock: Grade-1 wood, grade-2 wood, standard or thumbhole. Sights: Integrated Picatinny rail. Weight: 6.75 to 7.725 lbs. Features: Barrel-exchange system, adjustable trigger with trigger set, plasma-hardened bolt.

Price: .... **$3,452.00-$4,033.00**

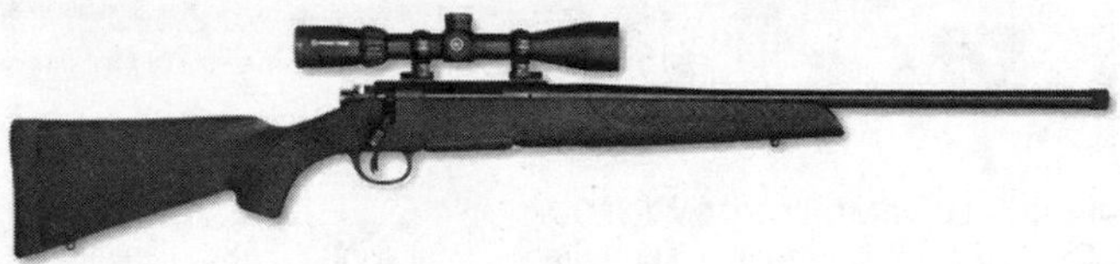

THOMPSON/CENTER COMPASS II

Calibers: .223 Rem., 5.56 NATO, .243 Win., .270 Win., .300 Win. Mag., .308 Win., .30-06, 6.5 Creedmoor, 7mm Rem. Mag. Capacity: 5 to 6. Barrel: 21.625 to 24 in., blued. Stock: Composite. Sights: Weaver bases or Crimson Trace scope combo. Weight: 8 lbs. Features: Threaded muzzle, three-lug bolt design, three-position safety.

Price: .... **$405.00 to $575.00**

THOMSON/CENTER COMPASS II COMPACT

Calibers: .223 Rem., 5.56 NATO, .243 Win., .308 Win., 6.5 Creedmoor. Capacity: 6. Barrel: 16.5 in., blued. Stock: Composite. Sights: Weaver bases or Crimson Trace scope combo. Weight: 6.5 lbs. Features: 5R rifling, compact size, Generation II trigger.

Price: .... **$405.00 to $575.00**

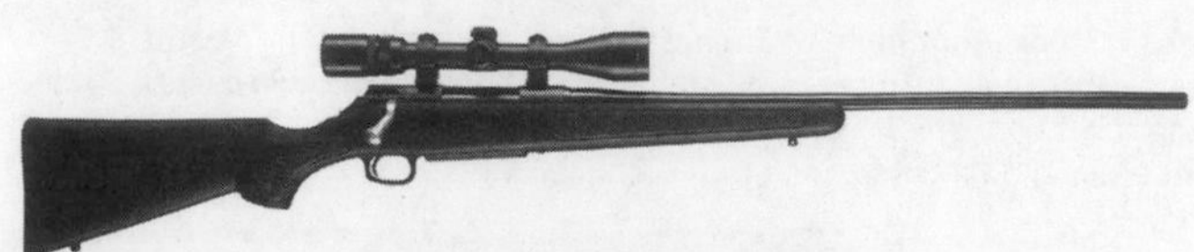

THOMPSON/CENTER VENTURE MEDIUM ACTION

Calibers: .204, .22-250, .223, .243, 7mm-08, .308 and 30TC. Capacity: 3+1 detachable nylon box magazine. Features: Bolt-action rifle with a 24-in. crowned medium weight barrel, classic-styled composite stock with inlaid traction grip panels, adjustable 3.5- to 5-pound trigger along with a drilled and tapped receiver (bases included). Weight: 7 lbs. Length: 43.5 in.

Price: **$537.00**

THOMPSON/CENTER VENTURE PREDATOR PDX

Calibers: .204, .22-250, .223, .243, .308. Weight: 8 lbs. Length: 41.5 in. Features: Bolt-action rifle similar to Venture medium action but with heavy, deep-fluted 22-in. barrel and Max-1 camo finish overall.

Price: **$638.00**

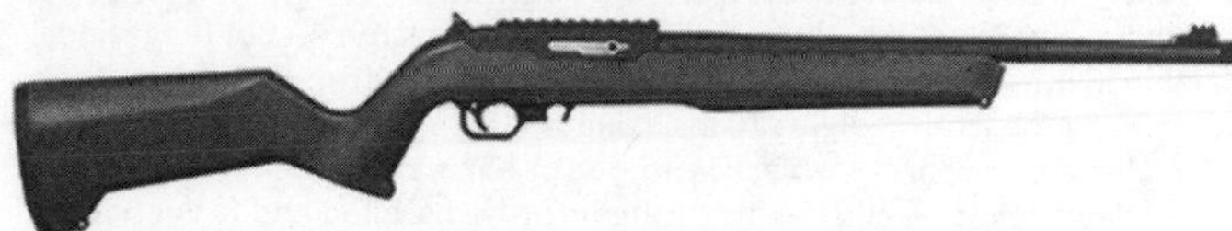

THOMPSON/CENTER LONG RANGE RIFLE

Calibers: .243 Win., 6.5 Creedmoor, .308 Win. Capacity: 10-round magazine. Barrel: 20 in. (.308), 22 in. (6.5), 24 in. (.243). Fluted and threaded with muzzle brake. Weight: 11-12 lbs. Stock: Composite black with adjustable cheek piece and buttplate, built-in Magpul M-LOK accessory slots. Finish: Black or Flat Dark Earth. Features: Picatinny-style rail, adjustable trigger, Caldwell Pic Rail XLA bipod. From the T/C Performance Center.

Price: **$1,211.00**

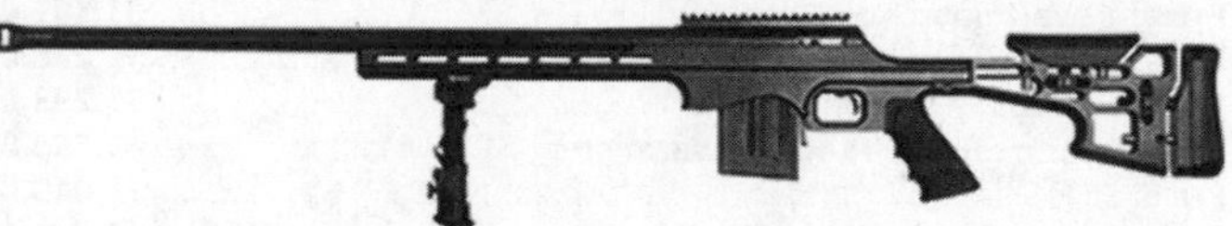

THOMPSON/CENTER COMPASS

Calibers: .204 Ruger, .223 Rem, .22-250 Rem., .243 Win., 6.5 Creedmoor, .270 Win., 7mm-08 Rem., 7mm Rem. Mag., .308 Win., .30-06, .300 Win. Mag. Capacity: 4-5-round detachable magazine. Barrel: Match-grade 22 in., (24 in. magnums.) with threaded muzzle. Weight: 7 ¼-7 1/2 lbs. Stock: Composite black with textured grip panels.

Price: **$399.00**

TIKKA T3X SERIES

Calibers: Virtually any popular chambering including .204 Ruger .222 Rem., .223 Rem., .243 Win., .25-06, 6.5x55 SE, .260 Rem, .270 Win., .260 WSM, 7mm-08, 7mm Rem. Mag., .308 Win., .30-06, .300 Win. Mag., .300 WSM. Barrels: 20, 22.4, 24.3 in. Stock: Checkered walnut, laminate or modular synthetic with interchangeable pistol grips. Newly designed recoil pad. Features: Offered in a variety of different models with many options. Left-hand models available. One minute-of-angle accuracy guaranteed. Introduced in 2016. Made in Finland by Sako. Imported by Beretta USA.

Price: Hunter **$875.00**
Price: Lite (shown) **$725.00**
Price: Varmint **$950.00**
Price: Laminate stainless.. **$1,050.00**
Price: Forest.. **$1,000.00**
Price: Tac A1 (shown).. **$1,899.00**
Price: Compact Tactical Rifle **$1,150.00**

WEATHERBY BACKCOUNTRY 2.0

Replaces the original Backcountry family. Upgraded with carbon-fiber Peak44 Blacktooth stock that weights under 20 oz. Other improvements include: second generation 3DHEX recoil pad, the first printed pad made. Deeper spiral fluting on the bolt and threaded bolt handle. Fit with Accubrake ST. Patriot Brown Cerakote finish. Weight from only 5.2 lbs. Carbon models include a carbon-fiber barrel. Ti models are built on a titanium action.

Price: Mark V Backcountry 2.0 .... **$2,699.00–$2,799.00**
Price: Mark V Backcountry 2.0 Carbon .... **$3,299.00–$3,399.00**
Price: Mark V Backcountry 2.0 Ti .... **$3,449.00–$3,599.00**
Price: Mark V Backcountry Ti Carbon $.......... **3,849.00–$3,949.00**

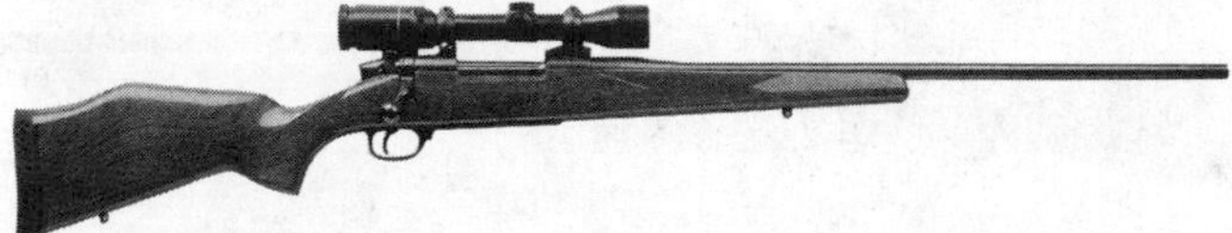

WEATHERBY MARK V

This classic action goes back more than 60 years to the late '50s. Several significant changes were made to the original design in 2016. Stocks have a slimmer fore-end and smaller grip, which has an added palm swell. The new LXX trigger is adjustable down to 2.5 lbs. and has precision ground and polished surfaces and a wider trigger face. All new Mark V rifles come with sub-MOA guarantee. Range Certified (RC) models are range tested and come with a certified ballistic data sheet and RC engraved floorplate. Calibers: Varies depending on model. Barrels: 22 in., 24 in., 26 in., 28 in. Weight: 5 3/4 to 10 lbs. Stock: Varies depending on model. Sights: None furnished. Features: Deluxe version comes in all Weatherby calibers plus .243 Win., .270 Win., 7mm-08 Rem., .30-06, .308 Win. Lazermark same as Mark V Deluxe except stock has extensive oak leaf pattern laser carving on pistol grip and fore-end; chambered in Wby. Magnums .257, .270 Win., 7mm., .300, .340, with 26 in. barrel. Sporter is same as the Mark V Deluxe without the embellishments. Metal has low-luster blue, stock is Claro walnut with matte finish, Monte Carlo comb, recoil pad. Chambered for these Wby. Mags: .257, .270 Win., 7mm, .300, .340. Other chamberings: 7mm Rem. Mag., .300 Win. Introduced 1993. Six Mark V models come with synthetic stocks. Ultra Lightweight rifles weigh 5.75 to 6.75 lbs.; 24 in., 26 in. fluted stainless barrels with recessed target crown; Bell & Carlson stock with CNC-machined aluminum bedding plate and tan "spider web" finish, skeletonized handle and sleeve. Available in .243 Win., .25-06 Rem., .270 Win., 7mm-08 Rem., 7mm Rem. Mag., .280 Rem, .308 Win., .30-06, .300 Win. Mag. Wby. Mag chamberings: .240, .257, .270 Win., 7mm, .300. Accumark uses Mark V action with heavy-contour 26 in. and 28 in. stainless barrels with black oxidized flutes, muzzle diameter of .705 in. No sights, drilled and tapped for scope mounting. Stock is composite with matte gel-coat finish, full-length aluminum bedding block. Weighs 8.5 lbs. Chambered for these Wby. Mags: .240, .257, .270, 7mm, .300, .340, .338-378, .30-378. Other chamberings: 6.5 Creedmoor, .270 Win., .308 Win., 7mm Rem. Mag., .300 Win. Mag. Altitude has 22-, 24-, 26-, 28-in. fluted stainless steel barrel, Monte Carlo carbon fiber composite stock with raised comb, Kryptek Altitude camo. Tacmark has 28-in. free floated fluted barrel with Accubrake, fully adjustable stock, black finish. Safari Grade has fancy grade checkered French walnut stock with ebony fore-end and grip cap, adjustable express rear and hooded front sights, from the Weatherby Custom Shop. Camilla series is lightweight model designed to fit a woman's anatomy. Offered in several variations chambered for .240 Wby. Mag., 6.5 Creedmoor, .270 Win., .308 Win., .30-06. Arroyo is available in Weatherby Magnums from .240 to .338-378, plus 6.5 Creedmoor, .300 Win. Mag., and .338 Lapua Mag. Finish is two-tone Cerakote with Brown Sand and FDE added flutes. Carbonmark has 26in. Proof Research carbon fiber threaded barrel and is chambered for .257 and .300 Wby. Mags. Outfitter is chambered for .240-.300 Wby. Magnums plus most popular calibers. Stock has Spiderweb accents. KCR model comes with Krieger Custom Match-grade barrel in .257, 6.5-300, .300 and .30-378 Wby. Magnums. Altitude is lightweight model (5 ¾-6 ¾ lbs.) and comes in Wby. Magnums from .240 to.300, plus 6.5 Creedmoor, .270 Win., .308, .30-06. Dangerous Game Rifle is offered in all Wby. Magnums from .300 to .450, plus .375 H&H. Hand laminated Monte Carlo composite stock. *Note: Most Mark V rifles are available in 6.5 Wby. RPM and 6.5-300 Wby. Mag. chamberings.* All Weatherby Mark V rifles are made in Sheridan, Wyoming.

Price: Mark V Backcountry **$2,499.00**
Price: Mark V Backcountry Ti .... **$3,349.00–$3,449.00**
Price: Mark V Deluxe **$2,700.00**
Price: Mark V Hunter **$1,499.00**
Price: Mark V Lazermark.......... **$2,800.00**
Price: Mark V Sporter **$1,800.00**
Price: Mark V Ultra Lightweight **$2,300.00**
Price: Mark V Accumark .... **$2,300.00–$2,700.00**
Price: Mark V Altitude .... **$3,000.00–$3,700.00**
Price: Mark V Safari Grade Custom.......... **$6,900.00–$7,600.00**
Price: Mark V Tacmark.......... **$4,100.00**
Price: Mark V Camilla Series.......... **$2,300.00–$2,700.00**
Price: Mark V Arroyo **$2,800.00**
Price: Mark V Carbonmark **$4,100.00**
Price: Mark V Outfitter .... **$2,600-$2,800.00***
Price: Mark V Krieger Custom Rifle (KCR).......... **$3,600-$4,100.00***
Price: Mark V Altitude **$2,700.00***
Price: Mark V Dangerous Game Rifle **$3,600.00**
Price: Mark V Weathermark.......... **$1,549.00–$1,749.00**
Price: Mark V Weathermark Bronze .... **$1,549.00–$1,749.00**
Price: Mark V Carbonmark Pro .... **$2,999.00–$3,099.00**
Price: Mark V Carbonmark Elite .... **$3,299.00–$3,399.00**
*Add ....$500 for optional Range Certified (RC) model with guaranteed sub-MOA accuracy certificate and target.

WEATHERBY VANGUARD II SERIES

Calibers: Varies depending on model. Most Weatherby Magnums and many standard calibers. Barrels: 20, 24, or 26 in. Weights: 7.5–8.75 lbs. Lengths: 44–46.75 in. overall. Stock: Raised comb, Monte Carlo, injection-molded composite stock. Sights: None furnished. Features: One-piece forged, fluted bolt body with three gas ports, forged and machined receiver, adjustable trigger, factory accuracy guarantee. Vanguard Stainless has 410-Series stainless steel barrel and action, bead blasted matte metal finish. Vanguard Deluxe has raised comb, semi-fancy-grade Monte Carlo walnut stock with maplewood spacers, rosewood fore-end and grip cap, polished action with high-gloss blued metalwork. Sporter has Monte Carlo walnut stock with satin urethane finish, fineline diamond point checkering, contrasting rosewood fore-end tip, matte-blued metalwork. Sporter SS metalwork is 410 Series bead-blasted stainless steel. Vanguard Youth/Compact has 20 in. No. 1 contour barrel, short action, scaled-down nonreflective matte black hardwood stock with 12.5-in. length of pull, and full-size, injection-molded composite stock. Chambered for .223 Rem., .22-250 Rem., .243 Win., 7mm-08 Rem., .308 Win. Weighs 6.75 lbs.; OAL 38.9 in. Sub-MOA Matte and Sub-MOA Stainless models have pillar-bedded Fiberguard composite stock (Aramid, graphite unidirectional fibers and fiberglass) with 24-in. barreled action; matte black metalwork, Pachmayr Decelerator recoil pad. Sub-MOA Stainless metalwork is 410 Series bead-blasted stainless steel. Sub-MOA Varmint guaranteed to shoot 3-shot group of .00 in. or less when used with specified Weatherby factory or premium (non-Weatherby calibers) ammunition. Hand-laminated, tan Monte Carlo composite stock with black spiderwebbing; CNC-machined aluminum bedding block, 22 in. No. 3 contour barrel, recessed target crown. Varmint Special has tan injection-molded Monte Carlo composite stock, pebble grain finish, black spiderwebbing. 22 in. No. 3 contour barrel (.740-in. muzzle dia.), bead blasted matte black finish, recessed target crown. Back Country has two-stage trigger, pillar-bedded Bell & Carlson stock, 24-in. fluted barrel, three-position safety.

Price: Vanguard Synthetic **$649.00**
Price: Vanguard Stainless **$799.00**
Price: Vanguard Deluxe, 7mm Rem. Mag., .300 Win. Mag. **$1,149.00**
Price: Vanguard Sporter **$849.00**
Price: Laminate Sporter.......... **$849.00**
Price: Vanguard Youth/Compact.......... **$599.00**
Price: Vanguard S2 Back Country.......... **$1,399.00**
Price: Vanguard RC (Range Certified).......... **$1,199.00**
Price: Vanguard Varmint Special.......... **$849.00**
Price: Camilla (designed for women shooters) **$849.00**
Price: Camilla Wilderness.......... **$899.00**
Price: Lazerguard (Laser carved AA-grade walnut stock).......... **$1,199.00**
Price: H-Bar (tactical series) .... **$1,149.00–$1,449.00**
Price: Weatherguard **$749.00**
Price: Modular Chassis **$1,519.00**
Price: Dangerous Game Rifle (DGR) .375 H&H.......... **$1,299.00**
Price: Safari (.375 or .30-06) **$1,199.00**

Price: First Lite Fusion Camo **$1,099.00**
Price: Badlands Camo **$849.00**
Price: Accuguard **$1,099.00**
Price: Select **$599.00**
Price: Wilderness **$999.00**
Price: High Country **$999.00**

WINCHESTER MODEL 70 SUPER GRADE
Calibers: .270 Win., .270 WSM, 7mm Rem. Mag., .30-06, .300 Win Mag., .300 WSM, .338 Win. Mag. Capacities: 5 rounds (short action) or 3 rounds (long action). Barrels: 24 in. or 26 in. blued. Weights: 8–8.5 lbs. Features: Full fancy Grade IV/V walnut stock with shadow-line cheekpiece, controlled round feed with claw extractor, Pachmayr Decelerator pad. No sights but drilled and tapped for scope mounts.
Price: .... **$1,440.00–$1,480.00**

WINCHESTER MODEL 70 ALASKAN
Calibers: .30-06, .300 Win. Mag., .338 Win. Mag., .375 H&H Magnum. Barrel: 25 in Weight: 8.8 lbs. Sights: Folding adjustable rear, hooded brass bead front. Stock: Satin finished Monte Carlo with cut checkering. Features: Integral recoil lug, Pachmayr Decelerator recoil pad.
Price: **$1,400.00**

WINCHESTER MODEL 70 COYOTE LIGHT SUPRESSOR READY
Calibers: .22-250, .243 Win., .308 Win., .270 WSM, .300 WSM and .325 WSM. Capacities: 5-round magazine (3-round mag. in .270 WSM, .300 WSM and .325 WSM). Barrel: 22-in. fluted stainless barrel (24 in. in .270 WSM, .300 WSM and .325 WSM). Threaded for suppressor or other muzzle device. Weight: 7.5 lbs. Length: NA. Features: Composite Bell and Carlson stock, Pachmayr Decelerator pad. Controlled round feeding. No sights but drilled and tapped for mounts.
Price: .... **$1,270.00–$1,310.00**

WINCHESTER MODEL 70 FEATHERWEIGHT
Calibers: .22-250, .243, 6.5 Creedmoor, 7mm-08, .308, .270 WSM, 7mm WSM, .300 WSM, .325 WSM, .25-06, .270, .30-06, 7mm Rem. Mag., .300 Win. Mag., .338 Win. Mag. Capacities: 5 rounds (short action) or 3 rounds (long action). Barrels: 22-in. blued (24 in. in magnum chamberings). Weights: 6.5–7.25 lbs. Length: NA. Features: Satin-finished checkered Grade I walnut stock, controlled round feeding. Pachmayr Decelerator pad. No sights but drilled and tapped for scope mounts.
Price: **$1,010.00**
Price: Magnum calibers **$1,050.00**
Price: Featherweight Stainless .... **$1,210.00-$1,250.00**

WINCHESTER MODEL 70 SPORTER
Calibers: .270 WSM, 7mm WSM, .300 WSM, .325 WSM, .25-06, .270, .30-06, 7mm Rem. Mag., .300 Win. Mag., .338 Win. Mag., 6.8 Western. Capacities: 5 rounds (short action) or 3 rounds (long action). Barrels: 22 in., 24 in. or 26 in. blued. Weights: 6.5–7.25 lbs. Length: NA. Features: Satin-finished checkered Grade I walnut stock with sculpted cheekpiece, controlled round feeding. Pachmayr Decelerator pad. No sights but drilled and tapped for scope mounts.
Price: **$1,010.00**

WINCHESTER MODEL 70 SAFARI EXPRESS
Calibers: .375 H&H Magnum, .416 Remington, .458 Win. Mag. Barrel: 24 in. Weight: 9 lbs. Sights: Fully adjustable rear, hooded brass bead front. Stock: Satin finished Monte Carlo with cut checkering, deluxe cheekpiece. Features: Forged steel receiver with double integral recoil lugs bedded front and rear, dual steel crossbolts, Pachmayr Decelerator recoil pad.
Price: **$1,560.00**

WINCHESTER MODEL 70 LONG RANGE MB
Calibers: .22-250 Rem., .243 Win., 6.5 Creedmoor, .308 Win., 6.5 PRC, .270 WSM, .300 WSM, 6.8 Western. Capacity: 3, 4, or 5-round internal magazine with hinged floorplate. Barrel: 24-in. matte blued, light varmint contour, fluted with muzzle brake. Weight: 7 lbs. 8oz. Length: 44 in. Stock: Bell & Carlson composite with tan/black spider web and Pachmayr Decelerator recoil pad. Sights: Drilled and tapped. Features: Bolt-action short action designed for long-range hunting and target shooting. Aluminum bedding block. Matte black finish. Controlled round feed with claw extractor. Three-position safety. Flat, bench-rest style fore-end with dual sling studs. Jeweled bolt. Recessed target crown.
Price: **$1,589.00**

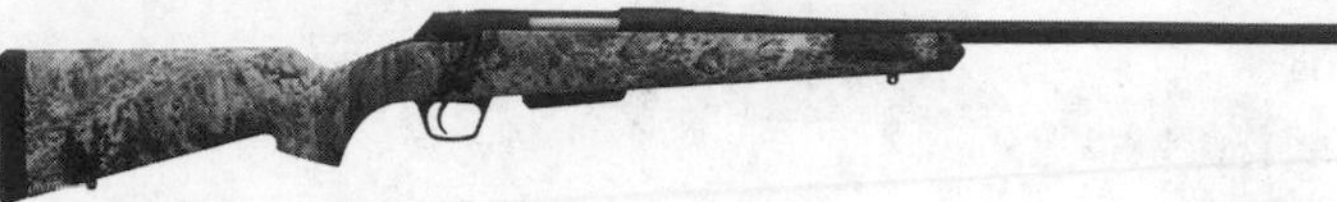

WINCHESTER XPR
Calibers: .243, 6.5 Creedmoor, 270 Win., .270 WSM, 7mm-08, 7mm Rem. Mag., .308 Win., .30-06, .300 Win. Mag., .300 WSM, .325 WSM, .338 Win. Mag.,.350 Legend, 6.8 Western. Capacities: Detachable box magazine holds 3 to 5 rounds. Barrels: 24 or 26 in. Stock: Black polymer with Inflex Technology recoil pad. Weight: Approx. 7 lbs. Finish: Matte blue. Features: Bolt unlock button, nickel coated Teflon bolt.
Price: **$549.00**
Price: Mossy Oak Break-Up Country camo stock **$600.00**
Price: With Vortex II 3-9x40 scope **$710.00**
Price: XPR Hunter Camo (shown) **$600.00**
Price: XPR Extreme Hunter Midnight MB w/True Timber Midnight camo **$769.00**
Price: XPR Hunter Strata MB w/True Timber Strata camo **$749.00**
Price: XPR Hunter w/ Mossy Oak DNA camo **$649.00**
Price: Sporter w/Grade 1 walnut stock **$600.00**
Price: True Timber Strata Camo **$600.00**
Price: Thumbhole Varmint Suppressor Ready **$800.00**
Price: Stealth SR **$669.00**

WINCHESTER XPC
Caliber: .243, 6.5 Creedmoor, 308 Winchester. Capacity: 3. Barrel: 20 in., free floating with target crown, threading for suppressor or muzzle brake. Stock: Cerakote fully machined alloy chassis frame, Magpul PRS Gen III fully adjustable buttstock. Weight: 10 lbs. Length: 40 in. Features: MOA Trigger System, two-position thumb safety. Full length Picatinny rail, M-LOK on fore-end and buttstock for attaching accessories.
Price: **$1,600.00**

BALLARD 1875 1 1/2 HUNTER
Caliber: Various calibers. Barrel: 26–30 in. Weight: NA Length: NA. Stock: Hand-selected classic American walnut. Sights: Blade front, Rocky Mountain rear. Features: Color casehardened receiver, breechblock and lever. Many options available. Made in USA by Ballard Rifle & Cartridge Co.
Price: **$3,250.00**

BALLARD 1875 #3 GALLERY SINGLE SHOT
Caliber: Various calibers. Barrel: 24–28 in. octagonal with tulip. Weight: NA. Length: NA. Stock: Hand-selected classic American walnut. Sights: Blade front, Rocky Mountain rear. Features: Color casehardened receiver, breechblock and lever. Many options available. Made in USA by Ballard Rifle & Cartridge Co.
Price: **$3,300.00**

BALLARD 1875 #4 PERFECTION
Caliber: Various calibers. Barrels: 30 in. or 32 in. octagon, standard or heavyweight. Weights: 10.5 lbs. (standard) or 11.75 lbs. (heavyweight bbl.) Length: NA. Stock: Smooth walnut. Sights: Blade front, Rocky Mountain rear. Features: Rifle or shotgun-style buttstock, straight grip action, single- or double-set trigger, "S" or right lever, hand polished and lapped Badger barrel. Made in USA by Ballard Rifle & Cartridge Co.
Price: **$3,950.00**

BALLARD MODEL 1885 LOW WALL SINGLE SHOT RIFLE
Calibers: Various calibers. Barrels: 24–28 in. Weight: NA. Length: NA. Stock: Hand-selected classic American walnut. Sights: Blade front, sporting rear. Features: Color casehardened receiver, breechblock and lever. Many options available. Made in USA by Ballard Rifle & Cartridge Co.
Price: **$3,300.00**

BALLARD MODEL 1885 HIGH WALL STANDARD SPORTING SINGLE SHOT
Calibers: Various calibers. Barrels: Lengths to 34 in. Weight: NA. Length: NA. Stock: Straight-grain American walnut. Sights: Buckhorn or flattop rear, blade front. Features: Faithful copy of original Model 1885 High Wall; parts interchange with original rifles; variety of options available. Introduced 2000. Made in USA by Ballard Rifle & Cartridge Co.
Price: **$3,300.00**

BALLARD MODEL 1885 HIGH WALL SPECIAL SPORTING SINGLE SHOT
Calibers: Various calibers. Barrels: 28–30 in. octagonal. Weight: NA. Length: NA. Stock: Hand-selected classic American walnut. Sights: Blade front, sporting rear. Features: Color casehardened receiver, breechblock and lever. Many options available. Made in USA by Ballard Rifle & Cartridge Co.
Price: **$3,600.00**

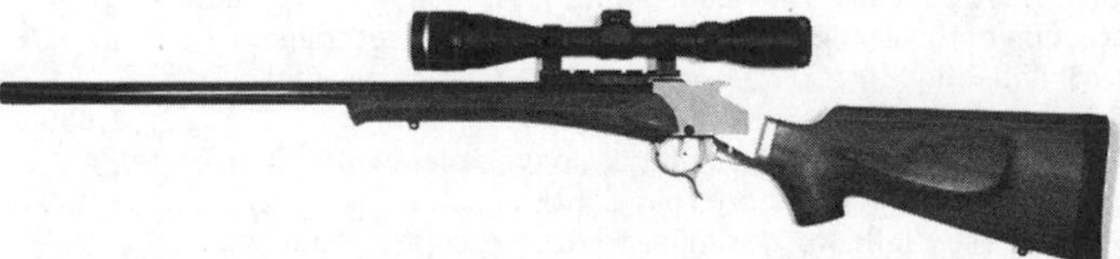

BROWN MODEL 97D SINGLE SHOT
Calibers: Available in most factory and wildcat calibers from .17 Ackley Hornet to .375 Winchester. Barrels: Up to 26 in., air-gauged match grade. Weight: About 5 lbs., 11 oz. Stock: Sporter style with pistol grip, cheekpiece and Schnabel fore-end. Sights: None furnished; drilled and tapped for scope mounting. Features: Falling-block action gives rigid barrel-receiver matting; polished blue/black finish. Hand-fitted action. Standard and custom made-to-order rifles with many options. Made in USA by E. Arthur Brown Co., Inc.
Price: Standard model **$1,695.00**

C. SHARPS ARMS 1874 BRIDGEPORT SPORTING
Calibers: .38-55 to .50-3.25. Barrel: 26 in., 28 in., 30-in. tapered octagon. Weight: 10.5 lbs. Length: 47 in. Stock: American black walnut; shotgun butt with checkered steel buttplate; straight grip, heavy fore-end with Schnabel tip. Sights: Blade front, buckhorn rear. Drilled and tapped for tang sight. Features: Double-set triggers. Made in USA by C. Sharps Arms.
Price: **$1,995.00**

C. SHARPS ARMS NEW MODEL 1885 HIGHWALL
Calibers: .22 LR, .22 Hornet, .219 Zipper, .25-35 WCF, .32-40 WCF, .38-55 WCF, .40-65, .30-40 Krag, .40-50 ST or BN, .40-70 ST or BN, .40-90 ST or BN, .45-70 Govt. 2-1/10 in. ST, .45-90 2-4/10 in. ST, .45-100 2-6/10 in. ST, .45-110 2-7/8 in. ST, .45-120 3-1/4 in. ST. Barrels: 26 in., 28 in., 30 in., tapered full octagon. Weight: About 9 lbs., 4 oz. Length: 47 in. overall. Stock: Oil-finished American walnut; Schnabel-style fore-end. Sights: Blade front, buckhorn rear. Drilled and tapped for optional tang sight. Features: Single trigger; octagonal receiver top; checkered steel buttplate; color casehardened receiver and buttplate, blued barrel. Many options available. Made in USA by C. Sharps Arms Co.
Price: **$1,975.00**

C. SHARPS ARMS 1885 HIGHWALL SCHUETZEN RIFLE
Calibers: .30-30, .32-40, .38-55, .40-50. Barrels: 24, 26, 28 or 30 in. Full tapered octagon. Stock: Straight grain American walnut with oil finish, pistol grip, cheek rest. Sights: Globe front with aperture set, long-range fully adjustable tang sight with Hadley eyecup. Finish: Color casehardened receiver group, buttplate and bottom tang, matte blue barrel. Single set trigger.
Price: **$2,875.00**

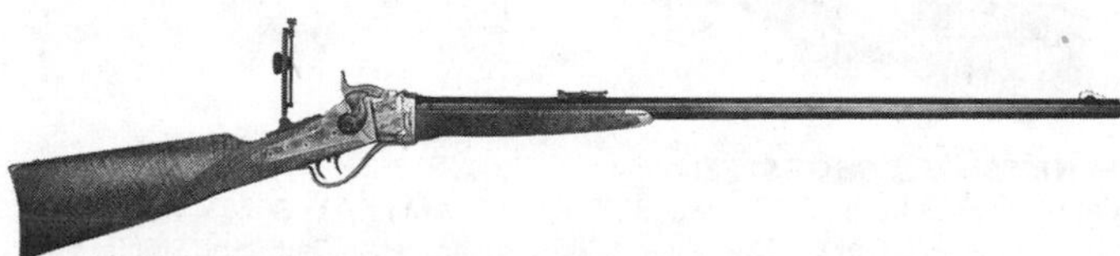

CIMARRON BILLY DIXON 1874 SHARPS SPORTING
Calibers: .45-70, .45-90, .50-70. Barrel: 32-in. tapered octagonal. Weight: NA. Length: NA. Stock: European walnut. Sights: Blade front, Creedmoor rear. Features: Color casehardened frame, blued barrel. Hand-checkered grip and fore-end; hand-rubbed oil finish. Made by Pedersoli. Imported by Cimarron F.A. Co.
Price: **$2,141.70**
Price: Officer's Trapdoor Carbine w/26-in. round barrel **$2,616.00**

CIMARRON ADOBE WALLS ROLLING BLOCK
Caliber: .45-70 Govt. Barrel: 30-in. octagonal. Weight: 10.33 lbs. Length: NA. Stock: Hand-checkered European walnut. Sights: Bead front, semi-buckhorn rear. Features: Color casehardened receiver, blued barrel. Curved buttplate. Double-set triggers. Made by Pedersoli. Imported by Cimarron F.A. Co.
Price: **$1,740.00**

DAKOTA ARMS SHARPS
Calibers: Virtually any caliber from .17 Ackley Hornet to .30-40 Krag. Features: 26-in. octagon barrel, XX-grade walnut stock with straight grip and tang sight. Many options and upgrades are available.
Price: **$4,490.00**

EMF PREMIER 1874 SHARPS
Calibers: .45-70, .45-110, .45-120. Barrel: 32 in., 34 in.. Weight: 11–13 lbs. Length: 49 in., 51 in. overall. Stock: Pistol grip, European walnut. Sights: Blade front, adjustable rear. Features: Superb quality reproductions of the 1874 Sharps Sporting Rifles; casehardened locks; double-set triggers; blue barrels. Imported from Pedersoli by EMF.
Price: Business Rifle **$1,585.00**
Price: Down Under Sporting Rifle, Patchbox, heavy barrel **$2,405.00**
Price: Silhouette, pistol-grip **$1,899.90**
Price: Super Deluxe Hand Engraved **$3,600.00**
Price: Competition Rifle **$2,200.00**

H&R BUFFALO CLASSIC
Calibers: .45 Colt or .45-70 Govt. Barrel: 32 in. heavy. Weight: 8 lbs. Length: 46 in. overall. Stock: Cut-checkered American black walnut. Sights: Williams receiver sight; Lyman target front sight with 8 aperture inserts. Features: Color casehardened Handi-Rifle action with exposed hammer; color casehardened crescent buttplate; 19th-century checkering pattern. Introduced 1995. Made in USA by H&R 1871, Inc.
Price: Buffalo Classic Rifle **$479.00**

HENRY SINGLE SHOT BRASS
Calibers: .44 Mag./.44 Spl., .357 Mag./.38 Spl., .45-70 Govt. Capacity: Single shot. Barrel: 22-in. round blued steel. Weight: 7.01–7.14 lbs. Length: 37.5 in. Stock: American Walnut with English-style straight buttstock. Sights: Fully adjustable folding leaf rear and brass bead front. Also drilled and tapped. Features: Polished brass receiver single-shot break actions built in a limited number of calibers. Sling studs. Brass buttplate. Rebounding hammer safety. Break-action lever can be moved either left or right to open, making it friendly for lefties.
Price: **$646.00**

HENRY SINGLE SHOT STEEL
Calibers: .223 Rem., .243 Win., .308 Win., .357 Mag./.38 Spl., .44 Mag., .30-30 Win., .45-70 Govt., .350 Legend, .450 Bushmaster. Capacity: Single-shot. Barrel: 22-in. round blued steel. Weight: 6.73–6.96 lbs. Length: 37.5 in. Stock: Checkered American Walnut, pistol grip style. Sights: Fully adjustable folding leaf rear and brass bead front. Also drilled and tapped. Features: Blued steel receiver single-shot rifles. Solid rubber recoil pad. Rebounding hammer safety. Sling studs. Break-action lever can be moved either left or right to open, making it friendly for lefties. Youth model uses shorter 13-inch LOP, standard model LOP is 14 inches.
Price: **$525.00**
Price: Youth Single Shot .243 Win. **$525.00**

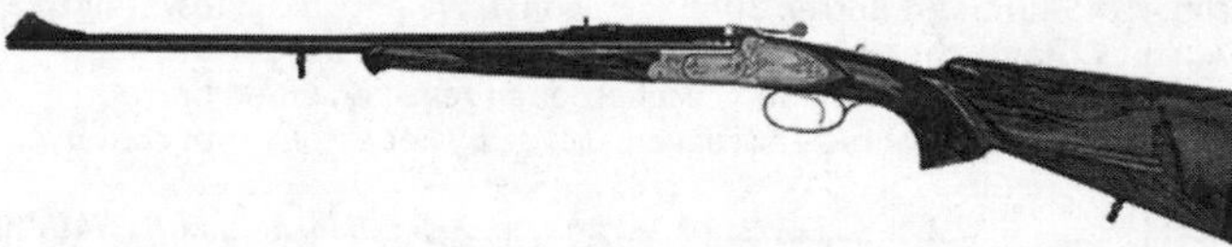

KRIEGHOFF HUBERTUS SINGLE-SHOT
Calibers: .222, .22-250, .243 Win., .270 Win., .308 Win., .30-06, 5.6x50R Mag., 5.6x52R, 6x62R Freres, 6.5x57R, 6.5x65R, 7x57R, 7x65R, 8x57JRS, 8x75RS, 9.3x74R, 7mm Rem. Mag., .300 Win. Mag. Barrels: 23.5 in. Shorter lengths available. Weight: 6.5 lbs. Length: 40.5 in. Stock: High-grade walnut. Sights: Blade front, open rear. Features: Break-open loading with manual cocking lever on top tang; takedown; extractor; Schnabel forearm; many options. Imported from Germany by Krieghoff International Inc.
Price: Hubertus single shot **$7,295.00**
Price: Hubertus, magnum calibers **$8,295.00**

MERKEL K1 MODEL LIGHTWEIGHT STALKING
Calibers: .243 Win., .270 Win., 7x57R, .308 Win., .30-06, 7mm Rem. Mag., .300 Win. Mag., 9.3x74R. Barrel: 23.6 in. Weight: 5.6 lbs. unscoped. Stock: Satin-finished walnut, fluted and checkered; sling-swivel studs. Sights: None (scope base furnished). Features: Franz Jager single-shot break-open action, cocking/uncocking slide-type safety, matte silver receiver, selectable trigger pull weights, integrated, quick detach 1 in. or 30mm optic mounts (optic not included). Extra barrels are an option. Imported from Germany by Merkel USA.
Price: Jagd Stalking Rifle **$3,795.00**
Price: Jagd Stutzen Carbine **$4,195.00**
Price: Extra barrels **$1,195.00**

MILLER ARMS
Calibers: Virtually any caliber from .17 Ackley Hornet to .416 Remington. Falling block design with 24-in. premium match-grade barrel, express sights, XXX-grade walnut stock and fore-end with 24 LPI checkering. Made in several styles including Classic, Target and Varmint. Many options and upgrades are available. From Dakota Arms.
Price: **$5,590.00**

ROSSI SINGLE-SHOT SERIES
Calibers: .223 Rem., .243 Win., .44 Magnum. Barrel: 22 in. Weight: 6.25 lbs. Stocks: Black Synthetic Synthetic with recoil pad and removable cheek piece. Sights: Adjustable rear, fiber optic front, scope rail. Some models have scope rail only. Features: Single-shot break open, positive ejection, internal transfer bar mechanism, manual external safety, trigger block system, Taurus Security System, Matte blue finish.
Price: **$238.00**

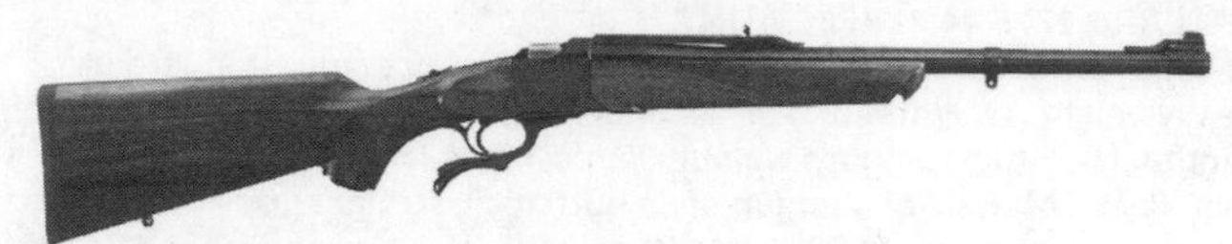

RUGER NO. 1 SERIES
This model is currently available only in select limited editions and chamberings each year. Features common to most variants of the No. 1 include a falling block mechanism and under lever, sliding tang safety, integral scope mounts machined on the steel quarter rib, sporting-style recoil pad, grip cap and sling swivel studs. Chamberings for 2018 and 2019 were .450 Bushmaster and .450 Marlin. In addition, many calibers are offered by Ruger distributors Lipsey's and Talo, usually limited production runs of approximately 250 rifles, including .204 Ruger, .22 Hornet, 6.5 Creedmoor, .250 Savage, .257 Roberts, .257 Weatherby Mag. and .30-30. For availability of specific variants and calibers contact www.lipseysguns.com or www.taloinc.com.
Price: .... **$1,899.00-$2,115.00**

SHILOH CO. SHARPS 1874 LONG RANGE EXPRESS
Calibers: .38-55, .40-50 BN, .40-70 BN, .40-90 BN, .40-70 ST, .40-90 ST, .45-70 Govt. ST, .45-90 ST, .45-110 ST, .50-70 ST, .50-90 ST. Barrel: 34-in. tapered octagon. Weight: 10.5 lbs. Length: 51 in. overall. Stock: Oil-finished walnut (upgrades available) with pistol grip, shotgun-style butt, traditional cheek rest, Schnabel fore-end. Sights: Customer's choice. Features: Re-creation of the Model 1874 Sharps rifle. Double-set triggers. Made in USA by Shiloh Rifle Mfg. Co.
Price: **$2,059.00**
Price: Sporter Rifle No. 1 (similar to above except with 30-in. barrel, blade front, buckhorn rear sight) **$2,059.00**
Price: Sporter Rifle No. 3 (similar to No. 1 except straight-grip stock, standard wood) **$1,949.00**

SHILOH CO. SHARPS 1874 QUIGLEY
Calibers: .45-70 Govt., .45-110. Barrel: 34-in. heavy octagon. Stock: Military-style with patch box, standard-grade American walnut. Sights: Semi-buckhorn, interchangeable front and midrange vernier tang sight with windage. Features: Gold inlay initials, pewter tip, Hartford collar, case color or antique finish. Double-set triggers.
Price: **$3,533.00**

SHILOH CO. SHARPS 1874 SADDLE
Calibers: .38-55, .40-50 BN, .40-65 Win., .40-70 BN, .40-70 ST, .40-90

Prices given are believed to be accurate at time of publication however, many factors affect retail pricing so exact prices are not possible.

BN, .40-90 ST, .44-77 BN, .44-90 BN, .45-70 Govt. ST, .45-90 ST, .45-100 ST, .45-110 ST, .45-120 ST, .50-70 ST, .50-90 ST. Barrels: 26 in. full or half octagon. Stock: Semi-fancy American walnut. Shotgun style with cheek rest. Sights: Buckhorn and blade. Features: Double-set trigger, numerous custom features can be added.

Price: **$2,044.00**

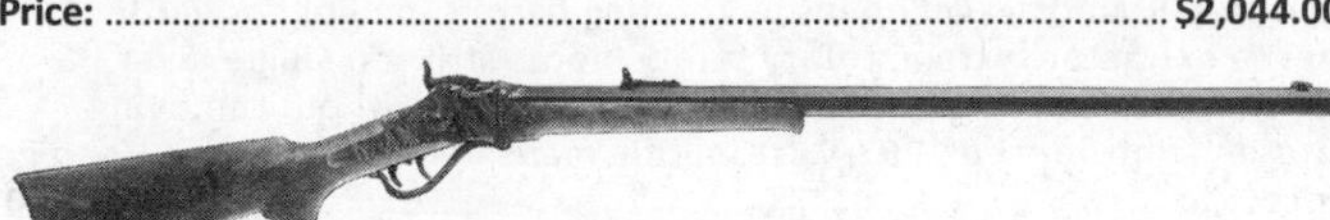

SHILOH CO. SHARPS 1874 MONTANA ROUGHRIDER

Calibers: .38-55, .40-50 BN, .40-65 Win., .40-70 BN, .40-70 ST, .40-90 BN, .40-90 ST, .44-77 BN, .44-90 BN, .45-70 Govt. ST, .45-90 ST, .45-100 ST, .45-110 ST, .45-120 ST, .50-70 ST, .50-90 ST. Barrels: 30 in. full or half octagon. Stock: American walnut in shotgun or military style. Sights: Buckhorn and blade. Features: Double-set triggers, numerous custom features can be added.

Price: **$2,059.00**

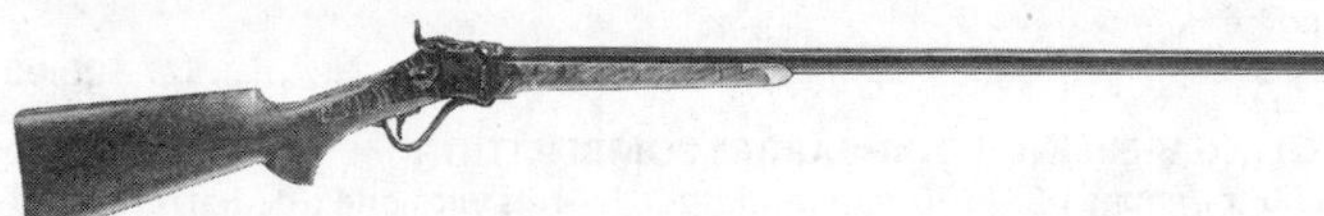

SHILOH CO. SHARPS CREEDMOOR TARGET

Calibers: .38-55, .40-50 BN, .40-65 Win., .40-70 BN, .40-70 ST, .40-90 BN, .40-90 ST, .44-77 BN, .44-90 BN, .45-70 Govt. ST, .45-90 ST, .45-100 ST, .45-110 ST, .45-120 ST, .50-70 ST, .50-90 ST. Barrel: 32 in. half round-half octagon. Stock: Extra fancy American walnut. Shotgun style with pistol grip. Sights: Customer's choice. Features: Single trigger, AA finish on stock, polished barrel and screws, pewter tip.

Price: **$3,105.00**

THOMPSON/CENTER ENCORE PRO HUNTER PREDATOR RIFLE

Calibers: .204 Ruger, .223 Remington, .22-250 and .308 Winchester. Barrel: 28-in. deep-fluted interchangeable. Length: 42.5 in. Weight: 7.75 lbs. Stock: Composite buttstock and fore-end with non-slip inserts in cheekpiece, pistol grip and fore-end. Realtree Advantage Max-1 camo finish overall. Scope is not included.

Price: **$882.00**

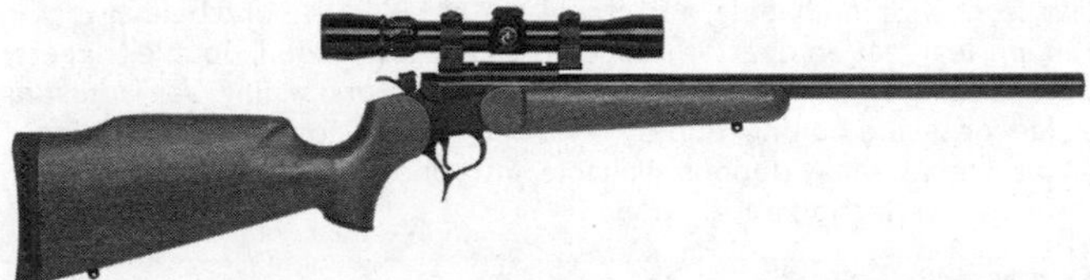

THOMPSON/CENTER G2 CONTENDER

Calibers: .204 Ruger, .223 Rem., 6.8 Rem. 7-30 Waters, .30-30 Win. Barrel: 23-in. interchangeable with blued finish. Length: 36.75 in. Stock: Walnut. Sights: None. Weight: 5.5 pounds. Reintroduced in 2015. Interchangeable barrels available in several centerfire and rimfire calibers.

Price: **$769.00**

UBERTI 1874 SHARPS SPORTING

Caliber: .45-70 Govt. Barrels: 30 in., 32 in., 34 in. octagonal. Weight: 10.57 lbs. with 32 in. barrel. Lengths: 48.9 in. with 32 in. barrel. Stock: Walnut. Sights: Dovetail front, Vernier tang rear. Features: Cut checkering, case-colored finish on frame, buttplate, and lever. Imported by Stoeger Industries.

Price: Standard Sharps **$1,919.00**
Price: Special Sharps **$2,019.00**
Price: Deluxe Sharps **$3,269.00**
Price: Down Under Sharps **$2,719.00**
Price: Long Range Sharps **$2,719.00**
Price: Buffalo Hunter Sharps **$2,620.00**
Price: Sharps Cavalry Carbine **$2,020.00**
Price: Sharps Extra Deluxe **$5,400.00**
Price: Sharps Hunter **$1,699.00**

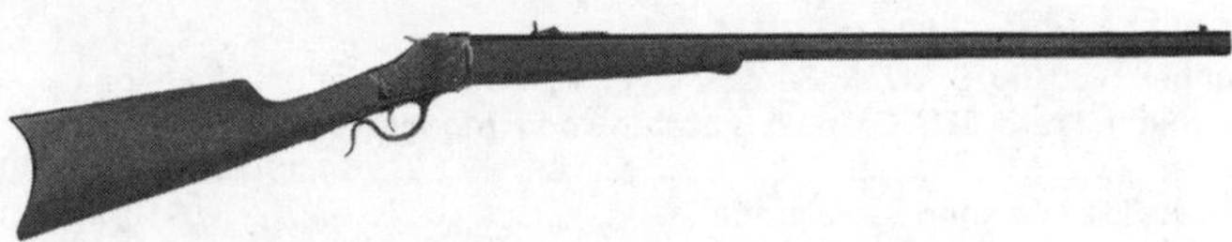

UBERTI 1885 HIGH-WALL SINGLE-SHOT

Calibers: .45-70 Govt., .45-90, .45-120. Barrels: 28–32 in. Weights: 9.3–9.9 lbs. Lengths: 44.5–47 in. overall. Stock: Walnut stock and fore-end. Sights: Blade front, fully adjustable open rear. Features: Based on Winchester High-Wall design by John Browning. Color casehardened frame and lever, blued barrel and buttplate. Imported by Stoeger Industries.

Price: .... **$1,079.00–$1,279.00**

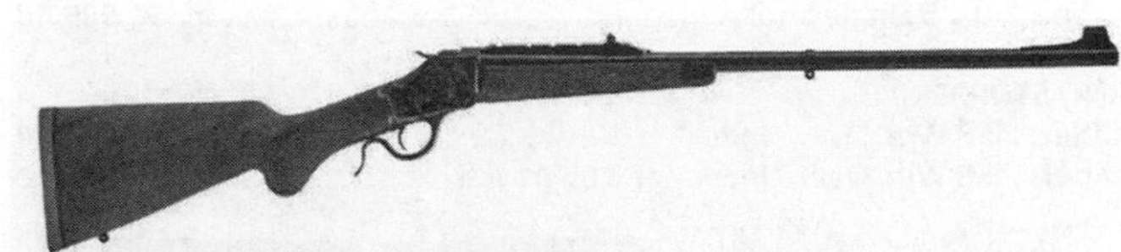

UBERTI 1885 COURTENEY STALKING RIFLE

Calibers: .303 British, .45-70 Gov't. Capacity: Single shot. Barrel: 24-in. round blued steel. Weight: 7.1 lbs. Length: 37.5 in. Stock: A-Grade Walnut, Prince of Wales buttstock and slim fore-end with African heartwood. Sights: Hooded front and V-style express rear with quarter-rib slot for Weaver rings. Features: Named after English hunter Courteney Selous, this single shot shows traditional British style. Casehardened receiver. Checkered pistol grip. Rubber buttpad. Sling swivels including barrel-mounted front.

Price: **$1,689.00**

UBERTI SPRINGFIELD TRAPDOOR RIFLE/CARBINE

Caliber: .45-70 Govt., single shot Barrel: 22 or 32.5 in. Features: Blued steel receiver and barrel, casehardened breechblock and buttplate. Sights: Creedmoor style.

Price: Springfield Trapdoor Carbine, 22 in. barrel **$1,749.00**
Price: Springfield Trapdoor Army, 32.5 in. barrel **$2,019.0**

Prices given are believed to be accurate at time of publication however, many factors affect retail pricing so exact prices are not possible.

BERETTA S686/S689 O/U RIFLE SERIES
Calibers: .30-06, 9.3x74R. Barrels: 23 in. O/U boxlock action. Single or double triggers. EELL Grade has better wood, moderate engraving.
Price: ....$4,200.00–$9,000.00
Price: EELL Diamond Sable grade $12,750.00

BRNO MODEL 802 COMBO GUN
Calibers/Gauges: .243 Win., .308 or .30-06/12 ga. Over/Under. Barrels: 23.6 in. Weight: 7.6 lbs. Length: 41 in. Stock: European walnut. Features: Double trigger, shotgun barrel is improved-modified chokes. Imported by CZ USA.
Price: $2,087.00

BRNO EFFECT
Caliber: .30-06 Single Shot....................$1,585.00

BRNO STOPPER
Caliber: .458 Win. Over/Under $5,554.00
Caliber: .458 Win. Over/Under hand engraved....................$8,072.00

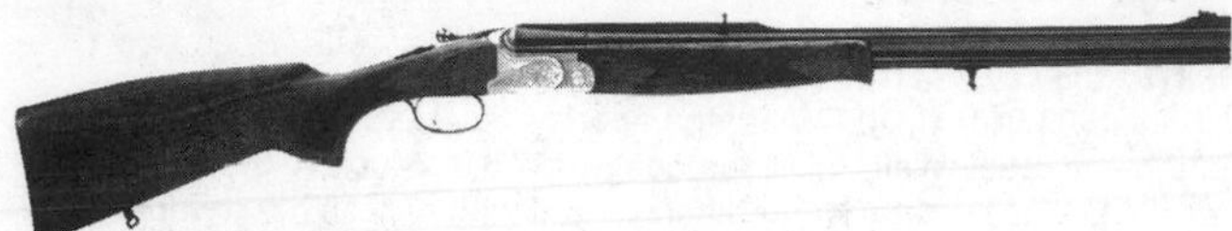

FAUSTI CLASS EXPRESS
Calibers: .243 Win., 6.5x55, 6.5x57R, 7x57R, .308 Win., .270 Win., .30-06, .30R Blaser, .45-70, .444 Marlin, 9.3x74, 8x57 JRS. Barrel: 24 in. Weight: 7.6 lbs. average. Stock: A-Grade Walnut with oil finish. Pistol grip style. Sights: Fiber-optic sight on ramp, adjustable for elevation. Features: O/U double rifle in a wide range of chamberings. LOP of 14.49 in. Choice of single or double triggers, no selector. Automatic ejectors. Includes VL151 gun case.
Price: $4,990.00
Price: CLASS SL EXPRESS $5,690.00

FAUSTI DEA EXPRESS
Calibers: .243 Win., 7x57R, .308 Win., .270 Win., .30-06, .30R Blaser, .45-70, .444 Marlin, 9.3x74, 8x57 JRS. Barrel: 24 in. Weight: 7 lbs. average. Stock: A-Grade Walnut with oil finish. Pistol grip style. Sights: Fiber-optic sight on ramp, adjustable for elevation. Features: SxS double rifle in a wide range of chamberings. LOP of 14.49 in. Choice of single or double triggers, no selector. Automatic ejectors. Includes VL151 gun case.
Price: $6,800.00

HEYM MODEL 88B SXS DOUBLE RIFLE
Calibers/Gauge: .22 Hornet, .300 Win. Mag., .375 H&H Belted Mag., .375 H&H Flanged Mag., .416 Rigby, .416/500 NE, .450/400 NE 3-in., .450 NE 3.25-in., .470 NE, .500 NE, .577 NE, .600 NE, 20 gauge, and more. Barrel: Up to 26 in., Krupp steel, hammer-forged. Stock: Custom select European walnut. Sights: V rear, bead front. Weight: 9 to 13 lbs. Features: Automatic ejectors, articulated front trigger, stocked-to-fit RH or LH, cocking indicators, engraving available.
Price: $18,000.00

HEYM MODEL 89B SXS DOUBLE RIFLE
Calibers/Gauge: .22 Hornet, .300 Win. Mag., .375 H&H Belted Mag., .375 H&H Flanged Mag., .416 Rigby, .416/500 NE, .450/400 NE 3-in., .450 NE 3.25-in., .470 NE, .500 NE, .577 NE, .600 NE, 20 gauge, and more. Barrel: Up to 26 in., Krupp steel, hammer-forged. Stock: Custom select European walnut. Sights: V rear, bead front. Weight: 9-13 lbs. Features: Five frame sizes, automatic ejectors, intercepting sears, stocked-to-fit RH or LH, engraving available.
Price: $23,000.00

HOENIG ROTARY ROUND ACTION DOUBLE
Calibers: Most popular calibers. Over/Under design. Barrels: 22–26 in. Stock: English Walnut; to customer specs. Sights: Swivel hood front with button release (extra bead stored in trap door grip cap), express-style rear on quarter-rib adjustable for windage and elevation; scope mount. Features: Round action opens by rotating barrels, pulling forward. Inertia extractor system, rotary safety blocks strikers. Single lever quick-detachable scope mount. Simple takedown without removing fore-end. Introduced 1997. Custom rifle made in USA by George Hoenig.
Price: $22,500.00

HOENIG ROTARY ROUND ACTION COMBINATION
Calibers: Most popular calibers and shotgun gauges. Over/Under design with rifle barrel atop shotgun barrel. Barrel: 26 in. Weight: 7 lbs. Stock: English Walnut to customer specs. Sights: Front ramp with button release blades. Foldable aperture tang sight windage and elevation adjustable. Quarter-rib with scope mount. Features: Round action opens by rotating barrels, pulling forward. Inertia extractor; rotary safety blocks strikers. Simple takedown without removing forend. Custom rifle made in USA by George Hoenig.
Price: $27,500.00

HOENIG VIERLING FOUR-BARREL COMBINATION
Calibers/gauges: Two 20-gauge shotgun barrels with one rifle barrel chambered for .22 Long Rifle and another for .223 Remington. Custom rifle made in USA by George Hoenig.
Price: $50,000.00

KRIEGHOFF CLASSIC DOUBLE
Calibers: 7x57R, 7x65R, .308 Win., .30-06, 8x57 JRS, 8x75RS, 9.3x74R, .375NE, .500/.416NE, .470NE, .500NE. Barrel: 23.5 in. Weight: 7.3–11 lbs. Stock: High grade European walnut. Standard model has conventional rounded cheekpiece, Bavaria model has Bavarian-style cheekpiece. Sights: Bead front with removable, adjustable wedge (.375 H&H and below), standing leaf rear on quarter-rib. Features: Boxlock action; double triggers; short opening angle for fast loading; quiet extractors; sliding, self-adjusting wedge for secure bolting; Purdey-style barrel extension; horizontal firing pin placement. Many options available. Introduced 1997. Imported from Germany by Krieghoff International.
Price: $10,995.00
Price: Engraved sideplates, add $4,000.00
Price: Extra set of rifle barrels, add....................$6,300.00
Price: Extra set of 20-ga., 28 in. shotgun barrels, add....................$4,400.00

KRIEGHOFF CLASSIC BIG FIVE DOUBLE RIFLE
Similar to the standard Classic except available in .375 H&H, .375 Flanged Mag. N.E., .416 Rigby, .458 Win., 500/416 NE, 470 NE, 500 NE. Has hinged front trigger, nonremovable muzzle wedge, Universal Trigger System, Combi Cocking Device, steel trigger guard, specially weighted stock bolt for weight and balance. Many options available. Introduced 1997. Imported from Germany by Krieghoff International.
Price: $13,995.00
Price: Engraved sideplates, add $4,000.00
Price: Extra set of 20-ga. shotgun barrels, add....................$5,000.00
Price: Extra set of rifle barrels, add....................$6,300.00

MERKEL BOXLOCK DOUBLE
Calibers: 5.6x52R, .243 Winchester, 6.5x55, 6.5x57R, 7x57R, 7x65R, .308 Win., .30-06, 8x57 IRS, 9.3x74R. Barrel: 23.6 in. Weight: 7.7 oz. Length: NA. Stock: Walnut, oil finished, pistol grip. Sights: Fixed 100 meter. Features: Anson & Deeley boxlock action with cocking indicators, double triggers, engraved color casehardened receiver. Introduced 1995. Imported from Germany by Merkel USA.
Price: Model 140-2 ....$13,255.00
Price: Model 141 Small Frame SXS Rifle; built on smaller frame, chambered for 7mm Mauser, .30-06, or 9.3x74R $11,825.00
Price: Model 141 Engraved; fine hand-engraved hunting scenes on silvered receiver. $13,500.00

Prices given are believed to be accurate at time of publication however, many factors affect retail pricing so exact prices are not possible.

BROWNING BUCK MARK SEMI-AUTO

Caliber: .22 LR. Capacity: 10+1. Action: A rifle version of the Buck Mark Pistol; straight blowback action; machined aluminum receiver with integral rail scope mount; manual thumb safety. Barrel: Recessed crowns. Stock: Stock and forearm with full pistol grip. Features: Action lock provided. Introduced 2001. Four model name variations for 2006, as noted below. Sights: FLD Target, FLD Carbon, and Target models have integrated scope rails. Sporter has Truglo/Marble fiber-optic sights. Imported from Japan by Browning.

Price: FLD Target, 5.5 lbs., bull barrel, laminated stock **$720.00**
Price: Target, 5.4 lbs., blued bull barrel, wood stock **$700.00**
Price: Sporter, 4.4 lbs., blued sporter barrel w/sights **$700.00**

BROWNING SA-22 SEMI-AUTO 22

Caliber: .22 LR. Capacity: Tubular magazine in buttstock holds 11 rounds. Barrel: 19.375 in. Weight: 5 lbs. 3 oz. Length: 37 in. overall. Stock: Checkered select walnut with pistol grip and semi-beavertail fore-end. Sights: Gold bead front, folding leaf rear. Features: Engraved receiver with polished blue finish; crossbolt safety; easy takedown for carrying or storage. The Grade VI is available with either grayed or blued receiver with extensive engraving with gold-plated animals: right side pictures a fox and squirrel in a woodland scene; left side shows a beagle chasing a rabbit. On top is a portrait of the beagle. Stock and fore-end are of high-grade walnut with a double-bordered cut checkering design. Introduced 1956. Made in Belgium until 1974. Currently made in Japan by Miroku.

Price: Grade I, scroll-engraved blued receiver **$700.00**
Price: Grade II, octagon barrel **$1,000.00**
Price: Grade VI BL, gold-plated engraved blued receiver **$1,640.00**
Price: Challenge w/Grade I Walnut, bull bbl **$959.00**

CITADEL M-1 CARBINE

Caliber: .22LR. Capacity: 10-round magazine. Barrel: 18 in. Weight: 4.8 lbs. Length: 35 in. Stock: Wood or synthetic in black or several camo patterns. Features: Built to the exacting specifications of the G.I. model used by U.S. infantrymen in both WWII theaters of battle and in Korea. Used by officers as well as tankers, drivers, artillery crews, mortar crews, and other personnel. Weight, barrel length and OAL are the same as the "United States Carbine, Caliber .30, M1," its official military designation. Made in Italy by Chiappa. Imported by Legacy Sports.

Price: Synthetic stock, black. **$316.00**
Price: Synthetic stock, camo. **$368.00**
Price: Wood stock. **$400.00**

CZ MODEL 512

Calibers: .22 LR/.22 WMR. Capacity: 5-round magazines. Barrel: 20.5 in. Weight: 5.9 lbs. Length: 39.3 in. Stock: Beech. Sights: Adjustable. Features: The modular design is easily maintained, requiring only a coin as a tool for field stripping. The action of the 512 is composed of an aluminum alloy upper receiver that secures the barrel and bolt assembly and a fiberglass reinforced polymer lower half that houses the trigger mechanism and detachable magazine. The 512 shares the same magazines and scope rings with the CZ 455 bolt-action rifle.

Price: .22 LR **$495.00**
Price: .22 WMR **$526.00**

H&K 416-22

Caliber: .22 LR. Capacity: 10- or 20-round magazine. Features: Blowback semi-auto rifle styled to resemble H&K 416 with metal upper and lower receivers; rail interface system; retractable stock; pistol grip with storage compartment; on-rail sights; rear sight adjustable for wind and elevation; 16.1-in. barrel. Also available in pistol version with 9-in. barrel. Made in Germany by Walther under license from Heckler & Koch and imported by Umarex.

Price: **$599.00**

H&K MP5 A5

Caliber: .22 LR. Capacity: 10- or 25-round magazine Features: Blowback semi-auto rifle styled to resemble H&K MP5 with metal receiver; compensator; bolt catch; NAVY pistol grip; on-rail sights; rear sight adjustable for wind and elevation; 16.1-in. barrel. Also available in pistol version with 9-in. barrel. Also available with SD-type fore-end. Made in Germany by Walther under license from Heckler & Koch. Imported by Umarex.

Price: **$499.00**
Price: MP5 SD **$599.00**

HENRY AR-7 SURVIVAL RIFLE

Caliber: .22 LR. Capacity: 8, detachable steel magazine. Barrel: 16.125-in. steel covered with ABS plastic. Weight: 3.5 lbs. Length: 35 in. Stock: ABS plastic, floating, hollow design allowing rifle to be disassembled and packed inside buttstock. Choice of Black, True Timber Kanati, or Viper Western camo. Sights: Peep rear with blaze orange blade front. Also 3/8-in. grooved receiver. Features: Henry's version of the AR-7 takedown rifle issued to U.S. Air Force pilots. Receiver, barrel, and spare mags stow inside the buttstock. Rubber buttpad. 14-inch LOP. Two 8-round magazines included. The US Survival Pack includes a black synthetic AR-7 rifle, zippered soft case, and a wide variety of survival gear, including a Henry-branded Buck knife.

Price: AR-7 Black **$319.00**
Price: AR-7 Camo **$388.00**
Price: AR-7 Survival Pack **$577.00**

HOWA GAMEPRO RIMFIRE

Calibers: .22 LR, .22 WMR, .17 HMR. Capacity: 10. Barrel: 18 in., threaded, blued. Stock: Composite Hogue over-molded. Sights: Picatinny rail. Weight: 9.35 lbs. Features: Guaranteed sub-MOA, two-stage HACT trigger.

Price: **$699.00**

KEL-TEC SU-22CA

Caliber: .22 LR. Capacity: 26-round magazine. Barrel: 16.1 in. Weight: 4 lbs. Length: 34 in. Features: Blowback action, crossbolt safety, adjustable front and rear sights with integral Picatinny rail. Threaded muzzle.

Price: **$547.00**

MAGNUM RESEARCH MAGNUM LITE RIMFIRE

Calibers: .22 LR or .22 WMR Capacity: 10 (.22 LR), 9 (.22 WMR) rotary magazine. Barrel: 17-, 18-, 18.5-, or 19-in. lengths with options of carbon, aluminum-tensioned, threaded, and integrally suppressed TTS-22. Weight: 4 lbs.–4 lbs. 8 oz. Length: 36-5/8–38-5/8 in. Stock: Multiple options including Hogue Overmolded and laminated Barracuda style. Sights: Integral scope base. Features: The Magnum Lite Rimfire (MLR) uses a one-piece forged 6061-T6 receivers that are black hardcoat anodized. Custom barrels. Integral Picatinny rail for easy optics mounting. Upgraded trigger. Multiple stock style and material options, as well as barrel types and lengths. Crossbolt safety and manual bolt hold-open catch. Made in the USA.

Price: Hogue Overmolded **$764.00**
Price: MLR .22 LR w/ aluminum-tensioned barrel **$641.00**
Price: MLR .22 WMR w/ Barracuda stock **$935.00**
Price: MLR .22 LR with Ultra barrel **$596.00**
Price: MLR .22 LR with TTS-22 suppressed barrel **$860.00**

Prices given are believed to be accurate at time of publication however, many factors affect retail pricing so exact prices are not possible.

MAGNUM RESEARCH SWITCHBOLT

Caliber: .22 LR. Capacity: 10-round rotary magazine. Barrel: 17-in. carbon. Weight: 4.25 lbs. Length: 35-1/8–35-1/2 in. Stock: Two models, one with Hogue Overmolded Black and the other with colored Ambidextrous Evolution laminate. Sights: Integral scope base. Features: Unique gas-assisted blowback operation. An extension of the lightweight MLR rifles, the Switchbolt was tested and perfected on the professional speed shooting circuit. Built in the USA. Integral Picatinny rail. Machined from 6061-T6, hardcoat anodized. Equipped with a bolt handle on the left side of a right-handed bolt, built for right-handed shooters so the trigger hand never has to leave the stock. Custom-designed Switchbolts are available from the Magnum Research Custom Shop.

Price: Hogue overmolded black stock **$731.00**
Price: Ambidextrous Evolution laminate stock **$893.00**

MARLIN MODEL 60

Caliber: .22 LR. Capacity: 14-round tubular magazine. Barrel: 19 in. round tapered. Weight: About 5.5 lbs. Length: 37.5 in. overall. Stock: Press-checkered, laminated Maine birch with Monte Carlo, full pistol grip; black synthetic or Realtree Camo. Sights: Ramp front, open adjustable rear. Matted receiver is grooved for scope mount. Features: Last-shot bolt hold-open. Available with factory mounted 4x scope.

Price: Laminate **$209.00**
Price: Model 60C camo **$246.00**
Price: Synthetic **$201.00**

MARLIN MODEL 60SS SELF-LOADING RIFLE

Same as the Model 60 except breech bolt, barrel and outer magazine tube are made of stainless steel; most other parts are either nickel-plated or coated to match the stainless finish. Monte Carlo stock is of black/gray Maine birch laminate, and has nickel-plated swivel studs, rubber buttpad. Introduced 1993.

Price: **$315.00**

MARLIN MODEL 795

Caliber: .22. Capacity: 10-round magazine. Barrel: 18 in. with 16-groove Micro-Groove rifling. Sights: Ramp front sight, adjustable rear. Receiver grooved for scope mount. Stock: Black synthetic, hardwood, synthetic thumbhole, solid pink, pink camo, or Mossy Oak New Break-up camo finish. Features: Last shot hold-open feature. Introduced 1997. SS is similar to Model 795 except stainless steel barrel. Most other parts nickel-plated. Adjustable folding semi-buckhorn rear sights, ramp front high-visibility post and removable cutaway wide scan hood. Made in USA by Marlin Firearms Co.

Price: **$183.00**
Price: Stainless **$262.00**

MOSSBERG BLAZE SERIES

Caliber: .22 LR. Capacities: 10 or 25 rounds. Barrel: 16.5 in. Sights: Adjustable. Weights: 3.5–4.75 lbs. Features: A series of lightweight polymer rifles with several finish options and styles. Green Dot Combo model has Dead Ringer greet dot sight. Blaze 47 has AK-profile with adjustable fiber optic rear and raised front sight, ambidextrous safety, and a choice of wood or synthetic stock.

Price: **$210.00**
Price: Muddy Girl camo **$269.00**
Price: Green Dot Combo **$281.00**
Price: Wildfire camo **$269.00**
Price: Kryptek Highlander camo **$283.00**
Price: Blaze 47 wood stock **$420.00**

MOSSBERG MODEL 702 PLINKSTER

Caliber: .22 LR. Capacity: 10-round magazine. Barrel: 18 in. free-floating. Weights: 4.1–4.6 lbs. Sights: Adjustable rifle. Receiver grooved for scope mount. Stock: Wood or black synthetic. Features: Ergonomically placed magazine release and safety buttons, crossbolt safety, free gun lock. Made in USA by O.F. Mossberg & Sons, Inc.

Price: From **$190.00**

MOSSBERG MODEL 715T SERIES

Caliber: .22 LR. Capacity: 10- or 25-round magazine. Barrel: 16.25 or 18 in. with A2-style muzzle brake. Weight: 5.5 lbs. Features: AR style offered in several models. Flattop or A2 style carry handle.

Price: Black finish **$326.00**
Price: Black finish, Red Dot sight **$375.00**
Price: Muddy Girl camo **$438.00**

REMINGTON MODEL 552 BDL DELUXE SPEEDMASTER

Calibers: .22 Short (20 rounds), Long (17) or LR (15) tubular magazine. Barrel: 21-in. round tapered. Weight: 5.75 lbs. Length: 40 in. overall. Stock: Walnut. Checkered grip and fore-end. Sights: Adjustable rear, ramp front. Features: Positive crossbolt safety in trigger guard, receiver grooved for tip-off mount. Operates with .22 Short, Long or Long Rifle cartridges. Classic design introduced in 1957.

Price: **$707.00**

ROSSI RS22

Caliber: .22 LR. Capacity: 10-round detachable magazine. Barrel: 18 in. Weight: 4.1 lbs. Length: 36 in. Stock: Black synthetic with impressed checkering. Sights: Adjustable fiber optic rear, hooded fiber optic front. Made in Brazil, imported by Rossi USA.

Price: Standard model, synthetic stock **$139.00**

RUGER 10/22 AUTOLOADING CARBINE

Caliber: .22 LR. Capacity: 10-round rotary magazine. Barrel: 18.5 in. round tapered (16.12 in. compact model). Weight: 5 lbs. (4.5, compact). Length: 37.25 in., 34 in. (compact) overall. Stock: American hardwood with pistol grip and barrel band, or synthetic. Sights: Brass bead front, folding leaf rear adjustable for elevation. Features: Available with satin black or stainless finish on receiver and barrel. Detachable rotary magazine fits flush into stock, crossbolt safety, receiver tapped and grooved for scope blocks or tip-off mount. Scope base adaptor furnished with each rifle. Made in USA by Sturm, Ruger & Co.

Price: Wood stock **$309.00**
Price: Synthetic stock **$309.00**
Price: Stainless, synthetic stock **$339.00**
Price: Compact model, fiber-optic front sight **$359.00**
Price: Go Wild Rockstar Camo **$399.00**
Price: Collector's Series Man's Best Friend **$399.00**
Price: Weaver 3-9x Scope **$399.00**

RUGER 10/22 TAKEDOWN RIFLE

Caliber: .22 LR. Capacity: 10-round rotary magazine. Barrels: 18.5 in. stainless, or 16.6 in. satin black threaded with suppressor. Easy takedown feature enables quick separation of the barrel from the action by way of a recessed locking lever, for ease of transportation and storage. Stock: Black synthetic. Sights: Adjustable rear, gold bead front. Weight: 4.66 pounds. Comes with backpack carrying bag.

Price: Stainless **$439.00**
Price: Satin black w/flash suppressor **$459.00**
Price: Threaded barrel **$629.00**
Price: With Silent-SR suppressor **$1,078.00**

RUGER 10/22 SPORTER

Same specifications as 10/22 Carbine except has American walnut stock with hand-checkered pistol grip and fore-end, straight buttplate, sling swivels, 18.9-in. barrel, and no barrel band.

Price: **$419.00**

RUGER 10/22 TARGET LITE

Features a 16 1/8-in. heavy, hammer-forged threaded barrel with tight chamber dimensions, black or red/black laminate stock with thumbhole and adjustable length-of-pull, BX Trigger with 2.5-3 lbs. pull weight, minimal overtravel and positive reset.

Price: **$649.00**

SAVAGE A17 SERIES
Calibers: .17 HMR, . Capacity: 10-round rotary magazine. Barrel: 22 in. Weight: 5.4–5.6 lbs. Features: Delayed blowback action, Savage AccuTrigger, synthetic or laminated stock. Target model has heavy barrel, sporter or thumbhole stock. Introduced in 2016.
Price: Standard model **$473.00**
Price: Sporter (Gray laminate stock) **$574.00**
Price: Target Sporter **$571.00**
Price: Target Thumbhole **$631.00**
Price: A17 Pro Varmint **$739.00**
Price: A17 Overwatch camo **$599.00**
Price: A17 HM2 chambered for 17HM2 with black synthetic stock **$409.00**

SAVAGE A22 SERIES
Caliber: .22 LR, .22 WMR. Capacity 10-round magazine. Similar to A17 series except for caliber.
Price: **$284.00**
Price: A22 SS stainless barrel **$419.00**
Price: Target Thumbhole stock, heavy barrel **$449.00**
Price: Pro Varmint w/Picatinny rail, heavy bbl., target stock **$409.00**
Price: 22 WMR **$479.00**
Price: A22 Pro Varmint **$569.00**
Price: A22 Pro Varmint Magnum in .22 WMR **$739.00**
Price: A22 FV-SR Overwatch Camo **$429.00**
Price: A22 Precision with MDT Chassis **$659.00**
Price: A22 Precision Lite with carbon-fiber stainless barrel **$949.00**

SAVAGE A22 BNS-SR
Caliber: .22 LR. Capacity: 10. Barrel: 18 In., carbon steel. Stock: Laminated wood. Sights: Two-piece Weaver bases, no scope included. Weight: 6.6 lbs. Features: Ergonomic stock, AccuTrigger, straight blowback semi-auto.
Price: **$479.00**

SAVAGE B-SERIES PRECISION
Calibers: .22 LR, .22 WMR, .17 HMR. Capacity: 10-round detachable magazine. Barrel: 18 in heavy carbon steel, threaded. Weight: from 5 lbs. 5 oz. Stock: MDT one-piece billet aluminum chassis with adjustable LOP and comb height. Sights: None. One-piece Picatinny rail. Features: B-Series Precision rifles are built for target performance. They include the B22 in .22 LR, B22 Magnum in .22 WMR, and B17 in .17 HMR. Adjustable AccuTrigger with red trigger detail.
Price: **$659.00**
Price: B-Series Precision Lite 18 in. carbon fiber bbl. wrap **$949.00**

SMITH & WESSON M&P15-22 SERIES
Caliber: .22 LR. Capacities: 10- or 25-round magazine. Barrel: 15.5 in., 16 in. or 16.5 in. Stock: 6-position telescoping or fixed. Features: A rimfire version of AR-derived M&P tactical autoloader. Operates with blowback action. Quad-mount Picatinny rails, plain barrel or compensator, alloy upper and lower, matte black metal finish. Kryptek Highlander or Muddy Girl camo finishes available.
Price: Standard **$449.00**
Price: Kryptek Highlander or Muddy Girl camo **$499.00**
Price: MOE Model with Magpul sights, stock and grip **$609.00**
Price: Performance Center upgrades, threaded barrel **$789.00**
Price: M&P 15 Sport w/Crimson Trace Red Dot sight **$759.00**

THOMPSON/CENTER T/CR22
Caliber: .22 LR. Capacities: 10-round rotary magazine. Barrel: 20 in. stainless steel, threaded muzzle. Stock: Hogue overmolded sculpted and ambidextrous thumbhole. Features: Picatinny top rail, sling swivel studs, push-button safety, fully machined aluminum receiver with hole to allow cleaning from rear. From the Smith & Wesson Performance Center.
Price: **$497.00**

VOLQUARTSEN CLASSIC
Calibers: .22 LR, .22 WMR, .17 HMR. Capacity: 10-round rotary magazine. Barrel: .920-in. stainless bull barrel threaded into receiver. Weight: from 5 lbs. 5oz. Stock: Choice of multiple options, including black Hogue or colored laminate wood sporter style. Sights: Integral Picatinny rail Features: Classic semi-automatic is the foundation of all subsequent models. Match bore and chamber tolerances for bolt-action accuracy from a repeater. Stainless steel CNC-machined receiver. TG2000 for crisp 2.25-lb. trigger pull.
Price: **$1,504.00**

VOLQUARTSEN VF-ORYX
Caliber: 22 LR Capacity: 10-round magazine. Barrel: 18.5-in. free-floating, snake-fluted. Weight: 9 lbs. 3 oz. Stock: MDT Oryx one-piece aluminum chassis. Sights: Integral 20 MOA rail. Features: CNC-machined stainless steel receiver. Barrel threaded into receiver for rigidity. CNC'ed bolt with round titanium firing pin and tuned extractor. TG2000 trigger group with crisp 2.25-lb. pull. Stock tailored for bench, bipod, and prone shooting. Adjustable cheek riser, overmolded pistol grip, and LOP spacer.
Price: **$1,944.00**
Price: VF-ORYX-S package with Zeiss Conquest **$3,269.00**

VOLQUARTSEN VT2
Caliber: .22 LR, .22 WMR, .17 HMR. Capacity: 9-shot detachable magazine. Barrel: 16.5-in. carbon-fiber tensioned with flush-fitting blow-forward compensator and aluminum thread protector. Stock: Magpul Milspec stock and MOE-K grip. Available in both 6 and 12-in. handguard lengths with M-LOK on both. Sights: Integral 0 MOA Picatinny rail. Features: VT2 semi-automatic takedown design utilizes a unique button and lever combination to slide the barrel out of the receiver for easy stowing. Unique new design VT2 rifles built for either .22 WMR and .17 HMR to swap calibers simply by changing the barrel. TG2000 trigger set at 2.5 lbs. Made in the USA.
Price: .22 LR **$2,207.00**
Price: .17 HMR, .22 WMR **$2,352.00**
Price: Short Handguard model **$2,207.00**
Price: .17 HMR, .22 WMR Combo **$2,871.00**

WINCHESTER WILDCAT 22 SR (SUPPRESSOR READY)
Caliber: .22 LR. Capacity: 10-round rotary magazine. Barrel: 16.5-in. precision button-rifled chromoly steel with threaded muzzle, thread protector, and recessed target crown. Weight: 4.0 lbs. Length: 34.75 in. Stock: Black polymer ambidextrous skeletonized buttstock with textured grip panels. Sights: Fully adjustable ghost ring rear and ramped post front. Also, integral Picatinny rail. Features: Suppressor-ready version of the company's lightweight repeating rimfire. Rotary magazine system with last round bolt hold open. Dual ambidextrous magazine releases. Reversible manual safety button. Suppressor not included.
Price: **$299.00**
Price: Wildcat SR True Timber Strata **$329.00**

Prices given are believed to be accurate at time of publication however, many factors affect retail pricing so exact prices are not possible.

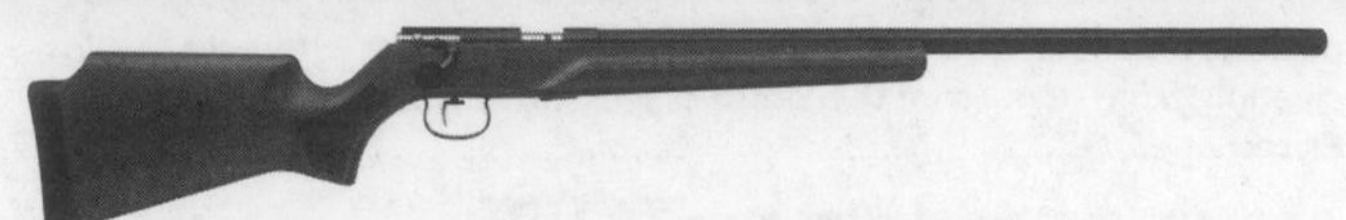

ANSCHUTZ MODEL 64 MP
Caliber: .22 LR. Capacity: 5-round magazine. Barrel: 25.6-in. heavy match. Weight: 9 lbs. Stock: Multipurpose hardwood with beavertail fore-end. Sights: None. Drilled and tapped for scope or receiver sights. Features: Model 64S BR (benchrest) has 20-in. heavy barrel, adjustable two-stage match-grade trigger, flat beavertail stock. Imported from Germany by Steyr Arms.
Price: **$1,399.00**

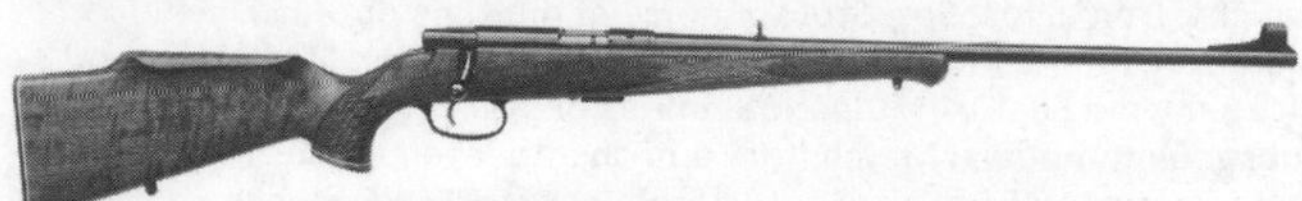

ANSCHUTZ 1416D/1516D CLASSIC
Calibers: .22 LR (1416D888), .22 WMR (1516D). Capacity: 5-round magazine. Barrel: 22.5 in. Weight: 6 lbs. Length: 41 in. overall. Stock: European hardwood with walnut finish; classic style with straight comb, checkered pistol grip and fore-end. Sights: Hooded ramp front, folding leaf rear. Features: Uses Match 64 action. Adjustable single-stage trigger. Receiver grooved for scope mounting. Imported from Germany by Steyr Arms.
Price: 1416D .22 LR **$1,199.00**
Price: 1416D Classic left-hand **$1,249.00**
Price: 1516D .22 WMR **$1,249.00**
Price: 1416D, thumbhole stock **$1,649.00**

ANSCHUTZ 1710D CUSTOM
Caliber:.22 LR. Capacity: 5-round magazine. Barrels: 23.75- or 24.25-in. heavy contour. Weights: 6.5–7.375 lbs. Length: 42.5 in. overall. Stock: Select European walnut. Sights: Hooded ramp front, folding leaf rear; drilled and tapped for scope mounting. Features: Match 54 action with adjustable single-stage trigger; roll-over Monte Carlo cheekpiece, slim fore-end with Schnabel tip, Wundhammer palm swell on pistol grip, rosewood grip cap with white diamond insert; skip-line checkering on grip and fore-end. Introduced 1988. Imported from Germany by Steyr Arms.
Price: **$2,195.00**

BERGARA B-14 RIMFIRE
Caliber: .22 LR. Capacity: 10. Barrel: 18 in., 4140 Bergara. Stock: HMR composite. Sights: None. Weight: 9.25 lbs. Features: Threaded muzzle, B-14R action, Remington 700 accessories compatible.
Price: **$1,150.00**

BROWNING BL-22
Caliber: .22 LR. Capacity: Tubular magazines, 15+1. Action: Short-throw lever action, side ejection. Rack-and-pinion lever. Barrel: Recessed muzzle. Stock: Walnut, two-piece straight-grip Western style. Trigger: Half-cock hammer safety; fold-down hammer. Sights: Bead post front, folding-leaf rear. Steel receiver grooved for scope mount. Weight: 5–5.4 lbs. Length: 36.75–40.75 in. overall. Features: Action lock provided. Introduced 1996. FLD Grade II Octagon has octagonal 24-in. barrel, silver nitride receiver with scroll engraving, gold-colored trigger. FLD Grade I has satin-nickel receiver, blued trigger, no stock checkering. FLD Grade II has satin-nickel receivers with scroll engraving; gold-colored trigger, cut checkering. Both introduced 2005. Grade I has blued receiver and trigger, no stock checkering. Grade II has gold-colored trigger, cut checkering, blued receiver with scroll engraving. Imported from Japan by Browning.
Price: BL-22 Grade I/II, From .... **$620.00–$700.00**
Price: BL-22 FLD Grade I/II, From .... **$660.00–$750.00**
Price: BL-22 FLD, Grade II Octagon **$980.00**

BROWNING T-BOLT RIMFIRE
Calibers: .22 LR, .17 HMR, .22 WMR. Capacity: 10-round rotary box double helix magazine. Barrel: 22-in. free-floating, semi-match chamber, target muzzle crown. Weight: 4.8 lbs. Length: 40.1 in. overall. Stock: Walnut, maple or composite. Sights: None. Features: Straight-pull bolt action, three-lever trigger adjustable for pull weight, dual action screws, sling swivel studs. Crossbolt lockup, enlarged bolt handle, one-piece dual extractor with integral spring and red cocking indicator band, gold-tone trigger. Top-tang, thumb-operated two-position safety, drilled and tapped for scope mounts. Varmint model has raised Monte Carlo comb, heavy barrel, wide forearm. Introduced 2006. Imported from Japan by Browning. Left-hand models added in 2009.
Price: .22 LR, From .... **$750.00–$780.00**
Price: Composite Target .... **$780.00–$800.00**
Price: .17 HMR/.22 WMR, From .... **$790.00–$830.00**

BROWNING T-BOLT TARGET W/ MUZZLE BRAKE
Calibers: .22 LR, .22 WMR, .17 HMR. Capacity: 10-round Double Helix box magazine. Barrel: 16.5-in. heavy bull. Sights: No iron sights. Drilled and tapped. Length: 34.75 in. Weight: 6 lbs. 2 oz. Stock: Black Walnut with satin-finish, checkered, Monte Carlo style. Features: Precision straight-pull bolt-action rimfire. Extra-wide fore-end. Free floating heavy bull target barrel threaded at 1/2x28. Includes removeable muzzle brake. Steel receiver with blued finish. Semi-match chamber and target crown. Top tang safety. Adjustable trigger. Sling studs. Plastic buttplate. Cut checkering at 20 LPI. Gold-plated trigger.
Price: .... **$699.00–$739.00**

CHIPMUNK SINGLE SHOT
Caliber: .22 Short, Long and Long Rifle or .22 WMR. Manually cocked single-shot bolt-action youth gun. Barrel: 16.125 in. blued or stainless. Weight: 2.6 lbs. Length: 30 in., LOP 11.6 in. Stock: Synthetic, American walnut or laminate. Barracuda model has ergonomic thumbhole stock with raised comb, accessory rail. Sights: Adjustable rear peep, fixed front. From Keystone Sporting Arms.
Price: Synthetic .... **$163.00-$250.00**
Price: Walnut .... **$209.00-$270.00**
Price: Barracuda .... **$258.00-$294.00**

COOPER MODEL 57-M REPEATER
Calibers: .22 LR, .22 WMR, .17 HMR, .17 Mach. Barrel: 22 in. or 24 in. Weight: 6.5–7.5 lbs. Stock: Claro walnut, 22 LPI hand checkering. Sights: None furnished. Features: Three rear locking lug, repeating bolt-action with 5-round magazine for .22 LR; 4-round magazine for .22 WMR and 17 HMR. Fully adjustable trigger. Left-hand models add $150 to base rifle price. 0.250-in. group rimfire accuracy guarantee at 50 yards; 0.5-in. group centerfire accuracy guarantee at 100 yards. Options include wood upgrades, case-color metalwork, barrel fluting, custom LOP, and many others.
Price: Classic **$2,495.00**
Price: Custom Classic **$2,995.00**
Price: Western Classic **$3,795.00**
Price: Schnabel **$2,595.00**
Price: Jackson Squirrel **$2,595.00**
Price: Jackson Hunter **$2,455.00**
Price: Mannlicher **$4,755.00**

CZ 457 AMERICAN

Calibers: .17 HMR, .22 LR, .22 WMR. Capacity: 5-round detachable magazine. Barrel: 24.8 in. Weight: 6.2 lbs. Stock: Turkish walnut American style with high flat comb. Sights: None. Integral 11mm dovetail scope base. Features: Adjustable trigger, push-to-fire safety, interchangeable barrel system.

Price: **$476.00**
Price: .17 HMR .22 WMR **$496.00**
Price: Varmint model........ **$660.00-$762.00**

CRICKETT SINGLE SHOT

Caliber: .22 Short, Long and Long Rifle or .22 WMR. Manually cocked single-shot bolt-action. Similar to Chipmunk but with more options and models. Barrel: 16.125 in. blued or stainless. Weight: 3 lbs. Length: 30 in., LOP 11.6 in. Stock: Synthetic, American walnut or laminate. Available in wide range of popular camo patterns and colors. Sights: Adjustable rear peep, fixed front. Drilled and tapped for scope mounting using special Chipmunk base. Alloy model has AR-style buttstock, XBR has target stock and bull barrel, Precision Rifle has bipod and fully adjustable thumbhole stock.

Price: Alloy **$300.00**
Price: XBR........ **$380.00-$400.00**
Price: Precision Rifle .... **$316.00-$416.00**
Price: Adult Rifle .... **$240.00-$280.00**

HENRY LEVER-ACTION RIFLES

Caliber: .22 Long Rifle (15 shot), .22 Magnum (11 shots), .17 HMR (11 shots). Barrel: 18.25 in. round. Weight: 5.5–5.75 lbs. Length: 34 in. overall (.22 LR). Stock: Walnut. Sights: Hooded blade front, open adjustable rear. Features: Polished blue finish; full-length tubular magazine; side ejection; receiver grooved for scope mounting. Introduced 1997. Made in USA by Henry Repeating Arms Co.

Price: H001 Carbine .22 LR **$378.00**
Price: H001L Carbine .22 LR, Large Loop Lever........ **$394.00**
Price: H001Y Youth model (33 in. overall, 11-round .22 LR) **$378.00**
Price: H001M .22 Magnum, 19.25 in. octagonal barrel, deluxe walnut stock **$525.00**
Price: H001V .17 HMR, 20 in. octagonal barrel, Williams Fire Sights **$578.00**
Price: Frontier Threaded Barrel, Suppressor-Ready .22 LR **$552.00**
Price: Frontier Threaded Barrel, Suppressor-Ready .22 WMR **$656.00**

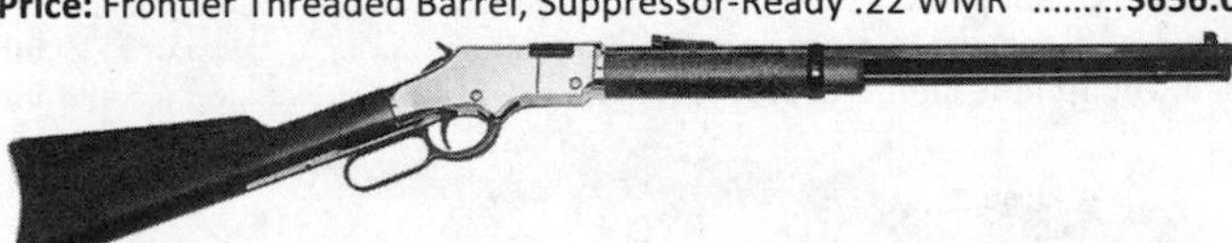

HENRY LEVER-ACTION OCTAGON FRONTIER MODEL

Same as lever rifles except chambered in .17 HMR, .22 Short/Long/LR, .22 Magnum. Barrel: 20 in. octagonal. Sights: Marble's fully adjustable semi-buckhorn rear, brass bead front. Weight: 6.25 lbs. Made in USA by Henry Repeating Arms Co.

Price: H001T Lever Octagon .22 S/L/R **$473.00**
Price: H001TM Lever Octagon .22 Magnum, .17 HMR **$578.00**

HENRY GOLDEN BOY SERIES

Calibers: .17 HMR, .22 LR (16-shot), .22 Magnum. Barrel: 20 in. octagonal. Weight: 6.25 lbs. Length: 38 in. overall. Stock: American walnut. Sights: Blade front, open rear. Features: Brasslite receiver, brass buttplate, blued barrel and lever. Introduced 1998. Made in USA from Henry Repeating Arms Co.

Price: H004 .22 LR........ **$578.00**
Price: H004M .22 Magnum **$625.00**
Price: H004V .17 HMR **$641.00**
Price: H004DD .22 LR Deluxe, engraved receiver........ **$1,575.00-1,654.00**

HENRY SILVER BOY

Calibers: 17 HMR, .22 S/L/LR, .22 WMR. Capacities: Tubular magazine. 12 rounds (.17 HMR and .22 WMR), 16 rounds (.22 LR), 21 rounds (.22 Short). Barrel: 20 in. Stock: American walnut with curved buttplate. Finish: Nickel receiver, barrel band and buttplate. Sights: Adjustable buckhorn rear, bead front. Silver Eagle model has engraved scroll pattern from early original Henry rifle. Offered in same calibers as Silver Boy. Made in USA from Henry Repeating Arms Company.

Price: .22 S/L/LR **$630.00**
Price: .22 WMR **$682.00**
Price: .17 HMR **$709.00**
Price: Silver Eagle........ **$892.00–$945.00**

HENRY PUMP ACTION

Caliber: .22 LR. Capacity: 15 rounds. Barrel: 18.25 in. Weight: 5.5 lbs. Length: NA. Stock: American walnut. Sights: Bead on ramp front, open adjustable rear. Features: Polished blue finish; receiver grooved for scope mount; grooved slide handle; two barrel bands. Introduced 1998. Made in USA from Henry Repeating Arms Co.

Price: H003T .22 LR........ **$578.00**
Price: H003TM .22 Magnum **$620.00**

MARLIN MODEL XT-17 SERIES

Caliber: .17 HRM. Capacity: 4- and 7-round, two magazines included. Barrel: 22 in. Weight: 6 lbs. Stock: Black synthetic with palm swell, stippled grip areas, or walnut-finished hardwood with Monte Carlo comb. Laminated stock available. Sights: Adjustable rear, ramp front. Drilled and tapped for scope mounts. Features: Adjustable trigger. Blue or stainless finish.

Price: .... **$269.00–$429.00**

MARLIN MODEL XT-22 SERIES

Calibers: .22 Short, .22 Long, .22 LR. Capacities: Available with 7-shot detachable box magazine or tubular magazine (17 to 22 rounds). Barrels: 22 in. Varmint model has heavy barrel. Weight: 6 lbs. Stock: Black synthetic, walnut-finished hardwood, walnut or camo. Tubular model available with two-tone brown laminated stock. Finish: Blued or stainless. Sights: Adjustable rear, ramp front. Some models have folding rear sight with a hooded or high-visibility orange front sight. Features: Pro-Fire Adjustable Trigger, Micro-Groove rifling, thumb safety with red cocking indicator. The XT-22M series is chambered for .22 WMR. Made in USA by Marlin Firearms Co.

Price: .... **$221.00–$340.00**
Price: XT-22M .... **$240.00–$270.00**

MEACHAM LOW-WALL

Calibers: Any rimfire cartridge. Barrels: 26–34 in. Weight: 7-15 lbs. Sights: none. Tang drilled for Win. base, .375 in. dovetail slot front. Stock: Fancy eastern walnut with cheekpiece; ebony insert in forearm tip. Features: Exact copy of 1885 Winchester. With most Winchester factory options available including double-set triggers. Introduced 1994. Made in USA by Meacham T&H Inc.

Price: From........ **$4,999.00**

MOSSBERG MODEL 464 RIMFIRE
Caliber: .22 LR. Capacity: 14-round tubular magazine. Barrel: 20-in. round blued. Weight: 5.6 lbs. Length: 35.75 in. overall. Features: Adjustable sights, straight grip stock, plain hardwood straight stock and fore-end. Lever-action model.
Price: **$503.00**
Price: SPX Tactical model, adjustable synthetic stock **$525.00**

MOSSBERG MODEL 801/802
Caliber: .22 LR Capacity: 10-round magazine. Barrel: 18 in. free-floating. Varmint model has 21-in. heavy barrel. Weight: 4.1–4.6 lbs. Sights: Adjustable rifle. Receiver grooved for scope mount. Stock: Black synthetic. Features: Ergonomically placed magazine release and safety buttons, crossbolt safety, free gun lock. 801 Half Pint has 12.25-in. LOP, 16-in. barrel and weighs 4 lbs. Hardwood stock; removable magazine plug.
Price: Plinkster **$242.00**
Price: Half Pint **$242.00**
Price: Varmint **$242.00**

NEW ULTRA LIGHT ARMS 20RF
Caliber: .22 LR, single-shot or repeater. Barrel: Douglas, length to order. Weight: 5.25 lbs. Length: Varies. Stock: Kevlar/graphite composite, variety of finishes. Sights: None furnished; drilled and tapped for scope mount. Features: Timney trigger, hand-lapped action, button-rifled barrel, hand-bedded action, recoil pad, sling-swivel studs, optional Jewell trigger. Made in USA by New Ultra Light Arms.
Price: 20 RF single shot **$1,800.00**
Price: 20 RF repeater **$1,850.00**

PEDERSOLI BLACK WIDOW
Calibers: .22 LR. Capacity: Single shot. Barrel: 19-in. round steel. Weight: 3.3 lbs. Stock: Black techno-polymer folder with skeletonized buttstock and removeable forend. Sights: Iron sights. Drilled and tapped for Picatinny rail mounting. Features: Folding-style, single-shot rimfire. Threaded barrel with knurled thread protector cap. Integral ammo storage along buttstock. Forward Picatinny rail at base of forend. Built to fit into medium-sized backpack. European model threaded at ½-20 UNF. American version threaded at ½"-28 TPI.
Price: **$400.00**

ROSSI GALLERY
Caliber: 22 LR. Capacity: 15-round tubular magazine. Barrel: 18-in. round. Weight: 5.3 lbs. Length: 36 in. Stock: Choice of either German Beechwood or black synthetic. Sights: Traditional Buckhorn iron sights on wood model; fiber optics on synthetic model. Features: Pump action reminiscent of classic gallery guns of the 1890s. Polished black metalwork. Hammer fired with cross-bolt safety. Sling studs.
Price: German Beechwood **$360.00**
Price: Black Polymer **$315.00**

ROSSI RIO BRAVO
Caliber: 22 LR. Capacity: 15-round tubular magazine. Barrel: 18-in. round. Weight: 5.5 lbs. Length: 36 in. Stock: Choice of either German Beechwood or black synthetic. Sights: Traditional Buckhorn iron sights on wood model; fiber optics on synthetic model. Features: Lever action rimfire based on the company's R92 centerfires. Polished black metal finish. Hammer fired with cross-bolt safety. Sling studs.
Price: German Beechwood **$370.00**
Price: Black Polymer **$370.00**

ROSSI RIO BRAVO GOLD
Caliber: .22 LR. Capacity: 15-round tubular magazine. Barrel: 18-in. round. Weight: 5.5 lbs. Length: 36 in. Stock: German Beechwood. Sights: Traditional Buckhorn iron sights. Features: New "Gold" version of Rossi's lever-action rimfire based on the R92 centerfire. PVD gold receiver and lever finish with polished black on remaining metalwork. Hammer fired with cross-bolt safety. Sling studs.
Price: **$465.00**

RUGER AMERICAN RIMFIRE RIFLE
Calibers: .17 HMR, .22 LR,.22 WMR. Capacity: 10-round rotary magazine. Barrels: 22-in., or 18-in. threaded. Sights: Williams fiber optic, adjustable. Stock: Composite with interchangeable comb adjustments, sling swivels. Adjustable trigger.
Price: **$359.00**

RUGER PRECISION RIMFIRE RIFLE
Calibers: .17 HMR, .22 LR, .22 HMR. Capacity: 9 to 15-round magazine. Barrel: 18 in. threaded. Weight: 6.8 lbs. Stock: Quick-fit adjustable with AR-pattern pistol grip, free-floated handguard with Magpul M-LOK slots. Features: Adjustable trigger, oversized bolt handle, Picatinny scope base.
Price: **$529.00**

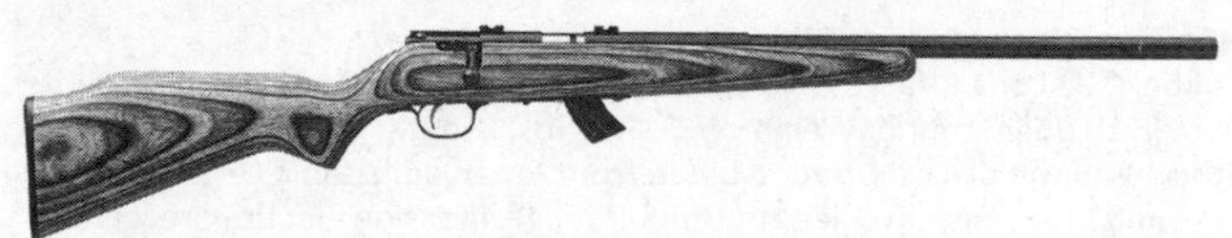

SAVAGE MARK II BOLT-ACTION
Calibers: .22 LR, .17 HMR. Capacity: 10-round magazine. Barrel: 20.5 in. Weight: 5.5 lbs. Length: 39.5 in. overall. Stock: Camo, laminate, thumbhole or OD Green stock available Sights: Bead front, open adjustable rear. Receiver grooved for scope mounting. Features: Thumb-operated rotating safety. Blue finish. Introduced 1990. Made in Canada, from Savage Arms, Inc.
Price: .... **$228.00–$280.00**
Price: Varmint w/heavy barrel **$242.00**
Price: Camo stock **$280.00**
Price: OD Green stock **$291.00**
Price: Multi-colored laminate stock **$529.00**
Price: Thumbhole laminate stock **$469.00**

SAVAGE MODEL 93FVSS MAGNUM
Similar to Model 93FSS Magnum except 21-in. heavy barrel with recessed target-style crown, satin-finished stainless barreled action, black graphite/fiberglass stock. Drilled and tapped for scope mounting; comes with Weaver-style bases. Introduced 1998. Imported from Canada by Savage Arms, Inc.
Price: **$364.00**

SAVAGE B SERIES
Calibers: .17 HMR, .22 LR, 22 WMR. Capacity: 10-round rotary magazine. Barrel: 21 in. (16.25 in. threaded heavy barrel on Magnum FV-SR Model). Stock: Black synthetic with target-style vertical pistol grip. Weight: 6 lbs. Features include top tang safety, Accutrigger. Introduced in 2017.
Price: .... **$281.00–$445.00**

Prices given are believed to be accurate at time of publication however, many factors affect retail pricing so exact prices are not possible.

SAVAGE MARK II MINIMALIST
Choice of Green or Brown Boyd's Minimalist laminate stock design.
Price: **$379.00**

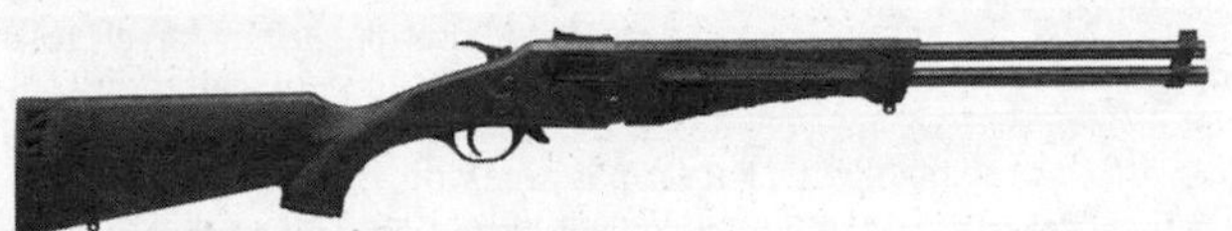

SAVAGE MODEL 42
Calibers/Gauges: Break-open over/under design with .22 LR or .22 WMR barrel over a .410 shotgun barrel. Under-lever operation. Barrel: 20 in. Stock: Synthetic black matte. Weight: 6.1 lbs. Sights: Adjustable rear, bead front. Updated variation of classic Stevens design from the 1940s.
Price **$509.00**

SAVAGE RASCAL
Caliber: .22 LR. Capacity: Single shot. Barrel: 16.125-in. carbon steel. Weight: 2.71 lbs. Length: 30.6 in. Stock: Synthetic sporter. Upgraded models available with different stock options. Sights: Adjustable peep sights. Features: Micro-rimfire bolt action with short 11.25-inch length of pull for the smallest framed shooters. Cocks by lifting the bolt and unloads without pulling the trigger. User-adjustable AccuTrigger. Feed ramp. Manual safety.
Price **$199.00**
Price Rascal FV-SR Left Hand **$249.00**
Price Rascal Target.. **$339.00**
Price Rascal Target XP.. **$429.00**

SAVAGE RASCAL MINIMALIST
Caliber: .22 LR. Capacity: single shot. Barrel: 16.125-in. carbon steel, threaded with protector. Length: 30.625 in. Weight: 3.5 lbs. Stock: Minimalist hybrid laminate design in two color options. Features: Addition to the micro-sized Rascal single shot, bolt-action family. Blued carbon steel receiver. Manual safety. Cocks by lifting the bolt. Unloads without pulling the trigger. 11-degree target crown. Adjustable peep sight. Sling studs. User-adjustable AccuTrigger. Feed ramp. ChevCore Laminate technology with Boyd's stock in two color options: Pink/Purple or Teal/Gray. Short 11.5-in length of pull. Package includes ear plugs and firearms lock.
Price: **$289.00**

STEYR ZEPHYR II
Calibers: .22 LR, .22 WMR, .17 HMR. Capacity: 5-round detachable magazine. Barrel: 19.7 in cold-hammer forged with Mannox finish. Option of standard or threaded. Weight: 5.8 lbs. Length: 39.2 in. Stock: European Walnut with Bavarian cheekpiece and fish scale checkering. Sights: No iron sights. 11mm receiver dovetail. Features: Rebirth of the original Zephyr rifle produced from 1955–1971. Single-stage trigger. Tang safety. Sling swivels. Gold trigger. Pistol grip features inset Steyr logo. Recessed target crown. Dual extractors.
Price **$1,099.00**

TIKKA T1x MTR
Calibers: .22 LR or .17 HMR. Capacity: 10-round polymer magazine. Barrel: 20-in. cold hammer forged, crossover profile. Weight: 5.7 lbs. Length: 39.6 in. Stock: Modular Black synthetic. Sights: No iron sights. Dovetailed and tapped. Features: Stainless steel bolt for smooth movement and weather resistance. Compatible with most T3x accessories. Action shares same bedding surfaces and inlay footprint with the T3x centerfire rifles. Threaded muzzle. Adjustable single-stage trigger.
Price **$529.00**

VOLQUARTSEN SUMMIT
Calibers: .22 LR or .17 Mach2. Capacity: 10-round rotary magazine. Barrel: 16.5-in. lightweight carbon fiber with threaded muzzle. Stainless steel tapered barrel also available. Weight: 4 lbs. 13 oz.–7 lbs. 11 oz. Stock: Available with multiple stock options, including black Hogue, colored Magpul, McMillan Sporter, or Laminated Silhouette Wood sporter. Sights: Integral 20 MOA Picatinny rail. Features: Unique straight-pull bolt-action rimfire inspired by the 10/22 platform. Built for both competition shooting and small game hunting. CNC-machined receiver with integral rail. Suppressor ready. Accepts 10/22-style magazines. Crisp 1.75-lb. trigger pull. Made in the USA.
Price **$1,252.00**

WINCHESTER XPERT
Calibers: .22 LR. Capacity: 10-round rotary detachable magazine, interchangeable with both Wildcat and Ruger 10/22. Barrel: 18-in. precision button rifled with recessed target crown. Weight: 4 lbs. 8 oz. Length: 36.25 in. Stock: Gray Synthetic skeletonized with optional LOP spacers and cheek riser. Sights: Adjustable rear and ramped post front. Drilled and tapped. Features: Bolt-action precision cousin to the Wildcat line of semi-auto rimfires. Xpert uses a rimfire version of the M.O.A. trigger found on Model 70 and XPR rifles. Semi-match Bentz chamber and hemispherical firing pin. Extended bolt handle. Ambidextrous side-mounted mag releases. Plastic butt plate.
Price: **$319.00**

Prices given are believed to be accurate at time of publication however, many factors affect retail pricing so exact prices are not possible.

ANSCHUTZ 1903 MATCH
Caliber: .22 LR. Capacity: Single-shot. Barrel: 21.25 in. Weight: 8 lbs. Length: 43.75 in. overall. Stock: Walnut-finished hardwood with adjustable cheekpiece; stippled grip and fore-end. Sights: None furnished. Features: Uses Anschutz Match 64 action. A medium weight rifle for intermediate and advanced Junior Match competition. Available from Champion's Choice.
Price: Right-hand $1,195.00

ANSCHUTZ 1912 SPORT
Caliber: .22 LR. Barrel: 26 in. match. Weight: 11.4 lbs. Length: 41.7 in. overall. Stock: Non-stained thumbhole stock adjustable in length with adjustable buttplate and cheekpiece adjustment. Flat fore-end raiser block 4856 adjustable in height. Hook buttplate. Sights: None furnished. Features: in. Free rifle in. for women. Smallbore model 1907 with 1912 stock: Match 54 action. Delivered with: Hand stop 6226, fore-end raiser block 4856, screwdriver, instruction leaflet with test target. Available from Champion's Choice.
Price: $2,995.00

ANSCHUTZ 1913 SUPER MATCH RIFLE
Same as the Model 1911 except European walnut International-type stock with adjustable cheekpiece, or color laminate, both available with straight or lowered fore-end, adjustable aluminum hook buttplate, adjustable hand stop, weighs 13 lbs., 46 in. overall. Stainless or blued barrel. Available from Champion's Choice.
Price: Right-hand, blued, no sights, walnut stock.. $3,799.00

ANSCHUTZ 1907 STANDARD MATCH RIFLE
Same action as Model 1913 but with 0.875-in. diameter 26-in. barrel (stainless or blues). Length: 44.5 in. overall. Weight: 10.5 lbs. Stock: Choice of stock configurations. Vented fore-end. Designed for prone and position shooting ISU requirements; suitable for NRA matches. Also available with walnut flat-forend stock for benchrest shooting. Available from Champion's Choice.
Price: Right-hand, blued, no sights.. $2,385.00

CADEX DEFENCE CDX-R7 CPS SERIES
Calibers: 6.5 Creedmoor, .308 Win. Capacity: Multiple magazine sleeves to fit most mags on the market. Barrel: 16.5-in. Bartlein heavy, straight-taper, fluted, threaded. Weight: 10.49 lbs. Length: 33.5 in. Stock: Lightweight with small contour forend tube and rail placement at 3, 6, and 9 o'clock. Takedown QD skeleton buttstock. Available in 14 color combinations. Cadex recoil pad, neoprene cheek pad, and rubberized grip panel. Sights: None. 0 MOA Picatinny rail standard, 20 or 30 MOA rails available. Features: Military-quality bolt-action platform for the civilian market. Spiral fluted bolt. DX2 Evo single-/two-stage selectable trigger. Optional MX2 muzzle brake. Hard case included.
Price: $4,479.00

CZ 457 VARMINT PRECISION CHASSIS
Caliber: .22 LR. Capacity: 5. Barrel: 16.5 or 24 in., suppressor ready, cold hammer-forged, heavy. Stock: Aluminum chassis. Sights: None, integral 11mm dovetail. Weight: 7 lbs. Features: Fully adjustable trigger, receiver mounted push-to-fire safety, swappable barrel system.
Price: $999.00

CZ 457 VARMINT PRECISION TRAINER MTR
Caliber: .22 LR. Capacity: 5-round detachable box magazine. Barrel: 16.2-in. cold hammer forged Varmint weight. Sights: No iron sights, integral 11mm Dovetail. Length: 33.5 in. Weight: 7.1 lbs. Stock: Manners carbon-fiber stock with colored highlights. Forearm is recessed, drilled, and threaded for ARCA rail. Features: The upgraded Varmint Precision Trainer makes use of a barrel borrowed from the Match Target Rifle (MTR). Match chamber. Heavy barrel threaded at 1/2x28. Designed to provide the same look and feel as a full-size tactical rifle but with more economical training. American-style, two position, push-to-fire safety. 60-degree bolt rotation. Fully adjustable trigger. Same swappable barrel system as the Model 455. Competition-grade rimfire rifle.
Price: $1,635.00

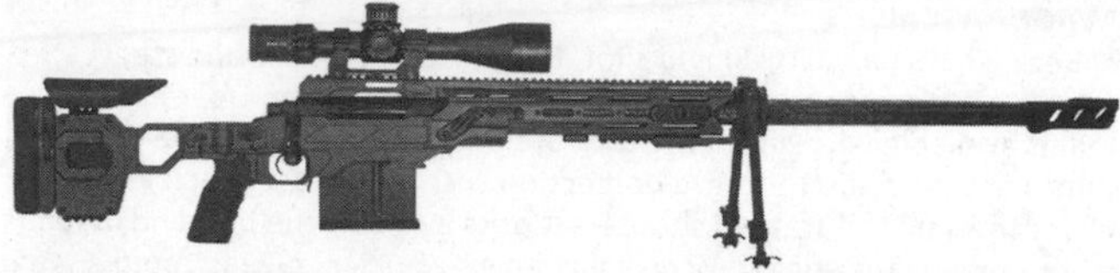

GUNWERKS HAMR 2.0
Calibers: .375 CheyTac. Barrel: 30 in. Carbon wrapped, threaded, with aggressive Cadex MX1 muzzle brake. Weight: 21.25 lbs. standard, total package. Stock: Cadex Defence Dual Strike tactical folding chassis-style with adjustable LOP. Sights: Comes standard with user option of scope (Kahles K525i, Leupold Mk 5HD, Revic PMR 428) on a 40 MOA mount. Features: Bolt-action ultra-long-range rifle built as a complete ELR system capable of shooting over two miles. The upgraded 2.0 version includes a carbon-wrapped barrel, new optic choices, and finish options. Included Elite Iron bipod encircles the centerline of the bore. Timney trigger set at 2.5 lbs. Prices increase significantly as options are added for custom factory builds. Long-range data package available.
Price: $9,150.00

HEYM HIGH PERFORMANCE PRECISION RIFLE (HPPR)
Calibers: Standard: .308 Win., 7mm Rem. Mag, .300 Win. Mag. Additional calibers available in 6.5 Creedmoor, 6.5x55, .270 Win., 7x64, .30-06 Spfld., and 8.5x63. Capacity: Detachable box magazine, varies by caliber. Barrel: 26-in. Krupp Steel, hammer forged, threaded, with protector. Sights: Top rail; available paired with Schmidt & Bender Precision Hunter scope. Weight: 8.0 lbs. Stock: PSE Carbon Precision with adjustable comb. Features: Precision shooting bolt actions from Heym built around two models, one SR21 with three-locking-lug turn bolt and the other SR30 straight pull. Single-stage trigger set at 3-lbs. with no creep or overtravel. Guaranteed 5-shot 20mm groups at 100 meters. Sling studs. Rubber recoil pad.
Price: $4,750.00

MASTERPIECE ARMS MPA BA PMR COMPETITION RIFLE
Calibers: .308 Win., 6mm Creedmoor, 6.5 Creedmoor. Capacity: 10. Barrel: 26 in., M24 stainless steel, polished. Stock: Aluminum chassis. Sights: None, optional package with MPA 30mm mount and Bushnell scope. Weight: 11.5 lbs. Features: Built-in inclinometer, MPA/Curtis action, match-grade chamber.
Price: .... $2,999.00-$3,459.00

ROCK RIVER ARMS RBG-1S
Calibers: .308 Win./7.62X51 NATO or 6.5 Creedmoor. Capacity: AICS/Magpul compatible box magazine. Barrel: 20-, 22-, or 24-in. stainless steel air-gauged, cryo-treated. Weight: 10.2 lbs. Length: 39.5–43.5 in.

Prices given are believed to be accurate at time of publication however, many factors affect retail pricing so exact prices are not possible.

Stock: KRG adjustable chassis in tan, black or green. Sights: 20 MOA rail. Also has standard scope base holes drilled for use with conventional ring mounts. Features: Rock River's first precision bolt-action rifles series. Precision aluminum bedding. One-piece, interchangeable two-lug bolt. Oversized knurled handle. TriggerTech trigger standard, with option of Timney upgrade. Toolless field adjustability. Guaranteed sub-MOA accuracy.
Price: **$4,235.00**

SAVAGE 110 ELITE PRECISION *(now adds LH)*
Calibers: .223 Rem., 6mm Creedmoor, 6.5 Creedmoor, .308 Win., .300 Win. Mag., .300 PRC, .338 Lapua. Capacity: 5- or 10-round AICS-pattern detachable box magazine. Barrel: 26 or 30 in stainless steel. Weight: 12.6–14.95 lbs. Stock: Modular Driven Technologies (MDT) Adjustable Core Competition aluminum chassis with Grey Cerakote finish. Sights: 20 MOA rail. Features: Factory blueprinted action. ARCA Rail along entire length of chassis. Titanium Nitride bolt body. User adjustable AccuTrigger. MDT vertical grip. Self-timing taper aligned muzzle brake on short action calibers only.
Price: ....**$1,999.00–$2,199.00**
Price: Left-hand model **$2,199.00**

SAVAGE IMPULSE ELITE PRECISION
Calibers: 6mm Creedmoor, 6.5 Creedmoor, .308 Win., 6.5 PRC, .300 Win. Mag., .300 PRC, .338 Lapua. Capacity: 5- or 10-round AICS magazine with ambidextrous release. Barrel: 26 or 30 in. precision button-rifled, stainless steel, modified Palma contour, with muzzle brake. Sights: Integral 20 MOA rail. Weight: 13.7 lbs. Stock: MDT Adjustable Core Competition chassis. Features: The straight-pull bolt action moves to Savage's Precision series rifles for faster split times. Action uses HexLock bolt system. Ambidextrous rotary bolt handle. Adjustable AccuTrigger. Matte black aluminum receiver. Removeable and user-adjustable round bolt knob handle. ARCA rail forend with M-LOK slots.
Price: **$2,499.00**

SEEKINS PRECISION HAVAK BRAVO
Calibers: 6mm Creedmoor, 6.5 Creedmoor, 6.5 PRC, .308 Win. Capacity: 5-round box magazine. Barrel: 24-in. 5R 416 stainless steel with threaded muzzle. Weight: 9.8 lbs. Stock: KRG Bravo Chassis in Black. OD Green, FDE, or Stealth Gray. Sights: 20 MOA Picatinny rail with five 8-32 screws. Features: Specialty bolt-action rifle built for hard-running, from SWAT to precision shooting. Matte black Cerakoted barreled action. Integrated recoil lug and M16-style extractor. Bolt with four locking lugs and 90-degree throw. Removeable bolt head. Extended magazine release.
Price: TRG-22..**$1,950.00**

SEEKINS PRECISION HAVAK ELEMENT
Calibers: .308 Win., 6mm Creedmoor, 6.5 PRC, 6.5 Creedmoor. Capacity: 3 to 5. Barrel: 21 in., Mountain Hunter contour, spiral fluted, threaded. Stock: Carbon composite. Sights: 20 MOA picatinny rail. Weight: 5.5 lbs. Features: Timney Elite Hunter trigger, M16-style extractor, 7075 aerospace aluminum/stainless steel body.
Price: **$2,795.00**

SEEKINS PRECISION HAVAK HIT
Calibers: 6mm GT, 6mm Creedmoor, 6.5 Creedmoor, .308 Win., 6.5 PRC. Capacity: Varies by chambering, compatible with single- or double-stack AICS magazines. Barrel: 24 in. 416 SS LT Tactical contour, threaded, with 5R rifling. Sights: 20 MOA rail. Length: 43.5 in; 34.5 in. folded. Weight: 11.5 lbs. Stock: Chassis-style, folding, available in black and FDE. Features: Bolt-action chassis rifle. A Pro version for competition is planned to follow. Changeable bolt head, M16-style extractor, integrated recoil lug. Quick-change barrel system. R700 trigger compatibility. Integral 20 MOA Picatinny rail. Carbon-fiber cheek piece, fully adjustable recoil pad, and toolless LOP adjustment.
Price: **$2,100.00**

SIG SAUER CROSS RIFLE
Calibers: .277 Sig Fury, .308 Win., 6.5 Creedmoor. Capacity: 5. Barrel: 16 to 18 in., stainless steel. Stock: Sig precision, polymer/alloy, folding. Sights: Picatinny rail. Weight: 6.5 to 6.8 lbs. Features: M-LOK rail, two-stage match trigger.
Price:..**$1,779.00**

SAKO TRG-22 BOLT-ACTION
Calibers: .308 Win., .260 Rem, 6.5 Creedmoor, .300 Win Mag, .338 Lapua. Capacity: 5-round magazine. Barrel: 26 in. Weight: 10.25 lbs. Length: 45.25 in. overall. Stock: Reinforced polyurethane with fully adjustable cheekpiece and buttplate. Sights: None furnished. Optional quick-detachable, one-piece scope mount base, 1 in. or 30mm rings. Features: Resistance-free bolt, free-floating heavy stainless barrel, 60-degree bolt lift. Two-stage trigger is adjustable for length, pull, horizontal or vertical pitch. TRG-42 has similar features but has long action and is chambered for .338 Lapua. Imported from Finland by Beretta USA.
Price: TRG-22 ....**$3,495.00**
Price: TRG-22 with folding stock **$6,400.00**
Price: TRG-42 ....**$4,445.00**
Price: TRG-42 with folding stock **$7,400.00**

SPRINGFIELD ARMORY M1A/M-21 TACTICAL MODEL
Similar to M1A Super Match except special sniper stock with adjustable cheekpiece and rubber recoil pad. Weighs 11.6 lbs. From Springfield Armory.
Price: **$3,619.00**
Price: Krieger stainless barrel..**$4,046.00**

ACCU-TEK AT-380 II ACP
Caliber: 380 ACP. Capacity: 6-round magazine. Barrel: 2.8 in. Weight: 23.5 oz. Length: 6.125 in. overall. Grips: Textured black composition. Sights: Blade front,rear adjustable for windage. Features: Made from 17-4 stainless steel, has an exposed hammer, manual firing-pin safety block and trigger disconnect. Magazine release located on the bottom of the grip. American made, lifetime warranty. Comes with two 6-round stainless steel magazines and a California-approved cable lock. Introduced 2006. Made in USA by Excel Industries.
Price: Satin stainless **$289.00**

ACCU-TEK HC-380
Similar to AT-380 II except has a 13-round magazine.
Price: **$330.00**

ACCU-TEK LT-380
Similar to AT-380 II except has a lightweight aluminum frame. Weight: 15 ounces.
Price: **$324.00**

AMERICAN CLASSIC 1911-A1 II SERIES
Caliber: .45 ACP, 9mm, .38 Super. Capacity: 8+1 magazine Barrel: 5 in. Grips: Checkered walnut. Sights: Novak-style rear, fixed front. Finish: Blue or hard chromed. Other variations include Trophy model with checkered mainspring housing, fiber optic front sight, hard-chrome finish.
Price: .... **$627-$700.00**

AMERICAN CLASSIC AMIGO SERIES
Caliber: .45 ACP. Capacity: 7+1. Same features as Commander size with 3.6-in. bull barrel and Officer-style frame.
Price: .... **$714.00-$813.00**

AMERICAN CLASSIC BX SERIES
Calibers: .45 ACP, 9mm. Capacity: 14- or 17-round magazine. Barrel: 5 in. Grips: Checkered aluminum. Sights: Mil-Spec style. Finish: Blue.
Price: **$774.00**

AMERICAN CLASSIC COMMANDER
Caliber: .45 ACP. Same features as 1911-A1 model except is Commander size with 4.25-in. barrel.
Price: .... **$624.00–$795.00**

AMERICAN CLASSIC COMPACT COMMANDER SERIES
Caliber: .45 ACP. Capacity: 7-round magazine. Barrel: 4.25 in. Grips: Textured hardwood. Sights: Fixed Novak style. Finish: Blue, hard chrome, two-tone.
Price: .... **$714.00-$812.00**

AMERICAN CLASSIC TROPHY
Caliber: .45 ACP. Capacity: 8-round magazine. Barrel: 5 in. Grips: Textured hardwood. Sights: Fixed, fiber-optic front/Novak rear. Finish: Hard chrome. Features: Front slide serrations, ambidextrous thumb safety.
Price: **$819.00**

AMERICAN TACTICAL IMPORTS MILITARY 1911
Caliber: .45 ACP. Capacity: 7+1 magazine. Barrel: 5 in. Grips: Textured mahogany. Sights: Fixed military style. Finish: Blue. Also offered in Commander and Officer's sizes and Enhanced model with additional features.
Price: .... **$500.00–$899.00**

AMERICAN TACTICAL IMPORTS GSG 1911
Caliber: .22 LR. Capacity: 10+1 magazine. Weight: 34 oz. Other features and dimensions similar to centerfire 1911.
Price: **$299.00**

AUTO-ORDNANCE 1911A1
Caliber: 45 ACP. Capacity: 7-round magazine. Barrel: 5 in. Weight: 39 oz. Length: 8.5 in. overall. Grips: Brown checkered plastic with medallion. Sights: Blade front, rear drift-adjustable for windage. Features: Same specs as 1911A1 military guns-parts interchangeable. Frame and slide blued; each radius has non-glare finish. Introduced 2002. Made in USA by Kahr Arms.
Price: 1911BKO Parkerized, plastic grips **$673.00**
Price: 1911BKOW Black matte finish, wood grips **$689.00**
Price: 1911BKOWWC1 Victory Girls Special **$750.00**

BAER 1911 BOSS .45
Caliber: .45 ACP. Capacity: 8+1 capacity. Barrel: 5 in. Weight: 37 oz. Length: 8.5 in. overall. Grips: Premium Checkered Cocobolo Grips. Sights: Low-Mount LBC Adj. Sight, Red Fiber Optic Front. Features: Speed Trigger, Beveled Mag Well, Rounded for Tactical. Rear cocking serrations on the slide, Baer fiber optic front sight (red), flat mainspring housing, checkered at 20 LPI, extended combat safety, Special tactical package, chromed complete lower, blued slide, (2) 8-round premium magazines.
Price: **$2,636.00**

BAER 1911 CUSTOM CARRY
Caliber: .45 ACP. Capacity: 7- or 10-round magazine. Barrel: 5 in. Weight: 37 oz. Length: 8.5 in. overall. Grips: Checkered walnut. Sights: Baer improved ramp-style dovetailed front, Novak low-mount rear. Features: Baer forged NM frame, slide and barrel with stainless bushing. Baer speed trigger with 4-lb. pull. Partial listing shown. Made in USA by Les Baer Custom, Inc.
Price: Custom Carry 5, blued **$2,190.00**
Price: Custom Carry 5, stainless **$2,290.00**
Price: Custom Carry 5, 9mm or .38 Super **$2,625.00**
Price: Custom Carry 4 Commanche-length, blued **$2,190.00**
Price: Custom Carry 4 Commanche-length, .38 Super **$2,550.00**

Prices given are believed to be accurate at time of publication however, many factors affect retail pricing so exact prices are not possible.

BAER 1911 PREMIER II

Calibers: .38 Super, .45 ACP. Capacity: 7- or 10-round magazine. Barrel: 5 in. Weight: 37 oz. Length: 8.5 in. overall. Grips: Checkered rosewood, double diamond pattern. Sights: Baer dovetailed front, low-mount Bo-Mar rear with hidden leaf. Features: Baer NM forged steel frame and barrel with stainless bushing, deluxe Commander hammer and sear, beavertail grip safety with pad, extended ambidextrous safety; flat mainspring housing; 30 LPI checkered front strap. Made in USA by Les Baer Custom, Inc.

Price: 5 in. .45 ACP **$2,2,245.00**
Price: 5 in. .38 Super, 9mm.......... **$2,968.00**
Price: 6 in. .45 ACP, .38 Super, 9mm.......... **$2,461.00-$2,925.00**
Price: Super-Tac, .45 ACP, .38 Super.......... **$2,729.00-3,917.00**
Price: 6-in Hunter 10mm.......... **$3090.00**

BAER 1911 S.R.P.

Caliber: .45 ACP. Barrel: 5 in. Weight: 37 oz. Length: 8.5 in. overall. Grips: Checkered walnut. Sights: Trijicon night sights. Features: Similar to the F.B.I. contract gun except uses Baer forged steel frame. Has Baer match barrel with supported chamber, complete tactical action. Has Baer Ultra Coat finish. Introduced 1996. Made in USA by Les Baer Custom, Inc.

Price: Government or Commanche Length **$2,925.00**

BAER 1911 STINGER

Calibers: .45 ACP or .38 Super. Capacity: 7-round magazine. Barrel: 5 in. Weight: 34 oz. Length: 8.5 in. overall. Grips: Checkered cocobolo. Sights: Baer dovetailed front, low-mount Bo-Mar rear with hidden leaf. Features: Baer NM frame. Baer Commanche slide, Officer's style grip frame, beveled mag well. Made in USA by Les Baer Custom, Inc.

Price: .45 ACP .... **$2,307.00–$2,379.00**
Price: .38 Super **$2,925.00**

BAER HEMI 572

Caliber: .45 ACP. Based on Les Baer's 1911 Premier I pistol and inspired by Chrysler 1970 Hemi Cuda muscle car. Features: Double serrated slide, Baer fiber optic front sight with green insert, VZ black recon grips with hex-head screws, hard chrome finish on all major components, Dupont S coating on barrel, trigger, hammer, ambi safety and other controls.

Price: **$2,770.00**

BAER ULTIMATE MASTER COMBAT

Calibers: .45 ACP or .38 Super. A full house competition 1911 offered in 8 variations including 5 or 6-inch barrel, PPC Distinguished or Open class, Bullseye Wadcutter class and others. Features include double serrated slide, fitted slide to frame, checkered front strap and trigger guard, serrated rear of slide, extended ejector, tuned extractor, premium checkered grips, blued finish and two 8-round magazines.

Price: Compensated .45 .... **$3,131.00**
Price: Compensated .38 Super **$3,234.00**

BAER 1911 MONOLITH S

Calibers: .45 ACP, .38 Super, 9mm, .40 S&W. A full house competition 1911 offered in 14 variations. Unique feature is extra-long dust cover that matches the length of the slide and reduces muzzle flip. Features include flat-bottom double serrated slide, low mount LBC adjustable sight with hidden rear leaf, dovetail front sight, flat serrated mainspring housing, premium checkered grips, blued finish and two 8-round magazines.

Price: .45 .... **From $2,419.00**
Price: .38 Super, .40 S&W .... **From $2,790.00**

BAER KENAI SPECIAL

Caliber: 10mm. Capacity: 9-round magazine. Barrel: 5 in. Features: Hard-chrome finish, double serrated slide, Baer fiber optic front sight with green or red insert, low-mount LBC adjustable rear sight, Baer black recon grips, special bear paw logo, flat serrated mainspring housing, lowered and flared ejection port, extended safety.

Price: **$3,630.00**

BAER GUNSITE PISTOL

Calibers: .45 ACP. Capacity: 8-round magazine. Barrel: 5 in. Features: double serrated slide, fitted slide to frame, flat serrated mainspring housing, flared and lowered ejection port, extended tactical thumb safety, fixed rear sight, dovetail front sight with night sight insert, all corners rounded, extended ejector, tuned extractor, premium checkered grips, blued finish and two 8-round magazines. Gunsite Raven logo on grips and slide.

Price: **$2,255.00**

BERETTA M92/96 A1 SERIES

Calibers: 9mm, .40 S&W. Capacities: 15-round magazine; .40 S&W, 12 rounds (M96 A1). Barrel: 4.9 in. Weight: 33-34 oz. Length: 8.5 in. Sights: Fiber optic front, adjustable rear. Features: Same as other models in 92/96 family except for addition of accessory rail.

Price: **$775.00**

BERETTA MODEL 92FS

Caliber: 9mm. Capacity: 10-round magazine. Barrels: 4.9 in., 4.25 in. (Compact). Weight: 34 oz. Length: 8.5 in. overall. Grips: Checkered black plastic. Sights: Blade front, rear adjustable for windage. Tritium night sights available. Features: Double action. Extractor acts as chamber loaded indicator, squared trigger guard, grooved front and backstraps, inertia firing pin. Matte or blued finish. Introduced 1977. Made in USA

Price: **$699.00**
Price: Inox **$850.00**

BERETTA MODEL 92G ELITE

Calibers: 9mm. Capacities: 15-round magazine. Barrel: 4.7 in. Weight: 33 oz. Length: 8.5 in. Sights: Fiber optic front, square notch rear. Features: M9A1 frame with M9A3 slide, front and rear serrations, ultra-thin VZ/LTT G10 grips, oversized mag release button, skeletonized trigger, ships with three magazines.

Price: **$1,100.00**

BERETTA M9 .22 LR

Caliber: .22 LR. Capacity: 10 or 15-round magazine. Features: Black Brunitron finish, interchangeable grip panels. Similar to centerfire 92/M9 with same operating controls, lighter weight (26 oz.).

Price: **$430.00**

BERETTA MODEL PX4 STORM

Calibers: 9mm, 40 S&W. Capacities: 17 (9mm Para.); 14 (40 S&W). Barrel: 4 in. Weight: 27.5 oz. Grips: Black checkered w/3 interchangeable backstraps. Sights: 3-dot system coated in Superluminova; removable front and rear sights. Features: DA/SA, manual safety/hammer decocking lever (ambi) and automatic firing pin block safety. Picatinny rail. Comes with two magazines (17/10 in 9mm Para. and 14/10 in 40 S&W). Removable hammer unit. American made by Beretta. Introduced 2005.

Price: 9mm or .40.......... **$650.00**
Price: .45 ACP **$700.00**
Price: .45 ACP SD (Special Duty).......... **$1,150.00**

BERETTA MODEL PX4 STORM SUB-COMPACT
Calibers: 9mm, 40 S&W. Capacities: 13 (9mm); 10 (40 S&W). Barrel: 3 in. Weight: 26.1 oz. Length: 6.2 in. overall. Grips: NA. Sights: NA. Features: Ambidextrous manual safety lever, interchangeable backstraps included, lock breech and tilt barrel system, stainless steel barrel, Picatinny rail.
Price: **$650.00**

BERETTA MODEL APX SERIES
Calibers: 9mm, 40 S&W. Capacities: 10, 17 (9mm); 10, 15 (40 S&W). Barrel: 4.25 or 3.7 in. (Centurion). Weight: 28, 29 oz. Length: 7.5 in. Sights: Fixed. Features: Striker fired, 3 interchangeable backstraps included, reversible mag release button, ambidextrous slide stop. Centurion is mid-size with shorter grip and barrel. Magazine capacity is two rounds shorter than standard model.
Price: **$575.00**

BERETTA MODEL M9
Caliber: 9mm. Capacity: 15. Barrel: 4.9 in. Weights: 32.2-35.3 oz. Grips: Plastic. Sights: Dot and post, low profile, windage adjustable rear. Features: DA/SA, forged aluminum alloy frame, delayed locking-bolt system, manual safety doubles as decocking lever, combat-style trigger guard, loaded chamber indicator. Comes with two magazines (15/10). American made by Beretta. Introduced 2005.
Price: **$675.00**

BERETTA MODEL M9A1
Caliber: 9mm. Capacity: 15. Barrel: 4.9 in. Weights: 32.2-35.3 oz. Grips: Plastic. Sights: Dot and post, low profile, windage adjustable rear. Features: Same as M9, but also includes integral Mil-Std-1913 Picatinny rail, has checkered front and backstrap. Comes with two magazines (15/10). American made by Beretta. Introduced 2005.
Price: **$775.00**

BERETTA M9A3
Caliber: 9mm. Capacity: 10 or 15. Features: Same general specifications as M9A1 with safety lever able to be converted to decocker configuration. Flat Dark Earth finish. Comes with three magazines, Vertec-style thin grip.
Price: **$1,100.00**

BERETTA BU9 NANO
Caliber: 9mm. Capacity: 6- or 8-round magazine. Barrel: 3.07 in. Weight: 17.7 oz. Length: 5.7 in. overall. Grips: Polymer. Sights: 3-dot low profile. Features: Double-action only, striker fired. Replaceable grip frames. Polymer frames offered in black, RE Blue, FDE, Rosa or Sniper Grey colors.
Price: **$450.00**

BERETTA PICO
Caliber: .380 ACP. Capacity: 6-round magazine. Barrel: 2.7 in. Weight: 11.5 oz. Length: 5.1 in. overall. Grips: Integral with polymer frame. Interchangeable backstrap. Sights: White outline rear. Features: Adjustable, quick-change. Striker-fired, double-action only operation. Ambidextrous magazine release and slide release. Available with Black, RE Blue, FDE or Lavender frame. Ships with two magazines, one flush, one with grip extension. Made in the USA.
Price: **$300.00**

BERSA THUNDER 45 ULTRA COMPACT
Caliber: .45 ACP. **Barrel:** 3.6 in. **Weight:** 27 oz. **Length:** 6.7 in. overall. **Grips:** Anatomically designed polymer. **Sights:** White outline rear. **Features:** Double action; firing pin safeties, integral locking system. Available in matte or duo-tone. Introduced 2003. Imported from Argentina by Eagle Imports, Inc.
Price: Thunder 45, matte blue **$500.00**

BERSA THUNDER 380 SERIES
Caliber: .380 ACP. **Capacity:** 7 rounds. **Barrel:** 3.5 in. **Weight:** 23 oz. **Length:** 6.6 in. overall. **Features:** Otherwise similar to Thunder 45 Ultra Compact. 380 DLX has 9-round capacity. 380 Concealed Carry has 8-round capacity. Imported from Argentina by Eagle Imports, Inc.
Price: Thunder Matte **$335.00**
Price: Thunder Satin Nickel **$355.00**
Price: Thunder Duo-Tone **$355.00**
Price: Thunder Duo-Tone with Crimson Trace Laser Grips **$555.00**
Price: Thunder CC Duo-Tone with aluminum frame.............................. **$346.00**

BERSA THUNDER 9 ULTRA COMPACT/40 SERIES
Calibers: 9mm, 40 S&W. Barrel: 3.5 in. Weight: 24.5 oz. Length: 6.6 in. overall. Features: Otherwise similar to Thunder 45 Ultra Compact. 9mm Para. High Capacity model has 17-round capacity. 40 High Capacity model has 13-round capacity. Imported from Argentina by Eagle Imports, Inc.
Price: **$500.00**

BERSA THUNDER 22
Caliber: .22 LR. Capacity: 10-round magazine. Weight: 19 oz. Features: Similar to Thunder .380 Series except for caliber. Alloy frame and slide. Finish: Matte black, satin nickel or duo-tone.
Price: **$320.00**

BERSA THUNDER PRO XT
Caliber: 9mm. Capacity: 17-round magazine. Barrel: 5 in. Weight: 34 oz. Grips: Checkered black polymer. Sights: Adjustable rear, dovetail fiber optic front. Features: Available with matte or duo-tone finish. Traditional double/single action design developed for competition. Comes with five magazines.
Price: **$923.00**

BROWNING 1911-22 COMPACT
Caliber: .22 LR Capacity: 10-round magazine. Barrel: 3.625 in. Weight: 15 oz. Length: 6.5 in. overall. Grips: Brown composite. Sights: Fixed. Features: Slide is machined aluminum with alloy frame and matte blue finish. Blowback action and single action trigger with manual thumb and grip safeties. Works, feels and functions just like a full-size 1911. It is simply scaled down and chambered in the best of all practice rounds: .22 LR for focus on the fundamentals.
Price: **$600.00**

BROWNING 1911-22 A1
Caliber: .22 LR, Capacity: 10-round magazine. Barrel: 4.25 in. Weight: 16 oz. Length: 7.0625 in. overall. Grips: Brown composite. Sights: Fixed. Features: Slide is machined aluminum with alloy frame and matte blue finish. Blowback action and single action trigger with manual thumb and grip safeties. Works, feels and functions just like a full-size 1911. It is simply scaled down and chambered in the best of all practice rounds: .22 LR for focus on the fundamentals.
Price: **$600.00**

BROWNING 1911-22 BLACK LABEL
Caliber: .22 LR. Capacity: 10-round magazine. Barrels: 4.25 in. or 3.625 in. (Compact model). Weight: 14 oz. overall. Features: Other features are similar to standard 1911-22 except for this model's composite/polymer frame, extended grip safety, stippled black laminated grip, skeleton trigger and hammer. Available with accessory rail (shown). Suppressor Ready model has threaded muzzle protector, 4.875-inch barrel.
Price: **$640.00**
Price: With Rail.. **$720.00**
Price: Suppressor Ready model.. **$800.00**

BROWNING 1911-22 POLYMER DESERT TAN
Caliber: .22 LR. Capacity: 10-round magazine. Barrels: 4.25 in. or 3.625 in. Weight: 13–14 oz. overall. Features: Other features are similar to standard 1911-22 except for this model's composite/polymer frame. Also available with pink composite grips.
Price: **$580.00**

BROWNING BUCK MARK CAMPER UFX
Caliber: .22 LR. Capacity: 10-round magazine. Barrel: 5.5-in. tapered bull. Weight: 34 oz. Length: 9.5 in. overall. Grips: Overmolded Ultragrip Ambidextrous. Sights: Pro-Target adjustable rear, ramp front. Features: Matte blue receiver, matte blue or stainless barrel.
Price: Camper UFX.. **$390.00**
Price: Camper UFX stainless **$430.00**

BROWNING BUCK MARK HUNTER
Caliber: .22 LR. Capacity: 10-round magazine. Barrel: 7.25-in. heavy tapered bull. Weight: 38 oz. Length: 11.3 in. overall. Grips: Cocobolo target. Sights: Pro-Target adjustable rear, Tru-Glo/Marble's fiber-optic front. Integral scope base on top rail. Scope in photo not included. Features: Matte blue.
Price: **$500.00**

Prices given are believed to be accurate at time of publication however, many factors affect retail pricing so exact prices are not possible.

BROWNING BUCK PRACTICAL URX
Caliber: .22 LR. Capacity: 10-round magazine. Barrels: 5.5-in. tapered bull or 4-in. slab-sided (Micro). Weight: 34 oz. Length: 9.5 in. overall. Grips: Ultragrip RX Ambidextrous. Sights: Pro-Target adjustable rear, Tru-Glo/Marble's fiber-optic front. Features: Matte gray receiver, matte blue barrel.
Price: **$479.00**
Price: Stainless **$470.00**
Price: Micro **$470.00**

BROWNING BUCK MARK MEDALLION ROSEWOOD
Caliber: .22 LR. Capacity: 10-round magazine. Barrel: 5.5-in. Grips: Laminate rosewood colored with gold Buckmark. Sights: Pro-Target adjustable rear, TruGlo/Marble's fiber-optic front. Finish: Matte black receiver, blackened stainless barrel with polished flats. Gold-plated trigger.
Price: **$510.00**

BROWNING BUCK MARK CONTOUR STAINLESS URX
Caliber: .22 LR. Capacity: 10-round magazine. Barrel: 5.5 or 7.25-in. special contour. Grips: Checkered, textured. Sights: Pro-Target adjustable rear, Pro-Target front. Integral scope base on top rail. Finish: Matte black receiver, blackened stainless barrel with polished flats. Gold-plated trigger.
Price: **$550.00**

BROWNING BUCK MARK FIELD TARGET SUPPRESSOR READY
Caliber: .22 LR. Capacity: 10-round magazine. Barrel: 5.5-in. heavy bull, suppressor ready. Grips: Cocobolo target. Sights: Pro-Target adjustable rear, Tru-Glo/Marble's fiber-optic front. Integral scope base on top rail. Scope in photo not included. Features: Matte blue.
Price: **$600.00**

CANIK TP9 SERIES
Caliber: 9mm. Capacity: 18-round magazine. Barrel: 4.07-in. Grip: Textured polymer, modular backstraps. Sights: White dot front, u-notch rear. Length: 7.1 in. overall. Weight: 27.8 oz. unloaded. Finish: Matte black, FDE. Features: DA/SA trigger with decocker.
Price: **$404.00**
Price: TP9SA Mod.2 .... **$379.00**
Price: TP9SF **$399.00**
Price: TP9SF Elite **$430.00**
Price: TP9SFx **$549.00**
Price: TP9 Elite Combat **$749.00**

CANIK METE SERIES
Caliber: 9mm. Capacity: 18- and 20-round magazine. Barrel: 4.46-in. Grip: Textured polymer, modular backstraps. Sights: White dot 3-dot, optics-ready. Length: 7.56 in. overall. Weight: 27.8 oz. unloaded. Finish: Matte black, FDE. Features: Striker fire.
Price: Mete SFT **$519.00**
Price: Mete SFX **$574.00**

CANIK RIVAL SERIES
Caliber: 9mm. Capacity: 18-round magazine. Barrel: 5-in. Grip: Textured polymer, modular backstraps. Sights: Fiber-optic front, adj. rear, optics-ready. Length: 8.1 in. overall. Weight: 29.5 oz. unloaded. Finish: Matte black, black with gold accents. Features: Striker fire.
Price: Mete SFT **$519.00**
Price: Mete SFX **$574.00**

CHIAPPA 1911-22
Caliber: .22 LR. Capacity: 10-round magazine. Barrel: 5 in. Weight: 33.5 oz. Length: 8.5 in. Grips: Two-piece wood. Sights: Fixed. Features: A faithful replica of the famous John Browning 1911A1 pistol. Fixed barrel design. Available in black, OD green or tan finish. Target and Tactical models have adjustable sights.
Price: From .... **$269.00–$408.00**

CHIAPPA M9-22 STANDARD
Caliber: .22 LR. Barrel: 5 in. Weight: 2.3 lbs. Length: 8.5 in. Grips: Black molded plastic or walnut. Sights: Fixed front sight and windage adjustable rear sight. Features: The M9 9mm has been a U.S. standard-issue service pistol since 1990. Chiappa's M9-22 is a replica of this pistol in 22 LR. The M9-22 has the same weight and feel as its 9mm counterpart but has an affordable 10-shot magazine for the .22 Long Rifle cartridge, which makes it a true rimfire reproduction. Comes standard with steel trigger, hammer assembly and a 1/2x28 threaded barrel.
Price: **$339.00**

CHIAPPA M9-22 TACTICAL
Caliber: .22 LR. Barrel: 5 in. Weight: 2.3 lbs. Length: 8.5 in. Grips: Black molded plastic. Sights: Fixed front sight and Novak-style rear sights. Features: The M9-22 Tactical model comes with a faux suppressor (this ups the "cool factor" on the range and extends the barrel to make it even more accurate). It also has a 1/2x28 thread adaptor that can be used with a legal suppressor.
Price: **$419.00**

Prices given are believed to be accurate at time of publication however, many factors affect retail pricing so exact prices are not possible.

CHRISTENSEN ARMS 1911 SERIES
Calibers: .45 ACP, 9mm. Barrels: 4.25 in., 5 or 5.5 in. Features: Models are offered with aluminum, stainless steel or titanium frame with hand-fitted slide, match-grade barrel, tritium night sights and G10 Operator grip panels.
Price: Aluminum frame **$1,995.00**
Price: Stainless **$2,895.00**
Price: Titanium .... **$4,795.00–$5,095.00**

CITADEL M-1911
Calibers: .45 ACP, 9mm. Capacity: 7 (.45), 8 (9mm). Barrels: 5 or 3.5 in. Weight: 2.3 lbs. Length: 8.5 in. Grips: Cocobolo. Sights: Low-profile combat fixed rear, blade front. Finish: Matte black. Features: Extended grip safety, lowered and flared ejection port, beveled mag well, Series 70 firing system. Built by Armscor (Rock Island Armory) in the Philippines and imported by Legacy Sports.
Price: **$599.00**

CIMARRON MODEL 1911
Caliber: .45 ACP. Barrel: 5 in. Weight: 37.5 oz. Length: 8.5 in. overall. Grips: Checkered walnut. Features: A faithful reproduction of the original pattern of the Model 1911 with Parkerized finish and lanyard ring. Polished or nickel finish available.
Price: **$571.00**
Price: Polished blue or nickel **$800.00**

CIMARRON MODEL 1911 WILD BUNCH
Caliber: .45 ACP. Barrel: 5 in. Weight: 37.5 oz. Length: 8.5 in. overall. Grips: Checkered walnut. Features: Original WWI 1911 frame with flat mainspring housing, correct markings, polished blue finish, comes with tanker shoulder holster.
Price: **$956.00**

COBRA ENTERPRISES FS32, FS380
Calibers: .32 ACP or .380 ACP. Capacity: 7 rounds. Barrel: 3.5 in. Weight: 2.1 lbs. Length: 6.375 in. overall. Grips: Black molded synthetic integral with frame. Sights: Fixed. Made in USA by Cobra Enterprises of Utah, Inc.
Price: .... **$138.00–$250.00**

COBRA ENTERPRISES PATRIOT SERIES
Calibers: .380, 9mm or .45 ACP. Capacities: 6-, 7- or 10-round magazine. Barrel: 3.3 in. Weight: 20 oz. Length: 6 in. overall. Grips: Black polymer. Sights: Fixed. Features: Bright chrome, satin nickel or black finish. Made in USA by Cobra Enterprises of Utah, Inc.
Price: .... **$349.00–$395.00**

COBRA DENALI
Caliber: .380 ACP. Capacity: 5 rounds. Barrel: 2.8 in. Weight: 22 oz. Length: 5.4 in. Grips: Black molded synthetic integral with frame. Sights: Fixed. Features: Made in USA by Cobra Enterprises of Utah, Inc.
Price: **$179.00**

COLT 1903 RE-ISSUE SERIES
Caliber: .32 ACP. Capacity: 8-round magazine. Barrel: 3.9 in. Grips: Checkered walnut. Sights: Fixed, round front/retro rear. Finish: Parkerized, Royal Blue, Blued or Chrome. Features: Reproduction of Colt 1903 pistol, marked "U.S. PROPERTY" on right side of frame.
Price: Blued **$1,338.00**
Price: Chrome **$1,647.00**
Price: Parkerized **$1,211.00**
Price: Royal Blue **$1,544.00**

COLT 1911 CLASSIC
Caliber: .45 ACP. Capacity: 7-round magazine. Barrel: 5 in. Grips: Double diamond checkered rosewood. Sights: Fixed-post front/retro rear. Finish: Blue. Features: Series 70 firing system.
Price: **$799.00**

COLT 1911 BLACK ARMY
Caliber: .45 ACP. Capacity: 7-round magazine. Barrel: 5 in. Grips: Double diamond checkered rosewood. Sights: Fixed, round front/retro rear. Finish: Matte blue. Features: Series 70 firing system, lanyard loop, reproduction of WWI U.S. Military model.
Price: **$999.00**

COLT MODEL 1991 MODEL O
Caliber: .45 ACP. Capacity: 7-round magazine. Barrel: 5 in. Weight: 38 oz. Length: 8.5 in. overall. Grips: Checkered black composition. Sights: Ramped blade front, fixed square notch rear, high profile. Features: Matte finish. Continuation of serial number range used on original G.I. 1911A1 guns. Comes with one magazine and molded carrying case. Introduced 1991. Series 80 firing system.
Price: Blue **$799.00**
Price: Stainless **$879.00**

COLT XSE SERIES MODEL O COMBAT ELITE
Caliber: .45 ACP. Capacity: 8-round magazine. Barrel: 5 in. Grips: Checkered, double-diamond rosewood. Sights: Three white-dot Novak. Features: Brushed stainless receiver with blued slide; adjustable, two-cut aluminum trigger; extended ambidextrous thumb safety; upswept beavertail with palm swell; elongated slot hammer.
Price: **$1,100.00**

COLT LIGHTWEIGHT COMMANDER
Calibers: .45 ACP, 8-shot, 9mm (9 shot). Barrel: 4.25 in. Weight: 26 oz. alloy frame, 33 oz. (steel frame). Length: 7.75 in. overall. Grips: G10 Checkered Black Cherry. Sights: Novak White Dot front, Low Mount Carry rear. Features: Blued slide, black anodized frame. Aluminum alloy frame.
Price: **$999.00**
Price: Combat Commander w/steel frame **$949.00**

Prices given are believed to be accurate at time of publication however, many factors affect retail pricing so exact prices are not possible.

COLT DEFENDER
Caliber: .45 ACP (7-round magazine), 9mm (8-round). Barrel: 3 in. Weight: 22.5 oz. Length: 6.75 in. overall. Grips: Pebble-finish rubber wraparound with finger grooves. Sights: White dot front, snag-free Colt competition rear. Features: Stainless or blued finish; aluminum frame; combat-style hammer; Hi-Ride grip safety, extended manual safety, disconnect safety. Introduced 1998. Made in USA by Colt's Mfg. Co., Inc.
Price: Stainless **$999.00**
Price: Blue **$999.00**

COLT SERIES 70
Caliber: .45 ACP. Barrel: 5 in. Weight: 37.5 oz. Length: 8.5 in. Grips: Rosewood with double diamond checkering pattern. Sights: Fixed. Features: Custom replica of the Original Series 70 pistol with a Series 70 firing system, original roll marks. Introduced 2002. Made in USA by Colt's Mfg. Co., Inc.
Price: Blued **$899.00**
Price: Stainless **$979.00**

COLT 38 SUPER CUSTOM SERIES
Caliber: .38 Super. Barrel: 5 in. Weight: 36.5 oz. Length: 8.5 in. Grips: Wood with double diamond checkering pattern. Finish: Bright stainless. Sights: 3-dot. Features: Beveled magazine well, standard thumb safety and service-style grip safety, flat mainspring housing. Introduced 2003. Made in USA. by Colt's Mfg. Co., Inc.
Price: **$1,549.00**

COLT MUSTANG POCKETLITE
Caliber: .380 ACP. Capacity: 6-round magazine. Barrel: 2.75 in. Weight: 12.5 oz. Length: 5.5 in. Grips: Black composite. Finish: Brushed stainless. Features: Thumb safety, firing-pin safety block. Introduced 2012.
Price: **$699.00**

COLT MUSTANG LITE
Caliber: .380 ACP. Similar to Mustang Pocketlite except has black polymer frame.
Price: **$599.00**

COLT MUSTANG XSP
Caliber: .380 ACP. Features: Similar to Mustang Pocketlite except has polymer frame, black diamond or bright stainless slide, squared trigger guard, accessory rail, electroless nickel finished controls.
Price: Bright Stainless **$528.00**
Price: Black Diamond-Like Carbon finish **$672.00**

COLT RAIL GUN
Caliber: .45 ACP. Capacity: (8+1). Barrel: 5 in. Weight: 40 oz. Length: 8.5 in. Grips: Rosewood double diamond. Sights: White dot front and Novak rear. Features: 1911-style semi-auto. Stainless steel frame and slide, front and rear slide serrations, skeletonized trigger, integral accessory rail, Smith & Alexander upswept beavertail grip palm swell safety, tactical thumb safety, National Match barrel.
Price: **$1,199.00**

COLT M45A1 MARINE PISTOL
Caliber: .45 ACP. Variant of Rail Gun series with features of that model plus Decobond Brown Coating, dual recoil springs system, Novak tritium front and rear 3-dot sights. Selected by U.S. Marine Corps as their Close Quarters Battle Pistol (CQBP).
Price: **$1,699.00**

COLT DELTA ELITE
Caliber: 10 mm. Capacity: 8+1. Barrel: 5 in. Grips: Black composite with Delta Medallions. Sights: Novak Low Mount Carry rear, Novak White Dot front. Finish: Two-tone stainless frame, black matte slide. Features: Upswept beavertail safety, extended thumb safety, 3-hole aluminum trigger.
Price: **$1,199.00**

COLT SPECIAL COMBAT GOVERNMENT CARRY MODEL
Calibers: .45 ACP (8+1), .38 Super (9+1). Barrel: 5 in. Weight: NA. Length: 8.5 in. Grips: Black/silver synthetic. Sights: Novak front and rear night sights. Features: 1911-style semi-auto. Skeletonized three-hole trigger, slotted hammer, Smith & Alexander upswept beavertail grip palm swell safety and extended magazine well, Wilson tactical ambidextrous safety. Available in blued, hard chrome, or blued/satin-nickel finish, depending on chambering. Marine pistol has desert tan Cerakote stainless steel finish, lanyard loop.
Price: **$2,095.00**

COLT GOVERNMENT MODEL 1911A1 .22
Caliber: .22 LR. Capacity: 12-round magazine. Barrel: 5 in. Weight: 36 oz. Features: Made in Germany by Walther under exclusive arrangement with Colt Manufacturing Company. Blowback operation. All other features identical to original, including manual and grip safeties, drift-adjustable sights.
Price: **$399.00**

COLT COMPETITION PISTOL

Calibers: .45 ACP, .38 Super or 9mm Para. Full-size Government Model with 5-inch national match barrel, dual-spring recoil operating system, adjustable rear and fiber optic front sights, custom G10 Colt logo grips blued or stainless steel finish.

Price: Blued finish.. **$949.00**
Price: Stainless steel.. **$999.00**
Price: 38 Super **$1,099.00**

COLT SERIES 70 NATIONAL MATCH GOLD CUP

Caliber: .45 ACP. Barrel: 5 in. national match. Weight: 37 oz. Length: 8.5 in. Grips: Checkered walnut with gold medallions. Sights: Adjustable Bomar rear, target post front. Finish: blued. Features: Flat top slide, flat mainspring housing. Wide three-hole aluminum trigger.

Price: **$1,299.00**

COLT GOLD CUP TROPHY

Calibers: .45 ACP or 9mm. Updated version of the classic Colt target and service pistol first introduced in the late 1950s to give shooters a serious competition pistol out of the box. Features include an undercut trigger guard, upswept beavertail grip safety and dual-spring recoil system. Checkering on the front and rear of the grip strap is 25 LPI with blue G10 grips. The new Gold Cup Trophy is built on the Series 70 firing system. Re-introduced to the Colt catalog in 2017.

Price: **$1,699.00**

CZ 75 B

Calibers: 9mm, .40 S&W. Capacity: 16-round magazine (9mm), 10-round (.40). Barrel: 4.7 In. Weight: 34.3 oz. Length: 8.1 in. overall. Grips: High impact checkered plastic. Sights: Square post front, rear adjustable for windage; 3-dot system. Features: Single action/double action; firing pin block safety; choice of black polymer, matte or high-polish blue finishes. All-steel frame. B-SA is a single action with a drop-free magazine. Imported from the Czech Republic by CZ-USA.

Price: 75 B **$625.00**
Price: 75 B, stainless **$783.00**
Price: 75 B-SA **$661.00**

CZ 75B 45TH ANNIVERSARY

Caliber: 9mm. Capacity: 16-round magazine. Barrel: 4.6 in. Grips: Engraved wood. Sights: Fixed, 3-dot tritium. Length: 8.1 in. overall. Weight: 35.2 oz. unloaded. Finish: Blued. Features: Limited edition pistol, only 1,000 produced. Engraved frame and slide.

Price: **$1,720.00**

CZ 75 BD DECOCKER

Similar to the CZ 75B except has a decocking lever in place of the safety lever. All other specifications are the same. Introduced 1999. Imported from the Czech Republic by CZ-USA.

Price: 9mm, black polymer **$612.00**

CZ 75 B COMPACT

Similar to the CZ 75 B except has 14-round magazine in 9mm, 3.9-in. barrel and weighs 32 oz. Has removable front sight, non-glare ribbed slide top. Trigger guard is squared and serrated; combat hammer. Introduced 1993. Imported from the Czech Republic by CZ-USA.

Price: 9mm, black polymer **$631.00**
Price: 9mm, dual tone or satin nickel **$651.00**
Price: 9mm. D PCR Compact, alloy frame **$651.00**

CZ P-07

Calibers: .40 S&W, 9mm. Capacity: 15 (9mm), 12 (.40). Barrel: 3.8 in. Weight: 27.2 oz. Length: 7.3 in. overall. Grips: Polymer black Polycoat. Sights: Blade front, fixed groove rear. Features: The ergonomics and accuracy of the CZ 75 with a totally new trigger system. The new Omega trigger system simplifies the CZ 75 trigger system, uses fewer parts and improves the trigger pull. In addition, it allows users to choose between using the handgun with a decocking lever (installed) or a manual safety (included) by a simple parts change. The polymer frame design and a new sleek slide profile (fully machined from bar stock) reduce weight, making the P-07 a great choice for concealed carry.

Price: **$524.00**

CZ P-09 DUTY

Calibers: 9mm, .40 S&W. Capacity: 19 (9mm), 15 (.40). Features: High-capacity version of P-07. Accessory rail, interchangeable grip backstraps, ambidextrous decocker can be converted to manual safety.

Price: **$544.00**
Price: Suppressor ready **$629.00**

Prices given are believed to be accurate at time of publication however, many factors affect retail pricing so exact prices are not possible.

CZ 75 SP-01

Similar to NATO-approved CZ 75 Compact P-01 model. Features an integral 1913 accessory rail on the dust cover, rubber grip panels, black Polycoat finish, extended beavertail, new grip geometry with checkering on front and back straps, and double or single action operation. Introduced 2005. The Shadow variant designed as an IPSC "production" division competition firearm. Includes competition hammer, competition rear sight and fiber-optic front sight, modified slide release, lighter recoil and mainspring for use with "minor power factor" competition ammunition. Includes Polycoat finish and slim walnut grips. Finished by CZ Custom Shop. Imported from the Czech Republic by CZ-USA.

Price: SP-01 Standard **$680.00**
Price: SP-01 Shadow Target II **$1,638.00**

CZ 97 B

Caliber: .45 ACP. Capacity: 10-round magazine. Barrel: 4.85 in. Weight: 40 oz. Length: 8.34 in. overall. Grips: Checkered walnut. Sights: Fixed. Features: Single action/double action; full-length slide rails; screw-in barrel bushing; linkless barrel; all-steel construction; chamber loaded indicator; dual transfer bars. Introduced 1999. Imported from the Czech Republic by CZ-USA.

Price: Black polymer **$707.00**
Price: Glossy blue **$727.00**

CZ 97 BD DECOCKER

Similar to the CZ 97 B except has a decocking lever in place of the safety lever. Tritium night sights. Rubber grips. All other specifications are the same. Introduced 1999. Imported from the Czech Republic by CZ-USA.

Price: **$816.00**

CZ 2075 RAMI

Calibers: 9mm. Barrel: 3 in. Weight: 25 oz. Length: 6.5 in. overall. Grips: Rubber. Sights: Blade front with dot, white outline rear drift adjustable for windage. Features: Single action/double action; alloy frame, steel slide; has laser sight mount. Rami BD has decocking system. Imported from the Czech Republic by CZ-USA.

Price: Rami Standard **$632.00**
Price: Rami Decocker version **$699.00**

CZ P-01

Caliber: 9mm. Capacity: 14-round magazine. Barrel: 3.85 in. Weight: 27 oz. Length: 7.2 in. overall. Grips: Checkered rubber. Sights: Blade front with dot, white outline rear drift adjustable for windage. Features: Based on the CZ 75, except with forged aircraft-grade aluminum alloy frame. Hammer forged barrel, decocker, firing-pin block, M3 rail, dual slide serrations, squared trigger guard, re-contoured trigger, lanyard loop on butt. Serrated front and backstrap. Introduced 2006. Imported from the Czech Republic by CZ-USA.

Price: CZ P-01 .... **$680.00**

CZ P-10 F

Caliber: 9mm. Capacity: 19-round magazine. Barrel: 4.5 in. Weight: 26 oz. Length: 8 in. overall. Grips: Textured polymer. Sights: Fixed, 3-dot. Features: Striker fire.

Price: **$524.00**
Price: CZ P-10 C **$579.00**
Price: CZ P-10 M **$505.00**
Price: CZ P-10 S .... **$619.00–$640.00**
Price: CZ P-10 C Suppressor Ready .... **$585.00–$649.00**

CZ P-10 F COMPETITION-READY

Caliber: 9mm. Capacity: 19-round magazine. Barrel: 5 in. Grip: Thin textured polymer. Sights: Fiber-optic front, serrated fixed rear; optic ready. Length: 8.5 in. overall. Weight: 30 oz. unloaded. Finish: Matte black, gold accents. Features: Striker-firer, competition ready, Apex Tactical extended magazine catch and extended slide stop, and HB Industries trigger.

Price: **$1,009.00**

CZ SCORPION EVO

Caliber: 9mm. Capacity: 20-round magazine. Features: Semi-automatic version of CZ Scorpion Evo submachine gun. Ambidextrous controls, adjustable sights, accessory rails.

Price: **$849.00**

CZ TS 2

Caliber: 9mm or 40 S&W. Capacity: 20-round magazine. Barrel: 5.28 in. Grip: Thin textured aluminum. Sights: Serrated fiber-optic front, serrated fixed rear. Length: 8.86 in. overall. Weight: 48.5 oz. unloaded. Finish: Blued. Features: Full dust cover, competition ready, improved ergonomics.

Price: **$1,699.00**

CZ TS 2 RACING GREEN

Caliber: 9mm. Capacity: 20-round magazine. Barrel: 5.28 in. Grip: Thin textured green anodized aluminum. Sights: Serrated fiber-optic front, serrated fixed rear. Length: 8.86 in. overall. Weight: 48.5 oz. unloaded. Finish: Blued. Features: Full dust cover, competition ready, improved ergonomics.

Price: **$1,699.00**

DAN WESSON DWX FULL SIZE
Calibers: 9mm, .40 S&W. **Capacity:** 19-round magazine (9mm), 15-round magazine (.40 S&W). **Barrel:** 5 in. **Grips:** Checkered red aluminum. **Sights:** Fixed fiber-optic front/adjustable rear. **Length:** 8.52 in. overall. **Weight:** 43 oz. unloaded. Finish: Black Duty Coat. **Features:** Hybrid pistol built using the single-action fire control group of a Dan Wesson 1911 and frame of a CZ 75 pistol. Compatible with CZ P-09 and CZ P-10 F magazines. Bull barrel and full dust cover with accessory rail. Flat red aluminum trigger. Oversized controls.
Price: **$1,799.00**

DAN WESSON DWX COMPACT
Caliber: 9mm. Capacity: 15-round magazine. Barrel: 5 in. Grips: Checkered red aluminum. Sights: Fixed, night-sight front/U-notch rear. Length: 7.47 in. overall. Weight: 28.5 oz. unloaded. Finish: Black Duty Coat. Features: Hybrid pistol built using the single-action fire control group of a Dan Wesson 1911 and frame of a CZ 75 pistol. With or without accessory rail. Full dust cover. Flat red aluminum trigger. Oversized controls.
Price: **$1,799.00**

DAN WESSON DW RZ-45 HERITAGE
Caliber: .45 ACP. Capacity: 7-round magazine. Weight: 36 oz. Length: 8.8 in. overall. Similar to the RZ-10 Auto except in .45 ACP.
Price: 10mm, 8+1 .... **$1,428.00**

DAN WESSON KODIAK
Caliber: 10mm. Capacity: 8-round magazine. Barrel: 6.03 in. Grips: Textured G10. Sights: Fixed, fiber-optic front/adjustable rear. Length: 9.7 in. overall. Weight: 47.1 oz. unloaded. Finish: Black or tri-tone. Features: 1911 platform with coarse slide serrations, mag well and ambidextrous safety. Black version has bronzed controls and barrel, and tri-tone with a matte gray slide.
Price: (tri-tone).. **$2,349.00**

DAN WESSON SPECIALIST
Caliber: .45 ACP. Capacity: 8-round magazine. Barrel: 5 in. Grips: G10 VZ Operator II. Sights: Single amber tritium dot rear, green lamp with white target ring front sight. Features: Integral Picatinny rail, 25 LPI frontstrap checkering, undercut trigger guard, ambidextrous thumb safety, extended mag release and detachable two-piece mag well.
Price: **$1,701.00**

DAN WESSON V-BOB
Caliber: .45 ACP. Capacity: 8-round magazine. Barrel: 4.25 in. Weight: 34 oz. Length: 8 in. Grips: Slim Line G10. Sights: Heinie Ledge Straight-Eight Night Sights. Features: Black matte or stainless finish. Bobtail forged grip frame with 25 LPI checkering front and rear.
Price: **$2,077.00**

DAN WESSON POINTMAN
Calibers: 9mm, .38 Super, .45 ACP. Capacity: 8 or 9-round magazine. Barrel: 5 in. Length: 8.5 in. Grips: Double-diamond cocobolo. Sights: Adjustable rear and fiber optic front. Features: Undercut trigger guard, checkered front strap, serrated rib on top of slide.
Price: .45, .38 Super **$1,597.00**
Price: 9mm **$1,558.00**

DAN WESSON A2
Caliber: .45 ACP. Capacity: 8-round magazine capacity. Limited production model based on traditional 1911A1 design. Features: Modern fixed combat sights, lowered/flared ejection port, double-diamond walnut grips. Introduced 2017.
Price: **$1,363.00**

DAN WESSON VALOR
Caliber: .45 ACP. Capacity: 8-round magazine. Barrel: 5 in. Grips: Textured G10. Sights: Fixed, night-sight front/U-notch rear. Length: 8.75 in. overall. Weight: 39.7 oz. unloaded. Finish: Matte stainless or black Duty Coat. Features: 1911 platform with GI style slide serrations, Stan Chen SI mag well, tapered grip and tactical ambidextrous safety.
Price: (stainless) **$1,864.00**

DAN WESSON VIGIL
Calibers: 9mm, .45 ACP. Capacity: 8 (.45) or 9 (9mm). Barrel: 4.25 or 5 in. Features: Forged aluminum frame with stainless round-top slide, serrated tactical rear and tritium front sight, checkered frontstrap and backstrap, walnut grips with rounded butt.
Price: **$1,298.00**

DAN WESSON WRAITH
Calibers: .45 ACP, 9m, 10mm. Capacity: 8 (.45), 9 (.40), 10 (9mm). Barrel: 5.75, threaded. Finish: Distressed Duty. Features: High profile fixed combat sights, lowered/flared ejection port, G10 grips, extended controls and grip safety.
Price: **$2,077.00**

DESERT EAGLE 1911 G
Caliber: .45 ACP. Capacity: 8-round magazine. Barrels: 5 in. or 4.33 in. (DE1911C Commander size), or 3.0 in. (DE1911U Undercover). Grips: Double diamond checkered wood. Features: Extended beavertail grip safety, checkered flat mainspring housing, skeletonized hammer and trigger, extended mag release and thumb safety, stainless full-length guide road, enlarged ejection port, beveled mag well and high-profile sights. Comes with two 8-round magazines.
Price: **$904.00**
Price: Undercover........ **$1,019.00**

DESERT EAGLE MARK XIX
Calibers: .357 Mag., 9 rounds; .44 Mag., 8 rounds; .50 AE, 7 rounds. Barrels: 6 in., 10 in., interchangeable. Weight: 62 oz. (.357 Mag.); 69 oz. (.44 Mag.); 72 oz. (.50 AE) Length: 10.25-in. overall (6-in. bbl.). Grips: Polymer; rubber available. Sights: Blade-on-ramp front, combat-style rear. Adjustable available. Features: Interchangeable barrels; rotating three-lug bolt; ambidextrous safety; adjustable trigger. Military epoxy finish. Satin, bright nickel, chrome, brushed, matte or black-oxide finishes available. 10-in. barrel extra. Imported from Israel by Magnum Research, Inc.
Price: .... **$1,572.00–$2,060.00**

BABY DESERT EAGLE III
Calibers: 9mm, .40 S&W, .45 ACP. Capacities: 10-, 12- or 15-round magazines. Barrels: 3.85 in. or 4.43 in. Weights: 28–37.9 oz. Length: 7.25–8.25 overall. Grips: Ergonomic polymer. Sights: White 3-dot system. Features: Choice of steel or polymer frame with integral rail; slide-mounted decocking safety. Upgraded design of Baby Eagle II series.
Price: .... **$646.00–$691.00**

DESERT EAGLE L5/L6
Caliber: .357 Magnum, .44 Magnum, .50 AE. Capacity: 7, 8 or 9+1. Barrel: 5 in. or 6 in (L6). Weight: 50 to 70 oz. Length: 9.7 in. (L5), 10.8, (L6). Features: Steel barrel, aluminum frame and stainless steel slide with full Weaver-style accessory rail and integral muzzle brake. Gas-operated rotating bolt, single-action trigger, fixed sights.
Price: From **$1,790.00**

DIAMONDBACK DB380
Caliber: .380 ACP. Capacity: 6+1. Barrel: 2.8 in. Weight: 8.8 oz. Features: ZERO-Energy striker firing system with a mechanical firing pin block, steel magazine catch, windage-adjustable sights. Frames available with several color finish options.
Price: .... **$290.00–$350.00**

DIAMONDBACK DB9
Caliber: 9mm. Capacity: 6+1. Barrel: 3 in. Weight: 11 oz. Length: 5.60 in. Features: Other features similar to DB380 model.
Price: .... **$290.00–$350.00**

DIAMONDBACK DB FS NINE
Caliber: 9mm. Capacity: 15+1. Barrel: 4.75 in. Weight: 21.5 oz. Length: 7.8 in. Features: Double-action, striker-fired model with polymer frame and stainless steel slide. Flared mag well, extended magazine base pad, ergonomically contoured grip, fixed 3-dot sights, front and rear slide serrations, integral MIL-STD 1913 Picatinny rail.
Price: **$483.00**

DIAMONDBACK FIREARMS DBX
Caliber: 5.7x28mm. Capacity: 20-round magazine. Barrel: 8 in. Grips: Magpul MOE-K. Sights: Optic-ready, Picatinny rail. Length: 16.9 in. overall, brace folded. Weight: 3 lbs. unloaded. Finish: Black hard coat anodized. Features: DBX muzzle brake, compatible with FN Five-seveN, side-folding brace. Uses AR15 Mil-Spec trigger.
Price: **$1,299.00**

DIAMONDBACK FIREARMS DBAM29
Caliber: 9mm. Capacity: 12- or 17-round magazine. Barrel: 3.5 in. Grips: Textured grip. Sights: Fixed, 3-dot. Length: 6.6 in. overall. Weight: 21 oz. unloaded. Finish: Black.
Price: **$350.00**

DOUBLESTAR 1911 SERIES
Caliber: .45 ACP. Capacity: 8-round magazine. Barrels: 3.5 in., 4.25 in., 5 in. Weights: 33–40 oz. Grips: Cocobolo wood. Sights: Novak LoMount 2 white-dot rear, Novak white-dot front. Features: Single action, M1911-style with forged frame and slide of 4140 steel, stainless steel barrel machined from bar stock by Storm Lake, funneled mag well, accessory rail, black Nitride finish. Optional features include bobtail grip frame, accessory rail.
Price: .... **$1,364.00–$2,242.00**

EAA WITNESS FULL SIZE
Calibers: 9mm, .38 Super. Capacity: 18-round magazine; .40 S&W, 10mm, 15-round magazine; .45 ACP, 10-round magazine. Barrel: 4.5 in. Weight: 35.33 oz. Length: 8.1 in. overall. Grips: Checkered rubber. Sights: Undercut blade front, open rear adjustable for windage. Features: Double-action/single-action trigger system; round trigger guard; frame-mounted safety. Available with steel or polymer frame. Also available with interchangeable .45 ACP and .22 LR slides. Steel frame introduced 1991. Polymer frame introduced 2005. Imported from Italy by European American Armory.
Price: Steel frame **$699.00**
Price: Polymer frame **$589.00**

EAA WITNESS COMPACT
Caliber: 9mm. Capacity: 14-round magazine; .40 S&W, 10mm, 12-round magazine; .45 ACP, 8-round magazine. Barrel: 3.6 in. Weight: 30 oz. Length: 7.3 in. overall. Features: Available with steel or polymer frame (shown). All polymer frame Witness pistols are capable of being converted to other calibers. Otherwise similar to full-size Witness. Imported from Italy by European American Armory.
Price: Polymer frame **$589.00**
Price: Steel frame **$699.00**

EAA WITNESS-P CARRY
Caliber: 9mm. Capacity: 17-round magazine; 10mm, 15-round magazine; .45 ACP, 10-round magazine. Barrel: 3.6 in. Weight: 27 oz. Length: 7.5 in. overall. Features: Otherwise similar to full-size Witness. Polymer frame introduced 2005. Imported from Italy by European American Armory.
Price: **$711.00**

EAA WITNESS PAVONA COMPACT POLYMER
Calibers: .380 ACP (13-round magazine), 9mm (13) or .40 S&W (9). Barrel: 3.6 in. Weight: 30 oz. Length: 7 in. overall. Features: Designed primarily for women with fine-tuned recoil and hammer springs for easier operation, a polymer frame with integral checkering, contoured lines and in black, charcoal, blue, purple or magenta with silver or gold sparkle.
Price: .... **$476.00–$528.00**

EAA WITNESS ELITE 1911
Caliber: .45 ACP. Capacity: 8-round magazine. Barrel: 5 in. Weight: 32 oz. Length: 8.58 in. overall. Features: Full-size 1911-style pistol with either steel or polymer frame. Also available in Commander or Officer's models with 4.25- or 3.5-in. barrel, polymer frame.
Price: **$580.00**
Price: Commander or Officer's Model........ **$627.00**
Price: Steel frame **$895.00**

EAA SAR B6P
Caliber: 9mm. Based on polymer frame variation of CZ 75 design. Manufactured by Sarsilmaz in Turkey. Features similar to Witness series.
Price: .... **$407.00–$453.00**

EAA SAR K2-45
Caliber: .45 ACP. Barrel: 4.7 in. Weight: 2.5 lbs. Features: Similar to B6P with upgraded features. Built by Sarsilmaz for the Turkish military. Features include a cocked and locked carry system, ergonomically designed grip, steel frame and slide construction, adjustable rear sight, extended beaver tail, serrated trigger guard and frame, removable dove-tail front sight, auto firing pin block and low barrel axis for reduced felt recoil.
Price: **$849.00**

EAA MC 1911 SERIES
Caliber: .45 ACP, 9mm. Capacity: 8-round magazine, 9+1 (9mm). Barrel: 5, 4.4, or 3.4 in. Weight: 26-39 oz. Sights: Novak-style rear, fixed front. Features: 1911-style pistol with either steel or polymer frame, ambidextrous safety, extended beavertail. Available in full-size, Commander or Officer's models. Manufactured by Girsan in Turkey.
Price: .... $572.00-$694.00

ED BROWN CLASSIC CUSTOM
Caliber: .45 ACP, 9mm, .38 Super. Capacity: 7-round magazine. Barrel: 5 in. Weight: 40 oz. Grips: Cocobolo wood. Sights: Bo-Mar adjustable rear, dovetail front. Features: Single action, M1911 style, custom made to order, stainless frame and slide available. Special mirror-finished slide.
Price: From $3,695.00

ED BROWN KOBRA CARRY
Caliber: .45 ACP. Capacity: 7-round magazine. Barrels: 4.25 in. Weight: 34 oz. Grips: Hogue exotic wood. Sights: Ramp, front; fixed Novak low-mount night sights, rear. Features: Snakeskin pattern serrations on forestrap and mainspring housing, dehorned edges, beavertail grip safety.
Price: .45 ACP From $2,995.00
Price: 9 mm From $3,095.00
Price: .38 Super From $3,095.00

ED BROWN KOBRA CARRY LIGHTWEIGHT
Caliber: .45 ACP, 9mm, .38 Super. Capacity: 7-round magazine. Barrel: 4.25 in. (Commander model slide). Weight: 27 oz. Grips: Hogue exotic wood. Sights: 10-8 Performance U-notch plain black rear sight with .156-in. notch for fast acquisition of close targets. Fixed dovetail front night sight with high-visibility white outlines. Features: Aluminum frame and bobtail housing. Matte finished Gen III coated slide for low glare, with snakeskin on rear of slide only. Snakeskin pattern serrations on forestrap and mainspring housing, dehorned edges, beavertail grip safety. LW insignia on slide, which stands for Lightweight.
Price: Kobra Carry Lightweight $3,495.00

ED BROWN EXECUTIVE SERIES
Similar to other Ed Brown products, but with 25-LPI checkered frame and mainspring housing. Various finish, sight and grip options.
Price: .... $3,170.00-$3,880.00

ED BROWN SPECIAL FORCES
Similar to other Ed Brown products, but with ChainLink treatment on forestrap and mainspring housing. Entire gun coated with Gen III finish. Square cut serrations on rear of slide only. Dehorned. Introduced 2006. Available with various finish, sight and grip options.
Price: From .... $2,770.00–$4,775.00

ED BROWN CCO SERIES
Caliber: .45 ACP, 9mm, .38 Super. Capacity: 7-round magazine. Barrel: 4.25 in. Built on Officer's size frame with Commander slide. Features: Snakeskin metal treatment on mainspring housing, front strap and slide, round butt housing, concealed-carry beavertail grip safety, fixed black rear sight, high visibility fiber optic front. Lightweight aluminum version available.
Price: From .... $3,070.00–$3,585.00

EXCEL ARMS MP-22
Caliber: .22 WMR. Capacity: 9-round magazine. Barrel: 8.5-in. bull barrel. Weight: 54 oz. Length: 12.875 in. overall. Grips: Textured black composition. Sights: Fully adjustable target sights. Features: Made from 17-4 stainless steel, comes with aluminum rib, integral Weaver base, internal hammer, firing pin block. American made, lifetime warranty. Comes with two 9-round stainless steel magazines and a California-approved cable lock. .22 WMR Introduced 2006. Made in USA by Excel Arms.
Price: $477.00

EXCEL ARMS MP-5.7
Caliber: 5.7x28mm. Capacity: 9-round magazine. Features: Blowback action. Other features similar to MP-22. Red-dot optic sights, scope and rings are optional.
Price: $615.00
Price: With optic sights $685.00
Price: With scope and rings $711.00

FIRESTORM 380
Caliber: .380 ACP. Capacity: 7+1. Barrel: 3.5 in. Weight: 20 oz. Length: 6.6 in. Sights: Fixed, white outline system. Grips: Rubber. Finish: Black matte. Features: Traditional DA/SA operation.
Price: $270.00

FMK 9C1 G2
Caliber: 9mm. Capacity: 10+1 or 14+1. Barrel: 4 in. Overall length: 6.85 in. Weight: 23.45 oz. Finish: Black, Flat Dark Earth or pink. Sights: Interchangeable Glock compatible. Features: Available in either single action or double action only. Polymer frame, high-carbon steel slide, stainless steel barrel. Very low bore axis and shock absorbing backstrap are said to result in low felt recoil. DAO model has Fast Action Trigger (FAT) with shorter pull and reset. Made in the USA.
Price: $409.00

FN 502 TACTICAL
Caliber: 22 LR. Capacity: 10- and 15- round magazine. Barrel: 4.6 in. threaded. Grip: Textured polymer. Sights: Suppressor height, fixed front and rear sights. Length: 7.6 in. overall. Weight: 23.7 oz. unloaded. Finish: Matte black or FDE. Features: Hammer-fire, accessory rail.
Price: $519.00

Prices given are believed to be accurate at time of publication however, many factors affect retail pricing so exact prices are not possible.

FN 509 COMPACT MRD
Caliber: 9mm. Capacity: 10-, 12- or 15-round magazine. Barrel: 3.7 in. Grips: Textured grip, interchangeable backstraps. Sights: Fixed, tall co-witness; FN Low Profile Optics Mounting System. Length: 6.8 in. overall. Weight: 25.5 oz. unloaded. Finish: Black or FDE.
Price: **$799.00**

FN FNX SERIES
Calibers: 9mm, .40 S&W. Capacities: 17-round magazine, .40 S&W (14 rounds), .45 ACP (10 or 14 rounds). Barrels: 4 in. (9mm and .40), 4.5 in. .45. Weights: 22–32 oz. (.45). Lengths: 7.4, 7.9 in. (.45). Features: DA/SA operation with decocking/manual safety lever. Has external extractor with loaded-chamber indicator, front and rear cocking serrations, fixed 3-dot combat sights.
Price: 9mm, .40 .... **$699.00**
Price: .45 ACP **$824.00**

FN FNX .45 TACTICAL
Similar to standard FNX .45 except with 5.3-in. barrel with threaded muzzle, polished chamber and feed ramp, enhanced high-profile night sights, slide cut and threaded for red-dot sight (not included), MIL-STD 1913 accessory rail, ring-style hammer.
Price: **$1,349.00**

FN FIVE-SEVEN
Caliber: 5.7x28mm. Capacity: 10- or 20-round magazine. Barrel: 4.8 in. Weight: 23 oz. Length: 8.2 in. Features: Adjustable three-dot system. Single-action polymer frame, chambered for low-recoil 5.7x28mm cartridge.
Price: **$1,435.00**

FN HIGH POWER
Caliber: 9mm. Capacity: 17-round magazine. Barrel: 4.7 in. Grip: Textured G10. Sights: Steel fixed front and rear. Length: 8 in. overall. Weight: 40 oz. unloaded. Finish: Stainless, Matte black or FDE. Features: Hammer-fire, based on classic High Power pistol.
Price: .... **$1,269.00–$1,369.00**

GLOCK 17/17C
Caliber: 9mm. Capacities: 17/19/33-round magazines. Barrel: 4.49 in. Weight: 22.04 oz. (without magazine). Length: 7.32 in. overall. Grips: Black polymer. Sights: Dot on front blade, white outline rear adjustable for windage. Features: Polymer frame, steel slide; double-action trigger with Safe Action system; mechanical firing pin safety, drop safety; simple takedown without tools; locked breech, recoil operated action. ILS designation refers to Internal Locking System. Adopted by Austrian armed forces 1983. NATO approved 1984. Model 17L has 6-inch barrel, ported or non-ported, slotted and relieved slide, checkered grip with finger grooves, no accessory rail. Imported from Austria by Glock, Inc. USA.
Price: From **$599.00**
Price: 17L.......... **$750.00**
Price: 17 Gen 4 .... **$649.00**
Price: 17 Gen 5 .... **$699.00**

GLOCK GEN4 SERIES
In 2010, a new series of Generation 4 pistols was introduced with several improved features. These included a multiple backstrap system offering three different size options, short, medium or large frame; reversible and enlarged magazine release; dual recoil springs; and RTF (Rough Textured Finish) surface. Some recent models are only available in Gen 4 configuration.

GEN 5 SERIES
A new frame design was introduced in 2017 named Generation 5. The finger grooves were removed for more versatility and the user can customize the grip by using different backstraps, as with the Gen 4 models. A flared mag well and a cutout at the front of the frame give the user more speed during reloading. There is a reversible and enlarged magazine catch, changeable by users, as well as the ambidextrous slide stop lever to accommodate left- and right-handed operators. The rifling and crown of the barrel are slightly modified for increased precision. As of 2019, Gen 5 variants are available in Glock Models 17, 19, 26, 34 and 45.

GLOCK 19/19C
Caliber: 9mm. Capacities: 15/17/19/33-round magazines. Barrel: 4.02 in. Weight: 20.99 oz. (without magazine). Length: 6.85 in. overall. Compact version of Glock 17. Imported from Austria by Glock, Inc.
Price: **$599.00**
Price: 19 Gen 4 .... **$649.00**
Price: 19 Gen 5 .... **$749.00**

GLOCK 20/20C 10MM
Caliber: 10mm. Capacity: 15-round magazine. Barrel: 4.6 in. Weight: 27.68 oz. (without magazine). Length: 7.59 in. overall. Features: Otherwise similar to Model 17. Imported from Austria by Glock, Inc. Introduced 1990.
Price: From **$637.00**
Price: 20 Gen 4 .... **$687.00**

GLOCK MODEL 20 SF SHORT FRAME
Caliber: 10mm. Barrel: 4.61 in. with hexagonal rifling. Weight: 27.51 oz. Length: 8.07 in. overall. Sights: Fixed. Features: Otherwise similar to the Model 20 but with short-frame design, extended sight radius.
Price: **$637.00**

GLOCK 21/21C
Caliber: .45 ACP. Capacity: 13-round magazine. Barrel: 4.6 in. Weight: 26.28 oz. (without magazine). Length: 7.59 in. overall. Features: Otherwise similar to the Model 17. Imported from Austria by Glock, Inc. Introduced 1991. SF version has tactical rail, smaller diameter grip, 10-round magazine capacity. Introduced 2007.
Price: From **$637.00**
Price: 21 Gen 4 .... **$687.00**

GLOCK 22/22C
Caliber: .40 S&W. Capacities: 15/17-round magazine. Barrel: 4.49 in. Weight: 22.92 oz. (without magazine). Length: 7.32 in. overall. Features: Otherwise similar to Model 17, including pricing. Imported from Austria by Glock, Inc. Introduced 1990.
Price: From **$599.00**
Price: 22C **$649.00**
Price: 22 Gen 4 .... **$649.00**

GLOCK 23/23C
Caliber: .40 S&W. Capacities: 13/15/17-round magazine. Barrel: 4.02 in. Weight: 21.16 oz. (without magazine). Length: 6.85 in. overall. Features: Otherwise similar to the Model 22, including pricing. Compact version of Glock 22. Imported from Austria by Glock, Inc. Introduced 1990.
Price: **$599.00**
Price: 23C Compensated **$621.00**
Price: 23 Gen 4 .... **$649.00**

GLOCK 24/24C
Caliber: .40 S&W. Capacities: 10/15/17 or 22-round magazine. Features: Similar to Model 22 except with 6.02-inch barrel, ported or non-ported, trigger pull recalibrated to 4.5 lbs.
Price: From **$750.00**

GLOCK 26
Caliber: 9mm. Capacities: 10/12/15/17/19/33-round magazine. Barrel: 3.46 in. Weight: 19.75 oz. Length: 6.29 in. overall. Subcompact version of Glock 17. Imported from Austria by Glock, Inc.
Price: **$599.00**
Price: 26 Gen 4 .... **$649.00**
Price: 26 Gen 5 .... **$749.00**

GLOCK 27
Caliber: .40 S&W. Capacities: 9/11/13/15/17-round magazine. Barrel: 3.46 in. Weight: 19.75 oz. (without magazine). Length: 6.29 overall. Features: Otherwise similar to the Model 22, including pricing. Subcompact version of Glock 22. Imported from Austria by Glock, Inc. Introduced 1996.
Price: From **$599.00**
Price: 27 Gen 4 .... **$649.00**

GLOCK 29 GEN 4
Caliber: 10mm. Capacities: 10/15-round magazine. Barrel: 3.78 in. Weight: 24.69 oz. (without magazine). Length: 6.77 in. overall. Features: Otherwise similar to the Model 20, including pricing. Subcompact version of the Glock 20. Imported from Austria by Glock, Inc. Introduced 1997.
Price: Fixed sight **$637.00**

GLOCK MODEL 29 SF SHORT FRAME
Caliber: 10mm. Barrel: 3.78 in. with hexagonal rifling. Weight: 24.52 oz. Length: 6.97 in. overall. Sights: Fixed. Features: Otherwise similar to the Model 29 but with short-frame design, extended sight radius.
Price: **$637.00**

GLOCK 30 GEN 4
Caliber: .45 ACP. Capacities: 9/10/13-round magazines. Barrel: 3.78 in. Weight: 23.99 oz. (without magazine). Length: 6.77 in. overall. Features: Otherwise similar to the Model 21, including pricing. Subcompact version of the Glock 21. Imported from Austria by Glock, Inc. Introduced 1997. SF version has tactical rail, octagonal rifled barrel with a 1:15.75 rate of twist, smaller diameter grip, 10-round magazine capacity. Introduced 2008.
Price: **$637.00**
Price: 30 SF (short frame) **$637.00**

GLOCK 30S
Caliber: .45 ACP. Capacity: 10-round magazine. Barrel: 3.78 in. Weight: 20 oz. Length: 7 in. Features: Variation of Glock 30 with a Model 36 slide on a Model 30SF frame (short frame).
Price: **$637.00**

GLOCK 31/31C
Caliber: .357 Auto. Capacities: 15/17-round magazine. Barrel: 4.49 in. Weight: 23.28 oz. (without magazine). Length: 7.32 in. overall. Features: Otherwise similar to the Model 17. Imported from Austria by Glock, Inc.
Price: From **$599.00**
Price: 31 Gen 4 .... **$649.00**

GLOCK 32/32C
Caliber: .357 Auto. Capacities: 13/15/17-round magazine. Barrel: 4.02 in. Weight: 21.52 oz. (without magazine). Length: 6.85 in. overall. Features: Otherwise similar to the Model 31. Compact. Imported from Austria by Glock, Inc.
Price: **$599.00**
Price: 32 Gen 4 .... **$649.00**

GLOCK 33
Caliber: .357 Auto. Capacities: 9/11/13/15/17-round magazine. Barrel: 3.46 in. Weight: 19.75 oz. (without magazine). Length: 6.29 in. overall. Features: Otherwise similar to the Model 31. Subcompact. Imported from Austria by Glock, Inc.
Price: From **$599.00**
Price: 33 Gen 4 .... **$614.00**

GLOCK 34
Caliber: 9mm. Capacities: 17/19/33-round magazine. Barrel: 5.32 in. Weight: 22.9 oz. Length: 8.15 in. overall. Features: Competition version of Glock 17 with extended barrel, slide, and sight radius dimensions. Available with MOS (Modular Optic System).
Price: From **$679.00**
Price: MOS **$840.00**
Price: 34 Gen 4 .... **$729.00**
Price: 34 Gen 5 .... **$899.00**

Prices given are believed to be accurate at time of publication however, many factors affect retail pricing so exact prices are not possible.

GLOCK 35
Caliber: .40 S&W. Capacities: 15/17-round magazine. Barrel: 5.32 in. Weight: 24.52 oz. (without magazine). Length: 8.15 in. overall. Sights: Adjustable. Features: Otherwise similar to the Model 22. Competition version of the Glock 22 with extended barrel, slide and sight radius dimensions. Available with MOS (Modular Optic System). Introduced 1996.
Price: From **$679.00**
Price: MOS.. **$840.00**
Price: 35 Gen 4 .... **$729.00**

GLOCK 36
Caliber: .45 ACP. Capacity: 6-round magazine. Barrel: 3.78 in. Weight: 20.11 oz. (without magazine). Length: 6.77 overall. Sights: Fixed. Features: Single-stack magazine, slimmer grip than Glock 21/30. Subcompact. Imported from Austria by Glock, Inc. Introduced 1997.
Price: **$637.00**

GLOCK 37
Caliber: .45 GAP. Capacity: 10-round magazine. Barrel: 4.49 in. Weight: 25.95 oz. (without magazine). Length: 7.32 overall. Features: Otherwise similar to the Model 17. Imported from Austria by Glock, Inc. Introduced 2005.
Price: **$614.00**
Price: 37 Gen 4 .... **$664.00**

GLOCK 38
Caliber: .45 GAP. Capacities: 8/10-round magazine. Barrel: 4.02 in. Weight: 24.16 oz. (without magazine). Length: 6.85 overall. Features: Otherwise similar to the Model 37. Compact. Imported from Austria by Glock, Inc.
Price: **$614.00**

GLOCK 39
Caliber: .45 GAP. Capacities: 6/8/10-round magazine. Barrel: 3.46 in. Weight: 19.33 oz. (without magazine). Length: 6.3 overall. Features: Otherwise similar to the Model 37. Subcompact. Imported from Austria by Glock, Inc.
Price: **$614.00**

GLOCK 40 GEN 4
Caliber: 10mm. Features: Similar features as the Model 41 except for 6.01-in. barrel. Includes MOS optics.
Price: **$840.00**

GLOCK 41 GEN 4
Caliber: .45 ACP. Capacity: 13-round magazine. Barrel: 5.31 in. Weight: 27 oz. Length: 8.9 in. overall. Features: This is a long-slide .45 ACP Gen4 model introduced in 2014. Operating features are the same as other Glock models. Available with MOS (Modular Optic System).
Price: **$749.00**
Price: MOS.. **$840.00**

GLOCK 42 GEN 4
Caliber: .380 ACP. Capacity: 6-round magazine. Barrel: 3.25 in. Weight: 13.8 oz. Length: 5.9 in. overall. Features: This single-stack, slimlline sub-compact is the smallest pistol Glock has ever made. This is also the first Glock pistol made in the USA.
Price: **$499.00**

GLOCK 43 GEN 4
Caliber: 9mm. Capacity: 6+1. Barrel: 3.39 in. Weight: 17.95 oz. Length: 6.26 in. Height: 4.25 in. Width: 1.02 in. Features: Newest member of Glock's Slimline series with single-stack magazine.
Price: **$599.00**

GLOCK 43X
Caliber: 9mm. Capacity: 17+1. Barrel: 4.02 in. Weight: 24.5 oz. Length: 7.4 in. Height: 5.5 in. Width: 1.3 in. Combines compact slide with full-size frame.
Price: **$580.00**

GLOCK G44

Caliber: .22 LR. Capacity: 10-round magazine. Barrel: 4.02 in. Grips: Textured grip, interchangeable backstraps. Sights: Fixed, dot front/notch rear. Length: 7.28 in. overall. Weight: 14.6 oz. unloaded. Finish: Black. Features: Same size as Glock G19, hybrid slide of polymer and steel.

Price: **$430.00**

GLOCK 45

Caliber: 9mm. Capacity: 10+1. Barrel: 3.41 in. Weight: 18.7 oz. Length: 6.5 in. Height: 5.04 in. Width: 1.1 in. Combines Glock 43 short and slim dimensions with extended frame size of G48.

Price: **$580.00**

GLOCK 48 GEN 4

Caliber: 9mm. Capacity: 10. Barrel: 3.41 in. Weight: 18.7 oz. Length: 6.05 in. Height: 5.04 in. Width: 1.1 in. Features: Silver-colored PVD coated slide with front serrations. Similar length and height as Model 19 with width reduced to 1.1 inch.

Price: **$580.00**

GRAND POWER P-1 MK7

Caliber: 9mm. Capacity: 15+1 magazine. Barrel: 3.7 in. Weight: 26 oz. Features: Compact DA/SA pistol featuring frame-mounted safety, steel slide and frame and polymer grips. Offered in several variations and sizes. Made in Slovakia

Price: **$449.00**

GUNCRAFTER INDUSTRIES

Calibers: 9mm, .38 Super, .45 ACP or .50 GI. Capacity: 7- or 8-round magazine. Features: 1911-style series of pistols best known for the proprietary .50 GI chambering. Offered in approximately 30 1911 variations. No. 1 has 5-inch heavy match-grade barrel, Parkerized or hard chrome finish, checkered grips and frontstrap, numerous sight options. Other models include Commander-style, Officer's Model, Long Slide w/6-inch barrel and several 9mm and .38 Super versions.

Price: .... **$2,795.00–$5,195.00**

HECKLER & KOCH USP

Calibers: 9mm, .40 S&W, .45 ACP. Capacities: 15-round magazine; .40 S&W, 13-shot magazine; 45 ACP, 12-shot magazine. Barrels: 4.25–4.41 in. Weight: 1.65 lbs. Length: 7.64–7.87 in. overall. Grips: Non-slip stippled black polymer. Sights: Blade front, rear adjustable for windage. Features: New HK design with polymer frame, modified Browning action with recoil reduction system, single control lever. Special "hostile environment" finish on all metal parts. Available in SA/DA, DAO, left- and right-hand versions. Introduced 1993. .45 ACP Introduced 1995. Imported from Germany by Heckler & Koch, Inc.

Price: USP .45 .... **$1,199.00**
Price: USP .40 and USP 9mm **$952.00**

HECKLER & KOCH USP COMPACT

Calibers: 9mm, .357 SIG, .40 S&W, .45 ACP. Capacities: 13-round magazine; .40 S&W and .357 SIG, 12-shot magazine; .45 ACP, 8-shot magazine. Features: Similar to the USP except the 9mm, .357 SIG and .40 S&W have 3.58-in. barrels, measure 6.81 in. overall and weigh 1.47 lbs. (9mm). Introduced 1996. .45 ACP measures 7.09 in. overall. Introduced 1998. Imported from Germany by Heckler & Koch, Inc.

Price: USP Compact .45 .... **$1,040.00**
Price: USP Compact 9mm, .40 S&W **$992.00**

HECKLER & KOCH USP45 TACTICAL

Calibers: .40 S&W, .45 ACP. Capacities: 13-round magazine; .45 ACP, 12-round magazine. Barrels: 4.90-5.09 in. Weight: 1.9 lbs. Length: 8.64 in. overall. Grips: Non-slip stippled polymer. Sights: Blade front, fully adjustable target rear. Features: Has extended threaded barrel with rubber O-ring; adjustable trigger; extended magazine floorplate; adjustable trigger stop; polymer frame. Introduced 1998. Imported from Germany by Heckler & Koch, Inc.

Price: USP Tactical .45 .... **$1,352.00**
Price: USP Tactical .40 .... **$1,333.00**

Prices given are believed to be accurate at time of publication however, many factors affect retail pricing so exact prices are not possible.

HECKLER & KOCH USP COMPACT TACTICAL

Caliber: .45 ACP. Capacity: 8-round magazine. Features: Similar to the USP Tactical except measures 7.72 in. overall, weighs 1.72 lbs. Introduced 2006. Imported from Germany by Heckler & Koch, Inc.

Price: USP Compact Tactical **$1,352.00**

HECKLER & KOCH HK45

Caliber: .45 ACP. Capacity: 10-round magazine. Barrel: 4.53 in. Weight: 1.73 lbs. Length: 7.52 in. overall. Grips: Ergonomic with adjustable grip panels. Sights: Low profile, drift adjustable. Features: Polygonal rifling, ambidextrous controls, operates on improved Browning linkless recoil system. Available in Tactical and Compact variations. Tactical models come with threaded barrel, adjustable TruGlo high-profile sights, Picatinny rail.

Price: HK45 .... **$819.00**
Price: HK45 Tactical **$919.00-999.00**

HECKLER & KOCH MARK 23 SPECIAL OPERATIONS

Caliber: .45 ACP. Capacity: 12-round magazine. Barrel: 5.87 in. Weight: 2.42 lbs. Length: 9.65 in. overall. Grips: Integral with frame; black polymer. Sights: Blade front, rear drift adjustable for windage; 3-dot. Features: Civilian version of the SOCOM pistol. Polymer frame; double action; exposed hammer; short recoil, modified Browning action. Introduced 1996. Imported from Germany by Heckler & Koch, Inc.

Price: **$2,299.00**

HECKLER & KOCH P30 AND P30L

Calibers: 9mm, .40 S&W. Capacities: 13- or 15-round magazines. Barrels: 3.86 in. or 4.45 in. (P30L) Weight: 26–27.5 oz. Length: 6.95, 7.56 in. overall. Grips: Interchangeable panels. Sights: Open rectangular notch rear sight with contrast points. Features: Ergonomic features include a special grip frame with interchangeable backstrap inserts and lateral plates, allowing the pistol to be individually adapted to any user. Browning-type action with modified short recoil operation. Ambidextrous controls include dual slide releases, magazine release levers and a serrated decocking button located on the rear of the frame (for applicable variants). A Picatinny rail molded into the front of the frame. The extractor serves as a loaded-chamber indicator.

Price: P30 .... **$1,099.00**
Price: P30L Variant 2 Law Enforcement Modification (LEM) enhanced DAO **$1,149.00**
Price: P30L Variant 3 Double Action/Single Action (DA/SA) with Decocker **$1,108.00**

HECKLER & KOCH P2000

Calibers: 9mm, .40 S&W. Capacities: 13-round magazine; .40 S&W, 12-shot magazine. Barrel: 3.62 in. Weight: 1.5 lbs. Length: 7 in. overall. Grips: Interchangeable panels. Sights: Fixed Patridge style, drift adjustable for windage, standard 3-dot. Features: Incorporates features of HK USP Compact pistol, including Law Enforcement Modification (LEM) trigger, double-action hammer system, ambidextrous magazine release, dual slide-release levers, accessory mounting rails, recurved, hook trigger guard, fiber-reinforced polymer frame, modular grip with exchangeable backstraps, nitro-carburized finish, lock-out safety device. Introduced 2003. Imported from Germany by Heckler & Koch, Inc.

Price: **$799.00**

HECKLER & KOCH P2000 SK

Calibers: 9mm, .357 SIG, .40 S&W. Capacities: 10-round magazine; .40 S&W and .357 SIG, 9-round magazine. Barrel: 3.27 in. Weight: 1.3 lbs. Length: 6.42 in. overall. Sights: Fixed Patridge style, drift adjustable. Features: Standard accessory rails, ambidextrous slide release, polymer frame, polygonal bore profile. Smaller version of P2000. Introduced 2005. Imported from Germany by Heckler & Koch, Inc.

Price: **$799.00**

HECKLER & KOCH VP9/VP 40

Calibers: 9mm, .40 S&W. Capacities: 10- or 15-round magazine. .40 S&W (10 or 13). Barrel: 4.09 in. Weight: 25.6 oz. Length: 7.34 in. overall. Sights: Fixed 3-dot, drift adjustable. Features: Striker-fired system with HK enhanced light pull trigger. Ergonomic grip design with interchangeable backstraps and side panels. VP9SK is compact model with 3.4-in. barrel.

Price: **$719.00**
Price: VP9 Match **$1,159.00**
Price: VP9L OR **$899.00**
Price: VP9SK **$849.00**
Price: VP9SK optic ready .... **$899.00–$999.00**
Price: VP9 Tactical OR **$1,059.00**

HI-POINT FIREARMS MODEL 9MM COMPACT

Caliber: 9mm. Capacity: 8-round magazine. Barrel: 3.5 in. Weight: 25 oz. Length: 6.75 in. overall. Grips: Textured plastic. Sights: Combat-style adjustable 3-dot system; low profile. Features: Single-action design; frame-mounted magazine release; polymer frame offered in black or several camo finishes. Scratch-resistant matte finish. Introduced 1993. Comps are similar except they have a 4-in. barrel with muzzle brake/compensator. Compensator is slotted for laser or flashlight mounting. Introduced 1998. Made in USA by MKS Supply, Inc.

Price: C-9 9mm **$199.00**

HI-POINT FIREARMS MODEL 380 POLYMER
Caliber: .380 ACP. Capacities: 10- and 8-round magazine. Weight: 25 oz. Features: Similar to the 9mm Compact model except chambered for adjustable 3-dot sights. Polymer frame with black or camo finish. Action locks open after last shot. Trigger lock.
Price: CF-380 .... **$179.00**

HI-POINT FIREARMS 40 AND 45 SW/POLYMER
Calibers: .40 S&W, .45 ACP. Capacities: .40 S&W, 8-round magazine; .45 ACP, 9 rounds. Barrel: 4.5 in. Weight: 32 oz. Length: 7.72 in. overall. Sights: Adjustable 3-dot. Features: Polymer frames, offered in black or several camo finishes, last round lock-open, grip-mounted magazine release, magazine disconnect safety, integrated accessory rail, trigger lock. Introduced 2002. Made in USA by MKS Supply, Inc.
Price: **$219.00**

ITHACA 1911
Caliber: .45 ACP. Capacity: 7-round capacity. Barrels: 4.25 or 5 in. Weight: 35 or 40 oz. Sights: Fixed combat or fully adjustable target. Grips: Checkered cocobolo with Ithaca logo. Classic 1911A1 style with enhanced features including match-grade barrel, lowered and flared ejection port, extended beavertail grip safety, hand-fitted barrel bushing, two-piece guide rod, checkered front strap.
Price: **$1,575.00**
Price: Hand fit **$2,375.00**

IVER JOHNSON EAGLE
Calibers: 9mm, .45 ACP, 10mm. Features: Series of 1911-style pistols made in typical variations including full-size (Eagle), Commander (Hawk), Officer's (Thrasher) sizes.
Price: Elite **$1,050.00**
Price: Elite w/tritium night sights **$1,185.00**
Price: Matte black w/tritium night sights **$1,146.00**
Price: Matte stainless **$1,107.00**

KAHR CM SERIES
Calibers: 9mm, .45 ACP. Capacities: 9mm (6+1), .45 ACP (5+1). CM45 Model is shown. Barrels: 3 in., 3.25 in. (45) Weights: 15.9–17.3 oz. Length: 5.42 in. overall. Grips: Textured polymer with integral steel rails molded into frame. Sights: Pinned in polymer sight; drift-adjustable, white bar-dot combat. Features: A conventional rifled barrel instead of the match-grade polygonal barrel on Kahr's PM series; the CM slide stop lever is MIM (metal-injection-molded) instead of machined; the CM series slide has fewer machining operations and uses simple engraved markings instead of roll marking. The CM series are shipped with one magazine instead of two. The slide is machined from solid 416 stainless with a matte finish, each gun is shipped with one 6-round stainless steel magazine with a flush baseplate. Magazines are U.S.-made, plasma welded, tumbled to remove burrs and feature Wolff springs. The magazine catch in the polymer frame is all metal and will not wear out on the stainless steel magazine after extended use.
Price: .... **$518.00–$565.00**

KAHR CT SERIES
Calibers: 9mm, .45 ACP. Capacities: 9mm (8+1), .45 ACP (7+1). Barrel: 4 in. Weights: 20–25 oz. Length: 5.42 in. overall. Grips: Textured polymer with integral steel rails molded into frame. Sights: Drift adjustable, white bar-dot combat.
Price: .... **$447.00–$530.00**

KAHR CT 380
Caliber: .380 ACP. Capacity: (7+1). Barrel: 3 in. Weight: 14 oz. Other features similar to CT 9/40/45 models.
Price: **$419.00**

KAHR K SERIES
Calibers: 9mm, 7-shot; .45 ACP 6-shot magazine. Barrel: 3.5 in. Weight: 25 oz. Length: 6 in. overall. Grips: Wraparound textured soft polymer. Sights: Blade front, rear drift adjustable for windage; bar-dot combat style. Features: Trigger-cocking double-action mechanism with passive firing pin block. Made of 4140 ordnance steel with matte black finish. Contact maker for complete price list. Introduced 1994. Made in USA by Kahr Arms.
Price: .... **$532.00–$959.00**

KAHR TP SERIES
Calibers: 9mm, .45 ACP. Capacities: TP9 9mm (8-shot magazine), TP45 .45 ACP (7 or 8 shots). Barrels: 4, 5, or 6 in. Features: Model with 4-inch barrel has features similar to KP GEN 2. The 5-inch model has front and rear slide serrations, white 3-dot sights, mount for reflex sights. The 6-inch model has the same features plus comes with Leupold Delta Point Reflex sight.
Price: .... **$679.00–$839.00**

Prices given are believed to be accurate at time of publication however, many factors affect retail pricing so exact prices are not possible.

KAHR MK SERIES MICRO

Similar to the K9/K40 except is 5.35 in. overall, 4 in. high, with a 3.08 in. barrel. Weighs 23.1 oz. Has snag-free bar-dot sights, polished feed ramp, dual recoil spring system, DAO trigger. Comes with 5-round flush baseplate and 6-shot grip extension magazine. Introduced 1998. Made in USA by Kahr Arms.

Price: M9093 MK9, matte stainless steel **$911.00**
Price: M9093N MK9, matte stainless steel, tritium night sights **$1,017.00**
Price: M9098 MK9 Elite 2003, stainless steel **$991.00**
Price: M4043 MK40, matte stainless steel **$911.00**
Price: M4043N MK40, matte stainless steel, tritium night sights **$1,115.00**
Price: M4048 MK40 Elite 2003, stainless steel **$991.00**

KAHR P SERIES

Calibers: .380 ACP, 9mm, .40 S&W, 45 ACP. Capacity: 7-shot magazine. Features: Similar to K9/K40 steel frame pistol except has polymer frame, matte stainless steel slide. Barrel length 3.5 in.; overall length 5.8 in.; weighs 17 oz. Includes two 7-shot magazines, hard polymer case, trigger lock. Introduced 2000. Made in USA by Kahr Arms.

Price: KP9093 9mm **$762.00**
Price: KP4043 .40 S&W **$762.00**
Price: KP4543 .45 ACP **$829.00**
Price: KP3833 .380 ACP (2008) **$667.00**

KAHR TP GEN 2 PREMIUM SERIES

Calibers: 9mm, .45 ACP. Capacities: TP9 9mm (8-shot magazine), TP45 .45 ACP (7 or 8 shots). Barrels: 4, 5, or 6 in. Features: Model with 4-inch barrel has features similar to KP GEN 2. The 5-inch model has front and rear slide serrations, white 3-dot sights, mount for reflex sights. The 6-inch model has the same features plus comes with Leupold Delta Point Reflex sight.

Price: **$976.00**
Price: 5-inch bbl **$1,015.00**
Price: 6-inch bbl **$1,566.00**

KAHR PM SERIES

Calibers: 9mm, .40 S&W, .45 ACP. Capacity: 7-round magazine. Features: Similar to P-Series pistols except has smaller polymer frame (Polymer Micro). Barrel length 3.08 in.; overall length 5.35 in.; weighs 17 oz. Includes two 7-shot magazines, hard polymer case, trigger lock. Introduced 2000. Made in USA by Kahr Arms.

Price: PM9093 PM9 .... **$810.00**
Price: PM4043 PM40 .... **$810.00**
Price: PM4543 PM45 .... **$880.00**

KAHR T SERIES

Calibers: 9mm, .40 S&W. Capacities: T9: 9mm, 8-round magazine; T40: .40 S&W, 7-round magazine. Barrel: 4 in. Weight: 28.1–29.1 oz. Length: 6.5 in. overall. Grips: Checkered Hogue Pau Ferro wood grips. Sights: Rear: Novak low-profile 2-dot tritium night sight, front tritium night sight. Features: Similar to other Kahr makes, but with longer slide and barrel upper, longer butt. Trigger cocking DAO; locking breech; Browning-type recoil lug; passive striker block; no magazine disconnect. Comes with two magazines. Introduced 2004. Made in USA by Kahr Arms.

Price: KT9093 T9 matte stainless steel **$857.00**
Price: KT9093-NOVAK T9, "Tactical 9," Novak night sight **$980.00**
Price: KT4043 40 S&W **$857.00**

KAHR CW SERIES

Caliber: 9mm or .45 ACP. Capacities: 9mm, 7-round magazine; .45 ACP, 6-round magazine. Barrels: 3.5 and 3.64 in. Weight: 17.7–18.7 oz. Length: 5.9–6.36 in. overall. Grips: Textured polymer. Similar to the P-Series, but CW Series have conventional rifling, metal-injection-molded slide stop lever, no front dovetail cut, one magazine. Made in USA.

Price: .... **$447.00–$502.00**

KAHR P380

Caliber: .380 ACP. Capacity: 6+1. Features: Very small DAO semi-auto pistol. Features include 2.5-in. Lothar Walther barrel; black polymer frame with stainless steel slide; drift adjustable white bar/dot combat/sights; optional tritium sights; two 6+1 magazines. Overall length 4.9 in., weight 10 oz. without magazine.

Price: Standard sights **$667.00**
Price: Night sights **$792.00**

KAHR CW380
Caliber: .380 ACP. Capacity: 6-round magazine. Barrel: 2.58 in. Weight: 11.5 oz. Length: 4.96 in. Grips: Textured integral polymer. Sights: Fixed white-bar combat style. Features: DAO. Black or purple polymer frame, stainless slide.
Price: **$419.00**

KAHR TIG SPECIAL EDITION
Caliber: 9mm. Capacity: 8 rounds. Weight: 18.5 oz. Barrel: 4 in. (Subcompact model). Features: Limited Special Edition to support Beyond the Battlefield Foundation founded by John "Tig" Tiegen and his wife to provide support for wounded veterans. Tiegen is one of the heroes of the Benghazi attack in 2012. Kryptek Typhon finish on frame, black Teracote finish on slide engraved with Tiegen signature, Tig logo and BTB logo. Production will be limited to 1,000 pistols. Part of the proceeds from the sale of each firearm will be donated to the Beyond the Battlefield Foundation by Kahr Firearms Group.
Price: **$541.00**

KEL-TEC P-11
Caliber: 9mm. Capacity: 10-round magazine. Barrel: 3.1 in. Weight: 14 oz. Length: 5.6 in. overall. Grips: Checkered black polymer. Sights: Blade front, rear adjustable for windage. Features: Ordnance steel slide, aluminum frame. DAO trigger mechanism. Introduced 1995. Made in USA by Kel-Tec CNC Industries, Inc.
Price: From **$340.00**

KEL-TEC PF-9
Caliber: 9mm. Capacity: 7 rounds. Weight: 12.7 oz. Sights: Rear sight adjustable for windage and elevation. Barrel: 3.1 in. Length: 5.85 in. Features: Barrel, locking system, slide stop, assembly pin, front sight, recoil springs and guide rod adapted from P-11. Trigger system with integral hammer block and the extraction system adapted from P-3AT. Mil-Std-1913 Picatinny rail. Made in USA by Kel-Tec CNC Industries, Inc.
Price: From **$425.00**

KELTEC P15
Caliber: 9mm. Capacity: 15-round magazine. Barrel: 4-in. bull. Grip: Textured polymer. Sights: Adjustable tritium and fiber optic. Length: 5.6 in. overall. Weight: 14 ozs. unloaded. Finish: Matte black. Features: Striker-fire, accessory rail, grip safety
Price: **$425.00**

KEL-TEC P17
Caliber: .22 LR. Capacity: 16-round magazine. Barrel: 3.8 in. Grips: Textured polymer. Sights: Fixed. Length: 6.7 in. overall. Weight: 11.2 oz. unloaded. Finish: Matte black.
Price: **$199.00**

KEL-TEC P-32
Caliber: .32 ACP. Capacity: 7-round magazine. Barrel: 2.68. Weight: 6.6 oz. Length: 5.07 overall. Grips: Checkered composite. Sights: Fixed. Features: Double-action-only mechanism with 6-lb. pull; internal slide stop. Textured composite grip/frame.
Price: From **$326.00**

KELTEC P50
Caliber: 5.7 x 28mm. Capacity: 20 round magazine. Barrel: 5-in. bull. Grip: Textured aluminum. Sights: Optic ready. Length: 15 in. overall. Weight: 3.2 lbs. unloaded. Finish: Matte black. Features: Uses FN P90 50-round double stack magazines, QD mount in butt.
Price: **$995.00**

KEL-TEC P-3AT
Caliber: .380 ACP. Capacity: 7-round magazine Weight: 7.2 oz. Length: 5.2. Features: Lightest .380 ACP made; aluminum frame, steel barrel.
Price: From **$331.00**

KEL-TEC PLR-16
Caliber: 5.56mm NATO. Capacity: 10-round magazine. Weight: 51 oz. Sights: Rear sight adjustable for windage, front sight is M-16 blade. Barrel: 9.2 in. Length: 18.5 in. Features: Muzzle is threaded 1/2x28 to accept standard attachments such as a muzzle brake. Except for the barrel, bolt, sights and mechanism, the PLR-16 pistol is made of high-impact glass fiber reinforced polymer. Gas-operated semi-auto. Conventional gas-piston operation with M-16 breech locking system. MIL-STD-1913 Picatinny rail. Made in USA by Kel-Tec CNC Industries, Inc.
Price: Blued **$682.00**

KEL-TEC PLR-22
Caliber: .22 LR. Capacity: 26-round magazine. Length: 18.5 in. overall. 40 oz. Features: Semi-auto pistol based on centerfire PLR-16 by same maker. Blowback action. Open sights and Picatinny rail for mounting accessories; threaded muzzle.
Price: **$400.00**

KEL-TEC PMR-30
Caliber: .22 Magnum (.22WMR). Capacity: 30 rounds. Barrel: 4.3 in. Weight: 13.6 oz. Length: 7.9 in. overall. Grips: Glass reinforced Nylon (Zytel). Sights: Dovetailed aluminum with front & rear fiber optics. Features: Operates on a unique hybrid blowback/locked-breech system. It uses a double-stack magazine of a new design that holds 30 rounds and fits completely in the grip of the pistol. Dual opposing extractors for reliability, heel magazine release to aid in magazine retention, Picatinny accessory rail under the barrel, Urethane recoil buffer, captive coaxial recoil springs. The barrel is fluted for light weight and effective heat dissipation. PMR30 disassembles for cleaning by removal of a single pin.
Price: **$455.00**

KIMBER COLLECTOR EDITION RAPTOR
Calibers: 9mm (Micro 9 and EVO), .45 ACP (1911) Capacity: 7- or 8-round magazine. Barrels: 3.15, 3.16 or 5 in. Weight: 15.6–38 oz. Grips: G10 smooth/scaled texture. Sights: Low profile, tritium. Finish: Two-tone bronze. Features: Scale-style slide serrations. Made in the Kimber Custom Shop.
Price: (1911 model).. **$1,524.00**
Price: (Micro 9 model)... **$951.00**
Price: (EVO SP model) **$999.00**

KIMBER MICRO CDP
Caliber: .380 ACP. Capacity: 6-round magazine. Barrel: 2.75 in. Weight: 17 oz. Grips: Double diamond rosewood. Mini 1911-style single action with no grip safety.
Price: **$869.00**

KIMBER MICRO CRIMSON CARRY
Caliber: .380 ACP. Capacity: 6-round magazine. Barrel: 2.75 in. Weight: 13.4 oz. Length: 5.6 in Grips: Black synthetic, double diamond. Sights: Fixed low profile. Finish: Matte black. Features: Aluminum frame with satin silver finish, steel slide, carry-melt treatment, full-length guide rod, rosewood Crimson Trace Lasergrips.
Price: **$839.00**

KIMBER MICRO TLE
Caliber: .380 ACP. Features: Similar to Micro Crimson Carry. Features: Black slide and frame. Green and black G10 grips.
Price: **$734.00**

KIMBER MICRO RAPTOR
Caliber: .380 ACP Capacity: 6-round magazine. Sights: Tritium night sights. Finish: Stainless. Features: Variation of Micro Carry with Raptor-style scalloped "feathered" slide serrations and grip panels.
Price: **$842.00**

KIMBER COVERT SERIES
Caliber: .45 ACP Capacity: 7-round magazine. Barrels: 3, 4 or 5 in. Weight: 25–31 oz. Grips: Crimson Trace laser with camo finish. Sights: Tactical wedge 3-dot night sights. Features: Made in the Kimber Custom Shop. Finish: Kimber Gray frame, matte black slide, black small parts. Carry Melt treatment. Available in three frame sizes: Custom, Pro and Ultra.
Price: **$1,457.00**

KIMBER CUSTOM II
Caliber: 9mm, .45 ACP. Barrel: 5 in. Weight: 38 oz. Length: 8.7 in. overall. Grips: Checkered black rubber, walnut, rosewood. Sights: Dovetailed front and rear, Kimber low profile adjustable or fixed sights. Features: Slide, frame and barrel machined from steel or stainless steel. Match-grade barrel, chamber and trigger group. Extended thumb safety, beveled magazine well, beveled front and rear slide serrations, high ride beavertail grip safety, checkered flat mainspring housing, kidney cut under trigger guard, high cut grip, match-grade stainless steel barrel bushing, polished breechface, Commander-style hammer, lowered and flared ejection port, Wolff springs, bead blasted black oxide or matte stainless finish. Introduced in 1996. Made in USA by Kimber Mfg., Inc.
Price: Custom II **$871.00**
Price: Two-Tone **$1,136.00**

Prices given are believed to be accurate at time of publication however, many factors affect retail pricing so exact prices are not possible.

KIMBER CUSTOM TLE II

Caliber: .45 ACP or 10mm. Features: TLE (Tactical Law Enforcement) version of Custom II model plus night sights, frontstrap checkering, threaded barrel, Picatinny rail.

Price: .45 ACP $1,007.00
Price: 10mm $1,028.00

KIMBER MICRO 9

Caliber: 9mm. Capacity: 7-round magazine. Barrel: 3.15 in. Weight: 15.6 oz. Features: The easily concealed Micro 9 features mild recoil, smooth trigger pull and the intuitive operation of a 1911 platform. Micro 9 slides are made to the tightest allowable tolerances, with barrels machined from stainless steel for superior resistance to moisture. All Micro 9 frames are shaped from the finest aluminum for integrity and strength. Lowered and flared ejection ports for flawless ejection and a beveled magazine well for fast, positive loading. In 2020, Kimber offered 15 different Micro 9 models with a total of 26 variations.

Prices:.. $654.00-$1,061.00

KIMBER STAINLESS II

Same features as Custom II except has stainless steel frame.

Price: Stainless II .45 ACP $998.00
Price: Stainless II 9mm $1,016.00
Price: Stainless II .45 ACP w/night sights.. $1,141.00
Price: Stainless II Target .45 ACP (stainless, adj. sight) $1,108.00

KIMBER PRO CARRY II

Calibers: 9mm, .45 ACP. Features: Similar to Custom II, has aluminum frame, 4-in. bull barrel fitted directly to the slide without bushing. Introduced 1998. Made in USA by Kimber Mfg., Inc.

Price: Pro Carry II, .45 ACP $837.00
Price: Pro Carry II, 9mm $857.00
Price: Pro Carry II w/night sights $977.00
Price: Two-Tone $1,136.00

KIMBER SAPPHIRE PRO II

Caliber: 9mm. Capacity: 9-round magazine. Features: Similar to Pro Carry II, 4-inch match-grade barrel. Striking two-tone appearance with satin silver aluminum frame and high polish bright blued slide. Grips are blue/black G-10 with grooved texture. Fixed Tactical Edge night sights. From the Kimber Custom Shop.

Price: $1,652.00

KIMBER RAPTOR II

Caliber: .45 ACP. Capacities: .45 ACP (8-round magazine, 7-round (Ultra and Pro models). Barrels: 3, 4 or 5 in. Weight: 25–31 oz. Grips: Thin milled rosewood. Sights: Tactical wedge 3-dot night sights. Features: Made in the Kimber Custom Shop. Matte black or satin silver finish. Available in three frame sizes: Custom (shown), Pro and Ultra.

Price: .... $1,192.00–$1,464.00

KIMBER ULTRA CARRY II

Calibers: 9mm, .45 ACP. Features: Lightweight aluminum frame, 3-in. match-grade bull barrel fitted to slide without bushing. Grips 0.4-in. shorter. Light recoil spring. Weighs 25 oz. Introduced in 1999. Made in USA by Kimber Mfg., Inc.

Price: Stainless Ultra Carry II .45 ACP $919.00
Price: Stainless Ultra Carry II 9mm $1,016.00
Price: Stainless Ultra Carry II .45 ACP with night sights $1,039.00
Price: Two-Tone.. $1,177.00

KIMBER GOLD MATCH II

Caliber: .45 ACP. Features: Similar to Custom II models. Includes stainless steel barrel with match-grade chamber and barrel bushing, ambidextrous thumb safety, adjustable sight, premium aluminum trigger, hand-checkered double diamond rosewood grips. Barrel hand-fitted for target accuracy. Made in USA by Kimber Mfg., Inc.

Price: Gold Match II .45 ACP.. $1,393.00
Price: Gold Match Stainless II .45 ACP $1,574.00

KIMBER CDP II SERIES

Calibers: 9mm, .45 ACP. Features: Similar to Custom II but designed for concealed carry. Aluminum frame. Standard features include stainless steel slide, fixed Meprolight tritium 3-dot (green) dovetail-mounted night sights, match-grade barrel and chamber, 30 LPI frontstrap checkering, two-tone finish, ambidextrous thumb safety, hand-checkered double diamond rosewood grips. Introduced in 2000. Made in USA by Kimber Mfg., Inc.

Price: Ultra CDP II 9mm (2008) $1,359.00
Price: Ultra CDP II .45 ACP $1,318.00
Price: Compact CDP II .45 ACP $1,318.00
Price: Pro CDP II .45 ACP $1,318.00
Price: Custom CDP II (5-in. barrel, full length grip) $1,318.00

KIMBER CDP

Calibers: 9mm, .45 ACP. Barrel: 3, 4 or 5 in. Weight: 25–31 oz. Features: Aluminum frame, stainless slide, 30 LPI checkering on backstrap and trigger guard, low profile tritium night sights, Carry Melt treatment. Sights: Hand checkered rosewood or Crimson Trace Lasergrips. Introduced in 2017.

Price: **$1,173.00**
Price: With Crimson Trace Lasergrips **$1,473.00**

KIMBER ECLIPSE II SERIES

Calibers: .38 Super, 10 mm, .45 ACP. Features: Similar to Custom II and other stainless Kimber pistols. Stainless slide and frame, black oxide, two-tone finish. Gray/black laminated grips. 30 LPI frontstrap checkering. All models have night sights; Target versions have Meprolight adjustable Bar/Dot version. Made in USA by Kimber Mfg., Inc.

Price: Eclipse Ultra II (3-in. barrel, short grip) **$1,350.00**
Price: Eclipse Pro II (4-in. barrel, full-length grip) **$1,350.00**
Price: Eclipse Custom II 10mm **$1,350.00**
Price: Eclipse Target II (5-in. barrel, full-length grip, adjustable sight) **$1,393.00**

KIMBER TACTICAL ENTRY II

Caliber: 45 ACP. Capacity: 7-round magazine. Barrel: 5 in. Weight: 40 oz. Length: 8.7 in. overall. Features: 1911-style semi-auto with checkered frontstrap, extended magazine well, night sights, heavy steel frame, tactical rail.

Price: **$1,490.00**

KIMBER TACTICAL CUSTOM HD II

Caliber: .45 ACP. Capacity: 7-round magazine. Barrel: 5 in. match-grade. Weight: 39 oz. Length: 8.7 in. overall. Features: 1911-style semiauto with night sights, heavy steel frame.

Price: **$1,387.00**

KIMBER ULTRA CDP II

Calibers: 9mm, .45 ACP. Capacities: 7-round magazine (9 in 9mm). Features: Compact 1911-style pistol; ambidextrous thumb safety; carry melt profiling; full-length guide rod; aluminum frame with stainless slide; satin silver finish; checkered frontstrap; 3-inch barrel; rosewood double diamond Crimson Trace laser grips; tritium 3-dot night sights.

Price: **$1,603.00**

KIMBER STAINLESS ULTRA TLE II

Caliber: .45 ACP. Capacity: 7-round magazine. Features: 1911-style semi-auto pistol. Features include full-length guide rod; aluminum frame with stainless slide; satin silver finish; checkered frontstrap; 3-in. barrel; tactical gray double diamond grips; tritium 3-dot night sights.

Price: **$1,136.00**

KIMBER ROYAL II

Caliber: .45 ACP. Capacity: 7-round magazine. Barrel: 5 in. Weight: 38 oz. Length: 8.7 in. overall. Grips: Solid bone-smooth. Sights: Fixed low profile. Features: A classic full-size pistol wearing a charcoal blue finish complimented with solid bone grip panels. Front and rear serrations. Aluminum match-grade trigger with a factory setting of approximately 4–5 pounds.

Price: **$1,785.00**

KIMBER MASTER CARRY SERIES

Caliber: .45 ACP. Capacity: 8-round magazine, 9mm (Pro only). Barrels: 5 in. (Custom), 4 in. (Pro), 3 in. (Ultra) Weight: 25–30 oz. Grips: Crimson Trace Laser. Sights: Fixed low profile. Features: Matte black KimPro slide, aluminum round heel frame, full-length guide rod.

Price: **$1,497.00**

KIMBER WARRIOR SOC

Caliber: .45 ACP. Capacity: 7-round magazine. Barrel: 5 in threaded for suppression. Sights: Fixed Tactical Wedge tritium. Finish: Dark Green frame, Flat Dark Earth slide. Features: Full-size 1911 based on special series of pistols made for USMC. Service melt, ambidextrous safety.

Price: **$1,392.00**

KIMBER SUPER JAGARE

Caliber: 10mm. Capacity: 8+1. Barrel: 6 in, ported. Weight: 42 oz. Finish: Stainless steel KimPro, Charcoal gray frame, diamond-like carbon coated slide. Slide is ported. Sights: Delta Point Pro Optic. Grips: Micarta. Frame has rounded heel, high cut trigger guard. Designed for hunting.

Price: **$2,688.00**

Prices given are believed to be accurate at time of publication however, many factors affect retail pricing so exact prices are not possible.

KIMBER KHX SERIES

Calibers: .45 ACP, 9mm. Capacity: 8+1. Features: This series is offered in Custom, Pro and Ultra sizes. Barrels: 5-, 4- or 3-inch match-grade stainless steel. Weights: 25–38 oz. Finishes: Stainless steel frame and slide with matte black KimPro II finish. Stepped hexagonal slide and top-strap serrations. Sights: Green and red fiber optic and Hogue Laser Enhanced MagGrip G10 grips and matching mainspring housings. Pro and Ultra models have rounded heel frames. Optics Ready (OR) models available in Custom and Pro sizes with milled slide that accepts optics plates for Vortex, Trijicon and Leupold red-dot sights.

Price: Custom OR .45 ACP **$1,087.00**
Price: Custom OR 9mm **$1,108.00**
Price: Custom, Pro or Ultra .45........ **$1,259.00**
Price: Custom, Pro or Ultra 9mm **$1,279.00**

KIMBER AEGIS ELITE SERIES

Calibers: 9mm, .45 ACP. Features: Offered in Custom, Pro and Ultra sizes with 5-, 4.25- or 3-in. barrels. Sights: Green or red fiber optic or Vortex Venom red dot on OI (Optics Installed) models (shown). Grips: G10. Features: Satin finish stainless steel frame, matte black or gray slide, front and rear AEX slide serrations.

Price: .45 ACP **$1,021.00**
Price: 9mm **$1,041.00**
Price: .45 OI **$1,375.00**
Price: 9mm OI **$1,395.00**

KIMBER EVO SERIES

Caliber: 9mm. Capacity: 7 rounds. Barrel: 3.16 in. Sights: Tritium night sights. Weight: 19 oz. Grips: G10. Features: Offered in TLE, CDP, Two Tone variants with stainless slide, aluminum frame.

Price: TLE **$925.00**
Price: CDP **$949.00**
Price: Two Tone **$856.00**

LIONHEART LH9 MKII

Caliber: 9mm. Capacities: 15-round magazine. LH9C Compact, 10 rounds. Barrel: 4.1 in. Weight: 26.5 oz. Length: 7.5 in Grips: One-piece black polymer with textured design. Sights: Fixed low profile. Novak LoMount sights available. Finish: Cerakote Graphite Black or Patriot Brown. Features: Hammer-forged heat-treated steel slide, hammer-forged aluminum frame. Double-action PLUS action.

Price: **$695.00**
Price: Novak sights .... **$749.**

LLAMA MAX-1

Calibers: .38 Super, .45 ACP. Barrel: 5 in. Weight: 37 oz. Sights: Mil-spec. fixed. Features: Standard size and features of the 1911A1 full-size model. Lowered ejection port, matte blue or hard chrome finish. Imported from the Philippines by Eagle Imports. Introduced in 2016.

Price: **$565.00**

LLAMA MICRO MAX

Caliber: .380 ACP. Capacity: 7-round magazine. Weight: 23 oz. Sights: Novak style rear, fiber optic front. Grips: Wood or black synthetic. Features: A compact 1911-style pistol with 3.75-in. barrel. Skeletonized hammer and trigger, double slide serrations, comes with two 7-shot magazines. Imported from the Philippines by Eagle Imports.

Price: **$468.00**

MAC 1911 BOB CUT

Caliber: .45 ACP. Capacity: 8+1 magazine. Barrel: 4.25 in. Commander-size 1911 design. Sights: Novak-type fully adjustable rear, dovetail front. Weight: 34.5 oz. Finish: Blue or hard chrome. Grips: Custom hardwood. Features: Stippled frontstrap, skeletonized trigger and hammer, flared and lowered ejection port, bobtail grip frame. Imported from the Philippines by Eagle Imports.

Price: **$902.00**

Prices given are believed to be accurate at time of publication however, many factors affect retail pricing so exact prices are not possible.

MAC 1911 BULLSEYE
Caliber: .45 ACP Capacity: 8+1 magazine. Barrel: 6-in. match-grade bull. Sights: Bomar-type fully adjustable rear, dovetail front. Weight: 46 oz. Finish: Blue or hard chrome. Grips: Hardwood. Features: Checkered frontstrap, skeletonized trigger and hammer, flared and lowered ejection port, wide front and rear slide serrations. Imported from the Philippines by Eagle Imports.
Price: **$1,219.00**

MAC 1911 CLASSIC
Caliber: .45 ACP. Capacity: 8-round magazine. Barrel: 5-in., match-grade bull. Sights: Bomar-type fully adjustable rear, fiber-optic front. Weight: 40.5 oz. Finish: Blue, black chrome or hard chrome. Grips: Hardwood. Features: Checkered frontstrap, skeletonized trigger and hammer, flared and lowered ejection port, wide front and rear slide serrations. Imported from the Philippines by Eagle Imports.
Price: **$1,045.00**

MAC 3011 SLD TACTICAL
Calibers: 9mm, .40 S&W, .45 ACP. Capacity: 14-, 15- or 17-round magazines. Barrel: 5 in.-, match-grade bull. Sights: Bomar-type fully adjustable rear, fiber-optic front. Weight: 46.5 oz. Finish: Blue. Grips: Aluminum. Features: Checkered frontstrap serrations, skeletonized trigger and hammer, flared and lowered ejection port, ambidextrous safety, full dust cover. Imported from the Philippines by Eagle Imports.
Price: **$1,136.00**

MOSSBERG MC1SC
Caliber: 9mm Capacity: 6+1 magazine. Barrel: 3.4 in. Sights: Three white-dot, snag free. TruGlo tritium Pro sights or Viridian E-Series Red Laser available as option. Weight: 22 oz., loaded. Grips: Integral with aggressive texturing and with palm swell. Features: Glass-reinforced polymer frame, stainless steel slide with multi-angle front and rear serrations, flat-profile trigger with integrated blade safety, ships with one 6-round and one 7-round magazine. Optional cross-bolt safety. Centennial Limited Edition (1,000 units) has 24k gold accents, tritium nitride finish on barrel, polished slide.
Price: **$421.00**
Price: Viridian laser sight........ **$514.00**
Price: TruGlo tritium sights........ **$526.00**
Price: Centennial Limited Edition **$686.00**
Price: FDE **$428.00**
Price: Two-Tone........ **$421.00**

MOSSBERG MC2C
Caliber: 9mm. Capacity: 10, 13- or 15-round magazine. Barrel: 3.9 in. Grips: Textured polymer. Sights: Fixed, 3-dot. Length: 7.1 in. overall. Weight: 21 oz. unloaded. Finish: Matte black. Features: Accessory rail, forward-slide serrations.
Price: **$505.00**
Price: Two Tone **$505.00**
Price: TruGlo tritium sights........ **$613.00**
Price: Cross Bolt Safety........ **$505.00**

MOSSBERG MC2SC
Caliber: 9mm. Capacity: 11- or 14-round magazine. Barrel: 3.4 in. Grips: Textured polymer. Sights: Fixed, 3-dot, optics-ready. Length: 6.2 in. overall. Weight: 19.5 oz. unloaded. Finish: Matte black. Features: Accessory rail, forward-slide serrations.
Price: **$556.00**
Price: TruGlo tritium sights........ **$662.00**
Price: Cross Bolt Safety **$556.00**

NIGHTHAWK CUSTOM AGENT2 COMMANDER
Calibers: 9mm, .45 ACP. Capacity: 10-round magazine. Barrel: 4.25 in. Grips: G10 Railscale texture. Sights: Fixed, Heinie Ledge Black rear/gold-bead front. Length: 7.85 in. overall. Weight: 38.6 oz. unloaded. Finish: Smoke Cerakote. Features: Accessory rail, faceted slide with side windows, one-piece mainspring housing/mag well, ultra-high-cut front grip strap.
Price: **$4,499.00**

NIGHTHAWK CUSTOM BULL OFFICER
Caliber: 9mm. Capacity: 8-round magazine. Barrel: 3.8 in. Grips: Textured carbon fiber. Sights: Fixed, Heinie Ledge Black rear/fiber-optic front. Length: 7.85 in. overall. Weight: 38.2 oz. unloaded. Finish: Black nitride. Features: Bull nose and French border on slide, ultra-high-cut front grip strap, dehorned.
Price: **$3,699.00**

NIGHTHAWK CUSTOM COLT SERIES 70
Caliber: .45 ACP. Capacity: 7-round magazine. Barrel: 5 in. Grips: Textured linen micarta. Sights: Fixed, retro rear/gold-bead front. Length: 8.75 in. overall. Weight: 39 oz. unloaded. Finish: Smoked nitride. Features: Match-grade solid short trigger, fully machined disconnector, retro hammer, Nighthawk Custom beavertail grip safety, mainspring housing and match barrel bushing.
Price: **$2,599.00**

NIGHTHAWK CUSTOM GRP
Calibers: 9mm, 10mm, .45 ACP. Capacity: 8-round magazine. Features: Global Response Pistol (GRP). Black, Sniper Gray, green, Coyote Tan or Titanium Blue finish. Match-grade barrel and trigger, choice of Heinie or Novak adjustable night sights.
Price: **$3,095.00**

Prices given are believed to be accurate at time of publication however, many factors affect retail pricing so exact prices are not possible.

NIGHTHAWK CUSTOM T4
Calibers: 9mm, .45 ACP Capacities: .45 ACP, 7- or 8-round magazine; 9mm, 9 or 10 rounds; 10mm, 9 or 10 rounds. Barrels: 3.8, 4.25 or 5 in. Weights: 28–41 ounces, depending on model. Features: Manufacturer of a wide range of 1911-style pistols in Government Model (full-size), Commander and Officer's frame sizes. Shown is T4 model, introduced in 2013 and available only in 9mm.
Price: From .... **$3,495.00–$3,695.00**

NIGHTHAWK CUSTOM THUNDER RANCH
Caliber: 9mm, .45 ACP. Capacity: 8-round (.45 ACP), 10-round (9mm) magazine. Barrel: 5 in. Grips: Textured linen micarta. Sights: Fixed, Heinie Black Ledge rear/gold-bead front. Length: 8.6 in. overall. Weight: 41.3 oz. unloaded. Finish: Smoked nitride. Features: Custom front- and rear-cocking serrations, lanyard-loop mainspring housing, GI-Style nub thumb safety and custom engraving.
Price: **$3,399.00**

NIGHTHAWK CUSTOM SHADOW HAWK
Caliber: 9mm. Barrels: 5 in. or 4.25 in. Features: Stainless steel frame with black Nitride finish, flat-faced trigger, high beavertail grip safety, checkered frontstrap, Heinie Straight Eight front and rear titanium night sights.
Price: **$3,795.00**

NIGHTHAWK CUSTOM VICE PRESIDENT
Caliber: 9mm. Capacity: 10-round magazine. Barrel: 4.25 in. Grips: G10 Railscale Ascend texture. Sights: Fixed, Heinie Straight Eight Ledge rear/tritium front. Length: 7.4 in. overall. Weight: 32 oz. unloaded. Finish: Black DLC. Features: Gold titanium nitride barrel, heavy angle slide-lightening cuts, one-piece mainspring housing/mag well, ultra-high-cut front grip strap, dehorned.
Price: **$4,199.00**

NIGHTHAWK CUSTOM WAR HAWK
Caliber: .45 ACP. Barrels: 5 in. or 4.25 in. Features: One-piece mainspring housing and mag well, Everlast Recoil System, Hyena Brown G10 grips.
Price: **$3,895.00**

NIGHTHAWK CUSTOM BOB MARVEL 1911
Calibers: 9mm or .45 ACP. Barrel: 4.25-in. bull barrel. Features: Everlast Recoil System, adjustable sights, match trigger, black Melonite finish.
Price: **$4,395.00**

NIGHTHAWK CUSTOM DOMINATOR
Caliber: .45 ACP. Capacity: 8-round magazine. Features: Stainless frame, black Perma Kote slide, cocobolo double-diamond grips,, front and rear slide serrations, adjustable sights.

Price: **$3,699.00**

NIGHTHAWK CUSTOM SILENT HAWK
Caliber: .45 ACP. Capacity: 8-round magazine. Barrel: 4.25 in. Features: Commander recon frame, G10 black and gray grips. Designed to match Silencerco silencer, not included with pistol.
Price: **$4,295.00**

NIGHTHAWK CUSTOM HEINIE LONG SLIDE
Calibers: 10mm, .45 ACP. Barrel: Long slide 6-in. Features: Cocobolo wood grips, black Perma Kote finish, adjustable or fixed sights, frontstrap checkering.
Price: **$3,895.00**

NIGHTHAWK CUSTOM BORDER SPECIAL
Caliber: .45 ACP Capacity: 8+1 magazine. Barrel: 4.25-in. match grade. Weight: 34 oz. Sights: Heinie Black Slant rear, gold bead front. Grips: Cocobolo double diamond. Finish: Cerakote Elite Midnight black. Features: Commander-size steel frame with bobtail concealed carry grip. Scalloped frontstrap and mainspring housing. Serrated slide top. Rear slide serrations only. Crowned barrel flush with bushing.
Price: **$3,699.00**

NIGHTHAWK VIP BLACK
Caliber: .45 ACP. Capacity: 8+1 magazine. Hand built with all Nighthawk 1911 features plus deep hand engraving throughout, black DLC finish, custom vertical frontstrap and mainspring serrations, 14k solid gold bead front sight, crowned barrel, giraffe bone grips, custom walnut hardwood presentation case.
Price: **$7,999.00**

NORTH AMERICAN ARMS GUARDIAN DAO
Calibers: .25 NAA, .32 ACP, .380 ACP, .32 NAA. Capacity: 6-round magazine. Barrel: 2.49 in. Weight: 20.8 oz. Length: 4.75 in. overall. Grips: Black polymer. Sights: Low-profile fixed. Features: DAO mechanism. All stainless steel construction. Introduced 1998. Made in USA by North American Arms. The .25 NAA is based on a bottle-necked .32 ACP case, and the .32 NAA is on a bottle-necked .380 ACP case. Custom model has roll-engraved slide, high-polish features, choice of grips.
Price: .25 NAA, .32 ACP **$409.00**
Price: .32 NAA, .380 ACP **$486.00**
Price: Engraved Custom Model .... **$575.00-$625.00**

PHOENIX ARMS HP22, HP25
Calibers: .22 LR, .25 ACP. Capacities: .22 LR, 10-shot (HP22), .25 ACP, 10-shot (HP25). Barrel: 3 in. Weight: 20 oz. Length: 5.5 in. overall. Grips: Checkered composition. Sights: Blade front, adjustable rear. Features: Single action, exposed hammer; manual hold-open; button magazine release. Available in satin nickel,matte blue finish. Introduced 1993. Made in USA by Phoenix Arms.
Price: With gun lock **$162.00**
Price: HP Range kit with 5-in. bbl., locking case and accessories (1 Mag) **$207.00**
Price: HP Deluxe Range kit with 3- and 5-in. bbls., 2 mags, case **$248.00**

REPUBLIC FORGE 1911
Calibers: .45 ACP, 9mm, .38 Super, .40 S&W, 10mm. Features: A manufacturer of custom 1911-style pistols offered in a variety of configurations, finishes and frame sizes, including single- and double-stack models with many options. Made in Texas.
Price: From **$2,795.00**

Prices given are believed to be accurate at time of publication however, many factors affect retail pricing so exact prices are not possible.

ROBERTS DEFENSE 1911 SERIES
Caliber: .45 ACP. Capacity: 8-round magazine. Barrels: 5, 4.25 or 3.5 in. Weights: 26–38 oz. Sights: Novak-type drift-adjustable rear, tritium-dot or fiber optic front sight. Features: Skeletonized trigger. Offered in four model variants with many custom features and options. Made in Wisconsin by Roberts Defense.
Price: Recon...... **$2,370.00**
Price: Super Grade **$2,270.00**
Price: Operator...... **$2,350.00**

ROCK ISLAND ARMORY 1911A1-45 FSP
Calibers: 9mm, .38 Super, .45 ACP. Capacities:.45 ACP (8 rounds), 9mm Parabellum, .38 Super (9 rounds). Features: 1911-style semi-auto pistol. Hard rubber grips, 5-inch barrel, blued, Duracoat or two-tone finish, drift-adjustable sights. Nickel finish or night sights available.
Price: From **$592.00**

ROCK ISLAND ARMORY 1911A1-FS MATCH
Caliber: .45 ACP. Barrels: 5 in. or 6 in. Features: 1911 match-style pistol. Features fiber optic front and adjustable rear sights, skeletonized trigger and hammer, extended beavertail, double diamond checkered walnut grips.
Price: **$877.00**

ROCK ISLAND ARMORY 1911A1-.22 TCM
Caliber: .22 TCM. Capacity: 17-round magazine. Barrel: 5 in. Weight: 36 oz. Length: 8.5 in. Grips: Polymer. Sights: Adjustable rear. Features: Chambered for high velocity .22 TCM rimfire cartridge. Comes with interchangeable 9mm barrel.
Price: From **$806.00**

ROCK ISLAND ARMORY PRO MATCH ULTRA "BIG ROCK"
Caliber: 10mm. Capacity: 8- or 16-round magazine. Barrel: 6 in. Weight: 40 oz. Length: 8.5 in. Grips: VZ G10. Sights: Fiber optic front, adjustable rear. Features: Two magazines, upper and lower accessory rails, extended beavertail safety.
Price: **$1,187.00**
Price: High capacity model...... **$1,340.00**

ROCK ISLAND ARMORY MAP & MAPP
Caliber: 9mm, .22 TCM. Capacity: 16-round magazine. Barrel: 3.5 (MAPP) or 4 in (MAP). Browning short recoil action-style pistols with: integrated front sight; snag-free rear sight; single- & double-action trigger; standard or ambidextrous rear safety; polymer frame with accessory rail.
Price: From **$429.00**

ROCK ISLAND ARMORY XT22
Calibers: .22 LR, .22 Magnum. Capacities: 10- or 15-round magazine. Barrel: 5 in. Weight: 38 oz. Features: The XT-22 is the only .22 1911 with a forged 4140 steel slide and a one piece 4140 chrome moly barrel. Available as a .22/.45 ACP combo.
Price: **$600.00**
Price: .22 LR/.45 combo **$900.00**

ROCK ISLAND ARMORY BABY ROCK 380
Caliber: .380 ACP. Capacity: 7-round magazine. Features: Blowback operation. An 85 percent-size version of 1911-A1 design with features identical to full-size model.
Price: **$460.00**

ROCK RIVER ARMS LAR-15/LAR-9
Calibers: .223/5.56mm NATO, 9mm. Barrels: 7 in., 10.5 in. Wilson chrome moly, 1:9 twist, A2 flash hider, 1/2x28 thread. Weights: 5.1 lbs. (7-in. barrel), 5.5 lbs. (10.5-in. barrel). Length: 23 in. overall. Stock: Hogue rubber grip. Sights: A2 front. Features: Forged A2 or A4 upper, single stage trigger, aluminum free-float tube, one magazine. Similar 9mm Para. LAR-9 also available. From Rock River Arms, Inc.
Price: LAR-15 7 in. A2 AR2115...... **$1,175.00**
Price: LAR-15 10.5 in. A4 AR2120...... **$1,055.00**
Price: LAR-9 7 in. A2 9mm2115...... **$1,320.00**

ROCK RIVER ARMS TACTICAL PISTOL
Caliber: .45 ACP. Features: Standard-size 1911 pistol with rosewood grips, Heinie or Novak sights, Black Cerakote finish.
Price: **$2,200.00**

ROCK RIVER ARMS LIMITED MATCH
Calibers: .45 ACP, 40 S&W, .38 Super, 9mm. Barrel: 5 in. Sights: Adjustable rear, blade front. Finish: Hard chrome. Features: National Match frame with beveled magazine well, front and rear slide serrations, Commander Hammer, G10 grips.
Price: **$3,600.00**

ROCK RIVER ARMS CARRY PISTOL
Caliber: .45 ACP. Barrel: 5 in. Sights: Heinie. Finish: Parkerized. Grips: Rosewood. Weight: 39 oz.
Price: **$1,600.00**

ROCK RIVER ARMS 1911 POLY
Caliber: .45 ACP. Capacity: 7-round magazine. Barrel: 5 in. Weight: 33 oz. Sights: Fixed. Features: Full-size 1911-style model with polymer frame and steel slide.
Price: **$925.00**

RUGER-57
Caliber: 5.7x28mm. Capacity: 20-round magazine. Barrel: 4.94 in. Grips: Textured polymer. Sights: Adjustable rear/fiber-optic front, optic ready. Length: 8.65 in. overall. Weight: 24.5 oz. unloaded. Finish: Black oxide. Features: 1911-style ambidextrous manual safety, Picatinny-style accessory rail, drilled and tapped for optics with optic-adapter plate. Made in the USA.
Price: **$799.00**

RUGER AR-556 PISTOL
Calibers: 5.56 NATO, .350 Legend, .300 BLK. Capacity: .350 Legend (5-round magazine), 5.56 NATO or .300 BLK (30-round magazine). Barrels: 9.5 - 10.5 in. Weight: 6.2 lbs. Sights: Optic-ready, Picatinny rail. Grips: AR15 A2 style. Features: SB Tactical SBA3 brace.
Price: ...... **$899.00-$949.00**

RUGER AMERICAN PISTOL
Calibers: 9mm, .45 ACP. Capacities: 10 or 17 (9mm), 10 (.45 ACP). Barrels: 4.2 in. (9), 4.5 in. (.45). Lengths: 7.5 or 8 in. Weights: 30–31.5 oz. Sights: Novak LoMount Carry 3-Dot. Finish: Stainless steel slide with black Nitride finish. Grip: One-piece ergonomic wrap-around module with adjustable palm swell and trigger reach. Features: Short take-up trigger with positive re-set, ambidextrous mag release and slide stop, integrated trigger safety, automatic sear block system, easy takedown. Introduced in 2016.
Price: **$579.00**

RUGER AMERICAN COMPACT PISTOL
Caliber: 9mm. Barrel: 3.5 in. Features: Compact version of American Pistol with same general specifications.
Price: **$579.00**

RUGER LITE RACK LCP II
Caliber: .22 LR. Capacity: 10-round magazine. Barrel: 2.75 in. Grips: Textured polymer. Sights: Integral-notch rear/post front. Length: 5.2 in. overall. Weight: 11.2 oz. unloaded. Finish: Black. Features: A good training/ practice pistol for anyone who carries a Ruger LCP or LCP II. Lite Rack system with refined slide serrations, cocking ears and lighter recoil spring. Made in the USA.
Price: **$349.00**

RUGER PC CHARGER
Caliber: 9mm. Capacity: 17-round magazine. Barrel: Threaded 6.5 in. Grips: AR15 A2 style. Sights: Optic-ready, Picatinny-style rail. Length: 16.5 in. overall. Weight: 5.2 lbs. unloaded. Finish: Blued. Features: Pistol version of the Ruger PC Carbine with a glass-filled polymer chassis system and M-LOK rail. Easy takedown system separates barrel/fore-end assembly from the action, and interchangeable magazine wells for Ruger American, Ruger Security-9 or Glock magazines. Made in the USA.
Price: **$799.00**

RUGER SECURITY-9 PRO
Caliber: 9mm. Capacity: 15-round magazine. Barrel: 4 in. Grips: Textured polymer. Sights: Fixed-steel tritium. Length: 7.24 in. overall. Weight: 23.8 oz. unloaded. Finish: Black oxide. Features: Rugged construction with black oxide, through-hardened, alloy-steel slide and barrel and high-performance, glass-filled nylon grip frame. Made in the USA.
Price: **$549.00**

RUGER SECURITY-9 COMPACT PRO
Caliber: 9mm. Capacity: 10-round magazine. Barrel: 3.42 in. Grips: Textured polymer. Sights: Fixed-steel tritium. Length: 6.52 in. overall. Weight: 21.9 oz. unloaded. Finish: Black oxide. Features: Similar to Ruger Security-9 Pro. Precision-machined, hard-coat, anodized-aluminum chassis with full-length guide rails. Made in the USA.
Price: **$549.00**

RUGER SR9 /SR40
Calibers: 9mm, .40 S&W. Capacities: 9mm (17-round magazine), .40 S&W (15). Barrel: 4.14 in. Weights: 26.25, 26.5 oz. Grips: Glass-filled nylon in two color options — black or OD Green, w/flat or arched reversible backstrap. Sights: Adjustable 3-dot, built-in Picatinny-style rail. Features: Semi-auto in six configurations, striker-fired, through-hardened stainless steel slide brushed or blackened stainless slide with black grip frame or blackened stainless slide with OD Green grip frame, ambidextrous manual 1911-style safety, ambi. mag release, mag disconnect, loaded chamber indicator, Ruger cam block design to absorb recoil, comes with two magazines. 10-shot mags available. Introduced 2008. Made in USA by Sturm, Ruger & Co.
Price: SR9 (17-Round), SR9-10 (SS) **$569.00**

RUGER SR9C/SR40C COMPACT
Calibers: 9mm, .40 S&W. Capacities: 10- and 17-round magazine. Barrels: 3.4 in. (SR9C), 3.5 in. (SR40C). Weight: 23.4 oz. Features: Features include 1911-style ambidextrous manual safety; internal trigger bar interlock and striker blocker; trigger safety; magazine disconnector; loaded chamber indicator; two magazines, one 10-round and the other 17-round; 3.5-in. barrel; 3-dot sights; accessory rail; brushed stainless or blackened allow finish.
Price: **$569.00**

RUGER SECURITY-9
Caliber: 9mm. Capacity: 10- or 15-round magazine. Barrel: 4 or 3.4 in. Weight: 21 oz. Sights: Drift-adjustable 3-dot. Viridian E-Series Red Laser available. Striker-fired polymer-frame compact model. Uses the same Secure Action as LCP II. Bladed trigger safety plus external manual safety.
Price: **$379.00**
Price: Viridian Laser sight **$439.00**

Prices given are believed to be accurate at time of publication however, many factors affect retail pricing so exact prices are not possible.

RUGER SR45
Caliber: .45 ACP. Capacity: 10-round magazine. Barrel: 4.5 in. Weight: 30 oz. Length: 8 in. Grips: Glass-filled nylon with reversible flat/arched backstrap. Sights: Adjustable 3-dot. Features: Same features as SR9.
Price: $569.00

RUGER LC9S
Caliber: 9mm. Capacity: 7+1. Barrel: 3.12 in. Grips: Glass-filled nylon. Sights: Adjustable 3-dot. Features: Brushed stainless slide, black glass-filled grip frame, blue alloy barrel finish. Striker-fired operation with smooth trigger pull. Integral safety plus manual safety. Aggressive frame checkering with smooth "melted" edges. Slightly larger than LCS380. LC9S Pro has no manual safety.
Price: $479.00

RUGER LC380
Caliber: .380 ACP. Other specifications and features identical to LC9.
Price: $479.00
Price: LaserMax laser grips $529.00
Price: Crimson Trace Laserguard $629.00

RUGER LCP
Caliber: .380. Capacity: 6-round magazine. Barrel: 2.75 in. Weight: 9.4 oz. Length: 5.16 in. Grips: Glass-filled nylon. Sights: Fixed, drift adjustable or integral Crimson Trace Laserguard.
Price: Blued $259.00
Price: Stainless steel slide $289.00
Price: Viridian-E Red Laser sight $349.00
Price: Custom w/drift adjustable rear sight $269.00

RUGER LCP II
Caliber: .380. Capacity: 6-round magazine. Barrel: 2.75 in. Weight: 10.6 oz. Length: 5.16 in. Grips: Glass-filled nylon. Sights: Fixed. Features: Last round fired holds action open. Larger grip frame surface provides better recoil distribution. Finger grip extension included. Improved sights for superior visibility. Sights are integral to the slide, hammer is recessed within slide.
Price: $349.00

RUGER EC9S
Caliber: 9mm. Capacity: 7-shot magazine. Barrel: 3.125 in. Striker-fired polymer frame. Weight: 17.2 oz.
Price: $299.00

RUGER CHARGER
Caliber: .22 LR. Capacity: 15-round BX-15 magazine. Features: Based on famous 10/22 rifle design with pistol grip stock and fore-end, scope rail, bipod. Black laminate stock. Silent-SR Suppressor available. Add $449. NFA regulations apply. Reintroduced with improvements and enhancements in 2015.
Price: Standard $309.00
Price: Takedown $419.00

RUGER MK IV COMPETITION

RUGER MARK IV SERIES
Caliber: .22 LR. Capacity: 10-round magazine. Barrels: 5.5 in, 6.875 in. Target model has 5.5-in. bull barrel, Hunter model 6.88-in. fluted bull, Competition model 6.88-in. slab-sided bull. Weight: 33–46 oz. Grips: Checkered or target laminate. Sights: Adjustable rear, blade or fiber-optic front (Hunter). Features: Updated design of Mark III series with one-button takedown. Introduced 2016. Modern successor of the first Ruger pistol of 1949.
Price: Standard $449.00
Price: Target (blue) $529.00
Price: Target (stainless) $689.00
Price: Hunter .... $769.00–$799.00
Price: Competition $749.00

Prices given are believed to be accurate at time of publication however, many factors affect retail pricing so exact prices are not possible.

RUGER 22/45 MARK IV PISTOL

Caliber: .22 LR. Features: Similar to other .22 Mark IV autos except has Zytel grip frame that matches angle and magazine latch of Model 1911 .45 ACP pistol. Available in 4.4-, 5.5-in. bull barrels. Comes with extra magazine, plastic case, lock. Molded polymer or replaceable laminate grips. Weight: 25–33 oz. Sights: Adjustable. Updated design of Mark III with one-button takedown. Introduced 2016.

Price: **$409.00**
Price: 4.4-in. bull threaded barrel w/rails **$529.00**
Price: Lite w/aluminum frame, rails **$549.00**

RUGER SR22

Caliber: .22 LR. Capacity: 10-round magazine. Barrel: 3.5 in. Weight: 17.5 oz. Length: 6.4 in. Sights: Adjustable 3-dot. Features: Ambidextrous manual safety/decocking lever and mag release. Comes with two interchangeable rubberized grips and two magazines. Black or silver anodize finish. Available with threaded barrel.

Price: Black **$439.00**
Price: Silver **$459.00**
Price: Threaded barrel **$479.00**

RUGER SR1911

Caliber: .45. Capacity: 8-round magazine. Barrel: 5 in. (3.5 in. Officer Model) Weight: 39 oz. Length: 8.6 in., 7.1 in. Grips: Slim checkered hardwood. Sights: Novak LoMount Carry rear, standard front. Features: Based on Series 70 design. Flared and lowered ejection port. Extended mag release, thumb safety and slide-stop lever, oversized grip safety, checkered backstrap on the flat mainspring housing. Comes with one 7-round and one 8-round magazine.

Price: **$939.00**

RUGER SR1911 CMD

Caliber: .45 ACP. Barrel: 4.25 in. Weight: 29.3 (aluminum), 36.4 oz. (stainless). Features: Commander-size version of SR1911. Other specifications and features are identical to SR1911. Lightweight Commander also offered in 9mm.

Price: Low glare stainless **$939.00**
Price: Anodized aluminum two-tone **$979.00**

RUGER SR1911 TARGET

Calibers: 9mm, 10mm, .45 ACP. Capacities: .45 and 10mm (8-round magazine), 9mm (9 shot). Barrel: 5 in. Weight: 39 oz. Sights: Bomar adjustable. Grips: G10 Deluxe checkered. Features: Skeletonized hammer and trigger, satin stainless finish. Introduced in 2016.

Price: **$1,019.00**

RUGER SR1911 COMPETITION

Calibers: 9mm. Capacities: .10+1. Barrel: 5 in. Weight: 39 oz. Sights: Fiber optic front, adjustable target rear. Grips: Hogue Piranha G10 Deluxe checkered. Features: Skeletonized hammer and trigger, satin stainless finish, hand-fitted frame and slide, competition trigger, competition barrel with polished feed ramp. From Ruger Competition Shop. Introduced in 2016.

Price: **$2,499.00**

RUGER SR1911 OFFICER

Caliber: .45 ACP, 9mm. Capacity: 8-round magazine. Barrel: 3.6 in. Weight: 27 oz. Features: Compact variation of SR1911 Series. Black anodized aluminum frame, stainless slide, skeletonized trigger, Novak 3-dot Night Sights, G10 deluxe checkered G10 grips.

Price: **$979.00**

SAVAGE STANCE

Calibers: 9mm. Capacity: 7-, 8- or 10-rounds. Barrel: 3-in. Grip: Textured polymer. Sights: 3 white-dot system. Finishes: Cerakote Black, gray or FDE. Features: Polymer frame with chassis system.

Price: **$479.00**

Prices given are believed to be accurate at time of publication however, many factors affect retail pricing so exact prices are not possible.

SCCY CPX

Caliber: 9mm. Capacity: 10-round magazine. Barrel: 3.1 in. Weight: 15 oz. Length: 5.7 in. overall. Grips: Integral with polymer frame. Sights: 3-dot system, rear adjustable for windage. Features: Zytel polymer frame, steel slide, aluminum alloy receiver machined from bar stock. DAO with consistent 9-pound trigger pull. Concealed hammer. Available with (CPX-1) or without (CPX-2) manual thumb safety. Introduced 2014. CPX-3 is chambered for .380 ACP. Made in USA by SCCY Industries.

Price: CPX-1 .... **$284.00**
Price: CPX-2 .... **$270.00**
Price: CPX-3 .... **$305.00**

SCCY DVG SERIES

Caliber: 9mm. Capacity: 10-round magazine. Barrel: 3.1 in. Weight: 15.5 oz. Length: 6 in. overall. Grips: Integral with polymer frame. Sights: white dot front and optic ready. Features: Zytel polymer frame, steel slide, aluminum alloy receiver machined from bar stock. Striker-fire with 5.5-pound trigger pull. Made in USA.

Price: DVG-1 .... **$370.00**
Price: DVG-1RDR **$399.00**
Price: DVG-1RD **$470.00**

SEECAMP LWS 32/380 STAINLESS DA

Calibers: .32 ACP, .380 ACP. Capacity: 6-round magazine. Barrel: 2 in., integral with frame. Weight: 10.5 oz. Length: 4.125 in. overall. Grips: Glass-filled nylon. Sights: Smooth, no-snag, contoured slide and barrel top. Features: Aircraft quality 17-4 PH stainless steel. Inertia-operated firing pin. Hammer fired DAO. Hammer automatically follows slide down to safety rest position after each shot, no manual safety needed. Magazine safety disconnector. Polished stainless. Introduced 1985. From L.W. Seecamp.

Price: .32 .... **$446.25**
Price: .380 .... **$795.00**

SIG SAUER 1911

Calibers: .45 ACP, .40 S&W. Capacities: .45 ACP, .40 S&W. 8- and 10-round magazine. Barrel: 5 in. Weight: 40.3 oz. Length: 8.65 in. overall. Grips: Checkered wood grips. Sights: Novak night sights. Blade front, drift adjustable rear for windage. Features: Single-action 1911. Hand-fitted dehorned stainless steel frame and slide; match-grade barrel, hammer/sear set and trigger; 25-LPI front strap checkering, 20-LPI mainspring housing checkering. Beavertail grip safety with speed bump, extended thumb safety, firing pin safety and hammer intercept notch. Introduced 2005. XO series has contrast sights, Ergo Grip XT textured polymer grips. STX line available from Sig Sauer Custom Shop; two-tone 1911, non-railed, Nitron slide, stainless frame, burled maple grips. Polished cocking serrations, flat-top slide, mag well. Carry line has Siglite night sights, lanyard attachment point, gray diamondwood or rosewood grips, 8+1 capacity. Compact series has 6+1 capacity, 7.7 OAL, 4.25-in. barrel, slim-profile wood grips, weighs 30.3 oz. Ultra Compact in 9mm or .45 ACP has 3.3-in. barrel, low-profile night sights, slim-profile gray diamondwood or rosewood grips. 6+1 capacity. 1911 C3 is a 6+1 compact .45 ACP, rosewood custom wood grips, two-tone and Nitron finishes. Weighs 30 oz. unloaded, lightweight alloy frame. Length is 7.7 in. Now offered in more than 30 different models with numerous options for frame size, grips, finishes, sight arrangements and other features. From SIG Sauer, Inc.

Price: STX **$1,050.00**
Price: Fastback Nightmare Carry **$1,484.00**
Price: Emperor Scorpion Full-Size **$1,225.00**
Price: Fastback Emperor Scorpion Carry **$1,650.00**

SIG SAUER P210 CARRY

Caliber: 9mm. Capacity: 8-round magazine. Barrel: 4.1 in. Grip: Checkered G10. Sights: SIGLITE night sights. Length: 7.5 in. overall. Weight: 32 ozs. unloaded. Finish: Nitron. Features: Conceal carry version of iconic P210.

Price: **$1,299.00**

SIG SAUER P220

Caliber: .45 ACP, 10mm. Capacity: 7- or 8-round magazine. Barrel: 4.4 in. Weight: 27.8 oz. Length: 7.8 in. overall. Grips: Checkered black plastic. Sights: Blade front, drift adjustable rear for windage. Optional Siglite night sights. Features: Double action. Stainless steel slide, Nitron finish, alloy frame, M1913 Picatinny rail; safety system of decocking lever, automatic firing pin safety block, safety intercept notch, and trigger bar disconnector. Squared combat-type trigger guard. Slide stays open after last shot. Introduced 1976. P220 SAS Anti-Snag has dehorned stainless steel slide, front Siglite night sight, rounded trigger guard, dust cover, Custom Shop wood grips. Equinox line is Custom Shop product with Nitron stainless slide with a black hard-anodized alloy frame, brush-polished flats and nickel accents. Truglo tritium fiber-optic front sight, rear Siglite night sight, gray laminated wood grips with checkering and stippling. From SIG Sauer, Inc.

Price: **$1,087.00**
Price: P220 Elite Stainless **$1,450.00**
Price: Hunter SAO **$1,629.00**
Price: Legion 45 ACP **$1,413.00**
Price: Legion 10mm **$1,904.00**

SIG SAUER P220 ELITE

Caliber: .45 ACP. Capacity: 8-round magazine. Barrel: 4.4 in. Grip: Textured polymer. Sights: SIGLITE night sights. Length: 7.7 in. overall. Weight: 30.4 ozs. unloaded. Finish: Nitron. Features: Accessory rail, extended beavertail.

Price: **$1,174.00**

SIG SAUER P226
Calibers: 9mm, .40 S&W. Barrel: 4.4 in. Length: 7.7 in. overall. Features: Similar to the P220 pistol except has 4.4-in. barrel, measures 7.7 in. overall, weighs 34 oz. DA/SA or DAO. Many variations available. Snap-on modular grips. Legion series has improved short reset trigger, contoured and shortened beavertail, relieved trigger guard, higher grip, other improvements. From SIG Sauer, Inc.
Price: From **$1,087.00**
Price: Elite Stainless.......... **$1,481.00**
Price: Legion.......... **$1,428.00**
Price: Legion RX w/Romeo 1 Reflex sight.......... **$1,685.00**
Price: MK25 Navy Version **$1,187.00**

SIG SAUER P226 ELITE
Caliber: 9mm. Capacity: 15-round magazine. Barrel: 4.4 in. Grip: Textured polymer. Sights: SIGLITE night sights. Length: 7.7 in. overall. Weight: 34 ozs. unloaded. Finish: Nitron. Features: Accessory rail, extended beavertail.
Price: **$800.00**

SIG SAUER P229 DA
Caliber: Similar to the P220 except chambered for 9mm (10- or 15-round magazines), .40 S&W, (10- or 12-round magazines). Barrels: 3.86-in. barrel, 7.1 in. overall length and 3.35 in. height. Weight: 32.4 oz. Features: Introduced 1991. Snap-on modular grips. Frame made in Germany, stainless steel slide assembly made in U.S.; pistol assembled in U.S. Many variations available. Legion series has improved short reset trigger, contoured and shortened beavertail, relieved trigger guard, higher grip, other improvements. Select has Nitron slide, Select G10 grips, Emperor Scorpion has accessory rail, FDE finish, G10 Piranha grips.
Price: P229, From **$1,085.00**
Price: P229 Emperor Scorpion **$1,282.00**
Price: P229 Legion **$1,413.00**
Price: P229 Select.......... **$1,195.00**

SIG SAUER P229 ELITE
Caliber: 9mm. Capacity: 15-round magazine. Barrel: 3.9-in. Grip: Textured polymer. Sights: SIGLITE night sights. Length: 7.1 in. overall. Weight: 32 ozs. unloaded. Finish: Nitron. Features: Accessory rail, extended beavertail.
Price: **$800.00**

SIG SAUER SP2022
Calibers: 9mm, .40 S&W. Capacities: 10-, 12-, or 15-round magazines. Barrel: 3.9 in. Weight: 30.2 oz. Length: 7.4 in. overall. Grips: Composite and rubberized one-piece. Sights: Blade front, rear adjustable for windage. Features: Polymer frame, stainless steel slide; integral frame accessory rail; replaceable steel frame rails; left- or right-handed magazine release, two interchangeable grips.
Price: **$642.00**

SIG SAUER P238
Caliber: .380 ACP. Capacity: 6-round magazine. Barrel: 2.7 in. Weight: 15.4 oz. Length: 5.5 in. overall. Grips: Hogue G-10 and Rosewood grips. Sights: Contrast/Siglite night sights. Features: All-metal beavertail-style frame.
Price: **$723.00**
Price: Desert Tan **$738.00**
Price: Polished.......... **$798.00**
Price: Rose Gold **$932.00**
Price: Emperor Scorpion **$801.00**

SIG SAUER P320
Calibers: 9mm, .357 SIG, .40 S&W, .45 ACP. Capacities: 15 or 16 rounds (9mm), 13 or 14 rounds (.357 or .40). Barrels: 3.6 in. (Subcompact), 3.9 in. (Carry model) or 4.7 in. (Full size). Weights: 26–30 oz. Lengths: 7.2 or 8.0 in overall. Grips: Interchangeable black composite. Sights: Blade front, rear adjustable for windage. Optional Siglite night sights. Features: Striker-fired DAO, Nitron finish slide, black polymer frame. Frame size and calibers are interchangeable. Introduced 2014. Made in USA by SIG Sauer, Inc.
Price: Full size **$679.00**
Price: Carry (shown) **$679.00**

SIG SAUER P320 SUBCOMPACT
Calibers: 9mm, .40 S&W. Barrel: 3.6 in. Features: Accessory rail. Other features similar to Full-Size and Carry models.
Price: **$679.00**

SIG SAUER MODEL 320 RX
Caliber: 9mm. Capacity: 17-round magazine. Barrels: 4.7 in. or 3.9 in. Features: Full and Compact size models with ROMEO1 Reflex sight, accessory rail, stainless steel frame and slide. XFive has improved control ergonomics, bull barrel, 21-round magazines.
Price: **$952.00**
Price: XFive.......... **$1,005.00**

SIG SAUER P365
Caliber: 9mm. Barrel: 3.1 in. Weight: 17.8 oz. Features: Micro-compact striker-fired model with 10-round magazine, stainless steel frame and slide, XRAY-3 day and night sights fully textured polymer grip.
Price: **$599.00**

SIG SAUER P365 XL
Caliber: 9mm. Capacity: 12-round magazine. Barrel: 3.7 in. Grips: Textured polymer. Sights: Optic-ready, Day/Night sights. Length: 6.6 in. overall. Weight: 20.7 oz. unloaded. Finish: Nitron. Features: Grip with integrated carry mag well and extended beavertail, flat trigger and optic-ready slide.
Price: **$605.00**

Prices given are believed to be accurate at time of publication however, many factors affect retail pricing so exact prices are not possible.

SIG SAUER P365 XL ROMEOZERO
Caliber: 9mm. Capacity: 12-round magazine. Barrel: 3.7 in. Grips: Textured polymer. Sights: RomeoZero red dot, Xray3 front sight. Length: 6.6 in. overall. Weight: 20.7 oz. unloaded. Finish: Nitron. Features: Grip with integrated carry mag well and extended beavertail, and flat trigger.
Price: **$749.00**

SIG SAUER P365SAS
Caliber: 9mm. Capacity: 10-round magazine. Barrel: 3.1 in. Grips: Textured polymer. Sights: Flush-mounted FT Bullseye fiber-tritium night sight. Length: 5.8 in. overall. Weight: 17.8 oz. unloaded. Finish: Nitron. Features: Ported slide and barrel, Sig Anti Snag (SAS) treatment.
Price: **$599.00**

SIG SAUER P320-M18
Caliber: 9mm. Capacity: 17-round magazine. Barrel: 3.9 in. Grips: Textured polymer. Sights: Siglite front/night rear, optic ready. Length: 7.2 in. overall. Weight: 28.1 oz. unloaded. Finish: Coyote tan. Features: Commercial version of U.S. Military M18, manual thumb safety.
Price: **$679.00**

SIG SAUER P320 RXP FULL-SIZE
Caliber: 9mm. Capacity: 17-round magazine. Barrel: 4.7 in. Grips: Textured polymer. Sights: Romeo1Pro red dot, suppressor contrast 3-dot. Length: 8 in. overall. Weight: 30 oz. unloaded. Finish: Nitron.
Price: **$899.00**

SIG SAUER P320 LEGION XCARRY
Caliber: 9mm. Capacity: 15-round magazine. Barrel: 3.6 in. Grip: TXG heavy XCARRY grip. Sights: XRAY3 day/night sights. Length: 7.0 in. overall. Weight: 40 ozs. unloaded. Finish: Matte black. Features: Threaded barrel.
Price: **$1099.00**

SIG SAUER P320 X MAX
Caliber: 9mm. Capacity: 21-round magazine. Barrel: 5 in. Grip: TXG heavy XCARRY grip. Sights: XRAY3 day/night sights, ROMEO red dot. Length: 8.5 in. overall. Weight: 40 ozs. unloaded. Finish: Matte black. Features: Flat trigger.
Price: **$1,658.00**

SIG SAUER CUSTOM WORKS AXG SCORPION
Caliber: 9mm. Capacity: 17-round magazine. Barrel: 3.9 in. Grip: Hogue Scorpion G10 grips. Sights: XRAY3 day/night sights, optic ready. Length: 7.4 in. overall. Weight: 31.3 ozs. unloaded. Finish: Cerakote FDE. Features: Accessory rail, extended beavertail, striker-fired, metal frame, flat trigger.
Price: **$1,299.00**

SIG SAUER P320 RXP COMPACT
Caliber: 9mm. Capacity: 15-round magazine. Barrel: 3.9 in. Grips: Textured polymer. Sights: Romeo1Pro red dot, suppressor contrast 3-dot. Length: 7.2 in. overall. Weight: 26 oz. unloaded. Finish: Nitron.
Price: **$899.00**

SIG SAUER P320 RXP XFULL-SIZE
Caliber: 9mm. Capacity: 17-round magazine. Barrel: 4.7 in. Grips: Textured polymer. Sights: Romeo1Pro red dot, suppressor contrast 3-dot. Length: 8 in. overall. Weight: 30 oz. unloaded. Finish: Nitron.
Price: **$899.00**

SIG SAUER MPX
Calibers: 9mm, .357 SIG, .40 S&W. Capacities: 10, 20 or 30 rounds. Barrel: 8 in. Weight: 5 lbs Features: Semi-auto AR-style gun with closed, fully locked short-stroke pushrod gas system.
Price: From **$2,016.00**

Prices given are believed to be accurate at time of publication however, many factors affect retail pricing so exact prices are not possible.

SIG SAUER P938
Calibers: 9mm, .22 LR. Capacities: 9mm (6-shot mag.), .22 LR (10-shot mag.). Barrel: 3.0 in. Weight: 16 oz. Length: 5.9 in. Grips: Rosewood, Blackwood, Hogue Extreme, Hogue Diamondwood. Sights: Siglite night sights or Siglite rear with Tru-Glo front. Features: Slightly larger version of P238.
Price: .... **$760.00–$1,195.00**
Price: .22 LR........ **$656.00**

SMITH & WESSON M&P SERIES
Calibers: .22 LR, 9mm, .40 S&W. Capacities, full-size models: 12 rounds (.22), 17 rounds (9mm), 15 rounds (.40). Compact models: 12 (9mm), 10 (.40). Barrels: 4.25, 3.5 in. Weights: 24, 22 oz. Lengths: 7.6, 6.7 in. Grips: Polymer with three interchangeable palm swell grip sizes. Sights: 3 white-dot system with low-profile rear. Features: Zytel polymer frame with stainless steel slide, barrel and structural components. VTAC (Viking Tactics) model has Flat Dark Earth finish, VTAC Warrior sights. Compact models available with Crimson Trace Lasergrips. Numerous options for finishes, sights, operating controls.
Price: **$569.00**
Price: VTAC **$799.00**
Price: Crimson Trace........ **$699.00–$829.00**
Price: M&P 22 .... **$389.00–$419.00**

SMITH & WESSON M&P 45
Caliber: .45 ACP. Capacity: 8 or 10 rounds. Barrel length: 4 or 4.5 in. Weight: 26, 28 or 30 oz. Features: Available with or without thumb safety. Finish: Black or Dark Earth Brown. Features: M&P model offered in three frame sizes.
Price: .... **$599.00–$619.00**
Price: Threaded Barrel Kit **$719.00**

SMITH & WESSON M&P SHIELD M2.0 SERIES
Calibers: 9mm, .40 S&W, .45 Auto and 10mm. Capacities, full-size models: 17 rounds (9mm), 15 rounds (.40). Compact models: 12 (9mm), 10 (.40). Barrels: 3.6-, 4.25-, 5- or 5.6-in. Weights: 22-24 oz. Lengths: 7.6, 6.7 in. Grips: Polymer with three interchangeable palm swell grip sizes. Sights: 3 white-dot system with low-profile rear or fiber optic. Finishes: Armornite Black or Flat Dark Earth. Features: Polymer frame with stainless steel slide, barrel and structural components. Numerous options for finishes, sights, operating controls.
Price: .... **$702.00–$914.00**
Price: Compact .... **$598.00–$654.00**
Price: Subcompact **$598.00**

SMITH & WESSON M&P SHIELD M2.0 SERIES
Calibers: 9mm, .40 S&W, .45 Auto. Capacities: 7- and 8-rounds (9mm), 6- and 7-rounds (.40). Barrel: 3.1-in. Weights: 18.3 oz. Lengths: 6.1 in. Grips: Polymer. Sights: 3 white-dot system with low-profile rear. Finishes: Armornite Black. Features: Polymer frame, micro-compact size.
Price: .... **$505.00–$710.00**
Price: Performance Center Edition .... **$577.00–$911.00**

SMITH & WESSON M&P 9/40 SHIELD
Calibers: 9mm, .40 S&W. Capacities: 7- and 8-round magazine (9mm); 6-round and 7-round magazine (.40). Barrel: 3.1 in. Length: 6.1 in. Weight: 19 oz. Sights: 3-white-dot system with low-profile rear. Features: Ultra-compact, single-stack variation of M&P series. Available with or without thumb safety. Crimson Trace Green Laserguard available.
Price: **$449.00**
Price: CT Green Laserguard **$589.00**

SMITH & WESSON M&P 45 SHIELD
Caliber: .45 ACP. Barrel: 3.3 in. Ported model available. Weight: 20–23 oz. Sights: White dot or tritium night sights. Comes with one 6-round and one 7-round magazine.
Price: **$479.00**
Price: Tritium Night Sights........ **$579.00**
Price: Ported Barrel **$609.00**

SMITH & WESSON MODEL SD9 VE/SD40 VE
Calibers: .40 S&W, 9mm. Capacities: 10+1, 14+1 and 16+1 Barrel: 4 in. Weight: 39 oz. Length: 8.7 in. Grips: Wood or rubber. Sights: Front: Tritium Night Sight, Rear: Steel Fixed 2-Dot. Features: SDT (Self Defense Trigger) for optimal, consistent pull first round to last, standard Picatinny-style rail, slim ergonomic textured grip, textured finger locator and aggressive front and backstrap texturing with front and rear slide serrations.
Price: **$389.00**

SMITH & WESSON MODEL SW1911
Calibers: .45 ACP, 9mm. Capacities: 8 rounds (.45), 7 rounds (subcompact .45), 10 rounds (9mm). Barrels: 3, 4.25, 5 in. Weights: 26.5–41.7 oz. Lengths: 6.9–8.7 in. Grips: Wood, wood laminate or synthetic. Crimson Trace Lasergrips available. Sights: Low-profile white dot, tritium night sights or adjustable. Finish: Black matte, stainless or two-tone. Features: Offered in three different frame sizes. Skeletonized trigger. Accessory rail on some models. Compact models have round-butt frame. Pro Series have 30 LPI checkered frontstrap, oversized external extractor, extended mag well, full-length guide rod, ambidextrous safety.
Price: Standard Model E Series, From **$979.00**
Price: Crimson Trace grips **$1,149.00**
Price: Pro Series .... **$1,459.00–$1,609.00**
Price: Scandium Frame E Series **$1,449.00**

Prices given are believed to be accurate at time of publication however, many factors affect retail pricing so exact prices are not possible.

SMITH & WESSON BODYGUARD 380
Caliber: .380 Auto. Capacity: 6+1. Barrel: 2.75 in. Weight: 11.85 oz. Length: 5.25 in. Grips: Polymer. Sights: Integrated laser plus drift-adjustable front and rear. Features: The frame of the Bodyguard is made of reinforced polymer, as is the magazine base plate and follower, magazine catch and trigger. The slide, sights and guide rod are made of stainless steel, with the slide and sights having a Melonite hardcoating.
Price: **$449.00**

SMITH & WESSON PERFORMANCE CENTER M&P380 SHIELD EZ
Caliber: .380 ACP. Capacity: 8-round magazine. Barrel: 3.67 in. Grips: Textured polymer. Sights: Fixed, HI-VIZ Litewave H3 Tritium/Litepipe. Length: 6.8 in. overall. Weight: 23 oz. unloaded. Finish: Black Armornite frame and black, silver or gold accents. Features: Easy to rack slide, grip safety, manual thumb safety, accessory rail, reversible magazine release, ported barrel and lightening cuts in slide.
Price: **$517.00**

SMITH & WESSON PERFORMANCE CENTER M&P9 AND M&P40 M2.0 C.O.R.E. PRO SERIES
Calibers: 9mm, .40 S&W. Capacity: 17-round (9mm) or 15-round (.40 S&W) magazine. Barrel: 4.25 or 5 in. Grips: Four interchangeable palm-swell inserts. Sights: Fixed, tall 3-dot/C.O.R.E. optics-ready system. Length: 7.5-8.5 in. overall. Weight: 23-27.2 oz. unloaded. Finish: Black Armornite. Features: Accessory rail, reversible magazine release and tuned action with audible trigger reset.
Price: 4.25-in. barrel.. **$700.00**
Price: 5-in. barrel... **$721.00**

SMITH & WESSON PERFORMANCE CENTER M&P9 AND M&P40 M2.0 PORTED SERIES
Calibers: 9mm, .40 S&W. Capacity: 17-round (9mm) or 15-round (.40 S&W) magazine. Barrel: 4.25 or 5 in. Grips: Four interchangeable palm-swell inserts. Sights: Fixed, fiber-optic front and rear. Length: 8.5 in. overall. Weight: 23 oz. unloaded. Finish: Black Armornite. Features: Accessory rail, reversible magazine release, ported barrel and slide and tuned action with audible trigger reset.
Price: 4.25-in. barrel.. **$700.00**
Price: 5-in. barrel... **$721.00**

SMITH & WESSON PERFORMANCE CENTER M&P9 AND M&P40 M2.0 PORTED C.O.R.E. SERIES
Calibers: 9mm, .40 S&W. Capacity: 17-round (9mm) or 15-round (.40 S&W) magazine. Barrel: 4.25 or 5 in. Grips: Four interchangeable palm-swell inserts. Sights: Fixed, tall 3-dot/C.O.R.E. optics-ready system. Length: 8.5 in. overall. Weight: 23 oz. unloaded. Finish: Black Armornite. Features: Accessory rail, reversible magazine release, oversized slide release, ported barrel and slide, and tuned action with audible trigger reset.
Price: 4.25-in. barrel.. **$714.00**
Price: 5-in. barrel... **$735.00**

SMITH & WESSON M&P9 SHIELD EZ M2.0
Caliber: 9mm. Capacity: 8-round magazine. Barrel: 3.67 in. Grips: Textured polymer. Sights: Fixed, 3-dot. Length: 6.8 in. overall. Weight: 23.2 oz. unloaded. Finish: Black Armornite. Features: Accessory rail and reversible magazine release, with or without manual thumb safety.
Price: **$479.00**
Price: Crimson Trace Laserguard **$575.00**

SMITH & WESSON M&P9 M2.0 COMPACT
Caliber: 9mm. Capacity: 15-round magazine. Barrel: 4 in. Grips: Four interchangeable palm-swell inserts. Sights: Fixed, steel 3-dot. Length: 7.3 in. overall. Weight: 26.6 oz. unloaded. Finish: FDE. Features: Accessory rail, with or without manual thumb safety.
Price: **$569.00**

SPHINX SDP
Caliber: 9mm. Capacity: 15-shot magazine. Barrel: 3.7 in. Weight: 27.5 oz. Length: 7.4 in. Sights: Defiance Day & Night Green fiber/tritium front, tritium 2-dot red rear. Features: DA/SA with ambidextrous decocker, integrated slide position safety, aluminum MIL-STD 1913 Picatinny rail, Blued alloy/steel or stainless. Aluminum and polymer frame, machined steel slide. Offered in several variations. Made in Switzerland and imported by Kriss USA.
Price: From **$999.00**

SPRINGFIELD ARMORY 1911 GARRISON
Calibers:.45 ACP. Capacity: 7-round magazine. Barrel: 5 in. Grips: Thinline checkered wood. Sights: Low profile, 3-dot. Length: 8.4 in. overall. Weight: 37 oz. unloaded. Finish: Blued or stainless. Features: Heirloom quality 1911.
Price: Blued **$849.00**
Price: Stainless **$899.00**

SPRINGFIELD ARMORY 1911 EMISARRY
Calibers: 9mm or .45 ACP. Capacity: 7-round (.45 ACP) or 9-round (9mm) magazine. Barrel: 4.25- or 5-in. Grips: Textured G10. Sights: Tactical Rack rear/tritium front sights. Length: 8.4 in. overall. Weight: 40 oz. unloaded. Finish: Two-tone, black slide/stainless frame. Features: Square triggerguard, custom milled slide, flat trigger.
Price: .... **.$1,349.00**
Price: Emissary 4.25 in. **$1,349.00**

SPRINGFIELD ARMORY EMP ENHANCED MICRO
Calibers: 9mm, 40 S&W. Capacity: 9-round magazine. Barrel: 3-inch stainless steel match grade, fully supported ramp, bull. Weight: 26 oz. Length: 6.5 in. overall. Grips: Thinline cocobolo hardwood. Sights: Fixed low-profile combat rear, dovetail front, 3-dot tritium. Features: Two 9-round stainless steel magazines with slam pads, long aluminum match-grade trigger adjusted to 5 to 6 lbs., forged aluminum alloy frame, black hardcoat anodized finish; dual spring full-length guide rod, forged satin-finish stainless steel slide. Introduced 2007. Champion has 4-inch barrel, fiber optic front sight, three 10-round magazines, Bi-Tone finish.
Price: .... **$1,104.00–$1,249.00**
Price: Champion **$1,179.00**

SPRINGFIELD ARMORY HELLCAT 3" MICRO COMPACT
Caliber: 9mm. Capacity: 11- and 13-round magazine. Barrel: 3 in. Grip: Textured polymer. Sights: Fixed, Tritium/Luminescent front, Tactical Rack U-Notch rear. Length: 6 in. overall. Weight: 18.3 oz. unloaded with flush magazine. Finish: Matte black or Desert FDE. Features: Dual captive recoil spring w/ full-length guide rod. With or without manual thumb safety.
Price: **$587.00**
Price: OSP with Optical Sight mount **$620.00M**

SPRINGFIELD ARMORY HELLCAT RDP (RAPID DEFENSE PACKAGE)
Caliber: 9mm. Capacity: 11- and 13-round magazine. Barrel: 3.8 in. Grip: Textured polymer. Sights: Fixed, Springfield Armory HEX micro red dot. Length: 7 in. overall. Weight: 19.3 oz. unloaded with flush magazine. Finish: Matte black. Features: Self-indexing single port compensator, with or without manual thumb safety.
Price: **$899.00**

SPRINGFIELD ARMORY XD SERIES
Calibers: 9mm, .40 S&W, .45 ACP. Barrels: 3, 4, 5 in. Weights: 20.5-31 oz. Lengths: 6.26-8 overall. Grips: Textured polymer. Sights: Varies by model; Fixed sights are dovetail front and rear steel 3-dot units. Features: Three sizes in X-Treme Duty (XD) line: Sub-Compact (3-in. barrel), Service (4-in. barrel), Tactical (5-in. barrel). Three ported models available. Ergonomic polymer frame, hammer-forged barrel, no-tool disassembly, ambidextrous magazine release, visual/tactile loaded chamber indicator, visual/tactile striker status indicator, grip safety, XD gear system included. Compact is shipped with one extended magazine (13) and one compact magazine (10). XD Mod.2 Sub-Compact has newly contoured slide and redesigned serrations, stippled grip panels, fiber-optic front sight. OSP has Vortex Venom Red Dot sight, and suppressor-height sights that co-witness with red dot. Non-threaded barrel is also included.
Price: Sub-Compact OD Green 9mm/40 S&W, fixed sights **$508.00**
Price: Compact .45 ACP, 4 barrel, Bi-Tone finish **$607.00**
Price: Service Black 9mm/.40 S&W, fixed sights **$541.00**
Price: Service Black .45 ACP, external thumb safety **$638.00**
Price: V-10 Ported Black 9mm/.40 S&W **$608.00**
Price: XD Mod.2 .... **$565.00**
Price: XD OSP w/Vortex Venom Red Dot Sight **$958.00**

SPRINGFIELD ARMORY XD(M) SERIES
Calibers: 9mm, .40 S&W, .45 ACP. Barrels: 3.8 or 4.5 in. Sights: Fiber optic front with interchangeable red and green filaments, adjustable target rear. Grips: Integral polymer with three optional backstrap designs. Features: Variation of XD design with improved ergonomics, deeper and longer slide serrations, slightly modified grip contours and texturing. Black polymer frame, forged steel slide. Black and two-tone finish options.
Price: .... **$623.00–$779.00**

Prices given are believed to be accurate at time of publication however, many factors affect retail pricing so exact prices are not possible.

SPRINGFIELD ARMORY XD-M ELITE 3.8" COMPACT
Caliber: 45 Auto or 10mm. Capacity: 10-round magazine. Barrel: 3.8 in. Grip: Textured polymer. Sights: Fixed, fiber-optic front, low profile U-Notch rear. Length: 6.75 in. overall. Weight: 25 oz. unloaded. Finish: Melonite. Features: Removable magwell.
Price: **$653.00**
Price: Hex Dragonfly Optic **$837.00**

SPRINGFIELD ARMORY XD-S MOD.2 SINGLE STACK
Caliber: 45 Auto or 9mm. Capacity: 10-round magazine. Barrel: 3.3 or 4 in. Grip: Textured polymer. Sights: Fixed, fiber-optic front, low profile U-Notch rear. Length: 6.3 in. overall with 3.3-in. barrel. Weight: 23 oz. unloaded with flush-mount magazine. Finish: Melonite. Features: Removable magwell.
Price: **$465.00**
Price: OSP Crimson Trace Optic **$568.00**

SPRINGFIELD ARMORY MIL-SPEC 1911A1
Caliber: .45 ACP. Capacity: 7-round magazine. Barrel: 5 in. Weights: 35.6–39 oz. Lengths: 8.5–8.625 in. overall. Finish: Stainless steel. Features: Similar to Government Model military .45.
Price: Mil-Spec Parkerized, 7+1, 35.6 oz. **$785.00**
Price: Mil-Spec Stainless Steel, 7+1, 36 oz. **$889.00**

SPRINGFIELD ARMORY 1911 LOADED
Caliber: .45 ACP. Capacity: 7-round magazine. Barrel: 5 in. Weight: 34 oz. Length: 8.6 in. overall. Similar to Mil-Spec 1911A1 with the following additional features: Lightweight Delta hammer, extended and ergonomic beavertail safety, ambidextrous thumb safety, and other features depending on the specific model. MC, Marine, LB and Lightweight models have match-grade barrels, low-profile 3-dot combat sights.
Price: Parkerized.......... **$950.00**
Price: Stainless **$1,004.00**
Price: MC Operator (shown).......... **$1,308.00**
Price: Marine Operator **$1,308.00**
Price: LB Operator **$1,409.00**
Price: Lightweight Operator **$1,210.00**
Price: 10mm TRP (Trijicon RMR Red Dot Sight).......... **$2,238.00**

SPRINGFIELD ARMORY TRP
Caliber: .45 ACP. Features: Similar to 1911A1, except checkered frontstrap and mainspring housing, Novak Night Sight combat rear sight and matching dovetailed front sight, tuned, polished extractor, oversize barrel link; lightweight speed trigger and combat action job, match barrel and bushing, extended ambidextrous thumb safety and fitted beavertail grip safety. Textured G10 grips. Finish: Blued or stainless.
Price: **$1,695.00**
Price: Adjustable rear sight and rail **$1,780.00**

SPRINGFIELD ARMORY RONIN OPERATOR
Calibers: 9mm, 10mm, or .45 ACP. Capacity: 7-round (.45 ACP) or 9-round (9mm) magazine. Barrel: 3-, 4-, 4.25- or 5-in. Grips: Checkered wood. Sights: Fiber-optic front, tactical rack, white-dot rear. Length: 8.6 in. overall. Weight: 40 oz. unloaded. Finish: Two-tone, black slide/stainless frame.
Price: **849.00**
Price: Ronin 4.25 in. **$899.00**
Price: Ronin EMP.......... **$899.00**

SPRINGFIELD ARMORY SA-35
Calibers: 9mm. Capacity: 13-round magazine. Barrel: 4.7 in. Grips: Checkered walnut. Sights: White dot front, tactical-rack rear. Length: 7.8 in. overall. Weight: 31.5 oz. unloaded. Finish: Matte blued. Features: Clone of Iconic Hi-Power pistol.
Price: **$699.00**

SPRINGFIELD ARMORY 911 9MM
Caliber: 9mm. Barrel: 3-in. stainless steel. Sights: Pro-Glo Tritium/luminescent front, white-dot outlined Tritium rear. Weight: 15.3 oz. Length: 5.9 in. Grips: Thin-line G10. Features: Alloy frame, stainless steel slide.
Price: **$659.00**
Price: Viridian Laser **$849.00**

SPRINGFIELD ARMORY VICKERS TACTICAL
Calibers: .45 Auto. Capacity: 8-round magazine. Barrel: 5 in. match grade. Grips: Textured G10. Sights: Tritium/Luminescent front, Vickers Elite Battle U-Notch rear. Length: 8.6 in. overall. Weight: 41.5 oz. unloaded. Finish: Black CeraKote. Features: Solid aluminum match trigger, woven slide serrations, two Vickeres Duty magazines, Wilson Combat hammer and safety.
Price: **$1,495.00**

STACCATO 2011 SERIES
Calibers: 9mm, .40 S&W, .38 Super. Capacity: 9-, 17- or 21-round magazine. Barrels: 3.9- or 5-in., match-grade. Sights: Optic-ready, Dawson Precision Perfect Impact. Weight: 38–46.5 oz. Finish: Carbon black. Grips: Textured polymer. Features: 4-lb. trigger pull, ambidextrous safety levers, single- or double-stack magazine.
Price: .... **$1,699.00–$4,299.00**

STANDARD MANUFACTURING 1911 SERIES
Caliber: .45 ACP. Capacity: 7-round magazine. Barrel: 5-inch stainless steel match grade. Weight: 38.4 oz. Length: 8.6 in. Grips: Checkered rosewood double diamond. Sights: Fixed, Warren Tactical blade front/U-notch rear. Finish: Blued, case color, or nickel. Features: Forged frame and slide, beavertail grip safety, extended magazine release and thumb safety, checkered mainspring housing and front grip strap.
Price: Blued **$1,295.00**
Price: Blued, Engraved.......... **$1,579.00**
Price: Case Color **$1,599.00**
Price: Case Color, Engraved **$1,899.00**
Price: Nickel.......... **$1,499.00**

STEYR L9-A2 MF

Calibers: 9mm. Capacities: 10 or 17-round. Barrels: 4.5 in. Weight: 27.2 oz. Sights: Trapizoid. Grips: Polymer, textured grip modules. Features: DAO striker-fired operation.

Price: **$745.00**

STOEGER STR-9 COMPACT

Caliber: 9mm. Capacity: 13-round magazine. Barrel: 3.8 in. Grips: Three interchangeable backstraps. Sights: 3-dot sights or tritium night sights. Length: 6.9 in. overall. Weight: 24 oz. unloaded. Finish: Matte black. Features: Compact version of the STR-9 striker-fire pistol. Aggressive forward and rear slide serrations and accessory rail. Made in Turkey.

Price: STR-9 Optic ready **$399.00**
Price: STR-9S Combat **$599.00**
Price: STR-9SC Subcompact **$329.00**
Price: STR-9SC Subcompact optic ready **$399.00**
Price: STR-9F Full Size **$329.00**

STI FIREARMS STACCATO SERIES

Calibers: 9mm, .40 S&W, .38 Super. Capacity: 9-, 17- or 21-round magazine. Barrels: 3.9- or 5-in., match-grade. Sights: Optic-ready, Dawson Precision Perfect Impact. Weight: 38 - 46.5 oz. Finish: Carbon black. Grips: Textured polymer. Features: 4-lb. trigger pull, ambidextrous safety levers, single- or double-stack magazine.

Price: .... **$1,699.00-$4,299.00**

TAURUS 22 POLY

Caliber: 22 LR. Capacity: 8-round magazine. Barrel: 2.34-in. Grip: Textured polymer. Sights: Integrated, fixed. Length: 4.9 in. overall. Weight: 11 oz. unloaded. Finish: Matte black, two-tone. Features: DAO trigger, tip-up barrel.

Price: **$280.00**

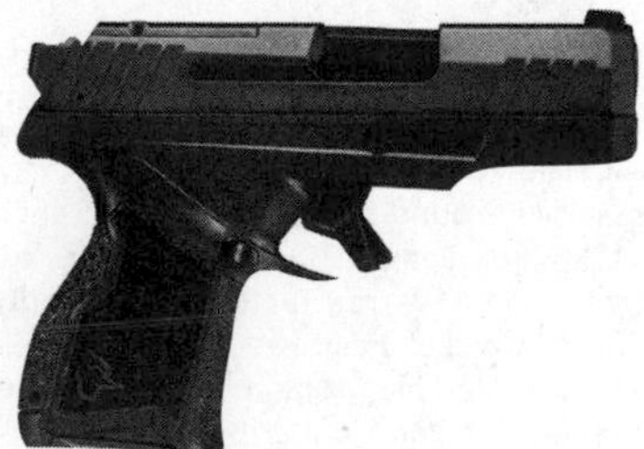

TAURUS GX4

Caliber: 9mm. Capacity: 11-round magazine. Barrel: 3.06-in. Grip: Textured polymer, modular back straps. Sights: White dot front, notch rear. Length: 5.8 in. overall with small backstrap. Weight: 18.7 oz. unloaded. Finish: Matte black. Features: T.O.R.O. model is optics-ready with mounting plates.

Price: **$392.00**
Price: T.O.R.O. **$468.00**

TAURUS G2S

Caliber: 9mm. Capacity: 6+1. Barrel: 3.2 in. Weight: 20 oz. Length: 6.3 in. Sights: Adjustable rear, fixed front. Features: Double/Single Action, polymer frame in blue with matte black or stainless slide, accessory rail, manual and trigger safeties.

Price: **$317.00**
Price: Two one with stainless slide **$333.00**

TAURUS G3

Caliber: 9mm. Capacity: 17-round magazine. Barrel: 4.0-in. Grip: Textured polymer. Sights: White dot front, notch rear. Length: 7.28 in. overall. Weight: 24.8 oz. unloaded. Finish: Matte black, gray, tan. Features: Re-strike trigger, accessory rail.

Price: **$339.00**
Price: T.O.R.O. **$449.00**
Price: G3c compact **$449.00**
Price: G3X **$342.00**

TAURUS TH9

Caliber: 9mm. Capacity: 16+1. Barrel: 4.3 in. Weight: 28 oz. Length: 7.7 in. Sights: Novak drift adjustable. Features: Full-size 9mm double-stack model with SA/DA action. Polymer frame has integral grips with finger grooves and stippling panels. Compact model has 3.8-in barrel, 6.8-in overall length.

Price: **$377.00**

TAURUS 22 POLY

Caliber: 22 LR. Capacity: 8-round magazine. Barrel: 2.34-in. Grip: Textured polymer. Sights: Integrated, fixed. Length: 4.9 in. overall. Weight: 11 oz. unloaded. Finish: Matte black, two-tone. Features: DAO trigger, tip-up barrel.

Price: **$280.00**

TAURUS TX22

Caliber: .22 LR. Capacity: 10- or 16-round magazine. Barrel: 4.1-in. Grip: Textured polymer, wrap around. Sights: Adjustable rear, white dot front. Length: 7.06 in. overall. Weight: 17.3 oz. unloaded. Finish: Matte black to tan.

Price: **$348.00**

TAURUS MODEL 1911

Calibers: 9mm, .45 ACP. Capacities: .45 ACP 8+1, 9mm 9+1. Barrel: 5 in. Weight: 33 oz. Length: 8.5 in. Grips: Checkered black. Sights: Heinie straight 8. Features: SA. Blued, stainless steel, duotone blue and blue/gray finish. Standard/Picatinny rail, standard frame, alloy frame and alloy/Picatinny rail. Introduced in 2007. Imported from Brazil by Taurus International.

Price: 1911B, Blue **$633.00**
Price: 1911B, Walnut grips **$685.00**
Price: 1911SS, Stainless Steel **$752.00**
Price: 1911SS-1, Stainless Steel w/rail **$769.00**
Price: 1911 DT, Duotone Blue **$727.00**

Prices given are believed to be accurate at time of publication however, many factors affect retail pricing so exact prices are not possible.

TAURUS MODEL 92
Caliber: 9mm. Capacity: 10- or 17-round magazine. Barrel: 5 in. Weight: 34 oz. Length: 8.5 in. overall. Grips: Checkered rubber, rosewood, mother of pearl. Sights: Fixed notch rear. 3-dot sight system. Also offered with micrometer-click adjustable night sights. Features: DA, ambidextrous 3-way hammer drop safety, allows cocked and locked carry. Blued, stainless steel, blued with gold highlights, stainless steel with gold highlights, forged aluminum frame, integral key-lock. .22 LR conversion kit available. Imported from Brazil by Taurus International.
Price: 92B **$433.00**
Price: 92SS **$550.00**

TAURUS SPECTRUM
Caliber: .380. Barrel: 2.8 in. Weight: 10 oz. Length: 5.4 in. Sights: Low-profile integrated with slide. Features: Polymer frame with stainless steel slide. Many finish combinations with various bright colors. Made in the USA. Introduced in 2017.
Price: .... **$289.00–$305.00**

TRISTAR AMERICAN CLASSIC II 1911
Calibers: 9mm, 10mm, or .45 ACP. Capacity: 7-round (.45 ACP) or 9-round (9mm) magazine. Barrel: 4.25- or 5-in. Grips: Checkered wood. Sights: Ramp front, low-profile rear. Length: 8.5 in. overall. Weight: 39.5 oz. unloaded. Finish: Hard chrome or blued.
Price: **$810.00**
Price: Commander **$730.00**
Price: Trophy **$945.00**

TURNBULL MODEL 1911
Caliber: .45 ACP. Features: An accurate reproduction of 1918-era Model 1911 pistol. Forged slide with appropriate shape and style. Late-style sight with semi-circle notch. Early-style safety lock with knurled undercut thumb piece. Short, wide checkered spur hammer. Hand-checkered double-diamond American Black Walnut grips. Hand polished with period correct Carbonia charcoal bluing. Custom made to order with many options. Made in the USA by Doug Turnbull Manufacturing Co.
Price: From **$2,625.00**

WALTHER PK380
Caliber: .380 ACP. Capacity: 8-round magazine. Barrel: 3.66 in. Weight: 19.4 oz. Length: 6.5 in. Sights: Three-dot system, drift adjustable rear. Features: DA with external hammer, ambidextrous mag release and manual safety. Picatinny rail. Black frame with black or nickel slide.
Price: **$399.00**
Price: Nickel slide **$449.00**

WALTHER PDP FULL SIZE
Caliber: 9mm. Capacity: 18-round magazine. Barrel: 4 in. Grip: Textured polymer, modular backstrap. Sights: 3-dot, optics ready. Length: 8 in. overall. Weight: 25.4 ozs. unloaded. Finish: Black. Features: Accessory rail.
Price: **$649.00**

WALTHER PDP COMPACT
Caliber: 9mm. Capacity: 15-round magazine. Barrel: 4 In. Grip: Textured polymer, modular backstrap. Sights: 3-dot, optic ready. Length: 7.5 in. overall. Weight: 24.4 ozs. unloaded. Finish: Black. Features: Accessory rail.
Price: **$649.00**

WALTHER PPK, PPK/S
Caliber: .380 ACP. Capacities: 6+1 (PPK), 7+1 (PPK/s). Barrel: 3.3 in. Weight: 21-26 oz. Length: 6.1 in. Grips: Checkered plastic. Sights: Fixed. New production in 2019. Made in Fort Smith, AR with German-made slide.
Price: **$749.00**

WALTHER PPQ M2
Calibers: 9mm, .40 S&W, .45 ACP, .22 LR. Capacities: 9mm, (15-round magazine), .40 S&W (11). .45 ACP, 22 LR (PPQ M2 .22). Barrels: 4 or 5 in. Weight: 24 oz. Lengths: 7.1, 8.1 in. Sights: Drift-adjustable. Features: Quick Defense trigger, firing pin block, ambidextrous slidelock and mag release, Picatinny rail. Comes with two extra magazines, two interchangeable frame backstraps and hard case. Navy SD model has threaded 4.6-in. barrel. M2 .22 has aluminum slide, blowback operation, weighs 19 ounces.
Price: 9mm, .40 .... **$649.00–$749.00**
Price: M2 .22 .... **$429.00**
Price: .45 .... **$699.00–$799.00**

WALTHER CCP
Caliber: 9mm. Capacity: 8-round magazine. Barrel: 3.5 in. Weight: 22 oz. Length: 6.4 in. Features: Thumb-operated safety, reversible mag release, loaded chamber indicator. Delayed blowback gas-operated action provides less recoil and muzzle jump, and easier slide operation. Available in all black or black/stainless two-tone finish.
Price: From .... **$469.00–$499.00**

WALTHER PPS M2 SERIES
Caliber: 9mm. Capacity: 6-, 7- or 8-round magazine. Barrel: 3.2 in. Sights: Optic-ready, fixed 3-dot, fixed 3-dot tritium or Crimson Trace Laserguard. Weight: 19.4 oz. Length: 6.3 in. Finish: Carbon black. Grips: Textured polymer. Features: Striker-fire, 6.1-lb. trigger pull.
Price: .... **$469.00-$560.00**

WALTHER P22
Caliber: .22 LR. Barrels: 3.4, 5 in. Weights: 19.6 oz. (3.4), 20.3 oz. (5). Lengths: 6.26, 7.83 in. Sights: Interchangeable white dot, front, 2-dot adjustable, rear. Features: A rimfire version of the Walther P99 pistol, available in nickel slide with black frame, Desert Camo or Digital Pink Camo frame with black slide.
Price: From **$379.00**
Price: Nickel slide/black frame, or black slide/camo frame **$449.00**

WALTHER Q4 STEEL FRAME
Caliber: 9mm. Capacity: 15-round magazine. Barrel: 4 in. Grips: Textured polymer, wrap around. Sights: 3-dot night. Length: 7.4 in. overall. Weight: 39.7 oz. unloaded. Finish: Matte black Tenifer. Features: Duty optimized beaver tail, Quick Defense trigger, accessory rail, oversized controls.
Price: **$1,399.00**
Price: Optic-ready model **$1,499.00**

WILSON COMBAT ELITE SERIES
Calibers: 9mm, .38 Super, .40 S&W; .45 ACP. Barrel: Compensated 4.1-in. hand-fit, heavy flanged cone match grade. Weight: 36.2 oz. Length: 7.7 in. overall. Grips: Cocobolo. Sights: Combat Tactical yellow rear tritium inserts, brighter green tritium front insert. Features: High-cut frontstrap, 30 LPI checkering on frontstrap and flat mainspring housing, High-Ride Beavertail grip safety. Dehorned, ambidextrous thumb safety, extended ejector, skeletonized ultra light hammer, ultralight trigger, Armor-Tuff finish on frame and slide. Introduced 1997. Made in USA by Wilson Combat. This manufacturer offers more than 100 different 1911 models ranging in price from about $2,800 to $5,000. XTAC and Classic 6-in. models shown. Prices show a small sampling of available models.
Price: Classic, From **$3,300.00**
Price: CQB, From **$2,865.00**
Price: Hackathorn Special **$3,750.00**
Price: Tactical Carry **$3,750.00**
Price: Tactical Supergrade **$5,045.00**
Price: Bill Wilson Carry Pistol **$3,850.00**
Price: Ms. Sentinel **$3,875.00**
Price: Hunter 10mm, .460 Rowland **$4,100.00**
Price: Beretta Brigadier Series, From **$1,195.00**
Price: X-Tac Series, From **$2,760.00**
Price: Texas BBQ Special, From **$4,960.00**

Prices given are believed to be accurate at time of publication however, many factors affect retail pricing so exact prices are not possible.

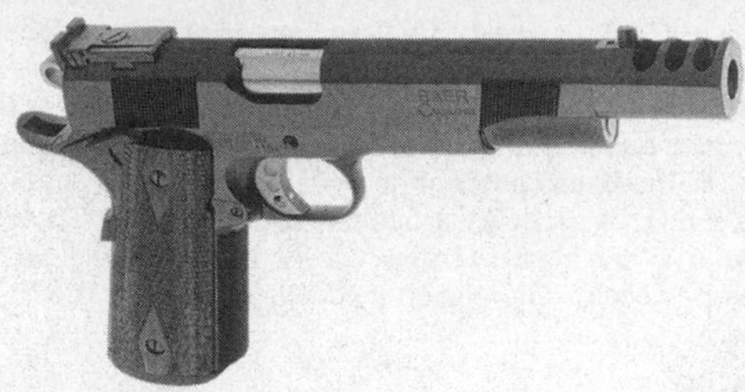

BAER 1911 ULTIMATE MASTER COMBAT
Calibers: .38 Super, 400 Cor-Bon, .45 ACP (others available). Capacity: 10-shot magazine. Barrels: 5, 6 in. Baer National Match. Weight: 37 oz. Length: 8.5 in. overall. Grips: Checkered cocobolo. Sights: Baer dovetail front, low-mount Bo-Mar rear with hidden leaf. Features: Full-house competition gun. Baer forged NM blued steel frame and double serrated slide; Baer triple port, tapered cone compensator; fitted slide to frame; lowered, flared ejection port; Baer reverse recoil plug; full-length guide rod; recoil buff; beveled magazine well; Baer Commander hammer, sear; Baer extended ambidextrous safety, extended ejector, checkered slide stop, beavertail grip safety with pad, extended magazine release button; Baer speed trigger. Made in USA by Les Baer Custom, Inc.
Price: .45 ACP Compensated **$3,240.00**
Price: .38 Super Compensated **$3,390.00**
Price: 5-in. Standard barrel **$3,040.00**
Price: 5-in. barrel .38 Super or 9mm **$3,140.00**
Price: 6-in. barrel **$3,234.00**
Price: 6-in. barrel .38 Super or 9mm **$3,316.00**

BAER 1911 NATIONAL MATCH HARDBALL
Caliber: .45 ACP. Capacity: 7-round magazine. Barrel: 5 in. Weight: 37 oz. Length: 8.5 in. overall. Grips: Checkered walnut. Sights: Baer dovetail front with under-cut post, low-mount Bo-Mar rear with hidden leaf. Features: Baer NM forged steel frame, double serrated slide and barrel with stainless bushing; slide fitted to frame; Baer match trigger with 4-lb. pull; polished feed ramp, throated barrel; checkered frontstrap, arched mainspring housing; Baer beveled magazine well; lowered, flared ejection port; tuned extractor; Baer extended ejector, checkered slide stop; recoil buff. Made in USA by Les Baer Custom, Inc.
Price: **$2,379.00**

BAER 1911 PPC OPEN CLASS
Caliber: .45 ACP, 9mm. Barrel: 6 in, fitted to frame. Sights: Adjustable PPC rear, dovetail front. Grips: Checkered Cocobola. Features: Designed for NRA Police Pistol Combat matches. Lowered and flared ejection port, extended ejector, polished feed ramp, throated barrel, frontstrap checkered at 30 LPI, flat serrated mainspring housing, Commander hammer, front and rear slide serrations. 9mm has supported chamber.
Price: **$2,775.00**
Price: 9mm w/supported chamber **$3,187.00**

BAER 1911 BULLSEYE WADCUTTER
Similar to National Match Hardball except designed for wadcutter loads only. Polished feed ramp and barrel throat; Bo-Mar rib on slide; full-length recoil rod; Baer speed trigger with 3.5-lb. pull; Baer deluxe hammer and sear; Baer beavertail grip safety with pad; flat mainspring housing checkered 20 LPI. Blue finish; checkered walnut grips. Made in USA by Les Baer Custom, Inc.
Price: From **$2,461.00**

BROWNING BUCK MARK PLUS VISION AMERICANA SUPPRESSOR READY
Caliber: .22 LR. Capacity: 10-round magazine. Barrel: 5.875-in. Grip: UFX rubber overmolded grips. Sights: Optics-ready, adjustable Pro-Target with fiber-optic front sight. Length: 9.9 in. overall. Weight: 27 oz. unloaded. Finish: anodized red, white and blue. Features: Blowback operating system, aluminum barrel sleeve with lightening cuts, removable muzzle brake.
Price: **$799.00**

BROWNING BUCK MARK PLUS VISION BLACK/GOLD SUPPRESSOR READY
Caliber: .22 LR. Capacity: 10-round magazine. Barrel: 5.875-in. Grip: UFX rubber overmolded grips. Sights: Optics-ready, adjustable Pro-Target with fiber-optic front sight. Length: 9.9 in. overall. Weight: 27 oz. unloaded. Finish: anodized black and gold. Features: Blowback operating system, aluminum barrel sleeve with lightening cuts, removable muzzle brake.
Price: **$749.00**

COLT GOLD CUP NM SERIES
Caliber: .45 ACP, 9mm, .38 Super. Capacity: 8-round magazine. Barrel: 5-inch National Match. Weight: 37 oz. Length: 8.5. Grips: Checkered wraparound rubber composite with silver-plated medallions or checkered walnut grips with gold medallions. Sights: Target post dovetail front, Bomar fully adjustable rear. Features: Adjustable aluminum wide target trigger, beavertail grip safety, full-length recoil spring and target recoil spring, available in blued finish or stainless steel.
Price: Blued **$1,299.00**
Price: Stainless **$1,350.00**
Price: Gold Cup Lite **$1,199.00**
Price: Gold Cup Trophy **$1,699.00**

COLT COMPETITION PISTOL
Calibers: .45 ACP, 9mm or .38 Super. Capacities: 8 or 9-shot magazine. Barrel: 5 in. National Match. Weight: 39 oz. Length: 8.5 In. Grips: Custom Blue Colt G10. Sights: Novak adjustable rear, fiber optic front. A competition-ready pistol out of the box at a moderate price. Blue or satin nickel finish. Series 80 firing system. O Series has stainless steel frame and slide with Cerakote gray frame and black slide, competition trigger, gray/black G-10 grips, front and rear slide serrations.
Price: .... **$949.00–$1,099.00**
Price: Competition O series **$2,499.00**

CZ 75 TS CZECHMATE
Caliber: 9mm. Capacity: 20-round magazine. Barrel: 130mm. Weight: 1360 g Length: 266mm overall. Features: The handgun is custom built, therefore the quality of workmanship is fully comparable with race pistols built directly to IPSC shooters' wishes. Individual parts and components are excellently match fitted, broke-in and tested. Every handgun is outfitted with a four-port compensator, nut for shooting without a compensator, the slide stop with an extended finger piece, the slide stop without a finger piece, ergonomic grip panels from aluminum with a new type pitting and side mounting provision with the C-More red-dot sight. For shooting without a red-dot sight there is included a standard target rear sight of Tactical Sports type, package contains also the front sight.
Price: **$3,416.00**

CZ 75 TACTICAL SPORTS
Calibers: 9mm,.40 S&W. Capacities: 17-20-round magazines. Barrel: 114mm. Weight: 1270 g Length: 225mm overall. Features: Semi-automatic handgun with a locked breech. This model is designed for competition shooting in accordance with world IPSC (International Practical Shooting Confederation) rules and regulations. The CZ 75 TS pistol model design stems from the standard CZ 75 model. However, this model features a number of special modifications, which are usually required for competitive handguns: SA trigger mechanism, match trigger made of plastic featuring option for trigger travel adjustments before discharge (using upper screw), and for overtravel (using bottom screw). The adjusting screws are set by the manufacturer — sporting hammer specially adapted for a reduced trigger pull weight, an extended magazine catch, grip panels made of walnut, guiding funnel made of plastic for quick inserting of the magazine into pistol's frame. Glossy blued slide, silver Polycoat frame. Packaging includes 3 magazines.
Price: $1,837.00

CZ SHADOW 2 SA
Caliber: 9mm. Capacity: 17-round magazine. Barrel: 4.89 in. Grips: Textured blue aluminum. Sights: Fiber-optic front, HAJO rear. Length: 8.53 in. overall. Weight: 46.5 oz. unloaded. Finish: Nitride black. Features: Single-action-only trigger. Swappable magazine release with adjustable, extended button with three settings. Ambidextrous manual thumb safety.
Price: $1,349.00

DAN WESSON CHAOS
Caliber: 9mm. Capacity: 21-round magazine. Barrel: 5 in. Weight: 3.20 lbs. Length: 8.75 in. overall. Features: A double-stack 9mm designed for 3-Gun competition.
Price: $3,829.00

DAN WESSON HAVOC
Calibers: 9mm, .38 Super. Capacity: 21-round magazine. Barrel: 4.25 in. Weight: 2.20 lbs. Length: 8 in. overall. Features: The Havoc is based on an "All Steel" Hi-capacity version of the 1911 frame. It comes ready to compete in Open IPSC/USPSA division. The C-more mounting system offers the lowest possible mounting configuration possible, enabling extremely fast target acquisition. The barrel and compensator arrangement pair the highest level of accuracy with the most effective compensator available.
Price: $4,299.00

DAN WESSON MAYHEM
Caliber: .40 S&W. Capacity: 18-round magazine. Barrel: 6 in. Weight: 2.42 lbs. Length: 8.75 in. overall. Features: The Mayhem is based on an "All-Steel" Hi-capacity version of the 1911 frame. It comes ready to compete in Limited IPSC/USPSA division or fulfill the needs of anyone looking for a superbly accurate target-grade 1911. The 6-in. bull barrel and tactical rail add to the static weight, or "good weight." A 6-in. long slide for added sight radius and enhanced pointability, but that would add to the "bad weight" so the 6-in. slide has been lightened to equal the weight of a 5 in. The result is a 6 in. long slide that balances and feels like a 5 in. but shoots like a 6 in. The combination of the all-steel frame with industry leading parts delivers the most well-balanced, softest shooting 6-in. limited gun on the market.
Price: $3,899.00

DAN WESSON TITAN
Caliber: 10mm. Capacity: 21-round magazine. Barrel: 4.25 in. Weight: 1.62 lbs. Length: 8 in. overall. Features: The Titan is based on an "All Steel" Hi-capacity version of the 1911 frame. The rugged HD night sights are moved forward and recessed deep into the slide yielding target accuracy and extreme durability. The Snake Scale serrations' aggressive 25 LPI checkering, and the custom competition G-10 grips ensure controllability even in the harshest of conditions. The combination of the all-steel frame, bull barrel and tactical rail enhance the balance and durability of this formidable target-grade Combat handgun.
Price: $3,829.00

DAN WESSON DISCRETION
Caliber: .45 ACP. Capacity: 8-round magazine. Barrel: 5.75 in. Match-grade stainless extended and threaded. Weight: 2.6 lbs. Features: Ported slide, serrated trigger, competition hammer, high tritium sights for sighting over the top of most suppressors.
Price: $2,142.00

EAA WITNESS ELITE GOLD TEAM
Calibers: 9mm, 9x21, .38 Super, .40 S&W, .45 ACP. Barrel: 5.1 in. Weight: 44 oz. Length: 10.5 in. overall. Grips: Checkered walnut, competition-style. Sights: Square post front, fully adjustable rear. Features: Triple-chamber cone compensator; competition SA trigger; extended safety and magazine release; competition hammer; beveled magazine well; beavertail grip. Hand-fitted major components. Hard chrome finish. Match-grade barrel. From EAA Custom Shop. Introduced 1992. Limited designed for IPSC Limited Class competition. Features include full-length dust-cover frame, funneled magazine well, interchangeable front sights. Stock (2005) designed for IPSC Production Class competition. Match introduced 2006. Made in Italy, imported by European American Armory.
Price: Gold Team $2,406.00
Price: Stock, 4.5 in. barrel, hard-chrome finish $1,263.00
Price: Limited Custom Xtreme $2,502.00
Price: Witness Match Xtreme $2,335.00
Price: Witness Stock III Xtreme $2.252.00

FREEDOM ARMS MODEL 83 .22 FIELD GRADE SILHOUETTE CLASS
Caliber: .22 LR. Capacity: 5-round cylinder. Barrel: 10 in. Weight: 63 oz. Length: 15.5 in. overall. Grips: Black Micarta. Sights: Removable Patridge front blade; Iron Sight Gun Works silhouette rear click-adjustable for windage and elevation (optional adj. front sight and hood). Features: Stainless steel, matte finish, manual sliding-bar safety system; dual firing pins, lightened hammer for fast lock time, pre-set trigger stop. Introduced 1991. Made in USA by Freedom Arms.
Price: Silhouette Class $2,762.00

FREEDOM ARMS MODEL 83 CENTERFIRE SILHOUETTE MODELS
Calibers: 357 Mag., .41 Mag., .44 Mag. Capacity: 5-round cylinder. Barrel: 10 in., 9 in. (.357 Mag. only). Weight: 63 oz. (41 Mag.). Length: 15.5 in., 14.5 in. (.357 only). Grips: Pachmayr Presentation. Sights: Iron Sight Gun Works silhouette rear sight, replaceable adjustable front sight blade with hood. Features: Stainless steel, matte finish, manual sliding-bar safety system. Made in USA by Freedom Arms.
Price: Silhouette Models, From $2,460.00

Prices given are believed to be accurate at time of publication however, many factors affect retail pricing so exact prices are not possible.

KIMBER SUPER MATCH II

Caliber: .45 ACP. Capacity: 8-round magazine. Barrel: 5 in. Weight: 38 oz. Length: 8.7 in. overall. Grips: Rosewood double diamond. Sights: Blade front, Kimber fully adjustable rear. Features: Guaranteed to shoot 1-in. groups at 25 yards. Stainless steel frame, black KimPro slide; two-piece magazine well; premium aluminum match-grade trigger; 30 LPI frontstrap checkering; stainless match-grade barrel; ambidextrous safety; special Custom Shop markings. Introduced 1999. Made in USA by Kimber Mfg., Inc.

Price: **$2,313.00**

MAC RAPIDO

Calibers: 9mm, .38 Super. Capacity: 17-round magazine. Barrels: 5- or 5.5-in., match-grade with compensator. Sights: Optic ready. Weight: 46.5 oz. Finish: Blue. Grips: Aluminum. Features: Checkered frontstrap serrations, combat trigger and hammer, flared and lowered ejection port, ambidextrous safety. Imported from the Philippines by Eagle Imports.

Price: **$1,725.00**

RUGER AMERICAN COMPETITION

Caliber: 9mm. Capacity: 17-round magazine. Barrel: 5 in. Grips: Three interchangeable grip inserts. Sights: Adjustable rear, fiber-optic front, optic ready. Length: 8.3 in. overall. Weight: 34.1 oz. unloaded. Finish: Black Nitrite. Features: Slide is drilled and tapped for mounting red-dot reflex optics, ported stainless steel slide. Made in the USA.

Price: **$579.00**

RUGER MARK IV TARGET

Caliber: .22 LR. Capacity: 10-round magazine. Barrel: 5.5-in. heavy bull. Weight: 35.6 oz. Grips: Checkered synthetic or laminate. Sights: .125 blade front, micro-click rear, adjustable for windage and elevation. Features: Loaded Chamber indicator; integral lock, magazine disconnect. Plastic case with lock included.

Price: Blued **$529.00**

Price: Stainless **$689.00**

SMITH & WESSON MODEL 41 TARGET

Caliber: .22 LR. Capacity: 10-round magazine. Barrels: 5.5 in., 7 in. Weight: 41 oz. (5.5-in. barrel). Length: 10.5 in. overall (5.5-in. barrel). Grips: Checkered walnut with modified thumb rest, usable with either hand. Sights: .125 in. Patridge on ramp base; micro-click rear-adjustable for windage and elevation. Features: .375 in. wide, grooved trigger; adjustable trigger stop drilled and tapped.

Price: .... **$1,369.00–$1,619.00**

SIG SAUER P320 XFIVE LEGION

Caliber: 9mm. Capacity: 17-round magazine. Barrel: 5 in. Grips: Textured polymer. Sights: Dawson Precision adjustable rear, fiber-optic front, optic ready. Length: 8.5 in. overall. Weight: 43.5 oz. unloaded. Finish: Legion gray. Features: TXG tungsten infused heavy XGrip module, slide has lightening cuts, Henning Group aluminum magazine basepads.

Price: **$999.00**

S.P.S. VISTA

Calibers: 9mm, .38 Super. Capacity: 17-round magazine. Barrels: 5- or 5.5-in., match-grade with compensator. Sights: Optic ready. Weight: 43 oz. Finish: Black chrome. Grips: Aluminum. Features: Polymer frame, checkered frontstrap serrations, skeletonized trigger and hammer, flared and lowered ejection port, ambidextrous safety, wide mag well. Imported from Spain by Eagle Imports.

Price: **$2,450.00**

S.P.S. PANTERA

Calibers: 9mm, .40 S&W, .45 ACP. Capacity: 12-, 16- or 18-round magazine. Barrel: 5-in., match-grade. Sights: Bomar-type, fully adjustable rear, fiber-optic front. Weight: 36.6 oz. Finish: Black, black chrome, chrome. Grips: Polymer. Features: Polymer frame, checkered frontstrap serrations, skeletonized trigger and hammer, flared and lowered ejection port, ambidextrous safety, wide mag well, full dust cover. Imported from Spain by Eagle Imports.

Price: **$1,730.00**

TAURUS TX22 COMPETITION

Caliber: .22 LR. Capacity: 10- or 16-round magazine. Barrel: 5.25 in. Grip: Textured polymer, wrap around. Sights: Adjustable rear, optics-ready. Length: 8.21 in. overall. Weight: 17.3 oz. unloaded. Finish: Matte black. Features: Red-dot optics-ready with mounting plates.

Price: **$485.00**

Price: SCR **$589.00**

WALTHER Q5 MATCH STEEL FRAME

Caliber: 9mm. Capacity: 15-round magazine. Barrel: 5 in. Grips: Textured polymer. Sights: LPA fiber optic front, adj. rear. Length: 8.7 in. overall. Weight: 41.6 oz. unloaded. Finish: Matte black. Features: Metal frame, optic ready, accessory rail.

Price: **$1,499.00**

WALTHER Q5 MATCH

Caliber: 9mm. Capacity: 15-round magazine. Barrel: 5 in. Grips: Textured polymer. Sights: LPA fiber-optic front, adj. rear. Length: 8.1 in. overall. Weight: 27.9 oz. unloaded. Finish: Matte black. Features: Polymer frame, optics-ready, accessory rail.

Price: **$1,300.00**

CHARTER ARMS BOOMER
Caliber: .44 Special. Capacity: 5-round cylinder. Barrel: 2 in., ported. Weight: 20 oz. Grips: Full rubber combat. Sights: Fixed.
Price: Blued **$443.00**

CHARTER ARMS POLICE BULLDOG
Caliber: .38 Special. Capacity: 6-round cylinder. Barrel: 4.2 in. Weight: 26 oz. Sights: Blade front, notch rear. Large frame version of Bulldog design.
Price: Blued **$408.00**

CHARTER ARMS CHIC LADY & CHIC LADY DAO
Caliber: .38 Special. Capacity: 5-round cylinder. Barrel: 2 in. Weight: 12 oz. Grip: Combat. Sights: Fixed. Features: 2-tone pink or lavender & stainless with aluminum frame. American made by Charter Arms.
Price: Chic Lady **$473.00**
Price: Chic Lady DAO **$483.00**

CHARTER ARMS CRIMSON UNDERCOVER
Caliber: .38 Special +P. Capacity: 5-round cylinder. Barrel: 2 in. Weight: 16 oz. Grip: Crimson Trace. Sights: Fixed. Features: Stainless finish and frame. American made by Charter Arms.
Price: **$577.00**

CHARTER ARMS OFF DUTY
Caliber: .38 Special. Barrel: 2 in. Weight: 12.5 oz. Sights: Blade front, notch rear. Features: 5-round cylinder, aluminum casting, DAO with concealed hammer. Also available with semi-concealed hammer. American made by Charter Arms.
Price: Aluminum **$404.00**
Price: Crimson Trace Laser grip **$657.00**

CHARTER ARMS MAG PUG
Caliber: .357 Mag. Capacity: 5-round cylinder. Barrel: 2.2 in. Weight: 23 oz. Sights: Blade front, notch rear. Features: American made by Charter Arms.
Price: Blued or stainless **$400.00**
Price: 4.4-in. full-lug barrel **$470.00**
Price: Crimson Trace Laser Grip **$609.00**

CHARTER ARMS PITBULL
Calibers: 9mm, 40 S&W, .45 ACP. Capacity: 5-round cylinder. Barrel: 2.2 in. Weights: 20–22 oz. Sights: Fixed rear, ramp front. Grips: Rubber. Features: Matte stainless steel frame or Nitride frame. Moon clips not required for 9mm, .45 ACP.
Price: 9mm **$502.00**
Price: .40 S&W **$489.00**
Price: .45 ACP **$489.00**
Price: 9mm Black Nitride finish **$522.00**
Price: .40, .45 Black Nitride finish **$509.00**

CHARTER ARMS PATHFINDER
Calibers: .22 LR or .22 Mag. Capacity: 6-round cylinder. Barrel: 2 in., 4 in. Weights: 20 oz. (12 oz. Lite model). Grips: Full. Sights: Fixed or adjustable (Target). Features: Stainless finish and frame.
Price .22 LR **$365.00**
Price .22 Mag **$367.00**
Price: Lite **$379.00**
Price: Target **$409.00**

CHARTER ARMS SOUTHPAW
Caliber: .38 Special +P. Capacity: 5-round cylinder. Barrel: 2 in. Weight: 12 oz. Grips: Rubber Pachmayr style. Features: Snubnose, matte black aluminum alloy frame with stainless steel cylinder. Cylinder latch and crane assembly are on right side of frame for convenience of left-hand shooters.
Price: **$419.00**

CHARTER ARMS THE PINK LADY
Caliber: .38 Special. Capacity: 6-round cylinder. Barrel: 2.2 in. Grips: Full. Sights: Fixed rear, LitePipe front. Weight: 12 oz. Features: As the name indicates, the Pink Lady has a pink and stainless steel finish. This is an aluminum-framed revolver from the Undercover Lite series.
Price: **$357.00**

CHARTER ARMS TARGET MAGNUM
Caliber: .357 Magnum. Capacity: 6-round cylinder. Barrel: 6 in. Grips: Full. Sights: Fully adjustable rear, fixed front. Features: This revolver of the Mag Pug series is built on Charter's XL frame. The 6-inch barrel and fully adjustable sights make this a great target piece that can also be used for hunting. Like all Charters, this one is made in the USA.
Price: **$476.00**

Prices given are believed to be accurate at time of publication however, many factors affect retail pricing so exact prices are not possible.

CHARTER ARMS THE PROFESSIONAL II
Caliber: .357 Magnum. Capacity: 6-round cylinder. Barrel: 3 in. Grips: Wood. Sights: Fixed rear, LitePipe front. Features: Built on Charter's large frame, the PROFESSIONAL II is a member of the PROFESSIONAL series of revolvers that is finished in a tough and attractive Blacknitride finish.
Price: **$406.00**

CHARTER ARMS THE PROFESSIONAL III
Caliber: .357 Magnum. Capacity: 6-round cylinder. Barrel: 4.2 in. Grips: Wood. Sights: Fixed rear, LitePipe front. Features: The PROFESSIONAL III is also a member of the PROFESSIONAL series of American-made revolvers from Charter Arms. This one, however, is built on Charter's XL frame, with a wood grip and a Blacknitride finish.
Price: **$470.00**

CHARTER ARMS THE PROFESSIONAL IV
Caliber: .32 Magnum. Capacity: 7-round cylinder. Barrel: 3 in. Grips: Wood. Sights: Fixed rear, LitePipe front. Features: A member of the PROFESSIONAL series, the PROFESSIONAL IV is manufactured on the large frame and features a 7-shot cylinder chambered in .32 Magnum. The finish is stainless steel.
Price: **$420.00**

CHARTER ARMS THE PROFESSIONAL V
Caliber: .357 Magnum. Capacity: 6-round cylinder. Barrel: 3 in. Grips: Wood. Sights: Fixed rear, LitePipe front. Features: A member of the PROFESSIONAL series, the PROFESSIONAL V is manufactured on the large frame and features a 6-shot cylinder chambered in .357 Magnum. The finish is stainless steel.
Price: **$399.00**

CHARTER ARMS THE PROFESSIONAL VI
Caliber: .357 Magnum. Capacity: 6-round cylinder. Barrel: 4.2 in. Grips: Wood. Sights: Fixed rear, LitePipe front. Features: The final model in the PROFESSIONAL series, the PROFESSIONAL VI is manufactured on Charter Arms' XL frame and features a 6-shot cylinder. The finish is stainless steel.
Price: **$420.00**

CHARTER ARMS UNDERCOVER
Caliber: .38 Special +P. Capacity: 6-round cylinder. Barrel: 2 in. Weight: 12 oz. Sights: Blade front, notch rear. Features: American made by Charter Arms.
Price: Blued **$346.00**

CHARTER ARMS UNDERCOVER LITE
Caliber: .38 Special. Capacity: 6-round cylinder. Barrel: 2.2 in. Grips: Full. Sights: Fixed rear, LitePipe front. Weight: 12 oz. Features: Aluminum-framed lightweight revolver with anodized finish. Lots of power in a feather-weight package.
Price: **$357.00**

CHARTER ARMS UNDERCOVER SOUTHPAW
Caliber: .38 Spec. +P. Capacity: 5-round cylinder. Barrel: 2 in. Weight: 12 oz. Sights: NA. Features: Cylinder release is on the right side and the cylinder opens to the right side. Exposed hammer for both SA and DA. American made by Charter Arms.
Price: **$419.00**

CHIAPPA RHINO
Calibers: .357 Magnum, 9mm, .40 S&W. Features: 2-, 4-, 5- or 6-inch barrel; fixed or adjustable sights; visible hammer or hammerless design. Weights: 24–33 oz. Walnut or synthetic grips with black frame; hexagonal-shaped cylinder. Unique design fires from bottom chamber of cylinder.
Price: From .... **$1,090.00-$1,465.00**

CHIAPPA RHINO REVOLVER 30DS NEBULA .357 MAG/3-INCH BBL (30SAR-CALIFORNIA COMPLIANT)
Type of Gun: Revolver, Caliber: .357 Magnum, Action: Single/Double, Barrel Length: 3 in. (76mm) Capacity: 6. Feed In: manual, Trigger System: Single. Grips: Blue laminate medium. Front Sight: Fixed red fiber optic. Rear Sight: Adjustable elevation and windage green fiber optic, Safety: Internal, Weight: 1.7 lbs. Length: 7.5 in. (190 mm) Material: Machined 7075-T6 alloy frame/ steel cylinder and barrel finish: Muti-Color PVD. Extraction: Manual. Notes: Includes three moon clips, removal tool, gun lock and black leather holster.
Price: **$1,912.00**

COBRA SHADOW
Caliber: .38 Special +P. Capacity: 5 rounds. Barrel: 1.875 in. Weight: 15 oz. Aluminum frame with stainless steel barrel and cylinder. Length: 6.375 in. Grips: Rosewood, black rubber or Crimson Trace Laser. Features: Black anodized, titanium anodized or custom colors including gold, red, pink and blue.
Price: **$369.00**
Price: Rosewood grips **$434.00**
Price: Crimson Trace Laser grips **$625.00**

COLT COBRA
Caliber: .38 Special. Capacity: 6 rounds. Sights: Fixed rear, fiber optic red front. Grips: Hogue rubbed stippled with finger grooves. Weight: 25 oz. Finish: Matte stainless. Same name as classic Colt model made from 1950–1986 but totally new design. Introduced in 2017. King Cobra has a heavy-duty frame and 3-inch barrel.
Price: **$699.00**
Price: King Cobra **$899.00**

COLT NIGHT COBRA
Caliber; .38 Special. Capacity: 6 rounds. Grips: Black synthetic VC G10. Sight: Tritium front night sight. DAO operation with bobbed hammer. Features a linear leaf spring design for smooth DA trigger pull.
Price: **$899.00**

COLT PYTHON
Caliber: .357 Magnum. Capacity: 6-round cylinder. Barrels: 4.25 and 6 in. Grips: Walnut. Sights: Fully adjustable rear, fixed red ramp interchangeable front. Weights: 42 oz. (4.25 in.), 46 oz. (6 in.). Features: New and improved and available only in stainless steel. Has recessed target crown and user-interchangeable front sight.
Price: **$1,499.00**

COLT PYTHON 3-INCH BARREL
Caliber: .357 Magnum. Capacity: 6-round cylinder. Barrels: 3, 4.25 and 6 in. Grips: Walnut. Sights: Fully adjustable rear, fixed red ramp interchangeable front. Weight: 42 oz. (4.25 in.), 46 oz. (6 in.). Features: New and improved and available only in stainless steel. Has recessed target crown and user-interchangeable front sight.
Price: **$1,499.00**

COLT ANACONDA
Caliber: .44 Magnum. Capacity: 6 rounds. Barrel: 6 and 8 in. Grip: Hogue Overmolded. Sights: Fully adjustable rear, fixed red ramp interchangeable front. Weight: 53 oz. (6 in.), 59 oz. (8 in.) Features: New and improved and available in stainless steel only. Has recessed target crown and user-interchangeable front sight.
Price: **$1,499.00**

COMANCHE II-A
Caliber: .38 Special. Capacity: 6-round cylinder. Barrels: 3 or 4 in. Weights: 33, 35 oz. Lengths: 8, 8.5 in. overall. Grips: Rubber. Sights: Fixed. Features: Blued finish, alloy frame. Distributed by SGS Importers.
Price: **$220.00**

DAN WESSON 715
Caliber: .357 Magnum. Capacity: 6-round cylinder. Barrel: 6-inch heavy barrel with full lug. Weight: 38 oz. Lengths: 8, 8.5 in. overall. Grips: Hogue rubber with finger grooves. Sights: Adjustable rear, interchangeable front blade. Features: Stainless steel. Interchangeable barrel assembly. Reintroduced in 2014. 715 Pistol Pack comes with 4-, 6- and 8-in. interchangeable barrels.
Price: From **$1,558.00**
Price: Pistol Pack **$1,999.00**

Prices given are believed to be accurate at time of publication however, many factors affect retail pricing so exact prices are not possible.

DIAMONDBACK SIDEKICK
Caliber: .22 LR/.22 Mag. Convertible. Action: Single & Double Grips: Checkered glass filled Nylon. Capacity: 9 rounds., Front Sight: Blade., Rear Sight: Integral., Barrel length: 4.5 inch. Overall Length: 9.875 in. Frame & Handle Material: Zinc., Frame & Handle Finish: Black Cerakote. Weight: 32.5 oz., Twist: 1:16 RH. Grooves: 6. The Sidekick is chambered in both .22 LR and .22 Mag with 9-shot cylinders. It has a 9-round capacity and weighs 32.5 ounces. Swing-out cylinders allow the user to switch between .22 LR and .22 Mag in seconds.
Price: **$320.00**

EAA WINDICATOR
Calibers: .38 Special, .357 Mag Capacity: 6-round cylinder. Barrels: 2 in., 4 in. Weight: 30 oz. (4 in.). Length: 8.5 in. overall (4 in. bbl.). Grips: Rubber with finger grooves. Sights: Blade front, fixed rear. Features: Swing-out cylinder; hammer block safety; blue or nickel finish. Introduced 1991. Imported from Germany by European American Armory.
Price: .38 Spec. from **$354.00**
Price: .357 Mag, steel frame from **$444.00**

KIMBER K6S
Caliber: .357 Magnum. Capacity: 6-round cylinder. Barrel: 2-inch full lug. Grips: Gray rubber. Finish: Satin stainless. Kimber's first revolver, claimed to be world's lightest production 6-shot .357 Magnum. DAO design with non-stacking match-grade trigger. Introduced 2016. CDP model has laminated checkered rosewood grips, Tritium night sights, two-tone black DLC/ brushed stainless finish, match grade trigger.
Price: **$878.00**
Price: 3-in. Barrel.. **$899.00**
Price: Deluxe Carry w/Medallion grips.. **$1,088.00**
Price: Custom Defense Package **$1,155.00**
Price: Crimson Trace Laser Grips **$1,177.00**
Price: TLE.. **$999.00**
Price: DA/SA **$949.00**

KIMBER K6s DASA TARGET
Caliber: .357 Magnum. Capacity: 6-round cylinder. Barrel: 4 in. Grips: Walnut laminate, oversized. Sights: Fully adjustable rear, fiber-optic front. Features: The DASA is the next evolution of the K6s. The DASA is outfitted with a double- and single-action trigger mechanism. Kimber's K6s revolvers feature the purportedly smallest cylinder capable of housing 6 rounds of .357 Magnum at 1.39-inch diameter, making for a very slim and streamlined package.
Price: **$989.00**

KIMBER K6s DASA COMBAT
Caliber: .357 Magnum. Capacity: 6-round cylinder. Barrel: 4 in. Grips: Walnut laminate, oversized with finger grooves. Sights: Fixed front and rear with white dots. Features: The DASA Combat is outfitted with a double- and single-action trigger mechanism. Kimber's K6s DASA revolvers have a smooth no-stack double-action trigger and a crisp 3.25- to 4.25-lb. single-action pull. The K6s DASA revolvers are equipped with knurled hammer spur.
Price: **$989.00**

KIMBER K6s DASA TEXAS EDITION

Caliber: .357 Magnum. Capacity: 6-round cylinder. Barrel: 2 in. Grips: Ivory G10. Sights: Fixed front and rear with white dots. Features: The Texas Edition is adorned with ivory G10 grips with the state moto, name and flag on this special edition. The satin finish has American Western cut scroll engraving on the barrel, frame and cylinder. The K6s DASA Texas Edition revolvers are equipped with knurled hammer spur.

Price: **$1,359.00**

KIMBER K6s ROYAL

Caliber: .357 Magnum. Capacity: 6-round cylinder. Barrel: 2 in. Grips: Walnut. Sights: Fixed brass-bead front and rear with white dots. Features: The K6s Royal features a 2-inch barrel for easy concealment. The dovetailed white-dot rear sight complements the brass-bead front sight. The Royal's stainless steel is hand polished to a high shine and a Dark Oil DLC is applied for a unique look.

Price: **$1,699.00**

KORTH USA

Calibers: .22 LR, .22 WMR, .32 S&W Long, .38 Special, .357 Mag., 9mm. Capacity: 6-shot. Barrels: 3, 4, 5.25, 6 in. Weights: 36–52 oz. Grips: Combat, Sport: Walnut, Palisander, Amboina, Ivory. Finish: German Walnut, matte with oil finish, adjustable ergonomic competition style. Sights: Adjustable Patridge (Sport) or Baughman (Combat), interchangeable and adjustable rear w/Patridge front (Target) in blue and matte. Features: DA/SA, 3 models, over 50 configurations, externally adjustable trigger stop and weight, interchangeable cylinder, removable wide-milled trigger shoe on Target model. Deluxe models are highly engraved editions. Available finishes include high polish blued finish, plasma coated in high polish or matte silver, gold, blue or charcoal. Many deluxe options available. From Korth USA.

Price: From **$8,000.00**
Price: Deluxe Editions, from **$12,000.00**

KORTH SKYHAWK

Caliber: 9mm. Barrels: 2 or 3 in. Sights: Adjustable rear with gold bead front. Grips: Hogue with finger grooves. Features: Polished trigger, skeletonized hammer. Imported by Nighthawk Custom.

Price: **$1,699.00**

NIGHTHAWK CUSTOM/KORTH-WAFFEN NXR

Caliber: .44 Magnum. Capacity: 6-round cylinder Barrel: 6 in. Grips: Ivory G10. Sights: Adjustable rear, fast-changeable front. Weight: 3.05 lbs. Features: The NXR is a futuristic looking stainless steel double-action revolver that is black DLC finished. Comes equipped with a removable under-barrel balancing lug/weight. Picatinny rail on top of barrel and underneath for easy accessory mounting.

Price: **$5,299.00**

RUGER (CUSTOM SHOP) SUPER GP100 COMPETITION REVOLVER

Calibers: .357 Magnum, 9mm. Capacity: 8-round cylinder. Barrels: 5.5 and 6 in. Grips: Hogue hand-finished hardwood. Sights: Adjustable rear, fiber-optic front. Weights: 47 oz., 45.6 oz. Features: Designed for competition, the new Super GP100 is essentially a Super Redhawk with the frame extension removed and replaced by a shrouded, cold hammer-forged barrel. The Super GP utilizes the superior action of the Super Redhawk. The high-strength stainless steel cylinder has a PVD finish and is extensively fluted for weight reduction. Comes with high-quality, impact-resistant case.

Price: **$1,549.00**

RUGER GP-100

Calibers: .357 Mag., .327 Federal Mag, .44 Special Capacities: 6- or 7-round cylinder, .327 Federal Mag (7-shot), .44 Special (5-shot), .22 LR, (10-shot). Barrels: 3-in. full shroud, 4-in. full shroud, 6-in. full shroud. (.44 Special offered only with 3-in. barrel.) Weights: 36–45 oz. Sights: Fixed; adjustable on 4- and 6-in. full shroud barrels. Grips: Ruger Santoprene Cushioned Grip with Goncalo Alves inserts. Features: Uses action, frame features of both the Security-Six and Redhawk revolvers. Full-length, short ejector shroud. Satin blue and stainless steel.

Price: Blued **$769.00**
Price: Satin stainless **$799.00**
Price: .22 LR **$829.00**
Price: .44 Spl. **$829.00**
Price: 7-round cylinder, 327 Fed or .357 Mag **$899.00**

RUGER GP-100 MATCH CHAMPION

Calibers: 10mm Magnum, .357 Mag. Capacity: 6-round cylinder. Barrel: 4.2-in. half shroud, slab-sided. Weight: 38 oz. Sights: Fixed rear, fiber optic front. Grips: Hogue Stippled Hardwood. Features: Satin stainless steel finish.

Price: Blued **$969.00**

Prices given are believed to be accurate at time of publication however, many factors affect retail pricing so exact prices are not possible.

RUGER LCR

Calibers: .22 LR (8-round cylinder), .22 WMR, .327 Fed. Mag, .38 Special and .357 Mag., 5-round cylinder. Barrel: 1.875 in. Weights: 13.5–17.10 oz. Length: 6.5 in. overall. Grips: Hogue Tamer or Crimson Trace Lasergrips. Sights: Pinned ramp front, U-notch integral rear. Features: The Ruger Lightweight Compact Revolver (LCR), a 13.5 ounce, small frame revolver with a smooth, easy-to-control trigger and highly manageable recoil.

Price: .22 LR, .22 WMR, .38 Spl., iron sights **$579.00**
Price: 9mm, .327, .357, iron sights.. **$669.00**
Price: .22 LR, .22WMR, .38 Spl. Crimson Trace Lasergrip.................... **$859.00**
Price: 9mm, .327, .357, Crimson Trace Lasergrip.................................. **$949.00**

RUGER LCRX

Calibers: .38 Special +P, 9mm, .327 Fed. Mag., .22 WMR. Barrels: 1.875 in. or 3 in. Features: Similar to LCR except this model has visible hammer, adjustable rear sight. The 3-inch barrel model has longer grip. 9mm comes with three moon clips.

Price: **$579.00**
Price: .327 Mag., .357 Mag., 9mm.. **$669.00**

RUGER SP-101

Calibers: .22 LR (8 shot); .327 Federal Mag. (6-shot), 9mm, .38 Spl, .357 Mag. (5-shot). Barrels: 2.25, 3 1/16, 4.2 in (.22 LR, .327 Mag., .357 Mag). Weights: 25–30 oz. Sights: Adjustable or fixed, rear; fiber-optic or black ramp front. Grips: Ruger Cushioned Grip with inserts. Features: Compact, small frame, double-action revolver. Full-length ejector shroud. Stainless steel only.

Price: Fixed sights **$719.00**
Price: Adjustable rear, fiber optic front sights **$769.00**
Price: .327 Fed Mag 3-in bbl **$769.00**
Price: .327 Fed Mag **$749.00**

RUGER REDHAWK

Calibers: .44 Rem. Mag., .45 Colt and .45 ACP/.45 Colt combo. Capacity: 6-round cylinder. Barrels: 2.75, 4.2, 5.5, 7.5 in. (.45 Colt in 4.2 in. only.) Weight: 54 oz. (7.5 bbl.). Length: 13 in. overall (7.5-in. barrel). Grips: Square butt cushioned grip panels. TALO Distributor exclusive 2.75-in. barrel stainless model has round butt, wood grips. Sights: Interchangeable Patridge-type front, rear adjustable for windage and elevation. Features: Stainless steel, brushed satin finish, blued ordnance steel. 9.5 sight radius. Introduced 1979.

Price: **$1,079.00**
Price: Hunter Model 7.5-in. bbl.. **$1,159.00**
Price: TALO 2.75 in. model **$1,069.00**

RUGER SUPER REDHAWK

Calibers: 10mm, .44 Rem. Mag., .454 Casull, .480 Ruger. Capacities: 5- or 6-round cylinder. Barrels: 2.5 in. (Alaskan), 5.5 in., 6.5 in. (10mm), 7.5 in. or 9.5 in. Weight: 44–58 oz. Length: 13 in. overall (7.5-in. barrel). Grips: Hogue Tamer Monogrip. Features: Similar to standard Redhawk except has heavy extended frame with Ruger Integral Scope Mounting System on wide topstrap. Wide hammer spur lowered for better scope clearance. Incorporates mechanical design features and improvements of GP-100. Ramp front sight base has Redhawk-style interchangeable insert sight blades, adjustable rear sight. Alaskan model has 2.5-inch barrel. Satin stainless steel and low-glare stainless finishes. Introduced 1987.

Price: .44 Magnum, 10mm.. **$1,159.00**
Price: .454 Casull, .480 Ruger.. **$1,199.00**
Price: Alaskan, .44 Mag, .454 Casull, .480 Ruger.............................. **$1,189.00**

SMITH & WESSON GOVERNOR

Calibers: .410 Shotshell (2.5 in.), .45 ACP, .45 Colt. Capacity: 6 rounds. Barrel: 2.75 in. Length: 7.5 in., (2.5 in. barrel). Grip: Synthetic. Sights: Front: Dovetailed tritium night sight or black ramp, rear: fixed. Grips: Synthetic. Finish: Matte black or matte silver (Silver Edition). Weight: 29.6 oz. Features: Capable of chambering a mixture of .45 Colt, .45 ACP and .410 gauge 2.5-inch shotshells, the Governor is suited for both close and distant encounters, allowing users to customize the load to their preference. Scandium alloy frame, stainless steel cylinder. Packaged with two full moon clips and three 2-shot clips.

Price: **$869.00**
Price: w/Crimson Trace Laser Grip **$1,179.00**

Prices given are believed to be accurate at time of publication however, many factors affect retail pricing so exact prices are not possible.

SMITH & WESSON J-FRAME
The J-frames are the smallest Smith & Wesson wheelguns and come in a variety of chamberings, barrel lengths and materials as noted in the individual model listings.

SMITH & WESSON 60LS/642LS LADYSMITH
Calibers: .38 Special +P, .357 Mag. Capacity: 5-round cylinder. Barrels: 1.875 in. (642LS); 2.125 in. (60LS) Weights: 14.5 oz. (642LS); 21.5 oz. (60LS); Length: 6.6 in. overall (60LS). Grips: Wood. Sights: Black blade, serrated ramp front, fixed notch rear. 642 CT has Crimson Trace Laser Grips. Features: 60LS model has a Chiefs Special-style frame. 642LS has Centennial-style frame, frosted matte finish, smooth combat wood grips. Introduced 1996. Comes in a fitted carry/storage case. Introduced 1989. Made in USA by Smith & Wesson.
Price: (642LS) **$499.00**
Price: (60LS) **$759.00**
Price: (642 CT) **$699.00**

SMITH & WESSON MODEL 63
Caliber: .22 LR Capacity: 8-round cylinder. Barrel: 3 in. Weight: 26 oz. Length: 7.25 in. overall. Grips: Black synthetic. Sights: Hi-Viz fiber optic front sight, adjustable black blade rear sight. Features: Stainless steel construction throughout. Made in USA by Smith & Wesson.
Price: **$769.00**

SMITH & WESSON MODEL 442/637/638/642 AIRWEIGHT
Caliber: .38 Special +P. Capacity: 5-round cylinder. Barrels: 1.875 in., 2.5 in. Weight: 15 oz. Length: 6.375 in. overall. Grips: Soft rubber. Sights: Fixed, serrated ramp front, square notch rear. Features: A family of J-frame .38 Special revolvers with aluminum-alloy frames. Model 637; Chiefs Special-style frame with exposed hammer. Introduced 1996. Models 442, 642; Centennial-style frame, enclosed hammer. Model 638, Bodyguard style, shrouded hammer. Comes in a fitted carry/storage case. Introduced 1989. Made in USA by Smith & Wesson.
Price: From **$469.00**
Price: Laser Max Frame Mounted Red Laser sight **$539.00**

SMITH & WESSON MODELS 637 CT/638 CT
Similar to Models 637, 638 and 642 but with Crimson Trace Laser Grips.
Price: **$699.00**

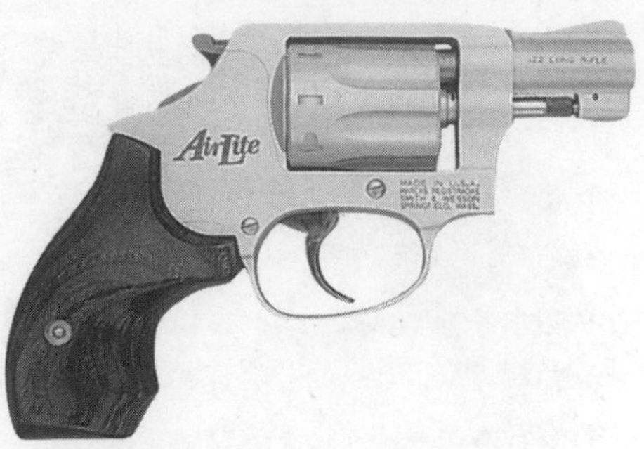

SMITH & WESSON MODEL 317 AIRLITE
Caliber: .22 LR. Capacity: 8-round cylinder. Barrel: 1.875 in. Weight: 10.5 oz. Length: 6.25 in. overall (1.875-in. barrel). Grips: Rubber. Sights: Serrated ramp front, fixed notch rear. Features: Aluminum alloy, carbon and stainless steels, Chiefs Special-style frame with exposed hammer. Smooth combat trigger. Clear Cote finish. Model 317 Kit Gun has adjustable rear sight, fiber optic front. Introduced 1997.
Price: **$759.00**

SMITH & WESSON MODEL 340/340PD AIRLITE SC CENTENNIAL
Calibers: .357 Mag., 38 Special +P. Capacity: 5-round cylinder. Barrel: 1.875 in. Weight: 12 oz. Length: 6.375 in. overall (1.875-in. barrel). Grips: Rounded butt rubber. Sights: Black blade front, rear notch Features: Centennial-style frame, enclosed hammer. Internal lock. Matte silver finish. Scandium alloy frame, titanium cylinder, stainless steel barrel liner. Made in USA by Smith & Wesson.
Price: **$1,019.00**

SMITH & WESSON MODEL 351PD
Caliber: .22 Mag. Capacity: 5-round cylinder. Barrel: 1.875 in. Weight: 10.6 oz. Length: 6.25 in. overall (1.875-in. barrel). Sights: HiViz front sight, rear notch. Grips: Wood. Features: 7-shot, aluminum-alloy frame. Chiefs Special-style frame with exposed hammer. Nonreflective matte-black finish. Internal lock. Made in USA by Smith & Wesson.
Price: **$759.00**

SMITH & WESSON MODEL 360/360PD AIRLITE CHIEF'S SPECIAL
Calibers: .357 Mag., .38 Special +P. Capacity: 5-round cylinder. Barrel: 1.875 in. Weight: 12 oz. Length: 6.375 in. overall (1.875-in. barrel). Grips: Rounded butt rubber. Sights: Red ramp front, fixed rear notch. Features: Chief's Special-style frame with exposed hammer. Internal lock. Scandium alloy frame, titanium cylinder, stainless steel barrel. Model 360 has unfluted cylinder. Made in USA by Smith & Wesson.
Price: 360 .... **$770.00**
Price: 360PD **$1,019.00**

SMITH & WESSON BODYGUARD 38
Caliber: .38 Special +P. Capacity: 5-round cylinder. Barrel: 1.9 in. Weight: 14.3 oz. Length: 6.6 in. Grip: Synthetic. Sights: Front: Black ramp, Rear: fixed, integral with backstrap. Plus: Integrated laser sight. Finish: Matte black. Features: The first personal protection series that comes with an integrated laser sight.
Price: **$539.00**

SMITH & WESSON MODEL 640 CENTENNIAL DA ONLY
Calibers: .357 Mag., .38 Special +P. Capacity: 5-round cylinder. Barrel: 2.125 in. Weight: 23 oz. Length: 6.75 in. overall. Grips: Uncle Mike's Boot grip. Sights: Tritium Night Sights. Features: Stainless steel. Fully concealed hammer, snag-proof smooth edges. Internal lock.
Price: **$839.00**

SMITH & WESSON MODEL 649 BODYGUARD
Caliber: .357 Mag., .38 Special +P. Capacity: 5-round cylinder. Barrel: 2.125 in. Weight: 23 oz. Length: 6.625 in. overall. Grips: Uncle Mike's Combat. Sights: Black pinned ramp front, fixed notch rear. Features: Stainless steel construction, satin finish. Internal lock. Bodyguard style, shrouded hammer. Made in USA by Smith & Wesson.
Price: **$729.00**

SMITH & WESSON K-FRAME/L-FRAME
The K-frame series are mid-size revolvers and the L-frames are slightly larger.

SMITH & WESSON MODEL 10 CLASSIC
Caliber: .38 Special. Capacity: 6-round cylinder. Features: Bright blued steel frame and cylinder, checkered wood grips, 4-inch barrel and fixed sights. The oldest model in the Smith & Wesson line, its basic design goes back to the original Military & Police Model of 1905.
Price: **$739.00**

SMITH & WESSON MODEL 17 MASTERPIECE CLASSIC
Caliber: .22 LR. Capacity: 6-round cylinder. Barrel: 6 in. Weight: 40 oz. Grips: Checkered wood. Sights: Pinned Patridge front, micro-adjustable rear. Updated variation of K-22 Masterpiece of the 1930s.
Price: **$989.00**

SMITH & WESSON MODEL 19 CLASSIC
Caliber: .357 Magnum. Capacity: 6-round cylinder Barrel: 4.25 in. Weight: 37.2 oz. Grips: Walnut. Sights: Adjustable rear, red ramp front. Finish: Polished blue. Classic-style thumbpiece. Reintroduced 2019.
Price: **$826.00**

SMITH & WESSON MODEL 48 CLASSIC
Same specifications as Model 17 except chambered in .22 Magnum (.22 WMR) and is available with a 4- or 6-inch barrel.
Price: .... **$949.00–$989.00**

SMITH & WESSON MODEL 64/67
Caliber: .38 Special +P. Capacity: 6-round cylinder Barrel: 3 in. Weight: 33 oz. Length: 8.875 in. overall. Grips: Soft rubber. Sights: Fixed, .125-in. serrated ramp front, square notch rear. Model 67 is similar to Model 64 except for adjustable sights. Features: Satin finished stainless steel, square butt.
Price: From .... **$689.00–$749.00**

SMITH & WESSON MODEL 66
Caliber: .357 Magnum. Capacity: 6-round cylinder. Barrel: 4.25 in. Weight: 36.6 oz. Grips: Synthetic. Sights: White outline adjustable rear, red ramp front. Features: Return in 2014 of the famous K-frame "Combat Magnum" with stainless finish.
Price: **$849.00**

SMITH & WESSON MODEL 69
Caliber: .44 Magnum. Capacity: 5-round cylinder. Barrel: 4.25 in. Weight: 37 oz. Grips: Checkered wood. Sights: White outline adjustable rear, red ramp front. Features: L-frame with stainless finish, 5-shot cylinder, introduced in 2014.
Price: **$989.00**

SMITH & WESSON MODEL 610
Caliber: 10mm. Capacity: 6-round cylinder. Barrels: 4.25 and 6 in. Grips: Walnut. Sights: Fully adjustable rear, fixed red ramp interchangeable front. Weights: 42.6 oz. (4.25 in.), 50.1 oz (6 in.). Features: Built on Smith & Wesson's large N-frame in stainless steel only. Will also fire .40 S&W ammunition. Comes with three moon clips.
Price: **$987.00**

SMITH & WESSON MODEL 617
Caliber: .22 LR. Capacity: 10-round cylinder. Barrel: 6 in. Weight: 44 oz. Length: 11.125 in. Grips: Soft rubber. Sights: Patridge front, adjustable rear. Drilled and tapped for scope mount. Features: Stainless steel with satin finish. Introduced 1990.
Price: From **$829.00**

SMITH & WESSON MODEL 648
Caliber: .22 Magnum. Capacity: 8-round cylinder. Barrel: 6 in. Grips: Walnut. Sights: Fully adjustable rear, Patridge front. Weight: 46.2 oz. Features: This reintroduction was originally released in 1989 and produced until 2005. Ideal for target shooting or small-game hunting.
Price: **$752.00**

SMITH & WESSON MODEL 686/686 PLUS
Caliber: .357 Mag/.38 Special. Capacity: 6 (686) or 7 (Plus). Barrels: 6 in. (686), 3 or 6 in. (686 Plus), 4 in. (SSR). Weight: 35 oz. (3 in. barrel). Grips: Rubber. Sights: White outline adjustable rear, red ramp front. Features: Satin stainless frame and cylinder. Stock Service Revolver (SSR) has tapered underlug, interchangeable front sight, high-hold ergonomic wood grips, chamfered charge holes, custom barrel w/recessed crown, bossed mainspring.
Price: 686 .... **$829.00**
Price: Plus **$849.00**
Price: SSR **$999.00**

SMITH & WESSON MODEL 986 PRO
Caliber: 9mm. Capacity: 7-round cylinder Barrel: 5-in. tapered underlug. Features: SA/DA L-frame revolver chambered in 9mm. Features similar to 686 PLUS Pro Series with 5-inch tapered underlug barrel, satin stainless finish, synthetic grips, adjustable rear and Patridge blade front sight.
Price: **$1,149.00**

SMITH & WESSON M&P R8
Caliber: .357 Mag. Capacity: 8-round cylinder. Barrel: 5-in. half lug with accessory rail. Weight: 36.3 oz. Length: 10.5 in. Grips: Black synthetic. Sights: Adjustable v-notch rear, interchangeable front. Features: Scandium alloy frame, stainless steel cylinder.
Price: **$1,329.00**

SMITH & WESSON N-FRAME
These large-frame models introduced the .357, .41 and .44 Magnums to the world.

SMITH & WESSON MODEL 25 CLASSIC
Calibers: .45 Colt or .45 ACP. Capacity: 6-round cylinder. Barrel: 6.5 in. Weight: 45 oz. Grips: Checkered wood. Sights: Pinned Patridge front, micro-adjustable rear.
Price: **$1,019.00**

SMITH & WESSON MODEL 27 CLASSIC
Caliber: .357 Magnum. Capacity: 6-round cylinder. Barrels: 4 or 6.5 in. Weight: 41.2 oz. Grips: Checkered wood. Sights: Pinned Patridge front, micro-adjustable rear. Updated variation of the first magnum revolver, the .357 Magnum of 1935.
Price: (4 in.) **$1,019.00**
Price: (6.5 in.) **$1,059.00**

SMITH & WESSON MODEL 29 CLASSIC
Caliber: .44 Magnum Capacity: 6-round cylinder. Barrel: 4 or 6.5 in. Weight: 48.5 oz. Length: 12 in. Grips: Altamont service walnut. Sights: Adjustable white-outline rear, red ramp front. Features: Carbon steel frame, polished-blued or nickel finish. Has integral key lock safety feature to prevent accidental discharges. Original Model 29 made famous by "Dirty Harry" character played in 1971 by Clint Eastwood.
Price: .... **$999.00–$1,169.00**

SMITH & WESSON MODEL 57 CLASSIC
Caliber: .41 Magnum. Capacity: 6-round cylinder. Barrel: 6 in. Weight: 48 oz. Grips: Checkered wood. Sights: Pinned red ramp, micro-adjustable rear.
Price: **$1,009.00**

Prices given are believed to be accurate at time of publication however, many factors affect retail pricing so exact prices are not possible.

SMITH & WESSON MODEL 329PD ALASKA BACKPACKER

Caliber: .44 Magnum. Capacity: 6-round cylinder. Barrel: 2.5 in. Weight: 26 oz. Length: 9.5 in. Grips: Synthetic. Sights: Adj. rear, HiViz orange-dot front. Features: Scandium alloy frame, blue/black finish, stainless steel cylinder.
Price: From **$1,159.00**

SMITH & WESSON MODEL 625/625JM

Caliber: .45 ACP. Capacity: 6-round cylinder. Barrels: 4 in., 5 in. Weight: 43 oz. (4-in. barrel). Length: 9.375 in. overall (4-in. barrel). Grips: Soft rubber; wood optional. Sights: Patridge front on ramp, S&W micrometer click rear adjustable for windage and elevation. Features: Stainless steel construction with .400-in. wide semi-target hammer, .312-in. smooth combat trigger; full lug barrel. Glass beaded finish. Introduced 1989. Jerry Miculek Professional (JM) Series has .265-in. wide grooved trigger, special wooden Miculek Grip, five full moon clips, gold bead Patridge front sight on interchangeable front sight base, bead blast finish. Unique serial number run. Mountain Gun has 4-in. tapered barrel, drilled and tapped, Hogue Rubber Monogrip, pinned black ramp front sight, micrometer click-adjustable rear sight, satin stainless frame and barrel weighs 39.5 oz.
Price: 625 or 625JM **$1,074.00**

SMITH & WESSON MODEL 629

Calibers: .44 Magnum, .44 S&W Special. Capacity: 6-round cylinder. Barrels: 4 in., 5 in., 6.5 in. Weight: 41.5 oz. (4-in. bbl.). Length: 9.625 in. overall (4-in. bbl.). Grips: Soft rubber; wood optional. Sights: .125-in. red ramp front, white outline rear, internal lock, adjustable for windage and elevation. Classic similar to standard Model 629, except Classic has full-lug 5-in. barrel, chamfered front of cylinder, interchangeable red ramp front sight with adjustable white outline rear, Hogue grips with S&W monogram, drilled and tapped for scope mounting. Factory accurizing and endurance packages. Introduced 1990. Classic Power Port has Patridge front sight and adjustable rear sight. Model 629CT has 5-in. barrel, Crimson Trace Hoghunter Lasergrips, 10.5 in. OAL, 45.5 oz. weight. Introduced 2006.
Price: From **$949.00**

SMITH & WESSON X-FRAME

These extra-large X-frame S&W revolvers push the limits of big-bore handgunning.

SMITH & WESSON MODEL 500

Caliber: 500 S&W Magnum. Capacity: 5-round cylinder. Barrels: 4 in., 6.5 in., 8.375 in. Weight: 72.5 oz. Length: 15 in. (8.375-in. barrel). Grips: Hogue Sorbothane Rubber. Sights: Interchangeable blade, front, adjustable rear. Features: Recoil compensator, ball detent cylinder latch, internal lock. 6.5-in.-barrel model has orange-ramp dovetail Millett front sight, adjustable black rear sight, Hogue Dual Density Monogrip, .312-in. chrome trigger with overtravel stop, chrome tear-drop hammer, glass bead finish. 10.5-in.-barrel model has red ramp front sight, adjustable rear sight, .312-in. chrome trigger with overtravel stop, chrome teardrop hammer with pinned sear, hunting sling. Compensated Hunter has .400-in. orange ramp dovetail front sight, adjustable black blade rear sight, Hogue Dual Density Monogrip, glass bead finish w/black clear coat. Made in USA by Smith & Wesson.
Price: From **$1,299.00**

SMITH & WESSON MODEL 460V

Caliber: 460 S&W Magnum (Also chambers .454 Casull, .45 Colt). Capacity: 5-round cylinder. Barrels: 7.5 in., 8.375-in. gain-twist rifling. Weight: 62.5 oz. Length: 11.25 in. Grips: Rubber. Sights: Adj. rear, red ramp front. Features: Satin stainless steel frame and cylinder, interchangeable compensator. 460XVR (X-treme Velocity Revolver) has black blade front sight with interchangeable green Hi-Viz tubes, adjustable rear sight. 7.5-in.-barrel version has Lothar-Walther barrel, 360-degree recoil compensator, tuned Performance Center action, pinned sear, integral Weaver base, non-glare surfaces, scope mount accessory kit for mounting full-size scopes, flashed-chromed hammer and trigger, Performance Center gun rug and shoulder sling. Interchangeable Hi-Viz green dot front sight, adjustable black rear sight, Hogue Dual Density Monogrip, matte-black frame and shroud finish with glass-bead cylinder finish, 72 oz. Compensated Hunter has teardrop chrome hammer, .312-in. chrome trigger, Hogue Dual Density Monogrip, satin/matte stainless finish, HiViz interchangeable front sight, adjustable black rear sight. XVR introduced 2006.
Price: 460V **$1,369.00**
Price: 460XVR, fr **$1,369.00**

STANDARD MANUFACTURING S333 THUNDERSTRUCK
Caliber: .22 Magnum. Capacity: 8-round cylinder. Barrel: 1.25 in. Grips: Polymer. Sights: Fixed front and rear. Weight: 18 oz. Features: Designed to be the ultimate in personal protection and featuring two-barrels that fire simultaneously with each trigger pull. The DA revolver has an 8-round, .22 Magnum capacity. Frame is constructed of 7075 aircraft-grade aluminum with anodized finish.
Price: **$429.00**

SUPER SIX CLASSIC BISON BULL
Caliber: .45-70 Government. Capacity: 6-round cylinder. Barrel: 10in. octagonal with 1:14 twist. Weight: 6 lbs. Length: 17.5 in. overall. Grips: NA. Sights: Ramp front sight with dovetailed blade, click-adjustable rear. Features: Manganese bronze frame. Integral scope mount, manual cross-bolt safety.
Price: **$1,500.00**

TAURUS 327
The new Taurus 327 is a double-action/single-action revolver, available with a 2- or 3-inch barrel that is multi-cartridge compatible, can accept .32 H&R Magnum and .32 S&W Long cartridges. The matte black carbon steel or stainless steel barrel, cylinder and frame are backed by a recoil-absorbing rubber grip that is comfortable and provides excellent retention in a compact handgun platform. The Taurus 327's front serrated ramp sight and no-snag rear sight channel provide quick and clear target acquisition.
Price: **$371.00**
Price: **$388.00**

TAURUS 942
Caliber: .22 LR. Capacity: 8-round cylinder. Barrels: 2 and 3 in. Grips: Soft rubber. Sights: Drift-adjustable rear, serrated-ramp front. Weight: 17.8, 25 oz. Features: The 942 is based closely on the Taurus 856 revolver, but chambered in .22 LR with an 8-shot cylinder. Eight models are available: 2- and 3-inch-barrel models with a steel-alloy frame and cylinder in matte-black finish, 2- and 3-inch-barrel models with an ultralight aluminum-alloy frame in hard-coat, black-anodized finish, 2- and 3-inch-barrel models with a stainless steel frame and cylinder in a matte finish, and 2- and 3-inch-barrel models with an ultralight aluminum-alloy frame in a stainless-matte finish. Imported by Taurus International.
Prce: .... **$369.52 - $384.97**

TAURUS 605 DEFENDER
Capacity: 5 Rounds, Action Type: Double Action/Single Action, Firing System: Hammer, Front Sight: Night Sight with orange outline, Rear Sight: Fixed, Grip: Hogue Rubber grips, VZ, Altamont. Caliber: .38 Spl. +P, .357 Mag, Frame Size: Small, Barrel Length: 3 in., Overall Length: 7.50 in., Overall Height: 4.80 in., Overall Width: 1.41 in. Weights: 23.52 to 25.52 oz., Features: Extended ejector rod, night sights, Safety: Transfer Bar. Finishes: Matte black oxide, matte stainless steel, tungsten Cerakote.
Price: .... **$472.00–$540.00**

TAURUS DEFENDER 856
Caliber: .38 Special +P. Capacity: 6-round cylinder. Barrel: 3 in. Grips: Hogue rubber, VZ black/gray, walnut. Sights: Fixed rear, tritium night sight with bright orange outline. Features: The Defender 856 is built on Taurus' small frame, making for a compact defensive revolver. Four standard models are available to include a stainless steel frame with matte finish, an ultralight aluminum-alloy frame with matte finish, stainless steel frame with black Tenifer finish, and an aluminum-alloy frame with hard-coat, black-anodized finish. Two upgrade versions are available with special grips and finish treatments. Imported by Taurus International.
Price: .... **$429.00 - $477.00**

TAURUS MODEL 17 TRACKER
Caliber: .17 HMR. Capacity: 7-round cylinder. Barrel: 6.5 in. Weight: 45.8 oz. Grips: Rubber. Sights: Adjustable. Features: Double action, matte stainless, integral key-lock.
Price: From **$539.00**

TAURUS MODEL 992 TRACKER
Calibers: .22 LR with interchangeable .22 WMR cylinder. Capacity: 9-round cylinder. Barrel: 4 or 6.5 in with ventilated rib. Features: Adjustable rear sight, blued or stainless finish.
Price: Blue **$640.00**
Price: Stainless **$692.00**

Prices given are believed to be accurate at time of publication however, many factors affect retail pricing so exact prices are not possible.

TAURUS MODEL 44SS
Caliber: .44 Magnum. Capacity: 5-round cylinder. Barrel: Ported, 4, 6.5, 8.4 in. Weight: 34 oz. Grips: Rubber. Sights: Adjustable. Features: Double action. Integral key-lock. Introduced 1994. Finish: Matte stainless. Imported from Brazil by Taurus International Manufacturing, Inc.
Price: From .... **$648.00-$664.00**

TAURUS MODEL 65
Caliber: .357 Magnum. Capacity: 6-round cylinder. Barrel: 4-in. full underlug. Weight: 38 oz. Length: 10.5 in. overall. Grips: Soft rubber. Sights: Fixed. Features: Double action, integral key-lock. Matte blued or stainless. Imported by Taurus International.
Price: Blued **$539.00**
Price: Stainless **$591.00**

TAURUS MODEL 66
Similar to Model 65, 4 in. or 6 in. barrel, 7-round cylinder, adjustable rear sight. Integral key-lock action. Imported by Taurus International.
Price: Blue **$599.00**
Price: Stainless **$652.00**

TAURUS MODEL 82 HEAVY BARREL
Caliber: .38 Special. Capacity: 6-round cylinder. Barrel: 4 in., heavy. Weight: 36.5 oz. Length: 9.25 in. overall. Grips: Soft black rubber. Sights: Serrated ramp front, square notch rear. Features: Double action, solid rib, integral key-lock. Imported by Taurus International.
Price: From **$521.00**

TAURUS MODEL 85FS
Caliber: .38 Special. Capacity: 5-round cylinder. Barrel: 2 in. Weights: 17–24.5 oz., titanium 13.5–15.4 oz. Grips: Rubber, rosewood or mother of pearl. Sights: Ramp front, square notch rear. Features: Spurred hammer. Blued, matte stainless, blue with gold accents, stainless with gold accents; rated for +P ammo. Integral keylock. Some models have titanium frame. Introduced 1980. Imported by Taurus International.
Price: From **$379.00**

TAURUS MODEL 856 ULTRALIGHT
Caliber: .38 Special. Capacity: 6-round cylinder. Barrel: 2 in. Matte black or stainless. Weights: 15.7 oz., titanium 13.5–15.4 oz. Grips: Rubber, rosewood or mother of pearl. Sights: Serrated ramp front, square notch rear. Features: Aluminum frame, matte black or stainless cylinder, azure blue, bronze, burnt orange or rouge finish.
Price: .... **$364.00-$461.00**

TAURUS 380 MINI
Caliber: .380 ACP. Capacity: 5-round cylinder w/moon clip. Barrel: 1.75 in. Weight: 15.5 oz. Length: 5.95 in. Grips: Rubber. Sights: Adjustable rear, fixed front. Features: DAO. Available in blued or stainless finish. Five Star (moon) clips included.
Price: Blued **$478.00**
Price: Stainless **$514.00**

TAURUS MODEL 45-410 JUDGE
Calibers: 2.5-in. .410/.45 Colt, 3-in. .410/.45 Colt. Barrels: 3 in., 6.5 in. (blued finish). Weights: 35.2 oz., 22.4 oz. Length: 7.5 in. Grips: Ribber rubber. Sights: Fiber Optic. Features: DA/SA. Matte stainless and ultra-lite stainless finish. Introduced in 2007. Imported from Brazil by Taurus International.
Price: From **$511.00**

TAURUS JUDGE PUBLIC DEFENDER POLYMER
Caliber: .45 Colt/.410 (2.5 in.). Capacity: 5-round cylinder. Barrel: 2.5-in. Weight: 27 oz. Features: SA/DA revolver with 5-round cylinder; polymer frame; Ribber rubber-feel grips; fiber-optic front sight; adjustable rear sight; blued or stainless cylinder; shrouded hammer with cocking spur; blued finish.
Price: From **$469.00**

TAURUS RAGING HUNTER
Calibers: .357 Magnum, .44 Magnum, .454 Casull, .460 Smith & Wesson Magnum. Capacity: 7 (.357), 6 (.44) and 5 (.454) rounds. Barrels: 5.12, 6.75, 8.37 in. Grips: Cushioned rubber. Sights: Adjustable rear, fixed front. Weight: 49 - 59.2 oz. Features: This is a DA/SA big-game-hunting revolver, available in three calibers and three barrel lengths, each featuring a Picatinny rail for easy optic mounting without removing the iron sights. All Raging Hunter models come with factory porting and cushioned rubber grips. Two finishes are available: matte black and two-tone matte stainless. Imported by Taurus International.
Prce: Black **$968.00**
Prce: Two Tone **$983.00**

TAURUS MODEL 627 TRACKER

Caliber: .357 Magnum. Capacity: 7-round cylinder. Barrels: 4 or 6.5 in. Weights: 28.8, 41 oz. Grips: Rubber. Sights: Fixed front, adjustable rear. Features: Double-action. Stainless steel, Shadow Gray or Total Titanium; vent rib (steel models only); integral key-lock action. Imported by Taurus International.

Price: From **$577.00**

TAURUS MODEL 444 ULTRA-LIGHT

Caliber: .44 Magnum. Capacity: 5-round cylinder. Barrels: 2.5 or 4 in. Weight: 28.3 oz. Grips: Cushioned inset rubber. Sights: Fixed red-fiber optic front, adjustable rear. Features: UltraLite titanium blue finish, titanium/alloy frame built on Raging Bull design. Smooth trigger shoe, 1.760-in. wide, 6.280-in. tall. Barrel rate of twist 1:16, 6 grooves. Introduced 2005. Imported by Taurus International.

Price: **$944.00**

TAURUS MODEL 444/454 RAGING BULL SERIES

Calibers: .44 Magnum, .454 Casull. Barrels: 2.25 in., 5 in., 6.5 in., 8.375 in. Weight: 53–63 oz. Length: 12 in. overall (6.5 in. barrel). Grips: Soft black rubber. Sights: Patridge front, adjustable rear. Features: DA, ventilated rib, integral key-lock. Most models have ported barrels. Introduced 1997. Imported by Taurus International.

Price: 444 .... **$900.00**
Price: 454 .... **$1,204.00.**

TAURUS MODEL 605 PLY

Caliber: .357 Magnum. **Capacity:** 5-round cylinder. **Barrel:** 2 in. **Weight:** 20 oz. **Grips:** Rubber. **Sights:** Fixed. **Features:** Polymer frame steel cylinder. Blued or stainless. Introduced 1995. Imported by Taurus International.

Price: Blued **$393.00**
Price: Stainless **$410.00**

TAURUS MODEL 905

Caliber: 9mm. **Capacity:** 5-round cylinder. **Barrel:** 2 in. **Features:** Small-frame revolver with rubber boot grips, fixed sights, choice of exposed or concealed hammer. Blued or stainless finish.

Price: Blued **$531.00**
Price: Stainless **$583.00**

TAURUS MODEL 692

Calibers: .38 Special/.357 Magnum or 9mm. **Capacity:** 7-round cylinder. **Barrels:** 3 or 6.5 in, ported. **Sights:** Adjustable rear, fixed front. **Grip:** "Ribber" textured. **Finish:** Matte blued or stainless. **Features:** Caliber can be changed with a swap of the cylinders which are non-fluted.

Price: **$659.00**

Prices given are believed to be accurate at time of publication however, many factors affect retail pricing so exact prices are not possible.

CIMARRON BISLEY MODEL SINGLE-ACTION

Calibers: .357 Magnum, .44 WCF, .44 Special, .45. Features: Similar to Colt Bisley, special grip frame and trigger guard, knurled wide-spur hammer, curved trigger. Introduced 1999. Imported by Cimarron F.A. Co.

Price: From **$636.00**

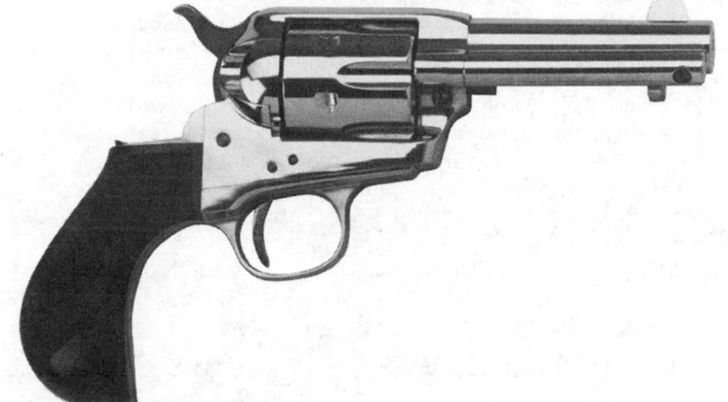

CIMARRON LIGHTNING SA

Calibers: .22 LR, .32-20/32 H&R dual cyl. combo, .38 Special, .41 Colt. Barrels: 3.5 in., 4.75 in., 5.5 in. Grips: Smooth or checkered walnut. Sights: Blade front. Features: Replica of the Colt 1877 Lightning DA. Similar to Cimarron Thunderer, except smaller grip frame to fit smaller hands. Standard blued, charcoal blued or nickel finish with forged, old model, or color casehardened frame. Dual cylinder model available with .32-30/.32 H&R chambering. Introduced 2001. From Cimarron F.A. Co.

Price: From .... **$503.00–$565.00**
Price: .32-20/.32 H&R dual cylinder **$649.00**

CIMARRON MODEL P SAA

Calibers: .32 WCF, .38 WCF, .357 Magnum, .44 WCF, .44 Special, .45 Colt and .45 ACP. Barrels: 4.75, 5.5, 7.5 in. Weight: 39 oz. Length: 10 in. overall (4.75-in. barrel). Grips: Walnut. Sights: Blade front. Features: Old model black-powder frame with Bullseye ejector, or New Model frame. Imported by Cimarron F.A. Co.

Price: From **$550.00**

CIMARRON MODEL "P" JR.

Calibers: .22 LR, .32-20, .32 H&R, 38 Special Barrels: 3.5, 4.75, 5.5 in. Grips: Checkered walnut. Sights: Blade front. Features: Styled after 1873 Colt Peacemaker, except 20 percent smaller. Blue finish with color case-hardened frame; Cowboy action. Introduced 2001. From Cimarron F.A. Co.

Price: From **$480.00**

CIMARRON U.S.V. ARTILLERY MODEL SINGLE-ACTION

Caliber: .45 Colt. Barrel: 5.5 in. Weight: 39 oz. Length: 11.5 in. overall. Grips: Walnut. Sights: Fixed. Features: U.S. markings and cartouche, casehardened frame and hammer. Imported by Cimarron F.A. Co.

Price: Blued finish.......... **$594.00**
Price: Original finish **$701.00**

CIMARRON BAD BOY

Calibers: .44 Magnum, 10mm. Capacity: 6-round cylinder. Barrel: 8 in. Grips: Walnut. Sights: Fully adjustable rear, fixed front. Features: Built on a replica Single Action Army Pre-War frame with an 1860 Army-style, one-piece walnut grip. The carbon-alloy steel frame is covered in a classic blue finish and it is fitted with an 8-inch octagon barrel and adjustable sights, and chambered in the popular semi-auto 10mm round in 2020.

Price: **$726.05**

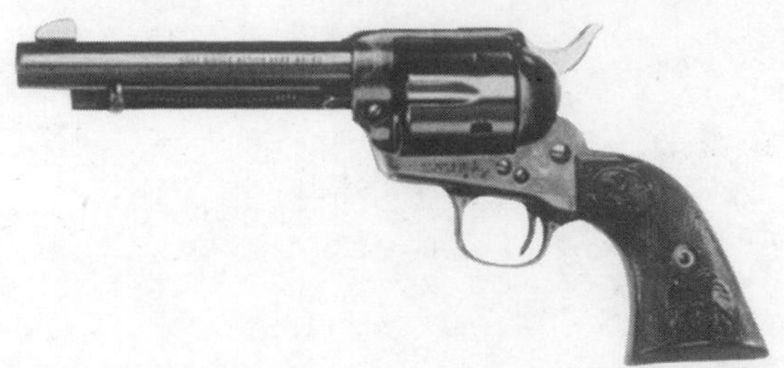

COLT SINGLE ACTION ARMY
Calibers: .357 Magnum, .45 Colt. Capacity: 6-round cylinder. Barrels: 4.75, 5.5, 7.5 in. Weight: 40 oz. (4.75-in. barrel). Length: 10.25 in. overall (4.75-in. barrel). Grips: Black Eagle composite. Sights: Blade front, notch rear. Features: Available in full nickel finish with nickel grip medallions, or Royal Blue with color casehardened frame. Reintroduced 1992. Additional calibers available through Colt Custom Shop.
Price: Blued **$1,599.00**
Price: Nickel **$1,799.00**

EAA BOUNTY HUNTER SA
Calibers: .22 LR/.22 WMR, .357 Mag., .44 Mag., .45 Colt. Capacities: 6. 10-round cylinder available for .22LR/.22WMR. Barrels: 4.5 in., 7.5 in. Weight: 2.5 lbs. Length: 11 in. overall (4.625 in. barrel). Grips: Smooth walnut. Sights: Blade front, grooved topstrap rear. Features: Transfer bar safety; 3-position hammer; hammer-forged barrel. Introduced 1992. Imported by European American Armory
Price: Centerfire, blued or case-hardened **$478.00**
Price: Centerfire, nickel **$515.00**
Price: .22 LR/.22 WMR, blued **$343.00**
Price: .22LR/.22WMR, nickel **$380.00**
Price: .22 LR/.22WMR, 10-round cylinder **$465.00**

EMF 1875 OUTLAW
Calibers: .357 Magnum, .44-40, .45 Colt. Barrels: 7.5 in., 9.5 in. Weight: 46 oz. Length: 13.5 in. overall. Grips: Smooth walnut. Sights: Blade front, fixed groove rear. Features: Authentic copy of 1875 Remington with firing pin in hammer; color casehardened frame, blued cylinder, barrel, steel backstrap and trigger guard. Also available in nickel, factory engraved. Imported by E.M.F. Co.
Price: All calibers **$520.00**
Price: Laser Engraved **$800.00**

EMF 1873 GREAT WESTERN II
Calibers: .357 Magnum, .45 Colt, .44/40. Barrels: 3.5 in., 4.75 in., 5.5 in., 7.5 in. Weight: 36 oz. Length: 11 in. (5.5-in. barrel). Grips: Walnut. Sights: Blade front, notch rear. Features: Authentic reproduction of the original 2nd Generation Colt single-action revolver. Standard and bone casehardening. Coil hammer spring. Hammer-forged barrel. Alchimista has case-hardened frame, brass backstrap, longer and wider 1860 grip.
Price: 1873 Californian .... **$545.00–$560.00**
Price: 1873 Custom series, bone or nickel, ivory-like grips **$689.90**
Price: 1873 Stainless steel, ivory-like grips **$589.90**
Price: 1873 Paladin **$560.00**
Price: Deluxe Californian with checkered walnut grips stainless.......... **$780.00**

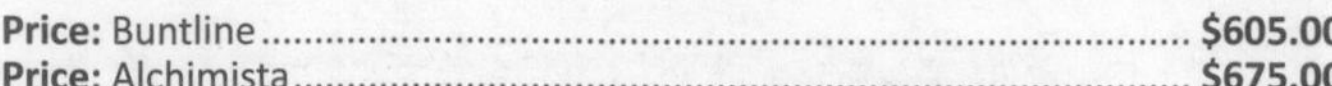

Price: Buntline **$605.00**
Price: Alchimista **$675.00**

EMF 1873 DAKOTA II
Caliber: .357 Magnum, 45 Colt. Barrel: 4.75 in. Grips: Walnut. Finish: black.
Price: **$460.00**

FREEDOM ARMS MODEL 83 PREMIER GRADE
Calibers: .357 Magnum, 41 Magnum, .44 Magnum, .454 Casull, .475 Linebaugh, .500 Wyo. Exp. Capacity: 5-round cylinder. Barrels: 4.75 in., 6 in., 7.5 in., 9 in. (.357 Mag. only), 10 in. (except .357 Mag. and 500 Wyo. Exp.) Weight: 53 oz. (7.5-in. bbl. in .454 Casull). Length: 13 in. (7.5 in. bbl.). Grips: Impregnatedhardwood. Sights: Adjustable rear with replaceable front sight. Fixed rear notch and front blade. Features: Stainless steel construction with brushed finish; manual sliding safety bar. Micarta grips optional. 500 Wyo. Exp. Introduced 2006. Lifetime warranty. Made in USA by Freedom Arms, Inc.
Price: From **$2,738.00**

FREEDOM ARMS MODEL 83 FIELD GRADE
Calibers: .22 LR, .357 Magnum, .41 Magnum, .44 Magnum, .454 Casull, .475 Linebaugh, .500 Wyo. Exp. Capacity: 5-round cylinder. Barrels: 4.75 in., 6 in., 7.5 in., 9 in. (.357 Mag. only), 10 in. (except .357 Mag. and .500 Wyo. Exp.) Weight: 56 oz. (7.5-in. bbl. in .454 Casull). Length: 13.1 in. (7.5 in. bbl.). Grips: Pachmayr standard, impregnated hardwood or Micarta optional. Sights: Adjustable rear with replaceable front sight. Model 83 frame. All stainless steel. Introduced 1988. Made in USA by Freedom Arms Inc.
Price: From **$2,332.00**

FREEDOM ARMS MODEL 97 PREMIER GRADE
Calibers: .17 HMR, .22 LR, .32 H&R, .327 Federal, .357 Magnum, 6 rounds; .41 Magnum, .44 Special, .45 Colt. Capacity: 5-round cylinder. Barrels: 4.25 in., 5.5 in., 7.5 in., 10 in. (.17 HMR, .22 LR, .32 H&R). Weight: 40 oz. (5.5 in. .357 Mag.). Length: 10.75 in. (5.5 in. bbl.). Grips: Impregnated hardwood; Micarta optional. Sights: Adjustable rear, replaceable blade front. Fixed

Prices given are believed to be accurate at time of publication however, many factors affect retail pricing so exact prices are not possible.

rear notch and front blade. Features: Stainless steel construction, brushed finish, automatic transfer bar safety system. Introduced in 1997. Lifetime warranty. Made in USA by Freedom Arms.
Price: From **$2,148.00**

HERITAGE ROUGH RIDER
Calibers: .22 LR, 22 LR/22 WMR combo, .357 Magnum .44-40, .45 Colt. Capacity: 6-round cylinder. Barrels: 3.5 in., 4.75 in., 5.5 in., 7.5 in. Weights: 31–38 oz. Grips: Exotic cocobolo laminated wood or mother of pearl; bird's head models offered. Sights: Blade front, fixed rear. Adjustable sight on 4.75 in. and 5.5 in. models. Features: Hammer block safety. Transfer bar with Big Bores. High polish blue, black satin, silver satin, casehardened and stainless finish. Introduced 1993. Made in USA by Heritage Mfg., Inc.
Price: Rimfire calibers, From **$200.00**
Price: Centerfire calibers, From.. **$450.00**

HERITAGE MANUFACTURING BARKEEP REVOLVER
Caliber: .22 LR. Capacity: 6 rounds. Barrel: 2, 3 in. Grip: Custom scroll wood or gray pearl. Sights: Fixed front and rear. Weight: 2.2 lbs. Features: Heritage Manufacturing's take on the 19th-Century "Storekeeper" single-action revolver. The new Barkeep is chambered in the economical .22 LR but is compatible with an optional interchangeable .22 WMR six-shot cylinder. Available with a black oxide or case-hardened finish. Two grips are also available — custom scroll wood or gray pearl.
Price: Custom wood scroll grips **$180.00**
Price: Gray pearl grips **$189.00**

HERITAGE MANUFACTURING BARKEEP BOOT
Caliber: .22 LR. Capacity: 6 Rounds. Finish: Black standard. Action Type: Single Action Only. Safety: Thumb/Hammer. Grips: Black, gray pearl, custom wood burnt snake. Weight: 25.5 oz. Barrel Length: 1.68 in. Overall Length: 6.38 in.
Price: .... **$196.00–$205.00**

HERITAGE ROUGH RIDER TACTICAL COWBOY
Chambered in .22 LR, is also compatible with the .22 WMR cylinder allowing you to shoot either .22 LR or .22 WMR ammo. The new Heritage Rough Rider Tactical Cowboy features modern day technology into an old classic world. The barrel is threaded for compensators and suppressors. Caliber: .22 LR, Capacity: 6 Rounds, Finish: Black standard. Action Type: Single Action Only. Lands & Grooves: 6. Front Sight: Fiber optic. Rear Sight: Picatinny rail. Safety: Thumb/hammer. Grips: Carbon fiber. Weight: 32.10 oz., Barrel Length: 6.5 in. Overall Length: 11.85 in.
Price: **$212.00**

MAGNUM RESEARCH BFR 20TH ANNIVERSARY
Each hand-crafted 20th Anniversary BFR is part of a limited series, with only 20 pistols to be produced. This custom gun is based on a .45-70 Government long frame model, the first production caliber. A full octagon barrel is added with a custom E-Rod Housing and base pin. Plow-style white polymer grips are hand fit. Exterior surfaces engraved with elegant scrollwork by the artists at Tyler Gun Works. Ships in a beautiful wood case, includes a signed letter of authenticity. Capacity: 5. Caliber: .45/70 Gov't. Barrel: 7.5 in. full octagon. Overall Length: 15 in. Height: 6 in. Cylinder Width: 1.75 in. Finish: Brushed stainless steel. Weight: 4.3 lbs. Sights: Factory black fixed front/rear adjustable. Grip: Plow-style white polymer.
Price: From **$7,000.00**

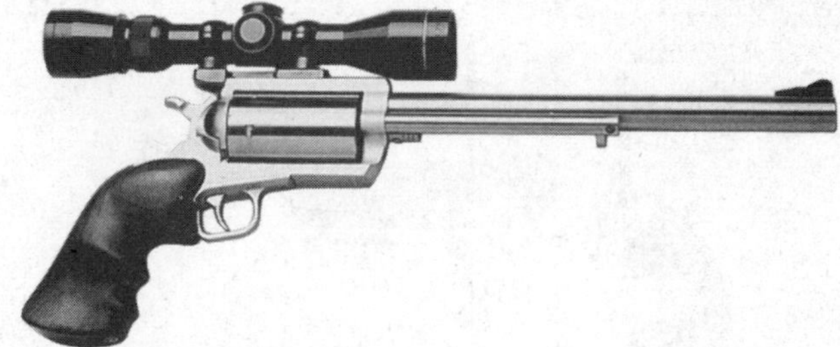

MAGNUM RESEARCH BFR SINGLE ACTION
Calibers: .44 Magnum, .444 Marlin, .45-70, .45 Colt/.410, .450 Marlin, .454 Casull, .460 S&W Magnum, .480 Ruger/.475 Linebaugh, .500 Linebaugh, .500 JRH, .500 S&W, .30-30. Barrels: 6.5 in., 7.5 in. and 10 in. Weights: 3.6–5.3 lbs. Grips: Black rubber. Sights: Rear sights are the same configuration as the Ruger revolvers. Many aftermarket rear sights will fit the BFR. Front sights are machined by Magnum in four heights and anodized flat black. The four heights accommodate all shooting styles, barrel lengths and calibers. All sights are interchangeable with each BFR's. Features: Crafted in the USA, the BFR single-action 5-shot stainless steel revolver frames are CNC machined inside and out from a pre-heat treated investment casting. This is done to prevent warping and dimensional changes or shifting that occurs during the heat treat process. Magnum Research designed the frame with large calibers and substantial recoil in mind, built to close tolerances to handle the pressure of true big-bore calibers. The BFR is equipped with a transfer bar safety feature that allows the gun to be carried safely with all five chambers loaded.
Price: .... **$1,218.00-$1,302.00**

MAGNUM RESEARCH BFR SHORT FRAME
Caliber: .357 Magnum, .44 Magnum. Capacity: 6-round cylinder. Barrels: 5 and 7.5 in. Grips: Standard rubber, Bisley, white polymer or black micarta. Sights: Adjustable rear, fixed front. Weights: 3.5, 3.65 lbs. Features: Made entirely of super tough 17-4PH stainless steel, BFRs are made in the United States and were designed from the outset to handle powerful revolver cartridges. The pre-eminent single-action hunting revolver. Two grip frame options available: a standard plow handle with rubber grip, and Magnum Research iteration of a Bisley with white polymer or black micarta grips.
Price: **$1,302.00**

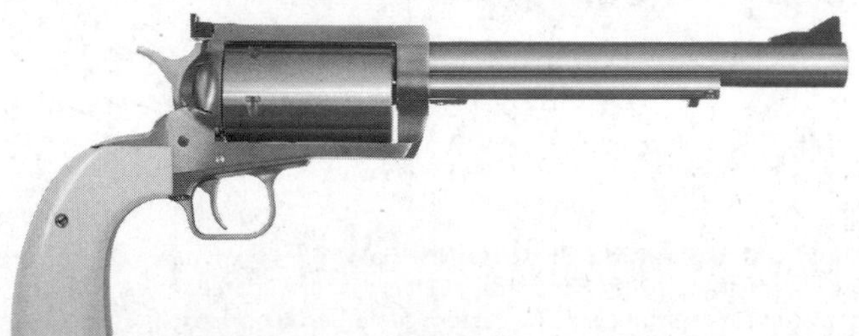

MAGNUM RESEARCH BFR LONG FRAME
Caliber: .350 Legend. Capacity: 6-round cylinder. Barrels: 7.5 and 10 in. Grips: Standard rubber, Bisley, white polymer or black micarta. Sights: Adjustable rear, fixed front. Weights: 4.8, 5 lbs. Features: Built on Magnum Research's long frame and made entirely of 17-4PH stainless steel. The first long frame in six-shot configuration. Two grip frame options available: a standard plow handle with rubber grip, and Magnum Research iteration of a Bisley with white polymer or black micarta grips.
Price: **$1,302.00**

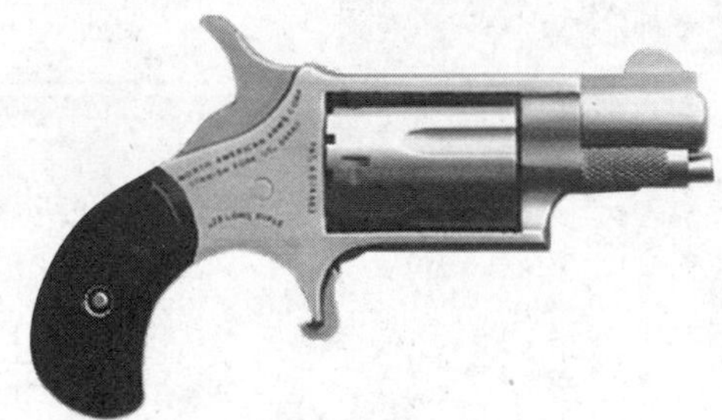

NORTH AMERICAN ARMS MINI
Calibers: .22 Short, 22 LR, 22 WMR. Capacity: 5-round cylinder. Barrels: 1.125 in., 1.625 in. Weight: 4–6.6 oz. Length: 3.625 in., 6.125 in. overall. Grips: Laminated wood. Sights: Blade front, notch fixed rear. Features: All stainless steel construction. Polished satin and matte finish. Engraved models available. From North American Arms.
Price: .22 Short, .22 LR **$226.00**
Price: .22 WMR **$236.00**

NORTH AMERICAN ARMS MINI-MASTER
Calibers: .22 LR, .22 WMR. Capacity: 5-round cylinder. Barrel: 4 in. Weight: 10.7 oz. Length: 7.75 in. overall. Grips: Checkered hard black rubber. Sights: Blade front, white outline rear adjustable for elevation, or fixed. Features: Heavy vented barrel; full-size grips. Non-fluted cylinder. Introduced 1989.
Price: .... **$284.00–$349.00**

NORTH AMERICAN ARMS BLACK WIDOW
Similar to Mini-Master, 2-in. heavy vent barrel. Built on .22 WMR frame. Non-fluted cylinder, black rubber grips. Available with Millett low-profile fixed sights or Millett sight adjustable for elevation only. Overall length 5.875 in., weighs 8.8 oz. From North American Arms.
Price: Adjustable sight, .22 LR or .22 WMR **$352.00**
Price: Fixed sight, .22 LR or .22 WMR **$288.00**

NORTH AMERICAN ARMS "THE EARL" SINGLE-ACTION
Calibers: .22 Magnum with .22 LR accessory cylinder. Capacity: 5-round cylinder. Barrel: 4 in. octagonal. Weight: 6.8 oz. Length: 7.75 in. overall. Grips: Wood. Sights: Barleycorn front and fixed notch rear. Features: Single-action mini-revolver patterned after 1858-style Remington percussion revolver. Includes a spur trigger and a faux loading lever that serves as cylinder pin release.
Price: .... **$298.00,$332.00 (convertible)**

RUGER NEW MODEL SINGLE-SIX SERIES
Calibers: .22 LR, .17 HMR. Convertible and Hunter models come with extra cylinder for .22 WMR. Capacity: 6. Barrels: 4.62 in., 5.5 in., 6.5 in. or 9.5 in. Weight: 35–42 oz. Finish: Blued or stainless. Grips: Black checkered hard rubber, black laminate or hardwood (stainless model only). Single-Six .17 Model available only with 6.5-in. barrel, blue finish, rubber grips. Hunter Model available only with 7.5-in. barrel, black laminate grips and stainless finish.
Price: (blued) **$629.00**
Price: (stainless) **$699.00**

RUGER SINGLE-TEN AND RUGER SINGLE-NINE SERIES
Calibers: .22 LR, .22 WMR. Capacities: 10 (.22 LR Single-Ten), 9 (.22 Mag Single-Nine). Barrels: 5.5 in. (Single-Ten), 6.5 in. (Single-Nine). Weight: 38–39 oz. Grips: Hardwood Gunfighter. Sights: Williams Adjustable Fiber Optic.
Price: **$699.00**

Prices given are believed to be accurate at time of publication however, many factors affect retail pricing so exact prices are not possible.

RUGER NEW MODEL BLACKHAWK/ BLACKHAWK CONVERTIBLE

Calibers: .30 Carbine, .357 Magnum/.38 Special, .41 Magnum, .44 Special, .45 Colt. Capacity: 6-round cylinder. Barrels: 4.625 in., 5.5 in., 6.5 in., 7.5 in. (.30 carbine and .45 Colt). Weights: 36–45 oz. Lengths: 10.375 in. to 13.5 in. Grips: Rosewood or black checkered. Sights: .125-in. ramp front, micro-click rear adjustable for windage and elevation. Features: Rosewood grips, Ruger transfer bar safety system, independent firing pin, hardened chrome-moly steel frame, music wire springs through-out. Case and lock included. Convertibles come with extra cylinder.

Price: Blued **$669.00**
Price: Convertible, .357/9mm **$749.00**
Price: Convertible, .45 Colt/.45 ACP **$749.00**
Price: Stainless, .357 only **$799.00**

RUGER BISLEY SINGLE ACTION

Calibers: .44 Magnum. and .45 Colt. Barrel: 7.5-in. barrel. Length: 13.5 in. Weight: 48–51 oz. Similar to standard Blackhawk, hammer is lower with smoothly curved, deeply checkered wide spur. The trigger is strongly curved with wide smooth surface. Longer grip frame. Adjustable rear sight, ramp-style front. Unfluted cylinder and roll engraving, adjustable sights. Plastic lockable case. Orig. fluted cylinder introduced 1985; discontinued 1991. Unfluted cylinder introduced 1986.

Price: **$899.00**

RUGER NEW MODEL SUPER BLACKHAWK

Caliber: .44 Magnum/.44 Special. Capacity: 6-round cylinder. Barrel: 4.625 in., 5.5 in., 7.5 in., 10.5 in. bull. Weight: 45–55 oz. Length: 10.5 in. to 16.5 in. overall. Grips: Rosewood. Sights: .125-in. ramp front, micro-click rear adjustable for windage and elevation. Features: Ruger transfer bar safety system, fluted or unfluted cylinder, steel grip and cylinder frame, round or square back trigger guard, wide serrated trigger, wide spur hammer. With case and lock.

Price: **$829.00**

RUGER NEW MODEL SUPER BLACKHAWK HUNTER

Caliber: .44 Magnum. Capacity: 6-round cylinder. Barrel: 7.5 in., full-length solid rib, unfluted cylinder. Weight: 52 oz. Length: 13.625 in. Grips: Black laminated wood. Sights: Adjustable rear, replaceable front blade. Features: Reintroduced Ultimate SA revolver. Includes instruction manual, high-impact case, set of medium scope rings, gun lock, ejector rod as standard. Bisley-style frame available.

Price: (Hunter, Bisley Hunter) **$959.00**

RUGER NEW VAQUERO SINGLE-ACTION

Calibers: .357 Magnum, .45 Colt. Capacity: 6-round cylinder. Barrel: 4.625 in., 5.5 in., 7.5 in. Weight: 39–45 oz. Length: 10.5 in. overall (4.625 in. barrel). Grips: Rubber with Ruger medallion. Sights: Fixed blade front, fixed notch rear. Features: Transfer bar safety system and loading gate interlock. Blued model color casehardened finish on frame, rest polished and blued. Engraved model available. Gloss stainless. Introduced 2005.

Price: **$829.00**

RUGER NEW MODEL BISLEY VAQUERO

Calibers: .357 Magnum, .45 Colt. Capacity: 6-round cylinder. Barrel: 5.5-in. Length: 11.12 in. Weight: 45 oz. Features: Similar to New Vaquero but with Bisley-style hammer and grip frame. Simulated ivory grips, fixed sights.

Price: **$899.00**

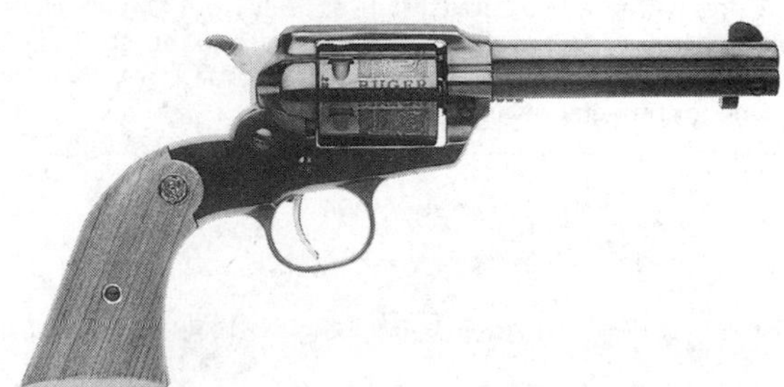

RUGER NEW BEARCAT SINGLE-ACTION

Caliber: .22 LR. Capacity: 6-round cylinder. Barrel: 4 in. Weight: 24 oz. Length: 9 in. overall. Grips: Smooth rosewood with Ruger medallion. Sights: Blade front, fixed notch rear. Distributor special edition available with adjustable sights. Features: Reintroduction of the Ruger Bearcat with slightly lengthened frame, Ruger transfer bar safety system. Available in blued finish only. Rosewood grips. Introduced 1996 (blued), 2003 (stainless). With case and lock.

Price: SBC-4, blued **$639.00**
Price: KSBC-4, satin stainless **$689.00**

RUGER WRANGLER

Caliber: .22 LR. Capacity: 6-round cylinder. Barrel: 4.62 in. Grips: Checkered synthetic. Sights: Fixed front and rear. Weight: 30 oz. Features: Inexpensive to own and inexpensive to shoot, this SA revolver is built on an aluminum-alloy frame and fitted with a cold hammer-forged barrel. Available in three models with three different finishes: Black Cerakote, Silver Cerakote or Burnt Bronze Cerakote. Equipped with transfer-bar mechanism and a free-wheeling pawl, allowing for easy loading and unloading.

Price: **$249.00**

RUGER WRANGLER BIRDSHEAD

Caliber: .22 LR, Grips: Birdshead synthetic. Capacity: 6. Front Sight: Blade. Barrel Length: 3.75 in. Overall Length: 8.62 in. Weight: 28 oz. Finish: Black Cerakote, silver Cerakote, burnt bronze Cerakote, Cylinder Frame Material: Aluminum alloy. Rear Sight: Integral. Twist 1:14 in. RH. Grooves: 6

Price: **$279.00**

STANDARD MANUFACTURING NICKEL SINGLE ACTION

Calibers: .38 Special, .45 Colt. Capacity: 6-round cylinder. Barrels: 4.75, 5.5 and 7.5 in. Grips: Walnut. Sights: Fixed front and rear. Weight: 40 oz. Features: This is one of the finest Single Action Army reproductions ever built, with great attention to detail. Made entirely from 4140 steel, the new nickel-plated revolvers are available in .38 special and the iconic .45 Colt. You can also opt for C-coverage engraving, making for a truly remarkable firearm. One- or two-piece walnut grips available.

Price: .... **$1,995.00 - $3,495.00**

TAYLOR'S CATTLEMAN SERIES

Calibers: .357 Magnum or 45 Colt. Barrels: 4.75 in., 5.5 in., or 7.5 in. Features: Series of Single Action Army-style revolvers made in many variations.

Price: Gunfighter w/blued & color case finish........ **$556.00**
Price: Stainless **$720.00**
Price: Nickel........ **$672.00**
Price: Charcoal blued **$647.00**
Price: Bird's Head 3.5- or 4.5-in. bbl., walnut grips **$603.00**
Price: Engraved (shown)........ **$925.00**

TAYLOR'S & COMPANY GUNFIGHTER

Caliber: .357 Magnum, .45 Colt. Capacity: 6 rounds. Barrel: 4.75, 5.5 in. Grip: Walnut. Checkered or smooth. Sights: Fixed front and rear. Weight: 2.4 lbs. Features: This 1873 Colt Single Action Army replica features an Army-sized grip for users with large hands. Casehardened finish. Available with Taylor Tuned action for additional cost.

Price: Smooth grip........ **$599.00**
Price: Checkered grip **$629.00**

TAYLOR'S & COMPANY GUNFIGHTER DEFENDER

Caliber: .357 Mag., .45 LC Capacity: 6. Weight: 4.75 in. 2.45 lb., 5.5 in. 2.50 lb. Finish: Blue with case hardened frame. Grip/Stock: Checkered walnut. Manufacturer: Uberti. Sights: Fixed front blade. Rear Frame Notch. Overall Length: 4.75 in. (10.35 in.), 5.5 in. (11.10 in.), Action: Taylor tuning available. The Gunfighter Defender with lowered Runnin' Iron hammer, 1860 Army grip is longer and slightly wider than the smaller Navy grip usually found on 1873 single-action models.

Price: .... **$695.00–$847.00**

TAYLOR'S & COMPANY 1860 ARMY SNUB NOSE

Caliber: .36 Caliber, .44 Caliber. Capacity: 6 rounds. Barrel: 3 in. Grip: Checkered flattop birdshead grip. Sights: Fixed front and rear. Weight: 2.3 lbs. Features: 1860 Army Snub Nose blackpowder percussion replica revolver. It features a steel frame, shoulder stock frame cuts and screws, and a round barrel. Barrel and cylinder are blued while the frame is casehardened. A conversion cylinder is available to shoot smokeless ammunition. Manufactured exclusively by Pietta for Taylor's & Company.

Price: **$379.00**

UBERTI 1851–1860 CONVERSION

Calibers: .38 Special, .45 Colt. Capacity: 6-round engraved cylinder. Barrels: 4.75 in., 5.5 in., 7.5 in., 8 in. Weight: 2.6 lbs. (5.5-in. bbl.). Length: 13 in. overall (5.5-in. bbl.). Grips: Walnut. Features: Brass backstrap, trigger guard; color casehardened frame, blued barrel, cylinder. Introduced 2007.

Price: 1851 Navy **$569.00**
Price: 1860 Army **$589.00**

Prices given are believed to be accurate at time of publication however, many factors affect retail pricing so exact prices are not possible.

UBERTI 1871–1872 OPEN TOP

Calibers: .38 Special, .45 Colt. Capacity: 6-round engraved cylinder. Barrels: 4.75 in., 5.5 in., 7.5 in. Weight: 2.6 lbs. (5.5-in. bbl.). Length: 13 in. overall (5.5-in. bbl.). Grips: Walnut. Features: Blued backstrap, trigger guard; color casehardened frame, blued barrel, cylinder. Introduced 2007.

Price: .... **$539.00–$569.00**

UBERTI 1873 CATTLEMAN SINGLE-ACTION

Caliber: .45 Colt. Capacity: 6-round cylinder. Barrels: 4.75 in., 5.5 in., 7.5 in. Weight: 2.3 lbs. (5.5-in. bbl.). Length: 11 in. overall (5.5-in. bbl.). Grips: Styles: Frisco (pearl styled); Desperado (buffalo horn styled); Chisholm (checkered walnut); Gunfighter (black checkered), Cody (ivory styled), one-piece walnut. Sights: Blade front, groove rear. Features: Steel or brass backstrap, trigger guard; color casehardened frame, blued barrel, cylinder. NM designates New Model plunger-style frame; OM designates Old Model screw cylinder pin retainer.

Price: 1873 Cattleman Frisco **$869.00**
Price: 1873 Cattleman Desperado (2006) **$889.00**
Price: 1873 Cattleman Chisholm (2006) **$599.00**
Price: 1873 Cattleman NM, blued 4.75 in. barrel **$669.00**
Price: 1873 Cattleman NM, Nickel finish, 7.5 in. barrel **$689.00**
Price: 1873 Cattleman Cody **$899.00**

UBERTI 1873 CATTLEMAN BIRD'S HEAD SINGLE ACTION

Calibers: .357 Magnum, .45 Colt. Capacity: 6-round cylinder. Barrels: 3.5 in., 4 in., 4.75 in., 5.5 in. Weight: 2.3 lbs. (5.5-in. bbl.). Length: 10.9 in. overall (5.5-in. bbl.). Grips: One-piece walnut. Sights: Blade front, groove rear. Features: Steel or brass backstrap, trigger guard; color casehardened frame, blued barrel, fluted cylinder.

Price: **$569.00**

UBERTI CATTLEMAN .22

Caliber: .22 LR. Capacity: 6- or 12-round cylinder. Barrel: 5.5 in. Grips: One-piece walnut. Sights: Fixed. Features: Blued and casehardened finish, steel or brass backstrap/trigger guard.

Price: (brass backstrap, trigger guard) **$539.00**
Price: (steel backstrap, trigger guard) **$559.00**
Price: (12-round model, steel backstrap, trigger guard) **$589.00**

UBERTI 1873 CATTLEMAN BRASS 9MM

Delivering the same performance and standout features as the 1873 Cattleman Brass 9mm, the 1873 Cattleman Brass Dual Cylinder ups the ante with two included cylinders — one chambered in 9mm Luger and the other in .357 Magnum.

Price: **$599.00**

UBERTI 1873 CATTLEMAN BRASS DUAL CYLINDER 9MM/.357 MAGNUM

Delivering the same performance and standout features as the 1873 Cattleman Brass 9mm, the 1873 Cattleman Brass Dual Cylinder ups the ante with two included cylinders — one chambered in 9mm Luger and the other in .357 Magnum.

Price: **$749.00**

UBERTI DALTON REVOLVER

Caliber: .45 Colt. Capacity: 6-round cylinder. Barrel: 5.5 in. Grips: Simulated pearl. Sights: Fixed front and rear. Weight: 2.3 lbs. Features: Uberti USA expands its Outlaws & Lawmen Series of revolvers with the addition of the Dalton Revolver, a faithful reproduction of the Colt Single Action Army revolver used by Dalton Gang leader Bob Dalton. Features hand-chased engraving from famed Italian engraving company, Atelier Giovanelli, on the receiver, grip frame and cylinder.

Price: **$1,109.00**

UBERTI 1873 BISLEY SINGLE-ACTION

Calibers: .357 Magnum, .45 Colt (Bisley); .22 LR and .38 Special. (Stallion), both with 6-round fluted cylinder. Barrels: 4.75 in., 5.5 in., 7.5 in. Weight: 2–2.5 lbs. Length: 12.7 in. overall (7.5-in. barrel). Grips: Two-piece walnut. Sights: Blade front, notch rear. Features: Replica of Colt's Bisley Model. Polished blued finish, color casehardened frame. Introduced 1997.

Price: 1873 Bisley, 7.5-in. barrel **$619.00**

UBERTI 1873 BUNTLINE AND REVOLVER CARBINE SINGLE-ACTION

Caliber: .357 Magnum, .44-40, .45 Colt. Capacity: 6. Barrel: 18 in. Length: 22.9–34 in. Grips: Walnut pistol grip or rifle stock. Sights: Fixed or adjustable.

Price: 1873 Revolver Carbine, 18-in. bbl., 34 in. OAL **$729.00**
Price: 1873 Cattleman Buntline Target, 18-in. bbl. 22.9 in. OAL **$639.00**

UBERTI 1873 EL PATRÓN 9MM

Presented with checkered walnut grips, case-hardened frame, 5.5-inch blued barrel, numbered cylinder, and EasyView sights, the El Patrón has the classic profile of the Old West SAA revolvers.

Price: **$729.00**

Prices given are believed to be accurate at time of publication however, many factors affect retail pricing so exact prices are not possible.

UBERTI 1870 SCHOFIELD-STYLE TOP BREAK
Calibers: .38 Special, .44 Russian, .44-40, .45 Colt. Capacity: 6-round cylinder. Barrels: 3.5 in., 5 in., 7 in. Weight: 2.4 lbs. (5-in. barrel) Length: 10.8 in. overall (5-in. barrel). Grips: Two-piece smooth walnut or pearl. Sights: Blade front, notch rear. Features: Replica of Smith & Wesson Model 3 Schofield. Single-action, top break with automatic ejection. Polished blued finish (first model). Introduced 1994.
Price: .... **$1,189.00-$1,599.00**

UBERTI STAINLESS STEEL SHORT STROKE CMS PRO
Caliber: .45 Colt. Capacity: 6-round cylinder. Barrel: 3.5 in. Grips: Synthetic traditional. Sights: Fixed front and rear. Weight: 2.1 lbs. Features: Made specifically for the rigors of Cowboy Mounted Shooting competition, and built entirely of stainless steel. Good for quick, one-handed shooting while riding a horse. Features low-profile, short-stroke hammer with 20-percent less travel. Extra-wide, deeply grooved hammer, and chambered in the classic .45 Colt.
Price: **$909.00**

UBERTI STAINLESS STEEL SHORT STROKE CMS KL PRO
Caliber: .45 Colt. Capacity: 6-round cylinder. Barrel: 3.5 in. Grips: Synthetic bird's head. Sights: Fixed front and rear. Weight: 2.1 lbs. Features: Made specifically for the rigors of Cowboy Mounted Shooting competition, and built entirely of stainless steel. This model is the result of the partnership between Uberti USA and legendary Cowboy Mounted Shooter competitor Kenda Lenseigne, winner of multiple world and national mounted shooting championships. It features a modified bird's-head grip with Lenseigne's brand on the grip and her signature engraved on the barrel. Features low-profile, short-stroke hammer with 20-percent less travel. Extra-wide, deeply grooved hammer, and chambered in the classic .45 Colt.
Price: **$909.00**

UBERTI USA DALTON
Caliber: .357 Magnum. Capacity: 6 rounds. Barrel: 5.5 in. Grip: Simulated pearl. Sights: Fixed front and rear. Weight: 2.3 lbs. Features: Uberti USA Outlaw & Lawmen Series of revolvers adds the Dalton — a faithful reproduction of the Colt Single Action Army revolver used by Dalton Gang leader Bob Dalton. Features hand-chased engraving from famed Italian engraving company, Atelier Giovanelli on the receiver, grip frame, and cylinder. This new version is chambered in .357 Magnum.
Price: **$1,109.00**

UBERTI USA FRANK
Caliber: .357 Magnum. Capacity: 6 rounds. Barrel: 7.5 in. Grip: Simulated ivory. Sights: Fixed front and rear. Weight: 2.3 lbs. Features: Uberti USA Outlaw & Lawmen Series of revolvers adds a .357 Magnum version of the Frank revolver, a faithful reproduction of the outlaw Frank James' 1875 Remington. Finished in nickel plating, the grip is simulated ivory with a lanyard loop.
Price: **$949.00**

UBERTI USA HARDIN
Caliber: .45 Colt. Capacity: 6 rounds. Barrel: 7 in. Grip: Simulated bison horn. Sights: Fixed front and rear. Weight: 2.6 lbs. Features: Uberti USA Outlaw & Lawmen Series adds the Hardin, a faithful reproduction of the Smith & Wesson Top-break revolver used by John Wesley Hardin. Features a case-colored frame and charcoal blue barrel and cylinder along with simulated bison-horn grip, chambered in .45 Colt.
Price: **$1,479.00**

UBERTI USA TEDDY
Caliber: .45 Colt. Capacity: 6 rounds. Barrel: 5.5 in. Grip: Simulated ivory. Sights: Fixed front and rear. Weight: 2.3 lbs. Features: Replica of the revolver Theodore Roosevelt carried on many of his adventures. A replica 1873 Colt, this one is chambered in .45 Colt, and features a nickel finish, full laser engraving along the frame, cylinder, and barrel, and simulated ivory grips.
Price: **$1,249.00**

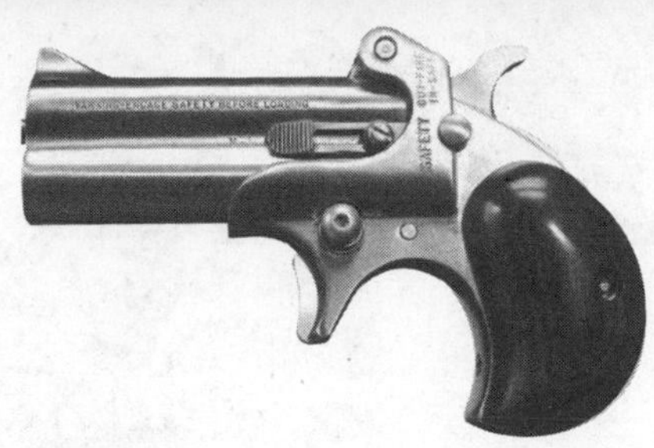

AMERICAN DERRINGER MODEL 1
Calibers: All popular handgun calibers plus .45 Colt/.410 Shotshell. Capacity: 2, (.45-70 model is single shot). Barrel: 3 in. Overall length: 4.82 in. Weight: 15 oz. Features: Manually operated hammer-block safety automatically disengages when hammer is cocked. Texas Commemorative has brass frame and is available in .38 Special, .44-40. or .45 Colt.
Price: .... **$635.00–$735.00**
Price: Texas Commemorative **$835.00**

AMERICAN DERRINGER MODEL 8
Calibers: .45 Colt/.410 shotshell. Capacity: 2. Barrel: 8 in. Weight: 24 oz.
Price: **$915.00**
Price: High polish finish **$1,070.00**

AMERICAN DERRINGER DA38
Calibers: .38 Special, .357 Magnum, 9mm Luger. Barrel: 3.3 in. Weight: 14.5 oz. Features: DA operation with hammer-block thumb safety. Barrel, receiver and all internal parts are made from stainless steel.
Price: .... **$690.00–$740.00**

BOND ARMS TEXAS DEFENDER DERRINGER
Calibers: Available in more than 10 calibers, from .22 LR to .45 LC/.410 shotshells. Barrel: 3 in. Weight: 20 oz. Length: 5 in. Grips: Rosewood. Sights: Blade front, fixed rear. Features: Interchangeable barrels, stainless steel firing pins, cross-bolt safety, automatic extractor for rimmed calibers. Stainless steel construction, brushed finish. Right or left hand.
Price: **$543.00**
Price: Interchangeable barrels, .22 LR thru .45 LC, 3 in. **$139.00**
Price: Interchangeable barrels, .45 LC, 3.5 in. .... **$159.00–$189.00**

BOND ARMS RANGER II
Caliber: .45 LC/.410 shotshells or .357 Magnum/.38 Special. Barrel: 4.25 in. Weight: 23.5 oz. Length: 6.25 in. Features: This model has a trigger guard. Intr. 2011. From Bond Arms.
Price: **$673.00**

BOND ARMS CENTURY 2000 DEFENDER
Calibers: .45 LC/.410 shotshells. or .357 Magnum/.38 Special. Barrel: 3.5 in. Weight: 21 oz. Length: 5.5 in. Features: Similar to Defender series.
Price: **$517.00**

BOND ARMS COWBOY DEFENDER
Calibers: From .22 LR to .45 LC/.410 shotshells. Barrel: 3 in. Weight: 19 oz. Length: 5.5 in. Features: Similar to Defender series. No trigger guard.
Price: **$493.00**

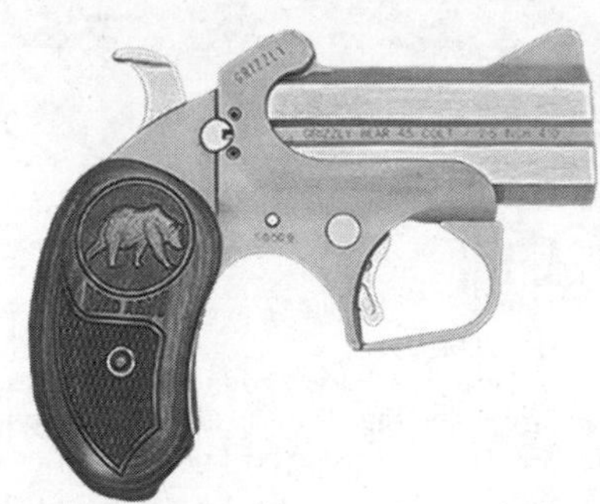

BOND ARMS GRIZZLY
Calibers: .45 Colt/.410 bore. Capacity: 2 rounds. Barrel: 3 in. Grips: Rosewood. Sights: Fixed front and rear. Features: Similar to other Bond Arms derringers, this model is chambered in .45 Colt and 2.5-inch, .410-bore shotshells. Vibrant rosewood grips with grizzly-bear artwork adorn the Grizzly. It includes a matching leather holster embossed with a grizzly bear.
Price: **$377.00**

BOND ARMS SNAKE SLAYER
Calibers: .45 LC/.410 shotshell (2.5 in. or 3 in.). Barrel: 3.5 in. Weight: 21 oz. Length: 5.5 in. Grips: Extended rosewood. Sights: Blade front, fixed rear. Features: Single-action; interchangeable barrels; stainless steel firing pin. Introduced 2005.
Price: **$603.00**

BOND ARMS ROUGHNECK
Calibers: 9mm, .357 Magnum, .45 ACP. Capacity: 2 rounds. Barrel: 2.5 in. Grips: Textured rubber. Sights: Fixed front and rear. Weight: 22 oz. Features: A member of the new Bond Arms Rough series of derringers that includes the premium features found in all Bond guns, including stainless steel barrel, cross-bolt safety, retracting firing pin, spring-loaded, cam-lock lever and rebounding hammer. Each gun of the new series undergoes a quick clean up and deburring and then is bead-blasted, giving it a rough finish. This lightweight tips the scales at 22 ounces.
Price: $269.00

BOND ARMS ROUGH N ROWDY

Calibers: .45 Colt/.410 bore. Capacity: 2 rounds. Barrel: 3 in. Grips: Black rubber. Sights: Fixed front and rear. Features: Similar to Bond Arms Roughneck, this model is chambered in .45 Colt and 2.5-inch, .410 bore shotshells.

Price: $299.00

BOND ARMS SNAKE SLAYER IV

Calibers: .45 LC/.410 shotshell (2.5 in. or 3 in.). Barrel: 4.25 in. Weight: 22 oz. Length: 6.25 in. Grips: Extended rosewood. Sights: Blade front, fixed rear. Features: Single-action; interchangeable barrels; stainless steel firing pin. Introduced 2006.

Price: $648.00

BOND ARMS STINGER

Calibers: 9mm, .380 ACP. The All-New Stinger has the same quality as Bond Arms' regular models but has half the weight and a slimmer profile. Features: Stainless steel matte barrel, 7075 anodized aluminum frame. Total weight: 12 oz. Rebounding hammer, retracting firing pins, cross-bolt safety. Comes with standard rubber grips and a slimmer set of polymer grips.

Price: **$379.00**

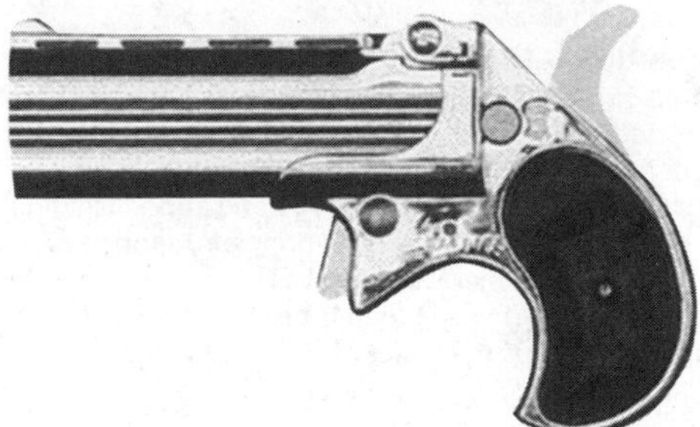

Calibers: .22 WMR, .32 H&R Mag., .38 Special, 9mm Para., .380 ACP. Barrel: 2.75 in. Weight: 14 oz. Length: 4.65 in. overall. Grips: Textured black or white synthetic or laminated rosewood. Sights: Blade front, fixed notch rear. Features: Alloy frame, steel-lined barrels, steel breechblock. Plunger-type safety with integral hammer block. Black, chrome or satin finish. Introduced 2002. Made in USA by Cobra Enterprises of Utah, Inc.

Price: $187.00

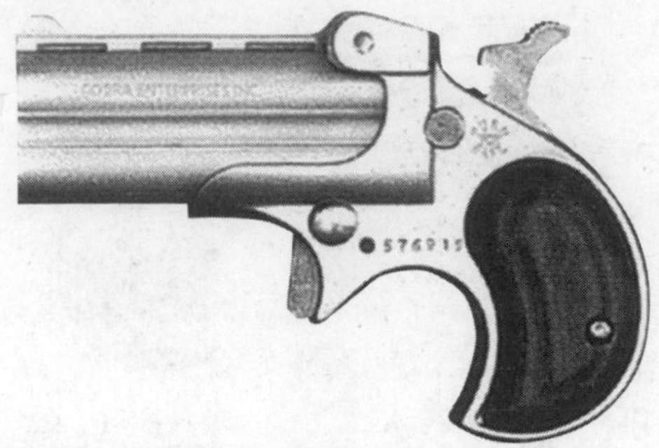

COBRA STANDARD SERIES DERRINGERS

Calibers: .22 LR, .22 WMR, .25 ACP, .32 ACP. Barrel: 2.4 in. Weight: 9.5 oz. Length: 4 in. overall. Grips: Laminated wood or pearl. Sights: Blade front, fixed notch rear. Features: Choice of black powder coat, satin nickel or chrome finish. Introduced 2002. Made in USA by Cobra Enterprises of Utah, Inc.

Price: $169.00

COBRA LONG-BORE DERRINGERS

Calibers: .22 WMR, .38 Special, 9mm. Barrel: 3.5 in. Weight: 16 oz. Length: 5.4 in. overall. Grips: Black or white synthetic or rosewood. Sights: Fixed. Features: Chrome, satin nickel, or black Teflon finish. Introduced 2002. Made in USA by Cobra Enterprises of Utah, Inc.

Price: $187.00

COBRA TITAN .45 LC/.410 DERRINGER

Calibers: .45 LC, .410 or 9mm, 2-round capacity. Barrel: 3.5 in. Weight: 16.4 oz. Grip: Rosewood. Features: Standard finishes include: satin stainless, black stainless and brushed stainless. Made in USA by Cobra Enterprises of Utah, Inc.

Price: $399.00

COMANCHE SUPER SINGLE-SHOT

Calibers: .45 LC/.410 Barrel: 10 in. Sights: Adjustable. Features: Blue finish, not available for sale in CA, MA. Distributed by SGS Importers International, Inc.

Price: $240.00

DOUBLETAP DERRINGER
Calibers: .45 Colt or 9mm Barrel: 3 in. Weight: 12 oz. Length: 5.5 in. Sights: Adjustable. Features: Over/under, two-barrel design. Rounds are fired individually with two separate trigger pulls. Tip-up design, aluminum frame.
Price: **$499.00**

HEIZER PAK1
Caliber: 7.2x39. Similar to Pocket AR but chambered for 7.62x39mm. Single shot. Barrel: 3.75 in., ported or unported. Length: 6.375 in. Weight: 23 oz.
Price: **$339.00**

HEIZER PS1 POCKET SHOTGUN
Calibers: .45 Colt or .410 shotshell. Single-shot. Barrel: Tip-up, 3.25 in. Weight: 22 oz. Length: 5.6 in. Width: .742 in Height: 3.81 in. Features: Available in several finishes. Standard model is matte stainless or black. Also offered in Hedy Jane series for the women in pink or in two-tone combinations of stainless and pink, blue, green, purple. Includes interchangeable AR .223 barrel. Made in the USA by Heizer Industries.
Price: **$499.00**

HEIZER POCKET AR
Caliber: .223 Rem./5.56 NATO. Single shot. Barrel: 3.75 in., ported or non-ported. Length: 6.375 in. Weight: 23 oz. Features: Similar to PS1 pocket shotgun but chambered for .223/5.56 rifle cartridge.
Price: **$339.00**

HENRY MARE'S LEG
Calibers: .22 LR, .22 WMR, .357 Magnum, .44 Magnum, .45 Colt. Capacities: 10 rounds (.22 LR), 8 rounds (.22 WMR), 5 rounds (others). Barrel: 12.9 in. Length: 25 in. Weight: 4.5 lbs. (rimfire) to 5.8 lbs. (centerfire calibers). Features: Lever-action operation based on Henry rifle series and patterned after gun made famous in Steve McQueen's 1950s TV show, "Wanted: Dead or Alive." Made in the USA.
Price: .22 LR.. **$462.00**
Price: .22 WMR **$473.00**
Price: Centerfire calibers **$1,024.00**

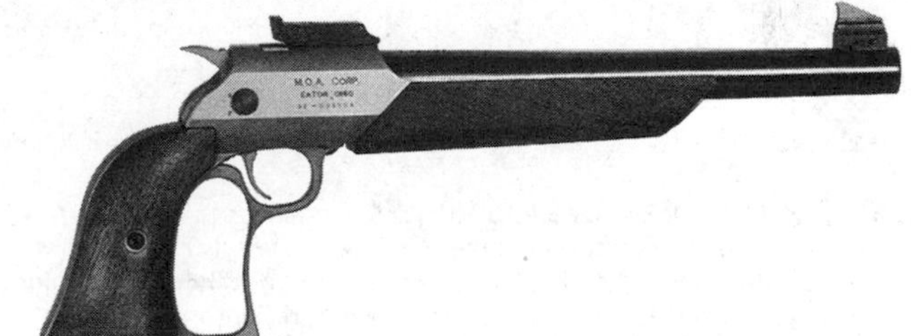

MAXIMUM SINGLE-SHOT
Calibers: .22 LR, .22 Hornet, .22 BR, .22 PPC, 223 Rem., .22-250, 6mm BR, 6mm PPC, .243, .250 Savage, 6.5mm-35M, .270 MAX, .270 Win., 7mm TCU, 7mm BR, 7mm-35, 7mm INT-R, 7mm-08, 7mm Rocket, 7mm Super-Mag., .30 Herrett, .30 Carbine, .30-30, .308 Win., 30x39, .32-20, .350 Rem. Mag., .357 Mag., .357 Maximum, .358 Win., .375 H&H, .44 Mag., .454 Casull. Barrel: 8.75 in., 10.5 in., 14 in. Weight: 61 oz. (10.5-in. bbl.); 78 oz. (14-in. bbl.). Length: 15 in., 18.5 in. overall (with 10.5- and 14-in. bbl., respectively). Grips: Smooth walnut stocks and fore-end. Also available with 17-finger-groove grip. Sights: Ramp front, fully adjustable open rear. Features: Falling block action; drilled and tapped for M.O.A. scope mounts; integral grip frame/receiver; adjustable trigger; Douglas barrel (interchangeable). Introduced 1983. Made in USA by M.O.A. Corp.
Price: **$1,062.00**

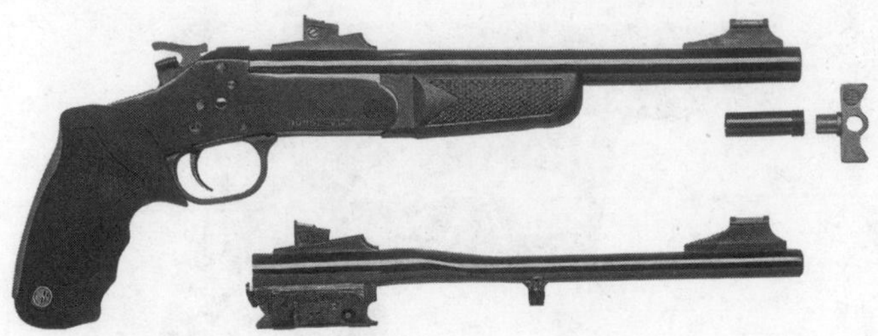

ROSSI MATCHED PAIR, "DUAL THREAT PERFORMER"
Calibers: .22LR, .44 Magnum, .223, .243. .410, 20 gauge, single shot. Interchangeable rifle and shotgun barrels in various combinations. Sights: Fiber optic front sights, adjustable rear. Features: Two-in-one pistol system with single-shot simplicity. Removable choke and cushioned grip with a Taurus Security System.
Price: .22/.410 from **$345.00**

SAVAGE ARMS 110 PCS (PISTOL CHASSIS SYSTEM)
Calibers: 6.5 Creedmoor, .308 Win., .350 Legend, .300 AAC BLK., .223 Rem. Features: Carbon steel, matte black, barrel and receiver. Medium-contour 10.5-in. barrel, with threaded muzzle (5/8x24). Machined aluminum, 1-piece chassis with 7-in. free-floating modular forend with M-LOK slots and Cerakote finish. 1-Piece 0 MOA rail. Left-hand bolt, right-side eject. Spiral fluted bolt body. 2.5 to 6-lb. user-adjustable AccuTrigger, Picatinny rail at rear of chassis. Accepts most AR-15 pistol grips. Barricade grooves milled into the front of the magazine well, ambidextrous magazine release and AICS magazine.
Price: From **$999.00**

THOMPSON/CENTER ENCORE PRO HUNTER
Calibers: .223, .308. Single shot, break-open design. Barrel: 15 in. Weight: 4.25–4.5 lbs. Grip: Walnut on blued models, rubber on stainless. Matching fore-end. Sights: Adjustable rear, ramp front. Features: Interchangeable barrels, adjustable trigger. Pro Hunter has "Swing Hammer" to allow reaching the hammer when the gun is scoped. Other Pro Hunter features include fluted barrel.
Price: From **$779.00**

THOMPSON/CENTER G2 CONTENDER
Calibers: .22 LR or .357 Magnum. A second generation Contender pistol maintaining the same barrel interchangeability with older Contender barrels and their corresponding forends (except Herrett fore-end). The G2 frame will not accept old-style grips due to the change in grip angle. Incorporates an automatic hammer block safety with built-in interlock. Features include trigger adjustable for overtravel, adjustable rear sight; ramp front sight blade, blued steel finish.
Price: From **$729.00**

Prices given are believed to be accurate at time of publication however, many factors affect retail pricing so exact prices are not possible.

BENELLI ETHOS
Gauges: 12 ga., 20 ga., 28 ga. 3 in. Capacity: 4+1. Barrel: 26 in. or 28 in. (Full, Mod., Imp. Cyl., Imp. Mod., Cylinder choke tubes). Weights: 6.5 lbs. (12 ga.), 5.3–5.7 (20 & 28 ga.). Length: 49.5 in. overall (28 in. barrel). Stock: Select AA European walnut with satin finish. Sights: Red bar fiber optic front, with three interchangeable inserts, metal middle bead. Features: Utilizes Benelli's Inertia Driven system. Recoil is reduced by Progressive Comfort recoil reduction system within the buttstock. Twelve and 20-gauge models cycle all 3-inch loads from light 7/8 oz. up to 3-inch magnums. Also available with nickel-plated engraved receiver. Imported from Italy by Benelli USA, Corp.
Price: **$1,999.00**
Price: Engraved nickel-plated (shown) **$2,149.00**
Price: 20 or 28 ga. (engraved, nickel plated only) **$2,149.00**

BENELLI ETHOS BE.S.T.
Benelli expands its Ethos line with the new BE.S.T. model, so named for the Benelli Surface Treatment, a proprietary coating that protects steel from rust and corrosion and was tested over several months in saltwater with no signs of corrosion. Parts treated with BE.S.T. are backed with a 25-year warranty against rust and corrosion.
Price: $2,199.00

BENELLI ETHOS CORDOBA BE.S.T.
Gauge: 12 ga. 3in., 20ga. 3in, 28ga. 3in. Barrel: 28 in. or 30 in. ventilated wide rib. Length: 49.5 –51.5 in. Weight: 5.4–7.0 lbs. Stock: Black Synthetic. Features: Benelli expands their Ethos line of Inertia-Driven semi-autos with the new BE.S.T. (Benelli Surface Treatment). This Cordoba version is designed for high-volume shooting like that of dove hunting in Argentina — the gun's namesake location. Specialty features include ported barrels, ComforTech recoil-reducing system, and lighter weight. Fiber optic front sight with mid-rib bead on a wide broadway sight channel. Shell View system places small windows in the magazine tube for quickly visualizing remaining shell count. Advertised to handle 3-inch magnum rounds down to the lightest 7/8-ounce loads. Ships with five extended Crio chokes (C, IC, M, IM, F).
Price: $2,349.00

BENELLI ETHOS SPORT
Gauges: 12 ga., 20 ga., 28 ga. 3 in. Capacity: 4+1. Barrel: Ported, 28 in. or 30 in. (12 ga. only). Full, Mod., Imp. Cyl., Imp. Mod., Cylinder extended choke tubes. Wide rib. Other features similar to Ethos model.
Price: **$2,269.00**

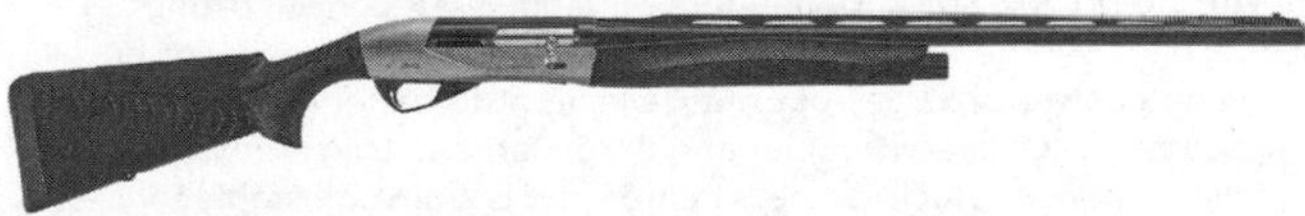

BENELLI ETHOS SUPER SPORT
Gauge: 12 ga. 3in., 20ga. 3in. Barrel: 26 in. or 28 in. ventilated wide rib. Length: 49.5–51.5 in. Weight: 5.4–7.0 lbs. Stock: Carbon-fiber finish composite stock and fore-end. Features: Benelli expands their Ethos semi-automatic line with the Super Sport competition-ready model. Lightweight, weather-resistant carbon-fiber finish furniture. Inertia-Driven semi-automatic with ComforTech recoil-reducing system. Ported Crio barrel. Fiber optic front sight and mid-barrel bead. Nickel-plated receiver. Capacity of 4+1 rounds. Ships with five extended Crio chokes (C, IC, M, IM, F).
Price: **$2,299.00**

BENELLI M2 FIELD
Gauges: 20 ga., 12 ga., 3 in. chamber. Barrels: 21 in., 24 in., 26 in., 28 in. Weights: 5.4–7.2 lbs. Length: 42.5–49.5 in. overall. Stock: Synthetic, Advantage Max-4 HD, Advantage Timber HD, APG HD. Sights: Red bar. Features: Uses the Inertia Driven bolt mechanism. Vent rib. Comes with set of five choke tubes. Imported from Italy by Benelli USA.
Price: Synthetic stock 12 ga. **$1,499.00**
Price: Camo stock 12 ga. **$1,549.00**
Price: Synthetic stock 20 ga. **$1,499.00**
Price: Camo stock 20 ga. **$1,599.00**
Price: Rifled slug .... **$1,469.00–$1,589.00**
Price: Left-hand 12 ga. **$1,409.00**
Price: Left-hand model 20 ga. **$1,519.00**
Price: Tactical **$1,249.00**

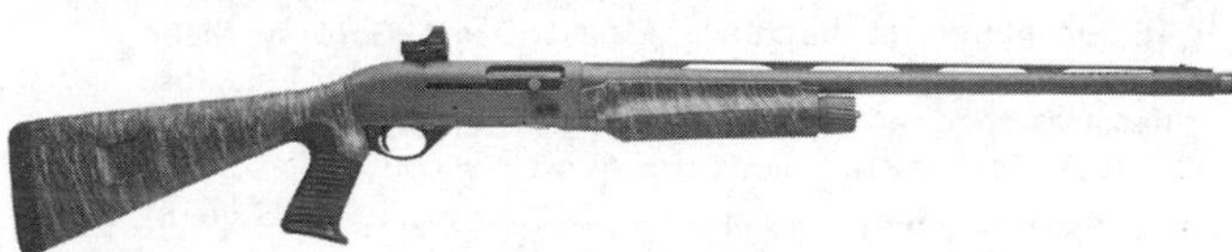

BENELLI M2 TURKEY EDITION
Gauges: 12 ga. and 20 ga., Full, Imp. Mod, Mod., Imp. Cyl., Cyl. choke tubes. Barrel: 24 in. Weight: 6-7 lbs. Stock: 12 ga. model has ComforTech with pistol grip, Bottomland/Cerakote finish. 20 ga. has standard stock with Realtree APG finish. Features: From the Benelli Performance Shop.
Price: 20 ga. standard stock **$3,199.00**
Price: 12 ga. pistol grip stock **$3,399.00**

BENELLI MONTEFELTRO
Gauges: 12 ga. and 20 ga. Full, Imp. Mod, Mod., Imp. Cyl., Cyl. choke tubes. Barrels: 24 in., 26 in., 28 in., 30 in. (Sporting). Weights: 5.3–7.1 lbs. Stock: Checkered walnut with satin finish. Lengths: 43.6–49.5 in. overall. Features: Burris FastFire II sight. Uses the Inertia Driven rotating bolt system with a simple inertia recoil design. Finish is blued. Introduced 1987.
Price: Standard Model **$1,129.00**
Price: Silver **$1,779.00**
Price: Sporting **$1,329.00**

BENELLI SUPER BLACK EAGLE III (SBE3)
Gauge: 12 ga. 3 in., 20 ga. 3 in., 28 ga. 3 in. Barrel: 26, 28 or 30-in. ventilated rib. Length: 47.5–49.5 in. Weight: 5.8–6.9 lbs. Stock: Synthetic with multiple finish choices. Features: Benelli expands their inertia-driven semi-automatic SBE III line by adding a 3-inch chambered 28-gauge model for 2022, which will have slimmer lines. Models available in Black synthetic, Realtree MAX-5, Gore OptiFade Timber, and Mossy Oak Bottomland. ComforTech stock for recoil reduction, Easy Locking bolt, and beveled loading port.
Price: **$1,699.00**
Price: 28 ga. **$1,799.00**

BENELLI SUPER BLACK EAGLE III BE.S.T.
Benelli expands its SBE III line with the new BE.S.T. model, so named for the Benelli Surface Treatment, a proprietary coating that protects steel from rust and corrosion and was tested over several months in saltwater with no signs of corrosion. Parts treated with BE.S.T. are backed with a 25-year warranty against rust and corrosion. The BE.S.T. package will be available on select SBE III models.
Price: **$2,199.00**

BENELLI SUPERSPORT & SPORT II
Gauges: 20 ga., 12 ga., 3-in. chamber. Capacity: 4+1. Barrels: 28 in., 30 in., ported, 10mm sporting rib. Weight: 7.2–7.3 lbs. Lengths: 49.6–51.6 in. Stock: Carbon fiber, ComforTech (Supersport) or walnut (Sport II). Sights: Red bar front, metal midbead. Sport II is similar to the Legacy model except has nonengraved dual tone blued/silver receiver, ported wide-rib barrel, adjustable buttstock, and functions with all loads. Walnut stock with satin finish. Introduced 1997. Features: Designed for high-volume sporting clays. Inertia-driven action, Extended CrioChokes. Ported. Imported from Italy by Benelli USA.
Price: SuperSport **$2,199.00**
Price: Sport II **$1,899.00**

BENELLI VINCI
Gauge: 12 ga., 3-in. Barrels: 26- or 28-inch ribbed. Tactical model available with 18.5-in. barrel. Finishes: Black, MAX-4HD or APG HD; synthetic contoured stocks; optional Steady-Grip model. Weight: 6.7–6.9 lbs. Features: Gas-operated action. Modular disassembly; interchangeable choke tubes. Picatinny rail, pistol grip, ghost ring sight.
Price: .... **$1,349.00–$1,469.00**

BENELLI SUPER VINCI
Gauge: 12 ga.. 2 3/4 in., 3 in. and 3 1/2 in. Capacity: 3+1. Barrels: 26 in., 28 in. Weights: 6.9–7 lbs. Lengths: 48.5–50.5 in. Stock: Black synthetic, Realtree Max4 and Realtree APG. Features: Crio Chokes: C,IC,M,IM,F. Length of Pull: 14.375 in. Drop at Heel: 2 in. Drop at Comb: 1.375 in. Sights: Red bar front sight and metal bead mid-sight. Minimum recommended load: 3-dram, 1 1/8 oz. loads (12 ga.). Receiver drilled and tapped for scope mounting. Imported from Italy by Benelli USA., Corp.
Price: Black Synthetic Comfortech **$1,799.00**
Price: Camo **$1,899.00**

BROWNING A5
Gauges: 12 ga, 3 or 3.5 in.; 16 ga., 2.75 in. Barrel: 26, 28, or 30 in. Weight: 5.95–7.0 lbs. Stock: Dependent on model, but current listings include high-gloss Walnut, black synthetic, or camouflage variants. Features: Operates on Kinematic short-recoil system, different from the classic Auto-5 long-recoil action built since 1903 and discontinued in the 1990's. New model features lengthened forcing cone, interchangeable choke tubes, and ventilated rib with multiple front sight options depending on model.
Price: A5 Wicked Wing with Vintage Tan camo **$2,159.00**
Price: A5 in Vintage Tan camo **$1,939.00**
Price: A5 Lightning Sweet 16 w/lightweight black anodized receiver .. **$1,819.00**
Price: A5 Sweet 16 w/ brushed nickel receiver & oil finish Walnut. **$2,029.00**
Price: A5 Sweet 16 with Mossy Oak Shadow Grass Habitat camo .. **$1,999.00**

BROWNING MAXUS HUNTER
Gauges: 12 ga., 3 in. and 3 1/2 in. Barrels: 26 in., 28 in. and 30 in. Flat ventilated rib with fixed cylinder choke; stainless steel; matte finish. Weight: 7 lbs. 2 oz. Length: 40.75 in. Stock: Gloss finish walnut stock with close radius pistol grip, sharp 22 LPI checkering, Speed Lock Forearm, shim adjustable for length of pull, cast and drop. Features: Vector Pro-lengthened forcing cone, three Invector-Plus choke tubes, Inflex Technology recoil pad, ivory front bead sight, One 1/4 in. stock spacer. Strong, lightweight aluminum alloy receiver with durable satin nickel finish & laser engraving (pheasant on the right, mallard on the left). All-Purpose Hunter has Mossy Oak Break-Up Country Camo, Duratouch coated composite stock. Wicked Wing has Cerakote Burnt Bronze finish on receiver and barrel, Mossy Oak Shadow Grass Blades camo on stock.
Price: 3 in. **$1,590.00**
Price: 3 1/2 in. **$1,740.00**
Price: All-Purpose Hunter **$1,780.00**
Price: Maxus Wicked Wing **$1,900.00**

BROWNING MAXUS SPORTING
Gauge: 12 ga., 3 in. Barrels: 28 in., 30 in. flat ventilated rib. Weight: 7 lbs. 2 oz. Length: 49.25 in.–51.25 in. Stock: Gloss finish high grade walnut stock with close radius pistol grip, Speed Lock forearm, shim adjustable for length of pull, cast and drop. Features: Laser engraving of game birds transforming into clay birds on the lightweight alloy receiver. Quail are on the right side, and a mallard duck on the left. The Power Drive Gas System reduces recoil and cycles a wide array of loads. It's available in a 28 in. or 30 in. barrel length. The high-grade walnut stock and forearm are generously checkered, finished with a deep, high gloss. The stock is adjustable and one .250-in. stock spacer is included. For picking up either clay or live birds quickly, the HiViz Tri-Comp fiber-optic front sight with mid-bead ivory sight does a great job, gathering light on the most overcast days. Vector Pro-lengthened forcing cone, five Invector-Plus choke tubes, Inflex Technology recoil pad, HiViz Tri-Comp fiber-optic front sight, ivory mid-bead sight, one .250-in. stock spacer.
Price: **$1,800.00**
Price: Golden Clays **$2,100.00**

BROWNING MAXUS SPORTING CARBON FIBER
Gauge: 12 ga., 3 in. Barrels: 28 in., 30 in. flat ventilated rib. Weights: 6 lbs. 15 oz.–7 lbs. Length: 49.25–51.25 in. Stock: Composite stock with close radius pistol grip, Speed Lock forearm, textured gripping surfaces, shim adjustable for length of pull, cast and drop, carbon fiber finish, Dura-Touch Armor Coating. Features: Strong, lightweight aluminum alloy, carbon fiber finish on top and bottom. The stock is finished with Dura-Touch Armor Coating for a secure, non-slip grip when the gun is wet. It has the Browning exclusive Magazine Cut-Off, a patented Turn-Key Magazine Plug and Speed Load Plus. Deeply finished look of carbon fiber and Dura-Touch Armor Coating. Vector Pro-lengthened forcing cone, five Invector-Plus choke tubes, Inflex Technology recoil pad, HiViz Tri-Comp fiber-optic front sight, ivory mid-bead sight, one .250-in. stock spacer.
Price: **$1,590.00**

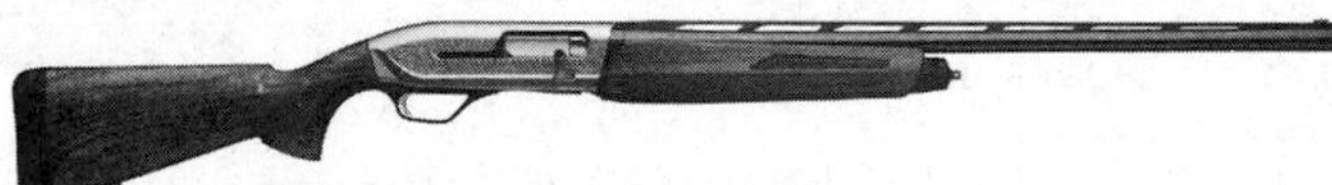

BROWNING MAXUS II
Gauge: 12 ga. With models in both 3 or 3.5 in. Barrel: 26, 28, or 30 in. Weight: 7.0–7.3 lbs. Stock: Dependent on model, but current listings include black synthetic and camouflaged variants. Features: Builds on Browning's Power Drive gas-operated Maxus autoloader in a II version with enhancements. Chrome chamber and bore. Ramped triggerguard for easier loading. Composite stock can be trimmed and is shim adjustable for cast, drop, and LOP. Rubber overmolding on the stock, including SoftFlex cheek pad and Inflex recoil pad. Oversized controls. New screw-on magazine cap design. Includes Invector-Plus choke tubes, extended on most models, as well as an ABS hard case.
Price: Maxus II Ultimate with nickel receiver & Grade III Walnut **$2,059.00**
Price: Maxus II Wicked Wing in Vintage Tan Camo **$2,159.00**
Price: Maxus II Camo in Vintage Tan **$1,979.00**
Price: Maxus II Hunter in matte black/ Satin finish Walnut **$1,669.00**

Prices given are believed to be accurate at time of publication however, many factors affect retail pricing so exact prices are not possible.

BROWNING GOLD LIGHT 10 GAUGE

Gauge: 10 ga. 3 1/2 in. Capacity: 4 rounds. Barrels: 24 (NWTF), 26 or 28 in. Stock: Composite with Dura-Cote Armor coating. Mossy Oak camo (Break-Up Country or Shadow Grass Blades). Weight: Approx. 9.5 pounds. Gas operated action, aluminum receiver, three standard Invector choke tubes. Receiver is drilled and tapped for scope mount. National Wild Turkey Foundation model has Hi-Viz 4-in-1 fiber optic sight, NWTF logo on buttstock.

Price: Mossy Oak Camo finishes **$1,780.00**
Price: NWTF Model **$1,900.00**

BROWNING GOLD 10 GAUGE FIELD

Gauge: 10 ga. 3.5 in. Barrel: 26 in. or 28 in. with ventilated rib. Weight: 9 lbs. 9 oz.–9 lbs. 10 oz. Length: 48.0–50.0 in. Stock: Composite with camouflage coverage in either Mossy Oak Shadow Grass Habitat or Mossy Oak Break-Up Country. Features: Browning's autoloading Gold Light 10-gauge shotgun is redesigned as the Gold 10 Gauge Field. The new style composite stock and forearm wear textured gripping surfaces with the buttstock able to be trimmed up to ¾-inch to shorten LOP. Added Inflex recoil pad. Silver bead front sight. Integral sling swivel studs. Capacity of 4+1 magnum shells. Standard Invector-style flush-mount interchangeable choke tubes with three included (F, M, IC).

Price: **$1,859.00**

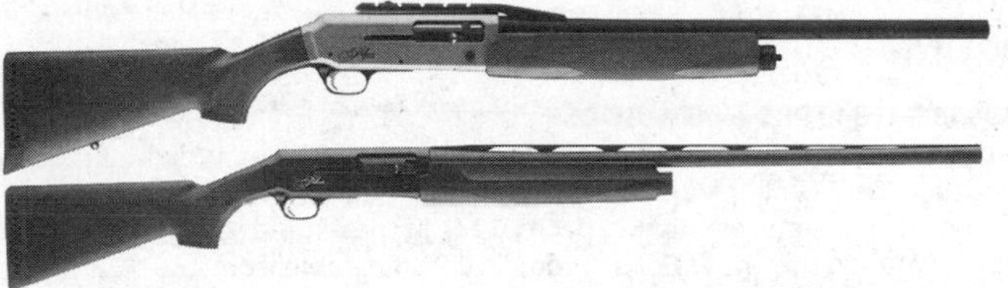

BROWNING SILVER

Gauges: 12 ga., 3 in. or 3 1/2 in.; 20 ga., 3 in. chamber. Barrels: 26 in., 28 in., 30 in. Invector Plus choke tubes. Weights: 7 lbs., 9 oz. (12 ga.), 6 lbs., 7 oz. (20 ga.). Stock: Satin finish walnut or composite. Features: Active Valve gas system, semi-humpback receiver. Invector Plus choke system, three choke tubes. Imported by Browning.

Price: Silver Field, 12 ga. **$1,070.00**
Price: Silver Field, 20 ga. **$1,140.00**
Price: Black Lightning, 12 ga. **$1,140.00**
Price: Silver Field Composite, 12 ga., 3 in. **$1,000.00**
Price: Silver Field Composite, 12 ga., 3 1/2 in. **$1,070.00**
Price: Silver Field Rifled Deer Matte, 20 ga. **$1,200.00**

CHARLES DALY MODEL 600

Gauges: 12 ga. or 20 ga. (3 in.) or 28 ga. (2 3/4 in.). Capacity: 5+1. Barrels: 26 in., 28 in. (20 and 28 ga.), 26 in., 28 in. or 30 in. (12 ga.). Three choke tubes provided (Rem-Choke pattern). Stock: Synthetic, wood or camo. Features: Comes in several variants including Field, Sporting Clays, Tactical and Trap. Left-hand models available. Uses gas-assisted recoil operation. Imported from Turkey.

Price: Field 12, 20 ga. **$480.00**
Price: Field 28 ga. **$531.00**
Price: Sporting **$858.00**
Price: Tactical **$685.00**

CZ MODEL 712/720

Gauges: 12 ga., 20 ga. Capacity: 4+1. Barrel: 26 in. Weight: 6.3 lbs. Stock: Turkish walnut with 14.5 in. length of pull. Features: Chrome-lined barrel with 3-inch chamber, ventilated rib, five choke tubes. Matte black finish.

Price: 712 12 ga. **$499.00–$699.00**
Price: 720 20 ga. **$516.00–$599.00**

CZ 1012

Gauge: 12 ga., 3 in. Capacity: 4+1. Barrel: 28 in., 8mm flat ventilated rib. Weight: 6.5-6.9 lbs. Length: 47 in. Stock: Options in either Turkish walnut or black synthetic. Features: The company's first gas-less, inertia-driven semi-automatic wears a gloss-black chrome barrel finish along with a choice of three receiver finishes: standard blued, bronze or gray. Oversized controls ideal for use when wearing gloves. Cross-bolt safety located at front of trigger guard. Addition of 26-inch barreled models to the existing 1012 inertia-driven repeater lineup. Includes two camouflaged synthetic stock options as well as checkered Walnut, consistent with the existing 1012 family. Includes five chokes (F, IM, M, IC, C).

Price: **$645.00**

EUROPEAN AMERICAN ARMORY (EAA) MC312 GOBBLER

Gauge: 12 ga., 3.5 in. Barrel: 24 in., with ventilated turkey rib. Length: 50 in. Stock: Synthetic camouflage with either straight or pistol-grip options. Features: The MC312 inertia-driven semi-auto produced by Girsan gets a turkey upgrade with a shorter barrel, mid-bead, Picatinny rail cut into the receiver, Cerakote finish receiver and barrel, cross-bolt safety, sling studs, rubber buttpad, fiber-optic front sight, and field-tested reflex optic. Includes flush mount choke tubes.

Price: **$600.00**

EUROPEAN AMERICAN ARMORY (EAA) AKKAR CHURCHILL 220

Gauge: 20 ga. Barrel: 18.5 in. Length: 37.5 in. Weight: 5.0 lbs. Stock: Black synthetic pistol grip style. Features: This Turkish-made semi-automatic springs from the Churchill 220 series of gas-driven repeaters is now re-vamped for home defense and tactical use. Optics rail machined into receiver for easy target acquisition with included red-dot optic on quick-release mount. Semi-enhanced loading port. Accessible controls. 5+1 round capacity. Checkered pistol grip stock. Black rubber recoil pad, sling swivels. Door-breaching choke tube and shrouded red fiber-optic front sight.

Price: **$561.00**

EAA/GIRSAN MC312

Gauge: 12 ga. Barrel: 28 in. vent rib. Length: 50 in. Weight: 6.95 lbs. Stock: Polymer in choice of either black or camo. Features: Inertia-driven single-action hunting autoloader. Lightweight aircraft aluminum receiver 5+1 round capacity. Fiber-optic front sight. Passed EAA's 5,000-round test with no cleaning and 10,000-round test with no parts replacement.

Price: **$431.00–$499.00**

EAA/GIRSAN MC312 GOOSE

Gauge: 12 ga. Barrel: 30-in. vent rib. Length: 52 in. Weight: 6.75 lbs. Stock: Black polymer. Features: Goose variant of the inertia-driven MC312 line. Lightweight aircraft aluminum receiver with machined integral accessory rail for the included red-dot optic. Fiber-optic front sight. Ships with five extended choke tubes. Same 5+1 capacity as the standard MC312.

Price: **$627.00**

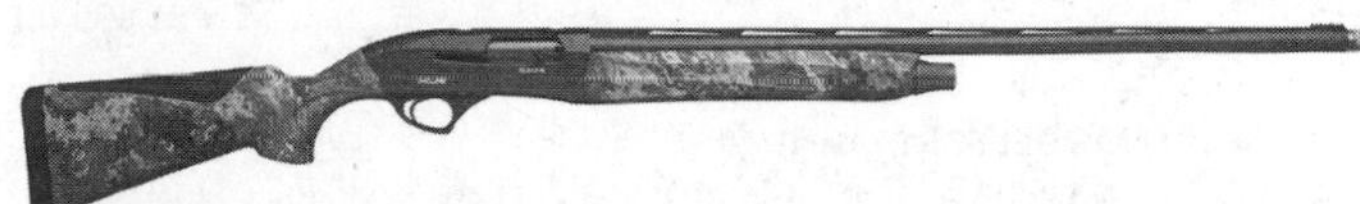

FABARM XLR5 VELOCITY AR

Gauge: 12 ga. 3 in. Barrel: 28 or 30 in. with flat rib. Stock: All-Terrain

Prices given are believed to be accurate at time of publication however, many factors affect retail pricing so exact prices are not possible.

camouflage composite with soft-touch finish. Both right- and left-handed option available for each model. Features: The Italian-made, gas-operated, semi-automatic XLR Chesapeake springs from Fabarm's XLR5 family of repeaters and is built for hunters. Pulse Pistol system acts as a brake, eliminating the valve system to cycle varying ammo types. Cerakote Midnight Bronze finish on action and barrel. Red fiber-optic bar front sight. Soft comb insert and rubberized buttpad. TriBore XP barrel with tapered bore for improved patterns and lower recoil. Inner HP extended choke tubes come standard.

Price: **$1,875.00**

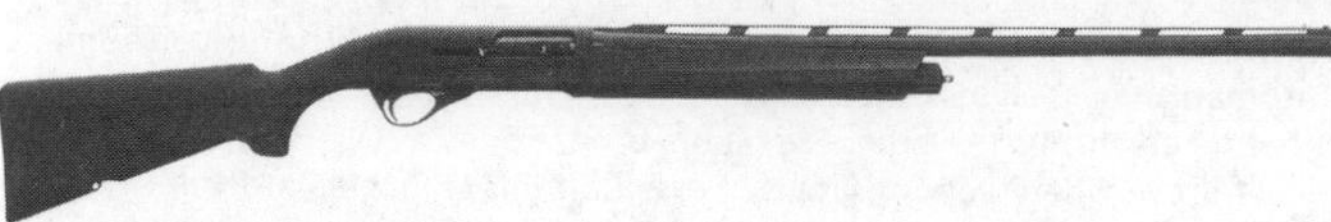

FRANCHI AFFINITY

Gauges: 12 ga., 20 ga. Three-inch chamber also handles 2 3/4-inch shells. Barrels: 26 in., 28 in., 30 in. (12 ga.), 26 in. (20 ga.). 30-in. barrel available only on 12-ga. Sporting model. Weights: 5.6–6.8 pounds. Stocks: Black synthetic or Realtree Camo. Left-hand versions available. Catalyst model has stock designed for women.

Price: Synthetic **$789.00**
Price: Synthetic left-hand action **$899.00**
Price: Camo **$949.00**
Price: Compact **$849.00**
Price: Catalyst **$969.00**
Price: Sporting **$1,149.00**
Price: Companion **$1,599.00**

FRANCHI AFFINITY 3

Price: Camo and Cerakote 12-ga. models **$1,099.00**
Price: Left-Hand Models in 12 or 20 Ga **$899.00**

FRANCHI AFFINITY ELITE

Gauges: 12ga. 3 in., 12ga. 3.5in., 20ga. 3 in. Barrel: 26 or 28 in. ventilated rib. Length: 48.5–50.75 in. Weight: 6.0–7.1 lbs. Stock: Synthetic with OptiFade Marsh or OptiFade Timber camo. Features: The Affinity Elite lineup offers semi-customized features building on the Affinity Italian-made family of Inertia-Drive semi-autos. Cerakote and OptiFade camo finishes. Oversized controls, lengthened forcing cone, TruGlo front sight. Oversized loading port, ambidextrous safety, chrome lined barrel. Drilled and tapped for optics mounting. Twin Shock Absorber (TSA) recoil pad allows for LOP adjustments. Capacity of 4+1 rounds. Includes shims for fitting drop and cast. Ships with three extended waterfowl chokes (Close, Mid, Long-Range).

Price: Synthetic **$1,249.00**

J.P. SAUER & SOHN SL5 TURKEY

Gauge: 12 ga. 3 in. Barrel: 18.5-in. deep-drilled, chrome-lined, with stepped rib. Weight: 7 lbs. Stock: Fixed synthetic pistol-grip style in choice of three Mossy Oak camo patterns: Obsession, Bottomland, or New Bottomland. Features: Durable inertia-driven semi-automatic with black anodized receiver. Oversized bolt handle and release button. Removeable Picatinny rail. Cervellati recoil pad and sling attachments. Red single-bead LPA front fiber-optic sight. Made in Italy and backed by 10-year warranty. Ships with three chokes: flush Cylinder, extender CRIO Plus Modified, and Carlson extended Turkey choke.

Price: **$1,199.00**

MOSSBERG MODEL 935 MAGNUM

Gauge: 12 ga. 3 in. and 3 1/2-in., interchangeable. Barrels: 22 in., 24 in., 26 in., 28in. Weights: 7.25–7.75 lbs. Lengths: 45–49 in. overall. Stock: Synthetic. Features: Gas-operated semi-auto models in blued or camo finish. Fiber-optics sights, drilled and tapped receiver, interchangeable Accu-Mag choke tubes.

Price: 935 Magnum Turkey Pistol grip; full pistol grip stock **$924.00**
Price: 935 Magnum Grand Slam: 22 in. barrel **$756.00**
Price: 935 Magnum Waterfowl: 26 in. or 28 in. barrel .... **$660.00–$735.00**
Price: 935 Pro Series Waterfowl **$875.00**

MOSSBERG 940 JM PRO

Gauge: 12 ga., 3 in. Capacity: 9+1. Barrel: 24 in., ventilated rib. Weight: 7.75 lbs. Length: 44.75 in. Stock: Choice of either black synthetic or Black Multicam. Features: Created in conjunction with speed shooter Jerry Miculek, the new 940 JM Pro uses a redesigned gas system built for fast-cycling competition. Adjustable for length of pull, cast and drop. Hi-Viz green front fiber-optic sight, oversized controls. Nickel-boron coated internal parts and anodized receivers in either tungsten gray or black. Competition-level loading port allows for quad loading, elongated pinch-free elevator, and anodized bright orange follower. Black synthetic model uses gold finish appointments and a tungsten-gray receiver. Multicam model wears black-anodized receiver. Ships with Briley Extended choke tube set.

Price: **$1,015.00**

MOSSBERG 940 PRO FIELD

Gauge: 12 ga. 3 in. Barrel: 28-in. vent rib. Length: 47.5 in. Weight: 7.75 lbs. Stock: Black synthetic, adjustable for LOP, cast and drop. Features: Field hunting variant of the 940 Pro lineup. Includes an Accu-Set of choke tubes. Fiber-optic front sight, matte blue metalwork finish. Oversized controls. Sling studs. LOP adjustable from 13–14.25 inches. 4+1-round capacity.

Price: **$903.00**

MOSSBERG 940 PRO SNOW GOOSE

Gauge: 12 ga. 3 in. Barrel: 28-in. vent rib. Length: 50.75 in. Weight: 8.25 lbs. Stock: True Timber Viper Snow camo synthetic, adjustable for LOP, cast and drop. Features: High-capacity 12+1 in the extended magazine tube, unique to the Snow Goose model. LOP adjustable from 13–14.25 in. TriComp fiber-optic front sight. X-Factor extended choke tube. Metalwork finished in Battleship Gray Cerakote.

Price: **$1,165.00**

MOSSBERG 940 PRO TURKEY

Gauge: 12 ga. 3 in. Barrel: 18 or 24-in. vent rib. Length: 39.25–44.75 in. Weight: 7.25–7.5 lbs. Stock: Synthetic in Mossy Oak Greenleaf camo, adjustable for LOP, cast and drop. Features: Turkey-specific variants of the 940 Pro lineup, these with shorter barrels, Greenleaf camo, and fitted with X-Factor XX-Full Turkey choke tubes. Optics-ready cutout. Compsight fiber optics. LOP adjustable from 13–14.25 in. Both models carry 4+1-round capacity.

Price: **$1,120.00**

MOSSBERG 940 PRO WATERFOWL

Gauge: 12 ga. 3 in. Barrel: 28-in. vent rib. Length: 48.75 in. Weight: 7.75 lbs. Stock: Synthetic in True Timber Prairie camo, adjustable for LOP, cast and drop. Features: Waterfowl-specific variant of the 940 Pro lineup. Includes a set of X-Factor extended choke tubes, TriComp fiber-optic front sight. Oversized controls. LOP adjustable from 13–14.25 inches. 4+1-round capacity.

Price: **$1,092.00**

Prices given are believed to be accurate at time of publication however, many factors affect retail pricing so exact prices are not possible.

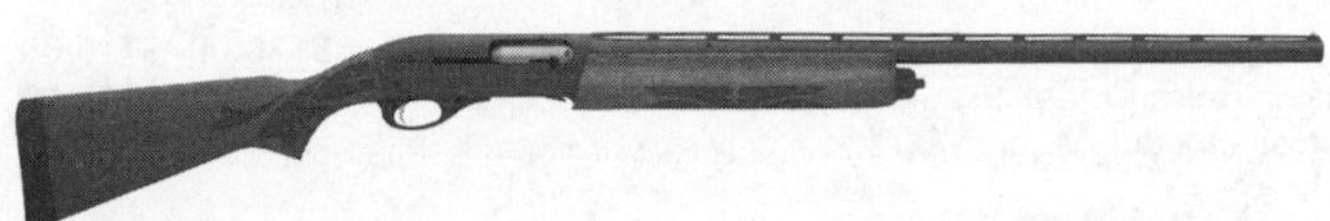

MOSSBERG SA-20
Gauge: 20 or 28 ga. Barrels: 20 in. (Tactical), 26 in. or 28 in. Weight: 5.5–6 lbs. Stock: Black synthetic. Gas operated action, matte blue finish. Tactical model has ghost-ring sight, accessory rail.
Price: 20 ga. .... **$592.00–$664.00**
Price: 28 ga. .... **$588.00–$675.00**

MOSSBERG SA-410 FIELD
Gauge: .410 bore, 3 in. Capacity: 4+1. Barrel: 26 in., ventilated rib. Weight: 6.5 lbs. Length: 46 in. Stock: Black synthetic. Features: Mossberg offers the baby bore for small-game and field hunters as well as light recoiling plinking with this lightweight gas-driven autoloader. Metalwork is finished in matte blue. Brass front bead, fixed 13.75 in. length of pull, ventilated rubber buttpad. Cross-bolt safety, easy-load elevator. Includes Sport Set flush fit chokes (F, IM, M, IC, C).
Price: **$616.00**

MOSSBERG SA-410 TURKEY
Gauge: .410 bore, 3 in. Capacity: 4+1. Barrel: 26 in., ventilated rib. Weight: 6.5 lbs. Length: 46 in. Stock: Synthetic stock with Mossy Oak Bottomland camouflage. Features: Mossberg expands its baby-bore turkey lineup with this gas-driven semi-automatic. Both the stocks and metalwork wear full camouflage coverage. Rear fiber-optic ghost-ring sight and front green fiber-optic. Top Picatinny rail for easy optics mounting. Cross-bolt safety, easy-load elevator. Ships with an XX-Full Extended Turkey choke.
Price: **$735.00**

RETAY GORDION
Gauge: 12 ga., 3 in. Barrels: 26 in., 28 in., ventilated rib. Weight: 6.5-6.75 lbs. Stock: Choice of black synthetic, several Realtree camo patterns, or Turkish walnut. Features: The Turkish-made Gordion line of semi-automatics uses an inertia-plus action and bolt system. Oversized SP controls, quick unload system, TruGlo red front sight. Choice of matte or polished black receiver and barrel, or full camouflage coverage. Easy-Load port as well as Easy Unload system that allows the magazine tube to be emptied without racking the action. Includes a stock adjustment ship kit, TSA airline-approved hard case, and five flush choke tubes (F, IM, M, IC, S).
Price: .... **$799.00–$899.00**
Price: Gordion Turkey 24-in. barrel, Realtree or Mossy Oak camo ... **$925.00**

RETAY MASAI MARA
Gauges: 12 ga., 3.5 in., 20 ga., 3 in. Barrels: 26 in., 28 in., ventilated rib. Weight: 6.5-6.75 lbs. Stock: Choice of synthetic in black or numerous camouflage patterns or two grades of Turkish walnut. Features: The Turkish-made Masai Mara line of semi-automatics uses an inertia-plus action and bolt system. Oversized controls, Easy Unload system, TruGlo red fiber-optic front sight. Options in Cerakote metalwork or anodized finishes. Push-button removeable trigger group for both safety and easy field cleaning. Microcell rubber recoil pad. Includes a TSA airline-approved hard case and ships with five flush choke tubes (F, IM, M, IC, S).
Price: **$1,099.00**
Price: Upland Grade 2.. **$1,399.00**
Price: Upland Grade 3.. **$1,900.00**
Price: Comfort Grade 2.. **$1,399.00**
Price: Comfort Grade 4.. **$1,999.00**
Price: SP Air King Waterfowl Camo/Cerakote.......................... **$1,600.00**
Price: SP Air King Waterfowl Cerakote.............................. **$1,600.00**

SAVAGE RENEGAUGE FIELD
Gauges: 12 ga. 3 in. Barrel: 26 or 28 in. fluted carbon steel with ventilated rib. Weight: 7.9–8.0 lbs. Length: 47.5–49.5 in. Stock: Grey synthetic stock with Monte Carlo-style cheekpiece. Adjustable for length of pull, comb height, drop and cast with included inserts. Features: American-made D.R.I.V. (Dual Regulating Inline Valve) gas system. Single-piece, chrome-plated action bar assembly and chrome-plated reciprocating components. Melonite-finished external metalwork. Stock rod buffer to reduce felt recoil. Red fiber-optic sight, competition-ready easy-loading port, oversized controls. 4+1 round capacity. Includes three Beretta/Benelli style chokes (IC, M, F) and hard case.
Price: **$1,489.00**

SAVAGE RENEGAUGE TURKEY
Gauge: 12 ga. 3 in. Barrel: 24-in. fluted carbon steel with ventilated rib. Weight: 7.8 lbs. Length: 49.5 in. Stock: Camo synthetic stock with Monte Carlo-style cheekpiece, adjustable for length of pull, comb height, drop and cast with included inserts. Choice of Mossy Oak Bottomland or Mossy Oak Obsession camouflage finishes. Features: American-made D.R.I.V. (Dual Regulating Inline Valve) gas system. Single-piece, chrome-plated action bar assembly and chrome-plated reciprocating components. Stock rod buffer to reduce felt recoil. Red fiber-optic front sight, competition-ready loading port, oversized controls. 4+1 round capacity. Includes four Beretta/Benelli style chokes (EF, F, IC, M) and hard case.
Price: **$1,599.00**

SAVAGE RENEGAUGE WATERFOWL
Gauge: 12 ga. 3 in. Barrel: 26- or 28-in. fluted carbon steel with ventilated rib. Weight: 7.8 lbs. Lengths: 47.5–49.5 in. Stock: Camouflage synthetic stock with Monte Carlo-style cheekpiece, adjustable for length of pull, comb height, drop and cast with included inserts. Mossy Oak Shadow Grass Blades camouflage. Features: American-made D.R.I.V. (Dual Regulating Inline Valve) gas system. Single-piece, chrome-plated action bar assembly and chrome-plated reciprocating components. Stock rod buffer to reduce felt recoil. Red fiber-optic sight, competition-ready easy loading port, oversized controls. 4+1 round capacity. Includes three Beretta/Benelli style chokes (IC, M, F) and hard case.
Price: **$1,959.00**

SAVAGE RENEGAUGE COMPETITION
Gauge: 12 ga. 3in. Barrel: 24-in. fluted carbon steel with ventilated rib. Weight: 8.2 lbs. Length: 46.2 in. Stock: Black synthetic Monte Carlo style, adjustable for length of pull, comb height, drop and cast. Features: American-made D.R.I.V. (Dual Regulating Inline Valve) gas system. Single-piece, chrome-plated action bar assembly and chrome-plated reciprocating components. Stock rod buffer to reduce felt recoil. Extended magazine tube with 9+1 capacity. Melonite finished barrel and Red Cerakote receiver. Hi-Viz Tri-Comp front sight. Competition-ready loading port, oversized controls. Extended Skeet2 Light Mod (.015-in.) choke tube of Beretta/Benelli-style.
Price: **$1,959.00**

SAVAGE RENEGAUGE PRAIRIE
Gauge: 12 ga. 3 in. Barrel: 28 in. fluted carbon steel with ventilated rib. Weight: 7.9 lbs. Length: 49.5 in. Stock: Camo synthetic sporter style, adjustable for length of pull, comb height, drop and cast with included inserts. Features: American-made D.R.I.V. (Dual Regulating Inline Valve) gas system. Single-piece, chrome plated action bar assembly and chrome-plated reciprocating components. True Timber Prairie camouflage stock finish with Brown Sand Cerakote metalwork. Stock rod buffer to reduce felt recoil. Red fiber-optic sight, competition-ready easy-loading port, oversized controls. 4+1 round capacity. Includes three Beretta/Benelli style chokes (IC, M, F) and hard case.
Price: **$1,599.00**

STANDARD MANUFACTURING SKO-12
Gauge: 12 ga., 3 in. Capacity: 5-round magazine. Barrel: 18-7/8-in. Weight: 7 lbs., 10 oz. Length: 38 in. Stock: Synthetic with six-position buttstock and will accept any Mil-Spec buttstock. Features: Gas-operated semi-automatic. Receivers machined from aircraft-grade aluminum and Mil-Spec hard anodized. Extended 22-inch Picatinny rail. Ambidextrous safety, AR-style mag and bolt release. MOE slots on fore-end. Tru-Choke thread pattern.
Price: **$1,100.00**

STANDARD MANUFACTURING SKO SHORTY
Gauge: 12 ga., 3 in. Capacity: 5-round magazine. Barrel: 18-7/8-in. Weight: 7.14 lbs. Length: 28.75 in. Stock: Black synthetic with forward vertical grip, but without a buttstock. Features: Gas-operated semi-automatic. Receivers machined from aircraft-grade aluminum and Mil-Spec hard anodized. Ambidextrous safety, AR-style mag and bolt release. MOE slots on fore-end. No sights or top rail. Tru-Choke thread pattern. Buttstock conversion kit available from manufacturer.
Price: $599.00

STOEGER M3500 PREDATOR/TURKEY
Gauge: 12 ga., 3.5 in. Capacity: 4+1. Barrel: 24 in., ventilated rib. Length: 46 in. Weight: 7.5 lbs. Stock: Synthetic Mossy Oak Overwatch. Features: Stoeger expands its M3500 line of inertia-driven autoloaders with a predator- and turkey-specific model with a shorter barrel and rubber pistol grip. Red bar fiber-optic front sight. Receiver drilled and tapped for optics mounting. Ships with a paracord sling and five extended chokes, including MOJO Predator and MOJO Turkey tubes.
Price: $929.00

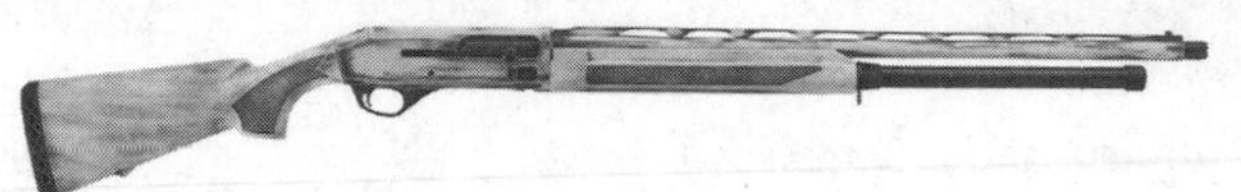

STOEGER M3500 WATERFOWL
Gauge: 12 ga. 3.5 in. Barrel: 28 in. ventilated rib. Length: 50 in. Weight: 8.2 lbs. Stock: Synthetic with distressed white Cerakote finish. Features: Stoeger combines the M3500 Waterfowl semi-auto with the 922R-compliant extended magazine Freedom Series to create the higher-capacity M3500 Snow Goose. Full 10+1 capacity. Inertia-driven autoloader with oversized controls. Beveled loading port. Distressed white Cerakote finish on stock, fore-end, receiver, and barrel act as winter camo. Red bar front sight. Includes paracord sling and shim kit for adjusting drop and cast. Ships with five extended choke tubes (IC, M, XFT, Close Range, Mid Range).
Price: $899.00

STOEGER MODEL 3000
Gauge: 12 ga., 2 3/4- and 3-in. loads. Minimum recommended load 3-dram, 1 1/8 ounces. Capacity: 4+1 magazine. Inertia-driven operating system. Barrels: 26 or 28 in. with 3 choke tubes IC, M, XF. Weights: 7.4–7.5 lbs. Finish: Black synthetic or camo (Realtree APG or Max-4). M3K model is designed for 3-Gun competition and has synthetic stock, 24-in. barrel, modified loading port.
Price: Synthetic $599.00
Price: Walnut or Camo $649.00
Price: M3K $699.00
Price: 3000R rifled slug model $649.00

STOEGER MODEL 3500
Gauge: 12 ga. 2 3/4-, 3- and 3 1/2-in. loads. Minimum recommended load 3-dram, 1-1/8 ounces. Barrels: 24 in., 26 in. or 28 in. Choke tubes for IC, M, XF. Weights: 7.4–7.5 pounds. Finish: Satin walnut, black synthetic or camo (Realtree APG or Max-4). Features: Other features similar to Model 3000.
Price: Synthetic $679.00
Price: Camo $799.00
Price: Satin Walnut (shown) $769.00

TRISTAR VIPER G2
Gauges: 12 ga., 20 ga. 2 3/4 in. or 3 in. interchangeably. Capacity: 5-round magazine. Barrels: 26 in., 28 in. (carbon fiber only offered in 12-ga. 28 in. and 20-ga. 26 in.). Stock: Wood, black synthetic, Mossy Oak Duck Blind camouflage, faux carbon fiber finish (2008) with the new Comfort Touch technology. Features: Magazine cutoff, vent rib with matted sight plane, brass front bead (camo models have fiber-optic front sight), shot plug included, and 3 Beretta-style choke tubes (IC, M, F). Viper synthetic, Viper camo have swivel studs. Five-year warranty. Viper Youth models have shortened length of pull and 24 in. barrel. Sporting model has ported barrel, checkered walnut stock with adjustable comb. Imported by Tristar Sporting Arms Ltd.
Price: $549.00
Price: Camo models $640.00
Price: Silver Model .... $670.00–$715.00
Price: Youth Model $565.00
Price: Sporting Model $825.00

TRISTAR VIPER MAX
Gauge: 12. 3 1/2 in. Barrel: 24–30 in., threaded to accept Benelli choke tubes. Gas-operated action. Offered in several model variants. Introduced in 2017.
Price: .... $630.00–$730.00

WEATHERBY SA-SERIES
Gauges: 12 ga., 20 ga., 3 in. Barrels: 26 in., 28 in. flat ventilated rib. Weight: 6.5 lbs. Stock: Wood and synthetic. Features: The SA-08 is a reliable workhorse that lets you move from early season dove loads to late fall's heaviest waterfowl loads in no time. Available with wood and synthetic stock options in 12- and 20-gauge models, including a scaled-down youth model to fit 28 ga. Comes with 3 application-specific choke tubes (SK/IC/M). Made in Turkey.
Price: SA-08 Synthetic $649.00
Price: SA-08 Synthetic Youth $649.00
Price: SA-08 Deluxe $849.00

WEATHERBY 18-I
Gauges: 12 ga., 20 ga., 3 in. Capacities: 4+1. Barrels: 26 or 28 in. Stock: Synthetic, camo or walnut. Features: Inertia-operated system. Mossy Oak Shadow Grass or Realtree Max-5 camo full coverage.
Price: Synthetic $1,099.00
Price: Waterfowler camo $1,199.00
Price: Deluxe model walnut stock $1,899.00

WINCHESTER SUPER X3
Gauge: 12 ga., 3 in. and 3 1/2 in. Barrels: 26 in., 28 in., .742-in. back-bored; Invector Plus choke tubes. Weights: 7–7.25 lbs. Stock: Composite, 14.25 in. x 1.75 in. x 2 in. Mossy Oak New Break-Up camo with Dura-Touch Armor Coating. Pachmayr Decelerator buttpad with hard heel insert, customizable length of pull. Features: Alloy magazine tube, gunmetal grey Perma-Cote UT finish, self-adjusting Active Valve gas action, lightweight recoil spring system. Electroless nickel-plated bolt, three choke tubes, two length-of-pull stock spacers, drop and cast adjustment spacers, sling swivel studs. Introduced 2006. Made in Belgium, assembled in Portugal.
Price: Field $1,140.00
Price: Sporting, adj. comb $1,700.00
Price: Long Beard, pistol grip camo stock $1,270.00
Price: Composite Sporting $1,740.00

WINCHESTER SX-4
Gauge: 12 ga., 3 in. and 3 1/2 in. Capacity: 4-round magazine. Barrels: 22 in., 24 in., 26 in. or 28 in. Invector Plus Flush choke tubes. Weight: 6 lbs. 10 oz. Stock: Synthetic with rounded pistol grip and textured gripping surfaces, or satin finished checkered grade II/III Turkish walnut. Length-of-pull spacers. Several camo finishes available. Features: TruGlo fiber optic front sight, Inflex Technology recoil pad, active valve system, matte blue barrel, matte black receiver. Offered in Standard, Field, Compact, Waterfowl, Cantilever Buck, Cantilever Turkey models.
Price: Synthetic $940.00
Price: Field .... $940.00–$1,070.00
Price: Upland Field $1,100.00
Price: Waterfowl Hunter .... $940.00–$1,070.00
Price: Waterfowl Hunter in Mossy Oak Shadow Grass Habitat $1,099.00
Price: Waterfowl Hunter Compact in Mossy Oak Shadow Grass Habitat ... $959.00
Price: Hybrid Hunter $1,040.00
Price: Hybrid Hunter in Mossy Oak Shadow Grass Habitat $1,079.00
Price: NWTF Cantilever Turkey, Mossy Oak Obsession $1,070.00
Price: 20-gauge, 3-inch models $939.00
Price: Universal Hunter in MOBU camo $1,069.00
Price: Universal Hunter 12 and 20 ga. in Mossy Oak DNA camo $1,149.00
Price: SX4 Left Hand 12 ga. in multiple variants $1,129.00

Prices given are believed to be accurate at time of publication however, many factors affect retail pricing so exact prices are not possible.

ARMSCOR/ROCK ISLAND ARMORY ALL GENERATION SERIES
Gauge: 12 ga. 3 in., 20 ga. 3 in., .410 bore 3 in. Barrel: 18.5, 26, 28 in. smoothbore contoured. Length: 41.0–48.2 in. Weight: 7.10–8.82 lbs. Stock: Black polymer with LOP spacers and adjustable cheek rest for customized fit. Features: Pump-action shotgun designed to accommodate a wide range of ages and physical sizes of shooters. The All Generation Series includes multiple models designed to customize the fit. Comes packaged with multiple stock spacers and an adjustable comb and ergonomic forend. Lightweight aluminum receiver with anodized finish. Magazine tube capacity 5+1 rounds in all chamberings. Bead front sight. Black rubber recoil pad. Interchangeable chokes (F, M, IM) except 18.5-inch barreled option, which has a Slug Choke.
Price: **$299.00**

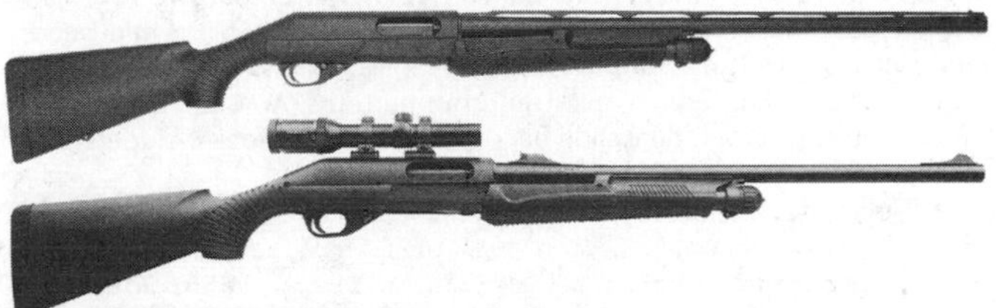

BENELLI SUPERNOVA
Gauge: 12 ga. 3 1/2 in. Capacity: 4-round magazine. Barrels: 24 in., 26 in., 28 in. Lengths: 45.5–49.5 in. Stock: Synthetic; Max-4, Timber, APG HD (2007). Sights: Red bar front, metal midbead. Features: 2 3/4 in., 3 in. chamber (3 1/2 in. 12 ga. only). Montefeltro rotating bolt design with dual action bars, magazine cutoff, synthetic trigger assembly, adjustable combs, shim kit, choice of buttstocks. Introduced 2006. Imported from Italy by Benelli USA.
Price: **$549.00**
Price: Camo stock **$669.00**
Price: Rifle slug model .... **$829.00–$929.00**
Price: Tactical model.. **$519.00–$549.00**

BENELLI NOVA
Gauges: 12 ga., 20 ga. Capacity: 4-round magazine. Barrels: 24 in., 26 in., 28 in. Stock: Black synthetic, Max-4, Timber and APG HD. Sights: Red bar. Features: 2 3/4 in., 3 in. (3 1/2 in. 12 ga. only). Montefeltro rotating bolt design with dual action bars, magazine cut-off, synthetic trigger assembly. Introduced 1999. Field & Slug Combo has 24 in. barrel and rifled bore; open rifle sights; synthetic stock; weighs 8.1 lbs. Imported from Italy by Benelli USA.
Price: Field Model.. **$449.00**
Price: Max-5 camo stock **$559.00**
Price: H20 model, black synthetic, matte nickel finish **$669.00**
Price: Tactical, 18.5-in. barrel, Ghost Ring sight.. **$459.00**
Price: Black synthetic youth stock, 20 ga... **$469.00**

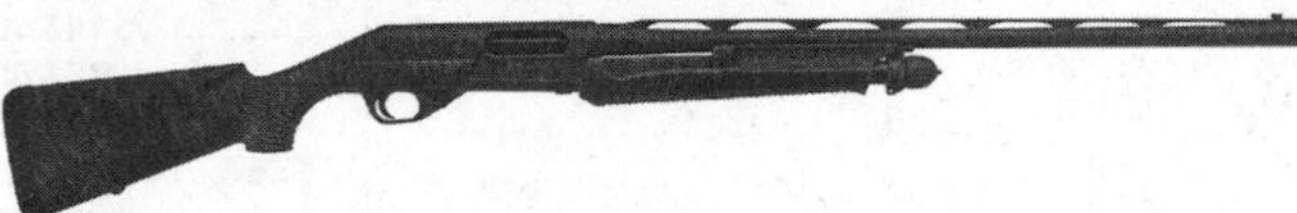

BENELLI NOVA TURKEY
Gauge: 20 ga. 3 in. Barrel: 24 in. with ventilated rib. Length: 45.5 in. Weight: 6.5 lbs. Stock: Synthetic with full Mossy Oak Bottomland camouflage. Features: Benelli's new addition to the Nova family targets run-and-gun hunters seeking a lighter-built and -recoiling turkey gun. Ergonomic forend. Red bar fiber-optic front sight. Magazine cutoff button. Ships with three chokes (IC, M, F).
Price:.. **$559.00**

BROWNING BPS
Gauges: 10 ga., 12 ga., 3 1/2 in.; 12 ga., 16 ga., or 20 ga., 3 in. (2 3/4 in. in target guns), 28 ga., 2 3/4 in., 5-shot magazine, .410, 3 in. chamber. Barrels: 10 ga. 24 in. Buck Special, 28 in., 30 in., 32 in. Invector; 12 ga., 20 ga. 22 in., 24 in., 26 in., 28 in., 30 in., 32 in. (Imp. Cyl., Mod. or Full), .410 26 in. (Imp. Cyl., Mod. and Full choke tubes.) Also available with Invector choke tubes, 12 or 20 ga. Upland Special has 22-in. barrel with Invector tubes. BPS 3 in. and 3 1/2 in. have back-bored barrel. Weight: 7 lbs., 8 oz. (28 in. barrel). Length: 48.75 in. overall (28 in. barrel). Stock: 14.25 in. x 1.5 in. x 2.5 in. Select walnut, semi-beavertail fore-end, full pistol grip stock. Features: All 12 ga. 3 in. guns except Buck Special and game guns have back-bored barrels with Invector Plus choke tubes. Bottom feeding and ejection, receiver top safety, high post vent rib. Double action bars eliminate binding. Vent rib barrels only. All 12 and 20 ga. guns with 3 in. chamber available with fully engraved receiver flats at no extra cost. Each gauge has its own unique game scene. Introduced 1977. Stalker is same gun as the standard BPS except all exposed metal parts have a matte blued finish and the stock has a black finish with a black recoil pad. Available in 10 ga. (3 1/2 in.) and 12 ga. with 3 in. or 3 1/2 in. chamber, 22 in., 28 in., 30 in. barrel with Invector choke system. Introduced 1987. Rifled Deer Hunter is similar to the standard BPS except has newly designed receiver/magazine tube/barrel mounting system to eliminate play, heavy 20.5-in. barrel with rifle-type sights with adjustable rear, solid receiver scope mount, "rifle" stock dimensions for scope or open sights, sling swivel studs. Gloss or matte finished wood with checkering, polished blue metal. Medallion model has additional engraving on receiver, polished blue finish, AA/AAA grade walnut stock with checkering. All-Purpose model has Realtree AP camo on stock and fore-end, HiVis fiber optic sights. Introduced 2013. Imported from Japan by Browning.
Price: Field, Stalker models .... **$600.00–$700.00**
Price: Camo coverage.. **$820.00**
Price: Deer Hunter.. **$830.00**
Price: Deer Hunter Camo **$870.00**
Price: Field Composite Field Composite in Mossy Oak Shadow Grass Habitat.. **$799.00**
Price: Field Composite in Mossy Oak Shadow Grass Habitat 10 ga. ..**$899.00**
Price: Field Composite in Mossy Oak Break-Up Country 10 ga. **$899.00**
Price: Field Composite Camo **$779.00**
Price: Magnum Hunter (3 1/2 in.) .... **$800.00–$1,030.00**
Price: Medallion **$830.00**
Price: Trap **$840.00**

BROWNING BPS 10 GAUGE SERIES
Similar to the standard BPS except completely covered with Mossy Oak Shadow Grass camouflage. Available with 26- and 28-in. barrel. Introduced 1999. Imported by Browning
Price: Mossy Oak camo **$950.00**
Price: Synthetic stock, Stalker **$800.00**

BROWNING BPS MICRO MIDAS
Gauges: 12 ga, 20 ga., 28 ga. or .410 bore. Barrels: 24 or 26 in. Three Invector choke tubes for 12 and 20 ga., standard tubes for 28 ga. and .410. Stock: Walnut with pistol grip and recoil pad. Satin finished and scaled down to fit smaller statured shooters. Length of pull is 13.25 in. Two spacers included for stock length adjustments. Weights: 7–7.8 lbs.
Price: .... **$700.00–$740.00**

CZ 612
Gauge: 12 ga. Chambered for all shells up to 3 1/2 in. Capacity: 5+1, magazine plug included with Wildfowl Magnum. Barrels: 18.5 in. (Home Defense), 20 in. (HC-P), 26 in. (Wildfowl Mag). Weights: 6–6.8 pounds. Stock: Polymer. Finish: Matte black or full camo (Wildfowl Mag.) HC-P model has pistol grip stock, fiber optic front sight and ghost-ring rear. Home Defense Combo comes with extra 26-in. barrel.
Price: Wildfowl Magnum **$428.00**
Price: Home Defense .... **$304.00–$409.00**
Price: Target.. **$549.00**

CZ MODEL 620/628 Field Select
Gauges: 20 ga. or 28 ga. Barrel: 28 inches. Weight: 5.4 lbs. Features: Similar to Model 612 except for chambering. Introduced in 2017.
Price: **$429.00**

ESCORT FIELDHUNTER TURKEY
Gauges: 12 ga., 3 in., 20 ga., 3 in, .410 bore, 3 in. Capacity: 4+1. Barrels: 22 in., 24 in., 26 in., ventilated rib. Length: 42-46 in. Weight: 6.0-6.9 lbs. Stock: Synthetic with camo finish. Features: The pump-action Turkey model addition to the FieldHunter family is built of aircraft alloy with a black chrome-finished steel barrel that is camo coated. Cantilever Weaver optics rail, fully adjustable green rear fiber-optic sight with windage-adjustable front red fiber-optic sight. Cross-bolt safety, rubber butt pad, sling studs. Includes three chokes (Ext Turkey, F, IM).
Price: **$399.00**

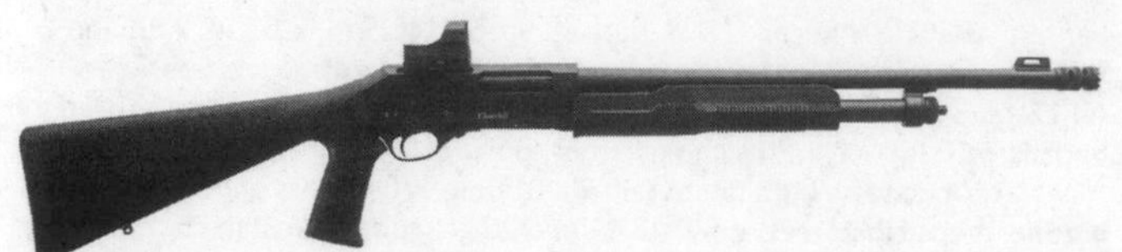

EUROPEAN AMERICAN ARMORY (EAA) AKKAR CHURCHILL 620
Gauge: 20 ga. Barrel: 18.5 in. Length: 37.5 in. Weight: 5.0 lbs. Stock: Black Synthetic pistol grip style. Features: This Turkish-made pump builds on the Churchill 620 series of slide actions now re-vamped for home defense and tactical use. Optics rail machined into receiver for easy target acquisition with included red-dot optic on quick-release mount. Semi-enhanced loading port. Accessible controls. Checkered pistol grip stock. Black rubber recoil pad, sling swivels. Door-breaching choke tube and shrouded red fiber-optic front sight.
Price: **$427.00**

HARRINGTON & RICHARDSON (H&R) PARDNER PUMP
Gauges: 12 ga., 20 ga. 3 in. Barrels: 21–28 in. Weight: 6.5–7.5 lbs. Stock: Synthetic or hardwood. Ventilated recoil pad and grooved fore-end. Features: Steel receiver, double action bars, cross-bolt safety, easy takedown, ventilated rib, screw-in choke tubes.
Price: .... **$231.00–$259.00**

IAC MODEL 97T TRENCH GUN
Gauge: 12 ga., 2 3/4 in. Barrel: 20 in. with cylinder choke. Stock: Hand rubbed American walnut. Features: Replica of Winchester Model 1897 Trench Gun. Metal handguard, bayonet lug. Imported from China by Interstate Arms Corp.
Price: **$465.00**

IAC HAWK SERIES
Gauge: 12, 2 3/4 in. Barrel: 18.5 in. with cylinder choke. Stock: Synthetic. Features: This series of tactical/home defense shotguns is based on the Remington 870 design. 981 model has top Picatinny rail and bead front sight. 982 has adjustable ghost ring sight with post front. 982T has same sights as 982 plus a pistol grip stock. Imported from China by Interstate Arms Corporation.
Price: 981 .... **$275.00**
Price: 982 .... **$285.00**
Price: 982T **$300.00**

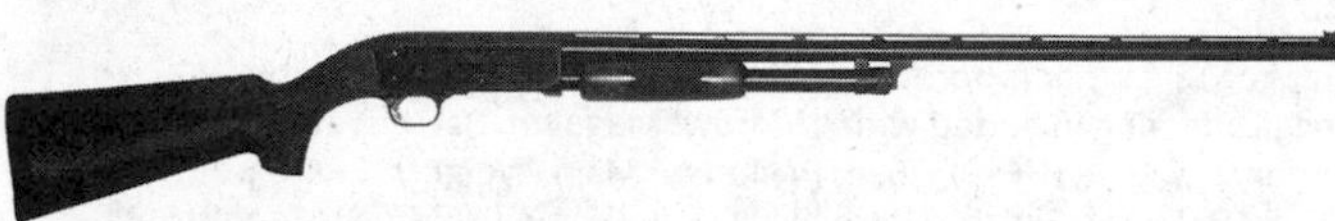

ITHACA MODEL 37 FEATHERLIGHT
Gauges: 12 ga., 20 ga., 16 ga., 28 ga. Capacity: 4+1. Barrels: 26 in., 28 in. or 30 in. with 3-in. chambers (12 and 20 ga.), plain or ventilated rib. Weights: 6.1–7.6 lbs. Stock: Fancy-grade black walnut with Pachmayr Decelerator recoil pad. Checkered fore-end made of matching walnut. Features: Receiver machined from a single block of steel or aluminum. Barrel is steel shot compatible. Three Briley choke tubes provided. Available in several variations including turkey, home defense, tactical and high-grade.
Price: 12 ga., 16 ga. or 20 ga. From **$895.00**
Price: 28 ga. **$1,149.00**
Price: Turkey Slayer w/synthetic stock **$925.00**
Price: Trap Series 12 ga. **$1,020.00**
Price: Waterfowl **$885.00**
Price: Home Defense 18- or 20-in. bbl **$784.00**

ITHACA DEERSLAYER III SLUG
Gauges: 12 ga., 20 ga. 3 in. Barrel: 26 in. fully rifled, heavy fluted with 1:28 twist for 12 ga. 1:24 for 20 ga. Weights: 8.14–9.5 lbs. with scope mounted. Length: 45.625 in. overall. Stock: Fancy black walnut stock and fore-end. Sights: NA. Features: Updated, slug-only version of the classic Model 37. Bottom ejection, blued barrel and receiver.
Price: **$1,350.00**

KEYSTONE SPORTING ARMS 4200 MY FIRST SHOTGUN
Gauges: .410 bore. 3 in. Barrel: 18.5 in. Length: 37 in. Stock: Turkish Walnut. Features: Marketed as a Crickett "My First Shotgun," this pump-action baby bore holds 5+1 rounds of 2.75-inch shells or 4+1 rounds of 3 inch. Aluminum receiver with matte blue metalwork. MC-1 choke. Blade-style front sight. Checkered stocks with rubber recoil pad. Length of pull built for small-frame shooters at only 12 in.
Price: **$399.00**

MOSSBERG MODEL 835 ULTI-MAG
Gauge: 12 ga., 3 1/2 in. Barrels: Ported 24 in. rifled bore, 24 in., 28 in., Accu-Mag choke tubes for steel or lead shot. Combo models come with interchangeable second barrel. Weight: 7.75 lbs. Length: 48.5 in. overall. Stock: 14 in. x 1.5 in. x 2.5 in. Dual Comb. Cut-checkered hardwood or camo synthetic; both have recoil pad. Sights: White bead front, brass mid-bead; fiber-optic rear. Features: Shoots 2 3/4-, 3- or 3 1/2-in. shells. Back-bored and ported barrel to reduce recoil, improve patterns. Ambidextrous thumb safety, twin extractors, dual slide bars. Mossberg Cablelock included. Introduced 1988.
Price: Turkey .... **$601.00–$617.00**
Price: Waterfowl .... **$518.00–$603.00**
Price: Turkey/Deer combo .... **$661.00–$701.00**
Price: Turkey/Waterfowl combo **$661.00**
Price: **Tactical** Turkey **$652.00**

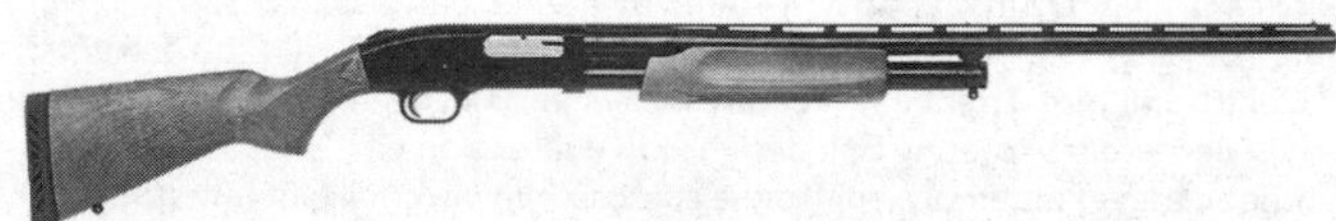

MOSSBERG MODEL 500 SPORTING SERIES
Gauges: 12 ga., 20 ga., .410 bore, 3 in. Barrels: 18.5 in. to 28 in. with fixed or Accu-Choke, plain or vent rib. Combo models come with interchangeable second barrel. Weight: 6.25 lbs. (.410), 7.25 lbs. (12). Length: 48 in. overall (28-in. barrel). Stock: 14 in. x 1.5 in. x 2.5 in. Walnut-stained hardwood, black synthetic, Mossy Oak Advantage camouflage. Cut-checkered grip and fore-end. Sights: White bead front, brass mid-bead; fiber-optic. Features: Ambidextrous thumb safety, twin extractors, disconnecting safety, dual action bars. Quiet Carry fore-end. Many barrels are ported. FLEX series has many modular options and accessories including barrels and stocks. From Mossberg. Left-hand versions (L-series) available in most models.
Price: Turkey **$486.00**
Price: Waterfowl **$537.00**
Price: Combo **$593.00**
Price: FLEX Hunting **$702.00**
Price: FLEX All Purpose **$561.00**
Price: Field **$419.00**
Price: Slugster **$447.00**
Price: FLEX Deer/Security combo **$787.00**
Price: Home Security 410 .... **$477.00**
Price: Tactical .... **$486.00–$602.00**

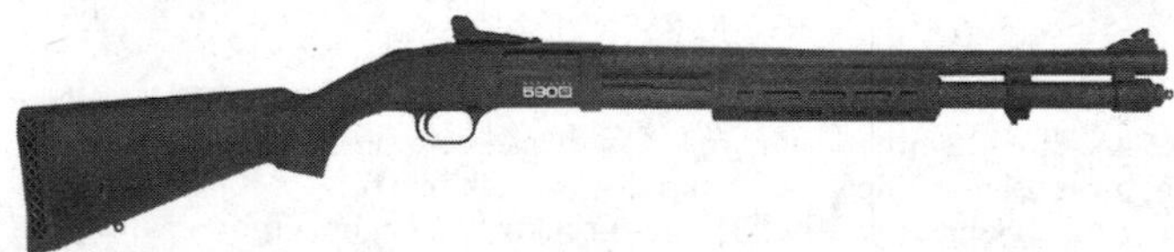

MOSSBERG 590S
Gauge: 12 ga. 3 in. with 1.75-in. short shell and 2.75 in. capability. Barrel: 18.5 or 20 in., matte blued. Length: 39.5–41 in. Weight: 6.75–7.25 lbs. Stock: Black Synthetic with fixed LOP; Model with Ghost ring sights uses tactical stock with M-LOK attachment points. Features: Standard model with 18.5-in. barrel allows capacities of 9+1, 6+1, or 5+1. Model with 20-in. barrel and ghost ring sights has capacities of 13+1, 8+1, or 7+1. The former uses a fixed cylinder bore. The latter features the Accu-Choke system with cylinder bore choke included. Both models cycle all length of shells without adapters or adjustment.
Price: Standard 18.5 in. **$623.00**
Price: Ghost Ring 20 in. **$731.00**

Prices given are believed to be accurate at time of publication however, many factors affect retail pricing so exact prices are not possible.

MOSSBERG SHOCKWAVE SERIES
Gauges: 12, 20 ga. or .410 cylinder bore, 3-inch chamber. Barrel: 14 3/8, 18.5 in. Weight: 5 – 5.5 lbs. Length: 26.4 - 30.75 in. Stock: Synthetic or wood. Raptor bird's-head type pistol grip. Nightstick has wood stock and fore-end.
Price: **$455.00**
Price: CTC Laser Saddle Model **$613.00**
Price: Ceracote finish **$504.00**
Price: Nightstick (shown **$539.00**
Price: Mag-Fed **$721.00**
Price: SPX w/heatshield .... **$560.00–$710.00**

RETAY GPS
Gauges: 12 ga. 3 in. Barrel: 18.5 in. Weight: 6 lbs. 9 oz. Stock: Black ABS synthetic. Features: Retay's first pump-action shotgun is the GPS, short for Geometric Pump System. Extra-short travel pump action. Anodized aluminum receiver. 5+1-round capacity. Chrome-lined barrel with elongated, back-bored forcing cones. Crossbolt safety. Milled aluminum trigger housing and guard. Integral sling swivel mounts. Beavertail adapter for optics mounting. High visibility front blade sight. Comfort rubber recoil pad. Ships with removeable MaraPro chokes (S, M, F).
Price: **$349.00**

RETAY GPS XL
Gauge: 12 ga. 3.5 in. Barrel: 28 in. Weight: oz. Stock: Black or camo ABS synthetic. Features: Retay's pump-action GPS expands to the XL, chambering magnum rounds. GPS, short for Geometric Pump System, uses a short-travel pump action with a frictionless forend design. Anodized aluminum receiver, chrome-lined barrel with elongated, back-bored forcing cones. Crossbolt safety. Milled aluminum trigger housing and guard. Integral sling swivel mounts. Red fiber-optic front sight. Rubber recoil pad. Ships with MaraPro chokes.
Price: **$419.00**

STEVENS MODEL 320
Gauges: 12 ga., or 20 ga. with 3-in. chamber. Capacity: 5+1. Barrels: 18.25 in., 20 in., 22 in., 26 in. or 28 in. with interchangeable choke tubes. Features include all-steel barrel and receiver; bottom-load and ejection design; black synthetic stock.
Price: Security Model **$276.00**
Price: Field Model 320 with 28-inch barrel **$251.00**
Price: Combo Model with Field and Security barrels **$307.00**

STEVENS 320 SECURITY THUMBHOLE
Gauges: 12 ga. 3 in., or 20 ga. 3in. Barrel: 18.5-in. chrome alloy steel matte black. Weight: 7.0–7.3 lbs. Length: 39.1 in. Stock: Black matte synthetic with thumbhole cutout. Features: Pump action with dual slide bars and rotary bolt. Thumbhole stock design with ambidextrous cheek riser and grip texture. Swivel studs. Bottom-loading tubular magazine with 5+1-round capacity. Black rubber recoil pad. Ghost Ring Sight or Front Bead Sight models available in both chamberings.
Price: 12-ga. Front Bead Sight Model **$275.00**
Price: 12-ga. Ghost Ring Sight Model **$305.00**
Price: 20-ga. Front Bead Sight Model **$275.00**
Price: 20-ga. Ghost Ring Sight Model **$305.00**

STEVENS 320 TURKEY THUMBHOLE
Gauges: 12 ga. 3 in., or 20 ga. 3 in. Barrel: 22-in. chrome alloy steel matte black with ventilated rib. Weight: 7.6 lbs. Length: 43.4 in. Stock: Olive drab green matte synthetic with thumbhole cutout. Features: Pump action with dual slide bars and rotary bolt. Thumbhole stock design with ambidextrous cheek riser and grip texture. Swivel studs. Bottom-loading tubular magazine with 5+1-round capacity. Black rubber recoil pad. Adjustable fiber-optic turkey sights. Extended Win-Choke-style Extra Full choke tube.
Price: 12-ga. Front Bead Sight Model **$323.00**

STOEGER P3000
Gauge: 12 ga. 3-in. Barrels: 18.5 in., 26 in., 28 in., with ventilated rib. Weight: 6.5–7 lbs. Stock: Black synthetic. Camo finish available. Defense Model available with or without pistol grip.
Price: **$299.00**
Price: Camo finish **$399.00**
Price: Defense model w/pistol grip **$349.00**

TRISTAR COBRA III FIELD
Gauges: 12 ga., 3 in., 20 ga., 3 in. Barrels: 26 in., 28 in., ventilated rib. Weight: 6.7-7.0 lbs. Length: 46.5-48.5 in. Stock: Field models available with either Turkish walnut or black synthetic furniture. Features: Third model upgrade to the Cobra pump-action line with extended fore-end. Rubber buttpad, cross-bolt safety, chrome-lined barrel, high-polish blue metalwork, sling studs. Includes three Beretta Mobil-style choke tubes (IC, M, F).
Price: .... **$305.00—$335.00**

TRISTAR COBRA III YOUTH
Gauge: 20 ga., 3 in. Barrel: 24 in., ventilated rib. Weight: 5.4-6.5 lbs. Length: 37.7 in. Stock: Version III youth models available with black synthetic, Realtree Max-5 camo or Turkish-walnut furniture. Features: Third iteration of the Cobra pump-action with extended fore-end. Ventilated rubber buttpad, cross-bolt safety, chrome-lined barrel, sling studs. Shorter length of pull on Youth model. Includes three Beretta Mobil-style choke tubes (IC, M, F).
Price: .... **$305.00—$365.00**

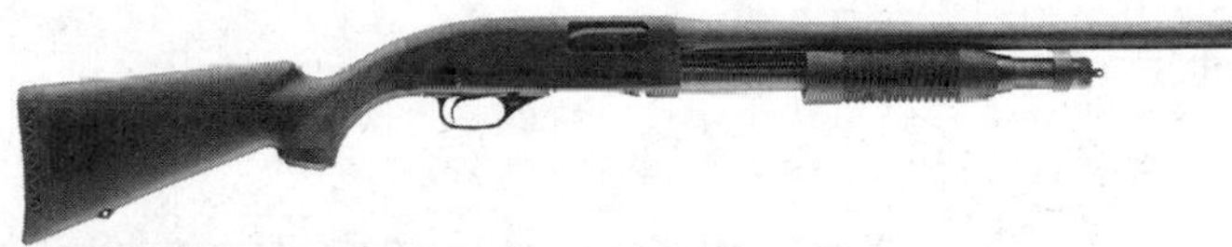

WINCHESTER SUPER X (SXP)
Gauges: 12 ga., 3 in. or 3 1/2 in. chambers; 20 ga., 3 in. Barrels: 18 in., 26 in., 28 in. Barrels .742-in. back-bored, chrome plated; Invector Plus choke tubes. Weights: 6.5–7 lbs. Stocks: Walnut or composite. Features: Rotary bolt, four lugs, dual steel action bars. Walnut Field has gloss-finished walnut stock and forearm, cut checkering. Black Shadow Field has composite stock and forearm, non-glare matte finish barrel and receiver. SXP Defender has composite stock and forearm, chromed plated, 18-in. cylinder choked barrel, non-glare metal surfaces, five-shot magazine, grooved forearm. Some models offered in left-hand versions. Reintroduced 2009. Made in USA by Winchester Repeating Arms Co.
Price: Black Shadow Field, 3 in. **$380.00**
Price: Black Shadow Field, 3 1/2 in. **$430.00**
Price: SXP Defender .... **$350.00–$400.00**
Price: SXP Universal Hunter 12 and 20 ga. Mossy Oak DNA camo **$509.00**
Price: Hybrid Hunter in Mossy Oak Shadow Grass Habitat **$449.00**
Price: Waterfowl Hunter 3 in. **$460.00**
Price: Waterfowl Hunter 3 1/2 in. **$500.00**
Price: Waterfowl Hunter in Mossy Oak Shadow Grass Habitat **$499.00**
Price: Turkey Hunter 3 1/2 in. **$520.00**
Price: Black Shadow Deer **$520.00**
Price: Trap **$480.00**
Price: Field, walnut stock .... **$400.00–$430.00**
Price: 20-ga., 3-in. models **$379.00**
Price: Extreme Defender FDE **$549.00**

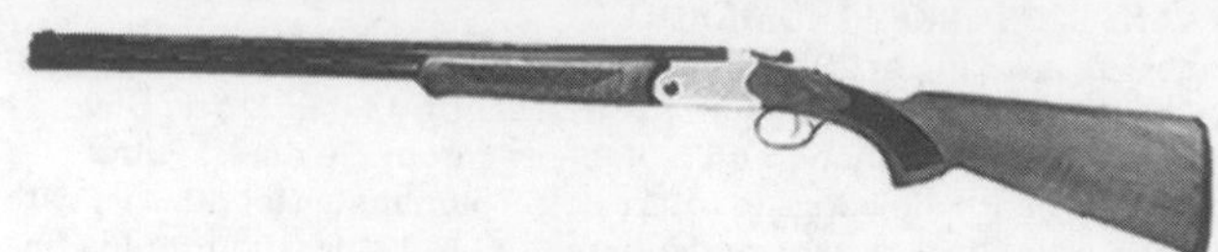

AMERICAN TACTICAL INC (ATI) CRUSADER
Gauges: 12 ga., 3 in., 20 ga., 3 in., 28 ga., 2.75 in, .410 bore, 3 in. Barrels: 26 in., 28 in., 30 in., ventilated rib. Weight: 6.0-6.5 lbs. Stock: Turkish walnut with oil finish. Features: ATI's new O/U line has both Field and Sport models. Made from 7075 aluminum with laser engraving on the receiver. Single selective trigger, fiber-optic front sight, extractors, chrome-moly steel barrel. Ships with five chokes: flush on the Field, extended on the Sport.
Price: Crusader Field **$499.00**
Price: Crusader Sport **$549.00**

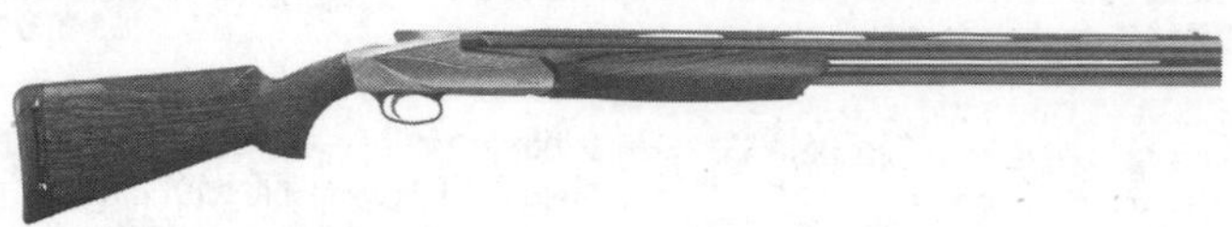

BENELLI 828U
Gauges: 12 ga. 3 in. Barrels: 26 in., 28 in. Weights: 6.5–7 lbs. Stock: AA-grade satin walnut, fully adjustable for both drop and cast. Features: New patented locking system allows use of aluminum frame. Features include carbon fiber rib, fiber-optic sight, removable trigger group, and Benelli's Progressive Comfort recoil reduction system.
Price: Matte black **$2,699.00**
Price: Nickel **$3,199.00**
Price: 20-gauge Nickel **$3,199.00**

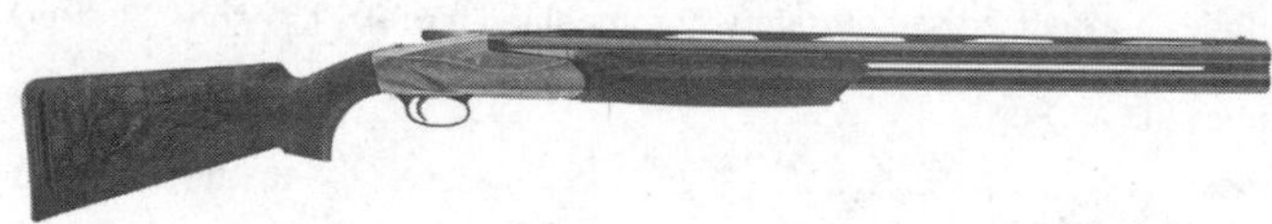

BENELLI 828U LIMITED EDITION
With nickel-plated steel frame, elegant engraved and gold inlayed game scene, and AA-grade Walnut. This 12 ga. with 28-in. barrel shows metalwork finished in B.E.S.T. coating. Limited to 200 units.
Price: **$6,499.00**

BERETTA 686/687 SILVER PIGEON SERIES
Gauges: 12 ga., 20 ga., 28 ga., 3 in. (2 3/4 in. 28 ga.). .410 bore, 3 in. Barrels: 26 in., 28 in. Weight: 6.8 lbs. Stock: Checkered walnut. Features: Interchangeable barrels (20 ga. and 28 ga.), single selective gold-plated trigger, boxlock action, auto safety, Schnabel fore-end.
Price: 686 Silver Pigeon Grade I **$2,350.00**
Price: 686 Silver Pigeon Grade I, Sporting **$2,400.00**
Price: 687 Silver Pigeon Grade III **$3,430.00**
Price: 687 Silver Pigeon Grade V **$4,075.00**

BERETTA 687 SILVER PIGEON III
Gauges: 12 ga. 3 in., 20 ga. 3 in., 28 ga. 2.75 in., .410 bore, 3 in. Barrels: 26, 28, 30 in. with 6x6 windowed rib. Stock: Class 2.5 Walnut with gloss finish. Features: The 687 Silver Pigeon III stems from the 680 series design. Trapezoid shoulders and dual conical locking lugs. Fine engraving with game scenes and floral motif done with 5-axis laser. MicroCore 20mm buttpad. The 28-gauge and .410-bore doubles are built on a smaller frame. Gold-colored single selective trigger. Tang safety selector. Steelium barrels. The 12, 20, and 28 gauges use 70mm Optima HP choke tubes while the .410 is equipped with 50mm Mobil Chokes.
Price: **$2,699.00**

BERETTA MODEL 687 EELL
Gauges: 12 ga., 20 ga., 28 ga., 410 bore. Features: Premium-grade model with decorative sideplates featuring lavish hand-chased engraving with a classic game scene enhanced by detailed leaves and flowers that also cover the trigger guard, trigger plate and fore-end lever. Stock has high-grade, specially selected European walnut with fine-line checkering. Offered in three action sizes with scaled-down 28 ga. and .410 receivers. Combo models are available with extra barrel sets in 20/28 or 28/.410.
Price: **$7,995.00**
Price: Combo model **$9,695.00**

BERETTA MODEL 690
Gauge: 12 ga. 3 in. Barrels: 26 in., 28 in., 30 in. with OptimaChoke HP system. Features: Similar to the 686/687 series with minor improvements. Stock has higher grade oil-finished walnut. Re-designed barrel/fore-end attachment reduces weight.
Price: .... **$2,650.00–$3,100.00**

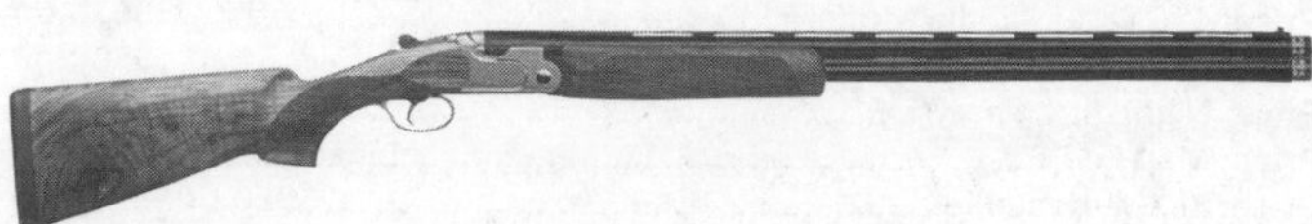

BERETTA MODEL 692 SPORTING
Gauge: 12 ga., 3 in. Barrels: 30 in. with long forcing cones of approximately 14 in.. Skeet model available with 28- or 30-in. barrel, Trap model with 30 in or 32 in. Receiver is .50-in. wider than 682 model for improved handling. Stock: Hand rubbed oil finished select walnut with Schnabel fore-end. Features include selective single adjustable trigger, manual safety, tapered 8mm to 10mm rib.
Price: **$4,800.00**
Price: Skeet **$5,275.00**
Price: Trap **$5,600.00**

BERETTA DT11
Gauge: 12 ga. 3 in. Barrels: 30 in., 32 in., 34 in. Top rib has hollowed bridges. Stock: Hand-checkered buttstock and fore-end. Hand-rubbed oil, Tru-Oil or wax finish. Adjustable comb on skeet and trap models. Features: Competition model offered in Sporting, Skeet and Trap models. Newly designed receiver, top lever, safety/selector button.
Price: Sporting **$8,650.00**
Price: Skeet **$8,650.00**
Price: Trap **$8,999.00**

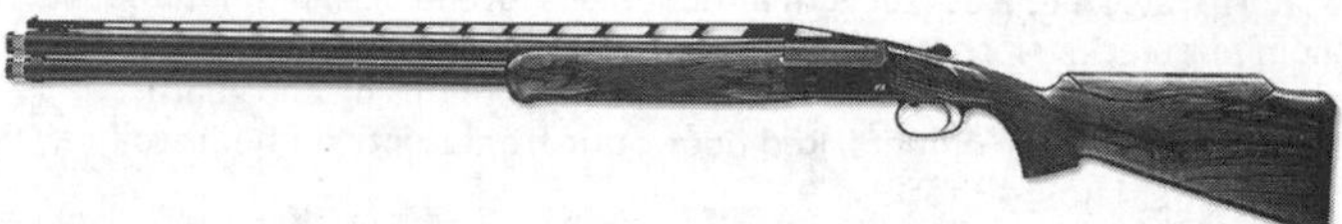

BLASER F3 SUPERSPORT
Gauge: 12 ga., 3 in. Barrel: 32 in. Weight: 9 lbs. Stock: Adjustable semi-custom, Turkish walnut wood grade: 4. Features: The latest addition to the F3 family is the F3 SuperSport. The perfect blend of overall weight, balance and weight distribution make the F3 SuperSport the ideal competitor. Briley Spectrum-5 chokes, free-floating barrels, adjustable barrel hanger system on o/u, chrome plated barrels full length, revolutionary ejector ball system, barrels finished in a powder coated nitride, selectable competition trigger.
Price: SuperSport **$9,076.00**
Price: Competition Sporting **$7,951.00**
Price: Superskeet **$9,076.00**
Price: American Super Trap **$9,530.00**

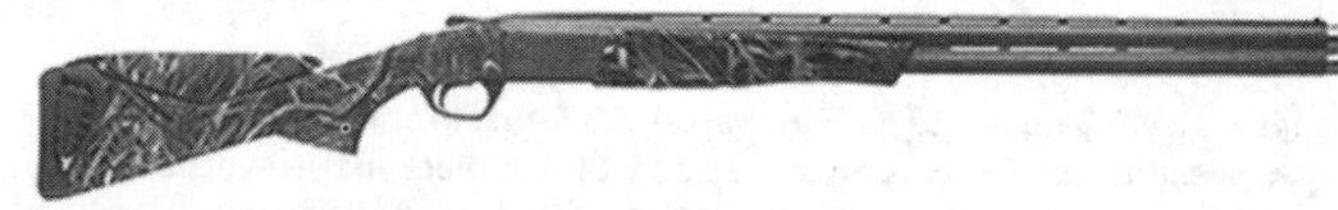

BROWNING CYNERGY
Gauges: .410 bore, 12 ga., 20 ga., 28 ga. Barrels: 26 in., 28 in., 30 in., 32 in. Stocks: Walnut or composite. Sights: White bead front most models; HiViz Pro-Comp sight on some models; mid bead. Features: Mono-Lock hinge, recoil-reducing interchangeable Inflex recoil pad, silver nitride receiver; striker-based trigger, ported barrel option. Imported from Japan by Browning.
Price: Field Grade Model, 12 ga. **$1,910.00**
Price: CX composite **$1,710.00**

Prices given are believed to be accurate at time of publication however, many factors affect retail pricing so exact prices are not possible.

Price: CX walnut stock $1,780.00
Price: Field, small gauges $1,940.00
Price: Ultimate Turkey, Mossy Oak Breakup camo $2,390.00
Price: Ultimate Turkey in Mossy Oak Bottomland camo $2,549.00
Price: Micro Midas $1,979.00
Price: Feather $2,269.00
Price: Wicked Wing $2,339.00
Price: Wicked Wing in Vintage Tan camo w/ Cerakote barrels $2,499.00

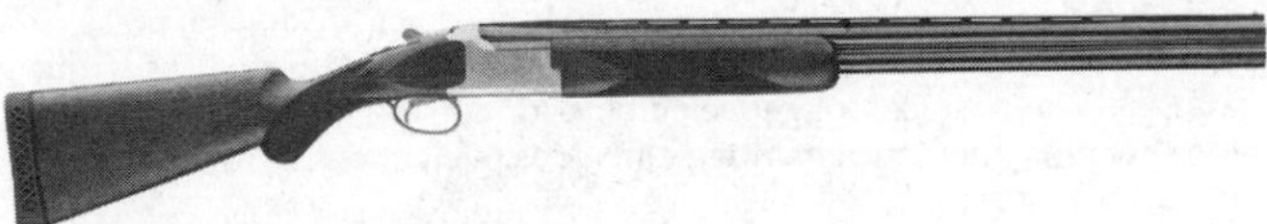

BROWNING CITORI SERIES
Gauges: 12 ga., 20 ga., 28 ga., .410 bore. Barrels: 26 in., 28 in. in 28 ga. and .410 bore. Offered with Invector choke tubes. All 12- and 20-ga. models have back-bored barrels and Invector Plus choke system. Weights: 6 lbs., 8 oz. (26 in. .410) to 7 lbs., 13 oz. (30 in. 12 ga.). Length: 43 in. overall (26-in. bbl.). Stock: Dense walnut, hand checkered, full pistol grip, beavertail fore-end. Field-type recoil pad on 12 ga. field guns and trap and skeet models. Sights: Medium-raised beads, German nickel silver. Features: Barrel selector integral with safety, automatic ejectors, three-piece takedown. Imported from Japan by Browning.
Price: White Lightning $2,670.00
Price: Feather Lightning $2,870.00
Price: Gran Lightning $3,300.00
Price: Crossover (CX) $2,140.00
Price: Crossover (CX) w/adjustable comb $2,560.00
Price: Crossover (CXS) $2,140.00
Price: Crossover Target (CXT) $2,260.00
Price: Crossover Target (CXT) w/adjustable comb $2,660.00
Price: Crossover (CXS) $2,190.00
Price: Crossover (CXS) w/adjustable comb $2,590.00
Price: Crossover (CXS Micro) $2,140.00
Price: White Lightning .410 bore and 28 ga. .... $2,669.00–$2,739.00
Price: CX White $2,379.00
Price: CX White Adjustable $2,939.00
Price: CX Micro $2,469.00
Price: CXS 20/28 Ga. Combo $3,939.00
Price: CXS White $2,439.00
Price: CXT White $2,499.00

BROWNING CITORI TRAP MAX
Gauge: 12 ga., 2.75 in. Barrels: 30 in., 32 in., ported with 5/16 to 7/16 adjustable ventilated rib. Weight: 9.0-9.2 lbs. Length: 47.75-49.75 in. Stock: Grade V/VI black walnut with gloss-oil finish. Features: Graco adjustable Monte Carlo comb. Buttplate adjusts for location and angle. GraCoil recoil reduction system increases comfort and offers length-of-pull adjustment. Adjustable rib allows for 50/50 or 90/10 POI. Semi-beavertail forearm with finger grooves, Pachmayr Decelerator XLT recoil pad. Close radius grip and palm swell. Triple Trigger System with three trigger shoes, gold-plated trigger, Hi-Viz Pro Comp sight, ivory mid-bead, polished blue barrels, Silver-Nitride receiver, chrome-plated chamber. Five Invector DS Extended choke tubes ideal for trap (F, LF, M, IM, IM).
Price: $5,859.00

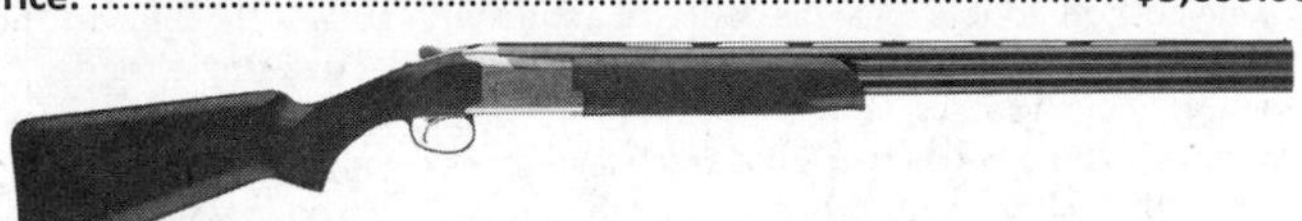

BROWNING 725 CITORI
Gauges: 12 ga., 20 ga., 28 ga. or .410 bore. Barrels: 26 in., 28 in., 30 in. Weights: 5.7–7.6 lbs. Length: 43.75–50 in. Stock: Gloss oil finish, grade II/III walnut. Features: New receiver that is significantly lower in profile than other 12-gauge Citori models. Mechanical trigger, Vector Pro lengthened forcing cones, three Invector-DS choke tubes, silver nitride finish with high relief engraving.
Price: 725 Field (12 ga. or 20 ga.) $2,560.00
Price: 725 Field (28 ga. or .410 bore) $2,590.00
Price: 725 Field Grade VI $6,000.00
Price: 725 Feather (12 ga. or 20 ga.) $2,670.00
Price: 725 Sporting $3,270.00
Price: 725 Sporting w/adjustable comb $3,600.00
Price: 725 Sporting Golden Clays $5,440.00
Price: 725 Trap $3,400.00

BROWNING CITORI 725 SPORTING MEDALLION HIGH GRADE
Gauge: 12 ga. 3 in. Barrels: 30 or 32 in., steel with floating 5/16 to 7/16-in. rib. Weight: 7 lbs. 8 oz.–7 lbs. 10 oz. Length: 48–50 in. Stock: Grade IV Turkish Walnut with gloss oil finish. Features: Browning expands the higher end of the Citori family. Extensive receiver engraving with gold enhancement. Cut checkering at 20 LPI and right-hand palm swell. HiViz Pro-Comp front sight. Chrome-plated chamber. Tapered locking bolt and full-width hinge pin. Triple trigger system with three included shoes. Blued receiver finish and polished blued barrels. Inflex recoil pad. Gold-plated trigger. Name plate inlay for owner's initials. Includes five Invector DS extended choke tubes (F, IM, M, IC, SK) and Negrini locking hard case.
Price: $7,069.00

CAESAR GUERINI
Gauges: 12 ga., 20 ga., 28 ga., also 20/28 gauge combo. Some models are available in .410 bore. Barrels: All standard lengths from 26–32 inches. Weights: 5.5–8.8 lbs. Stock: High-grade walnut with hand-rubbed oil finish. Features: A wide range of over/under models designed for the field, sporting clays, skeet and trap shooting. The models listed below are representative of some of the different models and variants. Many optional features are offered including high-grade wood and engraving, and extra sets of barrels. Made it Italy and imported by Caesar Guerini USA.
Price: Summit Sporting $3,995.00
Price: Summit Limited $4,895.00
Price: Summit Ascent $5,135.00
Price: Tempio $4,325.00
Price: Ellipse $4,650.00
Price: Ellipse Curve $7,500.00
Price: Ellipse EVO Sporting $6,950.00
Price: Magnus $5,075.00
Price: Maxum $6,825.00
Price: Forum $11,500.00
Price: Woodlander $3,795.00
Price: Invictus Sporting $7,400.00
Price: Maxum Trap $9,295.00
Price: Maxum Sporting $7,150.00

CAESAR GUERINI REVENANT
Addition of a new combo set to the high-grade 2019 Revenant O/U with a tapered, solid rib and highly engraved maple leaf and branch design receiver. Now with a 20/28-gauge combo barrel set.
Price: $13,495.00

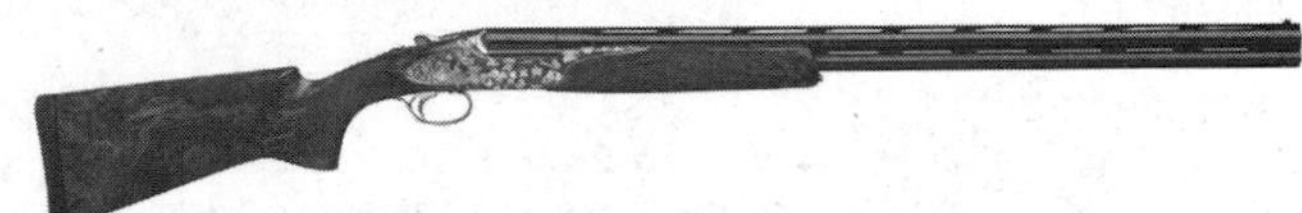

CAESAR GUERINI REVENANT SPORTING
Gauge: 20 ga. 3 in., 28 ga. 2.75 in. Barrels: 28 or 30 in. with non-ventilated center rib, tapered from 8–6mm. Weight: 6 lbs. 6 oz.–6 lbs. 11 oz. Stock: Extra-deluxe wood grade with hand-rubbed oil finish. Left-hand stock option available by special order. Features: Fine-grade over-under Sporting version of the Revenant. Hand-polished coin finish with Invisalloy protective finish. Long-tang triggerguard. Anson rod fore-end escutcheon. Intricate engraving and gold inlay that takes over 40-hours to produce each Revenant action. Wood butt plate. Silver front bead. Checkered at 26 LPI. Premium Revenant gun case included. Ships with five nickel-plated flush-fitting chokes.
Price: $14,750.00

CAESAR GUERINI SYREN JULIA SPORTING

Gauges: 12 ga. 2.75 in. Barrels: 30 in. ventilated rib tapered from 10–8mm. Weight: 7 lbs. 15 oz. Stock: Deluxe Turkish Walnut with hand-rubbed, semi-gloss oil finish. Left-hand stock option and adjustable comb (RH) available by special order Features: Named after Julia, daughter of Julius Caesar, as a top-tier, competition-grade target gun in the Syren line of shotguns for women. Fantasy-style receiver engraving depicting a woman's face evolving from floral scrollwork. Rich case color hardened finish. Checking cut at 26 LPI. Black rubber recoil pad. DuoCon forcing cones. White Bradley style front sight and silver center bead. DTS trigger system with take-up, over-travel, and LOP adjustments. Manual safety. Includes six MAXIS competition chokes as well as plastic hard case, combination locks, and velvet sleeves.

Price: $6,050.00

CHARLES DALY 202

Gauges: 12 ga., 3 in., 20 ga., 3 in., .410 bore, 3 in. Barrels: 26 in., 28 in., ventilated rib. Length: 43-45 in. Weight: 6.2-7.3 lbs. Stock: Checkered walnut. Features: The new Charles Daly 202 line of O/U shotguns are built of aluminum alloy. Silver receivers are engraved with a dog scene. Single selective mechanical reset trigger, fixed fiber-optic front sight, extractors, rubber buttpad. Includes five extended Mobil style chokes (SK, IC, M, IM, F).

Price: $499.00

CONNECTICUT SHOTGUN A10 AMERICAN

Gauges: 12 ga., 20 ga., 28 ga., .410 bore. 2 3/4, 3 in. Sidelock design. Barrels: 26 in., 28 in., 30 in. or 32 in. with choice of fixed or interchangeable chokes. Weight: 6.3 lbs. Stock: Hand rubbed oil finish, hand checkered at 24 LPI. Black, English or Turkish walnut offered in numerous grades. Pistol or Prince of Wales grip, short or long tang. Features: Low-profile, shallow frame full sidelock. Single-selective trigger, automatic ejectors. Engraved models available. Made in the USA by Connecticut Shotgun Mfg. Co.

Price: 12 ga. $9,999.00
Price: Smaller ga. $11,900.00
Price: Sporting Clays $14,950.00

CONNECTICUT SHOTGUN MODEL 21 O/U

Gauge: 20 ga., 3 in. Barrels: 26–32 in. chrome-lined, back-bored with extended forcing cones. Weight: 6.3 lbs. Stock: A Fancy (2X) American walnut, standard point checkering, choice of straight or pistol grip. Higher grade walnut is optional. Features: The over/under version of Conn. Shotgun's replica of the Winchester Model 21 side-by-side, built using the same machining, tooling, techniques and finishes. Low-profile shallow frame with blued receiver. Pigeon and Grand American grades are available. Made in the USA by Connecticut Shotgun Mfg. Co.

Price: $4,545.00

CZ ALL TERRAIN SERIES

Gauges: 12 ga., 3 in., 20 ga., 3 in. Barrels: 28 in., 30 in. Stock: Walnut, various styles. Features: CZ's new All-Terrain series encompasses five existing shotgun models. The new package includes upgraded wood, OD Green Cerakote finish on all metalwork, as well as a set of rare earth magnets added to the extractor/ejectors of the SxS and O/U models to keep shells from dropping out while handling a dog or working in the blind.

Price: Upland Ultralight All-Terrain 12 ga. or 20 ga. $890.00
Price: Redhead Premier All-Terrain 12 ga. or 20 ga. $1,123.00
Price: Drake All-Terrain 12 ga. or 20 ga. $791.00

CZ REDHEAD PREMIER

Gauges: 12 ga., 20 ga., (3 in. chambers), 28 ga. (2 3/4 in.). Barrel: 28 in. Weight: 7.4 lbs. Length: NA. Stock: Round-knob pistol grip, Schnabel fore-end, Turkish walnut. Features: Single selective triggers and extractors (12 & 20 ga.), screw-in chokes (12 ga., 20 ga., 28 ga.) choked IC and Mod (.410), coin-finished receiver, multi chokes. From CZ-USA.

Price: Deluxe $953.00
Price: Mini (28 ga., .410 bore) $1,057.00
Price: Target $1,389.00
Price: 16 ga., 28 in. barrel $988.00

CZ REDHEAD PREMIER PROJECT UPLAND

Gauge: 12, 20, 28 ga. Barrel: 28 in. with 8mm flat vent rib. Length: 43.75 in. Weight: 6.9–7.7 lbs. Stock: Grade III Turkish Walnut. Features: Project Upland hunting O/U with silver satin chrome receiver finish. One piece CNC'd action, 3-in. chamber. Gloss black chrome barrel finish. Brass front bead. Single mechanical trigger selectable for barrels. Manual tang safety. Patent pending magnetic chambers. Includes five chokes (F, IM, M, IC, C).

Price: 12 & 20 ga. $1,509.00
Price: 28 ga. $1,609.00

FABARM ELOS 2 ELITE

Gauge: 12 ga. 3 in., 20 ga. 3 in. Barrels: 28 in. ventilated rib. Stock: Deluxe-grade European Walnut with matte oil finish and pistol grip design. Features: Left-handed stock option available by special order. Rich case-colored action with gold inlay of sporting birds. Hand-cut checkering. Brass front bead. Single gold-plated trigger. TriBore HP barrel and Inner HP flush-fitting chokes. Ships with Integrale case.

Price: $3,325.00

FABARM ELOS N2 ALLSPORT COMBO

Gauge: 12 ga. Barrels: 30 in. O/U with 34 in. Unsingle combo; 32 in. O/U with 34 in. Unsingle combo. Stock: Turkish Walnut with TriWood enhanced finish. Available with left-hand stock option or Modified Compact Stock with shorter LOP. Features: The Elos N2 Allsport Type T Combo is built for competition shooting. Microcell 22mm recoil pad. Quick Release Rib (QRR) rib on O/U barrels. Adjustable competition trigger. Adjustable comb. TriBore HP barrel. Hand-cut checkering. Single trigger. Includes five EXIS HP Competition extended choke tubes. Ships with hard case.

Price: $3,325.00

F.A.I.R. CARRERA ONE

Gauge: 12 ga. 3 in. Barrels: 30 in. chrome-lined with flat 11mm vent rib. Optional 28, 30 in. Weight: 7 lbs. Stock: Selected European Walnut with ergonomic sporting design and XR-Stock adjustment system (comb/heel) in bright oil finish. Features: FAIR's latest sporting O/U with oversize cross-locking bolt on double lugs. Black bright action with golden clay pigeon and model names. Triple-depth laser engraving, black selective single trigger, top tang manual safety. Long-stroke automatic ejectors. Oil-resistant ventilated rubber recoil pad. Fine-pitch laser checkering. Red fiber-optic front sight. Technichoke XP70 system with 5 tubes. Packed in V500SP case.

Price: $1,988.00

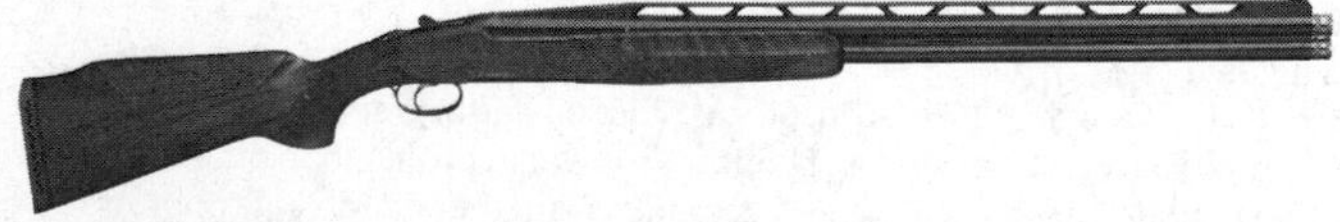

F.A.I.R. CARRERA ONE HR

Gauge: 12 ga. 3 in. Barrels: 30 in. chrome-lined with 15mm wide high vent rib. Optional 28, 30 in. Weight: 7.5 lbs. with mounted chokes. Stock: Selected European Walnut with ergonomic sporting design and XR-Stock adjustment system (comb/heel) Monte Carlo style, in bright oil finish. Features: FAIR's latest sporting O/U with oversize cross-locking bolt on double lugs, this HR variant with a high rib. Black bright action with golden clay pigeon and model names. Triple-depth laser engraving, black selective single trigger, top tang manual safety, long-stroke automatic ejectors. Oil-resistant ventilated rubber recoil pad. Fine-pitch laser checkering. Fiber-

Prices given are believed to be accurate at time of publication however, many factors affect retail pricing so exact prices are not possible.

optic front sight. Technichoke XP70 system with 5 tubes (F, IM, M, IC, C). Packed in V500SP case.
Price: **$2,198.00**

FAUSTI CLASS ROUND BODY
Gauges: 16 ga., 20 ga., 28 ga.. Barrels: 28 or 30 in. Weights: 5.8–6.3 lbs. Lengths: 45.5–47.5 in. Stock: Turkish walnut Prince of Wales style with oil finish. Features include automatic ejectors, single selective trigger, laser-engraved receiver.
Price: **$4,199.00**

FAUSTI CALEDON
Gauges: 12 ga., 16 ga., 20 ga., 28 ga. and .410 bore. Barrels: 26 in., 28 in., 30 in. Weights: 5.8–7.3 lbs. Stock: Turkish walnut with oil finish, round pistol grip. Features: Automatic ejectors, single selective trigger, laser-engraved receiver. Coin finish receiver with gold inlays.
Price: 12 ga. or 20 ga. **$1,999.00**
Price: 16 ga., 28 ga., .410 bore **$2,569.00**

FRANCHI INSTINCT SERIES
Gauges: 12 ga., 16 ga., 20 ga., 28 ga., .410 bore, 2 1/5 in. 2 3/4 in, 3 in." Barrels: 26 in., 28 in. Weight: 5.3–6.4 lbs. Lengths: 42.5–44.5 in. Stock: AA-grade satin walnut (LS), A-grade (L) with rounded pistol grip and recoil pad. Single trigger, automatic ejectors, tang safety, choke tubes. L model has steel receiver, SL has aluminum alloy receiver. Sporting model has higher grade wood, extended choke tubes. Catalyst model is designed for women, including stock dimensions for cast, drop, pitch, grip and length of pull.
Price: L **$1,299.00**
Price: SL **$1,599.00**
Price: Sporting **$1,999.00**
Price: Catalyst **$1,469.00**
Price: SL 28 ga. and .410 bore **$1,699.00**

FRANCHI INSTICT SIDEPLATE
Gauge: 12, 20 ga. 3 in. Barrel: 28 in. ventilated rib. Weight: 6.5–7.5 lbs. Length: 46.25 in. Stock: AA Grade Walnut. Features: Franchi's first sideplate-style shotgun. Fine engraving and gold inlays on the color case-hardened receiver. Prince of Wales stock and Schnabel forend with checkering. Red fiber-optic front bar, auto ejectors, top tang barrel selector and automatic safety. Five extended choke tubes (F, IM, M, IC, C) included, as well as custom-fitted hard case.
Price: **$2,229.00**

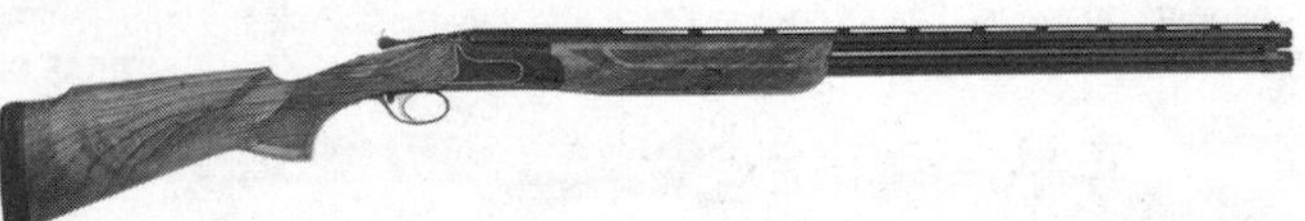

KOLAR SPORTING CLAYS
Gauge: 12 ga., 2 3/4 in. Barrels: 30 in., 32 in., 34 in.; extended choke tubes. Stock: 14.625 in. x 2.5 in. x 1.875 in. x 1.375 in. French walnut. Four stock versions available. Features: Single selective trigger, detachable, adjustable for length; overbored barrels with long forcing cones; flat tramline rib; matte blue finish. Made in U.S. by Kolar.
Price: Standard **$11,995.00**
Price: Prestige **$14,190.00**
Price: Elite Gold **$16,590.00**
Price: Legend **$17,090.00**
Price: Select **$22,590.00**
Price: Custom .... **Price on request**

KOLAR AAA COMPETITION TRAP
Gauge: 12 ga. Similar to the Sporting Clays gun except has 32 in. O/U 34 in. Unsingle or 30 in. O/U 34 in. Unsingle barrels as an over/under, unsingle, or combination set. Stock dimensions are 14.5 in. x 2.5 in. x 1.5 in.; American or French walnut; step parallel rib standard. Contact maker for full listings. Made in USA by Kolar.
Price: Single bbl. **$8,495.00**
Price: O/U **$11,695.00**

KOLAR AAA COMPETITION SKEET
Similar to the Sporting Clays gun except has 28 in. or 30 in. barrels with Kolarite AAA sub-gauge tubes; stock of American or French walnut with matte finish; flat tramline rib; under barrel adjustable for point of impact. Many options available. Contact maker for complete listing. Made in USA by Kolar.
Price: Max Lite **$13,995.00**

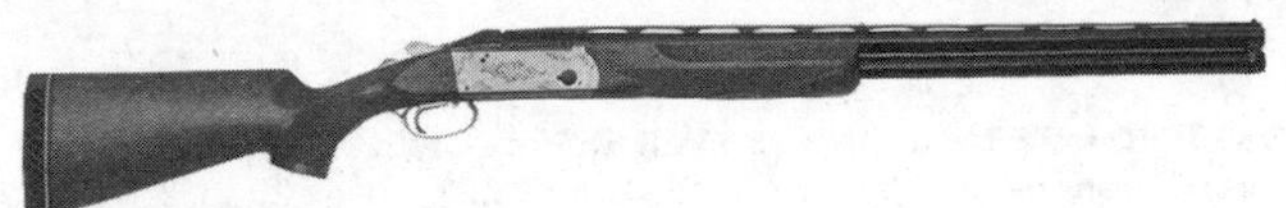

KRIEGHOFF K-80 SPORTING CLAYS
Gauge: 12 ga. Barrels: 28 in., 30 in., 32 in., 34 in. with choke tubes. Weight: About 8 lbs. Stock: #3 Sporting stock designed for gun-down shooting. Features: Standard receiver with satin nickel finish and classic scroll engraving. Selective mechanical trigger adjustable for position. Choice of tapered flat or 8mm parallel flat barrel rib. Free-floating barrels. Aluminum case. Imported from Germany by Krieghoff International, Inc.
Price: Standard grade with five choke tubes **$12,395.00**

KRIEGHOFF K-80 SKEET
Gauge: 12 ga., 2 3/4 in. Barrels: 28 in., 30 in., 32 in., (skeet & skeet), optional choke tubes. Weight: About 7.75 lbs. Stock: American skeet or straight skeet stocks, with palm-swell grips. Walnut. Features: Satin gray receiver finish. Selective mechanical trigger adjustable for position. Choice of ventilated 8mm parallel flat rib or ventilated 8–12mm tapered flat rib. Introduced 1980. Imported from Germany by Krieghoff International, Inc.
Price: Standard, skeet chokes **$11,795.00**

KRIEGHOFF K-80 TRAP
Gauge: 12 ga., 2 3/4 in. Barrels: 30 in., 32 in. (Imp. Mod. & Full or choke tubes). Weight: About 8.5 lbs. Stock: Four stock dimensions or adjustable stock available; all have palm-swell grips. Checkered European walnut. Features: Satin nickel receiver. Selective mechanical trigger, adjustable for position. Ventilated step rib. Introduced 1980. Imported from Germany by Krieghoff International, Inc.
Price: K-80 O/U (30 in., 32 in., Imp. Mod. & Full **$11,795.00**
Price: K-80 Unsingle (32 in., 34 in., Full), standard **$13,995.00**
Price: K-80 Combo (two-barrel set), standard **$17,995.00**

KRIEGHOFF K-20
Similar to the K-80 except built on a 20-ga. frame. Designed for skeet, sporting clays and field use. Offered in 20 ga., 28 ga. and .410; Barrels: 28 in., 30 in. and 32 in. Imported from Germany by Krieghoff International Inc.
Price: K-20, 20 ga. **$11,695.00**
Price: K-20, 28 ga. **$12,395.00**
Price: K-20, .410 .... **$12,395.00**
Price: K-20 Sporting or Parcours **$12,395.00**
Price: K-20 Victoria **$12,395.00**

MERKEL MODEL 2001EL O/U
Gauges: 12 ga., 20 ga., 3 in., 28 ga. 2-3/4 in. chambers. Barrels: 12 ga. 28 in.; 20 ga., 28 ga. 26.75 in. Weight: About 7 lbs. (12 ga.). Stock: Oil-finished walnut; English or pistol grip. Features: Self-cocking Blitz boxlock action with cocking indicators; Kersten double cross-bolt lock; silver-grayed receiver with engraved hunting scenes; coil spring ejectors; single selective or double triggers. Imported from Germany by Merkel USA.
Price: **$13,255.00**

MERKEL MODEL 2000CL
Similar to Model 2001EL except scroll-engraved casehardened receiver; 12 ga., 20 ga., 28 ga. Imported from Germany by Merkel USA.
Price: **$12,235.00**

MOSSBERG SILVER RESERVE II
Gauge: 12 ga., 3 in. Barrels: 28 in. with ventilated rib, choke tubes. Stock: Select black walnut with satin finish. Sights: Metal bead. Available with extractors or automatic ejectors. Also offered in Sport model with ported

barrels with wide rib, fiber optic front and middle bead sights. Super Sport has extra wide high rib, optional adjustable comb.
Price: Field $773.00
Price: Sport $950.00
Price: Sport w/ejectors $1,070.00
Price: Super Sport w/ejectors $1,163.00
Price: Super Sport w/ejectors, adj. comb $1,273.00

MOSSBERG INTERNATIONAL SILVER RESERVE FIELD SERIES
Gauge: Options depend on model, but include 12 ga. 3 in., 20 ga. 3 in., 28 ga. 2.75 in., and .410 bore 3 in., as well as a 20-ga. Youth. Barrels: 26- or 28-in. ventilated rib. Weight: 6.5–7.5 lbs. Length: 42.25–45 in. Stock: Choice of black synthetic or satin Black Walnut, depending upon model, as well as a Youth-sized model with shorter LOP. Features: Matte blue barrel finish. Satin silver receiver on all except the synthetic model with a matte blue receiver. Dual shell extractors. Tang-mounted safety/barrel selector. Includes flush-mount Field set of five chokes (Cyl, IC, M, IM, F).
Price: Eventide Black Synthetic 12-ga. $636.00
Price: Black Walnut Price 12, 20, 28 ga., .410 and 20-ga. Youth $692.00

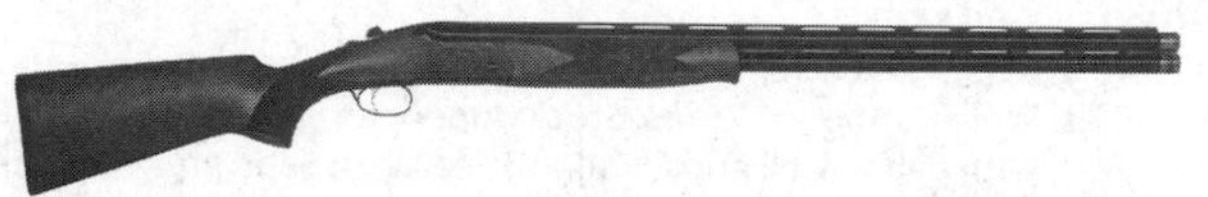

MOSSBERG INTERNATIONAL GOLD RESERVE SPORTING SERIES
Gauge: 12 ga. 3 in., 20 ga. 3 in., and .410 bore 3 in. Barrels: 28 or 30 in. ventilated rib. Weight: 6.5–7.5 lbs. Length: 45.0–48.0 in. Stock: Grade-A Satin Black Walnut. Adjustable stock on Super Sport model. Features: Dual locking lugs and Jeweled action. Chrome-lined bores and chambers. Competition-ready dual shell ejectors. Tang-mounted safety/barrel selector with scroll engraving. Polished silver receiver with scroll-engraved receiver with 24-Karat gold inlay on the underside receiver. Black Label variants wear polished black receiver with same embellishments. Includes set of five Extended Sport chokes (SK, IC, M, IM, F).
Price: Black Walnut 12 or 20 ga., .410 .... $983.00
Price: Black Label 12 ga. $983.00
Price: Super Sport in 12 ga with fully adjustable stock $1,221.00

PERAZZI HIGH TECH 2020
Gauge: 12 ga., 3 in. Barrels: 27-9/16 in., 28-3/8 in., 29-1/2 in., 30-3/4 in., 31-1/2 in., flat ramped stepped 9/32 x 3/8 in. rib. Weight: 8 lbs.-8 lbs., 8 oz. Stock: Oil-finish, high-grade walnut, HT design standard or custom adjustable. Features: The competition grade High Tech 2020 is made in Italy. Logo engraving across silver-finish receiver. Hand-cut checkering, blued-steel barrels. Removeable trigger group with coil or flat springs and selector. Ventilated mid-rib. Interchangeable chokes available on demand.
Price: $21,075.00

PERAZZI MX8/MX8 TRAP/SKEET
Gauge: 12 ga., 20 ga. 2 3/4 in. Barrels: Trap: 29.5 in. (Imp. Mod. & Extra Full), 31.5 in. (Full & Extra Full). Choke tubes optional. Skeet: 27.625 in. (skeet & skeet). Weights: About 8.5 lbs. (trap); 7 lbs., 15 oz. (skeet). Stock: Interchangeable and custom made to customer specs. Features: Has detachable and interchangeable trigger group with flat V springs. Flat .4375 in. vent rib. Many options available. Imported from Italy by Perazzi USA, Inc.
Price: Trap $11,760.00
Price: Skeet $11,760.00

PERAZZI MX8
Gauge: 12 ga., 20 ga. 2 3/4 in. Barrels: 28.375 in. (Imp. Mod. & Extra Full), 29.50 in. (choke tubes). Weight: 7 lbs., 12 oz. Stock: Special specifications. Features: Has single selective trigger; flat .4375 in. x .3125 in. vent rib. Many options available. Imported from Italy by Perazzi USA, Inc.
Price: Standard $11,760.00
Price: Sporting $11,760.00

Price: SC3 Grade (variety of engraving patterns) $21,000.00
Price: SCO Grade (more intricate engraving/inlays) $36,000.00

PIOTTI BOSS
Gauges: 12 ga., 16 ga., 20 ga., 28 ga., .410 bore. Barrels: 26–32 in., chokes as specified. Weight: 6.5–8 lbs. Stock: Dimensions to customer specs. Best quality figured walnut. Features: Essentially a custom-made gun with many options. Introduced 1993. SportingModel is production model with many features of custom series Imported from Italy by Wm. Larkin Moore.
Price: $78,000.00
Price: Sporting Model $27,200.00

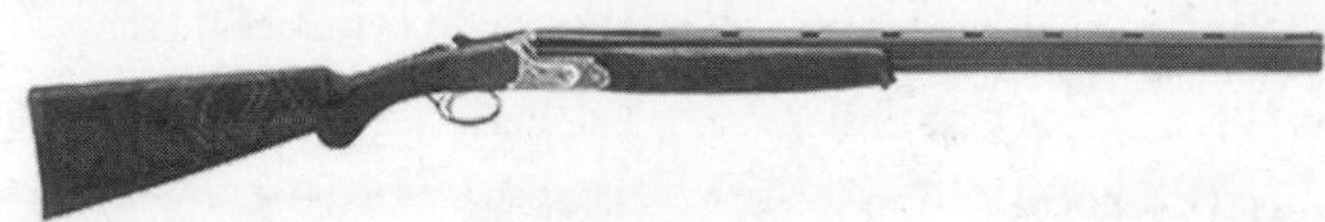

RIZZINI AURUM
Gauges: 12 ga., 16 ga., 20 ga., 28 ga., .410 bore. Barrels: 26, 28, 29 and 30, set of five choke tubes. Weight: 6.25 to 6.75 lbs. (Aurum Light 5.5 to 6.5 lbs.) Stock: Select Turkish walnut with Prince of Wales grip, rounded fore-end. Hand checkered with polished oil finish. Features: Boxlock low-profile action, single selective trigger, automatic ejectors, engraved game scenes in relief, light coin finish with gold inlay. Aurum Light has alloy receiver.
Price: 12, 16, 20 ga $3,425.00
Price: 28, .410 bore $3,625.00
Price: Aurum Light 12, 16, 20 ga $3,700.00
Price: Aurum Light 28, .410 bore $3,900.00

RIZZINI ARTEMIS
Gauges: 12 ga., 16 ga., 20 ga., 28 ga., .410 bore. Same as Upland EL model except dummy sideplates with extensive game scene engraving. Fancy European walnut stock. Fitted case. Introduced 1996. Imported from Italy by Fierce Products and by Wm. Larkin Moore & Co.
Price: $3,975.00
Price: Artemis Light $4,395.00

RIZZINI BR 460
Gauge: 12 ga., 3 in. Barrels: 30 in., 32 in., with 10mm x 6mm ventilated rib. Length: 43-45 in. Weight: 8.3 lbs. Stock: Walnut with hand-rubbed oil finish and adjustable comb. Features: These Rizzini O/U Competition guns are produced in Skeet, Sporting, Trap, and Double Trap, each with different characteristics. Choice of fixed or interchangeable chokes and fixed, adjustable or ramped rib. Stock checkered at 28 LPI. White rounded style front sight with silver mid-bead. Rubber buttpad. Either standard or long forcing cones depending on model. Ships with hard case and velvet stock sleeve.
Price: $7,045.00

RIZZINI FIERCE 1 COMPETITION
Gauges: 12 ga., 20 ga., 28 ga. Barrels: 28, 30 and 32 in. Five extended completion choke tubes. Weight: 6.6 to 8.1 lbs. Stock: Select Turkish walnut, hand checkered with polished oil finish. Features: Available in trap, skeet or sporting models. Adjustable stock and rib available. Boxlock low-profile action, single selective trigger, automatic ejectors, engraved game scenes in relief, light coin finish with gold inlay. Aurum Light has alloy receiver.
Price: $4,260.00

SKB 90TSS
Gauges: 12 ga., 20 ga., 2 3/4 in. Barrels: 28 in., 30 in., 32 in. Three SKB Competition choke tubes (SK, IC, M for Skeet and Sporting Models; IM, M, F for Trap). Lengthened forcing cones. Stock: Oil finished walnut with Pachmayr recoil pad. Weight: 7.1–7.9 lbs. Sights: Ventilated rib with target sights. Features: Boxlock action, bright blue finish with laser engraved receiver. Automatic ejectors, single trigger with selector switch incorporated in thumb-operated tang safety. Sporting and Trap models have adjustable

comb and buttpad system. Imported from Turkey by GU, Inc.
Price: Skeet $1,470.00
Price: Sporting Clays, Trap $1,800.00

SKB MODEL 690 FIELD
Gauge: 12, 20, 28 ga., .410 bore. Barrel: 26, 28 in. Weight: 6 lbs. 10 oz. –7 lbs. 14 oz. Stock: Grade II Turkish Walnut with pistol grip butt and Schnabel forend with high-gloss poly finish. Features: The 690 Field is built on a box lock receiver, cut with CNC machines from a solid billet of chrome-moly steel. White chrome receiver finish. Chrome lined barrels with 3-in. chambers and lengthened forcing cones and automatic ejectors. Also available as a 28-ga./.410 bore multi-gauge set. Youth model available in 12 and 20 ga. with 26-in. barrels and 13-in. LOP. Includes chokes in F, IM, M, IC, S.
Price: $1,369.00
Price: Multi-Gauge Set $2,169.00
Price: Youth Model $1,369.00

SKB MODEL 720 FIELD
Gauge: 12, 20, 28 ga., .410 bore. Barrel: 26, 28, 30 in. Weight: 6 lbs. 10 oz. –7 lbs. 14 oz. Stock: Select Grade II Turkish Walnut. Features: The 720 Field is built on a boxlock receiver, cut with CNC machines from a solid billet of chrome-moly steel. Brushed white chrome receiver is laser engraved with upland and waterfowl scenes and gold scroll. Chrome-lined barrels with 3-in. chambers (except 28 ga.) and lengthened forcing cones and automatic ejectors. Mechanical trigger. Also available as a 28-ga./.410-bore multi-gauge set with 28-in. barrels. Youth model available in 20 ga. with 26-in. barrels and 13-in. LOP. Includes top-thread internal chokes in F, IM, M, IC, S.
Price: $1,569.00
Price: Multi-Gauge Set $2,369.00
Price: Youth Model $1,569.00

STEVENS MODEL 555
Gauges: 12 ga., 20 ga., 28 ga., .410; 2 3/4 and 3 in. Barrels: 26 in., 28 in. Weights: 5.5–6 lbs. Features: Five screw-in choke tubes with 12 ga., 20 ga., and 28 ga.; .410 has fixed M/IC chokes. Turkish walnut stock and Schnabel fore-end. Single selective mechanical trigger with extractors.
Price: $705.00
Price: Enhanced Model $879.00

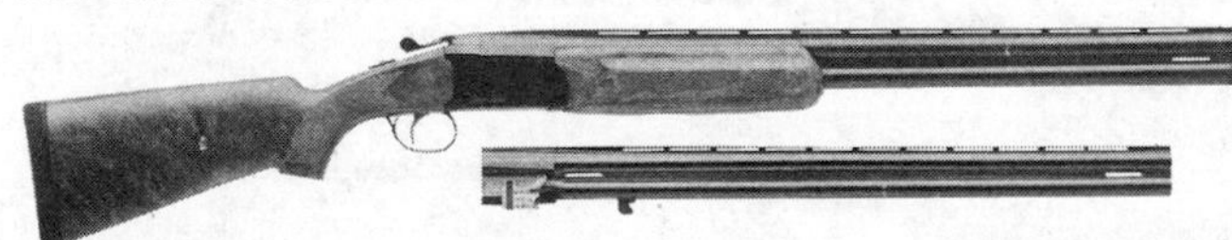

STOEGER CONDOR
Gauge: 12 ga., 20 ga., 2 3/4 in., 3 in.; 16 ga., .410. Barrels: 22 in., 24 in., 26 in., 28 in., 30 in. Weights: 5.5–7.8 lbs. Sights: Brass bead. Features: IC, M, or F screw-in choke tubes with each gun. Oil finished hardwood with pistol grip and fore-end. Auto safety, single trigger, automatic extractors.
Price: .... $449.00–$669.00
Price: Combo with 12 and 20 ga. barrel sets $899.00
Price: Competition $669.00

TRISTAR HUNTER MAG CAMO
Gauge: 12 ga., 3.5 in. Barrels: 26 in., 28 in., 30 in., ventilated rib. Length: 44-48 in. Weight: 7.3-7.9 lbs. Stock: Synthetic, with choice of black or numerous Mossy Oak patterns. Features: The 3.5-inch magnum chambered Hunter Mag O/U expands with the addition of Cerakote/Mossy Oak combination models. Steel mono-block construction, extractors, rubber recoil pad, fiber-optic front sight, single selective trigger, chrome-lined barrel, swivel studs. Includes five Mobil-style choke tubes (SK, IC, M, IM, F).
Price: .... $655.00–$760.00

TRISTAR SETTER
Gauge: 12 ga., 20 ga., 3-in. Barrels: 28 in. (12 ga.), 26 in. (20 ga.) with ventilated rib, three Beretta-style choke tubes. Weights: 6.3–7.2 pounds. Stock: High gloss wood. Single selective trigger, extractors.
Price: .... $535.00–$565.00
Price: Sporting Model .... $824.00–$915.00

TRISTAR TT-15 FIELD
Gauges: 12 ga., 3 in., 20 ga., 3 in., 28 ga., 2.75 in., .410 bore, 3 in. Barrel: 28 in., ventilated rib. Length: 45 in. Weight: 5.7-7.0 lbs. Stock: Turkish walnut. Features: Field hunting O/U model with steel mono-block construction, mid-rib, top-tang barrel selector and safety. Chrome-lined barrel and chamber, engraved silver receiver, single selective trigger, fiber-optic front sight, auto ejectors. Includes five Mobil-style extended, color-coded chokes (SK, IC, M, IM, F).
Price: $855.00

TRISTAR TRINITY
Gauges: 12 ga., 3 in., 16 ga., 2.75 in., 20 ga., 3 in. Barrels: 26 in., 28 in., steel ventilated rib. Weight: 6.3-6.9 lbs. Length: 43.5-45.5 in. Stock: Oil-finished Turkish walnut with checkering. Features: The CNC-machined all-steel receiver Trinity wears 24-karat gold inlay on the silver-finish engraved receiver. Barrels are blued steel. Single selective trigger, red fiber-optic front sight, rubber buttpad, dual extractors. Includes five Beretta Mobil-style chokes (SK, IC, M, IM, F).
Price: $685.00

TRISTAR TRINITY LT
Gauges: 12 ga., 3 in., 20 ga., 3 in., 28 ga., 2.75 in., .410 bore, 3 in. Barrels: 26 in., 28 in, ventilated rib. Weight: 5.3-6.3 lbs. Length: 43.5-45.5 in. Stock: Oil-finished Turkish walnut with checkering. Features: The CNC-machined lightweight aluminum-alloy receiver Trinity LT is engraved and wears a silver finish. Barrels are blued steel. Single selective trigger, red fiber-optic front sight, rubber buttpad, dual extractors. Includes five Beretta Mobil-style chokes (SK, IC, M, IM, F).
Price: .... $685.00–$700.00

WEATHERBY ORION
Gauge: 12, 20 ga. Barrel: 26, 28 in. ventilated rib. Weight: 6.2–7.0 lbs. Stock: Gloss-finished A-Grade Turkish Walnut. Features: The new line of Orion O/U shotguns are built at the new factory in Sheridan, WY. Ambidextrous top tang safety. Low-profile receiver, chrome-lined bores with automatic ejectors. Each ships with three interchangeable chokes (F, M, IC). 20-ga. versions introduced to each line in 2022. Sporting variant uses 30-in. barrels, adjustable comb, ported barrels, and five extended choke tubes.
Price: Orion I $1,049.00
Price: Orion Matte Blue $1,049.00
Price: Orion Sporting $1,149.00

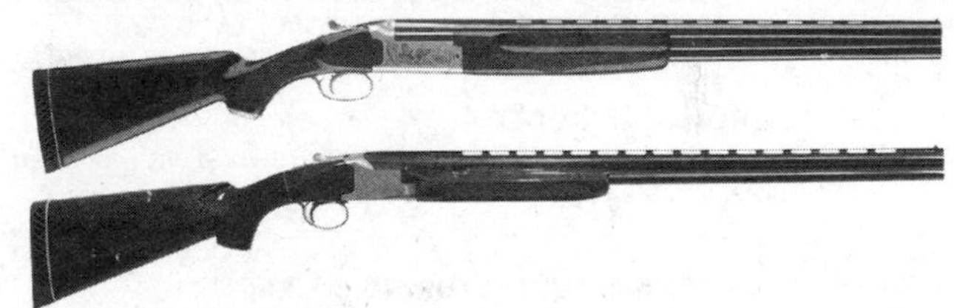

WINCHESTER MODEL 101
Gauge: 12 ga., 2 3/4 in., 3 in. Barrels: 28 in., 30 in., 32 in., ported, Invector Plus choke system. Weights: 7 lbs. 6 oz.–7 lbs. 12. oz. Stock: Checkered high-gloss grade II/III walnut stock, Pachmayr Decelerator sporting pad. Features: Chrome-plated chambers; back-bored barrels; tang barrel selector/safety; Signature extended choke tubes. Model 101 Field comes with solid brass bead front sight, three tubes, engraved receiver. Model 101 Sporting has adjustable trigger, 10mm runway rib, white mid-bead, Tru-Glo front sight, 30 in. and 32 in. barrels. Model 101 Pigeon Grade Trap has 10mm steel runway rib, mid-bead sight, interchangeable fiber-optic front sight, porting and vented side ribs, adjustable trigger shoe, fixed raised comb or adjustable comb, Grade III/IV walnut, 30 in. or 32 in. barrels, molded ABS hard case. Reintroduced 2008. Made in Belgium by FN. Winchester 150th Anniversary Commemorative model has grade IV/V stock, deep relief scrolling on a silver nitride finish receiver.
Price: Field $1,900.00
Price: Sporting $2,380.00
Price: Pigeon Grade Trap $2,520.00
Price: Pigeon Grade Trap w/adj. comb $2,680.00

ARRIETA SIDELOCK DOUBLE
Gauges: 12 ga., 16 ga., 20 ga., 28 ga., .410 bore. Barrels: Length and chokes to customer specs. Weight: To customer specs. Stock: To customer specs. Straight English with checkered butt (standard), or pistol grip. Select European walnut with oil finish. Features: Essentially custom gun with myriad options. H&H pattern hand-detachable sidelocks, selective automatic ejectors, double triggers (hinged front) standard. Some have self-opening action. Finish and engraving to customer specs. Imported from Spain by Quality Arms, Wm. Larking Moore and others.
Price: Model 557 .... **$6,970.00**
Price: Model 570 .... **$7,350.00**
Price: Model 578 .... **$12,200.00**
Price: Model 600 Imperial **$14,125.00**
Price: Model 803 .... **$17,000.00**
Price: Model 931 .... **$40,000.00**

BERETTA 486 PARALELLO
Gauges: 12 ga., 20 ga., 3 in., or 28 ga. 2 3/4 in. Barrels: 26 in., 28 in., 30 in. Weight: 7.1 lbs. Stock: English-style straight grip, splinter fore-end. Select European walnut, checkered, oil finish. Features: Round action, Optima-Choke Tubes. Automatic ejection or mechanical extraction. Firing-pin block safety, manual or automatic, open top-lever safety. Imported from Italy by Beretta USA
Price: **$5,350.00**

CHARLES DALY 500
Gauge: .410 bore, 3 in. Barrel: 28 in. Length: 43.25 in. Weight: 4.4 lbs. Stock: Checkered walnut English-style buttstock. Features: Charles Daly's new pair of baby-bore SxS Model 500 includes two versions, both steel, one with a black engraved receiver and the other black engraved with gold accents. Double triggers, extractors, manual safety, brass front bead. Includes five Mobil-style chokes (SK, IC, M, IM, F).
Price: .... **$725.00–$875.00**

CIMARRON 1878 COACH GUN
Gauge: 12 ga. 3 in. Barrels: 20 in., 26 in. Weights: 8–9 lbs. Stock: Hardwood. External hammers, double triggers. Finish: Blue, Cimarron "USA", Cimarron "Original."
Price: Blue .... **$597.00 (20 in.)–$623.00 (26 in.)**

CIMARRON DOC HOLLIDAY MODEL
Gauge: 12 ga. Barrels: 20 in., cylinder bore. Stock: Hardwood with rounded pistol grip. Features: Double triggers, hammers, false sideplates.
Price: **$1,581.00**

CONNECTICUT SHOTGUN MANUFACTURING CO. RBL
Gauges: 12 ga., 16 ga., 20 ga.. Barrels: 26 in., 28 in., 30 in., 32 in. Weight: NA. Length: NA. Stock: NA. Features: Round-action SxS shotguns made in the USA. Scaled frames, five TruLock choke tubes. Deluxe fancy grade walnut buttstock and fore-end. Quick Change recoil pad in two lengths. Various dimensions and options available depending on gauge.
Price: 12 ga. **$3,795.00**
Price: 16 ga. **$3,795.00**
Price: 20 ga. Special Custom Model **$7,995.00**

CONNECTICUT SHOTGUN MANUFACTURING CO. MODEL 21
Gauges: 12 ga., 16 ga., 20 ga., 28 ga., .410 bore. Features: A faithful re-creation of the famous Winchester Model 21. Many options and upgrades are available. Each frame is machined from specially produced proof steel. The 28 ga. and .410 guns are available on the standard frame or on a newly engineered small frame. These are custom guns and are made to order to the buyer's individual specifications, wood, stock dimensions, barrel lengths, chokes, finishes and engraving.
Price: 12 ga., 16 ga. or 20 ga **$15,000.00**
Price: 28 ga. or .410 .... **$18,000.00**

CZ ALL TERRAIN SERIES
Gauges: 12 ga., 3 in., 20 ga., 3 in. Barrels: 28 in., 30 in. Stock: Walnut, various styles. Features: CZ's new All-Terrain series encompasses five existing shotgun models. The new package includes upgraded wood, OD Green Cerakote finish on all metalwork, as well as a set of rare earth magnets added to the extractor/ejectors of the SxS and O/U models to keep shells from dropping out while handling a dog or working in the blind.
Price: Bobwhite G2 All-Terrain 12 ga. or 20 ga. **$828.00**

CZ BOBWHITE G2 INTERMEDIATE
Built on the Bobwhite G2 but with more compact dimensions for smaller-framed shooters.
The 26-in. barrel is 2 in. shorter than standard. Length of pull is also shorter at 14 in. even. Available only in 20 ga. Built for teens/smaller-stature shooters, as well as handling in tight spaces. All other features remain the same.
Price: **$709.00**

CZ BOBWHITE G2 PROJECT UPLAND
Gauge: 12, 20, 28 ga. Barrel: 28 in. with 8mm flat rib.Weight: 6.25–7.15 lbs. Stock: English-style straight grip with Grade III Turkish Walnut. Features: Project Upland hunting SxS designed with crowd-sourced input. Lovely color casehardened receiver finish, dual extractors, and gloss black chrome barrel finish. Splinter forend. Dual triggers and manual tang safety. Hand-engraving borrowed from Sharp Tail model. Includes five chokes (F, IM, M, IC, C).
Price: 12 & 20 ga. **$1,429.00**
Price: 28 ga. **$1,529.00**

CZ BOWWHITE G2 SOUTHPAW
Built on the Bobwhite G2 but the stock is "cast-on," or built in the opposite direction so it properly fits when brought up to the left shoulder. All other features remain, with the Southpaw using 28-in. barrels and available in 12 or 20 ga.
Price: **$709.00**

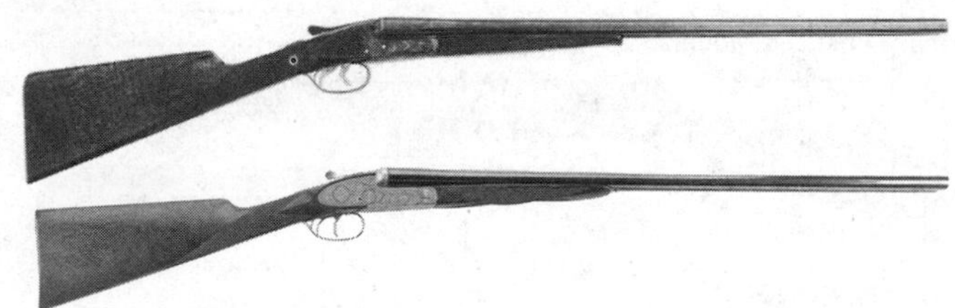

CZ SHARP-TAIL
Gauges: 12 ga., 20 ga., 28 ga., .410. (5 screw-in chokes in 12 and 20 ga. and fixed chokes in IC and Mod in .410). Barrels: 26 in. or 28 in. Weight: 6.5 lbs. Stock: Hand-checkered Turkish walnut with straight English-style grip and single selective trigger.
Price: Sharp-Tail **$1,022.00**
Price: Sharp-Tail Target **$1,298.00**

CZ HAMMER COACH
Gauge: 12 ga., 3 in. Barrel: 20 in. Weight: 6.7 lbs. Features: Following in the tradition of the guns used by the stagecoach guards of the 1880s, this cowboy gun features double triggers, 19th-century color casehardening and fully functional external hammers.
Price: **$922.00**
Price: Classic model w/30-in. bbls. **$963.00**

EMF MODEL 1878 WYATT EARP
Gauge: 12. Barrel: 20 in.. Weight: 8 lbs. Length: 37 in. overall. Stock: Smooth walnut with steel butt place. Sights: Large brass bead. Features: Colt-style exposed hammers rebounding type; blued receiver and

barrels; cylinder bore. Based on design of Colt Model 1878 shotgun. Made in Italy by Pedersoli.

Price: $1,590.00
Price: Hartford Coach Model $1,150.00

EUROPEAN AMERICAN ARMORY (EAA) CHURCHILL 512

Gauges: 12 ga., 3in., 20 ga., 3 in., 28 ga., 3 in., .410 bore. Barrels: 26 in., 28 in. Length: 45-47 in. Stock: Standard Turkish walnut. Features: These Turkish made Akkar side-by-sides have a Nitride-silver receiver, rubber buttpad, checkered stock, single selective gold-plated trigger, front bead, manual safety, chrome-lined barrels, extractors. Ships with three choke tubes.

Price: $1,355.00

FABARM AUTUMN

Gauges: 20 ga. 3 in. Barrels: 28 or 30 in. with textured top rib. Weight: 5 lbs. 9 oz.–6 lbs. 2 oz. Stock: Deluxe Turkish Walnut with hand-oiled matte finish. Available in either English-style straight stock or standard pistol grip style. Left-hand option available by special order. Features: Fine grade side-by-side built in Italy. Color casehardened receiver finish with ornamental scroll engraving. Four lug locking system. Monolithic action design machined from steel forging. Splinter fore-end with English stock or Semi-beavertail with pistol-grip stock. Hand-fit walnut buttplate. Single trigger, tang-mounted safety/selector, auto-ejectors. Ships with Integrale case. Includes five INNER HP long choke tubes.

Price: $4,095.00

FAUSTI DEA SERIES

Gauges: 12 ga., 16 ga., 20 ga., 28 ga., .410. Barrels: 26 in., 28 in., 30 in. Weight: 6–6.8 lbs. Stock: AAA walnut, oil finished. Straight grip, checkered butt, classic fore-end. Features: Automatic ejectors, single non-selective trigger. Duetto model is in 28 ga. with extra set of .410 barrels. Made in Italy and imported by Fausti, USA.

Price: 12 ga. or 20 ga. $5,590.00
Price: 16 ga., 28 ga., .410 .... $6,260.00
Price: Duetto $5,790.00

FOX, A.H.

Gauges: 16 ga., 20 ga., 28 ga., .410. Barrels: Length and chokes to customer specifications. Rust-blued Chromox or Krupp steel. Weight: 5.5–6.75 lbs. Stock: Dimensions to customer specifications. Hand-checkered Turkish Circassian walnut with hand-rubbed oil finish. Straight, semi or full pistol grip; splinter, Schnabel or beavertail fore-end; traditional pad, hard rubber buttplate or skeleton butt. Features: Boxlock action with automatic ejectors; double or Fox single selective trigger. Scalloped, rebated and color case-hardened receiver; hand finished and hand-engraved. Grades differ in engraving, inlays, grade of wood, amount of hand finishing. Introduced 1993. Made in U.S. by Connecticut Shotgun Mfg.

Price: CE Grade $19,500.00
Price: XE Grade $22,000.00
Price: DE Grade $25,000.00
Price: FE Grade $30,000.00
Price: 28 ga./.410 CE Grade $21,500.00
Price: 28 ga./.410 XE Grade $24,000.00
Price: 28 ga./.410 DE Grade $27,000.00
Price: 28 ga./.410 FE Grade $32,000.00

MERKEL MODEL 147SL

H&H style sidelock action with cocking indicators, ejectors. Silver-grayed receiver and sideplates have arabesque engraving, fine hunting scene engraving. Limited edition. Imported from Germany by Merkel USA.

Price: Model 147SL $13,255.00

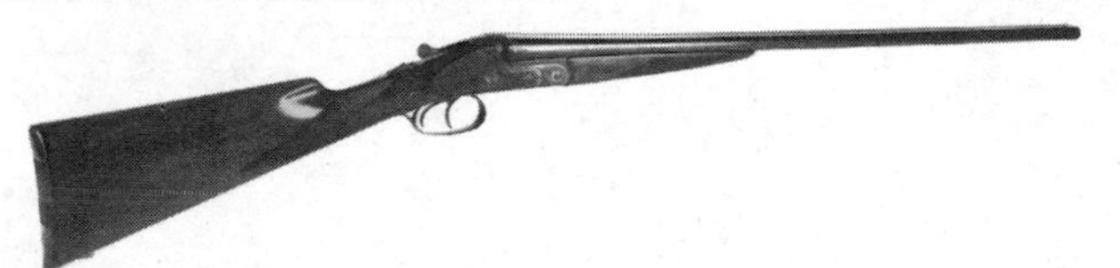

MERKEL MODEL 280EL, 360EL

Similar to Model 47E except smaller frame. Greener crossbolt with double under-barrel locking lugs, fine engraved hunting scenes on silver-grayed receiver, luxury-grade wood, Anson and Deeley boxlock action. H&H ejectors, single-selective or double triggers. Introduced 2000. Imported from Germany by Merkel USA.

Price: Model 280EL (28 ga., 28 in. barrel, Imp. Cyl. and Mod. chokes) $8,870.00
Price: Model 360EL (.410, 28 in. barrel, Mod. and Full chokes) $8,870.00

MERKEL MODEL 280SL AND 360SL

Similar to Model 280EL and 360EL except has sidelock action, double triggers, English-style arabesque engraving. Introduced 2000. Imported from Germany by Merkel USA.

Price: Model 280SL (28 ga., 28 in. barrel, Imp. Cyl. and Mod. chokes) $13,255.00
Price: Model 360SL (.410, 28 in. barrel, Mod. and Full chokes) $13,255.00

MERKEL MODEL 1620

Gauge: 16 ga. Features: Greener crossbolt with double under-barrel locking lugs, scroll-engraved casehardened receiver, Anson and Deeley boxlock action, Holland & Holland ejectors, English-style stock, single selective or double triggers, or pistol grip stock with single selective trigger. Imported from Germany by Merkel USA.

Price: Model 1620EL $8,870.00
Price: Model 1620EL Combo; 16- and 20-ga. two-barrel set $13,255.00

MERKEL MODEL 40E

Gauges: 12 ga., 20 ga. Barrels: 28 in. (12 ga.), 26.75 in. (20 ga.). Weight: 6.2 lbs. Features: Anson & Deeley locks, Greener-style crossbolt, automatic ejectors, choice of double or single trigger, blue finish, checkered walnut stock with cheekpiece.

Price: $4,795.00

PIOTTI KING NO. 1

Gauges: 12 ga., 16 ga., 20 ga., 28 ga., .410. Barrels: 25–30 in. (12 ga.), 25–28 in. (16 ga., 20 ga., 28 ga., .410). To customer specs. Chokes as specified. Weight: 6.5–8 lbs. (12 ga. to customer specs.). Stock: Dimensions to customer specs. Finely figured walnut; straight grip with checkered butt with classic splinter fore-end and hand-rubbed oil finish standard. Pistol grip, beavertail fore-end. Features: Holland & Holland pattern sidelock action, automatic ejectors. Double trigger; non-selective single trigger optional. Coin finish standard; color case-hardened optional. Top rib; level, file-cut; concave, ventilated optional. Very fine, full coverage scroll engraving with small floral bouquets. Imported from Italy by Wm. Larkin Moore.

Price: $42,800.00

PIOTTI LUNIK SIDE-BY-SIDE SHOTGUN

Similar to the Piotti King No. 1 in overall quality. Has Renaissance-style large scroll engraving in relief. Best quality Holland & Holland-pattern sidelock ejector double with chopper lump (demi-bloc) barrels. Other mechanical specifications remain the same. Imported from Italy by Wm. Larkin Moore.

Price: $46,000.00

PIOTTI PIUMA

Gauges: 12 ga., 16 ga., 20 ga., 28 ga., .410. Barrels: 25–30 in. (12 ga.), 25–28 in. (16 ga., 20 ga., 28 ga., .410). Weights: 5.5–6.25 lbs. (20 ga.). Stock: Dimensions to customer specs. Straight grip stock with walnut checkered butt, classic splinter fore-end, hand-rubbed oil finish are standard; pistol grip, beavertail fore-end, satin luster finish optional. Features: Anson & Deeley boxlock ejector double with chopper lump barrels. Level, file-cut rib, light scroll and rosette engraving, scalloped frame. Double triggers; single non-selective optional. Coin finish standard, color case-hardened optional. Imported from Italy by Wm. Larkin Moore.

Price: $25,000.00

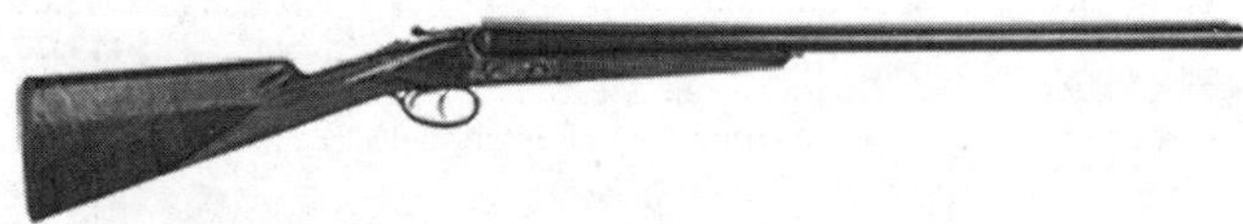

SAVAGE FOX A-GRADE

Gauge: 12 or 20. Barrels: 26 or 28 in. with solid rib and IC, M, and F choke tubes. Features: Straight-grip American walnut stock with splinter fore-end, oil finish and cut checkering. Anson & Deeley-style boxlock action, Holland & Holland-style ejectors, double triggers and brass bead sight. A re-creation of the famous Fox double gun, presented by Savage and made at the Connecticut Shotgun Manufacturing Co. plant.

Price: $5,375.00

SKB 200 SERIES

Prices given are believed to be accurate at time of publication however, many factors affect retail pricing so exact prices are not possible.

Gauges: 12 ga., 20 ga., .410, 3 in.; 28 ga., 2 3/4 in. Barrels: 26 in., 28 in. Five choke tubes provided (F, IM, M, IC, SK). Stock: Hand checkered and oil finished Turkish walnut. Prince of Wales grip and beavertail fore-end. Weight: 6–7 lbs. Sights: Brass bead. Features: Boxlock with platform lump barrel design. Polished bright blue finish with charcoal color case hardening on receiver. Manual safety, automatic ejectors, single selective trigger. 200 HR target model has high ventilated rib, full pistol grip. 250 model has decorative color casehardened sideplates. Imported from Turkey by GU, Inc.

Price: 12 ga., 20 ga. **$2,100.00**
Price: 28 ga., .410 .... **$2,250.00**
Price: 200 28 ga./.410 Combo **$3,300.00**
Price: 200 HR 12 ga., 20 ga. **$2,500.00**
Price: 200 HR 28 ga., .410 .... **$2,625.00**
Price: 200 HR 28 ga./.410 combo **$3,600.00**
Price: 250 12 ga., 20 ga. **$2,600.00**
Price: 250 28 ga., .410 .... **$2,725.00**
Price: 250 28 ga./.410 Combo **$3,700.00**

SKB 7000SL SIDELOCK

Gauges: 12 ga., 20 ga. Barrels: 28 in., 30 in. Five choke tubes provided (F, IM, M, IC, SK). Stock: Premium Turkish walnut with hand-rubbed oil finish, fine-line hand checkering, Prince of Wales grip and beavertail fore-end. Weights: 6–7 lbs. Sights: Brass bead. Features: Sidelock design with Holland & Holland style seven-pin removable locks with safety sears. Bison Bone Charcoal casehardening, hand engraved sculpted sidelock receiver. Manual safety, automatic ejectors, single selective trigger. Available by special order only. Imported from Turkey by GU, Inc.

Price: **$6,500.00**

STOEGER UPLANDER

Gauges: 12 ga., 20 ga., .410, 3 in.; 28 ga., 2 3/4. Barrels: 22 in., 24 in., 26 in., 28 in. Weights: 6.5–7.3 lbs. Sights: Brass bead. Features: Double trigger, IC & M choke tubes included with gun. Other choke tubes available. Tang auto safety, extractors, black plastic buttplate. Imported by Benelli USA.

Price: Standard **$449.00**
Price: Supreme (single trigger, AA-grade wood) **$549.00**
Price: Longfowler (12 ga., 30-in. bbl.) **$449.00**
Price: Home Defense (20 or 12 ga., 20-in. bbl., tactical sights) **$499.00**
Price: Double Defense (20 ga.) fiber-optic sight, accessory rail **$499.00**

STOEGER COACH GUN

Gauges: 12 ga., 20 ga., 2 3/4 in., 3 in., .410 bore, Barrel: 20 in. Weight: 6.5 lbs. Stock: Brown hardwood, classic beavertail fore-end. Sights: Brass bead. Features: Double or single trigger, IC & M choke tubes included, others available. Tang auto safety, extractors, black plastic buttplate. Imported by Benelli USA.

Price: **$549.00**
Price: **$449.00**
Price: .410 bore, 3-inch, 20-in. barrel **$449.00**
Price: Black-finished hardwood/polished-nickel model **$549.00**

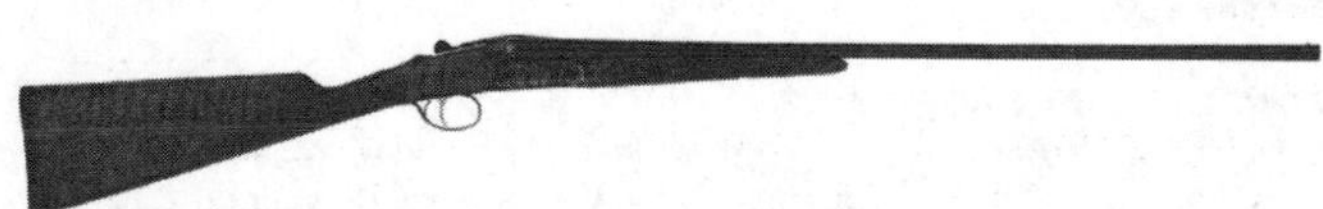

TRISTAR BRISTOL

Gauges: 12 ga. 3 in., 20 ga. 3 in., 28 ga. 2.75 in., .410 bore 3 in. Barrels: 28 in. Weight: 5.08–6.74 lbs. Stock: Select Turkish Walnut with oil finish, English style. Features: Side-by-side double available in four gauges, each built on a true steel frame. Laser-engraved detail. Features an English-style straight stock paired with case colored receiver. Dual-purpose tang safety/barrel selector. Auto-ejectors, brass front sight, single selective trigger. Chrome-lined chamber and barrel. Includes five Beretta-style choke tubes (SK, IC, M, IM, F).

Price: .... **$1,065.00–$1,100.00**

TRISTAR BRISTOL

Gauge: 12 ga. 3 in., 16 ga., 20 ga. 3 in., 28 ga. 2.75 in., .410 bore 3 in. Barrels: 28 in. Weight: 5.08–6.74 lbs. Stock: Select Turkish Walnut with oil finish, English style. Features: Side-by-side double available in four gauges, each built on a true steel frame. Laser engraved detail. Features an English-style straight stock paired with case colored receiver. Dual purpose tang safety/barrel selector. Auto-ejectors, brass front sight, single selective trigger. Chrome-lined chamber and barrel. Includes five Beretta-style choke tubes (SK, IC, M, IM, F).

Price: 12 and 20 ga. **$1,160.00**
Price: 16, 28 ga., and .410 bore **$1,190.00**

TRISTAR BRISTOL SILVER

Gauge: 12 ga. 3 in., 16 ga., 20 ga. 3 in., 28 ga. 2.75 in., .410 bore 3 in. Barrels: 28 in. Weight: 5.08–6.74 lbs. Stock: Select Turkish Walnut with oil finish, pistol grip style. Features: Side-by-side double available in four gauges, each built on a true steel frame. Laser engraved detail. Features a nickel-finished receiver with 24-Karat gold inlay on the bottom of the receiver, as well as semi-pistol grip-style stock. Dual-purpose tang safety/barrel selector. Auto-ejectors, brass front sight, single selective trigger. Chrome-lined chamber and barrel. Includes five Beretta-style choke tubes (SK, IC, M, IM, F).

Price: 12 and 20 ga. **$1,100.00**
Price: 16, 28 ga., and .410 bore **$1,130.00**

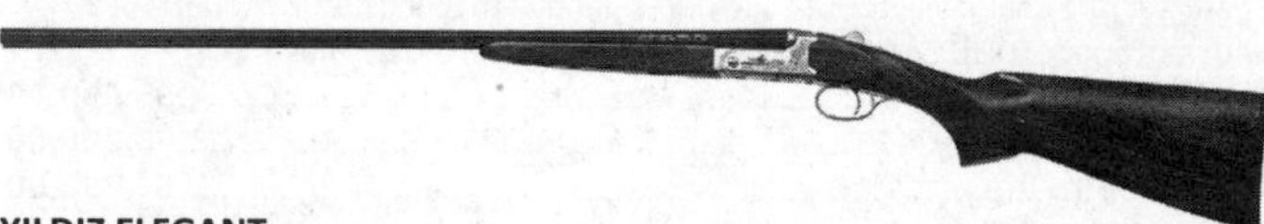

YILDIZ ELEGANT

Gauge: .410 bore, 3 in. Barrels: 26 in., 28 in., 30 in., with 7mm or 8mm rib. Weight: 4.8-6.0 lbs. Stock: Oil-finish selected walnut from standard through Grades 3 and 5, some pistol grip and others straight English-style. Features: Built of 4140 Steel, with varying degrees of receiver engraving. Manual or automatic safety, extractors or ejectors, depending on model. Single selective trigger, front bead, full black rubber recoil pad. Models include: A1, A3, A4, A5, and Special Lux. Includes five Mobil chokes. Manufactured in Turkey and imported/sold through Academy.

Price: **$479.00**

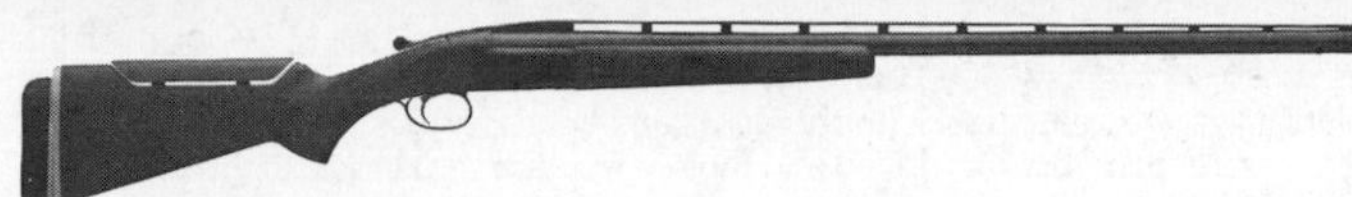

BROWNING BT-99 TRAP

Gauge: 12 ga. Barrels: 30 in., 32 in., 34 in. Stock: Walnut; standard or adjustable. Weights: 7 lbs. 11 oz.–9 lbs. Features: Back-bored single barrel; interchangeable chokes; beavertail forearm; extractor only; high rib.

Price: BT-99 w/conventional comb, 32- or 34-in. barrel....................**$1,470.00**
Price: BT-99 w/adjustable comb, 32- or 34-in. barrel....................**$1,840.00**
Price: BT-99 Max High Grade w/adjustable comb, 32- or 34-in. barrel....................**$5,340.00**
Price: Micro Adjustable LOP Model....................**$1,669.00**

CHARLES DALY 101

Gauges: 12 ga., 3 in., 20 ga., 3in., .410 bore. Barrels: 26 in., 28 in. Weight: 5.0-8.1 lbs. Length: 41.75-43.75 in. Stock: Choice of either checkered walnut or black synthetic stocks. Features: These updated break-action single shots have become more affordable than ever. Though built of steel, they're still quite light. Brass front bead, manual safety, single trigger, extractor, rubber butt pad. Includes a Modified Beretta/Benelli Mobil choke tube.

Price: ....**$119.00-$129.00**

HENRY .410 LEVER-ACTION SHOTGUN

Gauge: .410, 2 1/2 in. Capacity: 5. Barrels: 20 or 24 in. with either no choke (20 in.) or full choke (24 in.). Stock: American walnut. Sights: Gold bead front only. Finish: Blued. Introduced in 2017. Features: Design is based on the Henry .45-70 rifle.

Price: 20-in. bbl....................**$893.00**
Price: 24-in. bbl....................**$947.00**

HENRY SINGLE-SHOT SHOTGUN

Gauges: 12 ga., 20 ga. or .410 bore, 3 1/2 in. (12 ga.), 3 in. (20 ga. and 410). Barrels: 26 or 28 in. with either modified choke tube (12 ga., 20 ga., compatible with Rem-Choke tubes) or fixed full choke (.410). Stock: American walnut, straight or pistol grip. Sights: Gold bead front only. Weight: 6.33 lbs. Finish: Blued or brass receiver. Features: Break-open single-shot design. Introduced in 2017.

Price: **$448.00**
Price: Brass receiver, straight grip....................**$576.00**

HENRY SINGLE SHOT SLUG

Gauges: 12 ga. 3 in. Barrel: 24-in. round blued steel. Weight: 6.88 lbs. Length: 39.5 in. Stock: American Walnut. Features: The company's first slug-hunting shotgun, with a fully-rifled 1:35 twist barrel. This single shot is finished in traditional blued steel and checkered walnut with a black rubber recoil pad. Buttstock has a 14-inch LOP. Sling studs. Rebounding hammer safety. Fiber optic sights. Drilled and tapped for a Weaver 82 base.

Price: **$560.00**

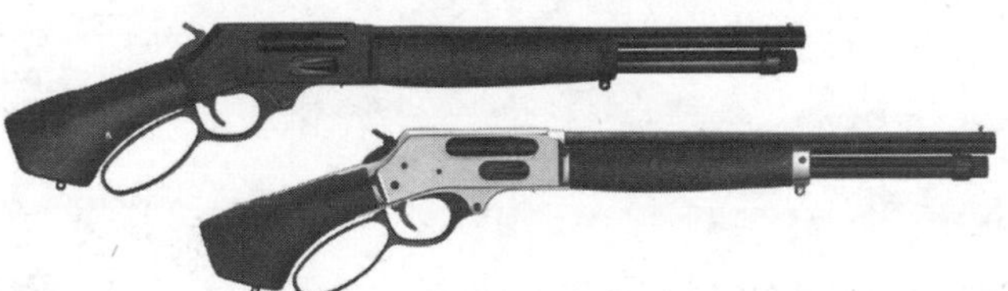

HENRY AXE

Gauge: .410 bore 2.5 in. Barrel: 15.14 in. smoothbore, round blued steel. Weight: 5.75 lbs. Length: 26.4 in. Stock: American Walnut with unique axe-handle-style rear grip. Features: Henry's Axe is most closely related to the handgun-chambered Mare's Leg platform, but this time with a slightly different design and firing .410 shotshells. Both the standard Steel and Brass Axe have a 5-round capacity with the addition of a loading gate. Short barrel takes interchangeable Invector-style chokes and ships with a full tube. Brass front bead, swivel studs, transfer bar safety. Drilled and tapped for optics mounting.

Price: **$1,049.00**
Price: Brass Axe....................**$1,132.00**

HENRY SINGLE SHOT TURKEY

Gauges: 12 ga. 3.5 in. Barrel: 24-in. round. Weight: 6.78 lbs. Length: 39.5 in. Stock: American Walnut covered in Mossy Oak Obsession camo. Features: The company's first dedicated turkey-hunting shotgun wears full-coverage Mossy Oak Obsession, the official camouflage pattern of the National Wild Turkey Federation. Fiber-optic front and rear sights. Drilled and tapped for a Weaver 82 base. Black solid rubber recoil pad creates a 14-inch LOP. Swivel studs. Rebounding hammer safety. Includes an extended Turkey choke.

Price: **$687.00**

KEYSTONE SPORTING ARMS 4100 My First Shotgun

Gauges: .410 bore 3 in. Barrel: 18.5 in. Length: 32 in. Weight: 4.2 lbs. Stock: Turkish Walnut. Features: Marketed as a Crickett "My First Shotgun," this single-shot baby bore uses a folding design. Recoil reducing chamber and soft rubber recoil pad. Aluminum receiver with matte blue metalwork. Blade-style front sight. Checkered stock. Length of pull built for small-frame shooters at 11 inches. Fixed modified choke.

Price: **$179.00**

KRIEGHOFF K-80 SINGLE BARREL TRAP GUN

Gauge: 12 ga., 2 3/4 in. Barrel: 32 in., 34 in. Unsingle. Fixed Full or choke tubes. Weight: About 8.75 lbs. Stock: Four stock dimensions or adjustable stock available. All hand-checkered European walnut. Features: Satin nickel finish. Selective mechanical trigger adjustable for finger position. Tapered step vent rib. Adjustable point of impact.

Price: Standard Grade Full Unsingle....................**$12,995.00**

KRIEGHOFF KX-6 SPECIAL TRAP GUN

Gauge: 12 ga., 2 3/4 in. Barrel: 32 in., 34 in.; choke tubes. Weight: About 8.5 lbs. Stock: Factory adjustable stock. European walnut. Features: Ventilated tapered step rib. Adjustable position trigger, optional release trigger. Fully adjustable rib. Satin gray electroless nickel receiver. Fitted aluminum case. Imported from Germany by Krieghoff International, Inc.

Price: **$5,995.00**

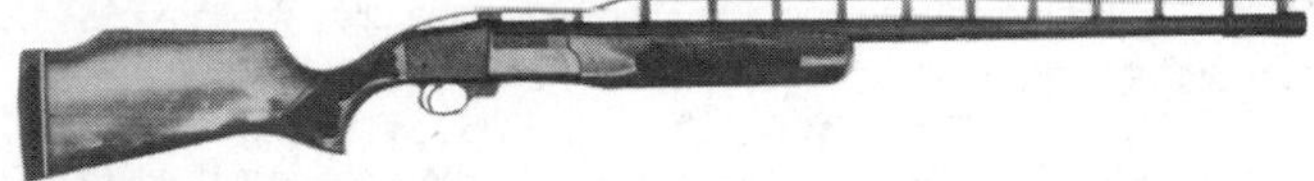

LJUTIC MONO GUN SINGLE BARREL

Gauge: 12 ga. Barrel: 34 in., choked to customer specs; hollow-milled rib, 35.5-in. sight plane. Weight: Approx. 9 lbs. Stock: To customer specs. Oil finish, hand checkered. Features: Custom gun. Pull or release trigger; removable trigger guard contains trigger and hammer mechanism; Ljutic pushbutton opener on front of trigger guard. From Ljutic Industries.

Price: Std., med. or Olympic rib, custom bbls., fixed choke. **$7,495.00**
Price: Stainless steel mono gun....................**$8,495.00**

LJUTIC LTX PRO 3 DELUXE MONO GUN

Deluxe, lightweight version of the Mono gun with high-quality wood, upgrade checkering, special rib height, screw-in chokes, ported and cased.

Price: **$8,995.00**
Price: Stainless steel model....................**$9,995.00**

ROSSI CIRCUIT JUDGE

Revolving shotgun chambered in .410 (2 1/2- or 3-in./.45 Colt. Based on Taurus Judge handgun. Features include 18.5-in. barrel; fiber-optic front sight; 5-round cylinder; hardwood Monte Carlo stock.

Price: **$689.00**

ROSSI TUFFY SINGLE SHOT 410 TURKEY

Gauge: .410 bore 3 in. Barrel: 26 in. Length: 41 in. Weight: 58.80 oz. Stock: Olive drab green polymer thumbhole-style with integral buttstock shell holders. Features: Part of Rossi's single-shot, break-action Tuffy family, the new 410 Turkey has an extended barrel length and gobbler-specific choke. Polymer receiver with steel frame structure. Matte black finish metalwork.

Bead front sight. Picatinny top rail for easy optics mounting. Sling swivels. Black rubber buttpad. Transfer bar safety. Extended Extra Full Turkey choke.
Price: Standard Grade Full Unsingle **$220.00**

SAVAGE 212/220

Gauges: 12 ga., 3 in., 20 ga., 3 in. Barrel: 22 in., carbon steel. Weight: 7.34-7.75 lbs. Length: 43 in. Stock: Synthetic AccuFit stock with included LOP and comb inserts. Thumbhole model uses gray wood laminate. Features: The bolt-action Savage models 212 and 220, so named for their chamberings, are available in Slug, Slug Camo, Thumbhole, Left-Handed and Turkey models. Choice of button-rifled slug barrels or smoothbore. Detachable box magazine, thread-in barrel headspacing. User adjustable AccuTrigger and AccuStock internal chassis. Oversized bolt handle, Picatinny optics rail, sling studs, rubber buttpad.
Price: .... **$629.00–$799.00**
Price: 212 Turkey w/extended X-Full choke.. **$779.00**
Price: 220 Turkey w/extended X-Full choke.. **$695.00**

STEVENS 301 TURKEY XP

Gauges: 20 ga., 3 in., .410 bore, 3 in. Barrel: 26 in., black matte. Weight: 5.07 lbs. Length: 41.5 in. Stock: Camouflage synthetic stock and fore-end with either Mossy Oak Obsession or Mossy Oak Bottomland pattern. Features: Single-shot break action with removable one-piece rail. XP variant includes mounted and bore-sighted 1x30 red-dot optic. Barrel optimized for Federal Premium TSS Heavyweight turkey loads. Swivel studs, front bead, manual hammer block safety, rubber recoil pad. Includes Winchoke pattern Extra Full turkey choke.
Price: **$239.00**

STEVENS 301 TURKEY THUMBHOLE

Gauges: .410 bore 3 in. Barrel: 26 in. chrome alloy steel black matte. Weight: 5.07 lbs. Length: 41.5 in. Stock: Olive drab green matte synthetic thumbhole style. Features: Continuation of the 301 single-shot break-action line with a removeable one-piece rail and gobbler-specific features. Ambidextrous cheek riser. Barrel optimized for Federal Premium Heavyweight TSS turkey loads. Swivel studs, front bead sight, manual hammer block safety, rubber recoil pad. Includes Win-Choke pattern Extra Full turkey choke.
Price: **$229.00**

STEVENS 555 TRAP

Gauges: 12 ga., 3 in., 20 ga., 3 in. Barrel: 30 in., raised ventilated rib. Weight: 6.6-6.8 lbs. Length: 47.5 in. Stock: Turkish walnut stock and fore-end with adjustable comb and oil finish. Features: Lightweight silver aluminum receiver scaled to gauge with steel breech reinforcement. Top single barrel with shell extractor. Manual tang safety, front bead, chrome-lined barrel, semi-gloss metalwork finish. Includes three chokes.
Price: **$689.00**

STEVENS 555 TRAP COMPACT

Gauges: 12 ga., 3 in., 20 ga., 3 in. Barrel: 26 in., raised ventilated rib. Weight: 7.3-7.5 lbs. Length: 42.5 in. Stock: Turkish walnut stock and fore-end with adjustable comb and oil finish. Features: Lightweight silver aluminum receiver scaled to gauge with steel breech reinforcement. Top single barrel with shell extractor. Manual tang safety, front bead, chrome-lined barrel, semi-gloss metalwork finish. Compact 13.5 in. length of pull. Includes three chokes.
Price: **$689.00**

TAR-HUNT RSG-12 PROFESSIONAL RIFLED SLUG GUN

Gauge: 12 ga., 2 3/4 in., 3 in., Capacity: 1-round magazine. Barrel: 23 in., fully rifled with muzzle brake. Weight: 7.75 lbs. Length: 41.5 in. overall. Stock: Matte black McMillan fiberglass with Pachmayr Decelerator pad. Sights: None furnished; comes with Leupold windage or Weaver bases. Features: Uses rifle-style action with two locking lugs; two-position safety; Shaw barrel; single-stage trigger; muzzle brake. Many options available. All models have area-controlled feed action. Introduced 1991. Made in U.S. by Tar-Hunt Custom Rifles, Inc.
Price: 12 ga. Professional model.. **$3,495.00**
Price: Left-hand model.. **$3,625.00**

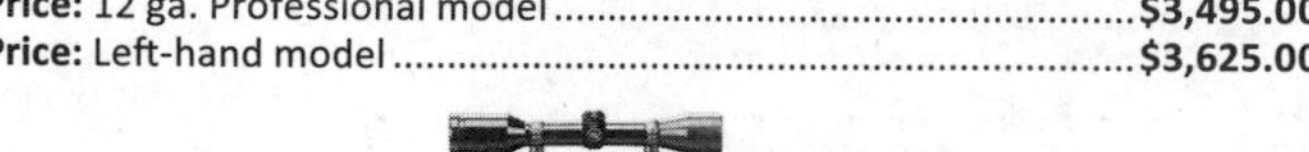

TAR-HUNT RSG-20 MOUNTAINEER SLUG GUN

Similar to the RSG-12 Professional except chambered for 20 ga. (2 3/4 in. and 3 in. shells); 23 in. Shaw rifled barrel, with muzzle brake; two-lug bolt; one-shot blind magazine; matte black finish; McMillan fiberglass stock with Pachmayr Decelerator pad; receiver drilled and tapped for Rem. 700 bases. Right- or left-hand versions. Weighs 6.5 lbs. Introduced 1997. Made in USA by Tar-Hunt Custom Rifles, Inc.
Price: **$3,495.00**

HENRY SIDE GATE LEVER ACTION 410 MODEL H018G-410R

Gauge: .410 bore 2.5in. Barrel: 19.75 in. smoothbore, round blued steel. Weight: 7.09 lbs. Length: 38.1 in. Stock: American Walnut with checkering. Features: This model launches as a blued steel companion to Henry's polished brass version last year. This is the more compact of the pair of lever action 410's. Has Henry's new side-loading gate in addition to the tubular loading port and magazine capacity of six rounds. Adjustable semi-buckhorn rear sight with diamond insert and brass bead front post sight. Black ventilated rubber recoil pad, transfer bar safety, sling swivel studs. Fixed cylinder bore choke.
Price: **$969.00**

HENRY SIDE GATE LEVER ACTION 410 Model H018G-410

Gauges: .410 bore, 2.5 in. Barrel: 24 in. smoothbore, round blued steel. Weight: 7.54 lbs. Length: 42.75 in. Stock: American Walnut with checkering. Features: The new-for-2021 model is blued steel instead of polished brass. Has Henry's side loading gate in addition to the tubular loading port and magazine capacity of six rounds. Brass bead front sight. Black ventilated rubber recoil pad, sling swivel studs. Transfer bar safety. LOP of 14-inches. Drilled and tapped for a Weaver 63B optics base. Threaded for Invector-style chokes with a Full choke supplied.
Price: **$1,012.00**

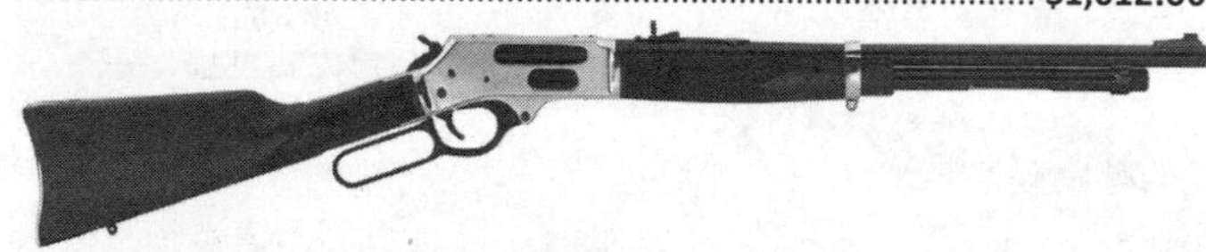

HENRY SIDE GATE LEVER ACTION 410 Model H024-410

Gauge: .410 bore 2.5 in. Barrel: 19.8 in. smoothbore, round blued steel. Weight: 7.09 lbs. Length: 38.1 in. Stock: American walnut with intricate floral and Henry logo checkering appointments. Features: Polished brass receiver with Henry's new side loading gate in addition to the tubular loading port. Magazine capacity of six rounds. Fully adjustable semi-buckhorn rear sight with diamond insert and ramp front with 0.62-inch ivory bead. Polished brass buttplate, transfer bar safety, sling swivel studs. Fixed cylinder bore choke.
Price: **$1,100.00**

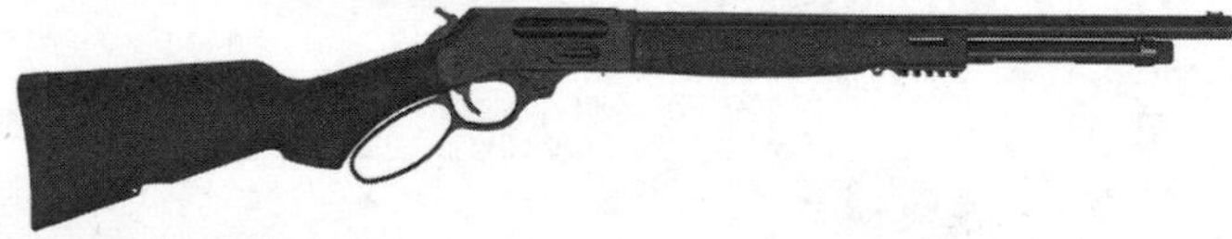

HENRY X-MODEL 410

Gauges: .410 bore 2.5 in. Barrel: 19.8 in. smoothbore, round blued steel. Weight: 7.5 lbs. Length: 38.6 in. Stock: Black synthetic with textured panels. Features: Henry's first blacked-out model with matte blued steel receiver. Side loading gate in addition to tubular port with magazine capacity of 6+1 rounds. Black solid rubber recoil pad. Green fiber-optic front sight, transfer bar safety, swivel studs, large loop lever. Tactical features include lower Picatinny rail and M-LOK attachment points at fore-end. Drilled and tapped for a Weaver 63B optics mount. Includes Invector choke.
Price: **$1,000.00**

AMERICAN TACTICAL BULLDOG
Gauge: 12 ga. 3 in., 20 ga. 3 in. Barrel: 16 and 18.5 in. with ported shroud. Length: 23.5–26 in. Weight: 4.5 lbs. Stock: Black synthetic with fixed bullpup style with adjustable cheek riser. Features: Gas-operated tactical bullpup shotgun with AR-style charging handle, adjustable cheek rest, and both Picatinny and M-LOK rails. Housing for spare five-round magazine. Extra magazine can also be attached to the bottom rail and used as a fore grip. Includes quick acquisition flip-up sights and three choke tubes.
Price: **$359.00**

ARMSCOR VRF-14
Gauge: 12 ga. Barrel: 14 in. Length: 26 in. Weight: 6.6 lbs. Stock: Black polymer with full-top forend and sling adapter rear. Features: Semi-automatic short-barreled firearm in 12-ga. Pistol-grip style designed to be fired from the hip. Built with a 7075 aluminum receiver, Bufferbolt system, and full-length top Picatinny rail. Flip-up front and rear sights. Five-round magazine included, but also compatible with VR-Series 9 and 19-round mags.
Price: **$599.00**

BENELLI M2 TACTICAL
Gauge: 12 ga., 2 3/4 in., 3 in. Capacity: 5-round magazine. Barrel: 18.5 in. IC, M, F choke tubes. Weight: 6.7 lbs. Length: 39.75 in. overall. Stock: Black polymer. Standard or pistol grip. Sights: Rifle type ghost ring system, tritium night sights optional. Features: Semi-auto inertia recoil action. Cross-bolt safety; bolt release button; matte-finish metal. Introduced 1993. Imported from Italy by Benelli USA.
Price: .... **$1,239.00–$1,359.00**

BENELLI M3 TACTICAL
Gauge: 12 ga., 3 in. Barrel: 20 in. Stock: Black synthetic w/pistol grip. Sights: Ghost ring rear, ramp front. Convertible dual-action operation (semi-auto or pump).
Price: **$1,599.00**

BENELLI M4 TACTICAL
Gauge: 12 ga., 3 in. Barrel: 18.5 in. Weight: 7.8 lbs. Length: 40 in. overall. Stock: Synthetic. Sights: Ghost Ring rear, fixed blade front. Features: Auto-regulating gas-operated (ARGO) action, choke tube, Picatinny rail, standard and collapsible stocks available, optional LE tactical gun case. Introduced 2006.
Price: **$1,999.00**
Price: M4 H20 Cerakote Finish **$2,269.00**

BENELLI NOVA TACTICAL
Gauge: 12 ga., 3 in. Barrel: 18.5 in. Stock: Black synthetic standard or pistol grip. Sights: Ghost ring rear, ramp front. Pump action.
Price: **$439.00**

BENELLI VINCI TACTICAL
Gauge: 12 ga., 3 in. Barrel: 18.5 in. Semi-auto operation. Stock: Black synthetic. Sights: Ghost ring rear, ramp front.
Price: **$1,349.00**
Price: ComforTech stock **$1,469.00**

CHARLES DALY AR 410 UPPER
Gauge: .410 bore 2.5 in. Barrel: 19 in. Length: 26.75 in. Weight: 4.9 lbs. Stock: Upper only with quad Picatinny rail fore-end. Features: Charles Daly enters the AR market with a .410 bore shotgun upper. Built of black anodized aluminum. Auto-ejection, gas-operated system. Windage-adjustable rear sight and elevation adjustable rear flip-up sights. Ships with a five-round magazine but compatible with 10 and 15 rounders. This upper must be used with a Mil-Spec lower and carbine-length buffer tube.
Price: **$415.00**

GARAYSAR FEAR 116
Gauge: 12 ga. 3 in. Barrel: 20 in. 4140 steel. Length: 39 in. Weight: 8.8 lbs. Stock: Synthetic available in a variety of colors and finishes. Features: Gas-operated semi-automatic with an aluminum receiver. Adjustable cheek rest. Front and rear flip-up sights. Ships with two five-round magazines, but also accepts 10-round mags. Includes five choke tubes (F, IM, M, IC, C), choke tube case, and hard case.
Price: **$589.00**

GARAYSAR FEAR BULLPUP
Gauge: 12 ga. 3 in. Barrel: 18.5 in. Length: 28.34 in. Stock: Black synthetic, with both green and FDE to follow. Features: Gas-regulated, semi-automatic bullpup-style shotgun. Built on an aluminum receiver with 4140 steel barrel. Bullpup family available in multiple model variants including 104, 105, 106, and 109, each with different options on a similar build. Ships with two five-round magazines, but also accepts 10- and 15-round mags. Adjustable cheek riser. Multiple choke options dependent on model; some fixed, others interchangeable.
Price: **$489.00**

IVER JOHNSON STRYKER-12
Gauge: 12 ga., 3 in. Barrel: 20 in., smoothbore with muzzle brake. Length: 43 in. Stock: Black synthetic two-piece, pistol-grip stock. Features: This AR15-style semi-auto shotgun uses a standard AR15 bolt and mag release. A2-style detachable carry handle with adjustable sight, fiber-optic front sight. Light rails on both sides and bottom of fore-end. Push button releases the stock and leaves the pistol grip for a modular platform. Cross-bolt safety, thick rubber buttpad. Ships with two MKA 1919 5-round box magazines.
Price: **$495.00**

IWI TAVOR TS-12
Gauge: 12 ga. 3 in. Barrel: 18.5 in. Length: 28.34 in. Weight: 8.9 lbs. Stock: Synthetic fixed bullpup style, with Black, OD green and FDE color options. Features: Gas-driven semi-automatic bullpup design that feeds from one of three magazine tubes. Each tube holds four 3-in. shells or five 2.75-in. rounds. Max capacity 15 rounds. Includes four sling attachment points, M-LOK rails, and extended Picatinny top rail. Crossbolt safety. Bullhead bolt system. Uses Benelli/Beretta-style Mobil choke tubes.
Price: **$1,399.00**

KALASHNIKOV KOMP12
Gauge: 12 ga. 3 in. Barrel: 18.25 in. with external threading. Weight: 17 lbs. Stock: Synthetic skeleton-style, collapsible. Features: The Kalashnikov USA x Dissident Arms KOMP12 is an American-made semi-automatic based on the Russian Saiga series. Adjustable gas system. Extended charging

Prices given are believed to be accurate at time of publication however, many factors affect retail pricing so exact prices are not possible.

handle, aluminum handguard rail, enhanced safety lever. Flared magazine well, tuned trigger. Top Picatinny rail for optics. Threaded flash suppressor. Magpul AK pistol grip. Zinc phosphate parkerized undercoat with Dissident Arms Black, Red, and Sniper Grey color scheme. Ships with Dissident SGM 12-round magazine.

Price: **$1,499.00**

KEL-TEC KSG BULL-PUP TWIN-TUBE

Gauge: 12 ga. Capacity: 13+1. Barrel: 18.5 in. Overall Length: 26.1 in. Weight: 8.5 lbs. (loaded). Features: Pump-action shotgun with two magazine tubes. The shotgun bears a resemblance to the South African designed Neostead pump-action gun. The operator is able to move a switch located near the top of the grip to select the right or left tube, or move the switch to the center to eject a shell without chambering another round. Optional accessories include a factory installed Picatinny rail with flip-up sights and a pistol grip. KSG-25 has 30-in. barrel and 20-round capacity magazine tubes.

Price: **$990.00**
Price: KSG-25 .... **$1400.00**

KEL-TEC KS7 BULLPUP

Gauge: 12 ga., 3 in. Capacity: 6+1. Barrel: 18.5 in. Length: 26.1 in. Weight: 5.9 lbs. Stock: Black synthetic bullpup. Features: The pump-action KS7 Bullpup is a compact self-defense shotgun. Carry handle, Picatinny rail, M-LOK mounting points. Rear loading, downward ejection, ambidextrous controls. Cylinder choke.

Price: **$495.00**

MOSSBERG MAVERICK 88 CRUISER

Gauges: 12 ga., 3 in., 20 ga., 3in. Capacity: 5+1 or 7+1 capacity. Barrels: 18.5 in., 20 in. Length: 28.125-30.375 in. Weight: 5.5-6.0 lbs. Stock: Black synthetic pistol grip. Features: Fixed cylinder bore choke, blued metalwork, bead front sight, cross-bolt safety.

Price: **$231.00**

MOSSBERG MODEL 500 SPECIAL PURPOSE

Gauges: 12 ga., 20 ga., .410, 3 in. Barrels: 18.5 in., 20 in. (Cyl.). Weight: 7 lbs. Stock: Walnut-finished hardwood or black synthetic. Sights: Metal bead front. Features: Slide-action operation. Available in 6- or 8-round models. Top-mounted safety, double action slide bars, swivel studs, rubber recoil pad. Blue, Parkerized, Marinecote finishes. Mossberg Cablelock included. The HS410 Home Security model chambered for .410 with 3 in. chamber; has pistol grip fore-end, thick recoil pad, muzzle brake and has special spreader choke on the 18.5-in. barrel. Overall length is 37.5 in. Blued finish; synthetic field stock. Mossberg Cablelock and video included. Mariner model has Marinecote metal finish to resist rust and corrosion. Synthetic field stock; pistol grip kit included. 500 Tactical 6-shot has black synthetic tactical stock. Introduced 1990.

Price: 500 Mariner **$636.00**
Price: HS410 Home Security **$477.00**
Price: Home Security 20 ga. **$631.00**
Price: FLEX Tactical **$672.00**
Price: 500 Chainsaw pistol grip only; removable top handle **$547.00**
Price: JIC (Just In Case) **$500.00**
Price: Thunder Ranch **$553.00**

MOSSBERG 590S SHOCKWAVE

Gauge: 12 ga. 1.7–3 in. Barrel: 14.375 and 18.5 in. Length: 26.37–30.75 in. Weight: 5.3–5.5 lbs. Stock: Black synthetic with Raptor grip and corn-cob forend with strap. Features: The upgraded 590S version of the pistol grip Shockwave is built to cycle any length shells without adapter or adjustment, from 1.75 to 3-in. Bead front sight, matte blued metalwork, shorter-barreled model uses heavy-walled barrel. Both feature fixed cylinder bore choke.

Price: **$623.00**

MOSSBERG MODEL 590 SPECIAL PURPOSE

Gauges: 12 ga., 20 ga., .410 3 in. Capacity: 9-round magazine. Barrel: 20 in. (Cyl.). Weight: 7.25 lbs. Stock: Synthetic field or Speedfeed. Sights: Metal bead front or Ghost Ring. Features: Slide action. Top-mounted safety, double slide action bars. Comes with heat shield, bayonet lug, swivel studs, rubber recoil pad. Blue, Parkerized or Marinecote finish. Shockwave has 14-inch heavy walled barrel, Raptor pistol grip, wrapped fore-end and is fully BATFE compliant. Magpul model has Magpul SGA stock with adjustable comb and length of pull. Mossberg Cablelock included. From Mossberg.

Price: **$559.00**
Price: Flex Tactical **$672.00**
Price: Tactical Tri-Rail Adjustable **$879.00**
Price: Mariner **$756.00**
Price: Shockwave .... **$455.00–$721.00**
Price: MagPul 9-shot **$836.00**

MOSSBERG 930 SPECIAL PURPOSE SERIES

Gauge: 12 ga., 3 in. Barrel: 18.5-28 in. flat ventilated rib. Weight: 7.3 lbs. Length: 49 in.. Stock: Composite stock with close radius pistol grip; Speed Lock forearm; textured gripping surfaces; shim adjustable for length of pull, cast and drop; Mossy Oak Bottomland camo finish; Dura-Touch Armor Coating. Features: 930 Special Purpose shotguns feature a self-regulating gas system that vents excess gas to aid in recoil reduction and eliminate stress on critical components. All 930 autoloaders chamber both 2 3/4 inch and 3-in. 12-ga. shotshells with ease — from target loads, to non-toxic magnum loads, to the latest sabot slug ammo. Magazine capacity is 7+1 on models with extended magazine tube, 4+1 on models without. To complete the package, each Mossberg 930 includes a set of specially designed spacers for quick adjustment of the horizontal and vertical angle of the stock, bringing a custom-feel fit to every shooter. All 930 Special Purpose models feature a drilled and tapped receiver, factory-ready for Picatinny rail, scope base or optics installation. 930 SPX models conveniently come with a factory-mounted Picatinny rail and LPA/M16-Style Ghost Ring combination sight right out of the box. Other sighting options include a basic front bead, or white-dot front sights. Mossberg 930 Special Purpose shotguns are available in a variety of configurations; 5-round tactical barrel, 5-round with muzzle brake, 8-round pistol-grip, and even a 5-round security/field combo.

Price: Tactical 5-Round **$612.00**
Price: Home Security **$662.00**
Price: Standard Stock **$787.00**
Price: Pistol Grip 8-Round **$1,046.00**
Price: 5-Round Combo w/extra 18.5-in. barrel **$693.00**
Price: Chainsaw **$564.00**

REMINGTON 870 DM SERIES

Gauge: 12 ga. (2 3/4 in., 3 in. interchangeably) Barrel: 18.5-in. cylinder bore. Detachable 6-round magazine. Stock: Hardwood or black synthetic with textured gripping surfaces. Tac-14 DM model features short pistol grip buttstock and 14-in. barrel.

Price: **$529.00**

REMINGTON 870 EXPRESS TACTICAL
Gauge: 12 ga., 2 3/4 and 3 in. Features: Pump-action shotgun; 18.5-in. barrel; extended ported Tactical RemChoke; SpeedFeed IV pistol-grip stock with SuperCell recoil pad; fully adjustable XS Ghost Ring Sight rail with removable white bead front sight; 7-round capacity with factory-installed 2-shot extension; drilled and tapped receiver; sling swivel stud.
Price: **$600.00**

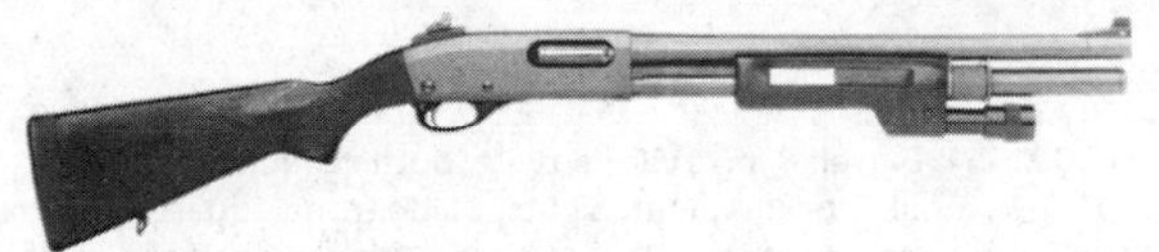

REMINGTON 887 NITRO MAG TACTICAL
Gauge: 12 ga., 2 3/4 to 3 1/2 in. Features: Pump-action shotgun,18.5-in. barrel with ported, extended tactical RemChoke; 2-shot magazine extension; barrel clamp with integral Picatinny rails; ArmorLokt coating; synthetic stock and fore-end with specially contour grip panels.
Price: **$534.00**

REMINGTON V3 TACTICAL
Addition of two tactical models to the V3 lineup with the same VersaPort self-regulating gas system that works with any shotshell from 2.75 in. to 3 in. Capacity: 6+1. Both wear an 18.5 in. barrel and oversized controls. One model with rifle sights, the other with a vent rib and bead sights.
Price: .... **$1,024.00–$1,076.00**

REMINGTON V3 COMPETITION TACTICAL
Addition of competition tactical model to the exiting V3 lineup. This 12 ga. uses the same Versa-Port technology to self-regulate for any shotshell from 2.75 in. to 3in. Capacity: 8+1. Features: 22-inch barrel with Hi-Viz front sight and low-profile, dovetail-rib mounting rear sight and oversized controls.
Price: **$1,128.00**

RETAY MASAI MARA WARDEN
Gauge: 12 ga., 3 in. Barrel: 18.5 in. Weight: 6.6 lbs. Stock: Black Synthetic. Features: The Turkish-made Masai Mara line of semi-automatics uses an inertia-plus action and bolt system. Oversized controls, quick unload system, Picatinny rail, extended charging handle, ghost-ring sights. Push-button removeable trigger group. Microcell rubber recoil pad. Includes a hard case and ships with five MaraPro choke tubes.
Price: **$1,099.00**

ROCK ISLAND ARMORY/ARMSCOR VRBP-100
Gauge: 12 ga., 3 in. Capacity: 5+1. Barrel: 20 in. contoured. Length: 32 in. Weight: 7.94 lbs. Stock: Black polymer bullpup design with pistol grip. Features: Semi-automatic bullpup design. Compatible with all VR Series magazines. Matte-black anodized finish. Includes rubber spacers to adjust length of pull. Full length top rail with flip-up sights, right-sided Picatinny accessory rail. Ships with three interchangeable chokes.
Price: **$774.00**

ROCK ISLAND ARMORY/ARMSCOR VRPA-40
Gauge: 12 ga., 3 in. Capacity: 5+1. Barrel: 20 in., contoured. Length: 55.11 in. Weight: 6.9 lbs. Stock: Black synthetic. Features: The VRPA40 marks the more affordable pump action addition to the VR family of shotguns. Magazine fed, aluminum heat shield, fiber-optic front sight, adjustable rear sight, Picatinny rail. Marine black anodized, compatible with VR series 9-round magazines. Mobil chokes.
Price: **$399.00**

ROCK ISLAND ARMORY/ARMSCOR VR82
Gauge: 20 ga. 3 in. Barrel: 18 in. contoured. Length: 38 in. Weight: 7.5 lbs. Stock: Black polymer thumbhole style. Features: The semi-automatic VR82 is the little brother of the VR80. Built of 7075 T6 aluminum for lighter weight. Magazine fed with 5+1 capacity but also accepts VR-series 10- and 20-round mags. Ambidextrous controls, flip-up sights, barrel shroud. Fore-end accepts most aftermarket accessories. Compatible with most buffer tube stocks and pistol grips. Black anodized finish. Mobil choke.
Price: **$729.00**

SAVAGE RENEGAUGE SECURITY
Gauge: 12 ga. 3 in. Barrel: 18.5 in. Melonite-treated, fluted, with ventilated rib. Length: 40 in. Weight: 7.3 lbs. Stock: Matte gray synthetic with adjustable LOP, comb height, and drop/cast. Features: Savage's self-regulating DRIV gas system. One-piece chrome-plated action bar and reciprocating components. Stock rod buffer to reduce recoil. Adjustable ghost ring sights and one-piece rail. Oversized controls. Includes three flush choke tubes (IC, M, F) and hard case.
Price: **$1,499.00**

SMITH & WESSON M&P-12
Gauge: 12 ga. 3 in. Barrel: 19 in. Length: 27.8 in. Weight: 8.3 lbs. Stock: Black synthetic with fixed stock. Features: Single barrel pump-action shotgun with two independent magazine tubes. Capacity of seven rounds of 2-3/4-in. shells or six rounds of 3-in. shells per tube. Vertical foregrip, action lock lever button, and push button mag tube selector. Ships with four interchangeable pistol grip palm swell inserts. Picatinny top rail, M-LOK barrel slots. Includes Rem-Choke-style choke tubes (M, C), choke wrench, and foam-lined hard gun case.
Price: **$1,185.00**

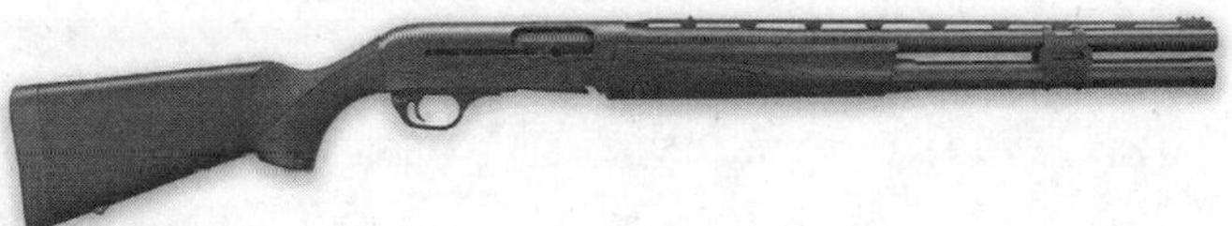

STANDARD MANUFACTURING DP-12 PROFESSIONAL
Gauge: 12 ga. 3 in. Barrels: 18-7/8 in. Length: 29.5 in. Weight: 9 lb. 12 oz. Stock: Synthetic with anodized aluminum. Features: Upgraded Professional version of the pump-action DP-12 high-capacity defense shotgun. Additions include an aluminum rail with front grip, which wears an integral laser and flashlight. Precision-honed bores and chambers finished with hand-lapping. PVD coating on all critical wear areas. Mil-spec hard anodized finish with accents in either Blue or OD Green. Includes Reflex Sight with multiple brightness levels. Ships with both soft and hard cases
Price: **$3,250.00**

TACTICAL RESPONSE STANDARD MODEL
Gauge: 12 ga., 3 in. Capacity: 7-round magazine. Barrel: 18 in. (Cyl.). Weight: 9 lbs. Length: 38 in. overall. Stock: Fiberglass-filled polypropylene with non-snag recoil absorbing butt pad. Nylon tactical fore-end houses flashlight. Sights: Trak-Lock ghost ring sight system. Front sight has Tritium insert. Features: Highly modified Remington 870P with Parkerized finish. Comes with nylon three-way adjustable sling, high visibility non-binding follower, high-performance magazine spring, Jumbo Head safety, and Side Saddle extended 6-shotshell carrier on left side of receiver. Introduced 1991. From Scattergun Technologies, Inc.
Price: Standard model **$1,540.00**
Price: Border Patrol model **$1,135.00**
Price: Professional Model 13-in. bbl. (Law enf., military only)........ **$1,550.00**

WINCHESTER SXP EXTREME DEFENDER
Gauge: 12 ga., 3 in. Barrel: 18 in., with Heat Shield. Length: 38.5 in. Weight: 7.0 lbs. Stock: Flat Dark Earth composite with textured grip panels and pistol grip. Features: Aluminum-alloy receiver, hard-chrome chamber and bore, Picatinny rail with ghost-ring sight, blade front sight. Two interchangeable comb pieces and two quarter-inch length-of-pull spacers for custom fit. Side-mounted Picatinny accessory rails, sling studs, Inflex recoil pad. Includes one Invector Plus cylinder choke and one Door Breacher choke.
Price: **$529.00**

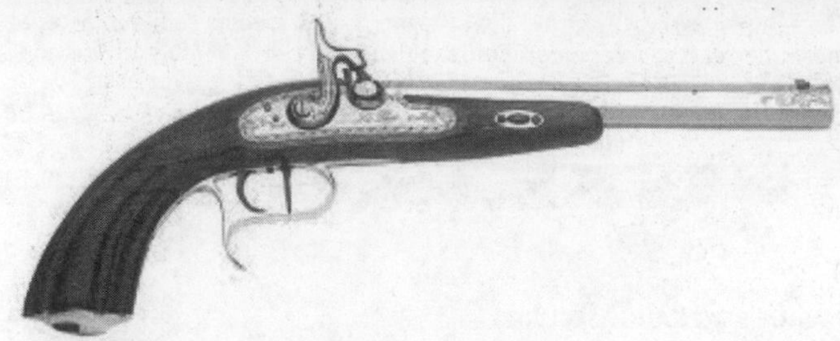

CHIAPPA LE PAGE PERCUSSION DUELING PISTOL
Caliber: .45. Barrel: 10 in. browned octagon, rifled. Weight: 2.5 lbs. Length: 16.6 in. overall. Stock: Walnut, rounded, fluted butt. Sights: Blade front, open-style rear. Features: Double set trigger. Bright barrel, silver-plated brass furniture. External ramrod. Made by Chiappa.
Price: Chiappa 940.001 .... **$779.00**

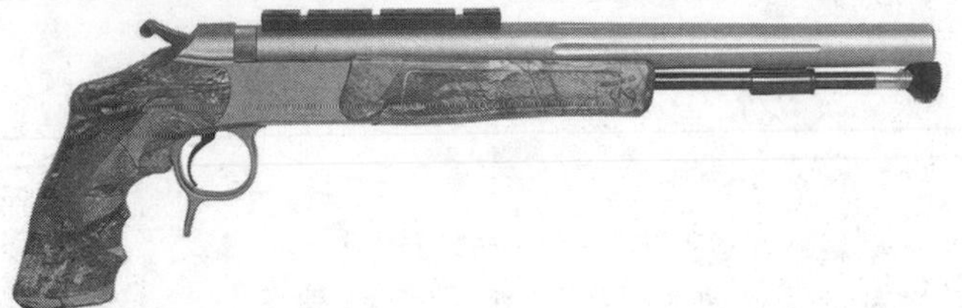

CVA OPTIMA PISTOL
Caliber: .50. Barrel: 14 in., 1:28-in. twist, Cerakote finish. Weight: 3.7 lbs. Length: 19 in. Stock: Black synthetic, Realtree Xtra Green. Sights: Scope base mounted. Features: Break-open action, all stainless construction, aluminum ramrod, quick-removal breech plug for 209 primer. From CVA.
Price: PP222SM Stainless/Realtree Xtra, rail mount **$354.00**
Price: PP221SM Stainless/black, rail mount **$307.00**

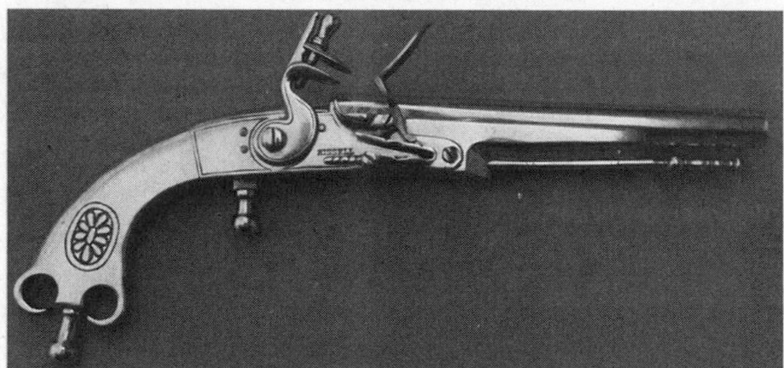

DIXIE MURDOCK SCOTTISH HIGHLANDER'S PISTOL
Caliber: .352. Barrel: 7.5 in., blued steel finish, round. Weight: 3.75 lbs. Length: 18.25 in. overall. Stock: Steel frame. Sights: None. Features: Flintlock, steel ramrod. An exact copy of an Alexander Murdock Scottish pistol of the 1770s. Made in India. Imported by Dixie Gun Works.
Price: Dixie Gun Works FH1040 .... **$425.00**

DIXIE MODEL 1855 U.S. DRAGOON PISTOL
Caliber: .58. Barrel: 12 in., bright finish, round. Weight: 2.25 lbs. Length: 16.75 in. overall. Stock: Walnut. Sights: Fixed rear and front sights. Features: Percussion, swivel-style, steel ramrod. Made by Palmetto Arms. Imported by Dixie Gun Works.
Price: Dixie Gun Works PH1000 .... **$650.00**

LYMAN PLAINS PISTOL
Caliber: .50 or .54. Barrel: 8 in.; 1:30-in. twist, both calibers. Weight: 3.1 lb. Length: 15 in. overall. Stock: Walnut. Sights: Blade front, square-notch rear adjustable for windage. Features: Polished brass triggerguard and ramrod tip, color case-hardened coil spring lock, spring-loaded trigger, stainless steel nipple, blackened iron furniture. Hooked patent breech, detachable belt hook. Introduced 1981. From Lyman Products.
Price: 6010608 .50-cal **$426.00**
Price: 6010609 .54-cal **$426.00**
Price: 6010610 .50-cal Kit **$349.00**
Price: 6010611 .54-cal. Kit **$349.00**

PEDERSOLI CARLETON UNDERHAMMER MATCH PERCUSSION PISTOL
Caliber: .36. Barrel: 9.5 in., browned octagonal, rifled. Weight: 2.25 lbs. Length: 16.75 in. overall. Stock: Walnut. Sights: Blade front, open rear, adjustable for elevation. Features: Percussion, under-hammer ignition, adjustable trigger, no half cock. No ramrod. Made by Pedersoli. Imported by Dixie Gun Works.
Price: Dixie Gun Works FH0332 .... **$925.00**

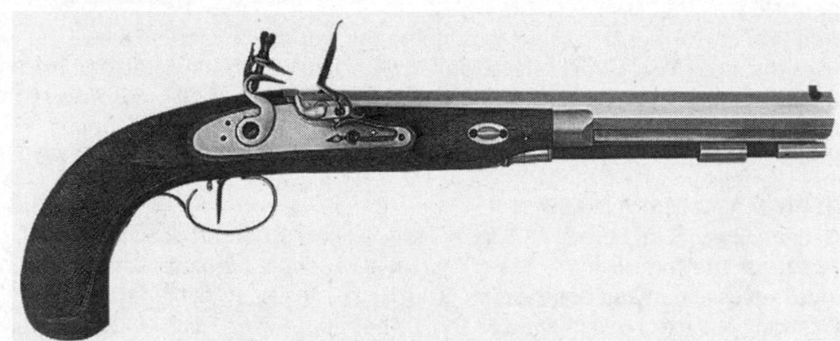

PEDERSOLI CHARLES MOORE ENGLISH DUELING PISTOL
Caliber: .45. Barrel: 11 in., 1:18 twist Weight: 2.5 lbs. Length: 16.5 in. overall. Stock: Walnut. Sights: Fixed. Features: Flintlock or percussion. Single set, adjustable trigger. Blued barrel and lock, steel furniture left in the white. Wooden ramrod. Replica of a fine British dueling pistol made by Charles Moore in London. Made by Pedersoli. Imported by Dixie Gun Works.
Price: Dixie Gun Works Flintlock FH0237 .... **$795.00**
Price: Dixie Gun Works Percussion PH0501 .... **$610.00**

PEDERSOLI FRENCH AN IX NAPOLEONIC PISTOL
Caliber: .69. Barrel: 8.25 in. Weight: 3 lbs. Length: 14 in. overall. Stock: Walnut. Sights: None. Features: Flintlock, case-hardened lock, brass furniture, buttcap, lock marked "Imperiale de S. Etienne." Steel ramrod. Made by Pedersoli. Imported by Dixie Gun Works.
Price: Dixie Gun Works FH0890 .... **$740.00**

PEDERSOLI FRENCH AN IX GENDARMERIE NAPOLEONIC PISTOL
Caliber: .69. Barrel: 5.25 in. Weight: 3 lbs. Length: 14 in. overall. Stock: Walnut. Sights: None. Features: Flintlock, case-hardened lock, brass furniture, buttcap, lock marked "Imperiale de S. Etienne." Steel ramrod. Imported by Dixie Gun Works.
Price: Dixie Gun Works Gendarmerie FHO954 .... **$725.00**

Prices given are believed to be accurate at time of publication however, many factors affect retail pricing so exact prices are not possible.

PEDERSOLI FRENCH AN XIII NAPOLEONIC PISTOL

Caliber: .69. Barrel: 8.25 in. Weight: 3 lbs. Length: 14 in. overall. Stock: Walnut half-stock. Sights: None. Features: Flintlock, case-hardened lock, brass furniture, butt cap, lock marked "Imperiale de S. Etienne." Steel ramrod. Made by Pedersoli. Imported by Dixie Gun Works.

Price: Dixie Gun Works AN XIII FHO895 .... **$725.00**

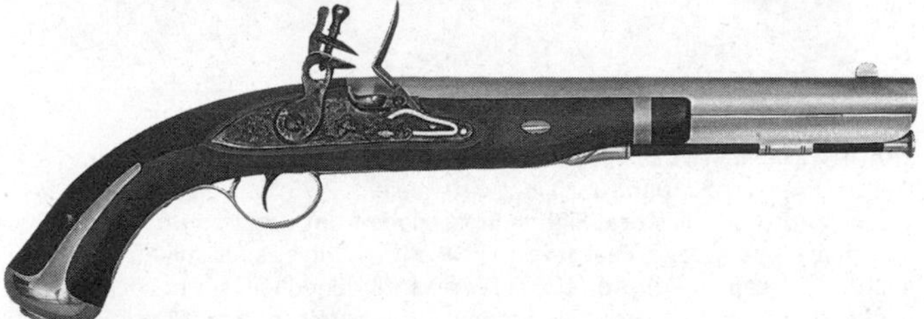

PEDERSOLI HARPER'S FERRY 1805 PISTOL

Caliber: .58. Barrel: 10 in. Weight: 2.5 lbs. Length: 16 in. overall. Stock: Walnut. Sights: Fixed. Features: Flintlock or percussion. Case-hardened lock, brass-mounted German silver-colored barrel. Wooden ramrod. Replica of the first U.S. government made flintlock pistol. Made by Pedersoli. Imported by Dixie Gun Works.

Price: Dixie Gun Works Flint RH0225 .... **$565.00**
Price: Dixie Gun Works Flint Kit RH0411 .... **$450.00**
Price: Dixie Gun Works Percussion RH0951 .... **$565.00**
Price: Dixie Gun Works Percussion Kit RH0937 .... **$395.00**

PEDERSOLI HOWDAH HUNTER PISTOLS

Caliber: .50, 20 gauge, .58. Barrels: 11.25 in., blued, rifled in .50 and .58 calibers. Weight: 4.25 to 5 lbs. Length: 17.25 in. Stock: American walnut with checkered grip. Sights: Brass bead front sight. Features: Blued barrels, swamped barrel rib, engraved, color case-hardened locks and hammers, captive steel ramrod. Available with detachable shoulder stock, case, holster and mold. Made by Pedersoli. Imported by Dixie Gun Works, Cabela's, Taylor's and others.

Price: Dixie Gun Works, 50X50, PH0572 .... **$895.00**
Price: Dixie Gun Works, 58XD58, PH09024 .... **$895.00**
Price: Dixie Gun Works, 20X20 gauge, PH0581 .... **$850.00**
Price: Dixie Gun Works, 50X20 gauge, PH0581 .... **$850.00**
Price: Dixie Gun Works, 50X50, Kit, PK0952 .... **$640.00**
Price: Dixie Gun Works, 50X20, Kit, PK1410 .... **$675.00**
Price: Dixie Gun Works, 20X20, Kit, PK0954 .... **$640.00**

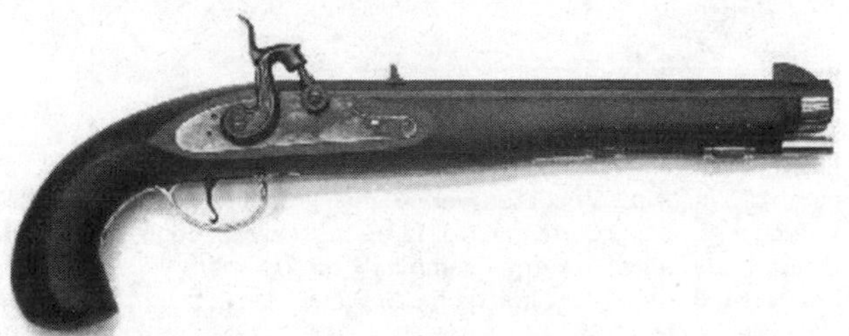

PEDERSOLI KENTUCKY PISTOL

Caliber: .45, .50, .54. Barrel: 10.33 in. Weight: 2.5 lbs. Length: 15.4 in. overall. Stock: Walnut with smooth rounded birds-head grip. Sights: Fixed. Features: Available in flint or percussion ignition in various calibers. Case-hardened lock, blued barrel, drift-adjustable rear sights, blade front. Wooden ramrod. Kit guns of all models available from Dixie Gun Works. Made by Pedersoli. Imported by Dixie Gun Works, EMF and others.

Price: Dixie Gun Works .45 Percussion, PH0440 .... **$395.00**
Price: Dixie Gun Works.45 Flint, PH0430 .... **$437.00**
Price: Dixie Gun Works .45 Flint, Kit FH0320 .... **$325.00**
Price: Dixie Gun Works .50 Flint, PH0935 .... **$495.00**
Price: Dixie Gun Works .50 Percussion, PH0930 .... **$450.00**
Price: Dixie Gun Works. 54 Flint, PH0080 .... **$495.00**
Price: Dixie Gun Works .54 Percussion, PH0330 .... **$450.00**
Price: Dixie Gun Works .54 Percussion, Kit PK0436 .... **$325.00**
Price: Dixie Gun Works .45, Navy Moll, brass buttcap, Flint PK0436 ...... **$650.00**
Price: .45, Navy Moll, brass buttcap, Percussion PK0903 .... **$595.00**

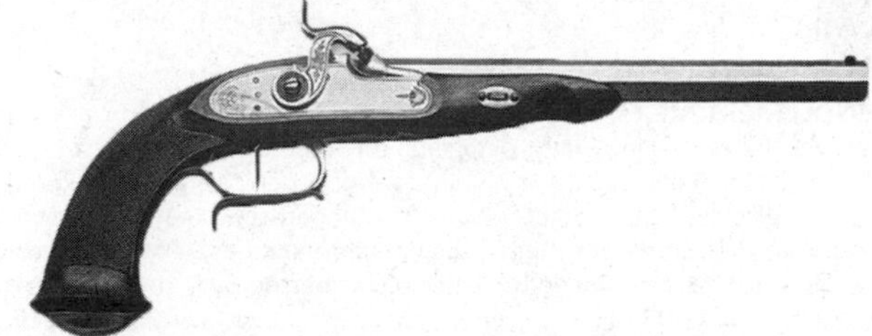

PEDERSOLI LE PAGE PERCUSSION DUELING PISTOL

Caliber: .44. Barrel: 10 inches, browned octagon, rifled. Weight: 2.5 lbs. Length: 16.75 inches overall. Stock: Walnut, rounded checkered butt. Sights: Blade front, open-style rear. Features: Single set trigger, external ramrod. Made by Pedersoli. Imported by Dixie Gun Works.

Price: Dixie, Pedersoli, PH0431 .... **$950.00**
Price: Dixie, International, Pedersoli, PH0231 .... **$1,250.00**

PEDERSOLI MAMELOUK

Caliber: .57. Barrel: 7-5/8 in., bright. Weight: 1.61 lbs. Length: 13 in. overall. Stock: Walnut, with brass end cap and medallion. Sights: Blade front. Features: Flint, lanyard ring, wooden ramrod. Made by Pedersoli. Available on special order from IFG (Italian Firearms Group)

Price: .... **TBD at time of order**

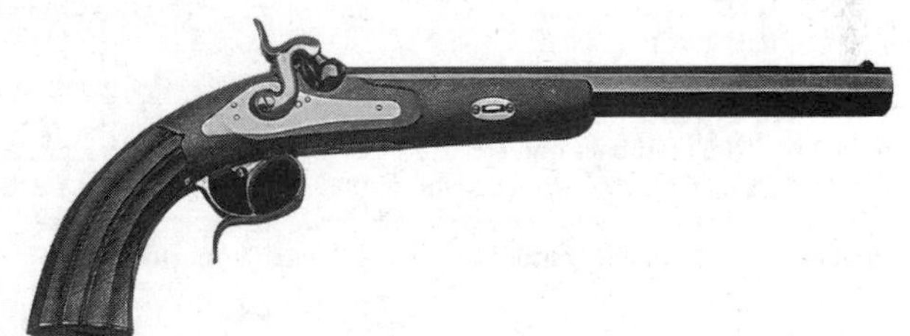

PEDERSOLI MANG TARGET PISTOL

Caliber: .38. Barrel: 11.5 in., octagonal, browned; 1:15-in. twist. Weight: 2.5 lbs. Length: 17. in. overall. Stock: Walnut with fluted grip. Sights: Blade front, open rear adjustable for windage. Features: Browned barrel, polished breech plug, remainder color case-hardened. Made by Pedersoli. Imported by Dixie Gun Works.

Price: PH0503 .... **$1,795.00**

Prices given are believed to be accurate at time of publication however, many factors affect retail pricing so exact prices are not possible.

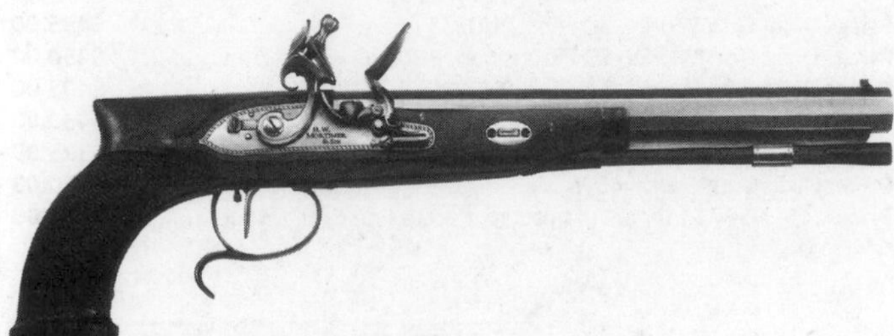

PEDERSOLI MORTIMER TARGET PISTOL
Caliber: .44. Barrel: 10 in., bright octagonal on Standard, browned on Deluxe, rifled. Weight: 2.55 lbs. Length: 15.75 in. overall. Stock: Walnut, checkered saw-handle grip on Deluxe. Sights: Blade front, open-style rear. Features: Percussion or flint, single set trigger, sliding hammer safety, engraved lock on Deluxe. Wooden ramrod. Made by Pedersoli. Imported by Dixie Gun Works.
Price: Dixie, Flint, FH0316 .... **$1,175.00**
Price: Dixie, Percussion, PH0231 .... **$1,095.00**
Price: Dixie, Deluxe, FH0950 .... **$2,220.00**

PEDERSOLI PHILADELPHIA DERRINGER
Caliber: .45. Barrel: 3.1 in., browned, rifled. Weight: 0.5 lbs. Length: 6.215 in. Stock: European walnut checkered. Sights: V-notch rear, blade front. Features: Back-hammer percussion lock with engraving, single trigger. Made by Pedersoli. Imported by Dixie Gun Works.
Price: Dixie, PH0913 .... **$550.00**
Price: Dixie, Kit PK0863 .... **$385.00**

PEDERSOLI QUEEN ANNE FLINTLOCK PISTOL
Caliber: .50. Barrel: 7.5 in., smoothbore. Stock: Walnut. Sights: None. Features: Flintlock, German silver-colored steel barrel, fluted brass triggerguard, brass mask on butt. Lockplate left in the white. No ramrod. Introduced 1983. Made by Pedersoli. Imported by Dixie Gun Works.
Price: Dixie, RH0211 .... **$495.00**
Price: Dixie, Kit, FH0421 .... **$375.00**

PEDERSOLI REMINGTON RIDER DERRINGER
Caliber: 4.3 mm (BB lead balls only). Barrel: 2.1 in., blued, rifled. Weight: 0.25 lbs. Length: 4.75 in. Grips: All-steel construction. Sights: V-notch rear, bead front. Features: Fires percussion cap only – no powder. Available as case-hardened frame or polished white. Made by Pedersoli. Imported by Dixie Gun Works.
Price: Dixie, Case-hardened PH0923. .... **$210.00**

PEDERSOLI SCREW BARREL PISTOL
Caliber: .44. Barrel: 2.35 in., blued, rifled. Weight: 0.5 lbs. Length: 6.5 in. Grips: European walnut. Sights: None. Features: Percussion, boxlock with center hammer, barrel unscrews for loading from rear, folding trigger, external hammer, combination barrel and nipple wrench furnished. Made by Pedersoli. Imported by Dixie Gun Works.
Price: Dixie, PH0530. .... **$225.00**
Price: Dixie, PH0545. .... **$175.00**

TRADITIONS KENTUCKY PISTOL
Caliber: .50. Barrel: 10 in., 1:20 in. twist. Weight: 2.75 lbs. Length: 15 in. Stock: Hardwood full stock. Sights: Brass blade front, square notch rear adjustable for windage. Features: Polished brass finger spur-style trigger guard, stock cap and ramrod tip, color case-hardened leaf spring lock, spring-loaded trigger, No. 11 percussion nipple, brass furniture. From Traditions, and as kit from Bass Pro and others.
Price: P1060 Finished **$244.00**
Price: KPC50602 Kit **$209.00**

TRADITIONS TRAPPER PISTOL
Caliber: .50. Barrel: 9.75 in., octagonal, blued, hooked patent breech, 1:20 in. twist. Weight: 2.75 lbs. Length: 15.5 in. Stock: Hardwood, modified saw-handle style grip, halfstock. Sights: Brass blade front, rear sight adjustable for windage and elevation. Features: Percussion or flint, double set triggers, polished brass triggerguard, stock cap and ramrod tip, color case-hardened leaf spring lock, spring-loaded trigger, No. 11 percussion nipple, brass furniture. From Traditions and as a kit from Bass Pro and others.
Price: P1100 Finished, percussion **$329.00**
Price: P1090 Finished, flint **$369.00**
Price: KPC51002 Kit, percussion **$299.00**
Price: KPC50902 Kit, flint **$359.00**

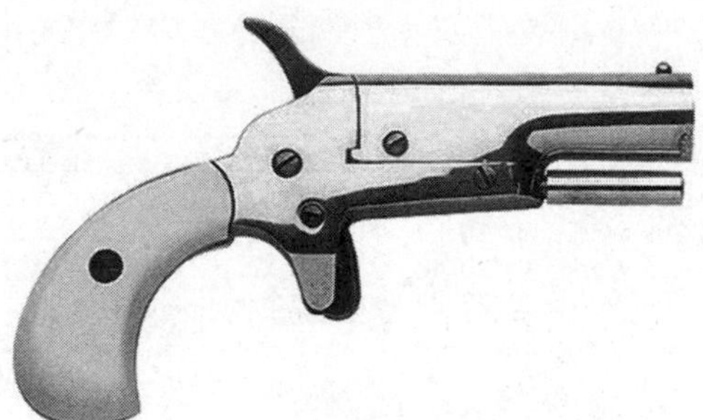

TRADITIONS VEST POCKET DERRINGER
Caliber: .31. Barrel: 2.35 in., round brass, smoothbore. Weight: .75 lbs. Length: 4.75 in. Grips: Simulated ivory. Sights: Front bead. Features: Replica of riverboat gambler's derringer. No. 11 percussion cap nipple, brass frame and barrel, spur trigger, external hammer. From Traditions.
Price: P1381, Brass **$194.00**
Price: Dixie, White, PH0920. .... **$175.00**

Prices given are believed to be accurate at time of publication however, many factors affect retail pricing so exact prices are not possible.

DANCE AND BROTHERS PERCUSSION REVOLVER
Caliber: .44. Barrel: 7.4 in., round. Weight: 2.5 lbs. Length: 13 in. overall. Grips: One-piece walnut. Sights: Brass blade front, hammer notch rear. Features: Reproduction of the C.S.A. revolver. Brass trigger guard. Color case-hardened frame Made by Pietta. Imported by Dixie Gun Works and others.
Price: Dixie Gun Works RH0344 .... **$350.00**

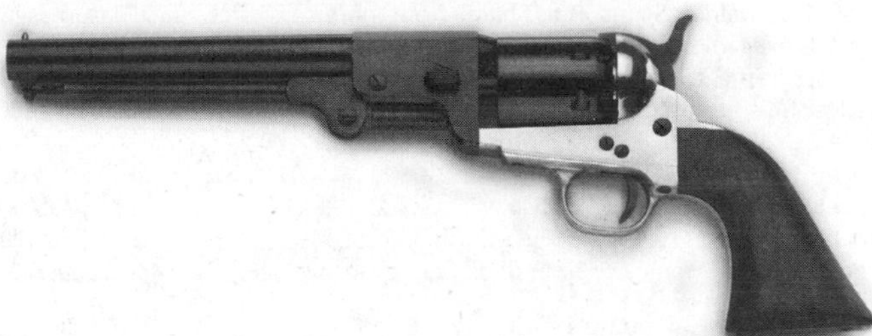

GRISWOLD AND GUNNISON PERCUSSION REVOLVER
Caliber: .36. Barrel: 7.5 in., round. Weight: 2.5 lbs. Length: 13.25 in. Grips: One-piece walnut. Sights: Fixed. Features: Reproduction of the C.S.A. revolver. Brass frame and triggerguard. Made by Pietta. Imported by EMF, Cabela's and others.
Price: EMF PF51BRGG36712 .... **$235.00**

NORTH AMERICAN COMPANION PERCUSSION REVOLVER
Caliber: .22. Barrel: 1-1/8 in. Weight: 5.1 oz. Length: 4 in. overall. Grips: Laminated wood. Sights: Blade front, notch rear. Features: All stainless steel construction. Uses No. 11 percussion caps. Comes with bullets, powder measure, bullet seater, leather clip holster, gun rag. Long Rifle frame. Introduced 1996. Made in U.S. by North American Arms.
Price: NAA-22LR-CB Long Rifle frame.. **$251.00**

NORTH AMERICAN SUPER COMPANION PERCUSSION REVOLVER
Caliber: .22. Barrel: 1-5/8 in. Weight: 7.2 oz. Length: 5-1/8 in. Grips: Laminated wood. Sights: Blade font, notched rear. Features: All stainless steel construction. No. 11 percussion caps. Comes with bullets, powder measure, bullet seater, leather clip holster, gun rag. Introduced 1996. Larger "Magnum" frame. Made in U.S. by North American Arms.
Price: NAA-Mag-CB Magnum frame.. **$296.00**

PEDERSOLI REMINGTON PATTERN TARGET REVOLVER
Caliber: .44. Barrel: 8 in., tapered octagon progressive twist. Weight: 2.75 lbs. Length: 13-3/4 in. overall. Grips: One-piece hardwood. Sights: V-notch on top strap, blued steel blade front. Features: Brass trigger guard, Non-reflective coating on the barrel and a wear resistant coating on the cylinder, blued steel frame, case-hardened hammer, trigger and loading lever. Made by Pedersoli. Imported by EMF, Dixie Gun Works, Cabela's and others.
Price: EMF Steel Frame PF58ST448.. **$1,010.00**

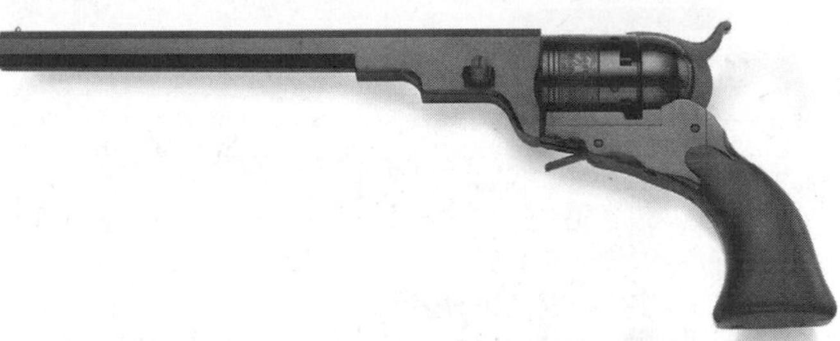

PIETTA TEXAS PATTERSON PERCUSSION REVOLVER
Caliber: .36. Barrel: 9 in. tapered octagon. Weight: 2.75 lbs. Length: 13.75 in. Grips: One-piece walnut. Sights: Brass pin front, hammer notch rear. Features: Folding trigger, blued steel furniture, frame and barrel; engraved scene on cylinder. Ramrod: Loading tool provided. Made by Pietta. Imported by E.M.F, Dixie Gun Works.
Price: EMF PF36ST36712... **$610.00**

PIETTA 1851 NAVY MODEL PERCUSSION REVOLVER
Caliber: .36, .44, 6-shot. Barrel: 7.5 in. Weight: 44 oz. Length: 13 in. overall. Grips: Walnut. Sights: Post front, hammer notch rear. Features: Available in brass-framed and steel-framed models. Made by Pietta. Imported by EMF, Dixie Gun Works, Cabela's, Cimarron, Taylor's, Traditions and others.
Price: Brass frame EMF PF51BR36712 ....**$230.00**
Price: Steel frame EMF PF51CH36712...**$275.00**

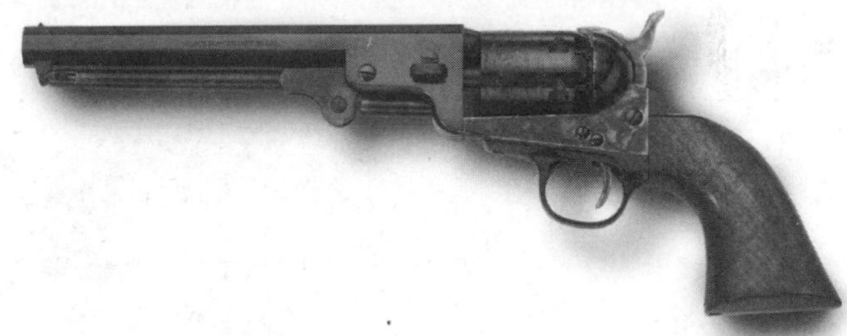

PIETTA 1851 NAVY LONDON MODEL PERCUSSION REVOLVER
Caliber: .36, 6-shot. Barrel: 7.5 In. Weight: 44 oz. Length: 13 in. overall. Grips: Walnut. Sights: Post front, hammer notch rear. Features: steel frame and steel trigger guard and back strap. Available with oval trigger guard or squared back trigger guard. Made by Pietta. Imported by EMF, Dixie, Gun Works, Cabela's, Cimarron, Taylor's, Traditions and others.
Price: EMF PF51CHS36712 ....**$275.00**

PIETTA 1851 NAVY SHERIFF'S MODEL PERCUSSION REVOLVER
Caliber: .44, 6-shot. Barrel: 5.5 in. Weight: 40 oz. Length: 11 in. overall. Grips: Walnut. Sights: Post front, hammer notch rear. Features: Available in brass-framed and steel-framed models. Made by Pietta. Imported by EMF, Dixie, Gun Works, Cabela's.
Price: Brass frame EMF PF51BR44512 ....**$235.00**
Price: Steel frame EMF PF51CH44512...**$275.00**

PIETTA 1851 NAVY CAPTAIN SCHAEFFER MODEL PERCUSSION REVOLVER
Caliber: .36, 6-shot. Barrel: 4 in. Weight: 40 oz. Length: 9.5 in. overall. Grips: Grips Ultra-ivory (polymer). Sights: Post front, hammer notch rear. Features: Polished steel finish, completely laser engraved. Made by Pietta. Imported by EMF
Price: EMF PF51LESS36312UI...**$395.00**

PIETTA 1851 NAVY YANK PEPPERBOX MODEL PERCUSSION REVOLVER
Caliber: .36, 6-shot. Barrel: No Barrel. Weight: 36 oz. Length: 7 in. overall. Grips: One-piece walnut. Sights: Post front, hammer notch rear. Features: There is no barrel. Rounds fire directly out of the chambers of the elongated cylinder. Made by Pietta. Imported by EMF, Dixie Gun Works and Taylor's & Co.
Price: EMF PF51PEPPER36 ....**$235.00**

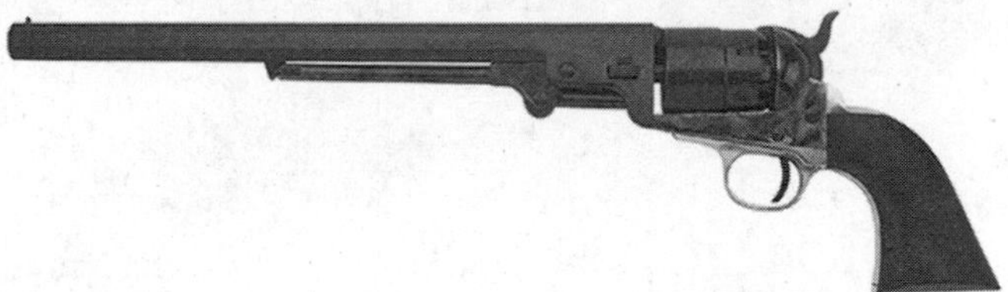

PIETTA 1851 NAVY BUNTLINE MODEL PERCUSSION REVOLVER
Caliber: .44, 6-shot. Barrel: 12 in. Weight: 36 oz. Length: 18.25 in. overall. Grips: Walnut. Sights: Post front, hammer notch rear. Features: Available in brass-framed and steel-framed models. Made by Pietta. Imported by EMF, Dixie Gun Works (Brass only).
Price: Brass frame EMF PF51BR4412 ....**$245.00**
Price: Steel frame EMF PF51CH4412...**$295.00**

PIETTA 1851 NAVY SNUBNOSE MODEL PERCUSSION REVOLVER
Caliber: .44, 6-shot. Barrel: 3 in. Weight: 36 oz. Length: 8.25 in. overall. Grips: Birds-head grip frame, one-piece checkered walnut. Sights: Post front, hammer notch rear. Features: Color case-hardened, steel-frame. Made by Pietta. Imported by Dixie Gun Works.
Price: Dixie SS1249...**$395.00**

PIETTA 1858 GENERAL CUSTER
Caliber: .44, 6-shot. Barrel: 8 in., blued. Grips: Two-piece wood. Sights: Open. Weight: 2.7 lbs. Features: Nickel-plated trigger guard, color case-hardened hammer, laser engraving.
Price: **$360.00**

PIETTA 1860 ARMY MODEL PERCUSSION REVOLVER
Caliber: .44. Barrel: 8 in. Weight: 2.75 lbs. Length: 13.25 in. overall. Grips: One-piece walnut. Sights: Brass blade front, hammer notch rear. Features: Models available with either case-hardened, steel frame, brass trigger guard, or brass frame, trigger guard and backstrap. EMF also offers a model with a silver finish on all the metal. Made by Pietta. Imported by EMF, Cabela's, Dixie Gun Works, Taylor's and others.
Price: EMF Brass Frame PF60BR448...**$260.00**
Price: EMF Steel Frame PF60CH448...**$295.00**
Price: EMF Steel Frame Old Silver finish PF60OS448 ....**$325.00**
Price: EMF Steel Frame Old Silver finish Deluxe Engraved PF60CHES448 ....**$350.00**

PIETTA 1860 ARMY SHERIFF'S MODEL PERCUSSION REVOLVER
Caliber: .44. Barrel: 5.5in. Weight: 40 oz. Length: 11.5 in. overall. Grips: One-piece walnut. Sights: Brass blade front, hammer notch rear. Features: Case-hardened, steel frame, brass trigger guard. Made by Pietta. Imported by EMF, Cabela's, Dixie Gun Works and others.
Price: EMF PF60CH44512...**$295.00**

PIETTA 1860 ARMY SNUBNOSE MODEL PERCUSSION REVOLVER
Caliber: .44. Barrel: 3 in. Weight: 36 oz. Length: 8.25 in. overall. Grips: Birds-head grip frame, one-piece, checkered walnut. Sights: Brass blade front, hammer notch rear. Features: Fluted cylinder, case-hardened, steel frame, brass trigger guard, Made by Pietta. Imported by EMF.
Price: EMF PF51CHLG44212CW **$385.00**

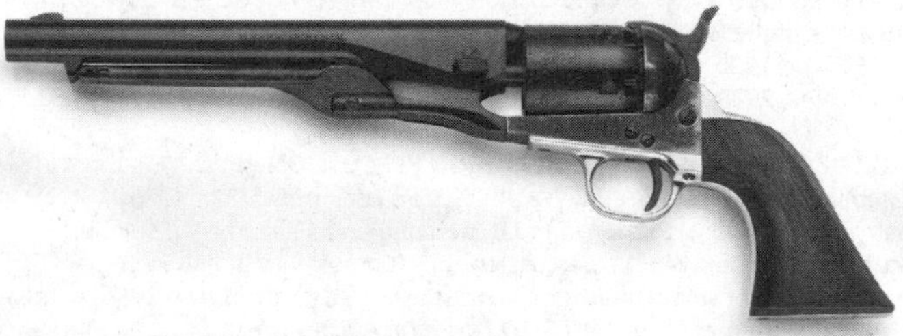

PIETTA NAVY 1861 PERCUSSION REVOLVER
Caliber: .36. Barrel: 8 in. Weight: 2.75 lbs. Length: 13.25 in. overall. Grips: One-piece walnut. Sights: Brass blade front, hammer notch rear. Features: Steel, case-hardened frame, brass-grip frame, or steel-grip frame (London Model), case-hardened creeping loading lever. Made by Pietta. Imported by EMF, Dixie Gun Works, Cabela's and others.
Price: EMF with brass triggerguard PF61CH368CIV **$300.00**
Price: EMF with steel triggerguard PF61CH368...**$300.00**

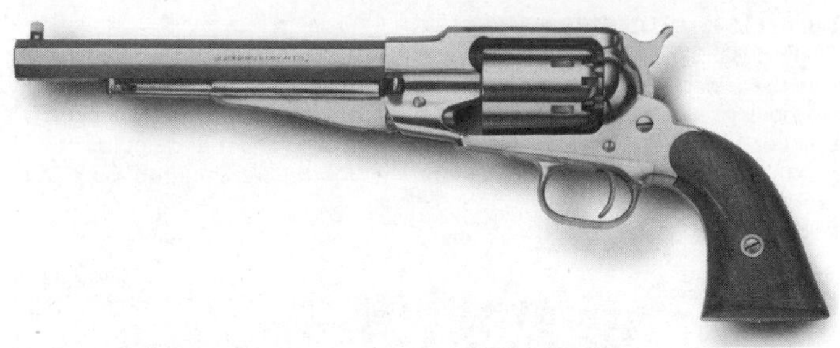

PIETTA 1858 REMINGTON ARMY REVOLVER
Caliber: .44. Barrel: 8 in., tapered octagon. Weight: 2.75 lbs. Length: 13.5 in. overall. Grips: Two-piece walnut. Sights: V-notch on top strap, blued steel blade front. Features: Brass triggerguard, blued steel backstrap and frame, case-hardened hammer and trigger. Also available, a brass-framed model, and an all stainless steel model. Made by Pietta. Imported by EMF, Dixie Gun Works, Cabela's and others.
Price: EMF Steel Frame PF58ST448 .... **$290.00**
Price: EMF Brass Frame PF58BR448 .... **$250.00**
Price: EMF Stainless Steel PF58SS448 .... **$430.00**

PIETTA 1858 REMINGTON TARGET REVOLVER
Caliber: .44. Barrel: 8 in., tapered octagon. Weight: 2.75 lbs. Length: 13.5 in. overall. Grips: Two-piece walnut. Sights: Adjustable rear, ramped blade front. Features: Brass triggerguard, blued steel frame, case-hardened hammer, and trigger. Also available, a brass-framed model. Made by Pietta. Imported by EMF, Dixie Gun Works, Cabela's and others.
Price: EMF PF58STT448 .... **$350.00**

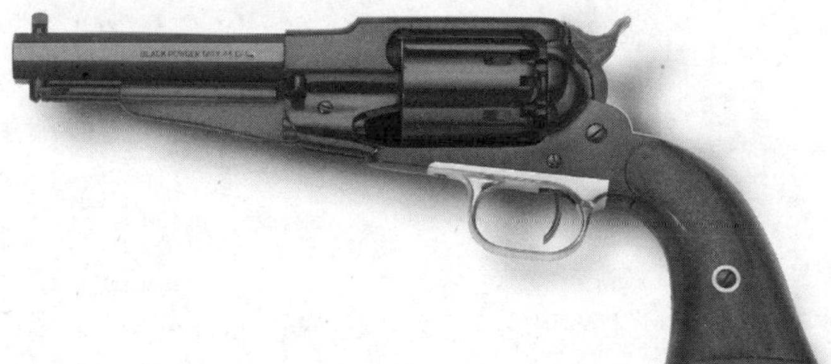

PIETTA 1858 REMINGTON SHIRIFF'S MODEL REVOLVER
Caliber: .36 and .44. Barrel: 5.5in., tapered octagon. Weight: 2.75 lbs. Length: 11.5 in. overall. Grips: Two-piece checkered walnut. Sights: V-notch on top strap, blued steel blade front. Features: Brass triggerguard, blued steel backstrap and frame, case-hardened hammer and trigger. Also available in a color case-hardened-framed model, and in an all stainless steel model. Made by Pietta. Imported by EMF, and others.
Price: EMF Blued Steel Frame PF58ST36612 .... **$290.00**
Price: EMF Color Case-Hardened frame PF58CH44512CW **$395.00**
Price: EMF Stainless Steel PF58SS44512CW **$490.00**

PIETTA 1858 REMINGTON BUFFALO BILL COMMEMORATIVE REVOLVER
Caliber: .44. Barrel: 8 in., tapered octagon. Weight: 2.75 lbs. Length: 13-3/4 in. overall. Grips: Two-piece walnut. Sights: V-notch on top strap, blued steel blade front. Features: Gold-filled engraving over dark blue steel. A higher-grade gun commemorating the life of Buffalo Bill Cody. Made by Pietta. Imported by EMF.
Price: EMF PF58BB448 .... **$695.00**

PIETTA REMINGTON BELT MODEL REVOLVER
Caliber: .36. Barrel: 6.5 in., octagon. Weight: 44 oz. Length: 12.5 in. overall. Grips: Two-piece walnut. Sights: V-notch on top strap, blued steel blade front. Features: Brass triggerguard, blued steel backstrap and frame, case-hardened hammer and trigger. Made by Pietta. Imported by Dixie Gun Works.
Price: Dixie RH0214 .... **$295.00**

PIETTA 1863 REMINGTON POCKET MODEL REVOLVER
Caliber: .31, 5-shot. Barrel: 3.5 in. Weight: 1 lb. Length: 7.6 in. Grips: Two-piece walnut. Sights: Pin front, groove-in-frame rear. Features: Spur trigger, iron-, brass- or nickel-plated frame. Made by Pietta. Imported by EMF (Steel Frame), Dixie Gun Works, Taylor's and others.
Price: Brass frame, Dixie PH0407 .... **$260.00**
Price: Steel frame, Dixie PH0370 .... **$295.00**
Price: Nickel-plated, Dixie PH0409 .... **$315.00**

PIETTA LEMATT REVOLVER
Caliber: .44/20 Ga. Barrel: 6.75 in. (revolver); 4-7/8 in. (single shot). Weight: 3 lbs., 7 oz. Length: 14 in. overall. Grips: Hand-checkered walnut. Sights: Post front, hammer notch rear. Features: Exact reproduction with all-steel construction; 44-cal., 9-shot cylinder, 20-gauge single barrel; color case-hardened hammer with selector; spur triggerguard; ring at butt; lever-type barrel release. Made by Pietta. Imported by EMF, Dixie Gun Works and others.
Price: EMF Navy PFLMSTN44634 .... **$1,075.00**
Price: EMF Cavalry PFLMST44712 .... **$1,100.00**
Price: EMF Army PFLMSTA44634 .... **$1,100.00**

PIETTA SPILLER & BURR PERCUSSION REVOLVER
Caliber: .36. Barrel: 7 in., octagon. Weight: 2.5 lbs. Length: 12.5 in. overall. Grips: Two-piece walnut. Sights: V-notch on top strap, blued steel blade front. Features: Reproduction of the C.S.A. revolver. Brass frame and trigger guard. Also available as a kit. Made by Pietta. Imported by Dixie Gun Works, Traditions, Midway USA and others.
Price: Dixie RH0120 .... **$275.00**
Price: Dixie kit RH0300 .... **$235.00**

PIETTA STARR DOUBLE-ACTION ARMY REVOLVER
Caliber: .44. Barrel: 6 in. tapered round. Weight: 3 lbs. Length: 11.75 in. Grips: One-piece walnut. Sights: Hammer notch rear, dovetailed front. Features: Double-action mechanism, round tapered barrel, all blued frame and barrel. Made by Pietta. Imported by Dixie Gun Works and others.
Price: Dixie RH460 .... **$565.00**

PIETTA STARR SINGLE-ACTION ARMY REVOLVER
Caliber: .44. Barrel: 8 in. tapered round. Weight: 3 lbs. Length: 13.5 in. Grips: One-piece walnut. Sights: Hammer notch rear, dovetailed front. Features: Single-action mechanism, round tapered barrel, all blued frame and barrel. Made by Pietta. Imported by Cabela's, Dixie Gun Works and others.
Price: Dixie RH460 .... **$550.00**

PIETTA 1873 PERCUSSION REVOLVER
Caliber: .44. Barrel: 5.5 in. Weight: 40 oz. Length: 11.25 in. overall. Grips: One-piece walnut. Sights: V-notch on top strap, blued steel blade front. Features: A cap-and-ball version of the Colt Single Action Army revolver. Made by Pietta. Imported by EMF, Cabela's, Dixie Gun Works and others.
Price: EMF PF73CHS434NM **$360.00**

TRADITIONS U.S. MARSHAL
Caliber: .36, 6-shot. Barrel: 8 in., blued. Grips: One-piece walnut. Sights: Open, hammer/blade. Weight: 2.61 lbs. Features: Case-hardened frame, single action, U.S. Marshal logo on grips.
Price: **$351.00**

TRADITIONS WILDCARD
Caliber: .36, 6-shot. Barrel: 7.375 in., blued octagon. Grips: Simulated stag. Sights: Open, hammer/blade. Weight: 2.5 lbs. Features: 1851 "Gunfighter," 13.5-in. overall length, case-hardened frame.
Price: **$409.00**

UBERTI 1847 WALKER PERCUSSION REVOLVER
Caliber: .44. Barrel: 9 in. Weight: 4.5 lbs. Length: 15.7 in. overall. Grips: One-piece hardwood. Sights: Brass blade front, hammer notch rear. Features: Copy of Sam Colt's first U.S. contract revolver. Engraved cylinder, case-hardened hammer and loading lever. Blued finish. Made by Uberti. Imported by Cabela's, Cimarron, Dixie Gun Works, EMF, Taylor's, Uberti U.S.A. and others.
Price: Uberti USA, standard model, blued steel 340200..................... **$429.00**

UBERTI DRAGOON PERCUSSION REVOLVERS
Caliber: .44. Barrel: 7.5 in. Weight: 4.1 lbs. Grips: One-piece walnut. Sights: Brass blade front, hammer notch rear. Features: Four models of the big .44 caliber revolvers that followed the massive Walker model and pre-dated the sleek 1860 Army model. Blued barrel, backstrap and trigger guard. Made by Uberti. Imported by Uberti USA, Dixie Gun Works, Taylor's and others.
Price: Uberti USA, Whitneyville Dragoon 340830.............................. **$429.00**
Price: Uberti USA, First Model Dragoon 340800................................ **$429.00**
Price: Uberti USA, Second Model Dragoon 340810............................ **$429.00**
Price: Uberti USA, Third Model Dragoon 340860................................ **$429.00**

UBERTI 1849 POCKET MODEL WELLS FARGO PERCUSSION REVOLVER
Caliber: .31. Barrel: 4 in., seven-groove, RH twist. Weight: About 24 oz. Grips: One-piece walnut. Sights: Brass pin front, hammer notch rear. Features: Unfluted cylinder with stagecoach holdup scene, cupped cylinder pin, no grease grooves, one safety pin on cylinder and slot in hammer face. Made by Uberti. Imported by Uberti USA, Cimarron, Dixie Gun Works and others.
Price: Uberti USA 340350... **$349.00**

UBERTI 1849 WELLS FARGO PERCUSSION REVOLVER
Caliber: .31. Barrel: 4 in.; seven-groove; RH twist. Weight: About 24 oz. Grips: One-piece walnut. Sights: Brass pin front, hammer notch rear. Features: No loading lever, Unfluted cylinder with stagecoach holdup scene, cupped cylinder pin, no grease grooves, one safety pin on cylinder and slot in hammer face. Made by Uberti. Imported by Uberti USA, Cimarron, Dixie Gun Works and others.
Price: Uberti USA 340380... **$349.00**

UBERTI NAVY MODEL 1851 PERCUSSION REVOLVER
Caliber: .36, 6-shot. Barrel: 7.5 in. Weight: 44 oz. Length: 13 in. overall. Grips: One-piece walnut. Sights: Post front, hammer notch rear. Features: Brass backstrap and trigger guard, or steel backstrap and trigger guard (London Model), engraved cylinder with navy battle scene; case-hardened hammer, loading lever. Made by Uberti and Pietta. Imported by Uberti USA, Cabela's, Cimarron, and others.
Price: Uberti USA Brass grip assembly 340000 ....**$329.00**
Price: Uberti USA London Model 340050 ....**$369.00**

UBERTI 1860 ARMY REVOLVER
Caliber: .44. Barrel: 8 in. Weight: 44 oz. Length: 13.25 in. overall. Grips: One-piece walnut. Sights: Brass blade front, hammer notch rear. Features: Steel or case-hardened frame, brass triggerguard, case-hardened creeping loading lever. Many models and finishes are available for this pistol. Made by Uberti. Imported by Cabela's, Cimarron, Dixie Gun Works, EMF, Taylor's, Uberti U.S.A. and others.
Price: Uberti USA, roll engraved cylinder 340400 .... **$349.00**
Price: Uberti USA, full fluted cylinder 340410 .... **$369.00**

UBERTI 1861 NAVY PERCUSSION REVOLVER
Caliber: .36 Barrel: 7.5 in. Weight: 44 oz. Length: 13.25 in. overall. Grips: One-piece walnut. Sights: Brass blade front, hammer notch rear. Features: Brass backstrap and trigger guard, or steel backstrap and trigger guard (London Model), engraved cylinder with navy battle scene; case-hardened hammer, loading lever. Made by Uberti. Imported by Uberti USA, Cabela's, Cimarron, Dixie Gun Works, Taylor's and others.
Price: Uberti USA Brass grip assembly 340630 ....**$349.00**
Price: Uberti USA London Model 340500 ....**$349.00**

Prices given are believed to be accurate at time of publication however, many factors affect retail pricing so exact prices are not possible.

UBERTI 1862 POLICE PERCUSSION REVOLVER
Caliber: .36, 5-shot. Barrel: 5.5 in., 6.5 in., 7.5 in. Weight: 26 oz. Length: 12 in. overall (6.5 in. bbl.). Grips: One-piece walnut. Sights: Fixed. Features: Round tapered barrel; half-fluted and rebated cylinder; case-hardened frame, loading lever and hammer; brass trigger guard and backstrap. Made by Uberti. Imported by Cimarron, Dixie Gun Works, Taylor's, Uberti U.S.A. and others.
Price: Uberti USA 340700 .... **$369.00**

UBERTI 1862 POCKET NAVY PERCUSSION REVOLVER
Caliber: .36, 5-shot. Barrel: 5.5 in., 6.5 in. Weight: 26 oz. Length: 12 in. overall (6.5 in. bbl.). Grips: One-piece walnut. Sights: Fixed. Features: Octagon barrel; case-hardened frame, loading lever and hammer; silver or brass trigger guard and backstrap; also available in an all stainless steel version. Made by Uberti. Imported by Uberti USA, Cimarron, Dixie Gun Works, Taylor's and others.
Price: Uberti USA 340750 .... **$369.00**

UBERTI LEACH AND RIGDON PERCUSSION REVOLVER
Caliber: .36. Barrel: 7.5 in., octagon to round. Weight: 2.75 lbs. Length: 13 in. Grips: One-piece walnut. Sights: Hammer notch and pin front. Features: Steel frame. Reproduction of the C.S.A. revolver. Brass backstrap and trigger guard. Made by Uberti. Imported by Uberti USA, Dixie Gun Works and others.
Price: Uberti USA 340030 .... **$349.00**

UBERTI NEW ARMY REMINGTON PERCUSSION REVOLVER
Caliber: .44, 6-shot. Barrel: Tapered octagon 8 in. Weight: 32 oz. Length: Standard 13.5 in. Grips: Two-piece walnut. Sights: Standard blade front, groove-in-frame rear; adjustable on some models. Features: Many variations of this gun are available. Target Model (Uberti U.S.A.) has fully adjustable target rear sight, target front, .36 or .44. Made by Uberti. Imported by Uberti USA, Cimarron F.A. Co., Taylor's and others.
Price: Uberti USA Steel frame, 341000 .... **$369.00**
Price: Uberti USA Stainless, 341020 .... **$449.00**

ARMI SPORT ENFIELD THREE-BAND P1853 RIFLE
Caliber: .58. Barrel: 39 in. Weight: 10.25 lbs. Length: 52 in. overall. Stock: European walnut. Sights: Blade front, flip-up rear with elevator marked to 800 yards. Features: Reproduction of the original three-band rifle. Percussion musket-cap ignition. Blued barrel with steel barrelbands, brass furniture. Case-hardened lock. Lockplate marked "London Armory Co. and Crown." Made by Euro Arms, Armi Sport (Chiappa). Imported by Dixie Gun Works and others.
Price: Dixie Gun Works rifled bore PR1130 .... **$895.00**
Price: Dixie Gun Work smooth bore PR1052 .... **$750.00**

CVA ACCURA IN-LINE BREAK-ACTION RIFLE
Caliber: .50. Barrel: 28 in. fluted. Weight: 7.5 lbs. Length: Standard 45 in. Stock: Ambidextrous solid composite in standard or thumbhole. Sights: Adj. fiber-optic. Features: Break-action, quick-release breech plug, aluminum loading rod, cocking spur, lifetime warranty. By CVA.
Price: CVA PR3120NM (Accura MR Nitride with Black Stocks and Scope Mount) **$493.00**

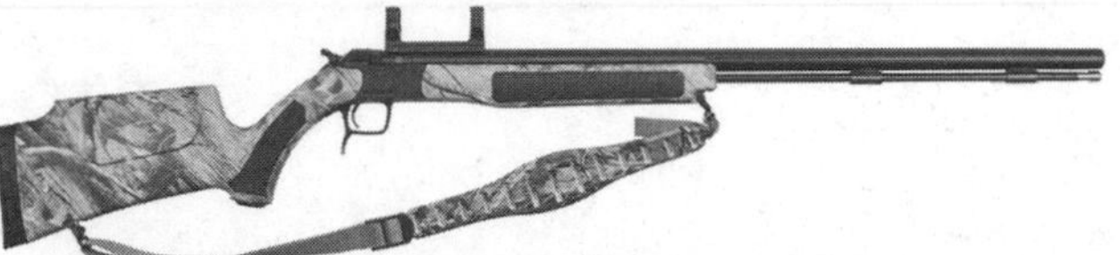

CVA ACCURA V2 LR NITRIDE "SPECIAL EDITION" IN-LINE BREAK-ACTION RIFLE
Caliber: .50. Barrel: 30 in. fluted. Weight: 7.5 lbs. Length: Standard 45 in. Stock: Ambidextrous solid composite. Sights: Adj. fiber-optic. Features: Break-action, quick-release breech plug, aluminum loading rod, cocking spur, equipped with a genuine, Nitride treated, 30-inch Bergara Barrel, and a deep pistol grip stock decorated in APG camo. Lifetime warranty. By CVA.
Price: CVA PR6124NM **$449.00**

CVA ACCURA LR
Caliber: .45, .50. Barrel: 30 in., Nitride-treated, 416 stainless steel Bergara. Stock: Ambidextrous thumbhole camo. Sights: DuraSight Dead-On one-piece scope mount, scope not included. Weight: 6.75 lbs. Features: Reversible hammer spur, CrushZone recoil pad, quick-release breech plug.
Price: **$605.00**

CVA ACCURA MR (MOUNTAIN RIFLE) IN-LINE BREAK-ACTION RIFLE
Caliber: .50. Barrel: 25 in. Weight: 6.35 lbs. Length: Standard 45 in. Stock: Ambidextrous solid composite. Sights: DuraSight DEAD-ON One-Piece Scope Mount. Features: Break-action, quick-release breech plug, aluminum loading rod, cocking spur, and a deep pistol grip stock decorated in Realtree APG camo. Lifetime warranty. By CVA.
Price: CVA PR3121SNM **$546.00**

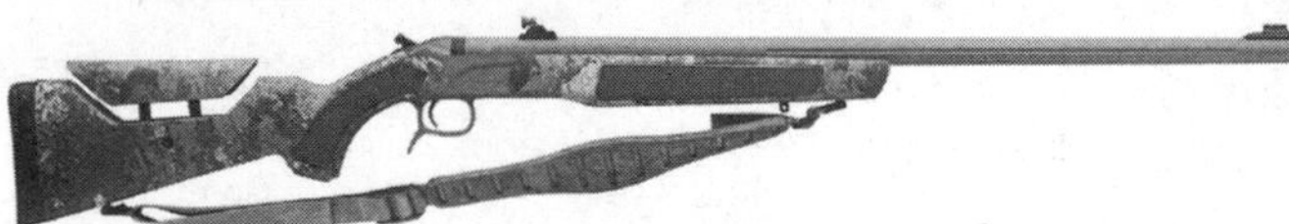

CVA ACCURA LRX
Caliber: .45 and .50. Barrel: 30 in. Nitride-treated stainless steel Bergara barrel. Comes with a carbon-fiber collapsible field rod, which you carry on your hip, a configuration that allows the barrel to be completely free-floated. The stock also wears a height-adjustable comb. Utilizes CVA's screw-in/out breech plug system.
Price: **$675.00**

CVA PLAINS RIFLE
Caliber: .50. Barrel: 28 in., Nitride, fluted, stainless steel Bergara. Stock: Ambidextrous composite Realtree MAX-1 XT. Sights: DuraSight Dead-On one-piece scope mount, scope not included. Weight: 7.2 lbs. Features: Solid aluminum PalmSaver ramrod, reversible cocking spur, Quake Claw sling.
Price: **$593.00**

CVA PARAMOUNT PRO
Caliber: .45, magnum. Barrel: Fluted Bergara free-floating, Cerakote/Nitride stainless steel/camo. Stock: Grayboe fiberglass. Sights: Threaded 3/4x20, scope not included. Weight: 8.75 lbs. Features: TriggerTech trigger, VariFlame breech plug, accessory trap door, self-deploying ramrod.
Price: **$1,667.00**

CVA PARAMOUNT PRO COLORADO
Caliber: .50, magnum. Barrel: Fluted Bergara free-floating, Cerakote/Nitride stainless steel/camo. Stock: Grayboe fiberglass. Sights: Williams peep sight. Weight: 8.75 lbs. Features: TriggerTech trigger, VariFlame breech plug, accessory trap door, self-deploying ramrod.
Price: **$1,667.00**

CVA PARAMOUNT HTR LONG RANGE MUZZLELOADER
Caliber: .40 and .45. Barrel: 26 in. Threaded 3/4x20 for muzzle brake. Twist rate: 1:20 (.40 cal.), 1:22 (.45 cal.). Weight: 9.6 lbs. Comes with a collapsible carbon-fiber ram rod. Features: Designed to handle "super-magnum" charges of Blackhorn 209 and capable of producing muzzle velocities comparable to centerfire rifles — eclipsing 2,700 fps.The HTR has a more hunting-focused stock design than the original Paramount model, featuring an adjustable comb and an internal aluminum chassis that provides a consistent shot-to-shot foundation for the action and free-floating barrel.
Price: **$1,225.00**

CVA OPTIMA IN-LINE BREAK-ACTION RIFLE
Caliber: .50. Barrel: 26 in., stainless steel. Weight: 6.65 lbs. Length: 41in. Stock: Ambidextrous solid composite. Available in pistol grip or thumbhole configurations. Sights: DuraSight DEAD-ON One-Piece Scope Mount. Features: Ambidextrous with rubber grip panels in black or Realtree APG camo, crush-zone recoil pad, reversible hammer spur, quake claw sling. Lifetime warranty. By CVA.
Price: CVA PR2020SM **$371.00**

CVA WOLF IN-LINE BREAK-ACTION RIFLE
Caliber: .50 Barrel: 24 in. Weight: 6.23 lbs. Stock: Ambidextrous composite. Sights: Dead-On Scope Mounts or Fiber Optic. Features: Break-action, quick-release breech plug for 209 primer, aluminum loading road, cocking spur. Lifetime warranty. By CVA.
Price: CVA PR2112SM (.50-cal, stainless/Realtree Hardwoods HD, scope mount) **$289.50**
Price: CVA PR2112S (50-cal, stainless/Realtree Hardwoods HD, fib. opt. sight) **$289.50**
Price: CVA PR2110SM (.50-cal, stainless/black, scope mount) **$240.50**

DIXIE DELUXE CUB RIFLE
Caliber: .32, .36. Barrel: 28 in. octagonal. Weight: 6.5 lbs. Length: 44 in. overall. Stock: Walnut. Sights: Fixed. Features: Each gun available in either flint or percussion ignition. Short rifle for small game and beginning shooters. Brass patchbox and furniture. Made by Pedersoli for Dixie Gun Works.
Price: Dixie Gun Works (.32-cal. flint) PR3130 .... **$890.00**
Price: Dixie Gun Works (.36-cal. flint) FR3135 .... **$890.00**
Price: Dixie Gun Works (.32-cal. Percussion kit) PK3360 .... **$690.00**
Price: Dixie Gun Works (.36-cal. Percussion kit) PK3365 .... **$690.00**
Price: Dixie Gun Works (.32-cal. Flint kit) PK3350 .... **$710.00**
Price: Dixie Gun Works (.36-cal. Flint kit) PK335 .... **$710.00**
Price: Dixie Gun Works (.32-cal. percussion) PR3140 .... **$850.00**
Price: Dixie Gun Works (.36-cal. percussion) PR3145 .... **$850.00**

Prices given are believed to be accurate at time of publication however, many factors affect retail pricing so exact prices are not possible.

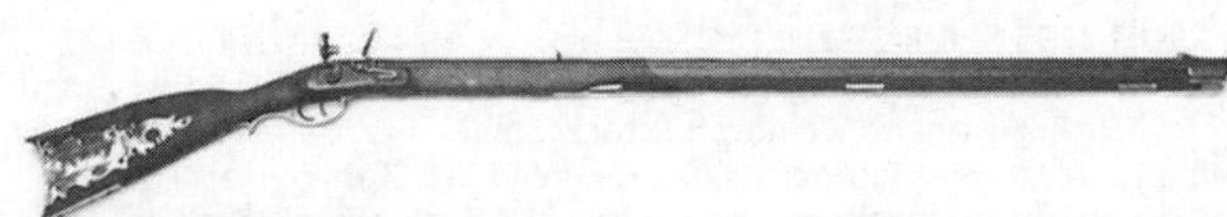

DIXIE PENNSYLVANIA RIFLE
Caliber: .45 and .50. Barrel: 41.5 in. octagonal, .45/1:48, .50/1:56 in. twist. Weight: 8.5, 8.75 lbs. Length: 56 in. overall. Stock: European walnut, full-length stock. Sights: Notch rear, blade front. Features: Flintlock or percussion, brass patchbox, double-set triggers. Also available as kit guns for both calibers and ignition systems. Made by Pedersoli for Dixie Gun Works.
Price: Dixie Gun Works (.45-cal. flint) FR1060 **$1,100.00**
Price: Dixie Gun Works (.50-cal. flint) FR3200 **$1,100.00**
Price: Dixie Gun Works (.45-cal. Percussion kit) PR1075 **$910.00**
Price: Dixie Gun Works (.50-cal. Percussion kit) PK3365 **$910.00**
Price: Dixie Gun Works (.45-cal. Flint kit) FR1065 **$910.00**
Price: Dixie Gun Works (.50-cal. Flint kit) FK3420 **$910.00**
Price: Dixie Gun Works (.45-cal. percussion) FR1070 **$1,050.00**
Price: Dixie Gun Works (.50-cal. percussion) PR3205 **$1,050.00**

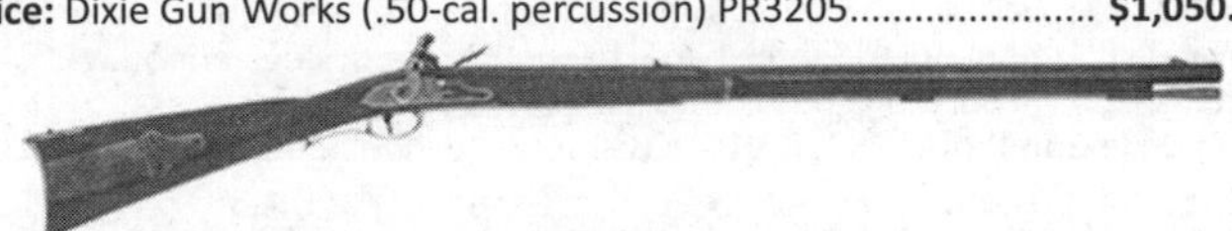

EUROARMS 1803 HARPER'S FERRY FLINTLOCK RIFLE
Caliber: .54. Barrel: 35.5 in., smoothbore. Weight: 9.5 lbs. Length: 50.5 in. overall. Stock: Half-stock, walnut w/oil finish. Sights: Blade front, notched rear. Features: Color case-hardened lock, browned barrel, with barrel key. Made by Euroarms. Imported by Dixie Gun Works.
Price: Dixie Gun Works FR0171 **$795.00**

EUROARMS J.P. MURRAY ARTILLERY CARBINE
Caliber: .58. Barrel: 23.5 in. Weight: 8 lbs. Length: 39.5 in. Stock: European walnut. Sights: Blade front, fixed notch rear. Features: Percussion musket-cap ignition. Reproduction of the original Confederate carbine. Lock marked "J.P. Murray, Columbus, Georgia." Blued barrel. Made by Euroarms. Imported by Dixie Gun Works and others.
Price: Dixie, Gun Works PR0173 **$1,100.00**

EUROARMS ENFIELD MUSKETOON P1861
Caliber: .58. Barrel: 24 in. Weight: 9 lbs. Length: 40 in. overall. Stock: European walnut. Sights: Blade front, flip-up rear with elevator marked to 700 yards. Features: Reproduction of the original cavalry version of the Enfield rifle. Percussion musket-cap ignition. Blued barrel with steel barrelbands, brass furniture. Case-hardened lock. Euroarms version marked London Armory with crown. Pedersoli version has Birmingham stamp on stock and Enfield and Crown on lockplate. Made by Euroarms. Imported by Dixie Gun Works and others.
Price: Dixie Gun Works PR0343 **$1,050.00**

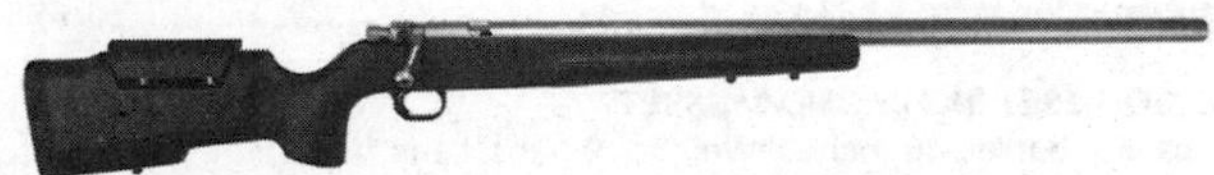

KNIGHT 500 IN-LINE RIFLE
Caliber: .50. Barrel: 28 in., custom Green Mountain. Weight: 10 lbs. Length: 46 in. overall. Stock: Boyd's custom stock with integrated aluminum bedding Sights: Not included. Features: Competition-grade muzzleloader that can be used as a hunting rifle, handcrafted Green Mountain barrel, the stock also features an adjustable cheek piece that gives you a clear view down range. Made in U.S. by Knight Rifles.
Price: Muzzleloaders.com MMTE758TAR **Starting at $2,080.00**

KNIGHT BIGHORN IN-LINE RIFLE
Caliber: .50. Barrel: 26 in., 1:28 in. twist. Weight: 7 lbs. 3 oz. Length: 44.5 in. overall. Stock: G2 straight or thumbhole, Carbon Knight straight or thumbhole or black composite thumbhole with recoil pad, sling swivel studs. Ramrod: Carbon core with solid brass extendable jag. Sights: Fully adjustable metallic fiber optic. Features: Uses four different ignition systems (included): #11 nipple, musket nipple, bare 208 shotgun primer and 209 Extreme shotgun primer system (Extreme weatherproof full plastic jacket system); vented breech plug, striker fired with one-piece removable hammer assembly. With recommended loads, guaranteed to have 4-inch, three-shot groups at 200 yards. Also available as Western gun with exposed ignition. Made in U.S. by Knight Rifles.
Price: Muzzleloaders.com MBH706C **$646.00**

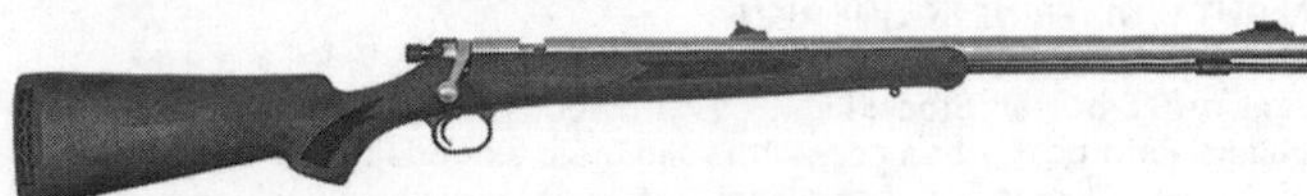

KNIGHT DISC EXTREME
Caliber: .50, .52. Barrel: 26 in., fluted stainless, 1:28 in. twist. Weight: 7 lbs. 14 oz. to 8 lbs. Length: 45 in. overall. Stock: Carbon Knight straight or thumbhole with blued or SS; G2 thumbhole; left-handed Nutmeg thumbhole. Ramrod: Solid brass extendable jag. Sights: Fully adjustable metallic fiber optics. Features: Bolt-action rifle, full plastic jacket ignition system, #11 nipple, musket nipple, bare 208 shotgun primer. With recommended loads, guaranteed to have 4-inch, three-shot groups at 200 yards. Also available as Western gun with exposed ignition. Made in U.S. by Knight Rifles.
Price: Muzzleloaders.com MDE706SMX **Starting at $721.00**

KNIGHT LITTLEHORN IN-LINE RIFLE
Caliber: .50. Barrel: 22 in., 1:28 in. twist. Weight: 6.7 lbs. Length: 39 in. overall. Stock: 12.5-in. length of pull, G2 straight or pink Realtree AP HD. Ramrod: Carbon core with solid brass extendable jag. Sights: Fully adjustable Williams fiber optic. Features: Uses four different ignition systems (included): Full Plastic Jacket, #11 nipple, musket nipple or bare 208 shotgun primer; vented breech plug, striker-fired with one-piece removable hammer assembly. Finish: Stainless steel. With recommended loads, guaranteed to have 4-inch, three-shot groups at 200 yards. Also available as Western gun with exposed ignition. Made in U.S. by Knight Rifles.
Price: Muzzleloaders.com MLHW702C **Starting at $390.00**

KNIGHT MOUNTAINEER IN-LINE RIFLE
Caliber: .45, .50, .52. Barrel: 27 in. fluted stainless steel, free floated. Weight: 8 lbs. (thumbhole stock), 8.3 lbs. (straight stock). Length: 45.5 inches. Sights: Fully adjustable metallic fiber optic. Features: Bolt-action rifle, adjustable match-grade trigger, aluminum ramrod with carbon core, solid brass extendable jag, vented breech plug. Ignition: Full plastic jacket, #11 nipple, musket nipple, bare 208 shotgun primer. With recommended loads, guaranteed to have 4-inch, three-shot groups at 200 yards. Also available as Western gun with exposed ignition. Made in U.S. by Knight Rifles.
Price: Muzzleloaders.com MMT707SNMNT **Starting at $1,016.00**

KNIGHT TK-2000 IN-LINE SHOTGUN
Gauge: 12. Barrel: 26 inches. Choke: Extra-full and improved cylinder available. Stock: Realtree Xtra Green straight or thumbhole. Weight: 7.7 pounds. Sights: Williams fully adjustable rear, fiber-optic front. Features: Striker-fired action, receiver is drilled and tapped for scope, adjustable trigger, removable breech plug, double-safety system. Ignition: #209 primer with Full Plastic Jacket, musket cap or No. 11. Striker-fired with one-piece removable hammer assembly. Made in U.S. by Knight Rifles.
Price: Muzzleloaders.com MTK2000SXG **Starting at $742.00**

KNIGHT ULTRA-LITE IN-LINE RIFLE
Caliber: .45 or .50. Barrel: 24 in. Stock: Black, tan or olive-green Kevlar spider web. Weight: 6 lbs. Features: Bolt-action rifle. Ramrod: Carbon core with solid brass extendable jag. Sights: With or without Williams fiber-optic sights, drilled and tapped for scope mounts. Finish: Stainless steel. Ignition: 209 Primer with Full Plastic Jacket, musket cap or #11 nipple, bare 208 shotgun primer; vented breech plug. With recommended loads, guaranteed to have 4-inch, three-shot groups at 200 yards. Also available as Western version with exposed ignition. Made in U.S. by Knight Rifles.
Price: Muzzleloaders.com MULE704TNT **Starting at $1,217.00**

KNIGHT VISION IN-LINE RIFLE
Caliber: .50. Barrel: 24 in. Length: 44 in. Stock: Black composite. Weight: 7.9 lbs. Features: Break-open rifle with carbon-steel barrel and all-new machined steel action. With recommended loads, guaranteed to have 4-inch, three-shot groups at 200 yards. Ramrod: Carbon core with solid brass extendable jag. Ignition: Full Plastic Jacket. Sights: Weaver sight bases attached, and Williams fiber-optic sights provided. Finish: Blued steel. Made in U.S. by Knight Rifles.
Price: Muzzleloaders.com MKVE04XT **Starting at $346.00**

Prices given are believed to be accurate at time of publication however, many factors affect retail pricing so exact prices are not possible.

KNIGHT WOLVERINE IN-LINE RIFLE
Caliber: .50. Barrel: 22 in. stainless steel, 1:28 in. twist. Weight: 6.9 lbs. Length: 40.5 overall. Stock: Realtree Hardwoods straight, CarbonKnight straight. Ramrod: Carbon core with solid brass extendable jag. Sights: Fully adjustable Williams fiber optic. Features: Ignition systems (included): #11 nipple, musket nipple, bare 208 shotgun primer; vented breech plug, striker-fired with one-piece removable hammer assembly. Finish: Stainless steel. With recommended loads, guaranteed to have 4-inch, three-shot groups at 200 yards. Also available as Western gun with exposed ignition. Made in U.S. by Knight Rifles.
Price: Muzzleloaders.com MWS702XT............................**Starting at $395.00**

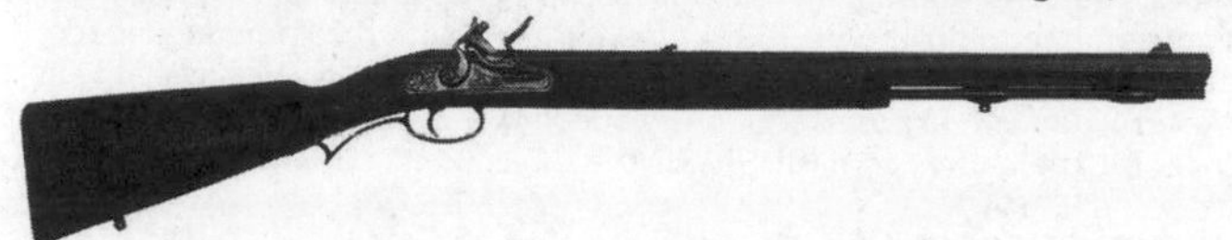

LYMAN DEERSTALKER RIFLE
Caliber: .50, .54. Barrel: 28 in. octagon, 1:48 in. twist. Weight: 10.8 lbs. Length: 45 in. overall. Stock: European walnut with black rubber recoil pad. Sights: Lyman's high visibility, fiber-optic sights. Features: Fast-twist rifling for conical bullets. Blackened metal parts to eliminate glare, stainless steel nipple. Hook breech, single trigger, coil spring lock. Steel barrel rib and ramrod ferrules. From Lyman.
Price: Muzzleloaders.com 6033146/7. 50-cal /.54-cal. flint............... **$448.00**
Price: Muzzleloaders.com 6033140/7 .50-cal /.54-cal. percussion **$398.00**

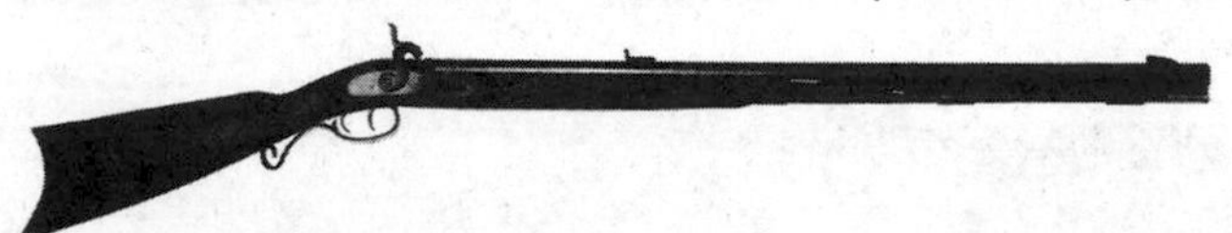

LYMAN GREAT PLAINS RIFLE
Caliber: .50, .54. Barrel: 32 in., 1:60 in. twist. Weight: 11.6 lbs. Stock: Walnut. Sights: Steel blade front, buckhorn rear adjustable for windage and elevation, and fixed notch primitive sight included. Features: Percussion or flint ignition. Blued steel furniture. Stainless steel nipple. Coil spring lock, Hawken-style triggerguard and double-set triggers. Round thimbles recessed and sweated into rib. Steel wedge plates and toe plate. Introduced 1979. From Lyman.
Price: 6031102/3 .50-cal./.54-cal percussion.......................................**$784.00**
Price: 6031105/6 .50-cal./.54-cal flintlock **$839.00**
Price: 6031125/6 .50-ca./.54-cal left-hand percussion **$824.00**
Price: 6031137 .50-cal. left-hand flintlock **$859.00**
Price: 6031111/2 .50/.54-cal. percussion kit..**$639.00**
Price: 6031114/5 .50/.54-cal. flintlock kit...**$689.00**

LYMAN GREAT PLAINS HUNTER MODEL
Similar to Great Plains model except 1:32 in. twist, shallow-groove barrel for conicals or sabots, and comes drilled and tapped for Lyman 57GPR peep sight.
Price: 6031120/1 .50-cal./.54-cal percussion.. **$791.00**
Price: 6031148/9 .50-cal/.54-cal flintlock **$839.00**
Price: 6031112 .50-cal/.54-cal percussion kit **$669.00**
Price: 6031115 .50-cal/.54-cal flintlock kit..**$729.00**

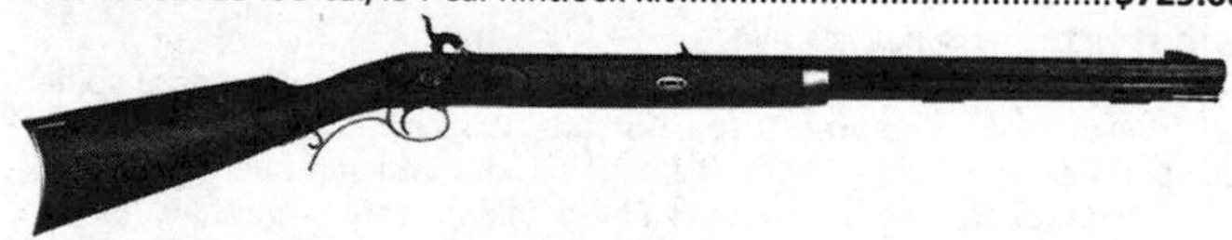

LYMAN TRADE RIFLE
Caliber: .50, .54. Barrel: 28 in. octagon, 1:48 in. twist. Weight: 10.8 lbs. Length: 45 in. overall. Stock: European walnut. Sights: Blade front, open rear adjustable for windage, or optional fixed sights. Features: Fast-twist rifling for conical bullets. Polished brass furniture with blue steel parts, stainless steel nipple. Hook breech, single trigger, coil spring percussion lock. Steel barrel rib and ramrod ferrules. Introduced 1980. From Lyman.
Price: 6032125/6 .50-cal./.54-cal. percussion **$565.00**
Price: 6032129/30 .50-cal./.54-cal. flintlock **$583.00**

PEDERSOLI 1777 CHARLEVILLE MUSKET
Caliber: .69. Barrel: 44.75 in. round, smoothbore. Weight: 10.5 lbs. Length: 57 in. Stock: European walnut, fullstock. Sights: Steel stud on upper barrelband. Features: Flintlock using one-inch flint. Steel parts all polished armory bright, brass furniture. Lock marked Charleville. Made by Pedersoli. Imported by Cabela's, Dixie Gun Works, others.
Price: Dixie Gun Works FR0930 .... **$1,450.00**

PEDERSOLI 1795 SPRINGFIELD MUSKET
Caliber: .69. Barrel: 44.75 in., round, smoothbore. Weight: 10.5 lbs. Length: 57.25 in. Stock: European walnut, fullstock. Sights: Brass stud on upper barrelband. Features: Flintlock using one-inch flint. Steel parts all polished armory bright, brass furniture. Lock marked US Springfield. Made by Pedersoli. Imported by Cabela's, Dixie Gun Works, others.
Price: Dixie Gun Works FR3210 .... **$1,495.00**

PEDERSOLI POTSDAM 1809 PRUSSIAN MUSKET
Caliber: .75. Barrel: 41.2 in. round, smoothbore. Weight: 9 lbs. Length: 56 in. Stock: European walnut, fullstock. Sights: Brass lug on upper barrelband. Features: Flintlock using one-inch flint. Steel parts all polished armory bright, brass furniture. Lock marked "Potsdam over G.S." Made by Pedersoli. Imported by Dixie Gun Works.
Price: Dixie Gun Works FR3175 .... **$1,575.00**

PEDERSOLI 1816 FLINTLOCK MUSKET
Caliber: .69. Barrel: 42 in., smoothbore. Weight: 9.75 lbs. Length: 56-7/8 in. overall. Stock: Walnut w/oil finish. Sights: Blade front. Features: All metal finished in "National Armory Bright," three barrel bands w/springs, steel ramrod w/ button-shaped head. Made by Pedersoli. Imported by Dixie Gun Works.
Price: Dixie Gun Works PR3180, Percussion conversion **$1,495.00**

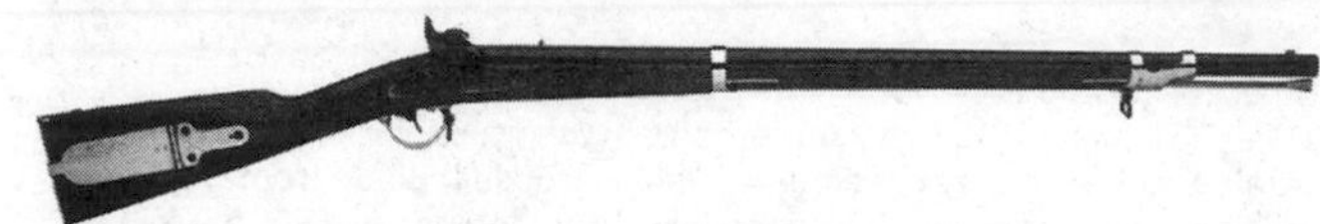

PEDERSOLI 1841 MISSISSIPPI RIFLE
Caliber: .54, .58. Barrel: 33 inches. Weight: 9.5 lbs. Length: 48.75 in. overall. Stock: European walnut. Sights: Blade front, notched rear. Features: Percussion musket-cap ignition. Reproduction of the original one-band rifle with large brass patchbox. Color case-hardened lockplate with browned barrel. Made by Pedersoli. Imported by Dixie Gun Works, Cabela's and others.
Price: Dixie Gun Works PR0870 (.54 caliber)....................................**$1,200.00**
Price: Dixie Gun Works PR3470 (.58 caliber)....................................**$1,100.00**

PEDERSOLI 1854 LORENZ RIFLE
Caliber: .54. Barrel: 37 in. Weight: 9 lbs. Length: 49 in. overall. Stock: European walnut. Sights: Blade front, rear steel open, flip-up style. Features: Percussion musket-cap ignition. Armory bright lockplate marked "Konigi. Wurt Fabrik." Armory bright steel barrel. Made by Pedersoli. Imported by Dixie Gun Works.
Price: Dixie Gun Works PR3156...**$1,500.00**

PEDERSOLI 1857 MAUSER RIFLE
Caliber: .54. Barrel: 39.75 in. Weight: 9.5 lbs. Length: 52 in. overall. Stock: European walnut. Sights: Blade front, rear steel adjustable for windage and elevation. Features: Percussion musket-cap ignition. Color case-hardened lockplate marked "Konigi. Wurt Fabrik." Armory bright steel barrel. Made by Pedersoli. Imported by Dixie Gun Works.
Price: Dixie Gun Works PR1330...**$1,695.00**

PEDERSOLI 1861 RICHMOND MUSKET
Caliber: .58. Barrel: 40 inches. Weight: 9.5 lbs. Length: 55.5 in. overall. Stock: European walnut. Sights: Blade front, three-leaf military rear. Features: Reproduction of the original three-band rifle. Percussion musket-cap ignition. Lock marked C. S. Richmond, Virginia. Armory bright. Made by Pedersoli. Imported by Dixie Gun Works and others.
Price: Dixie Gun Works PR4095...**$1,150.00**

PEDERSOLI 1861 SPRINGFIELD RIFLE
Caliber: .58. Barrel: 40 inches. Weight: 10 lbs. Length: 55.5 in. overall. Stock: European walnut. Sights: Blade front, three-leaf military rear. Features: Reproduction of the original three-band rifle. Percussion musket-cap ignition. Lockplate marked 1861 with eagle and U.S. Springfield. Armory bright steel. Made by Armi Sport/Chiappa, Pedersoli. Imported by Cabela's, Dixie Gun Works, others.
Price: Cabela's **$1,199.00**

PEDERSOLI BAKER CAVALRY SHOTGUN
Gauge: 20. Barrels: 11.25 inches. Weight: 5.75 pounds. Length: 27.5 in. overall. Stock: American walnut. Sights: Bead front. Features: Reproduction of shotguns carried by Confederate cavalry. Single non-selective trigger, back-action locks. No. 11 percussion musket-cap ignition. Blued barrel with steel furniture. Case-

hardened lock. Pedersoli also makes a 12-gauge coach-length version of this back-action-lock shotgun with 20-inch barrels, and a full-length version in 10, 12 and 20 gauge. Made by Pedersoli. Imported by Cabela's and others.
Price: Cabela's **$1,099.00**

PEDERSOLI BRISTLEN MORGES AND WAADTLANDER TARGET RIFLES
Caliber: .44, .45. Barrel: 29.5 in. tapered octagonal, hooked breech. Weight: 15.5 lbs. Length: 48.5 in. overall. Stock: European walnut, halfstock with hooked buttplate and detachable palm rest. Sights: Creedmoor rear on Morges, Swiss Diopter on Waadtlander, hooded front sight notch. Features: Percussion back-action lock, double set, double-phase triggers, one barrel key, muzzle protector. Specialized bullet molds for each gun. Made by Pedersoli. Imported by Dixie Gun Works and others.
Price: Dixie Gun Works, .44 Bristlen Morges PR0165 .... **$2,995.00**
Price: Dixie Gun Works, .45 Waadtlander PR0183 .... **$2,995.00**

PEDERSOLI BROWN BESS
Caliber: .75. Barrel: 42 in., round, smoothbore. Weight: 9 lbs. Length: 57.75 in. Stock: European walnut, fullstock. Sights: Steel stud on front serves as bayonet lug. Features: Flintlock using one-inch flint with optional brass flash guard (SCO203), steel parts all polished armory bright, brass furniture. Lock marked Grice, 1762 with crown and GR. Made by Pedersoli. Imported by Cabela's, Dixie Gun Works, others.
Price: Dixie Gun Works Complete Gun FR0810 .... **$1,350.00**
Price: Dixie Gun Works Kit Gun FR0825 .... **$1,050.00**
Price: Dixie Gun Works Trade Gun, 30.5-in. barrel FR0665 .... **$1,495.00**
Price: Dixie Gun Works Trade Gun Kit FR0600 .... **$975.00**

PEDERSOLI COOK & BROTHER CONFEDERATE CARBINE/ARTILLERY/RIFLE
Caliber: .58 Barrel: 24/33/39 inches. Weight: 7.5/8.4/8.6 lbs. Length: 40.5/48/54.5 in. Stock: Select oil-finished walnut. Features: Percussion musket-cap ignition. Color case-hardened lock, browned barrel. Buttplate, triggerguard, barrelbands, sling swivels and nose cap of polished brass. Lock marked with stars and bars flag on tail and Athens, Georgia. Made by Pedersoli. Imported by Dixie Gun Works, others.
Price: Dixie Gun Works Carbine PR0830 ....**$995.00**
Price: Dixie Gun Works Artillery/Rifle PR32165 .... **$995.00**

PEDERSOLI COUNTRY HUNTER
Caliber: .50. Barrel: 26 in. octagonal. Weight: 6 lbs. Length: 41.75 in. overall. Stock: European walnut, halfstock. Sights: Rear notch, blade front. Features: Percussion, one barrel key. Made by Pedersoli. Imported by Dixie Gun Works.
Price: Cherry's Fine Guns Percussion, .50 .... **$675.00**
Price: Cherry's Fine Guns Flint, .50.. **$688.00**

PEDERSOLI ENFIELD MUSKETOON P1861
Caliber: .58. Barrel: 33 in. Weight: 9 lbs. Length: 35 in. overall. Stock: European walnut. Sights: Blade front, flip-up rear with elevator marked to 700 yards. Features: Reproduction of the original cavalry version of the Enfield rifle. Percussion musket-cap ignition. Blued barrel with steel barrelbands, brass furniture. Case-hardened lock. Euroarms version marked London Armory with crown. Pedersoli version has Birmingham stamp on stock and Enfield and Crown on lockplate. Made by Euroarms, Pedersoli. Imported by Cabela's and others.
Price: Cabela's **$1,099.00**

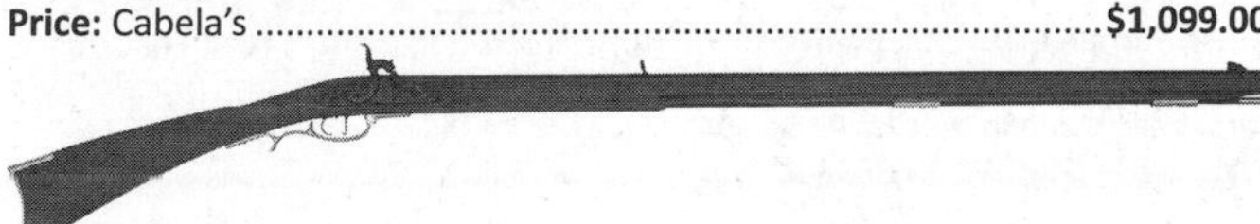

PEDERSOLI FRONTIER RIFLE
Caliber: .32, .36, .45, .50, .54. Barrel: 39 in., octagon, 1:48 twist. Weight: 7.75 lbs. Length: 54.5 in. overall. Stock: American black walnut. Sights: Blade front, rear drift adjustable for windage. Features: Color case-hardened lockplate and cock/hammer, brass triggerguard and buttplate; double set, double-phased triggers. Made by Pedersoli. Imported by Dixie Gun Works, and by Cabela's (as the Blue Ridge Rifle).
Price: Cabela's Percussion **$599.00**
Price: Cabela's Flintlock **$649.00**

PEDERSOLI ENFIELD THREE-BAND P1853 RIFLE
Caliber: .58. Barrel: 39 in. Weight: 10.25 lbs. Length: 52 in. overall. Stock: European walnut. Sights: Blade front, flip-up rear with elevator marked to 800 yards. Features: Reproduction of the original three-band rifle. Percussion musket-cap ignition. Blued barrel with steel barrelbands, brass furniture. Case-hardened lock. Lockplate marked "London Armory Co. and Crown." Made by Pedersoli. Imported by Cabela's.
Price: Cabela's **$1,149.00**

PEDERSOLI INDIAN TRADE MUSKET
Gauge: 20. Barrel: 36 in., octagon to round, smoothbore. Weight: 7.25 lbs. Length: 52 in. overall. Stock: American walnut. Sights: Blade front sight, no rear sight. Features: Flintlock. Kits version available. Made by Pedersoli. Imported by Dixie Gun Works.
Price: Dixie Gun Works, FR3170 .... **$1,095.00**
Price: Dixie Gun Works Kit, FK3370 .... **$995.00**

PEDERRSOLI JAEGER RIFLE
Caliber: .54. Barrel: 27.5 in. octagon, 1:24 in. twist. Weight: 8.25 lbs. Length: 43.5 in. overall. Stock: American walnut; sliding wooden patchbox on butt. Sights: Notch rear, blade front. Features: Flintlock or percussion. Conversion kits available, and recommended converting percussion guns to flintlocks using kit LO1102 at $209.00. Browned steel furniture. Made by Pedersoli. Imported by Dixie Gun Works.
Price: Dixie Gun Works Percussion, PR0835................................... **$1,350.00**
Price: Dixie Gun Works Flint, PR0835... **$1,450.00**
Price: Dixie Gun Works Percussion, kit gun, PK0146......................... **$1,075.00**
Price: Dixie Gun Works Flint, kit gun, PKO143.................................. **$1,100.00**

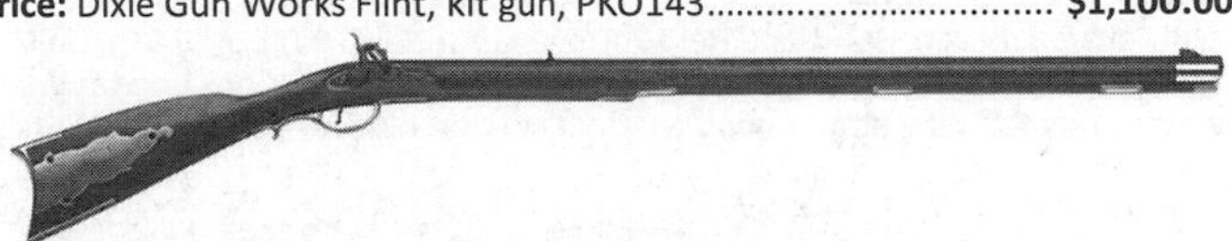

PEDERSOLI KENTUCKY RIFLE
Caliber: .32, .45 and .50. Barrel: 35.5 in. octagonal. Weight: 7.5 (.50 cal.) to 7.75 lbs. (.32 cal.) Length: 51 in. overall. Stock: European walnut, full-length stock. Sights: Notch rear, blade front. Features: Flintlock or percussion, brass patchbox, double-set triggers. Also available as kit guns for all calibers and ignition systems. Made by Pedersoli. Imported by Dixie Gun Works.
Price: Dixie Gun Works Percussion, .32, PR3115.............................. **$750.00**
Price: Dixie Gun Works Flint, .32, FR3100 .... **$775.00**
Price: Dixie Gun Works Percussion, .45, FR3120................................. **$750.00**
Price: Dixie Gun Works Flint, .45, FR3105 .... **$775.00**
Price: Dixie Gun Works Percussion, .50, FR3125................................. **$750.00**
Price: Dixie Gun Works Flint, .50, FR3110 .... **$775.00**

PEDERSOLI KODIAK DOUBLE RIFLES AND COMBINATION GUN.
Caliber: .50, .54 and .58. Barrel: 28.5 in.; 1:24/1:24/1:48 in. twist. Weight: 11.25/10.75/10 lbs. Stock: Straight grip European walnut. Sights: Two adjustable rear, steel ramp with brass bead front. Features: Percussion ignition, double triggers, sling swivels. A .72-caliber express rifle and a .50-caliber/12-gauge shotgun combination gun are also available. Blued steel furniture. Stainless steel nipple. Made by Pedersoli. Imported by Dixie Gun Works and some models by Cabela's and others.
Price: Dixie Gun Works Rifle 50X50 PR0970....................................**$1,525.00**
Price: Dixie Gun Works Rifle 54X54 PR0975 ....**$1,525.00**
Price: Dixie Gun Works Rifle 58X58 PR0980.....................................**$1,525.00**
Price: Dixie Gun Works Combo 50X12 gauge PR0990 ....**$1,350.00**
Price: Dixie Gun Works Express Rifle .72 caliber PR0916 ....**$1,550.00**

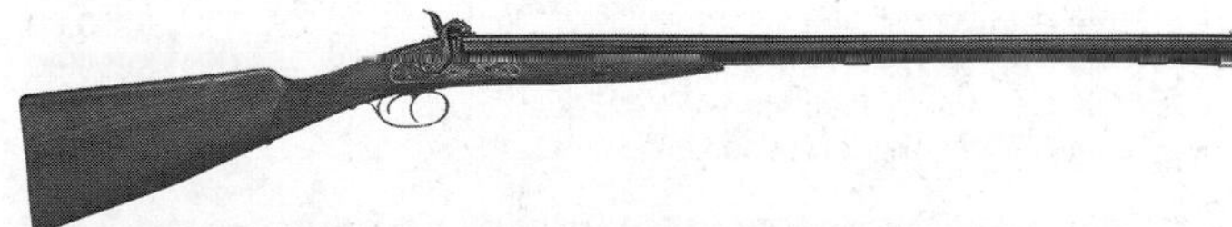

PEDERSOLI MAGNUM PERCUSSION SHOTGUN & COACH GUN
Gauge: 10, 12, 20 Barrel: Chrome-lined blued barrels, 25.5 in. Imp. Cyl. and Mod. Weight: 7.25, 7, 6.75 lbs. Length: 45 in. overall. Stock: Hand-checkered walnut, 14-in. pull. Features: Double triggers, light hand engraving, case-hardened locks, sling swivels. Made by Pedersoli. From Dixie Gun Works, others.
Price: Dixie Gun Works 10-ga. PS1030 .... **$1,250.00**
Price: Dixie Gun Works 10-ga. kit PS1040 .... **$975.00**
Price: Dixie Gun Works 12-ga. PS0930 .... **$1,175.00**
Price: Dixie Gun Works 12-ga. Kit PS0940 .... **$875.00**
Price: Dixie Gun Works 12-ga. Coach gun, CylXCyl, PS0914 ....**$1,150.00**
Price: Dixie Gun Works 20-ga. PS0334 .... **$1,175.00**

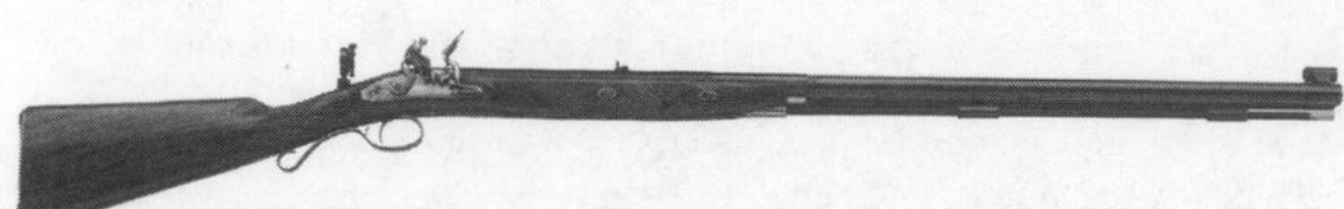

PEDERSOLI MORTIMER RIFLE & SHOTGUN
Caliber: .54, 12 gauge. Barrel: 36 in., 1:66 in. twist, and cylinder bore. Weight: 10 lbs. rifle, 9 lbs. shotgun. Length: 52.25 in. Stock: Halfstock walnut. Sights: Blued steel rear with flip-up leaf, blade front. Features: Percussion and flint ignition. Blued steel furniture. Single trigger. Lock with hammer safety and "waterproof pan" marked Mortimer. A percussion .45-caliber target version of this gun is available with a peep sight on the wrist, and a percussion shotgun version is also offered. Made by Pedersoli. Imported by Dixie Gun Works.
Price: Dixie Gun Works Flint Rifle, FR0151 .... **$1,575.00**
Price: Dixie Gun Works Flint Shotgun FS0155 .... **$1,525.00**

PEDERSOLI OLD ENGLISH SHOTGUN
Gauge: 12 Barrels: Browned, 28.5 in. Cyl. and Mod. Weight: 7.5 lbs. Length: 45 in. overall. Stock: Hand-checkered American maple, cap box, 14-in. pull. Features: Double triggers, light hand engraving on lock, cap box and tang, swivel studs for sling attachment. Made by Pedersoli. From Dixie Gun Works, others.
Price: Dixie Gun Works PR4090 .... **$1,750.00**

PEDERSOLI ROCKY MOUNTAIN & MISSOURI RIVER HAWKEN RIFLES
Caliber: .54 Rocky Mountain, .45 and .50 in Missouri River. Barrel: 34.75 in. octagonal with hooked breech; Rocky Mountain 1:65 in. twist; Missouri River 1:47 twist in .45 cal., and 1:24 twist in .50 cal. Weight: 10 lbs. Length: 52 in. overall. Stock: Maple or walnut, halfstock. Sights: Rear buckhorn with push elevator, silver blade front. Features: Available in Percussion, with brass furniture and double triggers. Made by Pedersoli. Imported by Dixie Gun Works and others.
Price: Dixie Gun Works Rocky Mountain, Maple PR3430 .... **$1,395.00**
Price: Dixie Gun Works Rocky Mountain, Walnut PR3435 .... **$1,195.00**
Price: Dixie Gun Works Missouri River, .50 Walnut PR3415 .... **$1,275.00**
Price: Dixie Gun Works Missouri River, .45 Walnut PR3405 .... **$1,275.00**

PEDERSOLI PENNSYLVANIA RIFLE
Caliber: .32, .45 and .50. Barrel: 41.5 in. browned, octagonal, 1:48 in. twist. Weight: 8.25 lbs. Length: 56 in. overall. Stock: American walnut. Sights: Rear semi-buckhorn with push elevator, steel blade front. Features: Available in flint or percussion, with brass furniture, and double triggers. Also available as a kit. Made by Pedersoli. Imported by Dixie Gun Works and others.
Price: Dixie Gun Works Flint .32 FR3040 .... **$950.00**
Price: Dixie Gun Works Percussion .32 PR3055.................................. **$900.00**
Price: Dixie Gun Works Flint .45 PR3045.. **$950.00**
Price: Dixie Gun Works Percussion .45 PR3060.................................. **$900.00**
Price: Dixie Gun Works Flint .50 PR3050.. **$950.00**
Price: Dixie Gun Works Percussion .50 PR3065.................................. **$900.00**
Price: Dixie Gun Works Flint Kit .32 FK3260 .... **$750.00**
Price: Dixie Gun Works Percussion kit .32 PK3275.............................. **$695.00**
Price: Dixie Gun Works Flint kit .45 FK3265 .... **$750.00**
Price: Dixie Gun Works Percussion kit .45 PR3280.............................. **$695.00**
Price: Dixie Gun Works Flint kit .50 FK3270 .... **$750.00**
Price: Dixie Gun Works Percussion kit .50 PK3285.............................. **$695.00**

PEDERSOLI SHARPS NEW MODEL 1859 MILITARY RIFLE AND CARBINE
Caliber: .54. Barrel: 30 in., 6-groove, 1:48 in. twist. Weight: 9 lbs. Length: 45.5 in. overall. Stock: Oiled walnut. Sights: Blade front, ladder-style rear. Features: Blued barrel, color case-hardened barrelbands, receiver, hammer, nose cap, lever, patchbox cover and buttplate. Introduced in 1995. Rifle made by Pedersoli. Rifle imported from Italy by Dixie Gun Works and others.
Price: Dixie Gun Work Rifle PR0862 .... **$1,650.00**
Price: Dixie Gun Work Carbine (22-in. barrel) PR0982.................... **$1,400.00**

PEDERSOLI SHARPS MODEL 1863 SPORTING RIFLE
Caliber: .45. Barrel: 32 in., octagon, 6-groove, 1:18 in. twist. Weight: 10.75 lbs. Length: 49 in. overall. Stock: Oiled walnut. Sights: Silver blade front, flip-up rear. Features: Browned octagon barrel, color case-hardened receiver, hammer and buttplate. Rifle made by Pedersoli. Imported by Dixie Gun Works and others.
Price: Dixie Gun Work Rifle PR5001 .... **$1,500.00**

PEDERSOLI SHARPS CONFEDERATE CARBINE
Caliber: .54. Barrel: 22 in., 6-groove, 1:48 in. twist. Weight: 8 lbs. Length: 39 in. overall. Stock: Oiled walnut. Sights: Blade front, dovetailed rear. Features: Browned barrel, color case-hardened receiver, hammer, and lever. Brass buttplate and barrel bands. Rifle made by Pedersoli. Imported by Dixie Gun Works and others.
Price: Dixie Gun Work Carbine PR3380.. **$1,395.00**

PEDERSOLI TRADITIONAL HAWKEN TARGET RIFLE
Caliber: .50 and .54. Barrel: 29.5 in. octagonal, 1:48 in. twist. Weight: 9 or 8.5 lbs. Length: 45.5 in. overall. Stock: European walnut, halfstock. Sights: Rear click adjustable for windage and elevation, blade front. Features: Percussion and flintlock, brass patchbox, double-set triggers, one barrel key. Flint gun available for left-handed shooters. Both flint and percussion guns available as kit guns. Made by Pedersoli. Imported by Dixie Gun Works.
Price: Dixie Gun Works Percussion, .50 PR0502................................ **$650.00**
Price: Dixie Gun Works Percussion, .54 PR0507................................ **$650.00**
Price: Dixie Gun Works Flint, .50 FR1332 .... **$725.00**
Price: Dixie Gun Works Flint, .54 FR3515 .... **$725.00**

PEDERSOLI TRYON RIFLE
Caliber: .50. Barrel: 32 in. octagonal, 1:48 in. twist. Weight: 9.5 lbs. Length: 49 in. overall. Stock: European walnut, halfstock. Sights: Elevation-adjustable rear with stair-step notches, blade front. Features: Percussion, brass patchbox, double-set triggers, two barrel keys. Made by Pedersoli. Imported by Dixie Gun Works.
Price: Percussion, PR0860 .... **$1,100.00**

PEDERSOLI VOLUNTEER RIFLE
Caliber: .451. Barrel: 33 in., round interior bore 1:21 in. twist. Weight: 9.5 lbs. Length: 49 in. Stock: Oiled Grade 1 American walnut. Sights: Blade front, ladder-style rear. Features: Checkered stock wrist and fore-end. Blued barrel, steel ramrod, bone charcoal case-hardened receiver and hammer. Designed for .451 conical bullets. Compare to hexagonal-bored Whitworth Rifle below. Hand-fitted and finished.
Price: Dixie Gun Works PR3150...... .... **$1,295.00**

PEDERSOLI WHITWORTH RIFLE
Caliber: .451. Barrel: 36 in., hexagonal interior bore 1:20 in. twist. Weight: 9.6 lbs. Length: 52.5 in. Stock: Oiled Grade 1 American walnut. Sights: Blade front, ladder-style rear. Features: Checkered stock wrist and fore-end. Blued barrel, steel ramrod, bone charcoal case-hardened receiver and hammer. Designed for .451 conical hexagonal bullet. Compare to round-bored Volunteer Rifle above. Hand-fitted to original specifications using original Enfield arsenal gauges.
Price: Dixie Gun Works PR3256...... .... **$1,750.00**

PEDERSOLI ZOUAVE RIFLE
Caliber: .58 percussion. Barrel: 33 inches. Weight: 9.5 lbs. Length: 49 inches. Stock: European walnut. Sights: Blade front, three-leaf military rear. Features: Percussion musket-cap ignition. One-piece solid barrel and bolster. Brass-plated patchbox. Made in Italy by Pedersoli. Imported by Dixie Gun Works, others.
Price: Dixie Gun Works PF0340. .... **$975.00**

REMINGTON MODEL 700 ULTIMATE MUZZLELOADER
Caliber: .50 percussion. Barrel: 26 in., 1:26 in. twist, satin stainless steel, fluted. Length: 47 in. Stock: Bell & Carlson black synthetic. Sights: None on synthetic-stocked model. Ramrod: Stainless steel. Weight: 8.5 lbs. Features: Remington single shot Model 700 bolt action, re-primable cartridge-case ignition using Remington Magnum Large Rifle Primer, sling studs.
Price: 86960 Starting at **$1,015.00**

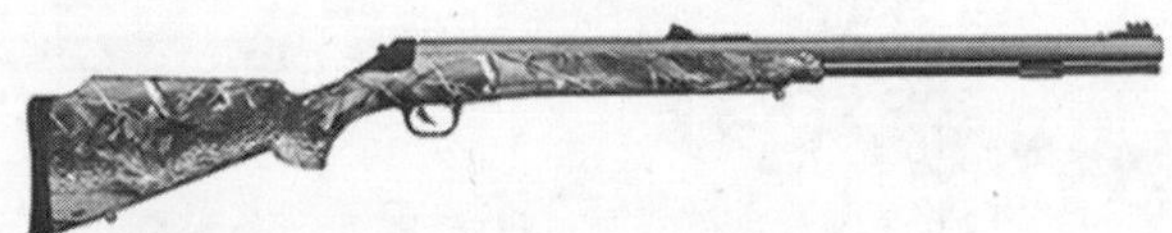

THOMPSON/CENTER IMPACT MUZZLELOADING RIFLE
Caliber: .50. Barrel: 26 in., 1:28 twist, Weather Shield finish. Weight: 6.5 lbs. Length: 41.5 in. Stock: Straight Realtree Hardwoods HD or black composite. Features: Sliding-hood, break-open action, #209 primer ignition, removable breech plug, synthetic stock adjustable from 12.5 to 13.5 in., adjustable fiber-optic sights, aluminum ramrod, camo, QLA relieved muzzle system.
Price: .50-cal Stainless/Realtree Hardwoods, Weather Shield **$324.00**
Price: .50-cal Blued/Black/scope, case..**$263.00**

THOMPSON/CENTER PRO HUNTER FX
Caliber: .50 as muzzleloading barrel. Barrel: 26 in., Weather Shield with relieved muzzle on muzzleloader; interchangeable with 14 centerfire calibers. Weight: 7 lbs. Length: 40.5 in. overall. Stock: Interchangeable American walnut butt and fore-end, black composite, FlexTech recoil-reducing camo stock as thumbhole or straight, rubber over-molded stock and fore-end. Ramrod: Solid aluminum. Sights: Tru-Glo fiber-optic front and rear. Features: Blue or stainless steel. Uses the frame of the Encore centerfire pistol; break-open design using triggerguard spur; stainless steel universal breech plug; uses #209 shotshell primers. Made in U.S. by Thompson/Center Arms.
Price: .50-cal Stainless/Black FlexTech Stock Model 5800.................. **$649.00**
Price: .50-cal Stainless/Engraved frame FlexTech RT-AP camo............**$709.00**

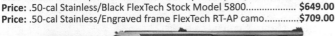

THOMPSON/CENTER TRIUMPH BONE COLLECTOR
Caliber: .50. Barrel: 28 in., Weather Shield coated. Weight: 6.5 lbs. Overall: 42 in. Stock: FlexTech recoil-reducing. Black composite or Realtree AP HD camo straight, rubber over-molded stock and fore-end. Sights: Fiber optic. Ramrod: Solid aluminum. Features: Break-open action. Quick Detachable Speed Breech XT plug, #209 shotshell primer ignition, easy loading QLA relieved muzzle. Made in U.S. by Thompson/Center Arms. Available from Cabela's, Bass Pro.
Price: .50-cal Synthetic Realtree AP, fiber optics.... .... **$720.00**
Price: .50-cal Synthetic/Weather Shield Black.................................. **$638.00**
Price: .50-cal. Weather Shield/AP Camo...**$679.00**
Price: .50 cal. Silver Weather Shield/AP Camo......................................**$689.00**

THOMPSON/CENTER STRIKE
Caliber: .50. Barrel: 24 or 20 in., nitride finished, tapered barrel. Weight: 6.75 or 6.25 lbs. Length: 44 in. or 40 in. Stock: Walnut, black synthetic, G2-Vista Camo. Finish: Armornite nitride. Features: Break-open action, sliding hammerless cocking mechanism, optional pellet or loose powder primer holders, easily removable breech plugs retained by external collar, aluminum frame with steel mono-block to retain barrel, recoil pad. Sights: Williams fiber-optic sights furnished, drilled and tapped for scope. Made in the U.S. by Thompson/Center.
Price: .50 cal. 24-in. barrel, black synthetic stock **$499.00**
Price: .50 cal. 24-in. barrel, walnut stock **$599.00**
Price: .50 cal. 24-in. barrel, G2 camo stock **$549.00**

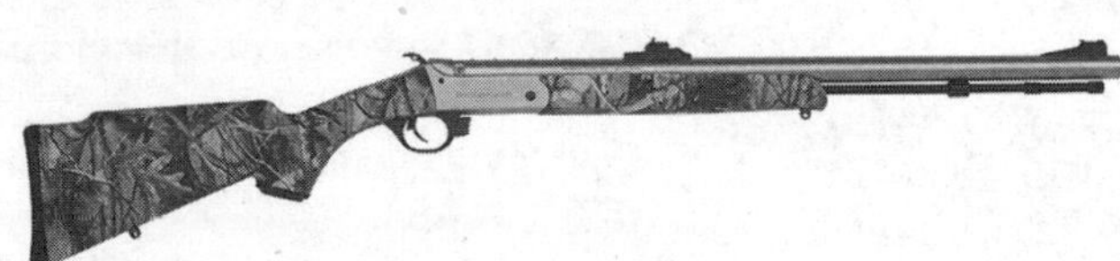

TRADITIONS BUCKSTALKER IN-LINE RIFLE
Caliber: .50. Barrel: 24 in., Cerakote finished, Accelerator Breech Plug. Weight: 6 lbs. Length: 40 in. Stock: Synthetic, G2 Vista camo or black. Sights: Fiber-optic rear. Features: Break-open action, matte-finished action and barrel. Ramrod: Solid aluminum. Imported by Traditions.
Price: R72003540 .50-cal. Youth Synthetic stock/blued.......................**$219.00**
Price: R72103540 .50-cal. Synthetic stock/Cerakote **$329.00**
Price: R5-72003540 .50-cal. Synthetic stock/blued, scope................. **$294.00**
Price: R5-72103547 .50-cal. Synthetic stock/Cerakote, scope **$369.00**

TRADITIONS BUCKSTALKER XT
Caliber: .50. Barrel: 24 in. Twist rate: 1:28 in. Ignition: 209 primer. Features: Upgraded premium-grade Chromoly steel barrel, Elite XT trigger system upgrade. Uses the Dual Safety System, Accelerator Breech Plug (the plug is removable by hand and allows the use of loose or pelletized powder), and what Traditions calls its Speed Load System. Variants include a G2 Vista camo or black stock, various finish options, and scoped and non-scoped versions. For Idaho and Oregon, the Buckstalker XT Northwest Magnum features the musket ignition, open breech, and open-sights.
Price: **$229.00**

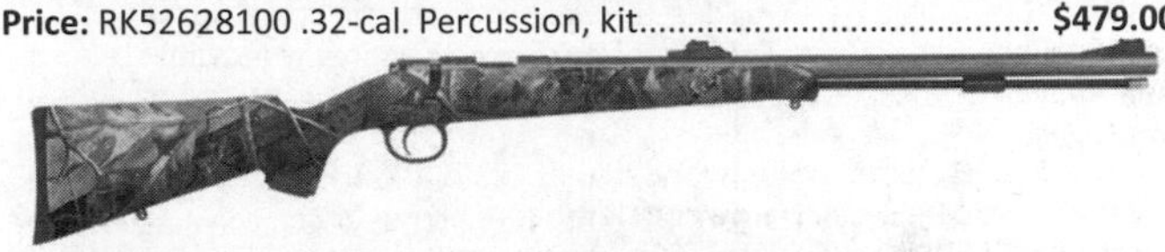

TRADITIONS CROCKETT RIFLE
Caliber: .32. Barrel: 32 in., 1:48 in. twist. Weight: 6.75 lbs. Length: 49 in. overall. Stock: Beech, inletted toe plate. Sights: Blade front, fixed rear. Features: Set triggers, hardwood halfstock, brass furniture, color case-hardened lock. Percussion. Imported by Traditions.
Price: R26128101 .32-cal. Percussion, finished **$543.00**
Price: RK52628100 .32-cal. Percussion, kit... **$479.00**

TRADITIONS EVOLUTION BOLT-ACTION BLACKPOWDER RIFLE
Caliber: .50 percussion. Barrel: 26 in., 1:28 in. twist, Cerakote finished barrel and action. Length: 39 in. Sights: Steel Williams fiber-optic sights. Weight: 7 to 7.25 lbs. Length: 45 in. overall. Features: Bolt action, cocking indicator, thumb safety, shipped with adaptors for No. 11 caps, musket caps and 209 shotgun primer ignition, sling swivels. Ramrod: Aluminum, sling studs. Available with exposed ignition as a Northwest gun. Imported by Traditions.
Price: R67113350 .50-cal. synthetic black, Cerakote.......................... **$250.00**
Price: R67113353 .50-cal. synthetic Realtree AP camo...... ....**$299.00**

TRADITIONS HAWKEN WOODSMAN RIFLE
Caliber: .50. Barrel: 28 in., blued, 15/16 in. flats. Weight: 7 lbs., 11 oz. Length: 44.5 in. overall. Stock: Walnut stained hardwood. Sights: Beaded blade front hunting-style open rear adjustable for windage and elevation. Features: Brass patchbox and furniture. Double-set triggers. Flint or percussion. Imported by Traditions.
Price: R2390801 .50-cal. Flintlock **$544.00**
Price: R24008 .50-cal. Percussion **$499.00**

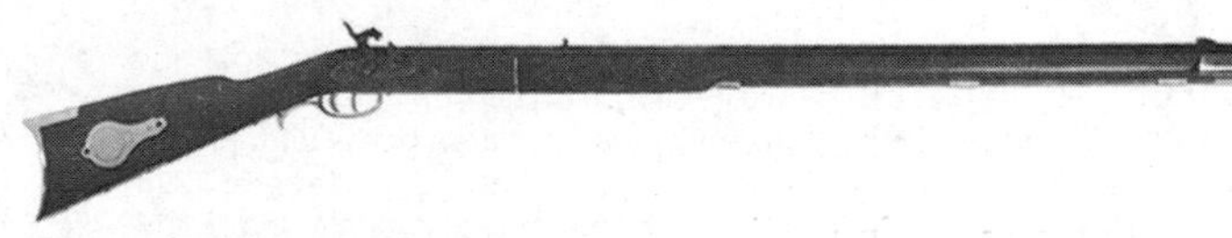

TRADITIONS KENTUCKY DELUXE
Caliber: .50. Barrel: 33.5 in., blued octagon. Stock: Walnut-finished select hardwood. Sights: Fixed blade. Weight: 7 lbs. Features: Double set trigger, brass patch box, available as a kit, authentic wooden ramrod.
Price: .... **$379.00-$485.00**

TRADITIONS KENTUCKY RIFLE
Caliber: .50. Barrel: 33.5 in., 7/8 in. flats, 1:66 in. twist. Weight: 7 lbs. Length: 49 in. overall. Stock: Beech, inletted toe plate. Sights: Blade front, fixed rear. Features: Full-length, two-piece stock; brass furniture; color case-hardened lock. Flint or percussion. Imported by Traditions.
Price: R2010 .50-cal. Flintlock,1:66 twist **$509.00**
Price: R2020 .50-cal. Percussion, 1:66 twist....................................... **$449.00**
Price: KRC52206 .50-cal. Percussion, kit... **$343.00**

Prices given are believed to be accurate at time of publication however, many factors affect retail pricing so exact prices are not possible.

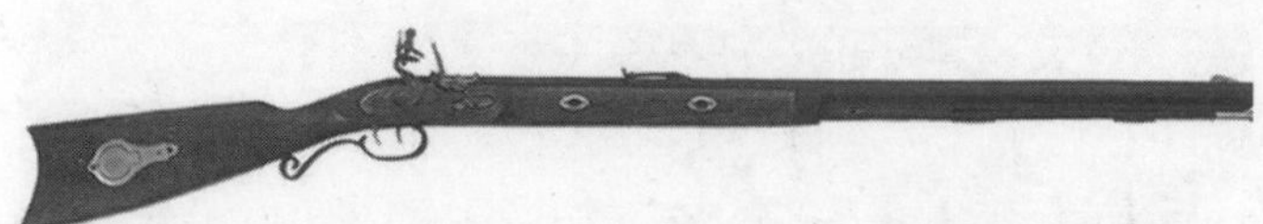

TRADITIONS MOUNTAIN RIFLE
Caliber: .50. Barrel: 32 in., octagon with brown Cerakote finish. Stock: Select hardwoods. Sights: Primitive, adjustable rear. Weight: 8.25 lbs. Features: Available in percussion or flintlock, case-hardened lock, wooden ramrod, available as a kit.
Price: .... **$494.00-$649.00**

TRADITIONS NITROFIRE
Caliber: .50. Barrel: 26 in., ultralight chromoly steel, tapered and fluted, premium Cerakote finish. Stock: Synthetic black or camo. Sights: Drilled and tapped, optional 3-9x40 scope. Weight: 6.5 lbs. Features: Several stock color options, Federal FireStick ignition system, no breech plug required, aluminum ramrod, sling swivel studs.
Price: .... **$549.00-$699.00**

TRADITIONS PA PELLET FLINTLOCK
Caliber: .50. Barrel: 26 in., blued, 1:28 in. twist., Cerakote. Weight: 7 lbs. Length: 45 in. Stock: Hardwood, synthetic and synthetic break-up, sling swivels. Fiber-optic sights. Features: New flintlock action, removable breech plug, available as left-hand model with hardwood stock. Imported by Traditions.
Price: R3800501 .50-cal. Hardwood, blued, fib. opt **$519.00**
Price: R3890501 .50-cal. Hardwood, left-hand, blued **$529.00**
Price: R3800550 .50-cal. Synthetic/blued, fib. opt........ **$497.00**

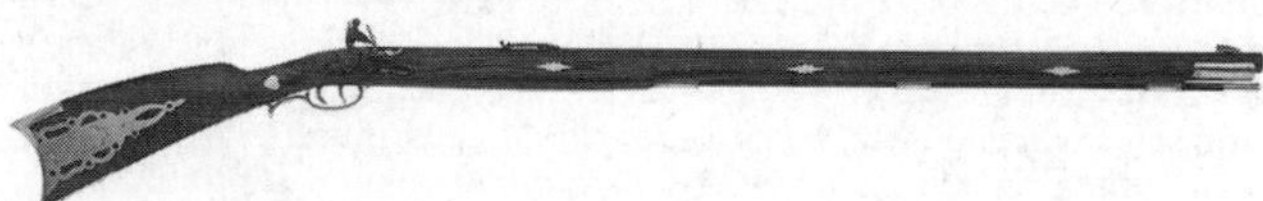

TRADITIONS PENNSYLVANIA RIFLE
Caliber: .50. Barrel: 40.25 in., 7/8 in. flats, 1:66 in. twist, octagon. Weight: 9 lbs. Length: 57.5 in. overall. Stock: Walnut. Sights: Blade front, adjustable rear. Features: Single-piece walnut stock, brass patchbox and ornamentation. Double-set triggers. Flint or percussion. Imported by Traditions.
Price: R2090 .50-cal. Flintlock **$865.00**
Price: R2100 .50-cal. Percussion........ **$834.00**

TRADITIONS PURSUIT ULTRALIGHT MUZZLELOADER
Caliber: .50. Barrel: 26 in., chromoly tapered, fluted barrel with premium Cerakote finish, Accelerator Breech Plug. Weight: 5.5 lbs. Length: 42 in. Stock: Rubber over-molded Soft Touch camouflage, straight and thumbhole stock options. Sights: Optional 3-9x40 scope with medium rings and bases, mounted and bore-sighted by a factory-trained technician. Features: Break-open action, Williams fiber-optic sights. Imported by Traditions.
Price: Pursuit G4 Ultralight .50 Cal. Select Hardwoods/ Cerakote R741101NS........ **$469.00**
Price: Pursuit G4 Ultralight .50 Cal. Mossy Oak Break Up Country Camo/ Cerakote R7411416........ **$404.00**
Price: Pursuit G4 Ultralight .50 Cal. Mossy Oak Break Up Country/Cerakote/ Scope/Carrying Case.... .... **$479.00**

TRADITIONS TRACKER IN-LINE RIFLE
Caliber: .50. Barrel: 24 in., blued or Cerakote, 1:28 in. twist. Weight: 6 lbs., 4 oz. Length: 43 in. Stock: Black synthetic. Ramrod: Synthetic, high-impact polymer. Sights: Lite Optic blade front, adjustable rear. Features: Striker-fired action, thumb safety, adjustable trigger, rubber buttpad, sling swivel studs. Takes 150 grains of Pyrodex pellets, one-piece musket cap and 209 ignition systems. Drilled and tapped for scope. Legal for use in Northwest. Imported by Traditions.
Price: R44003470 .50-cal. Synthetic/blued **$184.00**

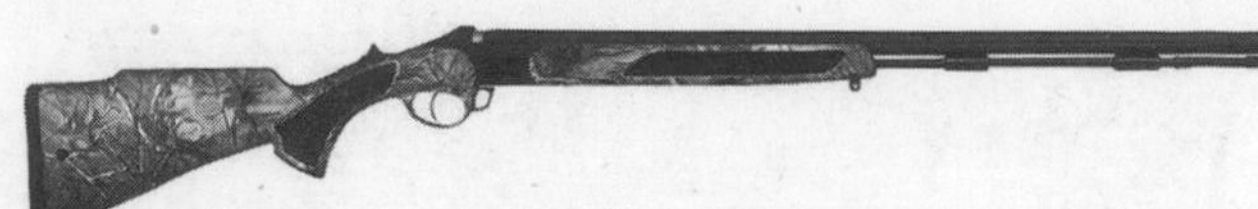

TRADITIONS VORTEK STRIKERFIRE
Caliber: .50 Barrel: 28 in., chromoly, tapered, fluted barrel. Weight: 6.25 lbs. Length: 44 in. Stock: Over-molded soft-touch straight stock, removable buttplate for in-stock storage. Finish: Premium Cerakote and Realtree Xtra. Features: Break-open action, sliding hammerless cocking mechanism, drop-out trigger assembly, speed load system, Accelerator Breech Plug, recoil pad. Sights: Optional 3-9x40 muzzleloader scope. Imported by Traditions. Recently upgraded with a VAPR twist barrel, 1:24-in-twist configuration. This faster twist rate stabilizes long bullets, increases accuracy, and expands the range of bullet options fueling the current long-range muzzleloading trends.
Price: Vortek StrikerFire with Nitride Coating Mossy Oak Break-Up Country Camo..... .... **$450.00**
Price: Vortek StrikerFire with 3-9x40 Sig Sauer Whisky 3 Scope, Sling & Case........ **$756.00**

TRADITIONS VORTEK STRIKERFIRE LDR
Caliber: .50. Barrel: 30 in., chromoly, tapered, fluted barrel. Weight: 6.8 lbs. Length: 46 in. Stock: Over-molded soft-touch straight stock, removable buttplate for in-stock storage. Finish: Premium Cerakote and Realtree Xtra. Features: Break-open action, sliding hammerless cocking mechanism, drop-out trigger assembly, speed load system, Accelerator Breech Plug, recoil pad. Sights: Optional 3-9x40 muzzleloader scope. Imported by Traditions.
Price: R491140WA Synthetic/black Hogue Over-mold, Cerakote barrel, no sights........ **$499.00**

WOODMAN ARMS PATRIOT
Caliber: .45, .50. Barrel: 24 in., nitride-coated, 416 stainless, 1:24 twist in .45, 1:28 twist in .50. Weight: 5.75 lbs. Length: 43-in. Stocks: Laminated, walnut or hydrographic dipped, synthetic black, over-molded soft-touch straight stock. Finish: Nitride black and black anodized. Features: Break-open action, hammerless cocking mechanism, match-grade patented trigger assembly, speed load system, recoil pad. Sights: Picatinny rail with built-in rear and 1-inch or 30 mm scope mounts, red fiber-optic front bead.
Price: Patriot .45 or .50-cal........ **$899.00**

UBERTI 1858 NEW ARMY REMINGTON TARGET CARBINE REVOLVER
Caliber: .44, 6-shot. Barrel: Tapered octagon, 18 in. Weight: 70.4 oz. Length: Standard 35.3 in. Stock: Walnut. Sights: Standard blade front, adjustable rear. Features: Replica of Remington's revolving rifle of 1866. Made by Uberti. Imported by Uberti USA, Cimarron F.A. Co., Taylor's and others.
Price: Uberti USA, 341200........ **$559.00**

Prices given are believed to be accurate at time of publication however, many factors affect retail pricing so exact prices are not possible.

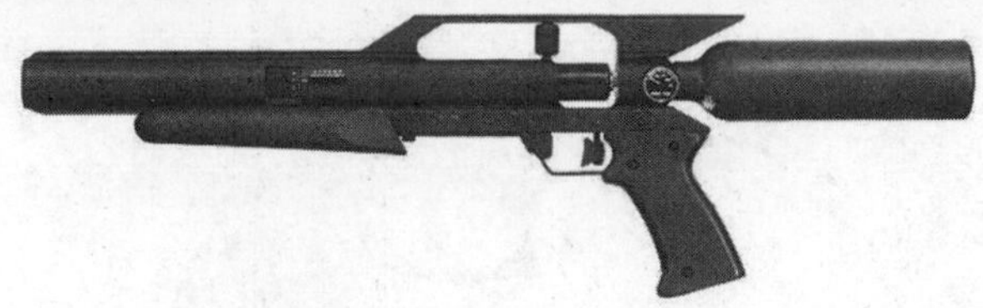

AIRFORCE TALON P PCP AIR PISTOL
Caliber: .25. Barrel: Rifled 12.0 in. Weight: 4.3 lbs. Length: 27.75–32.25 in. Sights: None, grooved for scope. Features: Quick-detachable air tank with adjustable power. Match-grade Lothar Walther barrel, massive power output in a highly compact size, two-stage trigger, single shot, open sights optional. Velocity: 500–900 fps.
Price: **$569.00**

AIR VENTURI V10 MATCH AIR PISTOL
Caliber: .177 pellets. Barrel: Rifled. Weight: 1.95 lbs. Length: 12.6 in. Power: Single stroke pneumatic. Sights: Front post, fully adjustable rear blade, Features: 10-Meter competition class pistol, fully adjustable trigger, 1.5-lb. trigger pull Velocity: 400 fps.
Price: **$300.00**

ALFA PROJ COMPETITION PCP PISTOL
Caliber: .177 pellets. Barrel: Rifled, 9.5 in. Weight: 2 lbs. Length: 15.5 inches. Power: Precharged pneumatic. Sights: Front adjustable width post, fully adjustable rear blade. Features: Single shot, 10-Meter competition class pistol, highly adjustable trigger, adjustable velocity, factory trigger pull set to 8 oz., ambidextrous grip. Velocity: 500 fps.
Price: **$1,109.00**

ASG STI DUTY ONE CO2 BB PISTOL
Caliber: .177 steel BBs. Barrel: Smoothbore Weight: 1.82 lbs. Length: 8.66 in. Power: CO2. Sights: Fixed. Features: Blowback, accessory rail, and metal slide. Velocity: 383 fps.
Price: **$120.00**

ATAMAN AP16 REGULATED COMPACT AIR PISTOL
Caliber: .177, .22 pellets. Barrel: Rifled Match Barrel Weight: 1.76 lbs. Length: 12.0 in. Power: Pre-Charged Pneumatic. Sights: Fixed Front Ramp, Adjustable Rear Notch. Features: 7 round Rotary Magazine, 300 Bar Max Fill, Regulated for hunting power, exceptional build quality, available in satin and blued finishes Velocity: 590 fps.
Price: **$1,049.00**

ATAMAN AP16 REGULATED STANDARD AIR PISTOL
Caliber: .177, .22 pellets. Barrel: Rifled Match Barrel Weight: 2.2 lbs. Length: 14.37 in. Power: Pre-Charged Pneumatic. Sights: Fixed Front Ramp, Adjustable Rear Notch. Features: 7-round Rotary Magazine, 300 Bar Max Fill, Regulated for hunting power, exceptional build quality, Velocity: 656 fps.
Price: **$1,049.00**

BEEMAN P17 AIR PISTOL
Caliber: .177 pellets. Barrel: Rifled. Weight: 1.7 lbs. Length: 9.6 in. Power: Single stroke pneumatic. Sights: Front and rear fiber-optic sights, rear sight fully adjustable. Features: Exceptional trigger, grooved for scope mounting with dry-fire feature for practice. Velocity: 410 fps.
Price: **$64.00**

BEEMAN P11 AIR PISTOL

BEEMAN P11 AIR PISTOL
Caliber: .177, .22. Barrel: Rifled. Weight: 2.6 lbs. Length: 10.75 in. Power: Single-stroke pneumatic with high and low settings. Sights: Front ramp sight, fully adjustable rear sight. Features: 2-stage adjustable trigger and automatic safety. Velocity: Up to 600 fps in .177 caliber and Up to 460 fps in .22 caliber.
Price: **$599.00**

BEEMAN 2027 PCP PISTOL
Caliber: .177 Barrel: Rifled. Weight: 1.7 lbs. Length: 9.25 in. Power: Single stroke pneumatic. Sights: Adjustable open sights. Features: Textured grip, 12-round magazine, adjustable velocity, 60 shots per fill (at 600 fps), adjustable trigger. Velocity: 600 fps.
Price: **$170.00**

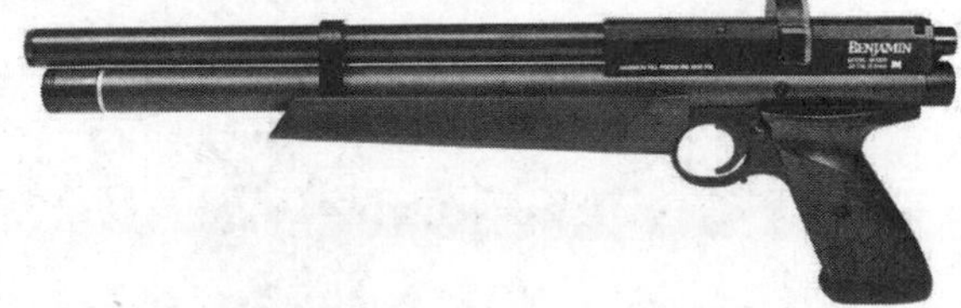

BENJAMIN MARAUDER PCP PISTOL
Caliber: .22 Barrel: Rifled. Weight: 2.7-3 lbs. Length: Pistol length 18 in./ Carbine length 29.75 in. Power: Pre-charged pneumatic Sights: None. Grooved for optics. Features: Multi-shot (8-round rotary magazine), bolt action, shrouded steel barrel, two-stage adjustable trigger, includes both pistol grips and a carbine stock and is built in America. Velocity: 700 fps.
Price: **$489.00**

Prices given are believed to be accurate at time of publication however, many factors affect retail pricing so exact prices are not possible.

BERETTA APX BLOWBACK AIR PISTOL

Caliber: .177 steel BBs. Barrel: Smoothbore. Weight: 1.47 lbs. Length: 7.48 in. Power: CO2. Sights: Fixed. Features: Highly accurate replica action pistol, 19-shot capacity, front accessory rail, metal and ABS plastic construction. Velocity: 400 fps.

Price: **$69.00**

BERETTA M84FS AIR PISTOL

Caliber: .177 steel BBs. Barrel: Smoothbore Weight: 1.4 lbs. Length: 7 in. Power: CO2. Sights: Fixed. Features: Highly realistic replica action pistol, blowback operation, full metal construction. Velocity: To 360 fps.

Price: **$119.00**

BERETTA PX4 Storm CO2 PISTOL

Caliber: .177 pellet /.177 steel BBs. Barrel: Rifled Weight: 1.6 lbs. Length: 7.6 in. Power: CO2. Sights: Blade front sight and fixed rear sight. Features: Semi-automatic, 16-shot capacity with maximum of 40-shots per fill, dual ammo capable. Velocity: To 380 fps.

Price: **$119.00**

BERETTA M9A3 FULL AUTO BB PISTOL

Caliber: .177 steel BBs. Barrel: Smoothbore Weight: NA. Length: NA. Power: CO2. Sights: Blade front sight and fixed rear sight. Features: Can operate as semi-automatic or fully automatic, full size 18-shot magazine, blowback slide, single/double action, ambidextrous safety. Velocity: To 380 fps.

Price: **$179.00**

BERETTA 92FS CO2 PELLET GUN

Caliber: .177 pellets. Barrel: Rifled Weight: 2.75 lbs. Length: 8.0 in. Power: CO2. Sights: Fixed front sight, rear adjustable for windage. Features: Highly realistic replica-action pistol, 8-shot semi-automatic, full metal construction, available in various finishes and grips. Velocity: To 425 fps.

Price: .... **$225.00-$289.00**

BERSA THUNDER 9 PRO BB PISTOL

Caliber: .177 steel BBs. Barrel: Smoothbore. Weight: 1.17 lbs. Length: 7.56 in. Power: CO2. Sights: Fixed, three-white-dot system. Features: Highly realistic replica action pistol, 19-shot semi-automatic, composite/synthetic construction. Velocity: To 400 fps.

Price: **$47.00**

BLACK OPS EXTERMINATOR CO2 REVOLVER

Caliber: .177 BBs. Barrel: Smoothbore Weight: 2.3 lbs. Length: NA. Power: CO2. Sights: Fixed front, adjustable rear. Features: 6-round cylinder with realistic shells, Weaver-style scope rail and under-barrel accessory rail, operates either double or single action, working ejector rod, black metal frame with black plastic grips, also available with 2.5 in. barrel and chrome finish. Velocity: 435 fps.

Price: **$119.00**

BROWNING BUCK MARK URX

BROWNING BUCK MARK AIR PISTOL

Caliber: .177 pellets. Barrel: Rifled Weight: 1.5 lbs. Length: 12.0 in. Power: Single cock, spring-piston. Sights: Front ramp sight, fully adjustable rear notch sight. Features: Weaver rail for scope mounting, light cocking force. Velocity: 360 fps.

Price: **$55.00**

Prices given are believed to be accurate at time of publication however, many factors affect retail pricing so exact prices are not possible.

CHIAPPA AG92 CO2 PISTOL
Caliber: .177 pellets. Barrel: Rifled, 4.8 in. Weight: 1.3 lbs. Length: 8.6 in. Power: CO2. Sights: Adjustable rear. Features: Powered by two 12 gram CO2 cylinders, holds two 7-round pellet cylinders, single/double action, polymer frame reinforced with fiberglass. Velocity: 330 fps.
Price: **$138.00**

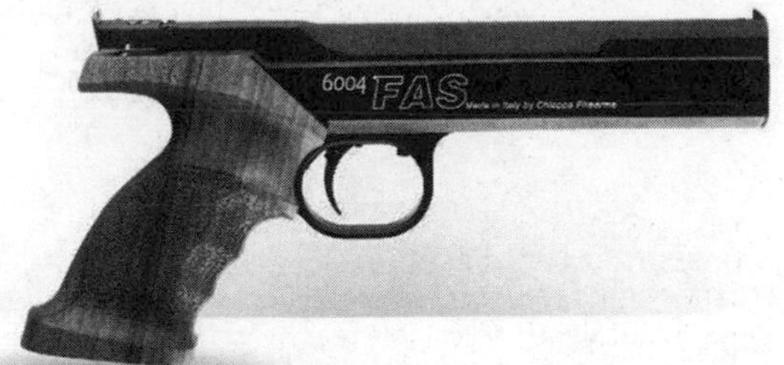

CHIAPPA FAS 6004 PNEUMATIC PISTOL
Caliber: .177 pellets. Barrel: Rifled. Weight: 2 lbs. Length: 11.0 in. Power: Single stroke pneumatic. Sights: Fully adjustable target rear sight. Features: Walnut ambidextrous grip, fully adjustable trigger. Also available with an adjustable target grip. Velocity: 330 fps.
Price: .... **$442.00–$569.00**

CHIAPPA RHINO 50DS CO2 REVOLVER
Caliber: .177 BBs. Barrel: Smoothbore, 5 in. Weight: 2.5 lbs. Length: 9.5 in. Power: CO2. Sights: Adjustable rear sight. Features: Single/double action, 6-shot capacity, black or silver frame, under barrel accessory rail. Velocity: 330 fps.
Price: .... **$159.00–$179.00**

COBRAY INGRAM M11 CO2 BB SUBMACHINE GUN
Caliber: .177 BBs. Barrel: Smoothbore. Weight: 1.2 lbs. Length: 10.0 in. Power: CO2. Sights: Fixed sights. Features: Semiautomatic, 39-shot capacity, folding metal stock. Velocity: 394 fps.
Price: **$89.00**

COLT DEFENDER BB PISTOL
Caliber: .177 steel BBs. Barrel: Smoothbore Weight: 1.6 lbs. Length: 6.75 in. Power: CO2. Sights: Fixed with blade ramp front sight. Features: Semi-automatic, 16-shot capacity, all metal construction, realistic weight and feel. Velocity: 410 fps.
Price: **$64.00**

COLT M45 QCBP CO2 PISTOL
Caliber: .177 steel BBs. Barrel: Smoothbore. Weight: 1.75 lbs. Length: 8.75 in. Power: CO2. Sights: Fixed three-dot sights, rear sight adjustable for windage. Features: Blowback action, 19-round drop-free magazine, desert tan steel slide, polymer frame, under barrel Picatinny rail. Velocity: 400 fps.
Price: **$88.00**

COLT PYTHON CO2 PISTOL
Caliber: .177 steel BBs. Barrel: Smoothbore Weight: 1.1 lbs. Length: 11.5 in. Power: CO2. Sights: Fixed front, adjustable rear. Features: Includes three 10-round removable clips, double/single action. Velocity: 410 fps.
Price: **$49.00**

COLT SAA CO2 PELLET REVOLVER
Caliber: .177 pellets. Barrel: Rifled. Weight: 2.1 lbs. Length: 11 in. Power: CO2. Sights: Blade front sight and fixed rear sight. Features: Full metal revolver with manual safety, realistic loading, 6 individual shells, highly accurate, full metal replica pistol, multiple finishes and grips available. Velocity: 380 fps.
Price: **$149.00**

COMETA INDIAN AIR PISTOL
Caliber: .177 pellets. Barrel: Rifled. Weight: 2.43 lbs. Length: 10.43 in. Power: Spring Powered. Sights: Blade front sight and adjustable rear sight. Features: Single shot, cold-hammered forged barrel, textured grips. Velocity: 492 fps.
Price: .... **$199.00–$219.00**

Prices given are believed to be accurate at time of publication however, many factors affect retail pricing so exact prices are not possible.

CROSMAN 2240 CO2 PISTOL
Caliber: .22. Barrel: Rifled. Weight: 1.8 lbs. Length: 11.13 in. Power: CO2. Sights: Blade front, rear adjustable. Features: Single shot bolt action, ambidextrous grip, all metal construction. Velocity: 460 fps.
Price: **$75.00**

CROSMAN 2300S TARGET PISTOL
Caliber: .177 pellets. Barrel: Rifled. Weight: 2.66 lbs. Length: 16 in. Power: CO2. Sights: Front fixed sight and Williams notched rear sight. Features: Meets IHMSA rules for Production Class Silhouette Competitions. Lothar Walter match-grade barrel, adjustable trigger, adjustable hammer, stainless steel bolt, 60 shots per CO2 cartridge. Velocity: 520 fps.
Price: **$366.00**

CROSMAN 1701P SILHOUETTE PCP AIR PISTOL
Caliber: .177 pellets. Barrel: Rifled Lothar Walther Match. Weight: 2.5 lbs. Length: 14.75 in. Power: Pre-charged Pneumatic. Sights: fixed front sight rear sight not included Features: Adjustable trigger, designed for shooting silhouette competition, 50 shots per fill. Velocity: 450 fps.
Price: **$477.00**

CROSMAN 1720T PCP TARGET PISTOL
Caliber: .177 pellets. Barrel: Rifled Lothar Walther Match. Weight: 2.96 lbs. Length: 18.00 in. Power: Pre-charged Pneumatic. Sights: Not included Features: Adjustable trigger, designed for shooting silhouettes, fully shrouded barrel, 50 shots per fill. Velocity: 750 fps.
Price: **$522.00**

CROSMAN SR.357S DUAL AMMO CO2 REVOLVER
Caliber: .177 steel BBs/.177 pellets. Barrel: Smoothbore Weight: 2.00 lbs. Length: 11.73 in. Power: CO2. Sights: Adjustable rear sight, Fixed Front Blade. Features: Full metal revolver in "stainless steel" finish. Comes with shells for BBs and .177 lead pellets Velocity: 400 fps. with steel BBs.
Price: **$136.00**

CROSMAN TRIPLE THREAT CO2 REVOLVER
Caliber: .177 steel BBs/.177 pellets. Barrel: Rifled. Weight: Variable. Length: Variable. Power: CO2. Sights: Adjustable rear sight. Features: Comes with three barrels (3 in., 6 in., and 8 in.) and six-shot BB clip and 10-shot .177 lead pellet clip, single/double action, die cast full metal frame. Velocity: Up to 425 fps. with steel BBs.
Price: **$92.00**

CROSMAN C11 CO2 BB GUN
Caliber: .177 steel BBs. Barrel: Smoothbore Weight: 1.4 lbs. Length: 7.0 in. Power: CO2. Sights: Fixed. Features: Compact semi-automatic BB pistol, front accessory rail. Velocity: 480 fps.
Price: **$44.00**

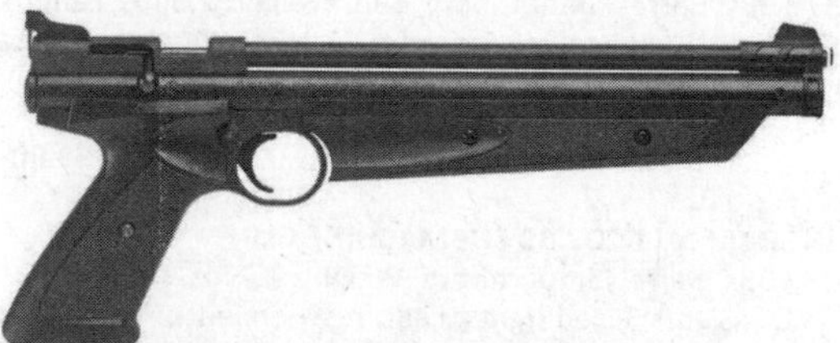

CROSMAN AMERICAN CLASSIC P1377/1322 AIR PISTOL
Caliber: .177 or .22. Barrel: Rifled Weight: 2 lbs. Length: 13.63 in. Power: Multi-pump pneumatic. Sights: Front Blade & Ramp, adjustable rear. Features: Single shot, bolt action, available with brown (.177 only) or black grips, pistol grip shoulder stock available separately. Velocities: To 695 fps (.177); to 460 fps (.22).
Price: **$69.00**

CROSMAN VIGILANTE CO2 REVOLVER
Caliber: .177 steel BBs/.177 pellets. Barrel: Rifled. Weight: 2 lbs. Length: 11.38 in. Power: CO2. Sights: Blade front, rear adjustable. Features: Single- and double-action revolver (10-shot pellet/6-shot BBs) synthetic frame and finger-molded grip design. Velocity: 465 fps.
Price: **$61.00**

Prices given are believed to be accurate at time of publication however, many factors affect retail pricing so exact prices are not possible.

CROSMAN 1911 CO2 BB PISTOL
Caliber: .177 steel BBs. Barrel: Smoothbore. Weight: 0.88 lbs. Length: 7.9 in. Power: CO2. Sights: Fixed. Features: 20-round capacity, double-action only, Picatinny under rail. Velocity: 480 fps.
Price: **$60.00**

CZ P-09 DUTY CO2 PISTOL
Caliber: .177 BBs/.177 flat-head pellets. Barrel: Rifled. Weight: 1.6 lbs. Length: 8.2 in. Power: CO2. Sights: Three-dot fixed sights. Features: Blowback action, manual safety, double-action-only trigger, 16-round capacity in a 2x8 shot stick magazine, Weaver-style accessory rail, threaded muzzle, blue or two-tone finish, ambidextrous safety with decocker. Velocity: 492 fps.
Price: **$129.00**

CZ-75 CO2 PISTOL
Caliber: .177 BBs. Barrel: Smooth. Weight: 2.1 lbs. Length: 8.2 in. Power: CO2. Sights: Fixed sights. Features: Blowback action, manual safety, full metal construction, single-action trigger, removable 17-round BB magazine, Weaver-style accessory rail, also available as a non-blowback compact version. Velocity: 312 fps.
Price: **$219.00**

CZ 75D COMPACT CO2 BB PISTOL
Caliber: .177 steel BBs. Barrel: Smoothbore. Weight: 1.5 lbs. Length: 7.4 in. Power: CO2. Sights: Adjustable rear sight and blade front sight. Features: Compact design, non-blowback action, blue or two-tone finish, accessory rail. Velocity: 380 fps.
Price: **$61.00**

DAISY POWERLINE 340 AIR PISTOL
Caliber: .177 steel BBs. Barrel: Smoothbore. Weight: 1.0 lbs. Length: 8.5 in. Power: Single cock, spring-piston. Sights: Rear sight Fixed Front blade. Features: Spring-air action, 200-shot BB reservoir with a 13-shot Speed-load Clip located in the grip. Velocity: 240 fps.
Price: **$24.00**

DAISY 408 CO2 PISTOL
Caliber: .177 steel BBs. Barrel: Rifled. Weight: 1.3 lbs. Length: 7.75 in. Power: CO2. Sights: Front blade, fixed open rear. Features: Semi-automatic, 8-shot removable clip, lower accessory rail. Velocity: 485 fps.
Price: **$64.00**

DAISY POWERLINE 415 CO2 BB PISTOL
Caliber: .177 steel BBs. Barrel: Smoothbore. Weight: 1 lb. Length: 8.6 in. Power: CO2. Sights: Front blade, fixed open rear. Features: Semi-automatic 21-shot BB pistol. Velocity: 500 fps.
Price: **$49.00**

DAISY POWERLINE 5501 CO2 PISTOL
Caliber: .177 steel BBs. Barrel: Smoothbore. Weight: 1.0 lbs. Length: 6.8 in. Power: CO2. Sights: Blade and ramp front, Fixed rear. Features: CO2 semi-automatic blowback action. 15-shot clip. Velocity: 430 fps.
Price: **$89.00**

DAN WESSON 2.5 in./4 in./6 in./8 in. PELLET REVOLVER
Caliber: .177 BBs or .177 pellets. Barrel: Smoothbore (BB version) or Rifled (Pellet version). Weights: 1.65–2.29 lbs. Lengths: 8.3–13.3 in. Power: CO2. Sights: Blade front and adjustable rear sight. Features: Highly realistic replica revolver with swing-out, six-shot cylinder, Weaver-style scope rail, multiple finishes and grip configurations, 6 realistic cartridges, includes a speed loader. Velocities: 318–426 fps.
Price: .... **$119.00–$159.00**

DAN WESSON 715 2.5 IN./4 IN./6 IN. REVOLVER
Caliber: .177 BBs or .177 pellets. Barrel: Smoothbore (BB Version) or Rifled (Pellet version). Weights: 2.2–2.7 lbs. Lengths: 8.3–11.7 in. Power: CO2. Sights: Blade front and adjustable rear sight. Features: Highly realistic replica revolver, accessory rail, multiple finishes and grip configurations, six realistic cartridges, includes a speed loader. Velocities: 318–426 fps.
Price: .... **$134.00–$159.00**

Prices given are believed to be accurate at time of publication however, many factors affect retail pricing so exact prices are not possible.

DAN WESSON VALOR 1911 PISTOL
Caliber: .177 pellets. Barrel: Rifled. Weight: 2.2 lbs. Length: 8.7 in. Power: CO2. Sights: Fixed. Features: Non-blowback, full metal construction, 12-round capacity in two six-round drum magazines. Velocities: 332 fps.
Price: **$129.00**

DIANA AIRBUG CO2 PISTOL
Caliber: .177, .22 pellets. Barrel: Rifled, 8.3 in. Weight: 2 lbs. Length: 14 in. Power: CO2. Sights: Front post, adjustable rear. Features: Hardwood, ambidextrous grip, bolt action, 9 shot (.117), 7 shot (.22), or single shot, comes with a soft-sided case. Velocities: 525 fps (.177), 460 fps (.22).
Price: **$139.00**

FEINWERKBAU P11 PICCOLO AIR PISTOL
Caliber: .177 pellets. Barrel: Rifled. Weight: 1.6 lbs. Length: 13.58 in. Power: Pre-charged pneumatic. Sights: Front post, fully adjustable rear blade, Features: 10-Meter competition class pistol, meets ISSF requirements, highly adjustable match trigger, Velocity: 492 fps.
Price: **$1,600.00**

FEINWERKBAU P8X PCP 10-METER AIR PISTOL
Caliber: .177 pellets. Barrel: Rifled. Weight: 2.09 lbs. Length: 16.33 in. Power: Pre-charged pneumatic. Sights: Front post, fully adjustable rear blade. Features: 10-Meter competition class pistol with highly customizable grip system, meets ISSF requirements, highly adjustable match trigger. Velocity: 508 fps.
Price: **$2,334.00**

GAMO GP-20 COMBAT CO2 BB PISTOL
Caliber: .177 BBs. Barrel: Smooth. Weight:1 lb. Length: 10 in. Power: CO2. Sights: Fixed with fiber optic rear. Features: Single/double action, manual safety, 20 BB magazine. Velocity: 400 fps.
Price: **$39.00**

GAMO P-27 AIR PISTOL
Caliber: .177 BB/.177 pellets. Barrel: Smooth. Weight: 1.5 lbs. Length: 7 in. Power: CO2. Sights: Fixed with white dots. Features: Single/double action, Semi-automatic, 16-shot capacity in two 8-round clips, non-blowback action, rail under barrel. Velocity: 400 fps.
Price: **$79.00**

GAMO PT-85 CO2 PISTOL
Caliber: .177 pellets. Barrel: Rifled. Weight: 1.5 lbs. Length: 7.8 in. Power: CO2. Sights: Fixed. Features: Semi-automatic, 16-shot capacity, realistic blowback action Velocity: 450 fps.
Price: **$129.00**

GLETCHER NGT F CO2 BB REVOLVER
Caliber: .177 steel BBs. Barrel: Smoothbore. Weight: 1.54 lbs. Length: 9.00 in. Power: CO2. Sights: Fixed Features: Full metal frame, highly realistic replica, 7-shot cylinder with realistic "shells," double action and single action, available in blued and polished silver finishes. Velocity: 403 fps..
Price: .... **$149.00–$159.00**

GLOCK 17 GEN 3/GEN 4/GEN 5 CO2 PISTOL
Caliber: .177 BBs. Barrel: Smoothbore. Weight: 1.6 lbs. Length: 7.75 in. Power: CO2. Sights: Fixed Features: Blowback action, metal slide and magazine, 18 BB capacity, manual safety, double-action trigger, replica of the Glock 17 firearm. Velocity: 365 fps..
Price: .... **$122.00–$155.00**

GLOCK 19 GEN3 CO2 PISTOL
Caliber: .177 BBs. Barrel: Smoothbore. Weight: 1.6 lbs. Length: 7.25 in. Power: CO2. Sights: Fixed Features: Non-blowback action, manual safety, 16 BB capacity, integrated Weaver-style accessory rail, double-action trigger, replica of the Glock 19 firearm. Velocity: 410 fps.
Price: **$89.00**

GLOCK 19 X CO2 PISTOL
Caliber: .177 BBs. Barrel: Smoothbore. Weight: 1.6 lbs. Length: 7.5 in. Power: CO2. Sights: Fixed Features: Blowback action, desert tan, metal

Prices given are believed to be accurate at time of publication however, many factors affect retail pricing so exact prices are not possible.

slide, manual safety, 18 BB magazine, integrated Weaver-style accessory rail, double-action trigger, replica of the Glock 19 firearm. Velocity: 377 fps.
Price: **$119.00**

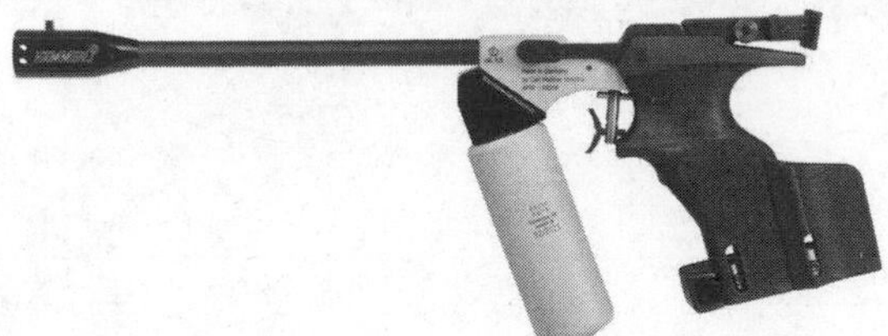

HAMMERLI AP-20 AIR PISTOL
Caliber: .177 pellets. Barrel: Rifled, match. Weight: 2.2 lbs. Length: 16.34 in. Power: Precharged pneumatic. Sights: Fully adjustable micrometer. Features: 2-stage adjustable trigger factory set to 500 grams pull weight, single shot, bolt action, up to 180 shots per fill, walnut grip with 3D adjustment, tunable front sight with three widths, adjustable width rear sight, comes with six barrel jackets in different colors. Velocity: 492 fps.
Price: **$1,149.00**

HATSAN MODEL 25 SUPERCHARGER QE AIR PISTOL
Caliber: .177 or .22 pellets. Barrel: Rifled. Weight: 3.9 lbs. Length: 20 in. Power: Single cock, air-piston. Sights: Fiber-optic front and fully adjustable fiber-optic rear sight. Features: Molded right-handed grips, fully adjustable "Quattro" two-stage trigger, Quiet Energy integrated sound moderator, 11mm dovetail grooves, XRS recoil reduction system. Velocity: 800 fps.
Price: **$119.00**

HATSAN USA AT P1 QUIET ENERGY PCP PISTOL

HATSAN USA AT P1 QUIET ENERGY PCP PISTOL
Calibers: .177, .22, .25. Barrel: Rifled. Weight: 4.7 lbs. Length: 23.2 in. Power: Pre-charged pneumatic. Sights: N/A. Grooved for scope mounting. Features: Multi-shot magazine feed, integrated suppressor, muzzle energy suitable for pest control and small game hunting. Velocity: .177, 870 fps/.22, 780 fps/.25, 710 fps.
Price: **$479.00**

H&K VP9 BB CO2 PISTOL
Caliber: .177 steel BBs. Barrel: Smoothbore. Weight: 1.42 lbs. Length: 7.2 in. Power: CO2. Sights: Fixed. Features: Highly realistic replica, blowback action, integrated front weaver accessory rail, 18-round magazine. Velocity: 350 fps.
Price: **$99.00**

H&K USP CO2 BB PISTOL
Caliber: .177 BBs. Barrel: Smoothbore. Weight: 2.15 lbs. Length: 7.75 in. Power: CO2. Sights: Fixed white dot. Features: Highly realistic replica, blowback, integrated front weaver accessory rail, single action/double action, realistic hammer movement, 16-shot drop-free magazine, metal barrel and slide. Velocity: 325 fps.
Price: **$55.00**

MORINI MOR-162EL AIR PISTOL
Caliber: .177 pellets. Barrel: Rifled. Weight: 2.25 lbs. Length: 16.14 in. Power: Precharged pneumatic. Sights: Front post, rear adjustable for windage. Features: Adjustable electronic trigger, single-shot bolt action, extreme match grade accuracy, over 200 regulated shots per 200 bar fill, available with different grip sizes. Velocity: 500 fps.
Price: **$2,250.00**

MORINI CM 200EI AIR PISTOL
Caliber: .177 pellets. Barrel: Rifled, Lothar Walther. Weight: 2.17 lbs. Length: 15.75 in. Power: Pre-charged pneumatic. Sights: Front post, rear diopter/micrometer adjustable. Features: Adjustable electronic trigger, single-shot bolt action, digital manometer, battery life of 15,000 shots, match-grade accuracy, available with medium or large grip size, muzzle compensator, 150 regulated shots per 200 bar fill, comes with two air cylinders. Velocity: 492 fps.
Price: **$2,439.00**

RUGER MARK IV PELLET PISTOL
Caliber: .177 pellets. Barrel: Rifled. Weight: 2.15 lbs. Length: 11 in. Power: Spring piston. Sights: Fiber optic fixed front, adjustable rear. Features: Single shot, single stage trigger, single stroke cocking. Velocity: 369 fps.
Price: **$59.00**

Prices given are believed to be accurate at time of publication however, many factors affect retail pricing so exact prices are not possible.

SCHOFIELD NO. 3 REVOLVER, FULL METAL
Caliber: .177 steel BBs or .177 pellets. Barrel: Smoothbore. Weight: 2.4 lbs. Length: 12.5 in. Power: CO2. Sights: Fixed. Features: Highly detailed replica top-break revolver, 6-shot capacity, realistic reusable cartridges, available in distressed black with imitation wood grips and plated steel with imitation ivory grips. Velocity: Up to 430 fps.
Price: .... **$159.00–$169.00**

SIG SAUER X-FIVE ASP .177 CO2 PISTOL
Caliber: .177 pellets. Barrel: Smoothbore. Weight: 2.75 lbs. Length: 9.75 in. Power: CO2. Sights: Fixed. Features: Realistic replica action pistol, 18-shot capacity, front accessory rail, full metal construction, metal slide with blowback action. Velocity: 300 fps.
Price: **$149.00**

SIG SAUER P320 CO2 PISTOL
Caliber: .177 BBs/.177 pellets. Barrel: Rifled. Weight: 2.2 lbs. Length: 9.6 in. Power: CO2. Sights: Fixed, white dot. Features: 30-round belt-fed magazine, front accessory rail, polymer frame, metal slide with blowback action, black or coyote tan finish. Velocity: 430 fps.
Price: **$129.00**

SIG SAUER P365 CO2 PISTOL
Caliber: .177 BBs. Barrel: Smoothbore. Weight: 0.8 lbs. Length: 5.75 in. Power: CO2. Sights: Fixed, white dot. Features: 12-round magazine, metal slide with blowback action, black finish, slide locks back after last shot. Velocity: 295 fps.
Price: **$119.00**

SMITH & WESSON MODEL 29 CO2 REVOLVER
Caliber: .177 BBs. Barrel: Smoothbore, 8.375 in. Weight: 2.65 lbs. with cartridges. Length: 12.14 in. Power: CO2. Sights: Fixed front, adjustable rear. Features: Brown faux wood grip, single/double action, approximately 60 shots per 12 gram cartridge, removable bullet casings. Velocity: 425 fps.
Price: **$179.00**

SMITH & WESSON M&P CO2 PISTOL
Caliber: .177 steel BBs. Barrel: Smoothbore. Weight: 1.5 lbs. Lengths: 7.5 in. Power: CO2. Sights: Blade front and ramp rear fiber optic. Features: Integrated accessory rail, removable 19-shot BB magazine, double-action only, synthetic frame available in dark earth brown or black color. Velocity: 300–480 fps.
Price: **$47.00**

SMITH & WESSON M&P 9 M2.0 CO2 PISTOL
Caliber: .177 steel BBs. Barrel: Smoothbore. Weight: 1.45 lbs. Length: 7.5 in. Power: CO2. Sights: Fixed front sight, fully adjustable rear sight. Features: Blowback action, full size drop free magazine with 18-round capacity, comes with three interchangeable backstraps, double- and single-action trigger, Picatinny accessory rail, last round hold open, ambidextrous slide release. Velocity: 400 fps.
Price: **$129.00**

SPRINGFIELD ARMORY 1911 MIL-SPEC C02 BB PISTOL
Caliber: .177 BBs. Barrel: Smoothbore, 4.1 in. Weight: 2.0 lbs. Length: 8.6 in. Power: CO2. Sights: Fixed 3-dot. Features: Full metal construction, blow-back slide, 18-round magazine, single action, checkered grips, approximately 65 shots per fill, slide locks back after last shot, functioning grip safety. Velocity: 320 fps.
Price: **$124.00**

Prices given are believed to be accurate at time of publication however, many factors affect retail pricing so exact prices are not possible.

SPRINGFIELD ARMORY XDE C02 BB PISTOL
Caliber: .177 BBs. Barrel: Smoothbore, 4.3 in. Weight: 1.95 lbs. Length: 7.75 in. Power: CO2. Sights: Fixed fiber optic. Features: Full metal construction, blow-back slide, 18-round drop-free magazine, double/single action, functional takedown lever, ambidextrous safety and magazine release, checkered grips, single slot Picatinny rail, front and rear slide serrations. Velocity: 380 fps.
Price: **$119.00**

SPRINGFIELD ARMORY XDM C02 BB PISTOL
Caliber: .177 BBs. Barrel: Smoothbore. Weight: 1.9 lbs. Length: 8 in. Power: CO2. Sights: Fixed fiber optic. Features: Blow-back metal slide, polymer frame, interchangeable backstraps, grip safety and trigger safety, functional striker status indicator, 20-round drop-free magazine, functional slide stop lever, fields strips like real XDM, Picatinny accessory rail, functional takedown lever, ambidextrous magazine release, slide locks back after last shot, available with 3.8- or 4.5-in. barrel, blue or two tone. Velocity: 325 fps.
Price: .... **$129.00–$149.00**

STEYR M9-A1 PISTOL
Caliber: .177 BBs. Barrel: Smoothbore. Weight: 1.2 lbs. Length: 7.5 in. Power: CO2. Sights: Fixed. Features: Non-blowback, accessory rail, metal slide, two-tone or blue finish, 19-round capacity. Velocity: 449 fps.
Price: Blue........ **$49.00**
Price: Two-tone........ **$69.00**

STI DUTY ONE CO2 BB PISTOL
Caliber: .177 steel BBs. Barrel: Smoothbore. Weight: 1.8 lbs. Length: 8.8 in. Power: CO2. Sights: Fixed. Features: Blowback, accessory rail, metal slide, threaded barrel, 20-round magazine. Velocity: 397 fps.
Price: **$109.00**

SWISS ARMS 18TH CENTURY PIRATE FLINTLOCK CO2 BB PISTOL
Caliber: .177 BBs. Barrel: Smoothbore. Weight: 2.7 lbs. Overall Length: 16.5 in. Power: CO2. Sights: None. Features: Detailed wood-grain polymer body, decorative embossed metal in either silver or gold tone, 30-round capacity, pirate's head buttcap, moving hammer and frizzen, includes imitation leather BB holder that resembles a powder flask and an instruction manual that resembles rolled parchment. The perfect air pistol for all pirate wannabes. Velocity: 415 fps.
Price: .... **$199.00–$229.00**

SWISS ARMS SA92 BB PISTOL
Caliber: .177 BBs. Barrel: Smoothbore. Weight: 2.5 lbs. Length: 8.5 in. Power: CO2. Sights: Fixed. Features: Blowback, accessory rail, full metal construction, stainless finish with brown grips, 20-round magazine. Velocity: 312 fps.
Price: **$139.00**

SWISS ARMS SA 1911 BB PISTOL
Caliber: .177 BBs. Barrel: Smoothbore. Weight: 2 lbs. Length: 8.6 in. Power: CO2. Sights: Fixed. Features: Blowback, slide locks back when empty, metal construction, single action only, desert tan, checkered grips, functional grip safety, accessory rail on some models, 18-round magazine. Velocity: 320 fps.
Price: **$139.00**

TANFOGLIO WITNESS 1911 CO2 BB PISTOL, BROWN GRIPS
Caliber: .177 steel BBs. Barrel: Smoothbore. Weight: 1.98 lbs. Length: 8.6 in. Power: CO2. Sights: Fixed. Features: Often recognized as the "standard" for 1911 replica action pistols, 18-shot capacity, full metal construction with metal slide with blowback action. Velocity: 320 fps.
Price: **$129.00**

UMAREX LEGENDS ACE-IN-THE-HOLE CO2 PELLET REVOLVER
Caliber: .177 pellets. Barrel: Rifled. Weight: 2.95 lbs. Length: 9.00 in. Power: CO2. Sights: Fixed. Features: Weathered plated finish, working ejector rod, 6-round cylinder with six shells, three removable plastic front sights, all-metal construction, black grip panels with ace of spades coin. Velocity: 340 fps.
Price: **$179.00**

UMAREX LEGENDS MAKAROV ULTRA BLOWBACK CO2 BB PISTOL
Caliber: .177 steel BBs. Barrel: Smoothbore. Weight: 1.40 lbs. Length: 6.38 in. Power: CO2. Sights: Fixed. Features: Highly realistic replica, all-metal

Prices given are believed to be accurate at time of publication however, many factors affect retail pricing so exact prices are not possible.

construction with blowback action, semi-automatic and fully-automatic capable, 16-round capacity. Velocity: 350 fps.
Price: **$69.00**

UMAREX LEGENDS M712 BROOM HANDLE FULL-AUTO CO2 BB PISTOL
Caliber: .177 steel BBs. Barrel: Smoothbore. Weight: 3.10 lbs. Length: 12.00 in. Power: CO2. Sights: Fixed front sight with rear sight adjustable for elevation. Features: Highly realistic replica that functions as the original, all-metal construction with blowback action, semi-automatic and fully-automatic capable, 18-round capacity. Velocity: 360 fps.
Price: **$139.00**

UMAREX 9XP/40XP CO2 PISTOL
Caliber: .177 BBs. Barrel: Smoothbore. Weight: 1.5 lbs. Length: 7.5 in. Power: CO2. Sights: Fixed. Features: Full metal slide with polymer grips, blowback action, double action, 20-round removable BB magazine, under barrel accessory rail. Velocity: 400 fps.
Price: **$66.00**

UMAREX BRODAX BB REVOLVER
Caliber: .177 steel BBs. Barrel: Smoothbore. Weight: 1.52 lbs. Length: 10.0 in. Power: CO2. Sights: Fixed. Features: Aggressively styled BB revolver, 10-shot capacity, top accessory rail, front accessory rail, synthetic construction. Velocity: 375 fps.
Price: **$44.00**

UMAREX D17 BB PISTOL
Caliber: .177 BBs. Barrel: Smoothbore. Weight: 1.6 lbs. Length: 9.5 in. Power: Spring piston. Sights: Fixed fiber optic. Features: Integrated accessory rail, 15 shot capacity. Velocity: 200 fps.
Price: **$22.00**

UZI (KWC) MINI CARBINE
Caliber: .177 steel BBs. Barrel: Smoothbore. Weight: 4.8 lbs. Length: 24/25 in. Power: CO2. Sights: Adjustable. Features: Realistic replica airgun, 25-shot capacity, foldable stock, semi-automatic with realistic blowback system, heavy bolt provides realistic "kick" when firing. Velocity: 344 fps.
Price: **$223.00**

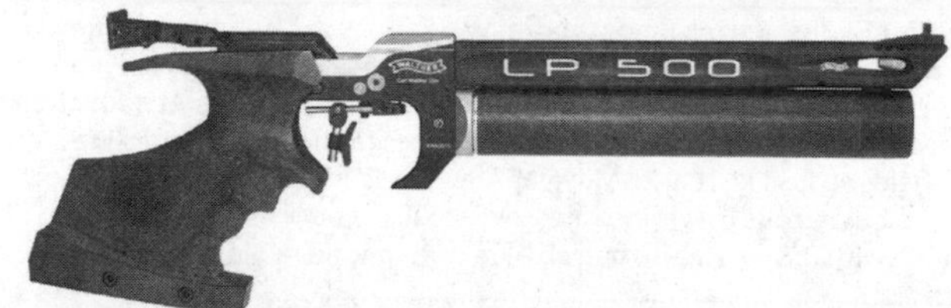

WALTHER LP500 COMPETITION PCP AIR PISTOL
Caliber: .177 pellets. Barrel: Rifled, match grade. Weight: 2 lbs. Length: 16.5 in. Power: Precharged pneumatic. Sights: Adjustable for windage and elevation. Features: Mechanical trigger, carbon-fiber air cylinder, up to 150 shots per fill, adjustable sight radius, walnut grip with adjustable palm shelf, single shot, five-way adjustable match trigger. Velocity: 500 fps.
Price: **$1,800.00**

WALTHER CP88 CO2 PISTOL
Caliber: .177 pellets. Barrel: Rifled. Weight: 2.3–2.5 lbs. Length: 7–9 in. Power: CO2. Sights: Blade ramp front sight and adjustable rear sight. Features: Manual safety, semi-auto repeater, single or double action, available with 4- or 6-in. barrel, available in multiple finishes and grip materials, 8-shot capacity. Velocity: 450 fps.
Price: .... **$266.00–$277.00**

Prices given are believed to be accurate at time of publication however, many factors affect retail pricing so exact prices are not possible.

WALTHER CP99 COMPACT

WALTHER CP99 COMPACT PISTOL
Caliber: .177 steel BBs. Barrel: Smoothbore. Weight: 1.7 lbs. Length: 6.6 in. Power: CO2. Sights: Fixed front and rear. Features: Extremely realistic replica pistol, semi-automatic 18-shot capacity, available in various configurations including a nickel slide. Velocity: 345 fps.
Price: .... **$99.00–$105.00**

WALTHER PPQ M2 CO2 PISTOL
Caliber: .177 pellets. Barrel: Rifled. Weight: 1.4 lbs. Length: 7.0 in. Power: CO2. Sights: Fixed front and rear sight adjustable for elevation. Features: Extremely realistic replica pistol, blowback action, 20-shot drop-free magazine, metal slide, polymer frame. Velocity: 380 fps.
Price: **$149.00**

WALTHER P38 CO2 BB PISTOL
Caliber: .177 steel BBs. Barrel: Smoothbore. Weight: 1.9 lbs. Length: 8.5 in. Power: CO2. Sights: Fixed. Features: Authentic replica action pistol, blowback action, semi-automatic 20-shot magazine. Velocity: 400 fps.
Price: **$120.00**

WALTHER PPK/S CO2 PISTOL
Caliber: .177 steel BBs. Barrel: Smoothbore. Weight: 3.7 lbs. Length: 6.1 in. Power: CO2. Sights: Fixed. Features: Authentic replica action pistol, blowback slide locks back after last shot, stick-style magazine with 15-shot capacity. Velocity: 295 fps.
Price: **$129.00**

WALTHER PPS M2 BLOWBACK COMPACT CO2 PISTOL
Caliber: .177 steel BBs. Barrel: Smoothbore. Weight: 1.2 lbs. Length: 6.38 in. Power: CO2. Sights: Fixed. Features: Authentic replica action pistol, blowback action, semi-automatic 18-shot capacity. Velocity: 390 fps.
Price: **$79.00**

WEBLEY AND SCOTT MKVI REVOLVER
Caliber: .177 pellets. Barrel: Rifled. Weight: 2.4 lbs. Length: 11.25 in. Power: CO2. Sights: Fixed. Features: Authentic replica pistol, single/double action, can be field-stripped, full metal construction, six-shot capacity, available in silver or distressed finish. Velocity: 430 fps.
Price: **$166.00**

WEBLEY AND SCOTT NEMESIS CO2 PISTOL
Caliber: .177 OR .22 pellets. Barrel: Rifled. Weight: 2 lbs. Length: 10.25 in. Power: CO2. Sights: Fiber optic fixed. Features: Bolt action, bolt can be swapped from right to left, tandem self-indexing magazine system (2x7 in .177 or 2x6 in .22), single-shot tray included, storage for magazine in grip, Picatinny rail for accessories, 3/8-in. dovetail for optics mounting, ambidextrous grip, ½-inch UNF threaded barrel, approximately 40 shots per CO2 cylinder, two-stage adjustable trigger. Velocities: 450 fps (.177), 370 fps (.22).
Price: .... **$111.00–$122.00**

WEIHRAUCH HW 40 AIR PISTOL
Caliber: .177, .20, .22. Barrel: Rifled. Weight: 1.7 lbs. Length: 9.5 in. Power: Single-stroke spring piston. Sights: Fiber-optic, fully adjustable. Features: Automatic safety, two-stage trigger, single shot. Velocity: 400 fps..
Price: **$323.00**

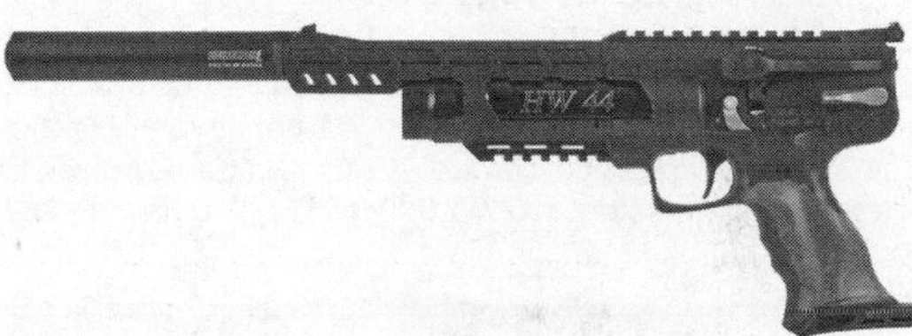

WEIHRAUCH HW 44 AIR PISTOL, FAC VERSION
Caliber: .177, .22. Barrel: Rifled. Weight: 2.9 lbs. Length: 19 in. Power: Pre-charged pneumatic. Sights: None. Features: Ambidextrous safety, two-stage adjustable match trigger, built in suppressor, Weaver-style scope rail, 10-shot magazine, built-in air cartridge with quick fill, internal pressure gauge. Velocity: 750 (.177), 570 (.22) fps.
Price: **$1,099.00**

WEIHRAUCH HW 45 AIR PISTOL
Caliber: .177, .20, .22. Barrel: Rifled. Weight: 2.5 lbs. Length: 10.9 in. Power: Single-stroke spring piston. Sights: Fiber-optic, fully adjustable. Features: Automatic safety, two-stage trigger, single shot, two power levels, blued or two tone. Velocity: 410/558 (.177), 394/492 (.20), 345/427 (.22) fps.
Price: **$578.00**

WEIHRAUCH HW 75 AIR PISTOL
Caliber: .177. Barrel: Rifled. Weight: 2.3 lbs. Length: 11 in. Power: Single-stroke spring piston. Sights: Micrometer adjustable rear. Features: Ambidextrous, adjustable match-type trigger, single shot. Velocity: 410 fps.
Price: **$554.00**

AIR ARMS TX200 MKIII AIR RIFLE
Calibers: .177, .22. Barrel: Rifled, Lothar Walter match-grade, 13.19 in. Weight: 9.3 lbs. Length: 41.34 in. Power: Single cock, spring-piston. Stock: Various; right- and left-handed versions, multiple wood options. Sights: 11mm dovetail. Features: Fixed barrel, heirloom quality craftsmanship, holds the record for the most winning spring powered airgun in international field target competitions. Velocities: .177, 930 fps/.22, 755 fps.
Price: .... **$799.00–$879.00**

AIR ARMS PRO-SPORT RIFLE
Calibers: .177, .22. Barrel: Rifled, Lothar Walter match-grade, 9.5 in. Weight: 9.03 lbs. Length: 40.5 in. Power: Single cock, spring-piston Stock: Various; right-and left-handed versions, multiple wood options. Sights: 11mm dovetail. Features: Fixed barrel, Heirloom quality craftsmanship, unique inset cocking arm. Velocities: .177, 950 fps/.22, 750 fps.
Price: .... **$924.00–$989.00**

AIR ARMS S510 XTRA FAC PCP AIR RIFLE
Calibers: .177, .22, .25. Barrel: Rifled, Lothar Walter match-grade, 19.45 in. Weight: 7.55 lbs. Length: 43.75 in. Power: Pre-charged pneumatic. Stock: Right-handed, multiple wood options. Sights: 11mm dovetail. Features: Side-lever action, 10-round magazine, shrouded barrel, variable power, Heirloom quality craftsmanship Velocities: .177, 1,050 fps/.22, 920 fps/.25, 850 fps.
Price: **$1,554.00**

AIR ARMS S510 XS ULTIMATE SPORTER
Calibers: .177, .22, .25. Barrel: Rifled, Lothar Walter match-grade, 19.75 in. Weight: 8.6 lbs. Length: 44.75 in. Power: Precharged pneumatic. Stock: Fully adjustable, ambidextrous black Soft-Touch stock. Sights: None, 11mm dovetail. Features: Side-lever action, two 10-shot magazines included, two-stage adjustable trigger, integrated suppressor, variable power, up to 40-60 shots per fill depending on caliber. Velocities: .177, 1,035 fps/.22, 950 fps/.25, 815 fps.
Price: **$1,724.00**

AIR ARMS S510 XS TDR RIFLE
Calibers: .177, .22. Barrel: Rifled, Lothar Walter match-grade, 15.55 in. Weight: 6.2 lbs. Length: 40.5 in. Power: Precharged pneumatic. Stock: Fully adjustable, ambidextrous black Soft-Touch. Sights: 11mm dovetail. Features: Takedown rifle breaks down in seconds, comes with a hard case with custom cut foam, side-lever action, 10-shot magazine, integrated suppressor, variable power, built-in manometer, adjustable two-stage trigger. Velocities: .177, 1,035 fps/.22, 950 fps.
Price: **$1,724.00**

AIR ARMS T200 SPORTER
Caliber: .177 pellets. Barrel: Hammer-forged, rifled 19.1 in. Weight: 6.6 lbs. Length: 35.5 in. Power: Pre-charged pneumatic. Stock: Hardwood. Sights: Globe front sight, fully adjustable diopter rear sight. Features: Aluminum muzzle brake, two-stage adjustable trigger, removable air tank, single shot, grooved receiver, made by CZ. Velocity: 575 fps.
Price: **$600.00**

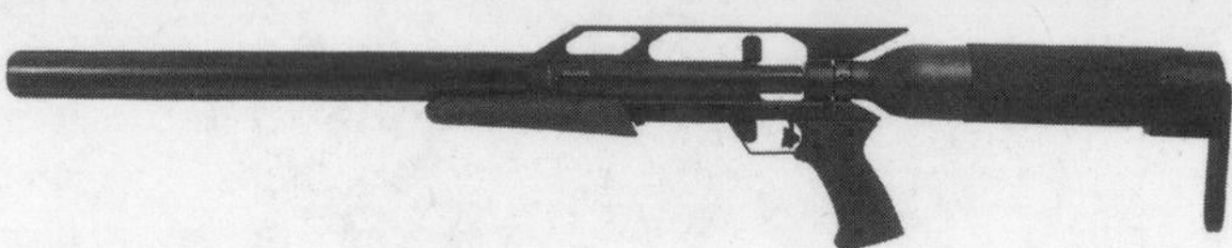

AIRFORCE CONDOR SS RIFLE
Calibers: .177, .20, .22, .25. Barrel: Rifled, Lothar Walther match-grade, 18 or 24 in. Weight: 6.1 lbs. Length: 38.1-38.75 in. Power: Pre-charged pneumatic. Stock: Synthetic pistol grip, tank acts as buttstock. Sights: Grooved for scope mounting. Features: Single shot, adjustable power, automatic safety, large 490cc tank volume, extended scope rail allows easy mounting of the largest air-gun scopes, optional CO2 power system available, manufactured in the USA by AirForce Airguns. Velocities: .177, 1,450 fps/.20, 1,150 fps/.22, 1,250 fps/.25, 1,100 fps.
Price: **$814.00**

AIRFORCE EDGE 10-METER AIR RIFLE
Caliber: .177. Barrel: Rifled, Lothar Walther match-grade, 12 in. Weight: 6.1 lbs. Length: 40.00 in. Power: Pre-charged pneumatic. Stock: Synthetic pistol grip, tank acts as buttstock. Sights: Front sight only or match front globe and rear micrometer adjustable diopter sight. Features: Single shot, automatic safety, two-stage adjustable trigger, accepted by CMP for completive shooting, available in multiple colors and configurations, manufactured in the USA. Velocity: .530 fps.
Price: .... **$639.00-$799.00**

AIRFORCE TALON SS PCP RIFLE
Calibers: .177, .20, .22, 25. Barrel: Rifled, Lothar Walther match-grade, 12 in. Weight: 5.25 lbs. Length: 32.75in. Power: Precharged pneumatic, Stock: Synthetic pistol grip. Sights: None, grooved for scope mounting. Features: Single shot, removable moderator to reduce noise, adjustable power, can be easily broken down for compact transport, red or blue anodized frame, automatic safety, two-stage nonadjustable trigger, 490 cc air tank, up to 50 ft-lbs of energy, manufactured in the USA. Velocities: 1,000 fps (.177), 800 fps (.20), 800 fps (.22), 665 fps (.25).
Price: **$689.00**

AIRFORCE INTERNATIONAL MODEL 94 SPRING AIR RIFLE
Calibers: .177, .22, 25. Barrel: Rifled, hammer forged, 18.75 in. Weight: 7.5 lbs. Length: 44.9 in. Power: Spring piston. Stock: Synthetic with textured grip and forearm. Sights: Fixed fiber-optic front and fully adjustable fiber-optic rear. Features: Single shot, adjustable two-stage trigger, 32-pound cocking effort, integral muzzle brake. Velocities: 1100 fps (.177)/900 fps (.22)/700 fps (.25).
Price: $249.00

AIRGUN TECHNOLOGY URAGAN KING RIFLE
Calibers: .25 or .30. Barrel: 19.6 in. Weight: 8 to 10 lbs. Length: 36 in. Power: Precharged pneumatic. Stock: Ambidextrous walnut or synthetic bullpup stock. Sights: None, Picatinny rail for scope mounting. Features: Has a reversible biathlon side lever, 10-shot (.25) or 9-shot (.30) magazine, dual air cylinders, bullpup design, sound moderator, approximately 100 shots per fill. Velocities: NA.
Price: .... **$1,889.00–$2,019.00**

Prices given are believed to be accurate at time of publication however, many factors affect retail pricing so exact prices are not possible.

AIRGUN TECHNOLOGY VULCAN 2 BULLPUP RIFLE
Calibers: .22 or .25. Barrel: 19.6 in. Weight: 7.25 lbs. Length: 29.75 in. Power: Precharged pneumatic. Stock: Ambidextrous walnut bullpup stock with polymer cheekpiece. Sights: Picatinny rail for scope mounting. Features: Has a biathlon side lever, comes with two 12-shot magazines, includes a hard case, side-lever action, shrouded barrel with M14 adapter, up to 60 shots per fill. Velocities: .22, 800 fps/.25, 600 fps.
Price: **$1,799.00**

AIR VENTURI AVENGER RIFLE
Caliber: .177, .22, .25. Barrel: Rifled, 22.75 in. Weight: 6.0 lbs. Length: 42.75 in. Power: Precharged pneumatic. Stock: Ambidextrous synthetic or wood stock. Sights: None, picatinny rail. Features: Side-lever cocking, externally adjustable regulator, hammer spring adjustment screw, two-stage adjustable trigger, shrouded barrel, easy access degassing screw, includes two magazines and a single shot loading tray, 8 (.25) or 10 shot (.177 and .22) capacity. Velocities: .177, 1000 fps; .22, 930 fps; .25, 900 fps.
Price: .... **$399.00–$479.00**

AIR VENTURI TR5 RIFLE
Caliber: .177. Barrel: Rifled, 18.75 in. Weight: 5.0 lbs. Length: 32.5-34.5 in. Power: Spring piston. Stock: Black or green synthetic stock. Sights: Fully adjustable rear sight, globe front sight, 11 mm dovetail. Features: Two-stage adjustable trigger, adjustable trigger blade position, five-position adjustable buttstock, includes two 5 round magazine, UIT accessory rail on underside of fore end. Velocity: 500 fps.
Price: **$109.00**

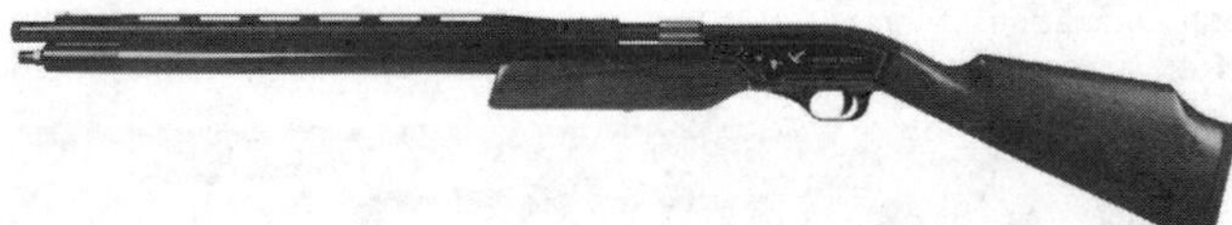

AIR VENTURI SENECA WING SHOT II SHOTGUN
Caliber: .50. Barrel: Smoothbore 22.5 in. Weight: 7.4 lbs. Length: 43.0 in. Power: Precharged pneumatic. Stock: Ambidextrous wood stock. Sights: Fixed bead shotgun-style sight. Features: 244cc reservoir delivers several powerful shots, shoots shot cartridges and round ball, exceptionally reliable. Use as a shotgun to hunt birds or small game or as a slug gun to hunt larger game. Velocity: 760 fps (with slug), 1,130 fps.
Price: **$924.00**

AMERICAN AIR ARMS EVOL CLASSIC CARBINE
Calibers: .22, .25, or .30. Barrel: Hammer forged, rifled, threaded, 15 in. (.22), 18 in (.25 or .30). Weight: 7-7.2 lbs. Length: 36-39 in with moderator. Power: Precharged pneumatic. Stock: Walnut. Sights: None, Picatinny rail. Features: Upper and lower chassis made from aluminum, titanium air cylinder, Picatinny underside accessory rail, adjustable two-stage trigger set to 10 ounces, 9-13 shot rotary magazine, Magpul stock and grip, manufactured in the USA in very limited quantities. Velocity: Adjustable.
Price: **$2,895.00**

AMERICAN AIR ARMS SLAYER HI-POWER BULLPUP RIFLE
Calibers: .308 or .357. Barrel: Rifled, threaded, 24 in (.357) or 26 in. (.308). Weight: 7.2 lbs. Length: 36-40 in with moderator. Power: Precharged pneumatic. Stock: Synthetic adjustable length stock. Sights: None, Picatinny rail. Features: Titanium reservoir, three pound cocking effort, 6 (.357 caliber) or 7 (.308 caliber) round rotary magazine, adjustable two-stage trigger, underside accessory rail, rear velocity adjuster, available in right or left hand, manufactured in the USA in very limited quantities. Velocity: 950 fps.
Price: **$2,795.00**

ANSCHUTZ 9015 AIR RIFLE
Caliber: .177. Barrel: Rifled, 16.5 in. Weight: Variable from 8.1 to 11 pounds. Length: Variable from 39.0 to 47 in. Power: Pre-charged pneumatic. Stock: Fully adjustable variable composition. Sights: Fully adjustable target sights with interchangeable inserts. Features: Single shot, ambidextrous grip, adjustable match trigger, exchangeable air cylinder with integrated manometer, approximately 200 shots per fill, available with a bewildering array of options. Velocity: 560 fps.
Price: .... **$2,545.00–$5,350.00**

ASG TAC-4.5 CO2 BB RIFLE
Caliber: .177 steel BBs. Barrel: Smoothbore. Weight: 3.5 lbs. Length: 36.0 in. Power: CO2 Stock: Synthetic thumbhole stock. Sights: Fixed fiber-optic front sight and fully adjustable fiber-optic rear sight/weaver rail for optics. Features: Semi-automatic action, includes bi-pod, 21-shot capacity. Velocity: 417 fps.
Price: **$119.00**

ATAMAN BP17 PCP AIR RIFLE
Calibers: .22. Barrel: Lothar Walther rifled match-grade, 14.5 in. Weight: 5.1 lbs. Length: 23.85 in. Power: Precharged pneumatic. Stock: Ambidextrous black Soft-Touch coated bullpup stock. Sights: Weaver/Picatinny rail for scope mounting. Features: Unique forward position cocking lever, cocking lever can be switched from right to left, 25 shots per fill, four magazine storage slots under Picatinny rail, includes two seven-round magazines, two-way adjustable trigger. Velocity: 840 fps.
Price: **$1,599.00**

ATAMAN M2R CARBINE ULTRA COMPACT AIR RIFLE
Caliber: .22. Barrel: Lothar Walther rifled match-grade, 15.39 in. Weight: 6.17 lbs. Length: 36.48 in. Power: Pre-charged pneumatic. Stock: Ambidextrous adjustable/foldable stock available in walnut or "soft touch" synthetic. Sights: Weaver rails for scope mounting. Features: Multi-shot side-lever action, 10-shot capacity, adjustable match trigger, finely tuned regulator matched to optimal velocity. Velocity: 850 fps.
Price: **$1,554.00**

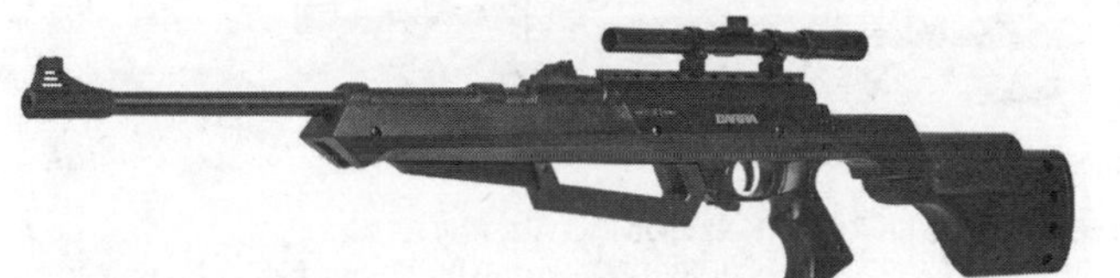

BARRA SPORTSMAN 900 RIFLE
Calibers: .177 BB or pellet. Barrel: Rifled, 20.1 in. Weight: 4.4 lbs. Length:

39.4in. Power: Multipump. Stock: Black synthetic. Sights: Fixed fiber-optic front, fully adjustable rear. Features: 50-round BB repeater or single shot pellet, 3/8-in. rail for mounting optics, Picatinny accessory rails on forearm sides, 6.25 lb trigger pull, 4x15 scope included. Velocity: 670 fps.
Price: **$72.00**

BEEMAN R9 AIR RIFLE
Calibers: .177, .20, .22. Barrel: Rifled 16.33 in. Weight: 7.3 lbs. Length: 43 in. Power: Break-barrel, spring-piston. Stock: Ambidextrous walnut-stained beech, cut-checkered pistol grip, Monte Carlo comb and rubber buttpad. Sights: None, grooved for scope. Features: German quality, limited lifetime warranty, highly adjustable match-grade trigger, extremely accurate. Velocities: .177, 935 fps/.20, 800 fps/.22, 740 fps.
Price: **$624.00**

BEEMAN AR2078A CO2 RIFLE
Calibers: .177, .22 pellets. Barrel: Rifled, 21.50 in. Weight: 7.5 lbs. Length: 38 in. Power: CO2. Stock: Beech. Sights: Competition diopter peep sight, 11 mm dovetail. Features: Bolt action, single shot, operates on two standard 12 gram CO2 cylinders or with tank adapter and connector, adjustable trigger, approximately 60 shots per fill. Velocities: .177, 650/.22, 500 fps.
Price: **$259.00**

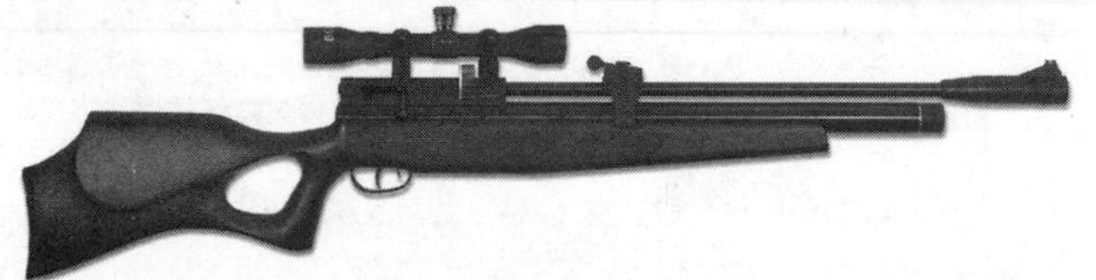

BEEMAN COMMANDER PCP RIFLE
Calibers: .177, .22 pellets. Barrel: Rifled. Weight: 8 lbs. Length: 43 in. Power: Precharged pneumatic. Stock: Hardwood thumbhole. Sights: Adjustable fiber optic, comes with a 4x32 scope. Features: Up to 100 shots per fill, 10-shot magazine, built in noise suppressor. Velocities: .177, 1100/.22, 1000 fps.
Price: **$269.00**

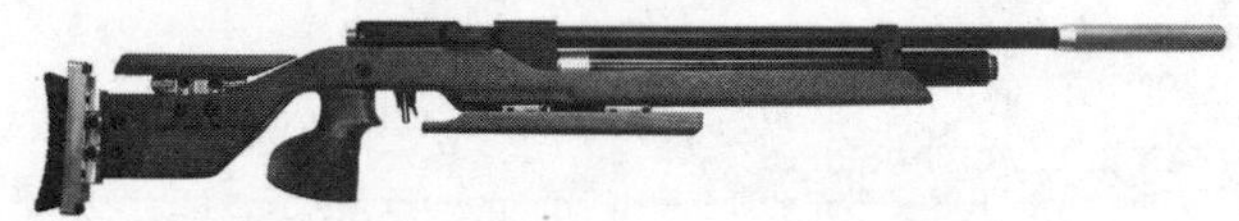

BEEMAN COMPETITION PCP RIFLE
Caliber: .177 pellets. Barrel: Rifled. Weight: 8.8 lbs. Length: 41.7 in. Power: Precharged pneumatic. Stock: Adjustable hardwood. Sights: None, dovetail grooves. Features: Side lever cocking, up to 200 shots per fill, single shot, built-in noise suppressor, 10-meter competition, adjustable trigger, adjustable pistol grip, comb, and buttplate. Velocity: 550 fps.
Price: **$1,059.00**

BEEMAN PCP UNDER LEVER RIFLE
Calibers: .177, .22 pellets. Barrel: Rifled. Weight: 7.3 lbs. Length: 32 in. Power: Precharged pneumatic. Stock: Bullpup style wood. Sights: Adjustable fiber optic. Features: 10 shot magazine, unique front under level cocking system, built in noise suppressor. Velocity: .177, 1000/.22, 830 fps.
Price: **$499.00**

BEEMAN SILVER KODIAK X2 COMBO AIR RIFLE
Calibers: .177, .22. Barrel: Rifled. Weight: 9 lbs. Length: 45.5 in. Power: Break-barrel, gas ram piston. Stock: Ambidextrous hardwood stock. Sights: Open includes 4x32 scope and rings. Features: Satin finish nickel plated receiver and barrels, single-shot, easily exchangeable .177 and .22 cal. barrels, two-stage trigger. Velocities: .177, 1,200 fps/.22, 830 fps.
Price: **$169.00**

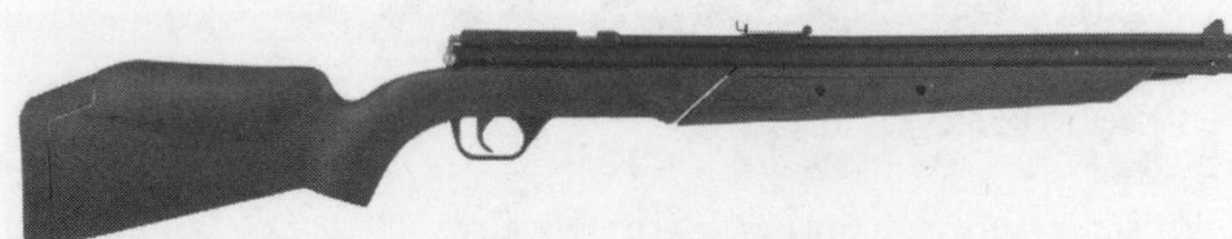

BENJAMIN 392 / 397 AIR RIFLE
Calibers: .177, .22. Barrel: Rifled 19.25 in. Weight: 5.5 lbs. Length: 36.25 in. Power: Multi-pump Pneumatic. Stock: Ambidextrous wood or synthetic stock. Sights: Front ramp and adjustable rear sight. Features: Multi-pump system provides variable power, single-shot bolt action. Velocities: .177, 800 fps/.20, 685 fps.
Price: **$236.00**

BENJAMIN ARMADA, BASE, TACTICAL, & MAGPUL EDITION AIR RIFLE

BENJAMIN ARMADA PCP RIFLE
Calibers: .177, .22, .25. Barrel: Rifled, 20 in. Weight: 7.3 lbs. (10.3 lbs. with scope and bipod). Length: 42.8 in. Power: Precharged pneumatic. Stock: Adjustable mil-spec AR-15-style buttstock, all metal M-LOK compatible handguard with 15 in. of Picatinny rail space. Sights: None, Weaver/Picatinny rail for scope mounting. Features: Fully shrouded barrel with integrated suppressor, dampener device, bolt action, multi shot, choked barrel for maximum accuracy. Velocities: .177, 1,100 fps/.22, 1,000 fps/.25, 900 fps.
Price: **$780.00**

BENJAMIN AKELA PCP AIR RIFLE
Calibers: .22. Barrel: Rifled. Weight: 7.7 lbs. Length: 32.9 in. Power: Precharged pneumatic. Stock: Bullpup style Turkish walnut stock. Sights: None, Picatinny rail for scope mounting. Features: Side cocking lever, adjustable trigger shoe, 3,000 psi pressure, up to 60 shots per fill, 12-shot rotary magazine. Velocity: 1,000 fps.
Price: **$649.00**

BENJAMIN CAYDEN PCP AIR RIFLE
Calibers: .22. Barrel: Rifled. Weight: 7.95 lbs. Length: 40.8 in. Power: Precharged Pneumatic. Stock: Turkish walnut stock with adjustable cheekpiece. Sights: None, grooved 11mm dovetail for scope mounting. Features: Side cocking lever, adjustable trigger shoe, 3,000 psi pressure, up to 60 shots per fill, 12-shot rotary magazine. Velocity: 1000 fps.
Price: **$699.00**

BENJAMIN FORTITUDE GEN 2 PCP RIFLE
Calibers: .177 or .22. Barrel: Rifled 24.25 in. Weight: 5.3 lbs. Length: 42.6 in. Power: Precharged Pneumatic. Stock: Synthetic, ambidextrous. Sights: None, grooved 11mm dovetail for scope mounting. Features: Shrouded barrel with integrated suppressor, 10-shot rotary magazine, 3,000 PSI pressure gauge with regulator, 60-200 shots per fill, adjustable hammer spring. Velocity: 950 fps (.177), 850 fps (.22).
Price: **$354.00**

Prices given are believed to be accurate at time of publication however, many factors affect retail pricing so exact prices are not possible.

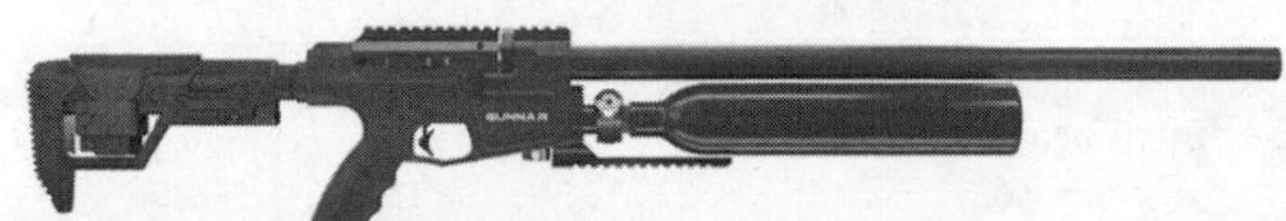

BENJAMIN GUNNAR AIR RIFLE
Calibers: .22 or .25. Barrel: Rifled. Weight: 9.8 lbs. Length: Adjustable. Power: Precharged Pneumatic. Stock: Synthetic, ambidextrous. Sights: None, Picatinny rail for scope mounting. Features: Bolt action, side lever cocking, adjustable AR-style stock, shrouded barrel with integrated suppressor, 500 cc reservoir, adjustable regulator and 5-position external power adjuster, Picatinny rail for monopod, multi-shot. Velocity: 1,000 fps (.22), 900 fps (.25).
Price: **$1,299.00**

BENJAMIN KRATOS PCP AIR RIFLE
Calibers: .22, .25. Barrel: Rifled. Weight: 8.26 lbs. Length: 43.35 in. Power: Precharged Pneumatic. Stock: Turkish walnut stock with adjustable cheekpiece. Sights: None, Picatinny rail for scope mounting. Features: Side cocking lever, adjustable trigger shoe, 3,000 psi pressure, up to 60 shots per fill, 12-shot rotary magazine in .22, 10-shot rotary magazine in .25. Velocities: 1,000 fps (.22), 900 fps (.25).
Price: **$724.00**

BENJAMIN MARAUDER PCP AIR RIFLE
Caliber: .177, .22, .25. Barrel: Rifled 20 in. Weight: Synthetic 7.3 lbs/Hardwood 8.2 lbs. Length: 42.8 in. Power: Precharged pneumatic. Stock: Ambidextrous stock available in hardwood or synthetic, adjustable cheek riser. Sights: None, grooved for scope mounting. Features: Multi-shot bolt action, 10-shot in .177 and .22, 8-shot in .25, user-adjustable performance settings for power and shot count, reversible bolt handle. Also available with options such as an integrated regulator for shot-to-shot consistency, a Picatinny rail, and Lothar Walther barrel. Velocities: .177, 1,100 fps/.22, 1,000 fps/.25, 900 fps.
Price: .... **$609.99–$709.99**

BENJAMIN MAXIMUS PCP AIR RIFLE
Calibers: .177, .22. Barrel: Rifled 26.25 in. Weight: 5.0 lbs. Length: 41.7 in. Power: Precharged Pneumatic. Stock: Ambidextrous synthetic stock. Sights: Front Fiber-optic and adjustable rear fiber-optic sight/grooved 11mm dovetail for scope mounting. Features: HPA required only 2,000 psi to operate, built in pressure gauge. Velocities: .177, 1,000 fps/.22, 850 fps.
Price: **$219.00**

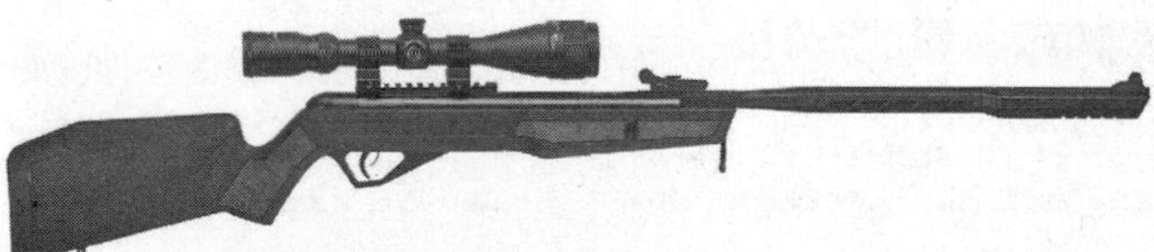

BENJAMIN VAPORIZER NITRO PISTON RIFLE
Calibers: .22. Barrel: Rifled 15 in. Weight: 8.5 lbs. Length: 46.5 in. Power: Break-barrel, Nitro Piston. Stock: Ambidextrous synthetic. Sights: Adjustable, Picatinny rail for scope mounting. Features: SBD sound suppression, shrouded barrel with integrated suppressor, single-shot, adjustable two-stage trigger. Velocity: 950 fps.
Price: **$265.00**

BLACK OPS TACTICAL SNIPER GAS-PISTON AIR RIFLE
Calibers: .22. Barrel: Rifled. Weight: 9.6 lbs. Length: 44.0 in. Power: Break-barrel, gas-piston. Stock: Ambidextrous pistol grip synthetic stock. Sights: none, Weaver rail for scope mounting, includes a 4x32 scope. Features: Muzzle brake helps with cocking force, single-shot, single cock delivers maximum power, adjustable single-stage trigger. Velocities: .177, 1,250 fps/.22, 1,000 fps.
Price: **$249.00**

BROCOCK BANTAM HI-LITE PCP RIFLE
Caliber: .25. Barrel: Rifled, Lothar Walther barrel. Weight: 6.4 lbs. Length: 34 in. Power: Pre-charged pneumatic. Stock: Semi-bullpup, beech wood. Sights: None, grooved for scope mounting. Features: 10-shot magazine, 480cc carbon-fiber air bottle, adjustable cheek piece and buttpad, three-step power adjuster. Velocities: NA.
Price: **$1,553.00**

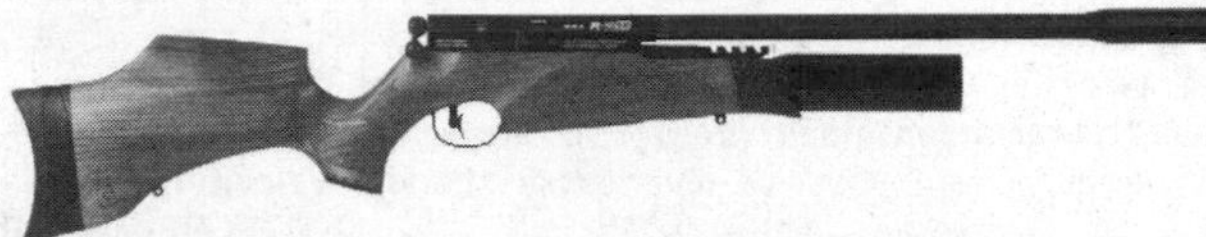

BSA R-10 SE PCP AIR RIFLE
Calibers: .177, .22. Barrel: Rifled, BSA-made cold hammer forged precision barrel, 19 in. Weight: 7.3 lbs. Length: 44 in. Power: Precharged pneumatic. Stock: Available right- or left-hand, walnut, laminate, camo or black synthetic. Sights: None, grooved for scope mounting. Features: Multi-shot bolt action, 10-shot magazine (8-shot for .25 caliber), fully regulated valve for maximum accuracy and shot consistency, free-floating, shrouded barrel, also available with lower power/velocity and as a shorter carbine. Velocities: 1,000 fps (.177)/980 fps (.22).
Price: .... **$1,299.00–$1,495.00**

BSA GOLD STAR SE HUNTER FIELD TARGET PCP AIR RIFLE
Caliber: .177. Barrel: Rifled, BSA-made enhanced cold hammer forged precision barrel, 15.2 in. Weight: 7 lbs. Length: 35.8 in. Power: Pre-charged pneumatic. Stock: Highly adjustable gray laminate field target competition stock. Sights: None, grooved for scope mounting. Features: Multi-shot boltaction, 10-shot magazine, fully regulated valve for maximum accuracy and shot consistency, 70 consistent shots per charge, free-floating barrel with 1/2 UNF threaded muzzle, includes adjustable air stripper, adjustable match-grade trigger. Velocity: 800 fps.
Price: **$1,499.00**

BSA SCORPION SE PCP AIR RIFLE
Calibers: .177, .22, .25. Barrel: Rifled, 15.2 in. Weight: 6.8 lbs. Length: 35 in. Power: Precharged pneumatic. Stock: Ambidextrous Monte Carlo stock in wood, camo or black. Sights: None, 11mm scope rail. Features: 10 shot (.177 and .22) or 8 shot (.25) magazine with last shot indicator, approximately 30-45 shots per fill depending on caliber, two-stage adjustable trigger. Velocity: 930 fps (.177), 770 fps (.22), 680 fps (.25).
Price: **$1,099.00**

BSA ULTRA CLX PCP RIFLE

Calibers: .177, .22. Barrel: Rifled, BSA-made cold hammer forged precision barrel, 12.5 in. Weight: 5.6 lbs. Length: 32 in. Power: Precharged pneumatic. Stock: Ambidextrous beech. Sights: None, grooved for scope mounting. Features: 12-shot magazine with shot countdown indicator, fully adjustable trigger, 60-72 shots per fill. Also available with a limited edition walnut stock. Velocities: 700 fps (.177)/570 fps (.22).

Price: **$1,080.00**

BSA ULTRA JSR AIR RIFLE

Calibers: .177, .22. Barrel: Rifled, BSA-made cold hammer forged precision barrel, 12 in. Weight: 4.95 lbs. Length: 27 in. Power: Precharged pneumatic. Stock: Beech. Sights: None, grooved for scope mounting. Features: Built for younger or smaller framed shooters, 10-shot magazine, fully regulated valve for maximum accuracy and shot consistency, free-floating, shrouded barrel, two-stage adjustable trigger, threaded muzzle, .177 available in two power configurations. Velocities: 560 or 800 fps (.177)/600 fps (.22).

Price: **$699.00**

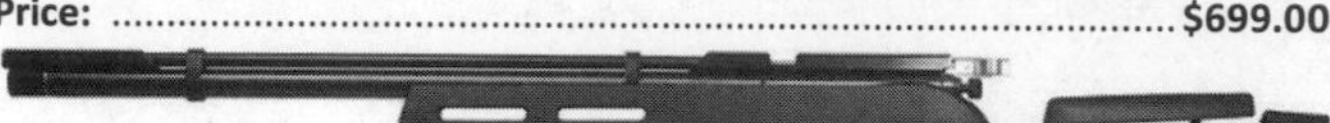

CROSMAN CHALLENGER PCP COMPETITION AIR RIFLE

Caliber: .177. Barrel: Match-grade Lothar Walther rifled barrel. Weight: 7.3 lbs. Length: 41.75 in. Power: Precharged pneumatic. Stock: Highly adjustable synthetic competition stock. Sights: Globe front sight and Precision Diopter rear sight. Features: Up to 200 shots per fill, single-shot, adjustable two-stage match-grade trigger with adjustable shoe, approved by the Civilian Marksmanship Program (CMP) for 3-position air rifle Sporter Class competition, swappable side-lever cocking handle. Velocity: 580 fps.

Price: .... **$699.00–$999.00**

CROSMAN M4-177

CROSMAN M4-177 RIFLE (various styles and kits available)

Caliber: .177 steel BBs, .177 pellets. Barrel: Rifled 17.25 in. Weight: 3.75 lbs. Length: 33.75 in. Power: Multi-pump pneumatic. Stock: M4-style adjustable plastic stock. Sights: Weaver/Picatinny rail for scope mounting and flip-up sights. Bundled packages include various included sighting options. Features: Single-shot bolt action, lightweight and very accurate, multiple colors available. "Ready to go" kits available complete with ammo, safety glasses, targets and extra 5-shot pellet magazines. Velocity: 660 fps.

Price: .... **$74.00-$139.00**

CROSMAN MODEL 760 PUMPMASTER AIR RIFLE

Caliber: .177 steel BBs, .177 pellets. Barrel: Rifled 16.75 in. Weight: 2.75 lbs. Length: 33.5 in. Power: Multi-pump pneumatic. Stock: Ambidextrous plastic stock. Sights: Blade and ramp, rear sight adjustable for elevation, grooved for scope mounting. Features: Single-shot pellet, BB repeater, bolt action, lightweight, accurate and easy to shoot. Multiple colors available and configurations available. "Ready to go" kits available complete with ammo, safety glasses, targets and extra 5-shot pellet magazines. Velocity: 625 fps.

Price: .... **$42.00–$54.00**

CROSMAN DIAMONDBACK SBD AIR RIFLE

Caliber: .22. Barrel: Rifled. Weight: 8.5 lbs. Length: 46.5 in. Power: Break-barrel, Nitro-piston. Stock: Synthetic with pistol grip. Sights: Open sights, dovetail for scope mounting, includes CenterPoint 4x32 scope and rings. Features: SBD sound-suppression system, sling mounts, single-shot, adjustable two-stage trigger. Velocities: 1,100 fps.

Price: **$139.00**

CROSMAN FIRE NITRO PISTON AIR RIFLE

Caliber: .177. Barrel: Rifled. Weight: 6.0 lbs. Length: 43.5 in. Power: Break-barrel, Nitro-piston. Stock: Synthetic thumbhole style. Sights: None, dovetail for scope mounting, includes CenterPoint 4x32 scope and rings. Features: Integrated muzzle brake for reduced recoil and noise, single-shot, adjustable two-stage trigger. Velocities: 1,200 fps.

Price: **$154.00**

CROSMAN MAG-FIRE EXTREME/ULTRA/MISSION BREAK BARREL AIR RIFLES

Caliber: .177, .22. Barrel: Rifled. Weight: 6.5 lbs. Length: 43 in. Power: Break-barrel. Stock: Ambidextrous synthetic. Sights: Adjustable rear sight, Picatinny rail for scope mounting, includes 3-9x40 scope and rings. Features: Extreme has a tactical-style stock with adjustable cheekpiece and pistol grip, Ultra has an all-weather stock with soft-touch inserts, Mission has a thumbhole-style stock, 12-shot magazine, QuietFire sound suppression, adjustable two-stage trigger, sling mount. Velocities: 1,300 fps (.177)/975 fps (.22).

Price: .... **$189.00–$249.00**

CROSMAN OPTIMUS AIR RIFLE COMBO

Caliber: .177, .22. Barrel: Rifled. Weight: 6.5 lbs. Length: 43 in. Power: Break-barrel. Stock: Ambidextrous wood. Sights: Fiber-optic with adjustable rear sight, dovetail for scope mounting, includes CenterPoint 4x32 scope and rings. Features: Single-shot, adjustable two-stage trigger. Velocities: 1,200 fps (.177)/950 fps (.22).

Price: **$144.00**

CROSMAN REPEATAIR 1077/1077 FREESTYLE CO2 RIFLE

Caliber: .177 pellets. Barrel: Rifled 20.38 in. Weight: 3.75 lbs. Length: 36.88 in. Power: CO2. Stock: Ambidextrous plastic stock. Sights: Blade and ramp, rear sight adjustable for windage and elevation, grooved for scope mounting. Features: Multi-shot, semi-automatic, 12-shot magazine, lightweight, fun and easy to shoot. "Ready to go" kits available complete with ammo, CO2, targets, target trap, etc. Velocity: 625 fps.

Price: .... **$89.00–$144.00**

CROSMAN TYRO AIR RIFLE

Calibers: .177. Barrel: Rifled. Weight: 4.9 lbs. Length: 37.5 in. Power: Break-barrel, spring-piston. Stock: Synthetic thumbhole with spacers to adjust length of pull. Sights: Front fiber-optic sight and adjustable rear sight. Features: Single shot, sized for smaller shooters. Velocities: 720 fps with alloy pellet.

Price: **$105.00**

CROSMAN VALIANT SBD NP AIR RIFLE

Calibers: .177, .22. Barrel: Rifled, 15.75 in. Weight: 7.95 lbs. Length: 46 in.

Power: Break-barrel, nitro-piston. Stock: Hardwood thumbhole. Sights: Adjustable rear, fixed front. Features: Adjustable two-stage trigger, 11 mm optics rail, comes with a CenterPoint 4X32 scope. Velocities: .177, 1,400 fps/.22, 1,100 fps. with alloy pellet.
Price: **$234.00**

DAISY 1938 RED RYDER AIR RIFLE
Caliber: .177 steel BBs. Barrel: Smoothbore 10.85 in. Weight: 2.2 lbs. Length: 35.4 in. Power: Single-cock, lever action, spring-piston. Stock: Solid wood stock and fore-end. Sights: Blade front sight, adjustable rear sight. Features: 650 BB reservoir, single-stage trigger, designed for all day fun and backyard plinking, exceptional first airgun for young shooters. Velocity: 350 fps.
Price: **$49.00**

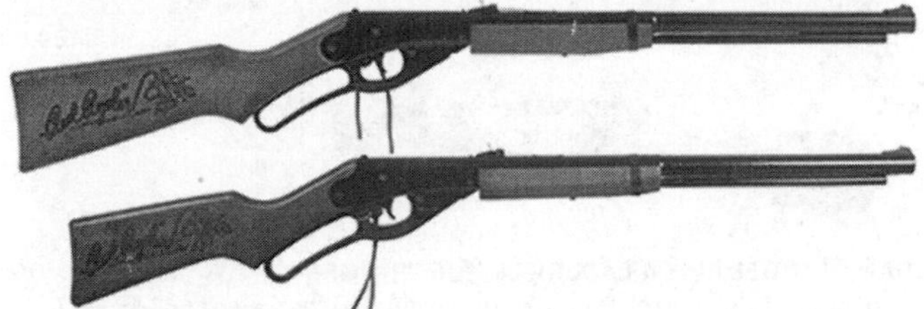

DAISY ADULT RED RYDER BB RIFLE
Caliber: .177 steel BBs. Barrel: Smoothbore, 10.85 in. Weight: 2.95 lbs. Length: 36.75 in. Power: Single-cock, lever-action, spring-piston. Stock: Solid wood stock and fore-end. Sights: Blade front sight, adjustable rear sight. Features: A larger, adult-size version of the classic youth Red Ryder with 650-shot reservoir. 18-pound cocking effort. Velocity: 350 fps.
Price: **$64.00**

DAISY MODEL 25 PUMP GUN
Caliber: .177 steel BBs. Barrel: Smoothbore. Weight: 3 lbs. Length: 37 in. Power: pump action, spring-air. Stock: Solid wood buttstock. Sights: Fixed front and rear sights. Features: 50 shot BB reservoir, removable screw out shot tube, decorative engraving on receiver, rear sight can be flipped over to change from open to peep sight. Velocity: 350 fps.
Price: **$49.00**

DAISY MODEL 105 BUCK AIR RIFLE
Caliber: .177 steel BBs. Barrel: Smoothbore 7.97 in. Weight: 1.6 lbs. Length: 29.8 in. Power: Single-cock, lever action, spring-piston. Stock: Solid wood buttstock. Sights: Fixed front and rear sights. Features: 400 BB reservoir, single-stage trigger, designed for all day fun and backyard plinking. Velocity: 275 fps.
Price: **$35.00**

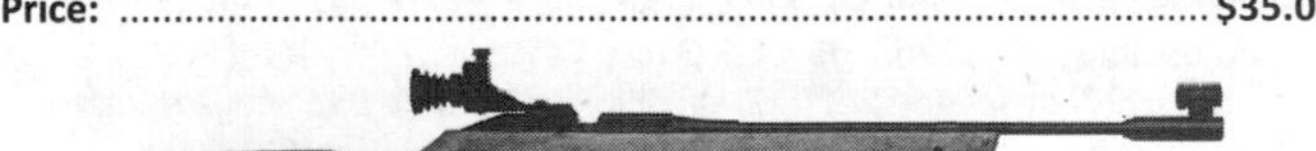

DAISY AVANTI MODEL 753S MATCH GRADE AVANTI
Caliber: .177 pellets. Barrel: Rifled, Lothar Walther, 19.5 in. Weight: 7.3 lbs. Length: 38.5 in. Power: Single-stroke pneumatic. Stock: Ambidextrous wood stock & Synthetic stock available Sights: Globe front sight and Precision Diopter rear sight. Features: Full-size wood stock, additional inserts available for front sight, fully self-contained power system, excellent "first" rifle for all 10-meter shooting disciplines. Velocity: 495 fps.
Price: .... **$300.00–$469.00**

DAISY POWERLINE MODEL 880 AIR RIFLE
Caliber: .177 steel BBs, .177 pellets. Barrel: Rifled, 21 in. Weight: 3.1 lbs. Length: 37.6 in. Power: Multi-pump pneumatic. Stock: Synthetic. Sights: Fiber-optic front sight, rear sight adjustable for elevation, grooved for scope mounting. Features: Single-shot pellet, 50 shot BB, lightweight, accurate and easy to shoot. Velocity: 800 fps (BBs), 665 fps (pellets).
Price: **$69.00**

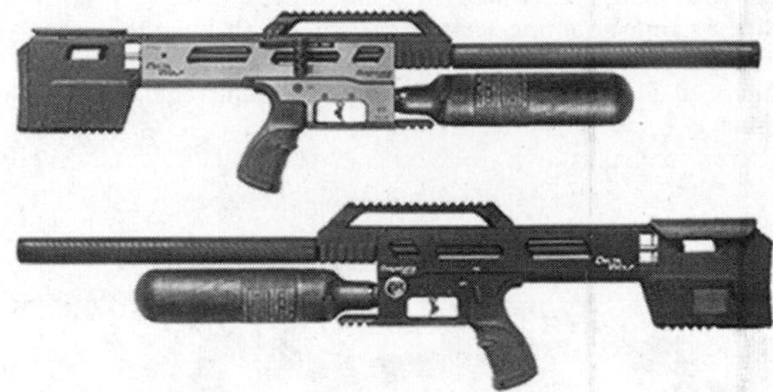

DAYSTATE DELTA WOLF RIFLE
Calibers: .177, .22, .25, .30. Barrel: Rifled 43 cm (.177 or .22) or 60 cm (.177, .22, .25, .30). Weight: 6.8 lbs. Length: 34 in. Power: Precharged pneumatic. Stock: AR style. Sights: None, 22mm Picatinny rail. Features: Advanced Velocity Technology with display touch screen, multi-caliber with fast-change barrel system, factory set power profiles for each caliber, built-in chronoscope that allows the shooter to dial in their preferred velocity, OEM Huma-Air regulated, large capacity (813-shot) magazine, Bluetooth connectivity, switchable side lever action, carbon-fiber shroud and optional silencer, removable air tank. Velocity: Adjustable.
Price: **$3,695.00**

DAYSTATE HUNTSMAN REVERE AIR RIFLE
Calibers: .177, .22, .25. Barrel: Match grade, rifled, 17 in. Weight: 6.4 lbs. Length: 36.5 in. Power: Precharged pneumatic. Stock: Right-handed Monte Carlo walnut. Sights: None, 11mm grooved dovetail for scope mounting. Features: Sidelever action, HUMA air regulator, 13 (.177), 11 (.22) or 10 (.25) shot rotary magazine, single shot loading tray, 20-46 shots per fill depending on caliber, adjustable two-stage trigger, shrouded barrel, available in a left-handed version. Velocity: Adjustable.
Price: **$1,499.00**

DAYSTATE RED WOLF HILITE HP RIFLE
Calibers: .177, .22, .25, .30. Barrel: Fully shrouded carbon fiber, 23 in. Weight: 8.5 lbs. Length: 45 in. Power: Precharged pneumatic. Stock: Ambidextrous walnut, red laminate, or blue laminate. Sights: None, 11mm grooved dovetail for scope mounting. Features: Three individual programmed energy and velocity settings, computer controlled state of the art MCT firing system, LCD screen displays air pressure, battery state, number of shots fired, 13- (.177), 11 (.22), 10 (.25) or 8- (.30) shot magazine or single shot tray for .177, .22, or .25, 30- 150 shots per fill depending on caliber, fully adjustable electronic release trigger from ounces to pounds, right or left hand reversible side cocking. Velocity: Adjustable.
Price: **$2,999.00**

DAYSTATE WOLVERINE 2 HUMA RIFLE
Calibers: .177 pellet, .22. Barrel: Match grade shrouded rifled, 23 in. Weight: 8.4 lbs. Length: 44 in. Power: Precharged pneumatic. Stock: Ambidextrous thumbhole walnut or laminate. Sights: None, 11mm grooved dovetail for scope mounting. Features: Right- or left-hand reversible side-lever cocking, HUMA air regulator, adjustable buttpad, 10-shot magazine, 120-140 shots per charge, two-stage adjustable trigger. Velocity: Adjustable.
Price: **$2,449.00**

DIANA CHASER CO2 AIR RIFLE/PISTOL KIT
Caliber: .177, .22. Barrel: Rifled, 17.7 in. Weight: 3.1 lbs. Length: 38.4 in. Power: CO2. Stock: Ambidextrous synthetic. Sights: Front fiber-optic sight and adjustable rear sight, 11 mm dovetail for scope mounting. Features: Shrouded barrel, two-stage adjustable trigger, single-shot (can use indexing 7-9 shot magazines from the Stormrider), approximately 50 shots per CO2 cylinder, kit includes soft case, Chaser pistol, buttstock, and rifle barrel. Velocities: 642 fps (.177 rifle), 500 fps (.22 rifle).
Price: **$84.00**

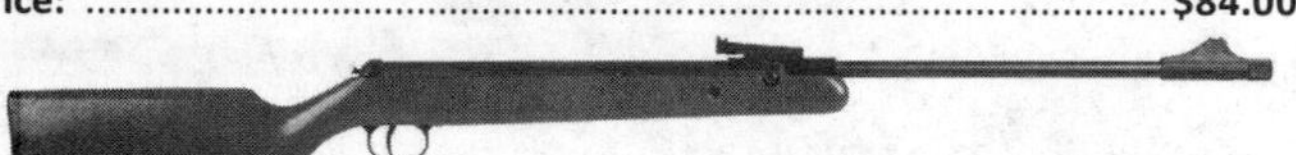

DIANA 34 EMS BREAK BARREL AIR RIFLE
Caliber: .177, .22. Barrel: Rifled, 19.5 in. Weight: 7.85 lbs. Length: 46.3 in. Power: Break-barrel, spring-piston, convertible to N-TEC gas piston. Stock: Ambidextrous wood or thumbhole synthetic. Sights: Front fiber-optic sight and micrometer adjustable rear sight, 11 mm dovetail. Features: Two-stage adjustable trigger, single-shot, removable ½ in UNF threaded barrel, EMS (easy modular system) allows for easy changing of barrels, adjustable barrel alignment, changeable front and rear sights, two piece cocking lever. Velocities: 890 fps (.177), 740 fps (.22).
Price: .... **$367.00–$398.00**

DIANA 54 AIRKING PRO LAMINATE AIR RIFLE
Caliber: .177, .22. Barrel: Rifled, 17.3 in. Weight: 10.25 lbs. Length: 44in. Power: Spring piston side lever. Stock: Red and black laminated. Sights: Adjustable rear sight, 11 mm dovetail. Features: Two-stage adjustable trigger, single-shot, forearm swivel stud to attach a bipod, adjustable barrel weight, checkered grip and forearm. Velocities: 1100 fps (.177), 990 fps (.22).
Price: **$749.00**

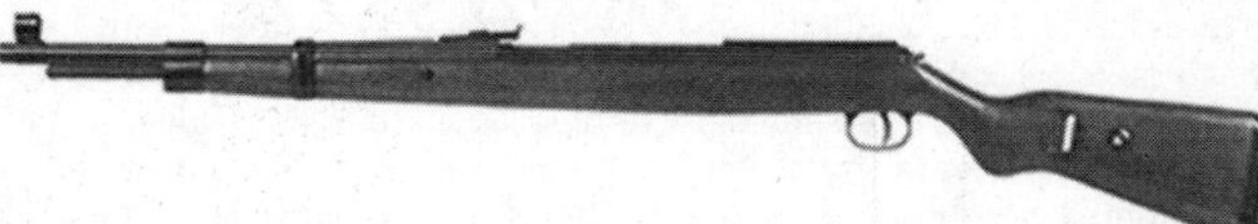

DIANA MAUSER K98 AIR RIFLE
Calibers: .177, .22. Barrel: Rifled 18.0 in. Weight: 9.5 lbs. Length: 44 in. Power: Break-barrel, spring-piston. Stock: Authentic Mauser K98 hardwood stock. Sights: Front post and fully adjustable rear sight, 11mm dovetail grooved for scope mounting. Features: European quality, fixed barrel with underlever cocking, exceptional two-stage adjustable match trigger, single-shot, German manufactured to stringent quality control and testing, limited lifetime warranty. Velocities: .177, 1,150 fps/.22, 850 fps.
Price: **$389.00**

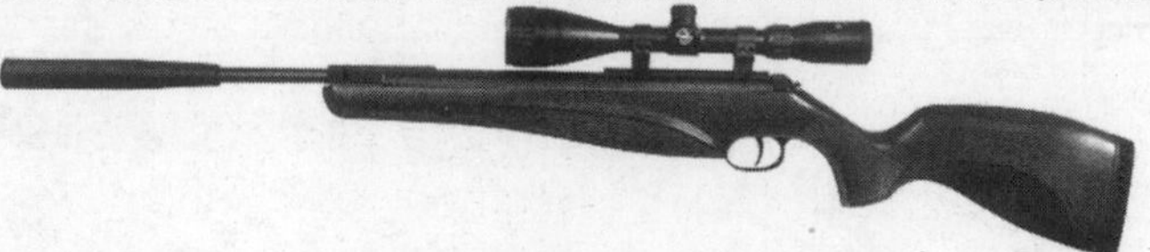

DIANA 340 N-TEC PREMIUM AIR RIFLE
Calibers: .177, .22. Barrel: Rifled 19.5 in. Weight: 7.9 lbs. Length: 46 in. Power: Break-barrel, German gas-piston. Stock: Ambidextrous beech stock. Sights: Front fiber-optic sight and fully adjustable rear fiber-optic sight, grooved for scope mounting. Features: European quality, exceptional two-stage adjustable match trigger, single-shot, German manufactured to stringent quality control and testing, limited lifetime warranty. The new N-TEC gas-piston power plant boasts smoother cocking and shooting, making the N-TEC line of Diana guns the most refined Diana airguns to date. Various bundled configurations available. Velocities: .177, 1,000 fps/.22, 800 fps.
Price: **$469.00**

DIANA MODEL RWS 48 AIR RIFLE, T06 TRIGGER
Calibers: .177, .22. Barrel: Rifled 17 in. Weight: 8.5 lbs. Length: 42.13 in. Power: Single-cock, side-lever, spring-piston. Stock: Ambidextrous beech thumbhole stock. Sights: Blade front sight, fully adjustable rear sight, grooved for scope mounting. Features: European quality, exceptional two-stage match trigger, single-shot, German manufactured to stringent quality control and testing, limited lifetime warranty. Velocities: .177, 1,100 fps/.22, 900 fps.
Price: **$499.00**

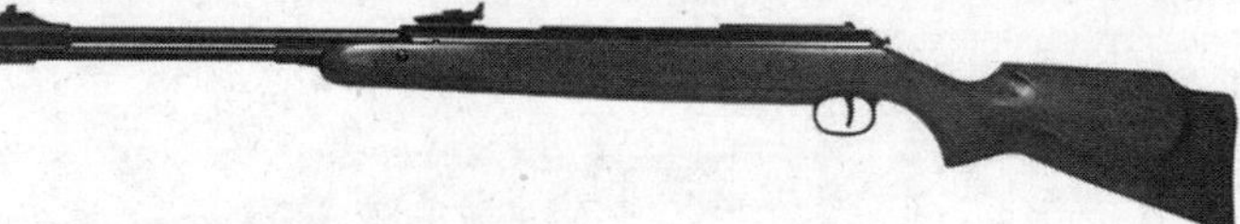

DIANA RWS 460 MAGNUM AIR RIFLE
Calibers: .177, .22. Barrel: Rifled 18.44 in. Weight: 8.3 lbs. Length: 45 in. Power: Under-lever, spring-piston. Stock: Right-hand hardwood stock with grip and fore-end checkering. Sights: Post front sight and fully adjustable rear sight, grooved for scope mounting. Features: European quality, exceptional two-stage adjustable match trigger, single-shot, German manufactured to stringent quality control and testing, limited lifetime warranty. Various bundled configurations available. Velocity: .177, 1,200 fps/.22, 1,000 fps.
Price: **$469.00**

DIANA STORMRIDER GEN 2 PCP RIFLE
Calibers: .177, .22. Barrel: Rifled 19 in. Weight: 5.0 lbs. Length: 40.5 in. Power: Pre-charged pneumatic. Stock: Checkered beech stock. Sights: Blade front, fully adjustable rear, 11 mm dovetail grove. Features: Entry level PCP rifle, nine-shot (.177) or seven-shot (.22) capacity, adjustable two-stage trigger, built-in muzzle brake, integrated pressure gauge. Velocities: 1,050 fps (.177)/900 fps (.22).
Price: **$299.00**

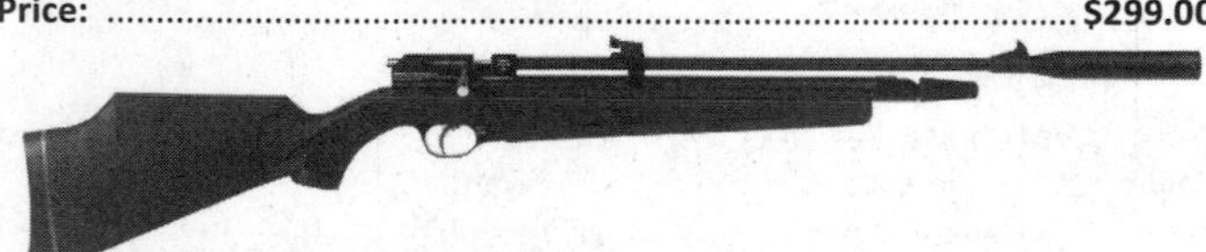

DIANA TRAILSCOUT CO2 RIFLE
Caliber: .177, .22 pellet. Barrel: Rifled, 19 in. Weight: 4.6 lbs. Length: 38.9 in. Power: CO2. Stock: Synthetic. Sights: Adjustable rear. Features: Uses three 12 g CO2 cylinders, can be used single shot or with a 7 (.22) or 9 (.177) shot magazine, bolt action, adjustable trigger, approximately 100 shots per fill.

Velocities: 660 fps (.177), 560 fps (.22).
Price: **$229.00**

EDGUN LELYA 2.0 PCP RIFLE
Calibers: .177, .22, or .25 pellet. Barrel: Rifled, Alfa Precision, 15.4 in. Weight: 6.4 lbs. Length: 23.5 in. Power: Precharged pneumatic. Stock: Walnut ambidextrous bullpup style. Sights: None, Weaver-style rail for scope mounting. Features: Dual side-lever cocking for ambidextrous cocking, adjustable hammer spring tension, two-stage adjustable trigger, 35–50 shots per fill depending on caliber, 10 round (in .177 or .22) or 9-round magazine (.25), sling loop in rear of stock, fully shrouded barrel. Velocities: Approximately 920 fps (.177), 900 fps (.22), 880 fps (.25).
Price: **$1,949.00**

EDGUN LESHIY 2 STANDARD PCP AIR RIFLE
Calibers: .177, .22, .25, or .30 pellets. Barrel: Rifled, 9.85 in. Weight: 5 lbs. Length: 25.5 in. overall. Power: Precharged pneumatic. Stock: Ambidextrous adjustable. Sights: None, Weaver-style rail for scope mounting Features: Semiautomatic, folding stock making it very compact to carry (13.5 in. when folded), red and gray laminate AR pistol grip, includes two 8-round magazines, single-stage trigger, Picatinny forearm accessory rail, unique hammerless design, 18-36 shots per fill depending on caliber. Velocities: 900 fps (.177), 870 fps (.22), 800 fps (.25), 740 fps (.30).
Price: **$2,399.00**

EDGUN MATADOR R5M STANDARD PCP RIFLE
Calibers: .177, .22, or .25. Barrel: Rifled, Lothar Walther, 18.75 in. Weight: 6.75 lbs. Length: 27.5 in. Power: Precharged pneumatic. Stock: Ambidextrous walnut thumbhole or synthetic. Sights: None, Weaver rail for scope mounting. Features: Adjustable trigger, adjustable hammer spring tension, designed and manufactured in Russia, 40-60 shots per fill depending on caliber, also available with a longer barrel, ambidextrous safety. Velocities: 950 fps (.177), 920 fps (.22 and .25)
Price: **$2,199.00**

EVANIX RAPTOR PCP AIR RIFLE
Calibers:.177, .22, .25, .30. Barrel: Rifled, 18.9 in. or 23.6 in. (.30 cal). Weight: 7.2 lbs. Length: 31.5 in. or 33.9 in. (.30) overall. Power: Precharged Pneumatic. Stock: Ambidextrous wood thumbhole stock. Sights: None, grooved 11mm dovetail for scope mounting Features: Multi-shot side-lever action, shot count varies based on caliber, very well made and versatile hunting airgun. Velocities: Variable.
Price: **$1,170.00**

EVANIX REX AIR RIFLE
Calibers: .22, .25, .35 (9mm), .45. Barrel: Rifled, 19.68 in. Weight: 5.51 lbs. Length: 35.82 in. overall. Power: Precharged Pneumatic. Sights: weaver rail for scope mounting Features: Lightweight, compact and massively powerful, single shot, capable of putting out well over 200 ft-lbs at the muzzle in .45 caliber, truly effective hunting power in a compact package Velocities: .22, 1,080 fps/.25, 970 fps/.35, 860 fps/.45, 700 fps.
Price: .... **$799.00–$1,149.00**

FEINWERKBAU 500 AIR RIFLE
Caliber: .177. Barrel: Rifled 13.8 in. Weight: 7.05 lbs. Length: 43.7 in. Power: Pre-charged pneumatic. Stock: Ambidextrous beech stock with adjustable cheekpiece and buttstock. Sights: Globe front sight and diopter rear. Features: Meets requirements for ISSF competition, trigger-pull weight adjusts from 3.9 to 7.8 ounces, bolt action, competition grade airgun. Velocity: 574 fps.
Price: **$1,439.00**

FEINWERKBAU 800X FIELD TARGET AIR RIFLE
Caliber: .177. Barrel: Rifled 16.73 in. Weight: 11.7–15.05 lbs. Length: 49.76 in. Power: Precharged pneumatic. Stock: Highly adaptable field target competition stock. Sights: None, 11mm grooved for scope mounting. Features: Approximately 100+ shots per fill, adjustable trigger shoe, adjustable hand rest, vertically adjustable butt pad, adjustable butt hook, vertically and laterally adjustable comb, 5-way adjustable match trigger, bolt action, competition grade airgun. Also available in a smaller, lower-priced model for Junior competition. Velocity: 825 fps.
Price: **$3,799.00**

FEINWERKBAU P75 BIATHLON AIR RIFLE
Caliber: .177. Barrel: Rifled 16.73 in. Weight: 9.26 lbs. Length: 42.91 in. Power: Pre-charged pneumatic. Stock: Highly adaptable laminate wood competition stock Sights: Front globe with aperture inserts and diopter micrometer rear. Features: 5-shot bolt action, competition grade airgun, inspired from airguns featuring Olympic accuracy, 5-way adjustable match trigger. Velocity: 564 fps.
Price: **$3,254.00**

FEINWERKBAU SPORT AIR RIFLE
Caliber: .177. Barrel: Rifled 18.31 in. Weight: 8.27 lbs. Length: 44.84 in. Power: Spring-piston break barrel. Stock: Ambidextrous wood stock with dual raised cheekpieces. Sights: Front globe, fully adjustable rear sight, grooved for scope mounting. Features: Lightweight, single-shot, easy cocking, adjustable two-stage trigger. Velocity: .177, 850 fps.
Price: **$999.00**

FX CROWN AIR RIFLE
Calibers: .177, .22, .25, .30. Barrel: Rifled 19-23.5 in. Weight: 6.5-7.5 lbs. Length: 38.5-43 in. Power: Precharged pneumatic. Stock: Ambidextrous stock in walnut, laminate, or synthetic. Sights: None, 11mm grooved for scope mounting. Features: Smooth Twist X barrels can be swapped to change not only caliber but also twist rate, adjustable 15 ounce two-stage trigger, externally adjustable regulator, adjustable power wheel and hammer spring, removable carbon fiber tank, dual air pressure gauges, multiple-shot magazine (14-18 shots depending on caliber). Velocities: .177, 1,000 fps/.22, 920 fps/.25, 900 fps/.30, 870 fps.
Price: .... **$1,649.00–$2,399.00**

FX IMPACT AIR RIFLE
Calibers: .25, .30. Barrel: Rifled 24.4 in. Weight: 7.0 lbs. Length: 34.0 in. Power: Pre-charged pneumatic. Stock: Compact bullpup stock in various materials and finishes Sights: None, 11mm grooved for scope mounting. Features: Premium airgun brand known for exceptional build quality and accuracy, regulated for consistent shots, adjustable two-stage trigger, FX smooth twist barrel, multi-shot side lever action, fully moderated barrel, highly adjustable and adaptable air rifle system. Velocities: .25, 900 fps/.30, 870 fps.
Price: .... **$2,099.00–$2,349.00**

FX MAVERICK SNIPER PCP AIR RIFLE

Calibers: .22, .25, .30. Barrel: Rifled 27.6 in. Weight: 7.2 lbs. Length: 36.0 in. Power: Precharged pneumatic. Stock: Tactical style with AR style grip. Sights: None, Picatinny rail with 20 MOA tilt for scope mounting. Features: Three Picatinny rails for accessories, adjustable match trigger, threaded barrel shroud, side lever action, dual AMP regulators, 580 cc carbon fiber air cylinder, dual manometers, 90 (.30), 170 (.25), 270 (.22) maximum shots per fill, 18 (.22), 16 (.25), 13 (.30) shot magazine, includes one magazine and a hard case, also available in a compact version. Velocities: .22, 1,000 fps/.25, 1,000 fps/.30, 900 fps.
Price: **$1,999.00**

FX WILDCAT MKIII SNIPER AIR RIFLE

Calibers: .22, .25, .30. Barrel: Rifled 23.6 in. Weight: 6.75 lbs. Length: 37.75 in. Power: Precharged pneumatic. Stock: Compact bullpup synthetic stock. Sights: None, Picatinny rail for scope mounting. Features: Externally adjustable regulator, adjustable two-stage trigger, FX Smooth Twist X barrel, multi-shot side lever action, 300cc aluminum air cylinder, adjustable hammer spring tension, comes standard with the Superior STX liner to swap calibers, threaded muzzle, up to 35-90 shots per fill depending on caliber, 18 round (.22), 16 round (.25) or 13 round (.30) capacity magazine. Velocity: .22, 950 fps/.25, 970 fps/.30, 930 fps.
Price: **$1,699.00**

FX .30 BOSS AIR RIFLE

Caliber: .30. Barrel: Rifled 24.4 in. Weight: 7.0 lbs. Length: 47.5 in. Power: Pre-charged pneumatic. Stock: Right-handed Monte Carlo Stock available in various materials and finishes. Sights: None. 11mm grooved for scope mounting. Features: Premium airgun brand known for exceptional build quality and accuracy, regulated for consistent shots, adjustable two-stage trigger, FX smooth twist barrel, multi-shot side lever action, fully moderated barrel. Velocities: .22, 1,200 fps/.25, 900 fps.
Price: **$2,099.00**

FX ROYALE 400 AIR RIFLE

Caliber: .177, .22. Barrel: Rifled 19.5 in. Weight: 7.5 lbs. Length: 40.25 in. Power: Precharged pneumatic. Stock: Ambidextrous laminated thumbhole. Sights: None. 11mm dovetailed for scope mounting. Features: FX smooth twist barrel, removable carbon fiber air cylinder, fully shrouded barrel, adjustable power, up to 100 shots per fill, side lever action, two-stage adjustable trigger, adjustable buttplate, 12-shot rotary magazine. Velocities: .177, 950 fps/.22, 950 fps.
Price: **$1,799.00**

* scope not included

GAMO COYOTE WHISPER FUSION PCP AIR RIFLE

Calibers: .177, .22. Barrel: Cold hammer-forged match-grade rifled barrel, 24.5 in. Weight: 6.6 lbs. Length: 42.9 in. Power: Pre-charged pneumatic. Stock: Ambidextrous hardwood stock. Sights: None, grooved for scope mounting, Features: European class airgun, highly accurate and powerful, adjustable two-stage trigger, integrated moderator, 10-shot bolt action. Velocities: .177, 1,200 fps/.22, 1,000 fps.
Price: **$569.00**

GAMO WILDCAT WHISPER BREAK BARREL AIR RIFLE

Calibers: .177, .22. Barrel: Rifled barrel, 19.1 in. Weight: 5.6 lbs. Length: 44.5 in. Power: Gas piston, break barrel. Stock: Ambidextrous synthetic stock. Sights: Fixed, grooved for scope mounting, includes a 4x32 scope. Features: Single shot, Inert Gas Technology (IGS), 30 pound cocking effort, Whisper noise suppression. Velocities: .177, 1,350 fps/.22, 975 fps.
Price: **$159.00**

GAMO SWARM MAXXIM 10X GEN2 MULTI-SHOT AIR RIFLE

Calibers: .177, .22. Barrel: Rifled 19.9 in. Weight: 5.64 lbs. Length: 45.3 in. Power: Break-barrel, gas-piston. Stock: Ambidextrous glass-filled nylon stock. Sights: None, grooved for scope mounting, includes recoil-reducing rail, 3-9x32 scope and mounts. Features: 10-shot multi-shot system allows for automatic loading with each cock of the barrel, easy cocking, adjustable two-stage trigger, all-weather fluted barrel, features integrated suppressor technology. Velocities: .177, 1,300 fps/.22, 1,000 fps.
Price: **$249.00**

GAMO SWARM MAGNUM 10X GEN 2 MULTI-SHOT AIR RIFLE

Caliber: .22. Barrel: Rifled 21.3 in. Weight: 6.88 lbs. Length: 49.2 in. Power: Break-barrel, gas-piston. Stock: Ambidextrous lightweight composite stock. Sights: None, grooved for scope mounting, includes recoil-reducing rail, 3-9x32 scope and mounts. Features: 10-shot multi-shot system allows for automatic loading with each cock of the barrel, easy cocking, adjustable two-stage trigger, steel barrel, features integrated suppressor technology. Velocity: 1,300 fps.
Price: **$339.00**

GAMO URBAN PCP AIR RIFLE

Caliber: .22. Barrel: Cold hammer forged match grade rifled barrel. Weight: 6.7 lbs. Length: 42.0 in. Power: Pre-charged pneumatic. Stock: Ambidextrous composite thumbhole stock. Sights: None, grooved for scope mounting, Features: European class airgun, highly accurate and powerful, adjustable two-stage trigger, integrated moderator, 10-shot bolt action. Velocity: 800 fps.
Price: **$449.00**

GAMO BIG BORE TC35 AIR RIFLE

Caliber: .35. Barrel: rifled, 14.96 in. Weight: 6.0 lbs. Length: 35.88 in. Power: Pre-charged pneumatic. Stock: Ambidextrous. Sights: None, weaver rail for scope mounting, Features: Very light and yet very powerful producing up to 170 ft-lbs of muzzle energy, adjustable trigger, two power settings, shrouded barrel, single-shot action allows for an extremely wide range of ammo choices.
Price: **$1,199.00**

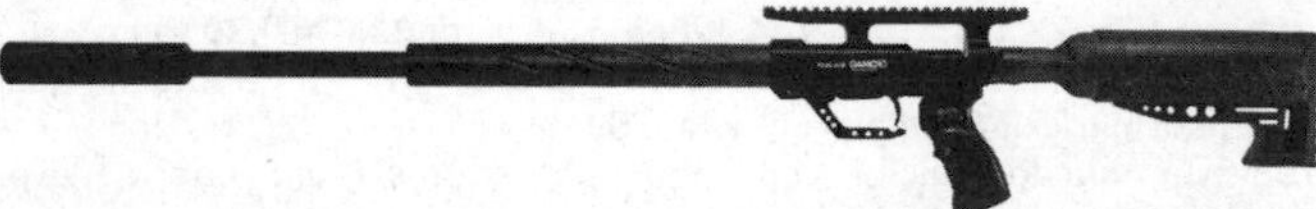

GAMO BIG BORE TC45 AIR RIFLE

Caliber: .45. Barrel: rifled, 24.24 in. Weight: 8.0 lbs. Length: 47.13 in. Power: Pre-charged pneumatic. Stock: Ambidextrous. Sights: None, weaver rail

Prices given are believed to be accurate at time of publication however, many factors affect retail pricing so exact prices are not possible.

for scope mounting. Features: Very light and yet very powerful producing over 400 ft-lbs of muzzle energy shooting 350-grain cast slugs, adjustable trigger, two power settings, shrouded barrel, single shot action allows for an extremely wide range of ammo choices.
Price: $1,099.00

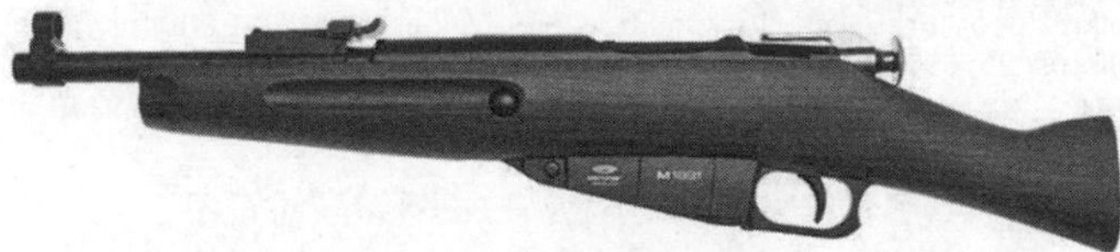

GLETCHER M1891 CO2 BB RIFLE
Caliber: .177 BBs. Barrel: Smooth, 16 in. Weight: 5.6 lbs. Length: 22.44 in. Power: CO2. Stock: Imitation wood. Sights: Adjustable rear with removable front globe. Features: Reproduction of the Mosin-Nagant sawed off rifle, working sliding metal bolt action, built in hex wrench for changing CO2 cylinders, 16 BB capacity, approximately 120 shots per fill. Velocity: 427 fps.
Price: $199.00

GLETCHER M1944 CO2 BB RIFLE
Caliber: .177 BBs. Barrel: Smooth, 16 in. Weight: 8.21 lbs. Length: 40.5 in with bayonet folded. Power: CO2. Stock: Imitation wood. Sights: Adjustable rear with removable front globe. Features: Reproduction of the Russian Mosin-Nagant rifle, working sliding metal bolt action, built in hex wrench for changing CO2 cylinders, 16 BB capacity, approximately 120 shots per fill, integral folding bayonet, reproduction sling included. Velocity: 427 fps.
Price: $329.00

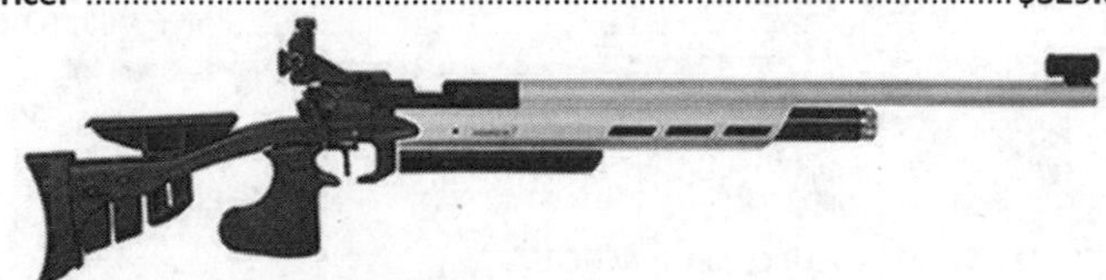

HAMMERLI AR20 SILVER AIR RIFLE
Calibers: .177. Barrel: Rifled Lothar Walther 19.7 in. Weight: 8.75 lbs. Length: 41.65-43.66 in. Power: Pre-charged pneumatic. Stock: Ambidextrous aluminum stock with vertically adjustable buttpad and spacers for adjusting length. Sights: Globe front sight and fully adjustable diopter rear sight, grooved for scope mounting. Features: Single shot, ambidextrous cocking piece, removable aluminum air cylinder, meets ISSF requirements, stock is available in several colors. Velocity: 557 fps.
Price: $995.00

H&K MP5-PCW CO2 BB RIFLE
Caliber: .177 BBs. Barrel: Smoothbore. Weight: 3.7 lbs. Length: 24.5 in. Power: CO2. Sights: Post globe front, adjustable rear. Features: 40-Round removable banana-style magazine, semiautomatic, recoils like a firearm, folding stock, forward grip. Velocity: 400 fps.
Price: $139.00

HATSAN USA EDGE CLASS AIRGUNS
Calibers: .177, .22, .25. Barrel: Rifled 17.7 in. Weight: 6.4–6.6 lbs. Length: 43 in. Power: Break-barrel, spring-piston and gas-spring variations. Stock: Multiple synthetic and synthetic skeleton stock options. Available in different colors such as black, muddy girl camo, moon camo, etc. Sights: Fiber-optic front sight and fully adjustable fiber-optic rear sight, grooved for scope mounting, includes 3-9x32 scope and mounts. Features: European manufacturing with German steel, single-shot, adjustable two-stage trigger, performance tested at the factory with lead pellets for accurate velocity specifications. Velocities: .177, 1,000 fps/.22, 800 fps/.25, 650 fps.
Price: ....$150.00–$180.00

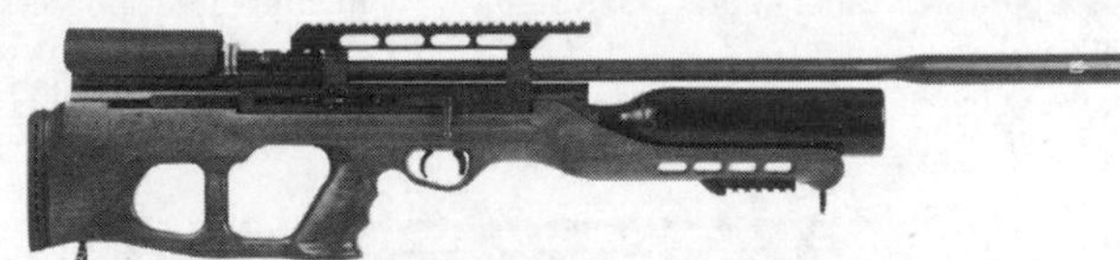

HATSAN USA AIRMAX PCP AIR RIFLE
Calibers: .177, .22, .25. Barrel: Rifled 23.0 in. Weight: 10.8 lbs. Length: 37 in. Power: Precharged pneumatic. Stock: Ambidextrous wood bullpup stock Sights: None, combination Picatinny rail and 11mm dovetail for scope mounting. Features: Multi-shot side-lever action, 10-shot .177 and .22 magazines/9-shot .25 magazine, "Quiet Energy" barrel shroud with integrated suppressor, removable air cylinder, fully adjustable two-stage "Quattro" trigger, "EasyAdjust" elevation comb, sling swivels, includes two magazines. Velocities: .177, 1,170 fps/.22, 1,070 fps/.25, 970 fps.
Price: $754.00

HATSAN USA BULLBOSS QE AIR RIFLE
Calibers: .177, .22, .25. Barrel: Rifled 23.0 in. Weight: 8.6 lbs. Length: 36.8 in. Power: Pre-charged pneumatic. Stock: Ambidextrous synthetic or hardwood bullpup stock Sights: None, innovative dual rail 11mm dovetail and Weaver compatible for scope mounting. Features: Multi-shot side-lever action, 10-shot .177 and .22 magazines/9-shot .25 magazine, "Quiet Energy" barrel shroud with integrated suppressor, European manufacturing with German steel, removable air cylinder, fully adjustable two-stage "Quattro" trigger, performance tested at the factory with lead pellets for accurate velocity specifications. Velocities: .177, 1,170 fps/.22, 1,070 fps/.25, 970 fps.
Price: $649.00–799.00

HATSAN USA BARRAGE SEMI-AUTOMATIC PCP AIR RIFLE
Calibers: .177, .22 .25. Barrel: Rifled, 19.7 in. Weight: 10.1 lbs. Length: 40.9 in. Power: Precharged pneumatic. Stock: Ambidextrous adjustable synthetic thumbhole stock with integrated magazine storage. Sights: None, innovative dual rail 11mm dovetail and Weaver compatible for scope mounting. Features: Air-driven true semi-automatic action, 14 shots in .177 and 12 shots in .22, "Quiet Energy" barrel shroud with integrated suppressor, 500cc cylinder with 250-BAR capacity, European manufacturing with German steel, performance tested at the factory with lead pellets for accurate velocity specifications. Velocities: .177, 1,100 fps/.22, 1,000 fps/.25, 900 fps.
Price: ....$1,099.00–$1,199.00

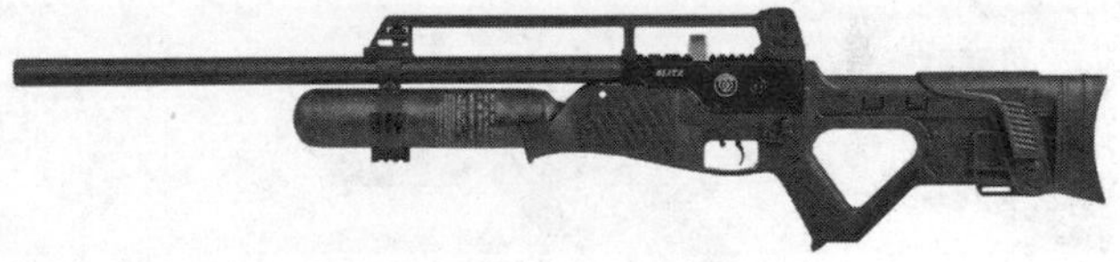

HATSAN BLITZ FULL AUTO PCP AIR RIFLE
Calibers: .22, .25, .30. Barrel: Rifled 23 in. Weight: 8.8 lbs. Length: 45.2 in. Power: Precharged pneumatic. Stock: Synthetic. Sights: Adjustable, innovative dual rail 11mm dovetail and Weaver compatible for scope mounting. Features: Full-/semi-automatic selector switch, 1,000 rounds per minute cyclic rate, includes two 21- (.22), 19- (.25), or 16-round (.30) SwingLoad magazines, 100-130 shots per fill depending on rate of fire and caliber, gas-operating cycling mechanism does not require batteries, "Quiet Energy" barrel shroud, adjustable cheekpiece and buttpad, carry handle, three Picatinny forearm accessory rails. Velocities: 1,050 fps (.22), 970 fps (.25), 730 fps (.30).
Price: $1,099.00

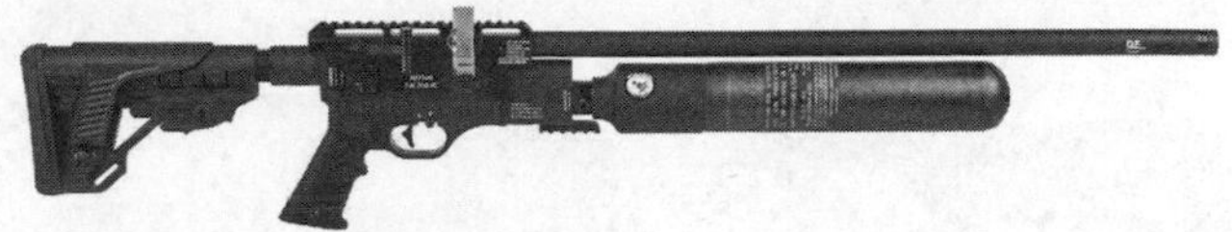

HATSAN USA FACTOR RC PCP RIFLE
Calibers: .177, .22, .25. Barrel: Rifled, 23 in. Weight: 7.9 lbs. Length: 40.3-42.9 in. Power: Precharged pneumatic. Stock: Ambidextrous adjustable synthetic tactical stock. Sights: None, innovative dual rail 11mm dovetail

and Weaver compatible for scope mounting. Features: Removable 580 cc carbon fiber air tank, two-stage adjustable trigger, right/left reversible side lever, threaded muzzle, externally adjustable regulator, up to 120-140 shots per fill depending on caliber, includes two 24- (.177), 21- (.22) or 19- (.25) round magazines, "Quiet Energy" barrel shroud with integrated suppressor. Velocities: .177, 1,010 fps/.22, 950 fps/.25 870 fps with lead pellets.
Price: **$1,099.00**

HATSAN USA HERCULES BULLY PCP AIR RIFLE
Calibers: .177, .22, .25, .30, .35, .45. Barrel: Rifled 23 in. Weight: 13 lbs. Length: 48.4 in. Power: Pre-charged pneumatic. Stock: Adjustable synthetic all-weather bullpup stock with, sling mounts. Sights: None, innovative dual rail 11mm dovetail and Weaver compatible for scope mounting. Features: Available in 6 calibers, 500cc of air via carbon fiber reservoir, multi-shot side-lever action, 17-shot .177 magazine, 14-shot .22 magazine, 13-shot .25 magazine, 10-shot .30 magazine, 9-shot .35 magazine, 7-shot .45 magazine. "Quiet Energy" barrel shroud with integrated suppressor, European manufacturing with German steel, fully adjustable two-stage "Quattro" trigger, performance tested at the factory with lead pellets for accurate velocity specifications. Velocities: .177, 1,450 fps/.22, 1,300 fps/.25, 1,200 fps/.30, 1,070 fps/.35, 910 fps/.45, 850 fps.
Price: **$999.00**

HATSAN USA FLASH QE PCP RIFLE
Calibers: .177, .22, .25. Barrel: Rifled, 17.7 in. Weight: 5.9 lbs. Length: 42.3 in. Power: Pre-charged pneumatic. Stock: Ambidextrous synthetic or hardwood thumbhole stock Sights: None, innovative dual rail 11mm dovetail and Weaver compatible for scope mounting. Features: Very lightweight, multi-shot side-lever action, multi-shot magazine (shot count varies by caliber). "Quiet Energy" barrel shroud with integrated suppressor, European manufacturing with German steel, fully adjustable two-stage "Quattro" trigger, performance tested at the factory with lead pellets for accurate velocity specifications. Velocities: .177, 1,250 fps/.22, 1,100 fps/.25, 900 fps.
Price: .... **$329.00–$399.00**

HATSAN USA FLASHPUP QE PCP RIFLE
Calibers: .177, .22, .25. Barrel: Rifled, 19.4 in. Weight: 6.1 lbs. Length: 32.0 in. Power: Pre-charged pneumatic. Stock: Ambidextrous hardwood bullpup stock Sights: None, innovative dual rail 11mm dovetail and Weaver compatible for scope mounting. Features: Very lightweight, multi-shot side-lever action, multi-shot magazine (shot count varies by caliber). "Quiet Energy" barrel shroud with integrated suppressor, European manufacturing with German steel, fully adjustable two-stage "Quattro" trigger, performance tested at the factory with lead pellets for accurate velocity specifications. Velocity: .177, 1,250 fps/.22, 1,100 fps/.25, 900 fps.
Price: .... **$399.00–$439.00**

HATSAN USA MOD 87 QE VORTEX AIR RIFLE
Calibers: .22 Barrel: Rifled 10.6 in. Weight: 7.4 lbs. Length: 44.5 in. Power: Break-barrel, gas-spring. Stock: Synthetic all-weather stock with adjustable cheekpiece. Sights: Fiber-optic front sight and fully adjustable fiber-optic rear sight, grooved for scope mounting, includes 3-9x32 scope and mounts. Features: "Quiet Energy" barrel shroud with integrated suppressor, European manufacturing with German steel, single-shot, fully adjustable two-stage "Quattro" trigger, performance tested at the factory with lead pellets for accurate velocity specifications. Velocities: .177, 1,000 fps/.22, 800 fps/.25, 650 fps.
Price: **$239.00**

HATSAN USA MOD 135 QE VORTEX AIRGUN

HATSAN USA MOD 135 QE VORTEX AIR RIFLE
Calibers: .177, .22, .25, .30. Barrel: Rifled 10.6 in. Weight: 9.9 lbs. Length: 47.2 in. Power: Break-barrel, gas-spring. Stock: Turkish walnut stock with grip and fore-end checkering, adjustable buttplate and cheekpiece. Sights: Fiber-optic front sight and fully adjustable fiber-optic rear sight, innovative dual rail 11mm dovetail and Weaver compatible for scope mounting. Features: The most powerful break barrel in the world. Worlds first "big-bore" break-barrel airgun, "Quiet Energy" barrel shroud with integrated suppressor, European manufacturing with German steel, single-shot, fully adjustable two-stage "Quattro" trigger, performance tested at the factory with lead pellets for accurate velocity specifications. Velocities: .177, 1,250 fps/.22, 1,000 fps/.25, 750 fps/.30, 550 fps.
Price: **$329.00**

HATSAN USA AT44 QE PCP AIRGUN

HATSAN USA AT44S-10 QE PCP AIRGUN
Calibers: .177, .22, .25. Barrel: Rifled 19.5 in. Weight: 8 lbs. Length: 45.4 in. Power: Pre-charged pneumatic. Stock: Various configurations, synthetic all-weather stock with front accessory rail and sling mounts. Turkish hardwood with sling mounts, full tactical stock with soft rubber grip inserts, adjustable buttstock and cheek riser. Sights: None, innovative dual rail 11mm dovetail and Weaver compatible for scope mounting. Features: Multi-shot side-lever action, 10-shot .177 and .22 magazines / 9-shot .25 magazine. "Quiet Energy" barrel shroud with integrated suppressor, European manufacturing with German steel, removable air cylinder, fully adjustable two-stage "Quattro" trigger, performance tested at the factory with lead pellets for accurate velocity specifications. Velocities: .177, 1,070 fps/.22, 970 fps/.25, 870 fps.
Price: **$499.00**

HATSAN USA ALPHA YOUTH QE AIR RIFLE
Caliber: .177. Barrel: Rifled, 15.4 in. Weight: 5.3 lbs. Length: 37.8 in. Power: Spring piston. Stock: Synthetic ambidextrous. Sights: Fiber-optic front sight and fully adjustable fiber-optic rear sight, dual-rail 11mm dovetail and Weaver compatible for scope mounting. Features: Easy cocking, designed for smaller, younger shooters, single-shot, integrated Quiet Energy sound-reducing moderator, adjustable trigger. Velocity: 600 fps with lead-free pellet.
Price: **$109.00**

HATSAN USA BT BIG BORE CARNIVORE QE AIR RIFLE
Calibers: .30, .35. Barrel: Rifled 23 in. Weight: 9.3 lbs. Length: 48.9 in. Power: Pre-charged pneumatic. Stock: Synthetic all-weather stock with sling mounts, front accessory rail, adjustable cheekpiece and buttpad. Sights: None, innovative dual rail 11mm dovetail and Weaver compatible for scope mounting. Features: Multi-shot bolt action, 6-shot .35 magazine / 7-shot .30 magazine. "Quiet Energy" barrel shroud with integrated suppressor, European manufacturing with German steel, removable air cylinder, fully adjustable two-stage "Quattro" trigger, performance tested at the factory with lead pellets for accurate velocity specifications. Velocities: .30, 860 fps/.35, 730 fps.
Price: **$599.00**

Prices given are believed to be accurate at time of publication however, many factors affect retail pricing so exact prices are not possible.

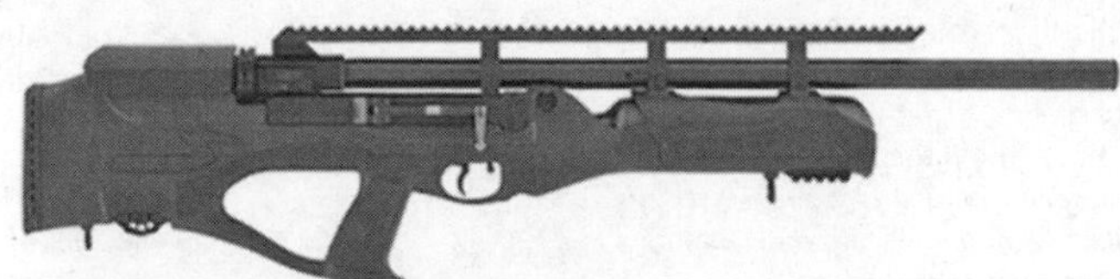

HATSAN USA HERCULES QE AIR RIFLE
Calibers: .177, .22, .25, .30, .35, .45. Barrel: Rifled 23 in. Weight: 13 lbs. Length: 48.4 in. Power: Pre-charged pneumatic. Stock: Fully adjustable synthetic all-weather stock with, sling mounts. Sights: None, innovative dual rail 11mm dovetail and Weaver compatible for scope mounting. Features: Available in 6 calibers, 1000cc of air on board provides industry leading shot count and energy on target. Multi-shot side-lever action, 17-shot .177 magazine, 14-shot .22 magazine, 13-shot .25 magazine, 10-shot .30 magazine, 9-shot .35 magazine, 7-shot .45 magazine. "Quiet Energy" barrel shroud with integrated suppressor, European manufacturing with German steel, fully adjustable two-stage "Quattro" trigger, performance tested at the factory with lead pellets for accurate velocity specifications. Velocities: .177, 1,300 fps/.22, 1,230 fps/.25, 1,200 fps/.30, 1,070 fps/.35, 930 fps/.45, 810 fps.
Price: **$1,399.00**

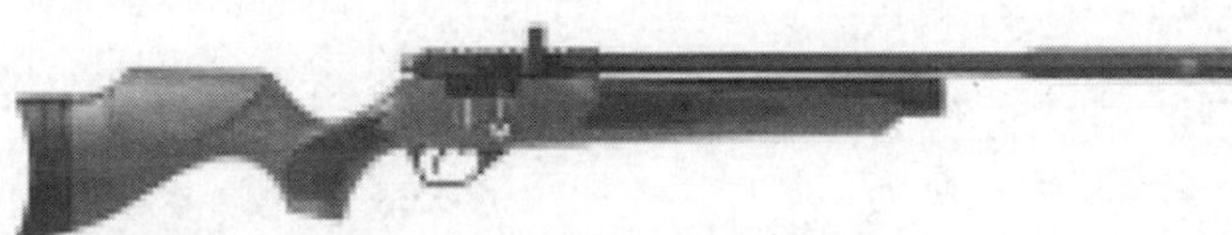

HATSAN USA HYDRA QE AIR RIFLE
Calibers: .177, .22, .25. Barrel: Rifled, 17.7 in. Weight: 6.8 lbs. Length: 42.7 in. Power: Pre-charged pneumatic. Stock: Turkish walnut. Sights: None, dual-rail 11mm dovetail and Weaver compatible for scope mounting. Features: Multi-caliber platform with Versi-Cal technology, swap calibers with a single thumb screw, extra barreled receivers sold separately, Quiet Energy fully shrouded barrel, fully adjustable two-stage "Quattro" trigger, multishot (14 rounds, .177; 12 rounds, .22; 10 rounds, .25). Velocities: .177, 1,250 fps/.22, 1,120 fps/.25, 900 fps (with lead-free pellets).
Price: **$429.00**

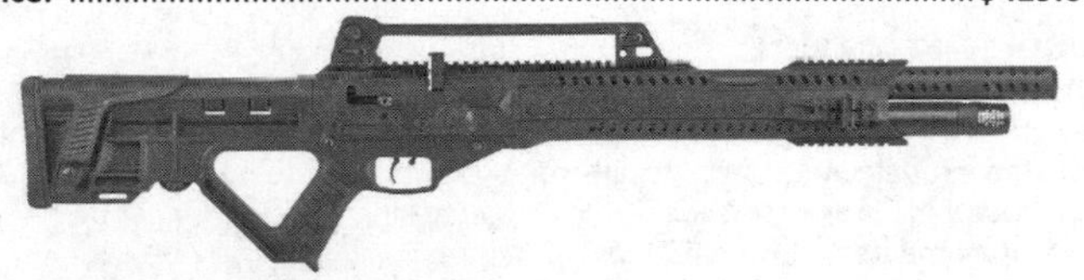

HATSAN USA INVADER AUTO AIR RIFLE
Calibers: .22, .25. Barrel: Rifled 19.7 in. Weight: 8.2 lbs. Length: 40.5 in. Power: Precharged pneumatic. Stock: Black ambidextrous thumbhole tactical style. Sights: Adjustable on removable carry handle, Picatinny rail for scope mounting. Features: Approximately 50 shots per fill, adjustable cheekpiece, built in magazine storage, three Picatinny rails for accessories, Quiet Energy fully shrouded barrel, multishot (12 rounds, .22; 10 rounds, .25). Velocities: .22, 1,100 fps/.25, 900 fps.
Price: **$669.00**

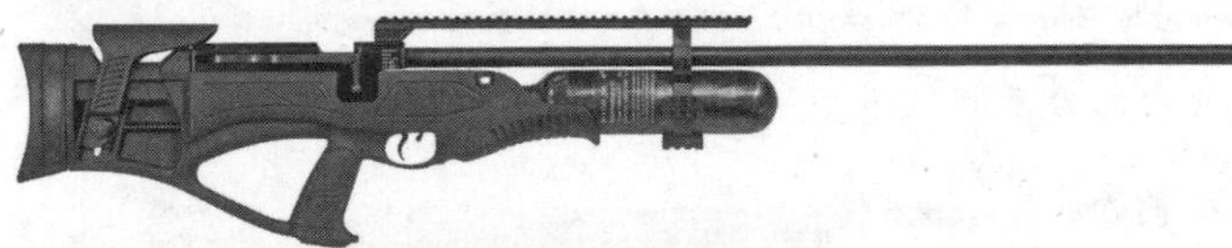

HATSAN USA PILEDRIVER BIG BORE PCP AIR RIFLE
Calibers: .45, .50. Barrel: Rifled 33 in. Weight: 10 lbs. Length: 46.5 in. Power: Precharged pneumatic. Stock: Bullpup style synthetic thumbhole stock with adjustable cheekpiece. Sights: None, dual rail 11mm dovetail and Weaver compatible for scope mounting. Features: 480 cc carbon fiber tank, long sidelever for easy cocking, three Picatinny accessory rails, 4-6 shots in .45 caliber, 3-5 shots in 50 caliber, fully adjustable two-stage "Quattro" trigger. Velocities: .45, 900 fps/.50, 850 fps.
Price: **$1,179.00**

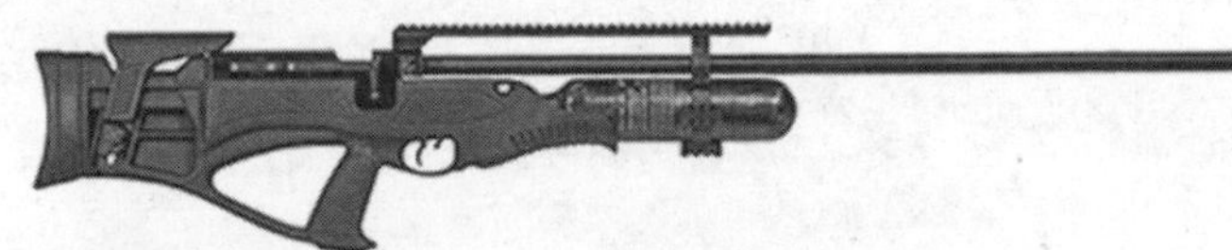

HATSAN USA PROXIMA MULTISHOT UNDERLEVER AIR RIFLE
Calibers: .177, .22, .25. Barrel: Rifled, 15.5 in. Weight: 9.3 lbs. Length: 45.4 in. Power: Gas piston. Stock: Turkish walnut ambidextrous stock with thumbhole and elevation-adjustable comb. Sights: Hooded TruGlo fiber-optic front sight, micro-adjustable rear sight. Features: Fixed barrel, underlever cocking system, shock-absorber system, fully adjustable two-stage "Quattro" trigger, 45-pound cocking effort. Velocities: .177, 820 fps/.22, 720 fps/.25, 620 fps.
Price: **$449.00**

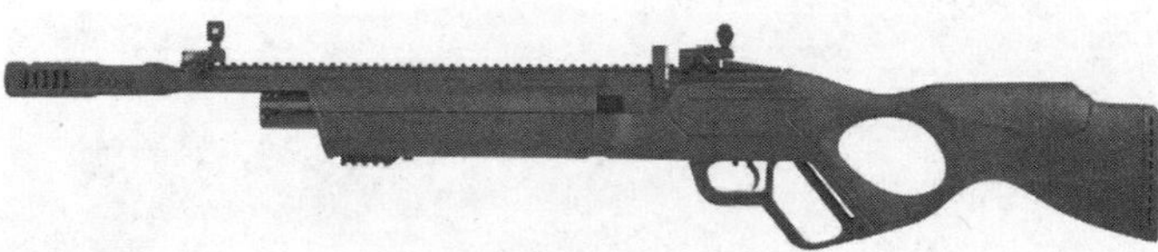

HATSAN USA VECTIS LEVER ACTION PCP AIR RIFLE
Calibers: .177, .22, .25. Barrel: Rifled 17.7 in. Weight: 7.1 lbs. Length: 41.3 in. Power: Pre-charged pneumatic. Stock: Synthetic all-weather stock. Sights: Fiber-optic front and rear, combination dual 11mm dovetail and Weaver compatible for scope mounting. Features: Multi-shot lever action, 14-shot .177 magazine, 12-shot .22 magazine, 10-shot .25 magazine. "Quiet Energy" barrel shroud with integrated suppressor, fully adjustable two-stage "Quattro" trigger, Picatinny under barrel accessory rail. Velocities: .177, 1,150 fps/.22, 1,000 fps/.25, 900 fps.
Price: **$399.00**

HELLRAISER HELLBOY RIFLE
Caliber: .177 BB. Barrel: 14.5 in. Weight: 5.2 lbs. Length: 30-33.5 in. Power: CO2 cartridge. Stock. Synthetic, tactical style. Sights: Open sights adjustable for windage and elevation, Picatinny rail for scope mounting. Features: Based on the M4 carbine, full-metal construction of barrel, magazine, and receiver, stock adjustable for length of pull, semiautomatic, 18 round magazine, removable carry handle, integrated sling swivels. Velocity: 495 fps.
Price: **$179.00**

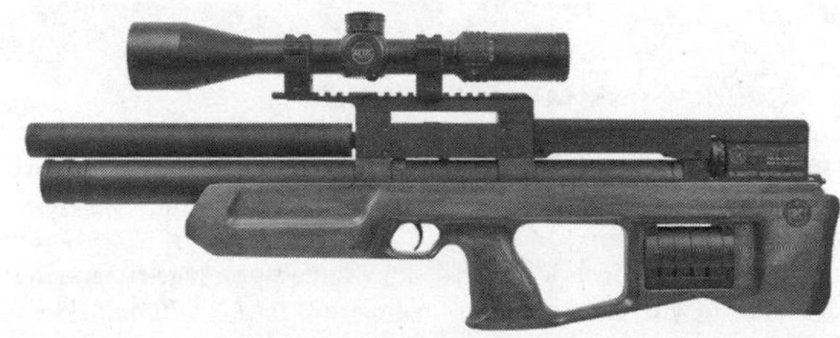

KALIBRGUN CRICKET 2 BULLPUP PCP AIR RIFLE
Caliber: .177 .22, .25, .30. Barrel: Rifled, Lothar Walther or CZ barrel (depending on caliber), 23.6 in. Weight: 7.5 lbs. Length: 33.1 in. Power: Precharged pneumatic. Stock: Ambidextrous wood or synthetic bullpup stock with synthetic cheek piece. Sights: None, Weaver rail for scope mounting. Features: Switchable (left/right) sidelever cocking system, adjustable power, 14-shot (.177 or .22), 12-shot (.25) or 10-shot magazine (.30), 35- 75 shots per fill depending on caliber, stock has integral magazine holder, adjustable two-stage trigger, also available in a tactical version. Velocity: Up to 915-970 fps depending on caliber.
Price: **$1,895.00**

Prices given are believed to be accurate at time of publication however, many factors affect retail pricing so exact prices are not possible.

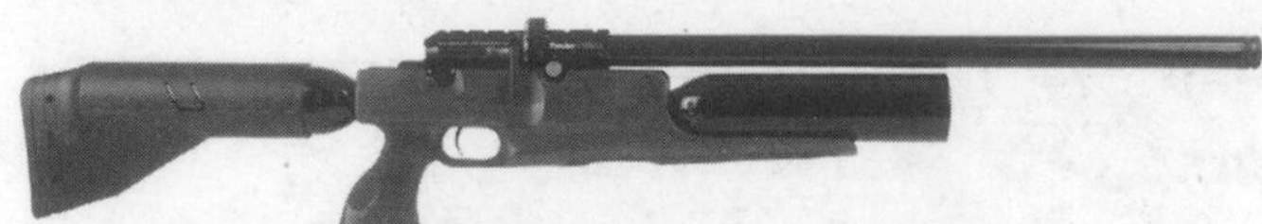

KRAL ARMS PUNCHER MEGA WALNUT SIDELEVER PCP AIR RIFLE
Calibers: .177, .22, .25. Barrel: Rifled 21.0 in. Weight: 8.35 lbs. Length: 42.0 in. Power: Pre-charged pneumatic. Stock: Ambidextrous stock available in synthetic with adjustable cheek piece, and Turkish walnut. Sights: None, 11mm grooved dovetail for scope mounting. Features: Multi-shot side-lever action, 14-shot .177 magazine, 12-shot .22 magazine, 10-shot .25 magazine, half shrouded barrel with integrated suppression technology, available in blue and satin marine finish, adjustable two-stage trigger. Velocities: .177, 1,070 fps/.22, 975 fps/.25, 825 fps.
Price: **$599.00**

KRAL ARMS PUNCHER PRO 500 PCP AIR RIFLE
Calibers: .177, .22, .25. Barrel: Rifled, 20.9 in. Weight: 8.5 lbs. Length: 41.3 in. Power: Precharged pneumatic. Stock: Monte Carlo hardwood right-handed stock. Sights: None, 11mm grooved dovetail for scope mounting. Features: Multi-shot rear bolt action, 14-shot .177 magazine, 12-shot .22 magazine, 10-shot .25 magazine, fully half shrouded barrel with integrated suppression technology, two-stage adjustable trigger, 70-80 shots per fill depending on caliber. Velocities: .177, 1,100 fps/.22, 900 fps/.25, 850 fps.
Price: **$724.00**

KRAL ARMS PUNCHER BREAKER SILENT SYNTHETIC SIDELEVER PCP AIR RIFLE
Calibers: .177, .22, .25. Barrel: Rifled 21.0 in. Weight: 7.4 lbs. Length: 29.0 in. Power: Pre-charged pneumatic. Stock: Ambidextrous bullpup stock available in synthetic and Turkish walnut. Sights: None, 11mm grooved dovetail for scope mounting. Features: Multi-shot side-lever action, 14-shot .177 magazine, 12-shot .22 magazine, 10-shot .25 magazine, half shrouded barrel with integrated suppression technology, available in blue and satin marine finish, adjustable two-stage trigger. Velocities: .177, 1,100 fps/.22, 975 fps/.25, 825 fps.
Price: **$599.00**

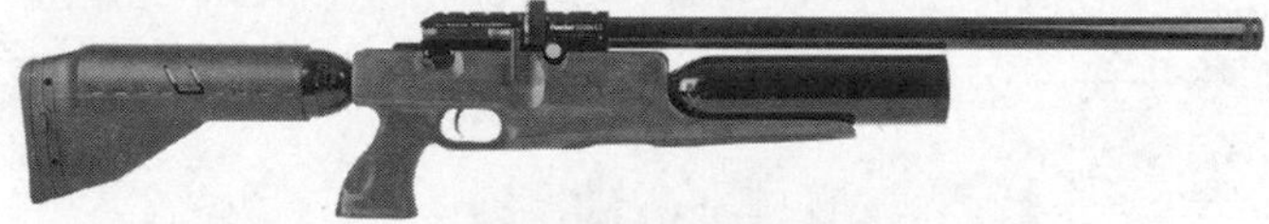

KRAL ARMS PUNCHER BIG MAX PCP AIR RIFLE
Calibers: .177, .22, .25. Barrel: Rifled 22.0 in. Weight: 9.5 lbs. Length: 42.1 in. Power: Pre-charged pneumatic. Stock: Ambidextrous Turkish walnut pistol grip. Sights: None, 11mm grooved dovetail for scope mounting. Features: Multi-shot side-lever action, 14-shot .177 magazine, 12-shot .22 magazine, 10-shot .25 magazine, shrouded barrel, adjustable two-stage trigger, massive dual air reservoirs with total of 850 CC. Velocities: .177, 1,070 fps/.22, 975 fps/.25, 825 fps.
Price: **$689.00**

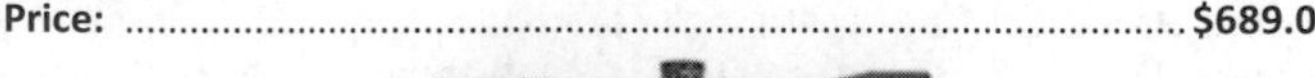

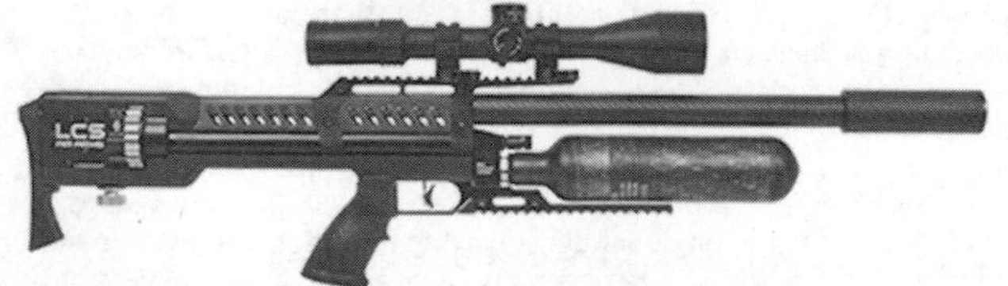

LCS AIR ARMS SK19 FULL AUTO AIRGUN
Calibers: .22, .25. Barrel: Lothar Walther match grade, 23 in. Weight: 7.75 lbs. Length: 35.0 in. Power: Precharged pneumatic. Stock: Laminate with adjustable cheek piece. Sights: None, Picatinny rail for scope mounting. Features: Made in USA, selector for semi-auto or full-auto rate of fire, tunable regulated action, carbon fiber barrel shroud, 480 or 580 cc removable tank, optional 580 cc tank available, hard case, 19 shot magazine. Velocity: 890-910 fps.
Price: .... **$2,089.00–$2,339.00**

RAPID AIR WEAPONS RAW HM1000X LRT RIFLE
Calibers: .22, .25, .30, .357. Barrel: Lothar Walther match grade with polygonal rifling, 24 in. Weight: 7 lbs., 13 oz. Length: 45.4 in. Power: Pre-charged pneumatic. Stock: Laminate with adjustable cheek piece. Sights: Grooved for scope mounting. Features: Picatinny rail and M-LOK mounting slots, match-grade trigger, multi-shot rotary magazine, adjustable power, side-lever cocking, regulated, quick-fill system, available with right- or left-hand actions. Velocities: .22, 950 fps/.25, 900 fps/.30, NA/.357, NA.
Price: **$2,199.00**

RAPID AIR WEAPONS RAW TM1000 BENCHREST RIFLE
Calibers: .177, .22. Barrel: Lothar Walther match grade with polygonal rifling, 24 in. Weight: 9.2 - 10.5 lbs. Length: 44 in. Power: Precharged pneumatic. Stock: Walnut or black laminate. Sights: Grooved for scope mounting. Features: Built to specifications, target model, internally fitted regulator, fixed bottle, quick fill coupling, approximately 80 shots depending on settings and caliber, Picatinny rail and M-LOK mounting slots, stainless steel ported shroud, adjustable cheek piece and buttpad, match grade trigger, single shot, 10 inch long accessory rail under barrel, side-lever cocking, right- or left-handed action. Velocities: Dependent on settings and caliber.
Price: **$2,199.00**

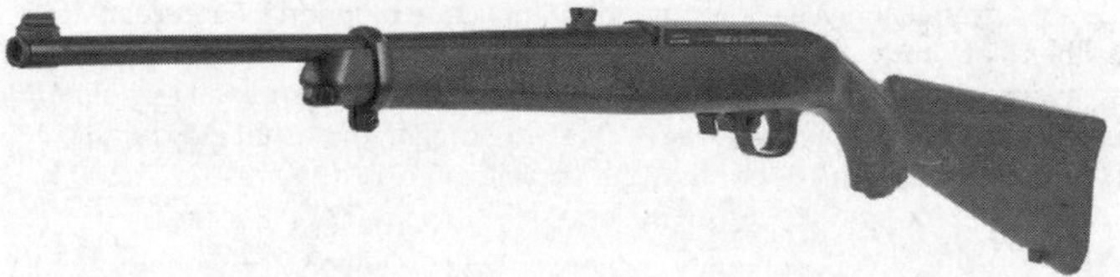

RUGER 10/22 CO2 RIFLE
Calibers: .177 pellets. Barrel: Rifled 18 in. Weight: 4.5 lbs. Length: 37.1 in. Power: Two 12-gram CO2 cylinders. Stock: Synthetic stock. Sights: Rear sight adjustable for elevation, accepts aftermarket rail. Features: 10-shot Ruger-style rotary magazine, bolt cocks rifle, 3-pound single-action trigger pull, sling attachments. Velocity: 650 fps.
Price: **$149.00**

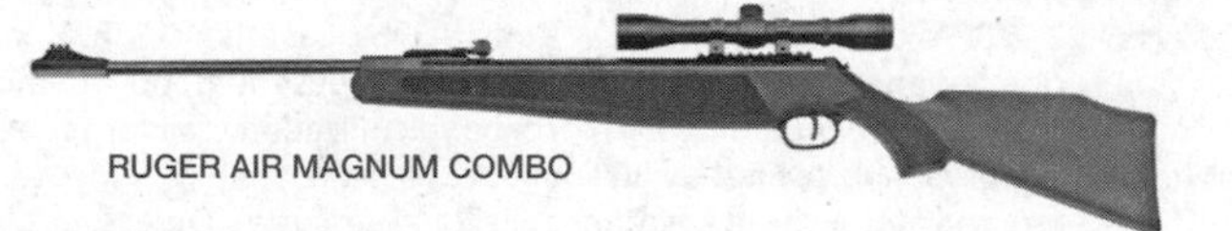

RUGER AIR MAGNUM COMBO

RUGER AIR MAGNUM COMBO
Calibers: .177, .22. Barrel: Rifled 19.5 in. Weight: 9.5 lbs. Length: 48.5 in. Power: Break-barrel, spring-piston. Stock: Ambidextrous Monte Carlo synthetic stock with textured grip and fore-end. Sights: Fiber-optic front sight and fully adjustable fiber-optic rear sight, Weaver scope rail, includes 4x32 scope and mounts. Features: Single-shot, two-stage trigger. Velocities: .177, 1,400 fps/.22, 1,200 fps.
Price: **$234.00**

RUGER EXPLORER RIFLE
Caliber: .177 pellets. Barrel: Rifled 15 in. Weight: 4.45 lbs. Length: 37.12 in. Power: Break-barrel, spring-piston Stock: Ambidextrous synthetic skeleton stock. Sights: Fiber-optic front sight and fully adjustable fiber-optic rear sight, grooved for scope mounting. Features: Designed as an entry level youth break-barrel rifle, easy to shoot and accurate, single-shot, two-stage trigger. Velocity: 495 fps.
Price: **$99.00**

Prices given are believed to be accurate at time of publication however, many factors affect retail pricing so exact prices are not possible.

RUGER IMPACT MAX ELITE RIFLE
Caliber: .22. Barrel: Rifled 15 in. Weight: 7.5 lbs. Length: 44.75 in. Power: Break-barrel, TNT gas-piston. Stock: Ambidextrous wood stock, includes rifle sling. Sights: Fiber-optic front sight and fully adjustable fiber-optic rear sight, Picatinny optics rail, includes scope and mounts. Features: Integrated "SilencAIR" suppressor. Velocity: 800 fps with lead pellet.
Price: **$169.00**

RUGER TARGIS HUNTER MAX AIR RIFLE COMBO
Caliber: .22. Barrel: Rifled 18.7 in. Weight: 9.85 lbs. Length: 44.85 in. Power: Break-barrel, spring-piston. Stock: Ambidextrous synthetic stock with texture grip and fore-end, includes rifle sling. Sights: Fiber-optic front sight and fully adjustable fiber-optic rear sight, Picatinny optics rail, includes scope and mounts. Features: Integrated "SilencAIR" suppressor, single-shot, two-stage trigger. Velocity: 1,000 fps.
Price: **$239.00**

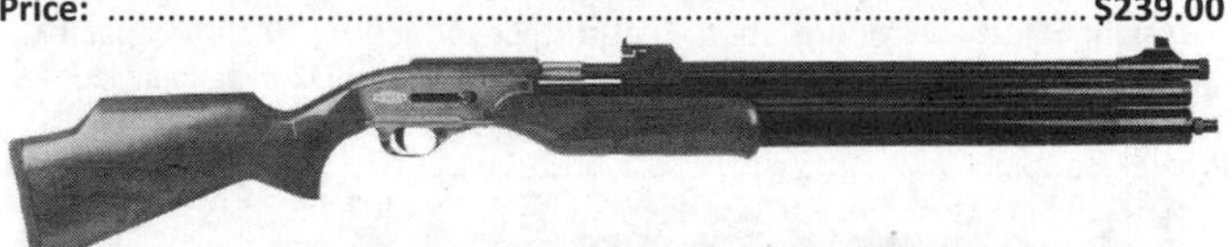

SENECA BIG BORE 44 909 LIGHT HUNTER 500CC TANK
Caliber: .45. Barrel: Rifled 21.65 in. Weight: 8.5 lbs. Length: 42.1 in. Power: Pre-charged pneumatic. Stock: Right-handed wood stock. Sights: Fixed front sight with fully adjustable rear sight. Features: Massive 500cc reservoir delivers several powerful shots, delivers well over 200 ft-lbs at the muzzle, long-range hunting accuracy, exceptionally reliable. Velocity: 730 fps.
Price: **$799.00**

SENECA DOUBLE SHOT .50 CAL DOUBLE BARREL AIR SHOTGUN
Caliber: .50. Barrel: Smooth, double barrel, 20.9 in. Weight: 8.55 Length: 43.5 in. Power: Precharged pneumatic. Stock: Ambidextrous wood stock. Sights: Front bead with no rear sight. Features: Up to five shots per fill, shoots shotshells, airbolts, or roundballs, thread on chokes, optional dovetail rail, two-stage nonadjustable trigger. Velocity: Up to 1,130 fps with shotshells.
Price: **$1,049.00**

SENECA DRAGON CLAW PCP AIR RIFLE
Caliber: .50. Barrel: Rifled, 21.65 in. Weight: 8.5 lbs. Length: 42.1 in. Power: Pre-charged pneumatic. Stock: Right-handed wood stock. Sights: Fixed front sight with fully adjustable rear sight. Features: Massive 500cc reservoir delivers several powerful shots, 230 ft-lbs energy at the muzzle on high setting, two power levels, dual air chambers, built-in manometer, 11mm scope rail. Velocity: 639 fps.
Price: **$799.00**

SENECA DRAGONFLY MK2 MULTI-PUMP AIR RIFLE
Calibers: .177, .22. Barrel: Rifled 22.75 in. Weight: 6.5 lbs. Length: 40 in. Power: Multi-Pump pneumatic. Stock: Ambidextrous wood stock. Sights: Fixed front sight with fully adjustable rear sight. Features: Butterfly High-Efficiency Pump System, threaded muzzle adapter, 11mm dovetail optics rail, variable power based on number of pumps, bolt action, single shot and multi-shot capability. Velocities: 850 fps (.177), 730 fps (.22).
Price: **$229.00**

SENECA RECLUSE AIR RIFLE
Caliber: .35 (9mm). Barrel: Rifled 21.60 in. Weight: 7.5 lbs. Length: 42.1 in. Power: Pre-charged pneumatic. Stock: Right-handed wood stock. Sights: Fixed front sight with fully adjustable rear sight. Features: Massive 500cc reservoir delivers several powerful shots, delivers well over 150 ft-lbs at the muzzle, long-range hunting accuracy, exceptionally reliable. Velocity: 983 fps.
Price: **$799.00**

SIG SAUER MCX CO2 RIFLE & SCOPE, BLACK
Caliber: .177. Barrel: Rifled 17.7 in. Weight: 7.9 lbs. Length: 34.7 in. Power: CO2. Stock: Synthetic stock, various color options. Sights: Varies with model, weaver rail system for iron sight systems, red dot systems, and traditional scope mounting. Features: 30-round semi-auto, reliable belt fed magazine system, available in various colors and sighting combination, very realistic replica. Velocity: 700 fps.
Price: **$299.00**

SIG SAUER MPX CO2 RIFLE, DOT SIGHT, BLACK
Caliber: .177. Barrel: Rifled 8 in. Weight: 6.6 lbs. Length: 25.8 in. Power: CO2. Stock: Synthetic stock, various color options. Sights: Varies with model, weaver rail system for iron sight systems, red dot systems, and traditional scope mounting. Features: 30-round semi-auto, reliable belt fed magazine system, available in various colors and sighting combination, very realistic replica. Velocity: 575 fps.
Price: **$269.00**

SIG SAUER ASP20 RIFLE
Caliber: .177 or .22 pellets. Barrel: Rifled 13.8 in. Weight: 8.5 pounds. Length: 45.6 in. Power: Break barrel. Stock: Black synthetic or black-stained beech wood. Sights: None, Picatinny rail. Features: Two-stage Matchlite trigger adjustable from 2.5-4 lbs., integrated suppressor, 33-lb. cocking effort. Velocity: 1,021 fps (.177), 841 fps (.22).
Price: .... **$399.00-$489.00**

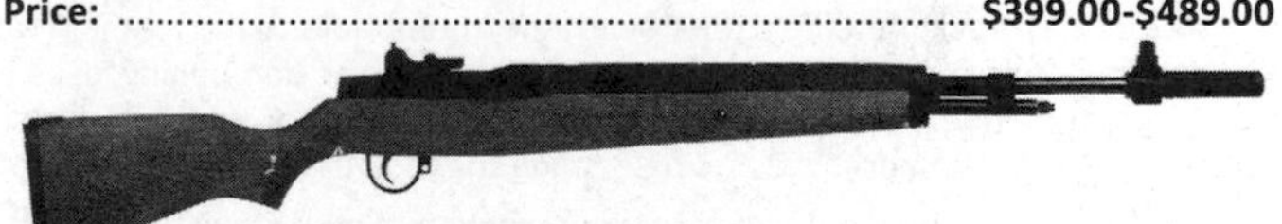

SPRINGFIELD ARMORY M1A UNDERLEVER RIFLE
Calibers: .177, .22. Barrel: Rifled, 18.9 in. Weight: 9.9 lbs. Length: 45.6 in. Power: Spring-piston underlever. Stock: Ambidextrous wood. Sights: Fixed front sight, rear peep sight adjustable for windage and elevation. Features: Fixed barrel, single shot, realistic replica of the National Match firearm, threaded holes on the left-hand side accept a traditional M1A/M14 mount for a scope, 35-pound cocking effort, two-stage nonadjustable trigger. Velocity: 1,000 fps (.177), 750 fps (.22).
Price: **$245.00**

STOEGER S4000-E PCP RIFLE COMBO
Caliber: .177 or .22 pellets. Barrel: Rifled, 18.5 in. Weight: 7.65 lbs. Length: 44.25 in. Power: Break action gas ram. Stock: Black or camo synthetic or hardwood. Sights: Adjustable fiber optic, 11mm dovetail. Features:

Automatic ambidextrous safety, interchangeable blue and orange embossed grips, includes a 4X32 scope, fully shrouded suppressed barrel, adjustable two-stage trigger, single shot. Velocities: 1,000 fps (.177), 800 fps (.22).
Price: **$179.00**

STOEGER XM1 PCP RIFLE
Caliber: .177 or .22 pellets. Barrel: Rifled, 22 in. Weight: 5.7 lbs. Length: 39 in. Power: Precharged pneumatic. Stock: Black or camo thumbhole synthetic. Sights: Adjustable fiber optic, 11 mm dovetail. Features: Approximately 50 shots per charge, 9-shot (.177) or 7-shot (.22) removable rotary magazine, available as a kit with a 4x32 scope, checkered stock, interchangeable cheekpiece, pistol grip, and buttpad, adjustable trigger, available as a suppressed model, Picatinny rails on each side, bolt action. Velocities: 1,200 fps (.177), 1,000 fps (.22).
Price: .... **$259.00–$299.00**

SWISS ARMS TAC1 AIR RIFLE COMBO
Caliber: .177 pellet. Barrel: Rifled 18.4 in. Weight: 7.8 lbs. (with scope and mount). Length: 43.75 in. Power: Spring piston. Stock: Ambidextrous tan thumbhole synthetic. Sights: None, grooved 11mm dovetail for scope mounting. Features: Comes with 4x32 scope and mount, single shot. Velocity: 1,200 fps.
Price: **$135.00**

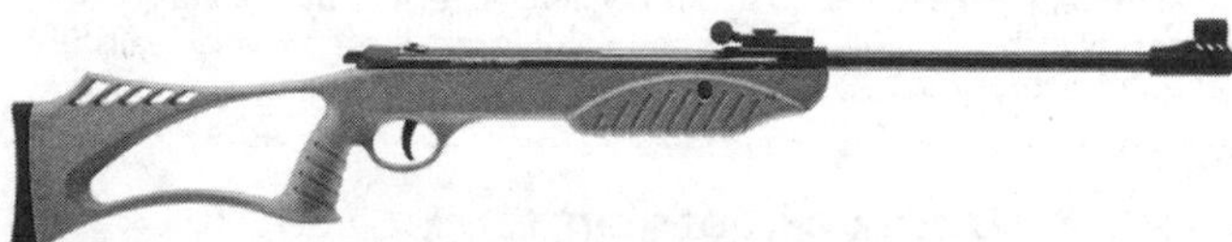

UMAREX EMBARK AIR RIFLE
Caliber: .177. Barrel: Rifled 15 in. Weight: 4.45 Length: 37.25 in. Power: Spring piston. Stock: Ambidextrous neon green thumbhole synthetic. Sights: Fully adjustable micrometer rear, grooved 11mm dovetail for scope mounting. Features: Official air rifle for the Student Air Rifle program, 12-inch length of pull, muzzle brake, 16.5-pound cocking effort, 4.25-pound trigger pull, automatic safety. Velocity: 510 fps.
Price: **$109.00**

UMAREX FUSION 2 CO2 RIFLE
Calibers: .177 pellets. Barrel: Rifled, 18.5 in. Weight: 5.95 lbs. Length: 40.55 in. Power: CO2. Stock: Ambidextrous, synthetic, thumbhole. Sights: None, Picatinny rail for scope mounting. Features: SilencAir noise dampening, uses two 12-gram cylinders or one 88-gram cylinder, 9-shot rotary magazine, bolt action, M-LOK slots on both sides, single-stage trigger. Velocity: 700 fps.
Price: **$159.00**

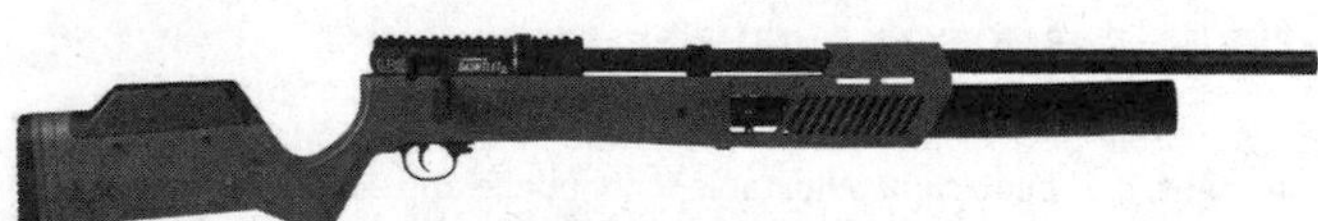

UMAREX GAUNTLET 2 PCP AIR RIFLE
Caliber: .22, .25, .30. Barrel: Rifled 28.25 in. Weight: 8.5 lbs. Length: 47 in. Power: Precharged pneumatic. Stock: Ambidextrous synthetic. Sights: None, grooved 11mm dovetail for scope mounting. Features: 10-shot (.177), 8-shot (.25) or 7-shot (.30) magazine, 25 (.30), 50 (.25), or 70 (.22) shots per fill, removable aluminum air cylinder, multi-shot bolt action, four baffle sound reduction, height-adjustable cheek comb, M-LOK accessory slots on sides and bottom or forearm, adjustable single-stage trigger. Velocities: 1,075 fps (.177), 985 fps (.25), 950 fps (.30).
Price: **$449.00**

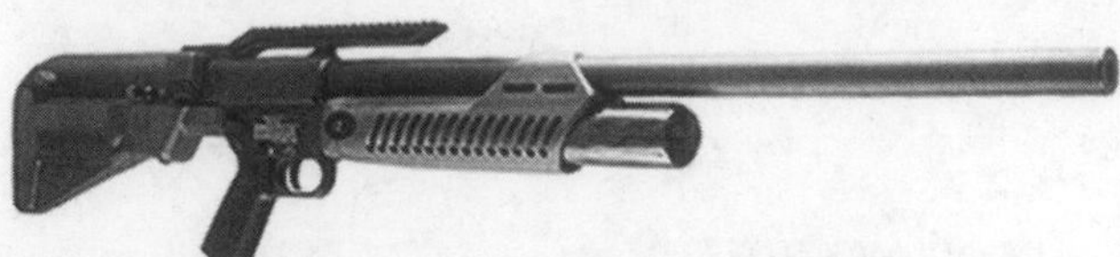

UMAREX HAMMER AIR RIFLE
Caliber: .50 Barrel: Rifled 29.5 in. Weight: 8.5 Length: 43.75 in. Power: Precharged pneumatic. Stock: Nymax synthetic. Sights: None, Picatinny rail for scope mounting. Features: Fires three full-power shots, two pound straight-pull bolt cocks the rifle and advances the magazine, 4,500 psi built-in carbon-fiber tank with quick disconnect Foster fitting, trigger-block safety, will not fire without magazine, Magpul AR grip, full-length composite barrel shroud, comes with two double chamber magazines. Velocities: 1,130 fps (180-gr. non-lead bullet), 760 fps (550-gr. lead slug).
Price: **$999.00**

UMAREX LEGENDS COWBOY LEVER ACTION RIFLE
Caliber: .177 BBs. Barrel: Smoothbore, 19.25 in. Weight: 7.75 lbs. Length: 38 in. Power: CO2. Stock: Faux wood polymer. Sights: Blade front sight with rear sight adjustable for elevation. Features: Lever-action, 10-shot capacity, ejectable cartridges, full metal frame, powered by two CO2 capsules, saddle ring. Velocity: 600 fps.
Price: **$209.00**

UMAREX LEGENDS M1A1 FULL AUTO BB GUN
Calibers: .177 BBs. Barrel: Smoothbore, 12.0 in. Weight: 7.75 lbs. Length: 31.75 in. Power: CO2. Stock: Synthetic. Sights: Fixed. Features: Semi-auto and full auto fire capability, 30-round drop free magazine with two CO2 cartridges, full metal frame, faux-wood polymer stock, blowback action, sling mounts. Velocity: 435 fps.
Price: **$279.00**

UMAREX LEGENDS M3 GREASE GUN
Calibers: .177 BBs. Barrel: Smoothbore. Weight: NA lbs. Length: NA in. Power: CO2. Stock: Synthetic with collapsible wire butt. Sights: Fixed. Features: Semi-auto and full-auto fire capability, operates on two 12-gram CO2 cylinders, 30-round drop-free magazine with 2 CO2 cartridges, full metal frame, blowback action, sling mounts. Velocity: 435 fps.
Price: **$249.00**

UMAREX NOTOS PCP CARBINE
Caliber: .22. Barrel: Rifled, 11.75 in. Weight: NA. Length: NA in. Power: Precharged pneumatic. Stock: Synthetic. Sights: None, Picatinny rail for

Prices given are believed to be accurate at time of publication however, many factors affect retail pricing so exact prices are not possible.

scope mounting. Features: Adjustable length buttstock, shrouded barrel, up to 40 shots per fill, 21 regulated shots per fill, 7-shot rotary-indexing magazine, single shot tray, side lever charging system. Velocity: 700 fps.
Price: **$259.00**

UMAREX ORIGIN PCP RIFLE
Caliber: .22 or .25 Barrel: Rifled, 22.9 in. Weight: 6.8 lbs. Length: 43.1 in. Power: Precharged pneumatic. Stock: Synthetic. Sights: None, Picatinny rail for scope mounting. Features: Hand-pump friendly Ever-Pressure pre-pressurized tank system, shoots at full power with approximately 100 pumps, up to 40 shots (.22) or 20 shots (.25) per fill, 8-shot (.25) or 10-shot (.22) rotary-indexing magazine, side lever charging system, two stage adjustable trigger, automatic overpressure air release, integrated sound suppressor. Velocity: 1,100 fps (.22), 950 fps (.25).
Price: **$329.00**

UMAREX PRIMAL 20 PCP AIR SHOTGUN
Caliber: 20 gauge. Barrel: Smoothbore with rifled choke tube. Weight: NA. Length: NA. Power: Precharged pneumatic. Stock: Ambidextrous synthetic thumbhole. Sights: None, Picatinny rail for scope mounting. Features: Ambidextrous reversible bolt action, two round sliding magazine, cocked bolt indicator, textured forearm and pistol grip, includes two magazines, sling stud hole in stock. Velocity: 700 fps with a 395 grain slug.
Price: **$649.00**

UMAREX SURGEMAX ELITE AIR RIFLE COMBO, GAS PISTON
Calibers: .177, .22. Barrel: Rifled 15.9 in. Weight: 7 lbs. Length: 45.3 in. Power: Break-barrel, gas-piston. Stock: Ambidextrous synthetic thumbhole. Sights: Adjustable, Weaver rail for scope mounting, includes 4X32 scope and mounts. Features: Single shot, two-stage adjustable trigger, sound suppression system. Velocities: .177, 1,050 fps/.22, 900 fps.
Price: **$159.00**

UMAREX SYNERGIS UNDER LEVER AIR RIFLE, COMBO
Calibers: .177, .22 pellets. Barrel: 18.5 in rifled. Weight: 8.3 lbs. Length: 45.3 in. Power: Gas piston under lever. Stock: Synthetic. Sights: None, Picatinny rail for scope mounting. Features: 3-9x32 scope, 2 magazines, 10-shot (.22) or 12-shot (.177) repeater, fixed barrel, removable magazine, integrated suppressor, two-stage nonadjustable trigger. Velocities: 1,000 fps (.177), 900 fps (.22).
Price: **$199.00**

UMAREX SYRIX AIR RIFLE
Calibers: .177, .22. Barrel: Rifled, 18.75 in. Weight: 8.6 lbs. Length: 46.1 in. Power: Break-barrel, gas-piston. Stock: Ambidextrous synthetic. Sights: Adjustable, Weaver rail for scope mounting, includes 4X32 scope and mounts. Features: Single shot. Velocities: .177, 1,000 fps/.22, 900 fps.
Price: **$124.00**

WALTHER LG400 UNIVERSAL AIR RIFLE, AMBI GRIP
Caliber: .177. Barrel: Advanced match-grade rifled barrel 16.53 in. Weight: 8.6 lbs. Length: 43.7 in. Power: Pre-charged pneumatic. Stock: Ambidextrous competition, highly adjustable wood stock. Sights: Olympic-grade, match Diopter/Micrometer adjustable sights. Features: True professional class 10-meter target rifle, meets ISSF requirements. Velocity: 557 fps.
Price: **$1,800.00**

WALTHER MAXIMATHOR AIR RIFLE
Calibers: .22, .25. Barrel: Advanced match-grade rifled barrel, 23.5 in. Weight: 9.6 lbs. Length: 41.75 in. Power: Pre-charged pneumatic. Stock: Ambidextrous wood stock. Sights: None, grooved 11mm dovetail for scope mounting. Features: Bolt action 8-shot magazine, pure hunting PCP with range and accuracy. Velocities: .22, 1,260 fps/.25, 1,000 fps.
Price: **$799.00**

WALTHER LEVER ACTION CO2 RIFLE, BLACK
Caliber: .177. Barrel: Rifled 18.9 in. Weight: 6.2 lbs. Length: 39.2 in. Power: CO2 Stock: Ambidextrous wood stock. Sights: Blade front sight, adjustable rear sight. Features: Lever-action repeater, 8-shot rotary magazine, great wild west replica airgun. Velocity: 600 fps.
Price: **$534.00**

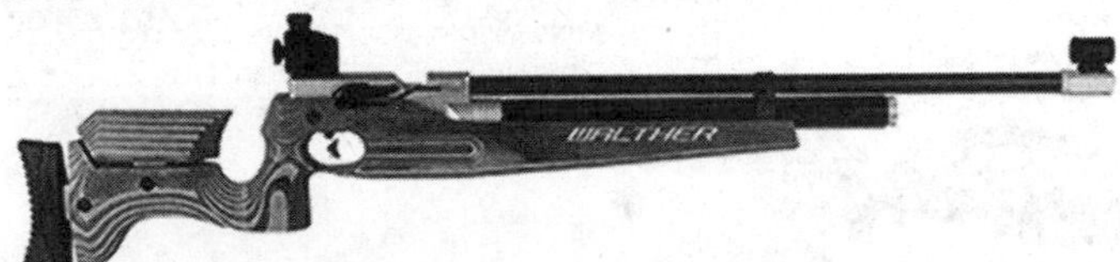

WALTHER LG400 JUNIOR AIR RIFLE
Caliber: .177. Barrel: Advanced match-grade rifled barrel, 16.53 in. Weight: 7.7 lbs. Length: 39.8 in. Power: Pre-charged pneumatic. Stock: Ambidextrous highly adjustable competition laminate wood stock. Sights: Olympic-grade, match Diopter/Micrometer adjustable sights. Features: 10-meter competition target rifle, meets ISSF requirements, removable air cylinder delivers up to 400 shots per fill. Velocity: 570 fps.
Price: **$1,800.00**

WALTHER REIGN UXT PCP BULLPUP RIFLE
Caliber: .22, .25. Barrel: Rifled, 23.6 in. Weight: 5.5 lbs. Length: 34 in. Power: Precharged pneumatic. Stock: Ambidextrous bullpup synthetic. Sights: None, Picatinny rail. Features: 10-shot (.22) or 9-shot (.25) auto indexing magazine, 40-60 shots per fill, adjustable trigger, ambidextrous cocking level, quick detach sling mount, muzzle shroud. Velocities: 975 fps (.22), 840 fps (.25).
Price: **$669.00**

Prices given are believed to be accurate at time of publication however, many factors affect retail pricing so exact prices are not possible.

WEIHRAUCH HW50S SPRING PISTON RIFLE
Caliber: .177, .22. Barrel: Rifled, 15.5 in. Weight: 6.8 lbs. Length: 40.5 in. Power: Spring-piston. Stock: Checkered beech wood. Sights: Front globe and adjustable rear. Features: Single shot, 24-lb. cocking effort, two-stage adjustable Rekord trigger. Velocity: 820 fps (.177), 574 fps (.22).
Price: $469.00

WEIHRAUCH HW90 SPRING PISTON RIFLE
Caliber: .177, .22, .25. Barrel: Rifled, 19.7 in. Weight: 6.8 lbs. Length: 45.3 in. Power: Spring-piston. Stock: Checkered beech wood. Sights: Front globe and adjustable rear, 11mm dovetail for scope mounting. Features: Single shot, 46-lb. cocking effort, 2-stage adjustable Rekord trigger. Velocity: 1,050 fps (.177), 853 fps (.22), 625 fps (.25).
Price: $834.00

WEIHRAUCH HW110 ST PCP RIFLE, FAC VERSION
Caliber: .177, .20, .22. Barrel: Rifled 30.5 in. Weight: 7.5 lbs. Length: 46 in. Power: Precharged pneumatic. Stock: Black Soft Touch coated wood. Sights: None, picatinny rail grooved for scope mounting. Features: Includes two 10-shot magazines, side lever action, fully regulated, internal pressure gauge, 2-stage adjustable match trigger, available in a shorter carbine version. Velocities: 1,050 fps (.177), 965 fps (.20), 1,025 fps (.22).
Price: $1,224.00

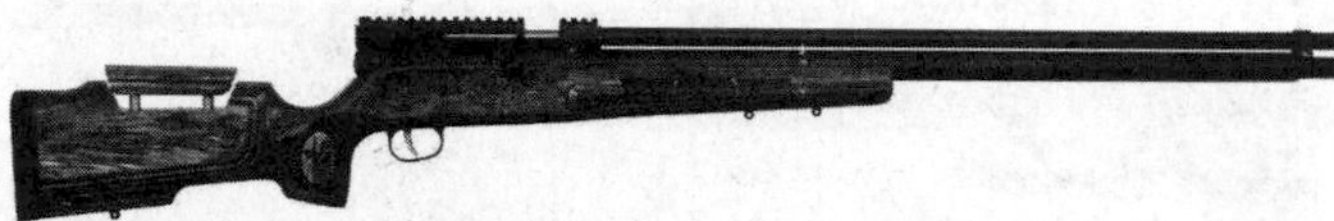

WESTERN BIG BORE BUSHBUCK PCP RIFLE
Calibers: .45. Barrel: Rifled, 30 in. Weight: 10.25 lbs. Length: 49.5 in. Power: Precharged pneumatic. Stock: Walnut or laminate. Sights: None, Picatinny rail for scope mounting. Features: One-piece aluminum receiver and Picatinny rail, all-steel air cylinder, accuracy tested to 250 yards, two 600 ft-lbs or four 400 ft lb shots per fill, accommodates extra-long bullets, approximately three pound trigger pull, sling studs, single shot, made in USA.
Price: .... $1,895.00–$2,154.00

WESTERN JUSTICE ANNIE OAKLEY LIL SURE SHOT/JOHN WAYNE LIL DUKE BB RIFLE
Caliber: .177 steel BBs. Barrel: Smooth. Weight: 2.6 lbs. Length: 34 in. Power: Spring piston, lever action. Stock: Hardwood stock. Sights: Adjustable for elevation, 11 mm dovetail mount. Features: 550-round BB reservoir, single stage trigger, 16 pound cocking effort, manual safety, available embossed with either Annie Oakley or John Wayne likeness. Velocity: 350 fps.
Price: $54.00

WINCHESTER MODEL 12 YOUTH PUMP ACTION BB GUN
Caliber: .177 steel BBs. Barrel: Smooth. Weight: 3.2 lbs. Length: 34.25 in. Power: Spring piston, pump action. Stock: Synthetic brown wood-look stock. Sights: Modeled after the famous Winchester Model 12 shotgun, adjustable for windage and elevation. Features: Single pump per shot, 250-round BB reservoir, 14 inch length of pull. Velocity: 350 fps.
Price: $54.00

WINCHESTER 77XS MULTI-PUMP AIR RIFLE
Caliber: .177 steel BBs, .177 Pellet. Barrel: Rifled 20.8 in. Weight: 3.1 lbs. Length: 37.6 in. Power: Multi-pump pneumatic. Stock: Ambidextrous synthetic thumbhole stock. Sights: Blade front sight, adjustable rear sight, grooved for scope mounting, includes 4x32 scope and mounts. Features: Single-shot pellet, 50-round BB repeater, bolt action, lightweight, accurate and easy to shoot. Velocity: 800 fps.
Price: $95.00

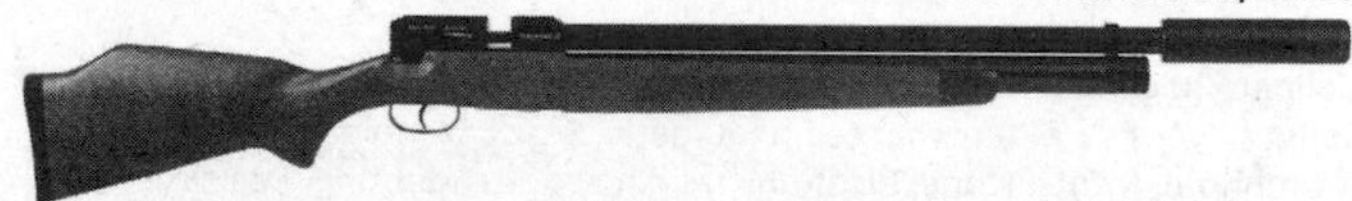

WINCHESTER MODEL 70 PCP RIFLE
Calibers: .35, .45. Barrel: Rifled, 20.87 in. Weight: 9.0 lbs. Length: 41.75 in. Power: Pre-charged pneumatic. Stock: Right handed hardwood. Sights: None, grooved for scope mounting. Features: Multi-Shot big bore (6 shots .35 / 5 shots .45), highly stable shot strings for maximum accuracy, traditional Winchester styling, .35 produces up to 134 ft-lbs, .45 produces over 200 ft-lbs. Velocities: .35, 865 fps/.45, 803 fps.
Price: $849.00

ZBROIA HORTIZIA PCP RIFLE
Calibers: .177, .22. Barrel: Rifled. Weight: NA. Length: NA. Power: Precharged pneumatic. Stock: Black stained ash Monte-Carlo style wood stock. Sights: None, grooved for scope mounting. Features: Up to 100 shots per fill in .177 caliber or 60 shots in .22 caliber, free floated barrel with 12 grooves, two-stage adjustable trigger that is detachable, side-lever cocking, 10- or 12-shot repeater, built in manometer with 4,351 psi fill, made in the Ukraine. Velocities: .177, 1,000 fps/.22, 980 fps.
Price: $849.00

ZBROIA KOZAK TACTICAL PCP RIFLE
Calibers: .177, .22. Barrel: Rifled. Weight: NA. Length: NA. Power: Precharged pneumatic. Stock: Black stained ash wood stock semi-bullpup design with adjustable cheekpiece. Sights: None, grooved for scope mounting. Features: Up to 100 shots per fill (.22 caliber), free floated barrel with 12 grooves, two stage adjustable trigger, side-lever cocking, 10- or 12-shot repeater, built in manometer with 4,351 psi fill, made in the Ukraine. Velocities: .177, 1,000 fps/.22, 980 fps.
Price: $869.00

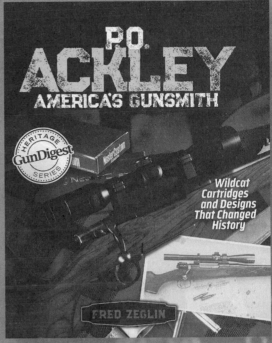

An * after the cartridge means these loads are available with Nosler Partition or Swift A-Frame bullets.
Wea. Mag.= Weatherby Magnum. Spfd. = Springfield. A-Sq. = A-Square. N.E.=Nitro Express.

Cartridge	Bullet Wgt. Grs.	VELOCITY (fps)					ENERGY (ft. lbs.)					TRAJ. (in.)			
		Muzzle	100 yds.	200 yds.	300 yds.	400 yds.	Muzzle	100 yds.	200 yds.	300 yds.	400 yds.	100 yds.	200 yds.	300 yds.	400 yds.
17, 22															
17 Hornet	15.5	3860	2924	2159	1531	1108	513	294	160	81	42	1.4	0	-9.1	-33.7
17 Hornet	20	3650	3078	2574	2122	1721	592	421	294	200	131	1.1	0	-6.4	-20.6
17 Hornet	25	3375	2842	2367	1940	1567	632	448	311	209	136	1.4	0	24.8	56.3
17 Remington Fireball	20	4000	3380	2840	2360	1930	710	507	358	247	165	1.6	1.5	-2.8	-13.5
17 Remington Fireball	25	3850	3280	2780	2330	1925	823	597	429	301	206	0.9	0	-5.4	NA
17 Remington	20	4200	3544	2978	2477	2029	783	558	394	272	183	0	-1.3	-6.6	-17.6
17 Remington	25	4040	3284	2644	2086	1606	906	599	388	242	143	2	1.7	-4	-17
4.6x30 H&K	30	2025	1662	1358	1135	1002	273	184	122	85	66	0	-12.7	-44.5	—
4.6x30 H&K	40	1900	1569	1297	1104	988	320	218	149	108	86	0	-14.3	-39.3	—
204 Ruger (Hor)	24	4400	3667	3046	2504	2023	1032	717	494	334	218	0.6	0	-4.3	-14.3
204 Ruger (Fed)	32 Green	4030	3320	2710	2170	1710	1155	780	520	335	205	0.9	0	-5.7	-19.1
204 Ruger	32	4125	3559	3061	2616	2212	1209	900	666	486	348	0	-1.3	-6.3	—
204 Ruger	32	4225	3632	3114	2652	2234	1268	937	689	500	355	0.6	0	-4.2	-13.4
204 Ruger	40	3900	3451	3046	2677	2336	1351	1058	824	636	485	0.7	0	-4.5	-13.9
204 Ruger	45	3625	3188	2792	2428	2093	1313	1015	778	589	438	1	0	-5.5	-16.9
5.45x39mm	60	2810	2495	2201	1927	1677	1052	829	645	445	374	1	0	-9.2	-27.7
221 Fireball	40	3100	2510	1991	1547	1209	853	559	352	212	129	0	-4.1	-17.3	-45.1
221 Fireball	50	2800	2137	1580	1180	988	870	507	277	155	109	0	-7	-28	0
22 Hornet (Fed)	30 Green	3150	2150	1390	990	830	660	310	130	65	45	0	-6.6	-32.7	NA
22 Hornet	34	3050	2132	1415	1017	852	700	343	151	78	55	0	-6.6	-15.5	-29.9
22 Hornet	35	3100	2278	1601	1135	929	747	403	199	100	67	2.75	0	-16.9	-60.4
22 Hornet	40	2800	2397	2029	1698	1413	696	510	366	256	177	0	-4.6	-17.8	-43.1
22 Hornet	45	2690	2042	1502	1128	948	723	417	225	127	90	0	-7.7	-31	0
218 Bee	46	2760	2102	1550	1155	961	788	451	245	136	94	0	-7.2	-29	0
222 Rem.	35	3760	3125	2574	2085	1656	1099	759	515	338	213	1	0	-6.3	-20.8
222 Rem.	50	3345	2930	2553	2205	1886	1242	953	723	540	395	1.3	0	-6.7	-20.6
222 Remington	40	3600	3117	2673	2269	1911	1151	863	634	457	324	1.07	0	-6.13	-18.9
222 Remington	50	3140	2602	2123	1700	1350	1094	752	500	321	202	2	-0.4	-11	-33
222 Remington	55	3020	2562	2147	1773	1451	1114	801	563	384	257	2	-0.4	-11	-33
222 Rem. Mag.	40	3600	3140	2726	2347	2000	1150	876	660	489	355	1	0	-5.7	-17.8
222 Rem. Mag.	50	3340	2917	2533	2179	1855	1238	945	712	527	382	1.3	0	-6.8	-20.9
222 Rem. Mag.	55	3240	2748	2305	1906	1556	1282	922	649	444	296	2	-0.2	-9	-27
22 PPC	52	3400	2930	2510	2130	NA	1335	990	730	525	NA	2	1.4	-5	0
223 Rem.	35	3750	3206	2725	2291	1899	1092	799	577	408	280	1	0	-5.7	-18.1
223 Rem.	35	4000	3353	2796	2302	1861	1243	874	607	412	269	0.8	0	-5.3	-17.3
223 Rem.	64	2750	2368	2018	1701	1427	1074	796	578	411	289	2.4	0	-11	-34.1
223 Rem.	75	2790	2562	2345	2139	1943	1296	1093	916	762	629	1.5	0	-8.2	-24.1
223 Remington	40	3650	3010	2450	1950	1530	1185	805	535	340	265	2	1	-6	-22
223 Remington	40	3800	3305	2845	2424	2044	1282	970	719	522	371	0.84	0	-5.34	-16.6
223 Remington (Rem)	45 Green	3550	2911	2355	1865	1451	1259	847	554	347	210	2.5	2.3	-4.3	-21.1
223 Remington	50	3300	2874	2484	2130	1809	1209	917	685	504	363	1.37	0	-7.05	-21.8
223 Remington	52/53	3330	2882	2477	2106	1770	1305	978	722	522	369	2	0.6	-6.5	-21.5
223 Remington (Win)	55 Green	3240	2747	2304	1905	1554	1282	921	648	443	295	1.9	0	-8.5	-26.7
223 Remington	55	3240	2748	2305	1906	1556	1282	922	649	444	296	2	-0.2	-9	-27
223 Remington	60	3100	2712	2355	2026	1726	1280	979	739	547	397	2	0.2	-8	-24.7
223 Remington	62	3000	2700	2410	2150	1900	1240	1000	800	635	495	1.6	0	-7.7	-22.8
223 Remington	64	3020	2621	2256	1920	1619	1296	977	723	524	373	2	-0.2	-9.3	-23
223 Remington	69	3000	2720	2460	2210	1980	1380	1135	925	750	600	2	0.8	-5.8	-17.5
223 Remington	75	2790	2554	2330	2119	1926	1296	1086	904	747	617	2.37	0	-8.75	-25.1
223 Rem. Super Match	75	2930	2694	2470	2257	2055	1429	1209	1016	848	703	1.2	0	-6.9	-20.7
223 Remington	77	2750	2584	2354	2169	1992	1293	1110	948	804	679	1.93	0	-8.2	-23.8
223 WSSM	55	3850	3438	3064	2721	2402	1810	1444	1147	904	704	0.7	0	-4.4	-13.6
223 WSSM	64	3600	3144	2732	2356	2011	1841	1404	1061	789	574	1	0	-5.7	-17.7
5.56 NATO	55	3130	2740	2382	2051	1750	1196	917	693	514	372	1.1	0	-7.3	-23
5.56 NATO	75	2910	2676	2543	2242	2041	1410	1192	1002	837	693	1.2	0	-7	-21
224 Wea. Mag.	55	3650	3192	2780	2403	2057	1627	1244	943	705	516	2	1.2	-4	-17
22 Nosler	55	3350	2965	2615	2286	1984	1370	1074	833	638	480	0	-2.5	-10.1	-24.4
22 Nosler	77	2950	2672	2410	2163	1931	1488	1220	993	800	637	0	-3.4	-12.8	-29.7
224 Valkyrie	90	2700	2542	2388	2241	2098	1457	1291	1140	1003	880	1.9	0	-8.1	-23.2

Cartridge	Bullet Wgt. Grs.	VELOCITY (fps)					ENERGY (ft. lbs.)					TRAJ. (in.)			
		Muzzle	100 yds.	200 yds.	300 yds.	400 yds.	Muzzle	100 yds.	200 yds.	300 yds.	400 yds.	100 yds.	200 yds.	300 yds.	400 yds.
224 Valkyrie	75	3000	2731	2477	2237	2010	1499	1242	1022	833	673	1.6	0	-7.3	-21.5
224 Valkyrie	60	3300	2930	2589	2273	1797	1451	1144	893	688	522	1.3	0	-6.5	-19.8
225 Winchester	55	3570	3066	2616	2208	1838	1556	1148	836	595	412	2	1	-5	-20
22-250 Rem.	35	4450	3736	3128	2598	2125	1539	1085	761	524	351	6.5	0	-4.1	-13.4
22-250 Rem.	40	4000	3320	2720	2200	1740	1420	980	660	430	265	2	1.8	-3	-16
22-250 Rem.	40	4150	3553	3033	2570	2151	1530	1121	817	587	411	0.6	0	-4.4	-14.2
22-250 Rem.	45 Green	4000	3293	2690	2159	1696	1598	1084	723	466	287	1.7	1.7	-3.2	-15.7
22-250 Rem.	50	3725	3264	2641	2455	2103	1540	1183	896	669	491	0.89	0	-5.23	-16.3
22-250 Rem.	52/55	3680	3137	2656	2222	1832	1654	1201	861	603	410	2	1.3	-4	-17
22-250 Rem.	60	3600	3195	2826	2485	2169	1727	1360	1064	823	627	2	2	-2.4	-12.3
22-250 Rem.	64	3425	2988	2591	2228	1897	1667	1269	954	705	511	1.2	0	-6.4	-20
220 Swift	40	4200	3678	3190	2739	2329	1566	1201	904	666	482	0.51	0	-4	-12.9
220 Swift	50	3780	3158	2617	2135	1710	1586	1107	760	506	325	2	1.4	-4.4	-17.9
220 Swift	50	3850	3396	2970	2576	2215	1645	1280	979	736	545	0.74	0	-4.84	-15.1
220 Swift	50	3900	3420	2990	2599	2240	1688	1298	992	750	557	0.7	0	-4.7	-14.5
220 Swift	55	3800	3370	2990	2630	2310	1765	1390	1090	850	650	0.8	0	-4.7	-14.4
220 Swift	55	3650	3194	2772	2384	2035	1627	1246	939	694	506	2	2	-2.6	-13.4
220 Swift	60	3600	3199	2824	2475	2156	1727	1364	1063	816	619	2	1.6	-4.1	-13.1
22 Savage H.P.	70	2868	2510	2179	1874	1600	1279	980	738	546	398	0	-4.1	-15.6	-37.1
22 Savage H.P.	71	2790	2340	1930	1570	1280	1225	860	585	390	190	2	-1	-10.4	-35.7
6mm (24)															
6mm BR Rem.	100	2550	2310	2083	1870	1671	1444	1185	963	776	620	2.5	-0.6	-11.8	0
6mm Norma BR	107	2822	2667	2517	2372	2229	1893	1690	1506	1337	1181	1.73	0	-7.24	-20.6
6mm Creedmoor	108	2786	2618	2456	2299	2149	1861	1643	1446	1267	1106	1.5	0	-6.6	-18.9
6mm PPC	70	3140	2750	2400	2070	NA	1535	1175	895	665	NA	2	1.4	-5	0
6mm ARC	103	2800	2623	2452	2288	2130	1793	1573	1375	1197	1038	1.8	0	-7.6	-21.8
6mm ARC	105	2750	2580	2417	2260	2108	1763	1552	1362	1190	1036	1.9	0	-7.8	-22.4
6mm ARC	108	2750	2582	2421	2265	2115	1813	1599	1405	1230	1072	1.9	0	-7.8	-22.4
243 Winchester	55	4025	3597	3209	2853	2525	1978	1579	1257	994	779	0.6	0	-4	-12.2
243 Win.	58	3925	3465	3052	2676	2330	1984	1546	1200	922	699	0.7	0	-4.4	-13.8
243 Winchester	60	3600	3110	2660	2260	1890	1725	1285	945	680	475	2	1.8	-3.3	-15.5
243 Win.	70	3400	3020	2672	2350	2050	1797	1418	1110	858	653	0	-2.5	-9.7	—
243 Winchester	70	3400	3040	2700	2390	2100	1795	1435	1135	890	685	1.1	0	-5.9	-18
243 Winchester	75/80	3350	2955	2593	2259	1951	1993	1551	1194	906	676	2	0.9	-5	-19
243 Win.	80	3425	3081	2763	2468	2190	2984	1686	1357	1082	852	1.1	0	-5.7	-17.1
243 Win.	87	2800	2574	2359	2155	1961	1514	1280	1075	897	743	1.9	0	-8.1	-23.8
243 Win.	95	3185	2908	2649	2404	2172	2140	1784	1480	1219	995	1.3	0	-6.3	-18.6
243 W. Superformance	80	3425	3080	2760	2463	2184	2083	1684	1353	1077	847	1.1	0	-5.7	-17.1
243 Winchester	85	3320	3070	2830	2600	2380	2080	1770	1510	1280	1070	2	1.2	-4	-14
243 Winchester	90	3120	2871	2635	2411	2199	1946	1647	1388	1162	966	1.4	0	-6.4	-18.8
243 Winchester*	100	2960	2697	2449	2215	1993	1945	1615	1332	1089	882	2.5	1.2	-6	-20
243 Winchester	105	2920	2689	2470	2261	2062	1988	1686	1422	1192	992	2.5	1.6	-5	-18.4
243 Light Mag.	100	3100	2839	2592	2358	2138	2133	1790	1491	1235	1014	1.5	0	-6.8	-19.8
243 WSSM	55	4060	3628	3237	2880	2550	2013	1607	1280	1013	794	0.6	0	-3.9	-12
243 WSSM	95	3250	3000	2763	2538	2325	2258	1898	1610	1359	1140	1.2	0	-5.7	-16.9
243 WSSM	100	3110	2838	2583	2341	2112	2147	1789	1481	1217	991	1.4	0	-6.6	-19.7
6mm Remington	80	3470	3064	2694	2352	2036	2139	1667	1289	982	736	2	1.1	-5	-17
6mm R. Superformance	95	3235	2955	2692	2443	3309	2207	1841	1528	1259	1028	1.2	0	-6.1	-18
6mm Remington	100	3100	2829	2573	2332	2104	2133	1777	1470	1207	983	2.5	1.6	-5	-17
6mm Remington	105	3060	2822	2596	2381	2177	2105	1788	1512	1270	1059	2.5	1.1	-3.3	-15
240 Wea. Mag.	87	3500	3202	2924	2663	2416	2366	1980	1651	1370	1127	2	2	-2	-12
240 Wea. Mag.	100	3150	2894	2653	2425	2207	2202	1860	1563	1395	1082	1.3	0	-6.3	-18.5
240 Wea. Mag.	100	3395	3106	2835	2581	2339	2559	2142	1785	1478	1215	2.5	2.8	-2	-11
25-20 Win.	86	1460	1194	1030	931	858	407	272	203	165	141	0	-23.5	0	0
25-45 Sharps	87	3000	2677	2385	2112	1859	1739	1384	1099	862	668	1.1	0	-7.4	-22.6
25-35 Win.	117	2230	1866	1545	1282	1097	1292	904	620	427	313	2.5	-4.2	-26	0
250 Savage	100	2820	2504	2210	1936	1684	1765	1392	1084	832	630	2.5	0.4	-9	-28
257 Roberts	100	2980	2661	2363	2085	1827	1972	1572	1240	965	741	2.5	-0.8	-5.2	-21.6
257 Roberts	122	2600	2331	2078	1842	1625	1831	1472	1169	919	715	2.5	0	-10.6	-31.4
257 Roberts+P	100	3000	2758	2529	2312	2105	1998	1689	1421	1187	984	1.5	0	-7	-20.5
257 Roberts+P	117	2780	2411	2071	1761	1488	2009	1511	1115	806	576	2.5	-0.2	-10.2	-32.6
257 Roberts+P	120	2780	2560	2360	2160	1970	2060	1750	1480	1240	1030	2.5	1.2	-6.4	-23.6
257 R. Superformance	117	2946	2705	2478	2265	2057	2253	1901	1595	1329	1099	1.1	0	-5.7	-17.1

Cartridge	Bullet Wgt. Grs.	VELOCITY (fps)					ENERGY (ft. lbs.)					TRAJ. (in.)			
		Muzzle	100 yds.	200 yds.	300 yds.	400 yds.	Muzzle	100 yds.	200 yds.	300 yds.	400 yds.	100 yds.	200 yds.	300 yds.	400 yds.
25-06 Rem.	87	3440	2995	2591	2222	1884	2286	1733	1297	954	686	2	1.1	-2.5	-14.4
25-06 Rem.	90	3350	3001	2679	2378	2098	2243	1790	1434	1130	879	1.2	0	-6	-18.3
25-06 Rem.	90	3440	3043	2680	2344	2034	2364	1850	1435	1098	827	2	1.8	-3.3	-15.6
25-06 Rem.	100	3230	2893	2580	2287	2014	2316	1858	1478	1161	901	2	0.8	-5.7	-18.9
25-06 Rem.	117	2990	2770	2570	2370	2190	2320	2000	1715	1465	1246	2.5	1	-7.9	-26.6
25-06 Rem.*	120	2990	2730	2484	2252	2032	2382	1985	1644	1351	1100	2.5	1.2	-5.3	-19.6
25-06 Rem.	122	2930	2706	2492	2289	2095	2325	1983	1683	1419	1189	2.5	1.8	-4.5	-17.5
25-06 R. Superformance	117	3110	2861	2626	2403	2191	2512	2127	1792	1500	1246	1.4	0	-6.4	-18.9
25 WSSM	85	3470	3156	2863	2589	2331	2273	1880	1548	1266	1026	1	0	-5.2	-15.7
25 WSSM	115	3060	2844	2639	2442	2254	2392	2066	1778	1523	1398	1.4	0	-6.4	-18.6
25 WSSM	120	2990	2717	2459	2216	1987	2383	1967	1612	1309	1053	1.6	0	-7.4	-21.8
257 Wea. Mag.	87	3825	3456	3118	2805	2513	2826	2308	1870	1520	1220	2	2.7	-0.3	-7.6
257 Wea. Mag.	90	3550	3184	2848	2537	2246	2518	2026	1621	1286	1008	1	0	-5.3	-16
257 Wea. Mag.	100	3555	3237	2941	2665	2404	2806	2326	1920	1576	1283	2.5	3.2	0	-8
257 Wea. Mag.	110	3330	3069	2823	2591	2370	2708	2300	1947	1639	1372	1.1	0	-5.5	-16.1
257 Scramjet	100	3745	3450	3173	2912	2666	3114	2643	2235	1883	1578	2.1	2.77	0	-6.93
6.5															
6.5 Grendel	123	2590	2420	2256	2099	1948	1832	1599	1390	1203	1037	1.8	0	-8.6	-25.1
6.5x47 Lapua	123	2887	NA	2554	NA	2244	2285	NA	1788	NA	1380	NA	4.53	0	-10.7
6.5x50mm Jap.	139	2360	2160	1970	1790	1620	1720	1440	1195	985	810	2.5	-1	-13.5	0
6.5x50mm Jap.	156	2070	1830	1610	1430	1260	1475	1155	900	695	550	2.5	-4	-23.8	0
6.5x52mm Car.	139	2580	2360	2160	1970	1790	2045	1725	1440	1195	985	2.5	0	-9.9	-29
6.5x52mm Car.	156	2430	2170	1930	1700	1500	2045	1630	1285	1005	780	2.5	-1	-13.9	0
6.5x52mm Carcano	160	2250	1963	1700	1467	1271	1798	1369	1027	764	574	3.8	0	-15.9	-48.1
6.5x55mm Swe.	93	2625	2350	2090	1850	1630	1425	1140	905	705	550	2.4	0	-10.3	-31.1
6.5x55 Swe.	93	3281	2952	2796	2359	-	2223	1799	1614	1149	-	1.2	0	-6.2	-
6.5x55mm Swe.	123	2750	2570	2400	2240	2080	2065	1810	1580	1370	1185	1.9	0	-7.9	-22.9
6.5x55mm Swe.	139/140	2850	2640	2440	2250	2070	2525	2170	1855	1575	1330	2.5	1.6	-5.4	-18.9
6.5x55mm Swe.	140	2550	NA	NA	NA	NA	2020	NA	NA	NA	NA	0	0	0	0
6.5x55mm Swe.	140	2735	2563	2397	2237	2084	2325	2041	1786	1556	1350	1.9	0	-8	-22.9
6.5x55mm Swe.	156	2650	2370	2110	1870	1650	2425	1950	1550	1215	945	2.5	0	-10.3	-30.6
260 Rem.	100	3200	2917	2652	2402	2165	2273	1889	1561	1281	1041	1.3	0	-6.3	-18.6
260 Rem.	130	2800	2613	2433	2261	2096	2262	1970	1709	1476	1268	1.8	0	-7.7	-22.2
260 Remington	125	2875	2669	2473	2285	2105	2294	1977	1697	1449	1230	1.71	0	-7.4	-21.4
260 Remington	140	2750	2544	2347	2158	1979	2351	2011	1712	1448	1217	2.2	0	-8.6	-24.6
6.5 Creedmoor	93	3314	2990	2689	2407	-	2267	1846	1493	1196	-	1.1	0	-5.9	-
6.5 Creedmoor	120	3020	2815	2619	2430	2251	2430	2111	1827	1574	1350	1.4	0	-6.5	-18.9
6.5 Creedmoor	120	3050	2850	2659	2476	2300	2479	2164	1884	1634	1310	1.4	0	-6.3	-18.3
6.5 Creedmoor	130	2875	2709	2550	2396	2247	2386	2119	1877	1657	1457	1.6	0	-6.9	-20
6.5 Creedmoor	140	2550	2380	2217	2060	1910	2021	1761	1527	1319	1134	2.3	0	-9.4	-27
6.5 Creedmoor	140	2710	2557	2410	2267	2129	2283	2033	1805	1598	1410	1.9	0	-7.9	-22.6
6.5 Creedmoor	140	2820	2654	2494	2339	2190	2472	2179	1915	1679	1467	1.7	0	-7.2	-20.6
6.5 C. Superformance	129	2950	2756	2570	2392	2221	2492	2175	1892	1639	1417	1.5	0	-6.8	-19.7
6.5x52R	117	2208	1856	1544	1287	1104	1267	895	620	431	317	0	-8.7	-32.2	—
6.5x57	131	2543	2295	2060	1841	1638	1882	1532	1235	986	780	0	-5.1	-18.5	-42.1
6.5 PRC	143	2960	2808	2661	2519	2381	2782	2503	2248	2014	1800	1.5	0	-6.4	-18.2
6.5 PRC	147	2910	2775	2645	2518	2395	2764	2514	2283	2069	1871	1.5	0	-6.5	-18.4
6.5-284 Norma	142	3025	2890	2758	2631	2507	2886	2634	2400	2183	1982	1.13	0	-5.7	-16.4
6.5-284 Norma	156	2790	2531	2287	2056	-	2697	2220	1812	1465	-	1.9	0	-8.6	-
6.5 Weatherby RPM	127	3225	3011	2809	2615	2429	2933	2554	2224	1928	1664	3	3.7	0	-8.8
6.5 Weatherby RPM	140	2975	2772	2579	2393	2215	2751	2389	2067	1780	1525	3.8	4.5	0	-10.6
6.5 Weatherby RPM	140	3075	2885	2703	2529	2361	2939	2587	2272	1988	1766	3.4	4.1	0	-9.5
6.71 (264) Phantom	120	3150	2929	2718	2517	2325	2645	2286	1969	1698	1440	1.3	0	-6	-17.5
6.5 Rem. Mag.	120	3210	2905	2621	2353	2102	2745	2248	1830	1475	1177	2.5	1.7	-4.1	-16.3
264 Win. Mag.	100	3400	3104	2828	2568	2322	2566	2139	1775	1464	1197	1.1	0	-5.4	-16.1
264 Win. Mag.	125	3200	2978	2767	2566	2373	2841	2461	2125	1827	1563	1.2	0	-5.8	-16.8
264 Win. Mag.	130	3100	2900	2709	2526	2350	2773	2427	2118	1841	1594	1.3	0	-6.1	-17.6
264 Win. Mag.	140	3030	2782	2548	2326	2114	2854	2406	2018	1682	1389	2.5	1.4	-5.1	-18
6.5 Nosler	129	3400	3213	3035	2863	2698	3310	2957	2638	2348	2085	0.9	0	-4.7	-13.6
6.5 Nosler	140	3300	3118	2943	2775	2613	3119	2784	2481	2205	1955	1	0	-5	-14.6
6.71 (264) Blackbird	140	3480	3261	3053	2855	2665	3766	3307	2899	2534	2208	2.4	3.1	0	-7.4
6.8 REM SPC	90	2840	2444	2083	1756	1469	1611	1194	867	616	431	2.2	0	-3.9	-32
6.8 REM SPC	110	2570	2338	2118	1910	1716	1613	1335	1095	891	719	2.4	0	-6.3	-20.8

Cartridge	Bullet Wgt. Grs.	VELOCITY (fps)					ENERGY (ft. lbs.)					TRAJ. (in.)			
		Muzzle	100 yds.	200 yds.	300 yds.	400 yds.	Muzzle	100 yds.	200 yds.	300 yds.	400 yds.	100 yds.	200 yds.	300 yds.	400 yds.
6.8 REM SPC	120	2460	2250	2051	1863	1687	1612	1349	1121	925	758	2.3	0	-10.5	-31.1
6.8mm Rem.	115	2775	2472	2190	1926	1683	1966	1561	1224	947	723	2.1	0	-3.7	-9.4
27															
270 Win.	96	3543	3173	2834	2519	-	2676	2146	1712	1352	-	0.9	0	-5.3	-
270 Win. (Rem.)	115	2710	2482	2265	2059	NA	1875	1485	1161	896	NA	0	4.8	-17.3	0
270 Win.	120	2675	2288	1935	1619	1351	1907	1395	998	699	486	2.6	0	-12	-37.4
270 Win.	140	2940	2747	2563	2386	2216	2687	2346	2042	1770	1526	1.8	0	-6.8	-19.8
270 Win. Supreme	130	3150	2881	2628	2388	2161	2865	2396	1993	1646	1348	1.3	0	-6.4	-18.9
270 Win. Supreme	150	2930	2693	2468	2254	2051	2860	2416	2030	1693	1402	1.7	0	-7.4	-21.6
270 W. Superformance	130	3200	2984	2788	2582	2393	2955	2570	2228	1924	1653	1.2	0	-5.7	-16.7
270 Winchester	100	3430	3021	2649	2305	1988	2612	2027	1557	1179	877	2	1	-4.9	-17.5
270 Winchester	130	3060	2776	2510	2259	2022	2702	2225	1818	1472	1180	2.5	1.4	-5.3	-18.2
270 Winchester	135	3000	2780	2570	2369	2178	2697	2315	1979	1682	1421	2.5	1.4	-6	-17.6
270 Winchester*	140	2940	2700	2480	2260	2060	2685	2270	1905	1590	1315	2.5	1.8	-4.6	-17.9
270 Winchester*	150	2850	2585	2336	2100	1879	2705	2226	1817	1468	1175	2.5	1.2	-6.5	-22
277 Fury	140	3000													
270 WSM	130	3275	3041	2820	2609	2408	3096	2669	2295	1564	1673	1.1	0	-5.5	-16.1
270 WSM	140	3125	2865	2619	2386	2165	3035	2559	2132	1769	1457	1.4	0	-6.5	-19
270 WSM	150	3000	2795	2599	2412	2232	2997	2601	2250	1937	1659	1.5	0	-6.6	-19.2
270 WSM	150	3120	2923	2734	2554	2380	3242	2845	2490	2172	1886	1.3	0	-5.9	-17.2
6.8 Western	162	2875	2711	2552	2399	2251	2973	2642	2342	2070	1823	1.6	0	-7	-20
6.8 Western	165	2970	2815	2667	2524	2385	3226	2902	2605	2333	2084	1.2	0	-6.3	-18.1
6.8 Western	170	2920	2754	2593	2439	2289	3218	2862	2538	2244	1978	1.3	0	-6.7	-19.3
6.8 Western	175	2835	2686	2541	2402	2266	3123	2803	2509	2241	1995	1.7	0	-7	-20.1
270 Wea. Mag.	100	3760	3380	3033	2712	2412	3139	2537	2042	1633	1292	2	2.4	-1.2	-10.1
270 Wea. Mag.	130	3375	3119	2878	2649	2432	3287	2808	2390	2026	1707	2.5	-2.9	-0.9	-9.9
270 Wea. Mag.	130	3450	3194	2958	2732	2517	3435	2949	2525	2143	1828	1	0	-4.9	-14.5
270 Wea. Mag.*	150	3245	3036	2837	2647	2465	3507	3070	2681	2334	2023	2.5	2.6	-1.8	-11.4
27 Nosler	150	3300	3143	2983	2828	2676	3638	3289	2964	2663	2385	1	0	-4.9	-14.2
7mm															
7mm BR	140	2216	2012	1821	1643	1481	1525	1259	1031	839	681	2	-3.7	-20	0
275 Rigby	140	2680	2455	2242	2040	1848	2233	1874	1563	1292	1062	2.2	0	-9.1	-26.5
7mm Mauser*	139/140	2660	2435	2221	2018	1827	2199	1843	1533	1266	1037	2.5	0	-9.6	-27.7
7mm Mauser	139	2740	2556	2379	2209	2046	2317	2016	1747	1506	1292	1.9	0	-8.1	-23.3
7mm Mauser	154	2600	2490	2300	2120	1940	2475	2120	1810	1530	1285	2.5	0.8	-7.5	-23.5
7mm Mauser	175	2440	2137	1857	1603	1382	2313	1774	1340	998	742	2.5	-1.7	-16.1	0
7x30 Waters	120	2700	2300	1930	1600	1330	1940	1405	990	685	470	2.5	-0.2	-12.3	0
7x30 Waters	120	2700	2425	2167	1926	1702	1942	1567	1251	988	772	2.2	0	-9.7	-28.8
7mm-08 Rem.	120	2675	2435	2207	1992	1790	1907	1579	1298	1057	854	2.2	0	-9.4	-27.5
7mm-08 Rem.	120	3000	2725	2467	2223	1992	2398	1979	1621	1316	1058	2	0	-7.6	-22.3
7mm-08 Rem.	139	2840	2608	2387	2177	1978	2489	2098	1758	1463	1207	1.8	0	-7.9	-23.2
7mm-08 Rem.*	140	2860	2625	2402	2189	1988	2542	2142	1793	1490	1228	2.5	0.8	-6.9	-21.9
7mm-08 Rem.	154	2715	2510	2315	2128	1950	2520	2155	1832	1548	1300	2.5	1	-7	-22.7
7-08 R. Superformance	139	2950	2857	2571	2393	2222	2686	2345	2040	1768	1524	1.5	0	-6.8	-19.7
7x64mm	173	2526	2260	2010	1777	1565	2452	1962	1552	1214	941	0	-5.3	-19.3	-44.4
7x64mm Bren.	140	2950	2710	2483	2266	2061	2705	2283	1910	1597	1320	1.5	0	-2.9	-7.3
7x64mm Bren.	154	2820	2610	2420	2230	2050	2720	2335	1995	1695	1430	2.5	1.4	-5.7	-19.9
7x64mm Bren.*	160	2850	2669	2495	2327	2166	2885	2530	2211	1924	1667	2.5	1.6	-4.8	-17.8
7x64mm Bren.	175	2650	2445	2248	2061	1883	2728	2322	1964	1650	1378	2.2	0	-9.1	-26.4
7x65mmR	173	2608	2337	2082	1844	1626	2613	2098	1666	1307	1015	0	-4.9	-17.9	-41.9
275 Rigby	139	2680	2456	2242	2040	1848	2217	1861	1552	1284	1054	2.2	0	-9.1	-26.5
284 Winchester	150	2860	2595	2344	2108	1886	2724	2243	1830	1480	1185	2.5	0.8	-7.3	-23.2
280 R. Superformance	139	3090	2890	2699	2516	2341	2946	2578	2249	1954	1691	1.3	0	-6.1	-17.7
280 Rem.	139	3090	2891	2700	2518	2343	2947	2579	2250	1957	1694	1.3	0	-6.1	-17.7
280 Remington	140	3000	2758	2528	2309	2102	2797	2363	1986	1657	1373	2.5	1.4	-5.2	-18.3
280 Remington*	150	2890	2624	2373	2135	1912	2781	2293	1875	1518	1217	2.5	0.8	-7.1	-22.6
280 Remington	160	2840	2637	2442	2556	2078	2866	2471	2120	1809	1535	2.5	0.8	-6.7	-21
280 Remington	165	2820	2510	2220	1950	1701	2913	2308	1805	1393	1060	2.5	0.4	-8.8	-26.5
280 Ack. Imp.	140	3150	2946	2752	2566	2387	3084	2698	2354	2047	1772	1.3	0	-5.8	-17
280 Ack. Imp.	150	2900	2712	2533	2360	2194	2800	2450	2136	1855	1603	1.6	0	-7	-20.3
280 Ack. Imp.	160	2950	2751	2561	2379	2205	3091	2686	2331	2011	1727	1.5	0	-6.9	-19.9
7x61mm S&H Sup.	154	3060	2720	2400	2100	1820	3200	2520	1965	1505	1135	2.5	1.8	-5	-19.8
7mm Dakota	160	3200	3001	2811	2630	2455	3637	3200	2808	2456	2140	2.1	1.9	-2.8	-12.5
7mm Rem. Mag.	127	3314	3050	2802	2567	-	3096	2623	2214	1858	-	1.1	0	-5.5	-
7mm Rem. Mag.	139	3190	2986	2791	2605	2427	3141	2752	2405	2095	1817	1.2	0	-5.7	-16.5
7mm Rem. Mag. (Rem.)	140	2710	2482	2265	2059	NA	2283	1915	1595	1318	NA	0	-4.5	-1.57	0

Cartridge	Bullet Wgt. Grs.	VELOCITY (fps)					ENERGY (ft. lbs.)					TRAJ. (in.)			
		Muzzle	100 yds.	200 yds.	300 yds.	400 yds.	Muzzle	100 yds.	200 yds.	300 yds.	400 yds.	100 yds.	200 yds.	300 yds.	400 yds.
7mm Rem. Mag.*	139/140	3150	2930	2710	2510	2320	3085	2660	2290	1960	1670	2.5	2.4	-2.4	-12.7
7mm Rem. Mag.	150/154	3110	2830	2568	2320	2085	3221	2667	2196	1792	1448	2.5	1.6	-4.6	-16.5
7mm Rem. Mag.*	160/162	2950	2730	2520	2320	2120	3090	2650	2250	1910	1600	2.5	1.8	-4.4	-17.8
7mm Rem. Mag.	165	2900	2699	2507	2324	2147	3081	2669	2303	1978	1689	2.5	1.2	-5.9	-19
7mm Rem Mag.	175	2860	2645	2440	2244	2057	3178	2718	2313	1956	1644	2.5	1	-6.5	-20.7
7 R.M. Superformance	139	3240	3033	2836	2648	2467	3239	2839	2482	2163	1877	1.1	0	-5.5	-15.9
7 R.M. Superformance	154	3100	2914	2736	2565	2401	3286	2904	2560	2250	1970	1.3	0	-5.9	-17.2
7mm Rem. SA ULTRA MAG	140	3175	2934	2707	2490	2283	3033	2676	2277	1927	1620	1.3	0	-6	-17.7
7mm Rem. SA ULTRA MAG	150	3110	2828	2563	2313	2077	3221	2663	2188	1782	1437	2.5	2.1	-3.6	-15.8
7mm Rem. SA ULTRA MAG	160	2850	2676	2508	2347	2192	2885	2543	2235	1957	1706	1.7	0	-7.2	-20.7
7mm Rem. SA ULTRA MAG	160	2960	2762	2572	2390	2215	3112	2709	2350	2029	1743	2.6	2.2	-3.6	-15.4
7mm Rem. WSM	140	3225	3008	2801	2603	2414	3233	2812	2438	2106	1812	1.2	0	-5.6	-16.4
7mm Rem. WSM	160	2990	2744	2512	2081	1883	3176	2675	2241	1864	1538	1.6	0	-7.1	-20.8
7mm Wea. Mag.	139	3300	3091	2891	2701	2519	3361	2948	2580	2252	1958	1.1	0	-5.2	-15.2
7mm Wea. Mag.	140	3225	2970	2729	2501	2283	3233	2741	2315	1943	1621	2.5	2	-3.2	-14
7mm Wea. Mag.	140	3340	3127	2925	2732	2546	3467	3040	2659	2320	2016	0	-2.1	-8.2	-19
7mm Wea. Mag.	150	3175	2957	2751	2553	2364	3357	2913	2520	2171	1861	0	-2.5	-9.6	-22
7mm Wea. Mag.	154	3260	3023	2799	2586	2382	3539	3044	2609	2227	1890	2.5	2.8	-1.5	-10.8
7mm Wea. Mag.*	160	3200	3004	2816	2637	2464	3637	3205	2817	2469	2156	2.5	2.7	-1.5	-10.6
7mm Wea. Mag.	165	2950	2747	2553	2367	2189	3188	2765	2388	2053	1756	2.5	1.8	-4.2	-16.4
7mm Wea. Mag.	175	2910	2693	2486	2288	2098	3293	2818	2401	2033	1711	2.5	1.2	-5.9	-19.4
7.21(.284) Tomahawk	140	3300	3118	2943	2774	2612	3386	3022	2693	2393	2122	2.3	3.2	0	-7.7
7mm STW	140	3300	3086	2889	2697	2513	3384	2966	2594	2261	1963	0	-2.1	-8.5	-19.6
7mm STW	140	3325	3064	2818	2585	2364	3436	2918	2468	2077	1737	2.3	1.8	-3	-13.1
7mm STW	150	3175	2957	2751	2553	2364	3357	2913	2520	2171	1861	0	-2.5	-9.6	-22
7mm STW	175	2900	2760	2625	2493	2366	3267	2960	2677	2416	2175	0	-3.1	-11.2	-24.9
7mm STW Supreme	160	3150	2894	2652	2422	2204	3526	2976	2499	2085	1727	1.3	0	-6.3	-18.5
7mm Rem. Ultra Mag.	140	3425	3184	2956	2740	2534	3646	3151	2715	2333	1995	1.7	1.6	-2.6	-11.4
7mm Rem. Ultra Mag.	160	3225	3035	2854	2680	2512	3694	3273	2894	2551	2242	0	-2.3	-8.8	-20.2
7mm Rem. Ultra Mag.	174	3040	2896	2756	2621	2490	3590	3258	2952	2669	2409	0	-2.6	-9.9	-22.2
7mm Firehawk	140	3625	3373	3135	2909	2695	4084	3536	3054	2631	2258	2.2	2.9	0	-7.03
7.21 (.284) Firebird	140	3750	3522	3306	3101	2905	4372	3857	3399	2990	2625	1.6	2.4	0	-6
.28 Nosler	160	3300	3114	2930	2753	2583	3883	3444	3049	2693	2371	1.1	0	-5.1	-14.9
30															
300 ACC Blackout	110	2150	1886	1646	1432	1254	1128	869	661	501	384	0	-8.3	-29.6	-67.8
300 AAC Blackout	125	2250	2031	1826	1636	1464	1404	1145	926	743	595	0	-7	-24.4	-54.8
300 AAC Blackout	220	1000	968	-	-	-	488	457	-	-	-	0	-	-	-
30 Carbine	110	1990	1567	1236	1035	923	977	600	373	262	208	0	-13.5	0	0
30 Carbine	110	2000	1601	1279	1067	—	977	626	399	278	—	0	-12.9	-47.2	—
300 Whisper	110	2375	2094	1834	1597	NA	1378	1071	822	623	NA	3.2	0	-13.6	NA
300 Whisper	208	1020	988	959	NA	NA	480	451	422	NA	NA	0	-34.1	NA	NA
303 Savage	190	1890	1612	1327	1183	1055	1507	1096	794	591	469	2.5	-7.6	0	0
30 Remington	170	2120	1822	1555	1328	1153	1696	1253	913	666	502	2.5	-4.7	-26.3	0
7.62x39mm Rus.	123	2360	2049	1764	1511	1296	1521	1147	850	623	459	3.4	0	-14.7	-44.7
7.62x39mm Rus.	123/125	2300	2030	1780	1550	1350	1445	1125	860	655	500	2.5	-2	-17.5	0
30-30 Win.	55	3400	2693	2085	1570	1187	1412	886	521	301	172	2	0	-10.2	-35
30-30 Win.	125	2570	2090	1660	1320	1080	1830	1210	770	480	320	-2	-2.6	-19.9	0
30-30 Win.	140	2500	2198	1918	1662	—	1943	1501	1143	858	—	2.9	0	-12.4	—
30-30 Win.	150	2390	2040	1723	1447	1225	1902	1386	989	697	499	0	-7.5	-27	-63
30-30 Win. Supreme	150	2480	2095	1747	1446	1209	2049	1462	1017	697	487	0	-6.5	-24.5	0
30-30 Win.	160	2300	1997	1719	1473	1268	1879	1416	1050	771	571	2.5	-2.9	-20.2	0
30-30 Win. Lever Evolution	160	2400	2150	1916	1699	NA	2046	1643	1304	1025	NA	3	0.2	-12.1	NA
30-30 PMC Cowboy	170	1300	1198	1121	—	—	638	474	—	—	—	0	-27	0	0
30-30 Win.*	170	2200	1895	1619	1381	1191	1827	1355	989	720	535	2.5	-5.8	-23.6	0
300 Savage	150	2630	2354	2094	1853	1631	2303	1845	1462	1143	886	2.5	-0.4	-10.1	-30.7
300 Savage	150	2740	2499	2272	2056	1852	2500	2081	1718	1407	1143	2.1	0	-8.8	-25.8
300 Savage	180	2350	2137	1935	1754	1570	2207	1825	1496	1217	985	2.5	-1.6	-15.2	0
30-40 Krag	180	2430	2213	2007	1813	1632	2360	1957	1610	1314	1064	2.5	-1.4	-13.8	0
7.65x53mm Arg.	180	2590	2390	2200	2010	1830	2685	2280	1925	1615	1345	2.5	0	-27.6	0
7.5x53mm Argentine	150	2785	2519	2269	2032	1814	2583	2113	1714	1376	1096	2	0	-8.8	-25.5
308 Marlin Express	140	2800	2532	2279	2040	1818	2437	1992	1614	1294	1207	2	0	-8.7	-25.8
308 Marlin Express	160	2660	2430	2226	2026	1836	2513	2111	1761	1457	1197	3	1.7	-6.7	-23.5
307 Winchester	150	2760	2321	1924	1575	1289	2530	1795	1233	826	554	2.5	-1.5	-13.6	0
307 WInchester	160	2650	2386	2137	1904	1688	2494	2022	1622	1287	1688	2.3	0	-10	-29.6
7.5x55 Swiss	180	2650	2450	2250	2060	1880	2805	2390	2020	1700	1415	2.5	0.6	-8.1	-24.9
7.5x55mm Swiss	165	2720	2515	2319	2132	1954	2710	2317	1970	1665	1398	2	0	-8.5	-24.6

Cartridge	Bullet Wgt. Grs.	VELOCITY (fps)					ENERGY (ft. lbs.)					TRAJ. (in.)			
		Muzzle	100 yds.	200 yds.	300 yds.	400 yds.	Muzzle	100 yds.	200 yds.	300 yds.	400 yds.	100 yds.	200 yds.	300 yds.	400 yds.
30 Remington AR	123/125	2800	2465	2154	1867	1606	2176	1686	1288	967	716	2.1	0	-9.7	-29.4
308 Winchester	55	3770	3215	2726	2286	1888	1735	1262	907	638	435	-2	1.4	-3.8	-15.8
308 Win.	110	3165	2830	2520	2230	1960	2447	1956	1551	1215	938	1.4	0	-6.9	-20.9
308 Win. PDX1	120	2850	2497	2171	NA	NA	2164	1662	1256	NA	NA	0	-2.8	NA	NA
308 Win.	139	2904	2609	2333	2074	-	2602	2101	1680	1327	-	1.7	0	-8.1	-
308 Winchester	150	2820	2533	2263	2009	1774	2648	2137	1705	1344	1048	2.5	0.4	-8.5	-26.1
308 W. Superformance	150	3000	2772	2555	2348	1962	2997	2558	2173	1836	1540	1.5	0	-6.9	-20
308 Win.	155	2775	2553	2342	2141	1950	2650	2243	1887	1577	1308	1.9	0	-8.3	-24.2
308 Win.	155	2850	2640	2438	2247	2064	2795	2398	2047	1737	1466	1.8	0	-7.5	-22.1
308 Winchester	165	2700	2440	2194	1963	1748	2670	2180	1763	1411	1199	2.5	0	-9.7	-28.5
308 Winchester	168	2680	2493	2314	2143	1979	2678	2318	1998	1713	1460	2.5	0	-8.9	-25.3
308 Win. Super Match	168	2870	2647	2462	2284	2114	3008	2613	2261	1946	1667	1.7	0	-7.5	-21.6
308 Win. (Fed.)	170	2000	1740	1510	NA	NA	1510	1145	860	NA	NA	0	0	0	0
308 Winchester	178	2620	2415	2220	2034	1857	2713	2306	1948	1635	1363	2.5	0	-9.6	-27.6
308 Win. Super Match	178	2780	2609	2444	2285	2132	3054	2690	2361	2064	1797	1.8	0	-7.6	-21.9
308 Winchester*	180	2620	2393	2178	1974	1782	2743	2288	1896	1557	1269	2.5	-0.2	-10.2	-28.5
30-06 Spfd.	55	4080	3485	2965	2502	2083	2033	1483	1074	764	530	2	1.9	-2.1	-11.7
30-06 Spfd. (Rem.)	125	2660	2335	2034	1757	NA	1964	1513	1148	856	NA	0	-5.2	-18.9	0
30-06 Spfd.	125	2700	2412	2143	1891	1660	2023	1615	1274	993	765	2.3	0	-9.9	-29.5
30-06 Spfd.	125	3140	2780	2447	2138	1853	2736	2145	1662	1279	953	2	1	-6.2	-21
30-06 Spfd.	139	2986	2686	2405	2142	-	2751	2227	1785	1416	-	1.6	0	-7.6	-
30-06 Spfd.	150	2910	2617	2342	2083	1853	2820	2281	1827	1445	1135	2.5	0.8	-7.2	-23.4
30-06 Superformance	150	3080	2848	2617	2417	2216	3159	2700	2298	1945	1636	1.4	0	-6.4	-18.9
30-06 Spfd.	152	2910	2654	2413	2184	1968	2858	2378	1965	1610	1307	2.5	1	-6.6	-21.3
30-06 Spfd.*	165	2800	2534	2283	2047	1825	2872	2352	1909	1534	1220	2.5	0.4	-8.4	-25.5
30-06 Spfd.	168	2710	2522	2346	2169	2003	2739	2372	2045	1754	1497	2.5	0.4	-8	-23.5
30-06 M1 Garand	168	2710	2523	2343	2171	2006	2739	2374	2048	1758	1501	2.3	0	-8.6	-24.6
30-06 Spfd. (Fed.)	170	2000	1740	1510	NA	NA	1510	1145	860	NA	NA	0	0	0	0
30-06 Spfd.	178	2720	2511	2311	2121	1939	2924	2491	2111	1777	1486	2.5	0.4	-8.2	-24.6
30-06 Spfd.*	180	2700	2469	2250	2042	1846	2913	2436	2023	1666	1362	-2.5	0	-9.3	-27
30-06 Superformance	180	2820	2630	2447	2272	2104	3178	2764	2393	2063	1769	1.8	0	-7.6	-21.9
30-06 Spfd.	220	2410	2130	1870	1632	1422	2837	2216	1708	1301	988	2.5	-1.7	-18	0
30-06 High Energy	180	2880	2690	2500	2320	2150	3315	2880	2495	2150	1845	1.7	0	-7.2	-21
30 T/C	150	2920	2696	2483	2280	2087	2849	2421	2054	1732	1450	1.7	0	-7.3	-21.3
30 T/C Superformance	150	3000	2772	2555	2348	2151	2997	2558	2173	1836	1540	1.5	0	-6.9	-20
30 T/C Superformance	165	2850	2644	2447	2258	2078	2975	2560	2193	1868	1582	1.7	0	-7.6	-22
300 Rem SA Ultra Mag	150	3200	2901	2622	2359	2112	3410	2803	2290	1854	1485	1.3	0	-6.4	-19.1
300 Rem SA Ultra Mag	165	3075	2792	2527	2276	2040	3464	2856	2339	1898	1525	1.5	0	-7	-20.7
300 Rem SA Ultra Mag	180	2960	2761	2571	2389	2214	3501	3047	2642	2280	1959	2.6	2.2	-3.6	-15.4
300 Rem. SA Ultra Mag	200	2800	2644	2494	2348	2208	3841	3104	2761	2449	2164	0	-3.5	-12.5	-27.9
7.82 (308) Patriot	150	3250	2999	2762	2537	2323	3519	2997	2542	2145	1798	1.2	0	-5.8	-16.9
300 RCM	150	3265	3023	2794	2577	2369	3550	3043	2600	2211	1870	1.2	0	-5.6	-16.5
300 RCM Superformance	150	3310	3065	2833	2613	2404	3648	3128	2673	2274	1924	1.1	0	-5.4	-16
300 RCM Superformance	165	3185	2964	2753	2552	2360	3716	3217	2776	2386	2040	1.2	0	-5.8	-17
300 RCM Superformance	180	3040	2840	2649	2466	2290	3693	3223	2804	2430	2096	1.4	0	-6.4	-18.5
300 WSM	150	3300	3061	2834	2619	2414	3628	3121	2676	2285	1941	1.1	0	-5.4	-15.9
300 WSM	180	2970	2741	2524	2317	2120	3526	3005	2547	2147	1797	1.6	0	-7	-20.5
300 WSM	180	3010	2923	2734	2554	2380	3242	2845	2490	2172	1886	1.3	0	-5.9	-17.2
300 WSM	190	2875	2729	2588	2451	2319	3486	3142	2826	2535	2269	0	3.2	-11.5	-25.7
308 Norma Mag.	180	2975	2787	2608	2435	2269	3536	3105	2718	2371	2058	0	-3	-11.1	-25
308 Norma Mag.	180	3020	2820	2630	2440	2270	3645	3175	2755	2385	2050	2.5	2	-3.5	-14.8
300 Dakota	200	3000	2824	2656	2493	2336	3996	3542	3131	2760	2423	2.2	1.5	-4	-15.2
300 H&H Mag.	180	2870	2678	2494	2318	2148	3292	2866	2486	2147	1844	1.7	0	-7.3	-21.6
300 H&H Magnum*	180	2880	2640	2412	2196	1990	3315	2785	2325	1927	1583	2.5	0.8	-6.8	-21.7
300 H&H Mag.	200	2750	2596	2447	2303	2164	3357	2992	2659	2355	2079	1.8	0	-7.6	-21.8
300 H&H Magnum	220	2550	2267	2002	1757	NA	3167	2510	1958	1508	NA	-2.5	-0.4	-12	0
300 Win. Mag.	139	3363	3036	2733	2449	-	3490	2845	2305	1851	-	1.1	0	-5.7	-
300 Win. Mag.	150	3290	2951	2636	2342	2068	3605	2900	2314	1827	1424	2.5	1.9	-3.8	-15.8
300 WM Superformance	150	3400	3150	2914	2690	2477	3850	3304	2817	2409	2043	1	0	-5.1	-15
300 Win. Mag.	165	3100	2877	2665	2462	2269	3522	3033	2603	2221	1897	2.5	2.4	-3	-16.9
300 Win. Mag.	178	2900	2760	2568	2375	2191	3509	3030	2606	2230	1897	2.5	1.4	-5	-17.6
300 Win. Mag.	178	2960	2770	2588	2413	2245	3463	3032	2647	2301	1992	1.5	0	-6.7	-19.4
300 WM Super Match	178	2960	2770	2587	2412	2243	3462	3031	2645	2298	1988	1.5	0	-6.7	-19.4
300 Win. Mag.*	180	2960	2745	2540	2344	2157	3501	3011	2578	2196	1859	2.5	1.2	-5.5	-18.5
300 WM Superformance	180	3130	2927	2732	2546	2366	3917	3424	2983	2589	2238	1.3	0	-5.9	-17.3
300 Win. Mag.	190	2885	1691	2506	2327	2156	3511	3055	2648	2285	1961	2.5	1.2	-5.7	-19

Cartridge	Bullet Wgt. Grs.	VELOCITY (fps)					ENERGY (ft. lbs.)					TRAJ. (in.)			
		Muzzle	100 yds.	200 yds.	300 yds.	400 yds.	Muzzle	100 yds.	200 yds.	300 yds.	400 yds.	100 yds.	200 yds.	300 yds.	400 yds.
300 Win. Mag.	195	2930	2760	2596	2438	2286	3717	3297	2918	2574	2262	1.5	0	-6.7	-19.4
300 Win. Mag.*	200	2825	2595	2376	2167	1970	3545	2991	2508	2086	1742	-2.5	1.6	-4.7	-17.2
300 Win. Mag.	220	2680	2448	2228	2020	1823	3508	2927	2424	1993	1623	2.5	0	-9.5	-27.5
300 Rem. Ultra Mag.	150	3450	3208	2980	2762	2556	3964	3427	2956	2541	2175	1.7	1.5	-2.6	-11.2
300 Rem. Ultra Mag.	150	2910	2686	2473	2279	2077	2820	2403	2037	1716	1436	1.7	0	-7.4	-21.5
300 Rem. Ultra Mag.	165	3350	3099	2862	2938	2424	4110	3518	3001	2549	2152	1.1	0	-5.3	-15.6
300 Rem. Ultra Mag.	180	3250	3037	2834	2640	2454	4221	3686	3201	2786	2407	2.4	0	-3	-12.7
300 Rem. Ultra Mag.	180	2960	2774	2505	2294	2093	3501	2971	2508	2103	1751	2.7	2.2	-3.8	-16.4
300 Rem. Ultra Mag.	200	3032	2791	2562	2345	2138	4083	3459	2916	2442	2030	1.5	0	-6.8	-19.9
300 Rem. Ultra Mag.	210	2920	2790	2665	2543	2424	3975	3631	3311	3015	2740	1.5	0	-6.4	-18.1
30 Nosler	180	3200	3004	2815	2635	2462	4092	3606	3168	2774	2422	0	-2.4	-9.1	-20.9
30 Nosler	210	3000	2868	2741	2617	2497	4196	3836	3502	3193	2906	0	-2.7	-10.1	-22.5
300 Wea. Mag.	100	3900	3441	3038	2652	2305	3714	2891	2239	1717	1297	2	2.6	-0.6	-8.7
300 Wea. Mag.	150	3375	3126	2892	2670	2459	3794	3255	2786	2374	2013	1	0	-5.2	-15.3
300 Wea. Mag.	150	3600	3307	3033	2776	2533	4316	3642	3064	2566	2137	2.5	3.2	0	-8.1
300 Wea. Mag.	165	3140	2921	2713	2515	2325	3612	3126	2697	2317	1980	1.3	0	-6	-17.5
300 Wea. Mag.	165	3450	3210	3000	2792	2593	4360	3796	3297	2855	2464	2.5	3.2	0	-7.8
300 Wea. Mag.	178	3120	2902	2695	2497	2308	3847	3329	2870	2464	2104	2.5	-1.7	-3.6	-14.7
300 Wea. Mag.	180	3330	3110	2910	2710	2520	4430	3875	3375	2935	2540	1	0	-5.2	-15.1
300 Wea. Mag.	190	3030	2830	2638	2455	2279	3873	3378	2936	2542	2190	2.5	1.6	-4.3	-16
300 Wea. Mag.	220	2850	2541	2283	1964	1736	3967	3155	2480	1922	1471	2.5	0.4	-8.5	-26.4
300 Pegasus	180	3500	3319	3145	2978	2817	4896	4401	3953	3544	3172	2.28	2.89	0	-6.79
300 Norma Magnum	215	3017	2881	2748	2618	2491	4346	3963	3605	3272	2963	NA	NA	NA	NA
300 Norma Magnum	230	2934	2805	2678	2555	2435	4397	4018	3664	3334	3028	NA	NA	NA	NA
300 Norma Magnum	225	2850	2731	2615	2502	2392	4058	3726	3417	3128	2859	1.6	0	-6.7	-18.9
300 PRC	212	2860	2723	2589	2849	2565	3850	3489	3156	2849	2565	1.6	0	-6.8	-19.3
300 PRC	225	2810	2692	2577	2465	2356	3945	3620	3318	3036	2773	1.7	0	-6.9	-19.5
31															
32-20 Win.	100	1210	1021	913	834	769	325	231	185	154	131	0	-32.3	0	0
303 British	150	2685	2441	2211	1993	1789	2401	1985	1628	1323	1066	2.2	0	-9.3	-27.4
303 British	180	2460	2124	1817	1542	1311	2418	1803	1319	950	687	2.5	-1.8	-16.8	0
303 Light Mag.	150	2830	2570	2325	2094	1884	2667	2199	1800	1461	1185	2	0	-8.4	-24.6
7.62x54mm Rus.	146	2950	2730	2520	2320	NA	2820	2415	2055	1740	NA	2.5	2	-4.4	-17.7
7.62x54mm Rus.	174	2800	2607	2422	2245	2075	3029	2626	2267	1947	1664	1.8	0	-7.8	-22.4
7.62x54mm Rus.	180	2580	2370	2180	2000	1820	2650	2250	1900	1590	1100	2.5	0	-9.8	-28.5
7.7x58mm Jap.	150	2640	2399	2170	1954	1752	2321	1916	1568	1271	1022	2.3	0	-9.7	-28.5
7.7x58mm Jap.	180	2500	2300	2100	1920	1750	2490	2105	1770	1475	1225	2.5	0	-10.4	-30.2
8mm															
8x56 R	205	2400	2188	1987	1797	1621	2621	2178	1796	1470	1196	2.9	0	-11.7	-34.3
8x57mm JS Mau.	139	3018	2724	2448	2189	-	2812	2290	1849	1479	-	1.5	0	-7.3	-
8x57mm JS Mau.	165	2850	2520	2210	1930	1670	2965	2330	1795	1360	1015	2.5	1	-7.7	0
32 Win. Special	165	2410	2145	1897	1669	NA	2128	1685	1318	1020	NA	2	0	-13	-19.9
32 Win. Special	170	2250	1921	1626	1372	1175	1911	1393	998	710	521	2.5	-3.5	-22.9	0
8mm Mauser	170	2360	1969	1622	1333	1123	2102	1464	993	671	476	2.5	-3.1	-22.2	0
8mm Mauser	196	2500	2338	2182	2032	1888	2720	2379	2072	1797	1552	2.4	0	-9.8	-27.9
325 WSM	180	3060	2841	2632	2432	2242	3743	3226	2769	2365	2009	1.4	0	-6.4	-18.7
325 WSM	200	2950	2753	2565	2384	2210	3866	3367	2922	2524	2170	1.5	0	-6.8	-19.8
325 WSM	220	2840	2605	2382	2169	1968	3941	3316	2772	2300	1893	1.8	0	-8	-23.3
8mm Rem. Mag.	185	3080	2761	2464	2186	1927	3896	3131	2494	1963	1525	2.5	1.4	-5.5	-19.7
8mm Rem. Mag.	220	2830	2581	2346	2123	1913	3912	3254	2688	2201	1787	2.5	0.6	-7.6	-23.5
33															
338 Federal	180	2830	2590	2350	2130	1930	3200	2670	2215	1820	1480	1.8	0	-8.2	-23.9
338 Marlin Express	200	2565	2365	2174	1992	1820	2922	2484	2099	1762	1471	3	1.2	-7.9	-25.9
338 Federal	185	2750	2550	2350	2160	1980	3105	2660	2265	1920	1615	1.9	0	-8.3	-24.1
338 Federal	210	2630	2410	2200	2010	1820	3225	2710	2265	1880	1545	2.3	0	-9.4	-27.3
338 Federal MSR	185	2680	2459	2230	2020	1820	2950	2460	2035	1670	1360	2.2	0	-9.2	-26.8
338-06	200	2750	2553	2364	2184	2011	3358	2894	2482	2118	1796	1.9	0	-8.22	-23.6
330 Dakota	250	2900	2719	2545	2378	2217	4668	4103	3595	3138	2727	2.3	1.3	-5	-17.5
338 Lapua	250	2900	2685	2481	2285	2098	4668	4002	2416	2899	2444	1.7	0	-7.3	-21.3
338 Lapua	250	2963	2795	2640	2493	NA	4842	4341	3881	3458	NA	1.9	0	-7.9	0
338 Lapua	285	2745	2616	2491	2369	2251	4768	4331	3926	3552	3206	1.8	0	-7.4	-21
338 Lapua	300	2660	2544	2432	2322	-	4715	4313	3940	3592	-	1.9	0	-7.8	-
338 RCM Superformance	185	2980	2755	2542	2338	2143	3647	3118	2653	2242	1887	1.5	0	-6.9	-20.3
338 RCM Superformance	200	2950	2744	2547	2358	2177	3846	3342	2879	2468	2104	1.6	0	-6.9	-20.1
338 RCM Superformance	225	2750	2575	2407	2245	2089	3778	3313	2894	2518	2180	1.9	0	-7.9	-22.7
338 WM Superformance	185	3080	2850	2632	2424	2226	3896	3337	2845	2413	2034	1.4	0	-6.4	-18.8

Cartridge	Bullet Wgt. Grs.	VELOCITY (fps)					ENERGY (ft. lbs.)					TRAJ. (in.)			
		Muzzle	100 yds.	200 yds.	300 yds.	400 yds.	Muzzle	100 yds.	200 yds.	300 yds.	400 yds.	100 yds.	200 yds.	300 yds.	400 yds.
338 Win. Mag.	200	3030	2820	2620	2429	2246	4077	3532	3049	2621	2240	1.4	0	-6.5	-18.9
338 Win. Mag.*	210	2830	2590	2370	2150	1940	3735	3130	2610	2155	1760	2.5	1.4	-6	-20.9
338 Win. Mag.*	225	2785	2517	2266	2029	1808	3871	3165	2565	2057	1633	2.5	0.4	-8.5	-25.9
338 WM Superformance	225	2840	2758	2582	2414	2252	4318	3798	3331	2911	2533	1.5	0	-6.8	-19.5
338 Win. Mag.	230	2780	2573	2375	2186	2005	3948	3382	2881	2441	2054	2.5	1.2	-6.3	-21
338 Win. Mag.*	250	2660	2456	2261	2075	1898	3927	3348	2837	2389	1999	2.5	0.2	-9	-26.2
338 Ultra Mag.	250	2860	2645	2440	2244	2057	4540	3882	3303	2794	2347	1.7	0	-7.6	-22.1
338 Lapua Match	250	2900	2760	2625	2494	2366	4668	4229	3825	3452	3108	1.5	0	-6.6	-18.8
338 Lapua Match	285	2745	2623	2504	2388	2275	4768	4352	3966	3608	3275	1.8	0	-7.3	-20.8
33 Nosler	225	3025	2856	2687	2525	2369	4589	4074	3608	3185	2803	0	-2.8	-10.4	-23.4
33 Nosler	265	2775	2661	2547	2435	2326	4543	4167	3816	3488	3183	0	-3.4	-12.2	-26.8
33 Nosler	300	2550	2445	2339	2235	2134	4343	3981	3643	3327	3033	0	-4.3	-15	-32.6
8.59(.338) Galaxy	200	3100	2899	2707	2524	2347	4269	3734	3256	2829	2446	3	3.8	0	-9.3
340 Wea. Mag.*	210	3250	2991	2746	2515	2295	4924	4170	3516	2948	2455	2.5	1.9	-1.8	-11.8
340 Wea. Mag.*	250	3000	2806	2621	2443	2272	4995	4371	3812	3311	2864	2.5	2	-3.5	-14.8
338 A-Square	250	3120	2799	2500	2220	1958	5403	4348	3469	2736	2128	2.5	2.7	-1.5	-10.5
338-378 Wea. Mag.	225	3180	2974	2778	2591	2410	5052	4420	3856	3353	2902	3.1	3.8	0	-8.9
338 Titan	225	3230	3010	2800	2600	2409	5211	4524	3916	3377	2898	3.07	3.8	0	-8.95
338 Excalibur	200	3600	3361	3134	2920	2715	5755	5015	4363	3785	3274	2.23	2.87	0	-6.99
338 Excalibur	250	3250	2922	2618	2333	2066	5863	4740	3804	3021	2370	1.3	0	-6.35	-19.2
34, 35															
348 Winchester	200	2520	2215	1931	1672	1443	2820	2178	1656	1241	925	2.5	-1.4	-14.7	0
348 Winchester LeveRevolution	200	2560	2294	2044	1811	1597	2910	2336	1855	1456	1133	2.6	0	-10.9	-32.6
357 Magnum	158	1830	1427	1138	980	883	1175	715	454	337	274	0		-33.1	0
350 Legend	145	2350	1916	1539	1241	n/a	1778	1182	763	496	n/a	0	-8.1	-31.2	NA
350 Legend	150	2325	1968	1647	1373	na	4800	1289	903	628	na	0	-7.6	-28.1	na
350 Legend	160	2225	1843	1509	1243	na	1759	1206	809	548	na	0	-8.9	-33.2	na
350 Legend	180	2100	1762	1466	1230	na	1762	1240	859	604	na	0	-9.8	-36	na
350 Legend	265	1060	990	936	890	na	661	577	515	466	na	0	-34.1	-107.4	na
35 Remington	150	2300	1874	1506	1218	1039	1762	1169	755	494	359	2.5	-4.1	-26.3	0
35 Remington	200	2080	1698	1376	1140	1001	1921	1280	841	577	445	2.5	-6.3	-17.1	-33.6
35 Remington	200	2225	1963	1722	1505	—	2198	1711	1317	1006	—	3.8	0	-15.6	—
35 Rem. Lever Evolution	200	2225	1963	1721	1503	NA	2198	1711	1315	1003	NA	3	-1.3	-17.5	NA
356 Winchester	200	2460	2114	1797	1517	1284	2688	1985	1434	1022	732	2.5	-1.8	-15.1	0
356 Winchester	250	2160	1911	1682	1476	1299	2591	2028	1571	1210	937	2.5	-3.7	-22.2	0
358 Winchester	200	2475	2180	1906	1655	1434	2720	2110	1612	1217	913	2.9	0	-12.6	-37.9
358 Winchester	200	2490	2171	1876	1619	1379	2753	2093	1563	1151	844	2.5	-1.6	-15.6	0
358 STA	275	2850	2562	2292	2039	NA	4958	4009	3208	2539	NA	1.9	0	-8.6	0
350 Rem. Mag.	200	2710	2410	2130	1870	1631	3261	2579	2014	1553	1181	2.5	-0.2	-10	-30.1
35 Whelen	200	2675	2378	2100	1842	1606	3177	2510	1958	1506	1145	2.5	-0.2	-10.3	-31.1
35 Whelen	200	2910	2585	2283	2001	1742	3760	2968	2314	1778	1347	1.9	0	-8.6	-25.9
35 Whelen	225	2500	2300	2110	1930	1770	3120	2650	2235	1870	1560	2.6	0	-10.2	-29.9
35 Whelen	250	2400	2197	2005	1823	1652	3197	2680	2230	1844	1515	2.5	-1.2	-13.7	0
358 Norma Mag.	250	2800	2510	2230	1970	1730	4350	3480	2750	2145	1655	2.5	1	-7.6	-25.2
358 STA	275	2850	2562	2292	2039	1764	4959	4009	3208	2539	1899	1.9	0	-8.58	-26.1
9.3mm															
9.3x57mm Mau.	232	2362	2058	1778	1528	NA	2875	2182	1630	1203	NA	0	-6.8	-24.6	NA
9.3x57mm Mau.	286	2070	1810	1590	1390	1110	2710	2090	1600	1220	955	2.5	-2.6	-22.5	0
370 Sako Mag.	286	3550	2370	2200	2040	2880	4130	3570	3075	2630	2240	2.4	0	-9.5	-27.2
9.3x62mm	184	2953	2650	2366	2100	-	3562	2869	2287	1802	-	1.7	0	-7.9	-
9.3x62mm	232	2625	2302	2002	1728	-	2551	2731	2066	1539	-	2.6	0	-11.3	-
9.3x62mm	250	2550	2376	2208	2048	—	3609	3133	2707	2328	—	0	-5.4	-17.9	—
9.3x62mm	286	2360	2155	1961	1778	1608	3537	2949	2442	2008	1642	0	-6	-21.1	-47.2
9.3x62mm	286	2400	2163	1941	1733	—	3657	2972	2392	1908	—	0	-6.7	-22.6	—
9.3x64mm	286	2700	2505	2318	2139	1968	4629	3984	3411	2906	2460	2.5	2.7	-4.5	-19.2
9.3x72mmR	193	1952	1610	1326	1120	996	1633	1112	754	538	425	0	-12.1	-44.1	—
9.3x74mmR	250	2550	2376	2208	2048	—	3609	3133	2707	2328	—	0	-5.4	-17.9	—
9.3x74Rmm	286	2360	2136	1924	1727	1545	3536	2896	2351	1893	1516	0	-6.1	-21.7	-49
375															
375 Winchester	200	2200	1841	1526	1268	1089	2150	1506	1034	714	527	2.5	-4	-26.2	0
375 Winchester	250	1900	1647	1424	1239	1103	2005	1506	1126	852	676	2.5	-6.9	-33.3	0
376 Steyr	225	2600	2331	2078	1842	1625	3377	2714	2157	1694	1319	2.5	0	-10.6	-31.4
376 Steyr	270	2600	2372	2156	1951	1759	4052	3373	2787	2283	1855	2.3	0	-9.9	-28.9
375 Dakota	300	2600	2316	2051	1804	1579	4502	3573	2800	2167	1661	2.4	0	-11	-32.7
375 N.E. 2-1/2"	270	2000	1740	1507	1310	NA	2398	1815	1362	1026	NA	2.5	-6	-30	0

Cartridge	Bullet Wgt. Grs.	VELOCITY (fps)					ENERGY (ft. lbs.)					TRAJ. (in.)			
		Muzzle	100 yds.	200 yds.	300 yds.	400 yds.	Muzzle	100 yds.	200 yds.	300 yds.	400 yds.	100 yds.	200 yds.	300 yds.	400 yds.
375 Flanged	300	2450	2150	1886	1640	NA	3998	3102	2369	1790	NA	2.5	-2.4	-17	0
375 Ruger	250	2890	2675	2471	2275	2088	4636	3973	3388	2873	2421	1.7	0	-7.4	-21.5
375 Ruger	260	2900	2703	2514	2333	—	4854	4217	3649	3143	—	0	-4	-13.4	—
375 Ruger	270	2840	2600	2372	2156	1951	4835	4052	3373	2786	2283	1.8	0	-8	-23.6
375 Ruger	300	2660	2344	2050	1780	1536	4713	3660	2800	2110	1572	2.4	0	-10.8	-32.6
375 H&H Magnum	250	2890	2675	2471	2275	2088	4636	3973	3388	2873	2421	1.7	0	-7.4	-21.5
375 H&H Magnum	250	2670	2450	2240	2040	1850	3955	3335	2790	2315	1905	2.5	-0.4	-10.2	-28.4
375 H&H Magnum	270	2690	2420	2166	1928	1707	4337	3510	2812	2228	1747	2.5	0	-10	-29.4
375 H&H Mag.	270	2800	2562	2337	2123	1921	4700	3936	3275	2703	2213	1.9	0	-8.3	-24.3
375 H&H Magnum*	300	2530	2245	1979	1733	1512	4263	3357	2608	2001	1523	2.5	-1	-10.5	-33.6
375 H&H Mag.	300	2660	2345	2052	1782	1539	4713	3662	2804	2114	1577	2.4	0	-10.8	-32.6
375 H&H Hvy. Mag.	270	2870	2628	2399	2182	1976	4937	4141	3451	2150	1845	1.7	0	-7.2	-21
375 H&H Hvy. Mag.	300	2705	2386	2090	1816	1568	4873	3793	2908	2195	1637	2.3	0	-10.4	-31.4
375 H&H Mag	350	2300	2052	1821	-	-	4112	3273	2578	-	-	0	-6.7	-	-
375 Rem. Ultra Mag.	270	2900	2558	2241	1947	1678	5041	3922	3010	2272	1689	1.9	2.7	-8.9	-27
375 Rem. Ultra Mag.	260	2950	2750	2560	2377	—	5023	4367	3783	3262	—	0	-3.8	-12.9	—
375 Rem. Ultra Mag.	300	2760	2505	2263	2035	1822	5073	4178	3412	2759	2210	2	0	-8.8	-26.1
375 Wea. Mag.	260	3000	2798	2606	2421	—	5195	4520	3920	3384	—	0	-3.6	-12.4	—
375 Wea. Mag.	300	2700	2420	2157	1911	1685	4856	3901	3100	2432	1891	2.5	-0.04	-10.7	0
378 Wea. Mag.	260	3100	2894	2697	2509	—	5547	4834	4199	3633	—	0	-4.2	-14.6	—
378 Wea. Mag.	270	3180	2976	2781	2594	2415	6062	5308	4635	4034	3495	2.5	2.6	-1.8	-11.3
378 Wea. Mag.	300	2929	2576	2252	1952	1680	5698	4419	3379	2538	1881	2.5	1.2	-7	-24.5
375 A-Square	300	2920	2626	2351	2093	1850	5679	4594	3681	2917	2281	2.5	1.4	-6	-21
38-40 Win.	180	1160	999	901	827	764	538	399	324	273	233	0	-33.9	0	0
40, 41															
400 A-Square DPM	400	2400	2146	1909	1689	NA	5116	2092	3236	2533	NA	2.98	0	-10	NA
400 A-Square DPM	170	2980	2463	2001	1598	NA	3352	2289	1512	964	NA	2.16	0	-11.1	NA
408 CheyTac	419	2850	2752	2657	2562	2470	7551	7048	6565	6108	5675	-1.02	0	1.9	4.2
405 Win.	300	2200	1851	1545	1296		3224	2282	1589	1119		4.6	0	-19.5	0
450/400-3"	400	2050	1815	1595	1402	NA	3732	2924	2259	1746	NA	0	NA	-33.4	NA
416 Ruger	400	2400	2151	1917	1700	NA	5116	4109	3264	2568	NA	0	-6	-21.6	0
416 Dakota	400	2450	2294	2143	1998	1859	5330	4671	4077	3544	3068	2.5	-0.2	-10.5	-29.4
416Taylor	375	2350	2021	1722	na	na	4600	3403	2470	NA	NA	0	-7	NA	NA
416 Taylor	400	2350	2117	1896	1693	NA	4905	3980	3194	2547	NA	2.5	-1.2	15	0
416 Hoffman	400	2380	2145	1923	1718	1529	5031	4087	3285	2620	2077	2.5	-1	-14.1	0
416 Rigby	350	2600	2449	2303	2162	2026	5253	4661	4122	3632	3189	2.5	-1.8	-10.2	-26
416 Rigby	400	2370	2210	2050	1900	NA	4990	4315	3720	3185	NA	2.5	-0.7	-12.1	0
416 Rigby	400	2400	2115	1851	1611	—	5115	3973	3043	2305	—	0	-6.5	-21.8	—
416 Rigby	400	2415	2156	1915	1691	—	5180	4130	3256	2540	—	0	-6	-21.6	—
416 Rigby	410	2370	2110	1870	1640	NA	5115	4050	3165	2455	NA	2.5	-2.4	-17.3	0
416 Rigby No. 2	400	2400	2115	1851	1611	—	5115	3973	3043	2305	—	0	-6.5	-21.8	—
416 Rem. Mag.*	350	2520	2270	2034	1814	1611	4935	4004	3216	2557	2017	2.5	-0.8	-12.6	-35
416 Rem. Mag.	400	2400	2142	1901	1679	—	5116	4076	3211	2504	—	3.1	0	-12.7	—
416 Rem. Mag	450	2150	1925	1716	-	-	4620	3702	2942	-	-	0	-7.8	-	-
416 Wea. Mag.*	400	2700	2397	2115	1852	1613	6474	5104	3971	3047	2310	2.5	0	-10.1	-30.4
10.57 (416) Meteor	400	2730	2532	2342	2161	1987	6621	5695	4874	4147	3508	1.9	0	-8.3	-24
500/416 N.E.	400	2300	2092	1895	1712	—	4697	3887	3191	2602	—	0	-7.2	-24	—
404 Jeffrey	400	2150	1924	1716	1525	NA	4105	3289	2614	2064	NA	2.5	-4	-22.1	0
404 Jeffrey	400	2300	2053	1823	1611	—	4698	3743	2950	2306	—	0	-6.8	-24.1	—
404 Jeffery	400	2350	2020	1720	1458	—	4904	3625	2629	1887	—	0	-6.5	-21.8	—
404 Jeffery	450	2150	1946	1755	-	-	4620	3784	3078	-	-	0	-7.6	-	-
425, 44															
425 Express	400	2400	2160	1934	1725	NA	5115	4145	3322	2641	NA	2.5	-1	-14	0
44-40 Win.	200	1190	1006	900	822	756	629	449	360	300	254	0	-33.3	0	0
44 Rem. Mag.	210	1920	1477	1155	982	880	1719	1017	622	450	361	0	-17.6	0	0
44 Rem. Mag.	240	1760	1380	1114	970	878	1650	1015	661	501	411	0	-17.6	0	0
444 Marlin	240	2350	1815	1377	1087	941	2942	1753	1001	630	472	2.5	-15.1	-31	0
444 Marlin	265	2120	1733	1405	1160	1012	2644	1768	1162	791	603	2.5	-6	-32.2	0
444 Mar. Lever Evolution	265	2325	1971	1652	1380	NA	3180	2285	1606	1120	NA	3	-1.4	-18.6	NA
444 Mar. Superformance	265	2400	1976	1603	1298	NA	3389	2298	1512	991	NA	4.1	0	-17.8	NA
45															
45-70 Govt.	250	2025	1616	1285	1068	—	2276	1449	917	634	—	6.1	0	-27.2	—
45-70 Govt.	300	1810	1497	1244	1073	969	2182	1492	1031	767	625	0	-14.8	0	0
45-70 Govt. Supreme	300	1880	1558	1292	1103	988	2355	1616	1112	811	651	0	-12.9	-46	-105
45-70 Govt.	325	2000	1685	1413	1197	—	2886	2049	1441	1035	—	5.5	0	-23	—

Cartridge	Bullet Wgt. Grs.	VELOCITY (fps)					ENERGY (ft. lbs.)					TRAJ. (in.)			
		Muzzle	100 yds.	200 yds.	300 yds.	400 yds.	Muzzle	100 yds.	200 yds.	300 yds.	400 yds.	100 yds.	200 yds.	300 yds.	400 yds.
45-70 Lever Evolution	325	2050	1729	1450	1225	NA	3032	2158	1516	1083	NA	3	-4.1	-27.8	NA
45-70 Govt. CorBon	350	1800	1526	1296			2519	1810	1307			0	-14.6	0	0
45-70 Govt.	405	1330	1168	1055	977	918	1590	1227	1001	858	758	0	-24.6	0	0
45-70 Govt. PMC Cowboy	405	1550	1193	—	—	—	1639	1280	—	—	—	0	-23.9	0	0
45-70 Govt. Garrett	415	1850	—	—	—	—	3150	—	—	—	—	3	-7	0	0
45-70 Govt. Garrett	530	1550	1343	1178	1062	982	2828	2123	1633	1327	1135	0	-17.8	0	0
450 Bushmaster	250	2200	1831	1508	1480	1073	2686	1860	1262	864	639	0	-9	-33.5	0
450 Marlin	325	2225	1887	1587	1332	—	3572	2570	1816	1280	—	4.2	0	-18.1	—
450 Marlin	350	2100	1774	1488	1254	1089	3427	2446	1720	1222	922	0	-9.7	-35.2	0
450 Mar. Lever Evolution	325	2225	1887	1585	1331	NA	3572	2569	1813	1278	NA	3	-2.2	-21.3	NA
457 Wild West Magnum	350	2150	1718	1348	NA	NA	3645	2293	1413	NA	NA	0	-10.5	NA	NA
450/500 N.E.	400	2050	1820	1609	1420	—	3732	2940	2298	1791	—	0	-9.7	-32.8	—
450 N.E. 3-1/4"	465	2190	1970	1765	1577	NA	4952	4009	3216	2567	NA	2.5	-3	-20	0
450 N.E.	480	2150	1881	1635	1418	—	4927	3769	2850	2144	—	0	-8.4	-29.8	—
450 N.E. 3-1/4"	500	2150	1920	1708	1514	NA	5132	4093	3238	2544	NA	2.5	-4	-22.9	0
450 No. 2	465	2190	1970	1765	1577	NA	4952	4009	3216	2567	NA	2.5	-3	-20	0
450 No. 2	500	2150	1920	1708	1514	NA	5132	4093	3238	2544	NA	2.5	-4	-22.9	0
450 Ackley Mag.	465	2400	2169	1950	1747	NA	5947	4857	3927	3150	NA	2.5	-1	-13.7	0
450 Ackley Mag.	500	2320	2081	1855	1649	NA	5975	4085	3820	3018	NA	2.5	-1.2	-15	0
450 Rigby	500	2350	2139	1939	1752	—	6130	5079	4176	3408	—	0	-6.8	-22.9	—
450 Rigby	550	2100	1866	1651	-	-	5387	4256	3330	-	-	-	-	-	-
458 Win. Magnum	400	2380	2170	1960	1770	NA	5030	4165	3415	2785	NA	2.5	-0.4	-13.4	0
458 Win. Magnum	465	2220	1999	1791	1601	NA	5088	4127	3312	2646	NA	2.5	-2	-17.7	0
458 Win. Magnum	500	2040	1823	1623	1442	1237	4620	3689	2924	2308	1839	2.5	-3.5	-22	0
458 Win. Mag.	500	2140	1880	1643	1432	—	5084	3294	2996	2276	—	0	-8.4	-29.8	—
458 Win. Magnum	510	2040	1770	1527	1319	1157	4712	3547	2640	1970	1516	2.5	-4.1	-25	0
458 Lott	465	2380	2150	1932	1730	NA	5848	4773	3855	3091	NA	2.5	-1	-14	0
458 Lott	500	2300	2029	1778	1551	—	5873	4569	3509	2671	—	0	-7	-25.1	—
458 Lott	500	2300	2062	1838	1633	NA	5873	4719	3748	2960	NA	2.5	-1.6	-16.4	0
460 Short A-Sq.	500	2420	2175	1943	1729	NA	6501	5250	4193	3319	NA	2.5	-0.8	-12.8	0
460 Wea. Mag.	500	2700	2404	2128	1869	1635	8092	6416	5026	3878	2969	2.5	0.6	-8.9	-28
475															
500/465 N.E.	480	2150	1917	1703	1507	NA	4926	3917	3089	2419	NA	2.5	-4	-22.2	0
470 Rigby	500	2150	1940	1740	1560	NA	5130	4170	3360	2695	NA	2.5	-2.8	-19.4	0
470 Nitro Ex.	480	2190	1954	1735	1536	NA	5111	4070	3210	2515	NA	2.5	-3.5	-20.8	0
470 N.E.	500	2150	1885	1643	1429	—	5132	3945	2998	2267	—	0	-8.9	-30.8	—
470 Nitro Ex.	500	2150	1890	1650	1440	1270	5130	3965	3040	2310	1790	2.5	-4.3	-24	0
475 No. 2	500	2200	1955	1728	1522	NA	5375	4243	3316	2573	NA	2.5	-3.2	-20.9	0
50, 58															
50 Alaskan	450	2000	1729	1492	NA	NA	3997	2987	2224	NA	NA	0	-11.25	NA	NA
500 Jeffery	570	2300	1979	1688	1434	—	6694	4958	3608	2604	—	0	-8.2	-28.6	—
505 Gibbs	525	2300	2063	1840	1637	NA	6166	4922	3948	3122	NA	2.5	-3	-18	0
505 Gibbs	570	2100	1893	1701	-	-	5583	4538	3664	-	-	0	-8.1	-	-
505 Gibbs	600	2100	1899	1711	-	-	5877	4805	3904	-	-	0	-8.1	-	-
500 N.E.	570	2150	1889	1651	1439	—	5850	4518	3450	2621	—	0	-8.9	-30.6	—
500 N.E.-3"	570	2150	1928	1722	1533	NA	5850	4703	3752	2975	NA	2.5	-3.7	-22	0
500 N.E.-3"	600	2150	1927	1721	1531	NA	6158	4947	3944	3124	NA	2.5	-4	-22	0
495 A-Square	570	2350	2117	1896	1693	NA	5850	4703	3752	2975	NA	2.5	-1	-14.5	0
495 A-Square	600	2280	2050	1833	1635	NA	6925	5598	4478	3562	NA	2.5	-2	-17	0
500 A-Square	600	2380	2144	1922	1766	NA	7546	6126	4920	3922	NA	2.5	-3	-17	0
500 A-Square	707	2250	2040	1841	1567	NA	7947	6530	5318	4311	NA	2.5	-2	-17	0
500 BMG PMC	660	3080	2854	2639	2444	2248	13688	500 yd. zero	3.1	3.9	4.7	2.8	NA		
577 Nitro Ex.	750	2050	1793	1562	1360	NA	6990	5356	4065	3079	NA	2.5	-5	-26	0
577 Tyrannosaur	750	2400	2141	1898	1675	NA	9591	7633	5996	4671	NA	3	0	-12.9	0
600, 700															
600 N.E.	900	1950	1680	1452	NA	NA	7596	5634	4212	NA	NA	5.6	0	0	0
700 N.E.	1200	1900	1676	1472	NA	NA	9618	7480	5774	NA	NA	5.7	0	0	0
50 BMG															
50 BMG	624	2952	2820	2691	2566	2444	12077	11028	10036	9125	8281	0	-2.9	-10.6	-23.5
50 BMG Match	750	2820	2728	2637	2549	2462	13241	12388	11580	10815	10090	1.5	0	-6.5	-18.3

Centerfire Handgun Cartridge Ballistics

Notes: Blanks are available in 32 S&W, 38 S&W and 38 Special. "V" after barrel length indicates test barrel was vented to produce ballistics similar to a revolver with a normal barrel-to-cylinder gap. Not all loads are available from all ammo manufacturers. Listed loads are those made by Remington, Winchester, Federal, and others. DISC. is a discontinued load.

Cartridge	Bullet Wgt. Grs.	VELOCITY (fps)			ENERGY (ft. lbs.)			Mid-Range Traj. (in.)		Bbl. Lgth. (in).
		Muzzle	50 yds.	100 yds.	Muzzle	50 yds.	100 yds.	50 yds.	100 yds.	
22, 25										
221 Rem. Fireball	50	2650	2380	2130	780	630	505	0.2	0.8	10.5"
25 Automatic	35	900	813	742	63	51	43	NA	NA	2"
25 Automatic	45	815	730	655	65	55	40	1.8	7.7	2"
25 Automatic	50	760	705	660	65	55	50	2	8.7	2"
30										
7.5mm Swiss	107	1010	NA	NA	240	NA	NA	NA	NA	NA
7.62x25 Tokarev	85	1647	1458	1295	512	401	317	0	-3.2	4.75
7.62mmTokarev	87	1390	NA	NA	365	NA	NA	0.6	NA	4.5"
7.62 Nagant	97	790	NA	NA	134	NA	NA	NA	NA	NA
7.63 Mauser	88	1440	NA	NA	405	NA	NA	NA	NA	NA
30 Luger	93	1220	1110	1040	305	255	225	0.9	3.5	4.5"
30 Carbine	110	1790	1600	1430	785	625	500	0.4	1.7	10"
30 Super Carry	100	1250	1129	1041	347	283	241	-0.6	-7.2	NA
30 Super Carry	115	1150	1044	970	338	278	240	-0.9	-8.9	4"
30-357 AeT	123	1992	NA	NA	1084	NA	NA	NA	NA	10"
32										
32 NAA	80	1000	933	880	178	155	137	NA	NA	4"
32 S&W	88	680	645	610	90	80	75	2.5	10.5	3"
32 S&W Long	98	705	670	635	115	100	90	2.3	10.5	4"
32 Short Colt	80	745	665	590	100	80	60	2.2	9.9	4"
32 H&R	80	1150	1039	963	235	192	165	NA	NA	4"
32 H&R Magnum	85	1100	1020	930	230	195	165	1	4.3	4.5"
32 H&R Magnum	95	1030	940	900	225	190	170	1.1	4.7	4.5"
327 Federal Magnum	85	1400	1220	1090	370	280	225	NA	NA	4-V
327 Federal Magnum	100	1500	1320	1180	500	390	310	-0.2	-4.5	4-V
32 Automatic	60	970	895	835	125	105	95	1.3	5.4	4"
32 Automatic	60	1000	917	849	133	112	96			4"
32 Automatic	65	950	890	830	130	115	100	1.3	5.6	NA
32 Automatic	71	905	855	810	130	115	95	1.4	5.8	4"
8mm Lebel Pistol	111	850	NA	NA	180	NA	NA	NA	NA	NA
8mm Steyr	112	1080	NA	NA	290	NA	NA	NA	NA	NA
8mm Gasser	126	850	NA	NA	200	NA	NA	NA	NA	NA
9mm, 38										
380 Automatic	60	1130	960	NA	170	120	NA	1	NA	NA
380 Automatic	75	950	NA	NA	183	NA	NA	NA	NA	3"
380 Automatic	85/88	990	920	870	190	165	145	1.2	5.1	4"
380 Automatic	90	1000	890	800	200	160	130	1.2	5.5	3.75"
380 Automatic	95/100	955	865	785	190	160	130	1.4	5.9	4"
38 Super Auto +P	115	1300	1145	1040	430	335	275	0.7	3.3	5"
38 Super Auto +P	125/130	1215	1100	1015	425	350	300	0.8	3.6	5"
38 Super Auto +P	147	1100	1050	1000	395	355	325	0.9	4	5"
38 Super Auto +P	115	1130	1016	938	326	264	225	1	-9.5	-
9x18mm Makarov	95	1000	930	874	211	182	161	NA	NA	4"
9x18mm Ultra	100	1050	NA	NA	240	NA	NA	NA	NA	NA
9x21	124	1150	1050	980	365	305	265	NA	NA	4"
9x21 IMI	123	1220	1095	1010	409	330	281	-3.15	—	5
9x23mm Largo	124	1190	1055	966	390	306	257	0.7	3.7	4"
9x23mm Win.	125	1450	1249	1103	583	433	338	0.6	2.8	NA
9mm Steyr	115	1180	NA	NA	350	NA	NA	NA	NA	NA
9mm Luger	88	1500	1190	1010	440	275	200	0.6	3.1	4"
9mm Luger	90	1360	1112	978	370	247	191	NA	NA	4"
9mm Luger	92	1325	1117	991	359	255	201	-3.2	—	4
9mm Luger	95	1300	1140	1010	350	275	215	0.8	3.4	4"
9mm Luger	100	1180	1080	NA	305	255	NA	0.9	NA	4"
9mm Luger Guard Dog	105	1230	1070	970	355	265	220	NA	NA	4"

Cartridge	Bullet Wgt. Grs.	VELOCITY (fps)			ENERGY (ft. lbs.)			Mid-Range Traj. (in.)		Bbl. Lgth. (in).
		Muzzle	50 yds.	100 yds.	Muzzle	50 yds.	100 yds.	50 yds.	100 yds.	
9mm Luger	115	1155	1045	970	340	280	240	0.9	3.9	4"
9mm Luger	123/125	1110	1030	970	340	290	260	1	4	4"
9mm Luger	124	1150	1040	965	364	298	256	-4.5	—	4
9mm Luger	135	1010	960	918	306	276	253	—	—	4
9mm Luger	140	935	890	850	270	245	225	1.3	5.5	4"
9mm Luger	147	990	940	900	320	290	265	1.1	4.9	4"
9mm Luger +P	90	1475	NA	NA	437	NA	NA	NA	NA	NA
9mm Luger +P	115	1250	1113	1019	399	316	265	0.8	3.5	4"
9mm Federal	115	1280	1130	1040	420	330	280	0.7	3.3	4"V
9mm Luger Vector	115	1155	1047	971	341	280	241	NA	NA	4"
9mm Luger +P	124	1180	1089	1021	384	327	287	0.8	3.8	4"
38										
38 S&W	146	685	650	620	150	135	125	2.4	10	4"
38 S&W Short	145	720	689	660	167	153	140	-8.5	—	5
38 Short Colt	125	730	685	645	150	130	115	2.2	9.4	6"
39 Special	100	950	900	NA	200	180	NA	1.3	NA	4"V
38 Special	110	945	895	850	220	195	175	1.3	5.4	4"V
38 Special	110	945	895	850	220	195	175	1.3	5.4	4"V
38 Special	130	775	745	710	175	160	120	1.9	7.9	4"V
38 Special Cowboy	140	800	767	735	199	183	168			7.5" V
38 (Multi-Ball)	140	830	730	505	215	130	80	2	10.6	4"V
38 Special	148	710	635	565	165	130	105	2.4	10.6	4"V
38 Special	158	755	725	690	200	185	170	2	8.3	4"V
38 Special +P	95	1175	1045	960	290	230	195	0.9	3.9	4"V
38 Special +P	110	995	925	870	240	210	185	1.2	5.1	4"V
38 Special +P	125	975	929	885	264	238	218	1	5.2	4"
38 Special +P	125	945	900	860	250	225	205	1.3	5.4	4"V
38 Special +P	129	945	910	870	255	235	215	1.3	5.3	4"V
38 Special +P	130	925	887	852	247	227	210	1.3	5.5	4"V
38 Special +P	147/150	884	NA	NA	264	NA	NA	NA	NA	4"V
38 Special +P	158	890	855	825	280	255	240	1.4	6	4"V
357										
357 SIG	115	1520	NA	NA	593	NA	NA	NA	NA	NA
357 SIG	124	1450	NA	NA	578	NA	NA	NA	NA	NA
357 SIG	125	1350	1190	1080	510	395	325	0.7	3.1	4"
357 SIG	135	1225	1112	1031	450	371	319	—	—	4
357 SIG	147	1225	1132	1060	490	418	367	—	—	4
357 SIG	150	1130	1030	970	420	355	310	0.9	4	NA
356 TSW	115	1520	NA	NA	593	NA	NA	NA	NA	NA
356 TSW	124	1450	NA	NA	578	NA	NA	NA	NA	NA
356 TSW	135	1280	1120	1010	490	375	310	0.8	3.5	NA
356 TSW	147	1220	1120	1040	485	410	355	0.8	3.5	5"
357 Mag., Super Clean	105	1650								
357 Magnum	110	1295	1095	975	410	290	230	0.8	3.5	4"V
357 (Med.Vel.)	125	1220	1075	985	415	315	270	0.8	3.7	4"V
357 Magnum	125	1450	1240	1090	585	425	330	0.6	2.8	4"V
357 Magnum	125	1500	1312	1163	624	478	376	—	—	8
357 (Multi-Ball)	140	1155	830	665	420	215	135	1.2	6.4	4"V
357 Magnum	140	1360	1195	1075	575	445	360	0.7	3	4"V
357 Magnum FlexTip	140	1440	1274	1143	644	504	406	NA	NA	NA
357 Magnum	145	1290	1155	1060	535	430	360	0.8	3.5	4"V
357 Magnum	150/158	1235	1105	1015	535	430	360	0.8	3.5	4"V
357 Mag. Cowboy	158	800	761	725	225	203	185			
357 Magnum	165	1290	1189	1108	610	518	450	0.7	3.1	8-3/8"
357 Magnum	180	1145	1055	985	525	445	390	0.9	3.9	4"V
357 Magnum	180	1180	1088	1020	557	473	416	0.8	3.6	8"V
357 Mag. CorBon F.A.	180	1650	1512	1386	1088	913	767	1.66	0	
357 Mag. CorBon	200	1200	1123	1061	640	560	500	3.19	0	
357 Rem. Maximum	158	1825	1590	1380	1170	885	670	0.4	1.7	10.5"
40, 10mm										
40 S&W	120	1150	-	-	352	-	-	-	-	-

Cartridge	Bullet Wgt. Grs.	VELOCITY (fps)			ENERGY (ft. lbs.)			Mid-Range Traj. (in.)		Bbl. Lgth. (in).
		Muzzle	50 yds.	100 yds.	Muzzle	50 yds.	100 yds.	50 yds.	100 yds.	
40 S&W	125	1265	1102	998	444	337	276	-3	—	4
40 S&W	135	1140	1070	NA	390	345	NA	0.9	NA	4"
40 S&W Guard Dog	135	1200	1040	940	430	325	265	NA	NA	4"
40 S&W	155	1140	1026	958	447	362	309	0.9	4.1	4"
40 S&W	165	1150	NA	NA	485	NA	NA	NA	NA	4"
40 S&W	175	1010	948	899	396	350	314	—	—	4
40 S&W	180	985	936	893	388	350	319	1.4	5	4"
40 S&W	180	1000	943	896	400	355	321	4.52	—	4
40 S&W	180	1015	960	914	412	368	334	1.3	4.5	4"
400 Cor-Bon	135	1450	NA	NA	630	NA	NA	NA	NA	5"
10mm Automatic	155	1125	1046	986	436	377	335	0.9	3.9	5"
10mm Automatic	155	1265	1118	1018	551	430	357	—	—	5
10mm Automatic	170	1340	1165	1145	680	510	415	0.7	3.2	5"
10mm Automatic	175	1290	1140	1035	650	505	420	0.7	3.3	5.5"
10mm Auto. (FBI)	180	950	905	865	361	327	299	1.5	5.4	4"
10mm Automatic	180	1030	970	920	425	375	340	1.1	4.7	5"
10mm Auto H.V.	180	1240	1124	1037	618	504	430	0.8	3.4	5"
10mm Auto	200	1100	1015	951	537	457	402	-1.1	-9.6	NA
10mm Automatic	200	1160	1070	1010	495	510	430	0.9	3.8	5"
10.4mm Italian	177	950	NA	NA	360	NA	NA	NA	NA	NA
41 Action Exp.	180	1000	947	903	400	359	326	0.5	4.2	5"
41 Rem. Magnum	170	1420	1165	1015	760	515	390	0.7	3.2	4"V
41 Rem. Magnum	175	1250	1120	1030	605	490	410	0.8	3.4	4"V
41 (Med. Vel.)	210	965	900	840	435	375	330	1.3	5.4	4"V
41 Rem. Magnum	210	1300	1160	1060	790	630	535	0.7	3.2	4"V
41 Rem. Magnum	240	1250	1151	1075	833	706	616	0.8	3.3	6.5V
44										
44 S&W Russian	247	780	NA	NA	335	NA	NA	NA	NA	NA
44 Special	210	900	861	825	360	329	302	5.57	—	6
44 Special FTX	165	900	848	802	297	263	235	NA	NA	2.5"
44 S&W Special	180	980	NA	NA	383	NA	NA	NA	NA	6.5"
44 S&W Special	180	1000	935	882	400	350	311	NA	NA	7.5"V
44 S&W Special	200	875	825	780	340	302	270	1.2	6	6"
44 S&W Special	200	1035	940	865	475	390	335	1.1	4.9	6.5"
44 S&W Special	240/246	755	725	695	310	285	265	2	8.3	6.5"
44-40 Win.	200	722	698	676	232	217	203	-3.4	-23.7	4
44-40 Win.	205	725	689	655	239	216	195	—	—	7.5
44-40 Win.	210	725	698	672	245	227	210	-11.6	—	5.5
44-40 Win.	225	725	697	670	263	243	225	-3.4	-23.8	4
44-40 Win. Cowboy	225	750	723	695	281	261	242			
44 Rem. Magnum	180	1610	1365	1175	1035	745	550	0.5	2.3	4"V
44 Rem. Magnum	200	1296	1193	1110	747	632	548	-0.5	-6.2	6
44 Rem. Magnum	200	1400	1192	1053	870	630	492	0.6	NA	6.5"
44 Rem. Magnum	200	1500	1332	1194	999	788	633	—	—	7.5
44 Rem. Magnum	210	1495	1310	1165	1040	805	635	0.6	2.5	6.5"
44 Rem. Mag. FlexTip	225	1410	1240	1111	993	768	617	NA	NA	NA
44 (Med. Vel.)	240	1000	945	900	535	475	435	1.1	4.8	6.5"
44 R.M. (Jacketed)	240	1180	1080	1010	740	625	545	0.9	3.7	4"V
44 R.M. (Lead)	240	1350	1185	1070	970	750	610	0.7	3.1	4"V
44 Rem. Magnum	250	1180	1100	1040	775	670	600	0.8	3.6	6.5"V
44 Rem. Magnum	250	1250	1148	1070	867	732	635	0.8	3.3	6.5"V
44 Rem. Magnum	275	1235	1142	1070	931	797	699	0.8	3.3	6.5"
44 Rem. Magnum	300	1150	1083	1030	881	781	706	—	—	7.5
44 Rem. Magnum	300	1200	1100	1026	959	806	702	NA	NA	7.5"
44 Rem. Magnum	330	1385	1297	1220	1406	1234	1090	1.83	0	NA
44 Webley	262	850	—	—	—	—	—	—	—	—
440 CorBon	260	1700	1544	1403	1669	1377	1136	1.58	NA	10"
45, 50										
450 Short Colt/450 Revolver	226	830	NA	NA	350	NA	NA	NA	NA	NA
45 S&W Schofield	180	730	NA	NA	213	NA	NA	NA	NA	NA
45 S&W Schofield	230	730	NA	NA	272	NA	NA	NA	NA	NA

Cartridge	Bullet Wgt. Grs.	VELOCITY (fps)			ENERGY (ft. lbs.)			Mid-Range Traj. (in.)		Bbl. Lgth. (in).
		Muzzle	50 yds.	100 yds.	Muzzle	50 yds.	100 yds.	50 yds.	100 yds.	
45 G.A.P.	165	1007	936	879	372	321	283	-1.4	-11.8	5
45 G.A.P.	185	1090	970	890	490	385	320	1	4.7	5"
45 G.A.P.	230	880	842	NA	396	363	NA	NA	NA	NA
45 Automatic	150	1050	NA	NA	403	NA	NA	NA	NA	NA
45 Automatic	165	1030	930	NA	385	315	NA	1.2	NA	5"
45 Automatic Guard Dog	165	1140	1030	950	475	390	335	NA	NA	5"
45 Automatic	185	1000	940	890	410	360	325	1.1	4.9	5"
45 Auto. (Match)	185	770	705	650	245	204	175	2	8.7	5"
45 Auto. (Match)	200	940	890	840	392	352	312	2	8.6	5"
45 Automatic	200	975	917	860	421	372	328	1.4	5	5"
45 Automatic	230	830	800	675	355	325	300	1.6	6.8	5"
45 Automatic	230	880	846	816	396	366	340	1.5	6.1	5"
45 Automatic +P	165	1250	NA	NA	573	NA	NA	NA	NA	NA
45 Automatic +P	185	1140	1040	970	535	445	385	0.9	4	5"
45 Automatic +P	200	1055	982	925	494	428	380	NA	NA	5"
45 Super	185	1300	1190	1108	694	582	504	NA	NA	5"
45 Win. Magnum	230	1400	1230	1105	1000	775	635	0.6	2.8	5"
45 Win. Magnum	260	1250	1137	1053	902	746	640	0.8	3.3	5"
45 Win. Mag. CorBon	320	1150	1080	1025	940	830	747	3.47		
455 Webley MKII	262	850	NA	NA	420	NA	NA	NA	NA	NA
45 Colt FTX	185	920	870	826	348	311	280	NA	NA	3"V
45 Colt	200	1000	938	889	444	391	351	1.3	4.8	5.5"
45 Colt	225	960	890	830	460	395	345	1.3	5.5	5.5"
45 Colt + P CorBon	265	1350	1225	1126	1073	884	746	2.65	0	
45 Colt + P CorBon	300	1300	1197	1114	1126	956	827	2.78	0	
45 Colt	250/255	860	820	780	410	375	340	1.6	6.6	5.5"
454 Casull	250	1300	1151	1047	938	735	608	0.7	3.2	7.5"V
454 Casull	260	1800	1577	1381	1871	1436	1101	0.4	1.8	7.5"V
454 Casull	300	1625	1451	1308	1759	1413	1141	0.5	2	7.5"V
454 Casull CorBon	360	1500	1387	1286	1800	1640	1323	2.01	0	
460 S&W	200	2300	2042	1801	2350	1851	1441	0	-1.6	NA
460 S&W	260	2000	1788	1592	2309	1845	1404	NA	NA	7.5"V
460 S&W	250	1450	1267	1127	1167	891	705	NA	NA	8.375-V
460 S&W	250	1900	1640	1412	2004	1494	1106	0	-2.75	NA
460 S&W	300	1750	1510	1300	2040	1510	1125	NA	NA	8.4-V
460 S&W	395	1550	1389	1249	2108	1691	1369	0	-4	NA
475 Linebaugh	400	1350	1217	1119	1618	1315	1112	NA	NA	NA
480 Ruger	325	1350	1191	1076	1315	1023	835	2.6	0	7.5"
50 Action Exp.	300	1475	1251	1092	1449	1043	795	-	-	6"
50 Action Exp.	325	1400	1209	1075	1414	1055	835	0.2	2.3	6"
500 S&W	275	1665	1392	1183	1693	1184	854	1.5	NA	8.375
500 S&W	300	1950	1653	1396	2533	1819	1298	—	—	8.5
500 S&W	325	1800	1560	1350	2340	1755	1315	NA	NA	8.4-V
500 S&W	350	1400	1231	1106	1523	1178	951	NA	NA	10"
500 S&W	400	1675	1472	1299	2493	1926	1499	1.3	NA	8.375
500 S&W	440	1625	1367	1169	2581	1825	1337	1.6	NA	8.375
500 S&W	500	1300	1178	1085	1876	1541	1308	—	—	8.5
500 S&W	500	1425	1281	1164	2254	1823	1505	NA	NA	10"

Rimfire Ammunition Ballistics

Note: The actual ballistics obtained with your firearm can vary considerably from the advertised ballistics. Also, ballistics can vary from lot to lot with the same brand and type load.

Cartridge	Bullet Wt. Grs.	Velocity (fps) 22-1/2" Bbl.		Energy (ft. lbs.) 22-1/2" Bbl.		Mid-Range Traj. (in.)	Muzzle Velocity
		Muzzle	100 yds.	Muzzle	100 yds.	100 yds.	6" Bbl.
17 Aguila	20	1850	1267	NA	NA	NA	NA
17 Hornady Mach 2	15.5	2050	1450	149	75	NA	NA
17 Hornady Mach 2	17	2100	1530	166	88	0.7	NA
17 HMR Lead Free	15.5	2550	1901	NA	NA	0.9	NA
17 HMR TNT Green	16	2500	1642	222	96	NA	NA
17 HMR	17	2550	1902	245	136	NA	NA
17 HMR	17	2650	na	na	na	na	NA
17 HMR	20	2375	1776	250	140	NA	NA
17 Win. Super Mag.	15	3300	2496	363	207	0	NA
17 Win. Super Mag.	20 Tipped	3000	2504	400	278	0	NA
17 Win. Super Mag.	20 JHP	3000	2309	400	237	0	NA
17 Win. Super Mag.	25 Tipped	2600	2230	375	276	0	NA
5mm Rem. Rimfire Mag.	30	2300	1669	352	188	NA	24
22 Short Blank	—	—	—	—	—	—	—
22 Short CB	29	727	610	33	24	NA	706
22 Short Target	29	830	695	44	31	6.8	786
22 Short HP	27	1164	920	81	50	4.3	1077
22 Colibri	20	375	183	6	1	NA	NA
22 Super Colibri	20	500	441	11	9	NA	NA
22 Long CB	29	727	610	33	24	NA	706
22 Long HV	29	1180	946	90	57	4.1	1031
22 LR Pistol Match	40	1070	890	100	70	4.6	940
22 LR Shrt. Range Green	21	1650	912	127	NA	NA	NA
CCI Quiet 22 LR	40	710	640	45	36	NA	NA
22 LR Sub Sonic HP	38	1050	901	93	69	4.7	NA
22 LR Segmented HP	40	1050	897	98	72	NA	NA
22 LR Standard Velocity	40	1070	890	100	70	4.6	940
22 LR AutoMatch	40	1200	990	130	85	NA	NA
22 LR HV	40	1255	1016	140	92	3.6	1060
22 LR Silhoutte	42	1220	1003	139	94	3.6	1025
22 SSS	60	950	802	120	86	NA	NA
22 LR HV HP	40	1280	1001	146	89	3.5	1085
22 Velocitor GDHP	40	1435	0	0	0	NA	NA
22 LR Segmented HP	37	1435	1080	169	96	2.9	NA
22 LR Hyper HP	32/33/34	1500	1075	165	85	2.8	NA
22 LR Expediter	32	1640	NA	191	NA	NA	NA
22 LR Stinger HP	32	1640	1132	191	91	2.6	1395
22 LR Lead Free	30	1650	NA	181	NA	NA	NA
22 LR Hyper Vel	30	1750	1191	204	93	NA	NA
22 LR Shot #12	31	950	NA	NA	NA	NA	NA
22 WRF LFN	45	1300	1015	169	103	3	NA
22 Win. Mag. Lead Free	28	2200	NA	301	NA	NA	NA
22 Win. Mag.	30	2200	1373	322	127	1.4	1610
22 Win. Mag. V-Max BT	33	2000	1495	293	164	0.6	NA
22 Win. Mag. JHP	34	2120	1435	338	155	1.4	NA
22 Win. Mag. JHP	40	1910	1326	324	156	1.7	1480
22 Win. Mag. FMJ	40	1910	1326	324	156	1.7	1480
22 Win. Mag. Dyna Point	45	1550	1147	240	131	2.6	NA
22 Win. Mag. JHP	50	1650	1280	300	180	1.3	NA
22 Win. Mag. Shot #11	52	1000	—	NA	—	—	NA

Shotshell Loads

Variations and number of rounds per box can occur with type and brand of ammunition.
Not every brand is available in all shot size variations. # = new load spec this year; "C" indicates a change in data.

Dram Equiv.	Shot Ozs.	Load Style	Shot Sizes	Brands	Velocity (fps)
10 Gauge 3-1/2" Magnum					
Max	2-3/8	magnum blend	5, 6, 7	Hevi-shot	1200
4-1/2	2-1/4	premium	BB, 2, 4, 5, 6	Win., Fed., Rem.	1205
Max	2	premium	4, 5, 6	Fed., Win.	1300
4-1/4	2	high velocity	BB, 2, 4	Rem.	1210
Max	18 pellets	premium	00 buck	Fed., Win.	1100
Max	1-7/8	Bismuth	BB, 2, 4	Bis.	1225
Max	1-3/4	high density	BB, 2	Rem.	1300
4-1/4	1-3/4	steel	TT, T, BBB, BB, 1, 2, 3	Win., Rem.	1260
Mag	1-5/8	steel	T, BBB, BB, 2	Win.	1285
Max	1-5/8	Bismuth	BB, 2, 4	Bismuth	1375
Max	1-1/2	hypersonic	BBB, BB, 2	Rem.	1700
Max	1-1/2	heavy metal	BB, 2, 3, 4	Hevi-Shot	1500
Max	1-1/2	steel	T, BBB, BB, 1, 2, 3	Fed.	1450
Max	1-3/8	steel	T, BBB, BB, 1, 2, 3	Fed., Rem.	1500
Max	1-3/8	steel	T, BBB, BB, 2	Fed., Win.	1450
Max	1-3/4	slug, rifled	slug	Fed.	1280
Max	24 pellets	Buckshot	1 Buck	Fed.	1100
Max	54 pellets	Super-X	4 Buck	Win.	1150
12 Gauge 3-1/2" Magnum					
Max	2-1/4	premium	4, 5, 6	Fed., Rem., Win.	1150
Max	2	Lead	4, 5, 6	Fed.	1300
Max	2	Copper plated turkey	4, 5	Rem.	1300
Max	18 pellets	premium	00 buck	Fed., Win., Rem.	1100
Max	1-7/8	Wingmaster HD	4, 6	Rem.	1225
Max	1-7/8	heavyweight	5, 6	Fed.	1300
Max	1-3/4	high density	BB, 2, 4, 6	Rem.	1300
Max	1-7/8	Bismuth	BB, 2, 4	Bis.	1225
Max	1-5/8	blind side	Hex, 1, 3	Win.	1400
Max	1-5/8	Hevi-shot	T	Hevi-shot	1350
Max	1-5/8	Wingmaster HD	T	Rem.	1350
Max	1-5/8	high density	BB, 2	Fed.	1450
Max	1-5/8	Blind side	Hex, BB, 2	Win.	1400
Max	1-3/8	Heavyweight	2, 4, 6	Fed.	1450

Dram Equiv.	Shot Ozs.	Load Style	Shot Sizes	Brands	Velocity (fps)
12 Gauge 3-1/2" Magnum (cont.)					
Max	1-3/8	steel	T, BBB, BB, 2, 4	Fed., Win., Rem.	1450
Max	1-1/2	FS steel	BBB, BB, 2	Fed.	1500
Max	1-1/2	Supreme H-V	BBB, BB, 2, 3	Win.	1475
Max	1-3/8	H-speed steel	BB, 2	Rem.	1550
Max	1-1/4	Steel	BB, 2	Win.	1625
Max	24 pellets	Premium	1 Buck	Fed.	1100
Max	54 pellets	Super-X	4 Buck	Win.	1050
12 Gauge 3" Magnum					
4	2	premium	BB, 2, 4, 5, 6	Win., Fed., Rem.	1175
4	1-7/8	premium	BB, 2, 4, 6	Win., Fed., Rem.	1210
4	1-7/8	duplex	4x6	Rem.	1210
Max	1-3/4	turkey	4, 5, 6	Fed., Fio.,	1450
Win., Rem.	NA	1300	4, 6	Rem.	1227
Max	1-3/4	high density	BB, 2, 4	Rem.	1450
Max	1-5/8	high density	BB, 2	Fed.	1450
Max	1-5/8	Wingmaster HD	4, 6	Rem.	1227
Max	1-5/8	high velocity	4, 5, 6	Fed.	1350
4	1-5/8	premium	2, 4, 5, 6	Win., Fed., Rem.	1290
Max	1-1/2	Wingmaster HD	T	Rem.	1300
Max	1-1/2	Hevi-shot	T	Hevi-shot	1300
Max	1-1/2	high density	BB, 2, 4	Rem.	1300
Max	1-5/8	Bismuth	BB, 2, 4, 5, 6	Bis.	1250
4	24 pellets	buffered	1 buck	Win., Fed., Rem.	1040
4	15 pellets	buffered	00 buck	Win., Fed., Rem.	1210
4	10 pellets	buffered	000 buck	Win., Fed., Rem.	1225
4	41 pellets	buffered	4 buck	Win., Fed., Rem.	1210
Max	1-3/8	heavyweight	5, 6	Fed.	1300
Max	1-3/8	high density	B, 2, 4, 6	Rem. Win.	1450
Max	1-3/8	slug	slug	Bren.	1476
Max	1-3/8	blind side	Hex, 1, 3, 5	Win.	1400
Max	1-1/4	slug, rifled	slug	Fed.	1600
Max	1-3/16	saboted	slug	Rem.	1875
slug	copper slug	Rem.	NA	1500	850

12 Gauge 3" Magnum (cont.)

Dram Equiv.	Shot Ozs.	Load Style	Shot Sizes	Brands	Velocity (fps)
Max	7/8	slug, rifled	slug	Rem.	1875
Max	1-1/8	low recoil	BB	Fed.	850
Max	1-1/8	steel	BB, 2, 3, 4	Fed., Win., Rem.	1550
Max	1	steel	4, 6	Fed.	1330
Max	1-3/8	buckhammer	slug	Rem.	1500
Max	1	TruBall slug	slug	Fed.	1700
Max	1	slug, rifled	slug, magnum	Win., Rem.	1760
Max	1	saboted	slug	Win.	2000
slug	slug	Rem., Win., Fed.	$10**	1550	1700
Max	385 grs.	partition	slug	Win.	2100
gold	slug	Win.	NA	2000	1275
Max	1-1/8	Rackmaster	slug	Win.	1700
Max	1-1/8	snow goose FS	BB, 2, 3, 4	Fed.	1635
Max	1-1/8	steel	BB, 2, 4	Rem.	1500
Max	1-1/8	steel	T, BBB, BB, 2, 4, 5, 6	Fed., Win.	1450
Max	1-1/8	steel	BB, 2	Fed.	1400
Max	1-1/8	FS lead	3, 4	Fed.	1600
Max	1-3/8	Blind side	Hex, BB, 2	Win.	1400
4	1-1/4	steel	T, BBB, BB, 1, 2, 3, 4, 6	Win., Fed., Rem.	1400
Max	1-1/4	FS steel	BBB, BB, 2	Fed.	1450

12 Gauge 2-3/4"

Dram Equiv.	Shot Ozs.	Load Style	Shot Sizes	Brands	Velocity (fps)
Max	1-5/8	magnum	4, 5, 6	Win., Fed.	1250
Max	1-3/8	lead	4, 5, 6	Fiocchi	1485
Max	1-3/8	turkey	4, 5, 6	Fio.	1250
Max	1-3/8	steel	4, 5, 6	Fed.	1400
Max	1-3/8	Bismuth	BB, 2, 4, 5, 6	Bis.	1300
3-3/4	1-1/2	magnum	BB, 2, 4, 5, 6	Win., Fed., Rem.	1260
Max	1-1/4	blind side	Hex, 2, 5	Win.	1400
Max	1-1/4	Supreme H-V	4, 5, 6, 7-1/2	Win.	1400
Rem.	NA	1400	BB, 2, 4, 5, 6, 7-1/2, 8, 9	Win., Fed., Rem., Fio.	1330
3-3/4	1-1/4	high velocity	BB, 2, 4, 5, 6,	Win., Fed., Rem., Fio.	1330
Max	1-1/4	high density	B, 2, 4	Win.	1450
Max	1-1/4	high density	4, 6	Rem.	1325
3-1/4	1-1/4	Standard velocity	6, 7-1/2, 8, 9	Win., Fed., Rem., Fio.	1220
Max	1-1/8	Hevi-shot	5	Hevi-shot	1350

12 Gauge 2-3/4" (cont.)

Dram Equiv.	Shot Ozs.	Load Style	Shot Sizes	Brands	Velocity (fps)
Max	1-1/8	steel	2, 4	Rem.	1390
Max	1	steel	BB, 2	Fed.	1450
3-1/4	1	standard velocity	6, 7-1/2, 8	Rem., Fed., Fio., Win.	1290
3-1/4	1-1/4	target	7-1/2, 8, 9	Win., Fed., Rem.	1220
3	1-1/8	spreader	7-1/2, 8, 8-1/2, 9	Fio.	1200
3	1-1/8	target	7-1/2, 8, 9, 7-1/2x8	Win., Fed., Rem., Fio.	1200
2-3/4	1-1/8	target	7-1/2, 8, 8-1/2, 9, 7-1/2x8	Win., Fed., Rem., Fio.	1145
2-3/4	1-1/8	low recoil	7-1/2, 8	Rem.	1145
2-1/2	26 grams	low recoil	8	Win.	980
2-1/4	1-1/8	target	7-1/2, 8, 8-1/2, 9	Rem., Fed.	1080
Max	1	spreader	7-1/2, 8, 8-1/2, 9	Fio.	1300
3-1/4	28 grams (1 oz)	target	7-1/2, 8, 9	Win., Fed., Rem., Fio.	1290
3	1	target	7-1/2, 8, 8-1/2, 9	Win., Fio.	1235
2-3/4	1	target	7-1/2, 8, 8-1/2, 9	Fed., Rem., Fio.	1180
3-1/4	24 grams	target	7-1/2, 8, 9	Fed., Win., Fio.	1325
3	7/8	light	8	Fio.	1200
3-3/4	8 pellets	buffered	000 buck	Win., Fed., Rem.	1325
4	12 pellets	premium	00 buck	Win., Fed., Rem.	1290
3-3/4	9 pellets	buffered	00 buck	Win., Fed., Rem., Fio.	1325
3-3/4	12 pellets	buffered	0 buck	Win., Fed., Rem.	1275
4	20 pellets	buffered	1 buck	Win., Fed., Rem.	1075
3-3/4	16 pellets	buffered	1 buck	Win., Fed., Rem.	1250
4	34 pellets	premium	4 buck	Fed., Rem.	1250
3-3/4	27 pellets	buffered	4 buck	Win., Fed., Rem., Fio.	1325
		PDX1	1 oz. slug, 3-00 buck	Win.	1150
Max	1 oz	segmenting, slug	slug	Win.	1600
Max	1	saboted slug	slug	Win., Fed., Rem.	1450
Max	1-1/4	slug, rifled	slug	Fed.	1520
Max	1-1/4	slug	slug	Lightfield	1440
Max	1-1/4	saboted slug	attached sabot	Rem.	1550
Max	1	slug, rifled	slug, magnum	Rem., Fio.	1680
Max	1	slug, rifled	slug	Win., Fed., Rem.	1610
Max	1	sabot slug	slug	Sauvestre	1640
Max	7/8	slug, rifled	slug	Rem.	1800
Max	400	plat. tip	sabot slug	Win.	1700

Dram Equiv.	Shot Ozs.	Load Style	Shot Sizes	Brands	Velocity (fps)
12 Gauge 2-3/4" (cont.)					
Max	385 grains	Partition Gold Slug	slug	Win.	1900
Max	385 grains	Core-Lokt bonded	sabot slug	Rem.	1900
Max	325 grains	Barnes Sabot	slug	Fed.	1900
Max	300 grains	SST Slug	sabot slug	Hornady	2050
Max	3/4	Tracer	#8 + tracer	Fio.	1150
Max	130 grains	Less Lethal	.73 rubber slug	Lightfield	600
Max	3/4	non-toxic	zinc slug	Win.	NA
3	1-1/8	steel target	6-1/2, 7	Rem.	1200
2-3/4	1-1/8	steel target	7	Rem.	1145
3	1#	steel	7	Win.	1235
3-1/2	1-1/4	steel	T, BBB, BB, 1, 2, 3, 4, 5, 6	Win., Fed., Rem.	1275
3-3/4	1-1/8	steel	BB, 1, 2, 3, 4, 5, 6	Win., Fed., Rem., Fio.	1365
3-3/4	1	steel	2, 3, 4, 5, 6, 7	Win., Fed., Rem., Fio.	1390
Max	7/8	steel	7	Fio.	1440
16 Gauge 2-3/4"					
3-1/4	1-1/4	magnum	2, 4, 6	Fed., Rem.	1260
3-1/4	1-1/8	high velocity	4, 6, 7-1/2	Win., Fed., Rem., Fio.	1295
Max	1-1/8	Bismuth	4, 5	Bis.	1200
2-3/4	1-1/8	Standard velocity	6, 7-1/2, 8	Fed., Rem., Fio.	1185
2-1/2	1	dove	6, 7-1/2, 8, 9	Fio., Win.	1165
2-3/4	1		6, 7-1/2, 8	Fio.	1200
Max	15/16	steel	2, 4	Fed., Rem.	1300
Max	7/8	steel	2, 4	Win.	1300
3	12 pellets	buffered	1 buck	Win., Fed., Rem.	1225
Max	4/5	slug, rifled	slug	Win., Fed., Rem.	1570
Max	.92	sabot slug	slug	Sauvestre	1560
20 Gauge 3" Magnum					
3	1-1/4	premium	2, 4, 5, 6, 7-1/2	Win., Fed., Rem.	1185
Max	1-1/4	Wingmaster HD	4, 6	Rem.	1185
3	1-1/4	turkey	4, 6	Fio.	1200
Max	1-1/4	Hevi-shot	2, 4, 6	Hevi-shot	1250
Max	1-1/8	high density	4, 6	Rem.	1300
Max	18 pellets	buck shot	2 buck	Fed.	1200
Max	24 pellets	buffered	3 buck	Win.	1150
2-3/4	20 pellets	buck	3 buck	Rem.	1200

Dram Equiv.	Shot Ozs.	Load Style	Shot Sizes	Brands	Velocity (fps)
20 Gauge 3" Magnum (cont.)					
Max	1	hypersonic	2, 3, 4	Rem.	Rem.
3-1/4	1	steel	1, 2, 3, 4, 5, 6	Win., Fed., Rem.	1330
Max	1	blind side	Hex, 2, 5	Win.	1300
Max	7/8	steel	2, 4	Win.	1300
Max	7/8	FS lead	3, 4	Fed.	1500
Max	1-1/16	high density	2, 4	Win.	1400
Max	1-1/16	Bismuth	2, 4, 5, 6	Bismuth	1250
Mag	5/8	saboted slug	275 gr.	Fed.	1900
Max	3/4	TruBall slug	slug	Fed.	1700
20 Gauge 2-3/4"					
2-3/4	1-1/8	magnum	4, 6, 7-1/2	Win., Fed., Rem.	1175
2-3/4	1	high velocity	4, 5, 6, 7-1/2, 8, 9	Win., Fed., Rem., Fio.	1220
Max	1	Bismuth	4, 6	Bis.	1200
Max	1	Hevi-shot	5	Hevi-shot	1250
Max	1	Supreme H-V	4, 6, 7-1/2	Win. Rem.	1300
Max	1	FS lead	4, 5, 6	Fed.	1350
Max	7/8	Steel	2, 3, 4	Fio.	1500
2-1/2	1	Standard velocity	6, 7-1/2, 8	Win., Rem., Fed., Fio.	1165
2-1/2	7/8	clays	8	Rem.	1200
2-1/2	7/8	promotional	6, 7-1/2, 8	Win., Rem., Fio.	1210
2-1/2	1	target	8, 9	Win., Rem.	1165
Max	7/8	clays	7-1/2, 8	Win.	1275
2-1/2	7/8	target	8, 9	Win., Fed., Rem.	1200
Max	3/4	steel	2, 4	Rem.	1425
2-1/2	7/8	steel - target	7	Rem.	1200
1-1/2	7/8	low recoil	8	Win.	980
Max	1	buckhammer	slug	Rem.	1500
Max	5/8	Saboted Slug	Copper Slug	Rem.	1500
Max	20 pellets	buffered	3 buck	Win., Fed.	1200
Max	5/8	slug, saboted	slug	Win.,	1400
2-3/4	5/8	slug, rifled	slug	Rem.	1580
Max	3/4	saboted slug	copper slug	Fed., Rem.	1450
Max	3/4	slug, rifled	slug	Win., Fed., Rem., Fio.	1570
Max	.9	sabot slug	slug	Sauvestre	1480
Max	260 grains	Partition Gold Slug	slug	Win.	1900

Dram Equiv.	Shot Ozs.	Load Style	Shot Sizes	Brands	Velocity (fps)
20 Gauge 2-3/4" (cont.)					
Max	260 grains	Core-Lokt Ultra	slug	Rem.	1900
Max	260 grains	saboted slug	platinum tip	Win.	1700
Max	3/4	steel	2, 3, 4, 6	Win., Fed., Rem.	1425
Max	250 grains	SST slug	slug	Hornady	1800
Max	1/2	rifled, slug	slug	Rem.	1800
Max	67 grains	Less lethal	2/.60 rubber balls	Lightfield	900
28 Gauge 3"					
Max	7/8	Tundra tungsten	4, 5, 6	Fiocchi	TBD
28 Gauge 2-3/4"					
2	1	high velocity	6, 7-1/2, 8	Win.	1125
2-1/4	3/4	high velocity	6, 7-1/2, 8, 9	Win., Fed., Rem., Fio.	1295
2	3/4	target	8, 9	Win., Fed., Rem.	1200
Max	3/4	sporting clays	7-1/2, 8-1/2	Win.	1300
Max	5/8	Bismuth	4, 6	Bis.	1250
Max	5/8	steel	6, 7	NA	1300
Max	5/8	slug		Bren.	1450

Dram Equiv.	Shot Ozs.	Load Style	Shot Sizes	Brands	Velocity (fps)
410 Bore 3"					
Max	11/16	high velocity	4, 5, 6, 7-1/2, 8, 9	Win., Fed., Rem., Fio.	1135
Max	9/16	Bismuth	4	Bis.	1175
Max	3/8	steel	6	NA	1400
		judge	5 pellets 000 Buck	Fed.	960
		judge	9 pellets #4 Buck	Fed.	1100
Max	Mixed	Per. Defense	3DD/12BB	Win.	750
410 Bore 2-1/2"					
Max	1/2	high velocity	4, 6, 7-1/2	Win., Fed., Rem.	1245
Max	1/5	slug, rifled	slug	Win., Fed., Rem.	1815
1-1/2	1/2	target	8, 8-1/2, 9	Win., Fed.,	1200
Rem., Fio.	$8	1200	7-1/2, 8, 8-1/2	Win.	1300
Max	1/2	sporting clays	7-1/2, 8, 8-1/2	Win.	1300
Max		Buckshot	5-000 Buck	Win.	1135
		judge	12-bb's, 3 disks	Win.	TBD
Max	Mixed	Per. Defense	4DD/16BB	Win.	750
Max	42 grains	Less lethai	4/.41 rubber balls	Lightfield	1150